Are A Click Away

with McGraw-Hill's Homework Management system

COMING FALL 2009...

The updated and enhanced version of McGraw-Hill's Homework Manager and Homework Manager Plus

Introducing...

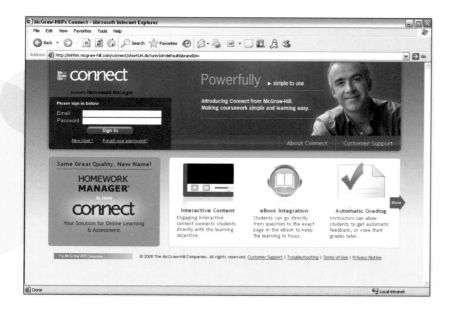

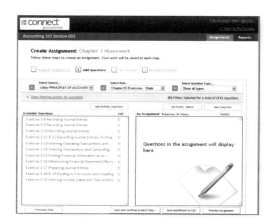

How did we improve our online homework and testing systems with Connect Accounting and Connect Accounting Plus*?

By listening to students and instructors who told us they wanted:

- Single entry point, registration and log on
- Better reports for instructors
- Enhanced ability to export reports and grades to Blackboard and WebCT
- Enhanced question selection including the ability to sort question by AACSB and learning objective tags
- Customizable assignment policies for instructors
- Student Assignment Preview for instructors
- Local time-zone support

*Connect Plus includes an interactive, integrated version of this textbook.

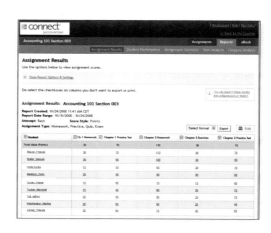

Are A Click Away

with McGraw-Hill's Web-Based Study Tools

Q Want an online, **searchable version** of your textbook?

Wish your textbook could be available online while you're doing your homework?

A ### Connect Plus eBook

If your instructor has chosen Homework Manager Plus (or the updated version, *Connect Plus*, available fall 2009), you have an affordable and searchable online version of your book integrated with your other online homework tools.

Connect Plus eBook offers features like:

- topic search
- adjustable text size
- jump to page number
- print by section

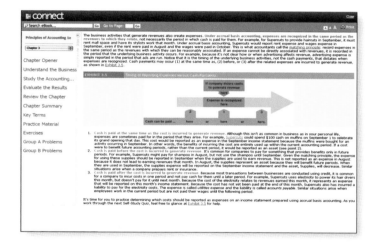

Q Want to get more **value** from your textbook purchase?

Think learning accounting should be a little bit more **interesting**?

A ### Check out the companion website for this textbook www.mhhe.com/LLPW1e

We put it there for you. Go online for test tips and practice problems whenever you study. The companion website for this book includes **games, quizzes, and outlines** to help you study. Get more from your textbook – use the Online Learning Center.

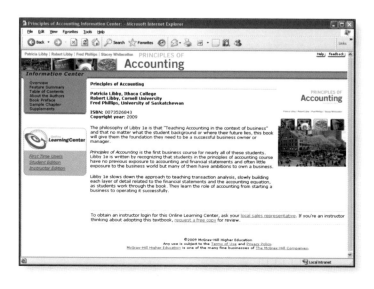

PRINCIPLES OF
Accounting

PRINCIPLES OF
Accounting

www.mhhe.com/LLPW1e

VOLUME 2, CHAPTERS 12–25

Patricia A. Libby
Ithaca College

Robert Libby
Cornell University

Fred Phillips
University of Saskatchewan

Stacey Whitecotton
Arizona State University

 **McGraw-Hill Irwin**

Boston Burr Ridge, IL Dubuque, IA New York San Francisco St. Louis
Bangkok Bogotá Caracas Kuala Lumpur Lisbon London Madrid Mexico City
Milan Montreal New Delhi Santiago Seoul Singapore Sydney Taipei Toronto

PRINCIPLES OF ACCOUNTING
Published by McGraw-Hill/Irwin, a business unit of The McGraw-Hill Companies, Inc., 1221 Avenue of the
Americas, New York, NY, 10020. Copyright © 2009 by The McGraw-Hill Companies, Inc. All rights reserved.
No part of this publication may be reproduced or distributed in any form or by any means, or stored in a
database or retrieval system, without the prior written consent of The McGraw-Hill Companies, Inc., including,
but not limited to, in any network or other electronic storage or transmission, or broadcast for distance learning.

Some ancillaries, including electronic and print components, may not be available to customers outside the
United States.

This book is printed on acid-free paper.

1 2 3 4 5 6 7 8 9 0 DOW/DOW 0 9 8

ISBN-13: 978-0-07-352684-3 (combined edition)
ISBN-10: 0-07-352684-3 (combined edition)
ISBN-13: 978-0-07-327395-2 (volume 1, chapters 1–12)
ISBN-10: 0-07-327395-3 (volume 1, chapters 1–12)
ISBN-13: 978-0-07-327396-9 (volume 2, chapters 12–25)
ISBN-10: 0-07-327396-1 (volume 2, chapters 12–25)
ISBN-13: 978-0-07-327408-9 (principles of financial accounting, chapters 1–17)
ISBN-10: 0-07-327408-9 (principles of financial accounting, chapters 1–17)

Vice president and editor-in-chief: *Brent Gordon*
Editorial director: *Stewart Mattson*
Publisher: *Tim Vertovec*
Senior sponsoring editor: *Alice Harra*
Senior developmental editor: *Kimberly D. Hooker*
Executive marketing manager: *Sankha Basu*
Manager of photo, design & publishing tools: *Mary Conzachi*
Full service project manager: *Elm Street Publishing Services*
Senior production supervisor: *Debra R. Sylvester*
Interior designer: *Pam Verros*
Senior photo research coordinator: *Jeremy Cheshareck*
Photo researcher: *Editorial Image, LLC*
Senior media project manager: *Susan Lombardi*
Cover design: *Cara Hawthorne*
Compositor: *Laserwords Private Limited*
Printer: *R. R. Donnelley*

The Library of Congress Cataloging-in-Publication Data

Principles of accounting / Patricia A. Libby . . . [et al.].
      p. cm.
   Includes index.
   ISBN-13: 978-0-07-352684-3 (combined edition : alk. paper)
   ISBN-10: 0-07-352684-3 (combined edition : alk. paper)
   ISBN-13: 978-0-07-327395-2 (volume 1, ch. 1–12 : alk. paper)
   ISBN-10: 0-07-327395-3 (volume 1, ch 1–12 : alk. paper)
   [etc.]
   1. Accounting. 2. Accounting—Textbooks. I. Libby, Patricia A.
HF5636.P75 2009
657—dc22

2008038810

DEDICATION

*Herman and Doris Hargenrater,
Laura Libby, Oscar and Selma Libby.*

–Patricia and Robert Libby

*To the best teachers I've ever had:
my Mom and Dad, Barb, Harrison,
and Daniel.*

–Fred Phillips

*This book is dedicated to Mark, Riley,
and Carley Drayna. Thanks for all your
love and support.*

–Stacey Whitecotton

MEET THE AUTHORS

Patricia A. Libby

Patricia Libby is Associate Professor of Accounting at Ithaca College, where she teaches the undergraduate Principles of Accounting course. She previously taught graduate and undergraduate Principles of Accounting at Eastern Michigan University and the University of Texas. Before entering academe, she was an auditor with Price Waterhouse (now PricewaterhouseCoopers) and a financial administrator at the University of Chicago. She is also faculty adviser to Beta Alpha Psi, Ithaca College Accounting Association, and Ithaca College National Association of Black Accountants. She received her B.S. from Pennsylvania State University, her M.B.A. from DePaul University, and her Ph.D. from the University of Michigan; she is also a CPA.

Pat conducts research on using cases in the introductory course and other parts of the accounting curriculum. She has published articles in *The Accounting Review, Issues in Accounting Education*, and *The Michigan CPA*.

Robert Libby

Robert Libby is the David A. Thomas Professor of Accounting at Cornell University, where he teaches the introductory Principles of Accounting course. He previously taught at the University of Illinois, Pennsylvania State University, the University of Texas at Austin, the University of Chicago, and the University of Michigan. He received his B.S. from Pennsylvania State University and his M.A.S. and Ph.D. from the University of Illinois; he is also a CPA.

Bob is a widely published author and researcher specializing in behavioral accounting. He was selected as the American Accounting Association (AAA) Outstanding Educator in 2000, received the AAA Outstanding Service Award in 2006, and received the AAA Notable Contributions to the Literature Award in 1985 and 1996. He is the only person to have received all three of the Association's highest awards for teaching, service, and research. He has published numerous articles in *The Accounting Review; Journal of Accounting Research; Accounting, Organizations, and Society;* and other accounting journals. He has held a variety of offices including Vice President of the American Accounting Association and is a member of the American Institute of CPAs and the editorial boards of *The Accounting Review; Accounting, Organizations, and Society; Journal of Accounting Literature;* and *Journal of Behavioral Decision Making.*

Fred Phillips

Fred Phillips is Professor and the George C. Baxter Scholar at the University of Saskatchewan, where he teaches introductory Principles of Accounting. He also has taught introductory accounting at the University of Texas at Austin and the University of Manitoba. Fred has an undergraduate accounting degree, a professional accounting designation, and a Ph.D. from the University of Texas at Austin. He previously worked as an audit manager at KPMG.

Fred's main interest is accounting education. He has won 11 teaching awards, including three national case-writing competitions. Recently, Fred won the 2007 Alpha Kappa Psi Outstanding Professor award at The University of Texas at Austin, and in 2006 he was awarded the title Master Teacher at the University of Saskatchewan. He has published instructional cases and numerous articles in journals such as *Issues in Accounting Education*, *Journal of Accounting Research*, and *Organizational Behavior and Human Decision Processes*. He received the American Accounting Association Outstanding Research in Accounting Education Award in 2006 and 2007 for his articles. Fred is a past Associate Editor of *Issues in Accounting Education* and a current member of the Teaching, Learning & Curriculum and Two-Year College sections of the American Accounting Association. In his spare time, he likes to work out, play video games, and drink iced cappuccinos.

Stacey Whitecotton

Stacey Whitecotton is Associate Professor in the School of Accountancy at Arizona State University. She received her Ph.D. and Masters of Accounting from The University of Oklahoma and her B.B.A. from Texas Tech University.

Stacey teaches managerial accounting topics at the undergraduate level and in the MBA program. She was recognized as the Outstanding Undergraduate Teacher by the School of Accountancy and Information Management in 1999 and was awarded the John W. Teets Outstanding Graduate Teacher award in 2000–2001. She is currently serving as the faculty director for the W. P. Carey Online MBA program.

Stacey's research interests center around the use of decision aids to improve the decision-making behavior of financial analysts, managers, and auditors. Her research has been published in *The Accounting Review*, *Organizational Behavior and Human Decision Processes*, *Behavioral Research in Accounting*, *Auditing: A Journal of Practice and Theory*, and *The Journal of Behavioral Decision Making*.

Stacey and her husband Mark enjoy traveling and the many outdoor activities Arizona has to offer with their two kids, Riley and Carley.

What Does Pizza Have to Do with Accounting?

Teaching challenge: Motivating students to read the book

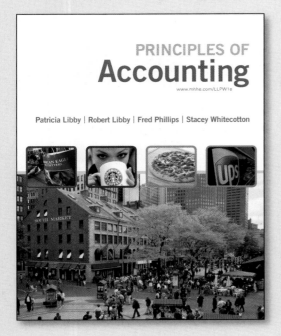

The number one challenge we hear from faculty is how to motivate students to read their textbook. Students taking Principles of Accounting don't yet know **why accounting matters** in their lives, so they aren't naturally drawn to reading their text.

However, most students do know about eating pizza, drinking Starbucks or their favorite coffee, shopping at retail stores like American Eagle, and shipping packages with UPS. Once they read about how these activities relate to accounting, they begin to see that **accounting is in their everyday lives.**

In addition, many of your students **imagine themselves starting and running a business** someday (or helping with a family business). So, our *Principles of Accounting* book opens with a novel idea: Chapters 1–4 are written around the true story of Mauricio Rosa, an immigrant from El Salvador who started Pizza Aroma, a small gourmet pizza restaurant in Ithaca, New York. Mauricio's actual experiences and decisions provide a consistent story line and create a framework for learning about accounting. In Chapter 1, Mauricio and his CPA discuss plans for starting his business, addressing topics such as choice of organizational form, accounting information needs, and financial statement reporting. In Chapter 2, Mauricio actually establishes Pizza Aroma by contributing capital, obtaining a bank loan, and investing in restaurant equipment. He learns how these activities affect Pizza Aroma's financial condition and how they are reported in the balance sheet. In Chapter 3, Pizza Aroma begins to earn revenue and incur expenses. He learns how these operating transactions affect the balance sheet and the income statement. Finally, in Chapter 4, Mauricio learns how the accounting records are adjusted prior to determining whether Pizza Aroma has been profitable.

The dialogue between Mauricio and Laurie in the first chapter invites students into a discussion like one they may have someday. Through this true story that

> The building cover has a busy marketplace that depicts the essence of business, accounting, free enterprise, etc., and the crowd rushing off to wherever indicates that business is alive and well . . .—Judy Daulton, Piedmont Technical College

> The examples follow through is an excellent case of how to close the books of accounts. The classifications of accounts make sense with easy understanding for the class. The accounting cycle is clearly explained and easy to understand for the class.—Shafi Ullah, Broward College

> The presentation of the pizza case is awesome . . . it lends itself to a mystery and drives you to find out the ending . . . excellent. . . .—David Laurel, South Texas College

"Others outside your business will also need financial information about your restaurant. For example, where will the money come from to start your business?"

"I'll contribute $30,000 from personal savings. But I'll still need to ask the bank for a $20,000 loan to buy equipment. What will the bank want to know?"

continues in the entire first 4 chapters (the accounting cycle), students see the relationship between accounting and business, and they get a mini-manual for how to start their own businesses. Students get captivated by the story and may not realize they are learning accounting principles in the process.

The choice of Pizza Aroma is purposeful: Students love pizza, they connect accounting to something in their everyday lives. More important, they learn to make the connection in the first few weeks that accounting can help them be successful. **When students understand why accounting matters to them, they want to read more.**

(Chapter One) is engaging with the interview approach. The business owner is at the same level of accounting knowledge as the students and asks the questions that are surely running through the students' minds. . . .
—Patricia Walczak, Lansing Community College

Since many (of my students) have worked in fast-food establishments and certainly all have eaten pizza, I think this should make it more interesting and understandable to them.—Sandra Augustine, Hilbert College

Introducing balance sheet accounts in Chapter 2 and, exclusively, income accounts in Chapter 3 is a dynamic idea that makes sense! The focus on a proprietorship selling pizza through the first 4 chapters is a topic students can identify with.—Marcia Sandvold, Des Moines Area Community College

Pizza Aroma: It's a true story

Pizza Aroma, Ithaca, NY

Author Patricia Libby and Owner Mauricio Rosa

Gourmet Pizza

How Can LLPW Ensure Students Will Master the Accounting Cycle?

Teaching challenge: Students struggle with the accounting cycle

Faculty understand that mastering the accounting cycle is essential to success in Principles of Accounting courses. The authors agree. They believe students struggle with the accounting cycle when transaction analysis is covered in one chapter. Students are often overwhelmed when they are exposed to the accounting equation, journal entries, and T-accounts for both balance sheet and income statement accounts in a single chapter.

Slowing down the material by breaking transaction analysis into two chapters is an excellent idea, which I think will help students greatly. That is one of my biggest complaints about my current text; it goes too fast.—Amy Haas, Kingsborough Community College

The Libby/Libby/Phillips/Whitecotton approach **covers transaction analysis over two chapters** so that students have the time to master the material. In Chapter 2 of *Principles of Accounting*, students are introduced to the accounting equation and transaction analysis for investing and financing transactions that affect only balance sheet accounts. This provides students the opportunity to learn the basic structure and tools used in accounting in a simpler setting than usual. Chapter 3 introduces operating transactions that affect income statement accounts. As a result of this slower building-block approach to transaction analysis, students are better prepared to learn adjustments, financial statement preparation, and more advanced topics.

It is presented in a very organized manner. The students are presented the journalizing/posting information (Chapters 2 and 3) at a slower pace, giving them the opportunity to absorb and comprehend this difficult information. Chapter 4 then wraps up the entire cycle all at once, instead of presenting adjusting entries in one chapter and then ending the accounting cycle in another. In other words, in a more efficient and easily understandable manner.—Carol Pace, Grayson Community College

The concentration and reinforcement of the basic accounting equation allow the student to master the equation before introducing the income statement concepts. Excellent idea.
—Patricia Holmes, Des Moines Area Community College

The following grid provides a detailed comparison of the Libby/Libby/Phillips/Whitecotton approach with the approach of other principles of accounting texts.

Accounting Cycle

Chapter	LLPW Approach	Other Approaches
1	Overview of Financial Statements and Users, Transaction Analysis with Accounting Equation	Overview of Financial Statements and Users, Transaction Analysis with Accounting Equation
2	Journal Entries and T-Accounts with Transactions affecting Balance Sheet Accounts only	Journal Entries and T-Accounts with Transactions affecting both Balance Sheet and Income Statement Accounts
3	Journal Entries and T-Accounts with Transactions affecting both Balance Sheet and Income Statement Accounts	Adjusting Entries, Financial Statement Preparation
4	Adjusting Entries, Financial Statement Preparation, Closing Process, (Worksheet)	Closing Process, Worksheet, (Reversing Entries), Financial Statement Preparation

First introducing income accounts in chapter 3 is great. I don't know any other text to do this.—Jeannie Harrington, Middle Tennessee State University

Learning accounting is like learning a foreign language where practice of new terms and concepts is essential. By taking a progressive building-block approach to Chapters 2 and 3, students have more time to master transaction analysis, which is the foundation for the rest of the course. Students have more time to practice and feel less overwhelmed.

It caught my attention from page 1 and I wanted to read on and find out how Pizza Aroma was going to do. The first four chapters simplify the accounting process and explain accounting on an entry level for first time accounting students. Great Job!!!—Susan Logorda, Lehigh Carbon Community College

How Can LLPW Help Students Learn Accounting in the Context of Business?

Teaching challenge: Many students don't have enough work experience to understand accounting in the context of business

Because many students don't have business experience, the authors teach accounting in the context of business by focusing each chapter on one well-known company and using that company as a consistent example throughout the chapter including the examples, financial statements, and data.

The authors focus every chapter of Principles of Accounting on a company that makes or provides something students use or see in their everyday lives. Chapters 1 through 4 focus on the true story of Pizza Aroma, a typical local small pizza restaurant. In Chapters 5–25, the authors profile well-known companies such as Starbucks (Chapter 21), American Eagle Outfitters (Chapter 7), Skechers (Chapter 9), Blockbuster (Chapter 25), General Mills (Chapter 14), Cedar Fair (Chapter 10), and Tombstone (Chapter 18).

> *Great explanations; fantastic use of the real world examples. . . .*—Shea Mears, Des Moines Area Community College

> *The use of Cedar Fair for (chapter 10) is great.* **How fascinating this was to use roller coasters for depreciation examples.**—Jeannie Harrington, Middle Tennessee State University

> *Authors did a nice job of making it easy to read and understand. Supplemental information with real company and use of extras like the coach's tips, self-study practice and exhibits, make this a better text than I currently use.*—Larry Dragosavac, Edison CC

LLPW is the only book that uses this unique "focus company approach" to teach accounting in the context of real business.

FOCUS COMPANIES

Ch 1: Introducing Accounting

Pizza Aroma

Ch 2: Balance Sheet

Pizza Aroma

Ch 3: Balance Sheet and Income Statement

Pizza Aroma

Ch 4: Adjusting and Closing the Books

Pizza Aroma

Ch 5: Accounting Systems

UPS

Ch 6: Merchandising

Wal-Mart

Ch 7: Inventories

American Eagle Outfitters

Ch 8: Internal Controls

The Home Depot

Ch 9: Receivables

Skechers

Ch 10: Long-lived Assets

Cedar Fair

Ch 11: Current Liabilities

General Mills

Ch 12: Partnerships

Bloom 'N Flowers

Ch 13: Corporations

Sonic Drive-In

Ch 14: Long-Term Liabilities

General Mills

Ch 15: Investments

Washington Post Companies

Ch 16: Statement of Cash Flows

Nautilus

Ch 17: Financial Statement Analysis

Lowe's

Ch 18: Managerial Accounting

Tombstone Pizza

Ch 19: Job Order Costing

Toll Brothers

Ch 20: Process Costing

CK Mondavi

Ch 21: Cost Behavior and Cost Volume Profit Analysis

Starbucks

Ch 22: Capital Budgeting

Mattel

Ch 23: Budgetary Planning

Cold Stone Creamery

Ch 24: Budgetary Control

Cold Stone Creamery

Ch 25: Standard Costing and Variance Analysis

Blockbuster

How Can LLPW Help Students Study and Practice?

Principles of Accounting offers a host of pedagogical tools that complement the different ways you like to teach and the ways your students like to learn. . . .

Coach's Tips

Every student needs encouragement, and inclusion of Coach's Tips is just one way Libby/Libby/Phillips/Whitecotton fulfills that need. Coach's Tips appear throughout the text offering tips, advice, and suggestions about how to learn principles of accounting.

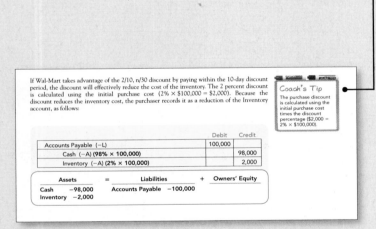

Self-Study Practice

Research shows that students learn best when they are actively engaged in the learning process. This active learning feature engages the student, provides interactivity, and promotes efficient learning. These practices ask students to pause at strategic points throughout each chapter to ensure they understand key points before moving ahead.

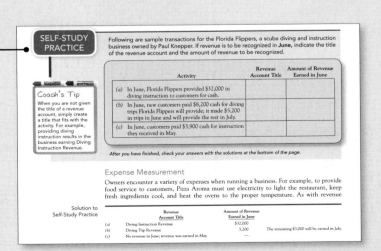

xiv

Spotlight On ETHICS

Accounting Scandals

Accounting scandals are driven by the fear of personal failure and greed. Initially, some people may appear to benefit from fraudulent reporting. In the long run, however, fraud harms most individuals and organizations. When it is uncovered, the corporation's stock price drops dramatically. In the case involving MicroStrategy, the stock price dropped 65 percent in a single day of trading, from $243 to $86 per share. Creditors are also harmed by fraud. WorldCom's creditors recovered only 42 percent of what they were owed. They lost $36 billion. Innocent employees also are harmed by fraud. At Enron, 5,600 employees lost their jobs and many lost all of their retirement savings.

Ethical conduct is just as important for small private businesses as it is for large public companies. Laurie's advice to Mauricio and to all managers is to strive to create an ethical environment and establish a strong system of checks and controls inside the company. Do not tolerate blatant acts of fraud, such as employees making up false expenses for reimbursement, punching in a time card belonging to a fellow employee who will be late for work, or copying

Spotlight On Ethics

This feature appears throughout the text stressing ethical issues that could be faced in relation to the chapter material and the importance of acting responsibly in business practice.

Spotlight On Business Decisions

Good decision making is essential in business whether you are preparing, using, or analyzing accounting information. Spotlight On Business Decisions helps students develop good decision-making skills by illustrating the relevance of accounting in real-world decision making.

If Wal-Mart paid for the inventory after the 10-day discount period, it would not be eligible for the 2 percent discount. Instead, it would pay the full $100,000 owed. The payment would be recorded as a decrease in Accounts Payable (debit) and a decrease in Cash (credit) of $100,000.²

Spotlight On BUSINESS DECISIONS

To Take or Not to Take the Discount, That Is the Question

Purchasers usually pay within the discount period because the savings are much larger than they may appear to you. Although 2 percent might seem a small discount, if taken consistently on all purchases made during the year, it can add up to substantial savings. All the purchaser must do to earn the 2 percent discount is to pay the bill 20 days early (on the 10th day instead of the 30th). Over a year (365 days), this discount is equivalent to a 37 percent annual interest rate.* So even if purchasers must borrow from the bank at a high rate, such as 15 percent, they will still save a great deal by taking the discount.

Spotlight On FINANCIAL REPORTING

Accrued Expenses in the Millions and Billions

Accrued expenses are significant liabilities for many companies. For example, Tootsie Roll Industries recently reported the following:

NOTE 2—ACCRUED LIABILITIES:
Accrued liabilities are comprised of the following:

(in thousands of dollars)	DECEMBER 31, 2006	2005
Compensation	$ 12,923	$ 15,756
Other employee benefits	5,631	5,213
Taxes, other than income	1,781	1,765
Advertising and promotions	17,854	14,701
Other	5,613	7,534
	$ 43,802	$ 44,969

The $43.8 million in total accrued liabilities represents 70 percent of Tootsie Roll's current liabilities and 27 percent of total liabilities.
Likewise, Wal-Mart Stores, Inc., reported approximately $14.7 billion in accrued liabilities, primarily from accrued wages and benefits owed to employees. This was 28 percent of current liabilities and 17 percent of total liabilities.

Spotlight On Financial Reporting

Concepts come to life when you see how well-known businesses apply them. Spotlight On Financial Reporting helps students to apply their knowledge to relevant, real-world financial reporting issues.

From Reading to Doing—Extensive End-of-Chapter Material to Help

Chapter Summary

End-of-chapter summaries complement the learning objectives outlined at the beginning of the chapter.

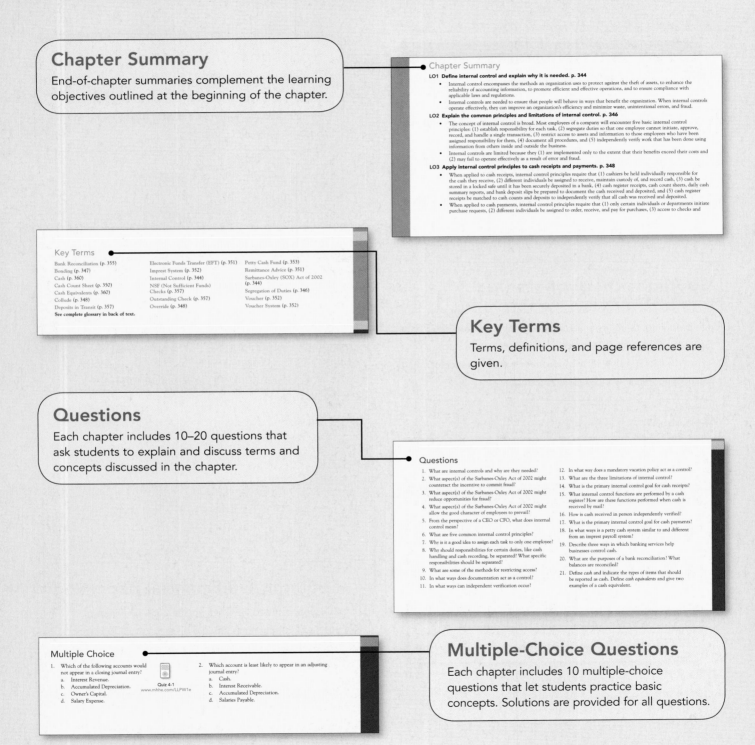

Chapter Summary

LO1 Define internal control and explain why it is needed. p. 344
- Internal control encompasses the methods an organization uses to protect against the theft of assets, to enhance the reliability of accounting information, to promote efficient and effective operations, and to ensure compliance with applicable laws and regulations.
- Internal controls are needed to ensure that people will behave in ways that benefit the organization. When internal controls operate effectively, they can improve an organization's efficiency and minimize waste, unintentional errors, and fraud.

LO2 Explain the common principles and limitations of internal control. p. 346
- The concept of internal control is broad. Most employees of a company will encounter five basic internal control principles: (1) establish responsibility for each task, (2) segregate duties so that one employee cannot initiate, approve, record, and handle a single transaction, (3) restrict access to assets and information to those employees who have been assigned responsibility for them, (4) document all procedures, and (5) independently verify work that has been done using information from others inside and outside the business.
- Internal controls are limited because they (1) are implemented only to the extent that their benefits exceed their costs and (2) may fail to operate effectively as a result of error and fraud.

LO3 Apply internal control principles to cash receipts and payments. p. 348
- When applied to cash receipts, internal control principles require that (1) cashiers be held individually responsible for the cash they receive, (2) different individuals be assigned to receive, maintain custody of, and record cash, (3) cash be stored in a locked safe until it has been securely deposited in a bank, (4) cash register receipts, cash count sheets, daily cash summary reports, and bank deposit slips be prepared to document the cash received and deposited, and (5) cash register receipts be matched to cash counts and deposits to independently verify that all cash was received and deposited.
- When applied to cash payments, internal control principles require that (1) only certain individuals or departments initiate purchase requests, (2) different individuals be assigned to order, receive, and pay for purchases, (3) access to checks and

Key Terms

Bank Reconciliation (p. 355)	Electronic Funds Transfer (EFT) (p. 351)	Petty Cash Fund (p. 353)
Bonding (p. 347)	Imprest System (p. 352)	Remittance Advice (p. 351)
Cash (p. 360)	Internal Control (p. 344)	Sarbanes-Oxley (SOX) Act of 2002
Cash Count Sheet (p. 350)	NSF (Not Sufficient Funds)	(p. 344)
Cash Equivalents (p. 360)	Checks (p. 357)	Segregation of Duties (p. 346)
Collude (p. 348)	Outstanding Check (p. 357)	Voucher (p. 352)
Deposits in Transit (p. 357)	Override (p. 348)	Voucher System (p. 352)
See complete glossary in back of text.		

Key Terms

Terms, definitions, and page references are given.

Questions

Each chapter includes 10–20 questions that ask students to explain and discuss terms and concepts discussed in the chapter.

Questions

1. What are internal controls and why are they needed?
2. What aspect(s) of the Sarbanes-Oxley Act of 2002 might counteract the incentive to commit fraud?
3. What aspect(s) of the Sarbanes-Oxley Act of 2002 might reduce opportunities for fraud?
4. What aspect(s) of the Sarbanes-Oxley Act of 2002 might allow the good character of employees to prevail?
5. From the perspective of a CEO or CFO, what does internal control mean?
6. What are five common internal control principles?
7. Why is it a good idea to assign each task to only one employee?
8. Why should responsibilities for certain duties, like cash handling and cash recording, be separated? What specific responsibilities should be separated?
9. What are some of the methods for restricting access?
10. In what ways does documentation act as a control?
11. In what ways can independent verification occur?
12. In what way does a mandatory vacation policy act as a control?
13. What are the three limitations of internal control?
14. What is the primary internal control goal for cash receipts?
15. What internal control functions are performed by a cash register? How are these functions performed when cash is received by mail?
16. How is cash received in person independently verified?
17. What is the primary internal control goal for cash payments?
18. In what ways is a petty cash system similar to and different from an imprest payroll system?
19. Describe three ways in which banking services help businesses control cash.
20. What are the purposes of a bank reconciliation? What balances are reconciled?
21. Define *cash* and indicate the types of items that should be reported as cash. Define *cash equivalents* and give two examples of a cash equivalent.

Multiple Choice

1. Which of the following accounts would not appear in a closing journal entry?
   a. Interest Revenue.
   b. Accumulated Depreciation.
   c. Owner's Capital.
   d. Salary Expense.

   Quiz 4-1
   www.mhhe.com/LLPW1e

2. Which account is least likely to appear in an adjusting journal entry?
   a. Cash.
   b. Interest Receivable.
   c. Accumulated Depreciation.
   d. Salaries Payable.

Multiple-Choice Questions

Each chapter includes 10 multiple-choice questions that let students practice basic concepts. Solutions are provided for all questions.

LLPW is written by best-selling authors whose books are well-known for the quality of their end-of-chapter problem material.

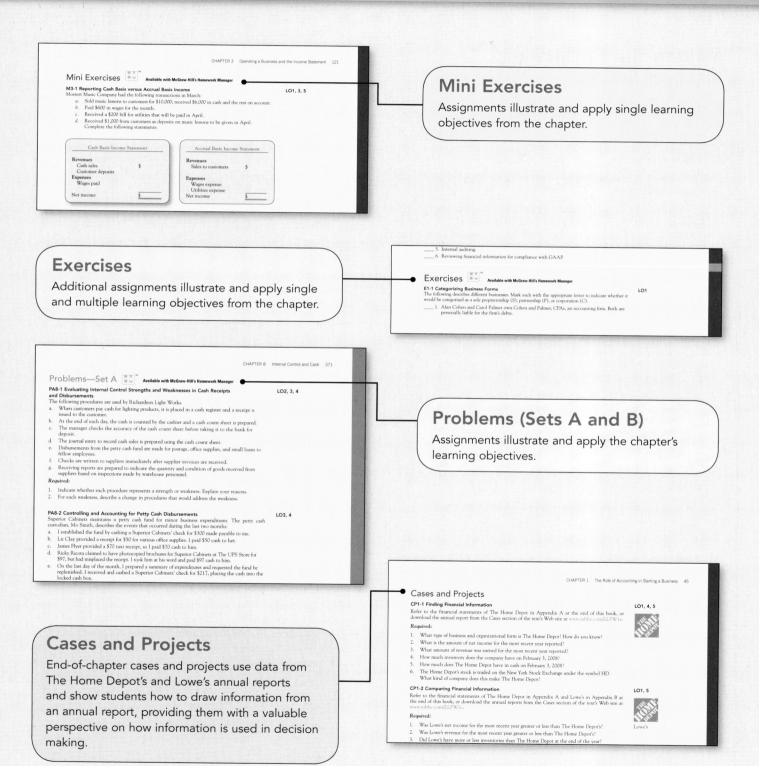

Mini Exercises

CHAPTER 3   Operating a Business and the Income Statement   121

Mini Exercises   Available with McGraw-Hill's Homework Manager

M3-1 Reporting Cash Basis versus Accrual Basis Income   LO1, 3, 5
Mostert Music Company had the following transactions in March:
a.   Sold music lessons to customers for $10,000; received $6,000 in cash and the rest on account.
b.   Paid $600 in wages for the month.
c.   Received a $200 bill for utilities that will be paid in April.
d.   Received $1,000 from customers as deposits on music lessons to be given in April.
     Complete the following statements:

Cash Basis Income Statement	
Revenues	
Cash sales	
Customer deposits	$
Expenses	
Wages paid	
Net income	$

Accrual Basis Income Statement	
Revenues	
Sales to customers	$
Expenses	
Wages expense	
Utilities expense	
Net income	$

Mini Exercises

Assignments illustrate and apply single learning objectives from the chapter.

Exercises

Additional assignments illustrate and apply single and multiple learning objectives from the chapter.

____ 5.   Internal auditing.
____ 6.   Reviewing financial information for compliance with GAAP.

Exercises   Available with McGraw-Hill's Homework Manager

E1-1 Categorizing Business Forms   LO1
The following describes different businesses. Mark each with the appropriate letter to indicate whether it
would be categorized as a sole proprietorship (S), partnership (P), or corporation (C).

____ 1.   Alan Cohen and Carol Palmer own Cohen and Palmer, CPAs, an accounting firm. Both are
          personally liable for the firm's debts.

Problems (Sets A and B)

CHAPTER 8   Internal Control and Cash   371

Problems—Set A   Available with McGraw-Hill's Homework Manager

**PA8-1 Evaluating Internal Control Strengths and Weaknesses in Cash Receipts
and Disbursements**   LO2, 3, 4
The following procedures are used by Richardson Light Works.
a.   When customers pay cash for lighting products, it is placed in a cash register and a receipt is
     issued to the customer.
b.   At the end of each day, the cash is counted by the cashier and a cash count sheet is prepared.
c.   The manager checks the accuracy of the cash count sheet before taking it to the bank for
     deposit.
d.   The journal entry to record cash sales is prepared using the cash count sheet.
e.   Disbursements from the petty cash fund are made for postage, office supplies, and small loans to
     fellow employees.
f.   Checks are written to suppliers immediately after supplier invoices are received.
g.   Receiving reports are prepared to indicate the quantity and condition of goods received from
     suppliers based on inspections made by warehouse personnel.

Required:
1.   Indicate whether each procedure represents a strength or weakness. Explain your reasons.
2.   For each weakness, describe a change in procedures that would address the weakness.

PA8-2 Controlling and Accounting for Petty Cash Disbursements   LO3, 4
Superior Cabinets maintains a petty cash fund for minor business expenditures. The petty cash
custodian, Mo Smith, describes the events that occurred during the last two months:
a.   I established the fund by cashing a Superior Cabinets' check for $300 made payable to me.
b.   Liz Clay provided a receipt for $50 for various office supplies. I paid $50 cash to her.
c.   James Flyer provided a $70 taxi receipt, so I paid $70 cash to him.
d.   Ricky Ricota claimed to have photocopied brochures for Superior Cabinets at The UPS Store for
     $97, but had misplaced the receipt. I took him at his word and paid $97 cash to him.
e.   On the last day of the month, I prepared a summary of expenditures and requested the fund be
     replenished. I received and cashed a Superior Cabinets' check for $217, placing the cash into the
     locked cash box.

Problems (Sets A and B)

Assignments illustrate and apply the chapter's learning objectives.

Cases and Projects

End-of-chapter cases and projects use data from The Home Depot's and Lowe's annual reports and show students how to draw information from an annual report, providing them with a valuable perspective on how information is used in decision making.

CHAPTER 1   The Role of Accounting in Starting a Business   45

Cases and Projects

CP1-1 Finding Financial Information   LO1, 4, 5
Refer to the financial statements of The Home Depot in Appendix A at the end of this book, or
download the annual report from the Cases section of the text's Web site at www.mhhe.com/LLPW1e.

Required:
1.   What type of business and organizational form is The Home Depot? How do you know?
2.   What is the amount of net income for the most recent year reported?
3.   What amount of revenue was earned for the most recent year reported?
4.   How much inventory does the company have on February 3, 2008?
5.   How much does The Home Depot have in cash on February 3, 2008?
6.   The Home Depot's stock is traded on the New York Stock Exchange under the symbol HD.
     What kind of company does this make The Home Depot?

CP1-2 Comparing Financial Information   LO1, 5
Refer to the financial statements of The Home Depot in Appendix A and Lowe's in Appendix B at
the end of this book, or download the annual reports from the Cases section of the text's Web site at
www.mhhe.com/LLPW1e.

Required:
1.   Was Lowe's net income for the most recent year greater or less than The Home Depot's?
2.   Was Lowe's revenue for the most recent year greater or less than The Home Depot's?
3.   Did Lowe's have more or less inventories than The Home Depot at the end of the year?

How Can McGraw-Hill Technology Help Students Study and Practice?

McGraw-Hill's Homework Manager System

Easy. Effective. Reliable.

McGraw-Hill's Homework Manager® and Homework Manager Plus.®

The #1 choice in web-based assessment, course management, and homework.

With Homework Manager and Homework Manager Plus system, instructors can create web-based assignments and assessments that can be customized to meet course needs. Assignments are based on content from the textbook, so terminology and problem styles are consistent, eliminating confusion for students.

Homework Manager and Homework Manager Plus include:

- Automatically graded homework
- Immediate student feedback
- Personalized gradebook
- Static and algorithmic exercises, problems, and select test bank questions
- Self-graded practice quizzes
- Online testbank
- Interactive, integrated eBook*

eBook available only with McGraw-Hill's Homework Manager Plus

EASY.

With a simple, four-step process and intuitive interface, Homework Manager and Homework Manager Plus system allows instructors to get their course online in less than an hour!

EFFECTIVE.

Instructors and students using McGraw-Hill's Homework Manager and Homework Manager Plus system report improved grades, greater retention, and increased student engagement.

RELIABLE.

Stability and support are as important to our customers as they are to us. Only Homework Manager and Homework Manager Plus offer a 24-hour support line to ensure you and your students stay connected.

To connect you with your students in even better ways, we're delighted to announce the new version of Homework Manager and Homework Manager Plus called CONNECT, coming in fall 2009. . . .

As with Homework Manager, Connect Accounting lets instructors easily deliver customized assignments, quizzes and tests online.

- Students can practice important skills on their own schedule and get instant feedback.
- Instructors get automatically graded homework, personalized student feedback and gradebook, static and algorithmic exercises, problems, and test questions.
- Access to an interactive eBook is available with Connect Accounting Plus.
- Continuous improvement: Homework Manager customers will find the following enhancements with CONNECT Accounting:
  - Single entry point, registration, and sign on
  - Enhanced gradebook reporting capabilities
  - The ability to export reports and grades to WebCT and Blackboard
  - Enhanced question selection including AACSB and learning objectives
  - Customizable assignment policies
  - Integrated, interactive eBook*
  - Student Assignment Preview for instructors
  - Local time-zone support

*eBook available only with McGraw-Hill CONNECT ACCOUNTING PLUS.

iPod Downloadable Content

Principles of Accounting gives students the option to download content for review and study to their Apple® iPods and most other MP3/MP4 devices. iPod icons appear throughout the text pointing students to chapter-specific audio lecture presentation slides and course-related videos.

McGraw-Hill has leading technology products for your classroom presentations, course management, labs, and self-study.

Carol Yacht's General Ledger and Peachtree

 From one of the most trusted names in computer accounting education, Carol Yacht, comes a general ledger package that's a perfect fit for your course no matter how you like to teach it.

Students using Carol Yacht's General Ledger (CYGL) can move from financial statements to the specific journal entries with just a click of the mouse; changing an entry updates the financial statements on the fly, allowing students to see instantly how journal entries impact financial statements.

If you want your students to practice on the same software the professionals use, the CYGL CD includes Peachtree for use on numerous problems from the text.

Excel Templates

eXcel If they are going to work in accounting (or business in general), students have to know Microsoft Excel. *Principles of Accounting* offers Excel templates tied to specific end-of-chapter problems and annual report cases. This allows students to experience problem solving as it truly happens in real companies. The templates are available on the text Web site www.mhhe.com/LLPW1e.

Online Learning Center

www.mhhe.com/LLPW1e

For instructors, *Principles of Accounting*'s Online Learning Center (OLC) includes the Instructor's Resource Manual, PowerPoint slides, Solutions Manual, and Excel Template solutions tied to the end-of-chapter material. There are also links to professional resources.

For students and instructors, the OLC includes multiple-choice quizzes, Excel templates, The Home Depot and Lowe's Companies annual reports, check figures, Web links, and McGraw-Hill's Homework Manager (see below). Instructors can pull all of this material as part of another online course management system.

ALEKS®

www.business.aleks.com

 ALEKS (Assessment and Learning in Knowledge Spaces) delivers precise, qualitative diagnostic assessments of students' knowledge, guides them in the selection of appropriate new study material, and records their progress toward mastery of curricular goals in a robust classroom management system.

ALEKS interacts with the student much as a skilled human tutor would, moving between explanation and practice as needed, correcting and analyzing errors, defining terms and chapter topics on request. By sophisticated modeling of a student's knowledge state for a given subject, ALEKS can focus clearly on what the student is most ready to learn next. When students focus on exactly what they are ready to learn, they build confidence and a learning momentum that fuels success.

ALEKS Math Prep for Accounting provides coverage of the basic math skills needed to succeed in introductory *Principles of Accounting,* while ALEKS for the Accounting Cycle provides a detailed, guided overview through every stage of the accounting cycle.

CourseSmart

http://www.coursesmart.com

 With the CourseSmart eTextbook, students can save up to 45 percent of the cost of a print book, reduce their impact on the environment, and access powerful Web tools for learning. CourseSmart is an online eTextbook, which means users access and view their textbook online when connected to the Internet. Students can also print sections of the book for maximum portability. CourseSmart eTextbooks are available in one standard online reader with full text search, notes and highlighting, and e-mail tools for sharing notes between classmates.

Quantum Tutors for the Accounting Cycle
Proven to Increase Test Scores by as Much as 50 percent

 The Quantum Tutors for the Accounting Cycle help tutor students on the fundamental accounting concepts and problem-solving skills needed for principles and financial accounting courses. Just like working with an excellent instructor, students can enter their own work into the software, ask questions, and receive step-by-step feedback at a detailed level not available with any other software or homework management system. The Quantum Tutors are ideal when the student needs immediate help and the instructor is not available to answer questions. Accessed over the Internet, it offers students unlimited, convenient access day or night. It also allows them to study independently at their own pace.

We are happy to help you integrate technology into your course. Please call your local McGraw-Hill representative to learn more.

Instructor Resources

☑ McGraw-Hill's Homework Manager

See page (xviii) for details.

☑ Instructor CD-ROM

ISBN 0073274038

This integrated CD-ROM allows you to access most of the text's ancillary materials. You no longer need to worry about the various supplements that accompany your text. Instead, almost everything is available on one convenient CD-ROM: PowerPoint slides, Solutions Manual, Instructor's Resource Manual, Test Bank, and Computerized Test Bank.

☑ Online Learning Center

www.mhhe.com/LLPW1e
See page (xix) for details.

☑ Solutions Manual

Prepared by Patricia Libby, Robert Libby, Fred Phillips, and Stacey Whitecotton, the manual provides solutions for end-of-chapter questions, mini exercises, exercises, problems, and cases and projects. Available on the Instructor CD-ROM and text Web site.

☑ Test Bank

Prepared by Laura Rickett, Kent State University, and Jay Holmen, University of Wisconsin–Eau Claire, this comprehensive Test Bank includes more than 2,000 true/false and multiple-choice questions, problems, essays, and matching questions. It is available on the Instructor CD-ROM.

☑ Presentation Slides

Prepared by Jon Booker and Charles Caldwell at Tennessee Technological University and Susan Galbreath at David Lipscomb University, this option provides completely customized PowerPoint presentations for use in your classroom. Available on the Instructor CD-ROM and text Web site.

☑ Instructor's Resource Manual

Prepared by J. Lowell Mooney, Georgia Southern University, supplements, including the Financial Accounting Videos, Study Guide, and PowerPoint slides, are topically cross-referenced in the Instructor's Manual to help instructors direct students to specific ancillaries to reinforce key concepts. Available on the Instructor CD-ROM and text Web site.

☑ Algorithmic-Diploma Testbank

ISBN 0073274054

This feature allows you to add and edit questions; create up to 99 versions of each chapter test; attach graphic files to questions; import and export ASCII files; and select questions based on type, level of difficulty, or learning objective. This software provides password protection for saved tests and question databases and can run on a network.

☑ EZ Test

McGraw-Hill's EZ Test is a flexible and easy-to-use electronic testing program that allows instructors to create tests from book-specific items. EZ Test accommodates a wide range of question types and allows instructors to add their own questions. Multiple versions of the test can be created, and any test can be exported for use with course management systems such as BlackBoard/WebCT. EZ Test Online is a new service that gives instructors a place to easily administer EZ Test–created exams and quizzes online. The program is available for Windows and Macintosh environments.

☑ Excel Templates

Available on the text Web site www.mhhe.com/LLPW1e, these templates are tied to selected end-of-chapter material.

☑ Instructor Excel Templates

This feature provides solutions to the student Excel Templates for selected end-of-chapter assignments. Available on the text Web site.

☑ Check Figures

Prepared by Lu Ann Bean, Florida Institute of Technology, it provides key numbers in the solutions to the problems at the end of each chapter. Available on the text Web site.

Student Resources

☑ Online Learning Center

www.mhhe.com/LLPW1e
Practice what you're learning. Lots of free practice problems are online whenever you're ready. Even at 1 A.M.

☑ McGraw-Hill's Homework Manager

See page (xviii) for details.

☑ Working Papers

Volume 1 (Chapters 1–12) 007327397X
Volume 2 (Chapters 12–25) 0073273988
Prepared by Jeannie Folk at College of DuPage, these items contain all of the forms necessary for completing end-of-chapter assignments.

☑ Study Guide

Volume 1 (Chapters 1–12) 0073273929
Volume 2 (Chapters 12–25) 0073273937
Prepared by Jeannie Folk at College of DuPage, this outstanding learning tool gives students a deeper understanding of the course material and reinforces, step by step, what they are learning in the main text.

☑ Check Figures

Available on the text Web site, www.mhhe.com/LLPW1e, check figures provide key numbers in solutions to end-of-chapter material.

☑ iPod Downloadable Content

See below for details.

☑ Excel Templates eXcel

Available on the text Web site www.mhhe.com/LLPW1e, these templates are tied to selected end-of-chapter material.

☑ Carol Yacht's General Ledger and Peachtree

 Carol Yacht's General Ledger Software is McGraw-Hill/Irwin's custom-built general ledger package. Carol Yacht's General Ledger can help you master every aspect of the general ledger, from inputting sales and cash receipts to calculating ratios for analysis or inventory valuations. Carol Yacht's General Ledger allows you to review an entire report and then double-click any single transaction to review or edit it. The report will then be updated on the fly to include the revised figures. When it comes to learning how an individual transaction affects the outcome of an entire report, no other approach matches that of Carol Yacht's General Ledger. Students can use Carol Yacht's General Ledger and Peachtree to solve numerous problems from the textbook.

iPod Downloadable Content

You are holding a media-integrated textbook that provides students portable educational content—just right for those students who want to study when and where it's most convenient for them. *Principles of Accounting* gives students the option to download content for review and study to their Apple® iPods and most other MP3/MP4 devices. iPod icons appear throughout the text pointing students to chapter-specific audio lecture presentation slides and course-related videos.

Quick Reference to iPod Icons

Photo Courtesy of Apple.®

Lectured slideshow–LP3-1
www.mhhe.com/LLPW1e

Lecture presentations available for download to your iPod, Zune, or MP3 device (audio and visual depending on your device)

Video 3-1
www.mhhe.com/LLPW1e

Topical videos available for download to your iPod, Zune, or MP3 (depending on your device)

Quiz 3-1
www.mhhe.com/LLPW1e

Multiple-choice quizzes available for download to your iPod, Zune, or MP3 (depending on your device)

Acknowledgments

Many dedicated instructors have devoted their time and effort to help us develop this text. We would like to acknowledge and thank all of our colleagues who helped guide our decisions. This text would not be what it is without the help of our dedicated contributors:

Reviewers

Alan Applebaum, Broward Community College
Leah Arrington, Northwest Mississippi Community College
Cynthia Ash, Davenport University
Sandy Augustine, Hilbert College
Collin Battle, Broward Community College
LuAnn Bean, Florida Institute of Technology
Sarah Beauchea, Berkeley College
Lisa Bernard, Pearl River Community College
Margaret Black, San Jacinto College
David Bland, Cape Fear Community College
Linda Bolduc, Mount Wachusett Community College
Patrick Borja, Citrus College
Thomas Branton, Alvin Community College
Gregory Brookins, Santa Monica College
Pennye Brown, Austin Peay State University
William P. Burke, Neumann College
Carla Cabarle, Minot State University
Michelle Cannon, Ivy Tech Community College of Indiana
Lloyd Carroll, Borough of Manhattan Community College
Lisa Cole, Johnson County Community College
Joan Cook, Milwaukee Area Technical College
Susan Cordes, Johnson County Community College
Christine Crosby, York Technical College
Judy Daulton, Piedmont Technical College
Passard Dean, Saint Leo University
Larry Dragosavac, Edison Community College
Karla Duckworth, Hinds Community College
Rebecca Evans, Blue Ridge Community College
Mary Falkey, Prince George Community College
John Gabeleman, Columbus State Community College
Patrick Geer, Hawkeye Community College
Gloria Grayless, Sam Houston State University
Joyce Griffin, Kansas City Kansas Community College
Amy Haas, Kingsborough Community College
Betty Harper, Middle Tennessee State University
Jeannie Harrington, Middle Tennessee State University
Paul Harris, Camden Community College
Patricia Holmes, Des Moines Area Community College
Robert Holtfreter, Central Washington University
Audrey Hunter, Broward Community College
Connie Hylton, George Mason University
Phillip Imel, Northern Virginia Community College
Thomas Kam, Hawaii Pacific University
Naomi Karolinski, Monroe Community College
Randy Kidd, Longview Community College
Thomas Knight, Borough of Manhattan Community College
Jerry Krueze, Western Michigan University
David Laurel, South Texas College
Susan Logorda, Lehigh Carbon Community College

Linda Mallory, Central Virginia Community College
Robert Mandau, Piedmont Technical College
Kenneth Mark, Kansas City Kansas Community College
Cynthia McCall, Des Moines Area Community College
Kevin McFarlane, Front Range Community College
Chris McNamara, Finger Lakes Community College
Shea Mears, Des Moines Area Community College
Terri Meta, Seminole Community College
Tammy Metzke, Milwaukee Area Technical College
Norma Montague, Central Carolina Community College
Karen Mozingo, Pitt Community College
Andrea Murowski, Brookdale Community College
Seved Noorian, Wentworth Institute of Technology
Shelly Ota, Leeward Community College
Carol Pace, Grayson Community College
Susan Pallas, Southeast Community College
Gregory L. Prescott, University of South Alabama
Timothy Prindle, Des Moines Area Community College
LaVonda Ramey, Schoolcraft College
Jenny Resnick, Santa Monica College
Carla Rich, Pensacola Junior College
Eric Rothenburg, Kingsborough Community College
Gary Rupp, SUNY–Farmingdale
Marcia Sandvold, Des Moines Area Community College
Richard Sarkisian, Camden Community College
Mona Seiler, Queensborough Community College
James Shimko, Sinclair Community College
Jay Siegel, Union County College
Alice Sineath, Forsyth Technical Community College
Lois Slutsky, Broward Community College–South Campus
Daniel Small, J. Sergeant Reynolds Community College
Robert Smolin, Citrus College
Laura Solano, Pueblo Community College
Laurel Stevenson, Seminole Community College
Janice Stoudemire, Midlands Technical College
Lynette Teal, Western Wisconsin Technical College
Lynda Thompson, Massasoit Community College
Judith Toland, Buck County Community College
Shafi Ullah, Broward Community College
Ski Vanderlaan, Delta College
Patricia Walczak, Lansing Community College
Scott Wallace, Blue Mountain Community College
Shane Warrick, Southern Arkansas University
Jack Wiehler, San Joaquin Delta College
Terrence Willyard, Baker College

TACTYC Focus Group Attendees (May 2006)

Patricia Walczak, Lansing Community College
Amy Haas, Kingsborough Community College
Mary Falkey, Prince George's Community College
Kenneth, Mark, Kansas City Kansas Community College
Allen Applebaum, Broward Community College
Audrey Hunter, Broward Community College
Scott Wallace, Blue Mountain Community College
Carla Rich, Pensacola Junior College
Marcia Sandvold, Des Moines Area Community College

TACTYC Focus Group Attendees (May 2007)

Amy Haas, Kingsborough Community College
Mary Falkey, Prince George Community College
Scott Wallace, Blue Mountain Community College
Patricia Holmes, Des Moines Area Community College
Ski Vanderlaan, Delta College
Lisa Cole, Johnson County Community College
Marcia Sandvold, Des Moines Area Community College

TACTYC Focus Group Attendees (May 2008)

Stanley Chapteru, Borough of Manhattan Community College
Paul Shinal, Cayuga Community College
Lois Slutsky, Broward Community College
Joan Cook, Milwaukee Area Technical College
John Gabelman, Columbus State Community College
Mary Halford, Prince George's Community College
Patty Holmes, Des Moines Area Community College
Marcia Sandvold, Des Moines Area Community College
Harvey Man, Manhattan Community College
Ron Dougherty, Tech Community College–Columbus
Natasha Librizzi, Milwaukee Area Technical College
Mary Falkey, Prince George's Community College
Melvin Williams, College of the Mainland
Carol Hutchinson, Asheville Buncombe Technical College

Principles of Accounting Symposium Attendees (March 2008)

Beverly Beatty, Anne Arundel Community College
George Bernard, Seminole Community College
Carla Cabarle, Minot State University
Chapterris Crosby, York Technical College
Steve Doster, Shawnee State University
Robert Dunlevy, Montgomery County Community College
Richard Fredericsk, Lasell College
John Gabelman, Columbus State Community College
Gloria Grayless, Sam Houston State University
Jeannie Harrington, Middle Tennessee State University
William Herd, Springfield Technical Community College
Susan Logorda, Lehigh Carbon Community College
Cathryn Nash, Dekalb Technical College
LaVonda Ramey, Schoolcraft College
Pamela Strysick, Broward Community College
Mario Tripaldi, Hudson County Community College
David Verduzco, University of Texas at Austin

Design Reviewers (WebEx, November 2007)

Paul Harris, Camden Community College
Audrey Hunter, Broward County Community College
Amy Haas, Kingsborough Community College
Kevin McFarlane, Front Range Community College
Patrick Geer, Hawkeye Community College
Patricia Holmes, Des Moines Area Community College
Sandra Augustine, Hilbert College

David Bland, Cape Fear Community College
David Laurel, South Texas College
Hoossein Noorian, Wentworth Institute of Technology
Margaret Black, San Jacinto College
Terri Meta, Seminole Community College
Lynda Thompson, Massasoit Community College
Jeannie Harrington, Middle Tennessee State University
John Gabelman, Columbus State Community College
Thomas Kam, Hawaii Pacific University
Tammy Metzke, Milwaukee Area Technical College
Chris McNamara, Finger Lakes Community College
Constance Hylton, George Mason University
Tom Branton, Alvin Community College
Lisa Cole, Johnson County Community College
Lois Slutksy, Broward Community College
Shane Warrick, South Arkansas University

We are grateful to the following individuals who helped develop, critique, and shape the text and ancillary package: Cheryl Bartlett, Central New Mexico Community College; Jeannie Folk, College of DuPage; Kimberly Temme, Maryville University of Saint Louis; Angela Sandberg, Jacksonville State University; Patricia Holmes, Des Moines Area Community College; LuAnn Bean, Florida Technical Institute; Beth Woods, Accuracy Counts; Laura Rickett, Kent State University; J. Lowell Mooney, Georgia Southern University; Rada Brooks, University of California–Berkeley; Jay Holmen, University of Wisconsin–Eau Claire; Susan Galbreath, David Lipscomb University; Jon Booker, Tennessee Technological University; Charles Caldwell, Tennessee Technological University; Matthew Muller, Adirondack Community College, Carol Yacht; Jack Terry, ComSource Associates, Inc.; and James Aitken, Central Michigan University.

Special thanks to Alan Cohen, Ithaca College, and John Gabelman, Columbus State Community College, and their Principles of Accounting Students, for class testing.

Last, we thank a talented group of individuals at McGraw-Hill/Irwin whose extraordinary efforts made all of this come together. We would especially like to thank our editorial director, Stewart Mattson; Tim Vertovec, our publisher; Alice Harra, our sponsoring editor; Kimberly Hooker, our developmental editor; Sankha Basu, our marketing manager; Mary Conzachi, our project manager; Martha Beyerlein, our freelance project manager; Pam Verros and Cara Hawthorne, our designers; Debra Sylvester, our production supervisor; Susan Lombardi, our media producer; Jeremy Cheshareck, our photo research coordinator; David Tietz, our photo researcher; and Marcy Lunetta, our permission researcher.

Patricia A. Libby
Robert Libby
Fred Philips
Stacey Whitecotton

Assurance of Accuracy

Dear Colleagues,

Accuracy has always been our top priority in producing a textbook. We test every word through your eyes and those of our many professional copy editors, line editors, accuracy checkers, and contributing supplement authors. We have taken every effort to ensure the accuracy of this first edition of *Principles of Accounting* including the following:

- *Three drafts of manuscript*: We wrote and edited the entire manuscript three times, reading each other's chapters and making sure our voices, vocabulary, and pedagogy were consistent throughout.

- *Three rounds of accuracy checking*: Three professional accuracy checkers individually tested every problem at different stages of the production so that you don't have any surprises.

- *Two rounds of professional line editing*: A large investment was made to ensure consistency of voice and appropriate reading level.

- *Two hundred and sixty reviews:* Detailed reviews of every chapter from principles instructors around the country were compiled, synthesized, studied, and acted upon during each draft of our manuscript.

- *Forty* students participated in a class test of Chapters 1–4.

- *Thirty-six* members at three different conferences of Teachers of Accounting at Two-Year Colleges participated in focus groups held in 2006 (Atlanta), 2007 (Indianapolis), and 2008 (San Antonio) where we spent several hours listening to their advice that helped us shape the content and pedagogy.

- *Twenty-six* faculty attendees of McGraw-Hill's Principles of Accounting Symposium in 2008 (Las Vegas) spent several days discussing the challenges of teaching principles of accounting.

- *Twenty-five* professors served as design reviewers via WebEx to critique the design and overall visual appeal of the text and challenged us to help their students with a book that says "You can do it!" through its design.

All of our editorial advisers, reviewers, and attendees are listed on page xxii.

You and your students can be assured that our dedication and commitment to producing an error-free text has gone into every page of *Principles of Accounting*.

| Patricia Libby | Robert Libby | Fred Phillips | Stacey Whitecotton |

To Our Students and Readers: Advice on How to Read Your Textbook

Dear Students,

The following advice is generated from an in-depth study of 172 undergraduate students of varying backgrounds, all of whom were enrolled in an introductory accounting course.

- **Read the chapters to learn rather than just to get through them.** Learning doesn't miraculously occur just because your eyes have skimmed all the assigned lines of the textbook. You have to think and focus while reading to ensure that you sink the material into your understanding and memory. Use the learning objectives in the text to focus on what's really important in each chapter.

- **Don't get discouraged if you initially find some material challenging to learn.** At various times, both the best and weakest students describe themselves as "confused" and "having a good grasp of the material," "anxious" and "confident," and "overwhelmed" and "comfortable." The simple fact is that learning new material can be challenging and initially confusing. Success doesn't appear to depend as much on whether you become confused as it does on what you do when you become confused.

- **Clear up confusion as it arises.** A key difference between the most and least successful students is how they respond to difficulty and confusion. When successful students are confused or anxious, they immediately try to enhance their understanding through rereading, self-testing, and seeking outside help if necessary. In contrast, unsuccessful students try to reduce anxiety by delaying further reading or by resorting to memorizing without understanding. Aim to clear up confusion when it arises because accounting in particular is a subject for which your understanding of later material depends on your understanding of earlier material.

- **Think of reading as the initial stage of studying.** Abandon the idea that "studying" occurs only during the final hours before an exam. By initially reading with the same intensity that occurs during later reviews for an exam, you can create extra time for practicing exercises and problems. This combination of concentrated reading and extensive practice is likely to contribute to better learning and superior exam scores.

To learn more about the study on which this advice is based, see B. J. Phillips and F. Phillips, "Sink or Skim: Textbook Reading Behaviors of Introductory Accounting Students," *Issues in Accounting Education* 22 (February 2007), pp. 21–44.

Brief Table of Contents

Chapter 12   **Partnerships**   504

Chapter 13   **Accounting for Corporations**   558

Chapter 14   **Long-Term Liabilities**   598

Chapter 15   **Accounting for Investments**   640

Chapter 16   **Reporting and Interpreting the Statement of Cash Flows**   680

Chapter 17   **Financial Statement Analysis**   728

Chapter 18   **Managerial Accounting**   764

Chapter 19   **Job Order Costing**   798

Chapter 20   **Process Costing and Activity Based Costing**   840

Chapter 21   **Cost Behavior and Cost-Volume-Profit Analysis**   882

Chapter 22   **Incremental Analysis and Capital Budgeting**   918

Chapter 23   **Budgetary Planning**   956

Chapter 24   **Budgetary Control**   986

Chapter 25   **Decentralized Performance Evaluation**   1026

Appendix A   A-1

Appendix B   B-1

Appendix C   C-1

Appendix D   D-1

Glossary   G-1

Credits   PC-1

Business Index   I-1

Subject Index   I-4

Table of Contents

Chapter **12**

Partnerships 504

BLOOM'N FLOWERS 505

Partnerships Compared to Similar Organizations 506
Characteristics of Partnerships 506
Similar Forms of Business 507

Accounting for Partnerships 509
Formation: Recording Cash and Noncash Contributions 509
Division of Income (or Loss): Four Methods 511
Preparation of Financial Statements 516

Changes of Ownerships in a Partnership 517
Admission of a Partner 517
Withdrawal of a Partner 521
Death of Partner 525

Liquidation of a Partnership 526
No Capital Deficiency 527
Capital Deficiency 529

Ratio Analysis 533
Partner Return on Equity 533

Demonstration Case A 534
Demonstration Case B 536
Demonstration Case C 538
Demonstration Case D 539
Chapter Summary 539
Key Terms 541
Questions 541
Multiple Choice 541
Mini Exercises 542
Exercises 545
Problems—Set A 549
Problems—Set B 552
Cases and Projects 555

Chapter **13**

Accounting for Corporations 558

SONIC CORP. 559

Characteristics of the Corporate Form 560
Ownership 560
Laws and Taxes 560
Formation 561
Financing 562

Accounting for Stock Transactions 562
Common and Preferred Stock 563
Treasury Stock 565
Financial Statement Reporting 567

Accounting for Dividends and Splits 568
Cash Dividends on Common Stock 568
Cash Dividends on Preferred Stock 570
Stock Dividends 572
Stock Splits 573
Statement of Retained Earnings 574

Financial Ratio Analysis 575
Earnings per Share (EPS) 576
Price/Earnings (P/E) Ratio 577

Demonstration Case A 577
Demonstration Case B 579
Chapter Summary 580
Key Terms 580
Questions 581
Multiple Choice 581
Mini Exercises 582
Exercises 584
Problems—Set A 590
Problems—Set B 593
Cases and Projects 595

Chapter 14

Long-Term Liabilities 598

GENERAL MILLS, INC. 599

Long-Term Liabilities 600
Making Financing Decisions 600
Measuring Liabilities 600

Accounting for Long-Term Liabilities 601
Discounted Notes 601
Bonds Payable 604
Lease Liabilities 610

Analyzing Long-Term Liabilities 611
Debt-to-Assets Ratio 611
Times Interest Earned Ratio 612

Demonstration Case A 613
Demonstration Case B 614
Demonstration Case C 615
Supplement 14A: Discounting Future Payments 616
Supplement 14B: Effective-Interest Method of Amortization 619
Supplement 14C: Straight-Line Method of Amortization 622
Chapter Summary 623
Key Terms 624
Questions 625
Multiple Choice 625
Mini Exercises 626
Exercises 628
Problems—Set A 631
Problems—Set B 634
Cases and Projects 637

Chapter 15

Accounting for Investments 640

THE WASHINGTON POST COMPANY 641

An Overview 642
Reasons Companies Invest 642

Identifying Investment Types and Accounting Methods 643

Accounting for Passive Investments 644
Debt Investments Held to Maturity: Amortized Cost Method 644

Investments in Stock of Significant Influence 645
Investments in Stock for Control 645
Securities Available for Sale: Market Value Method 646
Comparison of Available-for-Sale and Trading Securities 650

Accounting for Influential Investments 654
Investments for Significant Influence: Equity Method 654
Investments with Controlling Interests: Consolidated Statements 658

Evaluating Total Invested Capital 660
Return on Assets (ROA) 660
Comparison to Benchmarks 660

Demonstration Case A 661
Demonstration Case B 662
Demonstration Case C 663
Chapter Summary 664
Key Terms 665
Questions 665
Multiple Choice 666
Mini Exercises 667
Exercises 668
Problems—Set A 671
Problems—Set B 674
Cases and Projects 677

Chapter 16

Reporting and Interpreting the Statement of Cash Flows 680

NAUTILUS INC. 681

Classifications of the Statement of Cash Flows 682
The Relationship between Business Activities and Cash Flows 682
Cash Flows from Operating Activities 683
Cash Flows from Investing Activities 684
Cash Flows from Financing Activities 684

Net Increase (Decrease) in Cash   684

Relationships to the Balance Sheet and Income Statement   685

Reporting Cash Flows from Operating Activities—Indirect Method   687

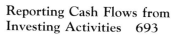

Depreciation and Gains and Losses on Sale of Long-Term Assets   689

Changes in Current Assets and Current Liabilities   689

Reporting Cash Flows from Investing Activities   693

Plant and Equipment   693

Land and Investments   694

Reporting Cash Flows from Financing Activities   694

Long-Term Debt   694

Contributed Capital   694

Retained Earnings   694

Preparing and Evaluating the Statement of Cash Flows   696

Format for the Statement of Cash Flows   696

Noncash Investing and Financing Activities   696

Supplemental Cash Flow Information   698

Free Cash Flow   698

Quality of Income Ratio   698

Demonstration Case A: Indirect Method   699

Supplement 16A: Reporting Cash Flows from Operating Activities—Direct Method   700

Demonstration Case B: Direct Method (Supplement A)   704

Supplement 16B: Spreadsheet Approach: Indirect Method   705

Chapter Summary   707

Key Terms   707

Questions   708

Multiple Choice   708

Mini Exercises   709

Exercises   712

Problems—Set A   719

Problems—Set B   721

Cases and Projects   723

Chapter **17**

Financial Statement Analysis   728

LOWE'S   729

Release of Financial Information   730

Preliminary Press Release   730

Quarterly and Annual Reports   730

Securities and Exchange Commission (SEC) Filings   731

Investor Information Web Sites   731

Horizontal (Trend) Analysis   732

Preparing Comparative Balance Sheets and Comparative Income Statements   732

Revealing Changes through Trend Analyses   732

Vertical (Common Size) Analysis   734

Preparing a Common Size Balance Sheet and Income Statement   735

Interpreting Common Size Statements   735

Financial Ratios   736

Profitability Ratios   736

Liquidity Ratios   740

Solvency Ratios   742

Accounting Decisions and Ratio Analysis   744

Demonstration Case   745

Supplement 17A: Nonrecurring and Other Special Items   746

Chapter Summary   747

Key Terms   747

Questions   747

Multiple Choice   747

Mini Exercises   748

Exercises   749

Problems—Set A   755

Problems—Set B   758

Cases and Projects   761

Chapter **18**

Managerial Accounting   764

TOMBSTONE PIZZA   765

Role of Managerial Accounting in Organizations   766

Decision-Making Orientation   766

Comparison of Financial and Managerial
Accounting   766

Functions of Management   767

Cost Classifications and Definitions   769

Definition of Cost   769

Out-of-Pocket versus
Opportunity Costs   770

Direct versus Indirect
Costs   770

Variable versus Fixed
Costs   771

Relevant versus
Irrelevant Costs   772

Manufacturing versus
Nonmanufacturing
Costs   772

Product versus Period Costs   773

**Costs in Manufacturing versus Nonmanufacturing
Firms   773**

Balance Sheets of Merchandising versus
Manufacturing Firms   775

Cost of Goods Manufactured Report   775

Income Statements of Merchandising versus
Manufacturing Firms   776

Demonstration Case   778

Chapter Summary   781

Key Terms   782

Questions   782

Multiple Choice   783

Mini Exercises   784

Exercises   789

Problems—Set A   791

Problems—Set B   793

Cases and Projects   796

Chapter **19**

Job Order Costing   798

TOLL BROTHERS INC.   799

Job Order versus Process Costing   800

Process Costing   800

Job Order Costing   801

Assignment of Manufacturing Costs to Jobs   801

Manufacturing Cost Categories   801

Materials Requisition Form   802

Direct Labor Time Tickets   803

Job Cost Sheet   803

Predetermined Overhead Rates   804

Journal Entries for Job Order Costing   806

Recording the Purchase and Issue of Materials   807

Recording Labor Costs   808

Recording Actual Manufacturing Overhead   809

Recording Applied Manufacturing Overhead   809

Transferring Costs to Finished Goods Inventory
and Cost of Goods Sold   811

Recording Nonmanufacturing Costs   812

**Overapplied or Underapplied Manufacturing
Overhead   812**

Calculating Overapplied and Underapplied
Overhead   812

Disposing of Overapplied or Underapplied
Overhead   813

Calculating Cost of Goods Manufactured and Cost
of Goods Sold   815

Demonstration Case   816

Chapter Summary   818

Key Terms   819

Questions   819

Multiple Choice   820

Mini Exercises   821

Exercises   823

Problems—Set A   828

Problems—Set B   832

Cases and Projects   835

Chapter **20**

Process Costing and Activity Based Costing   840

CK MONDAVI FAMILY VINYARDS   841

Basic Concepts in Process Costing   842

Job Order versus Process Costing   842

Flow of Costs in Process Costing   843

Journal Entries for Process Costing   844

Process Costing Production Report   849

Step 1: Reconcile the Number of Physical Units   850

Step 2: Translate Physical Units into Equivalent
Units   851

Step 3: Calculate Cost per Equivalent Unit   853

Step 4: Reconcile the Total Cost
of Work in Process   854

Step 5: Prepare a Production Report   855

Additional Factors in Process Costing   855

Activity Based Costing (ABC)   856

Step 1: Identify and Classify Activities   858

Step 2: Form Activity Cost Pools and Assign Indirect
Cost to Each Pool   858

Step 3: Select an Activity Cost Driver and Calculate
an Activity Rate for Each Cost Pool   859

Step 4: Assign Costs to Products or Services Based on
Their Activity Demands   860

Demonstration Case A (Process Costing)   862

Demonstration Case B (Activity Based Costing)   863

Supplement 20A: Weighted Average Method   865

Chapter Summary   869

Key Terms   870

Questions   870

Multiple Choice   871

Mini Exercises   872

Exercises   873

Problems—Set A   876

Problems—Set B   878

Cases and Projects   880

Chapter **21**

Cost Behavior and Cost-Volume-Profit Analysis   882

STARBUCKS COFFEE   883

Cost Behavior Patterns   884

Relevant Range   884

Variable Costs   884

Fixed Costs   884

Step Costs   885

Mixed Costs   886

**Estimating Cost
Behavior   887**

Preparing a
Scattergraph   887

Linear Approaches
to Analyzing Mixed
Costs   889

Contribution Margin   892

Contribution Margin Income Statement   892

Contribution Margin Formula   893

Unit Contribution Margin   893

Contribution Margin Ratio   893

Cost-Volume-Profit Analysis   894

Assumption of Cost-Volume-Profit   894

Break-Even Analysis   895

Margin of Safety   896

Target Profit Analysis   897

Cost-Volume-Profit Relationships
in Graphic Form   898

Multiproduct Cost-Volume-Profit Analysis   899

Demonstration Case   900

Supplement 21A   901

Chapter Summary   904

Key Terms   905

Questions   906

Multiple Choice   906

Mini Exercises   907

Exercises   909

Problems—Set A   911

Problems—Set B   913

Cases and Projects   915

Chapter **22**

Incremental Analysis and Capital Budgeting   918

MATTEL TOYS   919

Managerial Decision Making Process   920

Step 1: Identify the Decision to Be Made   920

Step 2: Determine the Decision Alternatives   920

Step 3: Evaluate the Costs and Benefits
of the Alternatives   921

Step 4: Make the Decision   921

Step 5: Review the Results of the Decision-Making
Process   922

Relevant versus Irrelevant Costs and Benefits   922

Relevant Costs   922

Irrelevant Costs   922

Incremental Analysis of Short-Term Decisions   923

Special-Order Decisions   923

Make-or-Buy Decisions   925

Keep-or-Drop Decisions   928

Sell-or-Process Further Decisions   930

Capital Budgeting for Long-Term Investment Decisions   931

Nondiscounting Methods   932

Discounted Cash Flow Methods   934

Demonstration Case A   937

Demonstration Case B   938

Chapter Summary   939

Key Terms   940

Questions   940

Multiple Choice   941

Mini Exercises   942

Exercises   944

Problems—Set A   948

Problems—Set B   950

Cases and Projects   953

Chapter **23**

Budgetary Planning   956

COLD STONE CREAMERY   957

Role of Budgets in the Planning and Control Cycles   958

Planning Process   959

Benefits of Budgeting   959

Behavioral Effects of Budgets   960

Components of the Master Budget   962

Preparation of the Operating Budget   964

Sales Budget   964

Production Budget   964

Raw Materials Purchases Budget   965

Direct Labor Budget   966

Manufacturing Overhead Budget   967

Budgeted Cost of Goods Sold   967

Selling and Administrative Expense Budget   968

Budgeted Income Statement   968

Preparation of the Financial Budgets   970

Cash Budget   970

Budgeted Balance Sheet   971

Budgeting in a Merchandising Company   972

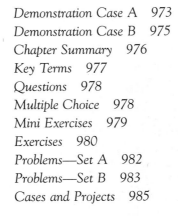

Demonstration Case A   973

Demonstration Case B   975

Chapter Summary   976

Key Terms   977

Questions   978

Multiple Choice   978

Mini Exercises   979

Exercises   980

Problems—Set A   982

Problems—Set B   983

Cases and Projects   985

Chapter **24**

Budgetary Control   986

COLD STONE CREAMERY   987

Standard Cost Systems   988

Ideal versus Attainable Standards   988

Types of Standard   988

Standard Cost Card   989

Favorable versus Unfavorable Variances   989

Use of Flexible Budgets to Calculate Cost Variances   990

Master Budgets versus Flexible Budgets   990

Flexible Budget as a Benchmark   992

Volume Variance versus Spending Variance   992

Direct Material and Direct Labor Variances   993

Variance Framework   993

Direct Materials Variances   994

Direct Labor Variances   996

Manufacturing Overhead Cost Variances   998

Variable Manufacturing Overhead Variances   998

Fixed Manufacturing Overhead Variances   1001

Summary of Variances   1003

Demonstration Case   1005

Supplement 24A: Recording Standard Costs and Variances in a Standard Cost System   1008

Chapter Summary   1012

Key Terms   1013

Questions   1013

Multiple Choice   1013

Mini Exercises   1014

Exercises   1015

Problems—Set A   1018

Problems—Set B   1021

Cases and Projects   1023

Chapter 25

Decentralized Performance Evaluation 1026

BLOCKBUSTER 1027

Decentralization of Responsibility 1028
Responsibility Centers   1030
Cost Centers   1030
Revenue Centers   1031
Profit Centers   1031
Investment Centers   1032

Evaluation of Investment Center Performance 1034
Return on Investment (ROI)   1034
Residual Income   1036
Return on Investment versus Residual Income   1038
Limitations of Financial Performance Measures   1038
Balanced Scorecard   1039

Transfer Pricing 1040
Market-Price Method   1041
Cost-Based Method   1042
Negotiation   1042

Demonstration Case   1043
Chapter Summary   1044
Key Terms   1045
Questions   1046
Multiple Choice   1046
Mini Exercises   1047
Exercises   1048
Problems—Set A   1050
Problems—Set B   1052
Cases and Projects   1054

Appendix A   A-1
Appendix B   B-1
Appendix C   C-1
Appendix D   D-1
Glossary   G-1
Credits   PC-1
Business Index   I-1
Subject Index   I-4

PRINCIPLES OF
Accounting

12 Partnerships

LEARNING OBJECTIVES

After completing this chapter, you should be able to:

LO1 Compare the partnership form of business with other forms.

LO2 Demonstrate how to account for partnerships.

LO3 Demonstrate the proper treatment for changes of ownership in a partnership.

LO4 Demonstrate the proper treatment for the liquidation of a partnership.

LO5 Calculate and interpret the partner return on equity ratio.

Lectured presentations–12-1
www.mhhe.com/LLPW1e

Focus Company: BLOOM 'N FLOWERS

Fabulously Fresh Flowers.

Perhaps the single most important decision the owners of a new business face is determining the appropriate form of the business. At one time, owners could choose from only three basic forms of business: corporation, general partnership, and sole proprietorship. These forms of business are still used today, but numerous others are now available. As a result, choosing the proper business form has become an increasingly complex decision requiring future owners to wade through mountains of information. Enlisting the services of a CPA or knowledgeable attorney in making this decision is highly advisable.

In this chapter, we investigate the advantages and disadvantages of two forms of business, the general partnership and a newer form called the limited liability company (LLC). We do so by following the story of Hal Flowers and Dawn Bloom, two friends who decided to start a business together.

Hal Flowers and Dawn Bloom both sold flowers to individuals and businesses in their respective neighborhoods. They wished to expand their customer base by moving their business into a large mall located in the center of the city. Because neither had the resources or the time to run a business this large by themselves, they decided to combine their resources and form a new business—Bloom 'N Flowers. The new business would serve more customers and carry a larger inventory of fresh cut flowers than was previously possible when operating separately as sole proprietors.

Hal and Dawn knew that their most important decision would be the form of business they chose for their enterprise. After doing a bit of research, they narrowed the choice to three possibilities: the general partnership, the limited liability company, and the S-corporation.

PARTNERSHIPS COMPARED TO SIMILAR ORGANIZATIONS	ACCOUNTING FOR PARTNERSHIPS	CHANGES OF OWNERSHIP IN A PARTNERSHIP	LIQUIDATION OF A PARTNERSHIP	RATIO ANALYSIS
• Characteristics of Partnerships • Similar Forms of Business	• Formation: Recording Cash and Noncash Contributions • Division of Income (or Loss): Four Methods • Preparation of Financial Statements	• Admission of a Partner • Withdrawal of a Partner • Death of a Partner	• No Capital Deficiency • Capital Deficiency	• Partner Return on Equity

PARTNERSHIPS COMPARED TO SIMILAR ORGANIZATIONS

Learning Objective 1

Compare the partnership form of business with other forms.

Because Hal and Dawn had little or no knowledge of the options available to them, they did some quick research. The two learned that each form of business has specific characteristics.

Characteristics of Partnerships

The Uniform Partnership Act defines partnership as "the association of two or more persons to carry on as co-owners of a business for profit, whether or not the persons intend to form a partnership." Because partnerships are so easy to form—no formal contract is required—this form of business has the greatest potential for disputes and lawsuits. **To prevent misunderstandings among partners, having a formal** partnership agreement, **preferably drafted by a lawyer, is advisable.**

Hal and Dawn decided to evaluate the partnership by listing its advantages and disadvantages. Later, they would weigh them against the advantages and disadvantages of other forms of business before deciding on the appropriate form for their own business.

Advantages of the Partnership

- **Pass-through taxation.** Profits from the business flow directly through to the partners' personal tax returns rather than being taxed first at the partnership level.
- **Ease of formation.** Partnerships are relatively easy and inexpensive to establish. In fact, some partnerships may be formed inadvertently through a handshake or a simple "OK."
- **Simplified recordkeeping.** No annual meetings are required and there are few recordkeeping requirements.
- **Favorable taxation.** Most small business partnerships receive favorable tax treatment and often do not have to pay the minimum taxes required of other business forms.
- **Increased ability to raise funds.** Generally, the more people involved in a business, the greater their collective ability to raise funds.

Disadvantages of the Partnership

- **Unlimited liability.** Business partners (both individually and as a group) are liable for all legal and financial obligations of the partnership.
- **Co-ownership of property.** Profits must be shared with the other partners.
- **Limited life.** A partnership ends when a partner dies or withdraws from the business.
- **Mutual agency.** Individual partners bear responsibility for the actions of all other partners.
- **Partner disagreements.** Poorly organized partnerships and those formed orally are susceptible to disputes among owners.

Clearly, a partnership has both significant benefits and serious drawbacks. The unlimited personal liability that each general partner bears for the legal and financial obligations of the business is especially important. Hal and Dawn realized that if they chose to form a partnership, they would need to develop a formal partnership agreement. Exhibit 12.1 lists the most important concerns to address in a partnership agreement.

Exhibit 12.1   **Essential Elements of a Partnership Agreement**

- Type of business
- Amount of equity invested by each partner
- Method for sharing profits and losses
- Partners' pay/compensation
- Distribution of assets on dissolution

- Provisions for changes to or dissolution of the partnership
- Provisions for settlement of disputes
- Settlement on death or incapacitation of partners
- Restrictions on partners' authority and expenditures
- Length of partnership's life

Similar Forms of Business

After the two friends gained a good understanding of the advantages and disadvantages of partnerships, they were ready to consider the other forms of business that interested them. They decided to look at one of the newest forms of business, the limited liability company.

Limited Liability Companies

The limited liability company (LLC) is a relatively new form of business organization created by state legislatures. Because this form of business is primarily state controlled, the laws regarding its formation, fees, and so on vary from state to state.

The LLC combines the most attractive features of a corporation with the best features of the partnership, creating a kind of hybrid business form. As the name suggests, it offers protection to members (owners of the LLC) against personal liability for company debts and other obligations. However, its formation is more complex and formal than that of a general partnership. The primary characteristics of the LLC follow.

> **Coach's Tip**
>
> Although some people mistakenly refer to an LLC as a limited liability corporation, the correct term is limited liability company.

Advantages of the Limited Liability Company

- **Limited liability.** If the LLC is properly structured and managed, each member's personal assets will be protected from lawsuits and judgments against the business. Thus, each member's liability is limited to the assets he or she has invested in the company. This statement is true even for owners who participate in the LLC's management.

- **Ease of formation.** An LLC is easier to form than a corporation. Rules regarding the formation of an LLC differ from state to state, but setting one up typically requires only one or two documents. First, every state requires the LLC to file its articles of organization and pay any required fees. The articles of organization set out important details such as the business name, purpose, and operating structure. Because of its importance, this document should be drawn up by a lawyer. A few states require a second document, an operating agreement. It helps to define the LLC's ownership, member responsibilities, and profit sharing. Much like a partnership agreement, it can be invaluable in the event of disagreements among members and is strongly recommended even if the state does not require it.

- **Simplified recordkeeping.** LLCs are not required to hold an annual meeting, keep formal minutes, record resolutions, or observe many other formalities required of corporations. However, they do require more paperwork than partnerships.

- **Favorable taxation.** If an LLC has only one member, the IRS automatically treats it as a sole proprietorship. Similarly, an LLC with multiple members is taxed by default as a partnership. Normal business expenses may be deducted from an LLC's profits before profits are allocated to members for tax purposes. Members report their share of the LLC's profits and losses on their personal tax returns. This arrangement, referred to as pass-through taxation, allows the business to avoid the double taxation to which corporations are subject. (Double taxation occurs when a corporation pays taxes on its corporate profits and then the individual owners pay taxes on any corporate profits distributed to them in the form of dividends. That is, the same profits are taxed twice, once at the corporate level and again at the personal level.)

- **Flexibility of operations.** An LLC allows members to allocate profits and losses as they see fit, to have great flexibility regarding the number of members, to elect to be managed as a partnership or as a corporation, and to admit new members or modify its membership and investment structure with ease.

Disadvantages of the Limited Liability Company

- **Limited corporate characteristics.** LLCs must not have more than two of the four favorable characteristics that define corporations, or they risk being taxed as a corporation. These characteristics are (1) owners' liability limited to business assets, (2) continuity of life, (3) centralization of (nonowner) management, and (4) free transferability of ownership interests.
- **Limited life.** LLCs dissolve with the death, incapacitation, bankruptcy, retirement, resignation, or expulsion of any member.
- **Lack of legal precedents.** Predicting how an LLC will be treated in the courts may be difficult. To date, relatively few legal cases have involved LLCs. However, as time goes on and LLCs become increasingly common, this disadvantage will become less significant.

Because of its long list of advantages and relatively few disadvantages, the LLC form has become a favorite choice among businesses that meet the following criteria:

- The business has one to three members.
- All members are active participants in a small local business.
- The business has no plans for significant growth.
- The business has no foreseeable need to raise significant amounts of capital.

S-Corporations

An S-corporation is a corporation with 1 to 100 shareholders that passes income (or loss) to shareholders, who are taxed at the individual shareholder level. This is a significant difference from a regular corporation, which is subject to double taxation. S-corporations enjoy many of the benefits of partnerships and LLCs, but the state requirements for forming a corporation, electing to be taxed as an S-corporation, and completing annual filings are complex and time consuming. Because of these complexities and required formalities, Dawn and Hal quickly discarded this form of business as a viable option. To compare the features of the two remaining forms of business, they set up the table in Exhibit 12.2.

Exhibit 12.2   Characteristics of Partnerships and LLCs

Characteristic	Partnership	Limited Liability Company
Ease of formation and recordkeeping	Less difficult	More difficult
Setup costs	Medium to high	High
Limited liability	No, unless limited partnership	Yes
Annual meetings	Recommended, not required	Recommended, not required
Limited life	Yes*	Yes
Corporate tax treatment permitted	No	Yes
Partnership tax treatment permitted	Yes, automatic	Yes, when there are two or more members
Annual state filings and fees	Almost never	Yes
Uniform state laws governing entity	Very little variation in laws	Moderate variation in laws

* Partnerships can appear to achieve unlimited lives if new partners are admitted as old partners exit, but technically these changes cause the dissolution of the existing partnership.

After careful consideration, the two friends decided to form a general partnership. Although the features of an LLC sounded great, they did not think they could limit themselves to only two of the four characteristics of a corporation, and they did not want to invest a lot of time and money in forming their business.

Indicate whether each of the following is a true (T) or false (F) statement regarding partnerships and other forms of business.

1. The partnership agreement is a required document; you will be unable to register your partnership without a properly documented partnership agreement. _____
2. A limited liability company must not have more than three of the four characteristics that define corporations, or it risks being taxed as a corporation. _____
3. One disadvantage of both partnerships and LLCs is pass-through taxation. _____
4. Because of its long list of disadvantages and relatively few advantages, the LLC is rarely the business form of choice for new businesses. _____
5. One disadvantage of the LLC is that it is subject to double taxation. _____

After you have finished, check your answers with the solution at the bottom of the page.

ACCOUNTING FOR PARTNERSHIPS

Because a partnership is a pass-through entity, each partner reports his or her share of the partnership's income (or loss) as an individual. In this respect, the accounting treatment is very much like that of a sole proprietorship. The only real difference is that the partners must determine how to divide the partnership's income (or loss) among themselves. To keep track of this information, accounting for a partnership requires:

1. A capital account for each partner.
2. A drawing account for each partner.
3. The allocation of the partnership's income (or loss) to each partner according to the terms of the partnership agreement.

Learning Objective 2

Demonstrate how to account for partnerships.

As we noted earlier, any new partnership is strongly encouraged to create a formal partnership agreement. Hal and Dawn took this recommendation seriously and asked a lawyer to draw up their partnership agreement. While they were discussing the agreement, the attorney spoke with them about some other matters including how to account for the formation of their partnership, how to allocate the partnership's income (or loss), and how to prepare the partnership's financial statements.

Formation: Recording Cash and Noncash Contributions

When a partnership is formed, the partners can invest any combination of assets and/or liabilities in it. Because both Hal and Dawn had sole proprietorships before forming their partnership, each contributed assets from the "proprietorships" as well as cash. Hal's entire investment in the partnership consisted of cash and accounts receivable; Dawn's included cash and equipment. The partnership did not take on liabilities from the sole proprietorships.

When a partner invests cash in a partnership, that partner's capital account is credited for the amount invested. Other investments are recorded at the fair market value of the assets on the date of transfer to the partnership. Each partner must agree to these assigned values. With

---

1. F—although partnerships may be fraught with disagreements among partners, having a partnership agreement is not required for forming a partnership.
2. F—a limited liability company must not have more than two of the four characteristics that define corporations.
3. F—pass-through taxation is a major advantage of the LLC and partnership forms of business.
4. F—the LLC is often the business form of choice for new businesses because of its long list of advantages and relatively few disadvantages.
5. F—the LLC form of business allows members to avoid double taxation.

Exhibit 12.3   Valuation of Contributed Assets

	BOOK VALUE		MARKET VALUE	
	Hal Flowers	Dawn Bloom	Hal Flowers	Dawn Bloom
Cash	$10,000	$ 9,000	$10,000	$ 9,000
Accounts receivable	3,800		3,800	
Allowance for doubtful accounts			(800)	
Store equipment		10,000		8,000
Accumulated depreciation		(1,000)		
	$13,800	$18,000	$13,000	$17,000

Coach's Tip

To record owner contributions of non-cash assets, use the market value of the assets rather than the book value.

the attorney's help, Hal and Dawn determined and agreed to the market values shown in the two right-hand columns of Exhibit 12.3. Although the table provides both the book values and market values of the contributed assets, **only the market values are used to record the investments.**

Note that the accounts receivable were brought into the partnership at net realizable value (the net amount of cash the partnership expects to collect) by establishing an allowance for doubtful accounts. This account is needed because no one knows which particular customer accounts will not be collected, but experience shows that some portion of the receivables would not be collected. Consequently, the estimated uncollectible portion was deducted from Hal's investment. Finally, note that Dawn's contribution of store equipment did not include the accumulated depreciation from her old business. Instead, its fair market value was used in recording her contribution to the partnership. In essence, the equipment contribution was treated as if the partnership purchased used equipment.

The following journal entries were made to record Hal and Dawn's investments. Once the partners' investments were recorded, the assets were treated just as any other business asset. The receivables were collected, and any uncollectible accounts were written off. At the end of the accounting period, the allowance account was re-evaluated and adjusted accordingly. The equipment was depreciated over its useful life using the method chosen by the partnership.

	Debit	Credit
Cash (+A) ($10,000 + $9,000)	19,000	
Accounts Receivable (+A)	3,800	
Store Equipment (+A)	8,000	
Allowance for Doubtful Accounts (+xA, −A)		800
Hal Flowers, Capital (+OE)		13,000
Dawn Bloom, Capital (+OE)		17,000

Assets		= Liabilities +	Owners' Equity	
Cash ($10,000 + $9,000)	+19,000		Hal Flowers, Capital	+13,000
Accounts Receivable	+3,800		Dawn Bloom, Capital	+17,000
Allowance for Doubtful Accounts (+xA)	−800			
Store Equipment	+8,000			

Division of Income (or Loss): Four Methods

A partnership's income (or loss) is divided according to the partnership agreement. Unfortunately, partners do not always draw up an agreement before forming their business. In such situations, the assumption is that the partners intend to share all profits and losses equally regardless of any oral agreements they may have made. To be legally enforceable, profit and loss allocations must be made in writing. When Hal and Dawn met with their attorney, he told them partners can use one of four methods to allocate income or loss among themselves.

1. **The fixed-ratio method** is often used when partners' initial financial contributions are the same or relatively close. This method bases income and loss allocations primarily on the amount of time each partner expects to devote to the business on a regular basis. For example, if partners expect to work equally, they may agree to split profits and losses equally. In this case, the fixed ratio can be stated in three ways: as a percentage (50 percent to 50 percent), as a proportion (1:1), or as a fraction (½ to ½).

2. **The interest on partners' capital balances method** may appeal to partners who wish to earn a specific return on their investments. This method sets a stated rate of interest partners will receive on their capital account balances; any remaining amounts are allocated on a fixed-ratio basis. This method is especially useful to partners who have invested large sums of cash in the partnership but have very little involvement in the business's day-to-day operations. Essentially, their entire return from the partnership hinges on the balances in their capital accounts.

3. **The salaries to partners method** appeals to partners who spend a great deal of time running the business on a daily basis and the partnership is their primary source of personal income. This method requires that the partners' salaries be distributed first; any remaining income (or loss) is allocated on a fixed-ratio basis.

4. **The salaries to partners and interest on partners' capital balances method** is the most complicated method. It is appropriate when the partners' needs, financial contributions, and time contributions are so diverse that some combination of each of the previous methods is necessary. With this method, the partners receive salaries and earn interest on their capital account balances. Any remaining amounts are allocated to them on a fixed-ratio basis.

Hal and Dawn asked the attorney to show them examples of each of these four allocation methods. The attorney was happy to oblige. **The following examples assume that Hal and Dawn's partnership earned a profit of $10,000 for the year and that Hal withdrew $2,600 from the partnership and Dawn withdrew $1,400.**

Fixed-Ratio Method

Assume that Hal and Dawn decided to share the $10,000 profit according to the fixed proportions of 8:2 (that is, $8 for Hal to every $2 for Dawn). These proportions are based on the relative time and effort each partner planned to contribute to the partnership. When you use proportions as the allocation basis, each partner's individual portion is divided by the total of the partners' numbers (8 + 2 = 10).

Hal's portion of the profit [$10,000 × (8 ÷ 10)]	$ 8,000
Dawn's portion of the profit [$10,000 × (2 ÷ 10)]	2,000
Total profit allocated	$10,000

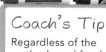

Coach's Tip

Regardless of the method used for the allocation, you should always verify that the amounts allocated to each partner equal the total amount of profit to be distributed.

Regardless of the allocation method used, the partners' capital accounts do not reflect the allocated amounts until the closing entries for the period have been made. The closing process for a partnership is nearly identical to that shown for a sole proprietorship in Chapter 4 on page 164. In this chapter, we assume that all revenues and expenses have been closed and that the net profit (or loss) of the business is now in the Income Summary account. In our example, the partnership had a $10,000 profit, so the Income Summary account needs to be debited and each individual partner's capital account credited for the amount of profit allocated to him or her. The entry to allocate the partnership profits to each partner under the fixed-ratio method follows.

	Debit	Credit
Income Summary (−OE)	10,000	
Hal Flowers, Capital (+OE)		8,000
Dawn Bloom, Capital (+OE)		2,000

Assets	=	Liabilities	+	Owners' Equity	
				Income Summary	−10,000
				Hal Flowers, Capital	+8,000
				Dawn Bloom, Capital	+2,000

Next the partners' drawing accounts must be closed. The balance in each partner's drawing account is credited with corresponding debits to the capital accounts. Because this entry remains the same regardless of the allocation method used, it is presented only once. However, recognize that this entry would be made for each of the allocation methods presented. The entry to close the partners' drawing accounts would be:

	Debit	Credit
Hal Flowers, Capital (−OE)	2,600	
Dawn Bloom, Capital (−OE)	1,400	
Hal Flowers, Drawing (+OE)		2,600
Dawn Bloom, Drawing (+OE)		1,400

Assets	=	Liabilities	+	Owners' Equity	
				Hal Flowers, Capital	−2,600
				Dawn Bloom, Capital	−1,400
				Hal Flowers, Drawing	+2,600
				Dawn Bloom, Drawing	+1,400

Coach's Tip

Do not confuse the allocation of income with the partners' withdrawals. The allocation represents how much profit each partner has **earned** from the business. The withdrawal represents how much of the partners' income has actually been taken out of the business (usually as cash).

Interest on Partners' Capital Balances Method

To illustrate this method, we will use Hal and Dawn's original capital contributions, $13,000 and $17,000, respectively. We also assume both Hal and Dawn wanted to earn 12 percent on their beginning capital balances. Under the interest on partners' capital balances method, **the interest must first be allocated to the partners.** Then, the remaining profit is allocated according to a fixed ratio. For this example, we will use a fixed ratio of 80 percent to Hal and 20 percent to Dawn. See Exhibit 12.4 for the way this method allocates the profit.

Exhibit 12.4 | Allocation of Income with Interest on Partners' Capital Balances

	Hal Flowers	Dawn Bloom	Total Allocated	Remainder to Allocate
Net income to allocate				$10,000
Interest				
Hal: $13,000 × 12%	$1,560		$ 1,560	(1,560)
Dawn: $17,000 × 12%		$2,040	2,040	(2,040)
Remainder (allocate on a fixed ratio)				6,400
Hal: $6,400 × 80%	5,120		5,120	(5,120)
Dawn: $6,400 × 20%		1,280	1,280	(1,280)
Total	$6,680	$3,320	$10,000	$ 0

When the partners' contributions of time and/or money differ significantly, this method or one of the remaining ones may be used to ensure that income allocation is based fairly on the individual partners' contributions of time and/or assets. The following entry records each partner's share of the partnership's income using the interest on partners' capital balances method.

	Debit	Credit
Income Summary (−OE)	10,000	
Hal Flowers, Capital (+OE)		6,680
Dawn Bloom, Capital (+OE)		3,320

Assets	=	Liabilities	+	Owners' Equity	
				Income Summary	−10,000
				Hal Flowers, Capital	+6,680
				Dawn Bloom, Capital	+3,320

SELF-STUDY PRACTICE

Jack Clumsy and Jill Mimic began the Hill Partnership on January 1, 2009. On December 31, 2009, the partnership has $18,000 of profit to allocate. Determine the amount of profit to be allocated to each partner under each of the following independent situations.

1. Fixed ratio of 3:6 to Jack and Jill, respectively.
2. Interest on capital balances of 12 percent with the remainder on a ratio of 3:6. Assume capital balances of $2,000 for Jack and $8,000 for Jill.

After you have finished, check your answers with the solution at the bottom of the page.

Salaries to Partners Method

The salaries to partners method allocates income first to cover the partners' salaries and then the remainder of the income according to a fixed ratio. Assume Hal and Dawn agreed to the following salaries and fixed ratios:

	Salaries	Fixed Ratio
Hal Flowers	$6,000	80%
Dawn Bloom	2,000	20

See Exhibit 12.5 for the allocation of the partnership's net income of $10,000.

Solution to Self-Study Practice

1. Jack receives $6,000 (=$18,000 × 3/9), and Jill receives $12,000 (=$18,000 × 6/9).
2. Jack and Jill receive the following:

	Jack	Jill	Total Allocated	Remainder to Allocate
Net income to allocate				$ 18,000
Interest	$2,000 × 12% = $ 240	$8,000 × 12% = $ 960	$ 1,200	(1,200)
				16,800
Remainder (allocate on a fixed ratio)	$16,800 × 3/9 = 5,600	$16,800 × 6/9 = 11,200	16,800	(16,800)
Total allocation	$ 5,840	$ 12,160	$18,000	$ 0

Exhibit 12.5 | Allocation of Income with Salaries to Partners

	Hal Flowers	Dawn Bloom	Total Allocated	Remainder to Allocate
Net income to allocate				$10,000
Salary allocations	$6,000	$2,000	$8,000	(8,000)
Remainder (allocate on a fixed ratio)				2,000
Hal: $2,000 × 80%	1,600		1,600	(1,600)
Dawn: $2,000 × 20%		400	400	(400)
Total	$7,600	$2,400	$10,000	$ 0

Coach's Tip

Partner salaries (if any) must *always* be allocated first.

Whenever salaries are allocated to the partners, they must be taken out of the partnership's income before any other allocations can be made. Once again, always verify that the total of the amounts allocated to each partner equals the total partnership income (or loss). The following journal entry would be used to allocate income under this method.

	Debit	Credit
Income Summary (−OE)	10,000	
Hal Flowers, Capital (+OE)		7,600
Dawn Bloom, Capital (+OE)		2,400

Assets	=	Liabilities	+	Owners' Equity	
				Income Summary	−10,000
				Hal Flowers, Capital	+7,600
				Dawn Bloom, Capital	+2,400

Salaries to Partners and Interest on Partners' Capital Balances Method

The salaries to partners and interest on partners' capital balances method allocates income first to the partners' salaries and second to the interest on the partners' capital accounts. Any remaining income is allocated according to a fixed ratio. Assume the following salaries, interest rate, and fixed ratios:

	Salaries	Interest	Fixed Ratio
Hal Flowers	$6,000	12%	80%
Dawn Bloom	2,000	12	20

See Exhibit 12.6 for the allocation of the partnership's $10,000 net income under this method. Study it carefully; it is tricky. Needless to say, this example illustrates why a proof of the allocation is so important. Sometimes allocating profit (or loss) according to the partnership agreement creates a situation in which the partnership's income is insufficient to give each partner the salaries and interest required in the partnership agreement. Nevertheless, **these amounts must be allocated** even if doing so results in the allocation of a negative amount. Any negative amount is allocated using the fixed ratio.

Exhibit 12.6	Allocation of Income under the Salaries to Partners and Interest on Partners' Capital Balances Method

	Hal Flowers	Dawn Bloom	Total Allocated	Remainder to Allocate
Net income to allocate				$10,000
Salary allocations	$6,000	$2,000	$ 8,000	(8,000)
Remaining after salary allocations				2,000
Interest				
Hal: $13,000 × 12%	$1,560		1,560	(1,560)
Dawn: $17,000 × 12%		$2,040	2,040	(2,040)
Remainder (overallocated)				(1,600)
Hal: ($1,600) × 80%	(1,280)		(1,280)	1,280
Dawn: ($1,600) × 20%		(320)	(320)	320
Total	$6,280	$3,720	$10,000	$ 0

The entry to record the allocation of income under this method would be:

	Debit	Credit
Income Summary (−OE)	10,000	
Hal Flowers, Capital (+OE)		6,280
Dawn Bloom, Capital (+OE)		3,720

Assets	=	Liabilities	+	Owners' Equity	
				Income Summary	−10,000
				Hal Flowers, Capital	+6,280
				Dawn Bloom, Capital	+3,720

Coach's Tip

A fixed ratio is used to allocate the remainder amount for every allocation method. So, it is important to select a fixed ratio for each partner even when the fixed ratio method is not used for allocating profit.

SELF-STUDY PRACTICE

Jack and Jill began the Hill Partnership on January 1, 2009. On December 31, 2009, the partnership has $18,000 profit to allocate. Determine the amount of profit to be allocated to each partner under the salaries to partners and interest on capital balances method using the following.

	Salaries	Interest	Capital	Fixed Ratio
Jack	$ 7,800	12%	$2,000	3
Jill	13,500	12	8,000	6

After you have finished, check your answers with the solution at the bottom of the page.

Solution to Self-Study Practice

	Jack		Jill		Total Allocated	Remainder to Allocate
Net income to allocate						$18,000
Salary		$ 7,800		$13,500	$21,300	(21,300)
Interest	$2,000 × 12% =	240	$8,000 × 12% =	960	1,200	(1,200)
						(4,500)
Remainder (overallocated)	($4,500) × 3/9 =	(1,500)	($4,500) × 6/9 =	(3,000)	(4,500)	4,500
Total/proof		$ 6,540		$11,460	$18,000	$ 0

After listening intently to their attorney's advice and carefully considering their options for allocating the partnership's income, Hal and Dawn asked the attorney to allocate all income (or loss) using the salaries to partners method (method 3). They chose this method because Hal agreed to take on more managerial responsibilities than Dawn, and this method rewards him for his commitment of additional time.

Preparation of Financial Statements

The financial statements of a partnership are very similar to those of a sole proprietorship. There are only three differences: (1) net income is allocated among the partners, (2) the balance sheet shows a capital account for each partner, and (3) the partners' capital statement replaces the owner's equity statement.

Net income on the partnership's income statement is calculated and reported in exactly the same way as for a sole proprietorship. The allocation of this net income to each partner's capital account is reported on the **partners' capital statement**. This statement begins with each partner's beginning capital account balance, which is increased by the portion of income allocated to each partner and reduced by withdrawals made by each partner. An illustration of this statement is shown in Exhibit 12.7, given the following assumptions.

	Capital Contributions	Net Income (allocated)	Partner Drawings
Hal Flowers	$13,000	$7,600	$2,600
Dawn Bloom	17,000	2,400	1,400

Exhibit 12.7   Partners' Capital Statement

Bloom 'N Flowers
Partners' Capital Statement
December 31, 2008

	Hal Flowers	Dawn Bloom	Total
Capital, January 1, 2008	$ 0	$ 0	$ 0
Add: Partner capital contributions	13,000	17,000	30,000
Net income	7,600	2,400	10,000
	20,600	19,400	40,000
Less: Partner drawings	2,600	1,400	4,000
Capital, December 31, 2008	$18,000	$18,000	$36,000

After the partners' capital statement is complete, the balance sheet can be prepared. See Exhibit 12.8 for the owners' equity section of the balance sheet for Bloom 'N Flowers partnership. Notice that the capital account balances in Exhibits 12.7 and 12.8 are equal.

Exhibit 12.8 Partial Balance Sheet

Bloom 'N Flowers
Balance Sheet (partial)
December 31, 2008

Total liabilities [for illustration purposes only]		$ 8,000
Owners' equity		
Hal Flowers, capital	$18,000	
Dawn Bloom, capital	18,000	
Total owners' equity		36,000
Total liabilities and owners' equity		$44,000

CHANGES OF OWNERSHIP IN A PARTNERSHIP

Hal and Dawn later toyed with the idea of admitting another partner to their business. Hal had a friend, Bud Green, who specialized in marketing—a field with which Hal and Dawn have little experience. The two partners knew that marketing would be critical to the success of their business, however.

Learning Objective 3

Demonstrate the proper treatment for changes of ownership in a partnership.

Admission of a Partner

The lawyer was pleased that Hal and Dawn had brought up the idea of admitting a new partner **before** actually going through with it. Although adding a new partner has little economic impact on a partnership, it does have a major legal effect called partnership dissolution. Specifically, adding a partner causes the dissolution of the existing partnership (consisting of the old partners) and the creation of a new partnership (consisting of the new partners).

Of course, additional capital and drawing accounts would need to be created for the new partner. Then the existing partners would need to decide how to complete the admission of the new partner. Legally, a new partner cannot be admitted into a partnership unless all existing partners agree to it. Assuming all current partners have agreed to admit a new partner, the new partner can be admitted in two ways: through a purchase made among partners or by the investment of additional assets.

Purchase among Partners

A purchase among partners transfers a portion of one or more existing partners' capital account balances to the new partner's capital account. This transaction is a **personal** transaction involving **only** those individuals involved in the purchase. The only impact on the partnership is that a journal entry is required to transfer amounts from the existing partners' capital accounts to the new partner's capital account.

Assume that on January 1, 2009, Bud was admitted to the partnership with a $33\frac{1}{3}$ percent ownership. Bud agreed to pay each partner $8,000 in exchange for 1/3 of each partner's capital account balance ($18,000 × 1/3 = $6,000). The following journal entry was made to record Bud's admission to the partnership, based on the capital balances on the balance sheet as of December 31, 2008 (see Exhibit 12.8).

	Debit	Credit
Hal Flowers, Capital (−OE)	6,000	
Dawn Bloom, Capital (−OE)	6,000	
Bud Green, Capital (+OE)		12,000

Assets	=	Liabilities	+	Owners' Equity	
				Hal Flowers, Capital	−6,000
				Dawn Bloom, Capital	−6,000
				Bud Green, Capital	+12,000

Hal and Dawn's attorney explained some important features of the purchase among partners method of admitting a new partner. First, the amount of money that each partner accepts in return for his or her capital is strictly a private matter between the new partner and the individuals who have agreed to give up a portion of their capital. Theoretically, neither Hal nor Dawn need to be aware of the amount the other receives for his or her share of the capital.

Furthermore, because the partnership is not involved in the transaction, the entry to record the transaction would be the same whether Bud paid each partner $100 or $100,000. The fact that Bud paid a total of $16,000 for a $12,000 capital account balance affects the partners' personal income tax returns but it does not affect the partnership's accounting records.

As the following T-accounts show, the **total** capital in the partnership would be the same **after** Bud's admission to the partnership as **before** he was admitted (that is, $36,000). After his admission, each **individual** partner's capital is $12,000 or exactly one-third of the total ($36,000 × 1/3). The three friends become equal partners, each of whom would own $33\frac{1}{3}$ percent of the partnership.

Hal Flowers, Capital		Dawn Bloom, Capital		Bud Green, Capital	
	Bal. 18,000		Bal. 18,000		Bal. 0
Jan.1 6,000		Jan.1 6,000			Jan. 1 12,000
	12,000		12,000		12,000

Investment of Additional Assets

The other way to admit a new partner is for the incoming partner to invest new assets into the partnership. Unlike the purchase among partners method, the investment method alters the partnership's assets.

Assume that Bud was admitted to Hal and Dawn's partnership as a new partner. Hal and Dawn's original capital balances did not change. They were still $18,000 each, or $36,000 in total. Bud invested $18,000 of additional cash in the partnership.

Under the investment of additional assets method, Bud's contribution affected only the partnership's net assets (cash) and Bud's capital account. The existing partners' capital accounts were unaffected. The journal entry made to record the admission of the new partner follows.

	Debit	Credit
Cash (+A)	18,000	
Bud Green, Capital (+OE)		18,000

Assets	=	Liabilities	+	Owners' Equity	
Cash +18,000				Bud Green, Capital	+18,000

After Bud's investment, the partners' capital accounts had the following balances:

Hal Flowers, Capital		Dawn Bloom, Capital		Bud Green, Capital	
	Bal. 18,000		Bal. 18,000		Bal. 0
					Jan. 1 18,000
					18,000

Bud's ownership of one-third of the partnership would not necessarily entitle him to one-third of the profits. Once again, the partnership agreement would dictate how to allocate profits (or losses) to the partners. The original partners may or may not have agreed to give him an equal share of the profits. If no written agreement exists, the profits would be allocated equally among all the partners whether or not that was their intention.

The example we have just presented assumed that the new partner's contribution **exactly equaled** his or her share of the partnership's total equity. Sometimes, however, the new partner contributes **more** or **less** than that amount. Let's see how these variations in the new partner's contribution affect the existing partners.

Bonus to the Existing Partners. In some situations, the existing partners require an extra contribution from the new partner in return for admission to the partnership. This situation is common when the fair market value of the partnership's assets is higher than the asset book value. When paying more than the book value of the assets he or she is acquiring, the new partner is effectively giving the existing partners a bonus.

Instead of contributing $18,000 to the partnership, let's assume that Bud contributed $24,000 in exchange for one-third of the partnership capital. The steps to determine the appropriate journal entry follow.

1. **Calculate the total capital in the partnership after the new partner's contribution.**

Total partnership capital before contribution	$36,000
New partner's contribution	24,000
Partnership capital after contribution	$60,000

2. **Calculate the amount of the new partner's capital account.** Multiply the result from Step 1 by the portion of the partnership that the new partner is purchasing.

Result from Step 1	$60,000
New partner's ownership portion	× 1/3
New partner's capital account balance	$20,000

3. **Calculate the total bonus to the existing partners.**

The total bonus to the existing partners is the difference between the amount contributed by the new partner and the amount of capital the new partner received.

Amount contributed by new partner	$24,000
Amount of capital given to the new partner	(20,000)
Total bonus to the existing partners	$ 4,000

4. **Allocate the bonus to the existing partners using their fixed ratios.** The existing partners' fixed ratios (after salaries) were 80 percent to Hal and 20 percent to Dawn. Therefore, the bonus allocation was as follows:

Hal's portion of the bonus ($4,000 × 80%)	$ 3,200
Dawn's portion of the bonus ($4,000 × 20%)	800
Total bonus allocated	$ 4,000

The following journal entry would be made to record the transaction.

	Debit	Credit
Cash (+A)	24,000	
Bud Green, Capital (+OE)		20,000
Hal Flowers, Capital (+OE)		3,200
Dawn Bloom, Capital (+OE)		800

Assets		=	Liabilities	+	Owners' Equity	
Cash	+24,000				Bud Green, Capital	+20,000
					Hal Flowers, Capital	+3,200
					Dawn Bloom, Capital	+800

Bonus to the New Partner. Sometimes the opposite situation occurs: The new partner may receive a capital account balance that exceeds the amount he or she invests in the partnership. This situation results in a bonus to the new partner. It can arise when the partnership desperately needs cash or the new partner has knowledge or skills that the original partners are eager to obtain. For example, Hal and Dawn may have needed Bud's marketing expertise so much that they were willing to give him a capital account that was **more** than his cash contribution.

To illustrate this situation, we assume that Bud contributed $9,000 (instead of $24,000) to the partnership in exchange for a one-third ownership interest. The steps required to determine the resulting journal entry are:

1. **Calculate the total capital in the partnership after the new partner's contribution.**

Total partnership capital before contribution	$36,000
New partner's contribution	9,000
Partnership capital after contribution	$45,000

2. **Calculate the amount of the new partner's capital account.** Multiply the result from Step 1 by the portion of the partnership that the new partner is purchasing.

Result from Step 1	$45,000
New partner's ownership portion	× 1/3
New partner's capital account balance	$15,000

3. **Calculate the total bonus to the new partner.** The total bonus to the new partner is the difference between the amount of capital the new partner received and the amount the new partner contributed.

Amount of capital given to the new partner	$15,000
Amount contributed by the new partner	(9,000)
Total bonus given by the existing partners	$ 6,000

4. **Allocate the bonus to the new partner using the fixed ratios.** The existing partners' fixed ratios (after their salaries) were 80 percent to Hal and 20 percent to Dawn. Therefore, the bonus given by the existing partners was allocated as follows:

Hal's portion of the bonus ($6,000 × 80%)	$4,800
Dawn's portion of the bonus ($6,000 × 20%)	1,200
Total bonus allocated	$6,000

In this case, the $6,000 bonus to the new partner was accomplished by removing a portion of the existing partners' capital balances. The entry that would be made to record the transaction is:

	Debit	Credit
Cash (+A)	9,000	
Hal Flowers, Capital (−OE)	4,800	
Dawn Bloom, Capital (−OE)	1,200	
Bud Green, Capital (+OE)		15,000

Assets		=	Liabilities	+	Owners' Equity	
Cash	+9,000				Hal Flowers, Capital	−4,800
					Dawn Bloom, Capital	−1,200
					Bud Green, Capital	+15,000

After Hal and Dawn's attorney had explained the ins and outs of admitting a new partner, the two friends decided to admit Bud in return for an $18,000 cash investment to the partnership. Following Bud's admission, each partner had a capital balance of $18,000, and each owned one-third of the partnership. The new partnership agreement specified that Hal, Dawn, and Bud would share the profits and losses according to a fixed ratio of 40 percent to 40 percent to 20 percent, respectively.

SELF-STUDY PRACTICE

Billie, Mandie, and Grimm agree to allow Crustie into their partnership and to give him a 25 percent ownership interest in the partnership on January 1, 2009. Prior to Crustie's entry, the following information was available.

	Capital	Fixed Ratio
Billie	$20,000	10%
Mandie	50,000	60
Grimm	30,000	30

1. Assume Crustie pays the partnership $30,000 for 25 percent of the partnership capital. Calculate the bonus to the new partner and the amounts that will be debited to the capital account for each of the existing partners.
2. Assume Crustie pays the partnership $40,000 for 25 percent of the partnership capital. Calculate the bonus to the existing partners and the amount that will be credited to Crustie's capital account.

After you have finished, check your answers with the solution at the bottom of the next page.

Withdrawal of a Partner

After his admission, Bud joined Hal and Dawn in all meetings with their attorney because he was a full partner. During one visit, Dawn asked the attorney to explain what would happen if one of the partners withdrew from the partnership. The attorney replied that as with the addition of a new partner, the withdrawal of a partner causes the immediate dissolution of the partnership. After dissolution, the remaining partners may carry on the business, but the partnership is legally new and different.

A partner can withdraw from a partnership in two ways: (1) voluntarily through the sale of his or her interest in the partnership to the remaining partner(s) or (2) involuntarily for one of several reasons. Death, insanity, mandatory retirement, and removal by the remaining partners (an unusual occurrence) can cause a partner's involuntary withdrawal from the partnership.

A properly prepared partnership agreement should cover the procedures, terms, and conditions for a partner's withdrawal. Similar to the admission of a new partner, certain options are available to the partners when a partner withdraws. Specifically, the remaining partners can purchase the exiting partner's capital account in one of two ways: They can pay the exiting partner with their own personal assets or with the partnership's assets. As we discuss in the following sections, the first option involves the partnership only insofar as a journal entry must be made to record the transfer of capital from the exiting partner to the remaining partner(s). The second option, in which the partnership uses its own assets to buy out the exiting partner, is more complicated.

Purchase among Partners

When partners use their own personal assets to pay the exiting partner, the partnership does nothing more than make a journal entry to transfer the balance in the exiting partner's capital account to the remaining partners' capital accounts. The dollar amount of the purchase and all other particulars are treated as personal transactions among the partners; the partnership itself is not involved.

Assume, for example, that on January 1, 2011 (after the partnership had been operating for several years), Dawn Bloom voluntarily withdrew from the partnership. At that time, each partner had a capital account balance of $30,000 (or a total of $90,000 for the partnership). Hal and Bud each agreed to purchase half of Dawn's interest in the partnership for $20,000. The entry made to record Dawn's withdrawal in this example follows:

	Debit	Credit
Dawn Bloom, Capital (−OE)	30,000	
Hal Flowers, Capital (+OE)		15,000
Bud Green, Capital (+OE)		15,000

Assets	=	Liabilities	+	Owners' Equity	
				Dawn Bloom, Capital	−30,000
				Hal Flowers, Capital	+15,000
				Bud Green, Capital	+15,000

In this case, the amount Dawn accepted for her capital account balance was strictly a private matter between her and the other partners. Theoretically, as in the admission of a new partner, each of the remaining partners may have been unaware of the amount the other paid

Solution to Self-Study Practice

1.
Step 1	Capital before contribution ($20,000 + $50,000 + $30,000)	$100,000
	Crustie's contribution	30,000
	New partnership capital	$130,000
2	New partner's capital account balance ($130,000 × 25%)	$ 32,500
3	Bonus to new partner ($32,500 − $30,000)	$ 2,500
4	Allocate bonus of new partner to existing partners	

Billie: $2,500 × 10% = $250

Mandie: $2,500 × 60% = $1,500

Grimm: $2,500 × 30% = $750

2.
Step 1	Capital before contribution ($20,000 + $50,000 + $30,000)	$100,000
	Crustie's contribution	40,000
	New partnership capital	$140,000
2	New partner's capital account balance ($140,000 × 25%)	$ 35,000
3	Bonus to existing partners ($40,000 − $35,000)	$ 5,000
4	Allocate bonus to existing partners	

Billie: $5,000 × 10% = $500

Mandie: $5,000 × 60% = $3,000

Grimm: $5,000 × 30% = $1,500

for his half of Dawn's capital account balance. The financial impact of the transaction, if any, is handled by the partners on their individual income tax returns, not by the partnership.

As the following T-accounts show, the **total** capital in the partnership was the same **before and after** Dawn's withdrawal from the partnership ($90,000). After the withdrawal, each **remaining** partner's capital was worth $45,000—exactly half the total ($90,000 × ½). The two remaining partners each own 50 percent of the partnership's net assets.

Hal Flowers, Capital		Dawn Bloom, Capital		Bud Green, Capital	
	Bal. 30,000		Bal. 30,000		Bal. 30,000
	Jan. 1 15,000	Jan. 1 30,000			Jan. 1 15,000
	45,000		0		45,000

Although each remaining partner owns one-half the partnership's net assets, that does not necessarily mean that each is entitled to half the partnership's profits. The allocation of the partnership's profit (or loss) is determined by the partnership agreement. The agreement may or may not state that profits will be split 50–50 after a partner exits. If no written agreement exists, the profits would be allocated equally among the partners whether or not that was their intention.

Withdrawal of Assets

The other means of a partner's withdrawal is to use the partnership's assets (usually cash) to purchase the exiting partner's capital account. Unlike the purchase among partners method, this method has an obvious impact on the partnership.

We assume, as before, that when Dawn withdrew from the partnership, all three partners had a capital account balance of $30,000. In this case, however, Dawn received $30,000 in cash from the partnership in return for her voluntary withdrawal. Under this method, only the partnership's net assets (cash) and Dawn's capital account were affected by her exit. The remaining partners' capital accounts were unaffected. The entry that would be made to record Dawn's withdrawal from the partnership follows.

	Debit	Credit
Dawn Bloom, Capital (−OE)	30,000	
Cash (−A)		30,000

Assets	=	Liabilities	+	Owners' Equity
Cash −30,000				Dawn Bloom, Capital −30,000

After the $30,000 payment to Dawn, the remaining partners' capital accounts had the following balances:

Hal Flowers, Capital		Dawn Bloom, Capital		Bud Green, Capital	
	Bal. 30,000		Bal. 30,000		Bal. 30,000
		Jan. 1 30,000			
			0		

As before, the remaining partners then owned 50 percent of the partnership's net assets except that those net assets have decreased by $30,000. Before Dawn's withdrawal, the partnership's net assets (Assets − Liabilities = Owners' Equity) were $90,000 (= $30,000 + $30,000 + $30,000). After her withdrawal, its net assets were $60,000 (= $30,000 + $30,000).

In this case, we assumed that the partnership paid Dawn the exact amount of her capital account—that is, one-third of the partnership's total capital. In some cases, however, the partnership may pay the exiting partner **more or less** than his or her capital account balance. In the following sections, we consider both possibilities.

Bonus to the Remaining Partners. Sometimes the cash payment to the exiting partner is less than that partner's capital balance. A reduced payment is possible for several reasons. The fair market value of the partnership's assets may be less than their book value, or the exiting partner may wish to leave the partnership as quickly as possible, no matter what payment is offered. Whatever the reason, the remaining partners effectively receive a bonus from the withdrawing partner.

Assume that instead of receiving $30,000 for her interest in the partnership, Dawn received only $24,000. The steps to follow in determining the journal entry to record the transaction are:

1. **Calculate the total bonus to the remaining partners.** The total bonus to the remaining partners is the difference between the amount in the exiting partner's capital account and the amount the exiting partner receives at withdrawal from the partnership.

Amount in exiting partner's capital account	$30,000
Amount of cash paid to the exiting partner	24,000
Total bonus to the remaining partners	$ 6,000

2. **Allocate the bonus to the remaining partners using their fixed ratios.** Referring to the partnership agreement that was drawn up after Bud's admission to the partnership, the fixed ratios for Hal, Dawn, and Bud were 40 percent, 40 percent, and 20 percent, respectively. With Dawn's withdrawal, the allocation was based on the remaining percentages, 40 percent and 20 percent.

Because the remaining percentages total 60 percent (= 40 percent + 20 percent), allocations were made on that basis. Therefore, the bonus was allocated as follows:

Hal's portion of the bonus [$6,000 × 40/60]	$4,000
Bud's portion of the bonus [$6,000 × 20/60]	2,000
Total bonus allocated	$6,000

The entry to record this transaction would be:

	Debit	Credit
Dawn Bloom, Capital (−OE)	30,000	
Cash (−A)		24,000
Hal Flowers, Capital (+OE)		4,000
Bud Green, Capital (+OE)		2,000

Assets	=	Liabilities	+	Owners' Equity
Cash −24,000				Dawn Bloom, Capital −30,000
				Hal Flowers, Capital + 4,000
				Bud Green, Capital + 2,000

Bonus to the Exiting Partner. Now let's examine the reverse situation. In this case, the partnership paid the exiting partner **more** than her capital account balance such that she received a bonus. This situation may occur for several reasons. The other partners may have been eager to see Dawn leave, the fair market value of the partnership's assets may have been higher than their book value, or the partnership may have enjoyed exceptional earnings and/or generated goodwill within the partnership.

To illustrate, assume that the partnership paid Dawn $33,000 (instead of $24,000) in exchange for her interest in the partnership. The procedure to account for this transaction is as follows:

1. **Calculate the bonus to the exiting partner.** The bonus to Dawn is the difference between the amount of cash she receives from the partnership and the balance in her capital account at the time of her withdrawal.

Amount of cash paid to the exiting partner	$33,000
Capital account balance of exiting partner	30,000
Total bonus to the exiting partner	$ 3,000

2. **Allocate the exiting partner's bonus to the remaining partners using their fixed ratios.** The remaining partner's fixed income ratios are the same as those shown in the last example. Therefore, the bonus would have been allocated as follows:

Hal's portion of the bonus [$3,000 × (40/60)]	$2,000
Bud's portion of the bonus [$3,000 × (20/60)]	1,000
Total bonus allocated	$3,000

The $3,000 bonus to the exiting partner came out of the remaining partners' capital accounts. The assumption is that the remaining partners are willing to give up some of their own capital account balances to obtain the exiting partner's withdrawal. The following entry would have been made to record this transaction.

	Debit	Credit
Dawn Bloom, Capital (–OE)	30,000	
Hal Flowers, Capital (–OE)	2,000	
Bud Green, Capital (–OE)	1,000	
Cash (–A)		33,000

Assets	=	Liabilities	+	Owners' Equity	
Cash −33,000				Dawn Bloom, Capital	−30,000
				Hal Flowers, Capital	−2,000
				Bud Green, Capital	−1,000

Death of a Partner

Although the death of a partner is not something most partners want to consider, the sobering fact is that no one knows when a partner's death might occur. When a partner dies, the existing partnership is dissolved. Because the partner's equity in the partnership will pass to his or her estate after death, the partnership agreement should include provisions for a settlement with the estate.

To determine the balance in the deceased partner's equity account on the date of death, the partnership is required to (1) calculate the partnership's net income up to the date of death, (2) close the books, and (3) prepare financial statements. If the partnership agreement requires it, the partnership's net assets may be restated at their fair market value, and an audit of the accounting records may be required.

In some cases, the remaining partners personally purchase the deceased partner's interest in the partnership. In other cases, the partnership's assets may be used to finance the buyout. Because a profitable and successful partnership can be worth hundreds of thousands, if not millions, of dollars, many partnerships purchase life insurance policies on all general partners to cover the potential cost of a buyout.

SELF-STUDY PRACTICE

Klock voluntarily withdraws from the 4K partnership on January 1, 2009. Prior to Klock's withdrawal, the following information is available.

	Capital	Fixed Ratio
Kharge	$15,000	10%
Klock	20,000	20
Knot	25,000	30
Katt	60,000	40

1. Assume the partnership pays Klock $18,000 for the balance in her capital account. Calculate the bonus allocated to each of the remaining partners.
2. Assume the partnership pays Klock $23,000 for the balance in her capital account. Calculate the bonus to her and the amount that will be debited to the capital accounts of each of the remaining partners.

After you have finished, check your answers with the solution at the bottom of the page.

LIQUIDATION OF A PARTNERSHIP

Learning Objective 4

Demonstrate the proper treatment for the liquidation of a partnership.

Although Hal, Dawn, and Bud's partnership had been successful for many years (Dawn never actually withdrew from the partnership), the three friends became weary of the time required and the stress involved in running a business. Increasingly, they talked of dissolving their partnership. As a result, they decided to meet with their attorney again to discuss the possibility of a dissolution—the process that ultimately ends in the liquidation and distribution of partnership assets.

A **partnership liquidation** may be caused by the death of a partner, the imminent bankruptcy of the partnership, or by mutual agreement among all partners. The attorney informed the three friends that when a partnership is liquidated, the assets are sold (for cash), any outstanding debts and liabilities are paid, and the remaining cash, if any, is distributed to the partners. Before the process begins, however, the accounting cycle should be completed. That is, adjustments should be made, financial statements prepared, and closing entries recorded and posted. At that point, only the permanent accounts reported on the balance sheet should contain balances.

Solution to Self-Study Practice

1.
Amount of Klock's capital account	$20,000
Cash paid to Klock	18,000
Bonus to remaining partners	$ 2,000

Kharge: $2,000 × [10/(10 + 30 + 40)] = $250

Knot: $2,000 × [30/(10 + 30 + 40)] = $750

Katt: $2,000 × [40/(10 + 30 + 40)] = $1,000

2.
Amount paid to Klock	$23,000
Capital balance of Klock	20,000
Bonus to Klock	$ 3,000

Kharge: $3,000 × [10/(10 + 30 + 40)] = $375

Knot: $3,000 × [30/(10 + 30 + 40)] = $1,125

Katt: $3,000 × [40/(10 + 30 + 40)] = $1,500

The four steps in the liquidation process follow.

1. **Sell.** All assets (except cash) must be sold for cash and the resulting gain or loss recognized.
2. **Allocate.** After all assets have been liquidated (that is, converted to cash), the gain or loss calculated in Step 1 must be allocated among the partners according to their fixed ratios.
3. **Pay.** The partnership's cash is then used to pay all of the partnership's liabilities.
4. **Distribute.** Any remaining cash can then be distributed to the partners according to their fixed ratios.

The attorney advised the partners that

- **These four steps must be performed in order.** Executing them in any other order could result in serious financial consequences to the partners.
- A journal entry must be recorded for each and every step in the liquidation process.
- All liabilities, debts, and/or other obligations **must** be paid before the partners receive anything.

After the business has been operating for several years, partners' capital account balances will differ from one another for several reasons. The partners may have received different percentages of the profit (or loss), or their drawings may have varied. Over the years, these additions and/or withdrawals may have greatly impacted their capital accounts. Two possibilities exist with regard to the partners' capital accounts: (1) no capital deficiency—that is, every partner has a credit balance in his or her capital account and (2) a capital deficiency—that is, one or more partners have a debit balance (deficit) in his or her capital account. These different situations dramatically affect the partnership liquidation process, as we show in the following examples.

Assume that after many years of successful operations, Hal, Dawn, and Bud decided to liquidate their partnership. Exhibit 12.9 shows the partnership's account balances just before liquidation. In the following sections, we investigate how the existence or nonexistence of a capital deficiency affects the liquidation of a partnership.

No Capital Deficiency

After deciding to liquidate the partnership, Hal, Dawn, and Bud followed their lawyer's instructions to the letter. They completed the four steps in the liquidation process in order, as follows.

1. **Sell the partnership's assets (except cash).** The partners accepted an offer from Plantland, Inc., to purchase the partnership's assets (except cash) for $240,000. The book value of these assets at the time of the transaction is $229,000 (=$94,000 − $8,000 + $85,000 + $105,000 − $47,000).

Exhibit 12.9　Partnership Account Balances before Liquidation

Assets		Liabilities and Owners' Equity	
Cash	$ 51,000	Accounts payable	$ 79,000
Accounts receivable	94,000	Notes payable	118,000
Allowance for doubtful accounts	(8,000)		
Inventory	85,000	Hal Flowers, capital	47,000
Store equipment	105,000	Dawn Bloom, capital	31,000
Accumulated depreciation	(47,000)	Bud Green, capital	5,000
	$280,000		$280,000

The entry to record the resulting $11,000 gain on the sale of the assets ($240,000 − $229,000) was:

	Debit	Credit
Cash (+A)	240,000	
Allowance for Doubtful Accounts (−xA, +A)	8,000	
Accumulated Depreciation (−xA, +A)	47,000	
Accounts Receivable (−A)		94,000
Inventory (−A)		85,000
Store Equipment (−A)		105,000
Gain on Liquidation (+OE)		11,000

Assets		=	Liabilities	+	Owners' Equity
Cash	+240,000				Gain on Liquidation +11,000
Allowance for Doubtful Accounts (−xA)	+8,000				
Accumulated Depreciation (−xA)	+47,000				
Accounts Receivable	−94,000				
Inventory	−85,000				
Store Equipment	−105,000				

2. **Allocate any gain or loss from the sale of the assets to the partners.** The partners allocated the $11,000 gain from Step 1 according to the partners' fixed ratios: 40 percent to Hal, 40 percent to Dawn, and 20 percent to Bud.

Hal's portion of the gain ($11,000 × 40%)	$ 4,400
Dawn's portion of the gain ($11,000 × 40%)	4,400
Bud's portion of the gain ($11,000 × 20%)	2,200
Total gain allocated	$11,000

The entry to record the allocation of the gain was:

	Debit	Credit
Gain on Liquidation (−OE)	11,000	
Hal Flowers, Capital (+OE)		4,400
Dawn Bloom, Capital (+OE)		4,400
Bud Green, Capital (+OE)		2,200

Assets	=	Liabilities	+	Owners' Equity	
				Hal Flowers, Capital	+ 4,400
				Dawn Bloom, Capital	+ 4,400
				Bud Green, Capital	+ 2,200
				Gain on Liquidation	−11,000

After posting the entry to allocate the gain, the partners' capital accounts appeared as follows.

Hal Flowers, Capital			Dawn Bloom, Capital			Bud Green, Capital	
	Bal. 47,000			Bal. 31,000			Bal. 5,000
	(2) 4,400			(2) 4,400			(2) 2,200
	51,400			35,400			7,200

3. **Pay all outstanding liabilities.** After the sale of assets, the partnership had $291,000 in cash ($51,000 + $240,000). This cash was used to pay the outstanding liabilities. The following entry was made to record the payment.

	Debit	Credit
Accounts Payable (–L)	79,000	
Notes Payable (–L)	118,000	
Cash (–A)		197,000

Assets		=	Liabilities		+	Owners' Equity
Cash	−197,000		Accounts Payable	−79,000		
			Notes Payable	−118,000		

4. **Distribute the remaining cash to the partners.** After paying all outstanding debts, the partnership had $94,000 cash remaining to distribute to the partners ($51,000 + $240,000 − $197,000). Because the partners completed each of the steps in the liquidation process properly and in sequence, the total balance in their capital accounts exactly equaled the amount of cash available for distribution ($51,400 + $35,400 + $7,200 = $94,000). The distribution of cash to the partners is shown in the following journal entry. After posting the entry, the balances in the capital accounts equaled zero, cash was zero, and the liquidation was complete.

	Debit	Credit
Hal Flowers, Capital (–OE)	51,400	
Dawn Bloom, Capital (–OE)	35,400	
Bud Green, Capital (–OE)	7,200	
Cash (–A)		94,000

Assets		=	Liabilities	+	Owners' Equity	
Cash	−94,000				Hal Flowers, Capital	−51,400
					Dawn Bloom, Capital	−35,400
					Bud Green, Capital	−7,200

Coach's Tip

A word of caution: Do not attempt to allocate cash to the partners on the basis of fixed ratios. It is not an appropriate basis for a final distribution of cash.

Capital Deficiency

The liquidation process is not always smooth. Sometimes one or more partners do not have a large enough balance in their capital accounts to cover all transactions the liquidation requires. This situation can occur when the partnership has suffered numerous losses over its life. It can also occur when one or more partners have made disproportionately large withdrawals or when the partnership incurs large losses in the liquidation process. The procedure for dealing with this situation is as follows.

1. **Sell the partnership's assets (except cash).** Assume that Hal, Dawn, and Bud could not find a buyer for the business's assets and were forced to auction them off for far less than their fair market value. In total, the partnership collected $150,000 for assets (except cash) whose book value was $229,000 (= $94,000 − $8,000 + $85,000 + $105,000 − $47,000). Because the partnership received only $150,000 for assets recorded on the books for $229,000, it incurred a loss on liquidation of $79,000 ($229,000 − $150,000). The following entry was made to record the loss and the sale of the assets.

	Debit	Credit
Cash (+A)	150,000	
Allowance for Doubtful Accounts (−xA, +A)	8,000	
Accumulated Depreciation (−xA, +A)	47,000	
Loss on Liquidation (−OE)	79,000	
Accounts Receivable (−A)		94,000
Inventory (−A)		85,000
Store Equipment (−A)		105,000

Assets		=	Liabilities	+	Owners' Equity	
Cash	+150,000				Loss on Liquidation	−79,000
Allowance for Doubtful Accounts (−xA)	+8,000					
Accumulated Depreciation (−xA)	+47,000					
Accounts Receivable	−94,000					
Inventory	−85,000					
Store Equipment	−105,000					

2. **Allocate any gain or loss from the sale of assets to the partners.** The loss was allocated according to the partners' fixed income ratios: 40 percent to Hal, 40 percent to Dawn, and 20 percent to Bud.

Hal's portion of the loss ($79,000 × 40%)	$ 31,600
Dawn's portion of the loss ($79,000 × 40%)	31,600
Bud's portion of the loss ($79,000 × 20%)	15,800
Total loss allocated	$ 79,000

This entry was made to record allocation of the loss.

	Debit	Credit
Hal Flowers, Capital (−OE)	31,600	
Dawn Bloom, Capital (−OE)	31,600	
Bud Green, Capital (−OE)	15,800	
Loss on Liquidation (+OE)		79,000

Assets	=	Liabilities	+	Owners' Equity	
				Hal Flowers, Capital	−31,600
				Dawn Bloom, Capital	−31,600
				Bud Green, Capital	−15,800
				Loss on Liquidation	+79,000

3. **Pay the partnership's outstanding liabilities.** After selling the assets, the partnership had cash of $201,000 (= $51,000 + $150,000). This cash was used to pay the outstanding liabilities. The following entry was made to record the payment.

	Debit	Credit
Accounts Payable (–L)	79,000	
Notes Payable (–L)	118,000	
Cash (–A)		197,000

Assets	=	Liabilities	+	Owners' Equity
Cash −197,000		Accounts Payable −79,000		
		Notes Payable −118,000		

4. Distribute the remaining cash to the partners. After paying all outstanding debts, the partnership had $4,000 cash (= $51,000 + $150,000 − $197,000) remaining to distribute to the partners. Normally, the partners receive the balances in their capital accounts after the first three transactions have been posted. However, as the debit balances in the following capital accounts show, both Bud and Dawn had a capital deficiency. Dawn owed the partnership $600, and Bud owed $10,800.

Hal Flowers, Capital		Dawn Bloom, Capital		Bud Green, Capital	
	Bal. 47,000		Bal. 31,000		Bal. 5,000
(2) 31,600		(2) 31,600		(2) 15,800	
	15,400	600		10,800	

The three friends realize that this was exactly the type of situation that a limited liability company (LLC) is formed to avoid. In a general partnership, each partner bears unlimited liability for the partnership's debts. So legally, Hal had an enforceable claim against both Dawn and Bud for the deficient funds. Hal could even have accessed their personal assets in an attempt to collect the deficiencies. Alternatively, Hal could have collected **the combined deficiency of both partners' capital accounts from just one of the two partners.** Often one partner has a great deal of personal wealth and another has very little. If Hal wanted, he could try to collect the entire amount from the wealthy partner. This ability to collect from any or all partners is called **joint** (all partners) **and several** (any partner) **liability.**

A capital deficiency can be resolved during the liquidation of a partnership in two ways: (1) the partner pays the deficiency and (2) the partner fails to pay the deficiency.

Deficiency Paid by Partner

Assume that Dawn decided to pay her $600 capital deficiency. The following entry was made to record the payment.

	Debit	Credit
Cash (+A)	600	
Dawn Bloom, Capital (+OE)		600

Assets	=	Liabilities	+	Owners' Equity
Cash +600				Dawn Bloom, Capital +600

As the following T-accounts show, after the entry was posted, Dawn's capital account had a zero balance. She received no cash when the final distribution was made, but she owed nothing more. The partnership's Cash account then had increased to $4,600 (= $4,000 + $600).

Hal Flowers, Capital		Dawn Bloom, Capital			Bud Green, Capital	
	Bal. 47,000			Bal. 31,000		Bal. 5,000
(2) 31,600		(2) 31,600	(4a) 600		(2) 15,800	
	15,400		0		10,800	

Deficiency Not Paid by Partner

Suppose that Bud could not pay his $10,800 capital deficiency. When a partner cannot pay the deficit in a capital account, the partners who have credit balances in their capital accounts must absorb the deficit. Normally, the partnership's fixed ratio would be used to allocate the deficit, but because Hal was the only partner with a credit balance, he had to absorb the entire deficit. The following entry was made to record the absorption of the deficit by the remaining partner.

	Debit	Credit
Hal Flowers, Capital (−OE)	10,800	
Bud Green, Capital (+OE)		10,800

Assets	=	Liabilities	+	Owners' Equity	
				Hal Flowers, Capital	−10,800
				Bud Green, Capital	+10,800

With the deficit resolved, the partners' capital accounts had the following balances after the entry was posted.

Hal Flowers, Capital

		Bal. 47,000
(2)	31,600	
(4b)	10,800	
		4,600

Dawn Bloom, Capital

		Bal. 31,000
(2)	31,600	(4a) 600
		0

Bud Green, Capital

		Bal. 5,000
(2)	15,800	(4b) 10,800
		0

The partnership had $4,600 cash, including the $600 that Dawn paid to resolve her deficit. Note that Hal's capital account **also** had a $4,600 balance. The final distribution to Hal could then be made. The final entry in the partnership liquidation was:

	Debit	Credit
Hal Flowers, Capital (−OE)	4,600	
Cash (−A)		4,600

Assets		=	Liabilities	+	Owners' Equity	
Cash	−4,600	=		+	Hal Flowers, Capital	−4,600

Even then, neither Bud nor Dawn was completely free of obligation to Hal. Hal had the right to collect the remaining $10,800 that he was owed from **either or both of them.** So even though Dawn may have thought she was in the clear because she paid her deficit, she still had unlimited liability.

SELF-STUDY PRACTICE

At the time of liquidation, AB Partners reported $2,000 in cash, $5,000 in other assets, $4,000 in liabilities, $2,600 in Ali Augo's capital account, and $400 in Bradyn Bad's capital account. For the following two independent cases, determine (a) the amount of cash available after the assets are sold and liabilities paid, and (b) the total balances in the partners' capital accounts after any gain (or loss) is allocated 50-50 between partners.

1. The assets (other than cash) are sold for $7,500.
2. The assets (other than cash) are sold for $3,000.

After you have finished, check your answers with the solution at the bottom of the next page.

RATIO ANALYSIS

Partner Return on Equity

Learning Objective 5
Calculate and interpret the partner return on equity ratio.

In our scenario, the partners certainly received their money's worth from their attorney, who gave them one last bit of information free of charge. He offered to provide the three partners a financial analysis tool called the **partner return on equity.**

Of the numerous financial measures used to analyze a business's performance, the partner return on equity is of particular interest to partnerships. An informative measure of profitability and managerial performance in a partnership, partner return on equity is calculated and interpreted as follows:

Financial Analysis Tools		
Name of Measure	Formula	What It Tells You
Partner Return on Equity Ratio	$\dfrac{\text{Net Income}}{\text{Average Partner Equity}}$	• Measures a company's efficiency at generating profits from every dollar of equity invested (or retained) in the partnership. • A higher ratio indicates a greater efficiency.

Take Hal, Dawn, and Bud's partnership, for example:

	Total	Hal Flowers	Dawn Bloom	Bud Green
Balance 1/1/2009	$54,000	$18,000	$18,000	$18,000
Net income	15,000	6,000	6,000	3,000
Drawings	(12,000)	(2,000)	(3,000)	(7,000)
Balance 12/31/2009	$57,000	$22,000	$21,000	$ 14,000
Partner Return on Equity:				
$\dfrac{\text{Net Income}}{\text{Average Partner Equity}}$	$\dfrac{\$15,000}{(\$54,000 + \$57,000)/2}$	$\dfrac{\$6,000}{(\$18,000 + \$22,000)/2}$	$\dfrac{\$6,000}{(\$18,000 + \$21,000)/2}$	$\dfrac{\$3,000}{(\$18,000 + \$14,000)/2}$
=	**0.270 or 27.0%**	**0.300 or 30.0%**	**0.308 or 30.8%**	**0.188 or 18.8%**

Notice that the partnership's return on equity (in the Total column) is vastly different from the individual return on equity (ROE) calculated for each partner. Bud's ROE, in particular, appears relatively low when compared to the others. This should not be a surprise, though, because Bud receives a smaller income allocation than the other partners.

---

1. (a) Cash = $2,000 + $7,500 − $4,000 = $5,500

   (b) Gain = $7,500 − $5,000 = $2,500 ($1,250 to Ali, $1,250 to Bradyn)

   A. Augo, Capital = $2,600 + $1,250 = $3,850

   B. Bad, Capital = $ 400 + $1,250 = 1,650

   Total $5,500

2. (a) Cash = $2,000 + $3,000 − $4,000 = $1,000

   (b) Gain (loss) = $3,000 − $5,000 = ($2,000) ($1,000 to Ali, $1,000 to Bradyn)

   A. Augo, Capital = $2,600 − $1,000 = $1,600

   B. Bad, Capital = $ 400 − $1,000 = (600)

   Total $1,000

Solution to
Self-Study Practice

In practice, very few businesses have a consistent return on equity of more than 30 percent. Moreover, maintaining ROE in a partnership at the same level over time is nearly impossible. That is because income is closed to the partners' equity accounts. Assuming the partners leave most of their earnings in the partnership to encourage its growth, the business's capital keeps increasing. To keep the partner ROE ratio high, then, income must also increase continually.

Another thing to watch for in relation to ROE is debt because a partnership can increase its ROE by relying more on debt. Assume, for example, that our partnership's beginning capital balance of $54,000 was made up entirely of partner contributions. Had the partnership instead borrowed $30,000 and required that much less in partner contributions, beginning capital would have been $24,000 rather than $54,000. In that situation, the ROE would have been a staggering 58.8%—[= $15,000/($24,000 + 27,000)/2]. But would you really want to take on all that debt just to achieve a high ROE? For this reason, the ROE should not be the only financial measure used to evaluate a business.

SELF-STUDY PRACTICE

Indicate whether each of the following is a true (T) or false (F) statement regarding partner return on equity.

1. Partner return on equity calculation is: Average Partner Equity ÷ Partner Net Income. _____

2. Each individual partner's ROE can vary substantially from the ROE of the partnership as a whole. _____

3. The ROE for most partnerships consistently exceeds 30 percent. _____

4. Assume a partner begins the year with $20,000 in partner equity and ends the year with $35,000. Her allocated net income for the year is $34,000. In this case, her ROE is 123.6 percent. _____

5. Replacing capital with debt can increase the ROE. _____

After you have finished, check your answers with the solution at the bottom of the page.

Demonstration Case A
Division of Partnership Income

Alwin and Teddy Ernest formed a partnership to provide accounting services. Assume that their partnership net income was $600,000, and other relevant information (immediately prior to allocating partnership net income) follows.

Partner	Capital Account Balances	Salaries	Interest	Fixed Ratio
Alwin Ernest	$200,000	$100,000	6%	1/3
Teddy Ernest	$300,000	$140,000	6%	2/3

Solution to Self-Study Practice

1. F—ROE is calculated as Partner Net Income ÷ Average Partner Equity.
2. T—Each partner's capital balance and allocated net income may be greater or less than others in the partnership.
3. F—It is rare for a partnership to consistently maintain an ROE in excess of 30 percent.
4. T—$34,000 / [($20,000 + $35,000) / 2] = 123.6%.
5. T—This reduces the bottom number in the ROE formula.

Required:

Allocate net income to each partner under the following four independent assumptions:

1. Fixed ratio.
2. Interest on partners' capital balances.
3. Salaries to partners.
4. Salaries to partners and interest on partners' capital balances.

Suggested Solution

1. Alwin Ernest: $600,000 × 1/3 = $200,000
   Teddy Ernest: $600,000 × 2/3 = $400,000

2.

	Alwin	Teddy	Total Allocated	Remainder to Allocate
Net income to allocate				$600,000
Interest:				
Alwin Ernest: $200,000 × 6%	$ 12,000		$ 12,000	(12,000)
Teddy Ernest: $300,000 × 6%		$ 18,000	18,000	(18,000)
Remainder (allocate on a fixed ratio):				570,000
Alwin Ernest: $570,000 × 1/3	190,000		190,000	(190,000)
Teddy Ernest: $570,000 × 2/3		380,000	380,000	(380,000)
Total	$202,000	$398,000	$600,000	$ 0

3.

	Alwin	Teddy	Total Allocated	Remainder to Allocate
Net income to allocate				$600,000
Salaries	$100,000	$140,000	$240,000	(240,000)
Remainder (allocate on a fixed ratio):				360,000
Alwin Ernest: $360,000 × 1/3	120,000		120,000	(120,000)
Teddy Ernest: $360,000 × 2/3		240,000	240,000	(240,000)
Total	$220,000	$380,000	$600,000	$ 0

4.

	Alwin	Teddy	Total Allocated	Remainder to Allocate
Net income to allocate				$600,000
Salaries	$100,000	$140,000	$240,000	(240,000)
Remainder				360,000
Interest:				
Alwin Ernest: $200,000 × 6%	12,000		12,000	(12,000)
Teddy Ernest: $300,000 × 6%		18,000	18,000	(18,000)
Remainder (allocate on a fixed ratio):				330,000
Alwin Ernest: $330,000 × 1/3	110,000		110,000	(110,000)
Teddy Ernest: $330,000 × 2/3		220,000	220,000	(220,000)
Total	$222,000	$378,000	$600,000	$ 0

Demonstration Case B

Admission and Withdrawal of Partners

In the year following Case A, Ernest & Ernest admits two new partners. Fred Whiney is admitted as an equal partner by purchasing half of Teddy's partnership interest. At the time, Teddy's capital account balance was $400,000 and Alwin's was $200,000. At the end of the year, Arthur Yong is admitted as an equal partner by investing $280,000 cash in the partnership and receiving a 25% partnership interest. At the time of Arthur's admission, the accounting records and partnership agreement contain the following information.

Partner	Capital Account Balances	Fixed Ratio
Alwin Ernest	$220,000	1/3
Teddy Ernest	250,000	1/3
Fred Whiney	250,000	1/3
Total	$720,000	

In the following year, Teddy Ernest retires and the partnership pays him $190,000 for his partnership interest. At the time, his capital account balance was $250,000.

Required:

Prepare the journal entry to record:

1. Admission of Fred Whiney.
2. Admission of Arthur Yong.
3. Withdrawal of Teddy Ernest.

Suggested Solution

1. Because Fred Whiney is admitted by a purchase among partners, the journal entry must only re-allocate the existing balances in capital accounts. The total in the capital accounts was $600,000 ($400,000 + $200,000). Equal partnership implies 1/3 of this amount for each partner, or $200,000 (= $600,000 × 1/3). Alwin's capital account balance already equals $200,000, so a portion of only Teddy's account is reallocated.

Teddy Ernest, Capital (−OE)	200,000	
Fred Whiney, Capital (+OE)		200,000

2. Arthur Yong is admitted by an investment of additional assets ($280,000 cash). The journal entry must record this additional investment, and account for any bonus to the new partner or to the existing partners.

Step 1   Calculate the total partnership capital after Arthur's investment.

Total partnership capital before contribution	$ 720,000
Arthur Yong's contribution	280,000
Partnership capital after contribution	$1,000,000

Step 2   Calculate the amount of Arthur's capital account.

Total partnership capital after contribution	$1,000,000
Arthur's ownership portion	× 25%
Arthur's capital account balance	$ 250,000

Step 3   Calculate the total bonus to existing partners.

Amount contributed by Arthur	$280,000
Amount of capital given to Arthur	(250,000)
Total bonus to existing partners	$ 30,000

Step 4   Allocate the bonus to existing partners.

Alwin's portion ($30,000 × 1/3)	$10,000
Teddy's portion ($30,000 × 1/3)	10,000
Fred's portion ($30,000 × 1/3)	10,000
Total bonus to existing partners	$30,000

Cash (+A)	280,000	
Alwin Ernest, Capital (+OE)		10,000
Teddy Ernest, Capital (+OE)		10,000
Fred Whiney, Capital (+OE)		10,000
Arthur Yong, Capital (+OE)		250,000

3. Upon his retirement, Teddy Ernest withdraws $190,000 of partnership assets (cash). The journal entry must record this asset distribution, and account for any bonus to the exiting partner or to the remaining partners.

Step 1   Calculate the total bonus to the remaining partners.

Amount in Teddy Ernest's capital account	$ 250,000
Amount of cash paid to Teddy Ernest	(190,000)
Total bonus to remaining partners	$ 60,000

Step 2   Allocate the bonus to remaining partners.

Alwin Ernest's portion ($60,000 × 1/3)	$20,000
Fred Whiney's portion ($60,000 × 1/3)	20,000
Arthur Yong's portion ($60,000 × 1/3)	20,000
Total bonus to existing partners	$60,000

Teddy Ernest, Capital (−OE)	250,000	
Alwin Ernest, Capital (+OE)		20,000
Fred Whiney, Capital (+OE)		20,000
Arthur Yong, Capital (+OE)		20,000
Cash (−A)		190,000

Demonstration Case C
Liquidation of Partnership

After many years of success, the partnership of Ernest, Whiney, & Yong is dissolved and liquidated. The partnership sold its assets (other than cash) to a competitor for $1,710,000, then paid its liabilities in full, and distributed the remaining cash to its three partners. The partnership reported the following book values at the time of liquidation.

Assets		Liabilities and Owners' Equity	
Cash	$ 50,000	Accounts payable	$ 80,000
Supplies	10,000	Alwin Ernest, Capital	450,000
Equipment	1,800,000	Fred Whiney, Capital	490,000
Accumulated depreciation	(400,000)	Arthur Yong, Capital	440,000
	$1,460,000		$1,460,000

Required:
Prepare journal entries for the partnership to record the:

1. Sale of assets.
2. Allocation of gain on sale. (Assume partners' fixed ratios remain at 1/3 each.)
3. Payment of liabilities.
4. Final cash distribution to partners.

Suggested Solution

1. **Sale of assets.** The partnership received $1,710,000 for assets with a total book value of $1,410,000, resulting in a gain on liquidation equal to $300,000 ($1,710,000 − $1,410,000). (The book value of assets sold includes supplies and equipment less accumulated depreciation, calculated as $10,000 + $1,800,000 − $400,000 = $1,410,000.) The journal entry to record the cash received, assets sold, and gain follows.

Cash (+A)	1,710,000	
Accumulated Depreciation (−xA, +A)	400,000	
Supplies (−A)		10,000
Equipment (−A)		1,800,000
Gain on Liquidation (+OE)		300,000

2. **Allocation of gain.** With a 1/3 fixed ratio for each partner, the $300,000 gain is allocated as $100,000 per partner (= $300,000 × 1/3).

Gain on Liquidation (−OE)	300,000	
Alwin Ernest, Capital (+OE)		100,000
Fred Whiney, Capital (+OE)		100,000
Arthur Yong, Capital (+OE)		100,000

3. **Payment of liabilities.** The journal entry to record payment for $80,000 of accounts payable follows.

Accounts Payable (−L)	80,000	
Cash (−A)		80,000

4. **Final cash distribution to partners.** The new balance in Cash, after receiving $1,710,000 (in step 1) and paying $80,000 (in step 3) is $1,680,000 (= $50,000 + $1,710,000 − $80,000). The new balances in the capital accounts (after step 2) include Alwin $550,000 (= $450,000 + $100,000), Fred $590,000 (= $490,000 + $100,000), and Arthur $540,000 (= $440,000 + $100,000), for a total of $1,680,000 (= $550,000 + $590,000 + $540,000). The journal entry to record the final cash distribution and liquidation of capital account balances follows.

Alwin Ernest, Capital (−OE)	550,000	
Fred Whiney, Capital (−OE)	590,000	
Arthur Yong, Capital (−OE)	540,000	
Cash (−A)		1,680,000

Demonstration Case D
Partner Return on Equity

Refer to Demonstration Case A. Assume partnership income is allocated using the fixed ratio method, and the partners did not make withdrawals or contributions during the year.

Required:
Calculate and interpret the return on equity (ROE) for the partnership as a whole and for each individual partner.

Suggested Solution

Remember to calculate the average balance in the Capital accounts using the beginning balances (provided in Case A) and the ending balances (after taking into account the allocated partnership income determined in Case A).

ROE formula:	$\dfrac{\text{Net income}}{[\text{Beginning capital} + \text{Ending capital}]/2}$	
Partnership:	$\dfrac{\$600,000}{[\$500,000 + (\$500,000 + \$600,000)]/2}$	= 0.750 or 75.0%
Alwin:	$\dfrac{\$200,000}{[\$200,000 + (\$200,000 + \$200,000)]/2}$	= 0.667 or 66.7%
Teddy:	$\dfrac{\$400,000}{[\$300,000 + (\$300,000 + \$400,000)]/2}$	= 0.800 or 80.0%

Because minimal amounts of cash and other assets are needed to start an accounting firm, the amount invested in the partnership is small relative to the amount of income generated. The very high ROEs are consistent with this. The ROE for Teddy is greater than for Alwin because Teddy receives twice as much partnership income as Alwin (2/3 versus 1/3), but Teddy did not contribute twice the amount of capital ($300,000 versus $200,000).

Chapter Summary

LO1 Compare the partnership form of business with other forms. p. 506

- A partnership is the association of two or more persons to carry on as co-owners of a business for profit, whether or not the persons intend to form a partnership.
- Advantages of partnerships include pass-through taxation, ease of formation, simplified recordkeeping, favorable taxation, and increased ability to raise funds.
- Disadvantages of partnerships include unlimited liability, co-ownership of property, limited life, mutual agency, and partner disagreements.

- The fees and procedures for forming a limited liability company (LLC) vary among states.
- Advantages of the LLC include limited liability, ease of formation, simplified recordkeeping, favorable taxation, and flexibility of operations.
- Disadvantages of LLCs include limited life, lack of legal precedents, limited corporate characteristics—no more than two of the following four corporate characteristics: (1) owners' liability limited to business assets, (2) continuity of life, (3) centralization of management, and (4) free transferability of assets.
- An S-Corporation is a corporation with 1 to 100 shareholders that enjoys pass-through taxation of profits. The formation requirements, annual filings, and required elections are complex and time consuming.

LO2 Demonstrate how to account for partnerships p. 509

- Partnership accounting requires a capital account for each partner, a drawing account for each partner, and an allocation of the partnership's income (or loss) to each partner based on the partnership agreement.
- Partner cash contributions are recorded at the amount of the cash contributed; noncash assets are recorded at the asset's market value. The contributing partner's capital account is credited for the net assets contributed.
- Partnership income (or loss) is allocated to the partners using one of four methods: (1) fixed-ratio method, (2) interest on partners' capital balances method, (3) salaries to partners method, or (4) salaries to partners and interest on partners' capital balances method.
- Closing entries must be made to transfer the allocated amounts of income (or loss) to each partner's capital account.
- The procedures for preparing financial statements is the same as for a proprietorship except a partnership (1) allocates net income among the partners, (2) shows a capital account on the balance sheet for each partner, and (3) replaces the owner's equity statement with the partners' capital statement.

LO3 Demonstrate the proper treatment for changes of ownership in a partnership. p. 517

- The admission of a new partner legally requires that all existing partners agree to it and causes the dissolution of the existing partnership and the creation of a new partnership.
- A new partner can be admitted in two ways: (1) a purchase among partners or (2) the investment of additional assets by the new partner. A purchase among partners is a personal transaction between individuals resulting in a journal entry made to transfer amounts from the original partners' capital accounts to the new partner's capital account. The investment of additional assets can result in a bonus to the new partner (or a bonus to existing partners) if the additional investment is less (or more) than the value of the partnership interest received.
- The withdrawal of a partner can also be accomplished in two ways: (1) a purchase among partners or (2) the withdrawal of assets. A purchase among partners is a personal transaction between individuals resulting in a journal entry made to transfer amounts from the exiting partner's capital account to the remaining partners' capital accounts. The withdrawal of assets can result in a bonus to the exiting partner (or the remaining partners) if the withdrawal is greater (or less) than the balance in the exiting partner's capital account.

LO4 Demonstrate the proper treatment for the liquidation of a partnership. p. 526

- The liquidation of a partnership may result from the death of a partner, the partnership's imminent bankruptcy, or mutual agreement among all partners.
- The four steps in the liquidation process that must be performed in sequence are (1) selling all assets (except cash) for cash and recognizing the resulting gain or loss, (2) allocating this gain or loss among the partners according to their fixed ratios, (3) using the cash in the partnership to pay off all partnership liabilities, (4) distributing any remaining cash according to the partners' fixed income ratios.
- The balance in the partners' capital accounts just before liquidation may have either no capital deficiency or a capital deficiency.
- If, after posting any gain or loss on the sale of the partnership assets, no capital deficiency exists in any of the partners' capital accounts, the outstanding debts of the partnership are paid. With the remaining cash, each partner receives a distribution equal to the balance in his or her capital account.
- If, after posting any gain or loss on the sale of the partnership assets, a capital deficiency exists in any of the partners' capital accounts, two possibilities exist: (1) that partner pays the deficiency or (2) that partner fails to pay the deficiency. When the partner pays the deficiency, the partnership has sufficient cash to pay the capital account balances of other partners. When the partner is unable to pay the capital deficiency, the partners who have credit balances in their capital accounts must absorb the deficit; the allocation of the deficit is based on the partners' fixed ratio.

LO5 Calculate and interpret the partner return on equity ratio. p. 533

- The partner return on equity ratio measures the profitability and managerial performance for each individual partner in a partnership.

Financial Analysis Tools		
Name of Measure	**Formula**	**What It Tells You**
Partner Return on Equity Ratio	$\dfrac{\text{Net Income}}{\text{Average Partner Equity}}$	• Measures a company's efficiency at generating profits from every dollar of equity invested (or retained) in the partnership. • A higher ratio indicates a greater efficiency.

Key Terms

Articles of Organization (p. 507)
Capital Deficiency (p. 531)
Limited Liability Company (LLC) (p. 507)
Operating Agreement (p. 507)

Partner Return on Equity (p. 533)
Partners' Capital Statement (p. 516)
Partnership (p. 506)
Partnership Agreement. (p. 506)

Partnership Dissolution (p. 517)
Partnership Liquidation (p. 526)
Pass-Through Taxation (p. 507)
S-Corporation (p. 508)

See complete glossary in back of text.

Questions

1. What is a partnership?

2. List at least two advantages and at least two disadvantages of a partnership.

3. Define unlimited liability and limited liability. Which would you prefer if you were starting a new business? Explain.

4. What is mutual agency? Is it considered an advantage or disadvantage of a partnership? Why?

5. What are the essential elements of a partnership agreement? Is this a required document? Why or why not?

6. Define limited liability company (LLC). Why is this new form of business so popular?

7. List the two documents often required to form a limited liability company (LLC). Which is always a requirement and which is often simply a recommended document?

8. What is double taxation? Which form of business is subject to double taxation?

9. List the four characteristics of a corporation used to evaluate a limited liability company (LLC). What is the maximum number of these characteristics that a limited liability company can possess without risking its status as an LLC? Explain.

10. List the three things necessary for partnership accounting.

11. What amount is used to record partner investments into the partnership?

12. List three ways that the fixed ratio for dividing partnership profits and losses can be expressed.

13. When a new partner is admitted using the purchase among partners method, who is (are) the other party(ies) to the transaction?

14. When a new partner is admitted using the investment of additional assets method and the existing partners' capital accounts are debited, do the existing partners or the new partner receive a bonus?

15. When a partner withdraws, why might the partnership give a bonus to the withdrawing partner?

16. A dissolution is the same as a liquidation. Do you agree with this statement? Why or why not?

17. What are the four steps in the liquidation process?

18. If a capital deficiency exists upon the liquidation of a partnership, what are two possible resolutions to the situation?

19. What is one thing that can cause partner ROE to increase?

Multiple Choice

1. Which of the following is not a disadvantage of the partnership form of business?
   a. Mutual agency.
   b. Pass-through taxation.
   c. Unlimited liability.
   d. Limited life.

Quiz 12-1
www.mhhe.com/LLPW1e

2. Which of the following is a disadvantage of the limited liability company form of business?
   a. Ease of formation.
   b. Limited liability.
   c. Simplified recordkeeping.
   d. Limited corporate characteristics.

3. The limited liability company (LLC) has become a favorite entity choice of businesses meeting all of the following criteria except:

    a. The business has plans for significant growth.

    b. All members are active participants in a small local business.

    c. The business will have one to three members.

    d. All of the above.

4. To accurately keep track of income and/or loss for individual partners, which of the following is not required for partnership accounting?

    a. Provisions for the addition or withdrawal of a partner.

    b. A drawings account for each partner.

    c. A capital account for each partner.

    d. An allocation of the partnership income/loss to each partner, according to the terms of the partnership agreement.

5. Which of the following is not a true statement regarding partnership formation?

    a. The partner's capital account is credited for the amount of assets invested.

    b. Partners can invest any combination of assets and/or liabilities into the partnership.

    c. Partnership investments are recorded at the book value of the assets on the date they are transferred into the partnership.

    d. Partnerships may be formed through a handshake.

6. A partnership has four partners who share income/loss on an 8:4:3:1 ratio according to the partnership agreement. Assuming the partnership has net income of $20,000, how much will be allocated to each partner, respectively?

    a. $8,000, $4,000, $3,000, and $1,000.

    b. $10,000, $5,000, $3,750, and $1,250.

    c. $12,000, $4,000, $3,000, and $1,000.

    d. None of the above is the correct allocation of net income.

7. Joe is admitted into a partnership with Jack and Jill. Joe invests $25,000 into the partnership in exchange for a $22,000 capital account balance. This transaction is referred to as:

    a. A purchase among partners with a bonus to the new partner.

    b. A purchase among partners with a bonus to the original partners.

    c. An investment of assets into the partnership with a bonus to the new partner.

    d. An investment of assets into the partnership with a bonus to the original partners.

8. Stan withdraws from the partnership of Stan, Lee, and Brick and the partnership pays him $54,000. Assuming the balance in his capital account at that time is $50,000, which of the following is true?

    a. There is no bonus because this transaction is personal between the withdrawing partner and each individual remaining partner.

    b. A bonus of $4,000 is allocated to Stan, Lee, and Brick.

    c. A bonus of $4,000 is allocated to Lee and Brick.

    d. A bonus of $4,000 goes to Stan.

9. Which of the following is not a true statement regarding a partnership liquidation?

    a. All liabilities, debts, and/or other obligations of the partnership must be paid before the partners receive anything.

    b. The steps in the liquidation process can be performed in any sequence.

    c. Liquidation may result from the death of a partner, partnership bankruptcy, or agreement among the partners.

    d. A journal entry must be recorded for each step in the liquidation process.

10. What is the partner return on equity for Greg assuming his average partnership equity is $62,800 and his allocated net income from the partnership is $24,000?

    a. 76.4 percent.

    b. 38.2 percent.

    c. 261.7 percent.

    d. Cannot be calculated without ending capital.

Multiple-Choice Solutions						
1. b	2. d	3. a	4. a	5. c	6. b	7. d
8. d	9. b	10. b				

Mini Exercises   Available with McGraw-Hill's Homework Manager

LO1, 2   **M12-1 Journalizing Partnership Formation**

Prepare the journal entry that would be made for the formation of the DL Partnership given the following information: Doe invests $10,000 cash and equipment with a book value of $7,000 (cost $9,000). Lee invests $12,000 cash and inventory with a cost of $6,000 to the partnership. Fair market values of the equipment and inventory are $6,500 and $4,500, respectively.

LO2   **M12-2 Dividing and Journalizing Income with Fixed Ratio**

Tram and Quyen share income and loss based on a fixed ratio of 5/8 and 3/8, respectively. Net income for the current year is $24,000. Determine the amount of net income allocated to each partner and prepare the corresponding journal entry to record the allocation.

M12-3 Dividing of Income with Salaries, Interest, and Fixed Ratio   LO2

Blaine Partnership earned $20,000 this year. The partnership agreement states that income should be allocated to Romine and Roach using the salaries to partners and interest on capital balances method. Calculate the amount of Blaine's net income that will be allocated to each partner, assuming the following for each partner.

	Romine	Roach
Salary	$ 8,000	$ 4,000
Interest	10%	10%
Fixed ratio	60%	40%
Capital account balance	$15,000	$22,000

M12-4 Dividing Income When Allocation Exceeds Net Income   LO2

Use the same facts as in M12-3 except that Blaine Partnership earned $14,000 this year. Calculate the amount of Blaine's net income that will be allocated to each partner.

M12-5 Journalizing the Division of Income (Various Situations)   LO2

Perform the following tasks:

1. Prepare the journal entry to record the division of income made in M12-3.
2. Prepare the journal entry to record the division of income made in M12-4.

M12-6 Preparing Partners' Capital Statement   LO2

A. Jel and O. Tin are partners in the Jel N Tin Partnership. Using the following information, prepare a partners' capital statement on December 31, 2009.

	Capital 1/1/09	Capital Contributions	Net Income (allocated)	Partner Drawings
A. Jel	$39,000	$8,000	$14,900	$16,400
O. Tin	27,000	6,000	11,200	7,700

M12-7 Journalizing Admission of Partner as a Purchase among Partners   LO3

Dot and Dash are equal partners in the DD partnership. They agree to admit Dee into the partnership. It is agreed that Dee will pay Dot and Dash $40,000 each in exchange for one-third of each partner's current capital balance. Currently, Dot and Dash each has a capital balance of $90,000. Prepare the journal entry to admit Dee as a partner.

M12-8 Admitting a Partner by Investment with Bonus to the Existing Partners   LO3

Calculate the bonus to each of the existing partners with the admission of a new partner in the following situation: Juniper, Pine, and Fir are equal partners in a partnership. They agree to admit Pinion into the partnership. Pinion invests $35,000 in the partnership in exchange for a 25 percent partnership interest. The partnership agreement stipulates that bonuses be allocated on the basis of the fixed ratios prior to the admission of a new partner. The following information is available prior to the admission of Pinion.

	Juniper	Pine	Fir
Capital balances	$25,000	$35,000	$40,000
Fixed ratio	30%	30%	40%

M12-9 Admitting a Partner by Investment with Bonus to the New Partner   LO3

Calculate the bonus to each of the existing partners with the admission of a new partner in the following situation: Juniper, Pine, and Fir are equal partners in a partnership. They agree to admit Pinion into the partnership. Pinion invests $20,000 into the partnership in exchange for a 25 percent partnership interest. The partnership agreement stipulates that bonuses be allocated on the basis of the fixed ratios prior to the admission of a new partner. The following information is available prior to the admission of Pinion.

	Juniper	Pine	Fir
Capital balances	$25,000	$35,000	$40,000
Fixed ratio	30%	30%	40%

LO3

M12-10 Journalizing the Admission of a Partner (Various Situations)

Perform the following tasks:

1. Prepare the journal entry to record the admission of the partner as calculated in M12-8.
2. Prepare the journal entry to record the admission of the partner as calculated in M12-9.

LO3

M12-11 Calculating Bonus to Remaining Partners upon Withdrawal of Partner (Payment from Partnership)

Calculate the bonus allocated to each remaining partner upon the withdrawal of a partner in the following situation: Ima, Owda, and Hier are equal partners in a partnership. Owda decides to withdraw from the partnership and is very eager to leave. The partnership agrees to pay Owda $76,000 for her partnership interest. The partnership agreement requires that bonuses be allocated on the basis of the partners' fixed ratios prior to the withdrawal. The following information is available prior to Owda's withdrawal:

	Ima	Owda	Hier
Capital balances	$96,000	$84,000	$108,000
Fixed ratio	25%	20%	55%

LO3

M12-12 Calculating Bonus to Exiting Partner upon Withdrawal of Partner (Payment from Partnership)

Assume the same facts as in M12-11 except that the partnership agrees to pay Owda $90,400 for her partnership interest. Calculate the bonus allocated to each remaining partner.

LO3

M12-13 Journalizing the Withdrawal of a Partner (Various Situations)

Perform the following tasks:

1. Prepare the journal entry to record the withdrawal of the partner as calculated in M12-11.
2. Prepare the journal entry to record the withdrawal of the partner as calculated in M12-12.

LO4

M12-14 Liquidating Partnership with No Capital Deficiency

For the liquidation of DDT partnership, calculate the final distribution to each partner. The partnership's net assets have been sold, and the gain/loss has been recorded. Assume the following information:

Assets		Liabilities and Owners' Equity	
Cash	$ 57,000	Notes payable	$ 40,000
		Doun, capital	9,000
		Da, capital	6,000
		Toobes, capital	2,000
	$ 57,000		$ 57,000

LO4

M12-15 Liquidating Partnership with Capital Deficiency

For the liquidation of DDT partnership, calculate the final distribution to each partner. The partnership's net assets have been sold, and the gain/loss has been recorded. Assume the following information and that Toobes does not pay the deficiency.

Assets		Liabilities and Owners' Equity	
Cash	$ 57,000	Notes payable	$ 40,000
		Doun, capital (fixed ratio: 20%)	12,000
		Da, capital (fixed ratio: 30%)	9,000
		Toobes, capital (fixed ratio: 50%)	(4,000)
	$ 57,000		$ 57,000

M12-16 Journalizing the Liquidation of a Partnership (Various Situations)

Perform the following tasks:

1. Prepare the journal entry to record the final payments to the partners of DDT partnership assuming the liquidation scenario in M12-14.
2. Prepare the journal entries to record the allocation of deficit and the final payments to the partners of DDT partnership assuming the liquidation scenario in M12-15.

M12-17 Calculating Partnership Return on Equity

Using the information in the following table, calculate the ROE for each partner.

	Capital 1/1/09	Capital Contributions	Net Income	Partner Drawings	Capital 12/31/09
A. Jel	$39,000	$8,000	$14,900	$16,400	$45,500
O. Tin	27,000	6,000	11,200	7,700	36,500

Exercises   Available with McGraw-Hill's Homework Manager

E12-1 Identifying Advantages and Disadvantages of a Partnership

The following are characteristics of a partnership. Determine whether each characteristic is an advantage (A) or a disadvantage (B).

Partnership Characteristic	Advantage or Disadvantage
___ 1. Limited life.	A. Advantage
___ 2. Co-ownership of property.	B. Disadvantage
___ 3. Mutual agency.	
___ 4. Ability to raise funds.	
___ 5. Partner disagreements.	
___ 6. Ease of formation.	
___ 7. Simplified recordkeeping.	
___ 8. Pass-through taxation.	

E12-2 Identifying Advantages and Disadvantages of a Limited Liability Company (LLC)

Following are characteristics of a limited liability company. Determine whether each characteristic is an advantage (A) or a disadvantage (B).

Limited Liability Company Characteristic	Advantage or Disadvantage
___ 1. Limited liability.	A. Advantage
___ 2. Limited life.	B. Disadvantage
___ 3. Ease of formation.	
___ 4. Limited corporate characteristics.	
___ 5. Flexible profit and loss allocations.	
___ 6. Limited legal precedents.	

E12-3 Journalizing Partnership Formation—Cash and Noncash Contributions

Georgy Cloon and Alfred Nunley form a partnership. The book and fair market values of the contributed assets follow:

	BOOK VALUE		FAIR MARKET VALUE	
	G. Cloon	A. Nunley	G. Cloon	A. Nunley
Cash	$11,000	$20,000	$11,000	$20,000
Accounts receivable		36,000		34,000
Allowance for doubtful accounts		(2,000)		(3,000)
Furniture and fixtures	54,000		42,000	
Accumulated depreciation	(5,000)			
	$60,000	$54,000	$53,000	$51,000

Required:
Based on the information presented, prepare the journal entry to record the contributions made by each partner to the partnership.

LO2   **E12-4 Journalizing Division of Income—Various Allocations**

Crane, Del, and Egbert are partners in the CDE partnership. Partnership net income for the current year is $70,000. Other relevant information appears in the following table.

	Capital Balance	Salary	Interest	Fixed Ratio
Crane	$65,000	$20,000	9%	5/8
Del	82,000	25,000	9	2/8
Egbert	53,000	18,000	9	1/8

Required:
Determine the allocation of net income to each partner under each of the following three independent assumptions:

1. Fixed-ratio method.
2. Interest on partners' capital balances and any remaining amounts on a fixed ratio.
3. Salaries to partners, interest on partners' capital balances, and any remaining on a fixed ratio.

LO2   **E12-5 Dividing Income and Preparing Partners' Capital Statement**

L. Len, S. Squigg, and S. Shirl are partners in the Shirl Len Squigg partnership. Partnership net income for the current year is $23,652. Other relevant information appears in the following table.

	Capital 1/1/08	Capital Contributions	Fixed Ratio	Partner Drawings
L. Len	$4,000	$2,500	1/6	$4,650
S. Squigg	5,000	1,500	2/6	5,200
S. Shirl	6,000	3,500	3/6	5,000

Required:

1. Allocate the net income to the partners using the fixed ratio method.
2. Prepare the partners' capital statement at December 31, 2008.

LO3   **E12-6 Journalizing Admission of a Partner—Investment with Bonus to Existing Partners**

Click and Clack are partners in the CC partnership. They agree to admit Cluck into the partnership. Cluck invests $45,000 into the partnership in exchange for a one-third interest in the partnership. Assume any bonuses will be allocated on the basis of the fixed ratios prior to the admission of the new partner.

Additional information prior to the admission of Cluck:

	Click	Clack
Capital account balance	$48,000	$21,000
Fixed ratio	70%	30%

Required:

1. Determine the capital account balance for each partner after the new partner is admitted.
2. Prepare the journal entry to admit the new partner.

E12-7 Journalizing Admission of a Partner—Investment with Bonus to New Partner

LO3

Assume the same facts as in E12-6 except that Cluck invests $31,950.

Required:

1. Determine the capital account balance for each partner after the new partner is admitted.
2. Prepare the journal entry to admit the new partner.

E12-8 Journalizing Withdrawal of Partner—Payment from Partnership with Bonus to Remaining Partners

LO3

Wallice, Gromett, Victer, and Warerabbit are partners in the Gromwell partnership. Warerabbit decides to withdraw from the partnership. Additional information available prior to the withdrawal follows:

	Wallice	Gromett	Victer	Warerabbit
Capital balances	$105,000	$122,000	$136,000	140,000
Fixed ratio	21%	28%	35%	14%

Required:

According to the partnership agreement, any bonuses resulting from a partner's withdrawal from the partnership should be allocated on the basis of fixed ratios prior to the withdrawal. Assuming the partnership pays Warerabbit $124,280 for his partnership interest,

1. Calculate the amount of the bonus allocated to each of the remaining partners.
2. Prepare the journal entry to record Warerabbit's withdrawal.
3. Determine the capital account balance for each remaining partner after the withdrawal.

E12-9 Journalizing Withdrawal of Partner—Payment from Partnership with Bonus to Exiting Partner

LO3

Assume the facts in E12-8.

Required:

According to the partnership agreement, any bonuses resulting from a partner's withdrawal from the partnership should be allocated on the basis of fixed ratios prior to the withdrawal. Assume the partnership pays Warerabbit $146,000 for his partnership interest.

1. Calculate the amount of the bonus allocated to each of the remaining partners.
2. Prepare the journal entry to record Warerabbit's withdrawal.
3. Determine the capital account balance for each remaining partner after the withdrawal.

E12-10 Journalizing Admission and Withdrawal of a Partner—Among Partners

LO3

Frey, Dones, and Bance are partners in the FDB partnership. Additional information available prior to the admission or withdrawal of any partners follows:

	Frey	Dones	Bance
Capital balances	$10,000	$20,000	$30,000
Fixed ratio	16%	39%	45%

Required:

Each of the following is an independent transaction.

1. Prepare the journal entry to admit a new partner given the following assumptions: Amos is admitted to the partnership with a 25 percent partnership interest and agrees to pay each partner $7,000 in exchange for receiving 25 percent of the capital account balances of Frey, Dones, and Bance.

2. Prepare the journal entry for the withdrawal of Frey assuming the following: Using the original information (i.e., assuming Amos was not admitted to the partnership), Frey decides to withdraw from the partnership. Dones and Bance agree to purchase one-half of Frey's capital account balance for $4,000 each.

LO4   **E12-11 Liquidating a Partnership—No Capital Deficiency**

The partnership of Law Dee Daw liquidates, and the account balances before liquidation follow.

Assets		Liabilities and Owners' Equity	
Cash	$ 6,000	Accounts payable	$19,000
Other partnership assets (net)	44,000	Notes payable	8,000
		L. Law, capital (3/5 fixed ratio)	4,000
		D. Dee capital (1/5 fixed ratio)	7,000
		D. Daw, capital (1/5 fixed ratio)	12,000
	$50,000		$50,000

Assume the assets of Law Dee Daw partnership (except cash) are sold for $40,000.

Required:

Determine the amount of cash to be distributed to the partners upon liquidation.

LO4   **E12-12 Liquidating a Partnership—Capital Deficiency (payment by partner)**

Refer to E12-11.

Assume the same facts except that the assets of Law Dee Daw partnership (except cash) are sold for $28,000.

Required:

Determine the amount of cash to be distributed to the remaining partners upon liquidation. Assume any capital deficiencies are paid to the partnership.

LO4   **E12-13 Liquidating a Partnership—Capital Deficiency (nonpayment by partner)**

Refer to E12-11.

Assume the same facts except that the assets of Law Dee Daw partnership (except cash) are sold for $28,000.

Required:

Determine the amount of cash to be distributed to the remaining partners upon liquidation. Assume any capital deficiencies are not paid but rather are absorbed by other partners.

LO5   **E12-14 Calculating Partnership Return on Equity**

Assume the following information for the partnership of Domee and Gleegal.

	Capital 1/1/08	Capital Contributions	Net Income	Partner Drawings
Domee	$28,000	$ 5,000	$16,500	$10,500
Gleegal	32,000	7,000	9,400	12,000
Total	$60,000	$12,000	$25,900	$22,500

Required:

1. Calculate the ending capital balance for each partner.
2. Calculate the return on equity (ROE) for each partner.
3. Explain the primary cause of any differences in the partners' ROE.

Problems—Set A Available with McGraw-Hill's Homework Manager

PA12-1 Identifying Characteristics of Partnerships and Limited Liability Companies (LLCs)

LO1

Following are various characteristics of partnerships and LLCs discussed in the chapter. For each characteristic, indicate the form(s) of business, partnership (A) or limited liability company (B), the characteristic describes. Some characteristics may describe more than one form of business.

Characteristic	Form of Business
___ 1. Ability to raise funds	A. Partnership
___ 2. Ease of formation	B. Limited Liability Company (LLC)
___ 3. Favorable tax treatment	
___ 4. Few legal precedents	
___ 5. Flexible profit/loss allocations	
___ 6. Limited corporate characteristics	
___ 7. Limited liabilities	
___ 8. Limited life	
___ 9. Pass-through taxation	
___ 10. Simplified recordedkeeping	
___ 11. Unlimited liability	

PA12-2 Forming a Partnership—Cash and Noncash Contributions, Making Journal Entries, and Creating Owners' Equity Section of the Balance Sheet

LO2

M. Arsee, P. Ann, and G. Tsosi form the MAT partnership on January 8, 2009. The book and fair market values of the contributed assets follow.

	BOOK VALUE			FAIR MARKET VALUE		
	M. Arsee	P. Ann	G. Tsosi	M. Arsee	P. Ann	G. Tsosi
Cash	$ 9,000	$ 6,000	$17,000	$ 9,000	$ 6,000	$17,000
Accounts receivable			19,000			18,000
Allowance for doubtful accounts			(900)			(1,000)
Inventory	26,000			25,000		
Furniture and fixtures		45,000			35,000	
Accumulated depreciation		(8,000)				
Notes payable		(7,000)			(7,000)	
Net assets contributed	$35,000	$36,000	$35,100	$34,000	$34,000	$34,000

Required:

1. Based on the information presented, prepare the journal entry to record the contributions each partner made to the partnership.
2. Prepare the Liabilities and Owners' Equity section of the partnership balance sheet immediately following the partner contributions on January 8, 2009.

PA12-3 Dividing Income—All Four Methods

LO2

www.mhhe.com/LLPW1e

Mills and Cross are partners in the MC partnership. Partnership net income for the current year is $52,200. Other relevant information follows.

	Capital Balances	Salaries	Interest	Fixed Ratio
Mills	$18,000	$21,000	7%	3/4
Cross	32,000	30,000	7	1/4

Required:
Determine the allocation of net income to each of the partners under each of the following four independent assumptions:

1. Fixed ratio.
2. Interest on partners' capital balances and any remaining amounts on a fixed ratio.
3. Salaries to partners and any remaining amounts on a fixed ratio.
4. Salaries to partners, interest on partners' capital balances, and any remaining amounts on a fixed ratio.

LO2

PA12-4 Dividing Income, Journalizing, and Preparing Partners' Capital Statement
A. Batt, B. Robbin, and F. Catt are partners in the Batt R Catt partnership. Partnership net income for 2009 is $46,000. Other relevant information follows:

	Capital 1/1/09	Capital Contributions	Fixed Ratio	Partner Drawings
A. Batt	$ 7,000	$4,400	25%	$4,000
B. Robbin	12,000	3,300	30	7,000
F. Catt	15,000	2,200	45	6,000

Required:

1. Allocate the net income to the partners based on fixed ratios.
2. Prepare the partners' capital statement at December 31, 2009.

LO3

www.mhhe.com/LLPW1e

PA12-5 Admitting a Partner—Journalizing Purchase and Investment Situations
Dick and Jane are partners in the DJ partnership. They agree to admit Spot into the partnership. According to the partnership agreement, any bonuses will be allocated on the basis of the fixed ratio prior to the admission of the new partner. Additional information available prior to Spot's admission follows.

	Dick	Jane
Capital account balance	$61,000	$57,000
Fixed ratio	58%	42%

Required:
Prepare journal entries to record the admission of Spot, under each of the following independent assumptions.

1. Spot pays Dick and Jane $19,000 each. In exchange he receives 30 percent of each partner's capital account balance.
2. Spot invests $25,000 into the partnership in exchange for a 25 percent interest in the partnership.
3. Spot invests $62,000 into the partnership in exchange for a 30 percent interest in the partnership.

LO2

PA12-6 Journalizing Partner Withdrawals
Carrtman, Kennie, and Kile are partners in the Southe Parke partnership. Kennie's death required his withdrawal from the partnership. According to the partnership agreement, any bonuses will be allocated on the basis of fixed ratios prior to the withdrawal. Additional information available prior to the withdrawal follows.

	Carrtman	Kennie	Kile
Capital account balance	$54,000	$64,000	$42,000
Fixed ratio	42%	30%	28%

Required:
Prepare journal entries to record the withdrawal of Kennie, under each of the following independent assumptions.

1. Carrtman and Kile agree to purchase ½ of Kennie's capital account balance for $40,000 each.
2. The partnership pays Kennie's estate $80,000 for his partnership interest.
3. The partnership pays Kennie's estate $59,000 for his partnership interest.

PA12-7 Liquidating a Partnership with No Capital Deficiency and Making Journal Entries

Assume when the partnership of Shasta, Sheba, Sheeva liquidates, account balances before liquidation are as follows.

LO4

www.mhhe.com/LLPW1e

Assets		Liabilities and Owners' Equity	
Cash	$ 4,000	Accounts payable	$ 3,000
Inventory	8,000	Notes payable	8,000
Furniture and fixtures	16,000	Shasta, capital (35% fixed ratio)	2,000
Accumulated depreciation	(4,000)	Sheba capital (13% fixed ratio)	5,000
		Sheeva, capital (52% fixed ratio)	6,000
	$24,000		$24,000

Required:

Assume the Shasta, Sheba, and Sheeva partnership sold its assets (except cash) for $18,000. Record the following entries:

1. Sale of the partnership assets (except cash).
2. Allocation of gain or loss to each of the partners.
3. Payment of outstanding partnership liabilities.
4. Distribution of remaining cash to partners.

PA12-8 Liquidating a Partnership with Capital Deficiency (payment and nonpayment by partner) and Making Journal Entries

LO4

Assume the same facts as in PA12-7.

Required:

Assume the Shasta, Sheba, and Sheeva partnership sold its assets (except cash) for $12,000. Record the following entries:

1. Sale of the partnership assets (except cash).
2. Allocation of gain or loss to each of the partners.
3. Payment of outstanding liabilities of partnership.
4. Distribution of remaining cash to partners assuming Shasta pays the deficiency.
5. Distribution of remaining cash to partners assuming Shasta does not pay the deficiency.

PA12-9 Calculating Partner Return on Equity (ROE)

LO5

Gren, Bare, and Rett are partners in the GBR partnership. Information related to the partners follows.

	Total	Gren	Bare	Rett
Balance 1/1/2008	$71,000	$20,000	$30,000	$21,000
Contributions	20,000	10,000	5,000	5,000
Net Income	33,000	11,000	11,000	11,000
Drawings	(30,000)	(2,000)	(20,000)	(8,000)
Balance 12/31/2008	$94,000	$39,000	$26,000	$29,000

Required:

1. Calculate the partnership ROE.
2. Calculate the ROE for each partner.
3. Which partner has the best ROE? Why?

Problems—Set B Available with McGraw-Hill's Homework Manager

PB12-1 Matching Terminology with Definitions

LO1

Following are the terms and definitions covered in Chapter 12. Match each term with its definition by entering the appropriate letter in the space provided. Use one letter for each blank.

Terms	Definitions
___ 1. Mutual agency	A. Lack of sufficient capital in a partner's capital account to absorb losses resulting from the liquidation of a partnership.
___ 2. Partners' capital statement	B. Document recommended when an LLC is formed to address potential problem areas in the LLC.
___ 3. Capital deficiency	C. Association of two or more persons to carry on as co-owners of a business for profit.
___ 4. Partnership agreement	D. Allows profits from a business to flow directly to the owners avoiding taxation at the business level.
___ 5. S-corporation	E. Document recommended when a partnership is formed to address potential problem areas in the partnership.
___ 6. Partner return on equity	F. Business form that offers its members limited liability protection and pass-through taxation.
___ 7. Partnership dissolution	G. Process of selling assets of the partnership, paying liabilities and distributing remaining cash to the partners.
___ 8. Articles of organization	H. Sufficient capital in a partner's capital account to absorb losses resulting from the liquidation of a partnership.
___ 9. Partnership	I. Shows all changes to capital for each partner in a partnership and replaces the owner's equity statement.
___ 10. Operating agreement	J. Occurs when a partner voluntarily or involuntarily leaves a partnership.
___ 11. Partnership liquidation	K. Corporation that allows profits to pass to the owners' personal income tax returns and provides owners limited liability.
___ 12. Pass-through taxation	L. Partnership characteristic that holds each partner accountable for the actions of all partners in the partnership.
___ 13. Limited liability company	M. Document required in states to form an LLC; provides important information about its operations and structure.
___ 14. No capital deficiency	N. Measures a company's efficiency in generating profits from every dollar of equity invested or retained by partners.

LO2

PB12-2 Forming a Partnership—Cash and Noncash Contributions, Making Journal Entries, and Creating Owners' Equity Section of the Balance Sheet

R. Tex, T. Ark, and L. Ana form the TexArkAna partnership on November 16, 2009. The book and fair market values of the contributed assets follow.

	BOOK VALUE			FAIR MARKET VALUE		
	R. Tex	T. Ark	L. Ana	R. Tex	T. Ark	L. Ana
Cash	$ 13,500	$ 9,000	$25,500	$13,500	$ 9,000	$25,500
Accounts receivable			28,500			27,000
Allowance for doubtful accounts			(1,350)			(1,500)
Inventory	39,000			37,500		
Furniture and fixtures		67,500			52,500	
Accumulated depreciation		(12,000)				
Notes payable		(10,500)			(10,500)	
Net assets contributed	$ 52,500	$54,000	$52,650	$51,000	$51,000	$51,000

Required:

1. Based on the information presented, prepare the journal entry to record the contributions each partner made to the partnership.
2. Prepare the Liabilities and Owners' Equity section of the partnership balance sheet immediately following the partner contributions on November 16, 2009.

PB12-3 Dividing Income—All Four Methods   LO2

Toffee and Bonnie are partners in the Toffnie partnership. Partnership net income for the current year is $81,000. Other relevant information follows.

	Capital Balances	Salaries	Interest	Fixed Ratio
Toffee	$27,000	$31,500	10%	1/3
Bonnie	48,000	45,000	10	2/3

Required:

Determine the allocation of net income to each of the partners under each of the following four independent assumptions:

1. Fixed Ratio.
2. Interest on partners' capital balances and any remaining amounts on a fixed ratio.
3. Salaries to partners and any remaining amounts on a fixed ratio.
4. Salaries to partners, interest on partners' capital balances and any remaining amounts on a fixed ratio.

PB12-4 Dividing Income, Journalizing, and Preparing Partners' Capital Statement   LO2

C. Crow, R. Beare, and K. Marin are partners in the CRM partnership. Partnership net income for 2009 is $59,000. Other relevant information follows.

	Capital 1/1/09	Capital Contributions	Fixed Ratio	Partner Drawings
C. Crow	$10,500	$6,000	32%	$ 8,000
R. Beare	18,000	4,500	17	7,000
K. Marin	22,500	3,000	51	10,000

Required:

1. Allocate the net income to the partners based on the fixed ratio.
2. Prepare the partners' capital statement at December 31, 2009.

LO3

PB12-5 Admitting a Partner—Journalizing Purchase and Investment Situations

Dott and Latta are partners in the DL partnership. They agree to admit Caspar into the partnership. Assume any bonuses will be allocated on the basis of the fixed ratio prior to the admission of the new partner. Additional information available prior to Caspar's admission follows.

	Dott	Latta
Capital account balance	$ 91,500	$ 85,500
Fixed ratio	60%	40%

Required:

Prepare journal entries to record the admission of Caspar, under each of the following independent assumptions.

1. Caspar pays Dott and Latta $28,500 each. In exchange he receives 25% of each partner's capital account balance.
2. Caspar invests $40,000 into the partnership in exchange for a 20% interest in the partnership.
3. Caspar invests $90,000 into the partnership in exchange for a 30% interest in the partnership.

LO3

PB12-6 Journalizing Partner Withdrawals

Pinkey, Brainne, and Snobal are partners in the Take Over partnership. Snobal decides to withdraw from the partnership. According to the partnership agreement, any bonuses will be allocated on the basis of fixed ratios prior to the withdrawal. Additional information available prior to the withdrawal follows.

	Pinkey	Brainne	Snobal
Capital account balance	$40,500	$48,000	$31,500
Fixed ratio	35%	45%	20%

Required:

Prepare journal entries to record the withdrawal of Snobal, under each of the following independent assumptions.

1. Pinkey and Brainne agree to purchase 50 percent of Snobal's capital account balance for $17,000 each.
2. The partnership pays Snobal $29,500 for his partnership interest.
3. The partnership pays Snobal $35,100 for his partnership interest.

LO4

PB12-7 Liquidating a Partnership with No Capital Deficiency and Making Journal Entries

Assume when the partnership of Flour, Rice, and Salt liquidates, account balances before liquidation are as follows.

Assets		Liabilities and Owners' Equity	
Cash	$ 16,000	Accounts payable	$ 12,000
Inventory	32,000	Notes payable	48,000
Furniture and fixtures	64,000	Flour, capital (30% fixed ratio)	5,000
Accumulated depreciation	(12,000)	Rice, capital (15% fixed ratio)	15,000
		Salt, capital (55% fixed ratio)	20,000
	$100,000		$100,000

Required:

Assume the Flour, Rice, and Salt partnership sold its assets (except cash) for $80,000. Record the following entries:

1. Sale of the partnership assets (except cash).
2. Allocation of gain or loss to each of the partners.
3. Payment of outstanding partnership liabilities.
4. Distribution of remaining cash to partners.

PB12-8 Liquidating a Partnership with Capital Deficiency (Payment and Nonpayment by Partner) and Making Journal Entries

LO4

Assume the same facts as in PB12-7, except that the fixed ratios for Flour, Rice, and Salt are 25%, 30%, and 45%, respectively.

Required:

Assume the assets of Flour, Rice, and Salt partnership sold all assets (except cash) for $60,000. Record the following entries:

1. Sale of the partnership assets (except cash).
2. Allocation of gain or loss to each of the partners.
3. Payment of outstanding liabilities of partnership
4. Distribution of remaining cash to partners assuming Flour pays the deficiency.
5. Distribution of the remaining cash to partners assuming Flour does not pay the deficiency.

PB12-9 Calculating Partner Return on Equity (ROE)

LO5

Preppen, Somme, and Allison are partners in the PSA partnership. Information related to the partners follows.

	Total	Preppen	Somme	Allison
Balance 1/1/2008	$40,000	$5,000	$10,000	$25,000
Contributions	6,000	2,000	2,000	2,000
Net income	25,000	8,000	10,000	7,000
Drawings	(18,000)	(6,000)	(9,000)	(3,000)
Balance 12/31/2008	$53,000	$9,000	$13,000	$31,000

Required:

1. Calculate the partnership ROE.
2. Calculate the ROE for each partner.
3. Which partner has the best ROE? Why?

Cases and Projects

CP12-1 Making Key Partnership Decisions

LO1, 2

Harrison and Daniel are two brothers who have been developing video games for several years as a hobby. Their games have proven to be very popular, so they recently decided to turn their hobby into a business venture. Harrison—the older and more responsible brother—has accumulated $30,000 to contribute to the business to get it started. Daniel, on the other hand, has relatively little capital to contribute ($3,000), but he has tremendous creativity and energy. After the business is established, Harrison is likely to work 20 hours per week developing games for the business and Daniel will work 40 hours per week. The brothers get along well, and do not anticipate any problems working together, however their oldest brother Tiger claims that eventually relationships change so they should plan for that possibility. Tiger claims that someday he might even be interested in joining them in running the business, or helping their kids to take over the business. Harrison and Daniel do not want to invest a lot of time or energy establishing the new business, so they have come to you for advice.

Required:

1. Should Harrison and Daniel form a partnership or limited liability company? List the differences between these two forms of business and then make a recommendation based on the facts you know about Harrison and Daniel.

2. Assume Harrison and Daniel decide to form a partnership. Explain the elements they should include in the partnership agreement. Provide specific advice for the division of profits and losses, taking into account the different contributions of capital and time that they plan to make.

CP12-2 Resolving Inequitable Partnership Contributions

LO2

Last year, Mick and Sayesha entered into a partnership to establish and run a local music promotions business called MuSick Promos (MSP). Both partners contributed $2,000 to the business to get MSP off the ground. They had verbally agreed to contribute their own special talents to MSP in approximately equal proportions. Mick was in his final year as a marketing major at a local university and Sayesha was a struggling musician who had many contacts in the local music scene. For that first year, Sayesha worked about 20 hours a week finding bands to represent and promoting to clubs and other venues in the city. Mick spent an equal amount of time building relationships with local clubs that would hire bands to play at weekend events. Both Mick and Sayesha succeeded in their efforts. Mick had found about 15 clubs that regularly hired the artists promoted by MSP, and Sayesha had signed an equal number of bands to represent.

As MSP entered its second year of operations, Mick and Sayesha started having problems. Sayesha complained that now that Mick had graduated and taken a full-time sales job with a newspaper company, he spent only a few hours a week on MSP business, yet she still spent about 15 hours a week drumming up bands to represent. Mick responded by explaining that his hard work during the first year had led to long-lasting relationships with the clubs, so he had little to do except occasionally keep in touch with the clubs' managers. In contrast, the bands signed by Sayesha frequently broke up or moved to other cities as their popularity fell or grew. Mick tried to further justify his situation by saying that his new job allowed him to leave his share of MSP's profits in the business. In contrast, he complained, Sayesha had withdrawn most of her share to pay her rent and other living costs. Mick said this imbalance in capital account balances caused differences in the partners' return on equity ratios, which were unfair to him.

Required:

1. Evaluate the validity of each argument expressed by Mick and Sayesha. Are these arguments reasonable and equally valid? With whom would you side if you were asked to reconcile their situation?

2. Could the conflict have been avoided? How? Can something be done now to improve the partners' future relations?

LO5

CP12-3 Making Ethical Decisions: A Mini-Case

Frank was recently hired as an accountant for the TMM Partnership. When the partnership published its quarterly figures, Frank noticed the return on equity figures seemed odd. After asking a few co-workers, he found that the figures were artificially and intentionally inflated each quarter. This type of reporting seemed to be a recurring event that co-workers questioned but accepted because they resulted in higher bonuses and "nobody" was hurt by it. The published results became a water cooler topic that Frank's co-workers were laughing about all the way to the bank. Frank saw the funding that the partnership was receiving based on the figures and realized that it was providing him and his co-workers with a great deal of job security. Frank thought, Who is it hurting anyway? Why should I put all of these benefits in jeopardy by saying something? With this reasoning, Frank decided to do nothing.

Required:

1. Describe the ethical dilemma that Frank faces.

2. Who benefits and who is harmed by reporting inflated ROE figures?

3. Do you think Frank handled the situation correctly? Would you have handled it differently?

LO1

CP12-4 Forming a Partnership or Limited Liability Company

Assume you are considering forming a general partnership or a limited liability company (LLC) in your state. Search the Internet for the required documents and forms needed to establish such business forms in your state. A good starting place for this search is the Web site smallbusiness.findlaw.com.

Required:

1. Prepare a checklist of key steps to follow when starting a partnership.

2. Locate and provide copies of any forms that must be filed to form a limited liability company (LLC).

13 Accounting for Corporations

LEARNING OBJECTIVES

After completing this chapter, you should be able to:

LO1 Describe the characteristics of corporations.

LO2 Demonstrate how to account for transactions involving common stock, preferred stock, and treasury stock.

Lectured presentations–13-1
www.mhhe.com/LLPW1e

LO3 Demonstrate how to account for cash dividends, stock dividends, and stock splits.

LO4 Analyze the earnings per share (EPS) and price/earnings (P/E) ratios.

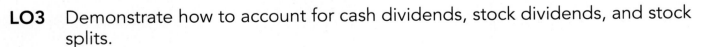

Focus Company: SONIC CORP.

America's Drive-In

www.sonicdrivein.com

N ews about shares of stock is everywhere. You can read it in the *Wall Street Journal,* listen to it on MSNBC, or search for it at Yahoo!Finance. Behind this fascination with stock is a dream many people share: taking a small amount of money and turning it into a fortune.

That is what Sonic Corp.—America's largest drive-in restaurant chain—has managed to do. When Sonic first started operations as a hamburger and root beer stand about 35 years ago, the company was selling 100 shares of stock to store owners for $100. As the company grew larger and more profitable, the value of its stock increased. By 1995, Sonic was selling 100 shares to investors for $2,125. Since then, those shares have split five times, causing 100 shares to multiply into 760 shares. Sonic is now buying back its stock at over $19 a share. That is more than $14,400 for the 100 shares bought in 1995, or an increase of nearly 700 percent in little more than a decade!

In this chapter, you will see how companies such as Sonic Corp. account for various stock transactions, including stock issues, stock splits, and stock dividends. Soon you'll understand many of the stock terms used in the financial news.

559

CHARACTERISTICS OF THE CORPORATE FORM	ACCOUNTING FOR STOCK TRANSACTIONS	ACCOUNTING FOR DIVIDENDS AND SPLITS	FINANCIAL RATIO ANALYSIS
• Ownership • Laws and Taxes • Formation • Financing	• Common and Preferred Stock • Treasury Stock • Financial Statement Reporting	• Cash Dividends on Common Stock • Cash Dividends on Preferred Stock • Stock Dividends • Stock Splits • Statement of Retained Earnings	• Earnings per Share (EPS) • Price/Earnings (P/E) Ratio

CHARACTERISTICS OF THE CORPORATE FORM

If you were to write down the names of 50 familiar businesses, probably all of them would be corporations. According to Bizstats.com, corporations account for 85 percent of the total sales reported by U.S. businesses. Furthermore, many people own shares in corporations, either directly or indirectly, through a mutual fund or pension program. You probably recall from Chapter 1 that the act of creating a corporation is costly. Why, then, is the corporate form so popular?

Ownership

The secret to the popularity of the corporate form is that investors both large and small can easily participate in a corporation's ownership. This widespread participation gives corporations one critical advantage over sole proprietorships and partnerships: They can raise large amounts of money. Several factors encourage investors to participate in corporate ownership:

1. **Shares of stock can be purchased in small amounts.** According to Yahoo!Finance, on January 21, 2008, you could have become one of Sonic Corp.'s owners by buying a single share of the company's stock for just $19. Owners of corporations are called stockholders or shareholders.

2. **Ownership interests are transferable.** Shares of a company's stock can be bought and sold, allowing new investors to become owners and existing owners to leave the business. If a corporation is a public company, any member of the public can buy or sell the company's shares through a stock market, such as the New York Stock Exchange. Sonic is a public company, but not all corporations are public companies. Chick-fil-A and Cargill, for example, are private companies whose shares are bought and sold privately.

3. **Stockholders are not liable for the corporation's debts.** Creditors have no legal claim on stockholders' personal assets as they do on the personal assets of those who own sole proprietorships and partnerships. So, if you owned stock in the old Montgomery Ward department store, which went bankrupt and was liquidated in 2000, you could lose only what you paid to buy the stock. You would not be liable for the hundreds of millions of dollars of debt that the company could not pay back.

Laws and Taxes

The law recognizes a corporation as a separate legal entity. It may own assets, incur liabilities, expand and contract in size, sue others and be sued, and enter into contracts independently of its owners. Because a corporation exists separate and apart from its owners, it does not die when its owners die. Thomas Edison died in 1931, but the company he founded—General Electric—continues in existence today.

As a separate legal entity, a corporation is obligated to pay taxes on the net income it generates. This obligation is reported on the balance sheet as the current liability Income Taxes

Payable. Because income taxes are a necessary cost of being a corporation, they are reported as an expense on the income statement.

Formation

To protect everyone's rights, the law tightly regulates the creation and oversight of corporations. Owners create corporations by submitting an application to a state government (not the federal government). Because laws vary from state to state, you might decide to create a corporation in a state that differs from the one(s) where it operates. Although Sonic has its headquarters in Oklahoma City, it was actually incorporated in Delaware. More than half of the largest corporations in the United States are incorporated in Delaware because it has some of the most favorable laws for establishing corporations. If the application is approved, the state issues a charter, which specifies the corporation's name and address, the nature of its business, and the type and number of shares that the corporation can issue.

The type and number of shares can vary greatly from one corporation to the next. In its most basic form, a corporation must have one type of share, appropriately called common stock. Owners of common stock usually enjoy the following benefits:

- **Voting rights.** For each share you own, you get one vote on major issues, such as which accounting firm will audit the company's books and who will serve on the board of directors. As Exhibit 13.1 illustrates, the board of directors appoints the corporation's executive officers and governs top management.
- **Dividends.** Dividends can be declared as a way of distributing the corporation's profits to its stockholders.
- **Residual claim.** If a corporation ceases to operate, stockholders share in any remaining assets after the company has paid all of its debts.
- **Preemptive rights.** Existing stockholders may be given the first chance to buy newly issued stock before it is offered to others.

In addition to common stock, corporations can issue preferred stock to a select group of investors. This special form of stock differs from common stock, typically in the following ways:

1. **Preferred stock generally does not include voting rights.** As a result, preferred stock does not appeal to investors who want some control over a company's operations. However, it does appeal to existing common stockholders because the company can sell preferred stock to raise funds without reducing common stockholders' voting control.

Exhibit 13.1   **Typical Organizational Structure of a Corporation**

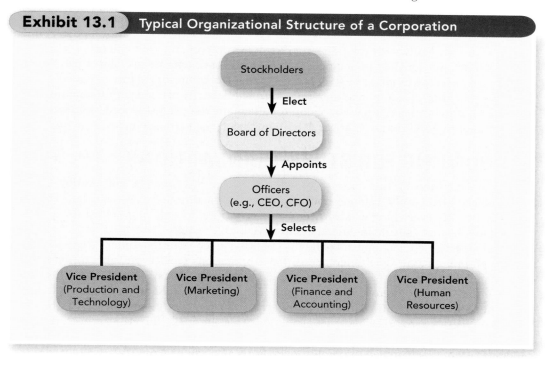

2. **Dividends on preferred stock, if any, are paid at a fixed rate,** specified as either a dollar amount or a percentage per share. For example, if dividends are declared on "6 percent preferred stock," the dividend will equal 6 percent of the stock's par value. A fixed dividend can be attractive to certain investors, such as retirees or company founders, who seek a stable income from their investments.

3. **Preferred stock carries priority over common stock.** Preferred stockholders have higher priority than common stockholders if a corporation distributes assets to its owners through dividends or at liquidation. That is, any dividends the corporation declares must be paid to preferred stockholders before they can be paid to common stockholders. Also, if the corporation goes out of business, its assets will be sold and used to pay creditors and then preferred stockholders. Common stockholders are paid last from whatever assets remain after paying preferred stockholders.

Financing

Whenever a corporation needs a large amount of long-term financing, its executives must decide whether to obtain it by issuing new stock to investors (equity financing) or by borrowing money from lenders (debt financing). Both these forms of financing have certain advantages as listed in Exhibit 13.2.

Exhibit 13.2	Advantages of Equity versus Debt Financing
Advantages of Equity Financing	**Advantages of Debt Financing**
1. Equity does not have to be repaid. Debt must be repaid or refinanced.	1. Interest on debt is tax deductible. Dividends on stock are not tax deductible.
2. Dividends are optional. Interest must be paid on debt.	2. Debt does not change stockholder control. In contrast, a stock issue gives new stockholders the right to vote and share in the earnings, diluting existing stockholders' control.

These relative advantages play a significant role in determining whether equity or debt financing is more appropriate for a particular corporation. One corporation's officers might be concerned primarily with the impact of financing on corporate income taxes. Thus, they might decide to rely on debt financing because interest payments are tax deductible. Another corporation's executives might be so concerned about the company's ability to pay off existing liabilities that they decide not to take on additional debt. By using equity financing, which does not need to be repaid, they can obtain the financing the company needs. Ultimately, the decision to pursue additional equity or debt financing depends on a company's circumstances.

ACCOUNTING FOR STOCK TRANSACTIONS

Learning Objective 2

Demonstrate how to account for transactions involving common stock, preferred stock, and treasury stock.

We should mention at the outset that **all transactions between a corporation and its stockholders affect only balance sheet accounts.** In addition, you should be pleased to know that nearly everything you learned about accounting for sole proprietorships applies to corporations as well. The main differences involve owner's equity.

See Exhibit 13.3 for a summary of how accounting for corporations differs from accounting for sole proprietorships. One difference is that corporations replace the label owner's equity with stockholders' equity to indicate that stockholders own the business. Another difference is that unlike sole proprietorships, which use just one capital account to accumulate all of the owner's investments and withdrawals and the company's net income, corporations use at least two types of capital account. Contributions that are made directly to the corporation by stockholders are referred to as Contributed Capital. The net income that the corporation generates each year through profitable operations is accumulated in a separate account,

Exhibit 13.3	Accounting Differences for Sole Proprietorships and Corporations

Sole Proprietorships

Owner's Equity

Joe Smith, Capital   =   Contributions   +   Net Income   –   Withdrawals

Corporations

Stockholders' Equity

| Contributed Capital | = | Contributions | | |
| Retained Earnings | = | | Net Income | – Dividends |

Retained Earnings. Unlike a sole proprietor, who may take money out of the business in the form of withdrawals, stockholders must rely on dividends. Dividends are subtracted from Retained Earnings as shown in Exhibit 13.3.

In the following section, we look more closely at transactions that affect Contributed Capital. Those transactions include issues of common stock and preferred stock and the repurchase of shares in the form of treasury stock.

Common and Preferred Stock

Stock Authorization

The corporate charter authorizes and defines the specific rights and characteristics of a corporation's stock. This authorization does not directly affect the accounting records, but it does establish certain characteristics that will later affect how to account for the stock.

One characteristic of importance is the stock's **par value.** Oddly enough, par value has little meaning today. It was originally introduced to prevent stockholders from removing their contributed capital after discovering that the business was going bankrupt. Today, stronger laws and regulations prevent that from happening, so the concept of par value is no longer critical to this aspect of the business.

Many states still require corporations to specify a par value for their stock. Typically, they set par value at a minimal amount, such as $0.01 per share, as Sonic did with its common stock. Other states have dropped the requirement to specify a par value and instead allow corporations to issue no-par value stock. **No-par value stock** is just like stock with par value except that it does not have a specified legal value per share. Although par value is a legal concept that is not related in any way to the share's market value, it does affect how to account for stock as you will see in the next section.

Stock Issues

Par Value Common Stock Issued for Cash.
The sale of stock from the corporation to an investor is called a stock issue. In most cases, these sales are cash transactions. To see how to account for an issue of par value stock, assume that during the next fiscal year, Sonic receives cash for 100,000 shares of its $0.01 par value common stock issued when the market price is $30 per share. This stock issue would be accounted for as follows:

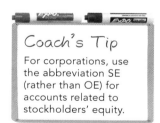

Coach's Tip

For corporations, use the abbreviation SE (rather than OE) for accounts related to stockholders' equity.

	Debit	Credit
Cash (+A) (100,000 × $30)	3,000,000	
Common Stock (+SE) (100,000 × $0.01)		1,000
Additional Paid-In Capital (+SE) ($3,000,000 – $1,000)		2,999,000

Assets	=	Liabilities	+	Stockholders' Equity	
Cash +3,000,000				Common Stock	+1,000
				Additional Paid-In Capital	+2,999,000

Notice that the account Common Stock is used to indicate the type of stock issued. The increase in the Common Stock account is the number of shares sold times the par value per share (100,000 × $0.01). Any amount received in excess of the par value is recorded in a separate account appropriately named Additional Paid-In Capital. These two accounts are reported in the Stockholders' Equity section of the balance sheet; together, they represent Contributed Capital.

No-Par Value Common Stock Issued for Cash.

If the corporate charter does not specify a par value for the stock, the total cash received from the sale of stock is entered in the Common Stock account. For example, if 100,000 shares of no-par common stock were issued for $30 per share, the journal entry would be:

	Debit	Credit
Cash (+A) (100,000 × $30)	3,000,000	
Common Stock (+SE) (100,000 × $30)		3,000,000

Assets	=	Liabilities	+	Stockholders' Equity
Cash +3,000,000				Common Stock +3,000,000

Common Stock Issued for Noncash Assets.

In some cases, a corporation might receive items other than cash in exchange for its shares. This situation occurs most often when someone starts a private company and contributes land, buildings, or equipment to the corporation.

Noncash transactions such as this are accounted for using the value of the items contributed to or given up by the corporation, whichever is easier to determine. Typically, the value of a private company's stock is difficult to determine because it is bought and sold infrequently. So usually the transaction is recorded using the value of the items contributed to the corporation. For example, if equipment valued at $50,000 were contributed to a private company in exchange for 10,000 common shares with a par value of $0.01 per share, the transaction would be recorded as:

	Debit	Credit
Equipment (+A)	50,000	
Common Stock (+SE) (10,000 × $0.01)		100
Additional Paid-In Capital (+SE) ($50,000 − $100)		49,900

Assets	=	Liabilities	+	Stockholders' Equity
Equipment +50,000				Common Stock +100
				Additional Paid-In Capital +49,900

Preferred Stock.

Just like common stock, preferred stock may be designated par value or no-par value and may be issued for cash or noncash assets. If preferred stock specifies a par value, any contributions in excess of par value are recorded as "Additional Paid-In Capital (APIC)—Preferred" to distinguish it from Additional Paid-In Capital related to common stock. In all other respects, **preferred stock issues are accounted for in the same way as common stock issues.** To illustrate, if Sonic issued 10,000 shares of $0.01 par value preferred stock for $40 per share, the company records the following journal entry:

	Debit	Credit
Cash (+A) (10,000 × $40)	400,000	
Preferred Stock (+SE) (10,000 × $0.01)		100
Additional Paid-In Capital— Preferred (+SE) ($400,000 − $100)		399,900

Assets		=	Liabilities	+	Stockholders' Equity	
Cash	+400,000				Preferred Stock	+100
					APIC—Preferred	+399,900

Stock Sold between Investors. When a company issues stock to an investor, the transaction is between the issuing corporation and the investor so it is recorded by the corporation. After the initial sale, investors can sell shares to other investors without directly affecting the corporation or its accounting records.

Assume, for example, that investor Aaron Cadieux sold 1,000 shares of Sonic stock to Tara Rink. Aaron received cash for the shares he sold, and Tara received shares for the cash she paid, but Sonic did not receive or pay anything. Following the separate entity assumption (see Chapter 1), Sonic would not record a journal entry on its books because the transaction involved only the stock's owners, not the corporation itself. (Think of an auto dealer who records the sale of a car to a customer but does nothing when the customer later sells the car to someone else.)

Stock Used to Compensate Employees. To encourage employees to work hard, many corporations offer a combination of base pay, cash bonuses, and stock options. Stock options allow employees to buy company stock at a predetermined price during a specified period. The idea is that if employees work hard to meet the company's goals, the stock price is likely to increase. If it increases before the options expire, employees can exercise their right to buy stock at the lower price and then sell it at the higher market price for an immediate profit. If the stock price declines, employees have not lost anything. Accounting rules require that when granting stock options, a company must report an expense for the estimated cost associated with stock options. The procedures for doing so are complex, so they are discussed in intermediate accounting courses.

Spotlight On ETHICS

Stock Options Motivate, but at Whose Expense?

Some critics claim that stock options, which are intended to give senior executives of a company the same goals as stockholders, are often granted at the expense of existing stockholders. When senior executives exercise their stock options to buy new stock, existing stockholders lose voting power because their percentage of ownership in the company is diluted. Furthermore, critics contend that stock options encourage senior executives to overstate financial results in an attempt to increase the company's stock price so they can reap huge personal gains.

Treasury Stock

Although corporations are never obligated to buy back their own stock, some companies find it desirable to do so. A corporation may repurchase its own stock (1) to signal to investors that the company believes its stock is worth purchasing, (2) to obtain shares that can be reissued as payment for purchases of other companies, or (3) to obtain shares to reissue to employees as part of stock option plans. When a corporation buys its own stock back from stockholders, the stock is called treasury stock. While the corporation holds these shares, they do not offer voting, dividend, or other stockholder rights.

Acquisition of Treasury Stock

Most companies record the purchase of treasury stock based on the cost of the shares that are purchased. This approach is called the cost method. If a company bought 50,000 shares of its common stock at a market price of $25 per share, the total cost of $1,250,000 (= 50,000 shares × $25) would be recorded as follows:

	Debit	Credit
Treasury Stock (+xSE, −SE)	1,250,000	
Cash (−A)		1,250,000

Assets	=	Liabilities	+	Stockholders' Equity	
Cash −1,250,000				Treasury Stock (+xSE) −1,250,000	

Coach's Tip

Treasury stock is not reported as an asset because it does not differ in substance from unissued stock certificates.

Treasury stock is recorded in a contra stockholders' equity account, which we indicate using the abbreviation xSE. Treasury Stock is subtracted from total stockholders' equity on the balance sheet as shown in the example in Exhibit 13.4.

Reissue of Treasury Stock

When a corporation reissues shares of treasury stock, the company receives cash. The amount of cash received may be more or less than the amount the company initially paid to acquire it, depending on the market price for the stock. The accounting effects depend on whether treasury stock is reissued above or below its initial cost.

Reissue above Cost. To illustrate this case, we extend the example in which the treasury stock was acquired at a cost of $25 per share. If the company resold 5,000 shares of the

Exhibit 13.4 Excerpt from Sonic Corp.'s Balance Sheet   SONIC DRIVE-IN

Sonic Corp.
Partial Balance Sheet
November 30, 2006
(dollars in thousands)

STOCKHOLDERS' EQUITY	
Contributed Capital	
Common Stock, Par Value $0.01 per share	
Authorized: 245,000,000 Shares	
Issued: 115,183,800 Shares	$ 1,152
Additional Paid-In Capital	178,115
Preferred Stock, Par Value $0.01 per share; none outstanding	—
Retained Earnings	491,980
Other	(4,035)
	667,212
Treasury Stock, at cost 47,171,602 Common Shares	(666,584)
Total Stockholders' Equity	$ 628

treasury stock for $27 per share, the required journal entry is:

	Debit	Credit
Cash (+A) (5,000 × $27)	135,000	
Treasury Stock (−xSE,+SE) (5,000 × $25)		125,000
Additional Paid-In Capital— Treasury (+SE) [5,000 × ($27 − $25)]		10,000

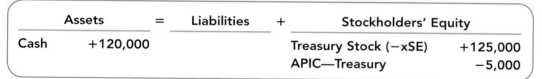

Assets	=	Liabilities	+	Stockholders' Equity	
Cash +135,000				Treasury Stock (−xSE)	+125,000
				APIC—Treasury	+10,000

Reissue below Cost. Assume the company resold 5,000 shares of treasury stock for $24 per share. Again, the company initially paid $25 per share to repurchase the stock. In this case, the required journal entry is:

	Debit	Credit
Cash (+A) (5,000 × $24)	120,000	
Additional Paid-In Capital—Treasury (−SE) [5,000 × ($25 − $24)]	5,000	
Treasury Stock (−xSE,+SE) (5,000 × $25)		125,000

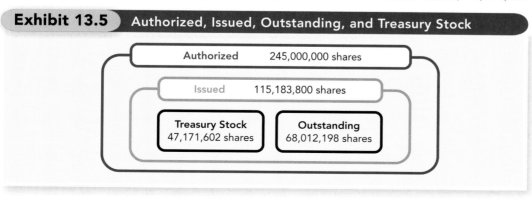

Assets	=	Liabilities	+	Stockholders' Equity	
Cash +120,000				Treasury Stock (−xSE)	+125,000
				APIC—Treasury	−5,000

Coach's Tip

As with all stock issues, the reissue of treasury stock affects only balance sheet accounts.

Coach's Tip

Additional Paid-In Capital never has a debit balance.

If a company fully depletes its balance in Additional Paid-In Capital—Treasury, any excess should be debited to Retained Earnings.

Financial Statement Reporting

In addition to reporting the dollar amounts for common stock, preferred stock, and treasury stock, corporations must disclose the number of shares related to those amounts. Most companies report this information on the balance sheet, as in Exhibit 13.4. Note in the exhibit that the authorized number of shares was 245 million common shares, but only 115,183,800 common shares had actually been issued. Unless the company buys them back, these shares will be owned forever by one investor or another. As you can see in the next-to-last line of Exhibit 13.4, Sonic held 47,171,602 shares of treasury stock that had been repurchased from the previously issued common shares.

Shares that have been issued but the corporation has not bought back are called outstanding shares. Based on Exhibit 13.4, you should be able to compute the number of Sonic shares still outstanding. As Exhibit 13.5 shows, of the 115,183,800 common shares issued, 47,171,602

Exhibit 13.5   Authorized, Issued, Outstanding, and Treasury Stock

Authorized	245,000,000 shares
Issued	115,183,800 shares
Treasury Stock 47,171,602 shares	Outstanding 68,012,198 shares

were repurchased, which means that 68,012,198 (= 115,183,800 − 47,171,602) were still outstanding. This number is important to financial analysts who need to express certain dollar amounts on a per share basis. Earnings per share (EPS)—a key financial ratio discussed later in this chapter—is expressed in terms of the number of outstanding shares.

SELF-STUDY PRACTICE

1. Assume that Aéropostale, Inc. issued 1,000 shares of its common stock, par value $0.01, for $21,900. Show the journal entry to record this transaction.

	Debit	Credit

2. Assume that Aéropostale, Inc. repurchased 500 of its common shares when the stock was selling for $20 per share. Show the journal entry to record this transaction at cost.

	Debit	Credit

3. Assume that Aéropostale, Inc. reissued 100 shares of its treasury stock at a market value of $25 per share. Show the journal entry to record this transaction.

	Debit	Credit

After you have finished, check your answers with the solution at the bottom of the page.

ACCOUNTING FOR DIVIDENDS AND SPLITS

Cash Dividends on Common Stock

Learning Objective 3

Demonstrate how to account for cash dividends, stock dividends, and stock splits.

Investors buy common stock because they expect a return on their investment. That return can come in two forms: dividends and increases in the stock price. Some investors prefer to buy stocks that pay little or no dividends (called "growth stocks") because companies that reinvest most of their earnings tend to increase their future earnings potential as well as their

Solution to Self-Study Practice

1.

	Debit	Credit
Cash (+A)	21,900	
Common Stock (+SE) (1,000 × $0.01)		10
Additional Paid-In Capital (+SE)		21,890

2.

	Debit	Credit
Treasury Stock (+xSE, −SE)	10,000	
Cash (−A) ($20 × 500)		10,000

3.

	Debit	Credit
Cash (+A) ($25 × 100)	2,500	
Treasury Stock (−xSE, +SE)		2,000
Additional Paid-In Capital—Treasury (+SE)		500

$2,000 = 100 shares × $20
$ 500 = 100 shares × ($25 − $20)

Video 13-2
www.mhhe.com/LLPW1e

stock prices. Dell Corporation, for example, has never paid a dividend, yet if you had bought 100 shares in Dell when they were first issued on June 22, 1988, for $850, your investment would have been worth about $200,000 when this chapter was written. Other investors, such as retired people who need a steady income, prefer to receive their return in the form of dividends. These people often seek stocks that pay dividends consistently (called "income stocks"), such as Coca-Cola, which has paid cash dividends each year since 1893.

A corporation does not have a legal obligation to pay dividends. The board of directors makes the decision each time a dividend is to be paid. Whenever the board of directors formally declares a dividend, a liability is created.

Dividend Dates

If Sonic were to declare a dividend, its press release would contain three important dates. In the following announcement, note the declaration date (May 20), the date of record (June 14), and the date of payment (July 1).

> **Sonic Corp. Announces Cash Dividend**
>
> Oklahoma City, Okla., May 20, 2008—Sonic Corp. (Nasdaq: SONC) announced today that the Company's Board of Directors declared a cash dividend of $.02 per common share, payable on or about July 1, 2008 to stockholders of record as of June 14, 2008.

SONIC DRIVE-IN

Declaration Date. The declaration date (in this case, May 20) is the date on which the board of directors officially approves the dividend. As soon as the board makes the declaration, the company records an increase in its liabilities and a corresponding decrease in Retained Earnings. **Dividends are distributions of a company's accumulated prior earnings,** so they are reported as a reduction in Retained Earnings on the balance sheet. **Dividends are not reported on the income statement because they are not expenses.**

With over 68 million common shares outstanding, the $0.02 dividend per share would equal $1,360,244 (= $0.02 × 68,012,198). The journal entry to record them is:

	Debit	Credit
Retained Earnings (−SE)	1,360,244	
Dividends Payable (+L)		1,360,244

Assets	=	Liabilities	+	Stockholders' Equity
		Dividends Payable +1,360,244		Retained Earnings −1,360,244

Date of Record. The next date, the record date (here, June 14), is the date on which the corporation prepares the list of current stockholders based on its records. The dividend is payable only to those names listed on the record date. Sonic makes no journal entry on this date.

Date of Payment. The third date, the payment date (July 1 in this example), is the date on which Sonic disburses cash to pay the dividend liability. When the dividend is paid and the liability is satisfied on July 1, the journal entry is:

	Debit	Credit
Dividends Payable (−L)	1,360,244	
Cash (−A)		1,360,244

Assets	=	Liabilities	+	Stockholders' Equity
Cash −1,360,244		Dividends Payable −1,360,244		

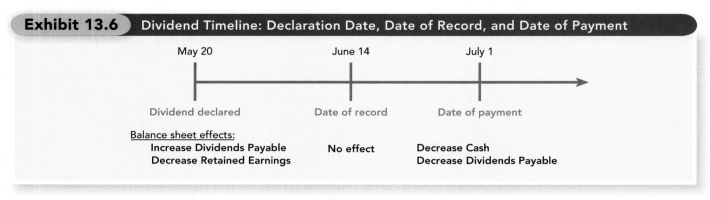

Exhibit 13.6   Dividend Timeline: Declaration Date, Date of Record, and Date of Payment

May 20	June 14	July 1
Dividend declared	Date of record	Date of payment

Balance sheet effects:

Increase Dividends Payable Decrease Retained Earnings	No effect	Decrease Cash Decrease Dividends Payable

The timeline in Exhibit 13.6 summarizes these three dates and the corresponding balance sheet effects.

Dividend Requirements

Notice in Exhibit 13.6 that the declaration of a cash dividend decreases Retained Earnings. Notice too that payment of the cash dividend later reduces the Cash account by the same amount. These two observations explain the **two fundamental requirements for payment of a cash dividend:** sufficient retained earnings and sufficient cash.

Sufficient Retained Earnings. The corporation must have accumulated a sufficient amount of retained earnings to cover the amount of the dividend. State laws often restrict cash dividends to the balance in the Retained Earnings account. The company may be further restricted by clauses in loan agreements that require an even larger minimum balance in Retained Earnings. If the company were to violate such a clause, a lender could demand immediate repayment of outstanding loans. Because such a restriction can severely limit a company's ability to pay dividends, accounting rules require that companies disclose it in their notes to the financial statements.

Sufficient Cash. The corporation must have sufficient cash to pay the dividend. The company can use cash for a variety of purposes other than just paying dividends. Sonic may use cash to install new debit machines at its drive-ins or to pay down some of its debt. So in addition to considering the balance in Retained Earnings, corporations must ensure that they have sufficient cash available to pay any dividends that are declared.

Coach's Tip

A lender imposes dividend restrictions because it does not want to lend money to a corporation and then have the corporation give it to stockholders via dividends rather than use it to grow the business.

SELF-STUDY PRACTICE

Answer the following questions concerning dividends:

1. On which dividend date is a liability created?
2. A cash outflow occurs on which dividend date?
3. What are the two fundamental requirements for paying a cash dividend?

After you have finished, check your answers with the solution at the bottom of the page.

Cash Dividends on Preferred Stock

Because purchasers of preferred stock give up the voting rights available to owners of common stock, preferred stock offers them dividend preferences in return. The two most common dividend preferences are called current and cumulative preferences.

Current Dividend Preference

A **current dividend preference** requires preferred dividends to be paid before paying any dividends to holders of common stock. This preference is a feature of all preferred stock. After

Solution to
Self-Study Practice

1. Declaration date.
2. Date of payment.
3. Dividends can be paid only if both sufficient retained earnings and sufficient cash are available.

the current dividend preference has been met, and if no other preference exists, dividends may be paid to the common stockholders.

When a company declares dividends, the current preferred dividend preference must be met first; then any remaining declared dividends go to common stockholders. Consider the following example:

> ## Checker Company
> Preferred stock outstanding, 6%, par $20; 2,000 shares
> Common stock outstanding, par $10; 5,000 shares

Assume the preferred stock carries only a current dividend preference and Checker declared dividends totaling $8,000 and $10,000 in 2009 and 2010, respectively. In each year, a portion of the total dividends would go first to the preferred stockholders; the remaining amount would go to the common stockholders, as follows.

Year	Total Dividends Declared	Dividends on 6% Preferred Stock*	Dividends on Common Stock†
2009	$ 8,000	$2,400	$5,600
2010	10,000	2,400	7,600

* Dividends on Preferred Stock = 2,000 Shares × $20 Par Value × 6% Dividend = $2,400
† Dividends on Common Stock = Total Dividends Declared − Dividends on Preferred Stock

If Checker Company did not declare dividends in 2009, preferred stockholders would have been entitled to dividends of $2,400 in 2010 only. The current dividend preference does not carry over to later years unless the preferred stock is designated as cumulative, as we discuss next.

Cumulative Dividend Preference

A cumulative dividend preference states that if a company does not pay all or part of the current dividend in full, the cumulative unpaid amount, known as dividends in arrears, must be paid in the future before any other dividends may be paid. To illustrate, assume Checker Company has the same amount of stock outstanding as in the previous example but dividends have been in arrears for two years. In this case, when Checker declares dividends in 2009, preferred stockholders first receive $4,800 for the dividends in arrears (2 years × $2,400) and then they receive $2,400 for the current year (2009). Any remaining dividend goes to common stockholders:

Year	Total Dividends Declared	DIVIDENDS ON 6% PREFERRED STOCK In Arrears*	Current†	Dividends on Common Stock‡
2009	$ 8,000	$4,800	$2,400	$ 800
2010	10,000	—	2,400	7,600

* Dividends in Arrears Preference = 2,000 Shares × $20 Par Value × 6% Dividend × 2 Years = $4,800
† Current Dividend Preference = 2,000 Shares × $20 Par Value × 6% Dividend = $2,400
‡ Dividends on Common Stock = Total Dividends Declared − Total Dividends on Preferred Stock

Notice that after the dividends in arrears have been satisfied (in 2009), the dividend preference reverts back to just a current dividend preference (in 2010).

Spotlight On **FINANCIAL REPORTING**

Dividends in Arrears

American Skiing

Because dividends do not represent a liability until the board of directors declares them, dividends in arrears are not reported on the balance sheet. Instead, they are disclosed in the notes to the financial statements. The following note from American Skiing, a company that operates ski, snowboard, and golf resorts throughout the United States, is typical:

> Cumulative dividends in arrears totaled approximately $23.7 million and $109.3 million for the Series C-1 Preferred Stock and Series C-2 Preferred Stock, respectively.

Stock Dividends

The term dividend, when used alone with no adjectives, implies a cash dividend. However, some dividends are not paid in cash but in additional shares of stock. These dividends, called stock dividends, are distributed to a corporation's stockholders on a pro rata basis at no cost to the stockholder. The phrase "pro rata basis" means that each stockholder receives additional shares based on the percentage of shares held. A stockholder who owns 10 percent of the outstanding shares would receive 10 percent of any additional shares issued as a stock dividend.

The value assigned to a stock dividend depends on whether it is large or small. If a stock dividend equals more than 20 to 25 percent of the currently outstanding shares, it is considered a large stock dividend and is recorded at the par value of the stock to be issued. If the stock dividend equals less than 20 to 25 percent of the outstanding shares, it is considered a small stock dividend and is recorded at the market value of the stock.

To illustrate, assume that on January 30, 2008, Sonic declared a 10 percent (small) stock dividend on its 68,012,198 shares of $0.01 par value common stock for stockholders of record on February 10, 2008. The dividend was distributed on February 21, 2008. **On the declaration date** (January 30), Sonic would record this small stock dividend at the shares' market value. Assuming that the stock price is $30 per share, the value of the dividend would be $204,036,594 (=$30 per share × 68,012,198 shares × 10% dividend). The par value of the stock to be issued would be $68,012 (=$0.01 per share × 68,012,198 shares × 10% dividend).

Until the stock is actually distributed, this amount would be recorded in the stockholders' equity account Common Stock Dividend Distributable. The difference between the total market value and the par value of the stock to be issued ($204,036,594 − $68,012 = $203,968,582) would be recorded as Additional Paid-In Capital, as follows:

	Debit	Credit
Retained Earnings (−SE)	204,036,594	
Common Stock Dividend Distributable (+SE)		68,012
Additional Paid-In Capital (+SE)		203,968,582

Assets	=	Liabilities	+	Stockholders' Equity	
				Retained Earnings	−204,036,594
				Common Stock	
				Dividend Distributable	+68,012
				Additional Paid-In Capital	+203,968,582

Along with Common Stock, Additional Paid-In Capital, and Retained Earnings, Common Stock Dividend Distributable is reported in the Stockholders' Equity section of the balance sheet. It is not reported as a liability because assets will not be used to pay the dividend. Notice in the accounting equation effects shown that the stock dividend does not change total stockholders' equity. It changes only the balances in some of the accounts that make up stockholders' equity.

On the date of record (February 10), no journal entry would be made. **On the date of distribution** (February 21), the following journal entry would be made:

	Debit	Credit
Common Stock Dividend Distributable (−SE)	68,012	
Common Stock (+SE)		68,012

Assets	=	Liabilities	+	Stockholders' Equity	
				Common Stock	+68,012
				Common Stock Dividend Distributable	−68,012

Large stock dividends (greater than 20 to 25 percent of the outstanding shares) are accounted for in the same way as small stock dividends, except that they are recorded at the stock's par value rather than its market value. Consequently, the Additional Paid-In Capital account is not affected when a large stock dividend is declared.

Stock Splits

Stock splits are not dividends. They are similar to a stock dividend, but they are quite different in terms of how they occur and how they affect the stockholders' equity accounts. With a stock split, the corporation increases the total number of authorized shares by a specified amount, such as 2 for 1. In this example, the corporation calls in each share and issues two new shares in its place. At the same time, the par value of each share decreases, so the total par value of the shares remains unchanged. For example, if a company with 1 million shares outstanding of $0.01 par value stock executes a 2-for-1 stock split, it decreases the par value of its stock from $0.01 to $0.005 and doubles the number of shares outstanding. (Think of taking a four-piece pizza and cutting each piece into two halves.)

Because the decrease in par value per share offsets the increase in the number of shares, the company's financial position does not change, and **no journal entry is needed when stock is split.** Similarly, the market price of each share will decrease to offset the increase in the number of shares, so investors are no wealthier after the split than they were before.

	Before a 2-for-1 Stock Split	After a 2-for-1 Stock Split
Number of shares outstanding	1,000,000	2,000,000
Par value per share	$ 0.01	$ 0.005
Total par value outstanding	$ 10,000	$ 10,000

If you are like most new financial managers, you are probably wondering how a company's board of directors chooses between a 2-for-1 stock split and a "large" 100 percent stock dividend when both have the same effect—that of doubling the number of shares outstanding

Exhibit 13.7   Comparison of a 2-for 1 Stock Split, a 100 percent Stock Dividend, and a Cash Dividend

Stockholders' Equity	BEFORE	AFTER		
		2-for-1 Stock Split	100% Stock Dividend	$10,000 Cash Dividend
Contributed capital				
Number of common shares outstanding	1,000,000	2,000,000	2,000,000	1,000,000
Par value per common share	$ 0.01	$ 0.005	$ 0.01	$ 0.01
Common stock, at par	$ 10,000	$ 10,000	$ 20,000	$ 10,000
Additional paid-in capital	30,000	30,000	30,000	30,000
Retained earnings	650,000	650,000	640,000	640,000
Total stockholders' equity	$ 690,000	$ 690,000	$ 690,000	$ 680,000

and reducing the per share market price. The answer, it seems, is closely related to the method of accounting for stock dividends and splits. A stock dividend causes a reduction in Retained Earnings, whereas a stock split does not (see Exhibit 13.7).

By itself, this accounting difference might not mean much. Remember, though, that to declare a cash dividend, a company must maintain an adequate balance in Retained Earnings. If you are managing a company that you expect will struggle financially in the future, you will prefer a 2-for-1 stock split rather than a 100 percent stock dividend because the stock split does not reduce Retained Earnings, so it does not reduce your ability to declare cash dividends in the future. On the other hand, if you expect your company to be financially successful in the near future, you will not care that a stock dividend reduces Retained Earnings because future earnings will rebuild that account to allow cash dividends to be declared. In fact, you will probably **want** to declare a stock dividend to show how confident you are of your company's financial outlook. This reasoning suggests that **a company's board of directors may declare a stock dividend rather than a stock split to signal to financial statement users that the company expects to be sufficiently profitable to replenish the reduction in Retained Earnings caused by the stock dividend.**

SELF-STUDY PRACTICE

To reduce the market price of its stock, which was $50 per share, Vandalay Industries declared a 10 percent (small) stock dividend on its 1,000,000 outstanding shares of common stock (par value $10).

1. Prepare the journal entry that Vandalay would use to record this transaction.
2. What journal entry would be required if the transaction instead involved a 2-for-1 split? Theoretically, what would be the new stock price after the split?

After you have finished, check your answers with the solution at the bottom of the page.

Statement of Retained Earnings

Retained Earnings represents the total earnings retained in the company after distributing dividends to stockholders. You have already seen that whenever the corporation declares a cash dividend or stock dividend, the balance in Retained Earnings decreases. Its balance increases each year the company reports net income, as you will see next.

Solution to Self-Study Practice

1.

Retained Earnings (−SE)	5,000,000	
Common Stock Dividend Distributable (+SE)		1,000,000
Additional Paid-in Capital (+SE)		4,000,000

($5,000,000 = 1,000,000 × 10% × $50; $1,000,000 = 1,000,000 × 10% × $10)

2. No journal entry is required in the case of a stock split. Theoretically, the new price would be one-half of what it was before the split ($50 × ½ = $25).

Assume, for example, Sonic determined it had $78 million of net income after closing revenues and expenses to the Income Summary account. Sonic records the following journal entry to transfer that amount to Retained Earnings:

	Debit	Credit
Income Summary (−SE)	78,000,000	
Retained Earnings (+SE)		78,000,000

Assets	=	Liabilities	+	Stockholders' Equity	
				Income Summary	−78,000,000
				Retained Earnings	+78,000,000

To report the causes of increases and decreases in Retained Earnings, a Statement of Retained Earnings is prepared each accounting period.[1] (This report replaces the Statement of Owner's Equity that is prepared for sole proprietorships.) Exhibit 13.8 shows an example of this statement for Sonic, assuming a net income of $78 million, cash dividends on common stock of $1,360,244, stock dividends on common stock of $204,036,594, no cash dividends or stock dividends on preferred stock, and a beginning balance in Retained Earnings of $476 million.

Exhibit 13.8   **Statement of Retained Earnings**   SONIC DRIVE-IN

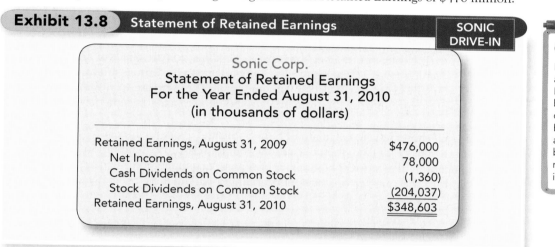

Sonic Corp.
Statement of Retained Earnings
For the Year Ended August 31, 2010
(in thousands of dollars)

Retained Earnings, August 31, 2009	$476,000
Net Income	78,000
Cash Dividends on Common Stock	(1,360)
Stock Dividends on Common Stock	(204,037)
Retained Earnings, August 31, 2010	$348,603

Coach's Tip

Like all permanent accounts, Retained Earnings carries its balance forward from one year to the next. In Exhibit 13.8, we have assumed an opening balance of $476 million for the sake of illustration.

FINANCIAL RATIO ANALYSIS

You have seen how, on the inside, a corporation accounts for stockholders' equity transactions. Now it is time to consider two ratios that outsiders use to evaluate how well a company has used its capital to generate returns for the company and its stockholders.

Financial Analysis Tools		
Name of Measure	Formula	What It Tells You
Earnings per share (EPS)	$\dfrac{\text{Net Income} - \text{Preferred Dividends}}{\text{Average Number of Common Shares Outstanding}}$	• The amount of income generated for each share of common stock owned by stockholders • The higher the number, the greater the profitability
Price/Earnings (P/E) ratio	$\dfrac{\text{Current Stock Price (per share)}}{\text{Earnings per Share (annual)}}$	• How many times more than the current year's earnings investors are willing to pay for a company's stock • The higher the number, the more investors anticipate an improvement in the company's future results

---

[1] A more comprehensive Statement of Stockholders' Equity may be presented instead of the Statement of Retained Earnings. A Statement of Stockholders' Equity shows the causes of increases and decreases in each stockholders' equity account, not just Retained Earnings. Preparing this statement is beyond the scope of this course.

Earnings Per Share (EPS)

Learning Objective 4

Analyze the earnings per share (EPS) and price/earnings (P/E) ratios.

The most famous of all financial ratios, earnings per share (EPS), reports how much profit is earned for each share of common stock outstanding. The calculation of EPS can involve many details and intricacies that are appropriately discussed in detail in intermediate accounting courses. In its basic form, EPS is computed by dividing net income by the average number of common shares outstanding. (If the company has declared dividends on preferred stock, they are first subtracted from net income.) Most companies report EPS on the income statement immediately below Net Income or in the notes to the financial statements.

You may be wondering why earnings per share is such a popular measure when dividends and stock prices ultimately determine the return to stockholders. The reason is that current earnings can predict future dividends and stock prices. If a company generates increased earnings in the current year, it will be able to pay higher dividends in future years. In other words, current EPS influences expectations about future dividends, which investors factor into the current stock price. That explains why Sonic Corp.'s stock price increased nearly 4 percent on January 4, 2008, immediately after the company announced that its EPS for the quarter was higher than in the preceding year.

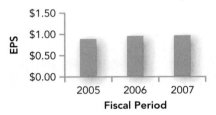

Another reason that EPS is such a popular measure is that it allows investors to make quick comparisons over time. Net income stated in dollars is more difficult to interpret. For example, in fiscal year 2007, Sonic earned a net income of $64 million compared to $78 million in the preceding year. It is hard to know whether that decrease was bad for stockholders because the decrease in Sonic's net income may have been accompanied by a decrease in the number of shares outstanding. By converting earnings to a per share basis, we adjust for the effect of any repurchased stock which gives a clearer picture of what decreased earnings might mean for each investor. As you can see from the accompanying graph, the decrease in net income in 2007 actually translated into higher EPS, from $0.91 to $0.94 per share, because fewer shares were outstanding.

Exhibit 13.9 shows how to calculate EPS for Sonic and a much larger fast food competitor, McDonald's Corporation. We should caution you to resist the temptation of comparing different companies' EPS ratios. The number of shares outstanding for one company can differ dramatically from the number of shares outstanding for a different company simply because

Exhibit 13.9   Earnings per Share (EPS) and Price/Earnings (P/E) Ratios

Company	Relevant Information (in millions)			2007 EPS	2007 P/E
		2007	2006		
	Net income	$64.2	$78.7	$\dfrac{\$64.2-0}{68.3}$	$\dfrac{\$24.59}{\$0.94}$
Sonic America's Drive-In	Preferred dividends	0.0	0.0		
	Average number of shares	68.3	86.5	=$0.94	=26.2
	Stock price	$24.59	$22.65		
		2007	2006		
	Net income	$2,395.1	$3,544.2	$\dfrac{\$2,395.1-0}{1,188.3}$	$\dfrac{\$56.00}{\$2.02}$
McDonald's	Preferred dividends	0.0	0.0		
	Average number of shares	1,188.3	1,234.0	=$2.02	=27.7
	Stock price	$56.00	$46.00		

one chooses to issue or repurchase more shares than the other. Also, as you have seen in earlier chapters, net income can be affected by more than just operating performance. Accounting differences in assigning inventory costs (Chapter 7), estimating bad debts (Chapter 9) and contingent liabilities (Chapter 11), and depreciating long-lived assets (Chapter 10) can reduce its comparability between companies. So while the EPS ratio is a useful measure for evaluating one company's performance over time, it is not appropriate for cross-company comparisons.

Price/Earnings (P/E) Ratio

The EPS ratio is useful for evaluating a company's ability to generate profits for stockholders, but it does not help investors determine a reasonable price for a company's stock. Advanced finance courses teach sophisticated techniques for valuing a company, but you will likely find it helpful to start with a much simpler tool. The price/earnings (P/E) ratio is the most basic way of determining the value investors place on a company's common stock. This ratio measures how many times more than the current year's earnings investors are willing to pay for a company's stock. The more they value the company, the more they will pay for its stock relative to the earnings the company generated. The P/E ratio is calculated by dividing a company's stock price by its earnings per share for the year (see Exhibit 13.9).

Generally, a relatively high P/E ratio means that investors expect the company to increase its profits in the future and they have factored those future earnings into the current stock price. A relatively low P/E ratio typically means that investors do not expect strong performance in the future. Because P/E ratios can vary significantly across industries, they are most meaningful when used to compare a company's performance over time or to compare competitors in the same industry. In 2007, Sonic's P/E ratio of 26.2 was similar to both McDonald's P/E ratio (27.7) and the overall industry average (24.6 according to Yahoo!Finance), suggesting that investors anticipated that Sonic would be at least as successful as other fast food restaurants.

SELF-STUDY PRACTICE

1. Use the information in Exhibit 13.9 to calculate Sonic's earnings per share (EPS) and price/earnings (P/E) ratio for 2006.

   2006 EPS   2006 P/E

   _____   _____

2. Did Sonic's EPS improve or decline from 2006 (calculated in part 1) to 2007 (shown in Exhibit 13.9)? Does Sonic's 2006 P/E ratio suggest that investors anticipated the changes that occurred in 2007? As a point of reference, the average P/E ratio for the industry was 19.5 in 2006.

After you have finished, check your answers with the solution at the bottom of the page.

Demonstration Case A

Stock Issue, Repurchase, and Financial Statement Reporting

This case focuses on selected transactions from the first year of operations of Zoogle Corporation, a lost-pet search business that became a public company on January 1, 2009. Zoogle's charter authorized it to issue the following:

   Common stock, $0.10 par value; 20,000 shares.
   Preferred stock, 5 percent cumulative, $100 par value; 5,000 shares.

Solution to Self-Study Practice

1. EPS: $78.7 / 86.5 = $0.91
    P/E: $22.65 / $0.91 = 24.9

2. Sonic's EPS improved, increasing from $0.91 in 2006 to $0.94 in 2007. Investors appeared to anticipate the improved performance because they were willing to pay 24.9 times earnings to buy a share of Sonic in 2006 when they were willing to pay only 19.5 times earnings for other companies in the industry.

The following transactions, selected from 2009, were completed on the dates indicated:

(a) Jan.   1   Issued a total of 8,000 shares of $0.10 par value common stock for cash at $50 per share.

(b) Feb.   1   Sold 2,000 shares of preferred stock at $100 per share; cash collected in full.

(c) July   1   Purchased 400 shares of common stock that had been issued earlier. Zoogle paid the stockholders $54 per share for the stock and currently holds the shares in treasury.

(d) Aug. 1   Sold 30 shares of the common treasury stock at $56 per share.

(e) Dec. 31   The board decided not to declare any dividends for the current year.

Required:

1.   Give the appropriate journal entries; show your calculations for each transaction.

2.   Prepare the Stockholders' Equity section of the balance sheet for Zoogle Corporation on December 31, 2009. Assume that the Retained Earnings account on that date totaled $31,000.

Suggested Solution

1.   **Journal entries:**

			Debit	Credit
(a)	Jan. 1, 2009	Cash (+A) ($50 × 8,000 shares)	400,000	
		Common Stock (+SE) ($0.10 × 8,000 shares)		800
		Additional Paid-In Capital—Common (+SE)		399,200
(b)	Feb. 1, 2009	Cash (+A) ($100 × 2,000 shares)	200,000	
		Preferred Stock (+SE) ($100 par × 2,000 shares)		200,000
(c)	July 1, 2009	Treasury Stock (+xSE, −SE)	21,600	
		Cash (−A) (400 shares × $54)		21,600
(d)	Aug. 1, 2009	Cash (+A) (30 × $56)	1,680	
		Treasury Stock (−xSE, +SE) (30 shares × $54)		1,620
		Additional Paid-In Capital—Treasury (+SE) ($1,680 − $1,620)		60
(e)	Dec. 31, 2009	No journal entry is required. Dividends in arrears from the current year (2,000 shares × $100 × 5% = $10,000) would be reported in the notes to Zoogle's financial statements.		

2.   **Stockholders' equity section of the balance sheet:**

Zoogle Corporation
Partial Balance Sheet
At December 31, 2009

Stockholders' Equity

Contributed capital

Common stock ($0.10 par value; authorized 20,000 shares, issued 8,000 shares of which 370 shares are held as treasury stock)	$ 800
Additional paid-in capital, common stock	399,200
Additional paid-in capital, treasury stock	60
Preferred stock, 5% cumulative (par value $100; 5,000 authorized shares, 2,000 issued and outstanding shares)	200,000
Total contributed capital	$600,060
Retained earnings	31,000
Treasury stock, at cost, 370 common shares	(19,980)
Total stockholders' equity	$611,080

Demonstration Case B

Dividends, Stock Split, and Retained Earnings

This case extends Demonstration Case A by focusing on dividends and other stock transactions that occurred during Zoogle Corporation's second year. The following transactions selected from 2010 were completed on the dates indicated:

(a) Nov. 1   The board declared a cash dividend on the preferred stock for the current year as well as payment of the prior year's dividends in arrears, payable on November 22 to stockholders of record as of November 15.

(b) Dec. 1   The board declared a 10 percent stock dividend on the outstanding common stock, distributable on December 18 to shareholders of record as of December 16. The stock price was $60 per share.

(c) Dec. 21   Zoogle Corporation completed a 2-for-1 stock split on its common stock.

(d) Dec. 31   The $50,000 balance in the Income Summary account was closed to Retained Earnings.

Required:

1. Give the appropriate journal entries; show your calculations for each transaction.
2. Prepare a Statement of Retained Earnings for the year ended December 31, 2010.

Suggested Solution

1.

			Debit	Credit
(a)	Nov. 1, 2010	Retained Earnings (−SE)	20,000	
		Dividends Payable (+L)		20,000
		(2,000 preferred shares × $100 par × 5% dividend rate × 2 years)		
	Nov. 15, 2010	No journal entry is required on the date of record.		
	Nov. 22, 2010	Dividends Payable (−L)	20,000	
		Cash (−A)		20,000
(b)	Dec. 1, 2010	Retained Earnings (−SE)	45,780	
		Common Stock Dividend Distributable (+SE)		76
		Additional Paid-In Capital (+SE)		45,704
		$45,780 = (8,000 common shares issued − 370 in treasury) × 10% × $60		
		$76 = (8,000 common shares issued − 370 in treasury) × 10% × $0.10		
		$45,704 = $45,780 − $76		
	Dec. 16, 2010	No journal entry is required on the date of record.		
	Dec. 18, 2010	Common Stock Dividend Distributable (−SE)	8	
		Common Stock (+SE)		8
(c)	Dec. 21, 2010	No journal entry is required to record a stock split.		
(d)	Dec. 31, 2010	Income Summary (−SE)	50,000	
		Retained Earnings (+SE)		50,000

2.

Zoogle Corporation
Statement of Retained Earnings
For the Year Ended December 31, 2010

Retained earnings, December 31, 2009	$31,000
Net income	50,000
Cash dividends on preferred stock	(20,000)
Stock dividends on common stock	(45,780)
Retained earnings, December 31, 2010	$15,220

Chapter Summary

LO1 Describe the characteristics of corporations. p. 560

- The law recognizes corporations as separate legal entities. Owners invest in a corporation and receive capital stock that can be bought from and sold to other investors.
- Common stock provides a number of rights, including the rights to vote, to receive dividends, to share in the corporation's residual assets at liquidation, and to preempt others from purchasing newly issued stock.
- Preferred stock gives investors certain advantages, including current dividend preferences and preference in asset distributions if the corporation is liquidated. If preferred stock carries cumulative dividend rights, any part of a current dividend that is not paid (dividends in arrears) must be paid in full before any additional dividends can be paid.

LO2 Demonstrate how to account for transactions involving common stock, preferred stock, and treasury stock. p. 562

- All transactions involving common stock, preferred stock, and treasury stock affect only the balance sheet. Corporations do not report income from gains or losses on transactions involving their own stock.
- If a stock specifies a par value, any amounts received in excess of par value are recorded in the stockholders' equity account Additional Paid-In Capital.
- If the corporation repurchases a stock, it is called treasury stock. The cost method records treasury stock at the cost to reacquire it in a contra-account that is subtracted from the Stockholders' Equity section on the balance sheet. If treasury stock is reissued, the treasury stock account is decreased by the cost of the treasury stock, and any excess amount received on reissue is recorded as Additional Paid-In Capital—Treasury.

LO3 Demonstrate how to account for cash dividends, stock dividends, and stock splits. p. 568

- Cash dividends reduce stockholders' equity (Retained Earnings) and create a liability (Dividends Payable) when the board of directors declares them. The liability is reduced when the dividends are paid.
- Stock dividends are pro rata distributions of a company's stock to existing owners. If the stock dividend is a small proportion of the outstanding stock, the transaction is accounted for by reducing Retained Earnings by the market value of the distributed stock, increasing Common Stock by the par value of the distributed stock, and increasing Additional Paid-In Capital for the excess of market value over par value. If the stock dividend is large (more than 20 to 25 percent), it is recorded at the par value of the stock.
- A stock split also involves the distribution of additional shares to owners, but no additional amount is transferred to Common Stock. Instead, the per share par value of the stock is reduced.

LO4 Analyze the earnings per share (EPS) and price/earnings (P/E) ratios. p. 576

- The earnings per share (EPS) ratio is calculated by dividing net income (less any dividends on preferred stock) by the average number of shares of common stock outstanding during the year. This ratio is helpful in comparing a corporation's earnings over time. It does not allow reliable comparisons across companies because it does not adjust for likely differences in the number of outstanding shares in each company and in the accounting methods used by each company.
- The price-earnings (P/E) ratio relates the corporation's current stock price to its most recent annual earnings per share. It indicates the value that investors place on the company's stock.

Financial Analysis Tools		
Name of Measure	Formula	What It Tells You
Earnings per share (EPS)	$\dfrac{\text{Net Income} - \text{Preferred Dividends}}{\text{Average Number of Common Shares Outstanding}}$	• The amount of income generated for each share of common stock owned by stockholders • The higher the number, the greater the profitability
Price/Earnings (P/E) ratio	$\dfrac{\text{Current Stock Price (per share)}}{\text{Earnings per Share (annual)}}$	• How many times more than the current year's earnings investors are willing to pay for a company's stock • The higher the number, the more investors anticipate an improvement in the company's future results

Key Terms

Authorized Shares (p. 567)

Common Stock (p. 561)

Contributed Capital (p. 562)

Cumulative Dividend Preference (p. 571)

Current Dividend Preference (p. 570)

Declaration Date (p. 569)

Dividends in Arrears (p. 571)

Issued Shares (p. 567)

No-Par Value Stock (p. 563)

Outstanding Shares (p. 567)   Public Companies (p. 560)   Stockholders' Equity (p. 562)
Par Value (p. 563)   Record Date (p. 569)   Stock Split (p. 573)
Payment Date (p. 569)   Retained Earnings (p. 563)   Treasury Stock (p. 565)
Preferred Stock (p. 561)   Stock Dividend (p. 572)
Private Companies (p. 560)   Stockholders (p. 560)

See complete glossary in the back of text.

Questions

1. Identify the primary advantages of the corporate form of business.

2. What four benefits do owners of common stock usually enjoy?

3. What are the differences between common stock and preferred stock?

4. What are the usual characteristics of preferred stock?

5. What are the relative advantages of equity versus debt financing?

6. In what ways does owner's equity differ for proprietorships and for corporations?

7. Explain each of the following terms: (a) authorized common stock, (b) issued common stock, and (c) outstanding common stock.

8. What is the distinction between par value and no-par value capital stock?

9. What is treasury stock? Why do corporations acquire treasury stock?

10. How is treasury stock reported on the balance sheet? How do the financial statements report the "gain or loss" on treasury stock reissued above or below cost?

11. What three dates are significant for dividends? What changes are made to the financial statement accounts on each of these three dates?

12. What are the two basic requirements to support the declaration of a cash dividend? What are the effects of a cash dividend on assets and stockholders' equity?

13. What is unique about cumulative preferred stock?

14. What is a stock dividend? How does a stock dividend differ from a cash dividend?

15. Why might a corporation's board declare a stock dividend rather than a stock split?

16. Why is the EPS number so popular? What are its limitations?

17. How do stock repurchases affect the EPS ratio?

18. Generally speaking, what does a high P/E ratio suggest?

Multiple Choice

Quiz 13-1
www.mhhe.com/LLPW1e

1. Which feature is not applicable to common stock ownership?
   a. Right to receive dividends before preferred stock shareholders.
   b. Right to vote on appointment of external auditor.
   c. Right to receive residual assets of the company should it cease operations.
   d. None of the above (all are applicable to common stock ownership).

2. Which statement regarding treasury stock is false?
   a. Treasury stock is considered to be issued but not outstanding.
   b. Treasury stock has no voting, dividend, or liquidation rights.
   c. Treasury stock reduces total stockholders' equity on the balance sheet.
   d. None of the above.

3. Which of the following statements about stock dividends is true?
   a. Stock dividends are reported on the income statement.
   b. Stock dividends increase total stockholders' equity.
   c. Stock dividends decrease total stockholders' equity.
   d. None of the above.

4. Which of the following is ordered from the largest number of shares to the smallest number of shares?
   a. Shares authorized, shares issued, shares outstanding.
   b. Shares issued, shares outstanding, shares authorized.
   c. Shares outstanding, shares issued, shares authorized.
   d. Shares in treasury, shares outstanding, shares issued.

5. Which of the following statements about the relative advantages of equity and debt financing is false?
   a. An advantage of equity financing is that it does not have to be repaid.
   b. An advantage of equity financing is that dividends are optional.
   c. An advantage of equity financing is that new stockholders get to vote and share in the earnings of the company.
   d. An advantage of debt financing is that interest is tax deductible.

6. A journal entry is not recorded on what date?
   a. Date of declaration.
   b. Date of record.
   c. Date of payment.
   d. None of the above. (A journal entry is recorded on all of the above dates.)

7. Which of the following transactions will increase the return on equity?
   a. Declare and issue a stock dividend.
   b. Split the stock 2-for-1.
   c. Repurchase the company's stock.
   d. None of the above.

8. Which statement regarding dividends is false?
   a. Dividends represent a sharing of corporate profits with owners.
   b. Both stock and cash dividends reduce retained earnings.
   c. Cash dividends paid to stockholders reduce net income.
   d. None of the above.
9. When treasury stock is purchased with cash, what is the impact on the balance sheet equation?
   a. No change—the reduction of the asset Cash is offset with the addition of the asset Treasury Stock.

b. Assets decrease and Stockholders' Equity increases.
c. Assets increase and Stockholders' Equity decreases.
d. Assets decrease and Stockholders' Equity decreases.

10. In what situation does an investor's personal wealth increase immediately?
   a. When receiving a cash dividend.
   b. When receiving a stock dividend.
   c. When a stock split is announced.
   d. In all of the above situations.

Solutions to Multiple-Choice Questions

1. a   2. d   3. d   4. a   5. c   6. b   7. c   8. c   9. d   10. a

---

Mini Exercises ▪▪▪ ™   Available with McGraw-Hill's Homework Manager

LO1   **M13-1 Favoring Equity versus Debt Financing**
Indicate whether each of the following favors the use of equity (E) or debt (D) financing.

____ 1. Interest is tax deductible.
____ 2. Dividends are optional.
____ 3. Debt must be repaid.
____ 4. Additional stock issuances dilute existing stockholders' control.

LO1   **M13-2 Evaluating Stockholders' Rights**
Name four rights of common stockholders. Which of these seems most important? Why?

LO2   **M13-3 Computing the Number of Unissued Shares**
The balance sheet for Crutcher Corporation reported 147,000 shares outstanding, 300,000 shares authorized, and 10,000 shares in treasury stock. Compute the maximum number of new shares that Crutcher could issue.

LO2   **M13-4 Recording the Sale of Common Stock**
To expand operations, Aragon Consulting issued 100,000 shares of previously unissued common stock with a par value of $1. The selling price for the stock was $75 per share. Record the journal entry for this sale of stock. Would your answer be different if the par value were $2 per share? If so, record the sale of stock with a par value of $2.

LO2   **M13-5 Recording the Sale of Common Stock**
Refer to M13-4. Assume the issued stock has no par value. Record the journal entry for the sale of no-par value stock at $75. Do the effects on total assets, total liabilities, and total stockholders' equity differ from those in M13-4?

LO2
Sonic Corporation   **M13-6 Comparing Common Stock and Preferred Stock**
Your parents have just retired and have asked you for some financial advice. They have decided to invest $100,000 in a company very similar to Sonic Corp. The company has issued both common and preferred stock. Which type of stock would you recommend? What factors would you consider in giving them advice?

LO2   **M13-7 Determining the Effects of Treasury Stock Transactions**
Trans Union Corporation sold 5,000 shares for $50 per share in 2007, and it sold 10,000 shares for $37 per share in 2008. In 2009, the company purchased 2,000 shares of its own stock for $45 per share. Determine the impact (increase, decrease, or no change) of each of these transactions on the following classifications:

1. Total assets.
2. Total liabilities.
3. Total stockholders' equity.
4. Net income.

M13-8 Comparing Stockholder's Equity to Owner's Equity
On January 1, Daniel Harrison contributed $20,000 to start his business. At the end of that year, the business had generated $30,000 in sales revenues, incurred $18,000 in operating expenses, and distributed $5,000 for Daniel to use to pay some personal expenses. Prepare the section of the balance sheet showing (a) his stockholder's equity, assuming this is a corporation with no-par value stock or (b) his owner's equity, assuming this is a sole proprietorship.

LO2

M13-9 Determining the Amount of a Dividend
Netpass Company has 300,000 shares of common stock authorized, 270,000 shares issued, and 50,000 shares of treasury stock. The company's board of directors declares a dividend of 50 cents per share on common stock. What is the total amount of the dividend that will be paid?

LO3

M13-10 Recording Dividends
On April 15, 2009, the board of directors for Auction.com declared a cash dividend of 40 cents per share payable to stockholders of record on May 20. The dividends will be paid on June 14. The company has 500,000 shares of stock outstanding. Prepare any necessary journal entries for each date.

LO3

M13-11 Determining the Impact of a Stock Dividend
Sturdy Stone Tools, Inc., announced a 100 percent stock dividend. Determine the impact (increase, decrease, no change) of this dividend on the following:

LO3

1. Total assets.
2. Total liabilities.
3. Common stock.
4. Total stockholders' equity.
5. Market value per share of common stock.

M13-12 Determining the Impact of a Stock Split
Complete the requirements of M13-11 assuming that the company announced a 2-for-1 stock split.

LO3

M13-13 Recording a Small Stock Dividend
Shriver Food Systems, Inc., declared a 10 percent stock dividend on May 1. The company has 800,000 shares authorized and 200,000 shares outstanding. The par value of the stock is $1 per share and the market value is $100 per share. The dividend was issued on May 21. Prepare the journal entries to record the declaration and issuance of this stock dividend.

LO3

M13-14 Recording a Large Stock Dividend
Refer to M13-13. Assume the company declared and issued a 50 percent stock dividend on the dates indicated. Prepare the journal entries to record the declaration and issuance.

LO3

M13-15 Determining the Amount of a Preferred Dividend
Colliers, Inc., has 100,000 shares of cumulative preferred stock outstanding. The preferred stock pays dividends in the amount of $2 per share but because of cash flow problems, the company did not pay any dividends last year. The board of directors plans to pay dividends in the amount of $1 million this year. What amount will go to preferred stockholders? How much will be available for common stock dividends?

LO3

M13-16 Calculating and Interpreting Earnings per Share (EPS)
Academy Driving School reported the following amount in its financial statements:

LO4

	2010	2009
Number of common shares	11,500	11,500
Net income	$23,000	$18,000
Cash dividends paid on common stock	$ 3,000	$ 3,000

Calculate 2010 EPS. Another driving school in the same city reported a higher net income ($45,000) in 2010, yet its EPS ratio was lower than that for the Academy Driving School. Explain how this apparent inconsistency could occur.

LO4   **M13-17 Determining the Impact of Transactions on Earnings per Share (EPS)**
Identify and explain the direction of effect (+ for increase, − for decrease, or NE for no effect) of each of the following transactions on EPS.

    a.   Purchased 50 shares into treasury.

    b.   Declared and paid a cash dividend.

    c.   Declared and issued a stock dividend.

    d.   Sold inventory at an amount more than cost.

    e.   Sold and issued 6,000 shares of common stock for cash.

LO4   **M13-18 Inferring Financial Information Using the P/E Ratio**
In 2008, Rec Room Sports reported earnings per share of $8.50 when its stock was selling for $212.50. In 2009, its earnings increased by 20 percent. If all other relationships remain constant, what is the price of the stock in 2009? Explain.

Exercises   Available with McGraw-Hill's Homework Manager

LO2   **E13-1 Computing Shares Outstanding**

Big Dog Holdings   Big Dog Holdings reported that, as of September 30, 2007, 30 million shares of common stock had been authorized. As of that date, 11,182,808 shares had been issued and 1,710,598 shares were held as treasury stock.

Required:
Determine the number of shares outstanding on September 30, 2007.

LO2, 3   **E13-2 Reporting Stockholders' Equity and Determining Dividend Policy**
Incentive Corporation was organized as a corporation in 2008 to operate a financial consulting business. The charter authorized the following capital stock: common stock, par value $4 per share, 12,000 shares. During the first year, the following selected transactions were completed:

    a.   Sold and issued 6,000 shares of common stock for cash at $20 per share.

    b.   Sold and issued 2,000 shares of common stock for cash at $23 per share.

Required:

1.   Give the journal entry required for each of these transactions.

2.   At year-end, the Income Summary account reflected a profit of $10,000. Give the journal entry to close this account to Retained Earnings.

3.   Prepare the Stockholders' Equity section as it should be reported on the 2008 year-end balance sheet.

4.   Incentive Corporation has $30,000 cash in the company's bank account. What is the maximum amount of cash dividends the company can declare at this time? Explain.

LO2   **E13-3 Reporting the Stockholders' Equity Section of the Balance Sheet**
North Wind Aviation received its corporate charter during January 2009. The charter authorized the following capital stock:

    Common stock: par $7, authorized 50,000 shares.

    Preferred stock: 8 percent, par $10, authorized 20,000 shares.

During 2009, the following transactions occurred in the order given:

    a.   Issued a total of 40,000 shares of the common stock to the company's founders for $11 per share.

    b.   Sold 5,000 shares of the preferred stock at $18 per share.

    c.   Sold 3,000 shares of the common stock at $14 per share and 1,000 shares of the preferred stock at $28.

    d.   Net income for the first year was $48,000, and no dividends were declared.

Required:
Prepare the Stockholders' Equity section of the balance sheet at December 31, 2009.

LO2, 3   **E13-4 Reporting the Stockholders' Equity Section of the Balance Sheet**
Shelby Corporation was organized in January 2010 by 10 stockholders to operate an air conditioning sales and service business. The charter issued by the state authorized the following capital stock:

    Common stock, $1 par value, 200,000 shares.

    Preferred stock, 6 percent, $8 par value, 50,000 shares.

During January and February 2010, the following stock transactions were completed:

  a.   Collected $40,000 cash from each of the 10 organizers and issued 2,000 shares of common stock to each of them.

  b.   Sold 15,000 shares of preferred stock at $25 per share; collected the cash and immediately issued the stock.

Net income for 2010 was $40,000; cash dividends declared and paid at year-end were $10,000.

Required:

Prepare the Stockholders' Equity section of the balance sheet at December 31, 2010.

E13-5 Determining the Effects of the Issuance of Common and Preferred Stock   LO2

Inside Incorporated was issued a charter on January 15, 2009, that authorized the following capital stock:

Common stock, $6 par, 100,000 shares, one vote per share.

Preferred stock, 7 percent, par value $10 per share, 5,000 shares, nonvoting.

During 2009, the following selected transactions were completed in the order given:

  a.   Sold and issued 20,000 shares of the $6 par common stock at $18 cash per share.
  b.   Sold and issued 3,000 shares of preferred stock at $22 cash per share.
  c.   At the end of 2009, the Income Summary account included net income of $38,000.

Required:

1.   Prepare journal entries to record transactions *a* and *b*, and to close Income Summary to Retained Earnings in *c*.

2.   Prepare the Stockholders' Equity section of the balance sheet at December 31, 2009.

3.   Assume that you are a common stockholder. If Inside Incorporated needed additional capital, would you prefer to have it issue additional common stock or additional preferred stock? Explain.

E13-6 Recording and Reporting Stockholders' Equity Transactions   LO2

AvA School of Learning obtained a charter at the start of 2009 that authorized 50,000 shares of no-par common stock and 20,000 shares of preferred stock, par value $10, 5% noncumulative dividend. During 2009, the following selected transactions occurred:

  a.   Collected $40 cash per share from four individuals and issued 5,000 shares of common stock to each.

  b.   Sold and issued 6,000 shares of common stock to an outside investor at $40 cash per share.

  c.   Sold and issued 8,000 shares of preferred stock at $15 cash per share.

Required:

1.   Give the journal entries indicated for each of these transactions.

2.   Prepare the Stockholders' Equity section of the balance sheet at December 31, 2009. At the end of 2009, the accounts reflected net income of $36,000.

E13-7 Finding Amounts Missing from the Stockholders' Equity Section   LO2

The Stockholders' Equity section on the December 31, 2009, balance sheet of Chemfast Corporation follows:

Stockholders' Equity	
Contributed capital	
Preferred stock (par $20; authorized 10,000 shares, ? issued,	
of which 500 shares are held as treasury stock)	$104,000
Additional paid-in capital, preferred	14,300
Common stock (no par; authorized 20,000 shares, issued and	
outstanding 8,000 shares)	600,000
Retained earnings	30,000
Cost of 500 shares of preferred treasury stock	9,500

Required:
Complete the following statements and show your computations.

1. The number of shares of preferred stock issued was _____.
2. The number of shares of preferred stock outstanding was _____.
3. The average sales price of the preferred stock when issued was $_____ per share.
4. The average issue price of the common stock was $_____.
5. The treasury stock transaction increased (decreased) stockholders' equity by _____.
6. How much did the treasury stock cost per share? $_____.
7. Total stockholders' equity is $_____.

LO2   **E13-8 Recording Treasury Stock Transactions and Analyzing Their Impact**
During 2009, the following selected transactions affecting stockholders' equity occurred for Corner Corporation:

    a. Feb. 1 Purchased 400 shares of the company's own common stock at $22 cash per share.
    b. Jul. 15 Sold 100 of the shares purchased on February 1, 2009, for $24 cash per share.
    c. Sept. 1 Sold 60 more of the shares purchased on February 1, 2009, for $20 cash per share.

Required:

1. Give journal entries for each of the transactions.
2. What impact does the purchase of treasury stock have on dividends paid?
3. What impact does the sale of treasury stock for an amount higher than the purchase price have on net income?

LO2, 3   **E13-9 Comparing Owners' Equity Sections for a Sole Proprietorship and Corporation**
Assume for each of the following independent cases that the annual accounting period ends on December 31, 2009, and that the Income Summary held a credit balance of $20,000.

    Case A: Assume that the company is a *sole proprietorship* owned by Proprietor A. Prior to the closing entries, the capital account reflected a credit balance of $50,000 and the drawings account a balance of $8,000.

    Case B: Assume that the company is a *corporation*. Prior to the closing entries, the stockholders' equity accounts showed the following: Common Stock, par $10, 30,000 shares authorized, 15,000 shares issued and outstanding; Additional Paid-In Capital, $5,000; Retained Earnings, $65,000. No dividends were declared.

Required:

1. Give all the closing entries required at December 31, 2009, for each case.
2. Show the body of (a) a statement of owner's equity and (b) a statement of retained earnings for the year ended December 31, 2009.
3. Show how the Equity section of the balance sheet would appear at December 31, 2009, for each case.

LO2, 3   **E13-10 Recording Stockholders' Equity Transactions**
The annual report for Malibu Beachwear reported the following transactions affecting stockholders' equity:

    a. Purchased $35,000 in treasury stock.
    b. Declared cash dividends in the amount of $25,420.
    c. Paid cash dividends in the amount of $25,420.
    d. Declared 10 percent common stock dividend, which would require issuing 20,000 additional $1 par value shares with a market price of $15 per share.
    e. Issued the stock dividend in transaction d.

Required:

1. Prepare journal entries to record each of these transactions.
2. Indicate the effect (increase, decrease, or no effect) of each of these transactions on total assets, liabilities, and stockholders' equity.

E13-11 Computing Dividends on Common and Preferred Stock and Analyzing Differences   LO3

The records of Hoffman Company reflected the following balances in the stockholders' equity accounts at December 31, 2009:

> Common stock, par $12 per share, 40,000 shares outstanding.
>
> Preferred stock, 8 percent, par $10 per share, 6,000 shares outstanding.
>
> Retained earnings, $220,000.

On January 1, 2010, the board of directors was considering the distribution of a $62,000 cash dividend. No dividends were paid during 2008 and 2009.

Required:

1. Determine the total and per share amounts that would be paid to the common stockholders and to the preferred stockholders under two independent assumptions:

    a.   The preferred stock is noncumulative.

    b.   The preferred stock is cumulative.

2. Briefly explain why the dividends per share of common stock were less for the second assumption.

3. What factors would cause a more favorable dividend for the common stockholders?

E13-12 Recording the Payment of Dividends and Preparing a Statement of Retained Earnings   LO3

The 2009 annual report for Sneers Corporation disclosed that the company declared and paid preferred dividends in the amount of $119.9 million in 2009. It also declared and paid dividends on common stock in the amount of $2 per share. During 2009, Sneers had 1,000,000,000 shares of common authorized; 387,570,300 shares had been issued; and 41,670,300 shares were in treasury stock. The balance in Retained Earnings was $1,554 million on December 31, 2008 and net income was $858 million for 2009.

Required:

1. Prepare journal entries to record the declaration of dividends on (a) preferred stock and (b) common stock.

2. Prepare journal entries to record the payment of dividends on (a) preferred stock and (b) common stock.

3. Prepare a journal entry to close 2009 net income into Retained Earnings from Income Summary.

4. Using the information given above, prepare a statement of retained earnings for the year ended December 31, 2009.

E13-13 Analyzing Stock Dividends   LO3

On December 31, 2008, the Stockholders' Equity section of the balance sheet of R & B Corporation reflected the following:

Common stock (par $10; authorized 60,000 shares, outstanding 25,000 shares)	$250,000
Additional paid-in capital	12,000
Retained earnings	75,000

On February 1, 2009, the board of directors declared a 12 percent stock dividend to be issued April 30, 2009. The market value of the stock on February 1, 2009, was $18 per share.

Required:

1. For comparative purposes, prepare the Stockholders' Equity section of the balance sheet both (a) immediately before the stock dividend and (b) immediately after the stock dividend. Consider using side-by-side columns for the amounts in parts (a) and (b).

2. Explain the effects of this stock dividend on the assets, liabilities, and stockholders' equity.

3. How would your answers to requirements 1 and 2 change if the stock dividend were 100 percent?

E13-14 Recording Dividends   LO3

Black & Decker is a leading global manufacturer and marketer of power tools, hardware, and home improvement products. A press release on October 17, 2007, contained the following announcement:

BLACK&DECKER.

> ... its Board of Directors declared a quarterly cash dividend of $0.42 per share on the Corporation's outstanding common stock payable December 28, 2007, to stockholders of record at the close of business on December 14, 2007.

At the time of the press release, Black & Decker had 150,000,000 shares authorized and 62,536,000 outstanding. The par value for the company's stock is $.50 per share.

Required:
Prepare journal entries as appropriate for each of the three dates mentioned above.

LO3

E13-15 Comparing Stock Dividends and Splits

On July 1, 2009, Jones Corporation had the following capital structure:

Common stock, $1 par, 200,000 authorized shares, 150,000 issued and outstanding	$150,000
Additional paid-in capital	88,000
Retained earnings	172,000
Treasury stock	None

Required:
Complete the following table based on three independent cases involving stock transactions:

Case 1: The board of directors declared and issued a 10 percent stock dividend when the stock was selling at $8 per share.

Case 2: The board of directors declared and issued a 100 percent stock dividend when the stock was selling at $8 per share.

Case 3: The board of directors voted a 2-for-1 stock split. The market price prior to the split was $8 per share.

Items	Before Stock Transactions	CASE 1 After 10% Stock Dividend	CASE 2 After 100% Stock Dividend	CASE 3 After Stock Split
Number of shares outstanding				
Par per share	$ 1	$	$	$
Common stock account	$	$	$	$
Additional paid-in capital	88,000			
Retained earnings	172,000			
Total stockholders' equity	$	$	$	$

LO2, 3

E13-16 Analyzing Dividends in Arrears

Mission Critical Software, Inc., was a leading provider of systems management software for Windows NT network and Internet infrastructure. Like many start-up companies, Mission Critical struggled with cash flows as it developed new business opportunities. A student found a financial statement for Mission Critical that stated that the increase in dividends in arrears on preferred stock this year was $264,000.

The student who read the note suggested that the Mission Critical preferred stock would be a good investment because of the large amount of dividend income that would be earned when the company started paying dividends again: "As the owner of the stock, I'll get dividends for the period I hold the stock plus some previous periods when I didn't even own the stock." Do you agree? Explain.

LO3

E13-17 Determining the Impact of Cash and Stock Dividends

Superior Corporation has the following capital stock outstanding on January 1, 2009:

Common stock, par $8, outstanding shares, 30,000.

Preferred stock, 6 percent, par $15, outstanding shares, 8,000.

On October 1, 2009, the board of directors declared dividends that would be paid, or issued, to stockholders of record on December 1, 2009:

Common stock: 10 percent common stock dividend, to be issued on December 20, 2009.

Preferred stock: Cash dividend, 6 percent, payable December 20, 2009.

On October 1, 2009, the market prices were preferred stock, $40, and common stock, $32. On December 20, 2009, the dividends were paid, or issued.

Required:

At each date indicated above, present journal entries for the dividends on (a) preferred stock and (b) common stock.

E13-18 Determining the Financial Statement Effects of Cash and Stock Dividends

LO3

Lynn Company has outstanding 60,000 shares of $10 par value common stock and 25,000 shares of $20 par value preferred stock (8 percent). On December 1, 2009, the board of directors voted an 8 percent cash dividend on the preferred stock and a 10 percent stock dividend on the common stock. At the date of declaration, the common stock was selling at $35 and the preferred at $20 per share. The dividends are to be paid, or issued, on February 15, 2010. The annual accounting period ends December 31.

Required:

Explain the comparative effects of the two dividends on the assets, liabilities, and stockholders' equity (*a*) through December 31, 2009, (*b*) on February 15, 2010, and (*c*) overall from December 1, 2009, through February 15, 2010. A schedule using the following structure might be helpful:

COMPARATIVE EFFECTS EXPLAINED

Item	Cash Dividend on Preferred	Stock Dividend on Common
(*a*) Through December 31, 2009:		
Effect on assets		
Effect on liabilities		
Effect on stockholders' equity		

E13-19 Preparing a Statement of Retained Earnings and Partial Balance Sheet and Evaluating Dividend Policy

LO2, 3, 4

The following account balances were selected from the records of Blake Corporation at December 31, 2009, after all adjusting entries were completed. The company had not issued or repurchased any additional shares this year.

Common stock (par $15; authorized 100,000 shares, issued 35,000 shares, of which 1,000 shares are held as treasury stock)	$525,000
Additional paid-in capital	180,000
Dividends on common stock declared and paid in 2009	28,000
Retained earnings, January 1, 2009	76,000
Treasury stock at cost (1,000 shares)	20,000
Net income for the year.	48,000

Required:

1. Prepare the statement of retained earnings for the year ended December 31, 2009, and the Stockholders' Equity section of the balance sheet at December 31, 2009.
2. Determine the number of shares of stock that received dividends.
3. Compute the EPS ratio for the year ended December 31, 2009. Is it better or worse than the $1.32 earnings per share in 2008?

E13-20 Analyzing Stock Repurchases and Stock Dividends

LO3, 4

Winnebago

Winnebago is a familiar name on vehicles traveling U.S. highways. The company manufactures and sells large motor homes for vacation travel. These motor homes can be quickly recognized because of the company's "flying W" trademark. An April 12, 2006, press release contained the following information:

> Winnebago Industries, Inc., (NYSE: WGO) announced that in a meeting held today, the Company's Board of Directors announced a new $60 million stock repurchase authorization. Winnebago Industries has repurchased approximately 24.4 million shares of common stock for approximately $356.8 million since December 31, 1997.

Required:

1. Explain the impact of a $60 million stock repurchase on the financial statements.
2. Why do you think the board decided to repurchase the stock?
3. Assuming that Winnebago continues its current level of annual dividend payments, what impact will this purchase have on Winnebago's future dividends per share?
4. On January 14, 2004, the company's board of directors declared a 100 percent stock dividend that was distributed on March 5, 2004. Why would Winnebago choose a stock dividend rather than a 2-for-1 stock split?
5. What impact would this stock dividend have had on Winnebago's financial statements? What impact would it have had on the EPS ratio?

Problems—Set A   **Available with McGraw-Hill's Homework Manager**

LO2

PA13-1 Recording Journal Entries and Preparing a Partial Balance Sheet after Stock Issue, Purchase, and Reissue Transactions

Worldwide Company obtained a charter from the state in January 2009, which authorized 200,000 shares of common stock, $10 par value. During the first year, the company earned $38,200, and the following selected transactions occurred in the order given:

a. Sold 60,000 shares of the common stock at $12 per share.
b. Purchased 2,000 shares at $15 cash per share from one of the 30 stockholders who needed cash and wanted to sell the stock back to the company.
c. Resold 1,000 of the shares of the treasury stock purchased in transaction *b* two months later to another individual at $18 cash per share.

Required:

1. Prepare journal entries to record each transaction.
2. Prepare the Stockholders' Equity section of the balance sheet at December 31, 2009. Because this is the first year of operations, Retained Earnings has a zero balance at the beginning of the year.

LO3

Macy's

PA13-2 Recording Dividends

Prior to changing its corporate name to Macy's, Inc., on June 1, 2007, Federated Department Stores issued a press release with the following information:

> CINCINNATI—May 19, 2006—The Board of Directors of Federated Department Stores, Inc. (NYSE:FD) today approved a split of the company's common stock on a two-for-one basis. Additional shares issued as a result of the stock dividend will be distributed after close of trading on June 9, 2006, to shareholders of record on May 26, 2006. At the company's Annual Meeting this morning, Federated shareholders approved an increase in the number of authorized shares of Federated common stock from 500 million to 1 billion. With the stock split, Federated's quarterly dividend will be 12.75 cents per outstanding common share, payable July 3, 2006, to Federated shareholders of record at the close of business on June 16, 2006.

Required:

1. Although the press release refers to a stock split, the transaction actually involved a 100 percent stock dividend, to be recorded at par value. Prepare any journal entries that Federated Department Stores should have made as the result of the stock dividend and the cash dividend. Assume that, at the time of the stock dividend, the company had 175 million shares outstanding, the par value was $0.01 per share, and the market value was $73 per share.

2. What two requirements would the board of directors have considered before making the dividend decision?

PA13-3 Finding Missing Amounts

At December 31, 2009, the records of Nortech Corporation provided the following selected and incomplete data:

LO2, 3, 4

> Authorized shares of common stock, 200,000.
>
> Balance in common stock account $1,250,000 (par $10; no changes during 2009).
>
> Common stock issued in prior year at a price of $17 per share.
>
> Shares held as treasury stock, 3,000 shares, cost $20 per share (no changes during 2009).
>
> Net income for 2009, $118,000.
>
> Dividends declared and paid during 2009, $73,200.
>
> Retained earnings balance, January 1, 2009, $155,000.

Required:

1. Complete the following:

    Shares authorized _____.

    Shares issued _____.

    Shares outstanding _____.

2. The balance in the Additional Paid-In Capital account would be $ _____.

3. Earnings per share is $ _____.

4. Dividends paid per share of common stock is $ _____.

5. Treasury stock should be reported in the Stockholders' Equity section of the balance sheet in the amount of $ _____.

6. Assume that the board of directors approved a 2-for-1 stock split. After the stock split, the par value per share will be $_____ and the number of outstanding shares will be _____. (The treasury stock was acquired after the split was issued.)

7. Disregard the stock split (assumed above). Assume instead a 100 percent stock dividend was declared and issued after the treasury stock was acquired, when the market price of the common stock was $21. Give any journal entry that should be made.

PA13-4 Recording Journal Entries and Preparing a Partial Balance Sheet after Common Stock Issue, Purchase, Reissue, and Cash Dividends

American Laser, Inc. reported the following stockholders' equity account balances on January 1, 2009.

LO2, 3

www.mhhe.com/LLPW1e

Common stock, 10,000 shares of $1 par	$ 10,000
Retained earnings	120,000
Additional paid-in capital—common	90,000
Treasury stock	0

The company entered into the following transactions during 2009.

Jan. 15   Issued 5,000 shares of $1 par common stock for $50,000 cash.

Feb. 15   Purchased 3,000 shares of $1 par common stock into treasury for $33,000 cash.

Mar. 15   Reissued 2,000 shares of treasury stock for $24,000 cash.

Aug. 15   Reissued 600 shares of treasury stock for $4,600 cash.

Sept. 15   Declared (but did not pay) a $1 cash dividend on each outstanding share of common stock.

Required:

1. Prepare journal entries to record each transaction.
2. Prepare the Stockholders' Equity section of the balance sheet at December 31, 2009. At the end of 2009, the accounts reflected net income of $20,000. The company was authorized to issue 200,000 shares.

LO2, 3

www.mhhe.com/LLPW1e

PA13-5 Comparing Stock and Cash Dividends

Water Tower Company had the following stock outstanding and retained earnings at December 31, 2009:

Common stock (par $8; outstanding, 30,000 shares)	$240,000
Preferred stock, 7% (par $10; outstanding, 6,000 shares)	60,000
Retained earnings	280,000

The board of directors is considering the distribution of a cash dividend to the common and preferred stockholders. No dividends were declared during 2007 or 2008. Three independent cases are assumed:

Case A: The preferred stock is noncumulative; the total amount of dividends is $30,000.

Case B: The preferred stock is cumulative; the total amount of dividends is $12,600.

Case C: Same as Case B, except the amount is $66,000.

Required:

1. Compute the amount of dividends, in total and per share (rounded to the nearest penny), that would be payable to each class of stockholders for each case. Show computations.
2. Assume that a 100 percent common stock dividend was issued when the market value per share was $24. Complete the following schedule.

	AMOUNT OF DOLLAR INCREASE (DECREASE)	
Item	Cash Dividend, Case C	Stock Dividend
Assets	$	$
Liabilities		
Stockholders' equity		

LO4

Aaron Rents, Inc.
Rent-A-Center, Inc.

www.mhhe.com/LLPW1e

PA13-6 Computing and Interpreting Earnings per Share (EPS) and Price/Earnings (P/E) Ratios

Aaron Rents, Inc., and Rent-A-Center, Inc., are two publicly traded rental companies. They reported the following in their 2006 financial statements (in thousands, except per share amounts):

	AARON RENTS, INC.		RENT-A-CENTER, INC.	
	2005	2006	2005	2006
Average number of common shares	49,994	52,423	72,977	69,657
Average number of preferred shares	0	0	0	0
Net income	$ 57,993	$ 78,635	$ 135,738	$ 103,092
Stock price when annual results reported	23.10	27.60	20.80	28.50

Required:

1. Compute the 2006 EPS for each company (rounded to the nearest penny). In 2005, Aaron Rents reported EPS of $1.16, whereas Rent-A-Center reported EPS of $1.86. Which company appears to have improved its performance in 2006?
2. Compute the 2006 P/E ratio for each company. Do investors appear to value one company more than the other? Explain.

Problems—Set B

PB13-1 Recording Journal Entries and Preparing a Partial Balance Sheet after Stock Issue and Purchase Transactions

LO2

Global Marine obtained a charter from the state in January 2009, which authorized 1,000,000 shares of common stock, $5 par value. During the first year of operations, the company earned $429,000, and the following selected transactions occurred in the order given:

    a. Sold 700,000 shares of the common stock at $54 per share. Collected the cash and issued the stock.

    b. Purchased 25,000 shares at $50 cash per share to use as stock incentives for senior management.

Required:

1. Prepare journal entries to record each transaction.
2. Prepare the Stockholders' Equity section of the balance sheet at December 31, 2009.

PB13-2 Recording Dividends

LO3
National Beverage Corp.

National Beverage Corp. produces soft drinks, bottled waters, and juices sold under the brand names Shasta, Faygo, and Everfresh. A press release contained the following information:

> March 5—National Beverage Corp. today announced that its Board of Directors has declared a special "one-time" cash dividend of $1.00 per share on approximately 36.6 million outstanding shares. The dividend will be paid on or before April 30 to shareholders of record at the close of business on March 26.

Required:

1. Prepare any journal entries that National Beverage Corp. should make to record the cash dividend.
2. On March 5, National Beverage Corp. also declared a 100 percent stock dividend, which was distributed on March 22. Prepare any journal entries that National Beverage Corp. should have made to record this stock dividend. Assume that the company had 18.3 million shares outstanding on March 5, the par value is $0.01 per share, and the market value is $10 per share.
3. What two requirements would the board of directors have considered before making the dividend decisions?

PB13-3 Finding Missing Amounts

LO2, 3, 4

At December 31, 2009, the records of Kozmetsky Corporation provided the following selected and incomplete data:

    Common stock (par $1; no changes during 2009).
    Shares authorized, 5,000,000.
    Shares issued, ___?___; issue price $80 per share.
    Shares held as treasury stock, 100,000 shares, cost $60 per share (no changes during 2009).
    Net income for 2009, $4,800,000.
    Common Stock account, $1,500,000.
    Dividends declared and paid during 2009, $2 per share.
    Retained Earnings balance, January 1, 2009, $82,900,000.

Required:

1. Complete the following:
   Shares issued _____.
   Shares outstanding_____.
2. The balance in the Additional Paid-In Capital account would be $_____.
3. Earnings per share is $_____.
4. Total dividends paid on common stock during 2009 is $_____.
5. Treasury stock should be reported in the Stockholders' Equity section of the balance sheet in the amount of $_____.

6. Assume that the board of directors voted a 2-for-1 stock split. After the stock split, the par value per share will be $_____, and the number of outstanding shares will be_____. The treasury stock was acquired after the split was issued.

7. Disregard the stock split (assumed above). Assume instead a 100 percent stock dividend was declared and issued after the treasury stock was acquired, when the market price of the common stock was $21. Explain how stockholders' equity will change.

LO2, 3   **PB13-4 Recording Journal Entries and Preparing a Partial Balance Sheet after Common Stock Issue, Purchase, Reissue, and Cash Dividends**

Waste Control, Inc. reported the following stockholders' equity account balances on January 1, 2009.

Common stock, 20,000 shares of $1 par	$ 20,000
Retained earnings	110,000
Additional paid-in capital—common	180,000
Treasury stock	0

The company entered into the following transactions during 2009.

Jan. 12 Issued 5,000 shares of $1 par common stock for $50,000 cash.

Feb. 3 Purchased 3,000 shares of $1 par common stock into treasury for $27,000 cash.

Mar. 4 Reissued 2,000 shares of treasury stock for $20,000 cash.

Aug. 5 Reissued 600 shares of treasury stock for $5,400 cash.

Sept. 15 Declared (but did not pay) a $2 cash dividend on each outstanding share of common stock.

Required:

1. Prepare journal entries to record each transaction.

2. Prepare the Stockholders' Equity section of the balance sheet at December 31, 2009. At the end of 2009, the accounts reflected net income of $50,000. The company was authorized to issue 500,000 shares.

LO2, 3   **PB13-5 Comparing Stock and Cash Dividends**

Ritz Company had the following stock outstanding and Retained Earnings at December 31, 2009:

Common stock (par $1; outstanding, 500,000 shares)	$500,000
Preferred stock, 8% (par $10; outstanding, 21,000 shares)	210,000
Retained earnings	900,000

The board of directors is considering the distribution of a cash dividend to the common and preferred stockholders. No dividends were declared during 2007 or 2008. Three independent cases are assumed:

Case A: The preferred stock is noncumulative; the total amount of dividends is $30,000.

Case B: The preferred stock is cumulative; the total amount of dividends is $30,000.

Case C: Same as Case B, except the amount is $75,000.

Required:

1. Compute the amount of dividends, in total and per share (rounded to the nearest penny), payable to each class of stockholders for each case. Show computations.

2. Assume that the company issued a 100 percent stock dividend on the outstanding common shares when the market value per share was $50. Complete the following schedule.

Item	AMOUNT OF DOLLAR INCREASE (DECREASE)	
	Cash Dividend, Case C	Stock Dividend
Assets	$	$
Liabilities		
Stockholders' equity		

PB13-6 Computing and Interpreting Earnings per Share (EPS) and Price/Earnings (P/E) Ratios   LO4

Two magazine companies reported the following in their 2008 financial statements:

	BUSINESSWORLD		FUN AND GAMES	
	2007	2008	2007	2008
Average number of common shares	20,000	22,000	40,000	45,000
Net income	$65,000	$76,000	$84,000	$180,000
Preferred dividends	10,000	10,000	0	0
Stock price when annual results reported	54.60	51.00	32.55	59.60

Required:

1. Compute the 2008 EPS for each company. In 2007, BusinessWorld reported EPS of $2.75, whereas Fun and Games reported EPS of $2.10. Which company appears to have improved its performance in 2008?

2. Compute the 2008 P/E ratio for each company. Do investors appear to value one company more than the other? Explain.

Cases and Projects

CP13-1 Finding Financial Information   LO2, 3, 4

Refer to the financial statements of The Home Depot in Appendix A at the end of this book, or download the annual report from the Cases and Projects section of the text's Web site at www.mhhe.com/LLPW1e.

Required:

1. As of February 3, 2008, how many shares of common stock were authorized? How many shares were issued? How many shares were held in treasury? What does this suggest to you about the number of shares outstanding?

2. According to the Retained Earnings column in the Statement of Stockholders' Equity, how much did the company declare in dividends during the year ended February 3, 2008?

3. According to the income statement, how has The Home Depot's net earnings changed over the past three years? Has the company's basic earnings per share changed over the past three years? How do you explain these seemingly inconsistent patterns?

CP13-2 Comparing Financial Information   LO2, 3, 4

Refer to the financial statements of The Home Depot in Appendix A and Lowe's in Appendix B at the end of this book, or download the annual reports from the Cases and Projects section of the text's Web site at www.mhhe.com/LLPW1e.

Lowe's

Required:

1. Did Lowe's have more or fewer authorized shares of common stock than The Home Depot at the beginning of February 2008?

2. From the Retained Earnings column in the statement of stockholders' equity, what total amount of cash dividends did Lowe's declare during the year ended February 1, 2008? Compared to The Home Depot, is Lowe's policy on dividends better, worse, or just different?

3. How have Lowe's net earnings changed over the past three years? How has the company's basic earnings per share changed over the past three years? According to financial statement note 11, were the changes in EPS caused only by changes in Lowe's net earnings?

CP13-3 Examining an Annual Report: Internet-Based Team Research   LO3, 4

As a team, select an industry to analyze. Using your Web browser, each team member should acquire the annual report or 10-K for one publicly traded company in the industry, with each member selecting a different company. (See CP1-3 in Chapter 1 for a description of possible resources for these tasks.)

Required:

1. On an individual basis, each team member should write a short report that incorporates the following:

   a. Has the company declared cash or stock dividends during the past three years?
   b. What is the trend in the company's EPS over the past three years?
   c. Compute and analyze the P/E ratio over the past two years.

2. Then, as a team, write a short report comparing and contrasting your companies using these attributes. Discuss any patterns across the companies that you as a team observe. Provide potential explanations for any differences discovered.

LO2

Activision, Inc.

CP13-4 Making Ethical Decisions: A Real-Life Example

Activision became a public company with an initial public offering of stock on June 9, 1983, at $12 per share. In June 2002, Activision issued 7.5 million additional shares to the public at approximately $33 per share. In October 2002, when its stock was trading at about $22 per share, Activision executives announced that the company would spend up to $150 million to buy back stock from investors. On January 8, 2003, *The Wall Street Journal* reported that several analysts were criticizing Activision's executives because the company had sold the shares to the public at a high price ($33) and then were offering to buy them back at the going market price, which was considerably lower than the issue price in 2002.

Required:

1. Do you think it was inappropriate for Activision to offer to buy back the stock at a lower price in October 2002?

2. Would your answer to requirement 1 be different if Activision had not issued additional stock in June 2002?

3. *The Wall Street Journal* article also reported that Activision executives had purchased over 530,000 shares of company stock in December 2002 at the then-current price of $13.32 per share. If you were an investor, how would you feel about executives buying stock in their own company?

4. Would your answer to requirement 3 be different if you also learned that the executives had sold nearly 2.5 million shares of Activision stock earlier that year, when the price was at least $26.08 per share?

LO3

CP13-5 Making Ethical Decisions: A Mini Case

You are the president of a very successful Internet company that has had a remarkably profitable year. You have determined that the company has more than $10 million in cash generated by operating activities not needed in the business. You are thinking about paying it out to stockholders as a special dividend. You discuss the idea with your vice president, who reacts angrily to your suggestion:

> Our stock price has gone up by 200 percent in the last year alone. What more do we have to do for the owners? The people who really earned that money are the employees who have been working 12 hours a day, six or seven days a week to make the company successful. Most of them didn't even take vacations last year. I say we have to pay out bonuses and nothing extra for the stockholders.

As president, you know that you are hired by the board of directors, which is elected by the stockholders.

Required:

What is your responsibility to both groups? To which group would you give the $10 million? Why?

LO3

CP13-6 Thinking Critically Making a Decision as an Investor

You have retired after a long and successful career as a business executive and now spend a good portion of your time managing your retirement portfolio. You are considering two basic investment alternatives. You can invest in (1) conservative stocks that pay substantial dividends (typically 5 percent of the stock price every year) or (2) growth-oriented technology stocks that pay no dividends.

Required:

Analyze each of these alternatives and select one. Justify your selection.

CP13-7 Charting Stock Price Movement around Important Announcement Dates

LO3

Using a Web search engine like Google, find either an earnings or dividend announcement for two different companies. Using a source such as bigcharts.com, determine the closing stock price for each company for each day during the five business days before and after the announcement. Using a separate worksheet for each company, prepare a line chart of its stock price movement.

Required:

Examine the charts for each company. Does the stock price appear to change as a consequence of their announcements? Explain why or why not.

14 Long-Term Liabilities

LEARNING OBJECTIVES

After completing this chapter, you should be able to:

LO1 Explain how to measure long-term liabilities.

LO2 Demonstrate how to account for discounted notes payable.

LO3 Demonstrate how to account for bonds payable.

LO4 Explain how to account for lease liabilities.

LO5 Calculate and interpret the debt-to-assets and times interest earned ratios.

Lectured presentation–14-1
www.mhhe.com/LLPW1e

Focus Company: GENERAL MILLS, INC.

Maker of Pillsbury, Green Giant, Cheerios, and More

www.generalmills.com

After turning in their report, they eagerly await their grade. They are expecting an A and would be devastated if they got a B. A group of high-achieving students waiting for their project grade? They could be, but these hopeful characters are actually the Jolly Green Giant, Lucky the Leprechaun, Poppin' Fresh, and their corporate bosses at General Mills.

That's right, this magically delicious company and all its brands receive a letter grade just as you do. The grading process is a bit different from yours because credit-rating agencies such as Standard & Poor's, Fitch, and Moody's assign their grades based on the company's ability to pay its liabilities on time. And instead of ranging from A to F, their grade can range from AAA to D. The AAA rating is given only to companies in rock-solid financial condition, and the D goes to those likely to pay less than half of what they owe. In general, any grade above a BB is considered a good to high-quality credit rating, which is what General Mills typically earns.

In this chapter, you will learn about the accounting procedures and financial ratios used to report and interpret long-term liabilities and how they influence a company's credit rating. Although we focus on business reporting and analysis, this chapter can also help you understand information that is used to assess your personal credit rating.

LONG-TERM LIABILITIES	ACCOUNTING FOR LONG-TERM LIABILITIES	ANALYZING LONG-TERM LIABILITIES
• Making Financing Decisions • Measuring Liabilities	• Discounted Notes • Bonds Payable • Lease Liabilities	• Debt-to-Assets Ratio • Times Interest Earned Ratio

LONG-TERM LIABILITIES

Learning Objective 1

Explain how to measure long-term liabilities.

Making Financing Decisions

Businesses of all forms, including sole proprietorships, partnerships, and corporations, usually require long-term financing at some time during their lives. This financing may be used to purchase new equipment, expand buildings, or acquire other businesses. Long-term financing generally involves borrowing money from lenders (debt) or obtaining money from owners (equity). Chapter 13 introduced the relative advantages of these two sources of financing when evaluated by corporations. See Exhibit 14.1 for similar ideas that apply to other organizational forms.

After a decision is made to rely on long-term debt financing, further decisions must be made about the type of debt to use. Long-term debt includes any liabilities that will require repayment over more than one year or if longer, the company's operating cycle. These long-term liabilities, which we explain in the following sections of this chapter, include notes payable, bonds payable, and lease liabilities. Although important differences for these types of debt exist, all liabilities are reported in the financial statements using the same principles, which we discuss next.

Measuring Liabilities

In Chapter 11, we noted that all liabilities are first recorded at their cash-equivalent amount—that is, the amount of cash that would be accepted in full settlement of the liability at the moment it is created. This amount excludes interest. Interest arises and is recorded as an expense as time passes.

In many instances, the cash-equivalent amount is readily apparent. For example, bank loans or interest-bearing notes (discussed in Chapter 11) refer specifically to separate principal and interest components. In these situations, the principal clearly represents the cash-equivalent amount. To illustrate, consider a $100,000 interest-bearing note that requires principal and

Exhibit 14.1 Reasons to Use Debt or Equity Financing

Reasons to Use Debt Financing	Reasons to Use Equity Financing
1. Owners may not have sufficient resources to contribute to the business. 2. Interest paid on business loans is tax deductible, but withdrawals paid to owners are not tax deductible. 3. Debt does not usually change an owner's control, but admitting new owners does.	1. A business must repay (or refinance) debt when it matures. Equity contributions by owners do not mature or require repayment. 2. Interest on debt must be repaid regardless of the financial condition of the business. Owners may forgo withdrawals to help the business survive its financial difficulties.

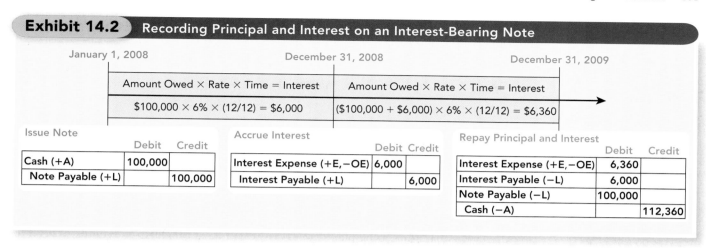

Exhibit 14.2   Recording Principal and Interest on an Interest-Bearing Note

January 1, 2008   December 31, 2008   December 31, 2009

Amount Owed × Rate × Time = Interest	Amount Owed × Rate × Time = Interest
$100,000 × 6% × (12/12) = $6,000	($100,000 + $6,000) × 6% × (12/12) = $6,360

Issue Note

	Debit	Credit
Cash (+A)	100,000	
Note Payable (+L)		100,000

Accrue Interest

	Debit	Credit
Interest Expense (+E, −OE)	6,000	
Interest Payable (+L)		6,000

Repay Principal and Interest

	Debit	Credit
Interest Expense (+E, −OE)	6,360	
Interest Payable (−L)	6,000	
Note Payable (−L)	100,000	
Cash (−A)		112,360

interest payments in two years with interest calculated at the rate of 6 percent of the unpaid balance each year. In this example, the principal is $100,000 and the total interest over the two years is $12,360. See Exhibit 14.2 for a review of how to calculate and record the principal and interest on the note. This long-term note is accounted for the same way as the short-term note payable you encountered in Chapter 11 except the long-term note is outstanding for two years rather than one.

The liabilities discussed in the remainder of this chapter apply these same principles, but they do not explicitly separate the principal and interest components. The separate components do exist, but they must be calculated before they can be recorded as principal or interest. A *discounted note payable*, for example, typically describes only the dollar amounts to be paid, such as requiring a payment of $112,360 in two years. Of this payment, part represents the principal and part is assumed to be built-in interest covering the two-year period. The accountant must determine what part is principal and what part is interest so that the cash-equivalent amount (the amount of the principal) can be initially recorded as a Note Payable. As time passes, interest is calculated and recorded, as you will see in the next section.

The procedures used for recording discounted notes are also used to record bonds and lease liabilities, as you will see in later sections. So take your time when learning about discounted notes, and you will find the other topics easier to learn.

The method that accountants use to determine the principal or cash-equivalent amount is called discounting or present value analysis. In effect, discounting allows accountants to remove the built-in interest component, leaving a **present value** that represents the note's principal (cash-equivalent) component on the date the liability was created. Supplement 14A explains the steps used in discounting various long-term liabilities.

ACCOUNTING FOR LONG-TERM LIABILITIES

Discounted Notes

Discounted notes are accounted for in the same way as interest-bearing notes with two exceptions. First, the accountant must discount the payments to be made on the note to determine the principal (cash-equivalent) amount to record in Notes Payable. Second, interest on a discounted note is accrued in the Notes Payable account. (Interest on interest-bearing notes is accrued in the Interest Payable account.)

Assume that on January 1, 2008, General Mills buys a new piece of equipment. Rather than pay cash, General Mills offers a note that promises to pay $112,360 on December 31, 2009. General Mills typically borrows at a 6 percent interest rate. Because this note does not explicitly state an interest rate, it must be discounted to remove the 6 percent interest that is presumed to be built into the $112,360 payment. By discounting the $112,360 payment using the steps explained in Supplement 14A (see page 616), we can determine that the note's present value on January 1, 2008, is $100,000. That amount is the principal, or

Learning Objective 2

Demonstrate how to account for discounted notes payable.

Video 14-1
www.mhhe.com/LLPW1e

cash-equivalent, amount of the note. The liability is recorded as a Note Payable using the following journal entry:

	Debit	Credit
Equipment (+A)	100,000	
Note Payable (+L)		100,000

Assets	=	Liabilities	+	Owners' Equity
Equipment +100,000		Note Payable +100,000		

Under the matching principle, General Mills **will need to adjust its records to account for the interest incurred each accounting period.** In reality, General Mills would make such an adjustment every month or quarter, but for the sake of simplicity, we assume that it occurs only once each year on December 31. Interest for the year ended December 31, 2008, is calculated by multiplying the amount of the liability by the interest rate for the full 12 months of the year ($100,000 × 6% × 12/12 = $6,000). This amount is an expense in 2008, and because it has not yet been paid, it also increases liabilities, as recorded in the following journal entry:

	Debit	Credit
Interest Expense (+E, −OE)	6,000	
Note Payable (+L)		6,000

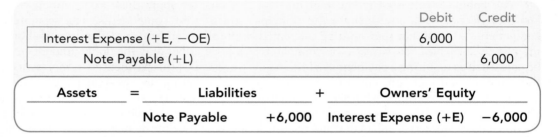

Assets	=	Liabilities	+	Owners' Equity
		Note Payable +6,000		Interest Expense (+E) −6,000

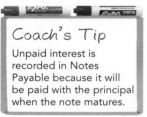

Coach's Tip

Unpaid interest is recorded in Notes Payable because it will be paid with the principal when the note matures.

After this journal entry has been recorded, the balance in the Note Payable account increases from $100,000 to $106,000. We use this new balance in calculating the interest for the following year ($106,000 × 6% × 12/12 = $6,360). This amount is matched to the period in which it was incurred by recording the following journal entry on December 31, 2009, when General Mills makes the required payment of $112,360:

	Debit	Credit
Interest Expense (+E, −OE)	6,360	
Note Payable (−L)	106,000	
Cash (−A)		112,360

Assets	=	Liabilities	+	Owners' Equity
Cash −112,360		Note Payable −106,000		Interest Expense (+E) −6,360

Refer to Exhibit 14.3 for a summary of these calculations and journal entries. If you compare Exhibit 14.3 to Exhibit 14.2 (page 601), you will see that recording the liability and interest on discounted notes is similar to recording them on interest-bearing notes.

Before moving to bonds payable, try the following Self-Study Practice to make sure you understand how to account for discounted notes.

Exhibit 14.3   Recording Principal and Interest on a Discounted Note

January 1, 2008	December 31, 2008	December 31, 2009
Amount Owed × Rate × Time = Interest	Amount Owed × Rate × Time = Interest	
$100,000 × 6% × (12/12) = $6,000	($100,000 + $6,000) × 6% × (12/12) = $6,360	

Issue Note

	Debit	Credit
Equipment	100,000	
Note Payable		100,000

Accrue Interest

	Debit	Credit
Interest Expense	6,000	
Note Payable		6,000

Repay Principal and Interest

	Debit	Credit
Interest Expense	6,360	
Note Payable	106,000	
Cash		112,360

After you have finished, check your answers with the solution at the bottom of the next page.

SELF-STUDY PRACTICE

Starbucks

Assume that Starbucks issued a discounted note on January 1, 2008, to acquire new equipment. The note requires a payment of $55,125 on December 31, 2009. Using an annual interest rate of 5 percent to discount the payment, you determine that the note's present value on January 1, 2008, was $50,000. Record the journal entries and accounting equation effects for (1) the equipment purchase, (2) the interest adjustment on December 31, 2008, and (3) the $55,125 payment on December 31, 2009.

1.

	Debit	Credit

Assets = Liabilities + Owners' Equity

2.

	Debit	Credit

Assets = Liabilities + Owners' Equity

3.

	Debit	Credit

Assets = Liabilities + Owners' Equity

Bonds Payable

Video 14-2
www.mhhe.com/LLPW1e

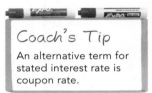

Coach's Tip

An alternative term for stated interest rate is coupon rate.

Occasionally, governments and very large companies such as General Mills need to borrow more money than any single lender can provide. In 2007, for example, General Mills needed to borrow $700 million. Because issuing a promissory note for such a large amount of money was impractical, the company instead issued bonds. A sample bond certificate is shown here.

Bonds are financial instruments that outline the future payments a company promises to make in exchange for receiving a sum of money now. From the company's perspective, the bond is a long-term liability. From the bondholder's perspective, the bond is an investment. After a company issues the bonds, they can be traded on established exchanges such as the New York Bond Exchange. The ability to sell a bond on the bond exchange is attractive to bondholders because it provides them liquidity, or the ability to receive cash for the bond whenever they wish to sell it. In return for this liquidity, bondholders will accept a lower interest rate, which benefits the company by lowering the cost of long-term borrowing.

As you can see from the sample bond certificate shown here, three key elements of a bond are (1) the maturity date, (2) the amount payable on the maturity date (often called the face value), and (3) the stated interest rate. In most cases, the face value of each bond is $1,000.

Solution to
Self-Study Practice

1.

	Debit	Credit
Equipment (+A)	50,000	
Note Payable (+L)		50,000

Assets	=	Liabilities	+	Owners' Equity
Equipment +50,000		Note Payable +50,000		

2.

	Debit	Credit
Interest Expense (+E, −OE)	2,500	
Note Payable (+L)		2,500
[$50,000 × 5% × 12/12 = $2,500]		

Assets	=	Liabilities	+	Owners' Equity
		Note Payable +2,500		Interest Expense (+E) −2,500

3.

	Debit	Debit
Interest Expense (+E, −OE)	2,625	
Note Payable (−L)	52,500	
Cash (−A)		55,125
[($50,000 + $2,500) × 5% × 12/12 = $2,625]		

Assets	=	Liabilities	+	Owners' Equity
Cash −55,125		Note Payable −52,500		Interest Expense (+E) −2,625

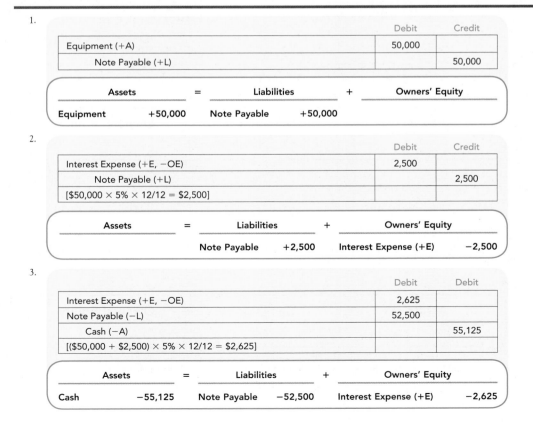

The stated interest rate is always expressed as an annual rate although some bonds require interest payments every six months (that is, semiannually). Each interest payment is computed by multiplying the face value times the stated interest rate (times the fraction of the year if payments are made semiannually). As you will see later, for good economic reasons, bonds may be sold at amounts above or below their face value. A bond's selling price does not affect the amount of each interest payment, however. For example, a 6 percent bond with a face value of $1,000 will always pay interest of $60 cash each year (= $1,000 × 6% × 12/12).

Spotlight On FINANCIAL REPORTING

The financial press reports bond prices each day based on transactions that occurred on the bond exchange. The following is typical of the information you will find:

Company Bond	Close	Yield	Volume	Change
Safeway 5.5 2013	97.2	6.80	58	−1/4
General Mills 6.0 2011	101.4	5.77	250	+3/8
Harrah's 7.0 2020	104.1	6.90	580	−7/8

GENERAL MILLS

This listing reports that the General Mills bond has a stated interest rate of 6.0 percent and will mature in the year 2011. The bond's price is quoted as a percentage of face value; in this case, 101.4 percent of face value, or $1,014 ($1,000 × 1.014). At this price, the bond payments represent a cash yield of 5.77 percent. On the date reported, 250 bonds were sold, and the price increased 3/8 of a point from the closing price on the day before (a point is 1 percent). **Daily changes in bond prices arise from transactions among bondholders, which do not directly involve the company. Consequently, they do not affect the company's financial statements.** The company accounts for its bonds using the historical face value and historical interest rates that existed when the bonds were first sold to the public.

Bond Pricing

Neither the company nor its financial advisers determine the price at which bonds sell. Instead, the market determines the price by discounting the cash payments that the company promises to make on the bond. Supplement 14A at the end of this chapter shows the calculations for the $1,000, 6 percent General Mills bond (see page 616). Although it is useful to know how to do these calculations, they are not a necessary step in accounting for a bond issue. Instead, what we really need to know is the amount of cash received from the market when the bonds were first sold. This cash-equivalent amount is the value at which the liability for the bonds is recorded.

Because the market determines the price at which bonds sell, the company may receive an amount of cash that is equal to the face value, above the face value, or below the face value. A bond issued for more than its face value is said to have been issued at a premium, which is the excess of the bond's issue price over its face value. A bond issued for less than its face value is said to have been issued at a discount, which is the amount by which the issue price falls short of the bond's face value. The following sections show how to account for bonds issued at face value, at a premium, and at a discount.

Coach's Tip

Bond prices are typically quoted as a percentage of face value (although the percentage symbol is often omitted).

Bonds Issued at Face Value. If General Mills receives $100,000 cash in exchange for issuing 100 bonds at their $1,000 face value, the company's accountants will record the following journal entry:

	Debit	Credit
Cash (+A)	100,000	
Bonds Payable (+L)		100,000

Assets		=	Liabilities		+	Owners' Equity
Cash	+100,000		Bonds Payable	+100,000		

Bonds Issued at a Premium.

If General Mills receives $107,260 for bonds with a total face value of $100,000, the cash-equivalent amount is $107,260, which represents the total liability on that date. The company's accountants will distinguish the $100,000 face value from the $7,260 premium by recording them in separate liability accounts as in the following journal entry:

	Debit	Credit
Cash (+A)	107,260	
Bonds Payable (+L)		100,000
Premium on Bonds Payable (+L)		7,260

Assets	=	Liabilities	+	Owners' Equity
Cash +107,260		Bonds Payable +100,000		
		Premium on Bonds Payable +7,260		

Why would bondholders be willing to pay a premium? For the same reason that you might pay a premium to acquire tickets to a great concert or a big game. If a bond offers something attractive, such as a high interest rate, bondholders may be willing to pay a premium to acquire it.

Bonds Issued at a Discount.

If General Mills receives $93,376 for bonds with a total face value of $100,000, the cash-equivalent amount is $93,376, which represents the liability on that date. The discount of $6,624 (= $100,000 − $93,376) offsets the face value, so accountants will record it in a contra-account. A contra-account to a liability is recorded as a debit as in the following journal entry:

	Debit	Credit
Cash (+A)	93,376	
Discount on Bonds Payable (+xL, −L)	6,624	
Bonds Payable (+L)		100,000

Assets	=	Liabilities	+	Owners' Equity
Cash +93,376		Bonds Payable +100,000		
		Discount on Bonds Payable (+xL) −6,624		

Why would companies such as General Mills be willing to discount a bond? The answer is that they must if they want to sell it. If a bond promises to pay interest at a stated rate of 6 percent when other financial instruments offer 8 percent, no one will be willing to buy the bond unless the company discounts it. The discount reduces the initial price of the bond without changing the interest payments and the face value to be paid at maturity. In effect, a discount increases the return that bondholders earn on their initial investment.

To illustrate, suppose you could buy a $1,000 bond that pays a stated interest rate of 6 percent and matures in one year. After one year, you would receive the stated interest of $60 ($1,000 × 6% × 12/12) plus the face value of $1,000. If you had paid $1,000 for the bond, you would receive 1.06 times as much as your initial investment [($60 + $1,000) ÷ $1,000]—a return of 6 percent. If instead the bond price were discounted $19, so that you paid only $981 for it, you would receive 1.08 times as much your initial investment [($60 + $1,000) ÷ $981 = 1.08]—a return of 8 percent. This percentage represents both the bondholder's rate of return and the company's cost of borrowing. It is commonly referred to as the market interest rate.

Exhibit 14.4   **Balance Sheet Reporting of Bond Liabilities**

Bonds issued at a premium		Bonds issued at face value		Bonds issued at a discount	
Bonds payable	$100,000	Bonds payable	$100,000	Bonds payable	$100,000
Premium on bonds payable	7,260			Discount on bonds payable	(6,624)
Unpaid bond liability	107,260			Unpaid bond liability	93,376

Reporting Bond Liabilities. The total face value of a bond plus any related premium or minus any related discount is reported in the liabilities section of the balance sheet as in Exhibit 14.4 for our three examples. The amount of the unpaid bond liability, after taking into account any premium or discount, is referred to as the bond's carrying value.

To determine whether a bond will be issued at a premium, at face value, or at a discount, you need consider only the relationship between the stated interest rate on the bond (what the bond pays in cash) and the market interest rate (the return that bondholders require). Exhibit 14.5 illustrates this relationship.

Exhibit 14.5   **Relationships between Interest Rates and Bond Pricing**

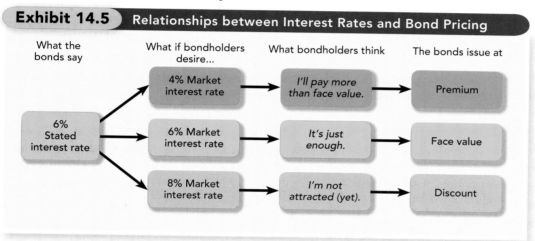

Before you continue, try the following Self-Study Practice to make sure you understand how bonds are priced.

For each of the following independent situations, indicate whether the bonds were issued at a premium, at a discount, or at face value.

1. Stated interest rate = 7% and market interest rate = 7%. _____
2. Stated interest rate = 5% and market interest rate = 6%. _____
3. Bond issue price = $10,100 and bond face value = $10,000. _____

After you have finished, check your answers with the solution at the bottom of the page.

Interest Expense

As time passes, a bond liability creates interest expense, which is matched to each period in which the liability is outstanding. Because interest expense arises from a financing decision (not an operating decision), it is reported below the Income from Operations line on the company's income statement as in Exhibit 14.6.

1. Face value.
2. Discount—the market requires a better rate of return than the interest stated on the bond.
3. Premium—the market is willing to pay more than face value to obtain the bond's higher interest rate.

Solution to
Self-Study Practice

GENERAL MILLS

Exhibit 14.6 | Reporting Interest Expense on the Income Statement

General Mills, Inc.
Income Statement
For the Quarter Ended August 26, 2007
(in millions)

Net sales	$3,072.0
Cost of sales	1,915.8
Selling, general, and administrative expenses	631.6
Other operating expenses	14.5
	2,561.9
Income from operations	510.1
Interest expense	113.3
Other expenses (revenues)	(22.4)
Income before income taxes	419.2
Income tax expense	130.3
Net income	$ 288.9

The process of calculating and recording interest on bonds is similar to that for notes payable, particularly when the bonds are issued at face value. Assume, for example, that General Mills issues bonds on July 1, 2009, at their total face value of $100,000. If the bonds carry an annual stated interest rate of 6 percent payable in cash on June 30 of each year, General Mills will need to accrue both an expense and a liability for interest at the end of each accounting period. On December 31, assuming no previous accrual of interest, General Mills would record interest of $3,000 (= $100,000 × 6% × 6/12) with the following entry:

	Debit	Credit
Interest Expense (+E, −OE)	3,000	
Interest Payable (+L)		3,000

Assets	=	Liabilities	+	Owners' Equity	
		Interest Payable +3,000		Interest Expense (+E)	−3,000

General Mills reports Interest Payable as a current liability because the company will pay this amount within the coming year. When it is paid, Interest Payable will be debited and Cash will be credited.

In comparison to this procedure for reporting interest expense on bonds issued at face value, the procedures for reporting interest expense on bonds issued at a premium or a discount are slightly more complicated. The complication arises because the premium or discount represents an adjustment to the interest rate stated on the bond. A premium reduces the company's cost of borrowing, so it reduces Interest Expense over the life of the bond. A discount increases the company's cost of borrowing, so it increases Interest Expense over the life of the bond. The process of recording these adjustments to interest expense is called amortization. Two methods may be used to amortize premiums and discounts, the effective-interest method (explained in Supplement 14B) and the straight-line method (explained in Supplement 14C).

Bond Retirement

Most bonds are retired (paid off) at maturity. If interest has been fully paid at the time of maturity, the only remaining account to settle will be Bonds Payable. Assuming the General

Mills bonds in our example were retired with a payment equal to their $100,000 face value, the following journal entry would be recorded:

	Debit	Credit
Bonds Payable (−L)	100,000	
Cash (−A)		100,000

Assets	=	Liabilities	+	Owners' Equity
Cash −100,000		Bonds Payable −100,000		

Rather than wait until the maturity date to retire the bonds, however, the company may retire them early. Companies with a lot of cash often retire their bonds early to reduce future interest expense and increase net income. Even companies that do not have extra cash may decide to retire their bonds early if interest rates have fallen since issuing the original bonds. In this case, the companies would issue new bonds at the lower interest rate and use the money they receive from the new bonds to retire the old ones before maturity. Again, this decision reduces future interest expense, which increases future earnings.

The early retirement of bonds has three financial effects. The company (1) pays cash, (2) eliminates the bond liability, and (3) reports either a gain or a loss. A gain arises if the cash paid to retire the bonds is less than the carrying value of the bond liability. A loss is incurred if the company pays more than the carrying value at the time of retirement.

To illustrate these effects, assume that in 2000, General Mills issued $100,000 of bonds at face value. Nine years later, in 2009, the company retired the bonds early. At the time, the bond price was 103, so General Mills made a payment of $103,000 (= $100,000 × 103%) to retire the bonds. The following journal entry recorded the retirement:

	Debit	Credit
Bonds Payable (−L)	100,000	
Loss on Bond Retirement (+E, −OE)	3,000	
Cash (−A)		103,000

Assets	=	Liabilities	+	Owners' Equity
				Loss on Bond
Cash −103,000		Bonds Payable −100,000		Retirement (+E) −3,000

Notice two features of this example. First, because the bond retirement is a financing decision, the loss would be reported after the Income from Operations line on the income statement. In Exhibit 14.6, this loss would be included in Other Expenses; a gain would be included in Other Revenues. Second, this retirement does not involve the removal of a bond discount or bond premium account because the bonds were issued at face value. If the bonds had been issued below or above face value, any premium or discount balance that existed at the time of retirement would need to be removed as well.

Types of Bonds

When you first start learning about bonds, it may seem the number of new terms that describe the bonds are limitless. These terms can generally be grouped into two categories: (1) those that describe the type of organization that issued the bonds and (2) those that describe specific features of the bond. In the first category are bonds issued by the U.S. Treasury Department ("treasuries"); municipal organizations such as states, cities, counties, and towns ("munis"); and corporations ("corporates"). In the second category are bonds that are backed by collateral ("secured") or not ("debentures"), that the issuing corporation can call in and exchange for cash ("callable") or convert into shares of its stock ("convertible"), and that mature in a series of installments ("serial bonds") or include no periodic interest payments ("zero-coupon bonds" and "strips"). The basic procedures shown in the previous sections for recording bond liabilities and interest expense apply equally to these various types of bonds.

Be sure you understand the basics of bond accounting by trying the following Self-Study Practice before you move to the next section.

In January 2008, Target Corporation issued bonds with a face value of $2,250,000, a stated interest rate of 7.0 percent, and a maturity date of January 15, 2038. The bonds issued at a price of 99.318. Based on this issue price, (1) indicate whether the market interest rate was higher or lower than the stated interest rate at the time of issue and (2) prepare the journal entry to record the bond issue.

After you have finished, check your answers with the solution at the bottom of the page.

Lease Liabilities

Learning Objective 4

Explain how to account for lease liabilities.

A lease is a rental agreement between the owner of property (the lessor) and the renter of that property (the lessee). Depending on the terms of the rental agreement, a lease may be accounted for as an operating lease or a capital lease.

Operating Leases

An operating lease allows a company to use property temporarily while the lessor continues to own it. An apartment lease and a daily or weekly car rental from Hertz or Avis are examples of operating leases.

When a company obtains the use of property through an operating lease, accountants record the payments made or owed to the lessor as an operating expense. For example, in 2007, General Mills rented warehouse space at a total cost of $46 million. Assuming that the company paid $40 million in cash and owed $6 million at the end of the year, accountants would record the following journal entry (in millions):

	Debit	Credit
Rent Expense (+E, −OE)	46	
Rent Payable (+L)		6
Cash (−A)		40

Assets	=	Liabilities	+	Owners' Equity
Cash −40		Rent Payable +6		Rent Expense (+E) −46

Capital Leases

A capital lease allows a lessee to use rented property in exchange for payments to the lessor, but unlike an operating lease, it transfers virtually all risks and rewards of owning the property to the lessee. In effect, the lessee purchases the property from the lessor through a series of payments made over the term of the lease. To account for this arrangement, the lessee records the property and the lease liability at the cash-equivalent amount. The cash-equivalent amount is calculated by discounting the payments the lessee will make over the term of the lease. Supplement 14A explains the procedure for discounting the payments (see page 616).

Solution to
Self-Study Practice

1. The bonds are issued at a discount (99.318 percent of face value), which implies that the stated interest rate was not as attractive as other interest rates available in the market. That is, the market interest rate was higher than the stated interest rate.

2. Issue price = $2,250,000 × .99318 = $2,234,655.

	Debit	Credit
Cash (+A)	2,234,655	
Discount on Bonds Payable (+xL, −L)	15,345	
Bonds Payable (+L)		2,250,000

General Mills obtains some of its equipment through capital leases. To illustrate the accounting, assume that the company has promised to make payments over a five-year period that equate to the cash-equivalent (discounted) amount of $42,124. When the equipment is obtained, General Mills would record the following journal entry:

	Debit	Credit
Equipment (+A)	42,124	
Lease Liability (+L)		42,124

Assets	=	Liabilities	+	Owners' Equity
Equipment +42,124		Lease Liability +42,124		

In the periods that follow, General Mills would record Depreciation Expense on the equipment and Interest Expense on the lease liability.

ANALYZING LONG-TERM LIABILITIES

In evaluating a company's ability to pay its liabilities, a good place to start is with the reports credit-rating agencies issue. These agencies do not report on all companies, however, particularly the smaller ones. Even if they did, their reports might not address your specific concerns. So, you need to know how to analyze a set of financial statements in the same way that a credit rater would.

Essentially, you want to assess what proportion of a company's assets are financed by liabilities and whether or not the company is likely to generate the resources needed to pay the interest on those liabilities. Two financial ratios are commonly used to make these assessments: the debt-to-assets ratio and the times interest earned ratio.

Learning Objective 5

Calculate and interpret the debt-to-assets and times interest earned ratios.

Financial Analysis Tools		
Name of Measure	Formula	What It Tells You
Debt-to-assets ratio	$\dfrac{\text{Total Liabilities}}{\text{Total Assets}}$	• The proportion of assets financed by liabilities • The higher the number the greater the financing risk
Times interest earned ratio	$\dfrac{(\text{Net Income} + \text{Interest Expense} + \text{Income Tax Expense})}{\text{Interest Expense}}$	• Whether sufficient resources are generated to cover interest costs • The higher the number the better the coverage

Debt-to-Assets Ratio

The debt-to-assets ratio compares total liabilities to total assets. Usually calculated to three decimal places, it can be expressed as a percentage by multiplying it by 100. This ratio indicates the proportion of total assets that are financed by debt. It is important to know how much debt is used to finance assets because debt must be repaid whether or not a company is doing well. If a company finances its assets mainly by debt rather than equity, then the debt-to-assets ratio will be high, suggesting that the company's financing strategy is risky. Ultimately, a company can be forced into bankruptcy if it takes on more debt than it could ever repay.

Refer to Exhibit 14.7 for an illustration of how debt plays a major role in financing General Mills' assets: 64.5 percent of the company's assets were financed by debt at the end of 2007. That percentage is not nearly as large, however, as the one for rival Kellogg's, whose debt-to-assets ratio was more than 80 percent. Although these ratios are typical of the food processing industry, they are high compared to other industries. Companies in the video game industry, for example, have much lower debt-to-assets ratios (Activision's is 13.7 percent).

| Exhibit 14.7 | Debt-to-Assets Ratios in the Food Processing Industry |

Company	Relevant Information (in millions)			2007 Debt-to-Assets Ratio	
GENERAL MILLS		2007	2006	$\frac{$11,726}{$18,184}$	= 0.645 or 64.5%
	Total liabilities	$11,726	$11,167		
	Total assets	18,184	18,075		
Kellogg's		2007	2006	$\frac{$8,645}{$10,714}$	= 0.807 or 80.7%
	Total liabilities	$ 8,645	$ 8,291		
	Total assets	10,714	10,575		

Spotlight on ETHICS

Doctoring the Debt-to-Assets Ratio

The debt-to-assets ratio can be a useful measure of the extent to which a company relies on debt to finance its assets. Analysts should be aware, however, that seemingly normal transactions that occur just before the end of an accounting period can influence this ratio. For example, the ratio can be reduced by repaying a loan just prior to the financial statement date. Although this transaction decreases total liabilities and total assets by the same amount, it has a greater impact on liabilities than on assets, thus reducing the ratio. If a company's debt-to-assets ratio is 10 to 15 (67 percent) before repayment of a $5 loan, it will be 5 to 10 (50 percent) after repayment.

Times Interest Earned Ratio

One way to judge a company's ability to pay interest is to ask whether it has generated enough income to cover its interest expense. The measure that most analysts use for this purpose is the times interest earned ratio.

The financial analysis tools box (on page 611) showed the formula for the times interest earned ratio. It is reproduced after the following paragraph. Notice that in this ratio, interest and income tax expenses are added back into net income. The reason for this is simple: Analysts want to know whether a company generates enough income to cover its interest expense **before the costs of financing and taxes.** In general, a high times interest earned ratio is viewed more favorably than a low one. A high ratio indicates an extra margin of protection should the company's profitability decline in the future.

Using the information in the income statement in Exhibit 14.6 on page 608, we can compute the times interest earned ratio for General Mills as follows.

$$\frac{\text{Net Income + Interest Expense + Income Tax Expense}}{\text{Interest Expense}} = \frac{$288.9 + $113.3 + $130.3}{$113.3} = 4.70$$

This ratio means that General Mills generates $4.70 of income (before the costs of financing and taxes) for each dollar of interest expense. No doubt this ratio is part of the reason that General Mills has earned a favorable credit rating of BBB or higher.

Every now and then you will see a times interest earned ratio that is less than 1.0 or even negative. **When the times interest earned ratio is less than 1.0, a company is not generating enough income to cover its interest expense.** Most companies with a negative times interest earned ratio survive only a couple of years before declaring bankruptcy.

Before you conclude your reading of this chapter, try the following Self-Study Practice to make sure you understand how to analyze long-term liabilities.

1. Use the information in Exhibit 14.7 to calculate the 2006 debt-to-assets ratios for General Mills and Kellogg's. Show the ratios as whole numbers calculated to three decimal places and as percentages.

2. Compare the ratios calculated in part (1) to the ratios in Exhibit 14.7. Did the two companies' financing risk increase or decrease in 2007 relative to 2006?

After you have finished, check your answers with the solutions at the bottom of the page.

Demonstration Case A
Discounted Notes

On January 1, 2008, Central University (CU) bought new gymnastics equipment. Rather than pay cash, CU gave a note that promised payment of $20,000 on January 1, 2011. CU typically borrows at a 4 percent interest rate. Using a 4 percent interest rate to discount the $20,000 payment, CU determined that the present value of this liability on January 1, 2008, was $17,780.

Required:

1. Give the journal entry required to record the equipment purchase on January 1, 2008.
2. Calculate the interest expense on the note in 2008. If this amount is added to the note amount on December 31, 2008, what will be the new balance in Note Payable on December 31, 2008? Continue these calculations for 2009 and 2010. What will be the balance in Notes Payable immediately prior to payment of the note on January 1, 2011? Round all calculations to the nearest dollar.
3. Assuming CU adjusts its accounting records once each year on December 31, give the journal entries required to accrue interest on the note on December 31, 2008, 2009, and 2010.

Suggested Solution

1.

	Debit	Credit
Equipment (+A)	17,780	
Note Payable (+L)		17,780

Assets	=	Liabilities	+	Owners' Equity
Equipment +17,780		Note Payable +17,780		

2.

	Note Payable, January 1	Interest Expense	Note Payable, December 31
2008	$17,780	$17,780 × 4% × 12/12 = $711	$17,780 + $711 = $18,491
2009	18,491	18,491 × 4% × 12/12 = 740	18,491 + 740 = 19,231
2010	19,231	19,231 × 4% × 12/12 = 769	19,231 + 769 = 20,000

---

1. General Mills = $11,167 / $18,075 = 0.618 or 61.8%.
   Kellogg's = $8,291 / $10,575 = 0.784 or 78.4%.

2. Both companies increased their reliance on debt in 2007, suggesting an increase in the risk that they would be unable to repay their borrowings.

Solution to
Self-Study Practice

3.   December 31, 2008:

	Debit	Credit
Interest Expense (+E, −OE)	711	
Note Payable (+L)		711

Assets	=	Liabilities	+	Owners' Equity
		Note Payable +711		Interest Expense (+E) −711

December 31, 2009:

	Debit	Credit
Interest Expense (+E, −OE)	740	
Note Payable (+L)		740

Assets	=	Liabilities	+	Owners' Equity
		Note Payable +740		Interest Expense (+E) −740

December 31, 2010:

	Debit	Credit
Interest Expense (+E, −OE)	769	
Note Payable (+L)		769

Assets	=	Liabilities	+	Owners' Equity
		Note Payable +769		Interest Expense (+E) −769

Demonstration Case B
Bonds

On February 1, 2006, Black & Decker Corporation issued 300,000 bonds at 5.75 percent, each with a face value of $1,000 and a maturity date of January 31, 2016. The bonds were issued at 99.6. Of the cash received from the issue, $154.6 million was used to retire some 7 percent bonds. Assume the 7 percent bonds had been previously issued at a face value of $155 million.

Required:

1.   How much cash did Black & Decker Corporation receive from the sale of the bonds payable? Show your computations.
2.   What was the amount of the premium or discount on the bonds payable?
3.   Give the journal entry for recording the issue of the 5.75 percent bonds on February 1, 2006.
4.   Show how the bonds would be reported on the balance sheet on February 1, 2006.
5.   Give the journal entry to record the retirement of the 7 percent bonds.

Suggested Solution

1.   Sale price of the bonds: 300,000 bonds × $1,000 face value × 99.6% = $298,800,000, or $298.8 million.
2.   Discount on the bonds payable: $300 million − $298.8 million = $1.2 million.

3.   February 1, 2006 (in millions):

	Debit	Credit
Cash (+A)	298.8	
Discount on Bonds Payable (+xL, −L)	1.2	
Bonds Payable (+L)		300.0

Assets	=	Liabilities	+	Owners' Equity
Cash +298.8		Bonds Payable +300.0		
		Discount on Bonds Payable (+xL) −1.2		

4.   Balance sheet reporting (long-term liabilities) (in millions):

Bonds Payable	$300.0
Discount on Bond Payable	(1.2)
Unpaid Bond Liability	298.8

5.   (in millions)

Face value	$ 155.0
Paid to retire	(154.6)
Gain	$ 0.4

	Debit	Credit
Bonds Payable (−L)	155.0	
Gain on Bond Retirement (+R, +OE)		0.4
Cash (−A)		154.6

Assets	=	Liabilities	+	Owners' Equity
Cash −154.6		Bonds Payable −155.0		Gain on Bond Retirement (+R) +0.4

Demonstration Case C

Leases

AMR Corporation provides air transportation to customers through its American Airlines and American Eagle business units. As of December 31, 2006, AMR operated 1,003 aircraft, 231 of which were obtained through operating leases and 90 through capital leases. For the year ended December 31, 2006, AMR incurred $606 million in aircraft rental expense. At the end of the year, the company owed $927 million for aircraft obtained via capital leases. The aircraft were capitalized as a noncurrent asset at a total cost of $1,744 million.

AMR

Required:

1.   Does the aircraft rental expense relate to operating leases or capital leases?
2.   Describe the two adjustments that would be made each year with respect to the aircraft and obligations related to capital leases.

Suggested Solution

1.   The aircraft rental expense relates to operating leases. (When payments are made for capital leases, they are reported as interest expense and reductions in the principal owed on the lease liability.)
2.   An adjustment would be recorded each accounting period for (a) depreciation on the aircraft obtained through capital leases and (b) interest on the lease liability. (Rent on the operating leases would be accrued as well.)

Supplement 14A
Discounting Future Payments

This supplement is based on the simple notion that you can invest cash today to earn interest over time, resulting in a larger amount in the future. The future value of your investment is larger than its present value because interest is added to the original investment, in a process called compounding. The following timeline shows how $1,000 invested today at a 10 percent interest rate becomes $1,100 one year from now ($1,000 × 1.10 = $1,100):

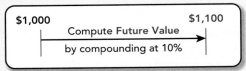

In finance, many problems involve determining the future value that can be generated from some present value. In accounting, however, our focus is just the opposite: We want to know the present (cash-equivalent) value today of amounts that will be paid in the future. This process of starting with the future value and working back to the present value is **discounting**. The following timeline shows the same situation as in the first timeline except that it works backward from the future value of $1,100 to a present value of $1,000, assuming a 10 percent discount rate:

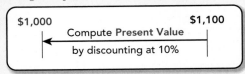

Two different discounting situations arise in business. The first involves discounting a **single amount** paid only once. This situation is illustrated in our timeline. To calculate the present value of a single amount, you divide the future payment by the rate at which interest accumulates in each period. Because our example involves only one period, the calculation is straightforward: $1,100 ÷ 1.10 = $1,000.

As the number of periods increases, this method becomes tiresome. An alternative approach is to use present value tables. Table 14A-1 shows the present value of $1 at various combinations of interest rates

| Table 14A-1 | Present Value of $1 |

Periods	2%	3%	3.75%	4%	4.25%	5%	6%	7%	8%
1	0.9804	0.9709	0.9639	0.9615	0.9592	0.9524	0.9434	0.9346	0.9259
2	0.9612	0.9426	0.9290	0.9246	0.9201	0.9070	0.8900	0.8734	0.8573
3	0.9423	0.9151	0.8954	0.8890	0.8826	0.8638	0.8396	0.8163	0.7938
4	0.9238	0.8885	0.8631	0.8548	0.8466	0.8227	0.7921	0.7629	0.7350
5	0.9057	0.8626	0.8319	0.8219	0.8121	0.7835	0.7473	0.7130	0.6806
6	0.8880	0.8375	0.8018	0.7903	0.7790	0.7462	0.7050	0.6663	0.6302
7	0.8706	0.8131	0.7728	0.7599	0.7473	0.7107	0.6651	0.6227	0.5835
8	0.8535	0.7894	0.7449	0.7307	0.7168	0.6768	0.6274	0.5820	0.5403
9	0.8368	0.7664	0.7180	0.7026	0.6876	0.6446	0.5919	0.5439	0.5002
10	0.8203	0.7441	0.6920	0.6756	0.6595	0.6139	0.5584	0.5083	0.4632
20	0.6730	0.5537	0.4789	0.4564	0.4350	0.3769	0.3118	0.2584	0.2145

Periods	9%	10%	11%	12%	13%	14%	15%	20%	25%
1	0.9174	0.9091	0.9009	0.8929	0.8850	0.8772	0.8696	0.8333	0.8000
2	0.8417	0.8264	0.8116	0.7972	0.7831	0.7695	0.7561	0.6944	0.6400
3	0.7722	0.7513	0.7312	0.7118	0.6931	0.6750	0.6575	0.5787	0.5120
4	0.7084	0.6830	0.6587	0.6355	0.6133	0.5921	0.5718	0.4823	0.4096
5	0.6499	0.6209	0.5935	0.5674	0.5428	0.5194	0.4972	0.4019	0.3277
6	0.5963	0.5645	0.5346	0.5066	0.4803	0.4556	0.4323	0.3349	0.2621
7	0.5470	0.5132	0.4817	0.4523	0.4251	0.3996	0.3759	0.2791	0.2097
8	0.5019	0.4665	0.4339	0.4039	0.3762	0.3506	0.3269	0.2326	0.1678
9	0.4604	0.4241	0.3909	0.3606	0.3329	0.3075	0.2843	0.1938	0.1342
10	0.4224	0.3855	0.3522	0.3220	0.2946	0.2697	0.2472	0.1615	0.1074
20	0.1784	0.1486	0.1240	0.1037	0.0868	0.0728	0.0611	0.0261	0.0115

and time periods. To solve the problem in our example, we would look for the value at the intersection of 10 percent and one period, which is 0.9091. This value implies that $1 paid one year from now equals $0.9091 today. To apply it to a $1,100 payment in one year, we would simply multiply it by $1,100 to obtain a present value of $1,000 (rounded).

The second type of discounting situation that arises in business involves a series of equal amounts, called an **annuity**. The following timeline illustrates an annuity:

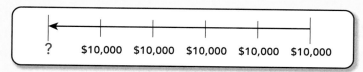

Although we could treat each payment in this annuity as a single amount to be discounted separately (and then totaled), such an approach would be cumbersome. To save time, we can use Table 14A-2, which shows the present value of a $1 annuity received at the end of several periods given various combinations of interest rates and periods. Assuming an interest rate of 6 percent for five years, we simply multiply the discounting factor in the table, 4.2124, by the annuity amount of $10,000 to obtain a present value of $42,124.

The following sections show how to apply these discounting techniques to discounted notes, bonds payable, and capital leases.

Discounted Notes

Assume that General Mills has just signed a note that requires a $112,360 payment in two years. The note does not state an interest rate, but General Mills typically incurs a 6 percent annual rate.

Table 14A-2   Present Value of Annuity of $1

Periods*	2%	3%	3.75%	4%	4.25%	5%	6%	7%	8%
1	0.9804	0.9709	0.9639	0.9615	0.9592	0.9524	0.9434	0.9346	0.9259
2	1.9416	1.9135	1.8929	1.8861	1.8794	1.8594	1.8334	1.8080	1.7833
3	2.8839	2.8286	2.7883	2.7751	2.7620	2.7232	2.6730	2.6243	2.5771
4	3.8077	3.7171	3.6514	3.6299	3.6086	3.5460	3.4651	3.3872	3.3121
5	4.7135	4.5797	4.4833	4.4518	4.4207	4.3295	4.2124	4.1002	3.9927
6	5.6014	5.4172	5.2851	5.2421	5.1997	5.0757	4.9173	4.7665	4.6229
7	6.4720	6.2303	6.0579	6.0021	5.9470	5.7864	5.5824	5.3893	5.2064
8	7.3255	7.0197	6.8028	6.7327	6.6638	6.4632	6.2098	5.9713	5.7466
9	8.1622	7.7861	7.5208	7.4353	7.3513	7.1078	6.8017	6.5152	6.2469
10	8.9826	8.5302	8.2128	8.1109	8.0109	7.7217	7.3601	7.0236	6.7101
20	16.3514	14.8775	13.8962	13.5903	13.2944	12.4622	11.4699	10.5940	9.8181

Periods*	9%	10%	11%	12%	13%	14%	15%	20%	25%
1	0.9174	0.9091	0.9009	0.8929	0.8550	0.8772	0.8696	0.8333	0.8000
2	1.7591	1.7355	1.7125	1.6901	1.6681	1.6467	1.6257	1.5278	1.4400
3	2.5313	2.4869	2.4437	2.4018	2.3612	2.3216	2.2832	2.1065	1.9520
4	3.2397	3.1699	3.1024	3.0373	2.9745	2.9137	2.8550	2.5887	2.3616
5	3.8897	3.7908	3.6959	3.6048	3.5172	3.4331	3.3522	2.9906	2.6893
6	4.4859	4.3553	4.2305	4.1114	3.9975	3.8887	3.7845	3.3255	2.9514
7	5.0330	4.8684	4.7122	4.5638	4.4226	4.2883	4.1604	3.6046	3.1611
8	5.5348	5.3349	5.1461	4.9676	4.7988	4.6389	4.4873	3.8372	3.3289
9	5.9952	5.7590	5.5370	5.3282	4.1317	4.9464	4.7716	4.0310	3.4631
10	6.4177	6.1446	5.8892	5.6502	5.4262	5.2161	5.0188	4.1925	3.5705
20	9.1285	8.5136	7.9633	7.4694	7.0248	6.6231	6.2593	4.8696	3.9539

*There is one payment each period.

We use that rate to discount the future payment of $112,360 to today's present value as in the following timeline:

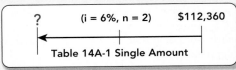

?   (i = 6%, n = 2) $112,360

Table 14A-1 Single Amount

Table 14A-1 shows that at an interest rate of 6 percent over two periods, the discounting factor we should use is 0.8900. So, we can compute the present value of the note as follows:

0.8900 × $112,360 = $100,000 Present Value

Bonds Payable

A bond represents a promise to pay a specified **face value** at maturity plus a **stated interest rate** each period until maturity. The following timeline illustrates these payments using the example in which General Mills issued 100 bonds, each with a face value of $1,000, to be repaid at maturity in four years. The stated interest rate of 6 percent is to be paid annually, which means a total annual interest payment of $6,000 (100 bonds × $1,000 × 6%). The two question marks on the timeline indicate that the $100,000 face value (a single amount) should be discounted separately from the $6,000 interest payments (an annuity). The total of the two present values will equal the value that the bond market places on these bonds.

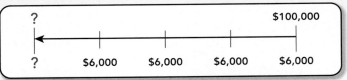

? $100,000

? $6,000 $6,000 $6,000 $6,000

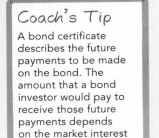

Coach's Tip

A bond certificate describes the future payments to be made on the bond. The amount that a bond investor would pay to receive those future payments depends on the market interest rate when the bond is issued.

The value the market places on bond payments depends on three factors: (1) the amount of the payments for face value and interest, (2) the period covered by each payment, and (3) the market interest rate when the bond is issued. The following examples show how differences in the market interest rate affect the computations.

Bonds Issued at Face Value.
Exhibit 14.5 (on page 607) shows that bonds will be issued at their face value if their stated interest rate (what the bond pays) equals the market interest rate (what the market demands). To illustrate, assume that the market interest rate is 6 percent, which equals the 6 percent stated interest rate used to compute the interest payments shown in the timeline. Table 14A-1 shows that the discounting factor for a single amount at 6 percent for four periods is 0.7921; Table 14A-2 shows that the discounting factor for an annuity at 6 percent for four periods 3.4651. We can multiply these factors by the future payments to get the present values:

Present value of $100,000 face value ($100,000 × 0.7921)	$ 79,210
Present value of $6,000 annuity ($6,000 × 3.4651)	20,790
Total present value of bond	$100,000

We should mention that, because the discounting factors are rounded to four decimal places, small rounding errors can arise. For example, if you calculate $6,000 × 3.4651 in the previous example, you will find it equals $20,790.60. We have rounded this down so that the total present value equals $100,000.

Bonds Issued above Face Value (at a Premium).
Bonds will be issued at a premium if their stated interest rate is higher than the market interest rate. Assume, for example, that the stated interest rate is 6 percent, but the market interest rate is only 4 percent. The discounting factor for a single amount at 4 percent for four periods is 0.8548 (see Table 14A-1); the discounting factor for an annuity at the same 4 percent interest rate for the same number of periods is 3.6299 (see Table 14A-2). If we multiply these factors by the future payments, we get the present values:

Present value of $100,000 face value ($100,000 × 0.8548)	$ 85,480
Present value of $6,000 annuity ($6,000 × 3.6299)	21,780
Total present value of bond	$107,260

Bonds Issued below Face Value (at a Discount).

Bonds will be issued at a discount if their stated interest rate is lower than the market interest rate. Assume, for example, that the stated interest rate is 6 percent, but the market interest rate is 8 percent. The discounting factor for a single amount at 8 percent for four periods is 0.7350 (see Table 14A-1); the discounting factor for an annuity at the same 8 percent rate for the same number of periods is 3.3121 (see Table 14A-2). If we multiply these factors by the future payments, we get the present values:

Present value of $100,000 face value ($100,000 × 0.7350)	$73,503
Present value of $6,000 annuity ($6,000 × 3.3121)	19,873
Total present value of bond	$93,376

Again, we need to mention that because the present value factors are rounded to four decimal places, small rounding differences may arise. In the preceding calculation, for example, we have shown $73,503, which is the actual present value unaffected by rounding, rather than the amount obtained by multiplying $100,000 by the rounded factor of 0.7350.

Capital Leases

A capital lease is a rental agreement that typically requires the lessee to make a series of equal payments over the term of the lease. Those payments represent an annuity. To compute the present (cash-equivalent) value of the annuity when a company enters into the lease, we can simply multiply the payment by the appropriate annuity factor in Table 14A-2.

To illustrate, assume General Mills has agreed to rent a piece of equipment for five years in return for five annual payments of $10,000 at an implied interest rate of 6 percent. The discounting factor for an annuity at 6 percent over five periods is 4.2124 (see Table 14A-2). We can use this factor to calculate the present (cash-equivalent) value of the five payments when a company enters into the agreement as follows:

$$\$10,000 \times 4.2124 = \$42,124 \text{ present value}$$

Interest Rates and Interest Periods

The preceding illustrations assumed annual interest periods. Although interest *rates* are always quoted on an annual basis, interest *periods* may cover less than a year. For example, semiannual interest implies two interest periods each year; quarterly interest implies four periods per year. When interest periods are less than a year, both the number of periods and the interest rate must be restated to be consistent with the length of the interest period.

To illustrate, 12 percent interest compounded annually for five years implies an interest rate of 12 percent and five periods. If interest is compounded quarterly, however, the interest period is one-quarter of a year (four periods per year), and the quarterly interest rate is one-quarter of the annual rate (3 percent per quarter). Therefore, 12 percent interest compounded quarterly for five years implies an interest rate of 3 percent per period over 20 interest periods (5 years × 4 periods per year).

Supplement 14B
Effective-Interest Method of Amortization

When a bond is issued at a premium or a discount, the amount of the bond premium or discount must be matched to the periods in which the bond is outstanding. This process, called bond amortization, may be accomplished using the effective-interest method, which ensures that interest expense represents the company's actual cost of borrowing. To calculate the interest expense for each interest period, accountants multiply the unpaid bond liability by the market interest rate that existed when the bonds were issued. Then they record the difference between the interest expense and the amount of interest paid (or accrued) that period as a reduction in the bond premium or discount as in the following examples.

Bond Premiums

A premium arises when the bond issuer receives more cash than the issuer repays at maturity. In effect, the premium reduces the company's cost of borrowing, so that in each accounting period, interest expense is lower than the actual interest payment. The excess of the interest payment over the interest expense is recorded as a reduction in the Premium on Bonds Payable liability account.

In our earlier example, General Mills received $107,260 for bonds with a total face value of $100,000. The company received a premium because the stated interest rate on the bonds (6 percent) was higher

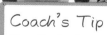

Coach's Tip

The effective-interest method computes interest expense by multiplying a **constant** interest rate (the market interest rate) by the unpaid bond liability.

than the market interest rate at the time the bonds were issued (4 percent). The stated interest rate determines the interest payment that is made each period ($100,000 × 6% × 12/12 = $6,000). Interest expense, however, is based on the market interest rate, as follows:

> **Interest Expense = Unpaid Bond Liability × Market Interest Rate × n/12**
>
> Unpaid Bond Liability = Bonds Payable + Premium on Bonds Payable
>
> n = Number of Months in Each Interest Period

For the first year ended December 31, 2007, interest expense for these bonds would be $4,290 ($107,260 × 4% × 12/12). The interest payment is $6,000 ($100,000 × 6% × 12/12). You can think of the difference between the $6,000 payment and the $4,290 interest expense ($6,000 − $4,290 = $1,710) as a partial repayment of the Premium on Bonds Payable. These effects would be recorded on December 31, 2007, in the following journal entry:

	Debit	Credit
Interest Expense (+E, −OE)	4,290	
Premium on Bonds Payable (−L)	1,710	
Cash (−A)		6,000

Assets	=	Liabilities	+	Owners' Equity
Cash −6,000		Premium on Bonds Payable −1,710		Interest Expense (+E) −4,290

Now that the journal entry has reduced the Premium on Bonds Payable, the unpaid bond liability in 2008 is smaller than it was in 2007 ($107,260 − $1,710 = $105,550). Thus, the calculation of Interest Expense in 2008 reflects this change, by multiplying the unpaid bond liability on January 1, 2008, by the market rate of interest for the full year ($105,550 × 4% × 12/12 = $4,222). Again, think of the difference between the $6,000 payment in 2008 and the $4,222 interest expense as another partial repayment of the Premium on Bonds Payable ($6,000 − $4,222 = $1,778). These effects would be recorded with the following journal entry:

	Debit	Credit
Interest Expense (+E, −OE)	4,222	
Premium on Bonds Payable (−L)	1,778	
Cash (−A)		6,000

Assets	=	Liabilities	+	Owners' Equity
Cash −6,000		Premium on Bonds Payable −1,778		Interest Expense (+E) −4,222

In each remaining year, General Mills will pay $6,000 as promised on the bond certificate. As you have just seen, a portion of that payment will represent Interest Expense and a portion reduces the original Premium on Bonds Payable. The following bond amortization schedule summarizes these effects:

BOND PREMIUM AMORTIZATION SCHEDULE: EFFECTIVE-INTEREST METHOD

	CHANGES DURING THE PERIOD			ENDING BOND LIABILITY BALANCES		
Period Ended	(A) Interest Expense	(B) Interest Payable	(C) (= B − A) Amortization of Premium	(D) Bonds Payable	(E) Premium on Bonds Payable	(F) (= D + E) Unpaid Bond Liability
01/01/07	—	—	—	$100,000	$7,260	$107,260
12/31/07	$4,290	$6,000	$1,710	100,000	5,550	105,550
12/31/08	4,222	6,000	1,778	100,000	3,772	103,772
12/31/09	4,151	6,000	1,849	100,000	1,923	101,923
12/31/10	4,077	6,000	1,923	100,000	0	100,000

Bond Discounts

A discount arises when the bond issuer receives less cash than the issuer must repay at maturity. In effect, the discount increases the company's cost of borrowing so that in each accounting period, interest expense is higher than the company's interest payment. The excess amount represents an increase in the unpaid bond liability, which will be paid at maturity. To report this effect, accountants record a decrease in the contra-liability account Discount on Bonds Payable. Decreasing this contra-liability increases the carrying value of the bond liability.

In our earlier example, General Mills received $93,376 for bonds with a total face value of $100,000. The company gave buyers a discount because the stated interest rate on the bonds (6 percent) was less than the market interest rate at the time the bonds were issued (8 percent). The stated interest rate determines the interest payment that must be made each period ($100,000 × 6% × 12/12 = $6,000). The interest expense is based on the market interest rate, as follows:

> **Interest Expense = Unpaid Bond Liability × Market Interest Rate × n/12**
>
> Unpaid Bond Liability = Bonds Payable − Discount on Bonds Payable
>
> n = Number of Months in Each Interest Period

For the first year ended December 31, 2007, interest expense on these bonds would be $7,470 ($93,376 × 8% × 12/12). The interest payment is $6,000 ($100,000 × 6% × 12/12). The difference between the interest expense and the payment ($7,470 − $6,000 = $1,470) represents the amortization of the bond discount in 2007. These effects would be recorded on December 31, 2007, in the following journal entry:

	Debit	Credit
Interest Expense (+E, −OE)	7,470	
Discount on Bonds Payable (−xL, +L)		1,470
Cash (−A)		6,000

Assets	=	Liabilities	+	Owners' Equity
Cash −6,000		Discount on Bonds Payable (−xL) +1,470		Interest Expense (+E) −7,470

Because the 2007 interest expense was not paid in full, the unpaid bond liability at the beginning of 2008 will be more than it was in the last year ($93,376 + $1,470 = $94,846). Interest expense for the following year will reflect this change in the unpaid bond liability. Interest expense in 2008 would be calculated by multiplying the unpaid bond liability on January 1, 2008, by the market rate of interest for the full year ($94,846 × 8% × 12/12 = $7,588). Again, the difference between the $7,588 interest expense and the $6,000 interest paid in 2008 represents amortization of the bond discount in 2008 ($7,588 − $6,000 = $1,588). These effects would be recorded with the following journal entry:

	Debit	Credit
Interest Expense (+E, −OE)	7,588	
Discount on Bonds Payable (−xL, +L)		1,588
Cash (−A)		6,000

Assets	=	Liabilities	+	Owners' Equity
Cash −6,000		Discount on Bonds Payable (−xL) +1,588		Interest Expense (+E) −7,588

> **Coach's Tip**
>
> The unpaid bond liability at the beginning of 2008 can also be computed by subtracting the balance in the Discount on Bonds Payable account from Bonds Payable.

In each remaining year, General Mills will pay $6,000 interest, as promised on the bond certificate. As we have seen, however, this payment will be less than the interest expense, so the unpaid bond liability will continue to increase (through decreases in the contra-liability account Discount on Bonds Payable). These effects are summarized in the following bond amortization schedule:

	BOND DISCOUNT AMORTIZATION SCHEDULE: EFFECTIVE-INTEREST METHOD					
	CHANGES DURING THE PERIOD			ENDING BOND LIABILITY BALANCES		
Period Ended	(A) Interest Expense	(B) Interest Payable	(C) (= A − B) Amortization of Discount	(D) Bonds Payable	(E) Discount on Bonds Payable	(F) (= D − E) Unpaid Bond Liability
01/01/07	—	—	—	$100,000	$6,624	$ 93,376
12/31/07	$7,470	$6,000	$1,470	100,000	5,154	94,846
12/31/08	7,588	6,000	1,588	100,000	3,566	96,434
12/31/09	7,715	6,000	1,715	100,000	1,851	98,149
12/31/10	7,851	6,000	1,851	100,000	0	100,000

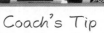

Coach's Tip

The straight-line method amortizes a bond premium or discount by adjusting Interest Expense each period by a **constant** dollar amount.

Supplement 14C
Straight-Line Method of Amortization

The aim of the straight-line method of amortization is to **match** any bond premium or discount to the periods in which the bond liability remains unpaid. Rather than adjust the rate used to calculate the interest expense, the straight-line method allocates the total premium or discount evenly over each year. Because this method results in an equal amount of interest expense each period, it is easy to apply. However, constant interest expense does not reflect reality because the bond liability changes each period. Consequently, the straight-line method may be used only when it does not materially differ from the effective-interest method of amortization (presented in Supplement 14B).

Bond Premiums

A premium arises when the bond issuer receives more cash than the issuer repays at maturity. In effect, a premium reduces the company's cost of borrowing, so amortization of the premium causes interest expense to be lower than the interest payment each period. The difference is recorded as a reduction in the Premium on Bonds Payable liability account.

In our earlier example, General Mills received $107,260 for four-year bonds with a total face value of $100,000, implying a premium of $7,260. Using the straight-line method, amortization of the premium in each of the four years that the bonds remain unpaid would be $1,815 (= $7,260 ÷ 4). This amount would be subtracted from the interest to be paid ($6,000) to arrive at the amount of interest expense ($4,185). The effects would be recorded in the following journal entry:

	Debit	Credit
Interest Expense (+E, −OE)	4,185	
Premium on Bonds Payable (−L)	1,185	
Cash (−A)		6,000

Assets	=	Liabilities	+	Owners' Equity
Cash −6,000		Premium on Bonds Payable −1,815		Interest Expense (+E) −4,185

This journal entry would be recorded each year on December 31 until the bonds mature. The following bond amortization schedule summarizes the effects:

	CHANGES DURING THE PERIOD			ENDING BOND LIABILITY BALANCES		
Period Ended	(A) Interest Payable	(B) Amortization of Premium	(C) (= A − B) Interest Expense	(D) Bonds Payable	(E) Premium on Bonds Payable	(F) (= D + E) Unpaid Bond Liability
01/01/07	—	—	—	$100,000	$7,260	$107,260
12/31/07	$6,000	$1,815	$4,185	100,000	5,445	105,445
12/31/08	6,000	1,815	4,185	100,000	3,630	103,630
12/31/09	6,000	1,815	4,185	100,000	1,815	101,815
12/31/10	6,000	1,815	4,185	100,000	0	100,000

BOND PREMIUM AMORTIZATION SCHEDULE: STRAIGHT-LINE METHOD

Bond Discounts

A discount arises when the bond issuer receives less cash than the issuer repays at maturity. In effect, a discount increases the company's cost of borrowing, so amortization of the discount causes interest expense to be higher than the interest payment each period. To report this effect, accountants record a decrease in Discount on Bonds Payable and an increase in Interest Expense.

In our earlier example, General Mills received $93,376 for four-year bonds with a total face value of $100,000, implying a discount of $6,624. Using the straight-line method, amortization of the discount in each of the four years that the bonds remain unpaid would be $1,656 (= $6,624 ÷ 4). This amount would be added to the interest to be paid ($6,000) to calculate the amount of Interest Expense ($7,656). The effects would be recorded in the following journal entry:

	Debit	Credit
Interest Expense (+E, −OE)	7,656	
Discount on Bonds Payable (−xL, +L)		1,656
Cash (−A)		6,000

Assets	=	Liabilities	+	Owners' Equity
Cash −6,000		Discount on Bonds Payable (−xL) +1,656		Interest Expense (+E) −7,656

This journal entry would be recorded each year on December 31 until the bonds mature. The effects are summarized in the following bond amortization schedule:

	CHANGES DURING THE PERIOD			ENDING BOND LIABILITY BALANCES		
Period Ended	(A) Interest Payable	(B) Amortization of Discount	(C) (= A + B) Interest Expense	(D) Bonds Payable	(E) Discount on Bonds Payable	(F) (= D − E) Unpaid Bond Liability
01/01/07	—	—	—	$100,000	$6,624	$ 93,376
12/31/07	$6,000	$1,656	$7,656	100,000	4,968	95,032
12/31/08	6,000	1,656	7,656	100,000	3,312	96,688
12/31/09	6,000	1,656	7,656	100,000	1,656	98,344
12/31/10	6,000	1,656	7,656	100,000	0	100,000

BOND DISCOUNT AMORTIZATION SCHEDULE: STRAIGHT-LINE METHOD

Chapter Summary

LO1 Explain how to measure long-term liabilities. p. 600

- Long-term liabilities are first recorded at their cash-equivalent amount, which is the amount of cash that would be accepted as full settlement of the liability at the moment it is created.

- The cash-equivalent amount is calculated using the discounting techniques explained in Supplement 14A. It excludes interest that arises (and is later recorded) with the passage of time.

LO2 Demonstrate how to account for discounted notes payable. p. 601

- Discounted notes are recorded at their cash-equivalent amount, which is computed using the discounting techniques explained in Supplement 14A.
- As time passes, interest on a discounted note is accrued in the Note Payable account.

LO3 Demonstrate how to account for bonds payable. p. 604

- The account Bonds Payable reports the face value of the bonds, which must be paid at maturity.
- If a company receives more cash when a bond is issued than the amount it promises to repay at maturity (perhaps because the bond pays an attractive rate of interest), the excess is recorded as a liability Premium on Bonds Payable.
- If the company receives less cash when a bond is issued than the amount it promises to repay at maturity (perhaps because the bond pays an unattractive rate of interest), the difference is recorded as a Discount on Bonds Payable, a contra-liability account that is deducted from Bonds Payable.
- Interest expense is the cost of borrowing; it equals the periodic interest payments plus (or minus) the amount of the bond discount (or premium) amortized in the current interest period.
- When a bond is retired, three financial effects are recorded: (1) a reduction in Cash for the amount paid, (2) the elimination of any balances in the bond liability account(s), and (3) a gain (or loss) if the amount paid is less (or more) than the carrying value of the bond liability accounts.

LO4 Explain how to account for lease liabilities. p. 610

- An operating lease allows a company (the lessee) to temporarily use property belonging to another company (the lessor) in exchange for payments that the lessee records as Rent Expense.
- A capital lease allows a lessee to use rented property in exchange for paying the lessor, but unlike an operating lease, it transfers virtually all risks and rewards of owning the property to the lessee. To account for a capital lease, the lessee records the property as an asset and a long-term lease liability equal to the cash-equivalent amount of the future lease payments.

LO5 Calculate and interpret the debt-to-assets and times interest earned ratios. p. 611

- The debt-to-assets ratio measures the extent to which a company's total assets have been financed by liabilities.
- The times interest earned ratio measures a company's ability to meet its interest obligations using resources generated by profit-making activities.

Financial Analysis Tools

Name of Measure	Formula	What It Tells You
Debt-to-assets ratio	$\dfrac{\text{Total Liabilities}}{\text{Total Assets}}$	• The proportion of assets financed by liabilities • The higher the number the greater the financing risk
Times interest earned ratio	$\dfrac{(\text{Net Income} + \text{Interest Expense} + \text{Income Tax Expense})}{\text{Interest Expense}}$	• Whether sufficient resources are generated to cover interest costs • The higher the number the greater the coverage

Key Terms

Bonds (p. 604)

Cash-Equivalent Amount (p. 600)

Capital Lease (p. 610)

Carrying Value (p. 607)

Debt-to-Assets Ratio (p. 611)

Discount (p. 605)

Discounting (p. 601)

Face Value (p. 604)

Long-term Debt (p. 600)

Market Interest Rate (p. 606)

Maturity Date (p. 604)

Operating Lease (p. 610)

Premium (p. 605)

Stated Interest Rate (p. 604)

Times Interest Earned Ratio (p. 612)

See complete glossary in back of text.

Questions

1. Why might a business finance using debt rather than equity? Why might a different business rely on equity rather than debt?

2. What term describes the amount at which liabilities are first recorded? Does this include interest? Why or why not?

3. How does a discounted note payable differ from an interest-bearing note payable, a topic introduced in Chapter 11? In what two ways does the accounting for these notes differ?

4. What accounting principle requires that interest expense be recorded each period even when interest has not been paid?

5. What are the three key elements of a bond, and which is/are indicated on the face of a bond certificate?

6. How are bond prices typically quoted? If an issuer sells 900 bonds, each with a face value of $1,000, at an issue price of 99.8, how much cash is received by the issuer? Describe how this would be reported by the issuer in the financial statements on the date of issue.

7. What are the reasons that some bonds are issued at a discount and others are issued at a premium?

8. Assuming simple annual compounding, how much should you pay for a one-year bond with a stated interest rate of 5 percent and a face value of $1,000 if you want to earn a return of 5 percent? What is the maximum you would be willing to pay if you want to earn a return of 8 percent? What is the maximum you would be willing to pay if you require a return of 4 percent?

9. What is the difference between the stated interest rate and the market interest rate on a bond?

10. Will the stated interest rate be higher than the market interest rate or will the market interest rate be higher than the stated interest rate when a bond is issued at (a) face value, (b) a discount, and (c) a premium?

11. In the context of bonds payable, to what does the term "carrying value" refer? In this same context, to what does the term "amortization" refer?

12. What three financial effects arise when a bond is retired early?

13. What two categories can be used to characterize seemingly limitless types of bonds?

14. What aspect of a lease agreement distinguishes a capital lease from an operating lease? In what ways does the accounting for capital leases differ from the accounting for operating leases?

15. If a company's debt-to-assets ratio increases, is it more or less likely to be able to pay the amounts it owes? If a company's times interest earned ratio decreases, has it become a better or worse credit risk?

16. (Supplement 14A) How does the purpose of compounding differ from the purpose of discounting? Which procedure (compounding or discounting) is more likely to be used in accounting?

17. (Supplement 14A) If you are asked to compute the present value of an amount compounded quarterly using an annual rate of 8 percent for five years, what combination of interest rates and interest periods should you use?

18. (Supplement 14B) How is interest expense calculated using the effective-interest method of amortization for a bond issued at (a) a discount and (b) a premium?

19. (Supplement 14C) How is interest expense calculated using the straight-line method of amortization for a bond issued at (a) a discount and (b) a premium?

Multiple Choice

1. Which of the following best describes a reason for using debt rather than equity financing?

   Quiz 14-1
   www.mhhe.com/LLPW1e

   a. Owners may not have sufficient resources available to contribute to the business.

   b. Debt must be repaid (or refinanced) when it matures.

   c. Owners may forgo withdrawals to help the business survive its financial difficulties.

   d. None of the above.

2. A company purchases a piece of equipment and pays for it by signing a discounted note payable that requires a single payment of $134,776 in three years. How does the company account for this transaction?

   a. The payment of $134,776 is reported as a noncurrent liability on the date of purchase.

   b. Nothing is reported until the payment of $134,776 is made.

   c. The accountant computes the present value of $134,776 and records that amount as a noncurrent liability on the date of purchase.

   d. The accountant computes the future value of $134,776 and records that amount as a noncurrent liability on the date of purchase.

3. A three-year discounted note payable, which requires a payment of $595,508 at maturity on December 31, 2010, had an adjusted balance of $530,000 at December 31, 2008. Assuming 6 percent annual interest, which of the following adjusting journal entries should be recorded on December 31, 2009?

a.	Interest Expense	31,800	
	Interest Payable		31,800
b.	Interest Expense	31,800	
	Cash		31,800
c.	Interest Expense	31,800	
	Note Payable		31,800
d.	Interest Expense	65,508	
	Note Payable	530,000	
	Cash		595,508

4. A corporate bond issued at 102 is currently trading at 97. Which of the following is true?
   a. The corporation reports a bond discount on the balance sheet.
   b. The corporation reports a bond premium on the income statement.
   c. The stated interest rate was less than the market interest rate on the date of issue.
   d. None of the above.

5. Which of the following does not impact the calculation of the cash interest payments to be made to bondholders?
   a. Face value of the bond.
   b. Stated interest rate.
   c. Market interest rate.
   d. Length of time between payments.

6. Which of the following is false when a bond is issued at a premium?
   a. The bond is issued at an amount above its face value.
   b. Interest expense will exceed the cash interest payments.
   c. The market interest rate is lower than the stated interest rate.
   d. The issue price will be quoted at a number more than 100.

7. Which of the following terms describes bonds that are issued without security?
   a. Zero coupon.   c. Serial.
   b. Debentures.   d. Callable.

8. To determine whether a bond will be issued at a premium, discount, or at face value, one must know which of the following pairs of information?
   a. The face value and the stated interest rate on the date the bonds were issued.
   b. The face value and the market interest rate on the date the bonds were issued.
   c. The stated interest rate and the market interest rate on the date the bonds were issued.
   d. You cannot tell without having more information.

9. For the year ended December 31, 2006, Land O' Lakes, Inc., reported income from operations of $124,195, net income of $88,666, interest expense of $58,360, and income tax expense of $7,806. What was this dairy company's times interest earned ratio for the year?
   a. 0.65   c. 2.13
   b. 1.51   d. 2.65

10. Which of the following expenses is recorded on an operating lease?
   a. Depreciation Expense.
   b. Interest Expense.
   c. Rent Expense.
   d. All of the above.

Solutions to Multiple-Choice Questions						
1. a	2. c	3. c	4. d	5. c	6. b	7. b
8. c	9. d	10. c				

Mini Exercises   Available with McGraw-Hill's Homework Manager

LO2   **M14-1 Recording Discounted Note Issue and Interest Accruals**
On January 1, 2008, Steelmet Furniture purchased new welding equipment by issuing a note that promises to pay $27,783 on December 31, 2010. Assuming a 5 percent annual interest rate, the cash-equivalent amount on January 1, 2008, is $24,000. Prepare journal entries needed on (a) January 1, 2008, (b) December 31, 2008, and (c) December 31, 2009.

LO2   **M14-2 Recording Discounted Note Issue and Interest Accruals**
On January 1, 2009, Shaw Cable purchased new computer switching equipment by issuing a note that promises to pay $115,762.50 on December 31, 2011. Assuming a 5 percent annual interest rate, the cash-equivalent amount on January 1, 2009, is $100,000. Prepare journal entries needed on (a) January 1, 2009, (b) December 31, 2009, and (c) December 31, 2010.

LO2   **M14-3 Recording Discounted Note Issue, Interest, and Maturity Repayment**
On January 1, 2008, Touchstone Developments purchased a new excavator by issuing a note that promises to pay $22,898 on December 31, 2009. Assuming a 7 percent annual interest rate, the cash-equivalent amount on January 1, 2008, is $20,000. Prepare journal entries needed on (a) January 1, 2008, (b) December 31, 2008, and (c) December 31, 2009.

LO2   **M14-4 Recording Discounted Note Issue, Interest, and Maturity Repayment**
On January 1, 2009, ACME Corporation purchased new aviation equipment by issuing a note that promises to pay $110,250 on December 31, 2010. Assuming a 5 percent annual interest rate, the cash-equivalent amount on January 1, 2009, is $100,000. Prepare journal entries needed on (a) January 1, 2009, (b) December 31, 2009, and (c) December 31, 2010.

LO3   **M14-5 Determining Bond Discount or Premium from Quoted Price**
Ford Motor Company   On October 1, 2006, biz.yahoo.com quoted a bond price of 101.5 for Ford Motor Company's 9.875 percent bonds maturing on August 10, 2011. Were the bonds selling at a discount or premium? Does this mean the market interest rate for comparable bonds was higher or lower than 9.875 percent?

M14-6 Computing and Reporting a Bond Liability at an Issuance Price of 98   LO3

E-Tech Initiatives Limited plans to issue $500,000, 10-year, 4 percent bonds. Interest is payable annually on December 31. All of the bonds will be issued on January 1, 2009. Show how the bonds would be reported on the January 2, 2009, balance sheet if they are issued at 98.

M14-7 Computing and Reporting a Bond Liability at an Issuance Price of 103   LO3

Repeat M14-6 assuming the bonds are issued at 103.

M14-8 Recording Bonds Issued at Face Value   LO3

Schlitterbahn Waterslide Company issued 25,000, 10-year, 6 percent, $100 bonds on January 1, 2009, at face value. Interest is payable each December 31. Show the journal entries and accounting equation effects for (a) the bond issue on January 1, 2009, and (b) the interest payment on December 31, 2009.

M14-9 Recording Bonds Issued at Face Value   LO3

Shark's Pool Company issued 2,000, 10-year, 6 percent, $1,000 bonds on July 1, 2009, at face value. Interest is payable each June 30. Show the journal entries and accounting equation effects for (a) the issuance of these bonds on July 1, 2009, and (b) accrual of interest on December 31, 2009.

M14-10 Determining Financial Statement Effects of an Early Retirement of Debt   LO3

If the market price of a bond increased after it was issued and the company decided to retire its debt early, would you expect the company to report a gain or loss on debt retirement? Describe the financial statement effects of a debt retirement under these circumstances.

M14-11 Recording Early Retirement of Bonds   LO3

Refer to M14-9. Prepare journal entries that would be recorded if the bonds were retired early by repurchasing them at a price of (a) 99 or (b) 100.5. Explain why an early bond retirement is likely to result in a gain or loss.

M14-12 Recording Operating and Capital Leases   LO4

Prepare the journal entries that Hamilton Property should make on June 30, 2008, to record the following transactions, in which Hamilton is the lessee.

a.   Made a lease payment of $8,000 on June 30, 2008, for equipment rented in June under an operating lease agreement.

b.   Leased a new building, which requires 10 annual payments of $50,000. Assuming an annual interest rate of 6 percent, the cash-equivalent amount on June 30, 2008, is $368,005.

M14-13 Computing the Debt-to-Assets Ratio and the Times Interest Earned Ratio   LO5

The balance sheet for Food Maker Corporation (FMC) reported the following: total assets, $250,000; noncurrent assets, $150,000; current liabilities, $40,000; total stockholders' equity, $90,000; net income, $3,320; interest expense, $4,400; and income before income taxes, $5,280. Compute FMC's debt-to-assets ratio and times interest earned ratio. Based on these calculations and the ratios reported in Exhibit 14.7, does it appear FMC will be able to meet its obligations to pay liabilities and interest obligations as they become payable?

M14-14 Analyzing the Impact of Transactions on the Debt-to-Assets Ratio   LO5

BSO, Inc., has total liabilities of $500,000 and total assets of $1,000,000, resulting in a debt-to-assets ratio of 0.50 (or 50 percent). For each of the following independent events, determine whether the debt-to-assets ratio will increase, decrease, or remain the same.

a.   Purchased $20,000 of new inventory on credit.
b.   Paid accounts payable in the amount of $50,000.
c.   Recorded accrued salaries in the amount of $10,000.
d.   Borrowed $250,000 from a local bank on an interest-bearing note to be repaid in 90 days.

M14-15 (Supplement 14A) Calculating Present Values

Refer to M14-1. Show how Steelmet's accountants determined that the cash-equivalent amount on January 1, 2008, was $24,000.

M14-16 (Supplement 14A) Calculating Present Values

Refer to M14-2. Show how Shaw's accountants determined that the cash-equivalent amount on January 1, 2009, was $100,000.

M14-17 (Supplement 14A) Calculating Present Values

Refer to M14-3. Show how Touchstone's accountants determined that the cash-equivalent amount on January 1, 2008, was $20,000.

M14-18 (Supplement 14A) Calculating Present Values

Refer to M14-4. Show how ACME's accountants determined that the cash-equivalent amount on January 1, 2009, was $100,000.

M14-19 (Supplement 14A) Calculating Present Values

Refer to M14-12. Show how Hamilton's accountants determined that the cash-equivalent amount on June 30, 2008, was $368,005.

M14-20 (Supplement 14B) Recording Bond Issuance and Interest Payment (Effective-Interest Amortization)

Clem Company issued $800,000, 10-year, 5 percent bonds on January 1, 2009. The bonds sold for $741,000. Interest is payable annually on January 1. Using effective-interest amortization, prepare journal entries to record (a) the bond issuance on January 1, 2009, and (b) the payment of interest on January 1, 2010. The market interest rate on the bonds is 6 percent.

M14-21 (Supplement 14C) Recording Bond Issuance and Interest Payment (Straight-Line Amortization)

Simko Company issued $600,000, 10-year, 5 percent bonds on January 1, 2009. The bonds were issued for $580,000. Interest is payable annually on January 1. Using straight-line amortization, prepare journal entries to record (a) the bond issuance on January 1, 2009, and (b) the payment of interest on January 1, 2010.

Exercises   Available with McGraw-Hill's Homework Manager

LO1

E14-1 Choosing between Debt and Equity Financing

Novelty Productions is operated as a sole proprietorship by its founder, Tina Wilkins. Tina is an inventor who recently created a new product that is growing in popularity. Tina needs to expand the business but has already contributed all personal resources to the business. Tina estimates that $100,000 is needed to purchase new equipment, and is confident that this investment will return about $25,000 cash each year for the next five years. Given the secret nature of the business, Tina is reluctant to admit partners. She rarely withdraws funds from the sole proprietorship.

Required:

How should Tina finance the expansion of her business? Provide reasons supporting your recommendation.

LO1

E14-2 Accounting for an Interest-Bearing Note Issue, Interest, and Maturity

Right Foot Shoes issued a two-year, $50,000 interest-bearing note on January 1, 2008, in exchange for new equipment. Interest accrues at 6 percent annually but is not paid until maturity.

Required:

Record the journal entries and accounting equation effects for each of the following.

1. The equipment purchase on January 1, 2008.
2. The interest adjustment on December 31, 2008.
3. The payment on December 31, 2009.

LO2

E14-3 Accounting for a Discounted Note Issue, Interest, and Maturity

Left Foot Shoes issued a discounted note on January 1, 2008, in exchange for new equipment. The note requires a payment of $56,180 on December 31, 2009. Using an annual interest rate of 6 percent to discount the payment, you determine that the note's present value on January 1, 2008, was $50,000.

Required:

Record the journal entries and accounting equation effects for each of the following.

1. The equipment purchase on January 1, 2008.
2. The interest adjustment on December 31, 2008.
3. The $56,180 payment on December 31, 2009.

LO2

E14-4 Accounting for a Discounted Note Issue, Interest, and Maturity

Deep Powder Corporation issued a discounted note on January 1, 2008, in exchange for new snow-making equipment. The note requires a $121,551 payment on December 31, 2011. Using an annual interest rate of 5 percent to discount the payment, you determine that the note's present value on January 1, 2008, was $100,000.

Required:

Record the journal entries for each of the following. (Round interest calculations to the nearest dollar.)

1. The equipment purchase on January 1, 2008.
2. The interest adjustments on December 31, 2008, 2009, and 2010.
3. The $121,551 payment on December 31, 2011.

E14-5 Accounting for Bonds Issued at Face Value with Interest Accrual and Early Retirement   LO3

On October 1, 2009, Garden Equipment Corporation issued 2,000 bonds at face value. The bond certificates indicate a face value of $1,000, a stated interest rate of 7 percent paid annually on September 30, and a September 30, 2020 maturity date.

Required:

1. Give the journal entry to record the bond issue on October 1, 2009.
2. Give the adjusting entry required on December 31, 2009.
3. Assume Garden Equipment retires the bond early on October 1, 2012, at a price of 103. Give the journal entry to record this early retirement.

E14-6 Accounting for Bonds Issued at Face Value with Interest Accrual and Maturity Repayment   LO3

On January 1, 2009, Arena Enterprises issued 300 bonds at face value. The bond certificates indicate a face value of $1,000, a stated interest rate of 6 percent paid annually on December 31, and a December 31, 2010, maturity date.

Required:

1. Give the journal entry to record the bond issue on January 1, 2009.
2. Give the journal entry required on December 31, 2009.
3. Give the journal entry to record the payment on December 31, 2010.

E14-7 Determining Bond Price and Preparing Journal Entries to Record Bond Issue and Interest Payment   LO3

On January 1, 2008, Applied Technologies Corporation (ATC) issued 600 bonds, each with a face value of $1,000 and a maturity date of December 31, 2017. The bonds have a stated interest rate of 10 percent. When the bonds were issued, the market interest rate was 10 percent. The bonds pay interest once per year on December 31.

Required:

1. Determine the price at which the bonds were issued and the amount of cash that ATC received.
2. Prepare the journal entry to record the bond issue.
3. Prepare the journal entry to record the interest payment on December 31, 2008.

E14-8 Preparing Journal Entries to Record Issuance of a Bond at Face Value, Payment of Interest, and Early Retirement   LO3

On January 1, 2009, Innovative Solutions, Inc., issued 200 bonds at face value ($1,000 each). The bonds have a stated interest rate of 6 percent, mature in 10 years, and pay interest annually on December 31.

Required:

1. Prepare the journal entry to record the bond issue.
2. Prepare the journal entry to record the interest payment on December 31, 2009.
3. Assume the bond was retired immediately after the first interest payment on January 1, 2010, at a quoted price of 102. Prepare the journal entry to record the early retirement of the bond.

E14-9 Describing the Effects of a Premium Bond Issue and Interest Payment on the Financial Statements, Debt-to-Assets Ratio, and Times Interest Earned Ratio   LO3, 5

Grocery Corporation received $300,328 for $250,000, 11 percent bonds issued on January 1, 2008, at a market interest rate of 8 percent. The bonds stated that interest would be paid each December 31 and that they mature on December 31, 2017.

Required:

1. Describe how the bond issue affects the balance sheet and income statement, specifically identifying the account names and direction of effects (ignore amounts). Also, describe its impact on the debt-to-assets ratio and times interest earned ratio.
2. Without doing calculations, describe which balance sheet and income statement accounts are affected by the recording of interest on December 31, 2008.

LO3

E14-10 Computing Price for One-Year Bond

Speedy Housing issued 200 bonds, each with a face value of $1,000 and stated interest rate of 5 percent to be paid out exactly one year after the issue date.

Required:

Determine your return on the 200 bonds if you purchased them all on the issue date for

1. $200,000.
2. $201,924.
3. $198,114.

LO4

E14-11 Recording Lease Transactions

On June 1, 2009, National Equipment Rental leased equipment to the Glendale Community Club and Craig Legal Services. Glendale signed a lease indicating the club would rent portable tables for the month of June 2009 at a cost of $1,000 to be paid in July 2009. Craig Legal Services signed a lease indicating that the business would rent computer equipment for the three-year period ended May 31, 2012. Craig is required to pay $10,000 at the end of each year; these payments equate to a present value of $26,730 on June 1, 2009.

Required:

1. Prepare the journal entry that Glendale Community Club should record on June 30, 2009.

2. Prepare the journal entry that Craig Legal Services should record on June 1, 2009.

LO5

Kraft

E14-12 Calculating and Interpreting the Debt-to-Assets Ratio and Times Interest Earned Ratio

According to its Web site, Kraft Foods Inc. sells enough Kool-Aid mix to make 1,000 gallons of the drink every minute during the summer and more than 560 million gallons each year. At December 31, 2007, the company reported the following amounts (in millions) in its financial statements:

	2007	2006
Total assets	$ 67,993	$ 55,574
Total liabilities	40,698	27,019
Interest expense	698	579
Income tax expense	1,137	951
Net income	2,590	3,060

Required:

1. Compute the debt-to-assets ratio (to three decimal places) and times interest earned ratio (to two decimal places) for 2007 and 2006.

2. Does the trend in these ratios suggest Kraft has relied more or less on debt financing? Is Kraft's financial position more or less risky than that for the companies in Exhibit 14.7?

LO5

TJX Companies Inc.

E14-13 Reporting Long-term Liabilities on a Classified Balance Sheet

TJX Companies, Inc., owns discount clothing stores operating in the United States under the store names Marshall's and TJ Maxx. For its year ended January 27, 2007, TJX Companies reported the following liabilities (all amounts in thousands). Prepare the Liabilities section of its classified balance sheet.

Accounts payable	$1,372,352	Bond debentures payable	$200,000
Accrued liabilities	1,008,774	Discount on bond debentures payable	183
Other long-term liabilities	604,572	Zero-coupon bonds payable	517,497
Lease liability, long-term	22,382	Discount on zero-coupon bonds payable	126,485
Lease liability, short-term	1,854	Other long-term borrowings	194,816

E14-14 (Supplement 14A) Calculating Present Values

Refer to E14-3. Show how, Left Foot Shoes determined that the cash-equivalent amount on January 1, 2008, was $50,000.

E14-15 (Supplement 14A) Calculating Present Values

Refer to E14-4. Show how Deep Powder's accountants determined that the cash-equivalent amount on January 1, 2008, was $100,000.

E14-16 (Supplement 14A) Calculating Present Values

Refer to E14-9. Show how investors determined the price of Grocery Corporation's bonds on January 1, 2008 to be $300,328.

E14-17 (Supplement 14A) Calculating Present Values

Refer to E14-11. Show how Craig Legal Services determined the cash-equivalent amount of $26,730 on June 1, 2009. What interest rate does this imply?

E14-18 (Supplement 14B) Recording the Effects of a Premium Bond Issue and First Interest Payment (Effective-Interest Amortization)

Refer to the information in E14-9 and assume Grocery Corporation uses the effective-interest method to amortize the bond premium.

Required:

1. Prepare the journal entry to record the bond issue.
2. Prepare the journal entries to record the December 31 interest payments in 2008 and 2009.

E14-19 (Supplement 14C) Recording the Effects of a Premium Bond Issue and First Interest Payment (Straight-Line Amortization)

Refer to the information in E14-9 and assume Grocery Corporation uses the straight-line method to amortize the bond premium.

Required:

1. Prepare the journal entry to record the bond issue.
2. Prepare the journal entries to record the December 31 interest payments in 2008 and 2009.

E14-20 (Supplement 14B) Recording the Effects of a Discount Bond Issue and First Interest Payment and Preparing a Discount Amortization Schedule (Effective-Interest Amortization)

On January 1, 2009, when the market interest rate was 9 percent, Seton Corporation sold a $200,000, 8 percent bond issue for $187,163. The bonds were dated January 1, 2009, pay interest each December 31, and mature December 31, 2018. Seton amortizes the bond discount using the effective-interest method.

Required:

1. Prepare the journal entry to record the bond issue.
2. Prepare the journal entry to record the interest payment on December 31, 2009.
3. Prepare a bond discount amortization schedule for these bonds using the format shown in Supplement 14B.

E14-21 (Supplement 14C) Recording the Effects of a Discount Bond Issue and First Interest Payment and Preparing a Discount Amortization Schedule (Straight-Line Amortization)

Refer to the information in E14-20 but assume Seton Corporation uses the straight-line method to amortize the bond discount.

Required:

1. Prepare the journal entry to record the bond issuance.
2. Prepare the journal entry to record the interest payment on December 31, 2009.
3. Prepare a bond discount amortization schedule for these bonds, using the format shown in Supplement 14C.

Problems—Set A   Available with McGraw-Hill's Homework Manager

PA14-1 Comparing and Recording a Discounted Note Payable and Capital Lease Liability

LO2, 4 ,5

Rockwell Industries is evaluating whether to purchase a piece of equipment or rent it. The company is a little short on cash, so a purchase would require Rockwell to finance the equipment's cost by signing a promissory note that requires a single payment of $100,000 three years after the purchase date. The present value of this payment is $83,960. If Rockwell were to rent the equipment, the company would pay $31,410.40 at the end of each of the following three years. This rental agreement would transfer to Rockwell virtually all risks and rewards of owning the equipment. The present value of these payments is $83,960. Rockwell's bank requires that the company's debt-to-assets ratio not exceed 0.50. Prior to acquiring the equipment, Rockwell has liabilities totaling $490,000 and assets totaling $1,000,000.

Required:

1.   Prepare the journal entry to record the purchase of the equipment by issuing a promissory note.
2.   Prepare the journal entry to record acquisition of the equipment through a capital lease.
3.   Describe any significant differences in your answers to requirements 1 and 2.
4.   Calculate the debt-to-assets ratio before and after the equipment acquisition. What are the possible consequences of acquiring the equipment through purchase or capital lease? How would you advise Rockwell to proceed?

LO3   **PA14-2 Comparing Bonds Issued at Face Value, Discount, and Premium**

Sikes Corporation, whose annual accounting period ends on December 31, issued the following bonds:

Date of bonds: January 1, 2008.

Maturity amount and date: $200,000 due in 10 years (December 31, 2017).

Interest: 10 percent per year payable each December 31.

Date issued: January 1, 2008.

Required:

1.   Provide the following amounts to be reported on the January 1, 2008, financial statements immediately after the bonds are issued:

	Case A (issued at 100)	Case B (issued at 96)	Case C (issued at 102)
a. Bonds payable	$	$	$
b. Unamortized premium or discount			
c. Unpaid bond liability			

2.   Assume that a retired person has written to you (an investment adviser) asking, "Why should I buy a bond at a premium when I can find one at a discount? Is it not the case that paying a premium is like paying list price for a car instead of negotiating a discount?" Write a brief message in response to the question.

PA14-3 (Supplement 14A) Comparing and Recording a Discounted Note Payable and Capital Lease Liability with Present Value Computations

Refer to PA14-1. Assume Rockwell Industries can acquire a comparable piece of equipment by signing a promissory note that requires a single payment of $80,000 three years after the purchase date or rent it by paying $25,128.32 at the end of each of the following three years. Rockwell typically borrows at a 6 percent annual interest rate.

Required:

1.   Calculate the present value of the promissory note, and prepare the journal entry to record the purchase of the equipment.
2.   Calculate the present value of the lease payments, and prepare the journal entry to record acquisition of the equipment through a capital lease.
3.   Describe any significant differences in your answers to requirements 1 and 2.
4.   Calculate the debt-to-assets ratio before and after the equipment acquisition. What are the possible consequences of acquiring the equipment through purchase or capital lease? How would you advise Rockwell to proceed?

PA14-4 (Supplement 14B) Recording Bond Issue, Interest Payments (Effective-Interest Amortization), and Early Retirement

Southwest Corporation issued bonds with the following details:

Face value: $600,000.

Interest: 9 percent per year paid each December 31.

Terms: Bonds issued January 1, 2009, maturing on December 31, 2013.

www.mhhe.com/LLPW1e

The annual accounting period ends December 31. The bonds were issued at 104 on January 1, 2009, implying an 8 percent market interest rate. Assume the company uses effective-interest amortization.

Required:

1.   Compute the bond issue price (show computations).
2.   Give the journal entry to record the bond issue.
3.   Give the journal entries to record the interest payments on December 31, 2009 and 2010.

4. How much interest expense would be reported on the income statements for 2009 and 2010? Show how the liability related to the bonds should be reported on the balance sheets at December 31, 2009 and 2010.

5. Assume the bonds are retired on January 1, 2011, at a price of 101. Give the journal entry to record the bond retirement.

PA14-5 (Supplement 14C) Recording Bond Issue, Interest Payments (Straight-Line Amortization), and Early Retirement

Complete the requirements of PA14-4, assuming Southwest Corporation uses straight-line amortization.

eXcel

www.mhhe.com/LLPW1e

PA14-6 (Supplement 14B) Interpreting and Completing an Amortization Schedule (Effective-Interest Amortization)

Hondor Corporation issued bonds and received cash for the issue price. The bonds were dated and issued on January 1, 2008. The stated interest rate was payable at the end of each year. The bonds mature at the end of four years. The following schedule has been completed (amounts in thousands):

Date	Cash Paid	Interest Expense	Amortization	Unpaid Bond Liability
January 1, 2008	—	—	—	$6,101
End of year 2008	$450	$427	$23	6,078
End of year 2009	450	426	24	6,054
End of year 2010	450	?	?	?
End of year 2011	450	?	28	6,000

Required:

1. What was the total face value to be paid at maturity?
2. How much cash was received at date of issuance (sale) of the bonds?
3. Was there a premium or a discount? If so, which was it and how much was it?
4. How much cash will be paid for interest each period and in total for the full life of the bond issue?
5. What is the stated interest rate?
6. What is the market interest rate?
7. Complete the amortization schedule by replacing the four ?s with appropriate amounts.
8. What amount should be reported on the income statement each year?
9. Show how the bonds should be reported on the balance sheet at the end of 2008 and 2009.

PA14-7 (Supplement 14C) Interpreting and Completing an Amortization Schedule (Straight-Line Amortization)

The Peg Corporation (TPC) issued bonds and received cash in full for the issue price. The bonds were dated and issued on January 1, 2009. The stated interest rate was payable at the end of each year. The bonds mature at the end of four years. The following schedule has been prepared (amounts in thousands):

Date	Cash Paid	Interest Expense	Amortization	Unpaid Bond Liability
January 1, 2009	—	—	—	$6,101
End of year 2009	$450	$425	$25	?
End of year 2010	450	?	25	6,051
End of year 2011	450	?	25	6,026
End of year 2012	450	424	26	6,000

Required:

1. What was the total face value to be paid at maturity?
2. How much cash was received at date of issuance (sale) of the bonds?
3. Was there a premium or a discount? If so, which was it and how much was it?
4. How much cash will be paid for interest each period and in total for the full life of the bond issue?
5. What is the stated interest rate?
6. Complete the amortization schedule by replacing the three ?s with appropriate amounts.
7. What amount should be reported on the income statement each year?
8. Show how the bonds should be reported on the balance sheet at the end of 2009 and 2010.

www.mhhe.com/LLPW1e

PA14-8 (Supplements 14A and 14B) Computing Bond Issue Price with Present Values, and Recording Bond Issue, Interest Payments (Effective-Interest Amortization), and Early Bond Retirement

On January 1, 2008, Surreal Manufacturing issued 600 bonds, each with a face value of $1,000, a stated interest rate of 3 percent paid annually on December 31, and a maturity date of December 31, 2010. On the issue date, the market interest rate was 4 percent. Surreal uses the effective-interest method of amortization.

Required:

1. Compute the bond issue price (show computations).
2. Prepare a bond amortization schedule similar to that shown in Supplement 14B.
3. Give the journal entry to record the bond issue.
4. Give the journal entries to record the interest payments on December 31, 2008 and 2009.
5. Give the journal entry to record the interest and face value payment on December 31, 2010.
6. Assume, instead, that the bonds are retired on January 1, 2010, at a price of 101. Give the journal entry to record the bond retirement.

PA14-9 (Supplements 14A and 14C) Computing Bonds Issue Price with Present Values, and Recording Bond Issue, Interest Payments (Straight-Line Amortization), and Early Bond Retirement

On January 1, 2008, Loop Raceway issued 600 bonds, each with a face value of $1,000, a stated interest rate of 5 percent paid annually on December 31, and a maturity date of December 31, 2010. On the issue date, the market interest rate was 6 percent. Loop uses the straight-line method of amortization.

Required:

1. Compute the bond issue price (show computations).
2. Prepare a bond amortization schedule similar to that shown in Supplement 14C.
3. Give the journal entry to record the bond issue.
4. Give the journal entries to record the interest payments on December 31, 2008 and 2009.
5. Give the journal entry to record the interest and face value payment on December 31, 2010.
6. Assume, instead, that the bonds are retired on January 1, 2010, at a price of 98. Give the journal entry to record the bond retirement.

Problems—Set B   Available with McGraw-Hill's Homework Manager

LO2, 4, 5

PB14-1 Comparing and Recording a Discounted Note Payable and Capital Lease Liability

Bridge Construction Company is evaluating whether to purchase a piece of equipment or rent it. The company is short on cash, so a purchase would require Bridge to finance the equipment's cost by signing a promissory note that requires a single payment of $200,000 three years after the purchase date. The present value of this payment is $167,920. If Bridge were to rent the equipment, the company would pay $62,820.80 at the end of each of the following three years. This rental agreement would transfer to Bridge virtually all risks and rewards of owning the equipment. The present value of these payments is $167,920. Bridge's bank requires that the company's debt-to-assets ratio not exceed 0.50. Prior to acquiring the equipment, Bridge has liabilities totaling $980,000 and assets totaling $2,000,000.

Required:

1. Prepare the journal entry to record the purchase of the equipment by issuing a promissory note.
2. Prepare the journal entry to record acquisition of the equipment through a capital lease.
3. Describe any significant differences in your answers to requirements 1 and 2.
4. Calculate the debt-to-assets ratio before and after the equipment acquisition. What are the possible consequences of acquiring the equipment through purchase or capital lease? How would you advise Bridge to proceed?

LO3

PB14-2 Comparing Bonds Issued at Par, Discount, and Premium

Net Work Corporation, whose annual accounting period ends on December 31, issued the following bonds:

Date of bonds: January 1, 2009.

Maturity amount and date: $200,000 due in 10 years (December 31, 2018).

Interest: 10 percent per year payable each December 31.

Date issued: January 1, 2009.

Required:

1. Provide the following amounts to be reported on the January 1, 2009, financial statements immediately after the bonds were issued:

	Case A (issued at 100)	Case B (issued at 97)	Case C (issued at 101)
a. Bonds payable	$	$	$
b. Unamortized premium or discount			
c. Unpaid bond liability			

2. Assume that a retired person has written to you (an investment adviser) asking, "Why did you encourage me to buy a bond at a premium when my friend bought a different one at a discount? Have I paid too much for the bond I bought?" Write a brief message in response to the question.

PB14-3 (Supplement 14A) Comparing and Recording a Discounted Note Payable and Capital Lease Liability with Present Value Computations

Refer to PB14-1. Assume that Bridge Construction Company can acquire a comparable piece of equipment by signing a promissory note that requires a single payment of $160,000 three years after the purchase date, or rent it by paying $50,256.64 at the end of each of the following three years. Bridge typically borrows at a 6% annual interest rate.

Required:

1. Calculate the present value of the promissory note, and prepare the journal entry to record the purchase of the equipment.
2. Calculate the present value of the lease payments, and prepare the journal entry to record acquisition of the equipment through a capital lease.
3. Describe any significant differences in your answers to requirements 1 and 2.
4. Calculate the debt-to-assets ratio before and after the equipment acquisition. What are the possible consequences of acquiring the equipment through purchase or capital lease? How would you advise Bridge to proceed?

PB14-4 (Supplement 14B) Recording Bond Issue, Interest Payments (Effective-Interest Amortization), and Early Retirement

WestCoast Airlines Corporation issued bonds with the following details:

Face value: $500,000.

Interest: 7 percent per year paid each December 31.

Terms: Bonds issued January 1, 2009, maturing on December 31, 2014.

The annual accounting period ends December 31. The bonds were issued at 95.38 on January 1, 2009, implying an 8 percent market interest rate. Assume the company uses effective-interest amortization.

Required:

1. Compute the bond issue price (show computations).
2. Give the journal entry to record the bond issue.
3. Give the journal entries to record the interest payments on December 31, 2009 and 2010.
4. How much interest expense would be reported on the income statements for 2009 and 2010? Show how the liability related to the bonds should be reported on the balance sheets at December 31, 2009 and 2010.
5. Assume the bonds are retired on January 1, 2011, at a price of 101. Give the journal entry to record the bond retirement.

PB14-5 (Supplement 14C) Recording Bond Issue, Interest Payments (Straight-Line Amortization), and Early Retirement

Complete the requirements of PA14-4, assuming WestCoast Airlines Corporation uses straight-line amortization.

PB14-6 (Supplement 14B) Interpreting and Completing an Amortization Schedule (Effective-Interest Amortization)

Amhert Corporation issued bonds and received cash for the issue price. The bonds were dated and issued on January 1, 2008. The stated interest rate was payable at the end of each year. The bonds mature at the end of four years. The following schedule has been completed (amounts in thousands):

Date	Cash Paid	Interest Expense	Amortization	Unpaid Bond Liability
January 1, 2008	—	—	—	$11,800
End of year 2008	$900	$944	$44	11,844
End of year 2009	900	?	48	11,892
End of year 2010	900	?	?	?
End of year 2011	900	957	57	12,000

Required:

1. What was the total face value to be paid at maturity?
2. How much cash was received at date of issuance (sale) of the bonds?
3. Was there a premium or a discount? If so, which was it and how much was it?
4. How much cash will be paid for interest each period and in total for the full life of the bond issue?
5. What is the stated interest rate?
6. What is the market interest rate?
7. Complete the amortization schedule by replacing the four ?s with appropriate amounts.
8. What amount should be reported on the income statement each year?
9. Show how the bonds should be reported on the balance sheet at the end of 2008 and 2009.

PB14-7 (Supplement 14C) Interpreting and Completing an Amortization Schedule (Straight-Line Amortization)

Toon Corporation (TC) issued bonds and received cash in full for the issue price. The bonds were dated and issued on January 1, 2009. The stated interest rate was payable at the end of each year. The bonds mature at the end of four years. The following schedule has been prepared (amounts in thousands):

Date	Cash Paid	Interest Expense	Amortization	Unpaid Bond Liability
January 1, 2009	—	—	—	$11,800
End of year 2009	$900	$950	$50	?
End of year 2010	900	?	50	11,900
End of year 2011	900	?	50	11,950
End of year 2012	900	950	50	12,000

Required:

1. What was the total face value to be paid at maturity?
2. How much cash was received at date of issuance (sale) of the bonds?
3. Was there a premium or a discount? If so, which was it and how much was it?
4. How much cash will be paid for interest each period and in total for the full life of the bond issue?
5. What is the stated interest rate?
6. Complete the amortization schedule by replacing the three ?s with appropriate amounts.
7. What amount should be reported on the income statement each year?
8. Show how the bonds should be reported on the balance sheet at the end of 2009 and 2010.

PB14-8 (Supplements 14A and 14B) Computing Bond Issue Price with Present Values, and Recording Bond Issue, Interest Payments (Effective-Interest Amortization), and Early Bond Retirement

On January 1, 2008, Methodical Manufacturing issued 100 bonds, each with a face value of $1,000, a stated interest rate of 5 percent paid annually on December 31, and a maturity date of December 31, 2010. On the issue date, the market interest rate was 4.25 percent. Methodical uses the effective-interest method of amortization.

Required:

1. Compute the bond issue price (show computations).
2. Prepare a bond amortization schedule similar to that shown in Supplement 14B.
3. Give the journal entry to record the bond issue.
4. Give the journal entries to record the interest payments on December 31, 2008 and 2009.
5. Give the journal entry to record the interest and face value payment on December 31, 2010.
6. Assume the bonds are retired on January 1, 2010, at a price of 101. Give the journal entries to record the bond retirement.

PB14-9 (Supplements 14A and 14C) Computing Bond Issue Price with Present Values, and Recording Bond Issue, Interest Payments (Straight-Line Amortization), and Early Bond Retirement
Refer to PB14-8. Assume Methodical uses the straight-line method of amortization.

Required:

1. Compute the bond issue price (show computations).
2. Prepare a bond amortization schedule similar to that shown in Supplement 14C.
3. Give the journal entry to record the bond issue.
4. Give the journal entries to record the interest payments on December 31, 2008 and 2009.
5. Give the journal entry to record the interest and face value payment on December 31, 2010.
6. Assume the bonds are retired on January 1, 2010, at a price of 102. Give the journal entry to record the bond retirement.

Cases and Projects

CP14-1 Finding Financial Information

Refer to the financial statements of The Home Depot in Appendix A at the end of this book, or download the annual report from the Cases and Projects section of the text's Web site at www.mhhe.com/LLPW1e.

LO5

Required:

1. Calculate, to two decimal places, the company's debt-to-assets ratio using amounts reported in its financial statements for the years ended February 3, 2008, and January 28, 2007. What do the changes in this ratio suggest about the company's ability to pay its liabilities?
2. Calculate, to two decimal places, the company's times interest earned ratio for the year ended February 3, 2008. Does this ratio cause you any concern about the company's ability to meet future interest obligations as they become due?

CP14-2 Comparing Financial Information

Refer to the financial statements of The Home Depot in Appendix A and Lowe's in Appendix B at the end of this book, or download the annual reports from the Cases and Projects section of the text's Web site at www.mhhe.com/LLPW1e.

LO5

Lowe's

Required:

1. Calculate, to two decimal places, the companies' debt-to-assets ratios using amounts reported in the financial statements for the years ending in early 2008 and 2007. What do the changes in this ratio suggest about the companies' ability to pay their liabilities? Does it appear that Lowe's or The Home Depot has a greater financing risk?
2. Calculate, to two decimal places, the companies' times interest earned ratios for the year ended in February 2008. Does it appear that Lowe's or The Home Depot will be better able to meet future interest obligations as they become payable?

CP14-3 Examining an Annual Report: Internet-Based Team Research

As a team, select an industry to analyze. Using your Web browser, each team member should acquire the annual report or 10-K for one publicly traded company in the industry, with each member selecting a different company. (See CP1-3 in Chapter 1 for a description of possible resources for these tasks.)

LO1, 5

Required:

1. On an individual basis, each team member should read the company's financial statement note regarding long-term debt and then write a short report that incorporates the following:

    a. What are the types of long-term debt owed by the company?

    b. Does the company have any significant amounts coming due in the next five years?

    c. Compute and analyze the debt-to-assets ratios and times interest earned ratios for the two most recent years.

2. Then, as a team, write a short report comparing and contrasting your companies using these attributes. Discuss any patterns across the companies that you as a team observe. Provide potential explanations for any differences discovered.

LO3   **CP14-4 Making Ethical Decisions: A Real-Life Example**

Many retired people invest a significant portion of their money in bonds of corporations because of their relatively low level of risk. During the 1980s, significant inflation caused some interest rates to rise to as high as 15 percent. Retired people who bought bonds that paid only 6 percent continued to earn at the lower rate. During the 1990s, inflation subsided and interest rates declined. Many corporations took advantage of the callability feature of these bonds and retired the bonds early. Many of these early retirements of high interest rate bonds were replaced with low interest rate bonds.

Required:

In your judgment, is it ethical for corporations to continue paying low interest rates when rates increase but to call bonds when rates decrease? Why or why not?

LO3   **CP14-5 Making Ethical Decisions: A Mini Case**

Assume you are a portfolio manager for a large insurance company. The majority of the money you manage is from retired school teachers who depend on the income you earn on their investments. You have invested a significant amount of money in the bonds of a large corporation and have just read a news release from the company's president explaining that it is unable to meet its current interest obligations because of deteriorating business operations related to increased international competition. The president has a recovery plan that will take at least two years. During that time, the company will not be able to pay interest on the bonds and, she admits, if the plan does not work, bondholders will probably lose more than half of their money. As a creditor, you can force the company into immediate bankruptcy and probably get back at least 90 percent of the bondholders' money. You also know that your decision will cause at least 10,000 people to lose their jobs if the company ceases operations.

Required:

Given only these two options, what should you do? Consider who would be helped or harmed by the two options.

LO1, 5   **CP14-6 Thinking Critically: Evaluating Effects on Debt-to-Assets Ratio**

Assume you work as an assistant to the chief financial officer (CFO) of Little Chip Company. The CFO reminds you that the fiscal year end is only one month away and that he is looking to you to ensure the company adheres to its loan covenant to maintain a debt-to-assets ratio of 0.50 or lower. A review of the general ledger indicates that assets total $1,690,000 and total liabilities are $820,000. Your company will soon need additional warehouse space that could be obtained by issuing a long-term, interest-bearing promissory note for $200,000 and using that money to purchase a nearby building. Alternatively, the building owner is willing to rent the space on either a long-term or month-to-month basis.

Required:

1. Determine whether the company is currently in compliance with its loan covenant. Show calculations (to three decimal places) in support of your answer.

2. Evaluate whether Little Chip should purchase the building before year-end. Show calculations in support of your answer.

3. Evaluate whether Little Chip should enter into a lease agreement before year-end. Explain your answer.

CP14-7 (Supplement 14B) Preparing a Bond Amortization Schedule (Effective-Interest Amortization)

Assume the authors of a popular accounting principles text have hired you to create spreadsheets that will calculate bond discount amortization schedules like those shown in Supplements 14B and 14C.

You e-mail your friend Sally for some guidance. Much to your disappointment, you receive an auto-reply message from Sally indicating that she's gone skiing in New Zealand. After a bit of panicking, you realize you can refer to Sally's previous e-mail messages for spreadsheet advice that will help you complete this task. From her advice for Chapter 10, you decide to create a data input section for the stated interest rate, market interest rate, face value, issue price, and years to maturity. The spreadsheet file also will have a separate amortization schedule worksheet that contains only formulas, references to the cells in the data input section, and references to other cells in the amortization schedule. All amounts will be rounded to the nearest dollar (using the Round function in Excel), which means the discount amortization in the final year might be off a few dollars (unless you use the If function in Excel to eliminate any remaining discount in the final year of the bond's life, in the same way that Sally showed in Chapter 10 for declining-balance depreciation).

Required:

Prepare a worksheet that reproduces the effective-interest bond discount amortization schedule shown in Supplement 14B (page 622). Provide a printout showing both the amortization schedule and the formulas underlying it. (Formulas can be revealed in Excel by entering Ctrl ~).

CP14-8 (Supplement 14C) Preparing a Bond Amortization Schedule (Straight-Line Amortization)

Refer to the information in CP14-7 and prepare a worksheet that reproduces the straight-line bond discount amortization schedule shown in Supplement 14C (page 623). Provide a printout showing both the amortization schedule and the formulas underlying it. (Formulas can be revealed in Excel by entering Ctrl ~).

15 Accounting for Investments

LEARNING OBJECTIVES

After studying this chapter, you should be able to:

Lectured presentations–15-1
www.mhhe.com/LLPW1e

LO1 Explain why companies invest in debt and stock securities.

LO2 Identify investment types and the related accounting methods.

LO3 Analyze and report bond investments held to maturity.

LO4 Analyze and report passive investments in securities using the market value method.

LO5 Analyze and report investments involving significant influence using the equity method.

LO6 Explain the reporting of investments in controlling interests.

LO7 Analyze and interpret the return on assets ratio.

Focus Company: THE WASHINGTON POST COMPANY

Investment Strategies

www.washpostco.com

Have you ever wondered how big companies become big? The answer, for many companies, is by investing in other companies. One such business is The Washington Post Company, best known for publishing the most important newspaper in our nation's capital. However, The Washington Post Company does much more than that. It owns television stations, *Newsweek* magazine, Cable One (a TV cable company), and a variety of community newspapers.

Many users of this text have already been Washington Post customers without knowing it. The company also owns Kaplan, Inc., the king of admissions test preparation services that will even help you prepare for the certified public accountant or chartered financial analyst exams. The Washington Post Company also recognizes that new technologies bring increased efficiency to its operations while expanding business opportunities. For example, it publishes electronic versions of *The Washington Post* and *Newsweek* and shares news resources with NBC News and MSNBC.

The company has achieved its diversity in part by investing in the stock of other companies. For example, it spent $350 million over the last three years to purchase other companies including the online magazine *Slate* and a variety of private education companies around the world. It jointly owns (with another publisher) the company that produces the European, Middle Eastern, and African editions of *Newsweek*. It also jointly owns one of the major providers of the paper on which *The Washington Post* is printed. In addition, the company's investment portfolio consists of more than $350 million worth of stock of other companies.

In this chapter, you will see how to account for four different types of investments. To understand these investments and the reasons why they are accounted for in certain ways, you first need to answer the following question: Why do companies invest in other companies?

AN OVERVIEW	ACCOUNTING FOR PASSIVE INVESTMENTS	ACCOUNTING FOR INFLUENTIAL INVESTMENTS	EVALUATING TOTAL INVESTED CAPITAL

• Reasons Companies Invest
• Identifying Investment Types and Accounting Methods
  • Passive Investments in Debt and Equity Securities
  • Investments in Stock for Significant Influence
  • Investments in Stock for Control
	• Debt Investments Held to Maturity: Amortized Cost Method
	• Securities Available for Sale: Market Value Method
	• Comparison of Available-for-Sale and Trading Securities
		• Investments for Significant Influence: Equity Method
		• Investments with Controlling Interests: Consolidated Statements
			• Return on Assets (ROA)
			• Comparison to Benchmarks

AN OVERVIEW

Reasons Companies Invest

Many factors motivate managers to invest in securities. Some do so **because the very nature of their business requires it.** For example, pension funds, insurance companies, and mutual funds receive large sums of cash from their clients. To generate earnings—an important source of revenue in these companies—they invest the cash in the securities of other companies. Investments are significant assets to these companies. State Farm Mutual Automobile Insurance Company, for example, holds more than $90 billion in securities that generate more than $3 billion in income each year.

Other managers invest in securities **to even out seasonal fluctuations in cash.** A manager whose company has extra cash at the end of a busy season may want to earn a return on the idle funds until they are needed for other purposes, such as repaying loans, purchasing property and equipment, or paying dividends. Excess cash can be invested in the stocks and bonds of other companies, either long or short term. Managers may also invest excess cash to provide a cushion against future downturns in the economy or unanticipated emergencies. Such investments in securities are referred to as **passive investments** because the investors are not interested in influencing or controlling the companies that issued the securities. The Washington Post Company's 2006 balance sheet in Exhibit 15.1 reflects both short-term and long-term Investments in Marketable Securities accounts—passive investments.

Sometimes managers want to expand their company's presence in a related industry or market. They do so by investing in another company **with the purpose of influencing, but not controlling, the company's policies and activities.** Washington Post's balance sheet reports these types of investments as Investments in Affiliates in Exhibit 15.1—investments for significant influence.

Finally, managers may want **to control another company,** either by purchasing it directly or by becoming the majority shareholder. In this case, the two companies combine their financial reports into **consolidated** financial statements, as Washington Post has done (see the title to its "consolidated" balance sheet). In the notes to the annual report, we find that Washington Post's recent acquisitions include PMBR, a bar exam test preparation company, and *Slate* magazine. As you saw in Chapter 10, when one company purchases another for more than the fair value of its assets and liabilities, the company records the difference as Goodwill (see Exhibit 15.1).

Exhibit 15.1   The Washington Post Company's Balance Sheet

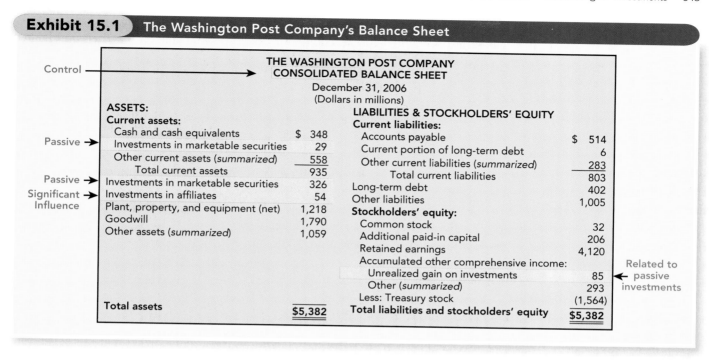

Control →

THE WASHINGTON POST COMPANY
CONSOLIDATED BALANCE SHEET
December 31, 2006
(Dollars in millions)

ASSETS:

Current assets:

Cash and cash equivalents	$ 348

Passive → Investments in marketable securities — 29

Other current assets (*summarized*)	558
Total current assets	935

Passive → Investments in marketable securities — 326
Significant Influence → Investments in affiliates — 54

Plant, property, and equipment (net)	1,218
Goodwill	1,790
Other assets (*summarized*)	1,059

Total assets $5,382

LIABILITIES & STOCKHOLDERS' EQUITY

Current liabilities:

Accounts payable	$ 514
Current portion of long-term debt	6
Other current liabilities (*summarized*)	283
Total current liabilities	803
Long-term debt	402
Other liabilities	1,005

Stockholders' equity:

Common stock	32
Additional paid-in capital	206
Retained earnings	4,120
Accumulated other comprehensive income:	
Unrealized gain on investments	85
Other (*summarized*)	293
Less: Treasury stock	(1,564)
Total liabilities and stockholders' equity	**$5,382**

Related to ← passive investments

Identifying Investment Types and Accounting Methods

The accounting methods used to record investments are directly related to the purpose of the investment.

Passive Investments in Debt and Equity Securities

Investors make **passive investments** to earn a high rate of return on funds that may be needed in the future for either short- or long-term purposes. This category includes investments in both debt securities (bonds and notes) and equity securities (stock):

- **Investments in equity securities** are presumed to be passive if the investing company owns less than 20 percent of the other company's outstanding voting shares or any amount of nonvoting shares. The market value method is used to measure and report these investments.

- **Investments in debt securities** are always considered to be passive. If they are meant to be sold before maturity, they are treated as equity securities and reported using the market value method (also called fair market value method). If the company intends and has the ability to hold them until the maturity date, however, the company measures and reports them at amortized cost.

Investments in Stock for Significant Influence

Active investments are those in which a company owns enough stock in another business to influence or control that business. An investor or company that owns enough shares of voting stock of another company to have an important impact on its operating and financing policies is said to have **significant influence.** Significant influence is presumed to exist if the investing company owns from 20 to 50 percent of the outstanding voting shares. However, other factors may also indicate significant influence, including membership on the board of directors of the other company, participation in its policy-making processes, evidence of material transactions between the two companies, an interchange of managerial personnel, and technological dependency. The equity method is used to measure and report this type of investment.

Investments in Stock for Control

Control is the ability to determine the operating and financial policies of another company through ownership of its voting stock. For all practical purposes, control is presumed when

Learning Objective 2

Identify investment types and the related accounting methods.

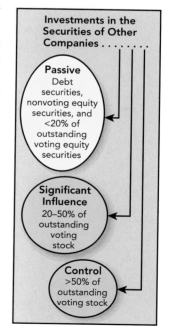

Investments in the Securities of Other Companies . . . .

Passive
Debt securities, nonvoting equity securities, and <20% of outstanding voting equity securities

Significant Influence
20–50% of outstanding voting stock

Control
>50% of outstanding voting stock

the investing company owns more than 50 percent of the outstanding voting stock. These investments are accounted for by combining the two companies using the consolidated statement method.

The three investment types and the appropriate measuring and reporting methods for each may be summarized as follows:

	Investment in Debt Securities of Another Entity		Investment in the Voting Common Stock of Another Entity		
Investment Category	Passive		Passive	Significant Influence	Control
Level of ownership	Held to maturity	Not held to maturity	<20% of outstanding shares	20–50% of outstanding shares	>50% of outstanding shares
Measuring and reporting method	Amortized cost method	Market value method		Equity method	Consolidation method

Let's look more closely at the accounting and reporting rules for each of these investment types.

ACCOUNTING FOR PASSIVE INVESTMENTS

Debt Investments Held to Maturity: Amortized Cost Method

Learning Objective 3

Analyze and report bond investments held to maturity.

When management plans to hold a bond investment until the maturity date (when the principal is due), it is reported in the account appropriately named Investments Held to Maturity. Bonds should be classified as investments held to maturity if management has both the intent and the ability to hold them until the maturity date. These bonds are reported at amortized cost—that is, at cost adjusted for the amortization of any bond discount or premium. We illustrate how to account for these investments from their purchase date through the maturity date.

Bond Purchases

On the date of purchase, a bond may be acquired at the maturity amount (at par), for less than the maturity amount (at a discount), or for more than the maturity amount (at a premium).[1] Following the cost principle, the bond's total cost, including all acquisition costs such as transfer fees and brokers' commissions, is debited to the Investments Held to Maturity account.

To illustrate, assume that on October 1, 2010, The Washington Post Company paid the par value of $100 million[2] for 8 percent bonds due to mature on October 1, 2015. The 8 percent interest is paid each September 30. Management plans and has the ability to hold the bonds for five years until their maturity date. The journal entry to record the purchase of the bonds on October 1, 2010, is:

(In millions)	Debit	Credit
Investments Held to Maturity (+A)	100	
Cash (−A)		100

Assets		=	Liabilities	+ Owners' Equity
Investments Held to Maturity	+100			
Cash	−100			

[1] The price of the bond is determined based on the present value techniques discussed in Chapter 14. Many analysts refer to a bond price as a percentage of par. For example, The Wall Street Journal might report that an ExxonMobil bond with a par value of $1,000 is selling at 82.97. This statement means that the bond costs $829.70 (82.97 percent of $1,000).

[2] When bond investors accept an interest rate that is the same as the rate stated on the bonds, the bonds will sell at par (that is, at 100 percent of face value).

Interest Earned

In this illustration, the company purchased the bonds at par, or face value. Because there is no premium or discount to amortize, the book value remains constant over the life of the investment. In such situations, the revenue earned on the investment each period is measured as the amount of interest collected in cash or accrued at year-end. The following journal entry records the accrual of $2 million in interest on December 31 [$100 million face value $\times$ 0.08 (or 8%) $\times$ 3/12 of a year (since the October 1 purchase)]:

(In millions)	Debit	Credit
Interest Receivable (+A)	2	
Interest Revenue (+R, +OE)		2

Assets		=	Liabilities	+	Owners' Equity	
Interest Receivable	+2				Interest Revenue (+R)	+2

On September 30, 2011, when the investor receives a full year of interest ($2 million each quarter $\times$ 4 quarters = $8 million), the following journal entry is made:

(In millions)	Debit	Credit
Cash (+A)	8	
Interest Receivable (−A)		2
Interest Revenue (+R, +OE)		6

Assets		=	Liabilities	+	Owners' Equity	
Cash	+8				Interest Revenue (+R)	+6
Interest Receivable	−2					

The same entry is made for succeeding interest payments. On the income statement, Interest Revenue is reported in the Other Items section.

Principal at Maturity

When the bonds mature on October 1, 2015, the journal entry to record receipt of the $100 million principal payment is:

(In millions)	Debit	Credit
Cash (+A)	100	
Investments Held to Maturity (−A)		100

Assets		=	Liabilities	+	Owners' Equity
Cash	+100				
Investments Held to Maturity	−100				

Note the following:

- If the bond investment is sold before maturity, any difference between the market value (the proceeds from the sale) and the net book value (the unamortized cost) is reported in the income statement as a gain or loss on the sale.
- If management intends to sell the bonds before (or is unable to hold them until) the maturity date, they should be treated in the same way as stock investments classified as securities available for sale, which we discuss in the next section.

SELF-STUDY PRACTICE

On February 1, 2011, Rodriguez Company had $200,000 in excess cash. The company invested it in a three-year bond, purchased at par, which pays 12 percent interest each year on January 31. Rodriguez expects and is able to hold the bond to maturity. Answer the following questions.

1. What type of investment is this, and how should Rodriguez account for it?
2. Record the journal entry on the purchase date, February 1, 2011.

	Debit	Credit

3. Record the journal entry on December 31, 2011, the company's year-end.

	Debit	Credit

4. Record the journal entry on the first interest payment date, January 31, 2012.

	Debit	Credit

5. Record the journal entry on the maturity date, February 1, 2014.

	Debit	Credit

After you have finished, check your answers with the solution at the bottom of the next page.

Securities Available for Sale: Market Value Method

Learning Objective 4

Analyze and report passive investments in securities using the market value method.

When the investing company owns less than 20 percent of the outstanding voting stock in another company or any level of nonvoting stock, its investment in equity securities is considered passive. Among the assets and liabilities shown on the balance sheet, only passive investments in marketable securities (that is, stock and debt that is not held to maturity) are reported using the market value method.

Classifying Passive Investments

Depending on management's intent, passive investments may be classified as either trading securities or securities available for sale:

Trading Securities. Trading securities are traded actively with the objective of generating short-term profits on changes in the securities' price. This approach is similar to the one taken by many mutual funds whose portfolio managers actively buy and sell securities. On the balance sheet, **Trading Securities** are classified as current assets.

Securities Available for Sale. Most companies do not actively trade the securities of other companies. Instead they invest in them to earn a return on funds they may need in the near future for operating purposes. These investments are called Securities Available for Sale.

On the balance sheet, they are classified as either current or noncurrent assets, depending on whether management intends to sell them within the next year.

Because securities available for sale are the most common type of passive investment, we focus on this category in the next section by analyzing Washington Post's investing activities.

Recording and Reporting Securities Available for Sale

Washington Post's Investments in Marketable Securities accounts are reported for the year 2006 at $29 million for the current asset and $326 million for the noncurrent asset (see Exhibit 15.1). The notes to Washington Post's annual report contain the following information concerning this investment portfolio:

NOTES TO CONSOLIDATED FINANCIAL STATEMENTS

A. SUMMARY OF SIGNIFICANT ACCOUNTING POLICIES

Investments in Marketable Equity Securities. The Company's investments in marketable equity securities are classified as **available-for-sale** and therefore are recorded at fair market value in the Consolidated Balance Sheets, with the change in fair market value during the period excluded from earnings and recorded net of tax as a separate component of comprehensive income. Marketable equity securities the Company expects to hold long term are classified as non-current assets. If the fair market value of a marketable equity security declines below its cost basis, and the decline is considered other than temporary, the Company will record a write-down, which is included in earnings [*emphasis added*].

WASHINGTON POST

2006 Annual Report

Here is how the market value method is applied:

- Washington Post invests in equity securities, acquiring a passive interest in the stock of other companies. These assets are reported on the balance sheet (Exhibit 15.1) as both current and noncurrent assets. The note to the annual report indicates both groups are accounted for as securities available for sale. Like most companies, Washington Post does not invest in trading securities.
- When the company purchases securities available for sale, accountants record them at cost in the account Securities Available for Sale (part of Investments in Marketable Securities on Washington Post's balance sheet).

Solution to
Self-Study Practice

1. Because Rodriguez intends to hold the bond until maturity, it is a passive investment called Investments Held to Maturity. It should be accounted for using the amortized cost method.

2.

	Debit	Credit
Investments Held to Maturity (+A)	200,000	
Cash (−A)		200,000

3.

	Debit	Credit
Interest Receivable (+A)	22,000	
Interest Revenue (+R, +OE)		22,000
[$200,000 × 0.12 × 11/12]		

4.

	Debit	Credit
Cash (+A)	24,000	
Interest Receivable (−A)		22,000
Interest Revenue (+R, +OE)		2,000

5.

	Debit	Credit
Cash (+A)	200,000	
Investments Held to Maturity (−A)		200,000

- In reporting the market value of the investments on the balance sheet at year-end, accountants record an adjusting entry for any temporary change up or down in the stock's market value since it was acquired. These changes are called unrealized holding gains or losses. Accountants use a special account, a valuation allowance, to show the change in the market value above or below acquisition cost. If the investments' market value has increased since they were purchased, the valuation allowance is added to the cost of the securities in the Securities Available for Sale account. If their market value has decreased, the valuation allowance is subtracted from the cost of the investments.

- Because a journal entry must affect at least two accounts, the other half of the adjusting entry is made to another account, reported in the Stockholders' Equity section of the balance sheet under Accumulated Other Comprehensive Income. Note in Exhibit 15.1 that Washington Post reported unrealized gains of $85 million in Stockholders' Equity. Because the amount reported for the long-term asset Investments in Marketable Securities was $326 million, the **cost** of the securities available for sale must have been $241 million with a valuation allowance of $85 million for unrealized gains ($326 million reported – $85 million unrealized gain = $241 million cost).

This process may sound complicated. To illustrate the market value method, let's assume that Washington Post had no passive investments at the end of 2009. In the following example, we apply the market value method, the accounting policy used by Washington Post, to a sample securities purchase.

Purchase of Stock. Assume that on January 2, 2010, Washington Post purchased 1,000,000 shares of Internet Financial News[3] (IFN) common stock for $60 per share, paying $60,000,000. On that date, 10,000,000 shares were outstanding, so Washington Post owned 10 percent of IFN (1,000,000 ÷ 10,000,000). This investment would be treated as a passive investment that is recorded initially (on January 2, 2010) at cost:

(In millions)	Debit	Credit
Securities Available for Sale (+A)	60	
Cash (−A)		60

Assets	=	Liabilities	+	Owners' Equity
Securities Available for Sale +60				
Cash −60				

See Exhibit 15.2 on page 651 for this entry and those that follow posted to T-accounts.

Dividends Earned. Investments in equity securities earn a return from two sources: (1) price increases and (2) dividend income. Price increases (or decreases) are analyzed both at year-end and when a security is sold. On the income statement, dividends earned are reported as Investment Income (or Dividend Revenue) and included in the computation of net income for the period. Let's assume that on December 15, 2010, Washington Post received a $1 per share cash dividend from IFN totaling $1,000,000 ($1 × 1,000,000 shares). The entry to record the receipt is:

(In millions)	Debit	Credit
Cash (+A)	1	
Investment Income (+R, +OE)		1

Assets	=	Liabilities	+	Owners' Equity
Cash +1				Investment Income (+R) +1

This entry is the same for both trading securities and available-for-sale securities.

---

[3] Internet Financial News is a fictitious company.

Year-End Valuation.

At the end of the accounting period, Washington Post reports passive investments on the balance sheet **at their market value.** Assume that IFN had a $58 per share market value at the end of the year. That is, the investment lost value ($60 − $58 = $2 per share). Because the shares were not sold, however, the loss is a holding loss, not a realized loss.

Reporting securities available for sale at market value requires adjusting the account to market value at the end of each period using the valuation account **Market Value Allowance.** The offset to the Market Value Allowance is the **Unrealized Gain (or Loss) on Investments** account. If the Market Value Allowance account has a **debit balance,** it is **added** to the Securities Available for Sale account. If it has a **credit balance,** it is **subtracted.** The Unrealized Gain (or Loss) on Investments account is then reported in the Stockholders' Equity section of the balance sheet under Accumulated Other Comprehensive Income. Thus, the balance sheet remains in balance.

The following chart shows the computation of any unrealized gain or loss in the securities available for sale portfolio. The amounts are given in millions of dollars:

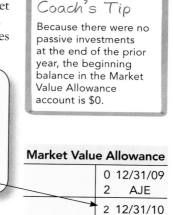

Coach's Tip

Because there were no passive investments at the end of the prior year, the beginning balance in the Market Value Allowance account is $0.

Year: 2010	*In millions*	
Market value	$58	($58 per share × 1 million shares)
− Cost	− 60	($60 per share × 1 million shares)
Balance needed in Market Value Allowance	(2)	A credit balance is needed.
− Unadjusted balance in Market Value Allowance	− 0	
Amount for adjusting entry	($ 2)	Credit

Market Value Allowance

	0 12/31/09
	2 AJE
	2 12/31/10

The adjusting entry on December 31, 2010, would be recorded as follows:

(In millions)	Debit	Credit
Unrealized Gain (Loss) on Investments (−OE)	2	
Market Value Allowance (−A)		2

Assets	=	Liabilities	+	Owners' Equity
Market Value Allowance −2				Unrealized Gain (Loss) on Investments −2

On the 2010 balance sheet under Investments in Marketable Securities, Washington Post reports securities available for sale of $58,000,000 ($60,000,000 cost − the $2,000,000 credit balance in the valuation allowance). The company also reports, under Accumulated Other Comprehensive Income (Stockholders' Equity), Unrealized Loss on Investments of $2,000,000 for securities available for sale. Because these investments are expected to be held into the future, the company does not report the unrealized holding loss as part of net income. (Recall that only when a security is sold are any realized gains or losses included in net income.) The only item that would be reported on the income statement for 2010 is investment income of $1,000,000 (from dividends earned), classified under Other Items.

On the Balance Sheet: *(in millions)*

Assets
Investments in Marketable Securities $ 60
   Market Value Allowance   (2)
      Net investment $ 58

Stockholders' Equity
   Other Comprehensive Income:
      Unrealized Loss on Investments $(2)

Now let's assume that Washington Post held the IFN securities through the year 2011. At the end of 2011, the stock had a market value of $61 per share. The adjustment for 2011 is computed as follows:

Year: 2011	*In millions*	
Market value	$ 61	($61 per share × 1 million shares)
− Cost	− 60	($60 per share × 1 million shares)
Balance needed in Market Value Allowance	1	
− Unadjusted balance in Market Value Allowance	− (2)	
Amount for adjusting entry	$ 3	Debit

Market Value Allowance

	0 12/31/09
	2 AJE
	2 12/31/10
AJE 3	
12/31/11 1	

The adjusting entry on December 31, 2011, is:

(in millions)	Debit	Credit
Market Value Allowance (+A)	3	
Unrealized Gain (Loss) on Investments (+OE)		3

Assets	=	Liabilities	+	Owners' Equity
				Unrealized Gain (Loss)
Market Value Allowance +3				**on Investments +3**

On the Balance Sheet: *(in millions)*

Assets
Investments in Marketable Securities $60
Market Value Allowance   1
Net investment $61

Stockholders' Equity
Other Comprehensive Income:
Unrealized Gain on Investments $ 1

Sale of Stock. Let's assume that on March 17, 2012, Washington Post sold all of its investment in IFN for $64 per share. The company receives $64,000,000 in cash ($64 × 1,000,000 shares) for stock purchased at $60,000,000 in 2010 ($60 × 1,000,000 shares). On that date, accountants record a $4,000,000 **realized gain** on the sale ($64 million − $60 million) and then eliminate the Securities Available for Sale account.

(in millions)	Debit	Credit
Cash (+A)	64	
Securities Available for Sale (−A)		60
Gain on Sale of Investments (+R, +OE)		4

Assets	=	Liabilities	+	Owners' Equity
Cash +64				**Gain on Sale**
Securities Available for Sale −60				**of Investments (+R) +4**

You may be wondering what a company does with the Market Value Allowance and the Unrealized Gain (Loss) on Investments accounts when investments are sold. The answer is that they adjust the account balances to $0 at the end of the year, similar to the process in the preceding example. Because Washington Post has no investment in IFN at December 31, 2012, it would eliminate the $1 balance in each account.

(in millions)	Debit	Credit
Unrealized Gain (Loss) on Investments (−OE)	1	
Market Value Allowance (−A)		1

Assets	=	Liabilities	+	Owners' Equity
				Unrealized Gain (Loss)
Market Value Allowance −1				**on Investments −1**

You now can review the T-accounts for all of the transactions from 2010 to 2012 in Exhibit 15.2.

Comparison of Available-for-Sale and Trading Securities

The impact of unrealized holding gains or losses on the financial statements depends on whether an investment is a trading security or a security available for sale.

Available-for-Sale Securities

As you learned in the last section, the balance in the Unrealized Gain (Loss) on Investments account is reported as a separate component of stockholders' equity under **Accumulated Other**

Exhibit 15.2 — T-Accounts for the Illustrated Transactions

Balance Sheet Accounts (in millions)

Securities Available for Sale (at cost) (A)		Market Value Allowance (A)		Unrealized Gain (Loss) on Investments (OE)	
12/31/09 0			0 12/31/09	12/31/09 0	
1/2/10 Purchase 60			2 AJE 12/31/10	12/31/10 AJE 2	
12/31/10 60		2 12/31/10		12/31/10 2	
		12/31/11 AJE 3			3 AJE 12/31/11
12/31/11 60		12/31/11 1			1 12/31/11
	60 Sale 3/17/12	1 AJE 12/31/12		12/31/12 AJE 1	
12/31/12 0		0 12/31/12		12/31/12 0	

Income Statement Accounts (in millions)

Investment Income (R)		Gain on Sale of Investments (R)	
	1 Earned 12/15/10		4 Sale 3/17/12
	1 12/31/10		4 12/31/12

Comprehensive Income. It is not reported on the income statement because it does not affect net income.

However, at the time of sale, the difference between the proceeds from the sale and the original cost of the investment is recorded as a gain or loss on the sale of investments. It is reported on the income statement because the gain has been realized. At the end of the year, the Unrealized Gain (Loss) on Investments account and the Market Value Allowance account are adjusted.

Trading Securities

For trading securities, the amount of the adjustment to record a holding gain or loss is included **in each period's income statement** (that is, it is treated as realized). Holding gains increase net income, and holding losses decrease net income. The amount that is recorded as Unrealized Gain (Loss) on Trading Securities is also closed to Retained Earnings at the end of the period as are other temporary accounts on the income statement. When a trading security is sold, the affected accounts are Cash, Trading Securities, and Market Value Allowance plus any additional Gain (Loss) on Sale of Investments.

See Exhibit 15.3 for a comparison of the treatment of trading securities and securities available for sale using Washington Post's transactions from 2010 to 2012. **Note that the total investment income reported for the three years is the same for both trading securities and securities available for sale ($5 million). Only the allocation across periods differs.**

	EFFECT ON INCOME STATEMENT (in millions)	
	Trading Securities	Securities Available for Sale
2010 Investment income	$1	$1
2010 Unrealized loss	(2)	—
2011 Unrealized gain	3	—
2012 Gain on sale	3	4
Total income	$5	$5

Spotlight On FINANCIAL REPORTING

Equity Securities and Earnings Management

Most managers prefer to treat passive investments as investments available for sale. This treatment generally reduces variations in reported earnings by avoiding recognition of unrealized holding gains and losses that result from quarter-to-quarter changes in stock prices. It also allows managers to smooth out fluctuations in earnings by selling securities with unrealized gains when earnings decline and securities with unrealized losses when earnings increase. Analysts can see through this strategy, however, by examining the required note on investments in the financial statements.

Exhibit 15.3   Comparison of Accounting for Trading and Available-for-Sale Securities

Part A: Journal Entries | Trading Securities **(in millions)** | Securities Available for Sale **(in millions)**

2010

- Purchase (for $60 million cash)

Trading Securities (+A)	60
Cash (−A)	60

Securities Available for Sale (+A)	60
Cash (−A)	60

- Receipt of dividends ($1 million cash)

Cash (+A)	1
Investment Income (+R, +OE)	1

Cash (+A)	1
Investment Income (+R, +OE)	1

- Year-end adjustment to market (market = $58 million)

Unrealized Loss on Trading Securities (+E, −OE)	2
Market Value Allowance (−A)	2

Unrealized Gain (Loss) on Investments (−OE)	2
Market Value Allowance (−A)	2

2011

- Year-end adjustment to market (market = $61 million)

Market Value Allowance (+A)	3
Unrealized Gain on Trading Securities (+R, + OE)	3

Market Value Allowance (+A)	3
Unrealized Gain (Loss) on Investments (+OE)	3

2012

- Sale (for $64 million)

Cash (+A)	64
Trading Securities (−A)	60
Market Value Allowance (−A)	1
Gain on Sale of Investments (+R, +OE)	3

Cash (+A)	64
Securities Available for Sale (−A)	60
Gain on Sale of Investments (+R, + OE)	4

- Year-end adjustment to market (market = $0 because investments have been sold)

None

Unrealized Gain (Loss) on Investments (−OE)	1
Market Value Allowance (−A)	1

Part B: Financial Statements | Trading Securities | | | | Securities Available for Sale | | |

Balance Sheet

Assets	2012	2011	2010	Assets	2012	2011	2010
Investment in marketable securities	—	$60	$60	Investment in marketable securities	—	$60	$60
Market value allowance	=	1	(2)	Market value allowance	—	1	(2)
Net investment in trading securities	=	$61	$58	Net investments available for sale	=	$61	$58
				Stockholders' Equity			
				Unrealized gain (loss) on investments	—	$ 1	$(2)

Income Statement

	2012	2011	2010		2012	2011	2010
Investment income	—	—	$ 1	Investment income	—	—	$1
Unrealized gain (loss) on trading securities.	—	$3	$(2)	Gain on sale of investments	$4	—	—
Gain on sale of investments	$3	—	—				

Let's reconstruct the investment activities Washington Post undertook in a recent year, with a few transactions assumed. Use the following T-accounts to infer the amounts. Then prepare journal entries and answer questions. The dollars are stated in millions.

Balance Sheet Accounts

(In Accumulated Other Comprehensive Income)

Securities Available for Sale

1/1	361		
Purchase	43	?	Sale
12/31	355		

Market Value Allowance

1/1	58	
AJE	?	
12/31	85	

Unrealized Gain (Loss) on Investments

	58	1/1
	?	AJE
	85	12/31

Income Statement Accounts

Investment Income

	?	Earned
	73	12/31

Gain on Sale of Investments

	34	Sale
	34	12/31

1. Purchased securities available for sale for cash as a noncurrent asset. Prepare the journal entry.
2. Received cash dividends on the investments. Prepare the journal entry.
3. Sold securities available for sale at a gain. Prepare the journal entry.
4. At year-end, the securities available for sale portfolio had a market value of $440. Prepare the adjusting entry.
5. What would be reported for investments on the balance sheet on December 31? On the income statement for the year? Indicate classifications, account titles, and amounts.
6. How would year-end reporting change if the investments were categorized as trading securities instead of securities available for sale? Assume the market value allowance for the trading securities sold was $20.

After you have finished, check your answers with the solution at the bottom of the page.

Solution to Self-Study Practice

1.	Securities Available for Sale (+A)	43	
	Cash (−A)		43
2.	Cash (+A)	73	
	Investment Income (+R, +OE)		73
3.	Cash (+A)	83	
	Gain on Sale of Investments (+R +OE)		34
	Securities Available for Sale (−A)		49
	(Beg. bal. $361 + purchase $43 − end. bal. $355 = $49 cost of securities sold)		
4.	Market Value Allowance (+A)	27	
	Unrealized Gain (Loss) on Investments (+OE)		27

	In Millions
Market value	$440
− Cost	− 355
Balance needed in Market Value Allowance	85
− Unadjusted balance in Market Value Allowance	− 58
Amount for adjusting entry	$ 27

5.

Balance Sheet
Assets (noncurrent)
　Investments in Marketable Securities $440
Stockholders' Equity
　Accumulated Other Comprehensive Income:
　　Unrealized Gain (Loss) on Investments   85

Income Statement
Other Items
　Gain on Sale of Investments $ 34
　Investment Income   73

6.

Balance Sheet
Assets (Current)
　Investments in Marketable Securities $440

Income Statement
Other Items
　Gain on Sale of Investments $ 14
　Investment Income   73

When trading securities were sold, the journal entry was:

Cash (+A)	83	
Investments in Marketable Securities (−A)		49
Market Value Allowance (−A)		20	Assumed
Gain on Sale of Investments (+R, +OE)		14

Spotlight On FINANCIAL REPORTING

Passive Investments and the Fair Value Option

Both U.S. GAAP and international financial reporting standards (IFRS) allow the option to account for bonds held to maturity and securities available for sale at **fair value.** Fair value is the price the seller would receive if the assets were sold. The election is made when each security is purchased. If a company decides to account for a held-to-maturity or available-for-sale security at fair value, it is transferred to the trading securities portfolio and is accounted for in the same manner as other trading securities.

ACCOUNTING FOR INFLUENTIAL INVESTMENTS

Investments for Significant Influence: Equity Method

Learning Objective 5

Analyze and report investments involving significant influence using the equity method.

For a variety of reasons, an investor may want to exert significant influence (by owning 20 to 50 percent of a company's outstanding voting stock) without becoming the controlling shareholder (by acquiring over 50 percent of the voting stock). For example:

- A retailer may want to influence a manufacturer to ensure obtaining certain products designed to its specifications.
- A manufacturer may want to influence a computer consulting firm to incorporate the firm's cutting-edge technology in its manufacturing processes.
- A manufacturer may recognize that a parts supplier lacks experienced management and could prosper with additional managerial support.

When an investor can exert **significant influence** over an **investee** (the company it partially owns), accountants must use the equity method to value the investment. As you have seen, when Washington Post invests in securities as a passive investor, the company reports those investments on the balance sheet as Investments in Marketable Securities. However, when Washington Post owns 20 to 50 percent of the outstanding voting stock, the company is presumed to be taking a more active role as an investor. On the balance sheet, Washington Post reports these long-term investments for significant influence as Investments in Affiliates (see Exhibit 15.1). Washington Post reported one primary investment in an affiliated company in its 2006 annual report. It sold another affiliated company during 2006:

WASHINGTON POST

2006 Annual Report

NOTES TO FINANCIAL STATEMENTS

A. SUMMARY OF SIGNIFICANT ACCOUNTING POLICIES

Investments in Affiliates. The Company uses the equity method of accounting for its investments in and earnings or losses of associated companies that it does not control, but over which it does exert significant influence. . . .

C. INVESTMENTS

. . .

Investments in Affiliates. The Company's investments in affiliates at December 31, 2006 and January 1, 2006 include the following (in millions):

	2006	2005
Bowater Mersey Paper Company	$49	$55
BrassRing	—	11
Other	5	1
	$54	$67

At the end of 2006, the Company's investments in affiliates consisted of a 49% interest in the common stock of Bowater Mersey Paper Company Limited, which owns and operates a newsprint mill in Nova Scotia, and other investments.

. . . On November 13, 2006, the Company sold its 49% interest in BrassRing and recorded a $43.2 million pre-tax gain that is included in "Other income (expense), net" in the Consolidated Statements of Income.

Recording Investments under the Equity Method

With a passive investment (less than 20 percent stock ownership), an investor usually cannot influence the investee's operating and financing activities—for example, by compelling the investee to pay dividends. So, the investor reports any dividends received from the investee as dividend revenue.

Under the equity method, however, the investor's 20 to 50 percent ownership in a company presumes significant influence over the investee's operating and financing policies. Often the investee's board of directors may include a representative of the investor who influences the investee's board to declare dividends among other decisions. Because of this influence, the investment is accounted for as if the two companies were one. That is, the net income the investee earned increases the investee's net assets (assets − liabilities). Likewise, the investor should report a portion of the investee's net income as its income and an increase in the investment account. Dividends paid by the investee decrease the investee's net assets. Similarly, the receipt of dividends by the investor is treated as a reduction of the investment account, not revenue. A summary follows:

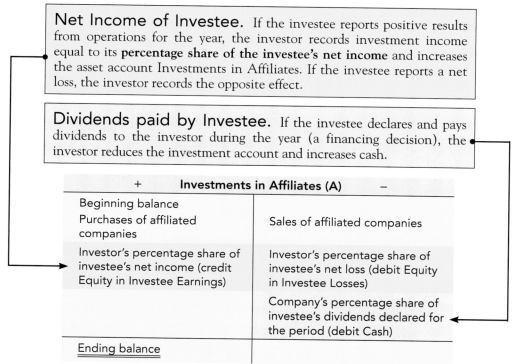

Net Income of Investee. If the investee reports positive results from operations for the year, the investor records investment income equal to its **percentage share of the investee's net income** and increases the asset account Investments in Affiliates. If the investee reports a net loss, the investor records the opposite effect.

Dividends paid by Investee. If the investee declares and pays dividends to the investor during the year (a financing decision), the investor reduces the investment account and increases cash.

+	Investments in Affiliates (A)	−
Beginning balance Purchases of affiliated companies	Sales of affiliated companies	
Investor's percentage share of investee's net income (credit Equity in Investee Earnings)	Investor's percentage share of investee's net loss (debit Equity in Investee Losses)	
	Company's percentage share of investee's dividends declared for the period (debit Cash)	
Ending balance		

Purchase of Stock. For simplicity, let's assume that at the end of 2009, Washington Post had no long-term investments in companies over which it exerted significant influence. On January 2, 2010, Washington Post purchased 4 million shares of the outstanding voting stock of IFN for $240,000,000 cash. Because IFN had 10 million shares of common stock outstanding, Washington Post acquired a 40 percent interest (4 million ÷ 10 million shares) and was presumed to have significant influence over the investee. Therefore, Washington Post must use the equity method to account for the investment. The purchase of the asset would be recorded on January 2, 2010, at cost in Investments in Affiliates.

(in millions)	Debit	Credit
Investments in Affiliates (+A)	240	
Cash (−A)		240

Assets		=	Liabilities	+	Owners' Equity
Investments in Affiliates	+240				
Cash	−240				

Investee Earnings. Because the investor can influence the investee's income-earning process, the investor bases its investment income on the investee's earnings rather than on the dividends paid. In 2010, IFN reported net income of $50,000,000. Washington Post's percentage share of that income, $20,000,000$ ($40\% \times \$50,000,000$), would be recorded on December 31, 2010, as follows:

(in millions)	Debit	Credit
Investments in Affiliates (+A)	20	
Equity in Investee Earnings (+R, +OE)		20

Assets	=	Liabilities	+	Owners' Equity	
Investments in Affiliates +20				Equity in Investee Earnings (+R)	+20

If reporting a net loss, the investor records its share of the loss by decreasing the investment account and recording the loss under Equity in Investee Losses. Equity in Investee Earnings (or Losses) is reported in the Other Items section of the income statement along with interest revenue, interest expense, and gains and losses on sales of assets.

Dividends Received. Because Washington Post can influence the dividend policies of its investees, the company should **not** record any dividends it receives as investment income. Instead, dividends reduce its investment account. On December 1, 2010, IFN declared and paid a cash dividend of $2 per share to stockholders. Washington Post received $8,000,000 in cash ($2 per share × 4,000,000 shares) from IFN, and recorded this on December 1, 2010, as follows:

(in millions)	Debit	Credit
Cash (+A)	8	
Investments in Affiliates (−A)		8

Assets	=	Liabilities	+	Owners' Equity
Investments in Affiliates −8				
Cash +8				

The cumulative effects of the IFN purchase, earnings, and dividends for 2010 are reflected in the following T-accounts (in millions of dollars):

Investments in Affiliates				Equity in Investee Earnings			
1/1/10	0					0	1/1/10
Purchases	240						
Share of investee net earnings	20	8	Share of investee dividends			20	Share of investee net earnings
12/31/10	252					20	12/31/10

Sale of Stock. Companies record any sale of stock in affiliated companies in the same way as sales of other assets. Investment in Affiliates is reduced by the percentage of stock sold, Cash is debited, and the difference is recorded as either a Gain (or Loss) on Sale of Investments.

Let's assume that on January 2, 2011, Washington Post decided to sell 1,000,000 of the 4,000,000 shares of stock it owned in IFN for $70 million. That represents 25 percent of Washington Post's Investment in Affiliates. One-fourth of the balance in the account is equal to $63 million ($252 million × ¼), so the entry in January 2011 is:

(in millions)	Debit	Credit
Cash (+A)	70	
Investments in Affiliates (−A)		63
Gain on Sale of Investments (+R, +OE)		7

Assets	=	Liabilities	+	Owners' Equity	
Cash +70				Gain on Sale of	
Investments in Affiliates −63				Investments (+R)	+7

Coach's Tip

Because Washington Post owned 40 percent of IFN prior to the sale (4 million of the 10 million shares outstanding), it will then own 30 percent (3 million of 10 million shares) after the sale. Thus, **it must still apply the equity method.**

Reporting Investments under the Equity Method

On the balance sheet, Investments in Affiliates is reported as a long-term asset. However, as the year-end entries show, the investment account does not reflect either cost or market value. Instead, the following occurs:

- The investment account increases with the cost of the purchased shares and the proportional share of the investee's income.
- The investment account decreases with the dividends received from the investee, the proportional share of any investee losses, and any sale of shares in the investee.

At the end of the accounting period, accountants **do not adjust the investment account to reflect changes in the market value** of the securities. When the securities are sold, accountants record the difference between the cash received and the book value of the investment as a Gain (Loss) on Sale of Investments and report the amount on the income statement in the Other Items section.

Spotlight On ETHICS

Improper Influence

A key assumption in accounting is that all transactions occur at "arm's length." That is, each party to the transaction is acting in his or her own self-interest. But when one company exerts significant influence over another (that is, when it owns 20 to 50 percent of the voting common stock), it is unreasonable to assume that transactions between the two companies are made at arm's length.

Consider what might happen if an investor company could affect the investee's dividend policy. If the investor reported dividends paid by the investee as dividend income, the investor could manipulate its own income by influencing the other company's dividend policy. In a bad year, the investor might request large dividend payments to bolster its income. In a good year, it might try to cut dividend payments to build up the investee's retained earnings, which would support large dividends in the future.

The equity method prevents this type of manipulation. Instead of recognizing dividends as income, this method bases income from the investment on a percentage of the affiliated company's reported net income.

SELF-STUDY PRACTICE

Let's reconstruct some actions Washington Post undertook recently regarding its investments in affiliated companies with a few transactions assumed. Prepare the following journal entries and answer the following questions. Use the T-accounts that follow to infer the amounts. The dollars are given in millions.

Investments in Affiliates				Equity in Investee Earnings		
1/1	67				0	1/1
Purchases	3	15	Sales of investments			
Share of investee earnings	?	2	Share of investee dividends		Share of investee earnings 1	
12/31	54				1 12/31	

1. Purchased additional investments in affiliated companies for cash. Prepare the journal entry.
2. Sold a portion of investments in affiliated companies for $58 cash. Prepare the journal entry.
3. Received cash dividends on the investments. Prepare the journal entry.
4. At year-end, the affiliated companies reported a total of $5 in net income, and investments in affiliates had a market value of $42. Prepare the adjusting entry. What percentage of the investee's stock is owned by the Washington Post?
5. What would be reported on the year-end balance sheet regarding the investments in affiliates? What would be reported on the income statement for the year?

After you have finished, check your answers with the solution at the bottom of the next page.

Spotlight On FINANCIAL REPORTING

Selecting Accounting Methods

Managers can choose freely between LIFO and FIFO for measuring inventory or between accelerated depreciation and straight-line depreciation for measuring the use of long-lived assets. In the case of minority investments (50 percent or less), however, they may **not** choose between the market value and equity methods. Investments in less than 20 percent of a company's outstanding stock are usually accounted for using the market value method. Investments of 20 to 50 percent are accounted for using the equity method.

However, managers may be able to structure acquisitions in a way that permits them to use the accounting methods they prefer. For example, a company that wants to use the market value method could purchase only 19.9 percent of the outstanding stock of another company and achieve essentially the same investment goals as it would with a 20 percent investment. Why might managers want to avoid using the equity method? Most managers prefer to minimize variations in reported earnings. If a company were planning to buy stock in a firm that reported large earnings in some years and large losses in others, it might want to use the market value method to avoid reporting its share of the investee's earnings and losses.

In short, analysts who compare companies must understand management's reporting choices and the way in which differences between the market value and equity methods can affect a company's earnings.

Investments with Controlling Interests: Consolidated Statements

Why Control Other Companies?

Learning Objective 6

Explain the reporting of investments in controlling interests.

Before we discuss financial reporting of investments that involve ownership of more than 50 percent of another company's outstanding voting stock, we should consider the reasons for acquiring this level of ownership. Following are some of these reasons:

1. **Vertical integration.** In this type of acquisition, one company acquires another company that operates on a different level in the distribution channel. For example, Washington Post owns a newsprint company that provides raw materials.

2. **Horizontal growth.** Horizontal acquisitions involve companies that operate on the same level of the distribution channel. For example, Washington Post has expanded internationally by creating or acquiring newspaper companies in major international markets.

Solution to
Self-Study Practice

1.	Investments in Affiliates (+A)	3	
	Cash (−A)		3
2.	Cash (+A)	58	
	Investments in Affiliates (−A)		15
	Gain on Sale of Investments (+R, +OE)		43
3.	Cash (+A)	2	
	Investments in Affiliates (−A)		2
4.	Investments in Affiliates (+A)	1	
	Equity in Investee Earnings (+R, +OE)		1
	Washington Post owns 20 percent of affiliates' stock (20% × $5 net income = $1 equity in investee earnings).		

Under the equity method, there is no entry at year-end to adjust the Investments in Affiliates account to market value.

5.

Balance Sheet		Income Statement	
Assets (under noncurrent assets)		*Other Items*	
Investments in Affiliates	$54	Equity in Investee Earnings	$ 1
		Gain on Sale of Investments	43

3. **Synergy.** Two companies operating together may be more profitable than two companies operating separately. Washington Post has created or purchased a number of broadcast and Internet services. Merging these companies and sharing news content may create more profits than operating separate entities could.

Understanding why one company has acquired control over other companies is a key factor in understanding that company's business strategy.

What Are Consolidated Statements?

Any corporate acquisition involves two companies. A merger occurs when one company purchases all assets and liabilities of another company and the **acquired company goes out of existence.** When the acquired company remains in business, the company that gains control over it by acquiring all or a majority of the voting stock is the parent company. The subsidiary company is the company that the parent acquired.[4] Following is a list of three corporations and some of the well-known companies they own:

The Gap, Inc.	YUM! Brands, Inc.	The Walt Disney Company
Gap	Pizza Hut	ABC Television Network
Old Navy	KFC	ESPN
Banana Republic	Taco Bell	Disneyland
Forth & Towne	Long John Silver's	Pixar Animation Studios
	A&W All-American Restaurants	Touchstone Pictures

> **Coach's Tip**
>
> Because a single set of financial statements covers both the parent company and its subsidiaries, external users such as stockholders and banks (and you) will not be able to obtain financial statements for individual subsidiaries.

When one company acquires another, the results of their operations must be reported together in consolidated statements. Consolidated financial statements **combine the operations of two or more companies into a single set of statements,** usually identified by the word consolidated in the statement titles. For example, the title of the statement in Exhibit 15.1 is *Consolidated* Balance Sheet. Consolidated statements may be thought of as adding together the financial statements for two or more companies so that they appear to be a single company. Thus, the cash accounts for the companies are summed, along with the inventory accounts, the land accounts, and all other accounts. Combining all financial information into one set of consolidated statements gives users better information on the size and scope of operations in companies controlled by the parent corporation.

The notes to Washington Post's 2006 annual report provide the following information:

> ### NOTES TO FINANCIAL STATEMENTS
>
> *A. SUMMARY OF SIGNIFICANT ACCOUNTING POLICIES*
>
> **Principles of Consolidation.** The accompanying financial statements include the accounts of the Company and its subsidiaries; significant intercompany transactions have been eliminated.

WASHINGTON POST

2006 Annual Report

As the note indicates, when consolidated statements are prepared, intercompany items such as loans from the parent company to the subsidiaries must be eliminated. Remember that consolidated statements imply that a single company exists when in fact there are two or more separate legal entities. Intercompany items do not exist in a single corporation. For example, a debt Washington Post (the parent) owes to its newsprint subsidiary is not reported

---

[4] The discussion assumes acquisition of 100 percent of another company. Any acquisition of 51 to 99 percent of another company creates a minority interest that is discussed in advanced accounting courses.

on a consolidated statement because a company cannot owe money to itself. Accounting for business acquisitions and preparing consolidated financial statements are discussed in detail in advanced accounting courses.

EVALUATING TOTAL INVESTED CAPITAL

Return on Assets (ROA)

Learning Objective 7

Analyze and interpret the return on assets ratio.

Investments are assets that are used to generate profits for their owners. To assess how well management has used the company's assets to earn income, analysts and managers compute the return on assets (ROA) ratio.

Accounting Decision Tools		
Name of Measure	**Formula**	**What It Tells You**
Return on assets (ROA)	$\dfrac{\text{Net Income*}}{\text{Average Total Assets}^\dagger} \times 100$	• The percentage of income earned on each dollar invested in assets • The higher the ratio, the more effectively managers are using total assets

* In more complicated analyses, interest expense (net of tax) and minority interest are added back to net income because the measure assesses return on assets independent of their source.

† Average Total Assets = (Beginning Total Assets + Ending Total Assets) ÷ 2

The ROA ratio measures how much the firm earned for each dollar invested in assets. It is the broadest measure of profitability and managerial effectiveness independent of financial strategy. Using the information from Washington Post's 2006 10-K report (with dollars given in thousands), the company's ROA is computed as follows:

$$\frac{\text{Return on}}{\text{Assets}} = \frac{\text{Net Income}}{\text{Average Total Assets}} \times 100 = \frac{\$324{,}469}{(\$5{,}381{,}372 + \$4{,}584{,}773) \div 2} \times 100 = 6.5\%$$

The return on assets ratio is helpful both in analyzing management's effectiveness in using assets to generate profits and in comparing one company or division to another. Companies often compute this measure on a division-by-division basis and then use it to evaluate divisional managers' performance. A higher ROA means that the managers are doing a better job at selecting new investments in assets, all other things held equal.

As you can see from the graph in the margin, Washington Post's ROA for 2006 was below its ROA for the preceding two years. In 2006, Washington Post generated 6.5 cents of income for every dollar of assets; in 2005 and 2004, the company generated 7.1 cents and 8.1 cents of income, respectively, for every dollar of assets. ROA allows investors to compare management's investment performance against alternative investment options. Firms with higher ROAs are doing a better job of selecting new investments, all other things equal.

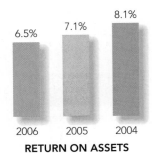

RETURN ON ASSETS

The Washington Post

Comparison to Benchmarks

Comparing a company's ROA ratio to those of competing companies provides additional information on management's effectiveness. As noted in Exhibit 15.4, in 2006, the Gannett Co., Inc., and the Tribune Company reported ROAs of 7.3 percent and 4.7 percent, respectively. By comparison, Washington Post's 2006 ROA of 6.5 percent was in the middle.

Be aware that ROAs can vary greatly from one industry to the next. As noted in Exhibit 15.4, footwear companies recently reported an average return on assets ratio of 16.4 percent compared to 1.0 percent for banks and 13.6 percent for nonalcoholic beverage companies.

Exhibit 15.4   Average Return on Assets Ratio by Industry

Publishing Industry

Tribune Co.	4.7%
Gannett	7.3%
All companies in industry	15.5%

Other Industries

Banks	1.0%
Nonalcoholic beverages	13.6%
Footwear	16.4%

Source: www.reuters.com/finance/industries

Spotlight On BUSINESS DECISIONS

The Big Get Bigger

We began this chapter by asking how big companies become big and suggesting that acquisitions of stock in other companies is a common strategy. As this chapter was being written, Dow Jones, another major player in the publishing industry, was acquired by News Corporation, a diversified entertainment company headquartered in Australia with worldwide operations in film (e.g., 20th Century Fox), television and cable network programming (e.g., Fox network), magazines (e.g., TV Guide), newspapers (e.g., New York Post), and other segments. News Corporation has more than $62 billion in total assets, and its annual revenues exceed $28 billion. With the $5 billion Dow Jones acquisition, News Corporation will grow by 8 percent. On December 13, 2007, Dow Jones issued the following press release:

> **NEW YORK** — Dow Jones & Company, Inc. (NYSE: DJ) announced today that its stockholders voted at a special meeting to approve the previously announced merger agreement with News Corporation. The stockholder vote satisfies the final condition for the completion of the transaction. The merger is expected to close and become effective at approximately the close of business on Dec. 13, 2007.

2007 Press Release

Demonstration Case A

(Try to resolve the following requirements before proceeding to the suggested solution that follows.) Howell Equipment Corporation sells and services a major line of farm equipment. Both sales and service operations have been profitable. The following transactions affected the company during 2009:

a. Jan. 1 Purchased 2,000 shares of common stock in Dear Company at $40 per share. Purchase represented 1 percent of the shares outstanding. Management intends to trade these shares actively.

b. Dec. 28 Received $4,000 cash dividend on Dear Company stock.

c. Dec. 31 Determined that the current market price of Dear stock was $39.

Required:

1. Prepare the journal entry for each of these transactions.
2. What accounts and amounts will be reported on the balance sheet at the end of 2009 and on the income statement for 2009?

Suggested Solution for Case A

1.

a.	Trading Securities (+A)	80,000	
	Cash (−A) (2,000 shares × $40)		80,000
b.	Cash (+A)	4,000	
	Investment Income (+R, +OE)		4,000
c.	Unrealized Loss on Trading Securities (+E −OE)	2,000	
	Market Value Allowance (−A)		2,000

Year: 2009

Market value	$78,000	($39 per share × 2,000 shares)
− Cost	−80,000	($40 per share × 2,000 shares)
Balance needed in Market Value Allowance	(2,000)	A credit balance
− Unadjusted balance in Market Value Allowance	− 0	
Amount for adjusting entry	$ (2,000)	An unrealized loss to income

2.   On the balance sheet   On the income statement

Current Assets		*Other Items*	
Investment in Marketable Securities	$78,000	Investment Income	$4,000
($80,000 cost − $2,000 allowance)		Unrealized Loss on	
		Trading Securities	(2,000)

Demonstration Case B

Assume the same facts as in Case A except that the shares were purchased as securities available for sale rather than as trading securities.

Required:

1. Prepare the journal entry for each of these transactions.
2. What accounts and amounts will be reported on the balance sheet at the end of 2009 and on the income statement for 2009?

Suggested Solution for Case B

1.

a.	Securities Available for Sale (+A)	80,000	
	Cash (−A) (2,000 shares × $40)		80,000
b.	Cash (+A)	4,000	
	Investment Income (+R, +OE)		4,000
c.	Unrealized Gain (Loss) on Investments (−OE)	2,000	
	Market Value Allowance (−A)		2,000

Year: 2009

Market value	$78,000	($39 per share × 2,000 shares)
− Cost	− 80,000	($40 per share × 2,000 shares)
Balance needed in Market Value Allowance	(2,000)	A credit balance
− Unadjusted balance in Market Value Allowance −	0	
Amount for adjusting entry	$ (2,000)	An unrealized loss to owners' equity

2.   On the balance sheet   On the income statement

Current or noncurrent assets		Other items	
Investments in marketable securities	$78,000	Investment income	$4,000
($80,000 cost − $2,000 allowance)			
Owners' equity			
Accumulated other comprehensive income:			
Unrealized loss on investments	(2,000)		

Demonstration Case C

On January 1, 2010, Connaught Company purchased 40 percent of the outstanding voting shares of London Company on the open market for $85,000 cash. London declared $10,000 in cash dividends on December 1, 2010, and reported net income of $60,000 for the year on December 31, 2010.

Required:

1.   Prepare the journal entries for 2010.
2.   What accounts and amounts were reported on Connaught's balance sheet at the end of 2010 and on Connaught's income statement for 2010?

Suggested Solution for Case C

1.

Jan. 1	Investments in Affiliates (+A)	85,000	
	Cash (−A)		85,000
Dec. 1	Cash (+A) (40% × $10,000)	4,000	
	Investments in Affiliates (−A)		4,000
Dec. 31	Investments in Affiliates (+A) (40% × $60,000)	24,000	
	Equity in Investee Earnings (+R, +OE)		24,000

2.   On the balance sheet   On the income statement

Noncurrent assets		Other items	
Investments in affiliates	$105,000	Equity in investee earnings	$24,000
$ 85,000 cost			
− 4,000 dividends			
+ 24,000 percentage of investee's net income			
$105,000 balance in Investments account			

Chapter Summary

LO1 Explain why companies invest in debt and stock securities. p. 642

- Businesses that receive large amounts of cash invest in the debt and stock securities of other companies to generate earnings.
- Companies with seasonal businesses that have extra cash on hand at the end of the busy season may invest in the stocks and bonds of other companies to earn a return on idle funds.
- Companies with a growth strategy may acquire the stock of other companies to significantly influence their financial and operating policies or to actually control their activities

LO2 Identify investment types and the related accounting methods. p. 643

- **Passive investments in debt and equity securities**
  - Debt securities that are accounted for and reported as
    - Held-to-maturity investments, accounted for under the cost method or
    - Investments not intended to be held to maturity, accounted for under the market value method.
  - Equity securities (stock) amounting to less than 20 percent of the outstanding voting stock of another company, accounted for and reported under the market value method.
- **Investments in stock for significant influence**
  - Investments that amount to 20 to 50 percent of the outstanding voting stock of another company are presumed to result in significant influence over the other company. These investments are accounted for and reported under the equity method.
- **Investments in stock for control**
  - Investments that amount to more than 50 percent of the outstanding voting stock of another company result in control over that company. These investments are combined with the parent company in consolidated financial statements.

LO3 Analyze and report bond investments held to maturity. p. 644

- **Debt investments held to maturity: Amortized cost**
  - When management intends to hold a bond investment until it matures, the bond is recorded at **cost** when acquired and at amortized cost on the balance sheet. Any interest earned during the period is reported on the income statement.

LO4 Analyze and report passive investments in securities using the market value method. p. 646

- **Securities available for sale: Market value method**
  - Depending on management's intent, passive investments may be classified as either
    - Trading securities (those that are actively traded to maximize their return) or
    - Securities available for sale (those that earn a return but are not as actively traded). Most companies classify investments as available for sale.
  - Debt securities that are not intended to be held to maturity and passive stock investments are recorded at cost and adjusted to market value at year-end. A valuation allowance is increased or decreased to arrive at the market value. The resulting unrealized holding gain or loss is recorded
    - For trading securities, in net income.
    - For securities available for sale, as a component of stockholders' equity in Accumulated Other Comprehensive Income.
  - Any dividends or interest earned are reported in the Other Items section of the income statement along with any gains or losses on sales of passive investments.
- **Comparing available-for-sale and trading securities**
  - Trading securities are always classified as current assets.
  - Accounting for trading securities is almost identical to accounting for securities available for sale. The primary difference is that any unrealized holding gains or losses are reported directly on the income statement.

LO5 Analyze and report investments involving significant influence using the equity method. p. 654

- **Investments for significant influence: Equity method**
  - Under the equity method, the investor records an investment at cost on the acquisition date. Each period after that, the investment's value is increased (or decreased) by the investor's percentage share of the investee's reported net income (or loss) and decreased by the investor's percentage share of the dividends declared by the investee. Each period, the investor recognizes as revenue its share of the net income (or loss) reported by the investee.
  - Equity in the investee's earnings or losses (that is, the investor's percentage share of the investee's net income or loss for the period) is reported in the Other Items section of the income statement along with any gains or losses on the sale of investments.

LO6 Explain the reporting of investments in controlling interests. p. 658

- **Investments with controlling interest: Consolidated statements**

    - A company acquires control of another company by purchasing more than 50 percent of the acquired company's outstanding voting shares. Often acquisitions are made to achieve vertical integration (with a different level in the distribution channel), horizontal growth (on the same level of the distribution channel), or synergy (more efficient operations, which increase profitability).

    - Mergers occur when one company purchases all net assets of another and the acquired company ceases to exist as a separate legal entity. When the acquired company remains in business, the purchaser is the parent company and the acquired company is the subsidiary.

    - The concept of consolidation is based on the view that a parent company and its subsidiaries constitute a single economic entity. Therefore, their separate income statements, balance sheets, and statements of cash flows should be combined each period on an item-by-item basis to form a single set of consolidated financial statements.

LO7 Analyze and interpret the return on assets ratio. p. 660

- **Return on assets (ROA)**

    - The return on assets ratio is computed by dividing net income by average total assets. This ratio measures how much income a company earned with each dollar of assets. It provides information on both a company's profitability and management's effectiveness in using assets. An increasing ratio suggests increased managerial efficiency.

Accounting Decision Tools		
Name of Measure	**Formula**	**What It Tells You**
Return on assets (ROA)	$\dfrac{\text{Net Income*}}{\text{Average Total Assets}^{\dagger}} \times 100$	• The percentage of income earned on each dollar invested in assets • The higher the ratio, the more effectively managers are using total assets

*In more complicated analyses, interest expense (net of tax) and minority interest are added back to net income because the measure assesses return on assets independent of their source.

†Average Total Assets = (Beginning Total Assets + Ending Total Assets) ÷ 2

Key Terms

Active Investments (p. 643)

Amortized Cost (p. 644)

Consolidated Financial Statements (p. 659)

Equity Method (p. 654)

Investments Held to Maturity (p. 644)

Investments for Significant Influence (p. 654)

Market Value Method (p. 646)

Merger (p. 659)

Parent Company (p. 659)

Passive Investments (p. 643)

Return on Assets (ROA) (p. 660)

Securities Available for Sale (p. 646)

Subsidiary Company (p. 659)

Trading Securities (p. 646)

Unrealized Holding Gains or Losses (p. 648)

See complete glossary in the back of text.

Questions

1. Explain the difference between a short-term investment and a long-term investment.

2. Why do companies invest in debt and stock securities?

3. What are
   a. Passive investments?
   b. Investments for significant influence?
   c. Investments for control?

4. What are the accounting methods used for passive investments, investments in which the investor can exert significant influence, and investments in which the investor has control over another entity?

5. Explain how to report bonds held to maturity on the balance sheet.

6. What are trading securities? How are they reported on the balance sheet, and how is income determined and reported on the income statement?

7. What are securities available for sale? How are they reported on the balance sheet, and how is income determined and reported on the income statement?

8. Under the market value method, when and how does the investor company measure investment revenue?

9. Under the equity method, why does the investor company measure revenue on a proportionate basis when the investee company reports income rather than when dividends are declared?

10. Under the equity method, dividends received from the investee company are not recorded as revenue. To record dividends as revenue involves double counting. Explain.

11. What is a parent–subsidiary relationship?

12. Explain the basic concept underlying consolidated statements.

Multiple Choice

1. Company A owns 40 percent of Company B and exercises significant influence over Company B management. Therefore, Company A uses what method of accounting for and reporting its ownership of stock in Company B?

   Quiz 15-1
   www.mhhe.com/LLPW1e

   a. Amortized cost method.
   b. Market-value method.
   c. Equity method.
   d. Consolidation of the financial statements of companies A and B.

2. Company A purchases 10 percent of Company X and intends to hold the stock for at least five years. At the end of the current year, how would Company A report on its December 31 (year-end) balance sheet its investment in Company X?

   a. At original cost in the Current Assets section.
   b. At the December 31 market value in the Current Assets section.
   c. At original cost in the Long-Term Assets section.
   d. At the December 31 market value in the Long-Term Assets section.

3. Dividends received from a stock that is reported as a security available for sale in the Long-Term Assets section of the balance sheet are reported as which of the following?

   a. Increase to cash and a decrease to the Investment in Marketable Securities account.
   b. Increase to cash and an unrealized gain on the balance sheet.
   c. Increase to cash and an increase to revenue.
   d. Increase to cash and an unrealized gain on the income statement.

4. Realized gains and losses are recorded on the income statement for which of the following transactions in Trading Securities and Securities Available for Sale?

   a. When adjusting a trading security to its market value.
   b. When adjusting a security available for sale to its market value.
   c. Only when recording the sale of a trading security.
   d. When recording the sale of either a trading security or an available-for-sale security.

5. When recording dividends received from a stock investment accounted for using the equity method, which of the following statements is true?

   a. Total assets are increased and net income is increased.
   b. Total assets are increased and total owners' equity is increased.

c. Total assets are decreased and total owners' equity is decreased.
   d. Total assets and total owners' equity do not change.

6. When using the equity method, when is revenue recorded on the books of the investor company?

   a. When the market value of the investee stock increases.
   b. When a dividend is received from the investee.
   c. When the investee company reports net income.
   d. Both (b) and (c).

7. Kelly Company acquired 500 shares of stock of Drucker Company at $60 per share as a long-term investment. This represents 10 percent of the outstanding voting shares of Drucker. During the year, Drucker paid stockholders $2 per share in dividends. At year-end, Drucker reported net income of $40,000. Drucker's stock price at year-end was $63 per share. The amount of investments reported on the balance sheet at year-end and the amount reported on the income statement for the year would be:

	Balance Sheet	Income Statement
a.	$31,500	$1,000
b.	$30,000	$1,000
c.	$33,000	$4,000
d.	$31,500	$4,000

8. Kelly Company acquired 500 shares of stock of Drucker Company at $60 per share as a long-term investment. This represents 40 percent of the outstanding voting shares of Drucker. During the year, Drucker paid stockholders $2 per share in dividends. At year-end, Drucker reported net income of $40,000. Drucker's stock price at year-end was $63 per share. The amount of investments reported on the balance sheet at year-end and the amount reported on the income statement for the year would be:

	Balance Sheet	Income Statement
a.	$31,500	$ 1,000
b.	$45,000	$16,000
c.	$31,000	$ 0
d.	$31,500	$16,000

9. Consolidated financial statements are required in which of the following situations?

   a. Only when a company can exert significant influence over another company.
   b. Only when a company acquires another company for more than it is valued.

c.   Only when a parent company can exercise control over its subsidiary.

d.   Only when a company acquires another company for passive investment.

10. Which of the following is true regarding the use of the return on assets ratio?

a.   Evaluates the efficiency of a company given the capital contributed by owners.

b.   Evaluates the financing strategy of a company.

c.   Evaluates the profit generated for every dollar of sales.

d.   Evaluates how efficiently a company uses its total assets to earn income.

Solutions to Multiple-Choice Questions

1. c   2. d   3. c   4. d   5. d   6. c   7. a   8. b   9. c   10. d

---

Mini Exercises

Available with McGraw-Hill's Homework Manager

M15-1 Matching Measurement and Reporting Methods

LO2

Match the following. Answers may be used more than once.

Measurement Method

A. Market value method

B. Equity method

C. Consolidation

D. Amortized cost

1. _____ More than 50 percent ownership

2. _____ Bonds held to maturity

3. _____ Less than 20 percent ownership

4. _____ At least 20 but not more than 50 percent ownership

5. _____ Current market value

6. _____ Original cost less any amortization of premium or discount associated with the purchase

7. _____ Original cost plus proportionate part of the income of the investee less proportionate part of the dividends declared by investee

M15-2 Recording a Bond Investment

LO3

Wall Company purchased $1,000,000, 8 percent bonds issued by Janice Company on January 1, 2010. The purchase price of the bonds was $1,070,000. Management plans and has the ability to hold bonds until their maturity date. Interest is payable semiannually each June 30 and December 31. Record the purchase of the bonds on January 1, 2010.

M15-3 Recording Trading Securities Transactions

LO4

During 2009, Princeton Company acquired some of the 50,000 outstanding shares of the common stock, par $10, of Cox Corporation as trading securities. The accounting period for both companies ends December 31. Give the journal entries for each of the following transactions that occurred during 2009:

July   2   Purchased 8,000 shares of Cox common stock at $28 per share.

Dec. 15   Recorded receipt of Cox Corporation's cash dividends of $2 per share.

    31   Determined the current market price of Cox stock to be $25 per share.

M15-4 Recording Available-for-Sale Securities Transactions

LO4

Using the data in M15-3, assume Princeton Company purchased the voting stock of Cox Corporation for the available-for-sale portfolio instead of the trading securities portfolio. Give the journal entries for each of the transactions listed.

M15-5 Determining Financial Statement Effects of Trading Securities Transactions

LO4

Using the information in M15-3, indicate in the following table the effects and amounts of each transaction listed. Use + for increase, − for decrease, and NE for no effect.

	BALANCE SHEET			INCOME STATEMENT		
Transaction	Assets	Liabilities	Owners' Equity	Revenues/ Gains	Expenses/ Losses	Net Income
July 2						
Dec. 15						
Dec. 31						

LO4

M15-6 Determining Financial Statement Effects of Available-for-Sale Securities Transactions

Using the information in M15-4, indicate in the following table the effects and amounts of each transaction listed. Use + for increase, − for decrease, and NE for no effect.

	BALANCE SHEET			INCOME STATEMENT		
Transaction	Assets	Liabilities	Owners' Equity	Revenues/ Gains	Expenses/ Losses	Net Income
July 2						
Dec. 15						
Dec. 31						

LO5

M15-7 Recording Equity Method Securities Transactions

On January 1, 2011, Ubuy.com acquired 25 percent (10,000 shares) of the common stock of E-Net Corporation. The accounting period for both companies ends December 31. Give the journal entries for each of the following transactions that occurred during 2011:

July   2   E-Net declared and paid a cash dividend of $3 per share.

Dec. 31   E-Net reported net income of $200,000.

LO5

M15-8 Determining Financial Statement Effects of Equity Method Securities

Using the information in M15-7, indicate in the following table the effects and amounts of each transaction listed. Use + for increase, − for decrease, and NE for no effect.

	BALANCE SHEET			INCOME STATEMENT		
Transaction	Assets	Liabilities	Owners' Equity	Revenues/ Gains	Expenses/ Losses	Net Income
July 2						
Dec. 31						

LO7

M15-9 Computing and Interpreting Return on Assets Ratio

M.A.D. Company reported the following information at the end of each year:

Year	Net Income	Total Assets
2008	$152,000	$ 52,000
2009	195,000	68,000
2010	201,000	134,000
2011	212,000	145,000

Compute return on assets for 2009, 2010, and 2011. What do the results suggest about M.A.D. Company?

Exercises   Available with McGraw-Hill's Homework Manager

LO3

Macy's, Inc.

E15-1 Explaining Investing Decisions and Recording Bonds Held to Maturity

Macy's, Inc. (formerly Federated Department Stores, Inc.) operates more than 880 department and furniture stores under the names of Macy's and Bloomingdales. The company does more than $20 billion in sales each year.

Assume that as part of its cash management strategy, Macy's purchased $10 million in bonds at par for cash on July 1, 2009. The bonds pay 10 percent annual interest each June 30 and December 31 and mature in 10 years. Macy's plans to hold the bonds until maturity.

Required:

1. Record the purchase of the bonds on July 1, 2009.
2. Record the receipt of interest on December 31, 2009.

E15-2 Comparing Market Value and Equity Methods

LO4, 5

Company A purchased a certain number of Company B's outstanding voting shares at $19 per share as a long-term investment. Company B had outstanding 20,000 shares of $10 par value stock.

Required:

Complete the following matrix relating to the measurement and reporting by Company A after the acquisition of the shares of Company B stock.

	Market Value Method	Equity Method
1. What is the applicable level of ownership by Company A of Company B to apply the method?	_____ %	_____ %
For 2, 3, 6, 7, and 8, assume the following:		
Number of shares acquired of Company B stock	1,000	5,000
Net income reported by Company B in the first year	$50,000	$50,000
Dividends declared by Company B in the first year	$10,000	$10,000
Market price at end of the first year, Company B stock	$ 15	$ 15
2. What is the percentage ownership of Company B by Company A?		
3. At acquisition, the investment account on the books of Company A should be debited at what amount?		
4. When should Company A recognize revenue earned on the stock of Company B? Explanation required.		
5. After the acquisition date, how should Company A change the balance of the investment account net of the allowance with respect to the stock owned in Company B (other than for disposal of the investment)? Explanation required.		
6. What is the net amount of investment reported on the balance sheet of Company A at the end of the first year?		
7. What amount of revenue from the investment in Company B should Company A report at the end of the first year?		
8. What amount of unrealized loss should Company A report at the end of the first year?		

E15-3 Recording Transactions in the Trading Securities Portfolio

LO4

On June 30, 2009, MetroMedia, Inc., purchased 10,000 shares of Mitek stock for $20 per share. Management purchased the stock for speculative purposes and recorded the stock in the trading securities portfolio. The following information pertains to the price per share of Mitek stock:

	Price
12/31/2009	$24
12/31/2010	31
12/31/2011	25

MetroMedia sold all of the Mitek stock on February 14, 2012, at a price of $22 per share. Prepare any journal entries that are required by the facts presented in this case.

E15-4 Recording Transactions in the Available-for-Sale Portfolio

LO4

Using the data in E15-3, assume MetroMedia's management purchased the Mitek stock for the available-for-sale portfolio instead of the trading securities portfolio. Prepare any journal entries required by the facts presented in the case.

E15-5 Recording Transactions in the Trading Securities Portfolio

LO4

On March 10, 2009, General Solutions, Inc., purchased 5,000 shares of MicroTech stock for $50 per share. Management purchased the stock for speculative purposes and recorded it in the trading securities portfolio. The following information pertains to the price per share of MicroTech stock:

	Price
12/31/2009	$55
12/31/2010	40
12/31/2011	42

General Solutions sold all of the MicroTech stock on September 12, 2012, at a price of $39 per share. Prepare any journal entries required by the facts presented in this case.

LO4

E15-6 Recording Transactions in the Available-for-Sale Portfolio

Using the data in E15-5, assume General Solutions' management purchased the MicroTech stock for the available-for-sale portfolio instead of the trading securities portfolio. Prepare any journal entries required by the facts presented in the case.

LO5

E15-7 Recording and Reporting an Equity Method Investment

Felicia Company acquired some of the 60,000 shares of outstanding common stock (no par) of Nueces Corporation during 2010 as a long-term investment. The annual accounting period for both companies ends December 31. The following transactions occurred during 2010:

Jan. 10 Purchased 21,000 shares of Nueces common stock at $12 per share.
Dec. 31 *a.* Received the 2010 financial statements of Nueces Corporation that reported net income of $90,000.
  b. Nueces Corporation declared and paid a cash dividend of $0.60 per share.
  c. Determined the market price of Nueces stock to be $11 per share.

Required:

1. What accounting method should the company use? Why?
2. Give the journal entries for each of these transactions. If no entry is required, explain why.
3. Show how the long-term investment and the related revenue should be reported in the 2010 financial statements of the company.

LO6

The Colgate-Palmolive Company

E15-8 Determining the Appropriate Accounting Treatment for an Acquisition

The notes of Colgate-Palmolive's recent financial statements contained the following information:

Note 3

Acquisitions

On May 1, 2006, the Company completed the purchase of 84% of the outstanding shares of Tom's of Maine, Inc., for approximately $100 plus transaction costs. Tom's of Maine gives Colgate the opportunity to enter the fast-growing health and specialty trade channel where Tom's of Maine toothpaste and deodorant are market leaders.

How would Colgate-Palmolive report the acquisition? Explain why.

LO7

Timberland ®

E15-9 Analyzing and Interpreting the Return on Assets Ratio

The Timberland Company is a leading designer of shoes and clothing. In a recent year, it reported the following (in thousands of dollars):

	Current Year	Prior Year
Revenue	$1,567,619	$1,565,681
Net income	106,432	164,624
Total assets	843,105	788,654
Total stockholders' equity	560,817	528,187

Required:

1. Determine the return on assets ratio for the current year.
2. Explain the meaning of the ratio.
3. The footwear industry ratio is 16.4 percent. What do your results for Timberland suggest about the company?

Problems—Set A Available with McGraw-Hill's Homework Manager

PA15-1 Determining Financial Statement Effects for Bonds Held to Maturity

Starbucks is a rapidly expanding company that provides high-quality coffee products. Assume as part of its expansion strategy, Starbucks plans to open numerous new stores in Mexico in five years. The company has $5 million to support the expansion and has decided to invest the funds in corporate bonds until the money is needed. Assume Starbucks purchased bonds with $5 million face value at par for cash on July 1, 2010. The bonds pay 8 percent interest each June 30 and December 31 and mature in five years. Starbucks plans to hold the bonds until maturity.

LO3

Starbucks Corporation

Required:

1. What accounts are affected when the bonds are purchased on July 1, 2010?
2. What accounts are affected when interest is received on December 31, 2010?
3. Should Starbucks prepare a journal entry if the market value of the bonds decreased to $4,000,000 on December 31, 2010? Explain.

PA15-2 Recording Passive Investments

On March 1, 2009, HiTech Industries purchased 10,000 shares of Integrated Services Company for $20 per share. The following information applies to the stock price of Integrated Services:

LO4

www.mhhe.com/LLPW1e

	Price
12/31/2009	$17
12/31/2010	24
12/31/2011	31

Required:

1. Prepare journal entries to record the facts in the case assuming HiTech purchased the shares for the trading portfolio.
2. Prepare journal entries to record the facts in the case assuming HiTech purchased the shares for the available-for-sale portfolio.

PA15-3 Reporting Passive Investments

During January 2010, Nash Glass Company purchased the following shares as a long-term investment:

LO4

Stock	Number of Shares Outstanding	Purchase	Cost per Share
Q Corporation Common (no par)	90,000	12,600	$ 5
R Corporation Preferred, nonvoting (par $10)	20,000	12,000	30

Subsequent to acquisition, the following data were available:

	2010	2011
Net income reported at December 31		
Q Corporation	$30,000	$36,000
R Corporation	40,000	48,000
Dividends declared and paid per share during the year		
Q Corporation common stock	$ 0.85	$ 0.90
R Corporation preferred stock	1.00	1.10
Market value per share at December 31		
Q Corporation common stock	$ 4.00	$ 4.00
R Corporation preferred stock	29.00	31.00

Required:

1. What accounting method should the company use for the investment in Q Corporation common stock? In R Corporation preferred stock? Why?
2. Give the journal entries for the company for each year in parallel columns (if none, explain why) for each of the following:
   a. Purchase of the investments.
   b. Income reported by Q and R corporations.

    c. Dividends received from Q and R corporations.

    d. Market value effects at year-end.

3. For each year, show how the following items and their balances should be reported on the financial statements:

    a. Long-term investments.

    b. Owners' equity—unrealized gains and losses.

    c. Revenues.

LO4, 5

www.mhhe.com/LLPW1e

PA15-4 Recording Passive Investments and Investments for Significant Influence

On August 4, 2009, Coffman Corporation purchased 1,000 shares of Dittman Company for $45,000. The following information applies to the stock price of Dittman Company:

	Price
12/31/2009	$52
12/31/2010	47
12/31/2011	38

Dittman Company declares and pays cash dividends of $2 per share on June 1 of each year.

Required:

1. Prepare journal entries to record the facts in the case assuming Coffman purchased the shares for the trading portfolio.

2. Prepare journal entries to record the facts in the case assuming Coffman purchased the shares for the available-for-sale portfolio.

3. Prepare journal entries to record the facts in the case assuming Coffman used the equity method to account for the investment. Coffman owns 30 percent of Dittman and Dittman reported $50,000 in income each year.

LO4, 5

PA15-5 Comparing Methods to Account for Various Levels of Ownership of Voting Stock

Company Chi had outstanding 30,000 shares of common stock, par value $10 per share. On January 1, 2009, Company Delta purchased some of these shares as a long-term investment at $25 per share. At the end of 2009, Company Chi reported the following: income, $50,000, and cash dividends declared and paid during the year, $25,500. The market value of Company Chi stock at the end of 2009 was $22 per share.

Required:

1. For each of the following cases (in the tabulation), identify the method of accounting that Company Delta should use. Explain why.

2. Give the journal entries for Company Delta at the dates indicated for each of the two independent cases, assuming that the investments will be held long term. If no entry is required, explain why. Use the following format:

Tabulation of Items	Case A: 3,600 Shares Purchased	Case B: 10,500 Shares Purchased

    1. Accounting method?

    2. Journal entries:

        a. To record the acquisition at January 1, 2009.

        b. To recognize the income reported by Company Chi for 2009.

        c. To recognize the dividends declared and paid by Company Chi.

        d. To recognize the market value effect at the end of 2009.

3. Complete the following schedule to show the separate amounts that should be reported on the 2009 financial statements of Company Delta:

DOLLAR AMOUNTS

	Case A	Case B

Balance sheet
   Investments
   Owners' equity
Income statement
   Investment income
   Equity in investee earnings

4.   Explain why assets, owners' equity, and revenues for the two cases are different.

PA15-6 Comparing the Market Value and Equity Methods

Ship Corporation had outstanding 100,000 shares of no-par common stock. On January 10, 2011, Shore Company purchased a block of these shares in the open market at $20 per share for long-term investment purposes. At the end of 2011, Ship reported net income of $300,000 and cash dividends of $.60 per share. At December 31, 2011, Ship's stock was selling at $18 per share. This problem involves two separate cases:

   Case A: Purchase of 10,000 shares of Ship common stock.
   Case B: Purchase of 40,000 shares of Ship common stock.

LO4, 5, 6

www.mhhe.com/LLPW1e

Required:

1.   For each case, identify the accounting method that Shore Company should use. Explain why.
2.   For each case, in parallel columns, give the journal entries for each of the following (if no entry is required, explain why):
   a.   Acquisition.
   b.   Revenue recognition.
   c.   Dividends received.
   d.   Market value effects.
3.   For each case, show how the following should be reported on the 2011 financial statements:
   a.   Long-term investments.
   b.   Owners' equity.
   c.   Revenues.
4.   Explain why the amounts reported for the two cases in requirement 3 differ.
5.   Explain whether either of the two cases requires preparing consolidated financial statements? Why?

PA15-7 Comparing Methods for Sales of Securities

Using the data in PA15-6, assume that Shore Company management sold 10,000 shares of its investment in Ship Corporation stock on January 10, 2012, at $19 per share. This problem involves two separate cases.

LO4, 5

Required:

1.   For each case, what level of ownership did Shore Company have in Ship Corporation after the sale?
2.   For each case, what method should Shore Company use for its investment in Ship Corporation after the sale?
3.   For each case, give the journal entry for the sale of the investment and any entry needed on December 31, 2012.

PA15-8 Interpreting the Return on Assets Ratio

The Cheesecake Factory Incorporated operates more than 120 upscale casual dining restaurants. The following information was reported in the company's 10-K annual report dated January 2, 2007:

LO7

(in thousands)	2006	2005	2004	2003
Net income	$ 81,282	$ 87,948	$ 65,366	$ 55,585
Total assets	1,039,731	926,250	758,994	610,116

Required:

1.   Compute the return on assets ratio for 2006, 2005, and 2004.
2.   What do the results in requirement 1 suggest about The Cheesecake Factory?

Problems—Set B   **Available with McGraw-Hill's Homework Manager**

LO3

Sonic Corporation

PB15-1 Determining Financial Statement Effects for Bonds Held to Maturity

Sonic Corporation operates and franchises a chain of quick-service drive-in restaurants in most of the United States and in Mexico. Customers drive up to a canopied parking space and order food through an intercom speaker system. A carhop then delivers the food to the customer. Assume Sonic has $10 million in cash to support future expansion and has decided to invest the funds in corporate bonds until the money is needed. Sonic purchases bonds with a face value of $10 million for $10.3 million cash on January 1, 2011. The bonds pay 8 percent interest each June 30 and December 31 and mature in four years. Sonic plans to hold the bonds until maturity.

Required:

1. What accounts were affected when the bonds were purchased on January 1, 2011?
2. What accounts were affected when interest was received on June 30, 2011?
3. Should Sonic prepare a journal entry if the market value of the bonds decreased to $9,700,000 on December 31, 2011? Explain.

LO4

PB15-2 Recording Passive Investments

On September 15, 2010, James Media Corporation purchased 5,000 shares of Community Broadcasting Company for $32 per share. The following information applies to the stock price of Community Broadcasting:

	Price
12/31/2010	$34
12/31/2011	25
12/31/2012	21

Required:

1. Prepare journal entries to record the facts in the case assuming James Media purchased the shares for the trading portfolio.
2. Prepare journal entries to record the facts in the case assuming James Media purchased the shares for the available-for-sale portfolio.

LO4

PB15-3 Reporting Passive Investments

During January 2009, Stevie's Bike Shop purchased the following shares as a long-term investment:

Stock	Number of Shares Outstanding	Purchase	Cost per Share
Chrome Corporation Common (no par)	100,000	15,000	$ 25
Leather Company Preferred, nonvoting (par $10)	30,000	20,000	10

Subsequent to acquisition, the following data were available:

	2009	2010
Net income reported at December 31		
Chrome Corporation	$60,000	$72,000
Leather Company	80,000	96,000
Dividends declared and paid per share during the year		
Chrome Corporation common stock	$ 1.20	$ 1.00
Leather Company preferred stock	2.00	1.20
Market value per share at December 31		
Chrome Corporation common stock	$ 24.00	$ 24.00
Leather Company preferred stock	9.00	11.00

Required:

1. What accounting method should Stevie's Bike Shop use for the investment in Chrome Corporation common stock? In Leather Company preferred stock? Why?

2. Give the journal entries for Stevie's Bike Shop for each year in parallel columns (if none, explain why) for each of the following:
    a. Purchase of the investments.
    b. Income reported by Chrome Corporation and Leather Company.
    c. Dividends received from Chrome Corporation and Leather Company.
    d. Market value effects at year-end.

3. For each year, show how the following amounts should be reported on the financial statements:
    a. Long-term investments.
    b. Owners' equity—unrealized gain/loss.
    c. Revenues.

PB15-4 Recording Passive Investments and Investments for Significant Influence

LO4, 5

On March 1, 2010, St. Denis Corporation purchased 10,000 shares of Carey Company for $520,000. The following information applies to the stock price of Carey Company:

	Price
12/31/2010	$54
12/31/2011	49
12/31/2012	40

Carey Company declares and pays cash dividends of $1.50 per share on June 1 of each year.

Required:

1. Prepare journal entries to record the facts in the case assuming St. Denis purchased the shares for the trading portfolio.

2. Prepare journal entries to record the facts in the case assuming St. Denis purchased the shares for the available-for-sale portfolio.

3. Prepare journal entries to record the facts in the case assuming St. Denis used the equity method to account for the investment. St. Denis owns 30 percent of Carey and Carey reported $150,000 in income each year.

PB15-5 Comparing Methods to Account for Various Levels of Ownership of Voting Stock

LO4, 5

Zeta Company had outstanding 100,000 shares of common stock, par-value $5 per share. On January 1, 2010, Beta Company purchased some of these shares as a long-term investment at $15 per share. At the end of 2010, Zeta Company reported the following: income, $100,000, and cash dividends declared and paid during the year, $2,500. The market value of Zeta Company stock at the end of 2010 was $12 per share.

Required:

1. For each of the following cases (in the tabulation), identify the method of accounting that Beta Company should use. Explain why.

2. Give the journal entries for Beta Company at the dates indicated for each of the two independent cases assuming the investments will be held long term. If no entry is required, explain why. Use the following format:

Tabulation of Items	Case A: 4,000 Shares Purchased	Case B: 40,000 Shares Purchased

1. Accounting method?
2. Journal entries:
   a. To record the acquisition at January 1, 2010.
   b. To recognize the income reported by Zeta Company for 2010.
   c. To recognize the dividends declared and paid by Zeta Company.
   d. To recognize the market value effect at the end of 2010.

3. Complete the following schedule to show the separate amounts that should be reported on the 2010 financial statements of Beta Company:

	DOLLAR AMOUNTS	
	Case A	Case B
Balance sheet		
Investments		
Owners' equity		
Income statement		
Investment income		
Equity in investee earnings		

4. Explain why assets, owners' equity, and revenues for the two cases are different.

LO4, 5, 6

PB15-6 Comparing the Market Value and Equity Methods

Boston Corporation had outstanding 200,000 shares of common stock. On October 1, 2009, Packer Company purchased a block of these shares in the open market at $15 per share for long-term investment purposes. At the end of 2009, Boston reported net income of $560,000 and cash dividends of $1.20 per share. At December 31, 2009, Boston's stock was selling at $17 per share. This problem involves two separate cases:

Case A: Purchase of 30,000 shares of Boston common stock.
Case B: Purchase of 80,000 shares of Boston common stock.

Required:

1. For each case, identify the accounting method that Packer Company should use. Explain why.
2. For each case, in parallel columns, give the journal entries for each of the following (if no entry is required, explain why).
   a. Acquisition.
   b. Revenue recognition.
   c. Dividends received.
   d. Market value effects.
3. For each case, show how the following should be reported on the 2009 financial statements:
   a. Long-term investments.
   b. Owners' equity.
   c. Revenues.
4. Explain why the amounts reported for the two cases in requirement 3 are different.
5. Explain whether either of the two cases requires preparing consolidated financial statements? Why?

LO4, 5

PB15-7 Comparing Methods for Sales of Securities

Using the data in PB15–6, assume that Packer Company's management sold 20,000 shares of its investment in Boston Corporation stock on January 10, 2010, at $16 per share. This problem involves two separate cases.

Required:

1. For each case, what level of ownership did Packer Company have in Boston Corporation after the sale?
2. For each case, what method should Packer Company use for its investment in Boston Corporation after the sale?
3. For each case, give the journal entry for the sale of the investment and any entry needed on December 31, 2010.

LO7

Marriott
International, Inc.

PB15-8 Interpreting the Return on Assets Ratio

Marriott International, Inc., is a global leader in the hospitality industry operating or franchising more than 2,800 lodging units and 2,000 furnished corporate housing units around the world. The following information was reported in the company's 2006 annual report (in millions of dollars):

(in millions)	2006	2005	2004	2003
Net income	$ 608	$ 669	$ 596	$ 502
Total assets	8,588	8,530	8,668	8,117

Required:

1. Compute the return on assets ratio for 2006, 2005, and 2004.
2. What do the results in requirement 1 suggest about Marriott?

Cases and Projects

CP15-1 Finding Financial Information

Refer to the financial statements of The Home Depot in Appendix A at the end of this book, or download the annual report from the *Cases* section of the text's Web site at www.mhhe.com/LLPW1e.

LO4, 5, 6

Required:

1. What was the balance in short-term investments reported by the company on February 3, 2008?
2. How much cash did the company realize from investments that matured or were sold during the year ended February 3, 2008?
3. What companies did The Home Depot acquire in 2007? What was the total purchase price of these acquisitions for the year?

CP15-2 Comparing Financial Information

Refer to the financial statements of The Home Depot in Appendix A and Lowe's in Appendix B at the end of this book, or download the annual reports from the *Cases* section of the text's Web site at www.mhhe.com/LLPW1e.

LO4, 5, 6, 7

Lowe's

Required:

1. What was the balance in short-term investments reported by Lowe's on February 1, 2008? By The Home Depot on February 3, 2008? What types of securities were included in short-term investments for each company?
2. Compute the net profit margin, total asset turnover, and return on assets ratios for both The Home Depot and Lowe's for the current year. Which company provided the higher return on its total investments during the current year?
3. Was the difference in ROA due primarily to profitability or efficiency differences? How did you know?

CP15-3 Examining an Annual Report: Internet-Based Team Research Project

As a team, select an industry to analyze. Using your Web browser, each team member should acquire the annual report or 10-K for one publicly traded company in the industry with each member selecting a different company.

LO2, 3, 4, 5, 6, 7

Required:

1. On an individual basis, each team member should write a short report that answers the following questions:

    a. Determine whether the company prepared consolidated financial statements. How do you know?

    b. Does the company use the equity method for any of its investments?

    c. Does the company hold any investments in securities? If so, what is their market value? Does the company have any unrealized gains or losses?

    d. Identify the company's lines of business. Why does management want to engage in these business activities?

    e. Compute the return on assets ratio for the two most recent years reported. What do the results suggest about your company?

2. Discuss any patterns that you as a team observe. Then, as a team, write a short report comparing and contrasting your companies according to the preceding attributes. Provide potential explanations for any differences discovered.

LO1

CP15-4 Evaluating an Ethical Dilemma: Using Inside Information

Assume you are on the board of directors of a company that has decided to buy 80 percent of the outstanding stock of another company within the next three or four months. The discussions have convinced you that this company is an excellent investment opportunity, so you decide to buy $10,000 worth of the company's stock.

Required:

1. Is there an ethical problem with your decision?
2. Would your answer be different if you planned to invest $500,000?
3. Are there different ethical considerations if you do not buy the stock but recommend that your brother do so?

LO6

CP15-5 Evaluating an Acquisition from the Standpoint of a Financial Analyst

Assume you are a financial analyst for a large investment banking firm. You are responsible for analyzing companies in the retail sales industry. You have just learned that a large West Coast retailer has acquired a large East Coast retail chain for a price more than the net book value of the acquired company. You have reviewed the separate financial statements for the two companies before the announcement of the acquisition.

Required:

Write a brief report explaining what will happen when the financial results of the companies are consolidated as well as the impact on the return on assets ratio.

16 Reporting and Interpreting the Statement of Cash Flows

LEARNING OBJECTIVES

After completing this chapter, you should be able to:

LO1 Identify cash flows from operating, investing, and financing activities.

Lectured presentation–16-1
www.mhhe.com/LLPW1e

LO2 Report cash flows from operating activities using the indirect method.

LO3 Report cash flows from investing activities.

LO4 Report cash flows from financing activities.

LO5 Prepare and evaluate the statement of cash flows.

Focus Company: NAUTILUS INC.

"Helping People Achieve a Fit and Healthy Lifestyle Through Proper Exercise, Rest and Nutrition."

www.nautilusinc.com

Have you ever studied your bank statements to see how much money you bring in and pay out during a typical month? You do not have to be a financial genius to know that if you are spending more than you earn, your savings will quickly disappear, and you will need to get a loan or some other source of financing to see you through.

Most businesses face the same issues you do. In 2005, for example, Nautilus Inc.—maker of Stairmaster and Bowflex fitness equipment—reported a net cash outflow from day-to-day operating activities. To ensure the company's long-term survival, managers had to stay on top of this change in the cash situation. Fortunately, the company had saved a great deal of cash in prior years. Managers were also able to negotiate some new loans to keep the business from running out of cash. By 2006, the company was again experiencing a positive net cash inflow from operating activities.

Investors and creditors also monitor a company's cash inflows and outflows to predict whether they are likely to receive dividends and other amounts they are owed. They can find the information they need to make such predictions reported in the statement of cash flows, which is similar to your bank statement in that it reports changes in the company's cash situation. In this chapter, we will investigate how cash flows from operating, investing, and financing activities are classified and reported on the statement of cash flows. We also examine some of the tools investors and creditors use to evaluate the statement of cash flows.

CLASSIFICATIONS OF THE STATEMENT OF CASH FLOWS	**REPORTING CASH FLOWS FROM OPERATING ACTIVITIES—INDIRECT METHOD**	**REPORTING CASH FLOWS FROM INVESTING ACTIVITIES**	**REPORTING CASH FLOWS FROM FINANCING ACTIVITIES**	**PREPARING AND EVALUATING THE STATEMENT OF CASH FLOWS**
• The Relationship between Business Activities and Cash Flows • Cash Flows from Operating Activities • Cash Flows from Investing Activities • Cash Flows from Financing Activities • Net Increase (Decrease) in Cash • Relationships to the Balance Sheet and Income Statement	• Depreciation and Gains and Losses on Sale of Long-Term Assets • Changes in Current Assets and Current Liabilities	• Plant and Equipment • Land and Investments	• Long-Term Debt • Contributed Capital • Retained Earnings	• Format for the Statement of Cash Flows • Noncash Investing and Financing Activities • Supplemental Cash Flow Information • Free Cash Flow • Quality of Income Ratio

CLASSIFICATIONS OF THE STATEMENT OF CASH FLOWS

Learning Objective 1

Identify cash flows from operating, investing, and financing activities.

Video 16-1
www.mhhe.com/LLPW1e

To this point, we have analyzed business activities to identify their financial effects on assets, liabilities, owners' equity, revenues, and expenses. We have emphasized that business activities have financial effects even when they do not involve cash. That is why accrual accounting exists. When accurately reported, accrual-based net income is the best measure of whether a company has been profitable during the period.

Despite the importance of net income as a measure of profit, however, companies cannot use net income to pay wages, dividends, or loans. Because those activities require cash, financial statement users need information about the company's cash situation.

The Relationship between Business Activities and Cash Flows

Neither the balance sheet nor the income statement provides all of the needed information about the company's cash situation. Although the balance sheet shows a company's cash balance at a point in time, it does not indicate where the cash came from. Cash might have been generated by the company's day-to-day operations, by the sale of the company's buildings, or by the negotiation of new loans. What financial statement users really need is a report that identifies the activities that produced the amount of cash reported on the balance sheet.

Furthermore, the timing of cash receipts and payments may differ from the items shown on the income statement, which reports revenues when they are earned and expenses when they are incurred. Nautilus, for example, reported a hefty amount of net income in each quarter of 2006, yet its cash flows were negative in two of those four quarters. Such differences between net income and cash flows are the reason that GAAP requires every company to report a statement of cash flows.

The statement of cash flows shows each major type of business activity that caused a company's cash to increase or decrease during the accounting period. For the purposes of this statement, cash is defined to include cash and cash equivalents. As you have seen before, cash equivalents are short-term, highly liquid investments that are both (1) readily convertible to known amounts of cash and (2) so near to maturity that there is little risk their value will change. All of a company's cash inflows and outflows must be classified under operating, investing, or financing activities. Exhibit 16.1 shows the general form of the statement. Note that each category of activities can result in net cash inflows (represented by a positive number)

| Exhibit 16.1 | Categories in the Statement of Cash Flows |

> Net cash provided by (used for) operating activities
> ± Net cash provided by (used for) investing activities
> ± Net cash provided by (used for) financing activities
>
> Net increase (decrease) in cash and cash equivalents
> + Cash and cash equivalents at beginning of period
> Cash and cash equivalents at end of period

or net cash outflows (represented by a negative number in brackets). The sum of the three categories of cash flows explains the change in cash on the balance sheet for the period.

Cash Flows from Operating Activities

Cash flows from operating activities (or cash flows from operations) are the cash inflows and outflows related directly to the revenues and expenses reported on the income statement. Operating activities involve day-to-day business activities with customers, suppliers, employees, landlords, and others. Typical cash flows from operating activities include:

> **Coach's Tip**
>
> Remember that each category of activities can show a positive or negative net cash flow. Use parentheses ($XXX) to denote a negative cash flow.

Inflows	Outflows
Cash provided by	**Cash used for**
Customers	Purchase of goods for resale and services (electricity, etc.)
Dividends and interest on investments	Salaries and wages
	Income taxes
	Interest on liabilities

The difference between these cash inflows and outflows is reported on the statement of cash flows as a subtotal, Net Cash Provided by (Used for) Operating Activities.

The two different methods for presenting the operating activities in the cash flow statement are:

1. The direct method reports the total cash inflow or outflow from each major type of transaction (that is, transactions with customers, suppliers, etc.). The difference between those cash inflows and outflows equals the Net Cash Provided by (Used for) Operating Activities.

2. The indirect method starts with net income from the income statement and adjusts it by removing items that do not involve cash and adding items that do involve cash. Adjusting net income for these items yields the amount of Net Cash Provided by (Used for) Operating Activities.

> Net income
> ± Adjustments
> Net cash provided by (used for) operating activities

The point to remember about these two methods is that they are simply different ways to arrive at the same number. **Net cash flows provided by (used for) operating activities is the same under both methods.** Also, the choice between the two methods affects only the operating activities section of the statement of cash flows, not the investing and financing sections.

Each company's management is allowed to choose which method to use. Nearly 99 percent of large U.S. companies, including Nautilus, choose the indirect method.[1] For this reason, we

---

[1] American Institute of Certified Public Accountants, *Accounting Trends & Techniques* (New York: AICPA, 2006). Some people have speculated that the indirect method is preferred so overwhelmingly because the FASB requires that companies using the direct method also report a reconciliation of net income to cash flow. That reconciliation is identical to the indirect method.

examine the indirect method in detail within this chapter. We present the less commonly used direct method in Supplement 16A at the end of the chapter.

Cash Flows from Investing Activities

Cash flows from investing activities are the cash inflows and outflows related to the purchase and disposal of investments and long-lived assets. Typical cash flows from investing activities include:

Inflows	Outflows
Cash provided by	*Cash used for*
Sale or disposal of property, plant, and equipment	Purchase of property, plant, and equipment
Sale or maturity of investments in securities	Purchase of investments in securities

The difference between these cash inflows and outflows is reported on the statement of cash flows as a subtotal, Net Cash Provided by (Used for) Investing Activities.

Cash Flows from Financing Activities

Cash flows from financing activities include exchanges of cash with stockholders and cash exchanges with lenders (for principal on loans). Common cash flows from financing activities include:

Inflows	Outflows
Cash provided by	*Cash used for*
Borrowing from lenders through formal debt contracts	Repaying principal to lenders
Issuing stock to owners	Repurchasing stock from owners
	Paying dividends to owners

The difference between these cash inflows and outflows is reported on the statement of cash flows as a subtotal, Net Cash Provided by (Used for) Financing Activities.

Net Increase (Decrease) in Cash

Together, **the net cash flows from operating activities, investing activities, and financing activities must equal the net increase (decrease) in cash** for the period. For 2006, Nautilus reported a net decrease in cash of $1,000. That explains the change in cash on the company's balance sheet from the beginning balance of $8,000 to the ending balance of $7,000 (all amounts in $thousands):

Net cash provided by operating activities	$29,000
− Net cash used for investing activities	(11,000)
− Net cash used for financing activities	(19,000)
Net decrease in cash and cash equivalents	(1,000)
+ Cash and cash equivalents at beginning of period	8,000
Cash and cash equivalents at end of period	$ 7,000

In the next section, we examine Nautilus's statement of cash flows in more detail, including the way in which it relates to the balance sheet and income statement. Then we see how each section of the statement describes a set of important decisions made by Nautilus's management, and how financial analysts use those sections to evaluate the company's performance. But first, to make sure you understand how to classify cash flows, complete the following Self-Study Practice.

Brunswick Corporation produces the Life Fitness line of gym equipment, which competes head to head with Nautilus. A list of some of the company's cash flows follows. Indicate whether each item should be disclosed in the operating activities (O), investing activities (I), or financing activities (F) section of the statement of cash flows.

Brunswick Corporation

_____ 1. Stock issued to owners for cash

_____ 2. Collections from customers

_____ 3. Interest paid on debt

_____ 4. Purchase of equipment

_____ 5. Purchase of investment securities

_____ 6. Dividends paid to owners

After you have finished, check your answers with the solution at the bottom of the page.

Spotlight On ETHICS

Cash Is Not Estimated

Critics of accrual-based net income claim that it can be manipulated because it includes many estimated amounts (for bad debts, the market values of inventory, and assets' useful lives, for example). Because cash flows are not estimated, these critics claim the cash flows are not so easily manipulated. Indeed, a cash balance changes only when cash has been received or paid.

One particularly dramatic illustration of the subjectivity of net income compared to cash is the bankruptcy of a department store chain operated by W. T. Grant Company. Through biased estimates, the company reported net income for nine consecutive years and then shocked everyone by declaring bankruptcy and closing. At the time, GAAP did not require a statement of cash flows. Had this been required, it would have shown that the company's operations led to net cash outflows in 7 of the company's last 10 years.

Relationships to the Balance Sheet and Income Statement

One way to classify cash flows into operating, investing, and financing categories is to think about the balance sheet accounts to which the cash flows relate. Although exceptions exist, the general rule is that operating cash flows cause changes in current assets and current liabilities; investing cash flows affect long-lived assets; and financing cash flows affect noncurrent liabilities or owners' equity accounts.[2] See Exhibit 16.2 for the way this general rule relates the three sections of the statement of cash flows to the main sections of the classified balance sheet.

The statement of cash flows is intended to provide a cash-based view of a company's business activities during the accounting period. So, a company cannot prepare this statement directly from the ledger accounts because those amounts are based on accrual accounting. Instead, the company must analyze the numbers recorded under the accrual method and convert them to a cash basis. To prepare a statement of cash flows, you need the following:

1. **Comparative balance sheets**, showing beginning and ending balances for use in calculating the cash flows from all activities (operating, investing, and financing).

2. **A complete income statement** for use primarily in calculating cash flows from operating activities.

3. **Additional details** concerning selected accounts that increase and decrease as a result of investing and/or financing activities.

---

[2] Intermediate accounting discusses exceptions to this general rule in detail. They include investing activities that affect current assets (for example, short-term investments) and financing activities that affect current liabilities (for example, dividends payable and short-term notes payable).

1. F	4. I
2. O	5. I
3. O	6. F

Solution to Self-Study Practice

Exhibit 16.2   Relationships between Balance Sheet and Cash Flow Categories

Operating Activities Affect	
Current assets	Current liabilities
Investing Activities Affect Noncurrent assets	**Financing Activities Affect** Noncurrent liabilities Owners' equity

This approach to preparing the cash flow statement focuses on changes in the balance sheet accounts. It relies on a simple rearrangement of the balance sheet equation:

$$\text{Assets} = \text{Liabilities} + \text{Owners' Equity}$$

First, assets can be separated into cash and all other assets, which we call noncash assets:

$$\text{Cash} + \text{Noncash Assets} = \text{Liabilities} + \text{Owners' Equity}$$

If we move the noncash assets to the right side of the equation, we get

$$\text{Cash} = \text{Liabilities} + \text{Owners' Equity} - \text{Noncash Assets}$$

Given this relationship, the changes (Δ) in cash from the beginning to the end of the period must equal the changes (Δ) in the amounts on the right side of the equation from the beginning to the end of the period:

$$\Delta \text{ Cash} = \Delta \text{ Liabilities} + \Delta \text{ Owners' Equity} - \Delta \text{ Noncash Assets}$$

This equation says that **changes in cash must be accompanied by, and can be explained by, changes in liabilities, owners' equity, and noncash assets.** See Exhibit 16.3 for examples of this basic idea using selected cash transactions.

Before beginning to prepare the statement of cash flows, it is helpful to compute the change in each balance sheet account (that is, the ending balance minus the beginning

Exhibit 16.3   Effects of Cash Transactions on Other Balance Sheet Accounts

Category	Transaction	Cash Effect	Other Account Affected
Operating	Collect accounts receivable	+ Cash	− Accounts Receivable (A)
	Pay accounts payable	− Cash	− Accounts Payable (L)
	Prepay rent	− Cash	+ Prepaid Rent (A)
	Pay interest	− Cash	− Retained Earnings (OE)
	Sell goods/services for cash	+ Cash	+ Retained Earnings (OE)
Investing	Purchase equipment for cash	− Cash	+ Equipment (A)
	Sell investment securities for cash	+ Cash	− Investments (A)
Financing	Pay back debt to bank	− Cash	− Bank Loan Payable (L)
	Issue stock for cash	+ Cash	+ Contributed Capital (OE)

balance). The next step is to relate each account to operating (O), investing (I), or financing (F) activities by marking it with the appropriate letter. **Operating activities** typically affect the following accounts:

- **Current assets** are used up or converted into cash through the company's regular operating activities. For example, the sale of inventories creates accounts receivable, which are turned into cash when they are collected. When marking an O beside the current assets related to operating activities, you should exclude cash (because the change in cash is what you are trying to explain).
- **Current liabilities** such as accounts payable and accrued liabilities arise from the purchase of goods or services that are used in the company's operations. Mark these items with an O.
- **Accumulated Depreciation** is a contra-asset account that increases each period by the amount of depreciation expense and decreases when the asset is sold. Because depreciation expense affects net income, this account is related to operating activities.
- **Retained Earnings** increases each period by the amount of net income, which is the starting point for the operating activities section. It decreases when dividends are declared and paid (a financing activity). To show that this account relates to both operating and financing activities, mark it with an O and an F.

After classifying all accounts related to operating activities, you should relate other balance sheet accounts to investing (I) or financing (F) activities. **All remaining asset accounts will be related to investing (I) and all remaining liability and owners' equity accounts will be related to financing (F).**

In Exhibit 16.4, the left-hand column shows how to classify the balance sheet accounts for Nautilus. The right-hand column shows the changes in the account balances, which we use in the following sections.

REPORTING CASH FLOWS FROM OPERATING ACTIVITIES—INDIRECT METHOD

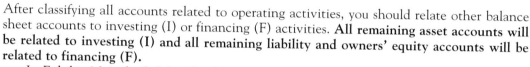

As we defined them earlier, operating cash flows are cash inflows and outflows that are directly related to the revenues and expenses reported on the income statement. These cash flows arise from transactions with customers, suppliers, employees, landlords, and others.

The indirect method begins with the creation of a schedule of operating activities in the following format:

> **Learning Objective 2**
> Report cash flows from operating activities using the indirect method.

Operating Activities
Net income
Add/Subtract to convert to cash basis
+ Depreciation expense
− Gain on sale of long-term assets
+ Loss on sale of long-term assets
+ Decreases in current assets
+ Increases in current liabilities
− Increases in current assets
− Decreases in current liabilities
Net cash flow from operating activities

As the format suggests, the conversion process begins with net income, which is taken from the bottom line of the company's income statement. The schedule for Nautilus is in Exhibit 16.5. Notice that the schedule begins with the $31,000 net income reported on the income statement in Exhibit 16.4.

Exhibit 16.4   Nautilus, Inc.: Comparative Balance Sheet and Current Income Statement   Nautilus

Nautilus, Inc.
Balance Sheet*
(in thousands)

Related Cash Flow Section		December 31, 2006	December 31, 2005	Change
Change in Cash	Assets			
	Current assets			
O	Cash and cash equivalents	$ 7,000	$ 8,000	−1,000
O	Accounts receivable	138,000	117,000	+21,000
O	Inventories	76,000	96,000	−20,000
O	Prepaid expenses	33,000	24,000	+9,000
	Total current assets	254,000	245,000	
I	Plant and equipment	219,000	203,000	+16,000
O	Less: Accumulated depreciation	(54,000)	(47,000)	−7,000
I	Land	10,000	12,000	−2,000
	Total assets	$429,000	$413,000	
	Liabilities and Stockholders' Equity			
	Current liabilities			
O	Accounts payable	$ 64,000	$ 61,000	+3,000
O	Accrued liabilities	38,000	37,000	+1,000
	Total current liabilities	102,000	98,000	
F	Long-term debt	67,000	63,000	+4,000
	Total liabilities	169,000	161,000	
	Stockholders' equity			
F	Contributed capital	5,000	4,000	+1,000
O, F	Retained earnings†	255,000	248,000	+7,000
	Total stockholders' equity	260,000	252,000	
	Total liabilities and stockholders' equity	$429,000	$413,000	

Nautilus, Inc.
Income Statement *
For the Year Ended December 31, 2006
(in thousands)

Net sales	$680,000
Cost of goods sold	382,000
Gross profit	298,000
Operating expenses	
Selling, general, and administrative expenses	250,000
Depreciation	7,000
Total operating expenses	257,000
Operating income	41,000
Gain on sale of land	3,000
Interest revenue (expense)	(1,000)
Net income before taxes	43,000
Income tax expense	12,000
Net income	$ 31,000

*Certain balances have been adjusted to simplify the presentation.
† This line item includes transactions related to both operating and financing activities.

Exhibit 16.5   **Schedule for Conversion of Net Income to Net Cash Flow from Operating Activities**

Items	Amount (in thousands)	Explanation
Net income	$31,000	From income statement.
Add (subtract) to convert to cash basis		
Depreciation	+7,000	Add because depreciation expense does not affect cash but was subtracted in computing net income.
Gain on sale of land	−3,000	Subtract because all cash collected from sale of long-lived assets are investing cash flows.
Accounts receivable increase	−21,000	Subtract because cash collected from customers was less than accrual-based revenues.
Inventory decrease	+20,000	Add because purchases were less than cost of goods sold expense.
Prepaid expense increase	−9,000	Subtract because cash prepayments for expenses were more than accrual-based expenses.
Accounts payable increase	+3,000	Add because amounts purchased on account (that is, borrowed from suppliers) were more than cash payments made to suppliers.
Accrued liabilities increase	+1,000	Add because accrual-based expenses were more than cash payments for expenses.
Net cash inflow (outflow)	$29,000	Subtotal for the operating cash flows section.

By starting with net income, it appears we are assuming all revenues resulted in cash inflows and all expenses resulted in cash outflows. Because we know that is not true, however, we must adjust net income for the effects of the items we marked with an O on the balance sheet (see Exhibit 16.4). Those items reflect differences in the timing of accrual-basis net income and cash flows. The process of adjusting net income has two steps.

Depreciation and Gains and Losses on Sale of Long-Term Assets

Step ① Adjust net income for depreciation expense and gains and losses on sale of long-term assets. On the income statement, depreciation is subtracted to determine net income. But depreciation does not affect cash, so we must eliminate its effect by adding it back to net income. In the case of Nautilus, we remove its effect by adding back the $7,000 of depreciation expense that had been subtracted to determine net income: See Exhibit 16.5.[3]

If Nautilus sells plant and equipment or land or investments at a gain or loss, the amount of cash received would be classified as an investing cash inflow. Because all of the cash received is an investing cash flow, an adjustment must also be made in the operating activities section to avoid double counting the gain or loss. **Gains on sales of property, plant, and equipment or investments are subtracted, and losses on such sales are added** to convert net income to cash flow from operating activities. Nautilus sold land at a gain of $3,000 ($5,000 cash received less cost of $2,000) that must be subtracted in Exhibit 16.5.

Changes in Current Assets and Current Liabilities

Step ② Adjust net income for changes in current assets and current liabilities. Each **change** in current assets (other than cash) and current liabilities causes a difference between

> **Coach's Tip**
> Adding back depreciation is not intended to suggest that depreciation creates an increase in cash. Rather, it shows that depreciation does not cause a decrease in cash. This is a subtle but very important point.

---

[3] Amortization expense for intangible assets and depletion expense for natural resources (discussed in Chapter 10) is handled in exactly the same way as depreciation expense.

net income and cash flow from operating activities. In converting net income to cash flow from operating activities, apply the following general rules:

- **Add the change when a current asset decreases or a current liability increases.**
- **Subtract the change when a current asset increases or a current liability decreases.**

Understanding what causes current assets and current liabilities to increase and decrease is the key to understanding the logic behind these additions and subtractions. Take your time reading the following explanations and make sure you understand the reasons for the changes.

Change in Accounts Receivable

The first operating item (O) listed on the Nautilus balance sheet in Exhibit 16.4 is Accounts Receivable. Remember that the income statement reflects sales revenue, but the cash flow statement must reflect cash collections from customers. As the following T-account for accounts receivable shows, when sales revenues are recorded, Accounts Receivable increases; when cash is collected from customers, the amount in the Accounts Receivable account decreases.

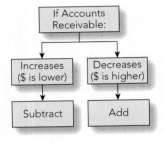

Accounts Receivable (A)		
Beginning balance	117,000	
Sales revenue (on account)	680,000	Cash collected from customers 659,000
Ending balance	138,000	

Change +$21,000

In the case of Nautilus, Accounts Receivable increased, which means that sales revenue was greater than cash collected from customers. To convert from the higher sales amount included in net income to the lower amount of cash collected from customers, we must subtract the difference ($680,000 − $659,000 = $21,000), which is the same as the change in Accounts Receivable.

Ending balance	$138,000
− Beginning balance	117,000
Change	$ 21,000

This procedure suggests a shortcut for determining adjustments to net income: Simply adjust for the **changes** in the current asset and current liability accounts that are related to operating activities. The sign of the adjustment fits the general rule just given. In the case of Nautilus, the net increase in Accounts Receivable is subtracted from net income. If Accounts Receivable had decreased, the net decrease would be added to net income.

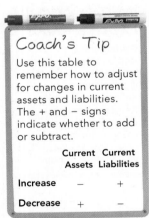

Coach's Tip

Use this table to remember how to adjust for changes in current assets and liabilities. The + and − signs indicate whether to add or subtract.

	Current Assets	Current Liabilities
Increase	−	+
Decrease	+	−

Accounts Receivable (A)		
Beg. bal.	117,000	
Increase	21,000	
End. bal.	138,000	

Cash Flows from Operating Activities	
Net income	31,000
Accts rec. increase	(21,000)
. . .	. . .
Net cash inflow	

Change in Inventory

The income statement reports the cost of merchandise sold during the period, but cash flow from operating activities must report cash purchases of inventory. As the following T-accounts show, recording purchases of goods (left) increases the balance in the Inventories account; recording cost of goods sold (right) decreases the balance in the Inventories account:

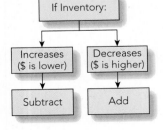

Inventories (A)		
Beg. bal.		
Purchases		Cost of goods sold
End. bal.		

Inventories (A)		
Beg. bal.	96,000	
		Decrease 20,000
End. bal.	76,000	

The balance sheet in Exhibit 16.4 indicates that Nautilus's inventory decreased by $20,000, which means that purchases were less than the amount of merchandise sold. This decrease (that is, the use of existing inventories) must be added to net income to convert to cash flow from operating activities: See Exhibit 16.5. (An increase in inventories would be subtracted.)

Change in Prepaid Expenses

The income statement reports expenses for the period, but cash flow from operating activities must report cash payments. As the following T-accounts show, cash prepayments increase the balance in Prepaid Expenses; the recording of expenses decreases the balance:

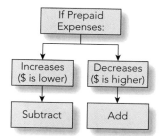

Prepaid Expenses (A)	
Beg. bal.	
Cash prepayments	Used up/expensed
End. bal.	

Prepaid Expenses (A)		
Beg. bal.	24,000	
Increase	9,000	
End. bal.	33,000	

The balance sheet for Nautilus (see Exhibit 16.4) shows a $9,000 increase in Prepaid Expenses, which means that new cash prepayments were more than recorded expenses. This increase (the extra cash prepayments) must be subtracted from net income in Exhibit 16.5. (A decrease in Prepaid Expenses would be added.)

Change in Accounts Payable

Cash flow from operations must reflect cash purchases, but not all purchases are paid for in cash. Purchases made on account increase Accounts Payable; cash paid to suppliers decreases Accounts Payable:

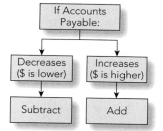

Accounts Payable (L)	
	Beg. bal.
Cash payments	Purchases on account
	End. bal.

Accounts Payable (L)		
	Beg. bal.	61,000
	Increase	3,000
	End. bal.	64,000

For Nautilus, Accounts Payable increased by $3,000 during the period (see Exhibit 16.4). That means cash payments to suppliers were less than purchases made on account. This increase in Accounts Payable must be added to net income in Exhibit 16.5. (A decrease in Accounts Payable would be subtracted.)

Change in Accrued Liabilities

The income statement reports all accrued expenses, but the cash flow statement must report actual payments for those expenses. Recording accrued expenses increases the balance in the Accrued Liabilities account; cash payments for these expenses decrease Accrued Liabilities:

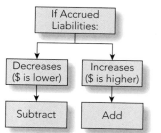

Accounts Liabilities (L)	
	Beg. bal.
Cash payments	Accrued expenses
	End. bal.

Accrued Liabilities (L)		
	Beg. bal.	37,000
	Increase	1,000
	End. bal.	38,000

According to Exhibit 16.4, Nautilus's Accrued Liabilities increased by $1,000, which means that cash payments were less than accrued expenses. This increase in Accrued Liabilities must be added to net income in Exhibit 16.5. (A decrease in Accrued Liabilities would be subtracted.)

Summary

We can summarize the typical additions and subtractions required to reconcile net income with cash flow from operating activities as follows:

	ADDITIONS AND SUBTRACTIONS TO RECONCILE NET INCOME TO CASH FLOW FROM OPERATING ACTIVITIES	
Item	When Item Increases	When Item Decreases
Depreciation and amortization	+	NA
Gain on sale of long-term asset	−	NA
Loss on sale of long-term asset	+	NA
Accounts receivable	−	+
Inventory	−	+
Prepaid expenses	−	+
Accounts payable	+	−
Accrued liabilities	+	−

Notice that to reconcile net income to cash flow from operations, you must:

- **Add the change when a current asset decreases or a current liability increases.**
- **Subtract the change when a current asset increases or a current liability decreases.**

Spotlight On BUSINESS DECISIONS

The Importance of Cash Flow from Operations

In an established business, operating activities are important to investors and creditors. Financial statement users are interested in a company's ability to generate enough cash flows from operations to continue investing in assets and repay its debt on time. Creditors and investors will tolerate poor operating cash flows only so long before they stop lending to or investing in a company. For a company to survive over the long run, then, the amount of cash generated by daily operating activities must exceed the amount of cash spent on them.

SELF-STUDY PRACTICE

Compute cash flow from operating activities assuming the following list includes all amounts related to operating activities.

Net income	$10,000	Inventory decrease	$ 300
Accounts receivable increase	600	Loss on sale of investments	100
Accounts payable decrease	700	Depreciation expense	3,000

After you have finished, check your answers with the solution at the bottom of the page.

Solution to Self-Study Practice

Net income	$10,000
+ Depreciation expense	3,000
+ Loss on sale of investments	100
− Accounts receivable increase	(600)
+ Inventory decrease	300
− Accounts payable decrease	(700)
Cash Flow from Operating Activities	$12,100

REPORTING CASH FLOWS FROM INVESTING ACTIVITIES

To prepare the second section of the statement of cash flows, we must analyze the accounts related to investments and to property, plant, and equipment.[4] In the operating activities section, we were concerned with only the **net** change in selected accounts. In the investing activities section, however (as well as in the financing activities section), we must identify the causes of **both** increases and decreases in selected accounts. The following activities and their related accounts are the ones you will encounter most often:

Related Balance Sheet Accounts	Investing Activity	Cash Flow Effect
Investments	Purchase of investment securities for cash	Outflow
	Sale (maturity) of investment securities for cash	Inflow
Property, Plant, and Equipment	Purchase of property, plant, and equipment for cash	Outflow
	Sale of property, plant, and equipment for cash	Inflow

In the case of Nautilus, the balance sheet in Exhibit 16.4 shows two investment-related accounts (noted with an I) that changed during the year: Plant and Equipment, and Land. To determine the cause(s) for the changes in these accounts, we need to examine the records for these accounts. Purchases of plant and equipment or land increase the account; sales decrease it.

Plant and Equipment

Assume Nautilus purchased equipment for $16,000 cash. This purchase caused a cash outflow, which we must subtract on the schedule of investing activities in Exhibit 16.6. This purchase explains the change in the Plant and Equipment account.

Plant and Equipment (A)			
Beg. bal.	203,000		
Purchases	16,000	Sales	0
End. bal.	219,000		

Exhibit 16.6	Nautilus, Inc.: Schedule for Net Cash Flow from Investing Activities

Items	Amount (in thousands)	Explanations
Purchases of plant and equipment	$(16,000)	Payment of cash for equipment
Sales of land	5,000	Sale of land for cash
Net cash inflow (outflow)	$(11,000)	Subtotal for the statement of cash flows

---

[4] Although they are not shown here, cash flows for intangible assets are similar to those for property, plant, and equipment.

If Nautilus had sold any plant and equipment during the period, regardless of the amount of any gain or loss on the sale, the total amount of cash received would have been an investing cash inflow.

Land and Investments

Nautilus sold land for $5,000 in cash. The land's book value on the balance sheet at the time of sale was $2,000. Consequently, a gain of $3,000 ($5,000 − $2,000) occurred on the sale. Regardless of the amount of any gain or loss on the sale, the total amount of cash received from the sale, $5,000, is an investing cash inflow.

Land (A)			
Beg. bal.	12,000		
Purchases	0	Sales	2,000
End. bal.	10,000		

If Nautilus had purchased or sold any investments during the period, they would be treated in the same manner as the land in this example.

SELF-STUDY PRACTICE

Compute cash flow from investing activities assuming the following list includes all amounts related to purchases and sales of plant and equipment, land, and investments.

a. Purchased investments for cash, $10,000.

b. Sold land with a book value of $17,000 for $18,000 cash.

c. Purchased plant and equipment for $25,000 cash.

d. Sold investments with a book value of $15,000 for $12,000 cash.

After you have finished, check your answers with the solution at the bottom of the page.

REPORTING CASH FLOWS FROM FINANCING ACTIVITIES

Learning Objective 4

Report cash flows from financing activities.

The third section of the statement of cash flows includes changes in the liabilities owed to owners (such as dividends payable) and financial institutions (such as bank loans payable, notes payable, and long-term debt) as well as changes in owners' equity. (Because earning interest is considered an operating activity, it is excluded from cash flows from financing.) The following activities and their related accounts are the ones you will encounter most often:

Coach's Tip

Remember that the dividends received from investing in other companies, as well as interest received and interest paid, affect net income. Thus, they are reported as **operating** (not investing or financing) cash flows.

Related Balance Sheet Accounts	Financing Activity	Cash Flow Effect
Notes Payable	Borrowing cash from banks or other financial institutions	Inflow
	Repayment of loan principal	Outflow
Long-Term Debt	Issuance of bonds for cash	Inflow
	Repayment of bond principal	Outflow
Contributed Capital	Issuance of stock for cash	Inflow
	Repurchase of stock with cash	Outflow
Retained Earnings	Payment of cash dividends	Outflow

Solution to
Self-Study Practice

Purchased plant and equipment	($25,000)
Purchased investments	(10,000)
Sold land	18,000
Sold investments	12,000
Cash flow from investing activities	($ 5,000)

To compute the cash flows from financing activities, we must review the changes in all debt and owners' equity accounts. Looking at changes in Nautilus's balance sheet (Exhibit 16.4), we find that the Long-Term Debt, Contributed Capital, and Retained Earnings accounts (noted with an F) all changed during the period. In the financing activities section (as in the investing activities section), we must **separately** identify the causes of both increases and decreases in selected accounts. This means that, in addition to the change in the balance sheet account, the accounting records related to the account must be examined.

Long-Term Debt

Suppose the accounting records indicate that the $4,000 increase in Long-Term Debt on the balance sheet resulted from a combination of new borrowing of $6,000 and repayment of $2,000 in **principal** on existing debt. We will include both the inflow and outflow in the schedule of financing activities in Exhibit 16.7.

Long-Term Debt (L)			
		Beg. bal.	63,000
Repayments	2,000	Borrowings	6,000
		End. bal.	67,000

Contributed Capital

The change in the Contributed Capital account resulted from an issue of company stock for $1,000 in cash, which produced a cash inflow. This $1,000 increase in contributed capital should be listed on the schedule of financing activities in Exhibit 16.7.

Contributed Capital (OE)		
	Beg. bal.	4,000
	Issuance of stock	1,000
	End. bal.	5,000

Retained Earnings

Net income increases the amount in the Retained Earnings account; dividends decrease Retained Earnings. We have already included the cash effects related to net income in the operating activities section of the statement of cash flows. The only change in retained earnings that remains to be accounted for is the cash outflow for any dividends paid.

From the income statement in Exhibit 16.4, we know that Nautilus reported net income of $31,000. From the statement of retained earnings (or statement of owners' equity), we know that Nautilus declared dividends of $24,000. The balance sheet does not report any dividends payable, so the full amount of dividends must have been paid in cash. This outflow is included in the schedule of financing activities in Exhibit 16.7. Together, net income

Exhibit 16.7   Nautilus, Inc.: Schedule for Net Cash Flow from Financing Activities

Items	Amount (in thousands)	Explanation
Additional borrowings of long-term debt	$ 6,000	Cash received when new loan obtained
Repayment of principal on existing debt	(2,000)	Cash paid to repay principal on existing debt
Issuance of company stock	1,000	Cash received from issuing stock
Cash dividends paid	(24,000)	Cash paid to stockholders as dividend
Net cash inflow (outflow)	$(19,000)	Subtotal for the statement of cash flows

and dividends account for the $7,000 increase in Retained Earnings as in the following T-account.

Retained Earnings (OE)			
		Beg. bal.	248,000
Dividends	24,000	Net Income	31,000
		End. bal.	255,000

SELF-STUDY PRACTICE

Compute cash flow from financing activities assuming the following list includes all financing activities of the period and some nonfinancing activities

Purchased investments for cash	$10,000	Additional short-term borrowing from bank	$19,000
Dividends paid	25,000	Interest paid	8,000

After you have finished, check your answers with the solution at the bottom of the page.

PREPARING AND EVALUATING THE STATEMENT OF CASH FLOWS

Format for the Statement of Cash Flows

Learning Objective 5

Prepare and evaluate the statement of cash flows.

Now that we have determined the cash flows for the three main types of business activity, we can prepare the statement of cash flows. In Exhibit 16.8, we show the format for the statement of cash flows using the indirect method. The statement of cash flows combines cash flows from operating, investing, and financing activities to produce an overall net increase (or decrease) in cash. This net change is added to the beginning cash balance to arrive at the ending cash balance, which is the same as the cash balance reported on the balance sheet.

Noncash Investing and Financing Activities

Certain transactions are important investing and financing activities but have no cash flow effects. These are called **noncash investing and financing activities.** For example, the purchase of a $100,000 building with a $100,000 mortgage given by the former owner does not cause either an inflow or an outflow of cash. As a result, these noncash activities are not listed in the three main sections of the cash flow statement. However, supplemental disclosure of these transactions is required, in either narrative or schedule form. Nautilus statement of cash flows does not list any noncash investing and financing activities. However, when Northwest Airlines purchases airplanes from AIRBUS or Boeing, the manufacturer provides some of the

Solution to Self-Study Practice

Dividends paid	($25,000)
Additional short-term borrowing from bank	19,000
Cash flow from financing activities	($6,000)

Exhibit 16.8   Format for the Statement of Cash Flows—Indirect Method

Nautilus

Nautilus, Inc.
Statement of Cash Flows*
For the Year Ended December 31, 2006
(in thousands)

Cash Flows from Operating Activities

Net income	$31,000
Adjustments to reconcile net income to net cash provided by operating activities:	
Depreciation	7,000
Gain on sale of land	(3,000)
Changes in assets and liabilities:	
Accounts receivable	(21,000)
Inventories	20,000
Prepaid expenses	(9,000)
Accounts payable	3,000
Accrued liabilities	1,000
Net cash provided by operating activities	29,000
Cash Flows from Investing Activities	
Purchases of plant and equipment	(16,000)
Sales of land	5,000
Net cash used by investing activities	(11,000)
Cash Flows from Financing Activities	
Additional borrowings of long-term debt	6,000
Repayment of principal on existing debt	(2,000)
Issuance of common stock	1,000
Cash dividends paid	(24,000)
Net cash used by financing activities	(19,000)
Net decrease in cash and cash equivalents	(1,000)
Cash and cash equivalents at beginning of period	8,000
Cash and cash equivalents at end of period	$ 7,000

*Certain amounts have been adjusted to simplify the presentation.

financing for those purchases. These amounts are disclosed as follows at the bottom of its cash flow statement:

NORTHWEST AIRLINES CORPORATION			
(in millions)	Year ended December 31,		
Investing and Financing Activities Not Affecting Cash:	2007	2006	2005
Manufacturer financing of aircraft and other non-cash transactions	$ 502	$ 280	$ 344

Northwest

Supplemental Cash Flow Information

Companies that use the indirect method of presenting cash flows from operations also must provide two other figures: cash paid for interest and cash paid for income taxes. These are normally listed at the bottom of the statement or in the notes.

Free Cash Flow

In evaluating the statement of cash flows, a good place to start is with the subtotals in each of the three main sections. Cash flow patterns differ from one company to the next, depending on how well established a company is. A healthy, well-established company will show positive cash flows from operations that are large enough to pay for the replacement of current property, plant, and equipment and pay dividends to stockholders.

Any additional cash beyond that required to meet a company's basic needs is called **free cash flow.** Free cash flow can be used (a) to expand the business through additional investing activities, (b) for financing (for example, to pay down debt or pay future dividends), or (c) simply to build the company's cash balance.

Financial Analysis Tools		
Name of Measure	Formula	What It Tells You
Free Cash Flow	Net Cash Flow from Operating Activities – Purchases of Property and Equipment – Dividends Paid	• Ability to make additional capital investments without external financing. • Ability to pay down debt or repurchase stock. • Ability to pay future dividends.

Nautilus's free cash flow would be computed as follows:

> **Free Cash Flow = Net Cash Flow from Operating Activities – Purchases of Property and Equipment – Dividends Paid**
> **= \$29,000 – \$16,000 – \$24,000 = (\$11,000)**

Quality of Income Ratio

The operating activities section of the statement of cash flows indicates how well a company can generate cash internally through its operations and its management of current assets and current liabilities. Most analysts believe this section is the most important one because in the long run, operations are the only continuing source of cash. Investors will not invest in a company if they do not believe that cash generated from operations will be available to pay dividends or expand the company. Similarly, creditors will not lend money if they believe that cash generated from operations will not be sufficient to repay them.

In evaluating the operating activities section of the statement of cash flows, consider the absolute amount of the cash flow; is it positive or negative? Keep in mind that for a company to be successful, operating cash flows must be positive over the long run. You can also look at the relationship between operating cash flows and net income by using the quality of income ratio. This ratio measures the portion of net income that was generated in cash. All other things held equal, a quality of income ratio near 1.0 indicates a high likelihood that revenues are realized in cash and that expenses are associated with cash outflows.

Financial Analysis Tools		
Name of Measure	Formula	What It Tells You
Quality of income ratio	Net Cash Flow from Operating Activities / Net Income	• Portion of net income generated in cash • Ratio near 1.0 means that operating cash flows and net income are in sync.

Nautilus's quality of income ratio would be computed as follows:

$$\text{Quality of Income Ratio} = \frac{\text{Net Cash Flow from Operating Activities}}{\text{Net Income}} = \frac{\$29,000}{\$31,000} = 0.94 \text{ times}$$

The quality of income ratio is most useful when it is compared to those of competitors in the same industry or to that of the same company in prior periods. Any major deviations—say, below 0.5 or above 1.5—should be investigated. In some cases, a deviation may be nothing to worry about, but in others it could be the first sign of serious problems.

There are three potential causes of deviations in this ratio. The first is **the corporate life cycle, or growth in sales.** New companies often experience rapid sales growth. When sales are increasing, accounts receivable and inventory normally increase faster than cash flows from sales. This lag in collections often reduces operating cash flows below net income, which in turn reduces the ratio. The problem is not serious provided that the company can get sufficient cash from financing activities to meet its needs until operating activities begin to generate positive cash flows.

A second potential cause of a deviation in the quality of income ratio is a **change in management of operating activities.** If a company's operating assets (such as Accounts Receivable and Inventories) are allowed to grow out of control, its operating cash flows and quality of income ratio will decrease. More efficient management will have the opposite effect. To investigate this potential cause more closely, use the inventory and accounts receivable turnover ratios covered in prior chapters

A third cause of deviation in this ratio is a **change in revenue and expense recognition.** Most cases of fraudulent financial reporting involve aggressive revenue recognition (that is, recording revenues before they are earned) or delayed expense recognition (that is, failing to report expenses). Both tactics cause net income to increase in the current period, suggesting that the company has improved its performance. However, neither of these tactics affects cash flows from operating activities. As a result, if revenue and expense recognition policies are used to artificially boost net income, the quality of income ratio will drop, providing one of the first warning signs that the financial statements might contain errors or fraud.

Demonstration Case A: Indirect Method

For a recent quarter ended March 31, Brunswick Corporation reported net income of $3,800 (all numbers in thousands). On December 31 of the year before, the balance in cash and cash equivalents had been $351,400; by March 31, it was $280,000. The company reported the following additional activities:

a. Received $2,200 from debt borrowings.
b. Accounts receivable increased by $40,300.
c. Paid $31,800 in cash for purchase of property, plant, and equipment.
d. Recorded depreciation of $35,600.
e. Salaries payable increased by $10,210.
f. Other accrued liabilities decreased by $35,000.
g. Prepaid expenses decreased by $14,500.

h. Inventories increased by $20,810.

i. Accounts payable decreased by $10,200.

j. Issued stock to employees for $400 in cash.

Required:

Based on this information, prepare the statement of cash flows using the indirect method. Evaluate the cash flows reported in the statement.

Suggested Solution

Brunswick Corporation
Statement of Cash Flows
For the Quarter Ended March 31
(in thousands)

Cash flows from operating activities	
Net income	$ 3,800
Adjustments	
Depreciation	35,600
Increase in accounts receivable	(40,300)
Increase in inventories	(20,810)
Decrease in prepaid expenses	14,500
Decrease in accounts payable	(10,200)
Increase in salaries payable	10,210
Decrease in other accrued liabilities	(35,000)
Net cash provided by (used for) operating activities	(42,200)
Cash flows from investing activities	
Additions to property, plant, and equipment	(31,800)
Net cash provided by (used for) investing activities	(31,800)
Cash flows from financing activities	
Proceeds from debt borrowings	2,200
Proceeds from issuance of stock to employees	400
Net cash provided by (used for) financing activities	2,600
Increase (decrease) in cash and cash equivalents	(71,400)
Cash and cash equivalents, December 31	351,400
Cash and cash equivalents, March 31	$280,000

Despite reporting a profit this quarter, the company has experienced negative cash flow from operations. The drop was caused primarily by a buildup of accounts receivable and inventories with no corresponding reduction in spending on accounts payable and other accrued liabilities. This negative cash flow from operations could be troublesome because it suggests that the company may be encountering difficulties in selling its products and collecting on past sales. In addition to the drain on cash for operating activities, the company spent more than $30 million for additional property, plant, and equipment. Financing activities had relatively little effect on cash flows during the period, however. The company entered the quarter with a lot of cash (more than $350 million). Despite the shortfall in cash flow, it still has a lot of cash remaining to finance future activities.

Supplement 16A

Reporting Cash Flows from Operating Activities—Direct Method

The direct method summarizes all operating transactions that result in either a debit or a credit to Cash. It is prepared by adjusting each revenue and expense on the income statement from an accrual basis to a cash basis. We demonstrate this process using the revenues and expenses reported in Nautilus's income statement (Exhibit 16.4). See Exhibit 16A.1 for the schedule for converting from an accrual to a cash basis using the direct method. Notice that in this method, we work directly with each revenue and expense listed on the income statement, ignoring any totals or subtotals (such as net income).

Exhibit 16A.1 Nautilus Inc.: Schedule for Net Cash Flow from Operating Activities—Direct Method

Cash flows from operating activities	
Cash collected from customers	$ 659,000
Cash payments to suppliers	(359,000)
Cash payments for operating expenses	(258,000)
Cash paid for interest	(1,000)
Cash payments for income taxes	(12,000)
Net cash inflow (outflow)	$ 29,000

Nautilus

Converting Sales Revenues to a Cash Inflow

When a company records sales, its Accounts Receivable increases; when the company collects cash, Accounts Receivable decreases. Thus, if Accounts Receivable increases by $21,000, sales on account must have been $21,000 more than cash collections. To convert sales revenue to cash collected, then, we need to subtract $21,000 from sales revenue. The following diagram shows this process:

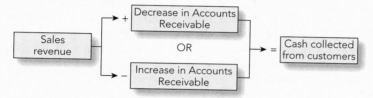

Using information from Nautilus's income statement and balance sheet in Exhibit 16.4, we can compute cash collected from customers as follows:

Net sales	$680,000
− Increase in accounts receivable	21,000
Cash collected from customers	$659,000

Accounts Receivable (A)		
Beg.	117,000	
Increase	21,000	
End.	138,000	

Converting Cost of Goods Sold to Cash Paid to Suppliers

Cost of goods sold represents the cost of merchandise sold during the accounting period. It may be more or less than the amount of cash paid to suppliers during the period. In the case of Nautilus, inventory decreased during the year because the company sold more merchandise than it purchased. If the company paid cash to inventory suppliers, it would have paid less cash than the amount of cost of goods sold. So, the decrease in inventory must be subtracted from the cost of goods sold to compute the cash paid to suppliers.

Typically, companies buy their inventory on account from suppliers (as indicated by an accounts payable balance on the balance sheet). Consequently, we need to consider more than just the change in Inventory to convert the cost of goods sold to cash paid to suppliers. We must also consider the credit purchases and payments recorded in Accounts Payable. Credit purchases increase Accounts Payable; cash payments decrease it. The overall increase in Accounts Payable reported by Nautilus in Exhibit 16.4 indicates that cash payments were less than credit purchases, so we must subtract the difference to compute the total cash payments to suppliers. In other words, to fully convert the cost of goods sold to a cash basis, we must consider the changes in both Inventory and Accounts Payable, in the following manner:

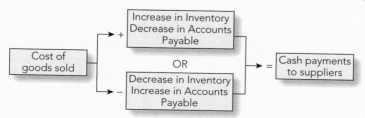

Using information from Exhibit 16.4, we can compute cash paid to suppliers as follows:

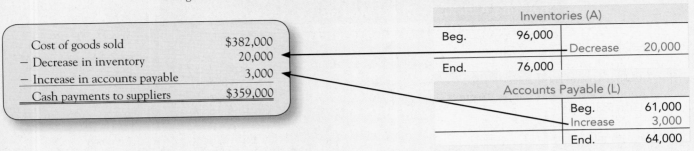

Cost of goods sold	$382,000
− Decrease in inventory	20,000
− Increase in accounts payable	3,000
Cash payments to suppliers	$359,000

Inventories (A)			
Beg.	96,000	Decrease	20,000
End.	76,000		

Accounts Payable (L)		
	Beg.	61,000
	Increase	3,000
	End.	64,000

Converting Operating Expenses to a Cash Outflow

The total amount of expense on the income statement may differ from the cash outflow associated with that activity. Some amounts, such as that for prepaid rent, are paid **before** they are recognized as expenses. When prepayments are made, the balance in the asset Prepaid Expenses increases. When expenses are recorded, Prepaid Expenses decreases. When Nautilus's Prepaid Expenses increase by $9,000, we know that the company paid more cash than it recorded in operating expenses. This increase in Prepaid Expenses must be added to net income to determine cash paid for operating expenses.

Some operating expenses, such as accrued wages, are paid **after** they are recorded. In that case, when the expenses are recorded, the balance in the Accrued Liabilities account increases. When the payments are made, Accrued Liabilities decreases. When Nautilus's Accrued Liabilities increase by $1,000, then we know the company paid that much less cash than it recorded as operating expenses. This amount must be subtracted in computing cash paid for expenses.

Generally, other operating expenses can be converted from an accrual basis to a cash basis in the following manner:

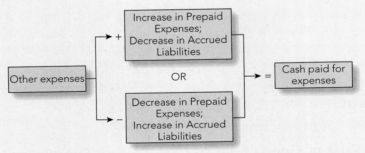

Using income statement information from Exhibit 16.4, we can compute cash paid for expenses as follows:

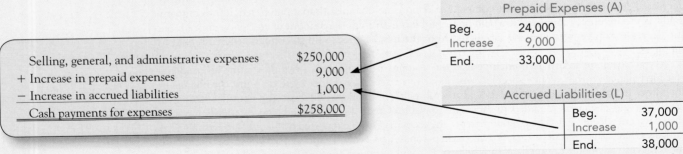

Selling, general, and administrative expenses	$250,000
+ Increase in prepaid expenses	9,000
− Increase in accrued liabilities	1,000
Cash payments for expenses	$258,000

Prepaid Expenses (A)		
Beg.	24,000	
Increase	9,000	
End.	33,000	

Accrued Liabilities (L)		
	Beg.	37,000
	Increase	1,000
	End.	38,000

It is easy to convert depreciation expense to a cash basis because depreciation does not involve cash. Thus, the direct method of preparing the statement of cash flows omits noncash expenses such as depreciation (as well as revenues, gains, and losses that do not affect cash).

The next line on the income statement in Exhibit 16.4 is interest expense of $1,000. Because the Interest Payable account has no balance, all interest expense must have been paid in cash. Thus, the interest expense equals the interest paid:

Interest expense	$1,000
No change in interest payable	0
Cash payments for interest	$1,000

The same logic can be applied to income taxes. Nautilus reported income tax expense of $12,000. Because Income Taxes Payable (or any other tax account) on the balance sheet in Exhibit 16.4 has no balance, the income tax paid must equal the income tax expense:

Income tax expense	$12,000
No change in taxes payable	0
Cash payments for income taxes	$12,000

Now that we have considered all of the line items shown on the income statement in Exhibit 16.4, it is time to gather all operating cash inflows and outflows that we have calculated (See Exhibit 16A.1). If Nautilus were to report its statement of cash flows using the direct method, Exhibit 16A.1 would replace the Cash Flows from Operating Activities section in Exhibit 16.8.

The following chart summarizes the adjustments that must be made to convert income statement items to operating cash flows. Before you move to the next section, review it carefully and then complete the self-study practice that follows to make sure you understand how to compute cash flow from operations (direct method).

Income Statement Account	± Change in Balance Sheet Account(s)	= Operating Cash Flow
Sales Revenue	+ Decrease in Accounts Receivable (A)	
	− Increase in Accounts Receivable (A)	= Collections from customers
Cost of Goods Sold	+ Increase in Inventory (A)	
	− Decrease in Inventory (A)	
	− Increase in Accounts Payable (L)	
	+ Decrease in Accounts Payable (L)	= Payments to suppliers of inventory
Other Expenses	+ Increase in Prepaid Expenses (A)	
	− Decrease in Prepaid Expenses (A)	
	− Increase in Accrued Expenses (L)	= Payments to suppliers of services
	+ Decrease in Accrued Expenses (L)	(e.g., rent, utilities, wages, interest)
Interest Expense	− Increase in Interest Payable (L)	
	+ Decrease in Interest Payable (L)	= Payments of interest
Income Tax Expense	+ Increase in Prepaid Income Taxes (Deferred Taxes) (A)	
	− Decrease in Prepaid Income Taxes (Deferred Taxes) (A)	
	− Increase in Income Taxes Payable (Deferred Taxes) (L)	
	+ Decrease in Income Taxes Payable (Deferred Taxes) (L)	= Payments of income taxes

Indicate which of the following items taken from a cash flow statement would be added (+), subtracted (−), or not included (0) when calculating cash flow from operations using the direct method.

____1. Payments to suppliers of inventories.

____2. Payment of dividends to stockholders.

____3. Cash collections from customers.

____4. Purchase of plant and equipment for cash.

____5. Payments of interest to lenders.

____6. Payment of taxes to the government.

After you have finished, check your answers with the solution at the bottom of the page.

1. −   2. 0   3. +   4. 0   5. −   6. −

Solution to
Self-Study Practice

Demonstration Case B: Direct Method (Supplement A)

During a recent quarter ended March 29, Cybex International reported that cash and cash equivalents had increased from $216 on December 31 to $469 on March 29 (all amounts in thousands). The company also reported the following:

a. Paid $13,229 to suppliers for inventory purchases.

b. Borrowed $2,400 from one of the company's main stockholders.

c. Paid $554 in cash for purchase of property, plant, and equipment.

d. Reported sales on account of $20,608 (accounts receivable were $13,628 at the beginning of the quarter and $12,386 at the end of the quarter).

e. Paid operating expenses totaling $6,188.

f. Made cash payments for interest totaling $1,060.

g. Made payments of $2,625 for principal owed on long-term debt.

h. Paid $284 cash for other financing activities.

i. Paid $57 cash for income taxes.

Required:
Based on this information, prepare the statement of cash flows using the direct method. Evaluate the cash flows reported in the statement.

Suggested Solution

Cybex International
Statement of Cash Flows
For the Quarter Ended March 29
(in thousands)

Operating activities	
Cash collected from customers ($20,608 + $13,628 − $12,386)	$ 21,850
Cash paid to suppliers	(13,229)
Cash paid for operating expenses	(6,188)
Cash paid for interest	(1,060)
Cash paid for income taxes	(57)
Net cash provided by operating activities	1,316
Investing activities	
Additions to property, plant, and equipment	(554)
Net cash used for investing activities	(554)
Financing activities	
Borrowed cash from related party (stockholder)	2,400
Repaid principal owed on long-term debt	(2,625)
Cash paid for other financing activities	(284)
Net cash used for financing activities	(509)
Increase in cash and cash equivalents	253
Cash and cash equivalents, December 31	216
Cash and cash equivalents, March 29	$ 469

Cybex reported a net cash inflow of $1,316 from operating activities during the quarter. This cash inflow was more than enough to pay for the property, plant, and equipment purchased during the quarter. Some of the extra cash from operations (that is, free cash flow) that was not needed to purchase property, plant, and equipment could have been used to pay down debt or increase the company's cash balance. The Financing Activities section suggests that the company did pay down a significant amount of long-term debt ($2,625) in part by borrowing funds from a related party ($2,400). Borrowing from a related party—particularly a major stockholder—is unusual, and would prompt analysts to investigate further. The company's quarterly report explains that lenders had demanded immediate repayment of their loans after the company violated its debt covenants. A major stockholder lent money to the company to make the repayment.

Supplement 16B

Spreadsheet Approach: Indirect Method

As a company's situation becomes more complex, the analytical approach that we used to prepare the statement of cash flows for Nautilus becomes cumbersome and inefficient. In practice, many companies use a spreadsheet to prepare the statement of cash flows. This approach is based on the same logic as our earlier approach. Its primary advantage is its systematic way of keeping track of detailed information. You may find it useful even in simple situations.

Exhibit 16B.1 is a spreadsheet for Nautilus, which we created using the following procedure:

1. Starting from the right side of the spreadsheet, set up four columns to record dollar amounts. The first column should hold the beginning balances for the items reported on the balance sheet. The next two columns should show debit and credit changes in those balances. The final column should show the ending balances in these balance sheet accounts.
2. On the top half of the spreadsheet, on the left side, enter each account name from the balance sheet.
3. On the bottom half of the spreadsheet, on the left side, enter the name of each item to be reported on the statement of cash flows. Do this as you analyze the change in each balance sheet account.

Coach's Tip

Think of the bottom half of the spreadsheet as a big Cash T-account.

Note that in the top half of the spreadsheet, you analyze changes in the balance sheet accounts in terms of debits and credits. In the bottom half of the spreadsheet, you record the offsetting debits and credits in terms of their impact on cash flows. Each change in the noncash balance sheet accounts explains part of the change in the Cash account.

Let's go through each of the entries in the spreadsheet in Exhibit 16B.1, starting with the first one in the bottom half:

a. Net income of $31,000 is shown as an inflow in the operating activities section. The corresponding credit in the top half of the spreadsheet goes to Retained Earnings (to show that net income increased Retained Earnings).

b. Depreciation expense of $7,000 is added back to net income because this expense does not cause a cash outflow. The corresponding credit explains the increase in the Accumulated Depreciation account during the period.

c. The $21,000 increase in Accounts Receivable means that cash collections from customers were less than sales made on account. Because net income includes the sales made on account, we must subtract that amount to adjust to the actual cash collected. This adjustment appears on the spreadsheet as a credit to Cash and a corresponding debit to Accounts Receivable.

d. This $20,000 entry reconciles purchases of inventory with the cost of goods sold. The amount is added to net income because more inventory was sold than was purchased.

e. This $9,000 entry reconciles the prepayment of expenses with their expiration. The amount is subtracted from net income because cash prepayments were more than the amounts reported as expired expenses.

f. This $3,000 entry reconciles cash paid to suppliers with purchases made on account. The amount is added because more was borrowed (by purchasing on account) than was paid in cash.

g. This $1,000 entry reconciles the accrual of liabilities for operating expenses with payments for those expenses. The amount is added because the cash paid for accrued liabilities was less than the expenses recorded for accrued liabilities. Note that the debit to Cash corresponds to the net credit to Accrued Liabilities.

h. This $16,000 entry records purchases of new equipment for cash.

i. This $5,000 entry records the sale of land for cash.

j. This $2,000 entry records cash repaid for principal on existing debt.

k. This $6,000 entry records cash obtained through additional long-term debt.

l. This $1,000 entry records cash received from an issue of company stock.

m. This $24,000 entry records the payment of dividends in cash.

n. This $1,000 entry shows that the change in cash (on the top part of the spreadsheet) is accounted for by the net cash flows listed on the bottom part of the spreadsheet.

Finally, check to make sure that the debits equal the credits on your spreadsheet. If they do not, you have missed something. If they do, you can then use the bottom part of the spreadsheet to prepare the statement of cash flows in Exhibit 16.8.

Exhibit 16B.1   Spreadsheet to Prepare Statement of Cash Flows, Indirect Method   Nautilus

Nautilus, Inc.
For the Year Ended December 31, 2006
(in thousands)

	Beginning Balances, December 31, 2005	ANALYSIS OF CHANGES Debit		ANALYSIS OF CHANGES Credit		Ending Balances, December 31, 2006
Items from Balance Sheet						
Cash and cash equivalents (A)	8,000			(n)	1,000	7,000
Accounts receivable (A)	117,000	(c)	21,000			138,000
Inventories (A)	96,000			(d)	20,000	76,000
Prepaid expenses (A)	24,000	(e)	9,000			33,000
Plant and Equipment (A)	203,000	(h)	16,000			219,000
Accumulated depreciation (xA)	(47,000)			(b)	7,000	(54,000)
Land (A)	12,000			(i)	2,000	10,000
Accounts payable (L)	(61,000)			(f)	3,000	(64,000)
Accrued liabilities (L)	(37,000)			(g)	1,000	(38,000)
Long-term debt (L)	(63,000)	(j)	2,000	(k)	6,000	(67,000)
Contributed capital (OE)	(4,000)			(l)	1,000	(5,000)
Retained earnings (OE)	(248,000)	(m)	24,000	(a)	31,000	(255,000)

		CASH Inflows		CASH Outflows		Subtotals
Statement of Cash Flows						
Cash flows from operating activities						
Net income		(a)	31,000			
Adjustments to reconcile net income to cash provided by operating activities						
Depreciation		(b)	7,000			
Gain on sale of land				(i)	3,000	
Changes in assets and liabilities						
Accounts receivable				(c)	21,000	
Inventories		(d)	20,000			
Prepaid expenses				(e)	9,000	
Accounts payable		(f)	3,000			
Accrued liabilities		(g)	1,000			
						29,000
Cash flows from investing activities						
Purchases of equipment				(h)	16,000	
Sale of land		(i)	5,000			
						(11,000)
Cash flows from financing activities						
Repayment of principal on existing debt				(j)	2,000	
Additional long-term debt borrowed		(k)	6,000			
Stock issuance		(l)	1,000			
Cash dividends paid				(m)	24,000	
						(19,000)
Net decrease in cash and cash equivalents		(n)	1,000			
			147,000		147,000	(1,000)

Chapter Summary

LO1 Identify cash flows from operating, investing, and financing activities. p. 682

- The statement of cash flows has three main sections: cash flows from operating activities, which are related to income earned from normal operations; cash flows from investing activities, which are related to the acquisition and sale of productive assets; and cash flows from financing activities, which are related to external financing of the enterprise.
- The net cash inflow or outflow for the period equals the increase or decrease in cash and cash equivalents on the balance sheet for the period. Cash equivalents are highly liquid investments with original maturities of less than three months.

LO2 Report cash flows from operating activities using the indirect method. p. 687

- The indirect method for reporting cash flows from operating activities converts net income to net cash flow from operating activities.
- The conversion involves additions and subtractions for (1) expenses (such as depreciation expense) and revenues that do not affect cash and gains and losses from sale of long-lived assets and (2) changes in each of the individual current assets (other than cash) and current liabilities that reflect differences in the timing of accrual-based net income and cash flows.

LO3 Report cash flows from investing activities. p. 693

- Investing activities reported on the statement of cash flows include cash payments to acquire property, plant, and equipment, investments, and cash proceeds from their sale.

LO4 Report cash flows from financing activities. p. 694

- Cash inflows from financing activities include cash proceeds from the issue of debt and common stock. Cash outflows include cash repayments of principal on debt, cash paid for the repurchase of the company's stock, and cash dividend payments. (Cash payments associated with interest are a cash flow from operating activities.)

LO5 Prepare and evaluate the statement of cash flows. p. 696

- A healthy company will generate positive cash flows from operations, some of which will be used to pay for purchases of property, plant, and equipment. Any additional cash, called free cash flow, can be used to further expand the business or pay down some of the company's debt, or it can be returned to owners. A company is in trouble if it cannot generate positive cash flows from operations over the long run because creditors will eventually stop lending to the company, and stockholders will stop investing in it.
- Two common measures for assessing operating, investing, and financing cash flows are free cash flow and the quality of income ratio.

Financial Analysis Tools		
Name of Measure	Formula	What It Tells You
Free Cash Flow	Net Cash Flow from Operating Activities – Purchases of Property and Equipment – Dividends Paid	• Ability to make additional capital investments without external financing. • Ability to pay down debt or repurchase stock. • Ability to pay future dividends.
Quality of income ratio	$\dfrac{\text{Net Cash Flow from Operating Activities}}{\text{Net Incomes}}$	• Portion of net income generated in cash • Ratio near 1.0 means that operating cash flows and net income are in sync.

Key Terms

Cash Equivalents (p. 682)

Cash Flows from Financing
Activities (p. 684)

Cash Flows from Investing Activities (p. 684)

Cash Flows from Operating Activities
(Cash Flows from Operations) (p. 683)

Direct Method (p. 683)

Indirect Method (p. 683)

See complete glossary in back of text.

Questions

1. Compare the purposes of the income statement, the balance sheet, and the statement of cash flows.

2. What information does the statement of cash flows report that is not reported on the other required financial statements?

3. What are cash equivalents? How are they reported on the statement of cash flows?

4. What are the major categories of business activities reported on the statement of cash flows? Define each of these activities.

5. What are the typical cash inflows from operating activities? What are the typical cash outflows from operating activities?

6. Describe the types of items used to compute cash flows from operating activities under the two alternative methods of reporting.

7. Under the indirect method, depreciation expense is added to net income to report cash flows from operating activities. Does depreciation cause an inflow of cash?

8. Explain why cash outflows during the period for purchases and salaries are not specifically reported on a statement of cash flows prepared using the indirect method.

9. Explain why a $50,000 increase in inventory during the year must be included in computing cash flows from operating activities under the indirect method.

10. What are the typical cash inflows from investing activities? What are the typical cash outflows from investing activities?

11. What are the typical cash inflows from financing activities? What are the typical cash outflows from financing activities?

12. What are noncash investing and financing activities? Give one example. How are noncash investing and financing activities reported on the statement of cash flows?

Multiple Choice

1. Where is the change in cash shown in the statement of cash flows?

   Quiz 16-1
   www.mhhe.com/LLPW1e

   a. In the top part, before the operating activities section.
   b. In one of the operating, investing, or financing activities sections.
   c. In the bottom part, following the financing activities section.
   d. None of the above.

2. In what order do the three sections of the statement of cash flows appear when reading from top to bottom?
   a. Financing, investing, operating.
   b. Investing, operating, financing.
   c. Operating, financing, investing.
   d. Operating, investing, financing.

3. Total cash inflow in the operating section of the statement of cash flows should include which of the following?
   a. Cash received from customers at the point of sale.
   b. Cash collections from customer accounts receivable.
   c. Cash received in advance of revenue recognition (unearned revenue).
   d. All of the above.

4. If the balance in Prepaid Expenses increased during the year, what action should be taken on the statement of cash flows when following the indirect method, and why?
   a. The change in the account balance should be subtracted from net income because the net increase in Prepaid Expenses did not impact net income but did reduce the Cash balance.
   b. The change in the account balance should be added to net income because the net increase in Prepaid Expenses did not impact net income but did increase the Cash balance.

   c. The net change in Prepaid Expenses should be subtracted from net income to reverse the income statement effect that had no impact on Cash.

   Coach's Tip

   To practice more multiple choice questions, go to www.mhhe.com/LLPW1e.

   d. The net change in Prepaid Expenses should be added to net income to reverse the income statement effect that had no impact on Cash.

5. Which of the following would not appear in the investing section of the statement of cash flows?
   a. Purchase of inventory.
   b. Sale of investments.
   c. Purchase of land.
   d. All of the above would appear in the investing section of the statement of cash flows.

6. Which of the following items would not appear in the financing section of the statement of cash flows?
   a. The issuance of the company's own stock.
   b. The repayment of debt.
   c. The payment of dividends.
   d. All of the above would appear in the financing section of the statement of cash flows.

7. Which of the following is not added when computing cash flows from operations using the indirect method?
   a. The net increase in Accounts Payable.
   b. The net decrease in Accounts Receivable.
   c. The net decrease in Inventory.
   d. None of the above.

8. If a company engages in a material transaction that is noncash, which of the following is required?

    a. The company must include an explanatory narrative or schedule accompanying the statement of cash flows.

    b. No disclosure is necessary.

    c. The company must include an explanatory narrative or schedule accompanying the balance sheet.

    d. It must be reported in the investing and financing sections of the statement of cash flows.

9. The **total** change in cash as shown near the bottom of the statement of cash flows for the year should agree with which of the following?

    a. The difference in retained earnings when reviewing the comparative balance sheet.

    b. Net income or net loss as found on the income statement.

    c. The difference in cash when reviewing the comparative balance sheet.

    d. None of the above.

10. Which of the following is a ratio or amount used to assess whether cash flows from operations are sufficiently large to pay for replacing current property, plant, and equipment and to pay dividends to stockholders?

    a. Free cash flow.

    b. Fixed asset turnover ratio.

    c. Cash coverage ratio.

    d. Quality of income ratio.

Solutions to Multiple-Choice Questions
1. c   2. d   3. d   4. a   5. a   6. d   7. d
8. a   9. c   10. a

Mini-Exercises Available with McGraw-Hill's Homework Manager

M16-1 Identifying Companies from Cash Flow Patterns
LO1, 5

Based on the cash flows shown, classify each of the following cases as a growing start-up company (S), a healthy established company (E), or an established company facing financial difficulties (F).

	Case 1	Case 2	Case 3
Cash provided by (used for) operating activities	$(120,000)	$ 3,000	$ 80,000
Cash provided by (used for) investing activities	10,000	(70,000)	(40,000)
Cash provided by (used for) financing activities	75,000	75,000	(30,000)
Net change in cash	(35,000)	8,000	10,000
Cash position at beginning of year	40,000	2,000	30,000
Cash position at end of year	$ 5,000	$10,000	$ 40,000

M16-2 Matching Items Reported to Cash Flow Statement Categories (Indirect Method)
LO1

Buckle

The Buckle, Inc., operates more than 330 stores in 38 states, selling brand name apparel such as Lucky Jeans and Fossil belts and watches. Some of the items included in its recent statement of cash flows presented using the indirect method are listed here. Indicate whether each item is disclosed in the operating activities (O), investing activities (I), or financing activities (F) section of the statement or (NA) if the item does not appear on the statement.

_____1. Purchase of investments.

_____2. Proceeds from issuance of stock.

_____3. Purchase of property and equipment.

_____4. Depreciation.

_____5. Accouts payable (decrease).

_____6. Inventories (increase).

M16-3 Determining the Effects of Account Changes on Cash Flows from Operating Activities (Indirect Method)
LO2

Indicate whether each item would be added (+) or subtracted (−) in the computation of cash flow from operating activities using the indirect method.

_____1. Depreciation.

_____2. Inventories (decrease).

_____3. Accounts payable (decrease).

_____4. Accounts receivable (increase).

_____5. Accrued liabilities (increase).

LO2

M16-4 Computing Cash Flows from Operating Activities (Indirect Method)

For each of the following independent cases, compute cash flows from operating activities. Assume the following list includes all balance sheet accounts related to operating activities.

	Case A	Case B
Net income	$ 200,000	$ 360,000
Depreciation expense	40,000	80,000
Accounts receivable increase (decrease)	100,000	(20,000)
Inventory increase (decrease)	(50,000)	50,000
Accounts payable increase (decrease)	(110,000)	70,000
Accrued liabilities increase (decrease)	60,000	(80,000)

LO2

M16-5 Computing Cash Flows from Operating Activities (Indirect Method)

For the following two independent cases, show the Cash Flows from Operating Activities section of the 2011 statement of cash flows using the indirect method.

	CASE A		CASE B	
	2011	2010	2011	2010
Sales revenue	$ 10,000	$ 9,000	$ 21,000	$ 18,000
Cost of goods sold	6,000	5,500	12,000	11,000
Gross profit	4,000	3,500	9,000	7,000
Depreciation expense	1,000	1,000	2,000	1,500
Salaries expense	2,500	2,000	5,000	5,000
Net income	500	500	2,000	500
Accounts receivable	300	400	750	600
Inventories	600	500	790	800
Accounts payable	800	700	800	850
Salaries payable	1,000	1,200	200	250

LO3

M16-6 Computing Cash Flows from Investing Activities

Based on the following information, compute cash flows from investing activities.

Cash collections from customers	$800
Purchase of used equipment	850
Depreciation expense	200
Proceeds from sale of investments	300

LO4

M16-7 Computing Cash Flows from Financing Activities

Based on the following information, compute cash flows from financing activities.

Purchase of investments	$ 250
Dividends paid	800
Interest paid	400
Additional short-term borrowing from bank	2,000

LO3, 4, 5

M16-8 Reporting Noncash Investing and Financing Activities

Which of the following transactions would be considered noncash investing and financing activities?

_____1. Additional borrowing from bank.

_____2. Purchase of equipment with investments.

_____3. Dividends paid in cash.

_____4. Purchase of building with promissory note.

LO5

M16-9 Interpreting Cash Flows from Operating, Investing, and Financing Activities

Quantum Dots, Inc., is a nanotechnology company that manufactures "quantum dots," which are tiny pieces of silicon consisting of 100 or more molecules. Quantum dots can be used to illuminate very small objects, enabling scientists to see the blood vessels beneath a mouse's skin ripple with each heartbeat, at the rate of 100 times per second. Evaluate this research intensive company's cash flows assuming the following was reported in its statement of cash flows.

	Current Year	Previous Year
Cash flows from operating activities		
Net cash provided by (used for) operating activities	$ (50,790)	$ (46,730)
Cash flows from investing activities		
Purchases of research equipment	(250,770)	(480,145)
Proceeds from selling all short-term investments	35,000	—
Net cash provided by (used for) investing activities	(215,770)	(480,145)
Cash flows from financing activities		
Additional long-term debt borrowed	100,000	200,000
Proceeds from stock issuance	140,000	200,000
Cash dividends paid	—	(10,000)
Net cash provided by (used for) financing activities	240,000	390,000
Net increase (decrease) in cash	(26,560)	(136,875)
Cash at beginning of period	29,025	165,900
Cash at end of period	$ 2,465	$ 29,025

M16-10 Calculating and Interpreting Free Cash Flow

LO5

Capital Corporation reported the following information in its statement of cash flows:

	2010	2011	2012
Net cash flow from operating activities	$35,000	$32,000	$23,000
Dividends paid	2,000	3,000	2,500
Income taxes paid	9,000	8,500	6,500
Purchases of property, plant, and equipment	31,818	22,857	20,325

Calculate the total free cash flow for the period covering 2010–2012 and the free cash flow for each year during the period. What does this analysis tell you about the company's need for using external financing to replace property, plant, and equipment and pay dividends?

M16-11 Calculating and Interpreting the Quality of Income Ratio

LO5

Dan's Products, Inc., reported net income of $80,000, depreciation expense of $2,000, and cash flow from operations of $60,000. Compute the quality of income ratio. What does the ratio tell you about the company's accrual of revenues and/or deferral of expenses?

M16-12 (Supplement A) Matching Items Reported to Cash Flow Statement Categories (Direct Method)

Prestige Manufacturing Corporation reports the following items in its 2011 statement of cash flows presented using the direct method. Indicate whether each item is disclosed in the operating activities (O), investing activities (I), or financing activities (F) section of the statement or (NA) if the item does not appear on the statement.

_____1. Payment for equipment purchase.   _____4. Proceeds from issuance of stock.

_____2. Repayments of bank loan.   _____5. Interest paid.

_____3. Dividends paid.   _____6. Receipts from customers.

M16-13 (Supplement A) Computing Cash Flows from Operating Activities (Direct Method)

For each of the following independent cases, compute cash flows from operating activities using the direct method. Assume the following list includes all items relevant to operating activities.

	Case A	Case B
Sales revenue	$ 70,000	$ 55,000
Cost of goods sold	35,000	32,000
Depreciation expense	10,000	2,000
Other operating expenses	5,000	13,000
Net income	20,000	8,000
Accounts receivable increase (decrease)	(1,000)	4,000
Inventory increase (decrease)	2,000	0
Accounts payable increase (decrease)	0	3,000
Accrued liabilities increase (decrease)	1,000	(2,000)

M16-14 (Supplement A) Computing Cash Flows from Operating Activities (Direct Method)
Refer to the two cases presented in M16-5, and show the Cash Flow from Operating Activities section of the 2011 statement of cash flows using the direct method.

Exercises   HM™   Available with McGraw-Hill's Homework Manager

LO1, 2

Nike

E16-1 Matching Items Reported to Cash Flow Statement Categories (Indirect Method)
Nike, Inc., is the best-known sports shoe, apparel, and equipment company in the world because of its association with sports stars such as LeBron James. Some of the items included in its recent statement of cash flows presented using the indirect method are listed here.

Indicate whether each item is disclosed in the operating activities (O), investing activities (I), or financing activities (F) section of the statement or (NA) if the item does not appear on the statement.

_____ 1. Additions to long-term debt (new borrowing).

_____ 2. Depreciation.

_____ 3. Additions to property, plant, and equipment (paid in cash).

_____ 4. Increase (decrease) in notes payable. (The amount is owed to financial institutions.)

_____ 5. (Increase) decrease in other current assets.

_____ 6. Cash received from disposal of property, plant, and equipment.

_____ 7. Reductions in long-term debt (repayment).

_____ 8. Issuance of stock (for cash).

_____ 9. (Increase) decrease in inventory.

_____ 10. Net income.

LO1, 2

E16-2 Comparing the Direct and Indirect Methods
To compare statement of cash flows reporting under the direct and indirect methods, enter check marks to indicate which line items are reported on the statement of cash flows with each method.

Cash Flows (and Related Changes)	Statement of Cash Flows Method	
	Direct	Indirect
1. Net income.	_____	_____
2. Receipts from customers.	_____	_____
3. Accounts receivable increase or decrease.	_____	_____
4. Payments to suppliers.	_____	_____
5. Inventory increase or decrease.	_____	_____
6. Accounts payable increase or decrease.	_____	_____
7. Payments to employees.	_____	_____
8. Wages payable, increase or decrease.	_____	_____
9. Depreciation expense.	_____	_____
10. Cash flows from operating activities.	_____	_____
11. Cash flows from investing activities.	_____	_____
12. Cash flows from financing activities.	_____	_____
13. Net increase or decrease in cash during the period.	_____	_____

LO2

E16-3 Reporting Cash Flows from Operating Activities (Indirect Method)
The following information pertains to Guy's Gear Company for 2010:

Sales		$80,000
Expenses		
Cost of goods sold	$50,000	
Depreciation expense	6,000	
Salaries expense	12,000	68,000
Net income		$12,000

Partial Balance Sheet	2010	2009
Accounts receivable	$ 15,000	$ 20,000
Merchandise inventory	18,000	10,000
Salaries payable	2,500	2,000

Required:

Present the operating activities section of the statement of cash flows for Guy's Gear Company using the indirect method.

E16-4 Reporting and Interpreting Cash Flows from Operating Activities from an Analyst's Perspective (Indirect Method)   LO2, 5

New Vision Company completed its income statement and balance sheet for 2010 and provided the following information:

Service revenue		$66,000
Expenses		
Salaries	$42,000	
Depreciation	7,300	
Utilities	7,000	
Loss on sale of machine	1,700	58,000
Net income		$ 8,000

Partial Balance Sheet	2010	2009
Accounts receivable	$12,000	$24,000
Salaries payable	19,000	10,000
Other accrued liabilities	5,000	9,000
Land	52,000	57,000

Required:

1. Present the operating activities section of the statement of cash flows for New Vision Company using the indirect method.

2. Of the potential causes of differences between cash flow from operations and net income, which are the most important to financial analysts?

E16-5 Reporting and Interpreting Cash Flows from Operating Activities from an Analyst's Perspective (Indirect Method)   LO2, 5

Sizzler, Inc., operates 700 family restaurants around the world. The company's annual report contained the following information (in thousands):

Operating Activities	
Net loss	$(9,482)
Depreciation	33,305
Increase in receivables	170
Decrease in inventories	643
Increase in prepaid expenses	664
Decrease in accounts payable	2,282
Decrease in accrued liabilities	719
Increase in income taxes payable	1,861
Reduction of long-term debt	12,691
Additions to equipment	29,073

Required:

1. Based on this information, compute cash flow from operating activities using the indirect method.

2. What were the major reasons that Sizzler was able to report a net loss but positive cash flow from operations?

3. Of the potential causes of differences between cash flow from operations and net income, which are the most important to financial analysts?

LO2, 3
AMC Theatres

E16-6 Determining Cash Flows from the Sale of Property (Indirect Method)

The first in the theatre industry to introduce a customer loyalty program (like frequent flyer miles for movie watchers) was AMC Theatres. During the prior year, the company sold property for $5,494,000 cash and recorded a gain on sale of $1,385,000. During the current year, the company sold property for $9,289,000 cash and recorded a gain on sale of $2,590,000.

Required:

For the property sold by AMC each year, show how the disposals would be reported on the comparative statements of cash flows using the following format (which assumes the indirect method). Indicate the sign and amount of the effects.

	Prior Year	Current Year
Cash flows from operating activities		
Gain on sale of property	_____	_____
Cash flows from investing activities		
Proceeds from disposition of property	_____	_____

LO2, 3
Gymboree

E16-7 Determining Cash Flows from the Sale of Property (Indirect Method)

The Gymboree Corporation, a specialty retailer, offers apparel, accessories, and play programs for children in the United States and Canada. During the prior year, the company sold property for $18,823,000 cash and recorded a loss on sale of $4,419,000. During the current year, the company sold property for $12,648,000 cash and recorded a loss on sale of $2,964,000.

Required:

For the property sold by Gymboree each year, show how the disposals would be reported on the comparative statements of cash flows, using the following format (which assumes the indirect method). Indicate the sign and amount of the effects.

	Prior Year	Current Year
Cash flows from operating activities		
Loss on sale of property	_____	_____
Cash flows from investing activities		
Proceeds from disposition of property	_____	_____

LO2
Colgate-Palmolive

E16-8 Inferring Balance Sheet Changes from the Cash Flow Statement (Indirect Method)

Colgate-Palmolive was founded in 1806. Its statement of cash flows for the first quarter of a recent year reported the following information (in millions):

Operating Activities	
Net income	$ 952.2
Depreciation	243.5
Cash effect of changes in	
Accounts receivable	(122.9)
Inventories	(128.9)
Accounts payable	122.8
Other	303.2
Net cash provided by operations	$1,369.9

Required:

Based on the information reported in the operating activities section of the statement of cash flows for Colgate-Palmolive, determine whether the following accounts increased or decreased during the period: Accounts Receivable, Inventories, and Accounts Payable.

LO2
Apple

E16-9 Inferring Balance Sheet Changes from the Cash Flow Statement (Indirect Method)

The statement of cash flows for Apple for the six-month period ended April 1 of a recent year contained the following information (in millions):

Operating Activities	
Net income	$975
Depreciation	102
Changes in assets and liabilities	
Accounts receivable	34
Inventories	(39)
Other current assets	(892)
Accounts payable	329
Other adjustments	(351)
Net cash provided by operations	$158

Required:

For each of the asset and liability accounts listed in the operating activities section of the statement of cash flows, determine whether the account balances increased or decreased during the period.

E16-10 Analyzing Cash Flows from Operating Activities (Indirect Method) and Calculating and Interpreting the Quality of Income Ratio

LO2, 5

PepsiCo

A recent annual report for PepsiCo contained the following information for the period (in millions):

Net income	$4,078
Cash dividends paid	1,642
Depreciation	1,308
Increase in accounts receivable	272
Increase in inventory	132
Increase in prepaid expense	56
Increase in accounts payable	188
Increase in taxes payable	609
Decrease in other liabilities related to operations	791

Required:

1. Compute cash flows from operating activities for PepsiCo using the indirect method.
2. Compute the quality of income ratio to one decimal place.
3. What was the main reason that PepsiCo's quality of income ratio did not equal 1.0?

E16-11 Calculating and Understanding Operating Cash Flows Relating to Inventory Purchases (Indirect Method)

LO2

The following information was reported by three companies. When completing the requirements, assume that any and all purchases on account are for inventory.

	Aztec Corporation	Bikes Unlimited	Campus Cycles
Cost of goods sold	$175	$175	$350
Inventory purchases from suppliers made using cash	200	0	200
Inventory purchases from suppliers made on account	0	200	200
Cash payments to suppliers on account	0	160	160
Beginning inventory	100	100	200
Ending inventory	125	125	250
Beginning accounts payable	0	80	80
Ending accounts payable	0	120	120

Required:

1. What amount did each company deduct on the income statement related to inventory?
2. What total amount did each company pay in cash during the period related to inventory?
3. By what amount do your answers in 1 and 2 differ for each company?

4. By what amount did each company's inventory increase (decrease)? By what amount did each company's accounts payable increase (decrease)?

5. Using the indirect method of presentation, what amount(s) must each company add (deduct) from net income to convert from accrual to cash basis?

6. Describe any similarities in your answers to requirements 3 and 5. Are these answers the same? Why or why not?

LO3, 4

E16-12 Reporting Cash Flows from Investing and Financing Activities

Randell Furniture Corporation is a North Carolina–based manufacturer of furniture. In a recent quarter, it reported the following activities:

Net income	$ 4,135
Purchase of property, plant, and equipment	871
Borrowings under line of credit (bank)	1,417
Proceeds from issuance of stock	11
Cash received from customers	29,164
Payments to reduce long-term debt	46
Sale of investments	134
Proceeds from sale of property and equipment	6,594
Dividends paid	277
Interest paid	90

Required:

Based on this information, present the cash flows from investing and financing activities sections of the cash flow statement.

LO3, 4, 5

GIBRALTAR
INDUSTRIES

E16-13 Reporting and Interpreting Cash Flows from Investing and Financing Activities with Discussion of Management Strategy

Gibraltar Steel Corporation is a Buffalo, New York–based manufacturer of steel products. In a recent year, it reported the following activities:

Net income	$ 5,213
Purchase of property, plant, and equipment	10,468
Payments of notes payable (bank)	8,598
Net proceeds of stock issuance	26,061
Depreciation	3,399
Long-term debt reduction	17,832
Proceeds from sale of investments	131
Proceeds from sale of property, plant, and equipment	1,817
Proceeds from long-term debt borrowed	10,242
Decrease in accounts receivable	1,137
Proceeds from notes payable (bank)	3,848

Required:

1. Based on this information, present the cash flows from investing and financing activities sections of the cash flow statement.

2. Referring to your response to requirement 1, comment on what you think Gibraltar's management plan was for the use of the cash generated by the stock issuance.

LO5

Disney

E16-14 Calculating and Interpreting Free Cash Flow

The Disney Company reported the following in its 2007 annual report.

	2007	2006	2005
Net income	$4,687	$3,374	$2,533
Net cash provided by operating activities	5,421	6,058	4,269
Purchase of parks, resorts, and other property	(1,566)	(1,299)	(1,823)
Cash paid for interest	551	617	641
Cash paid for income taxes	2,796	1,857	1,572
Cash paid for dividends	637	519	490

Required:

1.   Calculate the total free cash flow for the period covering 2005–2007 and the free cash flow for each year.

2.   Interpret the results of your calculation in requirement 1. What do they suggest about the company's need for external financing to acquire property and equipment and pay dividends?

E16-15 Calculating and Interpreting the Quality of Income Ratio

Refer to the information about the Disney Company in E16-14.

Required:

LO5

Disney

1.   Calculate to one decimal place the quality of income ratio for each year.

2.   Interpret the results of your calculations in requirement 1. Given what you know about the Walt Disney Company from your own personal observations, provide one reason that could explain the sizable difference between net income and net cash provided by operating activities.

E16-16 (Supplement A) Reporting and Interpreting Cash Flows from Operating Activities from an Analyst's Perspective (Direct Method)

Refer to the information for New Vision Company in E16-4.

Required:

1.   Present the operating activities section of the statement of cash flows for New Vision Company using the direct method. Assume other accrued liabilities relate to other expenses on the income statement.

2.   Of the potential causes of differences between cash flow from operations and net income, which are the most important to financial analysts?

E16-17 (Supplement A) Reporting and Interpreting Cash Flows from Operating Activities from an Analyst's Perspective (Direct Method)

Refer to the information given for E16-5 plus the following summarized income statement for Sizzler, Inc.:

Revenues	$136,500
Cost of sales	45,500
Gross margin	91,000
Salary expense	56,835
Depreciation	33,305
Other expenses	7,781
Net loss before income taxes	(6,921)
Income tax expense	2,561
Net loss	$ (9,482)

Required:

1.   Based on this information, compute the cash flow from operating activities using the direct method. Assume prepaid expenses and accrued liabilities relate to other expenses.

2.   What were the major reasons that Sizzler was able to report a net loss but positive cash flow from operations?

3.   Of the potential causes of differences between cash flow from operations and net income, which are the most important to financial analysts?

E16-18 (Supplement B) Preparing a Statement of Cash Flows, Indirect Method: Complete Spreadsheet

To prepare a statement of cash flows for Golf Champion Store, you examined the company's accounts, noting the following transactions:

a.   Purchased equipment, $20,000, and issued a promissory note in full payment.

b.   Purchased a long-term investment for cash, $15,000.

c. Paid cash dividend, $12,000.

d. Sold land for $24,000 cash (the land was purchased for $21,000).

e. Issued shares of stock, 500 shares at $12 per share cash.

You also created the following spreadsheet to use when preparing the statement of cash flows.

	ANALYSIS OF CHANGES			
	Beginning Balances, December 31, 2010	Debit	Credit	Ending Balances, December 31, 2011
Income statement items				
Sales			$140,000	
Cost of goods sold		$59,000		
Depreciation		3,000		
Wage expense		28,000		
Income tax expense		9,000		
Interest expense		5,000		
Other expenses		15,800		
Gain on the sale of land			3,000	
Net income		23,200		
Balance sheet items				
Cash	$ 20,500			$ 37,200
Accounts receivable	22,000			22,000
Merchandise inventory	68,000			75,000
Investments	0			15,000
Land	21,000			0
Equipment	114,500			134,500
Total debits	$246,000			$283,700
Accumulated depreciation	$ 32,000			$ 35,000
Accounts payable	17,000			14,000
Wages payable	2,500			1,500
Income taxes payable	3,000			4,500
Notes payable	75,000			95,000
Contributed capital	100,000			106,000
Retained earnings	16,500			27,700
Total credits	$246,000			$283,700
		Inflows	Outflows	
Statement of Cash Flows				
Cash flows from operating activities				
Cash flows from investing activities				
Cash flows from financing activities				
Net increase (decrease) in cash				
Totals				

Required:

Prepare a spreadsheet to prepare the statement of cash flows using the indirect method. Follow the format in Exhibit 16B.1.

Problems—Set A Available with McGraw-Hill's Homework Manager

PA16-1 Determining Cash Flow Statement Effects of Transactions

LO1

Motif Furniture is an Austin-based furniture company. For each of the following first-quarter transactions, indicate whether operating (O), investing (I), or financing activities (F) are affected and whether the effect is a cash inflow (+) or outflow (−), or (NE) if the transaction has no effect on cash.

_____1. Bought used equipment for cash.

_____2. Paid cash to purchase new equipment.

_____3. Declared and paid cash dividends to stockholders.

_____4. Collected payments on account from customers.

_____5. Recorded an adjusting entry to record accrued salaries expense.

_____6. Recorded and paid interest on debt to creditors.

_____7. Repaid principal on loan from bank.

_____8. Prepaid rent for the following period.

_____9. Made payment to suppliers on account.

PA16-2 Computing Cash Flows from Operating Activities (Indirect Method)

LO2

The income statement and selected balance sheet information for Direct Products Company for the year ended December 31, 2011, follow.

www.mhhe.com/LLPW1e

Income Statement	
Sales revenue	$49,600
Expenses	
Cost of goods sold	21,000
Depreciation expense	2,000
Salaries expense	9,000
Rent expense	4,500
Insurance expense	1,900
Interest expense	1,800
Utilities expense	1,400
Loss on sale of land	1,000
Net income	$ 7,000

Selected Balance Sheet Accounts		
	2011	2010
Accounts receivable	$560	$580
Merchandise inventory	990	770
Accounts payable	440	460
Salaries payable	100	70
Utilities payable	20	15
Prepaid rent	25	20
Prepaid insurance	25	28

Required:

Prepare the Cash Flows from Operating Activities section of the 2011 statement of cash flows using the indirect method.

PA16-3 Preparing a Statement of Cash Flows (Indirect Method)

LO2, 3, 4, 5

XS Supply Company is developing its annual financial statements at December 31, 2011. The statements are complete except for the statement of cash flows. The completed comparative balance sheets and income statement are summarized:

	2011	2010
Balance sheet at December 31		
Cash	$ 34,000	$ 29,000
Accounts receivable	35,000	28,000
Merchandise inventory	41,000	38,000
Property and equipment	121,000	100,000
Less: Accumulated depreciation	(30,000)	(25,000)
	$201,000	$170,000
Accounts payable	$ 36,000	$ 27,000
Wages payable	1,200	1,400
Note payable, long term	38,000	44,000
Contributed capital	88,600	72,600
Retained earnings	37,200	25,000
	$201,000	$170,000
Income statement for 2011		
Sales	$120,000	
Cost of goods sold	70,000	
Other expenses	37,800	
Net income	$ 12,200	

Additional Data:

a. Bought equipment for cash, $21,000.

b. Paid $6,000 on the long-term note payable.

c. Issued new shares of stock for $16,000 cash.

d. No dividends were declared or paid.

e. Other expenses included depreciation, $5,000; wages, $20,000; taxes, $6,000; other, $6,800.

f. Accounts Payable includes only inventory purchases made on credit. Because there are no liability accounts relating to taxes or other expenses, assume that these expenses were fully paid in cash.

Required:

1. Prepare the statement of cash flows for the year ended December 31, 2011, using the indirect method.

2. Evaluate the statement of cash flows.

LO2, 3, 4, 5

www.mhhe.com/LLPW1e

PA16-4 Preparing and Interpreting a Statement of Cash Flows (Indirect Method)

Heads Up Company was started several years ago by two hockey instructors. The company's comparative balance sheets and income statement with additional information follow.

	2012	2011
Balance sheet at December 31		
Cash	$ 6,000	$ 4,000
Accounts receivable	1,000	1,750
Equipment	5,500	5,000
Less: Accumulated depreciation	(1,500)	(1,250)
	$11,000	$ 9,500
Accounts payable	$ 500	$ 1,000
Wages payable	500	750
Bank loan payable	1,500	500
Contributed capital	5,000	5,000
Retained earnings	3,500	2,250
	$11,000	$ 9,500
Income statement for 2012		
Lessons revenue	$37,500	
Wages expense	35,000	
Other expenses	1,250	
Net income	$ 1,250	

Additional Data:

a. Bought new hockey equipment for cash, $500.

b. Borrowed $1,000 cash from the bank during the year.

c. Other expenses included depreciation, $250; rent, $500; taxes, $500.

d. Accounts Payable includes only purchases of services made on credit for operating purposes. Because there are no liability accounts relating to utilities or taxes, assume that these expenses were fully paid in cash.

Required:

1. Prepare the statement of cash flows for the year ended December 31, 2012, using the indirect method.

2. Use the statement of cash flows to evaluate the company's cash flows.

TIP: The demonstration cases provide good examples of information to consider when evaluating cash flows.

PA16-5 (Supplement A) Computing Cash Flows from Operating Activities (Direct Method)
Refer to the information in PA16-2.

www.mhhe.com/LLPW1e

Required:
Prepare the cash flows from the operating activities section of the 2011 statement of cash flows using the direct method.

PA16-6 (Supplement A) Preparing and Interpreting a Statement of Cash Flows (Direct Method)
Refer to PA16-4.

Required:
Complete requirements 1 and 2 using the direct method.

Problems—Set B   Available with McGraw-Hill's Homework Manager

PB16-1 Determining Cash Flow Statement Effects of Transactions   LO1
Fantatech Inc. designs, develops, and produces high-tech entertainment products, including VirtuaSports, that allow novice players to experience hazardous and difficult real-life sports in virtual reality. The company also produces a 4D theater system that combines 3D visual effects with special effects such as vibrating chairs, simulated drops, and scented air blasts. For each of the following transactions listed in Fantatech's annual report, indicate whether operating (O), investing (I), or financing activities (F) are affected and whether the effect is a cash inflow (+) or outflow (−), or (NE) if the transaction has no effect on cash.

_____1. Received deposits from customers for products to be delivered the following period.

_____2. Principal repayments on loan.

_____3. Paid cash to purchase new equipment.

_____4. Received proceeds from loan.

_____5. Collected payments on account from customers.

_____6. Recorded and paid salaries to employees.

_____7. Paid cash for building construction.

_____8. Recorded and paid interest to debt holders.

PB16-2 Computing Cash Flows from Operating Activities (Indirect Method)   LO2
The income statement and selected balance sheet information for Calendars Incorporated for the year ended December 31, 2011, follow.

Income Statement	
Sales revenue	$78,000
Expenses	
Cost of goods sold	36,000
Depreciation expense	16,000
Salaries expense	10,000
Rent expense	2,500
Insurance expense	1,300
Interest expense	1,200
Utilities expense	1,000
Net income	$10,000

Selected Balance Sheet Accounts

	2011	2010
Merchandise inventory	$ 430	$ 490
Accounts receivable	1,800	1,500
Accounts payable	1,200	1,300
Salaries payable	450	300
Utilities payable	100	0
Prepaid rent	50	100
Prepaid insurance	70	90

Required:
Prepare the Cash Flows from Operating Activities section of the 2011 statement of cash flows using the indirect method.

LO2, 3, 4, 5   **PB16-3 Preparing a Statement of Cash Flows (Indirect Method)**
Audio City, Inc., is developing its annual financial statements at December 31, 2011. The statements are complete except for the statement of cash flows. The completed comparative balance sheets and income statement are summarized:

	2011	2010
Balance sheet at December 31		
Cash	$ 63,000	$ 65,000
Accounts receivable	15,000	20,000
Merchandise inventory	22,000	20,000
Property and equipment	210,000	150,000
Less: Accumulated depreciation	(60,000)	(45,000)
	$250,000	$210,000
Accounts payable	$ 8,000	$ 19,000
Wages payable	2,000	1,000
Note payable, long term	60,000	75,000
Contributed capital	100,000	70,000
Retained earnings	80,000	45,000
	$250,000	$210,000
Income statement for 2011		
Sales	$190,000	
Cost of goods sold	90,000	
Other expenses	60,000	
Net income	$ 40,000	

Additional Data:
a.   Bought equipment for cash, $60,000.
b.   Paid $15,000 on the long-term note payable.
c.   Issued new shares of stock for $30,000 cash.
d.   Paid dividends of $5,000 in cash.
e.   Other expenses included depreciation, $15,000; wages, $20,000; taxes, $25,000.
f.   Accounts Payable includes only inventory purchases made on credit. Because a liability relating to taxes does not exist, assume they were fully paid in cash.

Required:
1. Prepare the statement of cash flows for the year ended December 31, 2011, using the indirect method.
2. Evaluate the statement of cash flows.

PB16-4 Preparing and Interpreting a Statement of Cash Flows (Indirect Method)   LO2, 3, 4, 5

Dive In Company was started several years ago by two diving instructors. The company's comparative balance sheets and income statement with additional information follow.

	2012	2011
Balance sheet at December 31		
Cash	$ 3,200	$ 4,000
Accounts receivable	1,000	500
Prepaid expenses	100	50
	$ 4,300	$ 4,550
Wages payable	$ 350	$ 1,100
Contributed capital	1,200	1,000
Retained earnings	2,750	2,450
	$ 4,300	$ 4,550
Income statement for 2012		
Lessons revenue	$33,950	
Wages expense	30,000	
Other expenses	3,650	
Net income	$ 300	

Additional Data:

a.   Prepaid expenses relate to rent paid in advance.
b.   Other operating expenses were paid in cash.
c.   An owner contributed capital by paying $200 cash in exchange for the company's stock.

Required:

1.   Prepare the statement of cash flows for the year ended December 31, 2012, using the indirect method.
2.   Use the statement of cash flows to evaluate the company's cash flows.

PB16-5 (Supplement A) Computing Cash Flows from Operating Activities (Direct Method)
Refer to the information in PB16-2.

Required:
Prepare the Cash Flows from Operating Activities section of the 2011 statement of cash flows using the direct method.

PB16-6 (Supplement A) Preparing and Interpreting a Statement of Cash Flows (Direct Method)
Refer to PB16-4.

Required:
Complete requirements 1 and 2 using the direct method.

Cases and Projects

CP16-1 Finding Financial Information   LO1, 5

Refer to the financial statements of The Home Depot in Appendix A at the end of this book, or download the annual report from the Cases section of the text's Web site at www.mhhe.com/LLPW1e.

Required:

1.   Which of the two basic reporting approaches for the cash flows from operating activities did The Home Depot use?
2.   What amount of tax payments did The Home Depot make during the current year? Where did you find this information?
3.   In the most recent year reported, The Home Depot generated $5,727 million from operating activities. Where did The Home Depot spend this money? List the two largest cash outflows.

LO1, 5

Lowe's

CP16-2 Comparing Financial Information

Refer to the financial statements of The Home Depot in Appendix A and Lowe's in Appendix B at the end of this book, or download the annual reports from the *Cases* section of the text's Web site at www.mhhe.com/LLPW1e.

Required:

1. Which of the two basic reporting approaches for the cash flows from operating activities did Lowe's use? Is this the same as what The Home Depot used?

2. What amount of cash did Lowe's receive during fiscal 2007 from issuing long-term debt?

3. In fiscal 2007, Lowe's generated $4,347 million from operating activities. Where did Lowe's spend this money? List the two largest cash outflows reported in the investing or financing activities sections. Do Lowe's uses differ significantly from The Home Depot's?

LO5

CP16-3 Examining an Annual Report: Internet-Based Team Research

As a team, select an industry to analyze. Using your Web browser, each team member should acquire the annual report or 10-K for one publicly traded company in the industry, with each member selecting a different company. (See CP1-3 in Chapter 1 for a description of possible resources for these tasks.)

Required:

1. On an individual basis, each team member should write a short report that incorporates the following:

    a. Has the company generated positive or negative operating cash flows during the past three years?

    b. Has the company been expanding over the period? If so, what appears to have been the source of financing for this expansion (operating cash flow, additional borrowing, issuance of stock)?

    c. Compute and analyze the quality of income ratio in each of the past three years.

2. Then, as a team, write a short report comparing and contrasting your companies using these attributes. Discuss any patterns across the companies that you as a team observe. Provide potential explanations for any differences discovered.

LO1, 2, 5

CP16-4 Making Ethical Decisions: A Mini Case

Assume you serve on the board of a local golf and country club. In preparation for renegotiating the club's bank loans, the president indicates that the club needs to increase its operating cash flows before the end of the current year. With a wink and sly smile, the club's treasurer reassures the president and other board members that he knows a couple of ways to boost the club's operating cash flows. First, he says, the club can sell some of its accounts receivable to a collections company that is willing to pay the club $97,000 up front for the right to collect $100,000 of the overdue accounts. That will immediately boost operating cash flows. Second, he indicates that the club paid about $200,000 last month to relocate the 18th fairway and green closer to the clubhouse. The treasurer indicates that although these costs have been reported as expenses in the club's own monthly financial statements, he feels an argument can be made for reporting them as part of land and land improvements (a long-lived asset) in the year-end financial statements that would be provided to the bank. He explains that, by recording these payments as an addition to a long-lived asset, they will not be shown as a reduction in operating cash flows.

Required:

1. Does the sale of accounts receivable to generate immediate cash harm or mislead anyone? Would you consider it an ethical business activity?

2. If cash is spent on long-lived assets, such as land improvements, how is it typically classified in the statement of cash flows? If cash is spent on expenses, such as costs for regular upkeep of the grounds, how is it typically classified in the statement of cash flows?

3. What facts are relevant to deciding whether the costs of the 18th hole relocation should be reported as an asset or as an expense? Is it appropriate to make this decision based on the impact it could have on operating cash flows?

4. As a member of the board, how would you ensure that an ethical decision is made?

LO2

CP16-5 Thinking Critically: Interpreting Adjustments Reported on the Statement of Cash Flows from a Management Perspective (Indirect Method)

QuickServe, a chain of convenience stores, was experiencing some serious cash flow difficulties because of rapid growth. The company did not generate sufficient cash from operating activities to finance its new stores, and creditors were not willing to lend money because the company had not produced any income for the previous three years. The new controller for QuickServe proposed a reduction in the estimated life of store equipment to increase depreciation expense; thus, "we can improve cash flows from operating activities because depreciation expense is added back on the statement of cash flows." Other executives were not sure that this was a good idea because the increase in depreciation would make it more difficult to have positive earnings: "Without income, the bank will never lend us money."

Required:

What action would you recommend for QuickServe? Why?

CP16-6 Using a Spreadsheet that Calculates Cash Flows from Operating Activities (Indirect Method)   LO2

You've recently been hired by B2B Consultants to provide financial advisory services to small business managers. B2B's clients often need advice on how to improve their operating cash flows and, given your accounting background, you are frequently called upon to show them how operating cash flows would change if they were to speed up their sales of inventory and their collections of accounts receivable or delay their payment of accounts payable. Each time you are asked to show the effects of these business decisions on the cash flows from operating activities, you get the uneasy feeling that you might inadvertently miscalculate their effects. To deal with this once and for all, you e-mail your friend Owen and ask him to prepare a template that automatically calculates the net operating cash flows from a simple comparative balance sheet. You received his reply today.

From: Owentheaccountant@yahoo.com
To: Helpme@hotmail.com
Cc:
Subject: Excel Help

Hey, pal. I like your idea of working smarter, not harder. Too bad it involved me doing the thinking. Anyhow, I've created a spreadsheet file that contains four worksheets. The first two tabs (labeled BS and IS) are the input sheets where you would enter the numbers from each client's comparative balance sheet and income statement. Your clients are small, so this template allows for only the usual accounts. Also, I've assumed that depreciation is the only reason for a change in accumulated depreciation. If your clients' business activities differ from these, you'll need to contact me for more complex templates. The third worksheet calculates the operating cash flows using the indirect method, and the fourth does this calculation using the direct method. I'll attach the screenshots of each of the worksheets so you can create your own. To answer "what if" questions, all you'll need to do is change selected amounts in the balance sheet and income statement.

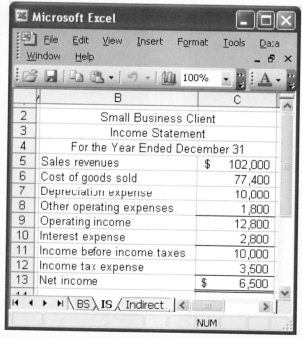

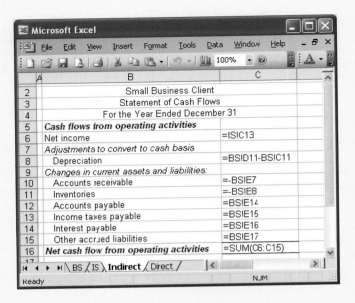

Required:

Copy the information from the worksheets for the balance sheet, income statement, and statement of cash flows (indirect method only) into a spreadsheet file. What was the net cash flow from operating activities?

17 Financial Statement Analysis

LEARNING OBJECTIVES

After completing this chapter, you should be able to:

LO1 Describe how financial statement information is communicated to external users.

Lectured presentations–17-1
www.mhhe.com/LLPW1e

LO2 Use horizontal (trend) analysis to recognize financial changes that unfold over time.

LO3 Use vertical (common size) analysis to understand important relationships within financial statements.

LO4 Calculate and use financial ratios to assess profitability, liquidity, and solvency.

Focus Company: LOWE'S

"Let's Build Something Together"

www.lowes.com

Measuring and evaluating financial performance is like judging gymnastics or figure skating at the Olympics. You have to know three things: (1) the general categories to evaluate for each event, (2) the particular elements to consider within each category, and (3) how to measure performance for each element. On the financial side, analysts follow the same process. They evaluate general categories such as profitability, liquidity, and solvency, which are separated into particular elements such as gross profit margin and net profit margin. For each of these elements, analysts measure performance by computing various percentages and ratios, which themselves are based on information reported in the financial statements.

In this chapter, we focus on Lowe's, the second largest home improvement retailer in the world. Lowe's is a giant with nearly 1,400 stores and 210,000 employees. Yet the company's continued success still requires innovations to increase sales in existing markets and to successfully enter new markets. At the same time, Lowe's must control costs while maintaining a high level of customer service in their stores. Finally, Lowe's management must anticipate the actions of its larger rival, The Home Depot, and deal with changes in overall demand for building products over which it has no control.

How do analysts, investors, and creditors assess Lowe's success in meeting these challenges? This is the purpose of financial statement analysis. Our discussion begins with an explanation of how companies release their financial statement information and where that information can be found. We then explain how to use trend and ratio analysis to understand the financial results of a company's business activities. We conclude the chapter with a review of the key accounting decisions analysts consider when evaluating financial statements.

RELEASE OF FINANCIAL INFORMATION	HORIZONTAL (TREND) ANALYSIS	VERTICAL (COMMON SIZE) ANALYSIS	FINANCIAL RATIOS
• Preliminary Press Release • Quarterly and Annual Reports • Securities and Exchange Commission (SEC) Filings • Investor Information Web Sites	• Preparing Comparative Balance Sheets and Comparative Income Statements • Revealing Changes through Trend Analyses	• Preparing a Common Size Balance Sheet and Income Statement • Interpreting Common Size Statements	• Profitability Ratios • Liquidity Ratios • Solvency Ratios • Accounting Decisions and Ratio Analysis

RELEASE OF FINANCIAL INFORMATION

Preliminary Press Release

Learning Objective 1

Describe how financial statement information is communicated to external users.

Video 17-1
www.mhhe.com/LLPW1e

To provide timely information to external users, public companies such as Lowe's announce their annual and quarterly financial results in a press release sent to news agencies three to five weeks after the accounting period ends. The press release typically includes key figures, a discussion of the results of the company's business activities, and a condensed income statement and balance sheet. During the time between the end of the company's year and the date of the press release, accountants are busy making adjusting journal entries and preparing the financial statements, and managers are preparing their analysis and discussion of the results.

Today, many companies, including Lowe's, follow up the press release with a conference call that is broadcast over the Internet. This call allows analysts to grill senior executives about the company's financial results. By listening to these calls, investors can learn much about a company's business strategy, its expectations for the future, and the key factors analysts consider when they evaluate a company. (To access this useful source of information, visit a company's Web site or check the archive of conference calls at biz.yahoo.com/cc.)

Quarterly and Annual Reports

Several weeks after the preliminary press release, public companies release their complete financial statements as part of the annual or quarterly report. The annual report has two main sections. The first half usually begins with a friendly letter to investors from the company's CEO followed by glossy photographs of the company's products and glowing commentaries on the company's brilliant future. After developing the right mood with these jazzy marketing tactics, the company then presents the financial section, the meat and potatoes of the report. See Exhibit 17.1 for a list of the typical elements of the financial section and the information they contain. The third column of the exhibit gives the pages in Appendix A (at the end of this book) where you will find an example of each element.

A company's quarterly report looks like a condensed version of its annual report. Following a short letter to stockholders and abbreviated discussion of the financial results, a quarterly report presents a condensed income statement for the quarter, a condensed balance sheet dated at the end of the quarter, and a condensed statement of cash flows. These condensed financial statements typically show less detail than the annual statements, often omitting the statement of retained earnings or stockholders' equity and many notes to the financial statements. Items 4, 7, 8, and 9 in Exhibit 17.1 are typically omitted. Because the quarterly financial statements are not audited, they are labeled unaudited. With these limitations, the quarterly reports are not as informative as the annual reports, but they are released on a timelier basis (every three months rather than every year). So, they also have a major impact on investor and creditor judgments about the company.

Exhibit 17.1	Typical Elements of the Financial Section of an Annual Report

Name of Financial Section	Information Presented
1. Summarized financial data	• Key figures covering a period of 5 or 10 years
2. Management's discussion and analysis (MD&A)	• Honest and detailed analysis of the company's financial condition and operating results—a must-read for any serious financial statement user
3. Management's report on internal control	• Statements that describe management's responsibility for ensuring adequate internal control over financial reporting and report on the effectiveness of those controls during the year
4. Auditor's report	• Auditor's conclusion about whether GAAP was followed (and for public companies, whether internal controls were effective)
5. Comparative financial statements	• Multiyear presentation of the four basic statements
6. Financial statement notes	• Further information about the financial statements, crucial to understanding the financial statement data
7. Recent stock price data	• Brief summary of highs and lows during the year
8. Unaudited quarterly data	• Condensed summary of each quarter's results
9. Directors and officers	• List of the individuals who are overseeing and running the company

Securities and Exchange Commission (SEC) Filings

To ensure that timely information is available to investors, the SEC requires public companies to file certain reports with the SEC electronically. These reports include an annual report on Form 10-K, quarterly reports on Form 10-Q, and current event reports on Form 8-K. Several of these reports include information beyond that reported in the quarterly or annual reports. For example, Lowe's 2006 10-K describes the significant business risks the company faces and outlines the strategies for addressing those risks. The 8-K reports significant business events that occurred between financial statement dates, such as the acquisition of another company or a change in auditor.

These filings are available to the public as soon as the SEC's Electronic Data Gathering and Retrieval Service (EDGAR) receives them. As a result, most users can get all the details of a company's financial results from the SEC filings several weeks before the company's glossy reports reach them in the mail. (To find a company's SEC filings, click on "Search for Company Filings" at www.sec.gov.)

Investor Information Web Sites

Investor information Web sites such as Hoovers.com, TheStreet.com, Fool.com, and Yahoo!Finance offer information about public companies. Some sections of these Web sites provide useful information for evaluating and predicting a company's financial performance. For example, at Yahoo!Finance, you can obtain valuable financial information about Lowe's and its industry sector including financial ratios similar to those you will read about later in this chapter. It is important to note that many Web sites do not show the formulas used to calculate the ratios. That can be a serious drawback because ratios and amounts with similar-sounding names may be calculated differently.

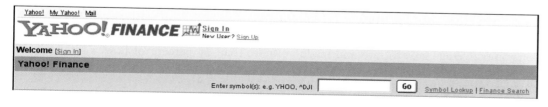

Most good stories have a plot, one the reader comes to understand as it unfolds over time. In the same way, the story of a business and its activities unfolds gradually. To understand and evaluate the results of business activities, then, you need to look at a company over time from many different angles. Only after you have combined the results of all your evaluations into a complete story will you understand whether or not a business is truly successful and why. The first financial analysis tool that we discuss is horizontal or trend analysis.

HORIZONTAL (TREND) ANALYSIS

Horizontal (trend) analysis helps financial statement users to recognize financial changes that unfold over time. This approach compares individual financial statement items from year to year with the general goal of identifying significant sustained changes or trends. For example, trend analysis can be used to determine the dollar and percentage changes in the cost of goods sold this year relative to prior years. Because this type of analysis compares the results on each line of the financial statements across several years, trend analysis is also known as horizontal analysis. Because it compares results over a series of periods, it is sometimes called **time-series analysis.**

Preparing Comparative Balance Sheets and Comparative Income Statements

Regardless of the name, trend analyses are usually calculated in terms of year-to-year dollar and percentage changes. A year-to-year percentage change expresses the current year's dollar change as a percentage of the prior year's total by using the following calculation:

$$\text{Year-to-Year Change (\%)} = \frac{\text{Change This Year}}{\text{Prior Year's Total}} \times 100 = \frac{(\text{Current Year's Total} - \text{Prior Year's Total})}{\text{Prior Year's Total}} \times 100$$

To demonstrate how to calculate a trend, we analyze Lowe's financial statements. Summaries of Lowe's balance sheets and income statements from three recent years appear in Exhibits 17.2 and 17.3. Dollar and percentage changes from fiscal year 2005 to 2006[1] are shown to the right of the balance sheet and income statement. The dollar changes were calculated by subtracting the 2005 balances from the 2006 balances. The percentage changes were calculated by dividing those differences by the 2005 balances. For example, according to Exhibit 17.2, Cash decreased by $59 = ($364 − $423) in 2006 relative to 2005 (all numbers in millions). That dollar amount represented a decrease of 13.9% [= ($59 ÷ $423) × 100]. To avoid focusing on unimportant changes, use the percentage changes to identify potentially significant changes and then check the dollar change to make sure that it too is significant.

Revealing Changes through Trend Analyses

Data in Exhibits 17.2 and 17.3 indicate that Lowe's grew significantly in 2006 despite a slowdown in the housing market. Exhibit 17.2, for example, shows that total assets increased approximately 12.7 percent in 2006. Similarly, Exhibit 17.3 shows that net sales revenues, gross profit, and net income also rose in 2006 by 8.5, 9.5, and 12.3 percent, respectively.

The major drivers of these changes are explained in the Management's Discussion and Analysis (MD&A) section of the company's 2006 annual report. Lowe's opened 155 new stores in 2006 and was planning to open more than 400 additional stores in the future. Installed sales, which reflect a trend away from do-it-yourself projects and toward do-it-for-me projects, increased by 9 percent in 2006, outpacing the company's overall sales growth. Even more impressive was growth in sales to commercial businesses, which grew at nearly double the company's average growth rate and made up more than 25 percent of Lowe's total sales in 2006. To expand online sales, the company also continued to refine the functionality and product offerings on its corporate Web site.

---

[1] Like many retail companies, Lowe's fiscal year ends at the end of January.

Exhibit 17.2   Trend (Horizontal) Analysis of Lowe's Summarized Balance Sheets   Lowe's

Lowe's
Balance Sheets
(in millions)

| | | | INCREASE (DECREASE) | |
Year Ended:	Fiscal 2006	Fiscal 2005	Amount	Percent
ASSETS				
Current assets				
Cash	$ 364	$ 423	$ (59)	(13.9)%
Short-term investments	432	453	(21)	(4.6)
Accounts receivable	—		—	0.0
Inventories	7,144	6,635	509	7.7
Other current assets	374	277	97	35.0
Total current assets	8,314	7,788	526	6.8
Property and equipment, net	18,971	16,354	2,617	16.0
Long-term Investments and other assets	482	497	(15)	(3.0)
Total assets	$27,767	$24,639	$3,128	12.7
LIABILITIES and STOCKHOLDERS' EQUITY				
Current liabilities	$ 6,539	$ 5,832	$ 707	12.1
Long-term liabilities	5,503	4,511	992	22.0
Total liabilities	12,042	10,343	1,699	16.4
Stockholders' equity	15,725	14,296	1,429	10.0
Total liabilities and stockholders' equity	$27,767	$24,639	$3,128	12.7

Exhibit 17.3   Trend (Horizontal) Analysis of Lowe's Summarized Income Statements   Lowe's

Lowe's
Income Statements
(in millions)

| | | | INCREASE (DECREASE) | |
Year Ended:	Fiscal 2006	Fiscal 2005	Amount	Percent
Net sales revenue	$46,927	$43,243	$3,684	8.5%
Cost of revenues	30,729	28,453	2,276	8.0
Gross profit	16,198	14,790	1,408	9.5
Operating and other expenses	11,046	10,136	910	9.0
Interest expense	154	158	(4)	(2.5)
Income tax expense	1,893	1,731	162	9.4
Net income	$ 3,105	$ 2,765	$ 340	12.3
Earnings per share	$ 2.02	$ 1.78	$ 0.24	13.5

In sum, the story told by our trend analysis is that Lowe's grew significantly from 2005 to 2006. While that growth increased sales and gross profit, it also increased operating expenses. Fortunately, the growth in sales more than offset the growth in expenses.

VERTICAL (COMMON SIZE) ANALYSIS

A second type of analysis, vertical (common size) analysis, focuses on important relationships within financial statements. When a company is growing or shrinking overall, it is difficult to tell from the dollar amounts whether the proportions within each statement category are changing. Common size financial statements provide this information by expressing each financial statement amount as a percentage of another amount on that statement. The usefulness of common size statements is illustrated by the fact that Lowe's presents its balance sheet and income statements in the common size format illustrated in Exhibits 17.4 and 17.5.

Exhibit 17.4   Vertical (Common Size) Analysis of Lowe's Summarized Balance Sheets   Lowe's

Lowe's
Balance Sheets
(in millions)

Year Ended	FISCAL 2006		FISCAL 2005	
	Amount	Percent	Amount	Percent
ASSETS				
Current assets				
Cash	$ 364	1.3%	$ 423	1.7%
Short-term investments	432	1.6	453	1.8
Inventories	7,144	25.7	6,635	26.9
Other current assets	374	1.3	277	1.1
Property and equipment, net	18,971	68.3	16,354	66.4
Long-term investments and other assets	482	1.7	497	2.0
Total assets	$27,767	100.0%	$24,639	100.0%
LIABILITIES and STOCKHOLDERS' EQUITY				
Current liabilities	$ 6,539	23.5%	$ 5,832	23.7%
Long-term liabilities	5,503	19.8	4,511	18.3
Stockholders' equity	15,725	56.6	14,296	58.0
Total liabilities and stockholders' equity	$27,767	100.0%	$24,639	100.0%

Exhibit 17.5   Vertical (Common Size) Analysis of Lowe's Summarized Income Statements   Lowe's

Lowe's
Income Statements
(in millions)

Year Ended	FISCAL 2006		FISCAL 2005	
	Amount	Percent	Amount	Percent
Net sales revenue	$46,927	100.0%	$43,243	100.0%
Cost of revenues	30,729	65.5	28,453	65.8
Gross profit	16,198	34.5	14,790	34.2
Operating and other expenses	11,046	23.5	10,136	23.4
Interest expense	154	0.3	158	0.4
Income tax expense	1,893	4.0	1,731	4.0
Net income	$ 3,105	6.6%	$ 2,765	6.4%

Preparing a Common Size Balance Sheet and Income Statement

In a common size balance sheet, each asset appears as a percent of total assets, and each liability or stockholders' equity item appears as a percent of total liabilities and stockholders' equity. For example, in Exhibit 17.4, which presents Lowe's common size balance sheets, cash was 1.3% of total assets [= ($364 ÷ $27,767) × 100] at the end of fiscal 2006.

The common size income statement reports each income statement item as a percentage of sales. For example, cost of revenues was equal to 65.5 percent of net sales revenue in 2006 [= ($30,729 ÷ $46,927) × 100]. Exhibit 17.5 presents common size income statements for Lowe's for 2005 and 2006.

Interpreting Common Size Statements

Although Lowe's balance sheet indicates growth during 2006, the common size balance sheet suggests that the increase on the assets side reflected relative increases in property and equipment resulting from the opening of new stores combined with relative declines in most other assets as a percentage of total assets. The decline in inventory reflects both lower costs of certain materials sold by Lowe's and the expected slowdown in the housing market in 2007. These increases in assets were financed more by increases in long-term liabilities than by current liabilities or stockholders' equity as evidenced by the increase in the long-term liabilities percentage.

The common size income statements tell us how Lowe's was able to increase its net income as a percent of sales from 6.4 percent to 6.6 percent. Lowe's accomplished this feat by reducing cost of goods sold as a percent of sales by 0.3 percent, which was partially offset by small increases in operating and other expenses. In its MD&A, Lowe's explains the improvement as resulting from a shift in sales mix to more profitable products and a switch to lower cost foreign-made products. A 0.3 percent decrease in cost of goods sold as a percent of sales may seem to be a small effect at first. But this improvement accounted for $141 million of Lowe's net income for 2006.

These findings from the vertical (common size) analysis are consistent with the results of the horizontal (trend) analysis discussed earlier. Opening 155 new stores involves a significant additional investment in property and equipment and start-up efforts at the new stores tend to add to other operating expenses.

SELF-STUDY PRACTICE

For the year ended January 28, 2007, The Home Depot reported net income of $5.76 billion on sales of $90.8 billion. If the company's cost of sales in fiscal 2006 was $61.1 billion, what percentages would be shown on a common size income statement for gross profit and net income? If sales were $81.5 billion in 2005, what was the year-to-year percentage increase in 2006? Round your answers to one decimal place.

$$\text{Gross Profit Percentage} = \frac{(\$\underline{} - \underline{}) \text{ billion}}{\$90.8 \text{ billion}} \times 100$$

$$\text{Net Profit Margin} = \frac{\$5.76 \text{ billion}}{\$\underline{}} \times 100$$

$$\text{Sales Increase (Percentage)} = \frac{(\$\underline{} - \underline{}) \text{ billion}}{\$\underline{} \text{ billion}} \times 100$$

After you have finished, check your answers with the solution at the bottom of the page.

Solution to
Self-Study Practice

Gross profit percentage = [($90.8 − $61.1) ÷ 90.8] × 100
    = 32.7%
Net profit margin = [$(5.76) ÷ 90.8] × 100 = 6.3%
Sales increase (percentage) = [($90.8 − $81.5) ÷ 81.5] ÷ 100
    = 11.4%

FINANCIAL RATIOS

Ratio analyses help financial statement users to understand relationships among various items reported in the financial statements. This type of analysis compares the amounts for one or more line items to the amounts for other line items in the same year. Like common size statements, ratio analyses are useful because they consider differences in the size of the amounts being compared, which allows users to evaluate how well a company has performed given the level of its other resources. In fact, some of the most popular ratios, such as net profit margin and debt to assets ratios, are taken directly from the common size statements.

Most analysts classify ratios into three categories:

1. Profitability ratios, which relate to the company's performance in the current period—in particular, the company's ability to generate income.
2. Liquidity ratios, which relate to the company's short-term survival—in particular, the company's ability to use current assets to repay liabilities as they become due.
3. Solvency ratios, which relate to the company's long-run survival—in particular, the company's ability to repay lenders when debt matures and to make the required interest payments prior to the date of maturity.

These three categories emphasize different aspects of a company's performance, which may or may not be important depending on the purpose of the analysis.

In the next section, we demonstrate how to calculate financial trends and ratios. We must emphasize at the start, however, that **no analysis is complete unless it leads to an interpretation that helps financial statement users to understand and evaluate a company's financial results.** Without interpretation, trends and ratios are nothing more than a list of apparently unrelated numbers. See Exhibit 17.6 for a summary of the most commonly used ratios, many of which were introduced in Chapters 4–16, categorized as profitability, liquidity, or solvency ratios.

As you have seen in other chapters, benchmarks help to interpret a company's ratios. Benchmarks can include the company's prior year results and those of close competitors, as well as industry averages. In a competitive economy, companies strive to outperform one another, so comparisons with other companies can suggest which are likely to survive and thrive in the long run.

For Lowe's, the industry average encompasses home improvement stores of all sizes and types. The Home Depot, the largest home improvement retailer in the world, is Lowe's closest competitor, with 2,147 stores located in the United States, Canada, China, and Mexico. (Both Lowe's and The Home Depot's annual reports for fiscal 2007 are reproduced in Appendix A and B at the end of this book.) Lowe's is the second largest company in the industry. Its customer-oriented marketing strategy focuses on attracting women. The Home Depot's marketing strategy focuses on contractors and other experienced builders as well as homeowners with a do-it-yourself attitude. In the following sections, we compare Lowe's financial ratios to the prior year and in some cases to those for The Home Depot and the industry as a whole.

Profitability Ratios

The financial analyses in this section focus on the level of profits Lowe's generated during the period. We will compute and interpret ratios (1) through (8) in Exhibit 17.6. The computation shown for each ratio is for 2006 and is based on the statements in Exhibits 17.4 and 17.5. Our first two profitability ratios come right from the common size income statement in Exhibit 17.5.

Net Profit Margin

Net profit margin indicates the percentage of sales revenues that remain in net income after expenses have been deducted. Using the equation in Exhibit 17.6, Lowe's net profit margin in each of the last two years was:

		2006	2005
Net Profit Margin $= \dfrac{\text{Net Income}}{\text{Net Sales Revenue}} \times 100 =$		6.6%	6.4%

$6.6\% = (\$3,105 \div \$46,927) \times 100\%$

Exhibit 17.6   Common Ratios Used in Financial Statement Analysis

Profitability Ratios

(1) Net Profit Margin = $\dfrac{\text{Net Income}}{\text{Net Sales Revenue}} \times 100$

(2) Gross Profit Percentage = $\dfrac{\text{Net Sales Revenue} - \text{Cost of Goods Sold}}{\text{Net Sales Revenue}} \times 100$

(3) Asset Turnover = $\dfrac{\text{Net Sales Revenue}}{\text{Average Total Assets}}$

(4) Fixed Asset Turnover = $\dfrac{\text{Net Sales Revenue}}{\text{Average Net Fixed Assets}}$

(5) Return on Assets (ROA) = $\dfrac{\text{Net Income*}}{\text{Average Total Assets}} \times 100$

(6) Return on Equity (ROE) = $\dfrac{\text{Net Income}}{\text{Average Stockholders' Equity}} \times 100$

(7) Earnings per Share (EPS) = $\dfrac{\text{Net Income} - \text{Preferred Dividends}}{\text{Average Number of Common Shares Outstanding}}$

(8) Price/Earnings = $\dfrac{\text{Stock Price}}{\text{EPS}}$

Liquidity Ratios

(9) Receivables Turnover = $\dfrac{\text{Net Sales Revenue}}{\text{Average Net Receivables}}$

Days to Collect = $\dfrac{365}{\text{Receivables Turnover Ratio}}$

(10) Inventory Turnover = $\dfrac{\text{Cost of Goods Sold}}{\text{Average Inventory}}$

Days to Sell = $\dfrac{365}{\text{Inventory Turnover Ratio}}$

(11) Current Ratio = $\dfrac{\text{Current Assets}}{\text{Current Liabilities}}$

(12) Quick Ratio = $\dfrac{\text{Quick Assets}}{\text{Current Liabilities}}$

Solvency Ratios

(13) Debt to Assets = $\dfrac{\text{Total Liabilities}}{\text{Total Assets}}$

(14) Times Interest Earned = $\dfrac{\text{Net Income} + \text{Interest Expense} + \text{Income Tax Expense}}{\text{Interest Expense}}$

(15) Free Cash Flow = Net Cash Flow from Operating Activities − Purchases of Property and Equipment − Dividends Paid

* In more complex ROA analyses, interest expense (net of tax) and minority interest are added back to net income in the numerator because the ratio assesses return on capital independent of source.

The net profit margin of 6.6 percent for 2006 indicates that for each dollar of sales, Lowe's generated 6.6 cents of net income. That is quite good compared to the average home improvement retailer, which according to Yahoo!Finance enjoyed a net profit margin of 5.9 percent that year. The seemingly small increase from 6.4 percent in 2005 to 6.6 percent in 2006 was significant, yielding an additional $94 million in profit on the company's $47 billion in sales.

Gross Profit Percentage

Our earlier analysis indicated that Lowe's gross profits from 2005 to 2006 increased in terms of total dollars, but it did not indicate whether those increases were caused by more total sales or more profit per sale. The gross profit percentage is particularly helpful in this kind of analysis because it indicates how much profit was made, on average, on each dollar of sales after deducting the cost of goods sold. Lowe's gross profit percentage for the last two years was:

	2006	2005
$\text{Gross Profit Percentage} = \dfrac{\text{Net Sales} - \text{Cost of Goods Sold}}{\text{Net Sales}} \times 100 =$	34.5%	34.2%

$$34.5\% = [(\$46,927 - \$30,729) \div \$46,927] \times 100$$

This analysis shows that in 2006, after payment of the cost of merchandise sold, 34.5 cents of each sales dollar were left to cover other costs, such as employee wages, advertising, and utilities and to provide profits to the stockholders. The increase in the gross profit percentage from 2005 to 2006 (34.5% − 34.2%) means that Lowe's made 0.3¢ more gross profit on each dollar of sales in 2006 than in 2005. There are two potential explanations for this increase: (1) Lowe's charged higher selling prices without paying a corresponding increase in the cost of merchandise and (2) Lowe's obtained merchandise at a lower unit cost. The MD&A section of Lowe's annual report explains that the increase in gross profit percentage came from a reduction in the cost of merchandise, primarily because of an increase in the proportion of imported goods.

Asset Turnover

The asset turnover ratio indicates the amount of sales revenue generated for each dollar invested in assets. Lowe's ratios for the two years were:

	2006	2005
$\text{Asset Turnover} = \dfrac{\text{Net Sales Revenue}}{\text{Average Total Assets}} =$	1.8	1.9

$$1.79 = \$46,927 \div [(\$27,767 + \$24,639) \div 2]$$

The asset turnover ratio suggests that Lowe's assets did not generate sales as efficiently in 2006 as in the prior year. To understand why, it is helpful to focus on the key assets used to generate sales. For a retailer such as Lowe's, the key asset is store properties, which we can compare to sales using the fixed asset turnover ratio, discussed next.

Fixed Asset Turnover

The fixed asset turnover ratio indicates how much revenue the company generates in sales for each dollar invested in fixed assets, such as store buildings and the property they sit on. Lowe's fixed asset turnover ratios for the two years were:

	2006	2005
$\text{Fixed Asset Turnover} = \dfrac{\text{Net Sales Revenue}}{\text{Average Net Fixed Assets}} =$	2.7	2.9

$$2.7 = \$46,927 \div [(\$18,971 + \$16,354) \div 2]$$

This analysis shows that Lowe's had $2.66 of sales in 2006 for each dollar invested in fixed assets. Although the decline from 2005 was not good, it is understandable because Lowe's added 155 stores during these two years. Those stores will likely need some time to establish a strong customer base and begin generating sales at full capacity. Moreover, as additional stores are opened, they are likely to be located in areas of greater competition. Still, Lowe's fixed asset turnover ratio is low compared to that of its main competitor, The Home Depot, whose fixed asset turnover ratio was 3.53 in 2006. In terms of using fixed assets to generate sales revenue, The Home Depot has a competitive advantage over Lowe's. In other words, Lowe's is operating less efficiently than its major competitor.

Return on Assets (ROA)

The return on assets ratio compares the amount of net income to average total assets. ROA measures how much the firm earned for each dollar of investment. It is the broadest measure of profitability and management effectiveness, independent of financing strategy. ROA allows investors to compare management's investment performance against alternative investment options. Firms with higher ROA are doing a better job of selecting new investments, all other things equal. Company managers often compute the measure on a division-by-division basis and use it to evaluate division managers' relative performance.[2]

		2006	2005
Return on Assets (ROA) = $\dfrac{\text{Net Income}}{\text{Average Total Assets}} \times 100 =$		11.8%	12.1%

$$11.8\% = (\$3,105 \div [(\$27,767 + \$24,639) \div 2]) \times 100$$

Even though Lowe's net income increased in 2006, its ROA fell slightly because of the increase in assets during the period. Net profit margin and total asset turnover affect return on assets in the following fashion:

$$\text{ROA} = \text{Net Profit Margin} \times \text{Asset Turnover}$$
$$11.8\% = 6.6\% \times 1.79$$

The decline resulted from the decline in total asset turnover discussed earlier, which was partially offset by the increase in net profit margin.

Return on Equity (ROE)

The return on equity ratio compares the amount of net income to average stockholders' equity. ROE reports the net amount earned during the period as a percentage of each dollar contributed by stockholders and retained in the business. Lowe's ROE ratios for the past two years were:

		2006	2005
Return on Equity (ROE) = $\dfrac{\text{Net Income}}{\text{Average Stockholders' Equity}} \times 100 =$		20.7%	21.4%

$$20.7\% = (\$3,105 \div [(\$15,725 + \$14,296) \div 2]) \times 100$$

Lowe's ROE fell to 20.7 percent because average stockholders' equity increased. Lowe's ROE was close to the industry average of 20.0 percent in 2006, but it lagged behind The Home Depot's, which was 22.2 percent. Lowe's ROE is higher than its ROA because it is earning a higher return on its borrowed funds than it is paying to creditors for interest.

---

[2] In more complex ROA analyses, interest expense (net of tax) and minority interest are added back to net income in the numerator because the ratio assesses return on capital independent of source.

Earnings Per Share (EPS)

Earnings per share (EPS) indicates the amount of earnings generated for each share of outstanding common stock. It is reported on the income statement. Lowe's reported average shares outstanding of 1,535 and 1,555 in 2006 and 2005, respectively. It has no preferred dividends. Despite the decline in Lowe's ROE, its EPS ratio increased in 2006 because the company repurchased some of its shares (which reduced the number of common shares outstanding). Lowe's EPS for the past two years was:

		2006	2005
Earnings per Share (EPS) $=$ $\dfrac{\text{Net Income} - \text{Preferred Dividends}}{\text{Average Number of Common Shares}}$ $=$		$2.02	$1.78

$$\$2.02 = \$3,105 \div 1,535$$

Price/Earnings (P/E) Ratio

The P/E ratio relates the company's stock price to its EPS, as follows:

		2006	2005
Price/earnings $=$ $\dfrac{\text{Stock Price}}{\text{EPS}}$ $=$		15.3	16.3

$$15.3 = \$31 \div \$2.02$$

Using the going price for Lowe's stock when its 2006 earnings were announced, its P/E ratio was 15.3, meaning that investors were willing to pay 15.3 times its earnings per share to buy a share of stock. According to Yahoo! Finance, the average P/E ratio for home improvement stores at that time was about 14.8, suggesting that investors were more willing to buy stock in Lowe's than in other home improvement retailers.

Let's pause to summarize what we have learned so far. Despite a slowdown in the housing market, Lowe's increased its profit margin in 2006. Management did so primarily by (1) reducing merchandise costs by importing more merchandise and (2) growing sales by opening new stores, increasing sales to commercial builders, and placing more emphasis on online sales. These increases in gross profit were partly eaten up by operating expenses, which grew at a rate of 9 percent. Despite a decline in ROE during 2006, the company's EPS ratio increased as a result of share repurchases. Asset turnover and fixed asset turnover both declined, meaning that the company was not using its assets to generate sales as efficiently as in the past. Lowe's P/E ratio, which was slightly higher than the industry average, suggests that investors were willing to overlook those declines and were more willing to buy stock in Lowe's than in other home improvement retailers. The bottom line is that Lowe's has fared reasonably well during the housing slump, although the company currently trails its main competitor, The Home Depot, on a number of key ratios.

Liquidity Ratios

The analyses in this section focus on Lowe's ability to survive in the short term by converting its assets to cash to pay current liabilities as they come due. We interpret ratios (9) through (12) from Exhibit 17.6.

Receivables Turnover

Most home improvement retailers have low levels of accounts receivable relative to sales revenue because they collect the majority of their sales immediately in cash. Lowe's sells its small amounts of accounts receivable to a bank. Although the formula for this ratio calls for net **credit** sales in the numerator, companies rarely report their credit sales and cash sales separately. Consequently, financial statement users must use total sales revenue in the numerator, which results in a receivables turnover ratio that is not terribly meaningful for businesses that make few sales on account. This ratio is presented in Exhibit 17.6 simply to remind you of how it is calculated.

Inventory Turnover

The inventory turnover ratio indicates how many times inventory is bought and sold during the year. The ratio "days to sell" converts inventory turnover into the number of days needed to sell each purchase of inventory.

		2006	2005
Inventory Turnover =	$\dfrac{\text{Cost of Goods Sold}}{\text{Average Inventory}}$ =	4.5	4.5
$4.5 = \$30,729 \div [(\$7,144 + \$6,635) \div 2]$			
Days to sell =	$\dfrac{365}{\text{Inventory Turnover Ratio}}$ =	81.1	81.1
$81.1 \text{ days} = 365 \div 4.5$			

The inventory turnover ratio is critical to Lowe's because the company wants to offer customers the right product when they need it at a price that beats the competition. Historically, The Home Depot has enjoyed a significant advantage over Lowe's in terms of inventory management. However, in recent years, Lowe's has been able to close the gap. In 2006, The Home Depot had an inventory turnover ratio of 5.04—only slightly better than Lowe's ratio of 4.5.

Turnover ratios vary significantly from one industry to the next. Companies in the food industry (restaurants and grocery stores) have high inventory turnover ratios because their inventory is subject to spoilage. Companies that sell expensive merchandise (automobiles and high-fashion clothes) have much lower ratios because sales of those items are infrequent, but customers want to have a wide selection to choose from when they do buy.

Current Ratio

The current ratio compares current assets to current liabilities, as follows:

		2006	2005
Current Ratio =	$\dfrac{\text{Current Assets}}{\text{Current Liabilities}}$ =	1.27	1.34
$1.27 = \$8,314 \div \$6,539$			

This ratio measures the company's ability to pay its current liabilities. The slight drop in Lowe's current ratio from 2005 to 2006 probably is not something to be concerned about so long as the decline does not continue. The 2006 current ratio of 1.27 indicates that the company's current assets were 127 percent of its current liabilities. Most analysts would judge that ratio to be very strong, especially considering Lowe's ability to generate cash. In this industry, a current ratio of more than 1.0 is considered to be acceptable.

Quick Ratio

The quick ratio compares the sum of cash, accounts receivable, and short-term investments to current liabilities as follows:

			2006	2005
Quick Ratio =	$\dfrac{\text{Quick Assets}}{\text{Current Liabilities}}$	=	0.12	0.15

$$0.12 = (\$364 + \$432) \div \$6{,}539$$

The quick ratio is a more stringent test of short-term liquidity than is the current ratio. The quick ratio compares quick assets, defined as cash and near-cash assets, to current liabilities. Quick assets include cash, short-term investments, and accounts receivable (net of the allowance for doubtful accounts). Inventory is omitted from quick assets because of the uncertainty of the timing of cash flows from its sale. Prepaid expenses are also excluded from quick assets.

Solvency Ratios

The analyses in this section focus on Lowe's ability to survive over the long term—that is, its ability to repay debt when it matures, pay interest until that time, and finance the replacement and/or expansion of long-term assets. We interpret ratios (13) through (15) from Exhibit 17.6.

Debt to Assets

The debt-to-assets ratio indicates the proportion of total assets that creditors finance. Remember that creditors must be paid regardless of how difficult a year the company may have had. The higher this ratio, the riskier is the company's financing strategy. Lowe's ratio for the two years was:

			2006	2005
Debt to Assets =	$\dfrac{\text{Total Liabilities}}{\text{Total Assets}}$	=	0.43	0.42

$$0.43 = \$12{,}042 \div \$27{,}767$$

Lowe's ratio of 0.43 in 2006 indicates that creditors contributed 43 percent of the company's financing, implying that stockholders' equity was the company's main source of financing at 57 percent. This ratio did not change significantly from 2005 to 2006. Lowe's currently relies less on debt financing than The Home Depot, which had a debt-to-assets ratio of 52 percent in 2006.

Times Interest Earned

The times interest earned ratio indicates how many times the company's interest expense was covered by its operating results. This ratio is calculated using accrual-based interest expense and net income before interest and income taxes, as follows:

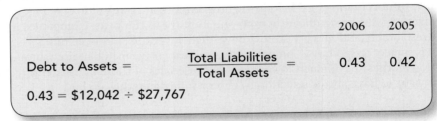

			2006	2005
Times Interest Earned =	$\dfrac{\text{Net Income} + \text{Interest Expense} + \text{Income Tax Expense}}{\text{Interest Expense}}$	=	33.5	29.5

$$33.5 = (\$3{,}105 + \$154 + \$1{,}893) \div \$154$$

A times interest earned ratio higher than 1.0 indicates that net income (before the costs of financing and taxes have been deducted) is sufficient to cover the company's interest expense. Lowe's ratio of 33.5 indicates that the company is generating more than enough profit to cover its interest expense.

Free Cash Flow

Free cash flow measures a company's ability to make capital investments and pay dividends from its operating cash flows. Lowe's free cash flow for the two years was:

		2006	2005
	Net Cash Flow from Operating Activities		
Free Cash Flow =	−Purchases of Property and Equipment =	$366	$323
	−Dividends Paid		

$366 = $4,502 − $3,860 − $276

The amounts in the computation come from the cash flow statement, which is not shown in this chapter. The positive free cash flow in the two years (in millions) indicates that Lowe's is a healthy company with enough cash flow from operations to purchase property, plant, and equipment and pay dividends to stockholders.

In sum, these solvency ratios suggest that Lowe's has grown significantly and has financed its growth through both operating cash flows and debt financing. Lowe's reliance on debt financing has remained relatively steady, and the company is in an excellent position to cover the interest expense associated with its debt. Overall, analysts would consider Lowe's to have a low-risk profile, one that bodes well for the company's long-term survival.

SELF-STUDY PRACTICE

Lowe's

1. Show the computations for the following two ratios for Lowe's for 2005. Use the information in Exhibits 17.2 and 17.3 (all numbers are in millions).

   a. Gross profit percentage ratio.
   b. Current ratio.

2. Assume that in 2006, Lowe's recorded a $25 (in millions) expiration of prepaid expenses. Complete the following table by showing its impact (+, −, or no change) on selected measures of profitability, and liquidity.

   Impact of Prepaid Expense Expiration

   a. Net profit margin ratio.
   b. Current ratio.

After you have finished, check your answers with the solution at the bottom of the page.

Solution to Self-Study Practice

1.

$$\frac{\text{Net Sales Revenue} - \text{Cost of Goods Sold}}{\text{Net Sales Revenue}} = \frac{\$43,243 - \$28,453}{\$43,243} \times 100 = 34.2\%$$

$$\frac{\text{Current Assets}}{\text{Current Liabilities}} = \frac{\$7,788}{\$5,832} = 1.34$$

2. The expiration of prepaid expenses would decrease prepaid expenses on the balance sheet and increase expenses on the income statement. The effects on the ratios are:

   a. "−" net income, the numerator of the ratio, decreases when expenses increase, so the ratio decreases

   b. "−" current assets, the numerator of the ratio, decreases when prepaid expenses decreases, so the ratio decreases

Exhibit 17.7	Comparison of Accounting Methods Used by Three Home Improvement Retailers

	Lowe's	The Home Depot	Builder's FirstSource
Inventory	FIFO	FIFO	Weighted Average Cost
Depreciation	Straight line Buildings: 10–40 yrs Equipment: 3–15 yrs	Straight line Buildings: 10–45 yrs Equipment: 3–20 yrs	Straight line Buildings: 20–40 yrs Equipment: 3–10 yrs

Accounting Decisions and Ratio Analysis

In the analyses just presented, we compared Lowe's results with those of The Home Depot. When appropriate, we discussed how differences in the two companies' strategies (for example, relying on debt versus equity financing) and business operations (for example, targeting do-it-yourselfers versus professionals) affected their financial ratios. We should also consider whether differences between the two companies' financial ratios might be caused by differences in their accounting decisions.

Information about a company's accounting decisions is presented in a note to the financial statements. Data in Exhibit 17.7 compare the policies that three home improvement retailers follow in accounting for inventory and depreciation—two line items that can have a noticeable impact on a retailer's results. Take a moment to study the exhibit.

As you can see, the three companies follow similar but not identical policies. Lowe's and The Home Depot use the FIFO method of accounting for ending inventory and the cost of goods sold; Builder's FirstSource uses the weighted average method. Although these two methods result in different numbers, the overall impact on the companies' financial ratios should be minor.

All three companies calculate depreciation using the straight-line method with a similar range of estimated useful lives for buildings and equipment. Because buildings and equipment make up such a large portion of each company's assets, these similarities go a long way toward making their financial results comparable. In conclusion, although the companies' accounting policies have some differences, they are unlikely to have a major impact on our comparisons.

Spotlight On FINANCIAL REPORTING

International Differences in Accounting Standards

Cross-national differences in accounting standards also create differences in the accounting methods different companies use. Many countries, including the members of the European Union, are committed to adopting the international financial reporting standards (IFRS) issued by the International Accounting Standards Board (IASB). Although IFRS are similar to GAAP, several important differences exist. Two of the differences relate to inventory accounting.

Difference	U.S. GAAP	IFRS
Last-in, first-out method for inventory	Permitted	Prohibited
Reversal of inventory write-downs	Prohibited	Required

These differences would make it difficult to compare a U.S. automaker such as Ford that follows U.S. GAAP with a European competitor such as BMW that follows IFRS.

Source: *Deloitte IAS Plus*, February 2007.

Demonstration Case

The following information was taken from The Home Depot's recent annual report.

(in millions of dollars)	Year ended January 28, 2007	
Net sales revenue	$90,837	
Cost of goods sold	61,054	
Net income	5,761	
	January 28, 2007	**January 29, 2006**
Inventory	$12,822	$11,401
Current assets	18,000	15,269
Net property and equipment	26,605	24,901
Total assets	52,263	44,405
Current liabilities	12,931	12,706
Total liabilities	27,233	17,496

Required:

1. Compute the following ratios for The Home Depot for the year ended January 28, 2007.

    Fixed Asset Turnover
    Return on Equity
    Days to Sell
    Current Ratio
    Debt to Assets

2. Interpret the meaning of the ratios you calculated in requirement 1.

Suggested Solution

1. Calculating ratios:

Fixed Asset Turnover
= Net Sales Revenue/Average Net Fixed Assets
= $90,837 ÷ [(26,605 + 24,901) ÷ 2]
= 3.53

Return on Equity
= Net Income/Average Stockholders' Equity
= $5,761 ÷ [(25,030 + 26,909) ÷ 2]
= 0.2218, or 22.2%

Days to Sell
= 365 ÷ Inventory Turnover Ratio
= 365 ÷ (Cost of Goods Sold/Average Inventory)
= 365 ÷ [61,054 ÷ [(12,822 + 11,401) ÷ 2]]
= 72

Current Ratio
= Current Assets/Current Liabilities
= $18,000 ÷ 12,931
= 1.39

Debt to Assets
= Total Liabilities/Total Assets
= $27,233 ÷ 52,263
= 0.52

2. Interpreting ratios

- The fixed asset turnover ratio of 3.53 means that on average, The Home Depot generated $3.53 of sales for each dollar of fixed assets.
- The return on equity of 22.2 percent means that The Home Depot's net income for the year was 22.2 percent of the amount investors contributed to and left in the company.
- The days to sell ratio of 72 means that on average, 72 days elapsed between the time The Home Depot acquired the inventory and the time the company sold it.

- The current ratio of 1.39 means that at year-end, The Home Depot had $1.39 of current assets for each dollar of current liabilities.
- The debt-to-assets ratio of 0.52 means that The Home Depot relied on short-term and long-term debt to finance 52 percent of its assets, implying that stockholders' equity financed 48 percent (=100 − 52) of its total assets.

Supplement 17A
Nonrecurring and Other Special Items

Until 2005, three different types of nonrecurring item were reported in income statements: discontinued operations, extraordinary items, and the cumulative effects of changes in accounting methods. Recently, however, **new accounting standards have nearly eliminated reporting of extraordinary items and the cumulative effects of changes in accounting methods.** In fact, the definition of the term **extraordinary** has become so restricted that few events—not even losses that arose from the terrorist attacks of September 11, 2001—now qualify as extraordinary. The cumulative effects of changes in accounting methods are reported as adjustments to retained earnings rather than as part of the income statement in the period when the change is made. That leaves only one remaining nonrecurring item, discontinued operations.

Discontinued operations result from the abandonment or sale of a major business component. The discontinued operations line on the income statement includes any gain or loss on the disposal of the discontinued operation as well as any operating income generated before its disposal. Because gains or losses from discontinued operations appear below the income tax expense line on the income statement, any additional tax effects related to those gains or losses are included in the reported amounts. Obviously, the sale of a particular business unit can happen only once, so these results are reported separately to inform users that they will not affect the company's future results. Exhibit 17A.1 shows how Newell Rubbermaid reported discontinued operations in 2005 and 2006 when the company divested its Little Tikes division and its Home Décor Europe and European Cookware operations.

In some cases, additional items may appear after the net income (loss) line on the income statement. Those items may be added to or subtracted from net income to arrive at the amount of **comprehensive income.** As you can learn in detail in intermediate financial accounting courses, those items represent gains or losses related to changes in the value of certain balance sheet accounts. While most gains and losses are included in the computation of net income, some (those related to changes in foreign currency exchange rates and the value of certain investments, for example) are excluded from net income and included only in comprehensive income. The main reason for excluding these gains and losses from net income is that the changes in value that created them may well disappear before the gains or losses are

---

Exhibit 17A.1 **Reporting of Nonrecurring Items on the Income Statement**   **Newell Rubbermaid**

Newell Rubbermaid
Condensed Income Statements
December 31,
(in millions)

	2006	2005
Net sales	$6,201.0	$5,717.2
Cost of products sold	4,131.0	3,959.1
Selling, general, and administrative expenses	1,347.0	1,117.7
Impairment charges and restructuring costs	66.4	73.0
Operating income (loss)	656.6	567.4
Interest and other expenses, net	141.7	104.0
Income (loss) before income taxes	514.9	463.4
Income tax expense (benefit)	44.2	57.1
Net income (loss) from continuing operations	470.7	406.3
Gain (loss) on sale of discontinued operations, net of income taxes	(85.7)	(155.0)
Net income (loss)	$ 385.0	$ 251.3

ever realized (when the company sells the related assets or liabilities). For this reason, most analysts will take a moment to consider the size of these special items in relation to net income. If the amount is not large, they will exclude the items in calculating profitability ratios.[3]

Chapter Summary

LO1 Describe how financial statement information is communicated to external users. p. 730

- The issuance of quarterly and annual reports is preceded by press releases containing preliminary results.
- Publicly owned companies file with the Securities and Exchange Commission more detailed information on Forms 10-Q, 10K, and 8-K, which are available first on the Web.

LO2 Use horizontal (trend) analysis to recognize financial changes that unfold over time. p. 732

- Horizontal analysis (also called trend analysis) compares financial statement items to comparable amounts in prior periods with the goal of identifying sustained changes, or trends.
- Trend analysis involves computing the dollar amount by which each account changes from one period to the next and expressing that change as a percentage of the balance for the prior period.

LO3 Use vertical (common size) analysis to understand important relationships within financial statements. p. 734

- Common size financial statements express each line of the income statement (or balance sheet) as a percentage of total sales (or total assets).
- The statements tell the reader whether the proportions within each statement category are changing.

LO4 Calculate and use financial ratios to assess profitability, liquidity, and solvency. p. 736

- Financial ratios are commonly classified with relation to profitability, liquidity, or solvency. Exhibit 17.6 lists common ratios in these three categories and shows how to compute them.
- Profitability ratios focus on measuring the adequacy of a company's income by comparing it to other items reported on the financial statements.
- Liquidity ratios measure a company's ability to meet its current debt obligations.
- Solvency ratios measure a company's ability to meet its long-term debt obligations.
- In comparing trends and ratios over time and across companies, watch for possible differences in accounting policies and nonrecurring events that could affect reported financial results.

Key Terms

Horizontal (Trend) Analysis (p. 732)

Liquidity (p. 736)

Profitability (p. 736)

Solvency (p. 736)

Vertical (Common Size)
Analysis (p. 734)

See complete glossary in back of text.

Questions

1. What are the major categories of information in the annual report financial section?
2. What is the general goal of trend analysis?
3. How is a year-to-year percentage change calculated?
4. What is ratio analysis? Why is it useful?
5. What benchmarks are commonly used for interpreting ratios?

6. Into what three categories of performance are most financial ratios classified? To what in particular does each of these categories relate?

7. (Supplement 17A) Name the most commonly reported nonrecurring item, and explain where and how it is reported on the income statement.

Multiple Choice

1. Which of the following ratios is not used to analyze profitability?
   a. Fixed asset turnover ratio.
   b. Gross profit percentage.
   c. Current ratio.
   d. Return on equity.

Quiz 17-1
www.mhhe.com/LLPW1e

2. Which of the following would not directly change the receivables turnover ratio for your company?
   a. Increases in the selling prices of your inventory.
   b. A change in your credit policy.
   c. Increases in the cost you incur to purchase inventory.
   d. None of the above.

---

[3] Instead of showing the computation of comprehensive income on the face of the income statement, companies are allowed to show it in either a statement of stockholders' equity or a separate statement of comprehensive income. One survey indicates that about 70 percent of companies show the computation in a statement of stockholders' equity. See American Institute of Public Accountants (New York: AICPA, 2006). *Accounting Trends & Techniques.*

3. Which of the following ratios is used to analyze liquidity?
   a. Earnings per share.
   b. Debt to assets.
   c. Current ratio.
   d. Both debt to assets and current ratio.

4. Analysts use ratios to
   a. Compare different companies in the same industry.
   b. Track a company's performance over time.
   c. Compare a company's performance to industry averages.
   d. All of the above.

5. Which of the following incorporates cash flows from operations?
   a. Inventory turnover.
   b. Earnings per share.
   c. Free cash flow.
   d. All of the above.

6. Given the following ratios for four companies, which company is least likely to experience problems paying its current liabilities promptly?

	Current Ratio	Receivables Turnover Ratio
a.	1.2	7.0
b.	1.2	6.0
c.	1.0	6.0
d.	0.5	7.0

7. A decrease in selling and administrative expenses would directly impact what ratio?
   a. Fixed asset turnover ratio.   c. Current ratio.
   b. Times interest earned.   d. Gross profit percentage.

8. A bank is least likely to use which of the following ratios when analyzing the likelihood that a borrower will pay interest and principal on its loans?
   a. Free cash flow.   c. Times interest earned ratio.
   b. Debt-to-assets ratio.   d. Return on equity ratio.

9. Which of the following accounting concepts do accountants and auditors assess by using financial analyses?
   a. Cost benefit.   c. Industry practices.
   b. Materiality.   d. Going-concern assumption.

10. (Supplement 17A) Which of the following items is reported net of related income taxes?
    a. Gain or loss from discontinued operations.
    b. Gain or loss from disposal of property, plant, and equipment.
    c. Interest on long-term debt.
    d. Gain or loss from early extinguishment of debt.

Solutions to Multiple-Choice Questions

1. c   2. c   3. c   4. d   5. c   6. a   7. b
8. d   9. d   10. a

Mini Exercises   Available with McGraw-Hill's Homework Manager

LO2   **M17-1 Calculations and Interpretations of Horizontal (Trend) Analyses**

Lockey Fencing Corporation
Income Statements
For the Years Ended December 31

	2009	2008
Net sales	$100,000	$75,000
Cost of goods sold	58,000	45,000
Gross profit	42,000	30,000
Selling, general, and administrative expenses	9,000	4,500
Interest expense	3,000	3,750
Income before income taxes	30,000	21,750
Income tax expense	9,000	6,525
Net income	$ 21,000	$15,225

What are the two most significant year-to-year changes in terms of dollars and in terms of percentages?

LO3   **M17-2 Calculations and Interpretations of Vertical (Common Size) Analyses**
Using the information in M17-1, prepare common size income statements to determine how the company increased its net income as a percent of revenues in 2009.

M17-3 Computing the Return on Equity Ratio

Given the following data, compute the 2008 return on equity ratio (expressed as a percentage to one decimal place).

LO4

	2008	2007
Net income	$ 1,850,000	$ 1,600,000
Stockholders' equity	10,000,000	13,125,000
Total assets	24,000,000	26,000,000
Interest expense	400,000	300,000

M17-4 Analyzing the Inventory Turnover Ratio

A manufacturer reported an inventory turnover ratio of 8.6 during 2009. During 2010, management introduced a new inventory control system that was expected to reduce average inventory levels by 25 percent without affecting sales volume or cost of goods sold. Given these circumstances, would you expect the inventory turnover ratio to increase or decrease during 2010? Explain.

LO4

M17-5 Analyzing the Impact of Accounting Alternatives

Nevis Corporation operates in an industry in which costs are falling. The company is considering changing its inventory method from FIFO to LIFO and wants to determine the impact that the change would have on selected accounting ratios in future years. In general, what impact would you expect on the following ratios: net profit margin, fixed asset turnover, and current ratio?

LO4

M17-6 Inferring Financial Information Using the P/E Ratio

In 2009, Big W Company reported earnings per share of $2.50 when its stock was selling for $50.00. In 2010, its earnings increased by 10 percent. If all other relationships remain constant, what is the price of the stock? Explain.

LO4

M17-7 Identifying Relevant Ratios

Identify the ratio that is relevant to answering each of the following questions.

LO4

1. How much net income does the company earn from each dollar of sales?
2. Is the company financed primarily by debt or equity?
3. How many dollars of sales were generated for each dollar invested in fixed assets?
4. How many days, on average, does it take the company to collect on credit sales made to customers?
5. How much net income does the company earn for each dollar owners have invested in it?
6. Does the company have sufficient assets to convert into cash for paying liabilities as they come due in the upcoming year?

M17-8 Interpreting Ratios

Generally speaking, do the following indicate good or bad news?

LO4

1. Increase in times interest earned ratio.
2. Decrease in days to sell.
3. Increase in gross profit percentage.
4. Decrease in EPS.
5. Increase in asset turnover ratio.

Exercises ™   Available with McGraw-Hill's Homework Manager

E17-1 Preparing and Interpreting a Horizontal (Trend) Analysis

The average price of a gallon of gas in 2005 jumped $0.43 (24 percent) from $1.81 in 2004 to $2.24 in 2005. Let's see whether these changes are reflected in the income statement of Chevron Corp. for the year ended December 31, 2005 (amounts in millions).

LO2

Chevron

	2005	2004
Total revenues	$198,200	$155,300
Costs of crude oil and products	140,902	104,948
Other operating costs	32,101	29,801
Income before income tax expense	25,197	20,551
Income tax expense	11,098	7,223
Net income	$ 14,099	$ 13,328

Required:

Conduct a horizontal analysis by calculating the year-to-year changes in each line item expressed in dollars and in percentages (rounded to one decimal place). How did the change in gas prices compare to the changes in Chevron Corp.'s total revenues and costs of crude oil and products?

LO3

Chevron

E17-2 Preparing and Interpreting a Vertical (Common Size) Analysis

Use the information for Chevron Corp. in E17-1 to conduct a vertical (common size) analysis of the income statements and then answer the following questions.

Required:

1. Was Chevron able to raise gas prices to offset the increase in its costs of crude oil and products?
2. How did you know?
3. Did other operating costs rise as fast as gas prices? How did you know? Why do you think this is so?

LO4

Chevron

E17-3 Computing and Interpreting Profitability Ratios

Use the information for Chevron Corp. in E17-1 to complete the following requirements.

Required:

1. Compute the gross profit percentage for each year (one decimal place). Assuming the change for 2004 to 2005 is the beginning of a sustained trend, is Chevron likely to earn more or less gross profit from each dollar of sales in 2006?
2. Compute the net profit margin for each year (expressed as a percentage with one decimal place). Given your calculations here and in requirement 1, explain whether Chevron did a better or worse job of controlling expenses other than the costs of crude oil and products in 2005 relative to 2004.
3. Chevron reported average net fixed assets of $54.2 billion in 2005 and $45.1 billion in 2004. Compute the fixed asset turnover ratios for both years (round to two decimal places). Did the company better utilize its investment in fixed assets to generate revenues in 2005 or 2004?
4. Chevron reported average stockholders' equity of $54.0 billion in 2005 and $40.8 billion in 2004. Compute the return on equity ratios for both years (expressed as a percentage with one decimal place). Did the company generate higher returns for stockholders in 2005 or 2004?

LO4

Chevron

E17-4 Computing a Commonly Used Solvency Ratio

Use the information for Chevron Corp. in E17-1 to complete the following requirement.

Required:

Interest expense in the amount of $482 million was included with Other Operating Costs in 2005 ($406 million in 2004). Compute the times interest earned ratios for each year (round to one decimal place). In your opinion, does Chevron generate sufficient net income (before taxes and interest) to cover the cost of debt financing?

LO2

E17-5 Preparing and Interpreting a Horizontal (Trend) Analysis

The average selling price of low-end laptops fell about $200 (25 percent) from $800 in 2008 to $600 in 2009. Let's see whether these changes are reflected in the income statement of Computer Tycoon Inc. for the year ended December 31, 2009.

	2008	2009
Sales revenues	$121,761	$98,913
Cost of goods sold	71,583	59,249
Operating expenses	36,934	36,943
Interest expense	474	565
Income before income tax expense	12,770	2,156
Income tax expense	5,540	1,024
Net income	$ 7,230	$ 1,132

Required:

Conduct a horizontal analysis by calculating the year-to-year changes in each line item expressed in dollars and in percentages (rounded to one decimal place). How did the change in computer prices compare to the changes in Computer Tycoon's sales revenues?

E17-6 Preparing and Interpreting a Vertical (Common Size) Analysis

LO3

Use the information in E17-5 to conduct a vertical (common size) analysis of Computer Tycoon's income statements and then answer the following questions.

Required:

1. Was Computer Tycoon able to lower its costs of goods to offset the decrease in selling price? How did you know?
2. What was the main reason Computer Tycoon's net income as a percent of revenues decreased?

E17-7 Computing Profitability Ratios

LO4

Use the information in E17-5 for Computer Tycoon to complete the following requirements.

Required:

1. Compute the gross profit percentage for each year (one decimal place). Assuming that the change for 2008 to 2009 is the beginning of a sustained trend, is Computer Tycoon likely to earn higher or lower gross profit from each dollar of sales in 2010?
2. Compute the net profit margin for each year (expressed as a percentage with one decimal place). Given your calculations here and in requirement 1, explain whether Computer Tycoon did a better or worse job of controlling operating expenses in 2009 relative to 2008.
3. Computer Tycoon reported average net fixed assets of $54,200 in 2009 and $45,100 in 2008. Compute the fixed asset turnover ratio for each year (round to two decimal places). Did the company better utilize its investment in fixed assets to generate revenues in 2009 or 2008?
4. Computer Tycoon reported average stockholders' equity of $54,000 in 2009 and $40,800 in 2008. Compute the return on equity ratio for each year (expressed as a percentage with one decimal place). Did the company generate greater returns for stockholders in 2009 or 2008?

E17-8 Computing a Commonly Used Solvency Ratio

LO4

Use the information in E17-5 for Computer Tycoon to complete the following requirement.

Required:

Compute the times interest earned ratios for 2009 and 2008. In your opinion, does Computer Tycoon generate sufficient net income (before taxes and interest) to cover the cost of debt financing?

E17-9 Matching Each Ratio with Its Computational Formula

LO4

Match each ratio or percentage with its formula by entering the appropriate letter for each numbered item.

Ratios or Percentages	Formula
___ 1. Current ratio	A. Net income ÷ Net sales revenue.
___ 2. Net profit margin	B. (Net sales revenue − Cost of goods sold) ÷ Net sales revenue.
___ 3. Inventory turnover	C. Current assets ÷ Current liabilities.
___ 4. Asset turnover	D. Cost of goods sold ÷ Average inventory.
___ 5. Fixed asset turnover	E. Net credit sales revenue ÷ Average net receivables.
___ 6. Free cash flow	F. Net income ÷ Average number of common shares outstanding.
___ 7. Return on equity	G. Total liabilities ÷ Total assets.
___ 8. Times interest earned	H. (Net income + Interest expense + Income tax expense) ÷ Interest expense.
___ 9. Debt to assets	I. Net cash flows from operating activities − Purchases of property and equipment − Dividends paid
___ 10. Price/earnings	J. Current stock price per share ÷ Earnings per share.
___ 11. Receivables turnover	K. Net income ÷ Average total stockholders' equity.
___ 12. Earnings per share	L. Net sales revenue ÷ Average total assets
___ 13. Gross profit percentage	M. Net sales revenue ÷ Average net fixed assets.

LO4

E17-10 Computing and Interpreting Selected Liquidity Ratios

DuckWing Stores (DWS) reported sales of $600,000 for the year; one-half of sales were on credit. The average gross profit percentage was 40 percent on sales. Account balances follow:

	Beginning	Ending
Accounts receivable (net)	$45,000	$55,000
Inventory	60,000	40,000

Required:

1. Compute the turnover ratios for accounts receivable and inventory (round to one decimal place).
2. Calculate the average days to collect receivables and the average days to sell inventory (round to one decimal place).
3. Explain what each of these ratios and measures means.

LO4

E17-11 Computing and Interpreting Liquidity Ratios

Cintas Corporation is the largest uniform supplier in North America. More than 5 million people wear Cintas clothing each day. Selected information from a recent balance sheet follows. For Year 2, the company reported sales revenue of $2,686,585 and cost of goods sold of $1,567,377 (in thousands).

Cintas	Year 2	Year 1
Balance Sheet (amounts in thousands)		
Cash	$ 32,239	$ 52,182
Accounts receivable, less allowance of $7,737 and $9,229	278,147	225,735
Inventories	228,410	164,906
Prepaid expenses	7,607	7,237
Other current assets	25,420	57,640
Accounts payable	53,909	60,393
Wages payable	25,252	29,004
Income taxes payable	69,545	73,163
Accrued liabilities	127,882	131,705
Long-term debt due within one year	28,251	18,369

Required:

Assuming that 60 percent of sales are on credit, compute the current ratio (two decimal places), inventory turnover ratio (one decimal place), and accounts receivable turnover ratio (one decimal place) for Year 2. Explain what each ratio means.

E17-12 Analyzing the Impact of Selected Transactions on the Current Ratio

In its most recent annual report, Appalachian Beverages reported current assets of $54,000 and a current ratio of 1.80. Assume that the following transactions were completed: (1) purchased merchandise for $6,000 on account and (2) purchased a delivery truck for $10,000, paying $1,000 cash and signing a two-year promissory note for the balance.

Required:

Compute the updated current ratio, rounded to two decimal places, after each transaction.

LO4

E17-13 Analyzing the Impact of Selected Transactions on the Current Ratio

In its most recent annual report, Sunrise Enterprises reported current assets of $1,090,000 and current liabilities of $602,000.

Required:

Determine the impact of the following transactions on the current ratio for Sunrise:

1. Sold long-term assets for cash.
2. Accrued severance pay for terminated employees.
3. Wrote down the carrying value of certain inventory items that were deemed to be obsolete.
4. Acquired new inventory by signing an 18-month promissory note (the supplier was not willing to provide normal credit terms).

LO4

E17-14 Analyzing the Impact of Selected Transactions on the Current Ratio

Sports Authority, Inc., is the country's largest private full-line sporting goods retailer. Stores are operated under four brand names: Sports Authority, Gart Sports, Oshman's, and Sportmart. Assume one of the Sports Authority stores reported current assets of $88,000 and its current ratio was 1.75. Assume also the following transactions were completed: (1) paid $6,000 on accounts payable, (2) purchased a delivery truck for $10,000 cash, (3) wrote off a bad account receivable for $2,000 under the allowance method, and (4) paid previously declared dividends in the amount of $25,000 (the dividends were declared in the prior period and paid in the current period).

Required:

Compute the updated current ratio, rounded to two decimal places, after each transaction.

LO4
Sports
Authority

E17-15 Analyzing the Impact of Selected Transactions on the Current Ratio

Current assets totaled $500,000, the current ratio was 2.00, and the company uses the perpetual inventory method. Assume that the following transactions were completed: (1) sold $12,000 in merchandise on short-term credit for $15,000, (2) declared but did not pay dividends of $50,000, (3) paid prepaid rent in the amount of $12,000, (4) paid previously declared dividends in the amount of $50,000, (5) collected an account receivable in the amount of $12,000, and (6) reclassified $40,000 of long-term debt as a current liability.

Required:

Compute the updated current ratio, rounded to two decimal places, after each transaction.

LO4

E17-16 Computing the Accounts Receivable and Inventory Turnover Ratios

Procter & Gamble is a multinational corporation that manufactures and markets many products that are probably in your home or dorm room. In 2006, sales for the company were $68,222 (all amounts in millions). The annual report did not report the amount of credit sales, so we assume all sales were on credit. The average gross profit percentage was 51 percent. Account balances follow:

LO4

P&G

	Beginning	Ending
Accounts receivable (net)	$5,266	$7,336
Inventory	5,006	6,291

Required:

1. Compute the turnover ratios (rounded to one decimal place) for accounts receivable and inventory.
2. Calculate the average days to collect receivables and the average days to sell inventory.
3. Interpret what these ratios and measures mean.

LO4

Dollar General

E17-17 Inferring Financial Information from Profitability and Liquidity Ratios

Dollar General Corporation operates approximately 8,250 general merchandise stores that feature quality merchandise at low prices to meet the needs of middle-, low-, and fixed-income families in southern, eastern, and midwestern states. For the year ended February 3, 2006, the company reported average inventories of $1,425 (in millions) and an inventory turnover of 4.3. Average total fixed assets were $1,137 (million), and the fixed asset turnover ratio was 7.5.

Required:

1. Calculate Dollar General's gross profit percentage (expressed as a percentage with one decimal place). What does this imply about the amount of gross profit made from each dollar of sales?
2. Is this an improvement from the gross profit percentage of 29.5 percent earned during the year ended January 28, 2005?

TIP: Work backward from the fixed asset turnover and inventory turnover ratios to compute the amounts needed for the gross profit percentage.

LO4

E17-18 Using Financial Information to Identify Mystery Companies

The following selected financial data pertain to four unidentified companies (balance sheet amounts reported in millions):

	COMPANY			
	1	2	3	4
Balance Sheet Data				
Cash	$ 5.1	$ 8.8	$ 6.3	$ 10.4
Accounts receivable	13.1	41.5	13.8	4.9
Inventory	4.6	3.6	65.1	35.8
Property and equipment	53.1	23.0	8.8	35.7
Selected Ratios				
Gross profit percentage	N/A*	N/A	45.2	22.5
Net profit margin ratio (%)	0.3	16.0	3.9	1.5
Current ratio	0.7	2.2	1.9	1.4
Inventory turnover	N/A	N/A	1.4	15.5
Debt to assets	0.7	0.5	0.6	0.7

* N/A = Not applicable.

This financial information pertains to the following companies:

a. Cable TV company.
b. Grocery store.
c. Accounting firm.
d. Retail jewelry store.

Required:
Match each company with its financial information, and explain the basis for your answers.

LO4

E17-19 Analyzing the Impact of Alternative Inventory Methods on Selected Ratios

Company A uses the FIFO method to cost inventory, and Company B uses the LIFO method. The two companies are exactly alike except for the difference in inventory costing methods. Costs of inventory items for both companies have been falling steadily in recent years, and each company has increased its inventory each year. Ignore income tax effects.

Required:
Identify which company will report the higher amount for each of the following ratios. If it is not possible to identify which will report the higher amount, explain why.

1. Current ratio.
2. Debt-to-assets ratio.
3. Earnings per share.

Problems—Set A ▦ ™ **Available with McGraw-Hill's Homework Manager**

PA17-1 Analyzing Financial Statements Using Horizontal (Trend) and Vertical (Common Size) Analysis

LO2, 3

The comparative financial statements prepared at December 31, 2009, for Pinnacle Plus showed the following summarized data:

eXcel
www.mhhe.com/LLPW1e

	2009	2008	INCREASE (DECREASE) 2009 OVER 2008 Amount	Percentage
Income Statement				
Sales revenue*	$110,000	$ 99,000		
Cost of goods sold	52,000	48,000		
Gross profit	58,000	51,000		
Operating expenses	36,000	33,000		
Interest expense	4,000	4,000		
Income before income taxes	18,000	14,000		
Income tax expense (30%)	5,400	4,200		
Net income	$ 12,600	$ 9,800		
Balance Sheet				
Cash	$ 49,500	$ 18,000		
Accounts receivable (net)	37,000	32,000		
Inventory	25,000	38,000		
Property and equipment (net)	95,000	105,000		
Total assets	$206,500	$193,000		
Accounts payable	$ 42,000	$ 35,000		
Income taxes payable	1,000	500		
Note payable, long term	40,000	40,000		
Total liabilities	83,000	75,500		
Common stock (par $10)	90,000	90,000		
Retained earnings†	33,500	27,500		
Total liabilities and stockholders' equity	$206,500	$193,000		

* One-half of all sales are on credit.
† During 2009, cash dividends amounting to $6,600 were declared and paid.

Required:

1. Complete the Amount and Percentage columns in Pinnacle Plus's comparative financial statements to prepare a horizontal (trend) analysis. Round the percentages to one decimal place. Does anything significant jump out at you from the year-to-year analyses?
2. Prepare common size income statements and balance sheets for the two years. Round the percentages to one decimal place. What significant changes have taken place in the relationship among items in the balance sheet and income statement?

PA17-2 Analyzing Comparative Financial Statements Using Selected Ratios

LO4

Use the data given in PA17-1 for Pinnacle Plus.

Required:

1. Compute the gross profit percentages in 2009 and 2008. Round the percentages to one decimal place. Is the trend going in the right direction?

2. Compute the net profit margin ratios in 2009 and 2008. Round the percentages to one decimal place. Is the trend going in the right direction?

3. Compute the earnings per share for 2009 and 2008. Does the trend look good or bad? Explain.

4. Stockholders' equity totaled $100,000 at the end of 2007. Compute the return on equity (ROE) ratios for 2008 and 2009. Express the ROE as percentages rounded to one decimal place. Is the trend going in the right direction?

5. Net property and equipment totaled $110,000 at the end of 2007. Compute the fixed asset turnover ratios for 2009 and 2008. Round the ratios to two decimal places. Is the trend going in the right direction?

6. Compute the debt-to-assets ratios for 2009 and 2008. Round the ratios to two decimal places. Is debt providing financing for a larger or smaller proportion of the company's asset growth? Explain.

7. Compute the times interest earned ratios for 2009 and 2008. Round the ratios to one decimal place. Do they look good or bad? Explain.

8. After Pinnacle Plus released its 2009 financial statements, the company's stock was trading at $18. After the release of its 2008 financial statements, the company's stock price was $15 per share. Compute the P/E ratios for both years rounded to one decimal place. Does it appear that investors have become more (or less) optimistic about Pinnacle's future success?

LO4

Coca-Cola &
Pepsico

PA17-3 Interpreting Profitability, Liquidity, Solvency, and P/E Ratios

Coke and Pepsi are well-known international brands. Coca-Cola sells more than $23 billion worth of beverages each year while annual sales of Pepsi products exceed $32 billion. Compare the two companies as a potential investment based on the following ratios:

Ratio	Coca-Cola	PepsiCo
Gross profit percentage	48.5 %	49.0 %
Net profit margin	2.6 %	4.1 %
Return on equity	66.2 %	23.3 %
EPS	$ 3.40	$ 1.54
Receivables turnover	11.5	9.8
Inventory turnover	15.1	12.8
Current ratio	1.47	1.40
Debt to assets	0.94	0.72
Price/Earnings	16.4	18.7

Required:

1. Which company appears more profitable? Describe the ratio(s) that you used to reach this decision.

2. Which company appears more liquid? Describe the ratio(s) that you used to reach this decision.

3. Which company appears more solvent? Describe the ratio(s) that you used to reach this decision.

4. Are the conclusions from your analyses in requirements 1–3 consistent with the value of the two companies suggested by the P/E ratio of each company? If not, offer one explanation for any apparent inconsistency.

LO4

PA17-4 Using Ratios to Compare Loan Requests from Two Companies

The 2008 financial statements for Royale and Cavalier companies are summarized here:

	Royale Company	Cavalier Company
Balance Sheet		
Cash	$ 25,000	$ 45,000
Accounts receivable (net)	55,000	5,000
Inventory	110,000	25,000
Property and equipment (net)	550,000	160,000
Other assets	140,000	57,000
Total assets	$880,000	$292,000
Current liabilities	$120,000	$ 15,000
Long-term debt	190,000	55,000
Capital stock (par $20)	480,000	210,000
Additional paid-in capital	50,000	4,000
Retained earnings	40,000	8,000
Total liabilities and stockholders' equity	$880,000	$292,000
Income Statement		
Sales revenue	$800,000	$280,000
Cost of goods sold	(480,000)	(150,000)
Expenses (including interest and income tax)	(240,000)	(95,000)
Net income	$ 80,000	$ 35,000
Selected Data from 2007 Statements		
Accounts receivable, net	$ 47,000	$ 11,000
Long-term debt	190,000	55,000
Property and equipment, net	550,000	160,000
Inventory	95,000	38,000
Total stockholders' equity	570,000	202,000
Other Data		
Per share price at end of 2008	$ 14.00	$ 11.00
Average income tax rate	30%	30%

These two companies are in the same line of business and in the same state but in different cities. One-half of Royale's sales are on credit whereas one-quarter of Cavalier's sales are on credit. Each company has been in operation for about 10 years. Both companies received an unqualified audit opinion on the financial statements, which means the independent auditors found nothing wrong. Royale Company wants to borrow $75,000 cash, and Cavalier Company is asking for $30,000. The loans will be for a two-year period. Both companies estimate bad debts based on an aging analysis, but Cavalier has estimated slightly higher uncollectible rates than Royale.

Required:

1. Complete a schedule that reflects the following ratios for each company: return on equity, gross profit percentage, net profit margin, earnings per share, fixed asset turnover, price earnings, current, receivables turnover, inventory turnover, debt to assets.

2. Assume you work in the loan department of a local bank. You have been asked to analyze the situation and recommend which loan is preferable. Based on the data given, your analysis prepared in requirement 1, and any other information, give your choice and the supporting explanation.

PA17-5 Analyzing an Investment by Comparing Selected Ratios   LO4

You have the opportunity to invest $10,000 in one of two companies from a single industry. The only information you have is shown here. The word *high* refers to the top third of the industry; *average* is the middle third; *low* is the bottom third.

Ratio	Company A	Company B
Current	Low	High
Inventory turnover	High	Low
Debt to assets	Low	Average
Times interest earned	High	Average
Price/earnings	High	Average

Required:

Which company would you select? Write a brief explanation for your recommendation.

Problems—Set B   Available with McGraw-Hill's Homework Manager

LO2, 3   **PB17-1 Analyzing Financial Statements Using Ratios and Percentage Changes**

The comparative financial statements prepared at December 31, 2010, for Tiger Audio showed the following summarized data:

	2010	2009	INCREASE (DECREASE) 2010 OVER 2009 Amount	Percentage
Income Statement				
Sales revenue*	$222,000	$185,000		
Cost of goods sold	127,650	111,000		
Gross profit	94,350	74,000		
Operating expenses	39,600	33,730		
Interest expense	4,000	3,270		
Income before income taxes	50,750	37,000		
Income tax expense (30%)	15,225	11,100		
Net income	$ 35,525	$ 25,900		
Balance Sheet				
Cash	$ 40,000	$ 38,000		
Accounts receivable (net)	18,500	16,000		
Inventory	25,000	22,000		
Property and equipment (net)	127,000	119,000		
Total assets	$210,500	$195,000		
Accounts payable	$ 27,000	$ 25,000		
Income taxes payable	3,000	2,800		
Note payable, long term	75,500	92,200		
Total liabilities	105,500	120,000		
Capital stock (par $1)	25,000	25,000		
Retained earnings†	80,000	50,000		
Total liabilities and stockholders' equity	$210,500	$195,000		

* One-half of all sales are on credit.

† During 2010, cash dividends amounting to $5,525 were declared and paid.

Required:

1. Complete the Amount and Percentage columns in Tiger Audio's comparative financial statements to prepare a horizontal (trend) analysis. Round the percentages to one decimal place. Does anything significant jump out at you from the year-to-year analyses?
2. Prepare common size income statements and balance sheets for the two years. Round the percentages to one decimal place. What significant changes have taken place in the relationship among items in the balance sheet and income statement?

PB17-2 Analyzing Comparative Financial Statements Using Selected Ratios

LO4

Use the data given in PB17-1 for Tiger Audio.

Required:

1. Compute the gross profit percentages in 2010 and 2009. Is the trend going in the right direction?
2. Compute the net profit margin ratios in 2010 and 2009. Is the trend going in the right direction?
3. Compute the earnings per share for 2010 and 2009. Does the trend look good or bad? Explain.
4. Stockholders' equity totaled $65,000 at the end of 2008. Compute the return on equity ratios for 2010 and 2009. Is the trend going in the right direction?
5. Net property and equipment totaled $115,000 at the end of 2008. Compute the fixed asset turnover ratios for 2010 and 2009. Is the trend going in the right direction?
6. Compute the debt-to-assets ratios for 2010 and 2009. Is debt providing financing for a larger or smaller proportion of the company's asset growth? Explain.
7. Compute the times interest earned ratios for 2010 and 2009. Do they look good or bad? Explain.
8. After Tiger released its 2010 financial statements, the company's stock was trading at $17. After the release of its 2009 financial statements, the company's stock price was $12 per share. Compute the P/E ratios for both years rounded to one decimal place. Does it appear that investors have become more (or less) optimistic about Tiger Audio's future success?

PB17-3 Interpreting Profitability, Liquidity, Solvency, and P/E Ratios

LO4

Mattel and Hasbro are the two largest makers of games and toys in the world. Mattel sells more than $5 billion of products each year while annual sales of Hasbro products exceed $3 billion. Compare the two companies as a potential investment based on the following ratios:

Hasbro

Ratio	Mattel	Hasbro
Gross profit percentage	48.3 %	58.7 %
Net profit margin	10.3 %	5.7 %
Return on equity	23.6 %	13.6 %
EPS	$ 1.23	$ 0.91
Receivables turnover	7.2	6.4
Inventory turnover	5.5	5.7
Current ratio	1.86	1.89
Debt to assets	0.24	0.33
Price/Earnings	15.2	18.9

Required:

1. Which company appears more profitable? Describe the ratio(s) that you used to reach this decision.
2. Which company appears more liquid? Describe the ratio(s) that you used to reach this decision.
3. Which company appears more solvent? Describe the ratio(s) that you used to reach this decision.
4. Are the conclusions from your analyses in requirements 1–3 consistent with the value of the two companies suggested by the P/E ratio of each company? If not, offer one explanation for any apparent inconsistency.

LO4   **PB17-4 Using Ratios to Compare Loan Requests from Two Companies**

The 2010 financial statements for Thor and Gunnar Companies are summarized here:

	Thor Company	Gunnar Company
Balance Sheet		
Cash	$ 35,000	$ 54,000
Accounts receivable (net)	77,000	6,000
Inventory	154,000	30,000
Property and equipment (net)	770,000	192,000
Other assets	196,000	68,400
Total assets	$1,232,000	$ 350,400
Current liabilities	$ 168,000	$ 18,000
Long-term debt (12% interest rate)	266,000	66,000
Capital stock (par $20)	672,000	252,000
Additional paid-in capital	70,000	4,800
Retained earnings	56,000	9,600
Total liabilities and stockholders' equity	$1,232,000	$ 350,400
Income Statement		
Sales revenue	$1,120,000	$ 336,000
Cost of goods sold	(672,000)	(180,000)
Expenses (including interest and income tax)	(336,000)	(114,000)
Net income	$ 112,000	$ 42,000
Selected Data from 2009 Statements		
Accounts receivable, net	$ 65,800	$ 13,200
Inventory	133,000	45,600
Property and equipment, net	770,000	192,000
Long-term debt (12% interest rate)	266,000	66,000
Total stockholders' equity	798,000	266,400
Other Data		
Per share price at end of 2010	$ 13.20	$ 19.60
Average income tax rate	30%	30%

These two companies are in the same line of business and in the same state but in different cities. One-half of Thor's sales are on credit, whereas one-quarter of Gunnar's sales are on credit. Each company has been in operation for about 10 years. Both companies received an unqualified audit opinion on the financial statements, which means the independent auditors found nothing wrong. Thor Company wants to borrow $105,000 cash, and Gunnar Company is asking for $36,000. The loans will be for a two-year period.

Required:

1. Complete a schedule that reflects the following ratios for each company: return on equity, gross profit percentage, net profit margin, earnings per share, fixed asset turnover, price earnings, current, receivables turnover, inventory turnover, debt to assets.

2. Assume you work in the loan department of a local bank. You have been asked to analyze the situation and recommend which loan is preferable. Based on the data given, your analysis prepared in requirement 1, and any other information, give your choice and the supporting explanation.

LO4   **PB17-5 Analyzing an Investment by Comparing Selected Ratios**

You have the opportunity to invest $10,000 in one of two companies from a single industry. The only information you have is shown here. The word *high* refers to the top third of the industry; *average* is the middle third; *low* is the bottom third.

Ratio	Company A	Company B
EPS	High	High
Return on equity	High	Average
Debt to assets	High	Low
Current	Low	Average
Price/Earnings	Low	High

Required:

Which company would you select? Write a brief explanation for your recommendation.

Cases and Projects

CP17-1 Finding Financial Information

Refer to the financial statements of The Home Depot in Appendix A at the end of this book, or download the annual report from the *Cases* section of the text's Web site at www.mhhe.com/LLPW1e. Compute and interpret the ratios discussed in the chapter for the most recent year presented. Assume that the stock price was $30.44.

LO4

CP17-2 Comparing Financial Information

Refer to the financial statements of Lowe's in Appendix B at the end of this book, or download the annual report from the *Cases* section of the text's Web site at www.mhhe.com/LLPW1e. From the list of ratios that were discussed in this chapter, compute and interpret the ratios that help you compare Lowe's to the results for The Home Depot for the most recent year presented. Assume that Lowe's stock price was $25.55 and The Home Depot's stock price was $30.44.

LO4

Lowe's

CP17-3 Examining an Annual Report: Internet-Based Team Research

As a team, select an industry to analyze. Using your Web browser, each team member should acquire the annual report or 10-K for one publicly traded company in the industry with each member selecting a different company. (See CP1-3 in Chapter 1 for a description of possible resources for these tasks.)

LO1, 2, 3, 4

Required:

1. On an individual basis, each team member should write a short report that incorporates trend analysis and as many of the ratios from the chapter as are applicable given the nature of the selected company.

2. Then, as a team, write a short report comparing and contrasting your companies using these attributes. Discuss any patterns across the companies that you as a team observe. Provide potential explanations for any differences discovered.

CP17-4 Making Ethical Decisions: A Real-Life Example

During its deliberations on the Sarbanes-Oxley Act, the U.S. Senate considered numerous reports evaluating the quality of work done by external auditors. One study by Weiss Ratings, Inc., focused on auditors' ability to predict bankruptcy. The study criticized auditors for failing to identify and report going-concern problems for audit clients that later went bankrupt. Based on a sample of 45 bankrupt companies, the Weiss study concluded that had auditors noted unusual levels for just two of seven typical financial ratios, they would have identified 89 percent of the sample companies that later went bankrupt. A follow-up to the Weiss study found that had the criteria in the Weiss study been applied to a larger sample of nonbankrupt companies, 46.9 percent of nonbankrupt companies would have been predicted to go bankrupt.* In other words, the Weiss criteria would have incorrectly predicted bankruptcy for nearly half of the companies in the follow-up study and would have led the auditors to report that these clients had substantial going-concern problems when, in fact, they did not.

LO4

---

* Michael D. Akers, Meredith A. Maher, and Don E. Giacomino, "Going-Concern Opinions: Broadening the Expectations Gap," *CPA Journal*, October 2003 (n. d.), www.nysscpa.org/cpajournal/2003/1003/features/f103803.htm (November 20, 2006).

Required:

Discuss the negative consequences that arise when auditors fail to predict companies that go bankrupt. Who is harmed by these failures? Discuss the negative consequences that arise when auditors incorrectly predict bankruptcy. Who is harmed by these errors? In your opinion, which of the potential consequences is worse?

LO4   **CP17-5 Making Ethical Decisions: A Mini Case**

Capital Investments Corporation (CIC) requested a sizable loan from First Federal Bank to acquire a large piece of land for future expansion. CIC reported current assets of $1,900,000 (including $430,000 in cash) and current liabilities of $1,075,000. First Federal denied the loan request for a number of reasons, including the fact that the current ratio was below 2:1. When CIC was informed of the loan denial, the controller of the company immediately paid $420,000 that was owed to several trade creditors. The controller then asked First Federal to reconsider the loan application.

Required:

Based on these abbreviated facts, would you recommend that First Federal approve the loan request? Why? Are the controller's actions ethical?

LO4   **CP17-6 Thinking Critically: Analyzing the Impact of Alternative Depreciation Methods on Ratio Analysis**

Speedy Company uses the double-declining-balance method to depreciate its property, plant, and equipment. Turtle Company uses the straight-line method. The two companies are exactly alike except for the difference in depreciation methods.

Required:

1. Identify the financial ratios discussed in this chapter that are likely to be affected by the difference in depreciation methods.

2. Which company will report the higher amount for each ratio that you have identified? If you cannot be certain, explain why.

LO4   **CP17-7 Using a Spreadsheet to Calculate Financial Statement Ratios**

Use the financial statement information from Exhibits 17.2, and 17.3.

Required:

Enter the financial information for each exhibit into two separate worksheets in one spreadsheet file. Create a third worksheet that uses the formulas in Exhibit 17.6 to recalculate ratios (1) through (14) for Lowe's for 2006. (For the EPS ratio, simply import the amount reported on the face of the income statement stock price is $31 per share.)

18 Managerial Accounting

LEARNING OBJECTIVES

After completing this chapter, you should be able to:

LO1 Describe the key differences between financial accounting and managerial accounting.

LO2 Explain the functions of management.

LO3 Define and give examples of different types of cost:

    a. Out-of-pocket and opportunity costs

    b. Direct and indirect costs

    c. Variable and fixed costs

    d. Relevant and irrelevant costs

    e. Manufacturing and nonmanufacturing costs

    f. Product and period costs

LO4 Compare the financial statements of merchandising and manufacturing firms.

LO5 Prepare a cost of goods manufactured report.

Lectured presentations 18-1
www.mhhe.com/LLPW1e

Focus Company: TOMBSTONE PIZZA

"What Do You Want On Your Tombstone?"

The past 17 chapters (and 700 plus pages) were devoted to preparing and interpreting financial accounting reports. The information provided in those reports is critical to small business owners such as Mauricio Rosa, owner of Pizza Aroma, as well as huge corporations such as Wal-Mart, which must report their financial and operating results to investors, creditors, and government regulators. In this chapter, we shift our focus to managerial accounting, the branch of accounting that specializes in meeting the information needs of internal business managers.

To illustrate the role of managerial accounting in organizations, we use the story of two brothers from Wisconsin who started out much like Mauricio Rosa, as owners of a small pizza business. In 1960, the Simek brothers began selling pizza at a small tavern across the street from the local cemetery, aptly named the Tombstone Tap. As the buzz about the Simeks' delicious pizza spread, other local businesses began to buy and serve it to their own customers. By 1966, the two brothers had bought the first in what would eventually become a fleet of refrigerated trucks that deliver Tombstone Pizza to small businesses and grocery stores across the country. In 1986, Kraft Foods made the brothers an offer they couldn't refuse, and Tombstone Pizza became a subsidiary—that is, a freestanding operating unit—of Kraft Foods.

As you read the chapter, try putting yourself in the shoes of one of the following managers at Tombstone Pizza:

- Regional sales manager responsible for sales and distribution to grocery stores in California, Nevada, Utah, and Arizona.
- Marketing manager responsible for pricing and promotion of existing products.
- New product development manager responsible for the development and introduction of a new whole wheat pizza.

- Production manager responsible for the rising-crust production line.
- Human resource manager responsible for hiring, training, and evaluating Tombstone employees.

Think about the activities you would engage in and the decisions you would make in your chosen role and, most of all, the information you would need as a manager. Chances are that much of that information would come from the company's managerial accounting system.

ORGANIZATION OF THE CHAPTER

ROLE OF MANAGERIAL ACCOUNTING IN ORGANIZATIONS	COST CLASSIFICATIONS AND DEFINITIONS	COSTS IN MANUFACTURING VERSUS NONMANUFACTURING FIRMS
• Decision-Making Orientation • Comparison of Financial and Managerial Accounting • Functions of Management	• Definition of Cost • Out-of-Pocket versus Opportunity Costs • Direct versus Indirect Costs • Variable versus Fixed Costs • Relevant versus Irrelevant Costs • Manufacturing versus Nonmanufacturing Costs • Product versus Period Costs	• Balance Sheets of Merchandising versus Manufacturing Firms • Cost of Goods Manufactured Report • Income Statements of Merchandising versus Manufacturing Firms

ROLE OF MANAGERIAL ACCOUNTING IN ORGANIZATIONS

Decision-Making Orientation

Video 18-1
www.mhhe.com/LLPW1e

The purpose of managerial accounting is to provide useful information to internal managers to help them make decisions that arise as they manage people, projects, products, or segments of the business. For example, managers at Tombstone Pizza might need to answer the following questions:

- How much should we charge for our pizza? Should we base the price on how much each pizza costs us to make or how much our competitors charge for their pizza?
- Should we make the pizza sauce ourselves or buy it in large quantities from a supplier?
- What kind of advertisements and promotions should we use to make consumers aware of our products?
- Should we invest in automated equipment or continue to make our pizza dough by hand?

Throughout this chapter, we focus on the role of managerial accounting in helping managers to answer questions such as these.

Comparison of Financial and Managerial Accounting

Learning Objective 1

Describe the key differences between financial accounting and managerial accounting.

The major difference between financial accounting and managerial accounting is the intended user of the information. Financial accounting information is used by external parties, such as investors, creditors, and regulators; managerial accounting information is used by internal managers. Of course, different users have different needs. Financial statements prepared

Exhibit 18.1   Differences between Financial and Managerial Accounting

	Financial Accounting	Managerial Accounting
User prespective	Used by external parties, such as investors, creditors, and regulators	Used by internal parties, such as managers and employees
Types of reports	Classified financial statements prepared according to GAAP	Various non-GAAP reports, such as budgets, performance evaluations, and cost reports
Nature of information	Objective, reliable, historical	Subjective, relevant, future oriented
Frequency of reporting	Prepared periodically (monthly, quarterly, annually)	Prepared as needed, perhaps day-to-day or even in real time
Level of detail	Information reported for the company as a whole	Information reported at the decision-making level (by product, region, customer, or other business segment)

according to generally accepted accounting principles (GAAP) provide external users certain advantages in terms of their comparability and objectivity. However, internal managers often need more detailed information that is not restricted by GAAP—information that is not captured in the financial reports prepared for external parties. More often than not, the information managers seek is relevant, future oriented, or subjective. See Exhibit 18.1 for a summary of these key differences between financial accounting and managerial accounting.

To illustrate these differences, let's return to Tombstone Pizza. For purposes of external financial reporting, Kraft Foods combines the Tombstone Pizza subsidiary with other well-known brands, such as DiGiorno pizza, Kraft macaroni and cheese, and Oscar Mayer hot dogs. At the end of the fiscal year, accountants at Kraft Foods prepare the company's annual report, including a consolidated income statement, balance sheet, and statement of cash flows, along with other relevant information and disclosures. These financial statements are audited by an independent public accounting firm, such as PricewaterhouseCoopers LLC. They are publicly available to anyone with an interest in Kraft Foods, including government regulators, financial analysts, and investors who are considering buying or selling stock in the company.

Although financial statements are an extremely important source of information to external decision makers, they probably are not that useful to individual managers responsible for making decisions in Kraft's Tombstone Pizza division. In particular, financial reports tend to be too focused on the past and too general for managerial decision making. Managers often need more detailed information related to their specific responsibilities—information that focuses on what will happen in the future rather than on what happened in the past. For example, a manager who is responsible for new product development must be able to predict, identify, and interpret consumers' ever-changing tastes to develop products that will appeal to consumer preferences.

To better understand the role of managerial accounting, let's consider the various functions that managers at Tombstone Pizza perform and the information they need to perform them.

Functions of Management

Regardless of the type of organization or size of the business unit they manage, all managers perform the same basic functions, which revolve around planning, organizing, leading/directing, and control. In the course of performing each of these functions, managers make a

Coach's Tip

Financial accounting is sometimes referred to as **external** reporting while managerial accounting is referred to as **internal** reporting. The difference is whether the intended users are inside or outside the company.

Learning Objective 2

Explain the functions of management.

Exhibit 18.2   Functions of Management

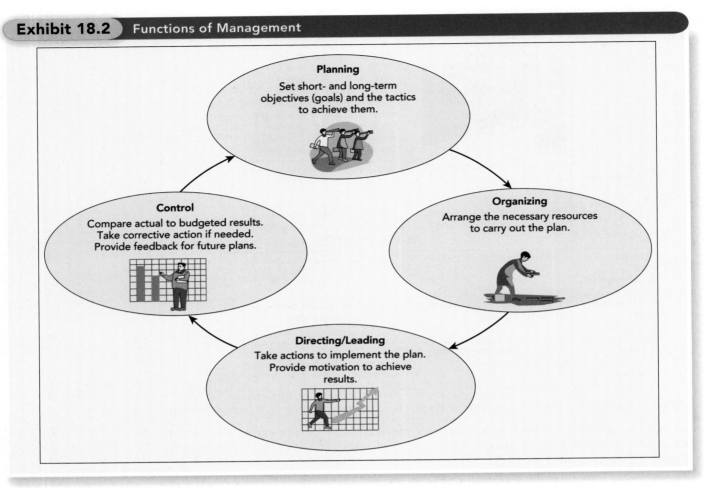

variety of decisions, many of which are based on managerial accounting information. Refer to Exhibit 18.2 for an illustration of the managerial process.

Planning is the future-oriented aspect of the managerial process. It involves setting long-term goals and objectives, along with the short-term tactics necessary to achieve them. Assume, for example, that Tombstone Pizza plans to introduce a new low-calorie pizza with a whole wheat crust to appeal to health-conscious consumers. The planning process would include setting long-term objectives for sales volume and market share over the first few years of the product's life cycle. Once the objectives have been set, managers would then identify and define the short-term tactics with which to achieve those objectives. Tactics would include the details of how to develop, test, produce, market, distribute, and sell the new product. Once the planning stage is complete, managers must begin organizing, or arranging for the necessary resources needed to achieve the plan. As part of the organization process, managers would need to develop a budget that details how much time and money should be spent on each of these critical tasks.

The next managerial function, directing/leading, relates to putting the plan into action and making all of the managerial decisions needed to implement the plan. In addition to leading, managers must motivate their employees to work toward the plan's success. For example, managers might offer bonuses for meeting project deadlines and staying within budget in each phase of the new product's development and introduction. They might also use incentives to motivate the sales force to sell the new whole wheat pizza as well as negotiate with retailers for shelf space for the product.

The final managerial function, control, involves comparing actual results to planned results, to see whether the company's objectives are being met. If not, managers must take corrective action to adjust the objectives and/or their implementation of the plan. For example, if managers determined that sales of Tombstone's whole wheat pizza were falling short of expectations, they might decide to spend more money on marketing to advertise the new product's health benefits.

As you can see, the managerial functions of planning, organizing, directing/leading, and control are interconnected: one function feeds into another, and feedback from the process is used to improve future decision making. Throughout, managers must make a variety of decisions based on relevant, up-to-date information including cost estimates, competitor pricing, market demand, and consumer preferences. Much of the information managers need to make these decisions comes from the managerial accounting system.

In the next section, we discuss the role of cost information in helping managers to make some of their decisions. But first take a moment to complete the following Self-Study Practice to make sure you understand the functions of management and the differences between financial and managerial accounting.

SELF-STUDY PRACTICE

1. Which of the following statements best describes the difference between financial accounting and managerial accounting?

   a. Managerial accounting is targeted at external stakeholders, while financial accounting is targeted at individuals within the company.

   b. Financial accounting relies more on subjective, future-oriented information than managerial accounting does.

   c. The major focus of managerial accounting is the preparation of the income statement, balance sheet, and statement of cash flows.

   d. Managerial accounting tends to focus on relevant, subjective, and future-oriented information while financial accounting relies primarily on objective, reliable, and historical information.

   e. All the above statements are false.

2. Which of the following statements regarding the key management functions is false? (You may select more than one answer.)

   a. Planning involves setting both long-term objectives and the short-term tactics necessary to achieve those objectives.

   b. Directing/leading involves comparing actual results to planned objectives and making any adjustments as necessary.

   c. Each of the management functions (planning, organizing, leading/directing, and controlling) is completely independent of the others.

   d. All of the above.

When you are have finished, check your answers with the solutions at the bottom of the page.

COST CLASSIFICATIONS AND DEFINITIONS

One of the key roles of managerial accounting is to measure the cost of various products, services, and customers. For example, a marketing manager at Tombstone Pizza would probably want to know how much each pizza costs to determine what price to charge. Similarly, a production manager might want to know how much it costs to make the pizza sauce in-house as opposed to buying it from a supplier. You may not realize it, but these two examples use the word **cost** in subtly different ways. Let's look more closely at the meaning of the word **cost.**

Video 18-2
www.mhhe.com/LLPW1e

Definition of Cost

When you incur a cost, you give up one thing, such as money or time, in exchange for something else. Cost is the value of what is given up during this exchange. Determining what something costs is fairly straightforward if you are paying cash or credit for an item. It is a

Learning Objective 3

Define and give examples of different types of cost.

1. D

2. B and C. (Item B describes control, not leading/directing. Item C is false because the management functions are interdependent).

Solution to
Self-Study Practice

lot trickier when you are giving up something of less obvious value, such as your time, your services, or your expertise. In this section, we classify and define various types of cost including those that are stated routinely in dollars and cents and those that are not.

Out-of-Pocket versus Opportunity Costs

Out-of-pocket costs involve an actual outlay of cash. In your personal life, these are the costs you pay "out of your pocket" for things such as food, clothing, and entertainment. For Tombstone Pizza, these costs would include payments for items such as rent, wages, utilities, advertising, and insurance.

Unlike an out-of-pocket cost which involves an outlay of cash, an opportunity cost is the cost of **not** doing something. In other words, it is the forgone benefit (or lost opportunity) of the path not taken. Anytime you choose to do one thing instead of another because of a limit on your time or money, you incur an opportunity cost. For example, if you are going to school full-time, you are giving up the opportunity to earn money by working full-time. The potential earnings you give up to go to school are an opportunity cost of pursuing your education.

Similarly, business managers incur an opportunity cost any time they are forced to choose between one alternative or another because of limited resources, such as cash, equipment, or space. If Tombstone Pizza has a limited number of ovens in which to bake its various pizza products, for example, managers may need to reduce production of an existing pizza product in order to produce the new whole wheat pizza. If so, the value of the lost sales from the existing product should be treated as an opportunity cost of introducing the new whole wheat pizza.

Spotlight On BUSINESS DECISIONS

Should You Continue Your Education?

You have obviously made the decision to further your education by taking this class. At some point in the future, you may even think of getting an advanced degree, such as an MBA, law degree, or medical degree.

The decision to pursue a degree is a very important one that should consider both the costs and benefits. As you know, the costs of education, including tuition, fees, and books, are very high. You also incur opportunity costs when you forgo working to go to school. These costs must be offset by the future career opportunities (and higher salary) the degree will bring.

If you ever consider getting an MBA, Forbes has an online decision tool that can help you weigh the costs and benefits of the advanced degree.* This tool estimates the five-year gain from getting an MBA as the difference between the salary and bonuses you would expect to earn in the five years after graduation minus the tuition and potential earnings you would give up while getting your MBA. Because these costs and benefits occur across a number of years, the online tool factors in the time value of money, or the opportunity cost of giving up cash today to earn cash at some point in the future.

This same approach can be applied to almost any decision so long as you can estimate the future costs and benefits of the particular decision you are trying to make.

_____
* http://www.forbes.com/2005/08/16/cz_05mba_business_schools_gain_calulator.html

Coach's Tip

Whether a cost is treated as direct or indirect depends on whether tracing it is both **possible** and **feasible.** Some minor costs, such as the cost of glue or other supplies, may not be worth the effort needed to trace to individual products. These costs are classified as **indirect costs.**

Direct versus Indirect Costs

When managers request cost information, they typically want to know the cost of something specific, whether it is a specific unit of product (such as a 16-inch pizza), a particular component of the product (such as the pizza dough), or an area or division in the company (such as the baking department). The item for which they are trying to determine cost is the cost object.

Costs that can be traced directly to a specific cost object are direct costs. Costs that cannot be traced to a specific cost object, or that are not worth the effort of tracing, are indirect costs. Assume, for example, you want to know the cost of taking a specific course, such as this accounting course. Some costs, such as those for tuition and books, can be traced directly to the course, so they would be considered direct costs. If you are taking multiple courses, some costs may not be directly traceable to a single course. Examples would be the cost of traveling to and from campus, the cost of your personal computer, and the supplies you use in class. These costs would be considered indirect costs.

For Tombstone Pizza, direct costs would include the costs of materials and labor that can be traced directly to each pizza produced. Indirect costs would include items such as depreciation on the ovens used to bake the pizzas as well as the costs of utilities, advertising, and plant supervision. See Exhibit 18.3 for some examples of direct and indirect costs at other real-world companies.

Exhibit 18.3   Real-World Examples of Direct versus Indirect Costs

Company	Cost Object	Direct Costs	Indirect Costs
Toni and Guy Hair Salons	Individual haircut and style	Stylist's time	Styling products, receptionist's service, depreciation on equipment
Federal Express	Package delivered	Packaging of materials (envelopes, etc.)	Planes, delivery personnel
GAP	Pair of blue jeans	Cost of the jeans, commissions paid to salesperson	Store supervision, rent, and inventory control
Dell Computer	Personal computer	Cost of the components, wages of workers who assembled the computer, and delivery costs	Production supervision, factory space, and quality control

Variable versus Fixed Costs

For internal decision making, managers are often interested in how costs will change with a change in activity level, such as the number of units produced or sold. Variable costs are those that change, in total, in direct proportion to changes in activity levels. For example, if Tombstone Pizza were to increase its production of pizzas by 20 percent, certain costs, such as those for direct materials, direct labor, and the power required to run the ovens, would increase proportionally.

Fixed costs are those that stay the same, in total, regardless of activity level, at least within some range of activity. For example, the costs of factory space, depreciation on equipment, insurance, and supervision probably would not increase as a result of a 20 percent increase in production. Because the distinction between fixed and variable costs is so important to many managerial decisions, we will analyze it in detail in Chapter 21.

Coach's Tip
In deciding whether a cost is variable or fixed, be sure to think about whether the **total cost** will change. Looking at average or unit cost will reveal an entirely different pattern, which we will examine more closely in Chapter 21.

Spotlight On BUSINESS DECISIONS

The Need to Understand Fixed and Variable Costs

Assume you are the treasurer of a university club and you are on the planning committee for the end-of-year social event. The committee is in charge of finding a location, renting tables and chairs, and hiring a DJ, photographer, and caterer for the event. Your responsibility as treasurer is to set the budget for the event and make sure the committee stays within that budget. One of the first questions you would need to know is how many people are likely to attend the event.

Which costs would you expect to vary with the number of people attending? Which costs will be the same regardless of how many people attend the event? Why is it important for you to know the answers to these questions to prepare a budget? Check the Coach's Tip on the next page for answers to these questions.

Managers must answer these same questions when making business decisions. They need to understand which costs will vary with the number of units produced or the number of customers served, and which will be incurred regardless of these factors.

Relevant versus Irrelevant Costs

Often managers are interested only in those costs that are relevant to a particular decision. A relevant cost is one that has the potential to influence a decision; an irrelevant cost is one that will not influence a decision. For a cost to be relevant, it must meet both of the following criteria:

- It must differ between the decision alternatives.
- It must be incurred in the future rather than in the past.

The first criterion means that the cost must change depending on the choice the manager makes. Costs that differ across decision alternatives are also called differential costs. The second criterion, that the cost must be incurred in the future, eliminates costs that have already been incurred or sunk costs. Because those costs have already been paid for (that is, they are sunk), they will not change with the manager's decision. Therefore, they are not relevant to future decisions.

Assume, for example, you are thinking of selling your old car and buying a new one. Is the amount you paid for your old car a relevant cost? The answer is no; it is a sunk cost that will not change regardless of what you do in the future. However, the amount of money you can get for your old car now (its current value) and the cost of the new car are relevant to your decision. Any difference in fuel costs and insurance for the old and the new cars would also be relevant. What about the parking fee you pay each semester—is that a relevant cost? The answer is no because you will have to pay for parking no matter which car you drive.

Now assume that you are thinking of getting rid of your car altogether and either riding a bike or relying on public transportation. Would the cost of on-campus parking be relevant to that decision? In this case, it would be relevant because it will change depending on whether or not you own a car. In Chapter 22, we rely heavily on this concept of relevant versus irrelevant costs to analyze a variety of managerial decisions.

Manufacturing versus Nonmanufacturing Costs

Another important distinction between costs is whether they are related to manufacturing or nonmanufacturing activities. This distinction is important only in companies that make a physical product, such as Apple (iPods), Toyota (cars and trucks), Harley Davidson (motorcycles), or Maytag (appliances). Businesses that sell services or purchased goods do not need to make this distinction.

Manufacturing costs include all costs incurred to produce the final product. They are generally classified into one of three categories:

Prime Cost =

**Direct Materials
+
Direct Labor**

Conversion Cost =

**Direct Labor
+
Manufacturing
Overhead**

- Direct materials are the major material inputs that can be physically and conveniently traced to the final product. For Tombstone Pizza, direct materials would include the major ingredients (dough, sauce, cheese, and meat), as well as packaging materials (plastic and cardboard). This category would not include minor materials that cannot be conveniently traced to individual units (such as seasoning and glue).
- Direct labor is the cost of labor that can be physically and conveniently traced to the product. This category includes all hands-on labor associated with making the physical product. It would not include the labor of those who do not touch the physical product, such as supervisors, maintenance workers, and engineers.
- Manufacturing overhead includes all manufacturing costs **other than direct materials and direct labor** that must be incurred to manufacture a physical product. For Tombstone Pizza, examples would include rent, insurance, utilities, and supervision at the manufacturing facility. Costs that are not related to manufacturing (such as distribution or marketing costs) should not be included in manufacturing overhead.

Taken together, direct materials and direct labor are referred to as prime cost because they represent the primary costs that can be traced to the end product. Similarly, direct labor and manufacturing overhead are referred to as conversion cost—that is, the total cost required to convert direct materials into the finished product.

Nonmanufacturing costs are the costs associated with running the business and selling the product, as opposed to manufacturing the product. They are generally classified into two groups:

- Marketing or selling costs are incurred to get the final product to the customer. For Tombstone Pizza, examples would include the cost of the trucks that deliver the pizzas to supermarkets, the sales managers' salaries, and advertising costs.

- **Administrative costs** are associated with running the overall organization. They include general management's salaries, rent and utilities for corporate headquarters, and corporate service functions, such as the accounting, payroll, and legal departments.

Product versus Period Costs

The distinction between product and period costs is closely tied to the distinction between manufacturing and nonmanufacturing costs. This terminology has to do with the way in which different costs are treated from a financial accounting perspective. Specifically, the distinction depends on **when** the cost is matched against revenue on the income statement.

For financial reporting purposes, GAAP requires that all manufacturing costs be treated as product costs, or costs that are attached to the product during production. Product costs are sometimes called inventoriable costs because they are initially counted as part of the cost of inventory. In contrast, period costs are never counted as inventory. Rather, they are expensed during the period they are incurred. For financial reporting purposes, GAAP requires that all nonmanufacturing costs be expensed in the period incurred. Note, however, that **these rules pertain only to external reporting.** For internal purposes, companies may use other accounting methods that are more useful in managerial decision making. Refer to Exhibit 18.4 for an illustration of the different treatment of product and period costs under GAAP.

> ### Coach's Tip
> The distinction between period and product costs is a matter of **when** the cost is matched against revenue on the income statement. Period costs are expensed as soon as they are incurred. Product costs are recorded initially as inventory; they do not appear on the income statement until the product is sold.

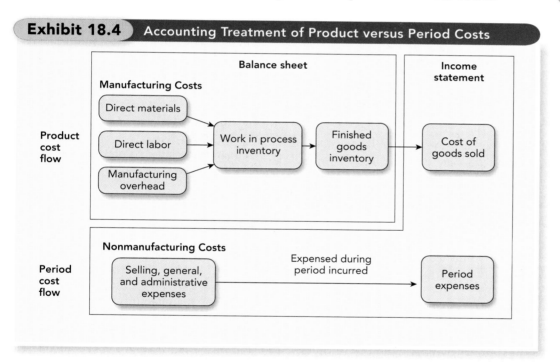

Exhibit 18.4   Accounting Treatment of Product versus Period Costs

In the next section, we see how various costs are reported in the financial statements. Chapter 19 will present costs in even more detail. For now, it is important that you understand the basic cost terminology and definitions. Before continuing take the Self-Study Practice on the next page to see how well you understand this terminology.

COSTS IN MANUFACTURING VERSUS NONMANUFACTURING FIRMS

Most businesses can be classified into one of three categories. Service companies provide services to other businesses or consumers. Examples of service companies include United Parcel Service (UPS), Regis hair salons, LA Fitness clubs, and Verizon Wireless. **Merchandising companies** purchase goods from others and sell them to other businesses or consumers. Examples of merchandising companies include Safeway, Sam's Club, Abercrombie and Fitch, and Amazon.com. **Manufacturing firms** purchase raw materials from suppliers and use them

SELF-STUDY PRACTICE

Match the appropriate description on the right to the terms on the left.

_____ 1. Cost

_____ 2. Product costs

_____ 3. Period costs

_____ 4. Manufacturing costs

_____ 5. Nonmanufacturing costs

_____ 6. Variable costs

_____ 7. Fixed costs

_____ 8. Direct costs

_____ 9. Indirect costs

_____10. Out-of-pocket costs

_____11. Opportunity cost

_____12. Sunk costs

A. Costs that remain the same in total regardless of the activity level

B. Costs that involve an outlay of cash for items such as rent, utilities, and salaries

C. The benefit that you forgo when you select one alternative over another

D. Costs that can be traced conveniently and physically to a specific cost object

E. Costs that have already been incurred and thus are not relevant to future decisions

F. Costs that are expensed in the period when they are incurred

G. Costs that are incurred while making a physical product, such as direct materials, direct labor, and manufacturing overhead

H. Costs that cannot be traced conveniently or physically to a specific cost object

I. Costs that change in total in direct proportion to a change in the activity level

J. Costs that are attached to the product being produced and are included in inventory until the product is sold

K. The value that is given up in an exchange of goods or services

L. Costs that are not related to producing a product, such as selling and administrative costs

When you have finished, check your answers with the solutions at the bottom of the page.

to make a finished product, which they sell to other businesses or consumers. Examples of manufacturing firms include Tombstone Pizza, Harley Davidson, Levis, and Ford Motor Company.

As you might expect, the financial statements of manufacturing firms are more complicated than those of service or merchandising companies because they must account for all costs of transforming raw materials into finished products. Because manufacturing firms play such an important (although diminishing) role in the U.S. economy, the remainder of this chapter will be devoted to issues that arise in manufacturing firms. To start, let's consider how a manufacturing firm's balance sheet differs from that of a merchandising firm.

Solution to Self-Study Practice

1. K
2. J
3. F
4. G
5. L
6. I
7. A
8. D
9. H
10. B
11. C
12. E

Balance Sheets of Merchandising versus Manufacturing Firms

Learning Objective 4

Compare the financial statements of merchandising and manufacturing firms.

The major difference between the balance sheets of merchandising and manufacturing firms is the treatment of inventory. Merchandisers report only one form of inventory (merchandise inventory) on their balance sheets; manufacturing firms report three types: raw materials, work in process, and finished goods (see Exhibit 18.5).

Exhibit 18.5   **Balance Sheets for Merchandising and Manufacturing Firms**

Merchandising Firm's Balance Sheet		Manufacturing Firm's Balance Sheet	
Assets		**Assets**	
Cash	$ 15,000	Cash	$ 20,000
Accounts receivable	35,000	Accounts receivable	30,000
Merchandise inventory	50,000	Raw materials inventory	15,000
Property, plant, and equipment	100,000	Work in process inventory	27,000
Total assets	$200,000	Finished goods inventory	40,000
		Property, plant, and equipment	78,000
		Total assets	$210,000

Raw Materials Inventory represents the cost of all materials purchased from suppliers but not yet used. For Tombstone Pizza, this amount would include the cost of all ingredients for making the pizza (cheese, dough, sauce, and spices) as well as the cost of all packaging materials (cardboard and plastic). As raw materials are used in production, these costs are transferred to the Work in Process Inventory account.

Work in Process Inventory represents the cost of units that have been started but are not yet complete. In addition to the cost of the direct materials transferred out of the raw materials account, this inventory account accumulates direct labor costs and manufacturing overhead costs, such as factory rent, depreciation, insurance, and utilities. Once the product is complete, these costs are transferred to the finished goods inventory account.

Finished Goods Inventory represents the cost of all units that have been completed but not yet sold. The cost of each unit manufactured remains in the Finished Goods Inventory account until the product is sold. After the product's sale, the cost is transferred to the Cost of Goods Sold account on the income statement.

Recall from our discussion of product costs (page 773) that GAAP requires all manufacturing costs initially be treated as part of the cost of inventory. As units make their way through the manufacturing process, the manufacturing costs flow into and out of the three inventory accounts (see Exhibit 18.6). At first, raw materials are recorded in the Raw Materials Inventory account. As materials are issued into production, their costs are transferred to the Work in Process Inventory account, which also accumulates direct labor and manufacturing overhead costs. When the product is complete, the total manufacturing cost is transferred out of the Work in Process Inventory account and into the Finished Goods Inventory account. Finally, when the product is sold, the manufacturing cost is transferred out of Finished Goods Inventory and into the Cost of Goods Sold account.

Cost of Goods Manufactured Report

The total cost that is transferred out of Work in Process and into Finished Goods is called the cost of goods manufactured. It represents the total cost of all units completed during a given period regardless of whether or not they have been sold. To calculate the cost of goods manufactured, accountants sum the direct materials, direct labor, and manufacturing overhead costs recorded during the period and then adjust them using the beginning and ending values in the Raw Materials Inventory and Work in Process Inventory accounts.

Learning Objective 5

Prepare a cost of goods manufactured report.

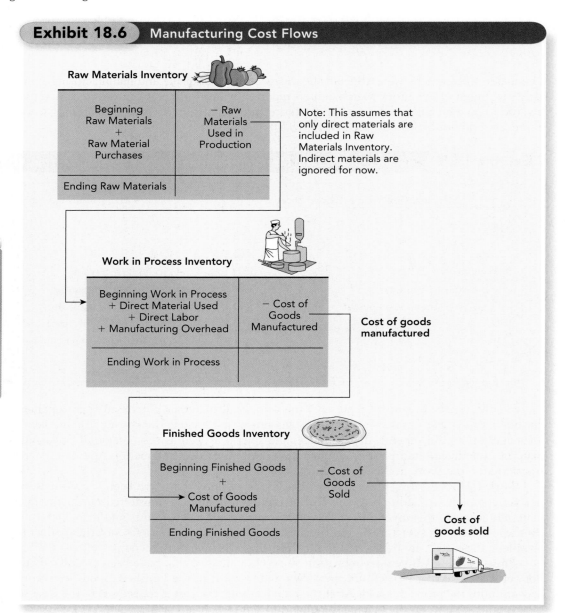

Exhibit 18.6 Manufacturing Cost Flows

Coach's Tip

Cost of goods manufactured is sometimes called cost of goods completed. It is the cost of the units completed during the period, regardless of whether or not they have been sold.

The total cost of goods manufactured or completed is reported in the cost of goods manufactured report. See Exhibit 18.7 for such a report.

Income Statements of Merchandising versus Manufacturing Firms

The main difference between the income statements of merchandising and manufacturing firms is the calculation of the cost of goods sold. These differences may be summarized as follows:

Merchandiser Cost of Goods Sold

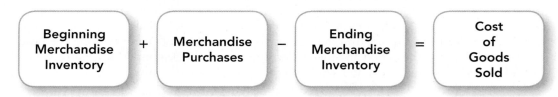

Manufacturer Cost of Goods Sold

| Beginning Finished Goods Inventory | + | Cost of Goods Manufactured | − | Ending Finished Goods Inventory | = | Cost of Goods Sold |

Exhibit 18.7   Cost of Goods Manufactured Report

Schedule of Cost of Goods Manufactured

Beginning raw materials inventory	$ 10,000	
Plus: Raw material purchases	95,000	
Total raw material available for use	105,000	
Less: Ending raw materials inventory	15,000	
Raw material used in production		$90,000
Direct labor		50,000
Manufacturing overhead costs		
Factory rent	25,000	
Supervisors' salaries	18,000	
Factory insurance	9,000	
Factory utilities	8,000	
Other manufacturing overhead cost	12,000	72,000
Total current manufacturing costs		$212,000
Plus: Beginning work in process inventory		15,000
Total work in process		227,000
Less: Ending work in process inventory		27,000
Cost of goods manufactured		$200,000

Because merchandising firms purchase finished goods from someone else (rather than making the products themselves), they calculate cost of goods sold by adding the value of the merchandise on hand at the beginning of the period to the value of goods purchased during the period and then subtracting the value of any merchandise remaining at the end of the period. Manufacturing firms make a similar calculation that considers the values of the beginning and ending finished goods inventory. However, because manufacturing firms make their products instead of purchasing them, they use the term **cost of goods manufactured** instead of **merchandise purchases.**

See Exhibit 18.8 for these differences in calculation, which are ultimately summarized in the Cost of Goods Sold section of the income statement. Notice that the only difference is

Exhibit 18.8   Income Statements for Merchandising and Manufacturing Firms

Merchandising Company Income Statement		Manufacturing Company Income Statement	
Sales	$200,000	Sales	$300,000
Less: Cost of goods sold		Less: Cost of goods sold	
Beginning merchandise inventory	40,000	Beginning finished goods inventory	50,000
Plus: Purchases	150,000	Plus: Cost of goods manufactured	200,000
Cost of goods available for sale	190,000	Cost of goods available for sale	250,000
Less: Ending merchandise inventory	50,000	Less: Ending finished goods inventory	40,000
Cost of goods sold	140,000	Cost of goods sold	210,000
Gross profit	60,000	Gross profit	90,000
Less: Operating expenses	20,000	Less: Operating expenses	40,000
Income from operations	$ 40,000	Income from operations	$ 50,000

that the merchandising firm bases cost of goods sold on purchases of merchandise, while the manufacturing firm bases cost of goods sold on the cost of goods manufactured.

To make sure you understand how to calculate a manufacturing firm's cost of goods manufactured and cost of goods sold, complete the following self-study practice.

SELF-STUDY PRACTICE

DiGiorno Pizza reported the following inventory balances at the beginning and end of January 2009.

	Beginning Inventory (1/1/2009)	Ending Inventory (1/31/2009)
Raw materials inventory	$15,000	$25,000
Work in process inventory	30,000	15,000
Finished goods inventory	50,000	40,000

Additional information for the month of January follows:

Raw material purchases	$ 80,000
Direct labor	50,000
Manufacturing overhead costs	100,000

Based on this information, compute the following:

1. Cost of raw material used in production.
2. Total current manufacturing costs.
3. Cost of goods manufactured.
4. Cost of goods sold.

When you have finished, check your answers with the solutions at the bottom of the page.

Demonstration Case

Barnaby's Bicycle Company manufactures high-quality mountain bikes. The company's managerial accountant has come to you for help. She needs to classify and identify each of the following costs before she can calculate the cost to produce each mountain bike.

Part 1: Classify each of the costs listed on the following chart into three categories based on the following questions.

1. Can this cost be directly and conveniently traced to each bicycle that is manufactured, or is doing so either not possible or not worth the effort?
2. Is this cost related to manufacturing the bicycles or to some other activity, such as selling them or managing the overall business?

Solution to Self-Study Practice

1. $ 15,000 + $80,000 − $ 25,000 = $ 70,000
2. $ 70,000 + $50,000 + $100,000 = $220,000
3. $220,000 + $30,000 − $ 15,000 = $235,000
4. $235,000 + $50,000 − $ 40,000 = $245,000

3. Will the total cost vary with the number of bicycles manufactured or sold, or will it remain the same regardless of how many bikes are produced and sold?

The first item in the chart is completed as an example.

| | QUESTION 1 | | QUESTION 2 | | | | QUESTION 3 | |
| | | | MANUFACTURING (PRODUCT) COSTS: | | | | COST BEHAVIOR | |
	Direct Cost	Indirect Cost	Direct Materials	Direct Labor	Mfg. Overhead	Nonmfg. (period) Expenses	Variable Cost	Fixed Cost
Alloy tubing used to make the bicycle frames	X		X				X	
Wages paid to employees who cut and weld the alloy tubing								
Factory rent								
Bicycle wheels and tires								
Miscellaneous bicycle components								
Insurance on the factory								
Insurance on the president's company car								

Part 2: On July 1, Barnaby's Bicycle Company had the following inventory on hand:

Raw materials inventory	$15,000
Work in process inventory	25,000
Finished goods inventory (500 bikes @ $90 each)	45,000

Additional information recorded during July follows.

Raw material purchases	$100,000
Raw materials used in production	105,000
Direct labor	30,000
Manufacturing overhead costs	40,000
Selling and administrative expenses	49,000

During July, workers completed 2,000 bikes and transferred $180,000 worth of goods from Work in Process to Finished Goods, leaving $20,000 worth of goods still in process. A monthly cost summary revealed that the average cost of each bike produced that month was $90. At the end of the month, 400 bikes, valued at a total cost of $36,000, were in finished goods inventory. The company sold 2,100 bikes in July at a retail price of $200 each.

Required:

1. Prepare a cost of goods manufactured report for the month of July.
2. Prepare the income statement for Barnaby's Bicycle Company for the month of July; include a detailed calculation of the cost of goods sold.

Suggested Solution

Part 1:

	QUESTION 1		QUESTION 2 MANUFACTURING (PRODUCT) COSTS:				QUESTION 3 COST BEHAVIOR	
Example:	Direct Cost	Indirect Cost	Direct Materials	Direct Labor	Mfg. Overhead	Nonmfg. (period) Expenses	Variable Cost	Fixed Cost
Alloy tubing used to make the bicycle frames	X		X				X	
Wages paid to employees who cut and weld the alloy tubing	X			X			X	
Factory rent		X			X			X
Bicycle wheels and tires	X		X				X	
Miscellaneous bicycle components		X			X		X	
Insurance on the factory		X			X			X
Insurance on the president's company car		X				X		X

Part 2:

1.

Barnaby's Bicycle Company
Cost of Goods Manufactured
for the Month of July

Beginning raw materials inventory	$ 15,000	
Plus: Raw material purchases	100,000	
Total raw materials available for use	115,000	
Less: Ending raw materials inventory	10,000	
Raw materials used in production		$105,000
Direct labor		30,000
Manufacturing overhead		40,000
Total current manufacturing costs		$175,000
Plus: Beginning work in process inventory		25,000
Total work in process		200,000
Less: Ending work in process inventory		20,000
Cost of goods manufactured		$180,000

2.

Barnaby's Bicycle Company
Income Statement
for the Month of July

Sales revenue (2,100 bikes × $200)		$420,000
Less: Cost of goods sold		
Beginning finished goods inventory	$ 45,000	
Plus: Cost of goods manufactured	180,000	
Cost of goods available for sale	225,000	
Less: Ending finished goods inventory	36,000	
Cost of goods sold		189,000
Gross profit		231,000
Less: Selling and administrative expenses		49,000
Income from operations		$182,000

Chapter Summary

LO1 Describe the key differences between financial accounting and managerial accounting. p. 766

- Financial accounting is used by external stakeholders, such as investors, creditors, and bankers.
- Managerial accounting is used by managers inside the organization.
- Other differences:
  - Financial accounting information tends to be reliable, objective, and historical in nature.
  - Managerial accounting information tends to be relevant, timely, and future oriented.
  - Financial accounting is reported through the income statement, balance sheet, and cash flow statement.
  - Managerial accounting relies on a variety of reports targeted at specific decisions, including budgets, cost reports, and performance evaluations.
  - Financial accounting reports are prepared on a monthly, quarterly, or annual basis.
  - Managerial accounting reports are prepared as needed.
  - Financial accounting reports are prepared at the company level.
  - Managerial accounting reports are prepared at the divisional or departmental level appropriate to the decision being made.

LO2 Explain the functions of management. p. 767

- The managerial decision making process can be described as including four interrelated functions:
- Planning, or the process of setting long-term objectives along with the short-term tactics needed to achieve those objectives.
- Organizing, or gathering the necessary resources to carry out the plan.
- Directing/Leading, or performing the steps involved in putting the plan into action.
- Control, or monitoring actual results against the plan and making any necessary adjustments.

LO3 Define and give examples of different types of costs. p. 769

- When you incur a cost, you give up something of value in exchange for something else.
- Costs can be classified in a variety of ways:
  - Out-of-pocket costs require a cash outlay.
  - Opportunity costs are the benefits you give up when you choose one alternative over another.
  - Direct costs can be traced directly to a specific cost object.
  - Indirect costs either cannot be traced to a specific cost object or are not worth the effort to do so.
  - Variable costs change in direct proportion to changes in the level of activity.
  - Fixed costs remain the same, in total, regardless of the level of activity.
  - Relevant costs are those that differ between alternatives.
  - Irrelevant costs are those that remain the same regardless of the alternatives and thus will not affect the decision.
  - Manufacturing costs are associated with making a physical product.
  - Nonmanufacturing costs are associated with selling a product or service or running the overall business.

- GAAP requires manufacturing costs to be treated as product costs and nonmanufacturing costs to be expensed as period costs.
- Product costs are assigned to a product as it is being produced; they accumulate in inventory accounts until the product is sold.
- Period costs are reported as expenses as they are incurred.

LO4 Compare the financial statements of merchandising and manufacturing firms. p. 775

- The major difference between the balance sheets of merchandising and manufacturing firms is the reporting of inventory: Merchandising firms report the total value of merchandise inventory; manufacturing firms break it down into three different categories.
- Manufacturing firms report three types of inventory on their balance sheets: Raw materials, Work in process, and Finished goods.
- The primary difference between the income statements of merchandising and manufacturing firms is the calculation of the cost of goods sold.
- Merchandising firms calculate cost of goods sold based on the cost of merchandise purchased adjusted for the beginning and ending values of merchandise inventory.
- Manufacturing firms calculate cost of goods sold based on the cost of goods manufactured adjusted for the beginning and ending values of finished goods inventory.

LO5 Prepare a cost of goods manufactured report. p. 775

- The cost of goods manufactured is the total cost to manufacture all units completed during the period; this amount is transferred out of the Work in Process Inventory account and into the Finished Goods Inventory account when the products are complete.
- To calculate the cost of goods manufactured, first account for the total manufacturing costs (direct materials, direct labor, and manufacturing overhead) and then make adjustments for the beginning and ending values of the raw materials and work in process inventories.
- The cost of goods completed remains on the balance sheet as part of Finished Goods Inventory until the products are sold, at which point it is reported as part of cost of goods sold on the income statement.

Key Terms

Administrative Costs (p. 773)
Budget (p. 768)
Control (p. 768)
Conversion Cost (p. 772)
Cost (p. 769)
Cost Object (p. 770)
Cost of Goods Manufactured (p. 775)
Differential Cost (p. 772)
Direct Costs (p. 770)
Directing/Leading (p. 768)
Direct Labor (p. 772)
Direct Materials (p. 772)
Financial Accounting (p. 776)

Finished Goods Inventory (p. 775)
Fixed Costs (p. 771)
Indirect Costs (p. 770)
Inventoriable Cost (p. 773)
Irrelevant Cost (p. 772)
Managerial Accounting (p. 766)
Manufacturing Costs (p. 772)
Manufacturing Overhead (p. 772)
Marketing or Selling Costs (p. 772)
Merchandising Company (p. 774)
Manufacturing Firm (p. 774)
Nonmanufacturing Costs (p. 772)
Opportunity Cost (p. 770)

Organizing (p. 768)
Out-of-Pocket Costs (p. 770)
Period Cost (p. 773)
Planning (p. 768)
Prime Cost (p. 772)
Product Costs (p. 773)
Raw Materials Inventory (p. 775)
Relevant Cost (p. 772)
Service Company (p. 783)
Sunk Cost (p. 772)
Variable Costs (p. 771)
Work in Process Inventory (p. 775)

See complete glossary in the back of text.

Questions

1. What is the primary difference between financial accounting and managerial accounting?

2. Explain how the primary difference between financial and managerial accounting results in other differences between the two.

3. Why are traditional, GAAP-based financial statements not necessarily useful to managers and other internal parties?

4. What are the four basic functions that all managers perform? How are these functions interrelated?

5. Think about all of the choices you make on a day-to-day basis: everything from driving versus riding a bike to school or deciding where to have lunch. Pick three decisions you have made today. Identify the out-of-pocket and opportunity costs of each decision.

6. Why is it important for managers to be able to cost a particular item? Name one decision that a company might make using cost information.

7. Explain the difference between a direct cost and an indirect cost. Look at the pen or pencil you are using to do your homework. Give an example of a direct cost that went into making that pen or pencil and an indirect cost of making the pen or pencil.

8. What types of costs are included in manufacturing overhead? Other than direct materials and direct labor, what costs would not be included in manufacturing overhead?

9. Why can't prime cost and conversion cost be added together to arrive at a total manufacturing cost?

10. Explain why product costs are also called inventoriable costs and how those costs move through a company's financial statements.

11. Explain the difference in fixed and variable costs. Give an example of a cost that varies with the number of miles you drive your car each week and an example of a cost that is fixed regardless of how many miles you drive your car each week.

12. Suppose you and your friends are planning a trip for spring break. You have narrowed the destination choices to Panama City, Florida, and Galveston Bay, Texas. List three relevant costs for this decision. List two costs that are irrelevant to this decision.

13. Explain the difference between service companies, merchandising companies, and manufacturing companies.

14. Consider the area in a 3-mile radius of your campus. What service companies, merchandising companies, and manufacturing firms are located within that area?

15. Suppose you have been given a balance sheet for Garcia Company. Without knowing any information about the company, how would the balance sheet help you determine what type of company Garcia is?

16. What are the three types of inventory accounts that you would expect to see on a manufacturing firm's balance sheet? Explain what each one represents and how a particular cost would move through these accounts.

17. What triggers the movement of product costs from an asset on the balance sheet to an expense on the income statement?

18. What is the cost of goods manufactured? What type of costs should be included in cost of goods manufactured?

19. Explain why ending work in process inventory is subtracted from total manufacturing costs to arrive at cost of goods manufactured.

20. Explain the relationship between cost of goods manufactured and cost of goods sold.

Multiple Choice

1. The **primary** difference between financial accounting and managerial accounting is that

Quiz 18-1
www.mhhe.com/LLPW1e

   a. Financial accounting is used by internal parties, while managerial accounting is used by external parties.
   b. Managerial accounting is future oriented, while financial accounting is historical in nature.
   c. Financial accounting is used by external parties, while managerial accounting is used by internal parties.
   d. Financial accounting is prepared as needed (perhaps even daily), but managerial accounting is prepared periodically (monthly, quarterly, annually).

2. Which of the following is not one of the four basic functions of management?
   a. Directing.   c. Planning.
   b. Control.   d. Customer service.

3. Which of the four basic functions of management involves monitoring actual results to see whether the objectives set in the planning stage are being met and, if necessary, taking corrective action to adjust the objectives or implementation of the plan?
   a. Directing.   c. Planning.
   b. Control.   d. Organizing.

4. Suppose you have decided that you would like to purchase a new home in five years. To do this, you will need a down payment of approximately $20,000, which means that you need to save $350 each month for the next five years. This is an example of
   a. Directing.   c. Planning.
   b. Control.   d. Organizing.

Use the following information regarding Garcia Company for questions 5–7.

Factory rent	$5,000
Direct labor	8,000
Indirect materials	1,000
Direct materials used	3,500
Sales commissions	2,500
Factory manager's salary	4,000
Advertising	1,500

5. What is Garcia's total current manufacturing cost?
   a. $25,500.
   b. $24,000.
   c. $21,500.
   d. $10,000.

6. What is Garcia's prime cost?
    a. $11,500.
    b. $12,500.
    c. $15,500.
    d. $21,500.

7. What is Garcia's manufacturing overhead?
    a. $24,000.
    b. $12,500.
    c. $14,000.
    d. $10,000.

8. Suppose you are trying to decide whether to sell your accounting book at the end of the semester or keep it for a reference book in future courses. If you decide to keep the book, the money you would have received from selling it is a(n)
    a. Sunk cost.
    b. Opportunity cost.
    c. Out-of-pocket cost.
    d. Indirect cost.

9. Work in Process Inventory would appear as an asset on the balance sheet for which type of company?
    a. Manufacturing.
    b. Merchandising.
    c. Service.
    d. All of the above.

10. Nguyen, Inc., has the following information available for January:

Cost of goods manufactured	$15,000
Finished goods inventory (1-31)	4,000
Finished goods inventory (1-1)	2,000

    What amount will appear on Nguyen's income statement as cost of goods sold?
    a. $21,000.
    b. $17,000.
    c. $13,000.
    d. $11,000.

Solutions to Multiple-Choice Questions

1. c   2. d   3. b   4. c   5. c   6. a   7. d   8. b   9. a   10. c

---

Mini Exercises Available with McGraw-Hill's Homework Manager

LO1

M18-1 Comparing Financial and Managerial Accounting
Match each of the following characteristics that describe **financial** accounting, **managerial** accounting, **both** financial and managerial accounting, or **neither** financial and managerial accounting.

_____ 1. Is future oriented.

_____ 2. Is used primarily by external parties.

_____ 3. Is relied on for making decisions.

_____ 4. Is historical in nature.

_____ 5. Can be obtained through the company Web site or requested from the company CFO.

_____ 6. Is reported in aggregate for the company as a whole.

_____ 7. May be reported daily or even in real time.

_____ 8. Is used mostly by managers within the company.

_____ 9. Must be accurate to help decision makers.

_____ 10. Is always available on the Internet to any interested party.

A. Financial accounting

B. Managerial accounting

C. Both financial and managerial accounting

D. Neither financial nor managerial accounting

LO2

M18-2 Identifying Management Functions
You were recently hired as a production manager for Medallion Company. You just received a memo regarding a company meeting being held this week. The memo stated that one topic of discussion will

be the basic management functions as they relate to the Production Department. You are expected to lead this discussion. To prepare for the discussion, briefly list the four basic functions of any management and how those functions might relate to your position as production manager.

M18-3 Classifying Costs

LO3

Top Shelf Company builds oak bookcases. Determine whether each of the following is a direct material (DM), direct labor (DL), manufacturing overhead (MOH), or a period cost (P) for Top Shelf.

_____ 1.   Depreciation on factory equipment.

_____ 2.   Depreciation on delivery trucks.

_____ 3.   Wood used to build a bookcase.

_____ 4.   Production supervisor's salary.

_____ 5.   Glue and screws used in the bookcases.

_____ 6.   Wages of persons who assemble the bookcases.

_____ 7.   Cost to run an ad on local radio stations.

_____ 8.   Rent for the factory.

_____ 9.   Accounts payable manager's salary.

_____10.   Wages of person who sands the wood after it is cut.

M18-4 Classifying and Calculating Cost

LO3, 5

Refer to M18-3. Assume that you have following about Top Shelf's costs for the most recent month.

Depreciation on factory equipment	$2,000
Depreciation on delivery trucks	900
Wood used to build bookcases	1,300
Production supervisor's salary	3,000
Glue and screws used in the bookcases	250
Wages of persons who assemble the bookcases	2,800
Cost to run an ad on local radio stations	1,200
Rent for the factory	4,000
Accounts payable manager's salary	1,500
Wages of person who sands the wood after it is cut	1,600

Determine each of the following costs for Top Shelf.

1.   Direct materials used.

2.   Direct labor.

3.   Manufacturing overhead.

4.   Prime.

5.   Conversion.

6.   Total current manufacturing.

7.   Total nonmanufacturing (period).

M18-5 Classifying Costs

LO3

You are considering the possibility of pursuing a master's degree after completing your undergraduate degree.

1.   List three costs (or benefits) that would be relevant to this decision including at least one opportunity cost.

2.   List two costs that would be irrelevant to this decision.

M18-6 Classifying Costs

LO3

Lighten Up Lamps, Inc., manufactures table lamps and other lighting products. For each of the following costs, use an X to indicate the category of product cost and whether it is a prime cost, conversion cost, or both.

	PRODUCT COSTS				
	Direct Materials	Direct Labor	Mfg. Overhead	Prime Cost	Conversion Cost
Production supervisor salary					
Cost of lamp shades					
Wages of person who assembles lamps					
Factory rent					
Wages of person who paints lamps					
Factory utilities					
Screws used to assemble lamps					

LO3

M18-7 Calculating Missing Amounts

For each of the following independent cases A–D, compute the missing values in the table below

Case	Direct Materials	Direct Labor	Manufacturing Overhead	Prime Cost	Conversion Cost
A	$800	$1,400	$2,100	$?	$?
B	400	?	1,325	2,550	?
C	?	675	1,500	2,880	?
D	?	750	?	1,500	2,000

LO4

M18-8 Classifying Type of Company

Indicate whether each of the following businesses would most likely be classified as a service company (S), merchandising company (Mer), or manufacturing company (Man).

_____ 1. Merry Maids.

_____ 2. Dell Computer.

_____ 3. Brinks Security.

_____ 4. Kmart.

_____ 5. PetSmart.

_____ 6. Ford Motor Company.

_____ 7. Bank One.

_____ 8. Ralph Lauren.

_____ 9. Dillard's.

_____10. Sam's Club.

LO4, 5

M18-9 Calculating Missing Amounts and Cost of Goods Manufactured

For each of the following independent cases A–D, compute the missing values in the table below.

Case	Total Current Manufacturing Costs	Beginning Work in Process Inventory	Ending Work in Process Inventory	Cost of Goods Manufactured
A	$4,800	$1,400	$1,100	$?
B	2,200	?	1,325	2,550
C	?	675	1,500	6,880
D	7,900	750	?	6.875

LO5

M18-10 Calculating Missing Amounts and Cost of Goods Sold

For each of the following independent cases A–D, compute the missing values in the table below.

Case	Cost of Goods Manufactured	Beginning Finished Goods Inventory	Ending Finished Goods Inventory	Cost of Goods Sold
A	$ 3,100	$ 400	$ 100	$?
B	4,250	?	1,325	4,550
C	?	950	500	4,375
D	10,900	2,200	?	9,750

Exercises

Available with McGraw-Hill's Homework Manager

E18-1 Making Decisions Using Managerial Accounting   LO1

Suppose you are a sales manager for Books on Wheels, Inc., which makes rolling book carts often used by libraries. The company is considering adding a new product aimed at university students. The new product will be a small, collapsible, wheeled tote designed specifically to aid students in transporting textbooks across campus.

Required:

1. List five questions you and the company would need to answer before proceeding with the development and marketing of this new product.

2. For each question identified in requirement 1, identify the information you would need to answer the question as well as the expected source of that information.

3. Identify three serious consequences of either not obtaining the information you need or obtaining inaccurate information.

E18-2 Identifying Management Functions   LO2

Refer to E18-1. Suppose that after a thorough investigation, Books on Wheels decided to go forward with the new product aimed at university students. The product, The Campus Cart, has gone into production and the first units have already been delivered to campuses across the country.

Required:

Match each of the following steps that took place as Books on Wheels moved through the decision making, production, marketing, and sale of The Campus Cart with the correct phase of the management process: planning (setting long- and short-term objectives), organizing (organizing the necessary resources to implement the plan), directing/leading (taking action to implement the plan), and control (making adjustments to the plan based on actual results).

____1. Identifying five college campuses to serve as test markets.

____2. Setting the goal of 1 million in annual sales by the year 2015.

____3. Hiring workers for the manufacturing facility.

____4. Overseeing the production and shipment of The Campus Cart.

____5. Preparing one-, three-, and five-year budgets that detail the necessary resources and costs that will be incurred to meet the projected sales forecasts.

____6. Deciding which new markets to expand into based on the first year's sales results.

____7. Implementing a bonus system to reward employees for meeting sales and production goals.

____8. Deciding to spend more advertising dollars in regions where sales were slower than expected.

A. Planning

B. Organizing

C. Directing/Leading

D. Control

E18-3 Classifying Costs   LO3

Suppose you have just finished your third year of college and expect to graduate with a bachelor's degree in accounting after completing two more semesters of coursework. The salary for entry-level positions with an accounting degree is approximately $48,000 in your area. Shelton Industries has just offered you a position in its northwest regional office. The position has an annual salary of $40,000 and would not require you to complete your undergraduate degree. If you accept the position, you would have to move to Seattle.

Required:

Identify with an X whether each of the following costs-benefits would be relevant to the decision to accept the offer from Shelton or stay in school. You may have more than one X for each item.

	Relevant Cost or Benefit	Irrelevant Cost or Benefit	Sunk Cost	Opportunity Cost
$40,000 salary from Shelton				
Anticipated $48,000 salary with an accounting degree				
Tuition and books for years 1–3 of college				
Cost to relocate to Seattle				
Tuition and books for remaining two semesters				
$19,000 from your part-time job, which you plan to keep until you graduate				
Cost to rent an apartment in Seattle (assume you are currently living at home with your parents)				
Food and entertainment expenses, which are expected to be the same in Seattle as where you currently live				
Increased promotional opportunities that will come from having a college degree				

LO3   **E18-4 Classifying Costs**

Seth's Skateboard Company has provided the following information about its company.

Required:

For each of the following costs, use an X to indicate the category of product cost and whether it is a prime cost, conversion cost, both or neither.

	PRODUCT COSTS					
	Direct Materials	Direct Labor	Mfg. Overhead	Period Cost	Prime Cost	Conversion Cost
Production supervisor salary						
Cost of fiberglass						
Wages of assembly person						
Sales commission						
Cost of high-grade wheels						
Screws						
Factory rent						
Wages of skateboard painter						
Factory utilities						
Utilities for corporate office						

LO3   **E18-5 Calculating Costs**

Cotton White, Inc. makes specialty clothing for chefs. The company reported the following costs for 2009:

Factory rent	$36,000
Company advertising	24,000
Wages paid to seamstresses	75,000
Depreciation on salespersons' vehicles	30,000
Thread	1,000
Utilities for factory	23,000
Cutting room supervisor's salary	30,000
President's salary	75,000
Premium quality cotton material	40,000
Buttons	750
Factory insurance	18,000
Depreciation on sewing machines	6,000
Wages paid to cutters	50,000

Required:
Compute the following for Cotton White:

1. Direct materials cost.
2. Direct labor cost.
3. Manufacturing overhead.
4. Total current manufacturing cost.
5. Prime cost.
6. Conversion cost.
7. Total period cost.

E18-6 Preparing an Income Statement

LO4

Refer to the information in E18-5 regarding Cotton White, Inc.

Required:
Prepare the company's income statement for 2009 assuming that all inventory accounts (Raw Materials, Work in Process, and Finished Goods) had a zero balance at both the beginning and end of the year. Cotton White's sales revenue for the year was $735,000.

E18-7 Calculating Missing Amounts

LO3, 5

Required:
For each of the following independent cases (A–E), compute the missing values in the table below.

Case	Prime Cost	Conversion Cost	Direct Materials	Direct Labor	Manufacturing Overhead	Total Manufacturing Cost
A	$?	$?	$2,000	$1,000	$3,500	$?
B	6,800	11,500	2,300	?	7,000	?
C	?	7,850	1,400	3,250	?	9,250
D	?	?	?	2,100	3,100	5,800
E	11,500	20,500	3,500	?	?	?

E18-8 Calculating Missing Amounts and Cost of Goods Manufactured and Sold

LO4, 5

Required:
For each of the following independent cases (A–D), compute the missing values in the table below.

	Case A	Case B	Case C	Case D
Beginning raw materials inventory	$ 5,000	?	$ 20,000	$110,000
Raw material purchases	45,000	12,250	41,640	?
Ending raw materials inventory	3,000	3,250	?	95,500
Raw materials used	?	13,500	33,720	?
Direct labor	29,000	?	?	123,250
Manufacturing overhead	52,000	40,350	31,080	541,730
Total current manufacturing costs	?	75,600	92,900	?
Beginning work in process inventory	41,000	32,600	?	102,520
Ending work in process inventory	?	?	41,250	236,100
Cost of goods manufactured	139,000	79,800	89,225	825,900
Beginning finished goods inventory	72,000	?	51,900	?
Ending finished goods inventory	80,000	30,100	?	397,200
Cost of goods sold	?	71,000	113,375	839,400

LO4, 5

E18-9 Classifying Costs and Calculating Cost of Goods Manufactured and Sold

The following information is available for Wonderway, Inc., for 2010.

Factory rent	$28,000
Company advertising	19,000
Wages paid to laborers	83,500
Depreciation for president's vehicle	8,000
Indirect production labor	1,800
Utilities for factory	30,000
Production supervisor salary	30,000
President's salary	60,000
Direct material purchases	32,500
Sales commissions	7,500
Factory insurance	12,000
Depreciation on factory equipment	26,000

Additionally, Wonderway provided the following:

Beginning raw materials inventory	$ 5,000
Ending raw materials inventory	3,000
Beginning work in process inventory	20,000
Ending work in process inventory	25,000
Beginning finished goods inventory	37,500
Ending finished goods inventory	45,000

Required:

Calculate the amount for each of the following for Wonderway:

1. Direct materials used (assume all material is direct).
2. Direct labor.
3. Manufacturing overhead.
4. Total current manufacturing costs.
5. Cost of goods manufactured.
6. Cost of goods sold.
7. Period expenses.

LO4

E18-10 Preparing an Income Statement

Refer to the information in E18-9 for Wonderway.

Required:

Prepare the company's income statement assuming sales revenue for the year was $500,000.

E18-11 Calculating Cost of Goods Manufactured and Sold and Preparing an Income Statement   LO4, 5

StorSmart Company makes plastic organizing bins. The company has the following inventory balances at the beginning and end of March.

	Beginning Inventory	Ending Inventory
Raw materials	$30,000	$25,000
Work in process	23,000	45,000
Finished goods	80,000	68,000

Additional information for the month of March follows.

Raw material purchases	$ 42,000
Direct labor	64,000
Manufacturing overhead	37,000
Selling and administrative expenses	25,000
Sales revenue	236,000

Required:

Based on this information, prepare the following for StorSmart:

1. Cost of goods manufactured report.
2. Income statement for the month of March.

Problems—Set A   Available with McGraw-Hill's Homework Manager

PA18-1 Comparing Financial and Managerial Accounting   LO1

You have been asked to take part in an upcoming Young Professionals meeting in your area. The program planned for the evening will cover many aspects of today's business world. Specifically, you have been asked to explain why there are two types of accounting—financial and managerial—and why they are both relevant to a company's employees. The program director would like for you to cover differences between the two types of accounting as well as how each type plays a role within today's competitive environment.

You will have 15 minutes for your presentation plus a 15-minute question-and-answer period at the end. Your audience is comprised primarily of entry-level managers from all fields (marketing, human resources, production, etc.). Assume that they all have some familiarity with accounting, but few are practicing accountants.

Required:

1. Prepare a detailed outline for your discussion identifying your topic of discussion.
2. List at least five questions you may be asked during the question-and-answer period. Briefly discuss your answers to these questions.

PA18-2 Identifying Management Functions   LO2

Your friend, Suzie Whitson, has designed a new type of outdoor children's toy that helps youngsters learn basic concepts such as colors, numbers, and shapes. Suzie's product will be targeted for two groups: day care centers in warm climates and home school programs for which few activity-intensive programs aim at toddlers' developmental processes. Suzie has come to you for help in getting her idea off the ground. She has never managed a business before and is not sure what functions she will need to perform to make her venture successful.

Required:

Briefly explain to Suzie the four major functions of management. For each function, give three examples of questions that Suzie will need to answer to make her business venture a success.

PA18-3 Classifying Costs; Calculating Total Costs; Identifying Impact of Misclassification   LO3

Assume that Suzie Whitson (PA18-2) has decided to begin production of her outdoor children's game. Her company is Jiffy Jet where costs for last month follow.

Factory rent	$3,000
Company advertising	1,000
Wages paid to assembly workers	30,000
Depreciation for salespersons' vehicles	2,000
Screws	500
Utilities for factory	800
Assembly supervisor's salary	3,500
Sandpaper	150
President's salary	5,000
Plastic tubing	4,000
Paint	250
Sales commissions	1,200
Factory insurance	1,000
Depreciation on cutting machines	2,000
Wages paid to painters	7,500

Required:

1. Identify each of the preceding costs as either a product or a period cost. If the cost is a product cost, decide whether it is direct materials (DM), direct labor (DL), or manufacturing overhead (MOH).

2. Determine the total amount for each of the following.

   a. Direct material.

   b. Direct labor.

   c. Manufacturing overhead.

   d. Prime cost.

   e. Conversion cost.

   f. Total product cost.

3. Suppose all period costs were incorrectly identified as product costs. What impact could that have on Jiffy Jet's financial statements? Be specific.

LO3, 4, 5

www.mhhe.com/LLPW1e

PA18-4 Identifying Types of Companies and Preparing Financial Statements

Following are the Assets section of comparative balance sheets for Dixie Industries for 2008 and 2009.

Dixie Industries Comparative Balance Sheet		
	12/31/2008	12/31/2009
Assets		
Cash	$130,400	$ 97,800
Accounts receivable	35,600	45,300
Merchandise inventory	59,200	51,700
Property, plant, & equipment	354,700	301,600
Total assets	$579,900	$496,400

Information available for Dixie's operations in 2009 includes the following.

President's salary	$ 78,000
Depreciation on office equipment	12,000
Merchandise purchases	205,800
Sales commissions	25,000
Utilities for corporate office	15,500
Sales revenue	763,900
Salaries for office personnel	225,000

Required:

1. Is Dixie a service, merchandising, or manufacturing firm? How can you tell?
2. Would Dixie have a cost of goods manufactured report?
3. Compute Dixie's cost of goods sold.
4. Prepare Dixie's income statement.

PA18-5 Identifying Types of Companies, and Preparing Financial Statements

Following are the Assets section of comparative balance sheets for Bettie Company for 2008 and 2009.

LO3, 4, 5

www.mhhe.com/LLPW1e

	12/31/2008	12/31/2009
Assets		
Cash	$ 30,300	$ 37,800
Accounts receivable	17,900	15,600
Direct materials inventory	12,900	13,850
Work in process inventory	21,450	25,190
Finished goods inventory	35,670	31,700
Property, plant, & equipment	138,200	143,600
Total assets	$256,420	$267,740

Information available for Bettie's operations in 2009 includes the following.

President's salary	$ 68,000
Direct material purchases	36,780
Depreciation on office equipment	12,000
Depreciation on factory equipment	62,400
Indirect materials	1,200
Direct labor	140,400
Sales commissions	17,200
Utilities on factory	17,230
Production supervisor's salary	38,500
Utilities for corporate office	9,300
Sales revenue	653,100
Salaries for office personnel	95,000

Required:

1. Is Bettie a service, merchandising, or manufacturing firm? How can you tell?
2. Prepare Bettie's cost of goods manufactured report.
3. Compute Bettie's cost of goods sold. Include any necessary supporting schedules.
4. Prepare Bettie's income statement.

Problems—Set B Available with McGraw-Hill's Homework Manager

PB18-1 Comparing Product and Period Costs

LO3

You have been asked to take part in an upcoming Young Professionals meeting in your area. The program planned for the evening focuses on today's manufacturing environment. Specifically, you have been asked to explain how manufacturing firms determine how much it costs to make their product and why some costs are initially recorded as inventory while other costs are expensed immediately. The program director would like for you to discuss (1) the rules for determining whether a cost should be treated as a product cost or period cost and (2) explain the types of costs that would be included in each category, how each flows through the accounting system, and the implications of the distinction between product costs and period costs for financial reporting (income statement versus balance sheet).

You will have 15 minutes for your presentation plus a 15-minute question-and-answer period at the end. Your audience is comprised primarily of entry-level production personnel although people from other fields (marketing, human resources, production, etc.) will be attending. Assume that they all have some familiarity with accounting but few are practicing accountants.

Required:

1. Prepare a detailed outline for your discussion identifying your topic of discussion.
2. List at least five questions you may be asked during the question-and-answer period. Briefly discuss your answers to these questions

LO2

PB18-2 Identifying Management Functions

Your friend, Maria Cottonwood, has designed a new type of fire extinguisher that is very small and easy to use. It will be targeted for two groups of people: elderly or people with disabilities who often have trouble operating the heavy traditional extinguishers and for people who need to store it in small spaces such as a vehicle or storage room where the size of traditional extinguishers makes them cumbersome. Maria has come to you for help in getting her idea off the ground. She has never managed a business before and she is not sure what functions she will need to perform to make her venture successful.

Required:

Briefly explain to Maria the four major functions of management. For each function, give three examples of questions that Maria will need to answer to make her business venture a success.

LO3

PB18-3 Classifying Costs, Calculating Total Costs, and Identifying Impact of Classifications

Assume that Maria Cottonwood (PB18-2) has decided to begin production of her fire extinguisher. Her company is Blaze Be Gone whose costs for last month follow.

Factory rent	$2,000
Company advertising	500
Wages paid to assembly workers	25,000
Depreciation for salespersons' vehicles	1,000
Screws	250
Utilities for factory	1,200
Production supervisor's salary	4,500
Sandpaper	150
President's salary	6,000
Sheet metal	8,000
Paint	750
Sales commissions	1,700
Factory insurance	3,000
Depreciation on factory machinery	5,000
Wages paid to painters	5,500

Required:

1. Identify each of the preceding costs as either a product or a period cost. If the cost is a product cost, decide whether it is direct materials (DM), direct labor (DL) or manufacturing overhead (MOH).
2. Determine the total amount for each of the following.
    a. Direct material.
    b. Direct labor.
    c. Manufacturing overhead.
    d. Prime cost.
    e. Conversion cost.
    f. Total product cost.
3. Assume that Maria wants you to explain why the depreciation on the salespersons' vehicles is treated differently than the depreciation on the factory machines. Explain why these costs are treated differently and what the implications are for Maria's financial statements in terms of the balance sheet and income statement.

LO3, 4, 5

PB18-4 Identifying Types of Companies Classifying Costs, and Preparing Financial Statements

Following are the Assets sections of comparative balance sheets for Wynflow Company for 2008 and 2009.

	2008	2009
Assets		
Cash	$ 90,300	$ 87,200
Accounts receivable	37,300	25,800
Direct materials inventory	22,500	19,530
Work in process inventory	40,150	55,000
Finished goods inventory	105,290	91,200
Property, plant, & equipment	278,100	288,600
Total assets	$573,640	$567,330

Information available for Wynflow's operations in 2009 includes the following.

President's salary	$ 72,000
Direct material purchases	56,870
Depreciation on office equipment	19,200
Depreciation on factory equipment	122,700
Indirect materials	2,150
Direct labor	187,900
Sales commissions	34,200
Utilities on factory	28,540
Production supervisor's salary	49,500
Utilities for corporate office	12,900
Sales revenue	788,100
Salaries for office personnel	106,500

Required:

1. Is Wynflow a service, merchandising, or manufacturing firm? How can you tell?
2. If possible, prepare Wynflow's cost of goods manufactured report.
3. Compute Wynflow's cost of goods sold. Include any necessary supporting schedules.
4. Prepare Wynflow's income statement.

PB18-5 Identifying Costs, Classifying Types of Companies, and Preparing Financial Statements   LO3, 4, 5

Following are the Assets sections of comparative balance sheets for Ratliff Industries the 2008 and 2009.

Ratliff Industries Comparative Balance Sheet

	12/31/2008	12/31/2009
Assets		
Cash	$ 69,600	$ 57,290
Accounts receivable	30,550	25,700
Merchandise inventory	24,500	31,100
Property, plant, & equipment	164,700	121,900
Total assets	$289,350	$235,990

Information available for Ratliff's operations in 2009 includes the following.

President's salary	$ 59,300
Depreciation on office equipment	4,000
Merchandise purchases	128,300
Sales commissions	6,300
Utilities for corporate office	7,500
Sales revenue	389,900
Salaries for office personnel	65,000

Required:

1. Is Ratliff a service, merchandising, or manufacturing firm? How can you tell?
2. If possible, prepare Ratliff's cost of goods manufactured report.
3. Compute Ratliff's cost of goods sold.
4. Prepare Ratliff's income statement.

Cases and Projects

LO1, 3   **CP18-1 Researching Cost Components of Everyday Item**

Choose one item that you use each day—anything from a toothbrush to your favorite soda to an automobile.

Required:

Research online the company that produces this item to find out as much information as you can about the manufacturing process used to create the product. Prepare a report on the product and its manufacturer including the following.

1. A summary of the company including information about its manufacturing facilities.
2. How the company's managerial accounting information would differ from its financial accounting information and specific users of each information type.
3. For the specific product you chose, provide three examples of each of the following.

   a. Direct costs.
   b. Indirect costs.
   c. Variable costs.
   d. Fixed costs.
   e. Product costs.
   f. Period costs.

4. At least two potential suppliers of raw materials used to manufacture the item.
5. The typical price that you pay for this item.

LO1, 3   **CP18-2 Identifying Changes in Manufacturing Process and Costs Due to Automation**

In recent years, many companies have converted from a labor-intensive manufacturing process to an automated one. As an example, think of a car wash company that used to wash cars by hand but has now invested in an automatic washing and drying system.

Required:

Think of another company that might upgrade to an automated system and answer the following questions.

1. What physical changes would the conversion to automation cause in the manufacturing process?
2. What impact, both positive and negative, might automation have on company morale?
3. What impact might automation have on the skill level of the company's workforce?
4. How might automation affect the quality of the product manufactured and the efficiency of the manufacturing process?
5. How would you expect automation to affect direct material, direct labor, and manufacturing overhead costs? Would you expect any of these costs to increase or decrease?
6. How would you expect automation to affect variable costs and fixed costs? Would you expect either of these costs to increase or decrease?
7. How might this change in manufacturing process affect the price consumers pay for the product?
8. How might this change in manufacturing process affect the company's bottom line both immediately and several years in the future?

LO1   **CP18-3 Finding Future-Oriented Information in Financial Statements**

Consider the following statement about the use of forward-looking information on Kraft's Web site.

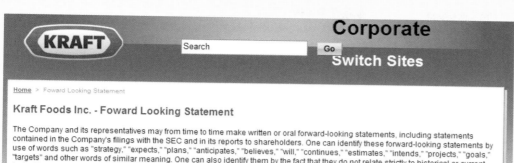

Home > Foward Looking Statement

Kraft Foods Inc. - Foward Looking Statement

The Company and its representatives may from time to time make written or oral forward-looking statements, including statements contained in the Company's filings with the SEC and in its reports to shareholders. One can identify these forward-looking statements by use of words such as "strategy," "expects," "plans," "anticipates," "believes," "will," "continues," "estimates," "intends," "projects," "goals," "targets" and other words of similar meaning. One can also identify them by the fact that they do not relate strictly to historical or current facts. These statements are based on our assumptions and estimates and are subject to risks and uncertainties. In connection with the "safe harbor" provisions of the Private Securities Litigation Reform Act of 1995, the Company is hereby identifying important factors that could cause actual results and outcomes to differ materially from those contained in any forward-looking statement made by or on behalf of the Company; any such statement is qualified by reference to the following cautionary statements.

Each of the Company's segments is subject to intense competition, changes in consumer preferences, the effects of changing prices for its raw materials and local economic conditions. Their results are dependent upon their continued ability to promote brand equity successfully, to anticipate and respond to new consumer trends, to develop new products and markets, to broaden brand portfolios in order to compete effectively with lower priced products in a consolidating environment at the retail and manufacturing levels, and to improve productivity. The Company's results are also dependent on its ability to consummate and successfully integrate acquisitions, including its ability to derive cost savings from the integration of Nabisco's operations with the Company. In addition, the Company is subject to the effects of foreign economies, currency movements and fluctuations in levels of customer inventories. The Company's benefit expense is subject to the investment performance of pension plan assets, interest rates and cost increases for medical benefits offered to employees and retirees. The food industry continues to be subject to recalls if products become adulterated or misbranded, liability if product consumption causes injury, ingredient disclosure and labeling laws and regulations and the possibility that consumers could lose confidence in the safety and quality of certain food products. Developments in any of these areas, which are more fully described elsewhere in this document and which descriptions are incorporated into this section by reference, could cause the Company's results to differ materially from results that have been or may be projected by or on behalf of the Company. The Company cautions that the foregoing list of important factors is not exclusive. Any forward-looking statements are made as of the date of the document in which they appear. The Company does not undertake to update any forward-looking statement that may be made from time to time by or on behalf of the Company.

Required:

1. What was the safe harbor provision of the Private Securities Litigation Reform Act of 1995? What was its intended purpose?

2. Does Kraft have to make similar statements about reports prepared for internal (managerial) use? Would you expect to see more or less forward-looking information in internal reports than external reports?

3. Can you think of other words that accountants might use to describe what they expect to happen in the future other than "strategy," "expects," "plans," "anticipates," "believes," "will," "continues," "estimates," "intends," "projects," "goals," or "targets"? (*Hint*: See the title to Chapter 23).

4. Go to the Web site of another public company and find a similar statement about the use of forward-looking information. Alternatively, you can search for "forward-looking information" and "safe harbor" using a search engine such as Google. What factors does the company list as potential reasons that actual results may differ from the "forward-looking" information. Why does the company list these factors?

CP18-4 Identifing Service, Merchandising, and Manufacturing Firms: Internet Research   LO4

As discussed in the chapter, companies can be classified into one of three categories: service, merchandising, and manufacturing.

Required:

1. Choose one publicly traded company from each category and explore that company's Web site. On the Web site, find a brief company description as well as the most recent published financial statements. Based on the company description, support your categorization of the company as service, merchandising, or manufacturing. If the company falls into more than one of these categories, describe how.

2. Look at the income statement and balance sheet for the company and list any factors that would support your categorization of the company as a service, merchandising, or manufacturing organization.

19 Job Order Costing

LEARNING OBJECTIVES

After completing this chapter, you should be able to:

LO1 Describe the key differences between job order costing and process costing.

LO2 Describe the source documents used to track direct materials and direct labor costs to the job cost sheet.

LO3 Calculate a predetermined overhead rate and use it to apply manufacturing overhead cost to jobs.

LO4 Prepare journal entries to record the flow of manufacturing and nonmanufacturing costs.

LO5 Calculate and dispose of overapplied or underapplied manufacturing overhead.

LO6 Calculate the cost of goods manufactured and cost of goods sold.

Lectured presentation–LP19-1
www.mhhe.com/LLPW1e

Focus Company: TOLL BROTHERS INC.

"America's Luxury Home Builder"

Toll Brothers
America's Luxury Home Builder®

www.tollbrothers.com

Consider the following situation. You go out to a trendy new restaurant with a group of friends. You are on a limited budget, so you order the cheapest dish on the menu and a glass of ice water. Meanwhile, your friends indulge in a full-course meal with drinks, appetizers, entrees, and dessert. When it is time to pay the bill, would you prefer to split the check or get a separate tab for each person at the table?

This common scenario illustrates the basic difference between the two costing systems discussed in the next two chapters. Process costing is similar to splitting the check, spreading the total cost over the number of units produced (or in the case of the restaurant meal, the number of customers at the table). This simple method works well as long as each unit (or customer) consumes about the same amount of cost (or food). Process costing will be covered in Chapter 20.

With job order costing, a separate cost record is kept for each individual product or customer, similar to getting separate checks at a restaurant. This method makes sense when products or customers consume vastly different resources and thus have different costs. Job order costing systems are used for companies that provide customized products or services, such as a custom home builder.

Imagine that you have just landed a great new job and are building your dream home with a luxury home builder such as Toll Brothers Inc. Founded by Bruce and Robert Toll in 1967, Toll Brothers has grown from a small family-owned business to become the nation's leading luxury home builder, with operations in all of the major regions throughout the United States. Toll Brothers prides itself on "building communities in picturesque settings where luxury meets convenience, and where neighbors become lifelong friends."

In this chapter, we track the cost of building a custom home using a job order costing system. Of course, we simplify many of the details, and the numbers we use are fictional. Nevertheless, this extended example should give you a good idea of how an actual job order costing system works—and how your dream home will be accounted for should you be fortunate enough to build one someday.

JOB ORDER VERSUS PROCESS COSTING	ASSIGNMENT OF MANUFACTURING COSTS TO JOBS	JOURNAL ENTRIES FOR JOB ORDER COSTING	OVERAPPLIED OR UNDERAPPLIED MANUFACTURING OVERHEAD
• Process Costing • Job Order Costing	• Manufacturing Cost Categories • Materials Requisition Form • Direct Labor Time Tickets • Job Cost Sheet • Predetermined Overhead Rates	• Recording the Purchase and Issue of Materials • Recording Labor Costs • Recording Actual Manufacturing Overhead • Recording Applied Manufacturing Overhead • Transferring Costs to Finished Goods Inventory and Cost of Goods Sold • Recording Nonmanufacturing Costs	• Calculating Overapplied and Underapplied Manufacturing Overhead • Disposing of Overapplied or Underapplied Manufacturing Overhead • Calculating Cost of Goods Manufactured and Cost of Goods Sold

JOB ORDER VERSUS PROCESS COSTING

Throughout the remainder of this book, you will learn about several different types of cost systems including job order cost systems, process cost systems, activity-based cost systems, full absorption cost systems, variable cost systems, and standard cost systems. Although this may sound a little overwhelming at this point, the most important thing to keep in mind is that these cost systems are not mutually exclusive. In other words, a company could use job order costing, activity-based costing, full absorption costing, and standard costing at the same time.

For now, we focus on the difference between job order and process costing. This distinction has to do with the type of product or service that the company provides and whether the product or service is highly standardized or unique.

Process Costing

Learning Objective 1

Describe the key differences between job order costing and process costing.

Video 19-1
www.mhhe.com/LLPW1e

Process costing is used by companies that make **homogeneous (standardized)** products or services, such as:

- Coca-Cola beverages.
- Kraft macaroni and cheese.
- Charmin toilet tissue.
- Exxon petroleum products.

These and many other common products are produced in a continuous manufacturing process in which raw materials are put through a standardized production process so that each unit of the final product comes out identical to the next. Process costing breaks the production process down into its basic steps, or processes, and then averages the total cost of the process over the number of units produced. The basic process costing formula is:

$$\text{Average Unit Cost} = \frac{\text{Total Manufacturing Cost}}{\text{Total Units Produced}}$$

Although this formula makes process costing sound simple, a few questions complicate its use in the real world. For example, how much cost should Coca-Cola assign to soft drinks that are still in process at the end of the month—that is, when all the ingredients have been added but the bottling process is not yet complete? These issues will be discussed in more detail in the next chapter, which focuses specifically on process costing.

Job Order Costing

Video 19-2
www.mhhe.com/LLPW1e

Job order costing is used in companies that offer **customized** or **unique** products or services. Unlike process costing, in which each unit is identical to the next, job order costing is used for situations in which each unit or customer tends to be very different from the next. Examples include:

- A custom home built by Toll Brothers.
- A skyscraper built by Trump Industries.
- A nuclear submarine built for the U.S. Department of Defense.
- A one-of-a-kind wedding gown designed by Vera Wang.

Job order costing is also common in service industries that serve clients or customers with unique needs. For example, the accounting firm Ernst and Young, LLP tracks the billable hours spent on each individual client's account. Law firms, architectural firms, and consulting firms also track the costs of serving individual clients.

In the next section, we illustrate the basics of job order costing using the example of a custom home built by Toll Brothers. First, to make sure you understand the difference between job order costing and process costing, take a moment to complete the following Self-Study Practice.

> **Coach's Tip**
>
> In job order costing, each unique product or customer order is called a **job**. The cost of each unique job is recorded on a document called a **job cost sheet**.

SELF-STUDY PRACTICE

Indicate which of the following statements are true (T) and which are false (F).

_____ 1. Job order costing systems are more appropriate for companies that produce many units of an identical product.

_____ 2. Job order costing is often used in service industries in which each client or customer has unique requirements.

_____ 3. A builder of custom pools is more likely to use process costing than job order costing.

_____ 4. A company such as Coca-Cola is more likely to use a process costing system than a job order costing system.

_____ 5. In process costing, costs are averaged to determine the unit cost of homogeneous goods and services.

After you have finished, check your answers with the solutions at the bottom of the page.

ASSIGNMENT OF MANUFACTURING COSTS TO JOBS
Manufacturing Cost Categories

As you learned in Chapter 18, the three categories of manufacturing cost are direct materials, direct labor, and manufacturing overhead. Recall that **direct materials** are the primary material inputs that can be directly and conveniently traced to each job. Examples of direct materials used in building a home include concrete, piping, lumber, drywall, fixtures, and appliances. **Direct labor** is the hands-on work that goes into producing a product or service. Examples of direct labor used in building a home include the work of pouring the foundation, framing the home, and installing the plumbing. **Manufacturing overhead** includes all other costs of producing a product that cannot be directly or

> **Coach's Tip**
>
> If you have ever done your own home improvement project, think of the direct materials as the materials you purchased at The Home Depot and the direct labor as the number of hours you put into the job. Unlike do-it-yourself enthusiasts, large construction companies also have many **indirect costs** including equipment, supervision, and insurance. These costs are called **manufacturing overhead**.

---

1. F   2. T   3. F   4. T   5. T

Solution to
Self-Study Practice

conveniently traced to an individual unit. Examples of the manufacturing overhead required to build (not sell) a home include the costs of site supervision, construction insurance, depreciation on construction equipment, and indirect materials (nails, screws, and so on).

All of these manufacturing costs are recorded on a document called the job cost sheet, which provides a detailed record of the cost incurred to complete a specific job. Refer to Exhibit 19.1 for an illustration of how the three types of manufacturing costs are assigned in a job order cost system.

The most important thing to notice in Exhibit 19.1 is that direct materials and direct labor costs are assigned to jobs differently than manufacturing overhead costs. For the direct costs, all that is needed to keep track of the costs of specific jobs is a set of records called **source documents.** These documents provide the detailed information needed to record direct materials and direct labor costs. In contrast, manufacturing overhead is made up of all the costs that **cannot** be directly or conveniently traced to specific jobs. To assign these indirect costs to jobs, accountants must use a predetermined overhead rate that is based on some secondary allocation measure, or cost driver.

Let's start by assigning the direct cost to specific jobs using materials requisition forms and direct labor time tickets.

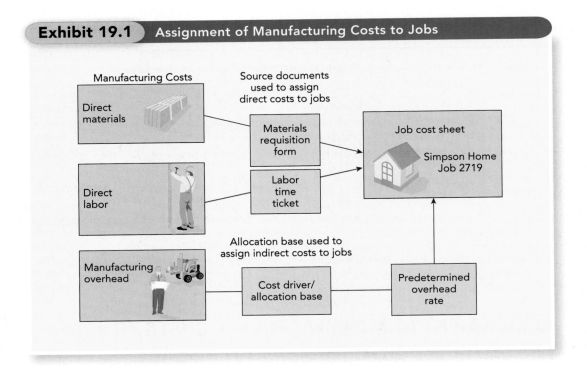

Exhibit 19.1   Assignment of Manufacturing Costs to Jobs

Materials Requisition Form

Learning Objective 2

Describe the source documents used to track direct material and direct labor costs to the job cost sheet.

Before materials can be used on a job, a materials requisition form—a form that lists the quantity and cost of the direct materials used on a specific job—must be filled out. This form is used to control the physical flow of materials out of inventory and into production. It is also the basis for the journal entries that record the costs of raw materials used in production.

Assume that Toll Brothers is getting ready to frame the interior and exterior walls of the Simpson family's new 2,500 square-foot custom home. The Simpson home has been assigned Job 2719. Before the lumber can be delivered to the job site, a materials requisition form like the one that follows must be completed.

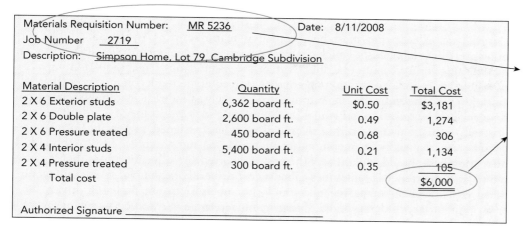

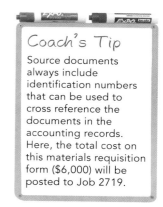

Coach's Tip

Source documents always include identification numbers that can be used to cross reference the documents in the accounting records. Here, the total cost on this materials requisition form ($6,000) will be posted to Job 2719.

Direct Labor Time Tickets

To determine how much direct labor cost is incurred on specific jobs, many companies use computers, bar codes, and handheld devices to track the time employees spend on various tasks. Others rely on the old-fashioned method, having employees record their time manually on labor time tickets. A direct labor time ticket is a source document that shows how much time a worker has spent on various jobs each week, as in the following illustration.

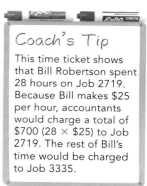

Coach's Tip

This time ticket shows that Bill Robertson spent 28 hours on Job 2719. Because Bill makes $25 per hour, accountants would charge a total of $700 (28 × $25) to Job 2719. The rest of Bill's time would be charged to Job 3335.

Job Cost Sheet

All costs assigned to an individual job are summarized on a source document called the **job cost sheet.** For example, the costs from the preceding materials requisition form and labor time ticket would be posted to the job cost sheet for the Simpson home (Job 2719).

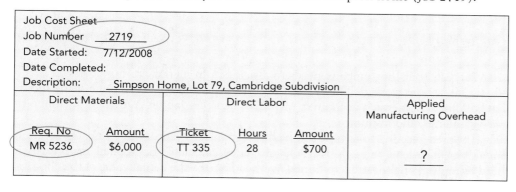

Learning Objective 3

Calculate a predetermined overhead rate and use it to apply manufacturing overhead cost to jobs.

Predetermined Overhead Rates

The third type of cost that must be recorded is **manufacturing overhead.** Unlike direct materials and direct labor costs, which can be traced to individual jobs using source documents, manufacturing overhead cannot be directly traced to specific jobs. The production supervisor's salary, for example, and depreciation on construction equipment are common costs that relate to multiple jobs. Theoretically, some indirect costs such as indirect materials (screws, nails, and so on) could be traced to individual jobs, but doing so is probably not worth the effort.

Instead, indirect manufacturing overhead costs are **assigned** to specific jobs using an allocation base, or a secondary measure that allocates, or assigns, indirect costs to jobs. Ideally, the allocation base should explain why the cost is incurred. An allocation base that is causally related to cost incurrence is sometimes called a **cost driver.** For example, some manufacturing overhead costs, such as employee taxes and site supervision, are probably driven by the number of direct labor hours worked. Other manufacturing overhead costs, such as machine maintenance and fuel, are driven by the length of time that construction equipment is used. The cost of indirect materials such as glue, sandpaper, and insulation might be driven by the square footage of the home under construction.

For the sake of simplicity, in this chapter, we use a single allocation base for assigning manufacturing overhead costs to jobs. Because home building is a labor-intensive business, let's assume that Toll Brothers uses direct labor hours as the single allocation base for assigning manufacturing overhead. (For a more accurate way to assign overhead cost using multiple cost drivers, see Chapter 20.)

Once an allocation base has been selected, the predetermined overhead rate is calculated as follows:

Coach's Tip

Manufacturing overhead costs are more difficult to assign than direct materials and direct labor costs, which can be traced directly to specific jobs. By definition, manufacturing overhead costs are not traceable to specific jobs, so they must be allocated or assigned to jobs using some observable measure.

$$\text{Predetermined Overhead Rate} = \frac{\text{Estimated Total Manufacturing Overhead Cost}}{\text{Estimated Units in the Allocation Base}}$$

This overhead rate is calculated for an entire accounting period (month, quarter, or year) and is based on **estimated** rather than actual values. We often do not know the actual manufacturing overhead cost until after the month, quarter, or year has ended. Thus, accountants must use their best estimate of manufacturing overhead based on past experience and any expectations they have about how the costs might change in the future.

Assume Toll Brothers estimates the total manufacturing overhead cost for the year to be $750,000 and direct labor hours to be 10,000. Based on these estimates, the predetermined overhead rate would be calculated as follows:

Coach's Tip

When you are asked to calculate a **predetermined overhead rate,** remember that it should be based on estimated rather than actual numbers. This rate is set **in advance,** before the actual numbers are known.

$$\frac{\text{Estimated Total Manufacturing Overhead Cost}}{\text{Estimated Direct Labor Hours}} = \frac{\$750,000}{10,000} = \begin{array}{c}\text{Predetermined Overhead Rate}\\ \text{(\$75 per direct labor hour)}\end{array}$$

This rate suggests that the company needs to assign $75 in manufacturing overhead cost for each direct labor hour worked. This is not the cost of the direct labor, but all of the **indirect costs** of building a home such as indirect materials, depreciation on construction equipment, supervisors' salaries, and insurance.

Once the predetermined overhead rate has been established, accountants use it to determine the amount of overhead to apply to each job. They calculate the **applied manufacturing overhead** by multiplying the predetermined overhead rate by the actual value of the allocation base used on the job, as follows:

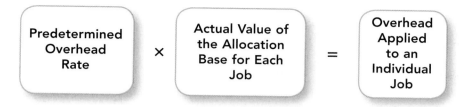

Assume that during the first week of construction, the Simpson home (Job 2719) required a total of 300 direct labor hours. Because the predetermined overhead rate is $75 per direct labor hour, the total applied manufacturing overhead for the week would be $22,500, calculated as follows:

Accountants can apply manufacturing overhead costs when they record direct labor hours, or they can wait until the job is completed and apply all of it at once. If some jobs are still in process at the end of an accounting period, however, accountants must make sure that all cost records are up to date by applying overhead to all jobs in process at the end of the period. The job cost sheet for the Simpson home at the end of the first week follows.

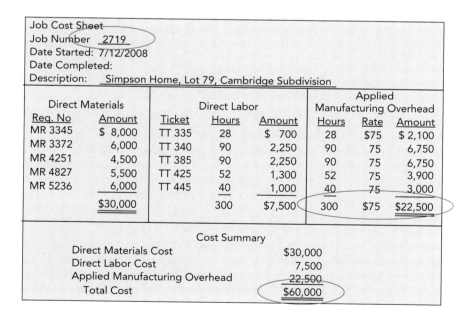

Coach's Tip

Notice that the overhead cost applied on the job cost sheet is based on the predetermined **(estimated)** overhead rate multiplied by the **actual** number of direct labor hours worked on that job.

Notice that manufacturing overhead was applied to the job cost sheet based on the predetermined overhead rate of $75 per direct labor hour. Because this rate was based on estimated data, applied manufacturing overhead is unlikely to be exactly the same as the actual manufacturing overhead cost incurred. You will see how to record actual manufacturing overhead cost and how to account for any difference between actual and applied manufacturing overhead later in this chapter. First, complete the following Self-Study Practice to make sure you know how to calculate the predetermined overhead rate and apply manufacturing overhead cost to jobs.

Carlton Brothers Construction Company applies manufacturing overhead to jobs on the basis of direct labor hours. The following estimated and actual information is available.

	Estimated	Actual
Total manufacturing overhead	$96,000	$90,000
Total direct labor hours	12,000	11,000

Based on these data, calculate the following:

1. Predetermined overhead rate.
2. Total amount of manufacturing overhead cost that would be applied during the period.

After you have finished, check your answers with the solutions at the bottom of the page.

JOURNAL ENTRIES FOR JOB ORDER COSTING

As you learned in Chapter 18, GAAP requires that all manufacturing costs be counted as inventory costs until a product is sold. The three inventory accounts that are used to record manufacturing costs are as follows:

- Raw Materials Inventory represents the cost of materials purchased but not yet issued to production. This account includes costs for both direct materials (lumber, piping) and indirect materials (screws, nails, and so on).
- Work in Process Inventory represents the cost of jobs still in process. Any cost that is added to work in process must also be added to the job cost sheet. Thus, the total cost of all jobs in process should equal the balance in the Work in Process Inventory account.
- Finished Goods Inventory represents the cost of jobs completed but not yet sold. Once a job has been sold, its total cost is transferred to Cost of Goods Sold, which is matched against sales revenue on the income statement.

See Exhibit 19.2 for an illustration of the flow of manufacturing costs through these inventory accounts before being recognized as part of the Cost of Goods Sold.

As the top row in Exhibit 19.2 shows, direct materials and direct labor are recorded directly into the Raw Materials Inventory and Work in Process Inventory accounts. Eventually, when the job is completed, they are transferred to the Finished Goods Inventory account. When the job is sold, the costs are moved to the Cost of Goods Sold account.

Manufacturing overhead costs, in contrast, are not added directly to the Work in Process Inventory account. The Manufacturing Overhead account is a temporary holding account that is used to accumulate actual and applied manufacturing overhead costs. Actual manufacturing overhead, or the actual **indirect** manufacturing costs incurred during the period, appears on the debit side of the Manufacturing Overhead account. **Applied manufacturing overhead,** or the amount that is applied to jobs based on the predetermined overhead rate and the allocation base, appears on the credit side of the Manufacturing Overhead account. The balance in the manufacturing Overhead account represents the difference between actual and applied manufacturing overhead, which is adjusted at the end of the accounting period.

Solution to Self-Study Practice

1.

$96,000 / 12,000 = $8.00 per Direct Labor Hour

2.

$8.00 × 11,000 Actual Direct Labor Hours = $88,000

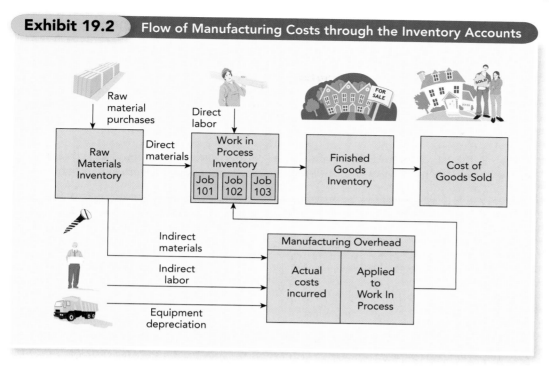

Exhibit 19.2   Flow of Manufacturing Costs through the Inventory Accounts

The journal entries to record manufacturing costs are described in the following sections. For the sake of simplicity, we assume that none of the accounts had a beginning balance, and that the company worked on only two jobs during the period.

Recording the Purchase and Issue of Materials

Learning Objective 4

Prepare journal entries to record the flow of manufacturing and nonmanufacturing costs.

When materials are purchased, the total cost is debited to the Raw Materials Inventory account. The credit should be to Cash or Accounts Payable, depending on the form of payment.

Assume that Toll Brothers purchased $150,000 in raw materials on account. The journal entry to record the purchase of raw materials follows:

	Debit	Credit
Raw Materials Inventory	150,000	
Accounts Payable		150,000

When materials are placed into production, the cost is debited to either Work in Process Inventory or Manufacturing Overhead, depending on whether the materials can be traced directly to a specific job. Only materials that can be traced directly to a specific job are debited to the Work in Process Inventory account, with a corresponding entry on the job cost sheet. Indirect materials—those that cannot be traced easily or conveniently to a specific job—are debited to the Manufacturing Overhead account. The credit entry should be to Raw Materials Inventory (if the materials come from inventory) or to Accounts Payable (if they are delivered directly from a supplier).

Assume that $150,000 worth of materials is withdrawn from inventory for the following uses:

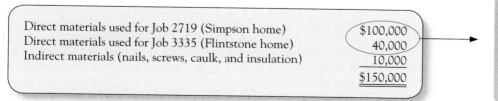

Direct materials used for Job 2719 (Simpson home)	$100,000
Direct materials used for Job 3335 (Flintstone home)	40,000
Indirect materials (nails, screws, caulk, and insulation)	10,000
	$150,000

Coach's Tip

Only **direct** materials are debited to Work in Process. **Indirect** materials are debited to Manufacturing Overhead because they cannot be traced to specific jobs.

The entry to record the issuance of direct and indirect materials follows:

	Debit	Credit
Work in Process Inventory ($100,000 + $40,000)	140,000	
Manufacturing Overhead	10,000	
Raw Materials Inventory		150,000

See Exhibit 19.3 for a summary of the flow of direct and indirect materials costs through the Raw Materials Inventory, Work in Process, and Manufacturing Overhead accounts.

Exhibit 19.3   **Recording Direct and Indirect Material Costs**

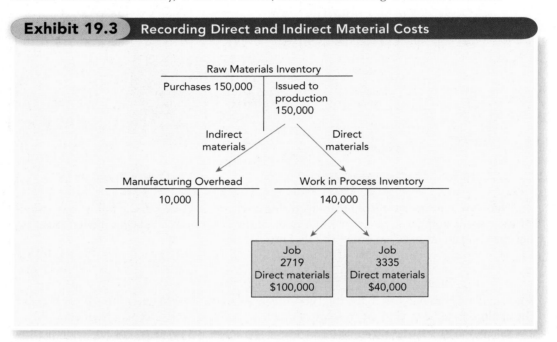

Recording Labor Costs

Labor costs are recorded in much the same way as direct materials: based on the direct labor time tickets that are filled out each week to show how much time was spent on each job. If the time can be traced directly to a specific job, the cost is added to the job cost sheet and debited to the Work in Process Inventory account. If it is not traceable directly to a specific job, the cost is considered indirect labor and is debited to the Manufacturing Overhead account. The corresponding credit should be to Wages Payable.

Assume Toll Brothers recorded the following information:

Direct labor on Job 2719 (Simpson home)	$30,000
Direct labor on Job 3335 (Flintstone home)	20,000
Indirect labor (such as maintenance and inspection work)	5,000
	$55,000

The journal entry to record the direct and indirect labor follows:

	Debit	Credit
Work in Process Inventory ($30,000 + $20,000)	50,000	
Manufacturing Overhead	5,000	
Wages Payable		55,000

See Exhibit 19.4 for a summary of the posting of this entry to the Manufacturing Overhead and Work in Process Inventory accounts.

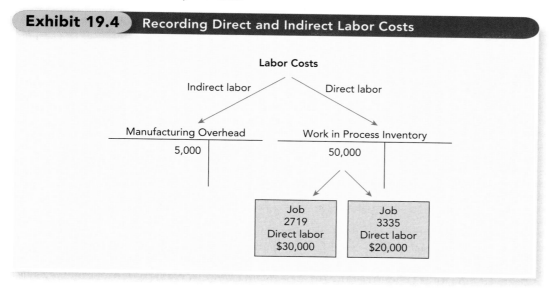

Exhibit 19.4   Recording Direct and Indirect Labor Costs

Recording Actual Manufacturing Overhead

Remember that actual manufacturing overhead costs are not recorded directly in the Work in Process Inventory account. Instead, these indirect costs are accumulated in the Manufacturing Overhead account.

We have already recorded the indirect materials and indirect labor costs in the Manufacturing Overhead account. Assume Toll Brothers recorded the following additional manufacturing overhead costs during the month:

Salary paid to construction site supervisor	$12,000
Salary owed to a construction engineer	8,000
Property taxes owed but not yet paid	6,000
Expired insurance premium for construction site	4,000
Depreciation on construction equipment	18,000
	$48,000

These actual manufacturing overhead costs would be debited to the Manufacturing Overhead account. The credit would be to Cash, Accounts Payable, Prepaid Assets, and/or Accumulated Depreciation, depending on the nature of the transaction. The journal entry to record these actual manufacturing overhead costs is:

	Debit	Credit
Manufacturing Overhead	48,000	
Cash		12,000
Salaries Payable		8,000
Taxes Payable		6,000
Prepaid Insurance		4,000
Accumulated Depreciation		18,000

Recording Applied Manufacturing Overhead

Manufacturing overhead costs are **applied** to jobs based on the predetermined overhead rate that was estimated at the beginning of the accounting period. As jobs are actually worked on during the period, accountants multiply that predetermined overhead rate by the actual number of direct labor hours worked to determine the amount of manufacturing overhead cost to apply to specific jobs.

In our home-building example, we estimated the manufacturing overhead rate to be $75 per direct labor hour. This rate is not the cost of the direct labor itself, but rather the amount of manufacturing overhead cost that needs to be added for each direct labor hour worked to cover the indirect costs of building the home (equipment depreciation, insurance, supervision, etc.). Assume Toll Brothers' labor time tickets for the month revealed the following:

	Job Number	Direct Labor Hours Spent
Simpson home	2719	600
Flintstone home	3335	200
Total direct labor hours		800

Because the overhead rate is $75 per direct labor hour, we need to apply a total of $60,000 (800 hours × $75 per direct labor hour) in manufacturing overhead costs to the Work in Process Inventory account. A corresponding credit should be made to the Manufacturing Overhead account. The journal entry to apply manufacturing overhead to work in process is:

	Debit	Credit
Work in Process Inventory	60,000	
Manufacturing Overhead		60,000

Again, anytime that we debit Work in Process Inventory, we must also update the individual job cost sheets. For the Simpson home, we would apply $45,000 (600 hours × $75 per hour) to Job 2719. For the Flintstone home, we would apply $15,000 (200 hours × $75) to Job 3335. See Exhibit 19.5 for a summary of the recording of actual and applied manufacturing overhead costs.

Exhibit 19.5   Recording Actual and Applied Manufacturing Overhead Costs

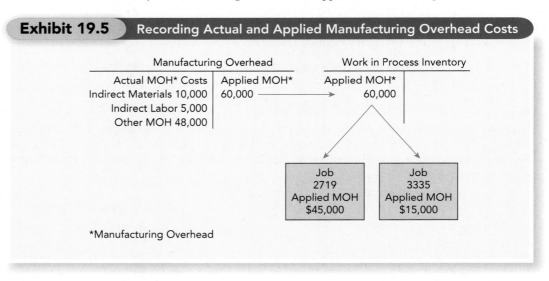

Notice that the amount of overhead that is applied to Work in Process Inventory of $60,000 is not equal to the actual manufacturing overhead cost incurred of $63,000 ($10,000 + $5,000 + $48,000). There are several reasons why the applied amount may be more or less than the actual amount; we discuss those reasons in detail in Chapter 24. For now, just remember that the applied amount is based on estimates made at the beginning of the period. We discuss how to handle the difference between actual and applied overhead costs later in this chapter.

Transferring Costs to Finished Goods Inventory and Cost of Goods Sold

When a job is finally completed, the job cost sheet must be updated to reflect all direct materials, direct labor, and applied overhead costs that should be charged to the job. Once all manufacturing costs for the Simpson home have been updated, the summary section of the final job cost sheet appears as follows:

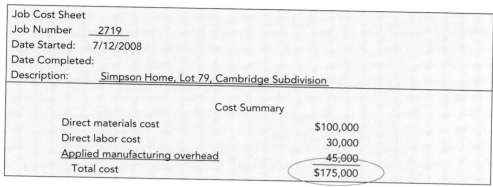

Job Cost Sheet
Job Number   2719
Date Started: 7/12/2008
Date Completed:
Description: Simpson Home, Lot 79, Cambridge Subdivision

Cost Summary

Direct materials cost	$100,000
Direct labor cost	30,000
Applied manufacturing overhead	45,000
Total cost	$175,000

The total cost to complete the job is referred to as the **cost of goods manufactured** or cost of goods completed. This is the total cost that must be transferred from the Work in Process Inventory account to the Finished Goods Inventory account. When Toll Brothers completes the Simpsons' home at a total cost of $175,000, the company's accountant should make the following journal entry to transfer the completed job from Work in Process Inventory to Finished Goods Inventory.

	Debit	Credit
Finished Goods Inventory	175,000	
Work in Process Inventory		175,000

The effect of this entry on the T-accounts follows.

Work in Process Inventory			
Direct material	140,000	When job is	
Direct labor	50,000	completed	
Applied MOH*	60,000	175,000	
Balance	75,000		

* Manufacturing overhead.

Job 2719

Finished Goods Inventory		
Cost of goods	When job	
completed	is sold	
175,000	175,000	

Job 2719

Cost of Goods Sold	
175,000	

Because this home was built for a specific customer, the new owners should take ownership shortly after construction is complete (and it passes the owners' inspection). Once the sale is final, accountants will move the total cost of the job from the Finished Goods Inventory account to Cost of Goods Sold. They will also make an entry to recognize the revenue that Toll Brothers earned on the sale. If the Simpsons agreed to pay $275,000 for their home, accountants would make the following journal entries to record the sales revenue and cost of the home.

	Debit	Credit
Cash or Accounts Receivable	275,000	
Sales Revenue		275,000
Cost of Goods Sold	175,000	
Finished Goods Inventory		175,000

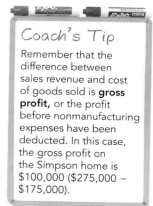

Coach's Tip

Remember that the difference between sales revenue and cost of goods sold is **gross profit**, or the profit before nonmanufacturing expenses have been deducted. In this case, the gross profit on the Simpson home is $100,000 ($275,000 − $175,000).

The $175,000 in the Cost of Goods Sold account includes all manufacturing costs of building the Simpson home. But we still need to account for the nonmanufacturing costs.

Recording Nonmanufacturing Costs

In addition to the manufacturing costs just described, companies incur many other **nonmanufacturing costs** to market their products and run their businesses. Nonmanufacturing costs are treated differently than manufacturing costs. Instead of being treated as part of the product cost (included in inventory and eventually the cost of goods sold), nonmanufacturing costs are expensed during the period in which they are incurred.

Assume Toll Brothers incurred the following nonmanufacturing expenses last month:

Commissions to sales agents	$20,000
Advertising expense	5,000
Depreciation on office equipment	6,000
Other selling and administrative expenses	4,000
Total	$35,000

The journal entries to record these nonmanufacturing costs are:

Coach's Tip

Notice that depreciation on office equipment is treated as a period expense while depreciation on construction equipment was treated as manufacturing overhead (a product cost). The difference has to do with whether the asset being depreciated is used for manufacturing or nonmanufacturing activities.

	Debit	Credit
Commissions Expense	20,000	
Cash or Commissions Payable		20,000
Advertising Expense	5,000	
Cash or Prepaid Advertising		5,000
Depreciation Expense	6,000	
Accumulated Depreciation		6,000
Selling and Administrative Expenses	4,000	
Cash, Prepaids, or Payables		4,000

OVERAPPLIED OR UNDERAPPLIED MANUFACTURING OVERHEAD

Calculating Overapplied and Underapplied Manufacturing Overhead

Because the amount of **applied** manufacturing overhead is based on a predetermined overhead rate that is estimated before the accounting period begins, it will probably differ from the **actual** manufacturing overhead cost incurred during the period. The difference between actual and applied overhead is called overapplied or underapplied overhead. Overhead cost is overapplied if the amount applied is more than the actual overhead cost. It is underapplied if the amount applied is less than the actual cost.

After recording the actual and applied manufacturing overhead in our home-building example, the Manufacturing Overhead account would appear as follows:

Manufacturing Overhead			
Actual Mfg. Overhead		Applied Mfg. Overhead	
Indirect Materials	10,000		
Indirect Labor	5,000		
Supervisor Salaries	12,000		
Engineering Salaries	8,000		
Property Taxes	6,000	$60,000	Applied Overhead
Plant Insurance	4,000		
Factory Depreciation	18,000		
Balance	3,000		

Coach's Tip

The debit balance in Manufacturing Overhead means that actual overhead cost was $3,000 more than the applied overhead cost. That is, overhead was **underapplied.** A credit balance will appear when actual overhead is less than applied overhead—that is, when overhead is **overapplied.**

Notice that actual overhead cost was $63,000, but applied overhead was only $60,000, resulting in $3,000 of **underapplied overhead.** We will see how to dispose of this overhead balance next.

Disposing of Overapplied or Underapplied Manufacturing Overhead

The most common method for disposing of the balance in Manufacturing Overhead is to make a direct adjustment to Cost of Goods Sold. Doing so makes sense as long as most of the jobs that were worked on during the period were completed and sold. However, if a significant amount of cost remains in the Work in Process Inventory or Finished Goods Inventory accounts, then part of the over- or underapplied manufacturing overhead technically should be adjusted to those accounts.

Learning Objective 5

Calculate and dispose of overapplied or underapplied manufacturing overhead.

In the example we just examined, the company worked on only two jobs. One was completed and sold, but the other was still in process. In reality, most companies complete and sell many more jobs during the accounting period. Thus, we demonstrate the simplest and most common method of transferring the balance in the Manufacturing Overhead account directly to Cost of Goods Sold. (The more complicated approach of adjusting multiple accounts is covered in advanced accounting textbooks.)

To eliminate the $3,000 debit balance in the Manufacturing Overhead account, we need to credit the Manufacturing Overhead account and debit the Cost of Goods Sold account. The journal entry to dispose of the underapplied overhead is:

	Debit	Credit
Cost of Goods Sold	3,000	
Manufacturing Overhead		3,000

The effect of this entry is to increase the Cost of Goods Sold account by $3,000. Increasing Cost of Goods Sold makes sense in this case because manufacturing overhead was underapplied. In other words, we did not apply enough cost to the jobs that were completed and eventually sold.

If Manufacturing Overhead had been overapplied (with a credit balance), we would have debited the Manufacturing Overhead account to eliminate the balance and credited the Cost of Goods Sold account. Crediting the Cost of Goods Sold account decreases the cost to reflect the fact that actual manufacturing overhead was less than applied overhead—that is, overhead was overapplied. The effect of disposing of the Manufacturing Overhead balance to the Cost of Goods Sold account is as follows:

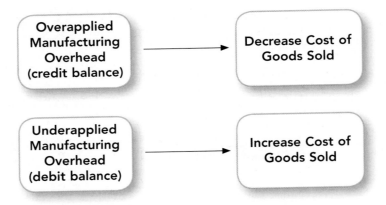

Take a moment to make sure you understand how to calculate over- and underapplied manufacturing overhead by completing this Self-Study Practice.

SELF-STUDY PRACTICE

Carlton Brothers Construction Company applies manufacturing overhead to jobs on the basis of direct labor hours. The following estimated and actual information is available.

	Estimated	Actual
Total manufacturing overhead	$96,000	$90,000
Total direct labor hours	12,000	11,000

1. Calculate the over- or underapplied overhead.
2. Show the journal entry needed to close that amount to the Cost of Goods Sold account.

After you have finished, check your answers with the solutions at the bottom of the page.

Solution to Self-Study Practice

1.

Predetermined Overhead Rate = $96,000 / 12,000 = $8.00 per Direct Labor (DL) Hour
Applied Overhead = $8.00 × 11,000 actual DL hours = $88,000

Applied overhead	=	$88,000 (credit)
Actual overhead	=	$90,000 (debit)
Underapplied overhead	=	$ 2,000 (debit balance)

2.

	Debit	Credit
Cost of Goods Sold	2,000	
Manufacturing Overhead		2,000

Coach's Tip

It is easy to become confused about whether to use actual or estimated data in calculating applied manufacturing overhead. Remember that applied overhead is calculated by multiplying the predetermined **(estimated)** overhead rate by the **actual** value of the allocation base.

Calculating the Cost of Goods Manufactured and Cost of Goods Sold

The preceding example illustrated how to record manufacturing and nonmanufacturing costs. See Exhibit 19.6 for the final balance in each of the major accounts after all of the previous transactions have been posted.

Recall that the company only worked on two jobs during the period. Because only one job (#3335) is still in process at the end of the accounting period, the balance in the Work in Process Inventory account will be equal to the total cost recorded on that job ($75,000). The ending balance in Finished Goods Inventory is zero because the only job completed during the period was also sold. The ending balance in Cost of Goods Sold represents the cost of Job #2719 ($175,000), plus the adjustment for underapplied manufacturing overhead ($3,000).

Exhibit 19.6   Summary of Recorded Manufacturing and Nonmanufacturing Costs

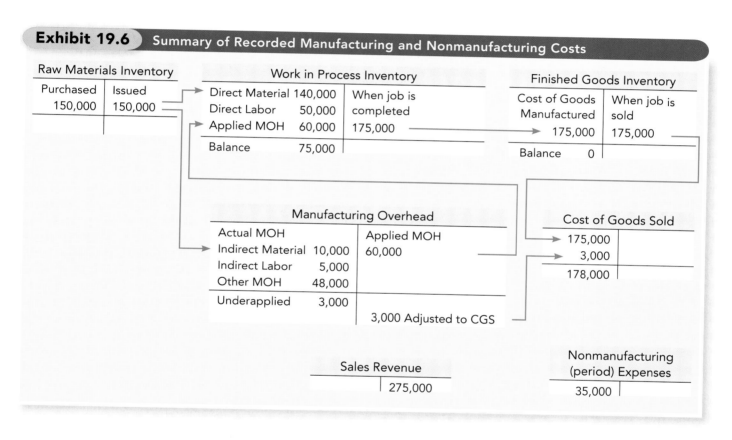

Using the T-accounts shown in Exhibit 19.6, we can prepare a cost of goods manufactured and sold report. The first part of this report is very similar to the one you learned to prepare in Chapter 18, with a few important differences:

- Because the Raw Materials Inventory account includes both direct and indirect materials, we need to subtract the indirect materials from the total materials purchased to determine how much direct materials were used in production. Remember that only direct materials will flow into the Work in Process Inventory account, while indirect materials will flow through the Manufacturing Overhead account.

- The total current manufacturing costs debited to Work in Process Inventory includes direct material, direct labor, and applied (not actual) manufacturing overhead. Any difference between actual and applied manufacturing overhead is made as a direct adjustment to Cost of Goods Sold.

The cost of goods manufactured and sold report for our home-building example follows, along with the resulting income statement.

Coach's Tip

Notice that cost of goods manufactured and cost of goods sold are initially based on the amount of overhead **applied** to Work in Process Inventory, Finished Goods Inventory, and Cost of Goods Sold. Any difference between the actual and applied overhead is adjusted directly to Cost of Goods Sold at the end of the year.

Toll Brothers Inc.
Cost of Goods Manufactured and Sold

Beginning raw materials inventory	0
Plus: Raw material purchases	$150,000
Less: Indirect materials used	− 10,000
Less: Ending raw materials inventory	0
Direct materials used in production	140,000
Direct labor	50,000
Manufacturing overhead applied	60,000
Total current manufacturing costs	250,000
Plus: Beginning work in process inventory	0
Less: Ending work in process inventory	− 75,000
Cost of goods manufactured	175,000
Plus: Beginning finished goods inventory	0
Less: Ending finished goods inventory	0
Unadjusted Cost of goods sold	175,000
Adjustment for underapplied manufacturing overhead	+ 3,000
Cost of Goods Sold	$178,000

Coach's Tip

Earlier in the chapter, we reported that the gross profit earned on the sale of the Simpson home was $100,000. The adjusted gross profit is less because we did not apply enough manufacturing overhead to the job.

Toll Brothers Inc.
Income Statement

Sales revenue	$275,000
Less: Cost of goods sold	178,000
Gross profit	97,000
Less: Selling and administrative expenses	35,000
Income from Operations	$ 62,000

Demonstration Case

Pacific Pool Company (PPC) builds custom swimming pools for homeowners in California, Arizona, and Nevada. PPC uses material requisition forms and direct labor time tickets to trace direct materials and direct labor costs to specific jobs. Manufacturing overhead is applied to jobs at a rate of $100 per direct labor hour. During the most recent month, the company recorded the following transactions:

a. Purchased $200,000 in raw materials on account.

b. Issued $150,000 in raw materials to production.
   - $130,000 of this cost was directly traceable to specific jobs;
   - $20,000 was not directly traceable to specific jobs.

c. Recorded the following labor costs (paid in cash):
   - Direct labor $50,000
   - Construction supervision   30,000

d. Recorded the following actual manufacturing overhead costs:
   - Construction insurance (prepaid) $ 5,000
   - Construction equipment depreciation   25,000
   - Pool permits and inspections   5,000

e. Recorded the following nonmanufacturing costs:
  • Office equipment depreciation $ 3,000
  • Rent and insurance on owner's company car   2,000
  • Advertising costs   10,000

f. Applied manufacturing overhead to jobs in process based on 900 actual direct labor hours.

g. Completed 15 pools at a total cost of $195,000.

h. Finalized the sale of 13 pools that cost $176,000. The other 2 pools are completed and awaiting inspection by the customer before the sale is finalized.

i. Recorded sales revenue of $325,000 on the 13 pools that were sold.

j. Closed the Manufacturing Overhead account balance to Cost of Goods Sold.

Required:

1. Prepare journal entries to record these transactions. Unless otherwise indicated, assume all expenses are paid in cash.

2. Assuming there were no beginning balances in any of the accounts, calculate the following:
  a. Ending Work in Process Inventory.
  b. Ending Finished Goods Inventory.
  c. Cost of Goods Sold (after the overhead adjustment).
  d. Gross profit (after the overhead adjustment).

Suggested Solution

1.

		Debit	Credit
a.	Raw Materials Inventory	200,000	
	Accounts Payable		200,000
b.	Work in Process Inventory	130,000	
	Manufacturing Overhead	20,000	
	Raw Materials Inventory		150,000
c.	Work in Process Inventory	50,000	
	Manufacturing Overhead	30,000	
	Cash		80,000
d.	Manufacturing Overhead	35,000	
	Prepaid Construction Insurance		5,000
	Accumulated Depreciation		25,000
	Cash		5,000
e.	Depreciation Expense	3,000	
	Rent and Insurance Expense	2,000	
	Advertising Expense	10,000	
	Accumulated Depreciation		3,000
	Cash		12,000
f.	Work in Process Inventory (900 × $100)	90,000	
	Manufacturing Overhead		90,000
g.	Finished Goods Inventory	195,000	
	Work in Process Inventory		195,000
h.	Cost of Goods Sold	176,000	
	Finished Goods Inventory		176,000
i.	Cash	325,000	
	Sales Revenue		325,000
j.	Manufacturing Overhead	5,000	
	Cost of Goods Sold		5,000

Manufacturing Overhead	
b. 20,000	f. 90,000
c. 30,000	
d. 35,000	
	Balance 5,000
j. 5,000 to remove	overapplied

2.

Work in Process Inventory	
b. 130,000	g. 195,000
c. 50,000	
f. 90,000	
Balance 75,000	

Finished Goods Inventory	
g. 195,000	h. 176,000
Balance 19,000	

Cost of Goods Sold	
h. 176,000	j. 5,000
Balance 171,000	

Sales revenue	325,000
Cost of goods sold	(171,000)
Gross profit	154,000

Chapter Summary

LO1 Describe the key differences between job order costing and process costing. p. 800

- Process costing is used in companies that make very homogeneous products using a continuous production process.
- Job order costing is used in companies that make unique products or provide specialized services.

LO2 Describe the source documents used to track direct materials and direct labor costs to the job cost sheet. p. 802

- Direct materials are issued to production by using a materials requisition form showing the costs and quantities of all materials requested and the job on which the materials were used.
- Direct labor costs are recorded using labor time tickets on which each worker records the amount of time spent on each specific job.
- The costs incurred for each job are recorded on a separate job cost sheet.

LO3 Calculate a predetermined overhead rate and use it to apply manufacturing overhead cost to jobs. p. 804

- Because manufacturing overhead costs cannot be traced directly to individual jobs, we must use an allocation base or cost driver to apply manufacturing overhead cost to specific jobs.
- The predetermined overhead rate is calculated by dividing the estimated total manufacturing overhead cost by the estimated value of the allocation base.
- Manufacturing overhead is applied to specific jobs by multiplying the predetermined overhead rate by the actual amount of the allocation base used on the job.

LO4 Prepare journal entries to record the flow of manufacturing and nonmanufacturing costs. p. 807

- Initially, raw material purchases are recorded in the Raw Materials Inventory account.
- When materials are placed into production, direct materials are recorded in the Work in Process Inventory account; indirect materials are recorded in the Manufacturing Overhead account.
- When labor costs are incurred, direct labor is recorded in the Work in Process Inventory account; indirect labor is recorded in the Manufacturing Overhead account.

- Actual manufacturing overhead costs are recorded with a debit to Manufacturing Overhead and a credit to the appropriate asset or liability account.
- When manufacturing overhead is applied to specific jobs, the Work in Process Inventory account is debited and the Manufacturing Overhead account is credited.
- When a job is completed, the total cost of goods completed is transferred from the Work in Process Inventory account to the Finished Goods Inventory account.
- When the job is delivered to the customer, the total cost is transferred from Finished Goods Inventory to Cost of Goods Sold.
- Nonmanufacturing costs are recorded as period expenses rather than as part of the manufacturing cost flow.

LO5 Calculate and dispose of overapplied or underapplied manufacturing overhead. p. 813

- Actual overhead costs are recorded on the debit side of the Manufacturing Overhead account; applied manufacturing overhead costs are recorded on the credit side. Thus, the balance in the Manufacturing Overhead account represents the amount of overapplied or underapplied overhead.
- If the overhead account has a debit balance, actual overhead costs were higher than applied overhead costs; that is, overhead was underapplied.
- If the overhead account has a credit balance, applied overhead costs were higher than actual overhead costs; that is, overhead was overapplied.
- At the end of the year, the remaining overhead balance is typically transferred to the Cost of Goods Sold account. Overapplied overhead decreases (credits) the Cost of Goods Sold account; underapplied overhead increases (debits) the Cost of Goods Sold account.

LO6 Calculate the cost of goods manufactured and cost of goods sold. p. 815

- The flow of manufacturing costs out of the Work in Process account and into the Finished Goods Inventory account is the cost of good manufactured. When the product is sold, this amount is transferred to the Cost of Goods Sold account.
- Initially, the cost of goods manufactured and the cost of goods sold are based on direct materials, direct labor, and **applied manufacturing overhead** costs.
- The cost of goods sold account is updated to reflect actual manufacturing overhead costs through an adjustment for overapplied or underapplied manufacturing overhead.

Key Formulas	
To Calculate	**Formula**
Predetermined overhead rate	$\dfrac{\text{Estimated Total Manufacturing Overhead Cost}}{\text{Estimated Units of the Allocation Base}}$
Applied overhead	Predetermined Overhead Rate $\times$ Actual Units of the Allocation Base
Overapplied or underapplied overhead	Applied Overhead $-$ Actual Overhead A positive value indicates that overhead cost was overapplied. A negative value indicates that overhead cost was underapplied.

Key Terms

Actual Manufacturing Overhead (p. 806)

Allocation Base (p. 804)

Cost of Goods Completed (p. 811)

Cost of Goods Sold (p. 806)

See complete glossary in the back of text.

Direct Labor Time Ticket (p. 803)

Indirect Materials (p. 807)

Job Cost Sheet (p. 802)

Job Order Costing (p. 801)

Materials Requisition Form (p. 802)

Overapplied Overhead (p. 812)

Predetermined Overhead Rate (p. 804)

Process Costing (p. 800)

Underapplied Overhead (p. 812)

Questions

1. What is the difference between job order and process costing?
2. What types of companies are likely to use job order costing? Give three examples.
3. What types of companies are likely to use process costing? Give three examples.
4. Many service industries use job order costing to keep track of the cost of serving clients. Can you think of a service industry that provides fairly homogeneous services? Describe the industry and explain why it might use process costing rather than job order costing.

5. Many companies use a modified costing system that blends certain elements of process costing and job order costing. Can you think of a company that makes products that have certain similarities from unit to unit (similar to process costing) but also allows a certain degree of customization (similar to job order costing)? Give an example.

6. Describe the three major types of manufacturing costs that are accounted for in a job order cost system. Give an example of each type of cost for an auto repair shop that uses job order costing.

7. What is the purpose of a job order cost sheet? What information should it contain?

8. The job order cost sheet serves as a subsidiary ledger to the Work in Process Inventory account. Explain what this means and how you would verify this.

9. What is the purpose of a materials requisition form? What information should it contain?

10. Explain why the cost of direct materials is debited to Work in Process Inventory while the cost of indirect materials is debited to Manufacturing Overhead.

11. What is the primary source document used to trace the cost of direct labor to specific jobs? What information should it contain?

12. Some would argue that costs would be more accurate if overhead costs were assigned to jobs using an overhead rate based on actual direct labor and actual value of the allocation base. Do you agree or disagree with this view? Explain.

13. Why is manufacturing overhead assigned to Work in Process Inventory in a different manner than direct materials and direct labor? Explain how it is different.

14. Explain how and why depreciation on office equipment is treated differently than depreciation on manufacturing equipment.

15. How is a predetermined overhead rate calculated? How does a company decide on an allocation base to use to calculate the rate?

16. How do you apply manufacturing overhead to the Work in Process Inventory account? Is it based on estimated or actual data?

17. Will the amount of manufacturing overhead that is applied to Work in Process Inventory be equal to the actual amount of manufacturing overhead costs incurred? Why or why not?

18. How do you know when manufacturing overhead is overapplied? What type of balance would you expect to see in the Manufacturing Overhead account?

19. How do you know when manufacturing overhead is underapplied? What type of balance would you expect to see in the Manufacturing Overhead account?

20. Explain the most common method of eliminating any balance in the Manufacturing Overhead account at year-end. What account(s) is (are) adjusted? What happens to the account(s) when manufacturing overhead is overapplied? Underapplied?

Multiple Choice

1. Why would a company choose to use process costing rather than job order costing to compute product cost?

Quiz 19-1
www.mhhe.com/LLPW1e

   a. The company produces units to customer specifications.
   b. The company manufactures a product using a series of continuous processes that results in units that are virtually identical from one to the next.
   c. The company wants to track the cost of material, labor, and overhead to specific customers.
   d. The company wants to allocate manufacturing overhead using an overhead application rate based on direct labor hours.
   e. All of the above.

2. The source document used to specify the quantity and unit costs of raw materials issued into production is called a:
   a. Production order form.
   b. Materials requisition form.
   c. Direct labor time ticket.
   d. Predetermined overhead rate.
   e. Job order cost sheet.

3. Which of the following source documents serves as a subsidiary ledger for the Work in Process Inventory account?
   a. Production order form.
   b. Materials requisition form.

   c. Direct labor time ticket.
   d. Predetermined overhead rate.
   e. Job order cost sheet.

4. Comstock Company uses a predetermined overhead rate based on machine hours to apply manufacturing overhead to jobs. Estimated and actual total manufacturing overhead costs and machine hours follow.

	Estimated	Actual
Total overhead cost	$100,000	$110,250
Machine hours	20,000	21,000

What is the predetermined overhead rate per machine hour?
   a. $4.75.   c. $5.25.
   b. $5.00.   d. $5.51.

5. Refer to the information in question 4 above. How much is over- or underapplied overhead?
   a. $10,250 overapplied.   d. $ 5,250 underapplied.
   b. $10,250 underapplied.   e. None of the above.
   c. $ 5,250 overapplied.

6. When raw materials are purchased on account, the journal entry would:
   a. Include a Debit to Work in Process Inventory.
   b. Include a Debit to Raw Materials Inventory.
   c. Include a Credit to Accounts Payable.
   d. Both A and C.
   e. Both B and C.

7. The journal entry to record actual overhead costs incurred would:
   a. Include a debit to Work in Process Inventory.
   b. Include a debit to Manufacturing Overhead.
   c. Include a credit to Manufacturing Overhead.
   d. Include both A and C.
   e. Not be recorded.

8. The journal entry to record applied manufacturing overhead costs would:
   a. Include a debit to Work in Process Inventory.
   b. Include a debit to Manufacturing Overhead.
   c. Include a credit to Manufacturing Overhead.
   d. Include both A and C.
   e. Not be recorded.

9. Carlton Construction Company sold a home that it built for a total cost of $150,000 for a sales price of $250,000. The journal entries to record the sales revenue and cost of the sale would include:
   a. A debit to Cost of Goods Sold for $150,000.
   b. A credit to Finished Goods for $150,000.
   c. A debit to Sales Revenue for $250,000.
   d. A credit to Accounts Receivable for $250,000.
   e. A and B.

10. Before disposing of its year-end manufacturing overhead balance, Delphi Corporation had the following amounts in Manufacturing Overhead and Cost of Goods Sold.

Applied manufacturing overhead	$100,000
Actual manufacturing overhead	90,000
Unadjusted cost of goods sold	800,000

    If Delphi closes the balance of its Manufacturing Overhead account directly to Cost of Goods Sold, how much is adjusted cost of goods sold?
    a. $790,000.
    b. $810,000.
    c. $890,000.
    d. $900,000.
    e. None of the above.

Solutions to Multiple-Choice Questions

1. b   2. b   3. e   4. b   5. d   6. e   7. b
8. d   9. e   10. a

Mini Exercises

Available with McGraw-Hill's Homework Manager

M19-1 Identifying Companies that Use Job Order versus Process Costing   LO1
Indicate whether each of the following companies is likely to use job order (j) or process costing (p).

_____ 1. Golf ball manufacturer.
_____ 2. Landscaping business.
_____ 3. Tile manufacturer.
_____ 4. Auto repair shop.
_____ 5. Pet food manufacturer.
_____ 6. Light bulb manufacturer.
_____ 7. Water bottling company.
_____ 8. Appliance repair business.
_____ 9. DVD manufacturer.
_____ 10. Music video production company.

M19-2 Calculating Total Current Manufacturing Cost   LO6
The following information is available for Carefree Industries.

Beginning work in process inventory	$ 75,000
Ending work in process inventory	90,000
Cost of goods manufactured	300,000

Compute total current manufacturing costs.

M19-3 Calculating Cost of Goods Sold   LO6
The following information is available for Carefree Industries.

Cost of goods manufactured	$300,000
Beginning finished goods inventory	140,000
Ending finished goods inventory	120,000

Compute cost of goods sold.

LO6

M19-4 Calculating Direct Material Used in Production

The following information is available for Carefree Industries.

Direct labor	$100,000
Total current manufacturing costs	370,000

Manufacturing overhead is applied to production at 150 percent of direct labor cost.
Determine how much direct material was used in production.

LO3

M19-5 Calculating Predetermined Overhead Rates

Willard Company applies manufacturing overhead costs to products as a percentage of direct labor dollars. Estimated and actual values of manufacturing overhead and direct labor costs are summarized here:

	Estimated	Actual
Direct labor cost	$400,000	$350,000
Manufacturing overhead	800,000	725,000

1. Compute the predetermined overhead rate.
2. Interpret this rate and explain how it will be used to apply manufacturing overhead to jobs.
3. Explain whether you used estimated or actual values to compute the rate, and why.

LO3

M19-6 Calculating Applied Manufacturing Overhead

Refer to M19-5 for Willard Company.

1. Determine how much overhead to apply to production.
2. Explain whether applied overhead was based on actual values, estimated values, or both.

LO4

M19-7 Calculating Over- or Underapplied Manufacturing Overhead

Refer to M19-5 for Willard Company.

1. Compute over- or underapplied overhead.
2. Explain how you would handle the over- or underapplied overhead at the end of the accounting period. Which accounts will be affected? Will the accounts be increased or decreased?

LO2, 4

M19-8 Recording the Purchase and Issue of Raw Materials

Kelly Company's raw materials inventory transactions for the most recent month are summarized here.

Beginning raw materials	$ 10,000	
Purchases of raw materials	100,000	
Raw materials issued		
Material Requisition #1445	50,000	For Job 101
Material Requisition #1446	40,000	For Job 102
Material Requisition #1447	15,000	Used on multiple jobs

1. Prepare the journal entries to record the purchase and issuance of raw materials.
2. In addition to the Work in Process Inventory account, on what subsidiary record would the $50,000 and $40,000 direct material costs be recorded?
3. Compute the ending balance in the Raw Materials Inventory account.

LO4

M19-9 Recording Direct and Indirect Labor Costs

Kelly Company's payroll costs for the most recent month are summarized here:

Item	Description		Total Cost
Hourly labor wages	750 hours @ $25 per hour		
	200 hours for Job 101 =	$5,000	
	300 hours for Job 102 =	7,500	
	250 hours for Job 103 =	6,250	$18,750
Factory supervision			4,250
Production engineer			6,000
Factory janitorial work			2,000
General and administrative salaries			8,000
Total payroll costs			$39,000

1. Prepare the journal entry to record the month's payroll costs.
2. Explain why some labor costs are recorded as work in process, some as manufacturing overhead, and some as period costs.

M19-10 Recording Applied Manufacturing Overhead Costs   LO3, 4
Refer to M19-9 for Kelly Company. The company applies manufacturing overhead to products at a predetermined rate of $50 per direct labor hour.

Prepare the journal entry to apply manufacturing overhead to production.

M19-11 Calculating Over- or Underapplied Overhead Costs   LO3, 4, 5
Refer to M19-10 for Kelly Company. Its actual manufacturing costs for the most recent period are summarized here:

Item	Description		Total Cost
Direct material	Used on Jobs 101 and 102		$90,000
Indirect material	Used on multiple jobs		15,000
Hourly labor wages	750 hours @ $25 per hour		
	200 hours for Job 101 =	$5,000	
	300 hours for Job 102 =	7,500	
	250 hours for Job 103 =	6,250	18,750
Factory supervision			4,250
Production engineer			6,000
Factory janitorial work			2,000
General and administrative salaries			8,000
Other manufacturing overhead costs (factory rent, insurance, depreciation, etc.)			7,000
Other general and administrative costs (office rent, insurance, depreciation, etc.)			5,000

1. Compute over- or underapplied manufacturing overhead.
2. Prepare the journal entry to close the Manufacturing Overhead account balance to Cost of Goods Sold.
3. Explain whether the entry in requirement 2 will increase or decrease Cost of Goods Sold and why.

Exercises ™   Available with McGraw-Hill's Homework Manager

E19-1 Recording Materials Based on Materials Requisitions   LO2, 4
A recent materials requisition form for Christopher Creek Furniture Manufacturers follows.

Requisition Number	Job Number	Item Description	Total Cost
MR 234	25	¼" maple planks	$400
MR 235	26	¼" cherry planks	500
MR 236	27	½" birch planks	450
MR 237	Indirect	Wood screws, etc	100

Required:
Prepare the journal entry to record the issuance of materials.

E19-2 Recording Direct Materials, Direct Labor, and Applied Overhead   LO2, 3, 4
Stone Creek Furniture Factory (SCFF), a custom furniture manufacturer, uses job order costing to keep track of the cost of each customer order. On March 1, SCFF had two jobs in process with the following costs:

Work in Process	Balance on 3/1
Job 33	$5,000
Job 34	4,000
	$9,000

Source documents revealed the following during March.

	Amount on Materials Requisitions Forms	Amount on Labor Time Tickets	Status of Job at Month-End
Job 33	$ 3,000	$ 5,000	Completed and sold
Job 34	3,000	4,000	Completed, but not sold
Job 35	4,000	3,000	In process
Indirect	1,000	2,000	
	$11,000	$14,000	

The company applies overhead to products at a rate of 75 percent of direct labor cost.

Required:

1. Prepare journal entries to record the material requisitions, labor costs, and applied overhead.
2. Calculate the balance in the Work in Process Inventory, Finished Goods Inventory, and Cost of Goods Sold accounts at month-end.

LO2,4   **E19-3 Analyzing Labor Time Tickets and Recording Labor Costs**

A weekly time ticket for Jim Bolton follows.

Direct Labor Time Ticket		Dates:	Monday 8/12 – Friday 8/16, 2008	
Ticket Number:	TT338			
Employee:	Jim Bolton			
Date	Time Started	Time Ended	Total Hours	Job Number
8/12/2008	7:00 AM	3:00 PM	8 hours	Job 271
8/13/2008	7:00 AM	3:00 PM	8 hours	Job 271
8/14/2008	7:00 AM	3:00 PM	8 hours	Job 272
8/15/2008	7:00 AM	11:00 AM	4 hours	Job 272
8/15/2008	12:00 PM	4:00 PM	4 hours	Maintenance
8/16/2008	7:00 AM	3:00 PM	8 hours	Job 273
		Weekly Total	40 hours	
		Hourly Labor Rate	$25	
		Total Wages Earned	$1,000	

Required:

1. Determine how much of the $1,000 that Jim earned during this week would be charged to Job 271, Job 272, and Job 273.
2. Explain how would the time spent doing maintenance work would be treated.
3. Prepare a journal entry to record the wages for Jim assuming they have not yet been paid.

LO3, 6   **E19-4 Finding Unknown Values in the Cost of Goods Manufactured and Sold Report**

Mulligan Manufacturing Company uses a job order cost system with overhead applied to products at a rate of 200 percent of direct labor cost. Selected manufacturing data follow.

	Case 1	Case 2	Case 3*
Direct material used	$ 10,000	f.	$15,000
Direct labor	15,000	e.	i.
Manufacturing overhead applied	a.	16,000	j.
Total current manufacturing costs	b.	35,000	27,000
Beginning work in process inventory	8,000	g.	7,000
Ending work in process inventory	6,000	8,000	k.
Cost of goods manufactured	c.	40,000	30,000
Beginning finished goods inventory	5,000	10,000	l.
Ending finished goods inventory	7,000	h.	5,000
Cost of goods sold	d.	42,000	33,000

* **Hint:** For Case 3 (parts i. and j.), first solve for conversion costs and then determine how much of that is direct labor and how much is manufacturing overhead.

Required:

Treat each case independently. Find the missing amounts for letters a–l. You should do them in the order listed.

E19-5 Calculating Overhead Rates, Recording Actual and Applied Manufacturing Overhead, and Analyzing Over- or Underapplied Manufacturing Overhead

LO3, 4, 5

Cayman Custom Manufacturing Company applies manufacturing overhead on the basis of machine hours. At the beginning of the year, the company estimated its total overhead cost to be $300,000 and machine hours to be 15,000. Actual manufacturing overhead and machine hours were $340,000 and 16,000, respectively.

Required:

1. Compute the predetermined overhead rate.
2. Compute applied manufacturing overhead.
3. Prepare the journal entries to record actual and applied manufacturing overhead.
4. Compute over- or underapplied manufacturing overhead.
5. Prepare the journal entry to transfer the overhead balance to Cost of Goods Sold.

E19-6 Calculating and Recording the Total Cost to Complete a Job and Sales Revenue

LO3, 4, 6

Aquazona Pool Company is a custom pool builder. It recently completed a pool for the Drayna family (Job 1324), as summarized on the following incomplete job cost sheet.

Job Cost Sheet
Job Number   1324
Date Started: 7/12/2008
Date Completed:
Description: Drayna Pool

Direct Materials		Direct Labor			Applied Manufacturing Overhead		
Req. No	Amount	Ticket	Hours	Amount	Hours	Rate	Amount
MR 3345	$1,500	TT 335	28	$ 600			
MR 3372	1,000	TT 340	40	800			
MR 4251	1,250	TT 385	30	600			
MR 4263	1,750	TT 425	35	700			
MR 5236	2,000	TT 445	25	500			
	$7,500		158	$3,200	?	?	?

Cost Summary	
Direct Material Cost	$7,500
Direct Labor Cost	3,200
Applied Manufacturing Overhead	
Total Cost	

The company applies overhead to jobs at a rate of $10 per direct labor hour.

Required:

1. Calculate how much overhead would be applied to Job 1324.
2. Compute the total cost of Job 1324.
3. Assume the company bids its pools at total manufacturing cost plus 30 percent. If actual costs were the same as estimated, determine how much revenue the company would report on the sale of Job 1324.
4. Prepare journal entries to show the completion of Job 1324 and to recognize the sales revenue. Assume the total cost of Job 1324 is currently in the Finished Goods Inventory Account and that the Draynas paid for the pool with cash.
5. Calculate how much gross profit Aquazona made on the sale of the Drayna pool.

E19-7 Recording Manufacturing Costs

LO4

The flow of costs through a company's cost accounting system is summarized in the following T-accounts.

Raw Materials Inventory		Manufacturing Overhead	
a.	b.	b.	d.
		c.	
		e.	

Work in Process Inventory		Finished Goods Inventory	
b.	g.	g.	h.
c.			
d.			

Sales Revenue		Cost of Goods Sold	
	i.	h.	

Selling and Administrative Expenses		Other Assets or Liabilities	
c.		i.	a.
f.			c.
			e.
			f.

Required:

Describe the transactions represented by letters a–i. When more than one debit appears in a single transaction, explain why the costs are debited to different accounts.

LO3, 4

E19-8 Preparing Entries for Manufacturing Costs

Roy's Appliance Repair Shop uses a job order costing system to keep track of the cost of each repair. Roy applies its "garage or shop" overhead at a rate of $25 per direct labor hour spent on each repair. Roy's uses the following accounts to keep track of the cost of all repairs.

Raw Materials (parts and supplies)	Repair Jobs in Process	Cost of Repairs Completed and Sold	Garage/Shop* Overhead Costs

* Because an auto shop does not manufacture a product, the overhead cost would include all of the indirect costs that are incurred in the "garage or shop" that cannot be traced to a specific repair job.

The following transactions occurred during the most recent month:

a. Purchased raw materials (parts and supplies) on account $21,000.

b. Used $16,000 in raw materials (parts and supplies). Of this, $14,000 was for major parts that were traceable to individual repair jobs, and the remainder was for incidental supplies such as lubricants, rags, fuel, and so on.

c. Recorded a total of $8,000 in direct labor cost (for 400 hours) that are owed but not yet paid.

d. Applied overhead to repair jobs at a rate of $25 per direct labor hour.

e. Recorded the following actual overhead costs:

Repair shop rent (prepaid)	$ 14,000
Depreciation on diagnostic equipment	2,000
Repair shop supervision (owed but not paid)	3,000

f. Completed repair jobs costing $45,000 and charged customers at cost plus 30 percent. (**Note:** You can bypass the Finished Goods Inventory account, which is not appropriate in this context).

Required:

Prepare journal entries for transactions a–f using the account names shown and other appropriate accounts such as Cash, Payables, Accumulated Depreciation, Prepaids, and Sales Revenue.

LO4, 5

E19-9 Recording Actual and Applied Manufacturing Overhead Costs, and Calculating Over- or Underapplied Overhead Costs

Verizox Company uses a job order costing system with manufacturing overhead applied to products based on direct labor hours. At the beginning of the most recent year, the company estimated its manufacturing overhead cost at $200,000. Estimated direct labor cost was $500,000 for 20,000 hours (average of $25 per hour). Actual costs for the most recent month are summarized here:

Item Description	Total Cost
Direct labor (2,000 hours @ $26 per hour)	$52,000
Indirect costs	
Indirect labor	2,400
Indirect material	3,300
Factory rent	3,200
Factory supervision	4,700
Factory depreciation	5,600
Factory janitorial work	1,100
Factory insurance	1,700
General and administrative salaries	4,100
Selling expenses	5,300

Required:

1. Calculate the predetermined overhead rate.
2. Prepare the journal entry to apply manufacturing overhead to Work in Process Inventory.
3. Calculate actual manufacturing overhead costs. Explain which costs you excluded and why.
4. Prepare the journal entry to record actual manufacturing overhead costs. The credit can be to a generic account titled Cash, Payables, etc.
5. Compute over- or underapplied overhead.
6. Prepare the journal entry to transfer the Manufacturing Overhead account balance to Cost of Goods Sold. Does this increase or decrease Cost of Goods Sold? Why?

E19-10 Recording Manufacturing and Nonmanufacturing Costs   LO4

Reyes Manufacturing Company uses a job order costing system. At the beginning of January, the company had one job in process (Job 201) and one job that was completed but not yet sold (Job 200). Other select account balances follow (ignore any accounts that are not listed).

Raw Materials Inventory		Work in Process Inventory		Finished Goods Inventory	
1/1 32,000		1/1 15,500		1/1 20,000	

Cost of Goods Sold		Manufacturing Overhead		Sales Revenue	

During January, the company had the following transactions.
  a.   Purchased $60,000 worth of material on account.
  b.   Recorded materials issued to production as follows:

Job Number	Total Cost
201	$ 10,000
202	20,000
Indirect materials	5,000
	$ 35,000

  c.   Recorded factory payroll costs from direct labor time tickets that revealed the following:

Job Number	Hours	Total Cost
201	120	$ 3,000
202	400	10,000
Factory supervision		4,000
		$ 17,000

d. Applied overhead to production at a rate of $30 per direct labor hour for 520 actual direct labor hours.

e. Recorded the following actual manufacturing overhead costs.

Item	Total Cost	Description
Factory rent	$ 2,000	Paid in cash
Depreciation	3,000	Factory equipment
Factory utilities	2,500	Incurred but not paid
Factory insurance	1,500	Prepaid policy
	$ 9,000	

f. Job 201 was completed and transferred to Finished Goods Inventory.

g. Sold Job 200 for $50,000.

Job 202 was still in process at the end of January.

Required:

1. Complete the following job cost summary to calculate the total cost of the jobs that were worked on during the period.

Job number	Beg. Balance (given)	Direct Material Cost	Direct Labor Cost	MOH* Applied @ $30 per DL† hour	Total Cost of Job
200	$20,000	$ 0	$ 0	$ 0	$20,000
201	15,500				
202	0				

* Manufacturing Overhead
† Direct labor

2. Post the preceding transactions to the T-accounts. Create an additional account called Miscellaneous to capture the offsetting debits and credits to other accounts such as Cash, Payables, Accumulated Depreciation, and so on.

3. Compute the ending balance in the following accounts:

Raw Materials Inventory
Work in Process Inventory
Finished Goods Inventory
Cost of Goods Sold
Manufacturing Overhead

4. Explain which jobs would appear in Work in Process Inventory, Finished Goods Inventory, and Cost of Goods Sold. Confirm that the total cost of each job is equal to the ending balance in its respective control accounts.

Problems—Set A Available with McGraw-Hill's Homework Manager

LO3, 4, 5

PA19-1 Calculating Predetermined Overhead Rates, Recording Manufacturing Cost Flows, and Analyzing Overhead

Tyler Tooling Company uses a job order costing system with overhead applied to products on the basis of machine hours. For the upcoming year, the company estimated its total manufacturing overhead cost at $250,000 and total machine hours at 62,500. During the first month of operations, the company worked on three jobs and recorded the following actual direct materials cost, direct labor cost, and machine hours for each job.

	Job 101	Job 102	Job 103	Total
Direct materials cost	$12,000	$9,000	$6,000	$27,000
Direct labor cost	$18,000	$7,000	$6,000	$31,000
Machine hours	2,000 hours	3,000 hours	1,000 hours	6,000 hours

Job 101 was completed and sold for $50,000.

Job 102 was completed but not sold.

Job 103 is still in process.

Actual overhead costs recorded during the first month of operations were $25,000.

Required:

1. Calculate the predetermined overhead rate.

2. Compute the total manufacturing overhead applied to the Work in Process Inventory account during the first month of operations.

3. Compute the balance in the Work in Process Inventory account at the end of the first month.

4. Prepare a journal entry showing the transfer of Job 102 into Finished Goods Inventory upon its completion.

5. Prepare the journal entries to recognize the sales revenue and cost of goods sold for Job 101. How much gross profit would the company report during the first month of operations before making an adjustment for over- or underapplied manufacturing overhead?

6. Determine the balance in the Manufacturing Overhead account at the end of the first month. Is it over or underapplied?

7. Prepare the journal entry to transfer the balance of the Manufacturing Overhead account to Cost of Goods Sold. How much is adjusted Cost of Goods Sold and adjusted gross profit?

PA19-2 Recording Manufacturing Costs and Analyzing Manufacturing Overhead

LO4, 5

Christopher's Custom Cabinet Company uses a job order costing system with overhead applied as a percentage of direct labor costs. Inventory balances at the beginning of 2009 follow:

eXcel

www.mhhe.com/LLPW1e

Raw materials inventory	$15,000
Work in process inventory	5,000
Finished goods inventory	20,000

The following transactions occurred during January.

a. Purchased materials on account for $26,000.

b. Issued materials to production totaling $22,000, 90 percent of which was traced to specific jobs and the remainder treated as indirect materials.

c. Payroll costs totaling $15,500 were recorded as follows:

$10,000 for assembly workers

3,000 for factory supervision

1,000 for administrative personnel

1,500 for sales commissions

d. Recorded depreciation: $6,000 for machines, $1,000 for office copier.

e. Had $2,000 in insurance expire, allocated equally between manufacturing and administrative expenses.

f. Paid $6,500 in other factory costs in cash.

g. Applied manufacturing overhead at a rate of 200 percent of direct labor cost.

h. Completed all jobs but one; the job cost sheet for this job shows $2,100 for direct materials, $2,000 for direct labor, and $4,000 for applied overhead.

i. Sold jobs costing $50,000; the company uses cost-plus pricing with a markup of 30 percent.

Required:

1. Set up T-accounts, record the beginning balances, post the January transactions, and compute the final balance for the following accounts:

Raw Materials Inventory

Work in Process Inventory

Finished Goods Inventory

Cost of Goods Sold

Manufacturing Overhead

Selling and Administrative Expenses

Sales Revenue

Other accounts (Cash, Payables, etc.)

2. Determine how much gross profit the company would report during the month of January **before** any adjustment is made for the overhead balance.

3. Determine the amount of over- or underapplied overhead.

4. Compute adjusted gross profit assuming that any over- or underapplied overhead balance is adjusted directly to Cost of Goods Sold.

LO4, 5

PA19-3 Finding Unknowns in the Cost of Goods Manufacturing and Sold Report and Analyzing Manufacturing Overhead

The following information was obtained from the records of Appleton Corporation during 2009.

1. Manufacturing Overhead was applied at a rate of 80 percent of direct labor dollars.

2. Beginning value of inventory follows:

    a. Beginning Work in Process, Inventory $10,000.

    b. Beginning Finished Goods, Inventory $20,000.

3. Work in Process Inventory increased by 20 percent during the period; Finished Goods Inventory decreased by 25 percent during the period.

4. Actual manufacturing overhead costs were $85,000.

5. Sales were $400,000.

6. Adjusted Cost of Goods Sold was $300,000.

Required:

Use the above information to find the missing values in the table below.

Item	Amount
Direct materials used in production	$?
Direct labor	?
Manufacturing overhead applied	80,000
Total current manufacturing costs	?
Plus: Beginning work in process inventory	10,000
Less: Ending work in process inventory	?
Cost of goods manufactured	?
Plus: Beginning finished goods inventory	20,000
Less: Ending finished goods inventory	?
Unadjusted cost of goods sold	?
Overhead adjustment	?
Adjusted cost of goods sold	$300,000

LO3, 5

PA19-4 Selecting Allocation Base and Analyzing Manufacturing Overhead

Amberjack Company is trying to decide on an allocation base to use to assign manufacturing overhead to jobs. In the past, the company has always used direct labor hours to assign manufacturing overhead to products, but it is trying to decide whether it should use a different allocation base such as direct labor dollars or machine hours.

Actual and estimated data for manufacturing overhead, direct labor cost, direct labor hours, and machine hours for the most recent fiscal year are summarized here:

	Estimated Value	Actual Value
Manufacturing overhead cost	$700,000	$655,000
Direct labor cost	$350,000	$360,000
Direct labor hours	17,500 hours	16,000 hours
Machine hours	14,000 hours	13,000 hours

Required:

1. Based on the company's current allocation base (direct labor hours), compute the following:

    a. Predetermined overhead rate.

    b. Applied manufacturing overhead.

    c. Over- or underapplied manufacturing overhead.

2. If the company had used direct labor dollars (instead of direct labor hours) as its allocation base, compute the following:

   a. Predetermined overhead rate.

   b. Applied manufacturing overhead.

   c. Over- or underapplied manufacturing overhead.

3. If the company had used machine hours (instead of direct labor hours) as its allocation base, compute the following:

   a. Predetermined overhead rate.

   b. Applied manufacturing overhead.

   c. Over- or underapplied manufacturing overhead.

4. Based on last year's data alone, which allocation base would have provided the most accurate measure for applying manufacturing overhead costs to production?

5. How does a company decide on an allocation base to use in applying manufacturing overhead? What factors should be considered?

PA19-5 Recording Manufacturing Costs, Preparing a Cost of Goods Manufactured and Sold Report, and Calculating Income from Operations

LO3, 4, 5, 6

Dobson Manufacturing Company uses a job order costing system with manufacturing overhead applied to products on the basis of direct labor dollars. At the beginning of the most recent period, the company estimated its total direct labor cost to be $50,000 and its total manufacturing overhead cost to be $75,000. Several incomplete general ledger accounts showing the transactions that occurred during the most recent accounting period follow.

Raw Materials Inventory

Beginning Balance	15,000	?
Purchases	95,000	
Ending Balance	30,000	

Work in Process Inventory

Beginning Balance	30,000	?
Direct Materials	70,000	
Direct Labor	40,000	
Applied Overhead	?	
Ending Balance	20,000	

Finished Goods Inventory

Beginning Balance	40,000	?
Cost of Goods Completed	?	
Ending Balance	50,000	

Cost of Goods Sold

Unadjusted Cost of Goods Sold	?
Adjusted Cost of Goods Sold	?

Manufacturing Overhead

Indirect Materials	10,000	?	Applied Overhead
Indirect Labor	15,000		
Factory Depreciation	13,000		
Factory Rent	7,000		
Factory Utilities	3,000		
Other Factory Costs	10,000		
Actual Overhead	58,000		

Sales Revenue

	300,000 Sales Revenue

Selling and Administrative Expenses

Adm. Salaries	28,000
Office Depreciation	20,000
Advertising	15,000
Ending balance	63,000

Required:

1. Calculate the predetermined overhead rate.
2. Fill in the missing values in the T-accounts.
3. Compute over- or underapplied overhead.
4. Prepare a statement of cost of goods manufactured and sold including the adjustment for over- or underapplied overhead.
5. Prepare a brief income statement for the company.

Problems—Set B   Available with McGraw-Hill's Homework Manager

LO3, 4, 5

PB19-1 Calculating Predetermined Overhead Rates, Recording Manufacturing and Cost Flows, and Analyzing Overhead

Babson Company uses a job order costing system with overhead applied to products on the basis of machine hours. For the upcoming year, Babson estimated its total manufacturing overhead cost at $360,000 and its total machine hours at 125,000. During the first month of operation, the company worked on three jobs and recorded the following actual direct materials cost, direct labor cost, and machine hours for each job.

	Job 101	Job 102	Job 103	Total
Direct materials cost	$15,000	$10,000	$5,000	$30,000
Direct labor cost	$ 7,000	$ 5,000	$8,000	$20,000
Machine hours	5,000 hours	4,000 hours	1,000 hours	10,000 hours

Job 101 was completed and sold for $50,000.

Job 102 was completed but not sold.

Job 103 is still in process.

Actual overhead costs recorded during the first month of operations were $28,000.

Required:

1. Calculate the predetermined overhead rate.
2. Compute the total overhead applied to the Work in Process Inventory account during the first month of operations.
3. Compute the balance in the Work in Process Inventory account at the end of the first month.
4. Prepare a journal entry showing the transfer of Job 102 into Finished Goods Inventory upon its completion.
5. Prepare the journal entries to recognize the sales revenue and cost of goods sold for Job 101. How much gross profit would the company report during the first month of operations before making an adjustment for over- or underapplied manufacturing overhead?
6. Determine the balance in the Manufacturing Overhead account at the end of the first month. Is it over- or underapplied?
7. Prepare the journal entry to close Manufacturing Overhead to the Cost of Goods Sold account. How much is adjusted Cost of Goods Sold and adjusted gross profit?

LO4, 5

PB19-2 Recording Manufacturing Costs and Analyzing Manufacturing Overhead

Carrington Custom Cabinet Company uses a job order costing system with overhead applied based on direct labor cost. Inventory balances at the beginning of 2009 follow.

Raw materials inventory	$25,000
Work in process inventory	30,000
Finished goods inventory	40,000

The following transactions occurred during January.

a. Purchased materials on account for $40,000.

b. Issued materials to production totaling $30,000, 80 percent of which was traced to specific jobs and the remainder treated as indirect materials.

c. Payroll costs totaling $25,500 were recorded as follows:

$15,000 for assembly workers

6,000 for factory supervision

2,000 for administrative personnel

2,500 for sales commissions

d. Recorded depreciation: $5,000 for machines, $2,000 for office copier.

e. Had $4,000 in insurance expire; allocated equally between manufacturing and administrative expenses.

f. Paid $8,500 in other factory costs in cash.

g. Applied manufacturing overhead at a rate of 150 percent of direct labor cost.

h. Completed all jobs but one; the job cost sheet for this job shows $7,000 for direct materials, $6,000 for direct labor, and $9,000 for applied overhead.

i. Sold jobs costing $60,000 during the period; the company uses cost-plus pricing with a markup of 35 percent.

Required:

1. Set up T-accounts, record the beginning balances, post the January transactions, and compute the final balance for the following accounts:

   Raw Materials Inventory

   Work in Process Inventory

   Finished Goods Inventory

   Cost of Goods Sold

   Manufacturing Overhead

   Selling and Administrative Expenses

   Sales Revenue

   Other accounts (Cash, payables, etc.)

2. Determine how much gross profit the company would report during the month of January **before** any adjustment is made for the overhead balance.

3. Determine the amount of over- or underapplied overhead.

4. Compute adjusted gross profit assuming that any over- or underapplied overhead is adjusted directly to Cost of Goods Sold.

PB19-3 Finding Unknowns in the Cost of Goods Manufacturing and Sold Report, and Analyzing Manufacturing Overhead

LO5, 6

The following information was obtained from the records of Carrington Corporation during 2009.

1. Manufacturing overhead was applied at a rate of 150 percent of direct labor dollars.
2. Beginning value of inventory follows:

   a. Beginning Work in Process Inventory $20,000.

   b. Beginning Finished Goods Inventory $10,000.

3. Work in Process Inventory decreased by 20 percent during the period; Finished Goods Inventory increased by 25 percent during the period.
4. Actual manufacturing overhead costs were $85,000.
5. Sales were $500,000.
6. Adjusted Cost of Goods Sold was $350,000.

Required:

Use the above information to find the missing values in the table below.

Item	Amount
Direct materials used in production	$?
Direct labor	?
Manufacturing overhead applied	90,000
Current manufacturing costs	?
Plus: Beginning work in process inventory	20,000
Less: Ending work in process inventory	?
Cost of goods manufactured	?
Plus: Beginning finished goods inventory	10,000
Less: Ending finished goods inventory	?
Unadjusted cost of goods sold	?
Overhead adjustment	?
Adjusted cost of goods sold	$350,000

PB19-4 Selecting Allocation Base and Analyzing Manufacturing Overhead

LO3, 5

Timberland Company is trying to decide on an allocation base to use to assign manufacturing overhead to jobs. In the past, the company has always used direct labor hours to assign manufacturing overhead to products, but it is trying to decide whether it should use a different allocation base such as direct labor dollars or machine hours.

Actual and estimated results for manufacturing overhead, direct labor cost, direct labor hours, and machine hours for the most recent fiscal year are summarized here:

	Estimated Value	Actual Value
Manufacturing overhead cost	$900,000	$890,000
Direct labor cost	$450,000	$464,000
Direct labor hours	30,000 hours	29,000 hours
Machine hours	15,000 hours	15,000 hours

Required:

1. Based on the company's current allocation base (direct labor hours), compute the following:

    a. Predetermined overhead rate.

    b. Applied manufacturing overhead.

    c. Over- or underapplied manufacturing overhead.

2. If the company had used direct labor dollars (instead of direct labor hours) as its allocation base, compute the following:

    a. Predetermined overhead rate.

    b. Applied manufacturing overhead.

    c. Over- or underapplied manufacturing overhead.

3. If the company had used machine hours (instead of direct labor hours) as its allocation base, compute the following:

    a. Predetermined overhead rate.

    b. Applied manufacturing overhead.

    c. Over- or underapplied manufacturing overhead

4. Based on last year's data alone, which allocation base would have provided the most accurate measure for applying manufacturing overhead costs to production?

5. How does a company decide on an allocation base to use in applying manufacturing overhead? What factors should be considered?

LO3, 4, 5, 6

PB19-5 Recording Manufacturing Costs, Preparing a Cost of Goods Manufactured, and Sold Report, and Calculating from Operations Income

Carlton Manufacturing Company uses a job order costing system with manufacturing overhead applied to products on the basis of direct labor dollars. At the beginning of the most recent period, the company estimated its total direct labor cost to be $30,000 and its total manufacturing overhead cost to be $60,000. Several incomplete general ledger accounts showing the transactions that occurred during the most recent accounting period follow.

Raw Materials Inventory

Beginning Balance	10,000	?
Purchases	85,000	
Ending Balance	20,000	

Work in Process Inventory

Beginning Balance	30,000	?
Direct Materials	?	
Direct Labor	35,000	
Applied Overhead	?	
Ending Balance	20,000	

Finished Goods Inventory

Beginning Balance	60,000	?
Cost of Goods Completed	?	
Ending Balance	40,000	

Cost of Goods Sold

Unadjusted Cost of Goods Sold	?
Adjusted Cost of Goods Sold	?

Manufacturing Overhead

Indirect Materials	10,000	?	Applied Overhead
Indirect Labor	20,000		
Factory Depreciation	13,000		
Factory Rent	12,000		
Factory Utilities	5,000		
Other Factory Costs	14,000		
Actual Overhead	74,000		

Sales Revenue

	280,000 Sales Revenue

Selling and Administrative Expenses

Adm. Salaries	30,000
Office Depreciation	20,000
Advertising	19,000
Ending Balance	69,000

Required:

1. Calculate the predetermined overhead rate.
2. Fill in the missing values in the T-accounts.
3. Compute over- or underapplied overhead.
4. Prepare a statement of cost of goods manufactured and sold including the adjustment for over- or underapplied overhead
5. Prepare a brief income statement for the company.

Cases and Projects

CP19-1 Multiple Allocation Bases and Ethical Dilemmas   LO3

Assume you recently accepted a job with a company that designs and builds helicopters for commercial and military use. The company has numerous contracts with the U.S. military that require the use of cost-plus pricing. In other words, the contracted price for each helicopter is calculated at a certain percentage (about 130 percent) of the total cost to produce it. Unlike the cost-plus pricing approach used for military contracts, the prices for civilian helicopters are based on the amount that individuals and corporations are willing to pay for a state-of-the-art helicopter.

As your first assignment, the company controller has asked you to reevaluate the costing system currently used to determine the cost of producing helicopters. Currently, the company assigns manufacturing overhead based on the number of units produced. The result is that every helicopter is assigned the same amount of overhead regardless of whether it is for military or civilian use.

As part of your assignment, you collected the following information about two other potential allocation bases (direct labor hours and machine hours) and how they differ for the two types of customers the company serves:

	MILITARY CONTRACTS		CIVILIAN CONTRACTS		
	Units in Allocation Base	Percent of Total	Units in Allocation Base	Percent of Total	Total
Units produced	1,000	50%	1,000	50%	2,000
Labor hours	800,000	40	1,200,000	60	2,000,000
Machine hours	700,000	70	300,000	30	1,000,000

These data show that while the company produces an equal number of military and civilian helicopters (1,000 of each), they require a different amount of direct labor and machine hours. In particular, civilian helicopters require relatively more direct labor hours (60 percent of the total) perhaps because of the labor required to install all of the "bells and whistles" that wealthy consumers expect on a luxury helicopter. However, military helicopters require more machine time (70 percent of the total) due to the precise machining and intensive instrument testing required to comply with the military contracts. Further analysis revealed that some of the manufacturing overhead items are logically related to labor hours (such as supervision and use of indirect materials) while other overhead items (such as machine depreciation and power) are more highly related to machine hours.

When you presented these data to the controller, you recommended that the company move to an allocation system whereby part of the overhead would be allocated based on direct labor hours and part of it based on machine hours. He responded that he wanted you to choose the system that would assign the highest percentage of the total overhead cost to the military contracts. His reasoning was that the cost-plus agreement with the U.S. government would result in a higher contract price for military helicopters without affecting the price of civilian helicopters, which are set by the market.

Required:

1. Explain how changing the allocation base can impact the profitability of the two types of products.
2. Which allocation base(s) do you think the company should use to apply manufacturing overhead to the two types of products?
3. Identify the ethical issues involved in this scenario. What are your potential courses of action for responding to the controller's request? What are the potential personal, professional, and legal implications of the alternative courses of action you considered? How would you ultimately respond to this situation?

LO1, 2, 3   **CP19-2 Applying Job Order Costing to an Entrepreneurial Business**

Assume you are going to become an entrepreneur and start your own business. Think about your talents and interests and come up with an idea for a small business venture that provides a unique product or service to local customers. You can select any business venture you want, but if you are struggling to come up with an idea, here are some examples:

> Catering
> Wedding-planning consulting
> Video production company
> Pool building company
> Personal shopping service
> Interior design business
> Flower shop
> Rock-climbing guide service
> River-rafting company
> Web design company

Required:

For whatever business venture you select, answer the following questions:

1. What would the major costs of your business be? Try to classify the costs into the areas of direct materials, direct labor, manufacturing overhead, general and administrative costs, and selling costs. (**Hint:** Not all businesses will have all of these cost classifications.)
2. Why would you need to determine the cost of providing your product or service to individual customers? In other words, what types of decisions would you expect to make based on job order cost information?
3. In general, would you expect your company's indirect (overhead) costs to be less or more than the direct costs (direct labor and materials)? What allocation base do you think you would use to charge overhead costs to individual customers? How much do you think the overhead rate would need to be?
4. Think about a hypothetical "average" customer and create a job cost sheet for this customer that includes estimates of the major costs of serving that customer. How much do you think you would need to charge the customer to cover all of the costs plus provide a reasonable profit for yourself?

LO3, 4, 5, 6   **CP19-3 Comprehensive Job Order Costing Case**

Sampson Company uses a job order cost system with overhead applied to products based on direct labor hours. Based on previous history, the company estimated its total overhead for the coming year (2009) to be $240,000 and its total direct labor hours to be 6,000.

On January 1, 2009, the general ledger of Sampson Company revealed that it had one job in process (Job 102) for which it had incurred a total cost of $15,000. Job 101 had been finished the previous month for a total cost of $30,000 but was not yet sold. The company had a contract for Job 103 but had not started working on it yet. Other balances in Raw Materials Inventory and other assets, liabilities and owner's equity accounts are summarized here:

Sampson Company
General Ledger Accounts

Raw Materials Inventory

1/1 Balance 10,000	

Work in Process Inventory

1/1 Balance 15,000	

Finished Goods Inventory

1/1 Balance 30,000	

Sales Revenue

Cash and Other Assets

1/1 Balance 100,000	

Manufacturing Overhead

Individual Job Cost Sheets (subsidiary ledgers to WIP)

	Job 102	Job 103
Beg. Balance	15,000	—
+ Direct Material		
+ Direct Labor		
+ Applied OH		
Total Mfg. Cost		

Cost of Goods Sold

Selling and Administrative Expenses

Payables and Other Liabilities

	85,000 1/1 Balance

Stockholder's Equity

	70,000 1/1 Balance

During January, the company had the following transactions:
a. Purchased $10,000 worth of raw materials on account.
b. Issued the following materials into production:

Item	Cost	Explanation
Direct materials	$7,000	Job 102, $2,000; Job 103, $5,000
Indirect materials	2,000	Used on both jobs
Total materials issued	$9,000	

c. Recorded salaries and wages payable as follows:

Item	Cost	Explanation
Direct labor	$10,000	Job 102, $6,000; Job 103, $4,000
Indirect labor	4,000	For factory supervision
Salaries	5,000	For administrative staff
Total payroll cost	$19,000	

d. Applied overhead to jobs based on the direct labor hours required:

Job Number	Direct Labor Hours
Job 102	300 hours
Job 103	200 hours
Total	500 hours

e. Recorded the following actual manufacturing costs:

Item	Cost	Explanation
Rent	$ 6,000	Paid factory rent in cash
Depreciation	5,000	Factory equipment
Insurance	3,000	Had one month of factory insurance policy expire
Utilities	2,000	Received factory utility bill but did not pay it
Total Cost	$16,000	

f. Recorded the following general and administrative costs:

Item	Cost	Explanation
Advertising	$ 2,000	Advertising paid in cash
Depreciation	3,000	Office equipment
Other expenses	1,000	Miscellaneous expenses owed but not paid
Total Cost	$ 6,000	

g. Sold Job 101, which is recorded in Finished Goods Inventory at a cost of $30,000, for $55,000.

h. Completed Job 102 but did not sell it; Job 103 is still in process at year-end.

Required:

1. Compute and interpret the predetermined overhead rate.
2. How much overhead would be applied to jobs during the period?
3. Compute the total cost of Jobs 102 and 103 at the end of the period. Where would the cost of each of these jobs appear on the year-end balance sheet?
4. Prepare journal entries to record the January transactions and post the entries to the general ledger T-accounts given earlier in the problem.
5. Calculate the amount of over- or underapplied overhead.
6. Prepare the journal entry to dispose of the overhead balance assuming that it had been a year-end balance instead of a month-end balance. Post the effect to the general ledger T-accounts.
7. Prepare a statement of cost of goods manufactured and sold report including the adjustment for over- or underapplied overhead.
8. Prepare a brief income statement for Sampson Company.

20 Process Costing and Activity Based Costing

LEARNING OBJECTIVES

After completing this chapter, you should be able to:

LO1   Describe the key features of a process costing system.

LO2   Prepare journal entries to record product costs using process costing.

LO3   Reconcile the number of physical units that were worked on during the period.

LO4   Calculate equivalent units of production using the FIFO method.

LO5   Prepare a process costing production report.

LO6   Calculate the cost of products using activity based costing.

Lectured presentation–LP20-1
www.mhhe.com/LLPW1e

Focus Company: CK MONDAVI FAMILY VINEYARDS

"Trust in a Family Name"

Why does a hamburger sell for $10 or more at an upscale restaurant when you can buy one at McDonald's for only a dollar or two? The same question can be asked about bottles of wine, which range in price from $5 to more than $50. While higher quality ingredients are used in the finer versions of these products, much of the difference in cost has to do with how the products are made. In other words, different resources, activities, and processes are used to create a dish in an upscale restaurant than to mass-produce standard variety fare at a fast-food franchise. Similarly, it takes different activities and processes to produce a truly outstanding bottle of wine than a more standard variety.

In this chapter, we study two methods that can be used to determine the cost of a product or service. **Process costing** is used to calculate the cost of highly similar (homogeneous) goods and services that are produced using standardized processes. McDonald's hamburgers and high-volume wine production would both fall into this category. Activity based costing (ABC) is appropriate for companies that offer a diverse range of products or services, some of which require more costly resources or activities than others. An example is a winery that produces its most popular wine in large batches using stainless steel containers, but also produces a small batch of "vintage reserve" that is aged in French oak barrels.

To illustrate these topics, we visit the CK Mondavi winery in Napa Valley, California. The Mondavi family history reads like a great American novel or soap opera.[1] In 1943, Italian immigrants Cesare and Rosa Mondavi purchased the Charles Krug (CK) winery, which had fallen on hard times during the depression. Sons Robert and Peter worked with their parents to turn the troubled winery into a successful business. Then in 1966, brotherly rivalry turned bitter when Peter took command of the family vineyards and Robert left, determined to build

[1] www.ckmondavi.com/family; www.charleskrug.com/familyhistory.

his own wine dynasty. Robert was extremely successful in that regard, turning the Mondavi name into a household brand. But he eventually lost control of his huge corporation and was forced to sell to Constellation Brands Inc.[2] Meanwhile, Peter Mondavi and his heirs continue to run the private family business (CK Mondavi) with an emphasis on quality and innovation.

Throughout this chapter, we use the CK Mondavi winery to demonstrate how to determine the cost of a bottle of wine. Although we will simplify things and the numbers we will use in our example are fictional, the accounting methods we show are actually used by wineries to determine the cost of their wines.

ORGANIZATION OF THE CHAPTER

BASIC CONCEPTS IN PROCESS COSTING	PROCESS COSTING PRODUCTION REPORT	ACTIVITY BASED COSTING (ABC)
• Job Order versus Process Costing • Flow of Costs in Process Costing • Journal Entries for Process Costing	• Step 1: Reconcile the Number of Physical Units • Step 2: Translate Physical Units into Equivalent Units • Step 3: Calculate Cost per Equivalent Unit • Step 4: Reconcile the Total Cost of Work in Process • Step 5: Prepare a Production Report • Additional Factors in Process Costing	• Step 1: Identify and Classify Activities • Step 2: Form Activity Cost Pools and Assign Indirect Costs to Each Pool • Step 3: Select an Activity Cost Driver and Calculate an Activity Rate for Each Cost Pool • Step 4: Assign Indirect Costs to Products or Services Based on Their Activity Demands

BASIC CONCEPTS IN PROCESS COSTING

In the last chapter, you learned about job order costing systems. This chapter introduces another type of costing system, process costing. Later in the chapter, you will also learn about a costing approach called activity based costing (ABC). ABC can be used with with either job order or process costing. For now, let's focus on the differences between job order and process costing.

Job Order versus Process Costing

Learning Objective 1

Describe the key features of a process costing system.

Job order costing is used by companies that offer **customized** products or services, such as a custom-built home, highway construction project, or legal defense. Because each individual product or customer is unique, a job cost sheet is used to keep track of the costs of each individual unit, or job, in a job order costing system.

Process costing is used by companies that produce **homogeneous** products or services using a series of standardized processes. Canned and bottled goods, frozen foods, paper products, and petroleum products are all examples of homogeneous products that result from a standardized process. Although process costing is most often identified with manufacturing companies, it can also be used in businesses that provide high-volume, standardized services, such as oil and filter changes at Jiffy Lube, standardized medical tests (X-rays, blood work at hospitals and clinics), and haircuts at Supercuts.

Because the products or services that result from standardized processes are the same, keeping a separate cost record for each individual unit is not necessary. Instead, process costing tracks the total cost of each production process and spreads that cost over the total number of units that flow through the process. See Exhibit 20.1 for a summary of the differences between job order and process costing.

Video 20-1
www.mhhe.com/LLPW1e

---

[2] Julia Flynn Siler, *The House of Mondavi: The Rise and Fall of an American Wine Dynasty*. New York: Gotham Books, 2007.

Exhibit 20.1	Job Order Costing versus Process Costing

	Job Order Costing	Process Costing
Type of product	Unique products and services, such as a custom-built ship	Homogeneous products and services, such as cans of soda
Manufacturing approach	Customized to the needs of the customer or client	Mass-production of products in series of standardized processes
Cost accumulation	Costs accumulated by job or customer	Costs accumulated by process
Major cost report	Job cost sheet for each unique unit, customer, or job	Production report for each major production process

Flow of Costs in Process Costing

Like job order costing, process costing relies on three inventory accounts to keep track of manufacturing costs:

- **Raw Materials Inventory** represents the cost of materials purchased from suppliers but not yet put into production.
- **Work in Process Inventory** represents the cost of units started in the manufacturing operation but not yet finished.
- **Finished Goods Inventory** represents the cost of units finished but not yet sold.

When the company sells the final product, it transfers the total manufacturing cost from Finished Goods Inventory to the **Cost of Goods Sold** account, where it will be reported as an expense and matched against sales revenue on the income statement. In terms of cost flows, the main difference between job order costing and process costing is that **process costing, has a different Work in Process Inventory account for each of the major processes the product must go through as it is being manufactured.**

See Exhibit 20.2 for an illustration of the process costing flow for a winery. As indicated, several production processes are required to convert raw materials (grapes) into the finished product (wine), including crushing, fermenting, aging, and bottling.

Wine making is an example of a **sequential** process. In other words, the grapes must be crushed before they can be fermented and then aged, which must occur before the wine can be bottled. Other companies may use a **parallel** processing approach in which more than one production process occurs at the same time. For example, Toyota Motor Company could have two different assembly processes running in parallel, one that produces engines and another that produces transmissions.

A process costing system will have a separate Work in Process Inventory account for each of the major processes the product must go through during production. To simplify our examples, we combine the crushing, fermenting, and aging processes into a single process, which we will refer to as the CFA process.

Recall from Chapter 19 that three categories of manufacturing cost must be traced to the product and recorded as inventory until the product is sold:

- **Direct materials** are the material inputs that can be traced directly to the product. For a winery, this category includes the cost of grapes and any other major material inputs, such as the bottles, labels, and boxes used in the packaging process.

Exhibit 20.2 Process Costing Flow for a Winery

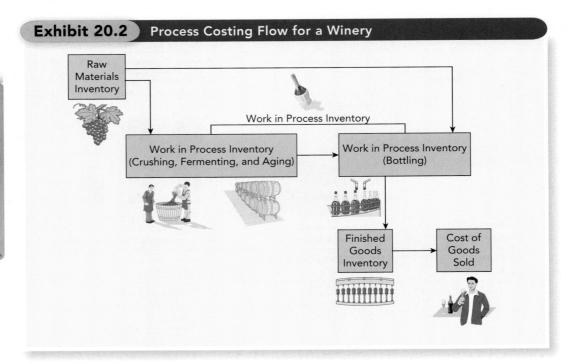

Conversion Cost =

Direct Labor
+
Manufacturing Overhead

- **Direct labor** is the cost of labor that can be traced directly to the product. This category includes the cost of manual labor involved in the process, such as the work of pouring the grapes into crushing bins, testing the fermenting mix, and bottling the wine.
- **Manufacturing overhead** includes all manufacturing costs **other than direct materials and direct labor** that must be incurred to make the final product. For a winery, this category includes rent or mortgage payments, insurance, utilities, equipment depreciation, and supervision.

Because today's wineries tend to be highly automated, direct labor is typically a very small portion of the total manufacturing cost. Thus, wineries and other process-oriented industries may combine direct labor and manufacturing overhead costs together in a single category called **conversion cost.** This category represents the total cost of converting raw materials (grapes) into the finished product (wine).

Remember that **nonmanufacturing costs,** including marketing, distribution, and general and administrative costs, are expensed during the period incurred rather than inventoried as part of the cost of the final product.

Journal Entries for Process Costing

Learning Objective 2

Prepare journal entries to record product costs using process costing.

In this section, we focus on the journal entries that record the flow of manufacturing costs in a process costing system. For the sake of simplicity, we begin our example on the first day of operations. Thus, there are no beginning balances in any of the accounts.

Purchase of Raw Materials

When materials are purchased, they are recorded in the Raw Materials Inventory account. Assume, for example, that CK Mondavi purchased $35,000 of direct materials (grapes, bottles, and corks) on account from various suppliers. The journal entry to record the purchase of raw materials is:

	Debit	Credit
Raw Materials Inventory	35,000	
Accounts Payable		35,000

Issue of Raw Materials into Production

When raw materials are taken out of storage and placed into production, the cost is debited to the Work in Process Inventory account for the first production process. Assume, for example, that $20,000 worth of grapes is added to the CFA process. The journal entry to record the issue of direct materials into production is:

	Debit	Credit
Work in Process Inventory (CFA)	20,000	
Raw Materials Inventory		20,000

Recording Actual and Applied Conversion Costs

Remember that conversion costs include direct labor and manufacturing overhead. Most accounting systems will maintain a separate general ledger account for each of these components. However, direct labor is likely to be a very small percentage of the total conversion cost in a winery and many other process-oriented industries. For this reason, we will combine direct labor and manufacturing overhead in a single account called Conversion Cost. This account is almost identical to the Manufacturing Overhead account we used in Chapter 19, except that it now includes a small amount of direct labor cost. We will use this account to record actual and applied conversion cost, just as we recorded actual and applied manufacturing overhead in Chapter 19. Actual costs will be debited to the Conversion Cost account and applied costs will be credited to the Conversion Cost account. Any difference between actual and applied conversion cost will be transferred to Cost of Goods Sold at the end of the accounting period.

To illustrate this process, assume that CK Mondavi incurred the following actual conversion costs:

Direct labor and supervision paid	$16,000
Winery utilities owed but not yet paid	5,000
Depreciation on winery equipment	15,250
Total conversion cost	$36,250

These actual conversion costs would be debited to the Conversion Cost account. Depending on the nature of the transaction, the credit would be to Cash, Payables, Prepaid Assets, or Accumulated Depreciation. The journal entry to record the actual conversion costs follows.

	Debit	Credit
Conversion Cost	36,250	
Cash		16,000
Utilities Payable		5,000
Accumulated Depreciation		15,250

Conversion costs are then applied to Work in Process Inventory using a predetermined allocation base. For example, a winery might apply conversion cost based on the number of barrels, the number of fermentation tanks, or the cost of the grapes that are processed. Direct labor hours and machine hours are also common allocation bases. Assume that CK Mondavi applies conversion cost in the CFA process at a rate equal to 125 percent of direct materials cost. In other words, for every $1.00 of direct materials cost, an additional $1.25 must be applied to cover the direct labor and manufacturing overhead costs. In a preceding transaction, we recorded the issue of $20,000 worth of direct materials into the CFA Work in Process account. Now we need to apply $25,000 ($20,000 × 125%) of conversion cost to Work in Process. The journal entry to apply the conversion cost to the Work in Process Inventory account follows.

	Debit	Credit
Work in Process Inventory (CFA)	25,000	
Conversion Cost		25,000

At the end of the accounting period, we will need to account for any difference in actual and applied conversion cost. We will do this after we have recorded all transactions for this example.

> **Coach's Tip**
>
> The process of accounting for conversion cost is the same as the process we used for manufacturing overhead in the last chapter. The only difference is that conversion cost also includes a small amount of direct labor. These costs were directly traced to jobs in the last chapter but are treated as indirect costs in this chapter.

Exhibit 20.3   Summary of Recorded Transactions

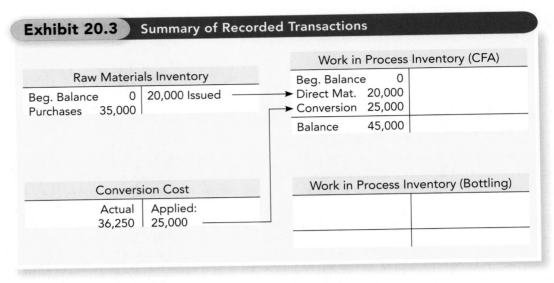

Transfer of Cost from One Work in Process Inventory Account to the Next

Once the wine has completed the CFA process, its total manufacturing cost must be transferred to the bottling process. See Exhibit 20.3 for a summary of the costs that have been recorded to this point.

Note that a total of $45,000 has been recorded in the CFA Work in Process Inventory account. This cost needs to be transferred out of Work in Process Inventory (CFA) and into the next process (Bottling), which will have its own Work in Process Inventory account. The journal entry to transfer the total manufacturing costs from one process to the other follows:

	Debit	Credit
Work in Process Inventory (Bottling)	45,000	
Work in Process Inventory (CFA)		45,000

Once the wine is in the bottling process, the company will incur more direct material costs for items such as bottles, corks, and boxes. Assume that CK Mondavi issues $10,000 worth of direct materials into the bottling process. The journal entry to record the issue of these direct materials into production is:

	Debit	Credit
Work in Process Inventory (Bottling)	10,000	
Raw Materials Inventory		10,000

Next we need to apply conversion cost to the bottling department's Work in Process Inventory account. Let's assume that the rate for applying conversion cost to the bottling process is 87.5 percent of direct materials cost. Because we just recorded $10,000 in direct materials cost, we need to apply an additional $8,750 ($10,000 × 87.5%) in conversion cost. The journal entry to apply conversion cost to the Work in Process Inventory account is:

	Debit	Credit
Work in Process Inventory (Bottling)	8,750	
Conversion Cost		8,750

Exhibit 20.4 shows the updated T-accounts.

Exhibit 20.4   Updated Summary of Recorded Transactions

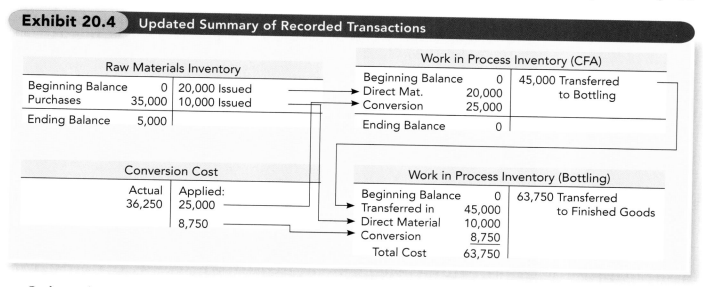

So far, we have recorded a total of $63,750 in the Work in Process Inventory (Bottling) account. Once the wine is through the bottling process, this amount will be transferred to Finished Goods Inventory. The journal entry to transfer cost from the last Work in Process account to Finished Goods Inventory is:

	Debit	Credit
Finished Goods Inventory	63,750	
Work in Process Inventory (Bottling)		63,750

Assuming that the $63,750 transferred to the Finished Goods Inventory account represents the cost of processing 15,000 bottles (or 1,250 cases) of wine, the costs per case and per bottle would be calculated as follows:

Total manufacturing cost	$63,750
Total number of cases	1,250
Total number of bottles	15,000
Cost per case ($63,750/1,250)	$ 51.00
Cost per bottle ($63,750/15,000)	$ 4.25

If CK Mondavi sold 12,000 bottles (1,000 cases) of this wine in the winery gift shop at a retail price of $8 per bottle, we would make additional journal entries to record cost of goods sold and sales revenue. The journal entry to record the cost of goods sold for 12,000 bottles at a cost of $4.25 per bottle is:

	Debit	Credit
Cost of Goods Sold (12,000 × $4.25)	51,000	
Finished Goods Inventory		51,000

The journal entry to record the sale of 12,000 bottles at a price of $8 per bottle is:

	Debit	Credit
Cash (12,000 × $8.00)	96,000	
Sales Revenue		96,000

Notice that the $4.25 cost per bottle was based on the amount of conversion cost **applied** to the Work in Process Inventory accounts, then transferred to Finished Goods Inventory and Cost of Goods Sold. But what if **actual** conversion costs was more or less than **applied** conversion cost? The Conversion Cost account for our example may be summarized as follows:

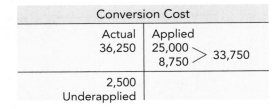

Conversion Cost	
Actual	Applied
36,250	25,000
	8,750 > 33,750
2,500	
Underapplied	

This account shows that actual conversion cost was $36,250, but only $33,750 was applied. In short, conversion cost was **underapplied** by $2,500.

Because most of the applied conversion cost is now in the Cost of Goods Sold account, the easiest way to handle the $2,500 in underapplied conversion cost is to increase Cost of Goods Sold. The journal entry to adjust for $2,500 in underapplied conversion cost is:

	Debit	Credit
Cost of Goods Sold	2,500	
Conversion Cost		2,500

If the conversion cost had been **overapplied,** we would have **decreased** Cost of Goods Sold. Thus, the journal entry just given would be reversed (that is, Conversion Cost would be debited and Cost of Goods Sold would be credited). See Exhibit 20.5 for the Cost of Goods Sold and Finished Goods Inventory accounts after these entries have been made.

Exhibit 20.5   **Final Summary of Recorded Transactions**

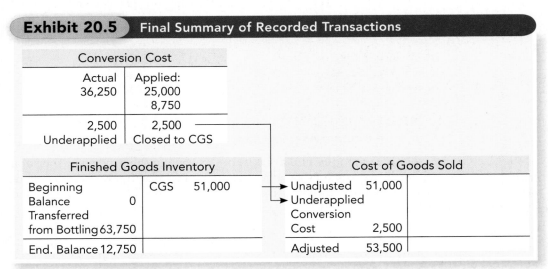

Conversion Cost	
Actual	Applied:
36,250	25,000
	8,750
2,500	2,500
Underapplied	Closed to CGS

Finished Goods Inventory		
Beginning Balance 0	CGS	51,000
Transferred from Bottling 63,750		
End. Balance 12,750		

Cost of Goods Sold	
Unadjusted 51,000	
Underapplied Conversion Cost 2,500	
Adjusted 53,500	

The example we have just illustrated shows how process costing works in a simplified production environment. Unfortunately, in the real world, production processes are not usually so simple. Specifically, the company may have units that are only partially complete at the end of an accounting period. For example, wine needs to age for months, or even years, before it is ready for bottling. How do we account for wine that is still in barrels at the end of an accounting period? According to Generally Accepted Accounting Principles (GAAP), the manufacturing cost of units that are not yet sold must be counted as inventory. But how do we value a partially complete unit? This question is the focus of the next section. First,

Coach's Tip

A debit balance indicates that actual conversion cost was more than applied conversion cost; that is, conversion cost was underapplied. Overapplied conversion cost would be reflected by a credit balance (because the applied cost was more than the actual cost).

Coach's Tip

For simplicity, we will close the entire amount of underapplied conversion cost to the Cost of Goods Sold account. A more precise approach would have been to adjust the Work in Process Inventory, Finished Goods Inventory, and Cost of Goods Sold accounts based on the amount of conversion cost in each (if any). This more complicated method is covered in intermediate-level accounting books.

make sure you understand the basic concepts of process costing by completing the following Self-Study Practice.

SELF-STUDY PRACTICE

1. Which of the following statements about process costing is false?

   a. Process costing is used in companies that produce very homogeneous products or services.

   b. Process costing uses the same type of inventory accounts as job order costing to record the flow of manufacturing costs.

   c. Process costing will typically have more Work in Process Inventory accounts than job order costing will.

   d. Process costing keeps a separate record, or cost sheet, for each unit produced.

   e. All of these statements are true.

2. The journal entry to apply conversion cost to Work in Process Inventory would include a:

   a. Debit to Work in Process Inventory.

   b. Debit to Conversion Cost.

   c. Credit to Conversion Cost.

   d. Credit to Cash, Accounts Payables, and other accounts.

   e. A and C.

   f. B and D.

3. The journal entry to record actual conversion costs would include a:

   a. Debit to Work in Process Inventory.

   b. Debit to Conversion Cost.

   c. Credit to Conversion Cost.

   d. Credit to Cash, Accounts Payables, and other accounts.

   e. A and C.

   f. B and D.

After you have finished, check your answers with the solutions at the bottom of the page.

PROCESS COSTING PRODUCTION REPORT

The production report is the main report in a process costing system. It provides information about manufacturing costs and the number of units that flowed into and out of the production process during a given period. A separate report is prepared for each production process on either a monthly or a quarterly basis.

In this section we discuss how to prepare a production report for the crushing, fermenting, and aging (CFA) process at CK Mondavi. For this process, we define a unit as one barrel of wine. About 740 pounds of crushed grapes are required to fill a standard barrel of wine. After the crushed grapes have been fermented and the wine aged for an appropriate period, the barrels are transferred to the next process (Bottling). Each barrel yields about 300 bottles, or 25 cases, of wine.

To prepare the production report we use four steps:

1. Reconcile the number of physical units worked on during the period.

2. Translate physical units into equivalent units.

1. d
2. e
3. f

Solution to
Self-Study Practice

3. Calculate the cost per equivalent unit.

4. Reconcile the total cost of Work in Process Inventory.

First, however, we must make an assumption about how the units flow through the production process. In this chapter, we assume that they follow a first-in, first-out (FIFO) pattern in which the units that were started first are also completed first. For most process-oriented industries, this assumption is a reasonable one.

An alternative approach, the weighted average method, averages the cost of units in beginning inventory with the cost of units started during the current period. This method works well for companies that do not maintain large amounts of inventory or have very stable inventory levels. We present the weighted average method in Supplement 20.

Step 1: Reconcile the Number of Physical Units

Learning Objective 3

Reconcile the number of physical units that were worked on during the period.

The first step in preparing a production report is to reconcile the number of physical units. To do so, we first calculate the total number of units worked on during the period by adding the number of units in beginning inventory to the number of units started during the current period. Then we determine whether those units were completed during the period or were still being worked on at the end of the period. The formula to reconcile the number of physical units is as follows:

Coach's Tip

This formula ignores any units that may have been lost due to spoilage or waste. Accounting for lost or spoiled units is covered in more advanced accounting texts.

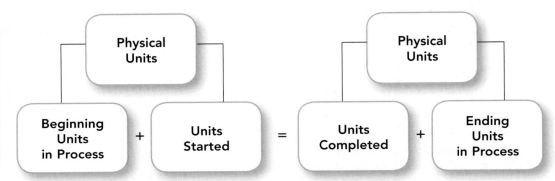

As an example, assume CK Mondavi had 200 barrels of wine in process at the start of a new accounting period. Last period's production report valued these partially complete units at $165,600. During the period, workers started another 1,800 barrels into the CFA process. At the end of the period, 400 barrels of wine were still in the CFA process. Based on this information, can you answer this question: How many barrels of wine were transferred out of the CFA process and into bottling during the current period?

To answer this question, we can prepare a reconciliation of physical units as follows:

Coach's Tip

The number of units completed is 1,600. A total of 2,000 units were worked on during the period, and 400 of them were still being worked on at the end of the period, so 1,600 of them must have been completed.

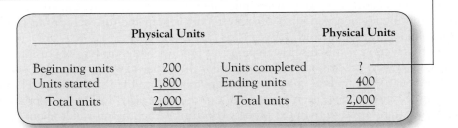

	Physical Units		Physical Units
Beginning units	200	Units completed	?
Units started	1,800	Ending units	400
Total units	2,000	Total units	2,000

We must account for a total of 2,000 units, 200 that were on hand at the beginning of the period plus 1,800 that were started this period. If we only have 400 on hand at the end of the period, we must have completed 1,600 units.

The next step is to determine how many units were both started **and** completed during the current period. Those units would have made it all the way through the CFA process during the current period, so they would not be part of either beginning or ending inventory, as the following formula shows:

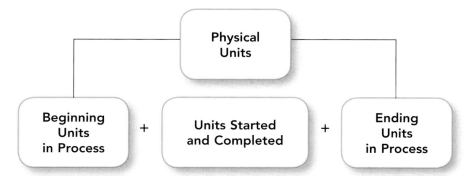

Remember that FIFO assumes that the units in beginning inventory were completed first. Thus, not all units that were completed during the current period were started during the current period; the units that were in the beginning inventory were started during the last period. Likewise, some of the units that were started during the period were not completed; they remain in the ending inventory.

In our example, we had a total of 2,000 physical units to account for: 200 from the beginning inventory plus 1,800 that were started during the period. During the period, 1,600 units were completed; 400 were still in process at the end of the period. How many units were both started **and** completed during the current period? The answer is 1,400 units, as shown in the following formulas:

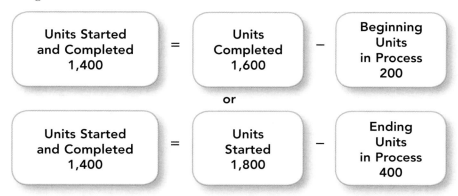

To summarize step 1, the number of physical units worked on during the period can be reconciled as follows:

	Physical Units
Beginning inventory	200
Started **and** completed	1,400
Ending inventory	400
Total units	2,000

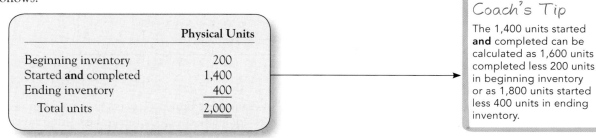

Coach's Tip

The 1,400 units started **and** completed can be calculated as 1,600 units completed less 200 units in beginning inventory or as 1,800 units started less 400 units in ending inventory.

Step 2: Translate Physical Units into Equivalent Units

The next step in preparing the production report is to calculate the number of equivalent units. An equivalent unit is a measure of the amount of work or effort expended during the current period to produce both fully and partially completed units. Why must we calculate equivalent units? Companies often have units in process at the beginning and end of an accounting period. Even though those units are incomplete, their cost must be recorded on the balance sheet as Work in Process Inventory. Remember that GAAP requires all manufacturing costs to be counted as part of the cost of the product and reported as inventory (an asset) until the product is sold. By converting partially completed units into equivalent units, we can assign an appropriate value to those units for financial statement reporting.

Learning Objective 4

Calculate equivalent units of production using the FIFO method.

To illustrate the calculation of equivalent units in our winery example, we assume the following additional details about the CFA process at CK Mondavi.

- Direct materials (grapes) are added at the beginning of the process. Thus, once a unit has started the CFA process, it will have 100 percent of the required direct materials.
- Conversion costs (direct labor and manufacturing overhead) are incurred uniformly throughout the process.
- The 200 units in beginning inventory were 70 percent through the CFA process. For these units, all direct materials and 70 percent of the conversion cost were incurred **in the last period.**
- Only 1,400 of the units that were started during the current period were completed during the current period. Thus, those units made it all the way through the CFA process without getting "stuck" in beginning or ending inventory.
- The 400 units in ending inventory were 60 percent through the CFA conversion process. Thus, these units have all required direct materials (crushed grapes) but only 60 percent of the conversion effort (fermenting and aging).

These details are presented in the form of a diagram of the production process in Exhibit 20.6.

Exhibit 20.6   Diagram of the Crushing, Fermenting, and Aging (CFA) Process, FIFO Method

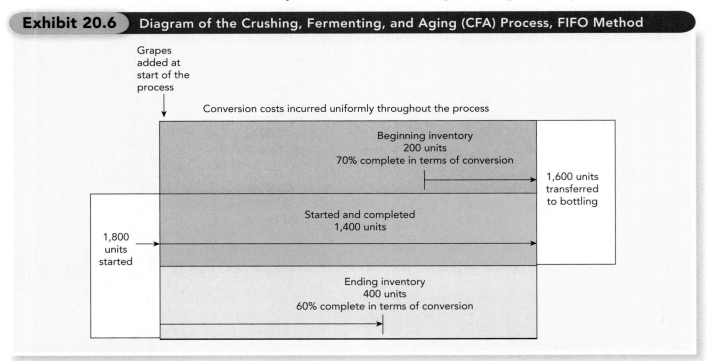

To calculate the number of equivalent units, we need to consider how much work was done during the **current** period to complete the 200 units in beginning inventory, to produce 1,400 units from start to finish, and to get the 400 units in ending inventory 60 percent complete with respect to conversion cost. This calculation must be made separately for direct materials and conversion costs because each of those costs are added at different points in the production process. See Exhibit 20.7 for a summary of the calculation of equivalent units.

Because direct materials are added at the beginning of the process, we did not need to add any direct materials to the beginning inventory during the current period. Thus, for the beginning inventory, we calculate zero equivalent units of direct materials. Because those units were already 70 percent of the way through the conversion process, they required only 30 percent conversion effort during the current period. So, we multiply the 200 physical units by 30 percent to arrive at 60 equivalent units of conversion cost for the beginning inventory units.

The 1,400 units that were started **and** completed went all the way through the CFA process during the current period. Because all work on those units happened during the current period, the number of equivalent units is the same as the number of physical units.

Exhibit 20.7   **Calculation of Equivalent Units, FIFO Method**

| | Physical Units | EQUIVALENT UNITS | |
		Direct Materials	Conversion Cost
Beginning inventory	200	0 (200 × (100% − 100%))	60 (200 × (100% − 70%))
Started and completed	1,400	1,400 (1,400 × 100%)	1,400 (1,400 × 100%)
Ending inventory	400	400 (400 × 100%)	240 (400 × 60%)
Total	2,000	1,800	1,700

The 400 units in ending inventory were started during the current period and received the entire amount of direct materials at the beginning of the process. Thus, the number of equivalent units for direct materials is the same as the 400 physical units in ending inventory. Those units went only 60 percent of the way through the conversion process during the current period, however. Therefore, the number of equivalent units for conversion would be 60 percent of the 400 units in ending inventory, or 240.

Finally, we calculate the number of total equivalent units by adding the number of equivalent units for beginning inventory, units started and completed, and ending inventory. This calculation gives us 1,800 equivalent units of direct materials and 1,700 equivalent units of conversion cost. In the next step of preparing the production report, we use these numbers to calculate the cost per equivalent unit.

> **Coach's Tip**
>
> To calculate the number of equivalent units, ask yourself the following questions: What did we do during the **current** period to get the beginning inventory units from 70 percent complete to fully complete? What did we do during the **current** period to start the ending inventory units and get them 60 percent complete?

Step 3: Calculate Cost per Equivalent Unit

To calculate the cost per equivalent unit under FIFO, we divide the current period's costs by the total number of equivalent units calculated in Step 2, as follows:

$$\text{Cost per Equivalent Unit} = \frac{\text{Current Period Costs}}{\text{Equivalent Units}}$$

Only current period costs are included in this calculation because **equivalent units relate only to work that was performed during the current period.** We do not include the cost of beginning inventory because those costs were incurred in a prior period. Because the number of equivalent units differs for direct materials and conversion cost, we must calculate each category separately.

Exhibit 20.8 shows the cost per equivalent unit calculations for our winery example. The cost per equivalent unit is $450 for direct materials and $540 for conversion. In the next step, we use these costs per equivalent unit to determine the cost of the units completed and transferred to bottling as well as the cost of the units that are still in process.

Exhibit 20.8   **Calculation of the Cost per Equivalent Unit, FIFO Method**

	Direct Materials	Conversion Cost
Current Period Cost (given)	$810,000	$918,000
Equivalent Units (from Exhibit 20.7)	÷ 1,800	÷ 1,700
Cost per Equivalent Unit	$ 450	$ 540

Step 4: Reconcile the Total Cost of Work in Process

The final step in preparing the production report is to reconcile the total cost recorded in the Work in Process account. Its total cost includes the cost that was already in the account at the beginning of the period plus the direct materials and conversion costs that were added to the process during the period. See the following T-account for the costs for our winery example.

Work in Process Inventory (CFA)			
Beginning Balance	165,600	Cost of Goods Completed	
Direct Materials	810,000	and Transferred to Bottling	?
Conversion Cost Applied	918,000		
	1,893,600		
Ending Balance	?		

In all, we need to account for a total cost of $1,893,600 for the CFA process. A portion of this cost will be transferred out of the CFA process and into the next department (Bottling), and part of it will remain in the CFA department as the ending balance in Work in Process Inventory.

Notice that $165,600 of this cost relates to the units that were already in process at the beginning of the period. Because FIFO assumes that these units are completed first, the cost of the beginning inventory is transferred out of the Work in Process Inventory account with the units that are completed and transferred. The $810,000 and $918,000 represent the current period's costs, which were included in the calculation of the cost per equivalent unit in Step 3. To determine how much of this cost should be transferred out and how much should remain in ending inventory, we must multiply the cost per equivalent unit (from Exhibit 20.8) by the number of equivalent units (calculated in Exhibit 20.7). See Exhibit 20.9 for the calculations.

- The 200 units in beginning inventory carried a cost of $165,600 from the prior period. During the current period, the company incurred an additional 60 equivalent units of conversion at a cost of $540 per equivalent unit, for a total cost of $32,400 (60 × $540). Under the FIFO cost assumption, the total cost of the beginning inventory $198,000 ($165,600 + $32,400) is transferred out of the department with the units completed.
- The 1,400 units that were started **and** completed during the current period would be transferred out at the full cost per equivalent unit of $450 for direct materials and $540 for conversion, for a total cost of $1,386,000 [1,400 × ($450 + $540)].

Exhibit 20.9	Calculation of the Cost of Goods Completed and Ending Inventory Costs, FIFO Method

CURRENT PERIOD COSTS

EQUIVALENT UNITS × COST PER EQUIVALENT UNIT

	Prior Period Costs	Direct Materials	Conversion Cost	Total Cost Accounted for	
Beginning inventory	$165,600	—	60 × $540 = $ 32,400	$ 198,000	$1,584,000 cost of goods completed and transferred
Started and completed	—	1,400 × $450 = $630,000	1,400 × $540 = 756,000	1,386,000	
Ending inventory	—	400 × $450 = 180,000	240 × $540 = 129,600	309,600	
Total cost to account for	$165,600	$810,000	$918,000	$1,893,600	

- The total cost transferred out of CFA work in process (for the units in beginning inventory plus the units started and completed) is $1,584,000 ($198,000 + $1,386,000). This cost would be debited to the next Work in Process Inventory account (bottling).
- The 400 units that remain in ending inventory are valued at the full $450 per equivalent unit for direct materials or $180,000 (400 × $450). The conversion cost attached to these units would be $129,600 (240 equivalent units × $540 per equivalent unit), for a total ending inventory cost of $309,600 ($180,000 + $129,600).

After we transfer $1,584,000 out of the Work in Process Inventory (CFA) account, the $309,600 cost of the ending inventory units remain in the Work in Process Inventory (CFA) account as in the following T-account.

Work in Process Inventory (CFA)			
Beginning Balance	165,600	Cost of Goods Completed	1,584,000
Direct Materials	810,000	and Transferred to Bottling	
Conversion Cost Applied	918,000		
Ending Balance	309,600		

Step 5: Prepare a Production Report

The final step in process costing is to summarize the results of Steps 1–4 into a single document called the production report. The production report is essentially a summary of what occurred in the production process during the accounting period. It includes information about the number of physical units (Step 1) and equivalent units (Step 2) as well as cost per equivalent unit (Step 3), and a reconciliation of the cost of work in process (Step 4).

Refer to Exhibit 20.10 for the production report based on Steps 1–4 for our winery example. This single document summarizes the four steps we followed to determine the cost of the CFA process.

> **Learning Objective 5**
>
> Prepare a process costing production report.

Exhibit 20.10   FIFO Process Costing Production Report

CK Mondavi Winery
Process Costing Production Report (FIFO Method)
Crushing, Fermenting and Aging (CFA) Department
For the Quarter Ended March 31, 2009

		Step 1 Reconcile Physical Units	Step 2 Calculate Equivalent Units		
UNITS			Direct Materials	Conversion	
1 Units to be accounted for:					
2 Beginning work in process		200			
3 Started into production		1,800			
4 Total units		2,000			
5					
6 Units accounted for as follows:					
7 Beginning work in process		200	0	60	
8 Started and completed		1,400	1,400	1,400	
9 Ending work in process		400	400	240	
10 Total units		2,000	1,800	1,700	
11 **COSTS**			Step 3: Calculate cost per equivalent unit		
12					
13			Direct Materials	Conversion	
14 Current period costs:			$ 810,000	$ 918,000	
15 Equivalent units (Row 10)			1,800	1,700	
16 Cost per equivalent unit			$ 450	$ 540	
17			Step 4: Reconcile the total cost of work in process		
Cost to be accounted for:			Direct Materials	Conversion	Total
18 Beginning work in process					$ 165,600
19 Current period costs			$ 810,000	$ 918,000	1,728,000
20 Total cost					$ 1,893,600
21					
22 Cost accounted for as follows:					
23 Beginning inventory balance (transferred out)					$ 165,600
24 Cost to complete beginning inentory (Row 7 x Row 16)			$ -	$ 32,400	32,400
25 Started and completed (Row 8 x Row 16)			630,000	756,000	1,386,000
26 Ending inventory (Row 9 x Row 16)			180,000	129,600	309,600
27 Total cost					$ 1,893,600

Additional Factors in Process Costing

The example you have just studied illustrates most aspects of process costing. However, you should be aware of two issues that were not included in the example. First, as was mentioned earlier, many process-oriented companies use an alternative method called weighted average process costing. The weighted average method does not separately account for the units in beginning inventory. Instead, it assumes that all units completed were started during the current period. As long as a company has minimal or very stable inventory levels, this method will approximate the results of FIFO.

Supplement 20 illustrates the weighted average method using the same data we used for our winery example. Your instructor may want you to learn the FIFO method, the weighted average method, or both. The steps for preparing the production report are the same. The only difference is how you treat the units and costs of the beginning inventory.

The second issue we did not consider is how to account for subsequent departments in process costing. We showed the first process in the production chain (CFA), but we did not extend the example to show how costs flow through the next process (Bottling). The cost of the wine transferred out of the CFA process ($1,584,000) would enter the Work in Process Inventory (Bottling) account in the same way that the cost of direct materials (grapes) were added to the Work in Process Inventory (CFA) account. Each subsequent department must then keep track of the costs that were transferred in from the prior departments in addition to the costs that are added during the process.

Before we move to activity based costing, make sure you understand the steps necessary to prepare a production report by completing the following Self-Study Practice.

SELF-STUDY PRACTICE

Aqua-Fit manufactures and sells fitness drinks (with added vitamins and minerals) to fitness clubs across the country. The company uses a FIFO process costing system to determine the cost of the fitness drinks. All materials (water, juice, vitamins, and bottles) are added at the beginning of the process, and conversion costs are added uniformly.

At the start of the most recent period, the company had 1,000 bottles that were about 40 percent through the conversion process. During the period, an additional 9,000 bottles were started in the process. The period ended with 3,000 bottles that were 20 percent of the way through the process.

1. How many units were **completed** during the period?
2. How many units were **started and completed** during the period?
3. How many equivalent units of conversion would be required to **complete** the beginning inventory?
4. Calculate the equivalent units of direct materials and conversion for the units in ending inventory.

After you have finished, check your answers with the solutions at the bottom of the page.

Video 20-2
www.mhhe.com/LLPW1e

ACTIVITY BASED COSTING (ABC)

We started this chapter by asking what makes a $5 bottle of wine different from a $50 bottle of wine. To answer this question, we expand our example to assume that CK Mondavi produces two types of wine. The first is a standard-variety chardonnay produced in large batches and aged for a relatively short period (about four months) in large metal containers called vats. The vats are very easy to clean and maintain and can be reused hundreds of times before they wear out. This wine is the company's highest volume product. Over the years, Mondavi has learned to produce it with a minimum of quality testing on each batch.

Solution to
Self-Study Practice

1. 7,000 (1,000 + 9,000 − 3,000)
2. 6,000 (7,000 − 1,000) or (9,000 − 3,000)
3. 600 [1,000 × (100% − 40%)]
4. 3,000 equivalent units of direct materials, 600 equivalent units of conversion (3,000 × 20%)

The second wine is a limited-edition cabernet that is made in very small batches from premium grapes and then aged for more than three years in special French oak barrels to provide a particular taste. The barrels require significant maintenance between batches and can be used only a few times before they lose some of the oak flavor that they transfer to the wine. The company maintains extremely tight quality control over this wine to ensure that it is produced to the most exacting standards.

In this scenario, averaging the manufacturing costs of the two products does not make sense. The chardonnay, which is produced in high volume, accumulates more of certain kinds of costs, but the limited-edition cabernet requires more care and attention. This situation is precisely what activity based costing was designed for.

Activity Based Costing (ABC) is a method of assigning indirect costs to products and services based on the underlying activities performed in the manufacturing process. Costs related to direct materials and direct labor can be traced directly to individual products or services so they are assigned directly to those products or services as they are incurred. Indirect costs, which cannot be directly traced to a specific product or service, are assigned using an **allocation base** or **cost driver**:

Learning Objective 6

Calculate the cost of products using activity based costing.

Most traditional (non-ABC) cost systems use measures such as number of direct labor hours, machine hours, or direct materials cost to apply indirect costs to products or services. We call these measures **volume-based allocation measures** because they are directly related to the number of units produced or the number of customers served. Volume-based allocation measures generally assign the highest cost to the products with the highest volume. In our example, a volume-based measure would assign higher cost to the standard chardonnay than to the limited-edition cabernet simply because the chardonnay is produced in higher volume and therefore requires more total labor hours, machine hours, and direct materials cost.

Unlike traditional cost systems which rely strictly on volume-based allocation measures, ABC systems include measures that capture something other than the volume of units produced or sold. These measures are called **nonvolume-based cost drivers**. Some common examples of volume-based and nonvolume-based measures are:

Volume-Based Allocation Measures (used in traditional cost systems)	Nonvolume-Based Cost Drivers (used in activity based costing)
Number of units produced	Number of batches or setup time
Number of direct labor hours	Processing time per unit
Number of machine hours	Number of quality inspections
Direct materials cost	Number of design changes

Coach's Tip

A traditional (non-ABC) costing system includes only volume-based measures such as those in the left column. An ABC system may include some volume measures, but it also includes nonvolume-based measures, such as those in the right column.

By incorporating allocation measures that capture other aspects of the production process besides volume, ABC can assign more cost to products that require more setup time, longer processing, more quality control, or more engineering. In our winery example, an ABC system would assign more cost to the limited edition cabernet than to the standard chardonnay because the cabernet is produced in small batches and requires more setups, longer aging, and more quality control.

Activity based costing involves four basic steps:

1. Identify and classify activities.
2. Form activity cost pools and assign indirect costs to each pool.
3. Select an activity cost driver and calculate an activity rate for each cost pool.
4. Assign indirect costs to products or services based on their activity demands.

Video 20-3
www.mhhe.com/LLPW1e

In the following sections, we use the example of CK Mondavi to complete these steps.

Step 1: Identify and Classify Activities

The first step in activity based costing is to identify all activities that must occur to make a product or provide a service and then classify them into one of the following categories:

- **Unit level activities** are performed for each unit or customer (one at a time).
- **Batch-level activities** are performed all at once for a group of units or customers.
- **Product-level activities** are performed to support a specific product line.
- **Customer-level activities** are performed for a specific customer.
- **Facility-level activities** are performed for the overall company to benefit multiple customers or product lines.

For a sample of activities as CK Mondavi would categorize them, see Exhibit 20.11.

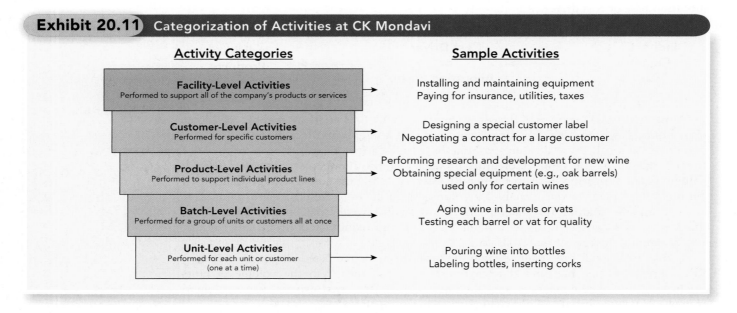

Exhibit 20.11 Categorization of Activities at CK Mondavi

Activity Categories

Facility-Level Activities	Sample Activities
Performed to support all of the company's products or services	Installing and maintaining equipment / Paying for insurance, utilities, taxes
Customer-Level Activities Performed for specific customers	Designing a special customer label / Negotiating a contract for a large customer
Product-Level Activities Performed to support individual product lines	Performing research and development for new wine / Obtaining special equipment (e.g., oak barrels) used only for certain wines
Batch-Level Activities Performed for a group of units or customers all at once	Aging wine in barrels or vats / Testing each barrel or vat for quality
Unit-Level Activities Performed for each unit or customer (one at a time)	Pouring wine into bottles / Labeling bottles, inserting corks

Step 2: Form Activity Cost Pools and Assign Indirect Costs to Each Pool

The next ABC step is to combine related activities into activity cost pools. The goal is to create as few activity cost pools as possible (to keep the approach manageable) while capturing the major activities identified in Step 1 (to provide useful information). Assume that CK Mondavi has determined that the following five categories capture its major production activities:

- Purchasing, receiving, and crushing grapes.
- Setting up and maintaining equipment.
- Fermenting and aging the wine in barrels.
- Performing quality control.
- Bottling and labeling the wine.

Next we must determine how much indirect cost CK Mondavi incurred to support each of these activities. Doing so means taking a detailed look at the Manufacturing Overhead Cost account to determine how much each activity costs. For example, managers at the winery might determine that the salary of a materials purchasing agent is related primarily to purchasing, receiving, and crushing the grapes. Similarly, the cost of setting up and maintaining the equipment would belong in the setup activity cost pool. The quality control supervisor's salary would be assigned to the quality control pool. Depreciation on the barrels used in the fermenting and aging process would be assigned to fermenting and aging, and the cost of the equipment used in bottling and packaging would be assigned to the bottling and packaging pool.

Some indirect costs may need to be spread over or allocated to more than one activity. For example, a production supervisor might be responsible for overseeing all five activities; thus, the supervisor's salary would be allocated to all five activities based on the amount of supervisory time spent on each. In this example, we assume CK Mondavi has divided a total of $880,000 in manufacturing overhead cost among the five activity cost pools as in the following diagram.

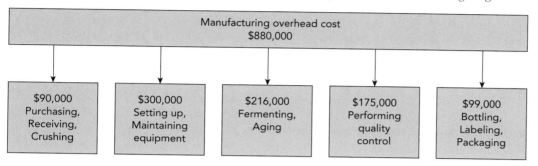

Step 3: Select an Activity Cost Driver and Calculate an Activity Rate for Each Cost Pool

The next step is to select an activity cost driver for each of the cost pools created in Step 2. An activity cost driver is an underlying measure that is used to assign the activity that occurs in an activity cost pool to individual products and services. Assume that CK Mondavi has identified the following cost drivers for its five activity cost pools:

- Purchasing, receiving, and crushing is driven by the weight (pounds) of grapes purchased, received, and then crushed.
- Setting up and maintaining equipment is driven by the number of setups.
- Fermenting and aging is driven by the number of days the wine remains in the vat or barrel.
- Quality control is driven by the number of quality inspections.
- Bottling, labeling and packaging is driven by the number of bottles processed.

We can incorporate these cost drivers in our diagram of the activity cost pools:

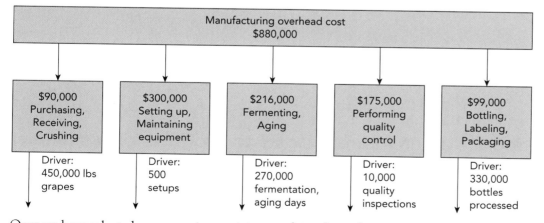

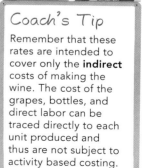

Once we have selected an appropriate activity cost driver for each cost pool, we can calculate the activity rate by dividing the total cost of each pool by the total activity cost driver, as follows:

$$\text{Activity Rate} = \frac{\text{Total Activity Cost}}{\text{Total Activity Driver}}$$

Coach's Tip

The process of assigning indirect costs to the activity cost pools is sometimes referred to as the first stage of allocation under activity based costing. In this chapter, our primary focus is on the second stage that assigns costs to products and services based on their activity cost drivers.

Coach's Tip

Remember that these rates are intended to cover only the **indirect** costs of making the wine. The cost of the grapes, bottles, and direct labor can be traced directly to each unit produced and thus are not subject to activity based costing.

Exhibit 20.12   Calculation of CK Mondavi's Activity Rates

Activity Cost Pool	Total Indirect Cost	/ Activity Cost Driver	=	Activity Rate
Purchasing, receiving, and crushing	$ 90,000	/ 450,000 pounds of grapes	=	$ 0.20 per pound
Setting up a production run	300,000	/ 500 setups	=	600.00 per setup
Fermenting, aging in barrels	216,000	/ 270,000 fermentating and aging days	=	0.80 per day
Performing quality control	175,000	/ 10,000 quality inspections	=	17.50 per inspection
Bottling, labeling, packaging	99,000	/ 330,000 bottles	=	0.30 per bottle

Refer to Exhibit 20.12 for the calculation of the activity rates for CK Mondavi's cost pools. Before we move to the final step in activity based costing, take the following Self-Study Practice to make sure you understand the first three steps.

SELF-STUDY PRACTICE

1. Which of the following would be classified as a unit-level activity by an ice cream manufacturer such as Ben & Jerry's?

   a. Purchasing the ingredients to make a batch of cookie dough ice cream.
   b. Performing quality checks on each batch produced to make sure the flavor is right.
   c. Conducting research and development on a new flavor of ice cream.
   d. Maintaining the equipment used to produce various flavors of ice cream.
   e. Pouring the ice cream into containers before freezing it.

2. Which of the activities in question 1 (a–e) would be classified as a product-level activity by an ice cream manufacturer such as Ben & Jerry's?

3. One of Ben & Jerry's major activities is changing over the equipment to produce a new flavor of ice cream. The total annual cost and the activity driver for this cost pool are:

Total annual cost of activity	$100,000
Activity driver	500 change-overs

What is the activity rate for this activity?

After you have finished, check your answers with the solutions at the bottom of the page.

Step 4: Assign Indirect Costs to Products or Services Based on Their Activity Demands

The final step in activity based costing is to use the activity rates developed in Step 3 to calculate the cost of individual products and services based on their activity demands. To see how this works, let's compare the activities needed for CK Mondavi to produce one batch of

Solution to Self-Study Practice

1. e
2. c
3. $200 per setup ($100,000/500)

standard chardonnay to the activities needed to produce one batch of vintage cabernet. We assume these two hypothetical products have the following activity requirements:

Activity Requirements	Standard Chardonnay	Vintage Cabernet
Pounds of grapes	1,250 pounds per batch	375 pounds per batch
Number of setups	1 setup per batch	1 setup per batch
Fermentation, aging days	150 days per batch	900 days per batch
Number of quality inspections	1 every 15 days (10 per batch)	1 every 10 days (90 per batch)
Number of bottles	1,000 bottles per batch	150 bottles per batch

To calculate the manufacturing overhead cost of each product, we simply multiply these activity requirements by the activity rates developed in Step 3 (see Exhibit 20.13).

Exhibit 20.13 Calculation of CK Mondavi's Activity-Based Costs

Activity Cost Pool	(From Exhibit 20.12) Activity Rate	STANDARD CHARDONNAY Activity Cost Driver	ABC Cost	VINTAGE CABERNET Activity Cost Driver	ABC Cost
Purchasing, receiving, crushing	$ 0.20 per pound	1,250 pounds	$250.00	375 pounds	$75.00
Setting up a production run	600.00 per set-up	1 setup	600.00	1 setup	600.00
Fermenting, aging in barrels	0.80 per day	150 days	120.00	900 days	720.00
Performing quality control	17.50 per inspection	10 inspections	175.00	90 inspections	1,575.00
Bottling, labeling, packaging	0.30 per bottle	1,000 bottles	300.00	150 bottles	45.00
Manufacturing overhead cost per batch			$1,445.00		$3,015.00
Number of bottles per batch			1,000		150
Manufacturing overhead cost per bottle			$1.45		$20.10

   The $1.45 and $20.10 in manufacturing overhead cost per bottle for the standard chardonnay and vintage cabernet represent only the indirect portion of the manufacturing costs. Direct materials costs and direct labor costs, which can be traced directly to each product, must still be added to the manufacturing overhead costs to determine the full manufacturing cost per unit under ABC. Assume the direct materials and direct labor costs per bottle follow:

Manufacturing Cost per Bottle	Standard Chardonnay	Vintage Cabernet
Direct materials cost	$2.00	$ 4.00
Direct labor cost	1.00	2.00
Manufacturing overhead (ABC) cost	1.45	20.10
Total manufacturing cost	$4.45	$26.10

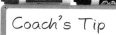

Coach's Tip

Why is the vintage cabernet so much more costly to produce? It is produced in smaller batches and requires more fermentation and aging as well as more frequent quality inspections.

This ABC analysis shows that it costs about $26.10 to produce a bottle of vintage cabernet compared to about $4.45 for a bottle of standard chardonnay. Although the cost of direct materials and direct labor for the two products differ, most of the difference in total cost is due to the manufacturing overhead cost per unit.

To summarize, activity based costing is a method of assigning indirect costs to products or services based on the activities required to produce them. ABC uses both volume-based cost drivers (such as the number of bottles produced or the number of pounds of materials used) and nonvolume-based cost drivers (such as the number of setups required, the number of days spent in fermentation and aging, and the number of quality inspections performed). The goal of ABC is to provide more valuable information about the cost of products and services so that managers can make better decisions about what prices to charge, whether to offer certain products or services, and how to reduce costs.

Demonstration Case A (Process Costing)

Bellagio Olive Oil Company manufactures extra virgin olive oil using a series of processes to convert olives into olive oil. These steps include cleaning the olives, grinding them into a paste, mixing to increase olive oil yield, separating the olive oil from the fruit, extracting the olive oil, storing, and bottling.

In the mixing department, direct materials (olives) are added at the beginning of the process, and conversion costs are incurred uniformly throughout the process. At the beginning of the most recent accounting period, Bellagio had 20,000 units in the mixing process, 30 percent complete. It started an additional 150,000 units into the process, and ended the period with 40,000 units in process, 40 percent complete. The mixing department's partially completed production report is shown below:

	A	B	C	D	E	F
1			Bellagio Olive Oil			
2			Process Costing Production Report (FIFO Method)			
3			Mixing Department			
4			For the Quarter Ended December 31, 2009			
5			Step 1			
6		UNITS	Reconcile			
7	1	Units to be accounted for:	Physical Units			
8	2	Beginning work in process	20,000			
9	3	Started into production	150,000			
10	4	Total units	170,000	Step 2		
11	5			Calculate Equivalent Units		
12	6	Units accounted for as follows:		Direct Materials	Conversion	
13	7	Beginning work in process	?	?	?	
14	8	Started and completed	?	?	?	
15	9	Ending work in process	40,000	?	?	
16	10	Total units	?	?	?	
17	11	COSTS		Step 3: Calculate cost per		
18	12			equivalent unit		
19	13			Direct Materials	Conversion	
20	14	Current period costs		$ 450,000	$ 679,000	
21	15	Equivalent units (from step 2 above)		?	?	
22	16	Cost per equivalent unit		?	?	
23	17			Step 4: Reconcile the total cost of work in process		
24	18	Costs to be accounted for:		Direct Materials	Conversion	Total
25	19	Beginning work in process				$ 301,000
26	20	Current period costs		$ 450,000	$ 679,000	1,129,000
27	21	Total cost				$ 1,430,000
28	22					
29	23	Costs accounted for as follows:				
30	24	Beginning inventory balance (transferred out)				?
31	25	Cost to complete beginning inentory (Row 7 x Row 16)		?	?	?
32	26	Started and completed (Row 8 x Row 16)		?	?	?
33	27	Ending inventory (Row 9 x Row 16)		?	?	?
34	28	Total cost				?

Required:

1. Complete steps 1–4 by filling in Bellagio's production report.
2. What is the balance in Work in Process Inventory (Mixing) at the end of the quarter?
3. Prepare the journal entry to show the transfer of cost from Work in Process Inventory (Mixing) to Work in Process Inventory (Separating) for all of the units completed during the quarter.

Suggested Solution

1.

	A	B	C	D	E	F
1			Bellagio Olive Oil			
2			Process Costing Production Report (FIFO Method)			
3			Mixing Department			
4			For the Quarter Ended December 31, 2009			
5			Step 1			
6		UNITS	Reconcile			
7	1 Units to be acccunted for:		Physical Units			
8	2	Beginning work in process	20,000			
9	3	Started into production	150,000			
10	4	Total units	170,000	Step 2		
11	5			Calculate Equivalent Units		
12	6 Units accounted for as follows:			Direct Materials	Conversion	
13	7	Beginning work in process	20,000	0	4,000	
14	8	Started and completed	110,000	110,000	110,000	
15	9	Ending work in process	40,000	40,000	6,000	
16	10	Total units	170,000	150,000	140,000	
17	11			Step 3: Calculate cost per		
18	12 COSTS			equivalent unit		
19	13			Direct Materials	Conversion	
20	14	Current period costs		$ 450,000	$ 679,000	
21	15	Equivalent units (from step 2 above)		150,000	140,000	
22	16	Cost per equivalent unit		$ 3.00	$ 4.85	
23	17			Step 4: Reconcile the total cost of work in process		
24	18 Costs to be accounted for:			Direct Materials	Conversion	Total
25	19	Beginning work in process				$ 301,000
26	20	Current period costs		$ 450,000	$ 679,000	1,129,000
27	21	Total costs				$ 1,430,000
28	22					
29	23 Costs accounted for as follows:					
30	24	Beginning inventory balance (transferred out)				$ 301,000
31	25	Cost to complete beginning inentory (Row 7 x Row 16)		$ -	$ 67,900	67,900
32	26	Started and completed (Row 8 x Row 16)		330,000	533,500	863,500
33	27	Ending inventory (Row 9 x Row 16)		120,000	77,600	197,600
34	28					$ 1,430,000

2. Ending balance in Work in Process Inventory (Mixing) is $197,600
3. Journal entry to transfer completed units from Mixing to Separating:

	Debit	Credit
Work in Process Inventory (Separating)	1,232,400	
Work in Process Inventory (Mixing)		1,232,400
$301,000 + $67,900 + $863,500 = $1,232,400		

Demonstration Case B (Activity Based Costing)

Tom and Terry's Ice Cream Company uses activity based costing to assign manufacturing overhead cost to various ice cream products. The company has completed the first few steps in the ABC process by identifying and pooling major activities, assigning manufacturing overhead cost to each pool, and developing an appropriate activity driver for each pool, as follows:

Activity Cost Pool	Total Cost	Total Activity Cost Driver
Purchasing ingredients	$200,000	400,000 pounds
Setting up equipment	150,000	500 setups
Performing quality testing	200,000	2,000 quality inspections
Packaging	40,000	200,000 pints

Using this information, the company is trying to determine how much it costs to manufacture chocolate chunk ice cream. The activity requirements for the chocolate chunk product follow.

Direct Costs	Chocolate Chunk per Pint
Direct materials cost	$0.75
Direct labor cost	0.25

Activity Requirements	Activity Drivers
Total pints produced	100,000
Pounds of materials required	15,000
Number of setups	1 per batch
Batch size	5,000 pints (20 batches)
Quality testing	6 times per batch (120 total)

Required:

1. Calculate an activity rate for each of the four activity cost pools.
2. Use the activity rates calculated in question 1 to assign manufacturing overhead cost to the chocolate chunk product.
3. Calculate the total manufacturing cost per pint of chocolate chunk ice cream.

Suggested Solution

1.

Activity	Total Cost	Total Activity Cost Driver	Activity Rate
Purchasing ingredients	$200,000	400,000 pounds	$ 0.50 per pound
Setting up equipment	150,000	500 setups	300.00 per setup
Performing quality testing	200,000	2,000 quality inspections	100.00 per quality inspection
Packaging	40,000	200,000 pints	0.20 per pint

2.

Activity Rate	Chocolate Chunk Requirements	ABC Cost Allocation
$ 0.50 per pound	15,000 pounds	$ 7,500
300.00 per setup	20 setups	6,000
100.00 per quality inspection	120 quality inspections	12,000
0.20 per pint	100,000 pints	20,000
Total manufacturing overhead cost (using ABC)		$45,500
		100,000 pints
Manufacturing overhead cost per pint (from ABC)		$0.455

3.

	Chocolate Chunk
Direct materials cost	$0.75 per pint
Direct labor cost	0.25 per pint
Manufacturing overhead per pint	0.46 (rounded from ABC in preceding table)
Total manufacturing cost per pint	$1.46

Supplement 20A
Weighted Average Method

This supplement demonstrates how to prepare a process costing production report using the weighted average method. The example used to demonstrate the weighted average method is the same as the one we used to prepare a production report using the FIFO method (see page 855).

The main difference between the FIFO and weighted average methods is that the FIFO method assumes that the units in beginning inventory are completed before any new units enter the process. The weighted average method assumes that all units completed during the current period were started in the current period. Thus, the weighted average method ignores the fact that the units in beginning inventory were partially complete at the start of the period. That is, the weighted average method ignores the percentage of completion of units in beginning inventory and instead treats them as if they were started in the current period.

Because the FIFO method pays more attention to how much work went into fully and partially completed units during the period, it is generally more accurate than the weighted average method. However, the weighted average method is simpler than the FIFO method and provides similar results for companies with minimal inventory or very stable production and inventory patterns. The weighted average method is used more often than the FIFO method and is expected to become even more common as companies move toward just-in-time inventory systems, which minimize inventory levels.

Regardless of whether a company uses the FIFO or weighted average method, the same four steps are followed in preparing the production report:

1. Reconcile the number of physical units.
2. Translate physical units into equivalent units.
3. Calculate the cost per equivalent unit.
4. Reconcile the total cost of Work in Process Inventory.

Step 1: Reconcile the Number of Physical Units

The first step in preparing the production report is to reconcile the number of physical units. First you calculate the total number of units that were worked on during the period by adding the number of units in beginning inventory to the number of units that were started in the current period. Then you determine whether those units were completed during the period or were still being worked on at the end of the period. The formula for reconciling the number of physical units is:

> **Coach's Tip**
>
> This formula ignores any units that may have been lost due to spoilage or waste. Accounting for lost or spoiled units is covered in more advanced texts.

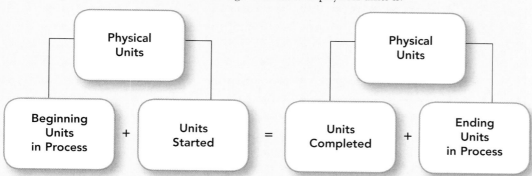

To apply this formula, let's return to the CFA process at CK Mondavi. For this example, assume the company had 200 barrels of wine in process at the start of a new accounting period. Last period's production report valued these partially complete units at $165,600 ($84,500 for direct materials + $81,100 for conversion cost). During the period, workers started another 1,800 barrels into the CFA process. At the end of the period, 400 barrels of wine were still in the CFA process. Based on this information, you can answer the following question: How many barrels of wine were transferred out of the CFA process and into bottling during the current period?

To answer this question, you can prepare a reconciliation of physical units, as follows:

> **Coach's Tip**
>
> The number of units completed and transferred to bottling is 1,600. During the period, 2,000 units were worked on and 400 units were still being worked on at the end of the period, so 1,600 units must have been completed.

	Physical Units		Physical Units
Beginning units	200	Units completed	?
Units started	1,800	Ending units	400
Total units	2,000	Total Units	2,000

Step 2: Translate Physical Units into Equivalent Units

The next step in preparing the production report is to calculate **equivalent units,** a measure of the amount of work or effort that occurred during the current period to produce full and partially completed units. Under the weighted average method, the only partially completed units we need to deal with are the units in inventory at the end of the period. The weighted average method ignores the beginning inventory, assuming that those units were started in the current period.

To determine the number of equivalent units in our winery example, we use the following additional details about CK Mondavi's production process.

- Direct materials (grapes) are added at the beginning of the process. Thus, once a unit has been started in the process, it has 100 percent of direct materials.
- Conversion costs (direct labor and manufacturing overhead) are incurred uniformly throughout the process.
- Although some units may have been in process at the beginning of the period, the weighted average method ignores that fact and assumes that the 1,600 units completed this period were all started in the current period.
- The 400 units in ending inventory were 60 percent of the way through the CFA process. Those units have all of the direct materials added but only 60 percent of the conversion cost.

See Exhibit 20A.1 for a summary of these details.

Exhibit 20A.1   Diagram of the Crushing, Fermenting, and Aging (CFA) Process, Weighted Average Method

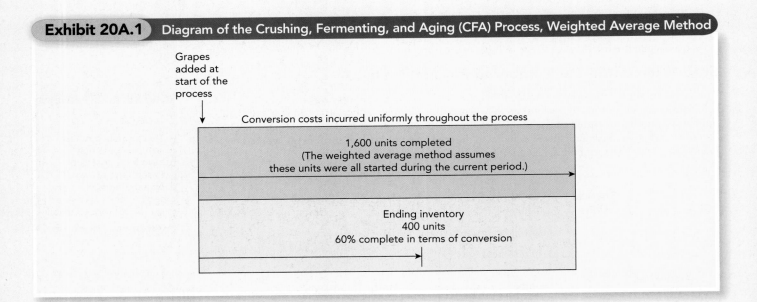

To determine the number of equivalent units, we must consider how much work went into the units that were completed in the current period and those that remain in ending inventory. We need to make separate calculations for direct materials and conversion cost because these costs are incurred at different points in the process. See Exhibit 20A.2 for a demonstration of the calculation of equivalent units. Notice that for the completed units, the equivalent units equal the physical units. That is because the weighted average method assumes that all units completed during the current period were started during the period. Thus, we ignore any units in beginning inventory.

The only adjustment we need to make is for the units in ending inventory. Remember that direct materials are added at the beginning of the process, so the 400 units in ending inventory are 100 percent complete with respect to direct materials. For direct materials, then, the number of equivalent units is the same as the number of physical units. For conversion cost, the units in ending inventory have gone only 60 percent of the way through the production process. Therefore,

Exhibit 20A.2   Calculation of Equivalent Units, Weighted Average Method

		EQUIVALENT UNITS			
	Number of Physical Units	Direct Materials		Conversion Cost	
Completed	1,600	1,600	(1,600 × 100%)	1,600	(1,600 × 100%)
Ending Inventory	400	400	(400 × 100%)	240	(400 × 60%)
Total	2,000	2,000		1,840	

the number of equivalent units for conversion cost would be 60 percent of the 400 units in ending inventory, or 240.

We can calculate the total number of equivalent units by summing the equivalent units for the units completed during the period and the units in ending inventory. The total equivalent units is 2,000 for direct materials and 1,840 for conversion cost. In the next step, we use these numbers to calculate the cost per equivalent unit.

Step 3: Calculate the Cost per Equivalent Unit

To calculate the cost per equivalent unit, we divide the total cost of work in process by the total number of equivalent units (calculated in Step 2):

$$\text{Cost per Equivalent Unit} = \frac{\text{Beginning Inventory + Current Costs}}{\text{Equivalent Units}}$$

> **Coach's Tip**
>
> To determine the number of equivalent units, ask yourself the following question: How much direct materials and conversion costs would be required to start the units in ending inventory and get them to the 60 percent point?

As this formula shows, the weighted average method combines the cost of the beginning inventory with the costs that were added to the process during the current period. This calculation should be done separately for direct materials and conversion costs.

In our winery example, the cost per equivalent unit is calculated as follows:

	Direct Materials	Conversion Cost
Beginning inventory costs	$ 84,500	$ 81,100
Current period cost	810,000	918,000
Total costs	$894,500	$999,100
Equivalent units (from Step 2)	2,000	1,840
Cost per equivalent unit	$ 447.25	$ 542.99

In the next section, we use the cost per equivalent unit of $447.25 for direct materials and $542.99 (rounded) for conversion to calculate the cost of units completed and transferred out of the process as well as the cost of units still in process at the end of the period.

Step 4: Reconcile the Total Cost of Work in Process

The final step in the preparation of the production report is to reconcile the total cost recorded in the Work in Process Inventory account. The total cost of Work in Process Inventory includes the cost that was already in the account at the beginning of the period plus the direct materials and conversion costs added to the process during the period. The following T-account shows the costs for our winery example:

Work In Process Inventory (CFA)			
Beginning balance		Cost of goods completed	?
Direct materials	84,500	(transferred to bottling)	
Conversion cost applied	81,100		
Current period costs			
Direct materials	810,000		
Conversion cost applied	918,000		
Total cost to account for	1,893,600		
Ending balance	?		

This T-account shows that we must account for a total cost of $1,893,600 for the CFA process. Some of that total cost will be transferred out of the Work in Process Inventory account with the units completed and transferred to the next department, and some will remain as Work in Process Inventory. To determine how much of the cost should be transferred out and how much should be kept with the ending inventory, we simply multiply the costs per equivalent unit of $447.25 for direct materials and $542.99 (rounded) for conversion by the number of equivalent units calculated in Step 2. See Exhibit 20A.3 for the calculations for our winery example.

Exhibit 20A.3 Reconciliation of the Total Cost of Work in Process, Weighted Average Method

	CURRENT PERIOD COSTS (EQUIVALENT UNITS × COST PER EQUIVALENT UNITS)		Total Cost Accounted for as Follows:
	Direct Materials	Conversion Cost	
Units completed	1,600 × $447.25 = $715,600	1,600 × $542.99* = $868,783	$1,584,383
Ending inventory	400 × $447.25 = $178,900	240 × $542.99* = $130,317	$ 309,217
Total cost to account for:			$1,893,600*

*$542.9891 is used to eliminate the rounding error.

After we transfer $1,584,383 out of the Work in Process account to reflect the cost of units completed and transferred to the next process, the T-account for the CFA process should appear as follows:

Work In Process Inventory (CFA)			
Beginning balance	165,600	Cost of goods completed	
Direct materials	810,000	(transferred to bottling)	$1,584,383
Conversion cost applied	918,000		
Total cost to account for	1,893,600		
Ending balance	309,217		

Step 5: Prepare a Production Report

The final step in process costing is to summarize the results of Steps 1–4 into a single document, the production report. The production report is essentially a summary of what occurred in the production process during the accounting period. It includes information about the number of physical units (Step 1) and equivalent units (Step 2) as well as the cost per equivalent unit (Step 3), and a reconciliation of the cost of work in process (Step 4).

Exhibit 20A.4 is a production report for the winery example. This single document summarizes the four steps used to determine the cost of the CFA process.

Exhibit 20A.4 — Weighted Average Process Costing Production Report

	A	B	C	D	E	F
1			CK Mondavi Winery			
2			Process Costing Production Report (Weighted Average Method)			
3			Crushing, Fermenting and Aging (CFA) Department			
4			For the Quarter Ended March 31, 2009			
5			Step 1			
6		UNITS	Reconcile			
7	1	Units to be accounted for:	Physical Units			
8	2	Beginning work in process	200			
9	3	Started into production	1,800			
10	4	Total units	2,000	Step 2		
11	5			Calculate Equivalent Units		
12	6	Units accounted for as follows:		Direct Materials	Conversion	
13	7	Completed and transferred	1,600	1,600	1,600	
14	8	Ending work in process	400	400	240	
15	9	Total units	2,000	2,000	1,840	
16	10	COSTS		Step 3: Calculate cost per		
17	11			equivalent unit		
18	12			Direct Materials	Conversion	
19	13	Cost of beginning inventory		$ 84,500 $	81,100	
20	14	Current period costs		810,000	918,000	
21	15	Total cost of units in process		$ 894,500 $	999,100	
22	16	Equivalent units (from step 2 above)		2,000	1,840	
23	17	Cost per equivalent unit		$ 447.25	$ 542.9891 *	
24	18			Step 4: Reconcile the total cost of work in process		
25	19	Costs to be accounted for:		Direct Materials	Conversion	Total
26	20	Beginning work in process		$ 84,500 $	81,100 $	165,600
27	21	Current period costs		$ 810,000 $	918,000	1,728,000
28	22	Total costs				$ 1,893,600
29	23					
30	24	Costs accounted for as follows:				
31	25	Units completed and transferred (Row 7 x Row 17)		715,600	868,783	1,584,383
32	26	Ending inventory (Row 8 x Row 17)		178,900	130,317	309,217
33	27					$ 1,893,600
34						
35		*This number must be kept to 4 decimal places for the the reconciliation in step 4 to balance.				

Chapter Summary

LO1 Describe the key features of a process costing system. (p. 842)

- Process costing is used by companies that produce homogeneous (similar) goods or services in a series of standardized processes.
- The flow of costs in process costing is very similar to that in job order costing. Manufacturing costs are recorded in the Raw Materials, Work in Process, and Finished Goods Inventory accounts until the product is sold, at which point they become part of the Cost of Goods Sold.
- Process costing systems maintain a separate Work in Process Inventory account for each major production process. As the product flows through the various production processes, the total cost is transferred from one Work in Process Inventory account to the next.

LO2 Prepare journal entries to record product costs using process costing. (p. 844)

- The three major categories of product costs are direct materials, direct labor, and manufacturing overhead. This chapter combined direct labor and manufacturing overhead into the single account Conversion Cost.
- Product costs are recorded in one of three inventory accounts: Raw Materials Inventory, Work in Process Inventory, or Finished Goods Inventory. Each major process has a separate Work in Process Inventory account, and the costs are transferred to the appropriate account as the product is manufactured.
- Actual and applied conversion costs can be recorded in a control account, much the same way that actual and applied manufacturing overhead costs were dealt with in Chapter 19. Any under- or overapplied balance is closed directly to Cost of Goods Sold at the end of the accounting period.

LO3 Reconcile the number of physical units that were worked on during the period. (p. 850)

- The first step in process costing is to reconcile the number of physical units.
- The number of units in beginning inventory plus the number of units started must equal the number of units completed plus the number of units in ending inventory.
- The number of units started and completed equals the number of units completed minus the number of units in beginning inventory or the number of units started minus the number of units in ending inventory.

LO4 Calculate equivalent units of production using the FIFO method. (p. 851)

- The second step is to translate physical units into equivalent units.
- An equivalent unit is an adjustment that is made to the number of physical units to reflect the amount of work or effort that went into full and partially completed units during the period.

LO5 Prepare a process costing production report. (p. 855)

- The production report summarizes the costs and units that flow into and out of the production process during a given period. It will summarize the following steps:
- Step 1: Reconcile the number of physical units.
- Step 2: Translate physical units into equivalent units.
- Step 3: Calculate cost per equivalent units.
- Step 4: Reconcile the total cost of work in process by multiplying the number of equivalent units by the cost per equivalent unit.
- Step 5: Prepare a production report by summarizing Steps 1–4.

LO6 Calculate the cost of products using activity based costing. (p. 857)

- Activity based costing is a method of assigning indirect costs to products or services based on their underlying activity requirements.
- Unlike traditional costing systems, which rely exclusively on volume-based cost drivers, ABC also incorporates nonvolume-based cost drivers, such as the number of setups, inspections, or design changes.
  ABC uses four steps
- Step 1: Identify the firm's key activities and classify them as either unit-level, batch-level, product-level, customer-level, or facility-level activities.
- Step 2: Form activity cost pools and assign the company's indirect costs to those cost pools.
- Step 3: Select an activity driver and calculate an activity rate for each pool by dividing the total cost by the total value of the activity driver.
- Step 4: Assign indirect costs to individual products or services by multiplying the activity rates by their activity requirements.

Key Terms

Activity Cost Driver (p. 859)

Activity Based Costing (p. 857)

Batch-Level Activities (p. 858)

Cost Driver (p. 857)

Customer-Level Activities (p. 858)

Equivalent Unit (p. 851)

Facility-Level Activities (p. 858)

Nonvolume Allocation Measures (p. 857)

Product-Level Activities (p. 858)

Production Report (p. 855)

Unit-Level Activities (p. 858)

Volume-Based Allocation Measures (p. 857)

See complete glossary in back of text.

Questions

1. Briefly describe the differences between job order, process, and activity based costing. Give an example of a type of company that would use each one.

2. Explain the differences between Raw Materials, Work in Process and Finished Goods inventories.

3. Explain the flow of costs in a manufacturing company including the type of account and the respective financial statement on which the cost appears.

4. What are the four steps to prepare a production report?

5. Why is a production report important to a company?

6. What is the difference between conversion cost and manufacturing overhead? Why would a company use a conversion cost account instead of a manufacturing overhead account?

7. How is the number of physical units reconciled in a production report?

8. Why must a company calculate equivalent units when using process costing?

9. How can a unit be 100% complete with respect to materials, but only partially complete in terms of conversion effort?

10. What does a credit to the Work in Process Inventory account represent?

11. What types of business might use activity based costing?

12. How does activity based costing differ from process costing in its assignment of overhead?

13. What is an allocation base? What is the difference between a volume-based allocation measure and a nonvolume-based allocation measure?

14. What are the advantages and disadvantages of an activity based costing system?

15. What are the four basic steps in ABC?

16. With ABC, why must costs be classified into different categories? What is the basis for these categories?

17. How do the weighted average and the FIFO methods treat beginning inventory.

18. Is the weighted average method or FIFO method usually more accurate? Why?

19. What are the four steps of preparing a weighted average production report? Is this different than the steps used for a FIFO production report?

Multiple Choice

1. The journal entry to record the issuance of direct materials into production includes
   a. A credit to cash.
   b. A debit to Work in Process Inventory.
   c. A credit to Finished Goods Inventory.
   d. A debit to Cost of Goods Sold.

   Quiz 20-1
   www.mhhe.com/LLPW1e

2. Which of the following is most likely to use a process costing system?
   a. A company that builds and installs custom cabinetry.
   b. A company that makes one style of office chair.
   c. A janitorial service.
   d. A paving company.

3. Suppose Shadow Company has 250 units in beginning inventory, 400 units started in production, and 175 units in ending inventory. How many units did Shadow complete?
   a. 25.   c. 475.
   b. 325.   d. Number cannot be determined.

4. If Wilson Corp. has 450 units that are estimated to be 60 percent complete, how many equivalent units are there?
   a. 270.   c. 100.
   b. 210.   d. 450.

5. Masterson Company has calculated a cost per unit of $4 for materials and $8.50 for conversion to manufacture a specific product. Ending work in process has 1,000 units that are fully complete for materials and 70 percent complete for conversion. What amount will Masterson have as ending Work in Process Inventory?
   a. $12,500.   c. $5,950.
   b. $8,750.   d. $9,950.

6. Which of the following is a nonvolume-based allocation measure?
   a. Machine hours.
   b. Direct labor hours.

   c. Number of batches.
   d. Direct labor cost.

7. Taylor Company has an overhead rate for machine setups of $200 per setup. Last month, Product A had 40 setups and Product B had 70 setups. How much overhead did Taylor assign to each product?
   a. $11,000 to Product A, $11,000 to Product B.
   b. $8,000 to Product A, $14,000 to Product B.
   c. $4,000 to Product A, $7,000 to Product B.
   d. Amount cannot be determined.

8. Which of the following is not a facility level activity?
   a. Maintenance on the factory building.
   b. Factory utilities.
   c. Research and development for a new product.
   d. Salaries for plant administration.

9. The primary difference between FIFO and weighted average methods of process costing has to do with the treatment of
   a. Beginning inventory.
   b. Ending inventory.
   c. Number of units started.
   d. Direct materials.

10. When calculating product cost using the weighted average method, which of the following amounts are combined?
    a. Ending finished goods and cost of goods sold.
    b. Beginning finished goods and cost of goods sold.
    c. Beginning work in process and beginning finished goods.
    d. Beginning work in process and current period costs.

Solutions to Multiple-Choice Questions
1. b   2. b   3. c   4. a   5. d   6. c   7. b
8. c   9. a   10. d

Mini Exercises **Available with McGraw-Hill's Homework Manager**

LO3   **M20-1 Calculating Physical Units**

Roundtree company had 575 units in work in process on January 1. During the month, Roundtree completed 2,400 units and had 1,000 units in process on January 31. Determine how many units Roundtree started during January.

LO3   **M20-2 Calculating Physical Units**

For each of the following independent cases (A–D), compute the missing value in the table.

Case	Beginning Units	Units Started	Units Completed	Ending Units
A	400	2,300	1,650	?
B	1,200	800	?	1,600
C	?	750	1,230	2,560
D	345	?	900	680

LO3, 4   **M20-3 Calculating Physical Units and Equivalent Units (FIFO)**

Bedford Company produces carrying cases for CDs. It has compiled the following information for the month of June.

	Physical Units	Percent Complete for Conversion
Beginning work in process	35,000	55%
Ending work in process	46,000	70

Bedford adds all materials at the beginning of its manufacturing process. During the month, it started 90,000 units.

Using the FIFO method, reconcile the number of physical units and calculate the number of equivalent units.

LO3, 4   **M20-4 Calculating Cost per Equivalent Unit (FIFO)**

Incontro Company manufactures file cabinets. The following cost information is available for the month of December.

Beginning work in process	
Direct materials	$ 34,000
Conversion cost	62,000
December costs	
Direct materials	68,000
Conversion cost	105,000

Incontro had 8,500 equivalent units of direct materials and 6,000 equivalent units of conversion activity during the month. Using the FIFO method, calculate Incontro's cost per equivalent unit for materials and conversion during December.

LO6   **M20-5 Classifying Activities in ABC**

For each of the following activities, indicate the appropriate category (unit, batch, product, customer, or facility level) and suggest a possible cost driver for each pool.

1. Factory utilities.
2. Machine setups.
3. Research and development for a new product.
4. Sanding rough edges of the product.
5. Packaging the product for shipment.
6. Developing new packaging for a special order of 200 units.
7. Maintaining equipment.
8. Assembling the product's component parts.
9. Materials-handling costs.
10. Quality control testing.

M20-6 Calculating Activity Rates and Assigning Costs to Products in ABC   LO6

Newkirk Co. has identified one of its cost pools to be quality control and assigned $50,000 to that pool. The number of inspections has been chosen as the cost driver for this pool. Newkirk performs 25,000 quality control inspections. Suppose Newkirk manufactures two products that consume 10,000 and 15,000 inspections each. Determine how much quality control cost will be assigned to each of Newkirk's product lines.

M20-7 Calculating Physical Units and Equivalent Units (Weighted Average) (Supplement)

Refer to M20-3 for information regarding Bedford Company. Using the weighted average method, reconcile the number of physical units and calculate the number of equivalent units.

M20-8 Calculating Cost per Equivalent Unit (Weighted average) (Supplement)

Refer to M20-4 for information regarding Incontro Company. Using the weighted average method, calculate Incontro's cost per equivalent unit for materials and conversion during December.

Exercises Available with McGraw-Hill's Homework Manager

E20-1 Recording Manufacturing Costs in Process Costing   LO2

Forrest Co. makes wooden tables.

Required:

Prepare the journal entries to record each of the following transactions.

 a. Purchased $20,000 of raw materials on credit.
 b. Issued $18,000 of direct materials into production.
 c. Applied $47,500 of conversion cost.
 d. Paid in full the raw materials purchased on credit.
 e. Completed $52,750 in tables.
 f. Recorded actual conversion costs of $42,000.
 g. Sold tables for $93,000 that cost $50,000 to produce.
 h. Disposed of any over- or underapplied conversion cost.

E20-2 Recording Manufacturing Costs in Process Costing   LO2

Rock-On Company produces wooden rocking chairs. The company has two sequential production departments, Cutting and Assembly. The wood is cut and sanded in Cutting, and then transferred to Assembly to be assembled and painted. From Assembly, the chairs are transferred to Finished Goods Inventory and then sold.

Rock-On has compiled the following information for the month of February.

	Cutting Department	Assembly Department
Direct materials	$ 75,000	$ 12,000
Direct labor	65,000	99,000
Applied manufacturing overhead	150,000	167,000
Cost of goods completed and transferred out	234,000	253,000

Required:

Prepare the following journal entries for Rock-On.

1. Amount of direct materials, direct labor, and manufacturing overhead incurred for the Cutting Department.
2. Transfer of products from Cutting to Assembly.
3. Amount of direct materials, direct labor, and manufacturing overhead incurred by the Assembly Department.
4. Transfer of chairs from Assembly to Finished Goods.

LO3, 4   **E20-3 Calculating Equivalent Units, Cost per Equivalent Unit and Reconciling the Cost of Work in Process (FIFO)**

GoFly Company manufactures kites and has the following information available for the month of April.

Work in process, April 1	
(100% complete for materials, 40% for conversion)	26,000 units
Direct materials	$ 40,000
Conversion cost	$ 55,000
Number of units started	79,000
April costs	
Direct materials	$113,000
Conversion cost	$168,000
Work in process, April 30	
(100% complete for materials, 20% for conversion)	40,000 units

Required:

Using the FIFO method of process costing, complete each of the following steps:

1. Reconcile the number of physical units worked on during the period.
2. Calculate the number of equivalent units.
3. Calculate the cost per equivalent unit, rounded to five decimal places.
4. Reconcile the total cost of work in process.

E20-4 Calculating Equivalent Units, Cost per Equivalent Unit and Reconciling the Cost of Work in Process (Weighted Average) (Supplement)

GoFly Company manufactures kites and has the following information available for the month of April.

Work in process, April 1	
(100% complete for materials, 40% for conversion)	26,000 units
Direct materials	$ 40,000
Conversion cost	$ 55,000
Number of units started	79,000
April costs	
Direct materials	$113,000
Conversion cost	$168,000
Work in process, April 30	
(100% complete for materials, 20% for conversion)	40,000 units

Required:

Using the weighted average method, complete each of the following steps:

1. Reconcile the number of physical units worked on during the period.
2. Calculate the number of equivalent units.
3. Calculate the cost per equivalent unit, rounded to five decimal places.
4. Reconcile the total cost of work in process.

LO3, 4   **E20-5 Calculating Equivalent Units, Cost per Equivalent Unit, and Reconciling the Cost of Work in Process (FIFO)**

Raindrop Company manufactures umbrellas and has the following information available for the month of May.

Work in process, May 1	
(100% complete for materials, 90% for conversion)	72,000 units
Direct materials	$129,000
Conversion cost	$175,000
Number of units started	181,000
May costs	
Direct materials	$206,000
Conversion cost	$379,000
Work in process, May 31	
(100% complete for materials, 20% for conversion)	67,000 units

Required:

Using the FIFO method of process costing, complete each of the following steps:

1. Reconcile the number of physical units worked on during the period.
2. Calculate the number of equivalent units.
3. Calculate the cost per equivalent unit, rounded to five decimal places.
4. Reconcile the total cost of work in process.

E20-6 Calculating Equivalent Units, Cost per Equivalent Unit, and Reconciling the Cost of Work in Process (Weighted Average) (Supplement)

Refer to E20-5 for information regarding Raindrop Company.

Required:

Using the weighted average method, complete each of the following steps:

1. Reconcile the number of physical units worked on during the period.
2. Calculate the number of equivalent units.
3. Calculate the cost per equivalent unit, rounded to five decimal places.
4. Reconcile the total cost of work in process.

E20-7 Calculating Activity Rates and Assigning Costs to Products in ABC

LO6

Titan Corp. has identified the following information about its cost pools and cost drivers.

Cost pools	
Materials handling	$40,000
Machine maintenance	25,500
Cost drivers	
Number of material moves	800
Number of machine hours	75,000

Required:

1. Calculate Titan's activity rate for each cost pool.
2. Determine the amount of overhead assigned to Titan's Product A and Product B if each has the following requirements:

	Product A	Product B
Number of material moves	500	300
Number of machine hours	42,000	33,000

E20-8 Calculating Activity Rates and Assigning Cost to Products in ABC

LO6

Matson Corp. manufactures automobile floor mats. It currently has two product lines, standard and deluxe. Matson has identified the following information about its overhead activity pools and the standard product line.

Activity Pools	Cost Driver	Activity Rate	Activity Cost Driver for Standard Floor Mat Line
Materials handling	Number of moves	$25 per move	40 moves
Quality control	Number of inspections	7 per inspection	600 inspections
Machine maintenance	Number of machine hours	2 per machine hour	3,000 machine hours

Required:

Calculate the amount of overhead that Matson will assign to the standard floor mat product line.

LO6

E20-9 Calculating Activity Rates and Assigning Costs to Products in ABC

Refer to the activity pool, cost driver, and activity rate information given in E20-8. Suppose Matson has compiled the following information for its deluxe floor mat line.

Activity Cost Driver for Deluxe Floor Mat Line
60 moves
720 inspections
4,150 machine hours

Required:

Calculate the amount of overhead that Matson will assign to the deluxe product line.

Problems—Set A ▪▪▪ ™   Available with McGraw-Hill's Homework Manager

LO3, 4, 5

PA20-1 Preparing a Process Costing Production Report (FIFO)

Boxer Corporation manufactures metal toolboxes. It adds all materials at the beginning of the manufacturing process. The company has provided the following information.

Beginning work in process	40,000 units
Direct materials (30% complete)	$ 40,000
Conversion cost	95,000
Total cost of beginning work in process	$ 135,000
Number of units started	76,000
Number of units completed and transferred to finished goods	82,000
Ending work in process: Conversion	50% complete
Direct materials cost incurred	$ 90,000
Conversion cost applied	157,000
Total cost added	$ 247,000

Required:

1. Using the FIFO method of process costing, complete each of the following steps:

    a. Reconcile the number of physical units worked on during the period.
    b. Calculate the number of equivalent units.
    c. Calculate the cost per equivalent unit, rounded to five decimal points.
    d. Reconcile the total cost of work in process.

2. Summarize the preceding steps in a production report for Boxer Corporation.

PA20-2 Preparing a Process Costing Production Report (Weighted Average) (Supplement)

Refer to the information for Boxer Corporation in PA20-1.

Required:

Complete all requirements for PA20-1 using the weighted average method.

PA20-3 Recording Manufacturing Costs and Preparing a Process Costing Production Report (FIFO)

LO2, 3, 4, 5

Seemore Company makes camping lanterns using a single production process. All direct materials are added at the beginning of the manufacturing process. Information for the month of March follows.

www.mhhe.com/LLPW1e

Beginning work in process (30% complete)	58,900 units
Direct materials	$ 96,000
Conversion cost	172,000
Total cost of beginning work in process	$ 268,000
Number of units started	121,500
Number of units completed and transferred to finished goods	167,400
Ending work in process (65% complete)	
Direct materials cost incurred	$ 253,700
Conversion cost applied	324,000
Total cost added	$ 577,700

Required:

1. Using the FIFO method of process costing, complete each of the following steps:

   a. Reconcile the number of physical units worked on during the period.
   b. Calculate the number of equivalent units.
   c. Calculate the cost per equivalent unit, rounded to five decimal places.
   d. Reconcile the total cost of work in process.

2. Summarize the preceding steps in a March production report for Seemore Company.
3. Prepare Seemore's journal entries to record each of the following transactions.

   a. Added direct materials to production during March.
   b. Applied conversion cost during March.
   c. Transferred completed units to Finished Goods Inventory.
   d. Sold units costing $650,000 for $1,000,000.
   e. Recorded $329,000 of actual conversion cost.
   f. Disposed of the ending balance in the Conversion Cost account.

PA20-4 Recording Manufacturing Costs and Preparing a Process Costing Production Report (Weighted Average) (Supplement)

eXcel

www.mhhe.com/LLPW1e

Refer to the information in PA20-3 for Seemore Company.

Required:

Complete all requirements for PA20-3 using the weighted average method.

PA20-5 Calculating Activity Rates and Assigning Costs to Products in ABC

LO6

Gutierrez Company makes two models of children's playhouses, the Castle and the Mansion. Information for Gutierrez follows.

	Castle	Mansion
Direct materials cost per unit	$45	$72
Direct labor cost per unit	$23	$35
Sales price per unit	$1,350	$1,565
Expected production per month	350 units	200 units

Gutierrez has monthly overhead of $219,000 that is divided into the following cost pools.

Setup costs		$ 85,000
Quality control		73,000
Maintenance		61,000
Total		$ 219,000

The company has also compiled the following information about its chosen cost drivers:

Number of	Castle	Mansion	Total
Setups required	42	58	100
Inspections	340	390	730
Machine hours	1,750	1,300	3,050

Required:
Complete the following for Gutierrez.

1. Select the appropriate cost driver for each cost pool and calculate the activity rates.
2. Assign overhead costs to each product based on activity demands.
3. Calculate the production cost per unit for each of Gutierrez's products.

Problems—Set B   Available with McGraw-Hill's Homework Manager

LO3, 4, 5   **PB20-1 Preparing a Process Costing Production Report (FIFO)**
Zoinks Inc. produces a popular brand of energy drink. It adds all materials at the beginning of the manufacturing process. The company has provided the following information.

Beginning work in process (30% complete)	20,000 units
Direct materials	$ 10,000
Conversion cost	46,000
Total cost of beginning work in process	$ 56,000
Number of units started	52,000
Number of units completed and transferred to finished goods	49,000
Ending work in process (70% complete)	
Direct materials cost incurred	$ 31,000
Conversion cost applied	82,000
Total cost added	$ 113,000

Required:

1. Using the FIFO method of process costing, complete each of the following steps:

    a. Reconcile the number of physical units worked on during the period.
    b. Calculate the number of equivalent units.
    c. Calculate the cost per equivalent unit, rounded to five decimal places.
    d. Reconcile the total cost of work in process.

2. Summarize the preceding steps in a production report for Zoinks Inc.

PB20-2 Preparing a Process Costing Production Report (Weighted Average) (Supplement)
Refer to the information about Zoinks Inc. in PB20-1.

Required:
Complete all requirements for PB20-1 using the weighted average method.

PB20-3 Recording Manufacturing Costs and Preparing a Process Costing Production Report (FIFO)

LO2, 3, 4, 5

Firelight Company makes camping tents in a single production department. All direct materials are added at the beginning of the manufacturing process. Information for the month of July follows.

Beginning work in process (30% complete)	23,100 units
Direct materials	$ 121,000
Conversion cost	184,000
Total cost of beginning work in process	$ 305,000
Number of units started	62,500
Number of units completed and transferred to finished goods	77,400
Ending work-in-process (35% complete)	
Direct materials cost incurred	$ 281,700
Conversion cost applied	386,200
Total cost added	$ 667,900

Required:

1. Using the FIFO method of process costing, complete each of the following steps:

    a.   Reconcile the number of physical units worked on during the period.
    b.   Calculate the number of equivalent units.
    c.   Calculate the cost per equivalent unit, rounded to five decimal places.
    d.   Reconcile the total cost of work in process.
2. Summarize the preceding steps in a July production report for Firelight Company.
3. Prepare Firelight's journal entries to record each of the following transactions.

    a.   Added direct materials to production during July.
    b.   Applied conversion cost during July.
    c.   Transferred completed units to Finished Goods Inventory.
    d.   Sold units costing $450,000 for $800,000.
    e.   Recorded $367,000 of actual conversion cost.
    f.   Disposed of ending the balance in the Conversion Cost account.

PB20-4 Recording Manufacturing Costs and Preparing a Process Costing Production Report (Weighted Average) (Supplement)

Refer to the information in PB20-3 for Firelight Company.

Required:

Complete all requirements for PB20-3 using the weighted average method.

PB20-5 Calculating Activity Rates and Assigning Costs to Products in ABC

LO5

Wayward Company makes two models of automobile navigation systems, the SeldomLost and the NeverLost.
Information for Wayward follows.

	SeldomLost	NeverLost
Direct materials cost per unit	$ 92	$ 115
Direct labor cost per unit	$ 51	$ 75
Sales price per unit	$850	$1,065
Expected production per month	400 units	900 units

Wayward has monthly overhead of $521,870 that is divided into the following cost pools.

Setup costs	$ 170,455
Quality control	203,775
Maintenance	65,700
Engineering	81,940
Total	$ 521,870

The company has also compiled the following information about its chosen cost drivers.

	ACTIVITY REQUIREMENTS		
	SeldomLost	NeverLost	Total
Number of setups required	60	86	146
Number of inspections	975	675	1,650
Number of machine hours	1,540	2,840	4,380
Number of engineering hours	352	612	964

Required:
Complete the following for Wayward.

1. Select the appropriate cost driver for each cost pool and calculate the activity rate.
2. Assign overhead costs to each product based on activity demands.
3. Calculate the production cost per unit for each of Wayward's products.

Cases and Projects

LO1   **CP20-1 Researching Companies That Use Process Costing**

Consider the many different manufactured products a person might use or consume in a typical day, everything from toothpaste to a custom-made Harley Davidson motorcycle.

Required:

Choose three items that you use regularly and whose manufacturer you believe is likely to use process costing. Investigate the manufacturing company of each item and its Web site for information to support or contradict your belief.

LO1   **CP20-2 Evaluating the Implications of Process Costing in a Service Industry**

Overnight package delivery is a multimillion dollar industry that has grown steadily since it began. The four largest carriers are the US Postal Service (USPS), Federal Express (FedEx), United Parcel Service (UPS), and Airborne Express. Suppose you have a document that must be delivered to each of the following cities by the close of business tomorrow. Using each company's Web site, determine the price to ship your letter and and record the information in the following table.

	Carefree, AZ	Happy Valley, TN	Experiment, PA	Opportunity, MT
USPS				
FedEx				
UPS				
Airborne				

To answer the following questions, assume that the prices charged by the companies are directly related to the cost of delivery.

Required:

1. Based on their pricing, which of the delivery companies appear(s) to use process costing?
2. For the companies that do(es) not appear to use process costing, what factors are likely to impact the cost (and thus pricing) of the overnight delivery service?
3. In this industry, what are the potential advantages and disadvantages of process costing?

CP20-3 Researching Companies That Have Implemented Activity Based Costing   LO6

Required:

Review recent issues of business publications (e.g., *BusinessWeek*, *The Wall Street Journal*) for information about companies that have implemented activity based costing. Choose one company to research in detail and then answer the following questions.

1. Give a brief description of the company, its products, and its history.
2. If the company has multiple divisions or segments, has one or more of them implemented ABC?
3. If one or more divisions or segments do use ABC, what factor(s) prompted the decision to do so?
4. What type of costing system was utilized prior to the conversion to ABC?
5. Were any specific difficulties experienced during the switch?
6. What benefits has the company or one or more of its divisions or segments identified as a result of implementing ABC?
7. Did the move to an ABC system impact other areas of the company and/or result in changes to other aspects of its operation?
8. Does the company view the ABC implementation as successful?

21 Cost Behavior and Cost-Volume-Profit Analysis

LEARNING OBJECTIVES

After completing this chapter, you should be able to:

LO1 Identify costs as either variable, fixed, step, or mixed.

LO2 Prepare a scattergraph to illustrate the relationship between total cost and activity.

LO3 Use the high-low method to analyze mixed costs.

LO4 Prepare and interpret a contribution margin income statement.

LO5 Use cost-volume-profit analysis to find the break-even point.

LO6 Use cost-volume-profit analysis to determine the sales needed to achieve a target profit.

Lectured slideshow—LP21-1
www.mhhe.com/LLPW1e

Focus Company: STARBUCKS COFFEE

"Beyond a Cup of Coffee"

www.starbucks.com

These days you don't have to go far to buy a cup of Starbucks coffee. Started as a small coffee shop in Seattle's Pike Place Market over three decades ago, Starbucks Coffee can now be found on street corners, college campuses, and airports across the country and abroad. Consider the following facts about Starbucks:

- From 2002–2007, Starbucks opened approximately five new locations every day. By 2008, the company realized it could not sustain that rate of growth and announced that it was closing 600 stores.
- The average customer spends $4.05 per visit at Starbucks.
- Starbucks spends more on employee health insurance than on coffee beans.
- When Starbucks eliminated the 8-ounce cup from its menu (making the "tall" the new "small"), it increased revenue by 25 cents per cup with only 2 cents of added product cost.[1]

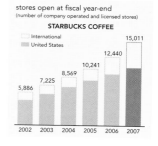

stores open at fiscal year-end
(number of company operated and licensed stores)

STARBUCKS COFFEE

☐ International
▨ United States

5,886 7,225 8,569 10,241 12,440 15,011

2002 2003 2004 2005 2006 2007

How does Starbucks decide how much to charge for a cup of coffee? How does the relationship between revenue, cost, and volume affect the bottom line, or profit?

This chapter illustrates two managerial accounting topics that can help managers answer these questions. The first topic, cost behavior, helps managers understand how total costs will change as the company's volume of activity changes. The second topic, cost-volume-profit analysis, focuses on the relationship among product prices, volume, costs, and profits. This approach allows managers to determine the number of units or customers needed to make a certain profit and to analyze how changing prices or costs will impact profit.

Throughout this chapter, we use a hypothetical Starbucks coffeeshop as our focus company, but we limit our analysis to the sale of coffee. So, forget about all of the other goodies that Starbucks sells, such as pastries, CDs, T-shirts, and appliances. To keep things simple, we have also made up some numbers for our examples—but that is only appropriate for the company that invented the words "venti" and "doppio."

---

[1] Taylor Clark, *Starbucked: A Double Tall Tale of Caffeine, Commerce, and Culture* (New York: Little, Brown and Company, 2007).

COST BEHAVIOR PATTERNS	ESTIMATING COST BEHAVIOR	CONTRIBUTION MARGIN	COST-VOLUME-PROFIT ANALYSIS
• Relevant Range • Variable Costs • Fixed Costs • Step Costs • Mixed Costs	• Preparing a Scattergraph • Linear Approaches to Analyzing Mixed Costs • High-low Method for Analyzing Mixed Costs	• Contribution Margin Income Statement • Contribution Margin Formula • Unit Contribution Margin • Contribution Margin Ratio	• Assumption of Cost-Volume-Profit • Break-Even Analysis • Margin of Safety • Target Profit Analysis • Cost-Volume-Profit Relationships in Graphic Form • Multiproduct Cost-Volume-Profit Analysis

COST BEHAVIOR PATTERNS

> **Coach's Tip**
>
> The terms cost and expense are used interchangeably in this chapter, although they have different meanings in financial accounting.

Cost behavior is defined as the way in which total costs change when some measure of activity changes. Activities that cause total cost to change are referred to as **cost drivers.** Some of the most common measures of activity include the number of direct labor hours, machine hours, units produced, and customers served.

Relevant Range

When we classify cost according to behavior, we must limit the range of activity, called the relevant range. The relevant range is the range of activity over which we expect our assumptions about cost behavior to hold true. For example, fixed costs will remain constant only over a limited range of activity. At some point, fixed costs must increase to accommodate more activity. In this chapter, we use a straight line to define the relationship between total cost and activity. In reality, the relationship between total cost and activity probably is not perfectly linear. However, so long as we limit our analysis to a fairly narrow range of activity—that is, the relevant range—we can **assume** that the relationship is linear and come close to estimating true cost behavior.

Variable Costs

> **Learning Objective 1**
>
> Identify costs as either variable, fixed, step, or mixed.

Recall from Chapter 18 that variable costs are those that change, in total, in direct proportion to changes in activity levels. If the activity level increases by 50 percent, total variable cost also increases by 50 percent. If the activity level decreases by 20 percent, total variable cost should decrease by 20 percent. Examples of variable costs for Starbucks Coffee include the cost of coffee beans, milk, sugar, cups, and other paper products. All of these costs will increase, in total, as Starbucks sells more coffee drinks.

Although **total** variable costs change with activity, variable cost **per unit** remains constant. For example, the cost of coffee used in each cup should be the same regardless of how many cups are served. This ignores any type of discount that a company may get by purchasing ingredients in large quantities.

See Exhibit 21.1 for charts of how the total and per unit cost of ingredients such as coffee beans change with the number of coffee drinks served.

As the graph on the left shows, the total cost of ingredients increases in direct proportion to increases in the number of coffee drinks served. As the graph on the right shows, however, the **per unit** cost of ingredients remains constant at about $0.50 per drink, regardless of how many drinks are served.

Fixed Costs

Fixed costs remain the same **in total** regardless of activity level. For a Starbucks Coffee shop, fixed costs include rent, the manager's salary, depreciation on equipment, and insurance. These costs

Exhibit 21.1   Variable Cost Behavior

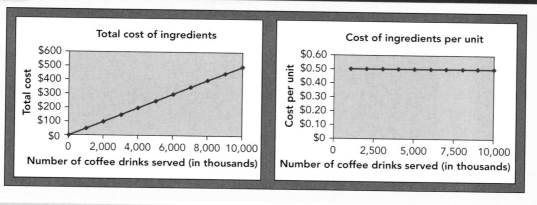

remain the same in total regardless of how many coffee drinks the shop serves each month. On a **per unit** basis, however, fixed costs decrease with increases in activity levels (see Exhibit 21.2).

The fact that per unit fixed cost decreases with increases in activity level does not mean that a manager can drive down costs simply by increasing the number of units produced. Imagine what would happen if a Starbucks manager decided to make as many cups of coffee as possible each day regardless of whether there were enough customers to buy them. Although doing so would drive down the per unit cost of each cup, it would also result in a lot of coffee being thrown away, with no revenue from customers to cover the cost.

Although this example may seem far fetched, it is not uncommon for managers to believe that they can drive down costs by producing as many units as possible. The difference is that in most companies, the unsold units are not thrown away at the end of the day like a cold cup of coffee. Instead, unsold units are stored in a warehouse as inventory—a solution that adds unnecessary costs for insurance, shipping and handling, and so on. The bottom line is that while increasing production lowers the average cost of each unit produced (because the fixed costs are spread over more units), it does not translate into increased profit without increased sales.

Exhibit 21.2   Fixed Cost Behavior

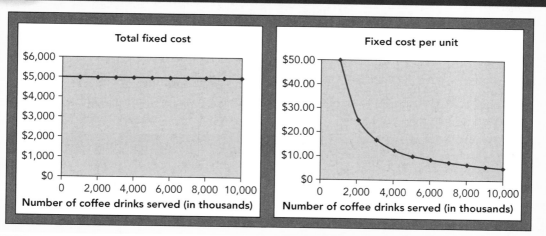

Step Costs

Step costs are fixed over some range of activity and then increase in a steplike fashion when a capacity limit is reached. Depending on the width of the steps, step costs may be treated as either step-variable or step-fixed costs as in Exhibit 21.3.

As the graph on the left shows, step-variable costs tend to be fixed over a fairly narrow range and rise in multiple steps across the relevant range. At Starbucks Coffee, a step-variable cost includes the wages paid to servers. Starbucks relies heavily on part-time labor, and managers try to schedule more workers when more customers are expected to arrive. Once employees are

Exhibit 21.3   Step Cost Behavior

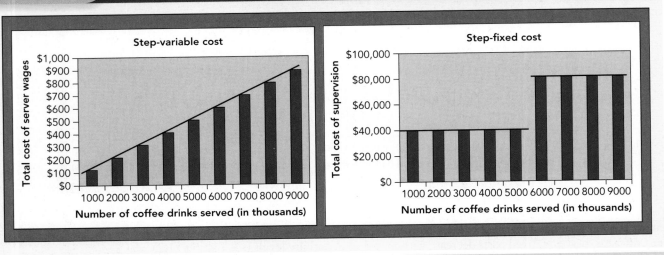

on the job, however, they must be paid regardless of how many customers they serve. Because the steps between servers' wages are so narrow and the total cost increases with the number of coffee drinks served, Starbucks can treat the cost of server wages as a variable cost.

As the graph on the right side of Exhibit 21.3 shows, step-fixed costs are fixed over a much wider range of activity than step-variable costs. To allow more customers to be served, for example, Starbucks might decide to hire an additional supervisor or rent additional space or equipment. Because these costs are fixed over a fairly wide range of activity, they are treated as fixed costs, at least within a limited range of activity.

Mixed Costs

Mixed costs, also known as semivariable costs, have both a fixed and a variable component. The fixed portion represents the base amount that is incurred regardless of activity. The variable cost is the amount that is based on activity or usage. An example of a mixed cost is a long-distance calling plan that has a fixed charge each month plus an additional charge for each minute of usage. Many utility expenses behave the same way. Most companies incur a minimum utility charge each month regardless of activity, but the total utility expense increases with increased activity. The activity driver for utility costs could be the number of hours a company is open or the number of hours that employees use electrical equipment.

Because mixed costs have both a fixed and a variable component, both the total cost and the per unit cost change with the level of activity (see Exhibit 21.4). Because part of the

Coach's Tip

When you see total cost increasing and per unit cost decreasing with activity level, you can conclude that the cost has both a fixed and a variable component. That is, it is a mixed cost.

Exhibit 21.4   Mixed Cost Behavior

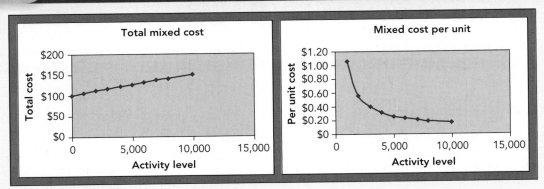

cost is variable, the total mixed cost rises with increases in activity as in the graph on the left. Because part of the cost is fixed, however, the mixed cost per unit falls with increases in activity as in the graph on the right.

The next section discusses how to separate the fixed and variable components of mixed costs. First take a moment to make sure you understand the difference between fixed, variable, step, and mixed costs by completing the following Self-Study Practice.

SELF-STUDY PRACTICE

1. Which of the following statements is true?

   a. If activity increases by 10 percent, total fixed cost will increase by 10 percent.
   b. If activity increases by 10 percent, per unit variable cost will increase by 10 percent.
   c. If activity increases by 10 percent, per unit fixed cost will decrease by 10 percent.
   d. If activity increases by 10 percent, total variable cost will increase by 10 percent.

2. For each row in the following table, indicate whether the cost is variable, fixed, step, or mixed.

| | UNITS OF ACTIVITY | | | | |
	0 Units	100 Units	200 Units	300 Units	400 Units
Total cost of A	$ 0	$200	$400	$600	$800
Total cost of B	500	500	500	750	750
Total cost of C	350	400	450	500	550
Total cost of D	750	750	750	750	750

After you have finished, check your answers with the solutions at the bottom of the page.

ESTIMATING COST BEHAVIOR

Preparing a Scattergraph

One of the easiest ways to identify cost behavior is by using a visual representation or graph. A scattergraph is a graph with total cost plotted on the vertical (Y) axis and some measure of activity on the horizontal (X) axis. It is useful for getting a "feel" for the data and helps answer preliminary questions about the nature of the relationship between total cost and activity and whether the data have any unusual patterns or blips.

A scattergraph can be created by manually plotting data points on graph paper, or by using the following steps in Excel:

1. Enter the data in Excel and highlight the data that you want to plot.
2. Select the Chart Wizard from the toolbar.
3. Select XY (Scatter) as the chart type. Be sure total cost is on the Y axis with the activity driver on the X axis.
4. Add a chart title and labels for the X and Y axes.

To apply these steps, consider the following data showing the total overhead cost (Y) and the number of customers served (X) for our hypothetical Starbucks location.

---

1. D.

2. A, variable cost; B, step cost; C, mixed cost; and D, fixed cost.

Solution to
Self-Study Practice

Learning Objective 2

Prepare a scattergraph to illustrate the relationship between total cost and activity.

Month	Number of Customers Served (X)	Total Overhead Cost (Y)
January	9,000	$15,000
February	15,000	15,750
March	12,500	16,000
April	6,000	12,500
May	5,000	13,250
June	10,000	13,000

See Exhibit 21.5 for an illustration of how to create a scattergraph of these data using Excel.

Exhibit 21.5   Creating a Scattergraph in Excel

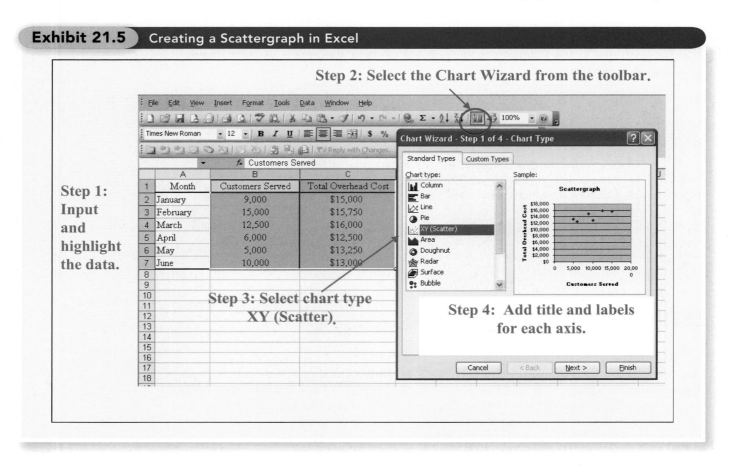

Refer to Exhibit 21.6 for the scattergraph that results from these steps. We have added a red line to the graph to show the general trend in the data. Although the data points do not fall in a perfect line, they are close enough so that we can use the line to approximate the relationship between total overhead cost (Y) and activity (X). In a later section, we discuss several ways to determine the line, but for now, let's focus on what the line reveals about the relationship between total overhead cost (Y) and the number of customers served (X).

This scattergraph reveals a slightly positive relationship between total overhead cost (Y) and the number of customers served (X). At least a portion of the overhead cost is variable. But we can also see that a large part of the overhead cost is fixed.

The slope of the red line represents the variable cost per unit of X. It indicates the amount by which total overhead will increase with each additional customer served. For Starbucks, the variable overhead cost would be for items such as paper supplies, sugar, cream, and power to run the coffee machines.

Exhibit 21.6   Scattergraph of Total Overhead Cost (Y) and Customers Served (X)

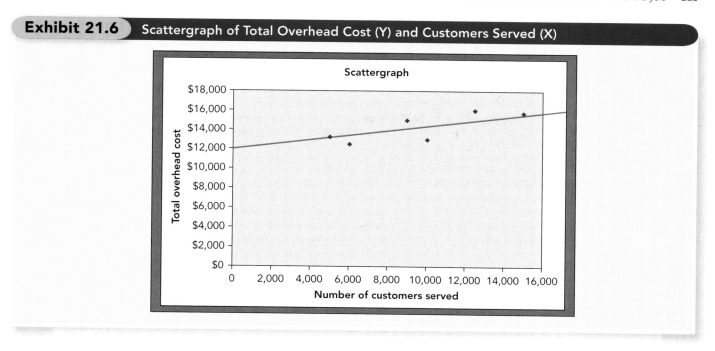

The intercept, or the point at which the red line connects with the Y axis, represents the fixed cost. This is also sometimes called the constant, because it reflects the amount of cost expected at zero activity. In this example, the fixed cost appears to be about $12,000. For Starbucks, the fixed overhead costs would be for items such as rent, insurance, the manager's salary, and other costs that will be incurred each month regardless of how many customers are served.

The next section discusses several methods for finding the variable cost per unit (slope of the line) and the total fixed cost (intercept).

Linear Approaches to Analyzing Mixed Costs

The linear approach to cost estimation is based on the following formulas:

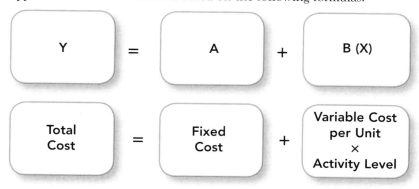

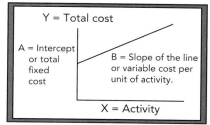

> **Coach's Tip**
>
> We often use a straight line to represent the relationship between total cost (Y) and activity (X). Although the data do not fall perfectly on the line, we can use a straight line to approximate or estimate the relationship. Of course, our estimates will be good only if our assumption of linearity is reasonable.

These terms are interpreted as follows.

- **Y** is total cost, which is shown on the vertical axis. It is called the **dependent variable** because we assume that Y is dependent on X.
- **X** is the activity that causes Y (total cost) to change. This variable is also called the **cost driver** or the independent variable.
- **A** is the amount of cost that will be incurred regardless of the activity level (X), or the **total fixed cost.** This term is also called the **intercept term** or the **constant.**
- **B** indicates how much Y (total cost) will increase with each additional unit of X (activity). In other words, it is the **variable cost per unit of X** and is represented by the **slope** of the line.

There are three linear approaches that can be used to analyze mixed costs: the visual fit method, regression analysis, and the high-low method. Although each method differs in terms of how the line is calculated, each provides an estimate of the intercept (total fixed cost) and slope of the line (variable cost per unit).

The **visual fit method** involves "eyeballing" the data on the scattergraph and drawing a line through the points to capture the relationship between total cost and activity. This method is simple and intuitive but is very subjective and does not provide very precise estimates of the intercept (fixed cost) and slope (variable cost per unit).

The **high-low method** uses the two most extreme activity (X) observations to "fit the line." This method uses only two data points to solve for variable cost per unit (slope) and total fixed cost (intercept). We illustrate this method in detail in the next section.

Regression analysis is a statistical technique for finding the best fitting line based on all available data points. Although it is more complicated than the high-low method, a spreadsheet program such as Excel can be used to do the calculations. The program's output will include an estimate of the intercept (total fixed cost) and X coefficient (variable cost per unit of X) as well as other statistical measures that are beyond the scope of this text. The regression method is covered in more detail in advanced managerial accounting books.

High-Low Method for Analyzing Mixed Costs

In this section, we apply the high-low method to Starbucks' overhead costs. Although the high-low method is less sophisticated than regression analysis, it provides a reasonable estimate of the fixed and variable costs as long as the high and low data points represent the trend in the overall data, which appears to be the case in this example.

The first step in the high-low method is to find the two most extreme activity (X) observations. The data we have been using for our Starbucks example follow:

Month	Number of Customers Served (X)	Total Overhead Cost (Y)	
January	9,000	$15,000	
February	15,000	15,750	High X
March	12,500	16,000	
April	6,000	12,500	
May	5,000	13,250	Low X
June	10,000	13,000	

The high-low method uses only the high (February) and low (May) data points to estimate the variable cost per unit and the total fixed cost.

The second step is to calculate the slope of the line based on the high and low data points. You may recall from your high school algebra class that the slope of the line is calculated as "rise over run," or the change in Y over the change in X. We use the same logic here to calculate how much total cost (Y) changes with a corresponding change in activity level (X).

$$\text{Variable Cost per Unit} = \frac{\text{Difference in Total Cost (Y)}}{\text{Difference in Activity (X)}}$$

Applying this formula to the data from February and May results in the following:

$$\text{Variable Cost} = \$0.25 \text{ per Unit} = \frac{(\$15,750 - \$13,250) = \$2,500}{(15,000 - 5,000) = 10,000}$$

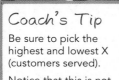

The high-low method shows that total overhead cost increased by $2,500 when the number of customers served increased by 10,000. This results in a variable overhead cost of $0.25 per customer served.

The third step is to solve for total fixed cost using the following equation:

| Total Fixed Cost | = | Total Cost | − | Total Variable Cost (Variable Cost per Unit × X) |

Because we now know that the variable cost is $0.25 per customer served and we know the total cost, we can solve for the fixed cost. To do this, we can use **EITHER** the high or the low data point to determine the fixed cost. The high and low data points for our Starbucks example follow.

Month	Number of Customers Served (X)	Total Overhead Cost (Y)	
February	15,000	$15,750	High X
May	5,000	13,250	Low X

First let's use the data from February to solve for the total fixed cost:

| Total Fixed Cost $12,000 | = | Total Cost (February) $15,750 | − | Total Variable Cost (February) $0.25 × 15,000 Customers Served $3,750 |

We get exactly the same result if we use May instead:

| Total Fixed Cost $12,000 | = | Total Cost (May) $13,250 | − | Total Variable Cost (May) $0.25 × 5,000 Customers Served $1,250 |

Regardless of whether we use the high (February) or low (May) data points, we arrive at a total fixed cost of $12,000. You should recall that this is the same estimate of fixed costs shown in Exhibit 21.6 where the red line intercepted the Y axis. If you look back to this exhibit, you will see that the red line was drawn so that it went through both the high and the low data points. Based on the high-low method, we now know that the red line can be more specifically defined as follows:

| Total Overhead Cost | = | Total Fixed Cost $12,000 | + | Total Variable Cost $.25 × Customers Served |

We can use this formula to predict total overhead cost in the future, so long as we have an estimate of the number of customers to be served. For example, if Starbucks expects to serve 8,000 customers in July, it would budget for $12,000 in fixed overhead cost plus $2,000 ($0.25 × 8,000 customers) in variable costs for a total of $14,000.

Before you continue, complete the following self-study practice to make sure you understand how to estimate fixed and variable cost using the high-low method.

A travel agent has collected the following information regarding the number of reservations made and the total cost of running the agency for the past four months:

Month	Number of Reservations Booked	Total Cost
January	600	$41,000
February	400	32,000
March	860	55,000
April	740	56,000

Using the high-low method, determine the variable cost per reservation and the total fixed cost.

After you have finished, check your answers with the solutions at the bottom of the page.

CONTRIBUTION MARGIN

Contribution Margin Income Statement

Learning Objective 4

Prepare and interpret a contribution margin income statement.

Now that you have learned how to separate mixed costs into their fixed and variable components, you can prepare a type of income statement called the **contribution margin income statement.** A contribution margin income statement categorizes costs as variable or fixed. Unlike financial statements meant for external users, which are prepared according to GAAP, a contribution margin income statement is used only for internal purposes. It is extremely useful for addressing a variety of managerial questions because cost behavior is the key to many managerial decisions.

To illustrate, let's construct a contribution margin income statement for our hypothetical Starbucks coffee shop for the month of February when it served 15,000 cups of coffee. For this analysis, we assume that the total variable cost per unit is $1.00. This includes not only the variable overhead calculated using the high-low method, but also the direct material cost (ingredients) and direct labor (server wages). We assume an average sales price of $2.50 per unit and total fixed overhead cost of $12,000. Based on this information, the contribution margin income statement would appear as follows:

Coach's Tip

Notice that fixed costs are stated on a total basis rather than per unit or as a percentage of sales because those measures will change as the sales volume changes. When you see fixed cost stated on a per unit basis, you should immediately calculate the total fixed cost because that is the number that is truly fixed.

Starbucks Coffee
Contribution Margin Income Statement
For the Month of February 2009

15,000 Units sold

	Total	Per Unit	Percent of Sales
Sales revenue	$37,500	$2.50	100%
Less: Variable costs	15,000	1.00	40
Contribution margin	22,500	$1.50	60%
Less: Fixed costs	12,000		
Profit (loss)	$10,500		

Solution to Self-Study Practice

High, March; Low, February

Variable Cost = ($55,000 − $32,000) / (860 − 400) = $23,000 / 460 = $50 per reservation
Total Fixed Cost = $55,000 − ($50 × 860) = $12,000, or $32,000 − ($50 × 400) = $12,000

Contribution Margin Formula

The key to the contribution margin income statement is the contribution margin, which is the difference between sales revenue and variable costs:

$$\boxed{\text{Contribution Margin}} \;=\; \boxed{\text{Sales Revenue}} \;-\; \boxed{\text{Variable Costs}}$$

The contribution margin represents the amount left over from sales revenue after variable costs have been covered to contribute to fixed costs and then provide a profit. In the preceding example, the total contribution margin was $22,500. Once the monthly fixed costs of $12,000 were deducted, $10,500 remained as profit.

What happens if the contribution margin is not enough to cover fixed costs? The company will incur a loss. If the contribution margin exactly equals fixed costs, the company earns zero profit. This concept lies at the heart of break-even analysis, which is covered later in this chapter.

As the next section discusses, the contribution margin formula can be used to find not only the total contribution margin but also the contribution margin per unit and as a percentage of sales.

Unit Contribution Margin

The contribution margin is often stated on a per unit basis. The unit contribution margin tells us how much each additional unit contributes to fixed costs and profit. It is very useful in solving cost-volume-profit questions involving the way changes in the number of units sold will affect the bottom line.

In our Starbucks example, each coffee drink provides $1.50 in contribution margin. Because fixed costs do not change with each additional unit sold, the contribution margin earned on each unit will have a direct effect on the bottom-line profit. What would happen if Starbucks sold 1,000 more coffee drinks in March than in February? Recall that the coffeehouse sold 15,000 units in February and made a profit of $10,500. Because the contribution margin per unit is $1.50, the profit would be $1,500 higher (1,000 × $1.50) than it was in February, or $12,000 ($10,500 + $1,500).

We can verify this answer by creating a new contribution margin income statement based on 16,000 units as follows:

Starbucks Coffee
Contribution Margin Income Statement
For the Month of March 2009

16,000 Units sold

	Total	Per Unit	Percent of Sales
Sales revenue	$40,000	$2.50	100%
Less: Variable costs	16,000	1.00	40
Contribution margin	24,000	$1.50	60%
Less: Fixed costs	12,000		
Net profit	$12,000		

STARBUCKS

Contribution Margin Ratio

The contribution margin can also be stated as percentage of sales, called the contribution margin ratio, that is calculated as follows:

$$\boxed{\text{Contribution Margin Ratio}} \;=\; \boxed{\dfrac{\text{Contribution Margin}}{\text{Sales Revenue}}}$$

The contribution margin ratio indicates how much additional contribution margin is generated by each dollar of sales. In our Starbucks example, the 60 percent contribution margin means that every

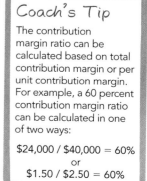

Coach's Tip

The contribution margin ratio can be calculated based on total contribution margin or per unit contribution margin. For example, a 60 percent contribution margin ratio can be calculated in one of two ways:

$24,000 / $40,000 = 60%

or

$1.50 / $2.50 = 60%

$1.00 in sales will generate $0.60 in contribution margin. Because fixed costs do not increase with increases in sales, this increased contribution margin will have a direct effect on the bottom line.

The contribution margin ratio is useful for answering cost-volume-profit questions involving how changes in total sales revenue will affect profitability. Assume, for example, Starbucks' manager is thinking of investing $2,000 per month in local advertising in hope of boosting monthly sales by $5,000. What effect would this decision have on profit? Because we know that the contribution margin ratio is 60 percent, we can quickly determine that a $5,000 increase in sales would increase the contribution margin by $3,000. Of course, fixed costs would go up by $2,000, so the net effect on profit would be a $1,000 increase, as follows:

Increased sales		$5,000
Increased contribution margin	($5,000 × 60%)	3,000
Increased fixed expenses		2,000
Increased profit		1,000

Before we continue on, take a moment to complete the following Self-Study Practice.

> ### Coach's Tip
>
> The contribution margin ratio provides a shortcut for determining the effect of an increase in sales on profit. Another way to find the effect is to prepare two contribution margin income statements and note whether profit increases or decreases. Although this approach takes longer, it is a good way to verify that your calculations are correct.

SELF-STUDY PRACTICE

In the same month that a company sold 750 units for $80 each, it reported total variable costs of $45,000 and total fixed expenses of $10,000.

Prepare a contribution margin income statement to calculate the following:

1. Total contribution margin.
2. Contribution margin per unit.
3. Contribution margin ratio.
4. Net profit.

After you have finished, check your answers with the solutions at the bottom of the page.

COST-VOLUME-PROFIT ANALYSIS

Video 21-1
www.mhhe.com/LLPW1e

This section extends the analysis of cost behavior to a specific application called cost-volume-profit analysis (CVP). Cost-volume-profit analysis is a managerial decision-making tool that focuses on the relationships among sales price, volume of units sold, fixed and variable costs, and profit. The basic approach allows managers to see how a change in any one of these variables will impact profitability while holding everything else constant.

Assumption of Cost-Volume-Profit

While CVP is very useful in answering certain questions, it requires managers to make several important assumptions. Like all business modeling approaches, the results are only as good as the underlying assumptions. The key assumptions of CVP analysis are:

1. A straight line can be used to model how total cost and total revenue change across the relevant range of activity.
2. All costs can be accurately described as either fixed or variable.
3. Changes in total cost are due strictly to changes in activity level rather than other factors, such as gains in efficiency.
4. Production and sales are equal so that inventory levels remain constant.
5. Companies that sell more than one product maintain a constant sales mix, or proportion of products sold.

If any of these assumptions are violated, the results of CVP analysis may not be accurate.

Solution to
Self-Study Practice

1. (750 × $80) − $45,000 = $15,000
2. $15,000/750 = $20
3. $20/$80 = 25%
4. $15,000 − $10,000 = $5,000

Break-Even Analysis

Break-even analysis is one of the most common applications of cost-volume-profit analysis. The goal of break-even analysis is to determine the level of sales (in either units or sales dollars) required for a company to break even, or earn zero profit.

Recall that contribution margin is the amount of sales revenue that remains after variable costs have been covered, and is available to cover fixed costs and provide a profit. The break-even point is the point at which the company would make zero profit. In terms of the contribution margin, the break-even point means that contribution margin must equal fixed costs so that nothing is left over as profit.

> **Learning Objective 5**
>
> Use cost-volume-profit analysis to find the break-even point.

| Total Contribution Margin | = | Total Fixed Costs | + | Profit |

Zero at break-even point

Recall too that we can express the contribution margin either on a per unit basis or as a percentage of sales. Let's state our formula for the contribution margin in terms of the number of units sold:

Unit Contribution Margin Approach

| Total Contribution Margin | = | Total Fixed Costs | + | Profit |

Zero at break-even point

Unit Contribution Margin × Number of Units Sold

> **Coach's Tip**
>
> This general framework can be used to solve many CVP problems. In break-even analysis, we set the profit equal to zero. If we want the profit to be something other than zero, we modify the equation to include the target profit.

To express the break-even point in terms of the number of units sold, we simply set the profit in this equation equal to zero. Then we rearrange the terms so that only the number of units sold appears to the left of the equal sign, which yields the following formula for the break-even point:

$$\text{Break-Even Units} = \frac{\text{Total Fixed Costs}}{\text{Unit Contribution Margin}}$$

Recall from our Starbucks example that monthly fixed costs were $12,000 and that each coffee drink provided a contribution margin of $1.50 ($2.50 price − $1.00 variable cost per unit). Thus, the number of coffee drinks that Starbucks needs to sell to break even would be calculated as follows:

$$\text{Break-Even Units} = \$12,000 \,/\, \$1.50 \text{ per drink}$$
$$\text{Break-Even Units} = 8,000 \text{ Coffee Drinks}$$

The break-even formula shows that Starbucks needs to sell 8,000 coffee drinks per month just to cover its fixed costs. Because we know that the average price of a coffee drink is $2.50, this result translates into $20,000 in total sales revenue (8,000 units × $2.50 price).

A more direct way to calculate the break-even point in total sales dollars is to use the contribution margin (CM) ratio. Recall that the CM ratio indicates how much total CM every dollar of sales generates. Thus, we can convert the total contribution margin to sales dollars using the CM ratio, as follows:

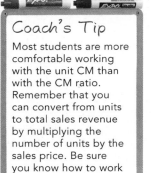

Coach's Tip

Most students are more comfortable working with the unit CM than with the CM ratio. Remember that you can convert from units to total sales revenue by multiplying the number of units by the sales price. Be sure you know how to work problems both ways, however, in case you are forced to work with missing information—as managers often are in the real world.

Contribution Margin Ratio Approach

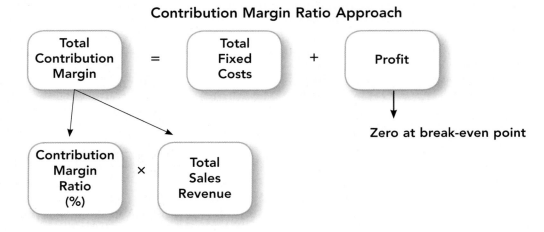

If we rearrange the terms of this equation so that only total sales dollars appears to the left of the equal sign, we arrive at the following formula:

$$\text{Break-Even Sales} = \frac{\text{Total Fixed Costs}}{\text{Contribution Margin Ratio (\%)}}$$

Because Starbucks' CM ratio is 60 percent, the total sales needed to break even can be calculated as follows:

> **Break-Even Units = $12,000 / 60%**
> **Break-Even Sales = $20,000**

Margin of Safety

The **margin of safety** is the difference between actual or budgeted sales and the break-even point. Think of the margin of safety as a buffer zone that identifies how much sales can drop before the business will begin operating at a loss. This application of CVP analysis is most relevant to companies that face a significant risk of **not** making a profit, such as start-up businesses or companies that face extreme competition or abrupt changes in demand. The formula for calculating the margin of safety is:

> **Margin of Safety** = **Actual or Budgeted Sales** − **Break-Even Sales**

Existing companies base the margin of safety on actual sales; new businesses or those in a new location base it on budgeted sales. For example, if you were thinking of opening a new Starbucks location and had developed a business plan based on an anticipated sales level, it would be wise to compare that level to the break-even point. Doing so would show you how much of a cushion you have between making a profit and suffering a loss.

To see how to apply the margin of safety to actual sales, let's return to the month of February when our Starbucks coffee location sold 15,000 coffee drinks:

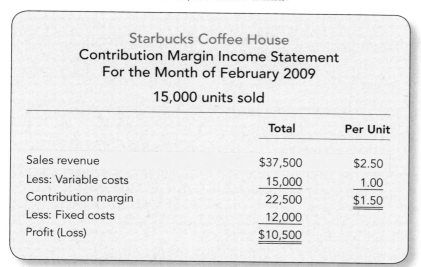

Starbucks Coffee House
Contribution Margin Income Statement
For the Month of February 2009

15,000 units sold

	Total	Per Unit
Sales revenue	$37,500	$2.50
Less: Variable costs	15,000	1.00
Contribution margin	22,500	$1.50
Less: Fixed costs	12,000	
Profit (Loss)	$10,500	

Notice that the company operated above the break-even point during February with sales of $37,500 and a profit of $10,500. Recall that the break-even point was 8,000 units, or $20,000 in total sales. Thus, the margin of safety is calculated as follows:

$$\begin{array}{ccccc} \textbf{Margin} & & \textbf{Actual or} & & \textbf{Break-} \\ \textbf{of} & = & \textbf{Budgeted} & - & \textbf{Even} \\ \textbf{Safety} & & \textbf{Sales} & & \textbf{Sales} \\ \\ \$17{,}500 & & \$37{,}500 & & \$20{,}000 \end{array}$$

Expressing the margin of safety as a percentage of actual sales provides a better idea of how large this buffer zone is. In this case, the margin of safety as a percentage of actual sales would be 46.7 percent ($17,500 / $37,500). That means that Starbucks' monthly sales could fall 46.7 percent below the February sales level before the company would begin to incur a loss.

Target Profit Analysis

Most managers want to do more than just break even; they want to earn a profit for the owners or shareholders. Target profit analysis is an extension of break-even analysis that allows managers to determine the number of units or total sales revenue needed to earn a target profit. To do so, the total contribution margin must be enough to cover the fixed costs plus the target profit as follows:

$$\boxed{\begin{array}{c} \textbf{Total} \\ \textbf{Contribution} \\ \textbf{Margin} \end{array}} \;=\; \boxed{\begin{array}{c} \textbf{Total} \\ \textbf{Fixed} \\ \textbf{Costs} \end{array}} \;+\; \boxed{\begin{array}{c} \textbf{Target} \\ \textbf{Profit} \end{array}}$$

We can easily modify the break-even formulas presented in the last section to incorporate a target profit as follows:

$$\text{Target Units} = \frac{\text{Total Fixed Costs} + \text{Target Profit}}{\text{Unit Contribution Margin}}$$

$$\text{Target Sales} = \frac{\text{Total Fixed Costs} + \text{Target Profit}}{\text{Contribution Margin Ratio (\%)}}$$

Learning Objective 6
Use cost-volume-profit analysis to determine the sales needed to achieve a target profit.

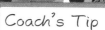

Coach's Tip

The only difference between the target profit formula and the break-even formula is that the target profit formula adds the target profit to fixed costs. The amount in the denominater depends on whether the purpose is to find the target in terms of units or total sales dollars.

For example, if the Starbucks' manager wants to earn $18,000 in profit each month, the target units and target sales would be calculated as follows:

$$\text{Target Units} = \frac{\$12{,}000 + \$18{,}000}{\$1.50 \text{ per Drink}} = 20{,}000 \text{ Coffee Drinks}$$

$$\text{Target Sales} = \frac{\$12{,}000 + \$18{,}000}{60\%} = \$50{,}000$$

Cost-Volume-Profit Relationships in Graphic Form

Cost-volume-profit relationships can be shown graphically. Sometimes called a break-even chart, a CVP graph is useful for visualizing the relationships among unit sales volume, total revenue, and total costs. It also shows how activity levels above or below the break-even point will produce a profit or loss. Refer to Exhibit 21.7 for a **CVP** graph based on the cost and revenue data we have been using for Starbucks Coffee.

You can quickly see that the company needs to sell 8,000 coffee drinks or earn $20,000 in total sales revenue to break even. The difference between the total revenue and total cost lines is the profit (or loss). For example, if Starbucks sells 20,000 coffee drinks, or $50,000 in sales, it will earn the target profit of $18,000.

CVP graphs are also useful for determining what will happen if different elements of the CVP relationship change—for example, the unit sales price, the variable cost, or the fixed costs. What would happen to the break-even point, for example, if fixed costs increased but the unit price and variable cost remained the same? The total cost line would shift upward by the amount of the added fixed cost, but its slope would remain the same because the variable cost per unit did not change. This change would shift the break-even point upward and to the right, raising the break-even point in terms of both units and total sales dollars, as shown in Exhibit 21.8.

Try visualizing how other changes to the CVP graph would affect the break-even point. For example, increasing the unit sales price would make the slope of the total revenue line steeper, which would lower the break-even point. Lowering the variable cost per unit would flatten the total cost line, which would also lower the break-even point.

Coach's Tip

The point where the total cost and total revenue lines cross is the break-even point. Activity levels below the break-even point will produce a loss; activity levels above the break-even point will generate a profit.

Exhibit 21.7   Cost-Volume-Profit Graph

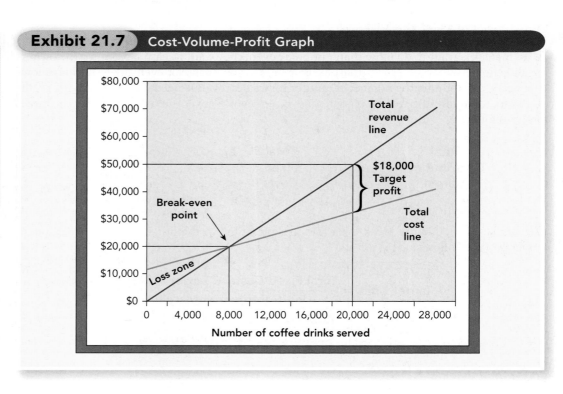

Exhibit 21.8   Effect of an Increase in Fixed Costs on the Break-Even Point

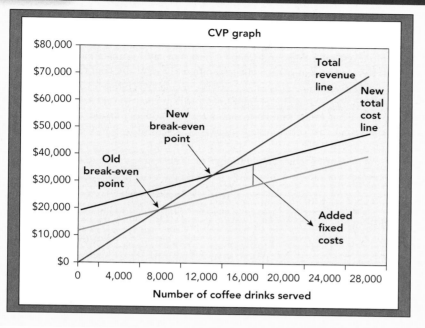

Multiproduct Cost-Volume-Profit Analysis

Throughout this chapter, we simplified the CVP analysis by assuming that Starbucks sells only a single product: coffee. But in reality Starbucks and most other businesses offer more than one product or service. For example, Starbucks sells various types of coffee and tea, as well as pastries, sandwiches, mugs, T-shirts, and other novelty items. The fact that each of these products has a different price (and different cost) makes the CVP analysis more complex.

To extend the single product CVP analysis to a multiproduct setting requires calculating an **average** contribution margin based on all of the products or services that the company offers. This average contribution margin should be weighted according to the volume of sales generated by the various products and services. For example, if 80 percent of a company's sales come from a particular product, that product's contribution margin should be weighted at 80 percent, with the other products receiving 20 percent of the weight. Once the average contribution margin is calculated, we can apply the same formulas we used to perform CVP analysis earlier in the chapter. Of course, the analysis will be valid only if the sales mix used to calculate the weighted average contribution margin remains constant.

The specific details for how to use the weighted average contribution margin to perform multiproduct cost-volume-profit analysis are covered in more advanced management accounting books.

To make sure you understand how to analyze cost-volume-profit for a single product company, complete the following Self-Study Practice.

SELF-STUDY PRACTICE

A company sells a product for $60 per unit. Variable costs per unit are $36, and monthly fixed costs are $120,000. Answer the following questions.

1. What is the break-even point in units and in total sales dollars?
2. What is the contribution margin ratio?
3. What level of total sales would be required to earn a target profit of $60,000?
4. Assuming the company achieves the level of sales required in part 3, what is the margin of safety as a percentage of sales?

After you have finished, check your answers with the solutions at the bottom of the next page.

Demonstration Case

In 2004, two young entrepreneurs realized that almost everyone loves cereal but no one ever eats it outside of their own home. So they opened Cereality, a cereal bar and café in the student union at Arizona State University. This innovative concept in fast food appealed to students and others who loved the idea of mixing Cocoa Puffs and Lucky Charms at almost any time of the day. Since then, Cereality franchises have opened at other college campuses around the country.

Based on market research, the young entrepreneurs decided to charge $3.75 for customers to create their own cereal combinations. But the entrepreneurs still needed to understand how much it would cost to run the business. They knew that costs such as cereal, milk, and paper products would vary with the number of customers but that other costs such as rent and insurance would be incurred each month even if the store were closed.

Assume the total operating costs and number of customers served during Cereality's first four months of operation were as follows:

Month	Total Operating Costs	Total Number of Customers
August	$7,500	2,000
September	8,000	2,600
October	8,700	3,600
November	8,800	3,400

Required:

1. Use the high-low method to determine the variable cost per customer and the total fixed operating costs.
2. Calculate and interpret the unit contribution margin and contribution margin ratio.
3. How many customers must Cereality serve each month to break even?
4. How much total sales revenue must Cereality earn each month to break even?
5. If the owners want to earn an operating profit of $7,500 per month, how many customers must they serve?

Suggested Solution

1. The high-low method should be based on the high and low × (total number of customers):

	Total Operating Cost (Y)	Total Number of Customers (X)	
August	$7,500	2,000	Low activity
October	8,700	3,600	High activity

Variable Cost = ($8,700 − $7,500)/(3,600 − 2,000) = $1,200/1,600 = $0.75 per Customer
Fixed Cost (based on August) = $7,500 − (2,000 × $0.75 per Customer) = $6,000
Fixed Cost (based on October) = $8,700 − (3,600 × $0.75 per Customer) = $6,000

2. Unit Contribution Margin = $3.75 Selling Price − $0.75 Variable Cost = $3.00 per Customer
Contribution Margin Ratio = $3.00 / $3.75 = 80%

The unit contribution margin of $3 means that each additional customer served generates $3 in contribution margin, which goes to cover fixed costs and then operating profit.
The contribution margin ratio of 80 percent means that each $1.00 of sales generates $0.80 in contribution margin, which goes to cover fixed costs and then operating profit.

Solution to
Self-Study Practice

1. Break-Even Units = Fixed Costs / CM per unit = $120,000 / ($60 − $36) = 5,000 units
   Break-Even Sales Dollars = 5,000 units × $60 price = $300,000

2. CM Ratio = $24 / $60 = 40%

3. Target Sales $ = (Fixed Costs + Target Profit) / CM Ratio = ($120,000 + 60,000) / 40% = $450,000

4. Margin of Safety = Actual Sales − Break-Even Sales = $450,000 − $300,000 = $150,000
   Margin of Safety Percentage = $150,000 / $450,000 = 33%

3. Break-Even Units = Fixed Cost / Unit Contribution Margin = $6,000 / $3.00 = 2,000 Customers

4. Break-Even Sales Dollar = Fixed Cost / Contribution Margin Ratio = $6,000 / 80% = $7,500

5. Target Units = (Fixed Costs + Target Profit) / Unit Contribution Margin
    = ($6,000 + $7,500) / $3.00 = 4,500 Units

Supplement 21A
Variable Costing

This chapter discussed how to prepare a contribution margin income statement. The statement categorizes costs according to their behavior based on how total costs respond to changes in the activity level. Because this approach classifies costs as either variable or fixed, it is called **variable costing.**

In the early chapters of this book, you learned to prepare financial statements for external users. Those statements were prepared to comply with the rules of GAAP, which does not distinguish between variable or fixed costs. Instead, GAAP requires that all manufacturing costs be treated as part of the cost of the product and inventoried until the product is sold. This approach is called **full absorption costing** because the product must "fully absorb" all costs incurred to produce it regardless of whether they are variable or fixed or whether units of the product have or have not been sold.

See Exhibit 21A.1 for a summary of the differences between variable costing and full absorption costing.

Exhibit 21A.1	Calculation and Uses of Full Absorption Costing and Variable Costing

	Full Absorption Costing	Variable Costing
Purpose	External financial reporting	Internal decision making
Cost classification	Manufacturing versus Nonmanufacturing costs	Variable versus fixed costs
Income statement formulas	Sales − Cost of goods sold Gross margin − Nonmanufacturing expenses Net income from operations	Sales − Variable costs Contribution margin − Fixed expenses Net income from operations
Treatment of fixed overhead	Divided between cost of goods sold and ending inventory	Expensed during the period incurred

Coach's Tip

Notice that gross margin and contribution margin are not the same. Contribution margin is the difference between sales revenue and variable costs; it is used only for internal reporting. Gross margin is the difference between sales revenue and the cost of goods sold; it appears on external financial statements.

Differences between Variable Costing and Full Absorption Costing

In terms of the effect on the bottom line, variable costing and full absorption costing have one critical difference: the treatment of fixed manufacturing overhead. Full absorption costing (GAAP) requires that fixed manufacturing overhead costs be treated as product cost, which means that the cost will be included as either cost of goods sold or inventory, depending on whether the product has been sold. Variable costing deducts all fixed costs, including fixed manufacturing overhead, during the period they are incurred.

To see how this difference can impact the bottom line, consider a company that produces and sells only one product. Assume this is the company's first month of operation, so no inventory was on hand at the beginning of the month. Costs and unit production follow.

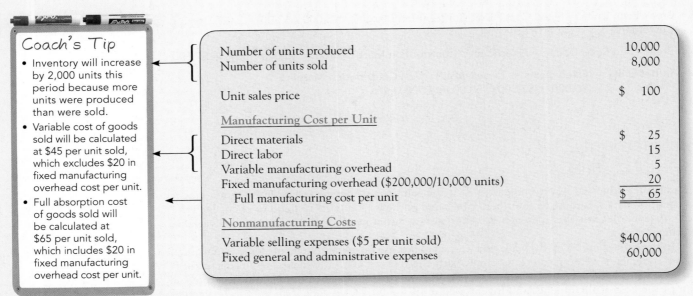

Coach's Tip

- Inventory will increase by 2,000 units this period because more units were produced than were sold.
- Variable cost of goods sold will be calculated at $45 per unit sold, which excludes $20 in fixed manufacturing overhead cost per unit.
- Full absorption cost of goods sold will be calculated at $65 per unit sold, which includes $20 in fixed manufacturing overhead cost per unit.

Number of units produced	10,000
Number of units sold	8,000
Unit sales price	$ 100
Manufacturing Cost per Unit	
Direct materials	$ 25
Direct labor	15
Variable manufacturing overhead	5
Fixed manufacturing overhead ($200,000/10,000 units)	20
Full manufacturing cost per unit	$ 65
Nonmanufacturing Costs	
Variable selling expenses ($5 per unit sold)	$40,000
Fixed general and administrative expenses	60,000

Refer to Exhibit 21A.2 for a comparison of the company's income statement under the two methods.

Reconciling Income under Full Absorption Costing and Variable Costing

The $40,000 difference in income between the two income statements in Exhibit 21A.2 is due to the different treatment of fixed manufacturing overhead under the two costing methods. Full absorption costing requires that this cost be spread over the number of units produced and then assigned either to the cost of goods sold or to ending inventory. As the cost and unit production data above indicate, the fixed manufacturing overhead cost of $200,000 is spread over the 10,000 units produced, for a fixed overhead rate of $20 per unit. This cost is then split between the 8,000 units sold and the 2,000 units remaining in ending inventory. Because the 2,000 units are not yet sold, full absorption costing reports

---

Exhibit 21A.2 Income Statement under Two Costing Approaches

Full Absorption Costing Income Statement

Sales ($100 × 8,000 units)		$800,000
Less: Cost of Goods Sold		
Inventory, January 1	$ —	
Cost of Goods Manufactured (10,000 × $65)	650,000	
Cost of Goods Available for Sale	650,000	
Less: Ending Inventory (2,000 × $65)	130,000	
Cost of Goods Sold (8,000 × $65)		520,000
Gross Margin		280,000
Less: Nonmanufacturing Expenses		
Variable Selling Expenses ($5 × 8,000)		40,000
Fixed General and Administrative Expenses		60,000
Income from Operations		$180,000

Variable Costing Income Statement

Sales ($100 × 8,000 units)		$ 800,000
Less: Variable Cost of Goods Sold		
Inventory, January 1	$ —	
Variable Manufacturing Costs (10,000 × $45)	450,000	
Cost of Goods Available for Sale	450,000	
Less: Ending Inventory (2,000 × $45)	90,000	
Variable Cost of Goods Sold (8,000 × $45)		360,000
Variable Selling Expenses (8,000 × $5)		40,000
Contribution Margin		400,000
Less: Fixed Expenses		
Fixed Manufacturing Overhead		200,000
Fixed General and Administrative Expenses		60,000
Income from Operations		$140,000

$40,000 Difference in income

$40,000 of the $200,000 in fixed overhead as an asset on the balance sheet rather than as an expense on the income statement. This cost will eventually be expensed but not until the units are sold.

In contrast, variable costing deducts the entire $200,000 in fixed manufacturing overhead as an expense during the current period. The rationale is that this cost is incurred regardless of how many units are produced and sold. Thus, variable costing assigns $20 less to each of the 2,000 units in ending inventory, or a total of $40,000. This difference in the treatment of fixed manufacturing overhead explains the $40,000 difference in income between the two methods.

In sum, the difference in income between full absorption costing and variable costing is directly related to the fixed manufacturing overhead cost per unit and the change in ending inventory, as in the following formula:

$$\text{Difference between Full Absorption and Variable Costing Income} = \text{Change in Units in Ending Inventory (Production − Sales)} \times \text{Fixed Manufacturing Overhead Cost per Unit}$$

The difference in income equals 2,000 units × $20 per unit, or $40,000. Income is higher under full absorption costing than under variable costing because full absorption costing counts a portion of the fixed manufacturing overhead as ending inventory instead of a period expense.

If the company had sold exactly the same number of units that it produced, the number of units in inventory would not change, and the two methods would give identical results. If production had been **lower** than sales, or the inventory level had **decreased,** variable costing would have produced a higher income than full absorption costing for exactly the opposite reason. Inventory units have a higher value under full absorption costing than under variable costing. Thus, when those units are finally sold, they must be deducted from income as part of the cost of goods sold at a higher value than under variable costing.

The illustration in Exhibit 21A.3 summarizes the effect of changes in inventory on income under full absorption versus variable costing.

Exhibit 21A.3 Effect of Changes in Inventory under Full Absorption Costing and Variable Costing

Chapter Summary

LO1 Identify costs as either variable, fixed, step, or mixed. p. 884
- Costs can be classified as either variable, fixed, step, or mixed.
- Variable costs increase in total in direct proportion to increases in the activity level.
- Fixed costs remain constant in total regardless of changes in the activity level.
- Step costs increase in a steplike fashion when a capacity constraint is reached.
- Mixed costs contain a fixed component plus a variable component that changes with the level of activity.

LO2 Prepare a scattergraph to illustrate the relationship between total cost and activity. p. 888
- A scattergraph provides a visual representation of the relationship between total cost and activity.
- A scattergraph is created by plotting the activity level on the horizontal (X) axis and the total cost on the vertical (Y) axis.
- If the scattergraph suggests that the relationship between cost and activity is roughly linear, a straight line can be used to approximate that relationship.
- The slope of the line represents the variable cost per unit of activity.
- The intercept of the line represents the total fixed cost.

LO3 Use the high-low method to analyze mixed costs. p. 890
- The high-low method is one of three linear methods that can be used to estimate the relationship between total cost and activity. The steps of the high-low method are:
- Identify the points that represent the highest and lowest activity (X) levels.
- Calculate the variable cost per unit by dividing the change in total cost across the high and low points by the change in activity level across the high and low points.
- Calculate the total fixed cost by subtracting the total variable cost from the total cost at either the high or low point.

LO4 Prepare and interpret a contribution margin income statement. p. 892
- Contribution margin is the difference between sales revenue and variable costs. The contribution margin can be expressed on a total, per unit, or percentage basis.
- The unit contribution margin, which is the difference between a unit's selling price and its variable cost, indicates how profit will change as a result of selling one more or one less unit.
- The contribution margin ratio is computed by dividing the unit contribution margin by the unit selling price or by dividing the total contribution margin by total sales. The contribution margin ratio shows how much a $1 increase in sales will affect the contribution margin and net operating income.

LO5 Use cost-volume-profit analysis to find the break-even point. p. 895
- The break-even point is that point at which contribution margin exactly equals fixed costs, indicating that the company is making zero profit.
- To find the break-even point in units, divide total fixed costs by the unit contribution margin. This is the number of units needed to break even.
- To find the break-even point in sales dollars, divide total fixed costs by the contribution margin ratio. This identifies the total sales that are needed to break even.
- The margin of safety is the difference between actual or budgeted sales and break-even sales. It indicates how much cushion there is between the current (or expected) level of sales and the break-even point.

LO6 Use cost-volume-profit analysis to determine the sales needed to achieve a target profit. p. 897
- For a business to earn a profit, the total contribution margin must be enough to cover fixed costs plus the desired target profit.
- To determine the number of units needed to earn a target profit, divide the target contribution margin (fixed cost plus target profit) by the unit contribution margin.
- To determine the total sales needed to earn a target profit, divide the target contribution margin (fixed cost plus target profit) by the contribution margin ratio.

Managerial Analysis Tools

Name of Measure	Formula
Variable cost (VC) per unit	$$\dfrac{\text{Difference in Total Cost (Y)}}{\text{Difference in Activity Level (X)}}$$
Total fixed costs	$$\text{Fixed Costs} = \text{Total Cost} - (\text{Variable Cost per Unit} \times \text{Activity})$$
Contribution margin per unit	$$\text{Unit Sales Price} - \text{Variable Cost per Unit}$$ or $$\dfrac{\text{Total Contribution Margin}}{\text{Number of Units Sold}}$$
Contribution margin ratio	$$\dfrac{\text{Unit Contribution Margin}}{\text{Unit Sales Price}}$$ or $$\dfrac{\text{Total Contribution Margin}}{\text{Total Sales Revenue}}$$
Break-even units	$$\dfrac{\text{Total Fixed Costs}}{\text{Unit Contribution Margin}}$$
Break-even sales	$$\text{Break-even Units} \times \text{Unit Sales Price}$$ or $$\dfrac{\text{Total Fixed Costs}}{\text{Contribution Margin Ratio}}$$
Target units	$$\dfrac{\text{Total Fixed Costs} + \text{Target Profit}}{\text{Unit Contribution Margin}}$$
Target sales revenue	$$\text{Target Units} \times \text{Unit Sales Price}$$ or $$\dfrac{\text{Total Fixed Costs} + \text{Target Profit}}{\text{Contribution Margin Ratio}}$$
Margin of safety	$$\text{Actual or Budgeted Sales} - \text{Break-Even Sales}$$
Margin of safety percentage	$$\dfrac{\text{Actual or Budgeted Sales} - \text{Break-Even Sales}}{\text{Actual or Budgeted Sales}}$$

Key Terms

Break-Even Analysis (p. 895)

Break-Even Point (p. 895)

Contribution Margin (p. 893)

Contribution Margin Income
Statement (p. 892)

Contribution Margin Ratio (p. 893)

Cost Behavior (p. 884)

Cost-Volume-Profit Analysis (p. 894)

See complete glossary in back of text.

CVP Graph (p. 898)

Dependent Variable (p. 889)

High-Low Method (p. 890)

Independent Variable (p. 889)

Margin of Safety (p. 896)

Mixed Costs (p. 886)

Regression Analysis (p. 890)

Relevant Range (p. 884)

Scattergraph (p. 887)

Step Costs (p. 885)

Step-Fixed Cost (p. 886)

Step-Variable Cost (p. 885)

Target Profit Analysis (p. 897)

Unit Contribution
Margin (p. 893)

Visual Fit Method (p. 890)

Questions

1. Explain the difference between variable cost, fixed cost, step cost, and mixed cost, and give an example of each.

2. When activity level decreases, explain what happens to:
   a. Total fixed cost.
   b. Total variable cost.
   c. Total mixed cost.
   d. Fixed cost per unit.
   e. Variable cost per unit.
   f. Mixed cost per unit.

3. What are the key assumptions of cost-volume-profit analysis? Why are they important?

4. Why is the relevant range important in cost-volume-profit analysis?

5. Why is separating the fixed and variable components of a mixed cost important? What might happen if that is not done?

6. The formula for analyzing mixed costs is $Y = A + B(X)$. Explain what each component represents.

7. Why is a scattergraph useful?

8. Describe the three methods of analyzing mixed costs. What are the strengths and weaknesses of each method? Will these methods always yield the same results?

9. Why is a contribution margin income statement more useful to managerial decision makers than an income statement intended for external users?

10. Explain how to calculate total contribution margin, contribution margin per unit, and the contribution margin ratio. What is the meaning of each?

11. When activity level increases, explain what happens to:
    a. Contribution margin per unit.
    b. Contribution margin ratio.
    c. Total contribution margin.
    d. Total fixed cost.
    e. Profit.

12. Why is it important for a company to know its break-even point? What happens to the break-even point if variable cost per unit decreases? If total fixed cost increases?

13. A company's cost structure can have a high proportion of fixed costs or a high proportion of variable costs. Which cost structure is more vulnerable to decreases in demand? Why?

14. Explain the difference in calculating the break-even point in units and in dollars. How can one be used to double-check the other?

15. Apple Company and Baker Company are competitors in the same industry. They produce the same product and have similar variable costs per unit and selling prices, but Baker has more fixed costs. Explain the impact of this on the break-even point of each company.

16. Bert Company and Ernie Company are competitors in the same industry. The companies produce the same product and have the same amount of fixed costs and the same selling price per unit. However, Bert has higher variable cost per unit. Compare the break-even point of each company.

17. Explain the difference between break-even analysis and target profit analysis.

18. Why is it important for managers to create a CVP graph?

19. Your supervisor has requested that you prepare a CVP graph for your company's product but does not understand its meaning or how changes would affect the graph. Explain to your supervisor how your graph would be affected by:
    a. an increase in the selling price.
    b. a decrease in variable cost per unit.
    c. an increase in fixed costs.

20. Explain margin of safety. Why is it important for managers to know their margin of safety? Give an example of a company to which margin of safety is particularly important.

21. Explain the difference between absorption costing and variable costing. Why do internal users need variable costing?

22. When will variable costing show the same income as absorption costing? When will they be different and why?

Multiple Choice

1. Which of the following would increase when the activity level increases?
   a. Total variable cost.
   b. Total fixed cost.
   c. Total mixed cost.
   d. Both a and c.

   Quiz 21-1
   www.mhhe.com/LLPW1e

2. Which of the following is **not** a method used to separate mixed costs?
   a. Regression analysis.   c. High-low method.
   b. Break-even analysis.   d. Visual fit method.

3. Consider the following information for a local concession stand's first four weeks of operation:

Week	Drinks Served	Total Cost
1	1,000	$2,500
2	2,000	3,250
3	1,750	3,000
4	2,250	3,200

Using the high-low method, what is the equation for total operating cost for this concession stand?

a. Operating Cost = $1,750 + $0.75 × (Number of drinks served).

b. Operating Cost = $1,000 + $1.75 × (Number of drinks served).

c. Operating Cost = $1,940 + $0.56 × (Number of drinks served).

d. Operating Cost = $1,750 + $0.56 × (Number of drinks served).

4. Bombay Co. sells handmade rugs. Bombay's variable cost per rug is $30 and each rug sells for $50. What are Bombay's contribution margin per unit and contribution margin ratio?

   a. $20 and 40 percent.   c. $20 and 60 percent.
   b. $30 and 60 percent.   d. $30 and 40 percent.

5. Whistler Co. sells one model of radio. Suppose its cost per radio is $125 and its total fixed costs are $4,130. Each radio sells for $195. How many radios must Whistler sell to break even?

   a. 33.   c. 45.
   b. 21.   d. 59.

6. Recent information for Shady Co., which makes automobile sunscreens, follows.

Selling price per screen	$ 18
Total fixed cost per month	1,225
Variable cost per screen	7

   If Shady wants to earn $1,250 profit next month, how many screens must it sell?

   a. 109.   c. 186.
   b. 136.   d. 225.

7. Various information for Happy Camper Co., which makes sleeping bags, follows.

Selling price per bag	$ 30
Total fixed cost per month	2,250
Variable cost per bag	21
Last month's profit	1,260

How many sleeping bags did the company sell last month?

   a. 159.   c. 140.
   b. 250.   d. 390.

8. Refer to the information in question 7 above. Suppose Happy Camper decides to lower its selling price to $27. How many sleeping bags must it sell to match last month's profit?

   a. 585.   c. 780.
   b. 375.   d. 130.

9. Which of the following statements about a CVP graph is true?

   a. Total revenue is a downward-sloping line.
   b. Break even is the point at which the total revenue and total cost lines intersect.
   c. The dollar value of sales revenue and total cost are plotted on the horizontal (X) axis.
   d. The total cost line includes only fixed costs.

10. Hathaway Corp. manufactures garden hoses. Last month its ending inventory level increased. In comparing absorption costing to variable costing,

   a. Both would show the same amount of profit.
   b. Variable costing would show more profit.
   c. Absorption costing would show more profit.
   d. Effect on income cannot be determined.

Solutions to Multiple-Choice Questions

1. d   2. b   3. c   4. a   5. d   6. d   7. d   8. a   9. b   10. c

---

Mini Exercises ™   Available with McGraw-Hill's Homework Manager

M21-1 Identifying Cost Behavior
Martha Trent is trying to prepare a budget and has come up with the following list of monthly costs. Identify each cost as fixed, variable, or mixed. Indicate a possible cost driver for any variable or mixed cost.

LO1

1. Rent.
2. Utilities.
3. Car payment.
4. Telephone.
5. Gasoline.
6. Cable bill.
7. Groceries.
8. Dining out.

M21-2 Identifying Cost Behavior
Steve's Snow Cones is a small refreshment stand located near a football stadium. Steve's fixed expenses total $300 per week, and the variable cost per snow cone is $0.35. Complete the following table for the various levels.

LO1

Number of snow cones	500	1,000	1,500
Total fixed cost			
Fixed cost per snow cone			
Total variable cost			
Variable cost per snow cone			
Total cost			
Cost per snow cone			

LO2

M21-3 Preparing a Scattergraph

Taylor's Tan-O-Rama is a local tanning salon. The information below reflects Taylor's number of appointments and total costs for the first half of the year:

Month	Number of Appointments	Total Cost
January	500	$5,400
February	600	5,900
March	1,000	6,700
April	450	5,675
May	300	5,328
June	350	5,325

Prepare a scattergraph by plotting Taylor's data on a graph. Then draw a line that you believe best fits the data points. Using the graph and line you have drawn, estimate Taylor's total fixed cost per month.

LO3

M21-4 Analyzing Mixed Costs Using High-Low Method

Refer to the Tan-O-Rama data in M21-3. Using the high-low method, calculate the fixed cost per month and the variable cost per tanning appointment. How does the estimate of fixed cost compare to what you estimated in M21-3?

LO3

M21-5 Analyzing Mixed Costs Using High-Low Method

Wendy's Widgits builds the world's best widgits. The information for the last eight months of Wendy's operations follows.

Month	Number of Widgits Produced	Total Cost
January	4,000	$7,000
February	2,250	5,000
March	3,500	6,250
April	4,300	7,750
May	1,875	5,000
June	3,000	6,250
July	1,500	4,250
August	2,500	5,750

Using the high-low method, calculate the fixed cost per month and the variable cost per widgit produced.

LO4

M21-6 Preparing a Contribution Margin Income Statement

Following is relevant information for Sunsplash Smoothie Shop, a small business that serves fruit drinks.

Total fixed cost per month	$1,200.00
Variable cost per drink	1.25
Sales price per drink	4.75

During the month of June, Sunsplash sold 500 smoothies. Using the preceding information, prepare Sunsplash's contribution margin income statement for the month of June.

LO4

M21-7 Calculating Contribution Margin and Contribution Margin Ratio

Lezoli Enterprises sells handmade clocks. Its variable cost per clock is $6, and each clock sells for $15. Calculate Lezoli's contribution margin per unit and contribution margin ratio. Suppose Lezoli sells 2,000 clocks this year. Calculate the total contribution margin.

M21-8 Calculating Break-Even Point

LO5

Refer to the information for Lezoli Enterprises in M21-7. If the company's fixed costs total $6,660 this year, determine how many clocks Lezoli must sell to break even.

M21-9 Calculating Target Profit

LO6

Theodora Patel makes stuffed teddy bears. Recent information for her business follows.

Selling price per bear	$ 25.00
Total fixed cost per month	1,500.00
Variable cost per bear	15.00

If Theodora wants to earn $1,250 profit next month, how many bears will she have to sell?

M21-10 Identifying Margin of Safety

LO5

Refer to the information in M21-9 for Theodora Patel. If Theodora sells 275 bears next month, what is the margin of safety in number of units? What is the margin of safety in sales dollars and as a percentage of sales?

Exercises _{TM}   Available with McGraw-Hill's Homework Manager

E21-1 Analyzing Mixed Costs Using High-Low Method

LO3

Valley Dental Services is a specialized dental practice whose only service is filling cavities. Valley has identified the following monthly costs.

Month	Number of Cavities Filled	Total Cost
January	625	$2,800
February	700	2,900
March	500	2,100
April	425	2,000
May	450	2,200
June	300	1,700
July	375	1,800
August	550	2,400
September	575	2,600

Required:

1. Use the high-low method to estimate the cost formula. Using this formula, calculate Valley's total cost for filling 500 cavities.
2. How closely does your estimate match the actual cost for March? Why would these be different?

E21-2 Analyzing Mixed Costs Using Scattergraph Method

LO2

Refer to the information in E21-1 regarding Valley Dental.

1. Create a scattergraph using Valley's activity and cost information and draw a line on the graph that you believe has the best fit.
2. Using this graph and best fitting line, estimate Valley Dental's total fixed cost.
3. Does your visual fit line differ from the one calculated using the high-low method? If so, why?

E21-3 Analyzing Mixed Costs Using High-Low Method and Scattergraph

LO2, 3

Aspen, Inc., manufactures one model of computer desk. The following data are available regarding units shipped and total shipping costs.

Month	Number of Units Shipped	Total Shipping Cost
January	30	$3,600
February	60	2,300
March	40	1,700
April	20	1,200
May	70	2,300
June	80	2,700
July	50	2,000

Required:

1. Prepare a scattergraph of Aspen's shipping cost and draw the line you believe best fits the data.
2. Based on this graph, estimate Aspen's total fixed shipping costs per month.
3. Using the high-low method, calculate Aspen's total fixed shipping costs and variable shipping cost per unit.

LO1, 4

E21-4 Determining Cost Behavior and Preparing Contribution Margin Income Statement

Paddle Away, Inc., makes one model of wooden canoe. Partial information for it follows.

	450	600	750
Number of canoes produced and sold	450	600	750
Total costs			
Variable costs	$ 67,500	?	?
Fixed costs	150,000	?	?
Total costs	$217,500	?	?
Cost per unit			
Variable cost per unit	?	?	?
Fixed cost per unit	?	?	?
Total cost per unit	?	?	?

Required:

1. Complete the preceding table.
2. Identify three costs that would be classified as fixed costs and three variable costs for Paddle Away.
3. Suppose Paddle Away sells its canoes for $500 each. Calculate the contribution margin per canoe and the contribution margin ratio.
4. This year Paddle Away expects to sell 800 canoes. Prepare a contribution margin income statement for the company.

LO5

E21- 5 Identifying Break-Even Point and Margin of Safety

Refer to the information in E21-4 regarding Paddle Away.

Required:

1. Calculate Paddle Away's break-even point in units and in sales dollars.
2. If Paddle Away sells 650 canoes, compute its margin of safety in units and as a percentage of sales.

LO3, 4, 5

E21-6 Analyzing Break Even and Preparing Contribution Margin Income Statement

Cory Bryant runs a courier service in downtown Phoenix. He charges clients $0.50 per mile driven. Cory has determined that if he drives 3,000 miles in a month, his total operating cost is $875. If he drives 4,000 miles in a month, his total operating cost is $1,025.

Required:

1. Using the high-low method, determine Cory's variable and fixed operating cost components. Show this as a cost formula.
2. Determine how many miles Cory will need to drive to break even.
3. Prepare a contribution margin income statement for Cory assuming he drove 2,400 miles last month.

LO5, 6

E21-7 Analyzing Break-Even Point and Preparing CVP Graph

Peggy's Ribbon World makes award rosettes. Following is information about the company.

Variable cost per rosette	$ 1.10
Sales price per rosette	2.50
Total fixed costs per month	889.00

Required:

1. Determine how many rosettes Peggy must sell to break even.
2. Calculate the break-even point in sales dollars.
3. Prepare a CVP graph for Peggy assuming the relevant range is zero to 1,500 rosettes.

E21-8 Identifying Target Profit and Margin of Safety

LO6

Refer to the information regarding Peggy's Ribbon World in E21-7.

Required:

1. Suppose Peggy would like to generate a profit of $800. Determine how many rosettes she must sell to achieve this target profit.

2. If Peggy sells 1,100 rosettes, compute her margin of safety in units, in sales dollers, and as a percentage of sales.

E21-9 (Supplement) Comparing Full Absorption Costing and Variable Costing

The following information pertains to Sonic Boom Radios, Inc. for its first year of operation:

Number of units produced	3,000
Number of units sold	2,500
Unit sales price	$ 350
Direct materials per unit	70
Direct labor per unit	60
Variable manufacturing overhead	10
Fixed manufacturing overhead ($225,000/3,000 units)	75
Variable selling expenses ($15/unit sold)	37,500
Fixed general and administrative expenses	65,000

Required:

Prepare Sonic Boom's full absorption costing income statement and variable costing income statement for the year.

Problems—Set A ™   Available with McGraw-Hill's Homework Manager

PA21-1 Analyzing Mixed Costs, Using High-Low Method, Preparing a Contribution Margin Income Statement, Analyzing Break-Even Point, and Setting Target Profit

LO3, 4, 5, 6

Fred Carson delivers parts for several local auto parts stores. He charges clients $0.75 per mile driven. Fred has determined that if he drives 2,000 miles in a month, his average operating cost is $0.55 per mile. If he drives 4,000 miles in a month, his average operating cost is $0.40 per mile.

Required:

1. Using the high-low method, determine Fred's variable and fixed operating cost components. Show this as a cost formula.
2. Determine how many miles Fred will need to drive to break even.
3. Assume Fred drove 1,500 miles last month. Without making any additional calculations, determine whether he earned a profit or a loss last month.
4. Prepare a contribution margin income statement for Fred's business last month.
5. If Fred wants to earn $1,000 a month, determine how many miles he must drive.

PA21-2 Preparing a Contribution Margin Income Statement and Analyzing Break-Even Point

LO1, 4, 5

Simpson Company produces one model of golf cart. A partially complete table of company costs follows.

	600	800	1,000
Number of golf carts produced and sold			
Total costs			
Variable costs	$?	$400,000	$?
Fixed costs per year	?	500,000	?
Total costs	?	$900,000	?
Cost per unit			
Variable cost per unit	?	?	?
Fixed cost per unit	?	?	?
Total cost per unit	?	?	?

Required:

1. Complete the table.
2. Simpson sells its carts for $1,200 each. Prepare a contribution margin income statement for each of the three production levels given in the table.
3. Based on these three statements (and without any additional calculations), estimate Simpson's break-even point in units.
4. Calculate Simpson's break-even point in number of units and in sales dollars.
5. Assume Simpson sold 700 carts last year. Without performing any calculations: determine whether Simpson earned a profit last year.

LO4, 5, 6

PA21-3 Preparing a CVP Graph and Calculating Contribution Margin, Contribution Margin Ratio, and Break-Even Point

Cardinal Castles, Inc. makes one type of birdhouse that it sells for $30 each. Its variable cost is $14 per house, and its fixed costs total $13,840 per year. Cardinal currently has the capacity to produce up to 2,000 birdhouses per year, so its relevant range is zero to 2,000 houses.

Required:

1. Prepare a contribution margin income statement for Cardinal assuming it sells 1,100 birdhouses this year.
2. Without any calculations, determine Cardinal's total contribution margin if the company breaks even.
3. Calculate Cardinal's contribution margin per unit and its contribution margin ratio.
4. Calculate Cardinal's break-even point in number of units and in sales dollars.
5. Suppose Cardinal wants to earn $20,000 this year. Determine how many birdhouses it must sell to generate this amount of profit. Is this possible?
6. Prepare a cost-volume-profit graph for Cardinal including lines for both total cost and sales revenue. Clearly identify fixed cost and the break-even point on your graph.

LO1, 5

www.mhhe.com/LLPW1e

PA21-4 Calculating Contribution Margin, Contribution Margin Ratio, and Break-Even Point

Overhill, Inc. produces one model of mountain bike. Partial information for the company follows.

	500	800	1,000
Number of bikes produced and sold	500	800	1,000
Total costs			
Variable costs	$125,000	$?	$?
Fixed costs per year	?	?	?
Total costs	?	?	?
Cost per unit			
Variable cost per unit	?	?	?
Fixed cost per unit	?	?	?
Total cost per unit	?	$543.75	?

Required:

1. Complete the table.
2. Calculate Overhill's contribution margin ratio and its total contribution margin at each sales level indicated in the table assuming the company sells each bike for $650.
3. Consider the contribution margins just calculated and total fixed costs. Determine whether Overhill's break-even point will be more or less than 500 units and 800 units.
4. Calculate Overhill's break-even point in units and sales dollars.

PA21-5 (Supplement) Determining Income Using Variable Costing

Refer to the information for Overhill, Inc., in PA21-4. Additional information available for Overhill's first year of operations follows.

Number of units produced	2,000
Number of units sold	1,300
Sales price per unit	$ 650.00
Direct materials per unit	110.00
Direct labor per unit	90.00
Variable manufacturing overhead	40.00
Fixed manufacturing overhead ($235,000/2,000 units)	117.50
Variable selling expenses ($10 per unit sold)	13,000.00
Fixed general and administrative expenses	70,000.00

Required:

1. Consider the computations performed in PA21-4 (and without further calculation). Explain whether Overhill earned a profit during its first year of operations.

2. Did Overhill's inventory increase or decrease last year? Without any calculation, explain whether Overhill's income will be higher with full absorption costing or variable costing.

3. Prepare a full absorption costing income statement and a variable costing income statement for Overhill.

4. Compute the difference in profit between full absorption costing and variable costing. Explain what is causing the difference.

Problems—Set B ™ Available with McGraw-Hill's Homework Manager

PB21-1 Analyzing Mixed Costs Using High-Low Method, Preparing a Contribution Margin Income Statement, Analyzing Break-Even Point, and Setting Target Profit   LO3, 4, 5

Tina Sutton delivers flowers for several local flower stores. She charges clients $0.85 per mile driven. Tina has determined that if she drives 1,200 miles in a month, her average operating cost is $0.70 per mile. If she drives 2,000 miles in a month, her average operating cost is $0.60 per mile.

Required:

1. Using the high-low method, determine Tina's variable and fixed operating cost components. Show this as a cost formula.

2. Determine how many miles Tina will need to drive to break even.

3. Assume Tina drove 900 miles last month. Without making any additional calculations, determine whether she earned a profit or a loss last month.

4. Prepare a contribution margin income statement for Tina's business last month.

5. If Tina wants to earn $800 a month, determine how many miles she must drive.

PB21-2 Preparing a Contribution Margin Income Statement and Analyzing Break-Even Point   LO1, 4, 5

StaySafe Company produces one model of security door. A partially complete table of company costs follows.

Number of doors produced and sold	400	500	700
Total costs			
Variable costs	$30,000	$?	$?
Fixed costs per year	65,000	?	?
Total costs	95,000	?	?
Cost per unit			
Variable cost per unit	?	?	?
Fixed cost per unit	?	?	?
Total cost per unit	?	?	?

Required:

1. Complete the table.
2. StaySafe sells its doors for $200 each. Prepare a contribution margin income statement for each of the three production levels in the table.
3. Based on these three statements (and without any additional calculations), estimate StaySafe's break-even point in units.
4. Calculate Staysafe's break-even point in number of units and in sales dollars.
5. Assume StaySafe sold 600 doors last year. Without performing any calculations, determine whether StaySafe earned a profit last year.

LO4, 5, 6   **PB21-3 Preparing a CVP Graph and Calculating Contribution Margin, Contribution Margin Ratio and Break-Even Point**

Hot Dog, Inc. makes one type of doggie sweater that it sells for $25 each. Its variable cost is $11 per sweater and its fixed costs total $8,600 per year. Hot Dog currently has the capacity to produce up to 1,000 sweaters per year, so its relevant range is zero to 1,000 sweaters.

Required:

1. Prepare a contribution margin income statement for Hot Dog assuming it sells 600 sweaters this year.
2. Without any calculations, determine Hot Dog's total contribution margin if the company breaks even.
3. Calculate Hot Dog's contribution margin per unit and its contribution margin ratio.
4. Calculate Hot Dog's break-even point in number of units and in sales dollars.
5. Suppose Hot Dog wants to earn $3,000 this year. Determine how many sweaters it must sell to generate this amount of profit. Is this possible?
6. Prepare a cost-volume-profit graph for Hot Dog including lines for both total cost and sales revenue. Clearly identify fixed cost and the break-even point on your graph.

LO1, 5   **PB21-4 Calculating Contribution Margin, Contribution Margin Ratio and Break-Even Point**

CoverUp, Inc. produces one model of seatcover. Partial information for the company follows:

	1,500	1,700	2,100
Number of seatcovers produced and sold			
Total costs			
Variable costs	$?	$?	$15,750
Fixed costs per year	?	?	?
Total costs	?	?	?
Cost per unit			
Variable cost per unit	?	?	?
Fixed cost per unit	?	?	?
Total cost per unit	$31.00	?	?

Required:

1. Complete the table.
2. Calculate CoverUp's contribution margin ratio and its total contribution margin at each sales level indicated in the table assuming the company sells each seatcover for $30.
3. Consider the contribution margins just calculated and total fixed costs for the company. Determine whether CoverUp's break-even point will be more or less than 1,500 units and 1,700 units.
4. Calculate CoverUp's break-even point in units and sales dollar.

PB21-5 (Supplement) Determining Variable Costing

Refer to the information for CoverUp in PB21-4. Additional information available for CoverUp's most recent year of operation follows.

Number of units produced	3,000
Number of units sold	2,800
Sales price per unit	$ 30.00
Direct materials per unit	3.00
Direct labor per unit	2.00
Variable manufacturing overhead	1.50
Fixed manufacturing overhead ($15,000/3,000 units)	5.00
Variable selling expenses ($1 per unit sold)	2,800.00
Fixed general and administrative expenses	20,250.00

Required:

1. Consider the computations performed in PB21-4 and without further calculation, explain whether CoverUp earned a profit during its first year of operations.

2. Did CoverUp's inventory increase or decrease last year? Without any calculation, explain whether CoverUp's income will be higher with full absorption costing or variable costing.

3. Prepare a full absorption costing income statement and a variable costing income statement for CoverUp.

4. Compute the difference in profit between full absorption costing and variable costing. Explain what is causing the difference.

Cases & Projects

CP21-1 Analyzing Cost Behavior and the Impact on Break-Even

LO1, 6

Ink Spot, Inc., is a new business located in upstate New York. It offers local businesses the service of printing and distributing promotional flyers at public places or events in the area. The flyers are either placed on the windshield of cars in parking lots or distributed by hand to people.

Ink Spot's owner, Dana Everhart, is facing a difficult decision. She could purchase a commercial printer and produce the flyers in-house. However, the machinery, costing approximately $20,000, is quite expensive. The printer has an estimated useful life of four years and would be depreciated using the straight-line method with no salvage value. If Dana purchases the printer, she would also have to buy paper and toner for the machine and pay for maintenance or repairs as needed. She estimates that it would cost $0.02 per page to print the flyers herself.

Alternatively, Dana could pay a local printing company $0.05 per copy to print the flyers. She would not incur any printing costs in addition to the $0.05 per page if she chooses this alternative. However, $0.05 per page is considerably more than Dana would have to pay for paper and toner if she owned a commercial printer.

Dana plans to charge customers $0.08 per page for each flyer Ink Spot distributes.

Required:

1. Name at least three other costs (other than the cost of producing the flyers) that a business such as Ink Spot would incur and identify the cost behavior of each one.

2. Considering the decision Dana must make, determine the cost behavior of each alternative. For any mixed cost, determine the amount of each component as much as possible.

3. Discuss whether Dana's choice will impact the break-even point for Ink Spot. Why might this be important?

4. Discuss other factors about Ink Spot's operating environment that Dana should consider.

5. Discuss factors other than cost that Dana should consider.

CP21-2 Evaluating the Effect of Decisions on Contribution Margin, Break-Even, and Margin of Safety

LO1, 5

Companies must make many decisions regarding day-to-day business activities. For each of the following decision-making situations, discuss the impact on a company's contribution margin (both total and per unit), break-even point, margin of safety, and ability to withstand fluctuation in product demand.

Required:

1. Whether to pay employees a fixed salary or an hourly wage.
2. Whether to pay commissions to salespeople.
3. Whether to purchase a building or rent space.
4. Whether to purchase component parts or manufacture them.
5. Whether to create its own delivery department (including the purchase and maintenance of delivery vehicles) or contract with a delivery company.

LO1, 5

CP21-3 Researching the Cost of Operating a Vending Machine and Performing Cost-Volume-Profit Analysis

Suppose that you have decided to start a small business selling snacks from vending machines. You have secured a location for one candy vending machine in a local bookstore. Rental for the space will cost $200 per month.

Vending machines can be purchased at wholesale clubs such as Sam's Club or Costco. You can also purchase the snacks to stock the machines in bulk at warehouse clubs.

Required:

1. Either visit a local warehouse club or review the club's Web site to determine the initial cost to purchase a snack vending machine.
2. Assume you are going to have only one type of snack bar in your machine initially. What type of snack bar will you choose? If you purchase the bars in bulk, what is your cost per bar?
3. How much will you charge for each bar sold?
4. What is your contribution margin per bar? How many bars must you sell to cover the cost of the vending machine?
5. Once you have covered the initial investment, what is the monthly break-even point in number of bars? In sales dollars?
6. Repeat requirements 2–5 assuming you decided to have a drink vending machine instead of a snack machine. Remember to look up the price for a beverage vending machine. You may assume rental for the vending machine space is $200 per month regardless of its type.

LO1, 5, 6

CP21-4 Researching a Company Web Site and Performing Cost-Volume-Profit Analysis

Pink Jeep Tours offers off-road tours to individuals and groups visiting the Southwestern U.S. hotspots of Sedona, Arizona, and Las Vegas, Nevada. Take a tour of the company's Web site at www.pinkjeep.com. Suppose you are a manager for the Pink Jeep office in Sedona. From the company Web site, choose two tours offered in Sedona. One tour should last all day and the other should be a shorter tour of 2–4 hours.

For the following requirements, assume that each Jeep tour has four adult passengers plus a tour guide.

Required:

1. Make a list of the various costs Pink Jeep would incur to offer each tour. Indicate whether each cost identified is variable, fixed, or mixed based on the number of tours offered.
2. Briefly research each cost listed in requirement 1 and estimate its amount. Estimate variable costs on a per Jeep tour basis and fixed costs on a monthly basis. Break any mixed cost into variable and fixed components. State any assumptions that you must make when estimating these costs (and be aware that many assumptions must be made).
3. What is Pink Jeep's total variable cost for each tour? Does this cost differ for each type of tour? Explain.
4. Using the current tour prices listed on Pink Jeep's Web site, determine the contribution margin per Jeep tour for each tour type.
5. Assume Pink Jeep ran **only** the all-day excursion tour in the month of August. In this case, how many tours must the company complete to break even?
6. Assume Pink Jeep ran **only** the shorter tour during August. In this case, how many tours must the company complete to earn $30,000 in profit for the month?

22 Incremental Analysis and Capital Budgeting

LEARNING OBJECTIVES

After completing this chapter, you should be able to:

LO1 Describe the five steps in the decision-making process.

LO2 Define and identify relevant costs and benefits.

LO3 Use incremental analysis to analyze the following managerial decisions:
    a. Special-order decisions.
    b. Make-or-buy decisions.
    c. Keep-or-drop decisions.
    d. Sell-or-process further decisions.

LO4 Analyze investment decisions using the following capital budgeting techniques:
    a. Accounting rate of return.
    b. Payback period.
    c. Net present value.
    d. Internal rate of return.

Lectured presentation–LP22-1
www.mhhe.com/LLPW1e

Focus Company: MATTEL TOYS

"The World's Premier Toy Brands"

www.mattel.com

In 1945, two friends named Matt and Elliot combined their names, money, and artistic skills to form a company called Mattel. They started out producing picture frames but quickly expanded into dollhouse furniture. Matt soon left the business and Elliot's wife, Ruth, joined the management team. Based on their early success with the dollhouse furniture, Elliot and Ruth decided to focus Mattel's efforts on the production and sale of toys.

After more than a decade of satisfactory but not stellar performance, Mattel struck it big in 1959 with the introduction of Barbie, a doll named after Ruth and Elliot's own daughter Barbara. Since then, Barbie and her fabulous friends, clothes, and accessories have entertained generations of young girls and, no doubt a few boys.

Today, Mattel's success hinges on much more than Barbie dolls. The company has a huge portfolio of products for children of all ages, including Fisher Price toys, Matchbox cars and trucks, Hot Wheels, Mattel classic games, and American Girl dolls. Mattel has also had its share of controversy over the years, including critics who question whether Barbie is an appropriate role model for young girls. More recently, Mattel experienced a wave of bad press when it recalled millions of toys that were manufactured in China and contained toxic levels of lead-based paint.

This chapter discusses how managers at Mattel use managerial accounting information to make both short- and long-term business decisions such as:

- Whether to accept an order from a large university to produce a special Barbie doll who wears the school logo and colors.
- Whether to make or buy the packaging materials for the American Girl doll collection.
- Whether to discontinue one of the Power Wheels products.
- Whether to add more features to a remote control toy.
- Whether to invest in a children's MP3 product that would allow parents to download children's books, music, and educational materials from Mattel's Web site.

To make these decisions, we use two different decision-making approaches. The first, incremental analysis, is a short-term analysis that compares the costs and benefits of different decision alternatives. The second technique, capital budgeting, is a long-term decision-making framework to help managers make decisions about the investment of assets. Although we will use fictitious scenarios and numbers to illustrate these techniques, we make them as realistic as possible to illustrate how Mattel's managers might approach these and other decisions.

Before we dive into these two topics, let's first discuss the decision-making process and some basic principles that apply to making any decision.

ORGANIZATION OF THE CHAPTER

MANAGERIAL DECISION-MAKING PROCESS	RELEVANT VERSUS IRRELEVANT COSTS AND BENEFITS	INCREMENTAL ANALYSIS OF SHORT-TERM DECISIONS	CAPITAL BUDGETING FOR LONG-TERM INVESTMENT DECISIONS
• Step 1: Identify the Decision Problem • Step 2: Determine the Decision Alternatives • Step 3: Evaluate the Costs and Benefits of the Alternatives • Step 4: Make the Decision • Step 5: Review the Results of the Decision-Making Process	• Relevant Costs • Irrelevant Costs	• Special-Order Decisions • Make-or-Buy Decisions • Keep-or-Drop Decisions • Sell-or-Process Further Decisions	• Nondiscounting Methods • Discounted Cash Flow Methods

MANAGERIAL DECISION-MAKING PROCESS

The managerial decision-making process has five basic steps (see Exhibit 22.1).

Step 1: Identify the Decision Problem

The first step in the decision-making process is to identify the decision problem. See Exhibit 22.2 for a description of a decision problem that you may have encountered yourself: deciding where to live. You can apply the same type of decision analysis to many other personal decisions, such as deciding where to go to college or what kind of vehicle to buy. Later in this chapter, we apply a similar process to a variety of problems that managers face in the business world.

Step 2: Determine the Decision Alternatives

Once managers have identified the problem, the next step is to determine the possible solutions to the problem, called decision alternatives. This is a critical step because the remainder of the decision process hinges on the decision alternatives identified here. If a potential alternative

Exhibit 22.1 Managerial Decision-Making Process

Step 1: Identify the decision problem	→	Step 2: Determine the decision alternatives	→	Step 3: Evaluate the costs and benefits of the alternatives	→	Step 4: Make the decision	→	Step 5: Review the results of the decision-making process

Improve future decisions

is not included in this initial stage, it will not be included in the later phases of the analysis. The housing decision described in Exhibit 22.2 identified two potential decision alternatives: lease a house with two roommates or rent a one-bedroom apartment on your own. We have eliminated other potential alternatives such as living with parents or buying your own home; thus, these alternatives will not be considered in the analysis.

Step 3: Evaluate the Costs and Benefits of the Alternatives

Our primary focus in this chapter is the third step of the decision process, which involves comparing the costs and benefits of the decision alternatives identified in Step 2. For decision making, we consider only those costs and benefits that differ between alternatives, an approach called incremental analysis or *differential analysis*. This approach is sometimes called relevant costing because it focuses only on those costs (and benefits) that are relevant to the decision to be made. The identification of relevant costs and benefits are discussed in more detail shortly.

Step 4: Make the Decision

Once managers have evaluated the costs and benefits of the decision alternatives, they are ready to make the decision. However, they will probably not base it strictly on the numerical analysis performed in Step 3. Managers should incorporate a variety of other factors, such

Exhibit 22.2	Application of the Five-Step Managerial Decision-Making Process to a Personal Decision
Step 1: Identify the decision problem.	Your freshman year living in the dorm is almost up and you must decide where you are going to live next year.
Step 2: Determine the decision alternatives.	You narrowed it down to two options: • Lease a 3-bedroom house with two roommates. • Lease a 1-bedroom apartment.
Step 3: Evaluate the costs and benefits of the alternatives.	After doing some research, you have gathered the following information. • The rent on the house is $1,800 per month ($600 per person). The rent on the apartment is $800 per month. Thus, sharing the house is $200 per month less expensive assuming you can find two roommates. • The monthly utility bills at the house are $450 ($150 per person). The monthly utilities at the apartment are $150. Because the cost to you is the same, it is not relevant to your decision, and you can ignore it. • Advertising in the student paper for two new roommates would cost you about $50. • The apartment is near the campus so you could bike to school. You estimate your monthly savings on fuel and parking to be about $75 per month. • The house is large and has a great backyard, but you are tired of sharing space with loud, messy roommates. You think you would enjoy the one-bedroom apartment, especially for studying and quiet entertaining. In summary, • The house is the less expensive alternative by about $125 per month ($200 in rent savings less $75 in additional vehicle expenses per month). However, you would need to spend some money ($50) to find new roommates. • The one-bedroom apartment has certain advantages that are more difficult to quantify (it is close to campus and very quiet).
Step 4: Make the decision.	You will have to make a trade-off between the cost advantages of the house and the qualitative advantages of the one-bedroom apartment. Let's assume you are on a very tight budget and have decided to sign the lease on the house and begin the search for new roommates.
Step 5: Review the results of the decision-making process.	Looking back on the outcome, you will later determine whether your decision was a good one. If you were unable to find two good roommates, the decision may prove to be a bad one. If you find that your roommates are great and will become lifelong friends, your decision was a good one. Either way, you are likely to learn something that will affect the way you make similar decisions in the future.

as strategic issues, quality considerations, legal and ethical issues, and the like. For all of the decisions that we analyze throughout this chapter, we first perform a numerical or quantitative analysis to determine which alternative is "best" based strictly on the numbers. We then discuss what qualitative factors might come into play to influence managers' decisions. For example, in the housing scenario illustrated in Exhibit 22.2, the numeric analysis showed that sharing a house with two roommates was the least costly alternative (by about $125 per month). However, the apartment may have other advantages (such as privacy and quiet) that might influence your decision about which housing alternative to choose.

Step 5: Review the Results of the Decision-Making Process

Once managers make the decision based on the relevant costs and benefits identified in Step 3 as well as any additional qualitative factors in Step 4, the managers will eventually need to review the results of the decision-making process to determine whether they made the correct decision, or did not make the correct decision and should use a different decision-making approach in the future. The role of managerial accounting in helping managers evaluate performance to improve future decisions is discussed in detail in Chapters 24 and 25.

RELEVANT VERSUS IRRELEVANT COSTS AND BENEFITS

Most of our attention throughout the remainder of this chapter focuses on the third step of the decision-making process, which involves comparing the costs and benefits of the decision alternatives. In particular, we want to compare only those costs and benefits that are **relevant** to the decision being made. Although the decision-making process should include consideration of both costs and benefits, our examples focus primarily on the **cost** side of the process. As you will see shortly, not all costs are relevant to a particular decision. Benefits are also incorporated only when they are relevant to the particular decision.

Relevant Costs

A relevant cost is one that will change depending on which alternative a manager selects. Costs that differ between alternatives are also called differential costs or incremental costs. In Exhibit 22.2, the difference in monthly rent between the house and the apartment was $200. This cost was relevant to the decision of whether to rent the house or the apartment.

Another term for relevant cost is avoidable cost—that is, a cost the manager can avoid by choosing one alternative instead of another. In Exhibit 22.2, the costs of fuel and on-campus parking could be avoided if you lived in an apartment near campus and could ride your bike to class. This cost was relevant to the decision because it differed between the two alternatives.

Managers must also identify any opportunity costs that are relevant to the decision. Recall from Chapter 18 that an opportunity cost is a benefit that you give up when you choose one alternative over another. Although opportunity costs are relevant for decision making, they are often difficult to estimate and measure because they are associated with the "path not taken." Whenever possible, however, managers should include opportunity costs in their analyses.

Irrelevant Costs

Irrelevant costs are those that do not differ between alternatives. Two types of cost do not change depending on the alternative selected, and should therefore be ignored:

- **Costs that have already been incurred, called** sunk costs. Because these costs have already been spent (that is, they are sunk), they will not change depending on which alternative the manager selects.

- **Costs that are the same regardless of the alternative the manager chooses.** In Exhibit 22.2, the monthly utility costs were the same regardless of whether you share the rental house or rent the apartment. You ignored that cost because it did not differ between the alternatives. In other words, it was an irrelevant cost.

Next we apply the concept of relevant costs, or incremental analysis, to Mattel, the world's leading toy company. First make sure that you understand the decision-making process and can correctly identify relevant costs by completing the following Self-Study Practice.

INCREMENTAL ANALYSIS OF SHORT-TERM DECISIONS

In this section, we illustrate how to use incremental analysis to make four common business decisions: special-order, make-or-buy, keep-or-drop, and sell or process further decisions. In the real world, the specific decisions managers need to make depend on a variety of factors, such as the type of business they are running, their level of responsibility, and the particular problems they are trying to solve. Nevertheless, the approach we use to address these problems can be applied to many other short-term managerial decisions.

Video 22-1
www.mhhe.com/LLPW1e

Special-Order Decisions

Managers must often decide whether to accept or reject an order that is outside the scope of normal sales. These so-called one-time or special orders often carry a lower sales price than the normal sales price of the product or service. The decision that managers must make is whether to accept or reject the offer. We can analyze this decision by comparing the incremental costs to the incremental benefits (revenue) of the special order.

As an example, assume that a major university has asked Mattel to produce a special **University Barbie** dressed in a sporty outfit and carrying a backpack with the school's logo and colors. The university bookstore has offered to buy 25,000 of these dolls at a price of $7 each,

Learning Objective 3a

Use incremental analysis to analyze special-order decisions.

Solution to
Self-Study Practice

which it would then sell in the bookstore and in alumni catalogues for a retail price of $15 each. Mattel has the capacity to fill the order without affecting production of other Barbie products, which are normally sold to toy stores and discount chains for about $9 each. Assume the estimated cost to produce the University Barbie is as follows:

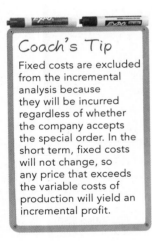

Coach's Tip

A key assumption in analyzing special orders is that it will not affect the production and sale of units that are sold through regular channels. That means the company must have the extra capacity (in terms of machines, people, etc.) to fill the special order without disrupting normal operations.

	Unit Cost
Direct materials (silicone rubber, clothing, accessories)	$3.50
Direct labor	1.00
Variable manufacturing overhead (indirect materials, power, etc.)	0.50
Fixed manufacturing overhead (factory rent, insurance, etc.)	2.50
Total manufacturing cost	$7.50

At first glance, it appears that Mattel should reject the offer because the $7.00 price is less than the $7.50 it will cost to make the University Barbie. But is that analysis correct?

Recall the relevant cost concept. Will **all** of the company's costs change if Mattel accepts the special order? To answer this question, we need to perform an incremental analysis below:

Quantitative Analysis

The incremental analysis of Mattel's special order decision is shown below:

Coach's Tip

Fixed costs are excluded from the incremental analysis because they will be incurred regardless of whether the company accepts the special order. In the short term, fixed costs will not change, so any price that exceeds the variable costs of production will yield an incremental profit.

Incremental Analysis of the Special Order for 25,000 University Barbie Dolls

	Per Unit	Total
Incremental revenue	$7.00	$175,000
Less: Incremental costs		
Direct materials	3.50	87,500
Direct labor	1.00	25,000
Variable overhead	0.50	12,500
Fixed overhead	—	—
Total incremental cost	5.00	125,000
Incremental profit	$2.00	$ 50,000

Notice that this incremental analysis does not include fixed manufacturing overhead costs. The reason these costs have been excluded is that fixed costs such as rent, insurance, and supervision will be incurred regardless of whether Mattel accepts the special order. Because the special order does not cause total fixed costs to increase, only the variable costs of producing the University Barbie are relevant. Compared to the special order price of $7, the $5 in variable cost per unit means that each Barbie sold would generate $2 in incremental profit, or a total of $50,000 in added profit.

Qualitative Analysis

Two important cautions should be kept in mind in doing this type of short-term analysis. First, this analysis is valid only for one-time or special orders. Managers would not want to use this type of analysis to make long-term pricing decisions because in the long run, prices must cover all costs, including fixed costs, if the company is to be profitable. They would also want to consider whether accepting the special order would have any effect on the price that regular customers are willing to pay for sales made through regular channels.

Second, this analysis is valid only if the company has excess, or idle, production capacity. If the company does not have the capacity to fill the order, it must either incur additional fixed costs (by renting more factory space, machines, etc.) or reduce the production and sale of other products, which would create an opportunity cost. Either way, the company would incur additional incremental costs that may make the special order unprofitable.

Before we discuss make-or-buy decisions, complete the following Self-Study Practice to make sure you understand how to analyze special-order decisions.

SELF-STUDY PRACTICE

Big Top Tent Company has received a special order for 10,000 units of its product at a discounted price of $100. The product, which normally sells for $150, has the following manufacturing costs.

	Cost per Unit
Direct materials	$ 40
Direct labor	20
Variable manufacturing overhead	20
Fixed manufacturing overhead	30
Unit cost	$110

Assume Big Top has enough extra capacity to fill the order without affecting the production or sale of its product to regular customers. If Big Top accepts the offer, what effect will the order have on the company's short-term profit?

a. $100,000 increase

b. $100,000 decrease

c. $200,000 increase

d. $400,000 decrease

After you have finished, check your answers with the solutions at the bottom of the page.

Make-or-Buy Decisions

The next managerial decision we analyze is whether to make certain parts of the product or provide a service in-house or to buy it from an outside supplier. Traditionally, these decisions have been called make-or-buy decisions, but more recently they have been referred to as insourcing versus outsourcing decisions.

In making this type of decision, we must compare the relevant costs of making a component or providing a service internally to the cost of buying it from an external supplier. To determine which costs to include in the analysis, we must again keep in mind the definition of a relevant cost. In other words, we want to include only those costs that will change depending on

Learning Objective 3b

Use incremental analysis to analyze make-or-buy decisions.

---

c.   ($100 price − $80 variable cost) = $20 incremental profit × 10,000 units = $200,000

Solution to Self-Study Practice

whether we make the item internally or buy it from an outside supplier. In addition, we should consider whether we give up any opportunity or benefits by choosing to make something internally instead of buying it externally (or vice versa).

Assume, for example, Mattel's managers are trying to decide whether to package the company's toys in-house or to outsource the packaging process to an external supplier. The design, marketing, and production of appealing toys are Mattel's competitive strengths, so outsourcing less critical activities may make sense. To see how Mattel might approach this decision, consider the following scenario in which Mattel currently performs all packaging of the American Girl dolls internally. Assume Mattel produces a total of 200,000 American Girl dolls annually; cost data for the product line follow:

> **Coach's Tip**
>
> When you see fixed costs stated on a per unit basis, be careful. What really counts is the **total** fixed cost and whether that total cost will change depending on the decision.

Internal Cost of Packaging
200,000 American Girl Dolls per Year

	Annual Cost	Cost per Unit
Packaging materials (cardboard, plastic, etc.)	$300,000	$1.50
Packaging direct labor	90,000	0.45
Indirect materials (e.g., glue)	60,000	0.30
Packaging supervision	50,000	0.25
Other fixed manufacturing overhead	200,000	1.00
Total packaging cost	$700,000	$3.50

Mattel has been negotiating with a reputable supplier to provide the packaging for the American Girl collection. After several discussions, the supplier has finally agreed to a price of $3 per unit for all packaging-related activities. The agreement includes a three-year contract for a minimum of 200,000 units per year. Should Mattel package the product internally or outsource this process to the supplier?

As you have seen, we cannot simply compare the internal cost of packaging of $3.50 per unit to the $3.00 price that the supplier will charge. Some of the costs included in the $3.50 per unit may not be relevant to the decision. We should also consider whether any opportunity costs are associated with continuing to package the product internally. After investigating the proposed agreement further, Mattel's managers learn the following:

Information Gathered	**Manager's Analysis**
• All costs directly related to the packaging activities including all direct and indirect materials, labor, and supervision could be avoided.	• Because these costs can be avoided, they should be considered a relevant cost of internal packaging.
• Other total fixed manufacturing overhead costs would remain unchanged.	• Because these costs will be incurred under either alternative, they should be excluded from the analysis.
• The factory space now used for packaging the American Girl collection could be used to expand production of a popular product line. The expansion would generate an additional $150,000 in profit per year.	• Mattel will receive this benefit by outsourcing the packaging but not if they keep the packaging in-house. This amount can be considered a benefit of outsourcing or an opportunity cost of insourcing, but not both.

Quantitative Analysis

Based on this information and analysis, the incremental cost of making the packaging versus buying it would be as follows:

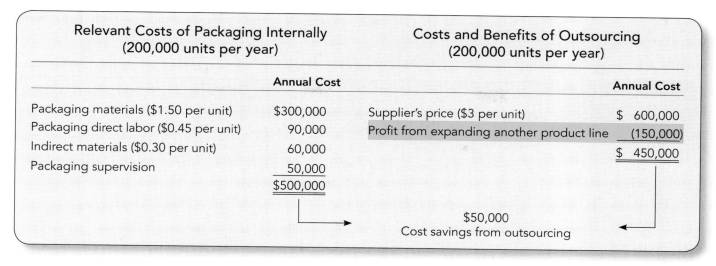

Relevant Costs of Packaging Internally (200,000 units per year)		Costs and Benefits of Outsourcing (200,000 units per year)	
	Annual Cost		**Annual Cost**
Packaging materials ($1.50 per unit)	$300,000	Supplier's price ($3 per unit)	$ 600,000
Packaging direct labor ($0.45 per unit)	90,000	Profit from expanding another product line	(150,000)
Indirect materials ($0.30 per unit)	60,000		$ 450,000
Packaging supervision	50,000		
	$500,000		

$50,000
Cost savings from outsourcing

The quantitative analysis suggests that Mattel will save $50,000 per year by outsourcing the packaging to the external supplier.

Qualitative Analysis

Of course, quantitative analysis has its limitations. Before making a final decision, Mattel's managers would want to consider other qualitative factors, such as the following:

- Will the quality of the packaging be as good as Mattel and its customers expect?
- Will the supplier be reliable in delivering the packaging?
- What will happen if demand for the product drops below 200,000 units or rises significantly higher than 200,000? Does the supplier have the capacity to meet the increased demand? Will the supplier charge a higher or lower price for the additional units?
- What will happen in three years? Will the price of packaging increase significantly? Going back to internal packaging would be difficult after the space has been converted for another purpose.
- What if the predicted profit from expanding the other product line has been substantially over- or underestimated?
- Does outsourcing the packaging create any additional risks, such as those described in the accompanying spotlight on business decisions?

Spotlight On BUSINESS DECISIONS

Mattel Becomes the Poster Child for the Dangers of Outsourcing to China

Outsourcing occurs when a company hires a third party to do part of its work. Often the third party is located in a foreign country, such as India or China, where labor is much less expensive.

Although many companies have recently started outsourcing to control costs, Mattel has been producing its toys overseas for almost 50 years. Most of its toys are produced in "company-owned" plants in China where Mattel can maintain strict quality standards. But the company also outsources production of some toys to other Chinese manufacturers that may not maintain the same quality standards.

This decision came back to haunt Mattel in the fall of 2007 when the company was forced to recall millions of "toxic toys" that contained unsafe levels of lead-based paint. The costs to Mattel were high including consumer lawsuits, a drop in the company's stock price, sanctions by Congress, and a general loss in consumer and investor confidence.

The lesson is that outsourcing decisions must be made carefully and include an analysis of both the benefits and risks. Mattel's experience also highlights the need to build strict quality control standards into outsourcing agreements regardless of whether the outsourcing contract is with a company overseas or in the United States.

> The New York Times, September 29, 2007
> **Recalls Make Toy Shopping a Source of Anxiety**
>
> **Mattel issues a third toy recall**
> Los Angeles Times, September 5, 2007
>
> St. Petersburg Times, August 15, 2007
> **Lead scare crosses all lines**
>
> Fisher-Price recalls IM toys
> CNN.com, August 1, 2007

To make sure you understand how to analyze make-or-buy decisions, complete the following self-study practice.

Keep-or-Drop Decisions

Learning Objective 3c

Use incremental analysis to analyze keep-or-drop decisions.

The next decision we consider is whether to continue or discontinue making a particular product or offering a specific service. Managers face this decision frequently, particularly when products and services are not generating as much profit as expected. Again, our approach determines which costs and benefits will change as a result of the decision. Because some of the costs of making a product or providing a service will be incurred regardless, we need to do an incremental analysis to determine the net effect on the bottom line.

Assume, for example, that Mattel has three versions of its Power-Wheels battery-powered vehicles sold under the Fisher Price brand. The hypothetical income statement in Exhibit 22.3 shows the revenues and costs for those product lines.

The company is considering eliminating the Barbie Ford Mustang product because it has shown a loss for the past few years.

Exhibit 22.3   Segmented Income Statement for the Power Wheels Product Lines

	Jeep Wrangler 4 × 4	Barbie Ford Mustang	Dora the Explorer Jeep	Total
Sales revenue	$500,000	$ 150,000	$350,000	$1,000,000
Variable costs	200,000	100,000	140,000	440,000
Contribution margin	300,000	50,000	210,000	560,000
Fixed costs*	200,000	60,000	140,000	400,000
Profit margin	$100,000	$ (10,000)	$ 70,000	$ 160,000

*Fixed costs are allocated based on total sales dollars.

Quantitative Analysis

What effect would the elimination of the Barbie Ford Mustang product have on the company's overall profitability? To answer this question, assume that managers have gathered the following additional information:

Solution to
Self-Study Practice

d   (The rent on the factory will remain unchanged and is therefore irrelevant.)

Information Gathered	Manager's Analysis	Differential Profit
Elimination of the Barbie Ford Mustang will reduce the revenue and variable costs that are directly attributable to this individual product line.	Lost sales = $(150,000) Reduced costs = $100,000 Lost contribution margin = ($50,000)	$(50,000)
Elimination of the Barbie Ford Mustang will increase sales of the Dora the Explorer Jeep by 20% with no effect on the Jeep 4 × 4.	Increased sales from the Dora line: $350,000 × 20% = $70,000	70,000
Total variable costs of the Dora the Explorer Jeep will increase as a result of the increased sales. Variable costs of the Dora Jeep are 40% of sales.	Increased variable costs of the Dora line: $70,000 × 40% = $28,000	(28,000)
Total fixed costs will not be affected by the elimination of the Barbie Ford Mustang. They will be reallocated to the remaining products based on total sales dollars.	Because the total cost will not change, it is not relevant to the decision.	—
Overall effect on profit of dropping the Barbie Ford Mustang:		$(8,000)

This differential analysis suggests that dropping the Barbie Ford Mustang will reduce Mattel's profit by $8,000. To confirm that the analysis is correct, we can recreate the income statement in Exhibit 22.3 without the Barbie Ford Mustang (see Exhibit 22.4). Notice that this new statement shows a profit of $152,000, which is $8,000 less than the company earned with the Barbie Ford Mustang line. The reason for the reduction in profit is that the elimination of the Barbie Ford Mustang reduced the overall contribution margin. However, the total fixed costs did not change with the elimination of the Barbie Ford Mustang. Instead, these costs were simply reallocated to the two remaining product lines:

Exhibit 22.4 — Segmented Income Statement for the Power Wheel Product Lines after Elimination of the Barbie Ford Mustang

	Jeep Wrangler 4 × 4	Dora the Explorer Jeep	Total after Elimination of Barbie Ford Mustang	Total before Elimination of Barbie Ford Mustang
Sales revenue	$500,000	$ 420,000 (350,000 × 120%)	$920,000	$1,000,000
Variable costs	200,000	168,000 (420,000 × 40%)	368,000	440,000
Contribution margin	300,000	252,000	552,000	560,000
Fixed costs*	216,000	184,000	400,000	400,000
Profit margin	$ 84,000	$ 68,000	$152,000	$160,000

* Fixed costs were reallocated based on the new sales revenue of the remaining products

$8,000 Reduction in Profit from Elimination of the Barbie Ford Mustang

Qualitative Analysis

As always, short-term quantitative analysis has its limitations, including these:

- What if the expected increase in sales of the Dora the Explorer product line has been underestimated?
- Will the elimination of the Barbie Ford Mustang free up resources (people, space, or machines) that could be used in another way?
- Can the company introduce another product that will yield more than $8,000 in incremental profit?
- Are there any other opportunity costs associated with keeping the Barbie Ford Mustang?

Before we continue, complete the following Self-Study Practice to make sure you can analyze keep-or-drop decisions correctly.

Big Top Tent Company is trying to decide whether to keep or drop one of its outdoor wedding tents. The company's segmented income statement shows that this product is generating a net loss, as follows:

	Total
Sales	$100,000
Variable cost (canvas, ropes, and direct labor)	70,000
Contribution margin	30,000
Fixed costs (allocated based on sales dollars)	40,000
Net loss	$ (10,000)

The company estimates that eliminating this product line will increase the contribution margin on a related product line by $20,000 and save $15,000 in allocated fixed costs. Based on this information, what impact would dropping the line have on the company's overall profitability?

a. $10,000 increase.

b. $25,000 increase.

c. $5,000 increase.

d. $5,000 decrease.

After you have finished, check your answers with the solutions at the bottom of the page.

Sell-or-Process Further Decisions

The next managerial decision we consider is whether to sell a product "as is," or spend additional money to process the product so that it can be sold for a higher price. Once again, we can analyze this decision by comparing the incremental costs and benefits of this decision. If the increased revenue is enough to offset the incremental cost, the company should process further; otherwise the company is better off selling the product "as is."

As an example, assume that Mattel has developed a remote control Hummer toy. So far, the company has spent a total of $250,000 on research and development. Based on the features that are currently included in the product, managers estimate that they could sell 100,000 units at a price of $15 each.

One of the product designers has proposed that additional features to be added to the Hummer, such as moveable parts, music, and lights. If the company spends an additional $100,000 on development, it could sell the enhanced product for $18 per unit. However, the enhanced product would have a slightly higher manufacturing cost because it would require additional components and more labor in the assembly and machining departments. The following table summarizes the expected costs and revenues from selling the product based on the current design versus selling it with the enhanced features.

Solution to
Self-Study Practice

c

Lost Contribution Margin	($30,000)
Gained Contribution Margin	20,000
Fixed Costs Avoided	15,000
Net Increase in Profit	$ 5,000

	Current Design	Enhanced Design
Estimated demand	100,000 units	100,000 units
Estimated sales price	$15 per unit	$18 per unit
Estimated manufacturing costs (per unit)		
Direct materials	$3.00	$4.25
Direct labor	1.50	1.75
Variable manufacturing overhead	0.50	0.75
Fixed manufacturing overhead	2.00	2.00
Unit manufacturing costs	$7.00	$8.75
Research and development costs	$250,000	$350,000

Should the company sell the product as it is currently designed or spend more money to create the enhanced design? To answer this question, we can compare the incremental revenue and incremental costs of the two alternatives as shown in the following table:

Increased sales revenue 100,000 units × $3 ($18 − $15)	$300,000
Increased manufacturing costs 100,000 units × $1.75 ($8.75 − $7.00)	(175,000)
Increased research and development costs	(100,000)
Increased profit	$ 25,000

This analysis suggests that the company would make an additional $25,000 in profit by incorporating additional features in the toy. The increase in development and manufacturing costs would be more than offset by the increased sales revenue generated by the higher sales price.

Notice, however, that no opportunity costs were incorporated in the analysis. By spending time on creating the enhanced design for the Hummer toy, Mattel's product designers may be sacrificing time that could be better spent designing new products that could be sold at an even higher profit. Whenever possible, managers need to incorporate these opportunity costs into the decision-making process.

CAPITAL BUDGETING FOR LONG-TERM INVESTMENT DECISIONS

Long-term capital investment decisions, called capital budgeting decisions, are decisions concerning major capital assets, including projects, production facilities, machines, land, and other assets. Examples include:

- Whether Mattel should replace old equipment with more modern and efficient equipment.
- Whether Mattel should invest in a new information system that will provide the company with more accurate and up-to-date information.
- Whether Mattel should automate part of the production process to save on long-term labor costs.
- How Mattel should invest its limited research and development budget when faced with multiple options for future products.

All of these decisions involve a significant up-front cash investment with the expectation of receiving future benefits in the form of either revenues or cost savings. Managers make two different types of capital investment decisions:

- Screening decisions require managers to evaluate a proposed capital investment to determine whether it meets some minimum criteria. In other words, they must decide whether a project is acceptable or not.

Video 22-2
www.mhhe.com/LLPW1e

• **Preference decisions** require managers to choose from among a set of alternative capital investment opportunities. Because companies typically have limited funds to invest in capital projects, managers must prioritize and select from the available options.

Several different capital budgeting techniques are available to help managers make these decisions. Some of those techniques are nondiscounting methods—that is, methods that do not consider the time value of money. We examine two nondiscounting methods, the annual rate of return and the payback period. Techniques that do incorporate the time value of money are called discounted cash flow methods. We consider two such methods, net present value and the internal rate of return. Because capital investment decisions affect a company's cash flow for many years, approaches that incorporate the time value of money are considered superior to the nondiscounting methods. To see how the various capital budgeting methods work, let's consider a possible scenario at Mattel.

Assume that Mattel's managers are evaluating a proposal to create a children's MP3 product that would allow parents to download children's music, books, and educational products from Mattel's Web site. This new product, the Learning Pod or L Pod, would require an up-front investment of $1,100,000. The product's estimated life cycle is five years, at which point the residual assets (equipment and so on) would have an estimated salvage value of about $100,000.

Based on preliminary market research and production cost estimates, Mattel has estimated the new product's net income over the next five years as follows:

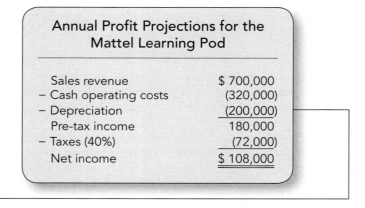

Annual Profit Projections for the Mattel Learning Pod	
Sales revenue	$ 700,000
− Cash operating costs	(320,000)
− Depreciation	(200,000)
Pre-tax income	180,000
− Taxes (40%)	(72,000)
Net income	$ 108,000

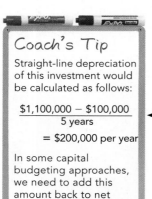

Coach's Tip

Straight-line depreciation of this investment would be calculated as follows:

$$\frac{\$1,100,000 - \$100,000}{5 \text{ years}}$$

$$= \$200,000 \text{ per year}$$

In some capital budgeting approaches, we need to add this amount back to net income to calculate cash flow.

Should Mattel invest in this project? Answering this question fully requires much more information and analysis than we can cover in this chapter. To illustrate how managers might begin to address this question, however, let's apply the four capital budgeting techniques.

Nondiscounting Methods

The two nondiscounting methods we will discuss are the accounting rate of return and the payback period. These methods are fairly simple to use but suffer from the limitation that they do not take into account the time value of money.

Accounting Rate of Return

Learning Objective 4a

Analyze investment decisions using the accounting rate of return.

The accounting rate of return, also called the annual rate of return, is an estimate of the average annual return on investment that a project is expected to generate over its life. It is calculated as follows:

$$\text{Accounting Rate of Return} = \text{Annual Net Income} \div \text{Average Investment Level}$$

To find the average investment level, we start with the original cost of $1,100,000, which will eventually be depreciated down to a salvage value of $100,000. Thus, the average investment is the average of these two numbers, or $600,000 (see Exhibit 22.5).

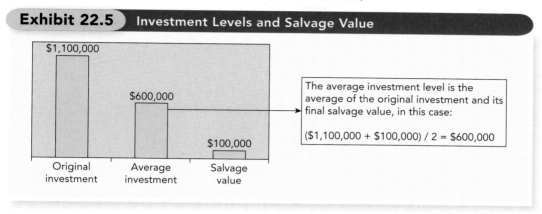

Exhibit 22.5   Investment Levels and Salvage Value

The average investment level is the average of the original investment and its final salvage value, in this case:

($1,100,000 + $100,000) / 2 = $600,000

In our example, the proposed project is expected to generate an annual net income of $108,000. So, the accounting rate of return is calculated as follows:

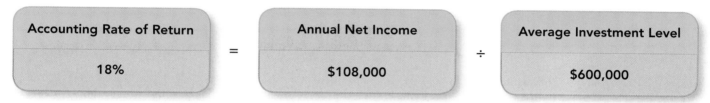

Accounting Rate of Return	=	Annual Net Income	÷	Average Investment Level
18%		$108,000		$600,000

To make a screening decision on this project, Mattel's managers would compare its 18 percent accounting rate of return to the company's minimum required rate of return, sometimes called the hurdle rate. The hurdle rate should reflect the company's cost of capital, which is a function of the interest rate the company pays on its debt as well as the cost of equity financing. If the accounting rate of return is higher than the hurdle rate, the project is acceptable; if not, it is unacceptable.

To make a preference decision on the project, managers would compare the project's accounting rate of return to the rate that could be earned on other potential projects. They would also need to consider other factors, such as the level of risk associated with each project.

The accounting rate of return is the only method we present that is based on the accounting measures of net income and investment. The other three methods focus on cash flows rather than net income.

Payback Period

The payback period is the amount of time needed for a capital investment to "pay for itself." The payback period is calculated as follows:

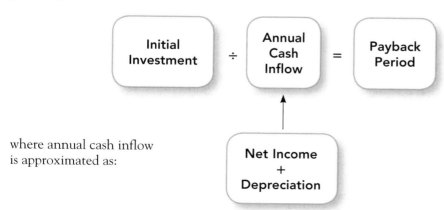

where annual cash inflow is approximated as:

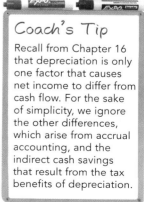

Coach's Tip

Recall from Chapter 16 that depreciation is only one factor that causes net income to differ from cash flow. For the sake of simplicity, we ignore the other differences, which arise from accrual accounting, and the indirect cash savings that result from the tax benefits of depreciation.

To apply these formulas, we must first calculate the annual cash flow from the investment. We estimated Mattel's annual net income to be $108,000 after a $200,000 deduction for depreciation expense. Because depreciation is a noncash expense that was deducted in the calculation of net income, we need to add this amount back to net income to get to cash flow. Adding $200,000 in depreciation to the $108,000 in net income provides an estimate of the project's annual cash inflow of $308,000. Because the initial investment requires a cash outflow of $1,100,000, the payback period would be calculated as follows.

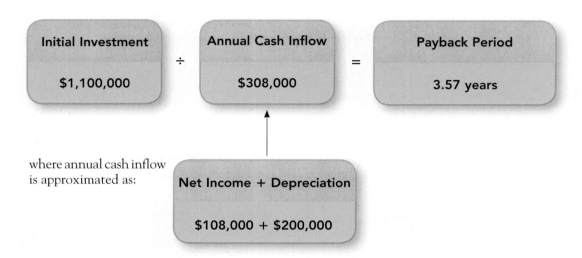

where annual cash inflow is approximated as:

This result tells managers that the project is expected to pay back the original cash investment in a little more than three and one-half years. In general, projects with short cash payback periods are considered safer investments than those with long payback periods. However, this approach is a very simplistic one that does not consider the timing of the cash flows or anything that happens after the payback period. For example, we completely ignored the salvage value of the equipment because that cash inflow does not occur until the end of the project, long after the cash inflows from the first three and one-half years are expected to pay back the original investment.

Discounted Cash Flow Methods

The next two methods we focus on consider the timing of all cash flows, recognizing that cash received today is more valuable than cash received in the future. Present value concepts lie at the heart of the discounted cash flow methods, so you may want to review the present value concepts discussed in Appendix C.

Net Present Value

Learning Objective 4c

Analyze investment decisions using the net present value method.

The **net present value (NPV) method** compares the present value of a project's future cash flows to the original investment made at the start of the project. The difference between the present value of the cash inflows and outflows over the life of the project is the net present value.

The discounting factor used to compute the net present value is called the required rate of return, hurdle rate, or cost of capital. In general terms, a positive NPV means that the project will generate a return in excess of the required rate of return; a negative net present value means that the project will not cover the required rate of return.

To compute the NPV for Mattel's project, let's assume that the required rate of return, or hurdle rate, is 12 percent. Recall that the project requires an initial investment of $1,100,000 and will generate $308,000 in cash flow each year. In addition, the assets have an estimated salvage value of $100,000, which will create a one-time cash inflow at the end of year 5. Based on this information and the present value factors for a 12 percent discount rate (which you will find in Appendix C), the NPV of this project would be calculated as follows:

Year	Cash Flow		Present Value Factor (12%)		Present Value
0	$(1,100,000)		—		$(1,100,000)
1	308,000	×	0.8929	=	275,013
2	308,000	×	0.7972	=	245,538
3	308,000	×	0.7118	=	219,234
4	308,000	×	0.6355	=	195,734
5	408,000	×	0.5674	=	231,499
			Net present value	=	$ 67,018

Coach's Tip

Notice that the original cash outflow happens at the beginning of the project and therefore does not need to be discounted. We assume that all other cash flows occur at the end of each year of the project. The cash inflow in year 5 is higher because of the equipment's $100,000 salvage value at the end of the project.

The resulting net present value of $67,018 indicates that the present value of the project's cash inflows is $67,018 more than the cost of the original investment. In general, a positive NPV indicates that a project is acceptable; a negative NPV indicates that it is not acceptable.

Since the $308,000 annual cash inflow happens in each of the five years of the project, we could have used the present value of an annuity (or stream of cash flows) to calculate the NPV of the project. But we would still need to do a separate calculation for the $100,000 salvage value, because this happens at only one point in the future (at the end of year five). This analysis, which yields the same NPV, is shown below.

Year	Cash Flow		Present Value Factor (12%)		Present Value
0	$(1,100,000)		—		$(1,100,000)
1–5	308,000	×	3.6048*	=	1,110,278
5	100,000	×	0.5674**	=	56,740
			Net present value	=	$ 67,018

* 3.6048 is the PV of an annuity for 5 years at 12%.
** 0.5674 is the PV of $1 in 5 years at 12%.

Coach's Tip

In practice, accountants usually use financial calculators or spreadsheet programs to calculate NPV rather than using PV tables.

Even so, it is important that you understand how to do the manual calculations so that you understand the logic behind the results you get from a calculator or spreadsheet.

Internal Rate of Return

We know from the positive NPV we just calculated that the expected cash flows from the proposed project will generate a return that is higher than the 12 percent required rate of return. It would be nice to have an exact number for the estimated return. We cannot rely on the 18 percent accounting rate of return we calculated earlier, however, because that approach was based on net income rather than cash flow and did not consider the time value of money. Instead, we need to find the discount rate that will equate the NPV of the future cash flows with the initial cash outflow. The rate at which the present value of the cash inflows exactly equals the present value of the cash outflows is called the **internal rate of return (IRR)**. It is also the discount rate at which the project's NPV would be zero.

Consider what would happen if we increased the discount rate used to evaluate the Mattel project from 12% to 13%, 14% and 15%:

Learning Objective 4d

Analyze investment decisions using the internal rate of return.

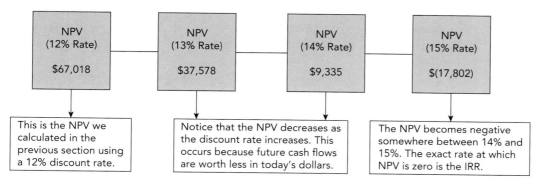

NPV (12% Rate)	NPV (13% Rate)	NPV (14% Rate)	NPV (15% Rate)
$67,018	$37,578	$9,335	$(17,802)

This is the NPV we calculated in the previous section using a 12% discount rate.

Notice that the NPV decreases as the discount rate increases. This occurs because future cash flows are worth less in today's dollars.

The NPV becomes negative somewhere between 14% and 15%. The exact rate at which NPV is zero is the IRR.

The previous diagram shows that the NPV is positive at a 14% discount rate, but becomes negative at a 15% discount rate. The point at which the NPV is zero is the internal rate of return (IRR).

To calculate the exact IRR, we would need to use a computer program such as Excel. These steps are illustrated in Exhibit 22.6

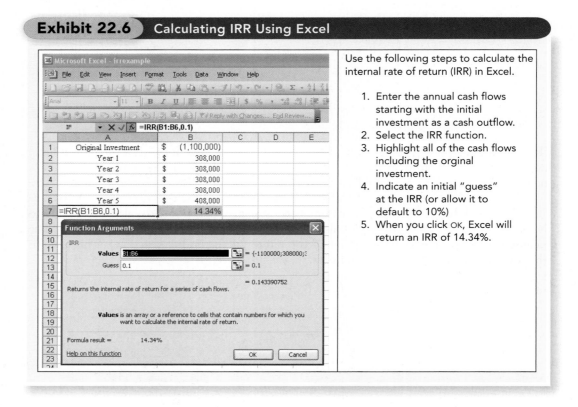

Exhibit 22.6   Calculating IRR Using Excel

Use the following steps to calculate the internal rate of return (IRR) in Excel.

1. Enter the annual cash flows starting with the initial investment as a cash outflow.
2. Select the IRR function.
3. Highlight all of the cash flows including the orginal investment.
4. Indicate an initial "guess" at the IRR (or allow it to default to 10%)
5. When you click OK, Excel will return an IRR of 14.34%.

Following these steps results in an IRR of 14.34 percent. As we predicted based on the NPV analysis, the IRR was between 14 percent and 15 percent.

As you can see, the IRR is closely related to the NPV method. The NPV uses the company's required rate of return as the discount rate to determine whether the present value of the project's expected cash flows is sufficient to cover the original investment. The IRR is the return that will yield a zero net present value. The following diagram summarizes the relationship between the IRR, the required rate of return, and the NPV.

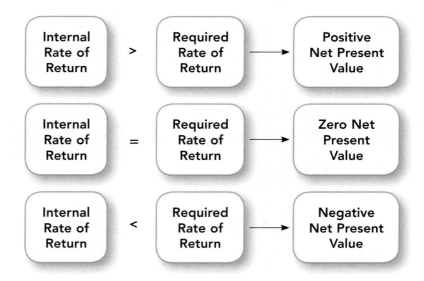

To make sure you understand the four capital budgeting techniques, complete the following Self-Study Practice.

1. Which of the following statements regarding the four capital budgeting techniques is **true?** You may select more than one answer.

   a. Both the accounting rate of return and the payback period consider the time value of money.

   b. Both the accounting rate of return and the payback period are based on net income rather than on cash flow.

   c. Both the NPV method and the IRR ignore the time value of money.

   d. The accounting rate of return is based on net income, the other three methods are based on cash flow.

   e. All of these statements are true.

2. Jackson Company's required rate of return is 10 percent. The NPV of a project using the 10 percent discount rate is $(15,333). Which of the following statements regarding the NPV and IRR is **true?** You may select more than one answer.

   a. The present value of the project's future cash flows is more than the original cost of the investment.

   b. The present value of the project's future cash flows is less than the original cost of the investment.

   c. The IRR on this project is less than 10 percent.

   d. The IRR on this project is more than 10 percent.

After you have finished, check your answers with the solutions at the bottom of the page.

Demonstration Case A

Assume you need to buy a new vehicle. The junker that you paid $5,000 for two years ago has a current value of $1,500. You have narrowed the choice down to a used 2002 Jeep Cherokee with a blue book value of $8,000 and a new Hyundai Elantra with a sticker price of $12,995. You plan to drive either vehicle for at least five more years.

Required:

1. List the five steps in the decision-making process and briefly describe the key factors you would consider at each step.

2. Indicate whether each of the following factors would be relevant or irrelevant to your decision:

> a. The $5,000 you paid for your junker two years ago.
> b. The $1,500 your vehicle is worth today.
> c. The blue book value of the Jeep Cherokee.
> d. The sticker price of the Hyundai Elantra.
> e. The difference in fuel economy for the Jeep and the Hyundai.
> f. The cost of on-campus parking.
> g. The difference in insurance cost for the Jeep and the Hyundai.
> h. The difference in resale value five years from now for the Jeep and the Hyundai.
> i. The fact that the Hyundai comes with a warranty but the Jeep does not.

1. d is the only true statement.
2. b and c are true statements.

Solution to
Self-Study Practice

3.   Consider only the costs you just classified as irrelevant.

   a.   Would any of these costs be relevant if you were deciding whether to keep your present vehicle or buy a new one?
   b.   Would any of these costs be relevant if you were deciding whether to get rid of your vehicle and ride your bike to work and school?

Suggested Solution

1.

Factors to Consider:	
Step 1: Identify the decision problem.	You need (or want) to buy a new vehicle, presumable because your old one is no longer fulfilling its purpose.
Step 2: Determine the decision alternatives.	What kind of vehicle should you buy (a car, a truck, an SUV)? Should you buy a new or a used vehicle? What is your price range? What kind of fuel economy should the vehicle you buy offer? What other features are important to you?
Step 3: Evaluate the costs and benefits of the alternatives.	What is the difference in price for each alternatives: fuel economy, the cost of insurance, the cost of maintenance, reliability ratings, future resale value, and other benefits or costs?
Step 4: Make the decision.	Which cost and qualitative considerations, such as style and function, outweigh the others?
Step 5: Review the results of the decision-making process.	Does the vehicle you selected meet your needs? Is it reliable? Are you comfortable in it? Can you make the payments?

2.
   a. Sunk cost.
   b. Same under both options.
   c. Relevant.
   d. Relevant.
   e. Relevant.
   f. Same under both options.
   g. Relevant.
   h. Relevant.
   i. Relevant.

3.
   a. Yes, the $1,500 value of your current vehicle would be relevant because you could sell it under one option but not the other.
   b. Yes, the cost of on-campus parking would be relevant because you could avoid it if you did not own a vehicle.

Demonstration Case B

Maddox Company is considering investing $800,000 in a new project. Projected annual revenues, expenses, and profit for the next four years follow:

Sales revenue	$ 600,000
−Cash operating costs	(300,000)
−Depreciation ($800,000 / 4)	(200,000)
Pre-Tax income	100,000
−Taxes (40%)	(40,000)
Net income	$ 60,000

The project's assets are expected to have no salvage value at the end of four years. The company's required rate of return is 12 percent.

Required:

1. Compute the accounting rate of return.
2. Compute the payback period.
3. Compute the four-year NPV using a 12 percent discount rate.
4. Without computing the exact IRR, explain whether it would be higher or lower than the 12 percent required rate of return.
5. Compute the exact IRR using Excel's IRR function.

Suggested Solution

1. Accounting rate of return = $60,000 / [($800,000 + 0) / 2] = 15%
2. Payback period = $800,000 / ($60,000 + $200,000) = 3.08 years
3.

Year	Cash Flow		PV Factor (12%)	Present Value
0	($ 800,000)		–	$(800,000)
1-4	$ 60,000 + $ 200,000 = $260,000	×	3.0373*	789,689
			Net Present Value =	$ (10,302)

*3.0373 is the PV of an annuity for 4 years at 12%.

4. Because the NPV is negative at a discount rate of 12 percent, the IRR must be less than 12 percent.
5. The exact IRR is 11.3879 percent.

Chapter Summary

LO1 Describe the five steps in the decision-making process. p. 920

- The managerial decision-making process has five steps:
  - Identify the decision problem.
  - Determine the decision alternatives.
  - Evaluate the costs and benefits of the alternatives.
  - Make the decision.
  - Review the results of the decision-making process.

LO2 Define and identify relevant costs and benefits. p. 922

- When making decisions, managers should focus only on costs and benefits that are relevant to the decision. To be relevant, a cost or benefit must meet the following criteria:
  - It must occur in the future, not the past. Sunk costs are never relevant.
  - The total amount of the cost or benefit must change depending on which alternative is selected.
  - Relevant costs are sometimes called **differential costs, incremental costs,** or **avoidable costs.** Costs that will not change regardless of the alternative that is selected are irrelevant and should be ignored.

LO3 Use incremental analysis to make short-term decisions. p. 923

- Incremental analysis is a short-term decision-making approach that compares the incremental costs and benefits of various alternatives. This approach can be used to address several common managerial decisions, including:
  - **Special-order decisions.** As long as the price of a special order is more than the incremental costs of filling it, a special order will contribute to short-term profit.
  - **Make-or-buy decisions.** Managers should compare the relevant (that is, differential) costs of making the product or providing the service internally to the cost of buying it from an outside supplier.

- **Keep-or-drop decisions.** In deciding whether to eliminate a product or service, managers should compare the lost revenue with the resulting reduction in cost to determine the overall impact on profit and should consider the effect of the decision on other product lines.
- **Sell-or-process further decisions.** To decide whether to sell a product "as is" or continue spending money to enhance it, managers should compare the incremental revenue with the incremental costs that will result from the additional processing.

- In making all of these decisions, it is important for managers to consider opportunity costs as well as factors that cannot be quantified, such as quality concerns.

LO4 Analyze investment decisions using four capital budgeting techniques. p. 932

- Managers use several approaches to make long-term capital budgeting decisions including the four considered here.
  - The accounting rate of return is a nondiscounting approach that estimates the average accounting rate of return on a project. This approach is the only one that focuses on net income rather than cash flow.
  - The payback period is the total amount of time needed for a capital investment project to pay back the company's original investment. This simple approach does not take into account the time value of money.
  - Net present value is a discounted cash flow technique that compares the present value of a project's future cash flows to the original investment.
  - The internal rate of return is related to the net present value. It is calculated by finding the discount rate that would generate a zero NPV. In other words, the IRR is the rate at which the present value of a project's future cash flows equals the original cash outflow. An IRR that is higher than the required rate of return will generate a positive net present value. An IRR that is lower than the required rate of return will generate a negative net present value.

Key Terms

Accounting Rate of Return (p. 932)
Annual Rate of Return (p. 932)
Avoidable Cost (p. 922)
Capital Budgeting (p. 920)
Capital Budgeting Decisions (p. 931)
Differential Analysis (p. 921)
Differential Cost (p. 922)

Discounted Cash Flow Method (p. 932)
Hurdle Rate (p. 933)
Incremental Analysis (p. 920)
Incremental Cost (p. 922)
Internal Rate of Return (IRR) (p. 935)
Irrelevant Cost (p. 922)

Net Present Value (NPV) Method (p. 934)
Nondiscounting Methods (p. 932)
Payback Period (p. 933)
Preference Decisions (p. 932)
Relevant Cost (p. 922)
Screening Decisions (p. 931)
Sunk Costs (p. 922)

See complete glossary in the back of text.

Questions

1. How do incremental analysis and capital budgeting differ? How are they similar?

2. Briefly describe the five steps of the management decision-making process.

3. Suppose you are considering a part-time job to earn some extra spending money. List four factors that could affect that decision and would be included in Step 3 of your decision-making process.

4. Tom Ellis recently bought a plasma television and has since stated that he would not recommend that brand to others. This indicates that Tom has completed which step of the decision-making process?

5. What are the criteria for a cost to be considered relevant to any decision?

6. How is an avoidable cost related to a relevant cost?

7. Explain opportunity cost and give two opportunity costs of your decision to enroll in classes this semester.

8. Why should opportunity costs be factored into the decision-making process and why is it often difficult to do?

9. What is a special-order decision? Why can managers ignore fixed overhead costs when making special-order decisions?

10. How might the acceptance of a special order have negative consequences for a company?

11. Briefly explain what excess capacity means. How does it impact a special-order decision?

12. Suppose that you are a manager of a local deli and sandwich shop. Give an example of each of the following decisions that

you might have to make and identify three factors that would be relevant to each decision.

   a.   Special order.

   b.   Make or buy.

   c.   Keep or drop.

13. Briefly describe three problems that might result from a decision to buy a component part from an external supplier. For each problem, identify one way to avoid or correct it.

14. How do opportunity costs affect make-or-buy decisions? How are opportunity costs shown in a make-or-buy analysis?

15. When a product line is eliminated, why are the fixed costs allocated to that line not automatically eliminated as well?

16. How might the decision to drop a product line affect a company's remaining products?

17. Briefly explain what happens to total variable costs when a product line is dropped.

18. Identify three opportunity costs that might be involved in a keep-or-drop decision.

19. Explain the difference between screening decisions and preference decisions.

20. How do nondiscounting methods and discounting methods of capital budgeting differ? Which is considered superior, and why?

21. Briefly explain what the time value of money means.

22. What is a company's hurdle rate? How is it relevant to capital budgeting?

23. In everyday terms, explain what information the payback period provides about an investment.

24. What do a positive net present value (NPV) and a negative NPV indicate about an investment?

25. When would you use an annuity factor in a net present value calculation instead of a present value factor for a single cash flow?

26. Explain how the internal rate of return and net present value are related. If a project has a net present value of $50,000 using a 10 percent discount factor, what does this imply about that project's IRR?

Multiple Choice

1. The decision-making approach in which a manager considers only costs and benefits that differ for alternatives is called:

Quiz 22-1

www.mhhe.com/LLPW1e

   a.   Incremental analysis.

   b.   Outsourcing.

   c.   Differential analysis.

   d.   Either a or c.

2. Which of the following is not a step of the management decision-making process?

   a.   Review results of the decision-making process.

   b.   Contact competitors who have made similar decisions.

   c.   Evaluate the costs and benefits of the alternatives.

   d.   Determine the decision alternatives.

3. Sunk costs are always

   a.   Opportunity costs.   c.   Relevant.

   b.   Avoidable.   d.   Irrelevant.

4. When making a one-time special-order decision, a company can ignore fixed overhead because

   a.   The cost is not avoidable.

   b.   The cost is avoidable.

   c.   The cost cannot be determined.

   d.   None of the above.

5. When making make-or-buy decisions, managers should consider

   a.   Alternate uses for any facility currently being used to make the item.

   b.   The costs of direct materials included in making the item.

   c.   Qualitative factors such as whether the supplier can deliver the item on time and to the company's quality standards.

   d.   All of the above.

6. Which of the following costs is not likely to be completely eliminated by a decision to drop a product line?

   a.   The variable overhead traced to that product line.

   b.   The cost of direct materials used to produce the product.

   c.   The portion of fixed overhead allocated to that product line.

   d.   All of the above will be completely eliminated.

7. Which of the following requires managers to determine whether a proposed capital investment meets some minimum criteria?

   a.   Preference decision.   c.   Cash payback period.

   b.   Screening decision.   d.   None of the above.

8. ABC Company is considering a $500,000 investment to automate its production process. The new equipment will allow ABC to save $75,000 each year in labor costs. What is this project's payback period?

   a.   4.00 years.   c.   6.67 years.

   b.   5.67 years.   d.   8.00 years.

9. Discounting methods of capital budgeting are considered superior to nondiscounting methods because

   a.   Discounting methods recognize the time value of money.

   b.   Discounting methods are simpler to calculate.

   c.   Discounting methods are always based on accounting measurements of net income and investment.

   d.   Both a and c are correct.

10. Jennings Company has evaluated a project and found that its internal rate of return is approximately 13.5 percent.

Suppose Jennings' cost of capital is 12 percent. What, if anything, can you infer about the net present value (NPV) of this project?

a.   The NPV is less than zero.

b.   The NPV is more than zero.

c.   The NPV is exactly zero.

d.   Nothing can be determined about the project's NPV.

Mini Exercises   ▪▪▪   Available with McGraw-Hill's Homework Manager

LO1, 2, 3, 4

M22-1 Matching Key Terms and Concepts to Definitions

A number of terms and concepts from this chapter and a list of descriptions, definitions, and explanations follow. For each term listed on the left, choose at least one corresponding item from the right. Note that a single term may have more than one description and a single description may be used more than once or not at all.

_____ 1.   Time value of money
_____ 2.   Identify the decision problem
_____ 3.   Payback period
_____ 4.   Special order decision
_____ 5.   Net present value method
_____ 6.   Differential costs
_____ 7.   Evaluate the costs and benefits of alternatives
_____ 8.   Make-or-buy decision
_____ 9.   Preference decision
_____10.   Sunk costs
_____11.   Opportunity costs
_____12.   Keep-or-drop decision
_____13.   Internal rate of return method
_____14.   Screening decision
_____15.   Accounting rate of return
_____16.   Avoidable costs

A.   Short-term management decision made using differential analysis.
B.   Discounting method of capital budgeting.
C.   Estimate of the average annual return on investment a project will generate.
D.   Management decision based on comparing lost revenue with the reduction of costs to determine the overall effect on profit.
E.   Capital budgeting method that finds the discount rate that generates a zero net present value.
F.   Decision made when managers evaluate potential capital investments to determine whether they meet a minimum criteria.
G.   The only capital budgeting method based on accounting measures of net income and investment.
H.   Costs that have already been incurred.
I.   Management decision based on ignoring fixed manufacturing overhead so long as there is enough excess capacity to meet the order.
J.   Costs that can be avoided by choosing one option over another.
K.   Concept recognizing that cash received today is more valuable than cash received in the future.
L.   Step 5 of the management decision-making process.
M.   Management decision based on the relevant costs of making a product internally compared with the cost of purchasing that product.
N.   Cost that is relevant to short-term decision making.
O.   Decision that requires a manager to choose from a set of alternatives.
P.   Step 1 of the management decision-making process.
Q.   Costs that are always irrelevant to management decisions.
R.   Method that calculates how long it will take for a particular capital investment to pay for itself.
S.   Benefits given up when one alternative is chosen over another.
T.   Capital budgeting technique that compares the present value of the future cash flows for a project to its original investment.
U.   Costs that change across decision alternatives.
V.   Nondiscounting method of capital budgeting.
W.   Step 3 of the management decision-making process.

M22-2 Identifying Relevant and Irrelevant Costs

LO2

Sarah Ramirez is considering taking a part-time job at a local clothing store. Sarah loves the store and shops there often, but unfortunately, employee discounts are given only to full-time employees. If Sarah takes this job, she will have to withdraw from her Tuesday night basket-weaving class to work. Accepting the job would also mean that Sarah must give up her volunteer work at the local animal sanctuary, an activity that she enjoys a great deal. The new job would pay approximately $125 per week but would cost Sarah $15 per week in gas. Sarah would be able to keep her Saturday afternoon job at the library that pays $40 per week.

A list of factors that Sarah has identified follows. For each one, indicate whether it is relevant or irrelevant to Sarah's decision.

1. The $125 income from the new job.
2. The $40 income from the library.
3. The $50 nonrefundable registration fee Sarah paid for the basket-weaving class.
4. The $15 cost for gas.
5. The $75 per month that Sarah spends for clothing.
6. The time Sarah spends volunteering at the animal sanctuary.

M22-3 Identifying Relevant and Irrelevant Costs

LO2

The local summer baseball league wants to buy new uniforms for its teams. The current uniforms are quite old and will require $400 in repairs before they can be handed out to players next week for the upcoming season. The old uniforms will be replaced as soon as new ones can be purchased. League leaders have investigated several possible fund-raisers and have narrowed the choice down to two options: candy sales or car washes. Each option can generate the $2,500 that the new uniforms would cost.

Option 1:

The candy sales option would require the league to purchase 2,000 candy bars at a cost of $0.75 each. The players and coaches would then sell the bars for $2.00 each. The league estimates that it would take about four weeks to sell the candy and collect all of the money.

Option 2:

The car wash option would require about $200 for buckets, sponges, soap, and towels. A local business has offered to donate the water (estimated at $300 total) and a location. The car washes would be held on Saturdays, and each team would be required to provide workers. Each car wash day is expected to generate $450 in proceeds, so the league expects that it would take six weeks to raise $2,500.

Required:

1. Several factors related to the league's choice follow. Indicate whether each factor is relevant or irrelevant to deciding which project to engage in and briefly explain your reason.

    a. Repair costs for the old uniforms, $400.
    b. Initial outlay to purchase the candy bars, $1,500.
    c. Initial outlay to purchase car wash supplies, $200.
    d. Cost of water for the car wash option, $300.
    e. Cost of the new uniforms, $2,500.
    f. Additional two weeks that the car wash option would require to raise the money.

2. List three qualitative factors that the league should consider in making its choice.

Questions M22-4–M22-6 refer to Flyaway Company, which produces window fans. Consider each question independently.

M22-4 Analyzing a Special-Order Decision

LO2, 3

Flyaway Company has just received a one-time offer to purchase 10,000 units of its Breezy model for a price of $20 each. The Breezy model costs $25 to produce ($17 in variable costs and $8 of fixed overhead). Because the offer came during a slow production month, Flyaway has enough excess capacity to accept the order.

Required:

1. Should Flyaway accept the special order offer?
2. Determine the impact the special order would have on Flyaway's net income.

M22-5 Analyzing a Keep-or-Drop Decision

LO2, 3

Suppose that Flyaway Company also produces the Windy model fan, which currently has a net loss of $40,000 as follows:

Sales	$ 160,000
Variable costs	(130,000)
Contribution margin	30,000
Allocated fixed costs	(70,000)
Profit (Loss)	$ (40,000)

Dropping the Windy product line will eliminate $20,000 of fixed costs. The remaining $50,000 will be redistributed to Flyaway's remaining product lines.

Determine whether Flyaway should drop the Windy fan line. Why or why not?

LO2, 3

M22-6 Analyzing a Make-or-Buy decision

Flyaway Company also has the Cyclone fan model. It is the company's top-selling model, with sales of 30,000 units per year. This model has a dual fan as well as a thermostat component that causes the fan to cycle on and off depending on the room temperature. Flyaway has always manufactured the thermostat component but is considering buying the part from a supplier.

It costs Flyaway $5 to make each thermostat ($3 variable and $2 fixed). Mostat Co. has offered to sell the component to Flyaway for $4. Flyaway's decision to purchase the part from Mostat will eliminate all variable costs but none of the fixed costs. Flyaway has no other possible uses for the area currently dedicated to the thermostat production.

Determine whether Flyaway should continue to make the thermostat or purchase the part from Mostat Co. Justify your answer.

LO4

M22-7 Calculating the Accounting Rate of Return and Payback Period

Milo Company is considering purchasing new equipment for its factory. The equipment will cost $250,000 and have a $50,000 salvage value in five years. The annual net income from the equipment is expected to be $30,000, and depreciation is $40,000 per year.

Calculate and evaluate Milo's:

Required:

1. Annual rate of return on the equipment.
2. Payback period for the equipment.

LO4

M22-8 Calculating Net Present Value and Predicting the Internal Rate of Return

Otis Company has the following information about a potential capital investment:

Initial investment	$400,000
Annual cash inflow	$ 70,000
Expected life	10 years
Cost of capital	11%

1. Calculate and evaluate the net present value of this project.
2. Without any calculations, explain whether the internal rate of return on this project is more or less than 11 percent.

Exercises ^{TM}   Available with McGraw-Hill's Homework Manager

LO1, 2

E22-1 Identifying Relevant Costs and Calculating Differential Costs

Maria Turner has just graduated from college with a degree in accounting. She had planned to enroll immediately in the master's program at her university but has been offered a lucrative job at a well-known company. The job is exactly what Maria had hoped to find after obtaining her graduate degree.

In anticipation of master's program classes, Maria has already spent $450 to apply for the program. Tuition for the master's program is $8,000 per year, and it will take two years to complete. Maria's expected salary after completing the master's program is approximately $60,000. If she pursues the master's degree, Maria would stay in her current home that is near the campus and costs $600 per month in rent. She would also remain at her current job that pays $25,000 per year. Additionally, Maria's immediate family is nearby.

She spends considerable time with family and friends, especially during the holidays. This would not be possible if she accepts the job offer because of the distance from her new location.

The job Maria has been offered includes a salary of $50,000. She would have to relocate to another state, but her employer would pay the $5,000 of moving expenses. Maria's rent in the new location would be approximately $800 per month. The new location is a fast-growing, active city that offers a number of cultural activities that Maria would enjoy. The city is also home to Maria's favorite Major League Baseball team, and she would expect to buy season tickets.

Required:

1. Help Maria make her decision by categorizing the factors involved in making her choice. Complete the following chart regarding the factors in Maria's decision. A single factor may have multiple columns checked.

	Relevant	Irrelevant	Sunk Cost	Qualitative
$450 spent on application fee				
$8,000 per year tuition				
$60,000 salary with master's degree				
$600 per month current rent				
$25,000 current salary				
Time spent with family and friends				
$50,000 new salary				
$5,000 moving expenses				
$800 rent per month in new location				
Cultural activities in the new location				
Ability to have MLB season tickets				

2. For each item following, determine the differential amount in Maria's alternatives. For example, the incremental cost of tuition is $16,000 if Maria chooses to pursue the master's degree.

    a.   Rent.
    b.   Salary for the next two years.
    c.   Salary after two years.
    d.   Moving expenses.

The following information pertains to E22-2 through E22-5.

Electronic Playground, Inc. (EPI) manufactures and sells computer games for children. The company has several product lines based on the age range of the target market and whether the games are marketed as educational or entertainment. EPI sells both individual games as well as packaged sets. All games are in CD format, and some utilize accessories such as steering wheels, electronic tablets, and hand controls. To date, EPI has developed and manufactured all CDs itself as well as the accessories and packaging for all of its products.

The gaming market has traditionally been targeted at teenagers and young adults. However, the increasing affordability of computers and the incorporation of computer activities into junior high and elementary school curriculums has led to a significant increase in sales to younger children. EPI has always included games for younger children but now wants to expand its business to capitalize on changes in the industry. The company currently has excess capacity and is investigating several possible ways to improve profitability.

E22-2 Analyzing a Special-Order Decision

LO2, 3

EPI has been approached by a fourth-grade teacher from Phoenix about the possibility of creating a specially designed game that would be customized for her classroom and environment. The teacher would like an educational game to correspond to her classroom coverage of the history of the desert Southwest and the state of Arizona in particular. EPI has not sold its products directly to teachers or school systems in the past, but that possibility was identified during a recent meeting of EPI's Marketing Department.

The teacher has offered to buy 1,000 copies of the CD at a price of $5 each. EPI could easily modify one of its existing educational programs about U.S. history to accommodate the request. The modifications would cost approximately $500. A summary of the information related to production of EPI's current history program follows.

Direct materials	$ 1.25
Direct labor	0.50
Variable manufacturing overhead	2.25
Fixed manufacturing overhead	2.00
Total cost per unit	$ 6.00
Sales price per unit	$12.00

Required:

1. Determine the impact this special order would have on EPI's total profit.

2. Should EPI accept the special order?

3. Suppose that the special offer had been to purchase 1,000 copies of the program for $4.50 each. What effect would that offer have on EPI's total profit?

4. Explain why a company might accept a special order that did not increase profits.

LO2, 3   **E22-3 Analyzing a Make-or-Buy Decision**

EPI is considering outsourcing the production of the handheld control module used with some of its products. The company has received a bid from Control Freak Co. (CFC) to produce 10,000 units of the module per year for $15 each. The following information pertains to EPI's production of the control modules.

Direct materials	$ 8
Direct labor	3
Variable manufacturing overhead	2
Fixed manufacturing overhead	3
Total cost per unit	$16

EPI has determined that it could eliminate all variable costs if the control modules were produced externally, but none of the fixed overhead is avoidable. At this time, EPI has no specific use in mind for the space that is currently dedicated to the control module production.

Required:

1. Determine the impact this decision will have on EPI's annual income.

2. Should EPI buy the modules from CFC or continue to make them?

3. Suppose that the EPI space currently used for the modules could be utilized by a new product line that would generate $35,000 in annual profit. Does this change your recommendation to EPI? If so, how?

LO2, 3   **E22-4 Analyzing a Keep-or-Drop Decision**

EPI is considering eliminating a product from its ToddleTown Tours collection. This collection is aimed at children one to three years of age and includes "tours" of a hypothetical town. Two products, The Pet Store Parade and The Grocery Getaway, have impressive sales. However, sales for the third CD in the collection, The Post Office Polka, have lagged the others. Several other CDs are planned for this collection, but none is ready for production.

EPI's information related to the ToddleTown Tours collection follows.

SEGMENTED INCOME STATEMENT FOR EPI'S TODDLETOWN TOURS PRODUCT LINES

	Pet Store Parade	Grocery Getaway	Post Office Polka	Total
Sales revenue	$50,000	$45,000	$15,000	$110,000
Variable costs	23,000	19,000	10,000	52,000
Contribution margin	27,000	26,000	5,000	58,000
Allocated fixed costs	19,200	15,600	5,200	40,000
Profit (loss)	$ 7,800	$10,400	$ (200)	$ 18,000

EPI has determined that elimination of the Post Office Polka (POP) program will not impact sales of the other two items. Additionally, total fixed cost will be reduced by only $1,500. The remaining fixed overhead currently allocated to the POP program will be redistributed to the remaining two products.

Required:

1. Determine what will happen to the company's total profit, if EPI drops the POP product. What is your recommendation about the elimination?
2. Suppose that the full amount of fixed overhead ($5,200) allocated to POP is avoidable. Would your recommendation to EPI change? Why or why not?

E22-5 Identifying Qualitative Factors in Short-Term Decision Making   LO2, 3
Refer to E22-2 through E22-4.

Required:

Identify at least three qualitative factors that EPI should consider when making each decision.

E22-6 Calculating the Accounting Rate of Return and Payback Period   LO4
Midway Printing Co. is considering the purchase of new electronic printing equipment. The new equipment would allow Midway to increase its annual before-tax profit by $100,000. Midway has a 40 percent tax rate. Other information about this proposed project follows:

Initial investment	$300,000
Useful life	5 years
Salvage value	$100,000

Required:
Calculate and evaluate Midway's

1. Annual rate of return.
2. Payback period.

E22-7 Calculating Net Present Value and Internal Rate of Return   LO4
Lancer Corp. has the following information available about a potential capital investment:

Initial investment	$1,300,000
Annual net income	$ 200,000
Expected life	8 years
Salvage value	$ 350,000
Lancer's cost of capital	10%

Required:

1. Calculate and evaluate the net present value of this project.
2. Without making any calculations, determine whether the internal rate of return on this project is more or less than 10 percent.

3. Calculate the net present value using a 20% discount rate.
4. Estimate the project's internal rate of return (IRR).

LO4

E22-8 Calculating the Accounting Rate of Return, Payback Period, and Net Present Value

Lenny's Limousine Service (LLS) is considering the purchase of two Hummer limousines. Various information about the proposed investment follows.

Initial investment (2 limos)	$600,000
Useful life	8 years
Salvage value	$100,000
Annual net income generated	$ 48,000
LLS's cost of capital	12%

Required:
Help LLS evaluate this project by calculating each of the following:

1. Annual rate of return.
2. Payback period.
3. Net present value.
4. Based on your calculation of net present value, what would you estimate the project's internal rate of return to be?

LO4

E22-9 Analyzing the Relationship between Net Present Value and Internal Rate of Return

Consider the relationship between a project's net present value (NPV), its internal rate of return (IRR), and a company's cost of capital. For each scenario that follows, indicate the relative value of the unknown. If cost of capital is unknown, indicate whether it would be higher or lower than the stated IRR. If NPV is unknown, indicate whether it would be higher or lower than zero. Project 1 is shown as an example.

	Net Present Value	Cost of Capital	Internal Rate of Return
Project 1	< 0	13%	<13%
Project 2	> 0	?	10
Project 3	?	14	12
Project 4	> 0	10	?
Project 5	< 0	?	9
Project 6	?	9	10

Problems—Set A ▪▼▪▪   **Available with McGraw-Hill's Homework Manager**

LO2, 3

PA22-1 Analyzing a Special-Order Decision

Sunblocker Corp. makes several varieties of beach umbrellas and accessories. It has been approached about producing a special order for custom umbrellas. The special-order umbrellas with logo of Randolph Industries would be distributed to participants at an upcoming convention sponsored by Randolph.

Randolph has offered to buy 1,500 of the No-More-Squint (NMS) model umbrellas at a price of $8 each. Sunblocker currently has the excess capacity necessary to accept the offer. The following information is related to production of Sunblocker's NMS umbrella.

Direct materials	$ 2.25
Direct labor	0.75
Variable manufacturing overhead	3.50
Fixed manufacturing overhead	2.50
Total cost	$ 9.00
Regular sales price	$19.00

Required:

1. Determine the impact this special order would have on Sunblocker's total profit.
2. Should Sunblocker accept the special order?
3. Suppose that the special offer had been to purchase 2,000 umbrellas for $7.50 each. What effect would that offer have on Sunblocker's total profit?

PA22-2 Analyzing a Make-or-Buy Decision

LO2, 3

Sunblocker Corp. (see PA22-1) is considering the possibility of outsourcing production of the umbrella tote bag included with some of its products. The company has received a bid from CarryAll Co. to produce 8,000 units per year for $6 each. Sunblocker has the following information about its own production of the tote bags:

Direct materials	$3
Direct labor	1
Variable manufacturing overhead	1
Fixed manufacturing overhead	2
Total cost per unit	$7

Sunblocker has determined that all variable costs could be eliminated by dropping production of the tote bags, but none of the fixed overhead is avoidable. At this time, Sunblocker has no specific use in mind for the space currently dedicated to producing the tote bags.

Required:

1. Determine the impact this decision will have on Sunblocker's annual income.
2. Should Sunblocker buy the tote bags from CarryAll or continue to make them?
3. Suppose that the space Sunblocker currently uses to make the bags could be utilized by a new product line that would generate $10,000 in annual profits. Does this change your recommendation to Sunblocker? If so, how?

PA22-3 Analyzing a Keep-or-Drop Decision

LO2, 3

Sunblocker Corp. (see PA22-1 and PA22-2) is considering eliminating a product from its Happy Sand line of beach umbrellas. This collection is aimed at people who spend time on the beach or have an outdoor patio near the beach. Two products, the Happy Day and Morning Sun umbrellas, have impressive sales. However, sales for another umbrella, the Rolling Surf model, have been dismal.

Sunblocker's information related to the Happy Sand line follows.

Segmented Income Statement for Sunblocker's Happy Sand Beach Umbrella Products

	Happy Day	Morning Sun	Rolling Surf	Total
Sales Revenue	$60,000	$60,000	$ 30,000	$150,000
Variable Costs	34,000	31,000	23,000	88,000
Contribution Margin	26,000	29,000	7,000	62,000
Allocated Fixed Costs*	20,000	20,000	10,000	50,000
Profit	$ 6,000	$ 9,000	$ (3,000)	$ 12,000

* Allocated based on total sales dollars.

Sunblocker has determined that eliminating the Rolling Surf model will cause sales of the Happy Day and the Morning Sun models to increase by 10 percent and 15 percent, respectively. Variable costs for these two models will increase proportionately. Additionally, none of the fixed cost allocated to the Rolling Surf model is avoidable. The fixed overhead currently allocated to the Rolling Surf model will be redistributed to the remaining two products.

Required:

1. Determine what will happen to the company's total profit, if Sunblocker drops the Rolling Surf product. What is your recommendation to Sunblocker?

2. Suppose that the full amount of fixed overhead allocated to Rolling Surf is avoidable. Would your recommendation to Sunblocker change? Why or why not?

LO4

www.mhhe.com/LLPW1e

PA22-4 Calculating the Accounting Rate of Return, Payback Period, and Net Present Value
Hot Air Highlights (HAH) is considering the purchase of two new hot air balloons so that it can expand its desert sunset tours. Various information about the proposed investment follows.

Initial investment (for two hot air balloons)	$500,000
Useful life	10 years
Salvage value	$ 50,000
Annual net income generated	$ 42,000
HAH's cost of capital	11%

Required:
Help HAH evaluate this project by calculating each of the following:

1. Annual rate of return.
2. Payback period.
3. Net present value (NPV).
4. Recalculate the NPV assuming HAH's cost of capital is 15 percent.
5. Based on your calculation of NPV, what would you estimate the project's internal rate of return to be?

LO4

www.mhhe.com/LLPW1e

PA22-5 Calculating the Accounting Rate of Return, Payback Period, and Net Present Value
Wing Walker Aces (WWA), Inc., is considering the purchase of a small plane to be used in its wing-walking demonstrations and aerial tour business. Various information about the proposed investment follows.

Initial investment	$110,000
Useful life	12 years
Salvage value	$ 10,000
Annual net income generated	$ 5,400
WWA's cost of capital	10%

Required:
Help WWA evaluate this project by calculating each of the following:

1. Annual rate of return.
2. Payback period.
3. Net present value (NPV).
4. Recalculate WWA's NPV assuming the cost of capital is 6 percent.
5. Based on your calculations of NPV, what would you estimate the project's internal rate of return to be?

Problems—Set B Available with McGraw-Hill's Homework Manager

LO2, 3

PB22-1 Analyzing a Special-Order Decision
Woodchuck Corp. makes several varieties of wooden furniture. It has been approached about producing a special order for rocking chairs. A local senior citizens group would use the special-order chairs in a newly remodeled activity center.

The senior citizens have offered to buy 80 of the Rock-On model chairs at a price of $70 each. Woodchuck currently has the excess capacity necessary to accept the offer. A summary of the information related to production of Woodchuck's Rock-On model follows.

Direct materials	$30
Direct labor	20
Variable manufacturing overhead	12
Fixed manufacturing overhead	11
Total cost	$73
Regular sales price	$99

Required:

1. What impact would this special order have on Woodchuck's total profit?
2. Should Woodchuck accept the special order?
3. Suppose that the special offer had been to purchase 100 rocking chairs for $65 each. What effect would that offer have on Woodchuck's total profit?

PB22-2 Analyzing a Make-or-Buy Decision   LO2, 3

Woodchuck Corp. (see PB22-1) is considering the possibility of outsourcing the production of upholstered chair pads that are included with some of its wooden chairs. The company has received a bid from Padalong Co. to produce 1,000 units per year for $9 each. Woodchuck has the following information about its own production of the chair pads:

Direct materials	$ 4
Direct labor	2
Variable manufacturing overhead	2
Fixed manufacturing overhead	3
Total cost per unit	$11

Woodchuck has determined that all variable costs could be eliminated by dropping production of the chair pads, but none of the fixed overhead is avoidable. At this time, Woodchuck has no specific use in mind for the space currently dedicated to producing the chair pads.

Required:

1. Determine the impact this decision will have on Woodchuck's annual income.
2. Should Woodchuck buy the chair pads from Padalong or continue to make them?
3. Suppose that a new product line that Woodchuck wants to develop could utilize the Woodchuck space currently used for the chair pads. What amount of income must be generated by the new product line for Woodchuck to outsource the chair pads?

PB22-3 Analyzing a Keep-or-Drop Decision   LO2, 3

Woodchuck Corp. (see PB22-1 and PB22-2) is considering eliminating a product from its line of outdoor tables. Two products, the Oak-A and Fiesta tables, have impressive sales. However, sales for the Studio model have been dismal.

Information related to Woodchuck's outdoor table line follows.

Segmented Income Statement for Woodchuck's Outdoor Table Products

	Oak-A	Fiesta	Studio	Total
Sales revenue	$110,000	$77,000	$33,000	$220,000
Variable costs	77,000	52,000	24,000	153,000
Contribution margin	33,000	25,000	9,000	67,000
Allocated fixed costs*	20,000	14,000	6,000	40,000
Profit	$ 13,000	$11,000	$ 3,000	$ 27,000

*Allocated based on total sales dollars

Woodchuck has determined that eliminating the Studio model will cause sales of the Oak-A and the Fiesta tables to increase by 20 percent and 5 percent, respectively. Variable costs for these two models will increase proportionately. Additionally, $1,000 of the fixed cost allocated to the Studio model is avoidable. The remaining fixed overhead currently allocated to the Studio model will be redistributed to the remaining two products.

Required:

1. Determine what will happen to the company's total profit, if Woodchuck drops the Studio product. What is your recommendation to Woodchuck?
2. Suppose that $4,000 of fixed overhead allocated to the Studio model is avoidable. Would your recommendation to Woodchuck change? Why or why not?

LO4   **PB22-4 Calculating the Accounting Rate of Return, Payback Period, and Net Present Value**
Ted's Taxi Company (TTC) is considering the purchase of four new taxi cabs. Various information about the proposed investment follows.

Initial investment (for 4 vehicles)	$220,000
Useful life	5 years
Salvage value	$ 20,000
Annual net income generated	$ 27,000
TTC's cost of capital	9%

Required:
Help TTC evaluate this project by calculating each of the following:

1. Annual rate of return.
2. Payback period.
3. Net present value (NPV).
4. Recalculate the NPV assuming the cost of capital is 15 percent.
5. Based on your calculations of NPV, what would you estimate the project's internal rate of return to be?

LO4   **PB22-5 Calculating the Accounting Rate of Return, Payback Period, and Net Present Value**
Titan Production Co. is considering an investment in new machinery for its factory. Various information about the proposed investment follows.

Initial investment	$750,000
Useful life	6 years
Salvage value	$120,000
Annual net income generated	$ 66,000
Titan's cost of capital	11%

Required:
Help Titan evaluate this project by calculating each of the following:

1. Annual rate of return.
2. Payback period.
3. Net present value (NPV).
4. Recalculate Titan's NPV assuming its cost of capital is 12 percent.
5. Based on your calculations of NPV, what would you estimate the project's internal rate of return to be?

Cases and Projects

CP22-1 Evaluating a University's Decision to Eliminate Collegiate Sports Programs: Quantitative and Qualitative Considerations

Due to budget cutbacks, colleges and universities across the country are struggling to cut expenses. Frequent casualties of these money-saving decisions are organized sport teams. Suppose that a fictional college, West Tennessee State (WTS), has identified three teams to be eliminated in its effort to cut costs: men's lacrosse, women's softball, and men's diving. A summary of each sport's annual revenue and costs follow:

	Men's Lacrosse	Women's Softball	Men's Diving
Revenue	$ 25,600	$ 37,800	$ 14,900
Less: Expenses			
Scholarships	150,000	130,000	40,000
Coaches' salaries	53,000	49,700	62,800
Team travel	21,100	28,500	13,200
Venue maintenance	15,000	20,000	35,000
Equipment	4,300	2,800	800
Team support	16,600	11,200	6,300
Net income (loss)	$(234,400)	$(204,400)	$(143,200)

The combined net loss from these three programs is $(582,000).

Required:

1. Do you think WTS will see an immediate improvement in the college's bottom line (loss) of $582,000? Why or why not?

2. Determine whether the decision for each individual line item will be completely eliminated, partially eliminated, or not eliminated. Label the items as avoidable, partially avoidable, or unavoidable and explain any assumptions you made in determining the classification.

3. Research actual examples of the colleges or universities that have eliminated sports programs. List five colleges or universities that have eliminated sports teams in the past three years and identify which teams were eliminated.

4. Major sports such as men's football and basketball are seldom, if ever, eliminated even though they generally have the highest dollar amount of expenses. Why are these sports retained? What other factors may affect which teams are eliminated?

5. Choose one of the institutions identified in requirement 3 to investigate in more detail. For that university, discuss the factors that led to its choice(s), the anticipated impact on direct participants (coaches, athletes, etc.), and the total amount of savings expected. Also include reactions from the student body and the local and college communities.

C22-2 Evaluating Wal-Mart's Decision to Eliminate Product Offerings: Quantitative and Qualitative Considerations

During 2006 and 2007, Wal-Mart decided to eliminate two long-standing components of its business: merchandise layaway and by-the-bolt sales of fabric. Each of these decisions was met with considerable controversy among Wal-Mart customers.

Required:

1. Research these two decisions by Wal-Mart and write a brief paragraph explaining the company's point of view in making each decision. Include any information you can find about the profitability of the segment and possible plans for an alternative in the fabric decision.

2. Describe the "typical" Wal-Mart customer who will be most impacted by these decisions.

3. Write a brief paragraph from this typical customer's point of view explaining how Wal-Mart's decision would impact the customer.

4. Identify three possible effects of each decision on other segments of Wal-Mart's business. Be specific in terms of both the segment and the possible impact.

5. Consider a small, rural community in an economically depressed area of the United States. How might each of these decisions impact the people in that community? Contrast this to the impact felt in larger, urban areas of the country.

LO3   **CP22-3 Researching Outsourcing Issues in the National and Local Press**

Outsourcing, particularly to overseas companies, is a hot-button topic that has garnered much attention in the academic, national, and local business media.

Required:

1. Do a quick search at www.wikipedia.org for a high-level overview of outsourcing. What are some of the major reasons that companies decide to follow this practice? What are the advantages and disadvantages to outsourcing from the perspective of the company and its stockholders, managers, employees, and local community?

2. Search for a recent article on outsourcing in a national business publication such as *Fortune*, *BusinessWeek*, or *The Wall Street Journal*. Briefly summarize the article's main points, including any outsourcing trends, companies making outsourcing decisions, or issues related to politics or the U.S. economy.

3. Search the archives of your local or regional newspaper for articles about outsourcing. Try to identify a specific company in your area that has outsourced part of its operations. Describe the part of the business that was outsourced. For example, did the company outsource part of its manufacturing operation or a support function such as information technology or customer support? What likely factors came into play in the decision? What impact, if any, will this decision have on customers, employees, and the local community?

4. Discuss whether you or someone you know has been personally affected by a company's decision to outsource.

LO4   **CP22-4 Analyzing a Personal Decision to Pursue a Graduate Degree**

Assume that your friend Greg Ellis is thinking of getting an MBA. He is a resident of Arizona and is currently earning $45,000 per year. One of the schools Greg is considering is Brigham Young University (BYU) in Provo, Utah. He went to the Forbes Web site and used the "Should You Get an M.B.A." decision tool to calculate the "five-year gain" from getting an MBA at BYU. The results of that analysis follow.

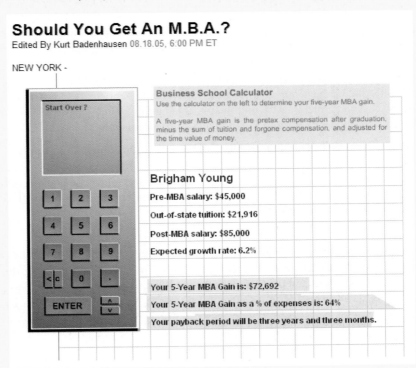

From: http://www.forbes.com/2005/08/16/cz_05mba_business_schools_gain_calulator.html

Greg was pleased to see that his five-year gain from getting an MBA was $72,692 and that the payback time on his investment would be just a little over three years. He is also considering a few other options:

- Getting a degree at Arizona State University (ASU) where he would qualify for in-state tuition. Greg believes his post-MBA salary would be the same with a degree from ASU as with one from BYU.

- Getting a degree at Harvard University. Greg believes he would be able to earn a higher starting salary coming out of Harvard (estimated at $100,000).

Required:

1. Go to the Forbes Web site and calculate the five-year gain from getting an MBA at ASU. State any assumption you are asked to make. Explain what factors caused the five-year gain to be higher or lower at ASU than at BYU.

2. Go to the Forbes Web site and calculate the five-year gain from getting an MBA at Harvard. State any assumption you are asked to make. Explain what factors caused the five-year gain to be higher or lower at Harvard than at BYU.

3. The Forbes decision tool takes into account both out-of-pocket costs and opportunity costs. Give examples of each.

4. The Forbes decision tool also takes into account the time value of money. Without making specific calculations, explain how the time value of money is likely to differ for the Harvard and ASU alternatives. Keep in mind that the up-front tuition is likely to be much lower at ASU than at Harvard, but the future benefits in terms of salary are likely to be higher at Harvard than ASU. How would these differences affect the time value of money?

5. Is the $45,000 pre-MBA salary relevant to Greg's decision about whether to go to Harvard, ASU, or BYU? Why or why not?

6. Suppose instead that Greg was trying to decide whether to continue with his current career path or get an MBA. Is his current salary relevant to this decision? Why or why not?

23 Budgetary Planning

LEARNING OBJECTIVES

After completing this chapter, you should be able to:

LO1 Describe the phases of the planning and control process.

LO2 List the key benefits of budgeting.

LO3 Explain the behavioral effects of budgets and provide guidelines for implementing a budget.

LO4 Describe the major components of the master budget and their interrelationships.

LO5 Prepare the following components of the operating budget:

    a. Sales budget.
    b. Production budget.
    c. Raw materials purchases budget.
    d. Direct labor budget.
    e. Manufacturing overhead budget.
    f. Selling and administrative expense budget.

LO6 Prepare the cash budget and describe the other financial budgets required to produce a budgeted balance sheet.

Lectured presentation–LP23-1
www.mhhe.com/LLPW1e

Focus Company: COLD STONE CREAMERY

"Because the world deserves better ice cream."

www.coldstonecreamery.com

Have you ever spent time planning a major event, such as a graduation party, bar or bat mitzvah, or wedding? If so, you probably realize the importance of having a **budget** to guide your decisions about where to hold the event, how many people to invite, and what food to serve. These and many other decisions affect the cost and success of any event.

Businesses use budgets in a similar way. Rather than budgeting for a one-time event, however, organizations use budgets to plan their ongoing operations so they will be able to meet their short-term and long-term objectives. Both profit-oriented and nonprofit organizations use budgets. The only difference is whether their short- and long-term objectives are oriented to earning a profit or reaching some nonprofit objective, such as providing education, feeding the poor, or improving health care.

In this chapter, we describe the budgeting process in a company that many of you may be familiar with, Cold Stone Creamery. Founded in 1988 by two ice cream lovers in Tempe, Arizona, Cold Stone Creamery now has more than 1,500 locations in countries around the world including Korea and Japan. The company's employees prepare delicious, custom-made ice cream creations on a piece of cold granite by mixing freshly made ice cream with a wide variety of high-quality ingredients. Consumers may choose one of Cold Stone's best-selling flavors, such as Peanut Butter Cup Perfection or Cheesecake Fantasy, or create their own unique flavor choosing from dozens of mix-ins, such as nuts, candy, cookies, and fruit. A Harvard business student has estimated that the average person would need more than 421 lifetimes to try all of the more than 11.5 million possible Cold Stone Creamery creations—but only by starting on the day he or she was born!

In this chapter, we prepare an entire master budget for a hypothetical Cold Stone Creamery location. In the next chapter, we determine whether Cold Stone Creamery achieved its budget by comparing actual to budgeted results. First, let's cover some basic concepts in budgeting.

ROLE OF BUDGETS IN THE PLANNING AND CONTROL CYCLE

- Planning Process
- Benefits of Budgeting
- Behavioral Effects of Budgets

COMPONENTS OF THE MASTER BUDGET

PREPARATION OF THE OPERATING BUDGETS

- Sales Budget
- Production Budget
- Raw Materials Purchases Budget
- Direct Labor Budget
- Manufacturing Overhead Budget
- Budgeted Cost of Goods Sold
- Selling and Administrative Expense Budget
- Budgeted Income Statement

PREPARATION OF FINANCIAL BUDGETS

- Cash Budget
- Budgeted Balance Sheet
- Budgeting in a Merchandising Company

ROLE OF BUDGETS IN THE PLANNING AND CONTROL CYCLE

Learning Objective 1

Describe the phases of the planning and control process.

Chapter 18 introduced the four functions of management: planning, organizing, directing/leading, and control. This process, which is illustrated in Exhibit 23.1, is sometimes referred to as the planning and control cycles.

Planning is the forward-looking phase of the planning and control process that involves setting long-term objectives and defining short-term tactics that will help to achieve them. Once the plan is in place, managers must beginning **organizing** or arranging for the necessary resources needed to achieve the plan. An important part of the organizing process is the

Exhibit 23.1 Planning and Control Cycles

Planning
Set short- and long-term objectives (goals) and the tactics to achieve them.

Organizing
Arrange the necessary resources to carry out the plan.

Directing/Leading
Take actions to implement the plan. Provide motivation to achieve results.

Control
Compare actual to budgeted results. Take corrective action if needed. Provide feedback for future plans.

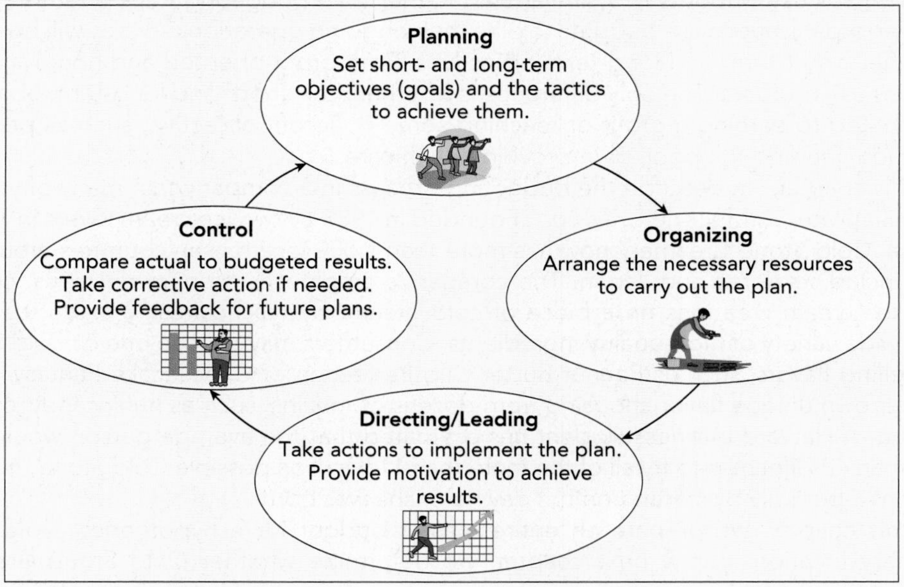

creation of a **budget,** a detailed plan that translates the company's objectives into financial terms, identifying the resources and expenditures that will be required over a limited planning horizon (typically a year) which can be broken into shorter periods (for example, months or quarters). The next step, **directing/leading,** involves all actions managers must take to implement the plan including motivating employees to achieve results. As you will see shortly, a budget can have either motivating or demotivating effects on behavior, depending on how it is implemented. As the plan is implemented, the managerial accounting system keeps track of the results, which are used later in the control process. The **control** function is the backward-looking part of the planning and control cycle. In this phase, managers compare actual to budgeted results to determine whether employees have met the objectives set during the planning stage. If not, managers should take corrective action where necessary. We focus more closely on the control process in Chapter 24, when we calculate variances that compare to budgeted results.

Planning Process

The starting point of the planning process is managers' strategic plan—their vision of what they want the organization to achieve over the long term. The strategic plan is then translated into long-term and short-term objectives (that is, goals) and the tactics necessary to achieve those objectives. A long-term objective is a specific goal that managers want to achieve over the long term, typically 5 to 10 years. A short-term objective is a specific goal that managers need to achieve in no more than a year to reach their long-term goals. Tactics are the specific actions or mechanisms managers plan to use to achieve their objectives.

For example, consider a company's long-term objective that is to gain a 50 percent share of the market over the next five years. A short-term objective might be to increase sales revenue by 10 percent during the next year. One possible tactic for achieving that goal would be to increase the amount spent on advertising and promotion to generate additional sales.

Consider Cold Stone Creamery's strategic vision, the "Pyramid of Success 2010" in Exhibit 23.2. It is a strategic plan that identifies what the company wants to achieve by the year 2010. The top of the pyramid shows the company's strategic vision, which is to become "the #1 best-selling ice cream brand in America by December 31, 2009." This goal, which was set in 2005, represents a specific long-term objective. To achieve this long-term goal, managers then set their short-term objectives and tactics. Although Cold Stone Creamery's objectives and tactics are not available to the general public (or to competitors), we can get a sense of their nature by examining the other levels of the pyramid.

The pyramid indicates that Cold Stone Creamery's daily purpose is to sell more ice cream to more people more often in more locations. Thus, we can assume that many of the company's short-term objectives are based on growth rates for sales revenue, the number of new stores opened, and the company's overall market share. In addition to these financial objectives, Cold Stone's success depends on its ability to introduce appealing new ice cream products and to hire and retain employees who can keep customers happy by providing the "ultimate ice cream experience." Thus, the company is likely to have objectives for new product development, employee training and retention, and customer satisfaction. In the last chapter of this book, we discuss the importance of developing nonfinancial measures to track performance in these areas.

Benefits of Budgeting

Budgeting has several benefits (see Exhibit 23.3). **One of the major advantages of budgeting is that it forces managers to look to the future.** In your own life, you or your parents may have prepared a budget to help save for college, a future vacation, or retirement. In business, budgets force managers to look ahead and address potential problems. For example, a budget can help managers plan to ensure they always have enough cash on hand to pay the company's bills or to avoid running out of inventory during periods of peak demand.

Budgets also play an important communication role within organizations. They provide a mechanism for managers to share expectations and priorities for the future. Because budgets span the entire organization, they also require managers from different functional areas to communicate and coordinate their activities.

Coach's Tip

The terms **budgeted, predicted, estimated, forecasted, anticipated, expected,** and **planned** are used interchangeably to reflect the future-oriented aspects of the budgeting process.

Video 23-1
www.mhhe.com/LLPW1e

Learning Objective 2

List the key benefits of budgeting.

Exhibit 23.2   Cold Stone Creamery's Strategic Vision: Pyramid of Success 2010

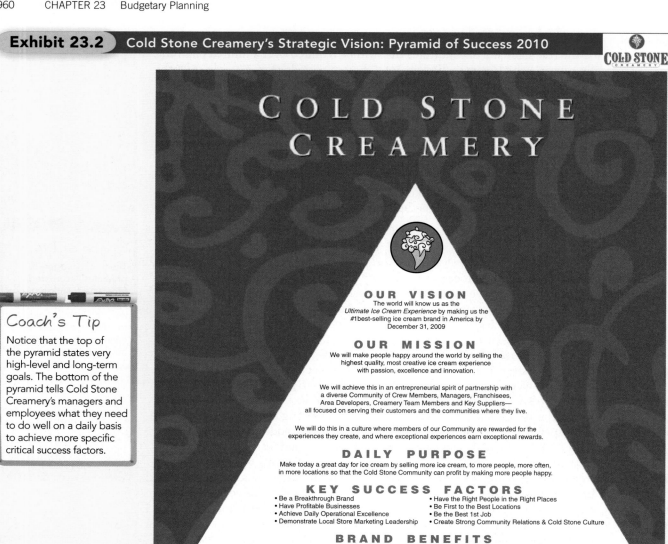

Source: http://www.coldstonecreamery.com/assets/pdf/secondary/Pyramid1.pdf.

Coach's Tip

Notice that the top of the pyramid states very high-level and long-term goals. The bottom of the pyramid tells Cold Stone Creamery's managers and employees what they need to do well on a daily basis to achieve more specific critical success factors.

Finally, **budgets serve an important role in motivating and rewarding employees.** If a budget is implemented correctly, it should motivate employees to work to meet the organization's objectives. **Budgets also provide a useful benchmark for evaluating and rewarding employee performance.** We discuss the motivational effects of budgets in the next section; their role in performance evaluation is addressed in the next two chapters.

Behavioral Effects of Budgets

Although budgets are intended to motivate employees to work to achieve the organization's goals, they can sometimes create unintended effects. The way in which managers and employees behave in response to budgets depends, in large part, on how goals and budgets are set. Two considerations are especially critical: the relative difficulty of meeting goals and the degree of employee participation in establishing goals.

In setting budgetary goals, finding the right level of difficulty is important. Research suggests that **budgets that are tight but attainable are more likely to motivate people** than

Exhibit 23.3   Benefits of Budgeting

Thinking ahead	Communication	Motivation
• Forcing managers to look ahead and state their goals for the future • Providing lead time to solve potential problems	• Communicating management's expectations and priorities • Promoting cooperation and coordination between functional areas of the organization	• Providing motivation for employees to work toward organizational objectives • Providing a benchmark for evaluating performance

budgets that are either too easy or too difficult to achieve. Think about your own personal goals. If your goal is too easy, you will not have to work very hard to achieve it. If you set your goal too high, however, you will quickly become frustrated and give up. Similarly, managers must try to find the just-right level of difficulty in setting an organization's budgetary goals to have a motivating rather than a demotivating effect on employee behavior.

Involving employees at all levels of the organization in the budgeting process is also important. Participative budgeting allows employees throughout the organization to have input into the budget-setting process. This bottom-up approach to budgeting can be contrasted with a top-down approach in which top management sets the budget and imposes it on lower levels of the organization. In general, **a participative approach is more likely to motivate people to work toward an organization's goals than a top-down approach.**

One downside to participative budgeting is that managers may try to build a little extra cushion, or budget slack, into their budgets. They can do so by understating expected sales or overstating budgeted expenses, making it more likely that they will come in under budget for expenses or over budget for revenues. Budgets can also create a "use-it-or-lose-it" mentality that encourages managers to spend their entire budgets to avoid a reduction in the next budget period. Some of these dysfunctional behaviors can be minimized by implementing the following budget-setting guidelines:

- **Use different budgets for planning and for performance evaluation.** Although budget slack causes problems in planning, it provides a way for managers to hedge against uncertainty. In organizations that face major fluctuations in demand or costs that are beyond the manager's control, some slack can be beneficial.

- **Use a continuous, or rolling budget, approach.** Under continuous budgeting, the company maintains a rolling budget that always extends a certain period into the future. When one budget period passes, another is automatically added at the end. This approach keeps managers in a continuous planning mode, always looking into the future rather than at the end of a specific budget period.

- **Use a zero-based budgeting approach.** Under zero-based budgeting, the entire budget must be constructed from zero each period rather than starting with the last period's actual results.

As this discussion indicates, managers must take a variety of behavioral factors into account in designing and implementing a budget system. There is not a "one-size-fits-all" solution to

Learning Objective 3

Explain the behavioral effects of budgets and provide guidelines for implementing a budget.

Spotlight On ETHICS

Playing Budget Games

Managers who are evaluated and rewarded for meeting budgetary goals may engage in game playing. For example, a sales manager who has reached his or her sales quota for the week may try to defer sales to a future period by telling customers to come back later to make their purchases. Managers may even be tempted to post-date purchase orders so that purchases **appear** to have been made in a later period. Alternatively, a salesperson who has not met his or her quota may cut prices at the end of the period to increase sales volume and meet the sales goal.

By engaging in these tactics, managers are putting their own self-interest ahead of the organization's objectives. Although the complete elimination of such budget games is difficult to achieve, organizations must try to design their budgets and control systems to minimize these dysfunctional behaviors.

budgeting. The best approach depends on the nature of the business environment, type of organization, and tasks managers must perform within the organization.

Before continuing, take a moment to make sure you understand the basic principles of budgeting by completing the following Self-Study Practice.

SELF-STUDY PRACTICE

Which of the following statements is false? (You may select more than one answer.)

1. Planning is the forward-looking phase of the planning and control cycle; control is the backward-looking phase of the cycle.
2. Short-term objectives are the specific goals that managers would like to achieve; tactics are the specific mechanisms they will use to achieve those goals.
3. Employees are more likely to be motivated by a top-down approach to budgeting than by a participative approach.
4. The creation of budget slack is not a problem for planning purposes, but it does cause problems in evaluating employees' performance.

After you have finished, check your answers with the solutions at the bottom of the page.

COMPONENTS OF THE MASTER BUDGET

A master budget is a comprehensive set of budgets that covers all phases of an organization's planned activities for a specific period. Within the master budget, individual budgets can be classified as either operating budgets or financial budgets. See Exhibit 23.4 for an illustration of the components of the master budget. Note that each component is either based on or provides input for another component.

Operating budgets cover the organization's planned operating activities for a particular period including expected sales, production, raw materials purchases, direct labor, manufacturing overhead, and selling and administrative expenses. When all of these individual budgets are combined, they form a budgeted income statement.

Financial budgets focus on the financial resources needed to support operations including cash receipts and disbursements, inventory, capital expenditures, and financing. Note that each of these budgets relates in some way either to an asset (for example, cash, inventory, and capital investments) or to liabilities and equity (for example, the way operating activities are financed). Thus, the financial budgets can be combined to form a budgeted balance sheet.

Learning Objective 4

Describe the major components of the master budget and their interrelationships.

Solution to
Self-Study Practice   Statements 3 and 4 are false.

Exhibit 23.4   Components of the Master Budget

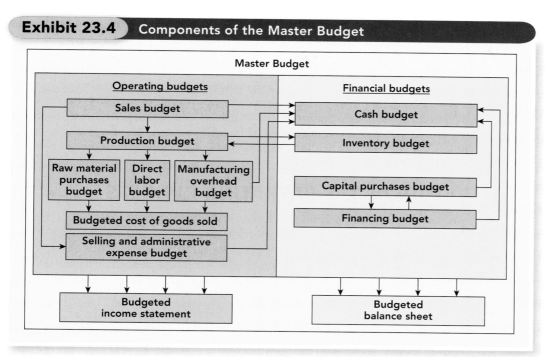

Coach's Tip

Notice that the sales budget affects almost all other budgets in the master budget. If the sales forecast is wrong, the rest of the master budget will be incorrect.

The starting point for preparing the master budget is the sales budget, or sales forecast, an estimate of the number of units to be sold and the total sales revenue to be generated each period. Various sources are used to determine the sales forecast including:

- Actual sales for the preceding period.
- Research on overall industry trends.
- Input from top management about overall sales objectives (for example, market share goals).
- Input from research and development about new product introductions, new features of existing products, and so on.
- Planned marketing activities (for example, advertising and sales promotions).

By considering all of these factors, sales managers determine their best estimate of future sales, which is reflected in the sales budget.

When the sales budget has been set, managers prepare the production budget, which shows how many units must be produced each period. The number of units to be produced may differ from the number of units to be sold depending on the company's inventory budget, which shows planned levels of the finished goods, work in process, and raw materials inventories at the beginning and end of each period.

When managers know how many units to produce, they can prepare budgets estimating the materials, labor, and manufacturing overhead costs they will need to produce those units.

- The raw materials purchases budget indicates the amount of raw materials needed to meet production goals and allow for planned levels of raw materials inventory.
- The direct labor budget identifies the amount of direct labor needed to meet production needs.
- The manufacturing overhead budget indicates the manufacturing overhead cost needed to support budgeted production.

All of these manufacturing budgets are combined to calculate the budgeted manufacturing cost per unit, which is used to determine the budgeted cost of goods sold. This cost is calculated by multiplying the budgeted cost per unit by the number of units of expected sales. Based on the sales forecast, managers can also prepare a selling and administrative expense budget, which identifies how much they need to spend on selling and administrative costs to support planned sales levels.

The operating budgets in turn are used to prepare the budgeted income statement. Essentially, each of the operating budgets, starting with the sales budget, becomes a line item in the budgeted income statement. Managers then subtract the budgeted cost of goods sold, which incorporates all budgeted manufacturing costs, to arrive at the budgeted gross margin. Finally, managers subtract budgeted selling and administrative expenses to arrive at the budgeted operating profit (before taxes).

Note in Exhibit 23.4 that all operating budgets are connected in some way to one or more financial budgets. The primary financial budget that we prepare in this chapter is the cash budget, which provides information about budgeted cash receipts and disbursements. Based on the cash budget and the other financial budgets, we can then prepare a **budgeted balance sheet** to show the balances of all of the company's assets, liabilities, and owners' equity accounts at the end of the period.

PREPARATION OF THE OPERATING BUDGETS

In this section, we prepare the operating budgets for a hypothetical Cold Stone Creamery location. Although we make a number of simplifying assumptions and the numbers do not necessarily represent Cold Stone's actual cost of operations, the objective of this example is to show the key components of the various operating budgets and how they relate to one another.

Sales Budget

Learning Objective 5a

Prepare the sales budget.

As mentioned, the starting point for the master budget is the sales forecast or sales budget. The sales department typically provides this information based on a variety of sources, including prior sales, industry trends, and marketing activities.

Preparation of the sales budget requires multiplying the number of units expected to be sold each period by the budgeted sales price. See Exhibit 23.5 for Cold Stone Creamery's quarter-by-quarter estimate of unit sales for the year 2010.

Notice that budgeted unit sales are high during the summer months and low during the winter months. The budgeted sales price is expected to remain constant at an average of $5 per unit, for a total budgeted sales revenue of $425,000.

Exhibit 23.5   Sales Budget

	Quarter 1 Jan.–Mar.	Quarter 2 Apr.–June	Quarter 3 July–Sept.	Quarter 4 Oct.–Dec.	Yearly Total
Budgeted unit sales	15,000	20,000	27,000	23,000	85,000
Budgeted sales price	× $ 5.00	× $ 5.00	× $ 5.00	× $ 5.00	× $ 5.00
Budgeted sales revenue	$75,000	$100,000	$135,000	$115,000	$425,000

Production Budget

Coach's Tip

Today, many service businesses and manufacturing companies produce their products and services to order. These companies have no finished goods inventory, so the sales budget and the production budget are identical.

The production budget is directly related to the sales budget and to the amount of inventory the company wants to have on hand at the beginning and end of each period. If the company is planning to build inventory, production needs to exceed sales. If the company is planning to reduce its inventory, sales should be more than production. The relationship between budgeted production, sales, and inventory is summarized in the following formula:

Budgeted Production Units	=	Budgeted Unit Sales	+	Budgeted Ending Finished Goods Inventory	−	Budgeted Beginning Finished Goods Inventory

In the past, manufacturing companies held substantial inventories of finished goods, which created a marked difference between the sales budget and the production budget. Today, however, companies such as Dell and Nike are moving toward a make-to-order approach in which the final product is manufactured to fill a specific customer order.

Cold Stone Creamery is a make-to-order company that produces its ice cream creations at the customer's request. Thus, the company holds virtually no finished goods inventory. The only exception is the "grab and go" containers that Cold Stone stocks for customers who want to enjoy a frozen creation at home. Traditional manufacturing companies maintain a much larger finished goods inventory as a buffer between expected sales and production. To make our example more consistent with that of a traditional manufacturing company, we assume that **Cold Stone Creamery maintains a small stock of finished goods inventory equal to 5 percent of the current period's budgeted sales.** See Exhibit 23.6 for the resulting production budget for Cold Stone Creamery based on this assumption and on the sales budget in Exhibit 23.5.

> **Learning Objective 5b**
> Prepare the production budget.

As expected, production is budgeted to be highest during the summer months when budgeted sales are at their highest. Notice that the ending finished goods inventory is calculated as 5 percent of the current period sales. In quarter 1, ending inventory is budgeted at 750 units (15,000 units × 5 percent). This ending inventory value becomes the beginning inventory value for the next quarter.

Exhibit 23.6   Production Budget

	Quarter 1 Jan.–Mar.	Quarter 2 Apr.–June	Quarter 3 July–Sept.	Quarter 4 Oct.–Dec.	Yearly Total
Budgeted unit sales (from Exhibit 23.5)	15,000	20,000	27,000	23,000	85,000
+ Budgeted ending inventory 5% of current period budgeted sales	+ 750*	+ 1,000	+ 1,350	+ 1,150	+ 1,150
− Budgeted beginning inventory	− 900†	− 750	− 1,000	− 1,350	− 900
Budgeted production	14,850	20,250	27,350	22,800	85,250

* Ending inventory for quarter 1 = 15,000 × 5% = 750
† Beginning inventory for quarter 1 is assumed to be 900 units.

Raw Materials Purchases Budget

Next managers must determine what amount of raw materials to purchase. Budgeted purchases depend on budgeted production needs and on the planned levels for beginning and ending raw materials inventory. The formula follows:

> **Learning Objective 5c**
> Prepare the raw materials purchases budget.

$$\text{Budgeted Raw Material Purchases} = \text{Budgeted Production Needs} + \text{Budgeted Ending Raw Materials Inventory} - \text{Budgeted Beginning Raw Materials Inventory}$$

Let's apply this formula to the primary ingredients used to make ice cream: milk, cream, and sugar. The super-premium ice cream made at Cold Stone Creamery contains a relatively high proportion of cream (as opposed to milk) compared to most commercially manufactured ice cream. The specific mix of ingredients is what creates the rich and creamy taste of the ice cream, as well as the relatively high price (since cream is much more expensive than milk). In reality, Cold Stone Creamery would prepare a separate budget for each of these major ingredients. However, for simplicity we will combine the purchase of milk, cream, and sugar into a single budget. We assume that each Cold Stone creation requires a total of 10 ounces of milk, cream, and sugar, and that the average price of this ingredient mix is $.05 per ounce. Because of the company's emphasis on freshness and quality, managers will want to keep the inventory of raw materials to a minimum. For this example, we assume that Cold Stone Creamery plans its purchase of raw materials so that the ending inventory is equal to 3 percent of **next period's** production needs. Exhibit 23.7 shows Cold Stone Creamery's raw materials purchases budget based on these assumptions.

Notice that raw materials purchases are based on budgeted **production** levels (not sales levels). We multiply budgeted production by the materials requirement per unit (10 ounces)

> **Coach's Tip**
>
> Notice that the formula for budgeted raw material purchases is very similar to the one for budgeted production. The only difference is that it starts with production (not sales) and adjusts for beginning and ending raw materials inventory.
>
> In these formulas, always add the ending inventory and subtract the beginning inventory.

Exhibit 23.7　Raw Materials Purchases Budget (Milk, Sugar, and Cream)

	Quarter 1 Jan.–Mar.	Quarter 2 Apr.–June	Quarter 3 July–Sept.	Quarter 4 Oct.–Dec.	Yearly Total
Budgeted production (from Exhibit 23.6)	14,850	20,250	27,350	22,800	85,250
Materials requirement (10 oz. per unit)	× 10 oz.	× 10 oz.	× 10 oz.	× 10 oz.	× 10 oz.
Total material needed for production	148,500	202,500	273,500	228,000	852,500
+ Planned ending inventory (3% of next month's production needs)	+ 6,075*	+ 8,205	+ 6,840	+ 3,510‡	+ 3,510
− Planned beginning inventory (3% of current month's production needs)	− 4,455†	− 6,075	− 8,205	− 6,840	− 4,455
Total purchases of raw materials	150,120	204,630	272,135	224,670	851,555
Average cost per ounce	× $ 0.05	× $ 0.05	× $ 0.05	× $ 0.05	× $ 0.05
Budgeted cost of raw materials purchases	$ 7,506	$ 10,232	$ 13,607	$ 11,233	$ 42,578

* Ending inventory for quarter 1 = 202,500 × 3% = 6,075
† Beginning inventory for quarter 1 = 148,500 × 3% = 4,455
‡ Ending inventory for quarter 4 is assumed to be 3,510 ounces. Cannot determine based on information given.

to find the total amount of materials needed for production. Then we add the budgeted ending raw materials inventory and subtract the beginning raw materials inventory to determine how much ice cream to purchase. In this case, the ending inventory is based on 3 percent of the **next period's** production needs, so the first quarter ending inventory equals 3 percent of 202,500, or 6,075 ounces. This value becomes the beginning inventory for the next period.

Cold Stone Creamery would construct similar budgets for all other raw materials including the various candies and nuts used to make its ice cream creations. For this example, we assume the purchase cost of these additional ingredients is about 40 percent of the cost of the milk, sugar, and cream (see Exhibit 23.8).

Exhibit 23.8　Total Raw Materials Purchases

	Quarter 1 Jan.–Mar.	Quarter 2 Apr.–June	Quarter 3 July–Sept.	Quarter 4 Oct.–Dec.	Yearly Total
Total purchases of milk, sugar, and cream	$ 7,506	$10,232	$13,607	$11,233	$42,578
Total purchases of mix-in ingredients*	3,002	4,093	5,443	4,493	17,031
Total cost of raw materials purchased	$10,508	$14,325	$19,050	$15,726	$59,609

* Assumed to be 40 percent of the cost of milk, sugar, and cream.

Direct Labor Budget

Learning Objective 5d

Prepare the direct labor budget.

Next we can determine how much direct labor will be needed to support budgeted production levels. We assume each Cold Stone Creamery creation requires .10 hour (6 minutes) of labor time including the time needed to take customers' orders, mix and serve the ice cream, take customers' payments, as well as cleanup time and employee breaks. See Exhibit 23.9 for the resulting direct labor budget based on budgeted production levels and an average labor rate of $8 per hour.

Exhibit 23.9 **Direct Labor Budget**

	Quarter 1 Jan.–Mar.	Quarter 2 Apr.–June	Quarter 3 July–Sept.	Quarter 4 Oct.–Dec.	Yearly Total
Budgeted production (from Exhibit 23.6)	14,850	20,250	27,350	22,800	85,250
Direct labor requirements (.10 hour per unit)	× .10 hr.	× .10 hr.	× .10 hr.	× .10 hr.	× .10 hr.
Total direct labor hours required	1,485	2,025	2,735	2,280	8,525
Direct labor cost per hour	× $ 8	× $ 8	× $ 8	× $ 8	× $ 8
Total direct labor cost	$11,880	$16,200	$21,880	$18,240	$68,200

Manufacturing Overhead Budget

Next we can prepare the manufacturing overhead budget. Although Cold Stone Creamery is not a traditional manufacturing company, it does create and serve a physical product. Thus, we define manufacturing overhead as all costs other than direct materials and direct labor that the company must incur to make the ice cream and serve it to customers. This amount includes the costs of rent, depreciation on equipment, and other indirect costs such as utilities, paper supplies, and the like. It does not include selling costs, such as advertising and promotion, or administrative costs for legal counsel, accounting services, insurance, franchise fees, and so on.

Some manufacturing overhead costs, such as those for indirect materials and paper supplies, vary with the number of units produced. Other costs, such as those for rent and depreciation, are incurred regardless of the number of units produced. We assume Cold Stone Creamery's variable manufacturing overhead cost is $0.10 per unit produced and the fixed manufacturing overhead cost is $8,525 per quarter. Refer to Exhibit 23.10 for the resulting manufacturing overhead cost budget.

Notice that the variable manufacturing overhead cost is highest during the summer, when production is highest but fixed manufacturing overhead cost is constant each period.

Learning Objective 5e

Prepare the manufacturing overhead budget.

Exhibit 23.10 **Manufacturing Overhead Budget**

	Quarter 1 Jan.–Mar.	Quarter 2 Apr.–June	Quarter 3 July–Sept.	Quarter 4 Oct.–Dec.	Yearly Total
Budgeted production	14,850	20,250	27,350	22,800	85,250
Variable overhead rate	× $ 0.10	× $ 0.10	× $ 0.10	× $ 0.10	× $ 0.10
Total variable manufacturing overhead cost	$ 1,485	$ 2,025	$ 2,735	$ 2,280	$ 8,525
Fixed manufacturing overhead	8,525	8,525	8,525	8,525	34,100
Total budgeted manufacturing overhead cost	$10,010	$ 10,550	$ 11,260	$10,805	$42,625

Budgeted Cost of Goods Sold

The budgeted cost of goods sold should reflect all costs required to manufacture the product including raw materials, direct labor, and manufacturing overhead. See Exhibit 23.11 for the calculation of the budgeted cost of each ice cream creation using information from the manufacturing cost budgets in Exhibits 23.8 through 23.10.

Notice that all variable manufacturing costs were calculated based on the variable manufacturing overhead cost per unit, but fixed manufacturing overhead cost was calculated

Exhibit 23.11 **Budgeted Manufacturing Cost Per Unit**

Budgeted cost of milk, sugar and cream (10 ounces × $0.05 per ounce)	$0.50
Budgeted cost of mix-in ingredients (40% of the cost of milk, sugar and cream)	0.20
Budgeted direct labor (.10 hours × $8.00 per hour)	0.80
Budgeted variable manufacturing overhead ($.10 per unit)	0.10
Budgeted fixed manufacturing overhead ($34,100 per year / 85,250 units)	0.40
Budgeted manufacturing cost per unit	$2.00

based on the total annual cost and yearly production. Fixed manufacturing overhead costs do not change with production levels. Calculating the fixed manufacturing overhead cost in this way avoids the changes in unit cost that occur from quarter to quarter due to seasonal fluctuations in production levels.

Using the budgeted manufacturing cost of $2 per unit calculated in Exhibit 23.11, we can calculate the budgeted cost of goods sold for each period (Exhibit 23.12).

Notice that budgeted cost of goods sold is calculated based on the sales budget (Exhibit 23.5), not the production budgeted (Exhibit 23.6). The cost of the units produced but not sold appears on the budgeted balance sheet as inventory.

Exhibit 23.12 **Budget Cost of Goods Sold**

	Quarter 1 Jan.–Mar.	Quarter 2 Apr.–June	Quarter 3 July–Sept.	Quarter 4 Oct.–Dec.	Yearly Total
Budgeted unit sales (from Exhibit 23.5)	15,000	20,000	27,000	23,000	85,000
Budgeted manufacturing cost per unit	× $ 2.00	× $ 2.00	× $ 2.00	× $ 2.00	× $ 2.00
Budgeted cost of goods sold	$30,000	$40,000	$54,000	$46,000	$170,000

Selling and Administrative Expense Budget

Learning Objective 5f

Prepare the selling and administrative expense budget.

The last operating budget we need to prepare is the selling and administrative expense budget, which includes all the costs related to selling the product (such as advertising and promotion) and managing the business (such as franchise fees, legal counsel, accounting services, and insurance). We assume that Cold Stone Creamery's selling costs are budgeted at 5 percent of sales revenue. Fixed administrative expenses are estimated to be $10,000 per quarter. The resulting selling and administrative expense budget is in Exhibit 23.13.

Budgeted Income Statement

Finally, we can combine all of the operating budgets we just prepared to form a budgeted income statement for Cold Stone Creamery (Exhibit 23.14).

Exhibit 23.13 **Selling and Administrative Expense Budget**

	Quarter 1 Jan.–Mar.	Quarter 2 Apr.–June	Quarter 3 July–Sept.	Quarter 4 Oct.–Dec.	Yearly Total
Budgeted sales revenue (from Exhibit 23.5)	$75,000	$100,000	$135,000	$115,000	$425,000
5% of sales revenue	× $ .05	× .05	× .05	× .05	× .05
Variable selling expenses	3,750	5,000	6,750	5,750	21,250
Fixed administrative expenses	10,000	10,000	10,000	10,000	40,000
Budgeted selling and administrative expense	$13,750	$ 15,000	$ 16,750	$ 15,750	$ 61,250

Exhibit 23.14 **Budgeted Income Statement**

Cold Stone Creamery
Budgeted Income Statement
For the Year Ended December 31, 2010

	Quarter 1 Jan.–Mar.	Quarter 2 Apr.–June	Quarter 3 July–Sept.	Quarter 4 Oct.–Dec.	Yearly Total
Budgeted sales revenue (from Exhibit 23.5)	$75,000	$100,000	$135,000	$115,000	$425,000
Less: Budgeted cost of goods sold (from Exhibit 23.12)	30,000	40,000	54,000	46,000	170,000
Budgeted gross margin	45,000	60,000	81,000	69,000	255,000
Less: Budgeted selling and administrative expenses (from Exhibit 23.13)	13,750	15,000	16,750	15,750	61,250
Budgeted operating income	$31,250	$ 45,000	$ 64,250	$ 53,250	$193,750

Before you move to the financial budgets, take a moment to make sure you understand the key relationships among the operating budgets by completing the following Self-Study Practice.

SELF-STUDY PRACTICE

1. Taylor Made's sales forecast for the next four quarters follows:

	Quarter 1	Quarter 2	Quarter 3	Quarter 4
Sales forecast (units)	12,000	14,000	15,000	18,000

If the company wants to maintain a finished goods inventory equal to 20 percent of sales for the next quarter, how many units should it produce during the second quarter?

2. Calico Coat Company's production budget follows:

	Quater 1	Quarter 2	Quarter 3	Quarter 4
Production budget (units)	15,000	13,000	14,000	12,000

Each unit requires 5 yards of raw materials at a cost of $3 per yard. The company plans its raw materials purchases so that ending raw materials inventory equals 10 percent of the production needs for the current quarter. At the beginning of the first quarter, 5,000 yards of materials were on hand.

What is the budgeted cost of raw materials purchases during the first quarter?

After you have finished, check your answers with the solutions at the bottom of the page.

Solution to
Self-Study Practice

1. $14,200 = 14,000 + (.20 \times 15,000) - (.20 \times 14,000)$
2.   Current production needs $= 15,000 \times 5 = 75,000$ yards
    Ending raw materials inventory $= 75,000 \times .10 = 7,500$
    Beginning raw materials inventory $= 5,000$
    $75,000 + 7,500 - 5,000 = 77,500 \times \$3.00$ per yard $= \$232,500$

PREPARATION OF THE FINANCIAL BUDGETS

As mentioned earlier, the financial budgets focus on the financial resources needed to support the company's operations including cash receipts and disbursements, inventory, capital purchases, and financing. To review the relationship between the financial budgets and the operating budgets, take a moment to review Exhibit 23.4 on page 963. In this section, we concentrate on two financial budgets, the cash budget and the budgeted balance sheet.

Cash Budget

> **Learning Objective 6**
>
> Prepare the cash budget and describe the other financial budgets required to produce a budgeted balance sheet.

The **cash budget** is a future-oriented version of the statement of cash flows, which you learned about in Chapter 16. Recall that cash inflows (receipts) can come from operating activities or from financing and investing activities. Similarly, cash outflows (disbursements) can be made for operating activities or for investing and financing activities. In this chapter, we focus strictly on cash flows that arise from operating activities, which are directly related to the operating budgets described previously. We do not consider cash flows that arise from investing or financing activities, which would appear in the capital purchases budget (for investing activities) and the financing budget (for financing).

The basic formula for the cash budget follows:

$$\boxed{\text{Ending Cash Balance}} = \boxed{\text{Beginning Cash Balance}} + \boxed{\text{Budgeted Cash Receipts}} - \boxed{\text{Budgeted Cash Disbursements}}$$

Because we are focusing strictly on operating activities, all budgeted cash receipts come from sales revenue. Remember, however, that sales revenue is not the same as cash. Sales are recognized when revenue is earned, not when cash is received. Thus, to calculate the budgeted cash receipts, we need to know what type of sales are made (cash or credit) and how credit sales are collected.

We assume 60 percent of Cold Stone Creamery's sales are paid for in cash and 40 percent are paid with credit cards. Credit card sales are collected immediately subject to a 5 percent transaction fee. Cold Stone's cash receipts budget is in Exhibit 23.15.

Exhibit 23.15   Cash Receipts Budget

	Quarter 1 Jan.–Mar.	Quarter 2 Apr.–June	Quarter 3 July–Sept.	Quarter 4 Oct.–Dec.	Yearly Total
Budgeted sales revenue (from Exhibit 23.5)	$ 75,000	$100,000	$135,000	$115,000	$425,000
Cash collections (60% of sales)	45,000*	60,000	81,000	69,000	255,000
Credit card collections (40% of sales less a 5% service fee)	28,500†	38,000	51,300	43,700	161,500
Budgeted cash (receipts)	$ 73,500	$ 98,000	$132,300	$112,700	$416,500

* Quarter 1 cash collections = $75,000 × 60% = $45,000
† Quarter 1 credit collections = $75,000 × 40% × (100% − 5%) = $28,500

As you can see, budgeted cash receipts are not the same thing as budgeted sales. Similarly, cash disbursements do not necessarily equal budgeted expenses. To calculate budgeted cash disbursements it is necessary to know when the company pays for raw materials purchases, direct labor costs, manufacturing overhead costs, and selling and administrative costs. To continue our Cold Stone Creamery example, assume the following:

- Of raw materials purchases, 70 percent is paid for during the quarter purchased; 30 percent is paid for in the following quarter. Assume last year's quarter 4 raw materials purchases totaled $10,000.
- Direct labor, manufacturing overhead costs, and selling and administrative costs are paid for during the quarter in which they are incurred.
- The fixed manufacturing overhead cost budget includes $3,000 in depreciation (a noncash expense).

See Exhibit 23.16 for the Cold Stone Creamery's budgeted cash disbursements using this information.

Exhibit 23.16   Cash Disbursements Budget

	Quarter 1 Jan.–March	Quarter 2 April–June	Quarter 3 July–Sept.	Quarter 4 Oct.–Dec.	Yearly Total
Budgeted direct materials purchased (from Exhibit 23.8)	$10,508	$14,325	$19,050	$15,726	$ 59,609
Budgeted Cash Payments:					
70% of raw materials purchases paid for in current quarter	7,356*	10,028	13,335	11,008	41,727
30% of raw materials purchases paid for in the next quarter	3,000	3,152†	4,298	5,715	16,165
Budgeted payments for raw materials purchases	10,356	13,180	17,633	16,723	57,892
Budgeted direct labor costs (from Exhibit 23.9)	11,880	16,200	21,880	18,240	68,200
Budgeted manufacturing overhead costs (from Exhibit 23.10)	10,010	10,550	11,260	10,805	42,625
Less depreciation (noncash expense)	(3,000)	(3,000)	(3,000)	(3,000)	(12,000)
Budgeted selling and administrative expenses (from Exhibit 23.13)	13,750	15,000	16,750	15,750	61,250
Budgeted cash disbursements	$42,996	$51,930	$64,523	$58,518	$217,967

*Quarter 1 cash paid for current quarter's materials purchases = $10,508 × 70% = $7,356
†Quarter 2 cash paid for previous quarter raw materials purchases =$10,508 × 30% = $3,152

The cash receipts and cash disbursements can then be combined into a summary cash budget. Cold Stone Creamery's cash budget for the year, assuming it had $100,000 cash on hand at the beginning of the year is in Exhibit 23.17.

Exhibit 23.17   Cash Budget

	Quarter 1 Jan.–Mar.	Quarter 2 Apr.–June	Quarter 3 July–Sept.	Quarter 4 Oct.–Dec.	Yearly Total
Beginning balance of cash	$ 100,000	$130,504	$176,574	$244,351	$100,000
Plus: Budgeted cash receipts (from Exhibit 23.15)	73,500	98,000	132,300	112,700	416,500
Less: Budgeted cash disbursements (from Exhibit 23.16)	(42,996)	(51,930)	(64,523)	(58,518)	(217,967)
Ending Balance of Cash	$ 130,504	$176,574	$244,351	$298,533	$ 298,533

Believe it or not, Cold Stone Creamery's cash budget is relatively straightforward because most customers pay in cash at the time of sale. Sales made on credit card are collected almost instantaneously minus the fee the credit card company charges. But some businesses sell goods or services on credit terms that allow the customer to take weeks or even months to pay. In these situations, the cash receipts component of the cash budget is slightly more complicated because part of the cash receipts are based on the previous period sales number rather than the current period sales. To see whether you can complete a cash budget when credit sales are collected in a later period, complete the Self-Study Practice on the next page.

Budgeted Balance Sheet

The final financial budget that we discuss is the budgeted balance sheet. Just as the operating budgets were combined into a pro forma (forward-looking) income statement, all of the financial budgets can be combined into a pro forma (forward-looking) balance sheet. A number of financial budgets including the inventory budget, the capital expenditures budget, and the financing budget must be created before we can prepare a complete balance sheet. For the sake of simplicity, we do not show how to prepare those budgets. Just make sure you understand the structure of the **budgeted balance sheet** (Exhibit 23.18).

Exhibit 23.18 Budgeted Balance Sheet

COLD STONE CREAMERY

Cold Stone Creamery
Budgeted Balance Sheet
December 31, 2010

Assets		Liabilities	
Cash (from Exhibit 23.17)	$298,533	Accounts payable	$ 4,718
Accounts receivable	13,274	Long-term liability	250,000
Inventory	2,300	Total liabilities	254,718
Long-term assets	170,000	**Owners' Equity**	229,389
Total assets	$484,107	Total liabilities and owners' equity	$484,107

Budgeting in a Merchandising Company

Throughout this chapter, we have used Cold Stone Creamery to illustrate how to prepare the operating and financial budgets for a manufacturing company that purchases raw materials and converts them into a final product.

The budgets for a merchandising company differ slightly from those of a manufacturing firm. Recall that a merchandising company purchases finished goods for resale. As such, one of the primary operating budgets a merchandiser needs to prepare is the merchandise purchases budget. This budget is very similar to the raw materials purchases budget in Exhibit 23.7. However, instead of considering production needs and raw materials inventory, this budget is based on budgeted sales and the need to maintain adequate levels of finished goods inventory as in the following formula:

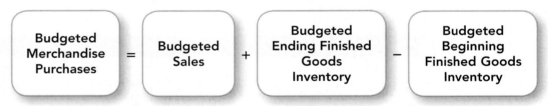

The other major difference between merchandising and manufacturing firms' budgets is that merchandising firms do not have a raw materials, direct labor, or manufacturing overhead expense budget. Remember that these are all categories of manufacturing costs and apply only to manufacturing companies.

SELF-STUDY PRACTICE

Big Ben Clock Company's total sales for the first two quarters of the year are budgeted as follows:

	Quarter 1	Quarter 2
Total sales budget	$120,000	$140,000

Of total sales, 60 percent is expected to be cash with the remaining 40 percent on credit. Of the credit sales, 30 percent will be collected in the quarter in which the sales are made, 65 percent the following quarter, and 5 percent will never be collected.

Based on this information, calculate Big Ben's budgeted cash receipts for Quarter 2 only.

After you have finished, check your answers with the solutions at the bottom of the page.

Solution to Self-Study Practice

Cash Sales (Quarter 2) = $140,000 × .60 = $84,000
Credit Sales (Quarter 2) = $140,000 × .40 × .30 = $16,800
Credit Sales (Quarter 1) = $120,000 × .40 × .65 = $31,200
Budgeted Cash Receipts (Quarter 2) = $132,000

Demonstration Case A
Operating Budgets

Sky High Parachute Company manufactures and sells parachutes to adventure companies. The company's sales forecast for the coming year is as follows:

	Quarter 1	Quarter 2	Quarter 3	Quarter 4
Sales (units)	40,000	35,000	45,000	50,000

Other budgeted information follows:

- The budgeted sales price for each parachute is $1,000 per unit.
- The company budgets production so that ending finished goods inventory equals 10 percent of the next quarter's budgeted sales.
- Each parachute requires 20 square yards of specialty material at a price of $15 per square yard.
- The company purchases raw materials so that about 10 percent of each quarter's production needs are left over at the end of the quarter to be used as beginning inventory in the next quarter. At the beginning of the first quarter, 70,000 square yards of material were on hand.
- Each parachute requires 15 hours of direct labor at a rate of $12 per hour.
- Manufacturing overhead costs are budgeted at $1,000,000 per quarter plus $50 per unit produced.
- Selling and administrative expenses are budgeted at $500,000 per quarter plus 10 percent of total sales revenue.

Required:
Prepare the following operating budgets for quarters 1–3. (You do not have enough information to prepare all of the budgets, for quarter 4.)

1. Sales budget.
2. Production budget.
3. Raw materials purchases budget.
4. Direct labor budget.
5. Manufacturing overhead budget.
6. Selling and administrative expense budget.

Suggested Solution

1.

	Quarter 1	Quarter 2	Quarter 3	Quarter 4
Sales forecast (units)	40,000	35,000	45,000	50,000
Price per unit	× $ 1,000	× $ 1,000	× $ 1,000	× $ 1,000
Sales budget (dollars)	$40,000,000	$35,000,000	$45,000,000	$50,000,000

2.

	Quarter 1	Quarter 2	Quarter 3	Quarter 4
Unit sales forecast (from requirement 1)	40,000	35,000	45,000	50,000
Plus: Desired ending inventory	3,500	4,500	5,000	
Less: Planned beginning inventory	4,000	3,500	4,500	
Production budget (units)	39,500	36,000	45,500	

3.

	Quarter 1	Quarter 2	Quarter 3
Production budget (from requirement 2 in units)	39,500	36,000	45,500
Raw materials requirements (per unit in sq. yards)	× 20	× 20	× 20
Total raw materials needed for production (sq. yards)	790,000	720,000	910,000
Plus: Desired ending inventory	79,000	72,000	91,000
Less: Planned beginning inventory	70,000	79,000	72,000
Budgeted raw materials purchases (sq. yards)	799,000	713,000	929,000
Budgeted cost per square yard	× $ 15	× $ 15	× $ 15
Total raw materials purchases	$11,985,000	$10,695,000	$13,935,000

4.

	Quarter 1	Quarter 2	Quarter 3
Production budget (from requirement 2 in units)	39,500	36,000	45,500
Direct labor requirements (hours per unit)	× 15	× 15	× 15
Total labor hours required	592,500	540,000	682,500
Direct labor rate (per hour)	× $ 12	× $ 12	× $ 12
Total direct labor cost	$7,110,000	$6,480,000	$8,190,000

5.

	Quarter 1	Quarter 2	Quarter 3
Production budget (from requirement 2 in units)	39,500	36,000	45,500
Variable overhead rate ($50 per unit)	× $ 50	× $ 50	× $ 50
Variable overhead budget	$1,975,000	$1,800,000	$2,275,000
Fixed overhead budget	1,000,000	1,000,000	1,000,000
Total manufacturing overhead budget	$2,975,000	$2,800,000	$3,275,000

6.

	Quarter 1	Quarter 2	Quarter 3
Sales budget (from requirement 1)	$40,000,000	$35,000,000	$45,000,000
	× .10	× .10	× .10
Variable selling expenses (10% of sales dollars)	4,000,000	3,500,000	4,500,000
Fixed selling expenses	500,000	500,000	500,000
Budgeted selling and administrative expenses	$ 4,500,000	$ 4,000,000	$ 5,000,000

Demonstration Case B
Cash Budget

Assume that Sky High Parachute Company's budgeted income statement is as follows:

	Quarter 1	Quarter 2	Quarter 3	Quarter 4
Budgeted sales revenue	$40,000,000	$35,000,000	$45,000,000	$50,000,000
Budgeted cost of goods sold	15,600,000	13,650,000	17,550,000	19,500,000
Budgeted gross margin	24,400,000	21,350,000	27,450,000	30,500,000
Budgeted selling and administrative expenses	4,500,000	4,000,000	5,000,000	5,500,000
Budgeted income from operations	$19,900,000	$17,350,000	$22,450,000	$25,000,000

Budgeted sales revenue is collected as follows:

- 60 percent of sales revenue is collected in cash.
- The remainder of sales is on credit and is collected as follows:
  - During the quarter of sale, 35 percent.
  - During the quarter following the sale 60 percent.
  - Uncollected, 5 percent.

Cost of goods sold (manufacturing costs) consists of the following:

- Materials purchases represent 70 percent of cost of goods sold. The company pays for 40 percent of materials during the quarter of purchase and the remainder the next quarter.
- The remaining 30 percent of cost of goods sold is made up of direct labor and manufacturing overhead including $400,000 in depreciation (a noncash expense). All of the cash disbursements for direct labor and overhead are paid during the quarter incurred.
- Selling and administrative expenses are paid in the next quarter.

Required:
Prepare the following schedules for quarters 2, 3, and 4.

1. Cash receipts budget.
2. Cash disbursements budget.
3. Cash budget.

Note: You do not have enough information to prepare the cash budget for quarter 1, so assume its ending cash balance is $500,000.

Suggested Solution

1.

	Quarter 1	Quarter 2	Quarter 3	Quarter 4
Budgetes sales revenue (given)	$40,000,000	$35,000,000	$45,000,000	$50,000,000
Budgeted cash receipts				
Cash sales (60% of current quarter sales)		$21,000,000	$27,000,000	$30,000,000
Credit sales collected in current quarter (40% of current quarter sales × 35%)		4,900,000	6,300,000	7,000,000
Credit sales collected in following quarter (40% of previous quarter sales × 60%)		9,600,000	8,400,000	10,800,000
Budgeted cash receipts		$35,500,000	$41,700,000	$47,800,000

2.

	Quarter 1	Quarter 2	Quarter 3	Quarter 4
Budgeted cost of goods sold (given)	$15,600,000	$13,650,000	$17,550,000	$19,500,000
Raw materials purchases (70% of cost of goods sold)	10,920,000	9,555,000	12,285,000	13,650,000
Direct labor and manufacturing overhead (30% of cost of goods sold)	4,680,000	4,095,000	5,265,000	5,850,000
Budgeted selling and administrative expenses (given)	4,500,000	4,000,000	5,000,000	5,500,000
Raw materials paid for in current quarter (40% of current quarter purchases)		3,822,000	4,914,000	5,460,000
Raw materials paid for in next quarter (60% of previous quarter purchases)		6,552,000	5,733,000	7,371,000
Cash paid for direct labor and overhead (Less: $400,000 in depreciation)		3,695,000	4,865,000	5,450,000
Cash paid for selling and administrative expenses		4,500,000	4,000,000	5,000,000
Budgeted cash disbursements		$18,569,000	$19,512,000	$23,281,000

3.

	Quarter 1	Quarter 2	Quarter 3	Quarter 4
Beginning balance of cash		$ 500,000	$ 17,431,000	$ 39,619,000
Plus: Budgeted cash receipts		35,500,000	41,700,000	47,800,000
Less: Budgeted cash disbursements		(18,569,000)	(19,512,000)	(23,281,000)
Ending balance of cash	$500,000	$17,431,000	$39,619,000	$64,138,000

Chapter Summary

LO1 Describe the phases of the planning and control process. p. 958

- Planning is the forward-looking phase of the managerial process. It involves setting both long- and short-term objectives and identifying the tactics used to achieve them.
- Organizing involves arranging for the necessary resources needed to achieve the plan, including the preparation of a budget.
- Directing/leading is the action phase of the managerial process. It involves implementing the objectives developed in the planning phase including motivating employees to achieve the objectives.
- Control is the backward-looking phase of the managerial process. It involves comparing actual results to budgeted figures and taking corrective action if necessary.

LO2 List the key benefits of budgeting. p. 959

Budgeting has several benefits:
- Forces managers to plan ahead.
- Serves as a basis for communication throughout the organization.
- Motivates employees to work toward the organization's goals.

LO3 Explain the behavioral effects of budgets and provide guidelines for implementing a budget. p. 961

- Budgets can create a number of behavioral effects that should be considered in designing and implementing a budgetary control system.
- Budgets that are "tight but attainable" are more likely to motivate people to work harder than budgets that are either too easy or impossible to achieve.

- Participative budgeting allows individuals to provide input into the budget-setting process. However, it may lead to the creation of budget slack.
- Using different budgets for planning than for performance evaluations, rolling budgets, or zero-based budgets can mitigate some of the game playing that occurs in the budgeting process.

LO4 Describe the major components of the master budget and their interrelationships. p. 962

- The master budget is a comprehensive set of budgets that covers all phases of an organization's planned activities for a specific period.
- The master budget contains two types of budgets: operatings budgets and financial budgets.
- Operating budgets include all budgets needed to prepare a budgeted income statement including the sales budget, production budget, raw materials purchases budget, direct labor budget, manufacturing overhead cost budget, and selling and administrative expense budget.
- Financial budgets provide the information on financial resources and obligations needed to prepare a budgeted balance sheet. These budgets include the cash budget, inventory budget, capital expenditures budget, and financing budget.

LO5 Prepare the following components of the operating budget. p. 964

- **Sales budget.** The starting point for the operating budget is the sales budget. It is based on a variety of inputs and affects all other components of the master budget.
- **Production budget.** This budget is based on the sales budget and the planned levels of beginning and ending finished goods inventory.
- **Raw materials purchases budget.** This budget is based on the production budget and the planned levels of the beginning and ending raw materials inventory.
- **Direct labor budget.** It is based on the production budget and shows how much labor is required to produce (or serve) each unit.
- **Manufacturing overhead cost budget.** This budget provides information about expected variable and fixed manufacturing overhead costs.
- **Selling and administrative expense budget.** Information about expected selling and administrative expenses is in this budget.
- Information from all operating budgets can be combined to prepare a budgeted income statement.

LO6 Prepare the cash budget and describe the other financial budgets required to produce a budgeted balance sheet. p. 976

- The cash budget is a future-oriented version of the statement of cash flows; it includes budgeted cash receipts and budgeted cash disbursements.
- The ending balance of the cash budget appears on the budgeted balance sheet along with the budgeted balances for all other asset, liability, and equity accounts.
- Other financial budgets needed to prepare a comprehensive budgeted balance sheet include the inventory budget, capital purchases budget, and financing budget.

Key Terms

Budgeted Balance Sheet (p.962)

Budgeted Cost of Goods Sold (p. 963)

Budgeted Gross Margin (p. 964)

Budgeted Manufacturing Cost
 per Unit (p. 963)

Budgeted Income Statement (p. 962)

Budget Slack (p. 961)

Cash Budget (p. 964)

Direct Labor Budget (p. 963)

See complete glossary in back of text.

Financial Budget (p. 962)

Inventory Budget (p. 963)

Long-Term Objective (p. 959)

Manufacturing Overhead Budget (p. 963)

Master Budget (p. 962)

Operating Budgets (p. 962)

Participative Budgeting (p. 961)

Production Budget (p. 963)

Raw Materials Purchases Budget (p. 963)

Sales Forecast Budget (p. 963)

Selling and Administrative Expense
 Budget (p. 963)

Short-Term Objective (p. 959)

Strategic Plan (p. 959)

Tactics (p. 959)

Top-Down Approach (p. 961)

Questions

1. Briefly describe why budgetary planning is crucial to companies.

2. What role do budgets play in the planning and control cycle?

3. What is a strategic plan? How does a strategic plan involve both short- and long-term goals?

4. Suppose that your strategic plan is to retire comfortably at the age of 55. List several long-term objectives, short-term objectives, and tactics that will enable you to accomplish this goal.

5. Identify and briefly discuss the benefits of budgeting.

6. Suppose a company chooses not to develop budgets. Describe three potential negative consequences of this decision.

7. What are the advantages and disadvantages of participative budgeting over top-down budgeting?

8. Explain the concept of budgetary slack. How might budgetary slack be detrimental to a company?

9. Briefly explain how each of the following helps to minimize dysfunctional behaviors caused by budgeting:
   a. Different budgets for different purposes.
   b. Continuous budgeting.
   c. Zero-based budgeting.

10. What is the master budget? What are its components?

11. Explain why the sales budget is the starting point for a company's budgeting process. Which budgets does the sales budget affect? Which budgets does the sales budget not affect?

12. What sources does a company utilize to determine its sales forecast? What could happen if one of the sources used is inaccurate?

13. What are the components of the operating budget?

14. What are the components of the financial budget?

Multiple Choice

1. Budgets help companies
   a. Meet short-term objectives.
   b. Meet long-term objectives.
   c. Both a and b.
   d. None of the above.

Quiz 23-1
www.mhhe.com/LLPW1e

2. Which phases of the management process does budgeting impact?
   a. Planning.   c. Control.
   b. Directing/leading. d. All of the above.

3. Which of the following statements is true?
   a. GAAP requires all companies to prepare budgets.
   b. Only newly formed companies need budgets.
   c. Budgets are used by all companies.
   d. Most companies would benefit from budgeting.

4. Shasta Company plans to double profits in five years. This is an example of a
   a. Long-term objective.   c. Tactic.
   b. Short-term objective. d. Sales forecast.

5. Which of the following is not considered a direct benefit of budgeting?
   a. Better communication.
   b. Motivating employees.
   c. Developing new product lines.
   d. Forcing managers to think ahead.

6. Which of the following budgets would be prepared earliest in a company's budgeting process?
   a. Budgeted income statement.
   b. Budgeted balance sheet.
   c. Raw materials purchases budget.
   d. Production budget.

7. Which of the following budgets does the sales budget impact?
   a. Direct labor budget.
   b. Cash receipts and disbursements budget.
   c. Selling and administrative budget.
   d. All of the above.

8. ABC Company expects to sell 100,000 units of its primary product in January. Expected beginning and ending finished goods inventory for January are 20,000 and 45,000 units, respectively. How many units should ABC produce?
   a. 100,000.   c. 75,000.
   b. 125,000.   d. 35,000.

9. Which of the following is not considered an operating budget?
   a. Cash budget.
   b. Budgeted income statement.
   c. Selling and administrative expense budget.
   d. Raw materials purchases budget.

10. Raya Company is calculating its expected cash receipts for the month of June. This should not include
    a. Cash sales made during June.
    b. Credit sales made during May.
    c. Credit sales made during June.
    d. Credit sales made during July.

Solutions to Multiple-Choice Questions						
1. c	2. d	3. d	4. a	5. c	6. d	7. d
8. b	9. a	10. d				

Mini Exercises Available with McGraw-Hill's Homework Manager

M23-1 Explaining the Role of Managerial Accounting in the Planning and Control Cycle
Your boss believes that the three management functions of planning, directing/leading, and control are unrelated. He also thinks that managerial accounting has no role in any of the functions. Is your boss correct? Explain why or why not.

LO1

M23-2 Describing the Advantages of Budgetary Planning
Calypso Cal (CC) has a "Live today, worry about tomorrow later" motto. In keeping with this philosophy, CC has not set any long-term or short-term objectives or budgets for the company, which manufactures surfboards. Describe three potential consequences of CC's philosophy.

LO2

M23-3 Classifying and Ordering the Components of the Master Budget
Indicate whether each of the following budgets is an operating (O) or financing (F) budget and the order in which they would be prepared.

LO4

	O or F	Order of Preparation
Cash receipts and disbursements budget		
Sales budget		
Raw materials purchases budget		
Selling and administrative expense budget		
Budgeted balance sheet		
Manufacturing overhead budget		
Direct labor budget		
Budgeted income statement		
Production budget		

M23-4 Preparing a Sales Budget
Ranger Company estimates that unit sales of its weather radios will be 8,000 in October; 8,200 in November; and 9,350 in December. Prepare Ranger's sales budget for the fourth quarter assuming each unit sells for $27.50.

LO5

M23-5 Preparing a Purchases Budget
Pascall Corp. expects to sell 1,300 units of its camera bags in March and 900 units in April. Each unit sells for $110. Pascall's ending inventory policy is 40 percent of the following month's sales. Pascall pays its supplier $50 per unit. Prepare Pascall's purchases budget for March.

LO5

M23-6 Preparing a Raw Materials Purchases Budget
CubbyHole, Inc., manufactures wooden shelving units for collecting and sorting mail. The company expects to produce 310 units in July and 400 units in August. Each unit requires 10 feet of wood at a cost of $1.20 per foot. CubbyHole wants to always have 300 feet of wood on hand in materials inventory. Prepare CubbyHole's raw materials purchases budget for July and August.

LO5

M23-7 Preparing a Direct Labor Budget
Refer to the information in M23-6 for CubbyHole, Inc. Each unit requires 1.5 hours of direct labor, and labor wages average $9 per hour. Prepare CubbyHole's direct labor budget for July and August.

LO5

M23-8 Preparing a Manufacturing Overhead Cost Budget
Damon Company expects sales of its headphones to be $200,000 in the first quarter and $236,000 in the second quarter. Its variable overhead is approximately 17 percent of sales, and fixed overhead costs are $52,000 per quarter. Prepare Damon's manufacturing overhead cost budgets for the first two quarters.

LO5

M23-9 Preparing a Selling and Administrative Expense Budget
Affleck, Inc., expects sales of its housing for electric motors to be $83,000, $79,000 and $88,000 for January, February, and March, respectively. Its variable selling and administrative expenses are 9 percent of sales, and fixed selling and administrative expenses are $11,000 per month. Prepare Affleck's selling and administrative expense budget for January, February, and March.

LO5

Exercises   ᴴᴹ™   **Available with McGraw-Hill's Homework Manager**

LO4

E23-1 Classifying and Ordering the Components of the Master Budget

Organize the following budgets in order of preparation by placing the number before it and indicate how each would be affected by a sales forecast that is understated.

_____ Cash receipts and disbursements budget.

_____ Selling and administrative expense budget.

_____ Manufacturing overhead budget.

_____ Raw materials purchases budget.

_____ Budgeted balance sheet.

_____ Sales budget.

_____ Direct labor budget.

_____ Budgeted income statement.

_____ Budgeted cost of goods sold.

_____ Production budget.

LO5

E23-2 Calculating Unknowns Based on Production, Sales, and Beginning and Ending Inventory Values

Complete the following table.

	NUMBER OF UNITS		
Production	Sales	Ending Inventory	Beginning Inventory
?	500	100	75
800	?	90	125
750	675	?	80
900	1,200	100	?
665	?	225	160
845	795	305	?

LO5

E23-3 Calculating the Sales and Production Budgets

Rainwater Corp. expects to sell 600 umbrellas in January and 400 umbrellas in February. Each umbrella sells for $15. Rainwater's beginning and ending finished goods inventories for January are 75 and 50 units, respectively. Ending finished goods inventory for February will be 60 units.

Required:

1. Prepare Rainwater's sales budget for January and February.
2. Prepare Rainwater's production budget for January and February.

LO5

E23-4 Preparing the Raw Materials Purchases and Manufacturing Overhead Cost Budgets

Refer to the information in E23-3 for Rainwater Corp. Assume its production budget calls for production of 605 umbrellas in May and 530 umbrellas in June. Each umbrella requires an opening mechanism that the company purchases from a supplier at a cost of $2 each. Rainwater wants to have 30 mechanisms on hand at May 1, 20 mechanisms at May 31, and 25 mechanisms at June 30. Additionally, Rainwater's fixed manufacturing overhead is $1,000 per month, and variable manufacturing overhead is $1.25 per unit produced.

Required:

1. Prepare Rainwater's May and June raw materials purchases budget for these mechanisms.
2. Prepare Rainwater's manufacturing overhead budget for May and June.

E23-5 Calculating Cash Receipts

LO6

Refer to information in E23-3 and E23-4 for Rainwater Corp. It expects the following unit sales for the third quarter.

July	525
August	490
September	450

Sixty percent of Rainwater's sales are cash. Of the credit sales, one-half is collected in the month of the sale, 45 percent is collected during the following month, and 5 percent is never collected.

Required:
Calculate Rainwater's total cash receipts for sales for August and September.

E23-6 Preparing a Selling and Administrative Expense Budget

LO5

The following information is available for Revelle Company.

- Sales price per unit is $80.
- In November and December, sales were 3,100 and 3,550 units, respectively.
- Variable costs are 11 percent of sales (6 percent commission, 2 percent advertising, 3 percent shipping).
- Fixed costs per month are sales salaries, $5,000; office salaries, $2,500; depreciation, $2,500; building rent, $3,500; insurance, $1,500; and utilities, $800.

Required:
Prepare Revelle's selling and administrative expense budgets for November and December.

E23-7 Preparing a Cash Budget

LO6

Garcia Company has the following information for the month of March.

Cash balance, March 1	$15,575
Collections from customers	34,650
Paid to suppliers	22,300
Manufacturing overhead	6,100
Direct labor	8,250
Selling and administrative expenses	4,200

Wages are paid in the month incurred. Manufacturing overhead includes $1,200 for machinery depreciation, but the amount for selling and administrative expenses is exclusive of depreciation. Additionally, Garcia also expects to sell a piece of property for $15,000 during March.

Required:
Prepare Garcia's cash budget for the month of March.

E23-8 Calculating Cash Receipts

LO6

For Wright Company, 75 percent of sales are cash. Credit sales are collected as follows: 65 percent in the month of the sale and 35 percent in the month following the sale.

Wright's budgeted sales for upcoming months are:

June	$22,500
July	25,000
August	23,000
September	21,000

Required:
Compute Wright's expected cash receipts for August.

Problems—Set A   **Available with McGraw-Hill's Homework Manager**

For problems PA23-1 through PA23-3, refer to the following information about Bamboo You, Inc., which manufactures bamboo picture frames that sell for $20 each. Each frame requires 4 linear feet of bamboo, which costs $1.50 per foot. Each frame takes approximately 30 minutes to build, and the labor rate averages $10.00 per hour.

Bamboo You has the following inventory policies:

Ending finished goods inventory should be 40 percent of the next month's sales.

Ending raw materials inventory should be 30 percent of the next month's production.

Expected sales in number of frames for the upcoming months are:

March	275
April	250
May	300
June	400
July	375
August	425

Variable manufacturing overhead is incurred at a rate of $0.25 per unit produced. Annual fixed manufacturing overhead is estimated to be $7,200 ($600 per month) for an expected production of 4,000 units for the year. Selling and administrative expenses are estimated at $650 per month plus $0.60 per unit sold.

LO5

www.mhhe.com/LLPW1e

PA23-1 Preparing the Components of the Operating Budget

Required:

Prepare the following for Bamboo You, Inc., for the second quarter. Include each month (April–June) as well as the quarter 2 total in your budgets.

1. Sales budget.
2. Production budget.
3. Raw materials purchases budget.
4. Direct labor budget.
5. Manufacturing overhead cost budget.
6. Budgeted cost of goods sold.
7. Selling and administrative expense budget.

LO5

www.mhhe.com/LLPW1e

PA23-2 Preparing a Budgeted Income Statement

Refer to the information in PA23-1.

Required:

Prepare Bamboo You's budgeted income statement for Quarter 2.

LO6

www.mhhe.com/LLPW1e

PA23-3 Preparing a Cash Budget

Refer to the information in PA23-1. Bamboo You, Inc., had $9,800 cash on hand at April 1. Seventy percent of sales are cash. Of the credit sales, 40 percent is collected during the month of the sale and 60 percent is collected during the month following the sale.

Eighty percent of direct material purchases is paid for during the month purchased. Twenty percent is paid in the following month. Raw materials purchases for March 1 totaled $2,000. All other operating costs are paid during the month incurred. Monthly fixed manufacturing overhead includes $150 in depreciation.

Required:

Prepare the following for Bamboo You.

1. Budgeted cash receipts for Quarter 2. Include each month (April–June) as well as quarter 2 totals.
2. Budgeted cash disbursements for Quarter 2.
3. Cash budget for Quarter 2.

LO5

PA23-4 Preparing the Components of the Operating Budget

Black & Decker (B&D) manufactures a wide variety of tools and accessories. One of its more popular items is a cordless power Handisaw. Use the following fictitious information about this product line to complete the problem requirements. Each Handisaw sells for $40. B&D expects the following sales in number of units.

January	2,000
February	2,200
March	2,700
April	2,500
May	1,900

B&D's ending finished goods inventory policy is 25 percent of the following month's sales.

Suppose each Handisaw takes approximately 0.75 hours to manufacture, and B&D pays an average labor wage of $16.50 per hour.

Each Handisaw requires a plastic housing. B&D purchases these housings from a supplier at a cost of $7 each. The company has a raw materials inventory policy of 20 percent of the following month's production requirements. Materials other than the housing unit total $4.50 per Handisaw.

Manufacturing overhead for this product includes $72,000 annual fixed overhead (based on production of 27,000 units) and $1.10 per unit variable manufacturing overhead. B&D's selling expenses are 7 percent of sales dollars, and administrative expenses are fixed at $18,000 per month.

Required:
Prepare the following for B&D.
1. Sales budget for the first quarter.
2. First quarter production budget.
3. B&D's First quarter raw materials purchases budget for the plastic housings.
4. First quarter direct labor budget.
5. Cost of goods sold budget for the first quarter.
6. First quarter selling and administrative expense budget.

Problems—Set B ░░ Available with McGraw-Hill's Homework Manager

For problems PB23-1 through PB23-3, refer to the following information about Flying High Company, which manufactures kites that sell for $15 each. Each kite requires 2 yards of lightweight canvas, which costs $0.50 per yard. Each kite takes approximately 45 minutes to build, and the labor rate averages $8.00 per hour.

Flying High has the following inventory policies:

Ending finished goods inventory should be 30 percent of next month's sales.

Ending raw materials inventory should be 20 percent of next month's production.

Expected sales in number of kites for the upcoming months are:

March	850
April	700
May	650
June	720
July	830
August	760

Variable manufacturing overhead is incurred at a rate of $0.30 per unit produced. Annual fixed manufacturing overhead is estimated to be $9,000 ($750 per month) for an expected production of 9,000 units for the year. Selling and administrative expenses are estimated at $820 per month plus $0.75 per unit sold.

PB23-1 Preparing the Components of the Operating Budget   LO5
Required:
Prepare the following for Flying High for the second quarter. Include each month (April–June) as well as the quarter 2 total in your budgets.
1. Sales budget.
2. Production budget.
3. Raw materials purchases budget.

4. Direct labor budget.
5. Manufacturing overhead cost budget.
6. Budgeted cost of goods sold.
7. Selling and administrative expenses budget.

LO5

PB23-2 Preparing a Budgeted Income Statement
Refer to the information in PB23-1.

Required:
Prepare Flying High's budgeted income statement for Quarter 2.

LO6

PB23-3 Preparing a Cash Budget
Refer to the information in PB23-1. Flying High Company had $12,200 cash on hand at April 1. Eighty percent of sales are cash. Of the credit sales, 60 percent is collected during the month of the sale and 40 percent is collected during the month following the sale.

Seventy percent of raw material purchases is paid for during the month purchased. Thirty percent is paid in the following month. Raw materials purchases for March totaled $800. All other operating costs are paid during the month incurred. Monthly fixed manufacturing overhead includes $280 in depreciation.

Required:
Prepare the following for Flying High.
1. Budgeted cash receipts for Quarter 2. Include each month (April–June) as well as quarter 2 totals.
2. Budgeted cash disbursements for Quarter 2.
3. Cash budget for Quarter 2.

LO5

PB23-4 Preparing the Components of the Operating Budget
Black & Decker (B&D) manufactures a wide variety of tools and accessories. One of its more popular craft-related items is the Cord Free Glue Gun. Use the following fictitious information about this product to complete the problem requirements. Each glue gun sells for $25. B&D expects the following sales in number of glue guns.

January	8,000
February	7,400
March	8,700
April	9,500
May	9,150

B&D's ending finished goods inventory policy is 30 percent of the following month's sales.

Suppose each glue gun takes approximately 0.5 hours to manufacture, and B&D pays an average labor wage of $16.50 per hour.

Each glue gun requires a heating element. B&D purchases these heating elements from a supplier at a cost of $1.25 each. The company has a raw materials inventory policy of 40 percent of the following month's production requirements. Materials other than the heating elements total $3.25 per glue gun.

Manufacturing overhead for this product includes $96,900 annual fixed overhead (based on production of 102,000 units) and variable manufacturing overhead of 0.80 per unit. B&D's selling expenses are 5 percent of sales dollars, and administrative expenses for this product are fixed at $17,500 per month.

Required:
Prepare the following for B&D.
1. Sales budget for the first quarter.
2. First quarter production budget.
3. First quarter raw materials purchases budget for the heating element.
4. First quarter direct labor budget.
5. Cost of goods sold budget for the first quarter.
6. First quarter selling and administrative expense budget.

Cases and Projects

CP23-1 Evaluating the Impact of Corporate Culture and Pressure to Meet the Numbers in the Accounting Reporting Environment

LO3

In 1995, *BusinessWeek* ran a cover story entitled "Blind Ambition: How the Pursuit of Results Got Out of Hand at Bausch and Lomb." The two-part article details a number of games Bausch and Lomb (B&L) managers played to artificially achieve short-term results at the expense of long-term value.

The "numbers-oriented" culture at B&L was far from unique, as evidenced by the high-profile accounting scandals that occurred over the past decade. Since then, numerous reforms, including the Sarbanes-Oxley Act of 2002, have been implemented to improve the corporate reporting environment.

Required:

1. Find *BusinessWeek's* "Blind Ambition" article on the Internet. Read it and list five specific examples of actions that B&L managers took to artificially boost short-term results.
2. Were the actions taken at B&L unethical, illegal, or both? What was the likely impact on long-term results and stockholder value?
3. Explain how the corporate culture at B&L may have contributed to managers' pressure to achieve budgetary results.
4. How did the bonus and compensation systems affect the behavior of individual B&L managers?
5. Conduct an Internet search on the Sarbanes-Oxley Act. What was its intent? Did it include any requirements aimed at improving corporate culture as a means to reduce fraudulent reporting?

CP23-2 Interviewing and Writing a Report on a Real-World Budget Process.

LO2, 3

Budgets can be used in almost any type of organization including large corporations, small businesses, government organizations, universities, churches, and student clubs.

Required:

Choose any organization and interview two people who are involved in its budget process. Try to choose one person who actually worked on preparing the budget (e.g., an accountant or treasurer of the organization) and another person who is affected by the budget (e.g., a person in charge of spending the budget, or an employee who is evaluated based on his or her ability to meet budgetary goals).

1. Based on your interviews, write a brief description of the budgeting process within this organization. The description should be a factual account of the steps taken to develop and distribute the budget without any qualitative evaluations of the process. You should identify the type of budgeting (top down or participative) and the personnel involved in the budgeting procedure as well as any recent and/or anticipated adjustments to the process and the overall importance management place on budgets.
2. Separately consider each of the people you interviewed. How satisfied does each seem with the organization's budgeting process? With what step(s) of the process were they the most and least satisfied? Did either of your interviewees identify a particular step of the process that has been troublesome?
3. Suppose the organization you investigated has retained you as a consultant. Based on the information compiled from the organization and your knowledge from this course, what recommendations would you make to this organization regarding its budgeting process?

CP23-3 Researching Online Budget Tools.

LO2, 3

Numerous personal financial planning or budgeting tools are available on the Internet, many of them free. Choose at least two different online budgeting calculators and input information for a typical person of your age. (**Note:** You may either create a fictitious profile or use your own personal information. If you choose to use your personal data, be sure to read the sites' privacy policies.)

Required:

1. Develop weekly, monthly, and annual budgets.
2. Compare and contrast the two online budgeting tools. Do you prefer aspects of one over the other? Are there things that you dislike?
3. What tools other than budgeting calculators are available online?
4. How helpful do you think such tools are in personal financial management?

24 Budgetary Control

LEARNING OBJECTIVES

After completing this chapter, you should be able to:

LO1 Describe the standard-setting process and explain how standard costs relate to budgets and variances.

LO2 Prepare a flexible budget and show how total costs change with sales volume.

LO3 Calculate and interpret the direct materials price and quantity variances.

LO4 Calculate and interpret the direct labor rate and efficiency variances.

LO5 Calculate and interpret the variable overhead rate and efficiency variances.

LO6 Calculate and interpret the fixed overhead spending and volume variances.

Lectured slideshow—LP24-1
www.mhhe.com/LLPW1e

Focus Company: COLD STONE CREAMERY

"Because the World Deserves Better Ice Cream."

The last chapter focused on the role of budgets in the planning and control process. This chapter discusses the use of variances in the control phase of that process. A **variance** is simply the difference between actual costs and budgeted or standard costs. Variances act as signals to managers that their planned results are (or are not) being achieved.

Think of the planning and control process in terms of flying an airplane. Before takeoff, the pilot must file a flight plan that states where the plane is going and how it will get there. The flight plan is similar to the role of a budget in business. The budget states where the business is going and how managers plan to get it there.

Likewise, the system of signals that guides pilots and air traffic controllers during the flight serves as an aviation control process. Just as the pilot monitors the plane's instrument panel to follow these signals, managers keep a close eye on key indicators, including variances, to determine whether they are on track to achieve their plan. If they go too far off course, managers need a signal that they should take corrective action.

In the last chapter, you began the study of the planning and control process by preparing a master budget for a hypothetical Cold Stone Creamery location. In this chapter, we continue this example to calculate Cold Stone's cost variances for direct materials, direct labor, and manufacturing overhead. We also discuss how to prepare a different kind of budget, the **flexible budget.** First, we need to become familiar with **standard cost systems,** the basis for these budgets and variances.

STANDARD COST SYSTEMS	USE OF FLEXIBLE BUDGETS TO CALCULATE COST VARIANCES	DIRECT MATERIALS AND DIRECT LABOR VARIANCES	MANUFACTURING OVERHEAD COST VARIANCES
• Ideal versus Attainable Standards • Types of Standard • Standard Cost Card • Favorable versus Unfavorable Variances	• Master Budgets versus Flexible Budgets • Flexible Budget as a Benchmark • Volume Variance versus Spending Variance	• Variance Framework • Direct Materials Variances • Direct Labor Variances	• Variable Manufacturing Overhead Variances • Fixed Manufacturing Overhead Variances • Summary of Variances

STANDARD COST SYSTEMS

A standard cost system is the foundation of a managerial control system. The key difference between a standard cost system and the cost systems covered in earlier chapters is that a standard cost system records cost at standard rather than actual amounts. The standards are set in advance to reflect what managers think a particular cost **should** be. Managers can then use these standards to create budgets, set prices for products and services, and make a variety of other decisions.

Ideal versus Attainable Standards

Standards can be set at varying levels of difficulty or achievability. The most extreme case is an ideal standard, or one that can be achieved only under perfect or ideal conditions. An example is the performance standard of a world-class athlete, such as a 4-minute mile. Standards that are almost impossible to achieve are unlikely to motivate people to work hard to try to achieve the standards. At the other end of the spectrum is an easily attainable standard, or one that can be met without much effort. Research suggests that **tight but attainable standards**—the happy medium between these two extremes—are best for motivating individuals to work hard.

What these general guidelines mean to a particular business depends on the type of task and the person performing it. Imagine, for example, that you just started training for a 10-K charity run. You can run a 10-minute mile with relative ease but would like to improve your running time. It probably would not be realistic to set a 4-minute mile as your performance standard because most people are not physically capable of achieving that ideal standard. What standard would motivate you to train harder without being so difficult that it would cause you to give up? This type of standard is sometimes called a "stretch goal"—one you must stretch yourself to achieve. Similarly, organizations should set standard costs so that they are difficult but not impossible to achieve. To foster continuous improvement, the standards should increase in difficulty over time, just as you would decrease your target running time as your strength and training improve.

Types of Standard

Standard cost systems rely on two types of standard, quantity standards and price standards:

	Definition	Examples
Quantity standard	The amount of **input** that should go into a single unit of the product	Number of ounces of aluminum in a Coca Cola can Number of tons of steel in a Ford F-150 truck Number of yards of denim in a pair of Levi's 550 jeans
Price standard	The price that should be paid for a specific quantity of **input**	Price per ounce of aluminum Price per ton of steel Price per yard of denim

Coach's Tip

Managers should set standards at realistic levels that allow a certain amount of downtime for preventive maintenance, employee breaks and training, and the like. Failure to build these factors into the standards can reduce performance over the long run because of machine breakdowns, low employee morale, and high turnover rates.

Video 24-1
www.mhhe.com/LLPW1e

Coach's Tip

You may wonder how companies set their price and quantity standards. Managers use many types of information including historical data, industry averages, and the results of process studies to determine how much time and money they **should** spend to make a product.

Notice that these standards are stated in terms of the quantity and price of the **input** (ounces, tons, or yards) that **should** be used to create a single unit of output. Similar quantity and price standards are developed for direct labor cost. The quantity standard for direct labor is the amount of time (in hours, minutes, or seconds) that workers **should** take to produce a single unit of product. The price standard for labor, called the **standard labor rate,** is the expected hourly cost of labor including employee taxes and benefits.

Standard Cost Card

The price standard is multiplied by the quantity standard for each input to get the standard unit cost. Then all standard costs are summarized on a standard cost card, a form that shows what the company **should** spend to make a single unit of product based on expected production and sales for the coming period. Exhibit 24.1 shows a hypothetical standard cost card for Cold Stone Creamery.

Exhibit 24.1	Standard Cost Card for Cold Stone Creamery		
	Standard Quantity	**Standard Price (Rate)**	**Standard Unit Cost**
Direct costs			
Ice cream*	10 oz.	$0.05 per oz.	$ 0.50
Mix-in ingredients	2 oz.	0.10 per oz.	0.20
Direct labor	.10 hrs.	8.00 per hr.	0.80
Manufacturing overhead costs			
Variable manufacturing overhead (based on number of direct labor hours)	.10 hrs.	1.00 per hr.	0.10
Fixed manufacturing overhead $6,000 / 15,000 units = $0.40 per unit			.40
Standard manufacturing cost per unit			$2.00

*In reality, Cold Stone Creamery purchases milk, cream, and sugar and uses these raw ingredients to make fresh ice cream at each individual store. For simplicity, we assume that the ice cream is purchased from a regional distribution center. The standard cost card focuses only on mixing the ice cream with ingredients to create and serve a Cold Stone Creation to customers.

According to the standard cost card, Cold Stone should use 10 ounces of ice cream and 2 ounces of mix-in ingredients (fruits, candy, nuts) to make each unit of product. The standard price is $0.05 per ounce for ice cream and $0.10 per ounce for mix-ins, which results in a standard unit cost for materials of $0.70 ($0.50 + $0.20).

The direct labor standard assumes that employees can produce and serve an average of 10 units per hour—including the time needed to prepare, serve, and clean up after each unit, as well as an allowance for training time, breaks, and the like. Converting this direct labor standard to a per unit basis produces a standard amount of time to produce each unit of .10 hours (6 minutes). Because the standard labor rate (including taxes and benefits) is $8.00 per hour, the standard direct labor cost per unit is $0.80.

Variable manufacturing costs are applied to the product at a rate of $1.00 per direct labor hour. When this standard variable overhead rate is multiplied by the standard quantity of .10 labor hours per unit, we get a standard unit cost of $0.10 for variable overhead. Fixed overhead costs are budgeted at $6,000 per month. If that amount is spread over the 15,000 units we expect to produce and sell, we get a fixed manufacturing overhead cost of $0.40 per unit. Adding all of these standard cost components, we arrive at a standard manufacturing cost of $2.00 per unit.

Learning Objective 1

Describe the standard-setting process and explain how standard costs relate to budgets and variances.

Favorable versus Unfavorable Variances

Cost variances are calculated by comparing actual costs to budgeted or standard costs. A favorable variance (F) occurs when actual costs are less than budgeted or standard costs. An unfavorable variance (U) occurs when actual costs are more than budgeted or standard costs. Common causes of favorable and unfavorable variances include the following:

Causes of Favorable Variances	Causes of Unfavorable Variances
• Paying a **lower price** than expected for direct materials	• Paying a **higher price** than expected for direct materials
• Using **less** direct materials than expected	• Using **more** direct materials than expected
• Paying a **lower** rate than expected for direct labor	• Paying a **higher** rate than expected for direct labor
• Producing a unit in **less** time than expected	• Producing a unit in **more** time than expected
• Paying **less** than expected for manufacturing overhead costs	• Paying **more** than expected for manufacturing overhead costs
• Using **less** of a variable overhead resource than expected	• Using **more** of a variable overhead resource than expected
• Using **more** of a fixed overhead resource than expected	• Using **less** of a fixed overhead resource than expected

In the remainder of this chapter, we calculate cost variances that illustrate each of these potential causes. First, we need to discuss and develop a flexible budget.

USE OF FLEXIBLE BUDGETS TO CALCULATE COST VARIANCES

Video 24-2
www.mhhe.com/LLPW1e

As mentioned in the previous section, we calculate variances by comparing actual costs to budgeted or standard costs. Although we often use the terms **standard** and **budget** interchangeably, they have slightly different meanings. Standards are expressed at a very detailed level to reflect the cost and quantity of the **inputs** that go into a product or service. A simple example of an input is the amount of flour that is needed to make a cake. A budget, on the other hand, is the total dollar amount that we expect to spend to achieve a certain level of **output.** In other words, a budget depends not only on the standards that are stated in terms of the input but also on the level of output, such as the number of cakes that will be made. As you will see shortly, we can develop different budgets for different levels of output, but the standards we use to develop those budgets remain the same.

Master Budgets versus Flexible Budgets

In the last chapter, you prepared an entire master budget for Cold Stone Creamery. Recall that the master budget is an integrated set of operating and financial budgets that reflects what managers expect to achieve in a future accounting period. The starting point for preparing the master budget is the sales forecast, or the company's best estimate of future sales. All other components of the master budget are based on the sales forecast, including the production budget, the raw materials purchases budget, the direct labor budget, the manufacturing overhead budget, and the selling and administrative expense budget.

The master budget is an example of a static budget—that is, a budget that is based on a single (fixed) estimate of sales volume. Because predicting sales volume with 100 percent certainty is impossible, managers often find it useful to prepare a flexible budget that shows how budgeted costs and revenues will change across different levels of sales volume. As you should recall from Chapter 21, variable costs are those that change (in total) in response to a change in production or sales volume. Fixed costs are those that remain the same (in total) regardless of production or sales volume. For the sake of simplicity, we assume that production and sales are equal throughout this chapter. See Exhibit 24.2 for a flexible budget for Cold Stone Creamery's manufacturing costs.

Two points are important to keep in mind when preparing a flexible budget. **First, total variable costs change in direct proportion to changes in volume.** For example, if Cold Stone's sales volume increases from 15,000 units to 18,000 units (see Exhibit 24.2), the total cost of ice cream should increase from $7,500 to $9,000. The 20 percent increase in sales

Exhibit 24.2   Preparation of the Master and Flexible Budgets

The master budget is based on managers' best estimate of sales volume (15,000 units) multiplied by the standard unit cost.

	Standard Unit Cost	Flexible Budget (12,000 Units)	Master Budget (15,000 Units)	Flexible Budget (18,000 Units)
Variable manufacturing costs:				
Ice cream	$ 0.50	$ 6,000	$ 7,500	$ 9,000
Mix-in ingredients	0.20	2,400	3,000	3,600
Direct labor	0.80	9,600	12,000	14,400
Variable manufacturing overhead	0.10	1,200	1,500	1,800
Fixed manufacturing overhead	0.40	6,000	6,000	6,000
Total manufacturing costs	$ 2.00	$ 25,200	$ 30,000	$ 34,800

The flexible budget shows how total costs are expected to change if sales are lower (12,000 units) or higher (18,000 units) than expected.

volume (3,000 / 15,000 = 20%) produces a 20 percent increase in the total cost of ice cream ($1,500 / $7,500 = 20%). The same effect will occur for all other variable costs.

Second, total fixed costs should remain the same, regardless of volume. Cold Stone's budgeted fixed cost is $6,000 regardless of the number of units produced or sold. Thus, the fixed cost of $0.40 per unit shown in the standard unit cost column is valid only for the master budget of 15,000 units ($6,000 / 15,000 = $0.40).

Before we continue, complete the following Self-Study Practice to make sure you understand how to prepare a flexible budget.

SELF-STUDY PRACTICE

Assume that Papa John's standard unit cost and master budget for 20,000 units are as follows.

	Standard Unit Cost	Master Budget (20,000 units)	Flexible Budget (25,000 units)
1. Pizza dough	$0.80	$16,000	
2. Pizza sauce	0.20	4,000	
3. Direct labor	1.00	20,000	
4. Variable manufacturing overhead	0.25	5,000	
5. Fixed manufacturing overhead	0.50	10,000	
	$2.75	$55,000	

Calculate a flexible budget for 25,000 units and enter the amounts in the Flexible Budget column.

After you have finished, check your answers with the solutions at the bottom of the page.

Solution to Self-Study Practice

1. $20,000 (25,000 × $0.80)
2. $ 5,000 (25,000 × $0.20)
3. $25,000 (25,000 × $1.00)
4. $ 6,250 (25,000 × $0.25)
5. $10,000 (remains the same)
   $66,250

Flexible Budget as a Benchmark

The flexible budget is a useful benchmark for evaluating managerial performance. In general, we rely on the master budget for planning, or forward-looking purposes, and on the flexible budget for control, or backward-looking purposes. See Exhibit 24.3.

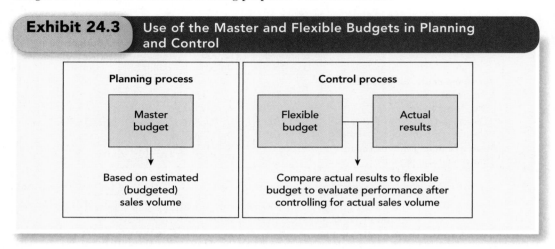

Exhibit 24.3 Use of the Master and Flexible Budgets in Planning and Control

To illustrate the use of a flexible budget for performance evaluation, assume you are a store manager at Cold Stone Creamery and part of your responsibility is to control the cost of the ice cream used to make Cold Stone Creations. Based on the master budget sales forecast of 15,000 units, your ice cream budget was set at $7,500 ($0.50 per unit × 15,000 units). After the budget period, you learned that the actual cost of ice cream was $8,000, or $500 higher than budgeted. Based on this information, how should the company evaluate your performance at controlling ice cream costs?

To answer this question, we need to think about the two possible reasons that the cost might have been higher than budgeted:

- You may have spent more than $0.50 per unit for ice cream.
- You may have produced more than 15,000 units.

Now we learn that the company actually produced and sold 18,000 units for the period. Would that knowledge change how we should evaluate your performance at controlling direct materials costs? In this case, we can blame the increased cost on the increase in volume. In fact, when we compare the budgeted cost for 18,000 units in Exhibit 24.2 to the actual cost, we can see that you spent **less** than $0.50 per unit on ice cream.

The lesson here is that to evaluate cost control, we cannot just compare actual results to the master budget. Although the master budget is very useful in planning, a flexible budget is more useful in evaluating past managerial performance because it helps separate the effects that are due to spending from those that are due to volume.

Volume Variance versus Spending Variance

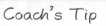

Coach's Tip

Some volume variances are driven by the difference in actual and budgeted **sales** volume, while others are driven by the difference in actual and budgeted **production** volume. To keep things simple, we assume that sales and production are equal.

Using the flexible budget for performance evaluation allows us to separate the effect of volume from the effect of spending. The only difference between the master budget and the flexible budget, in fact, is the volume used to create each budget. Thus, any comparison of the master budget to the flexible budget creates a volume variance that represents the difference between actual and budgeted volume. Spending variances are calculated by comparing actual costs to the flexible budget (not the master budget). Because both numbers are based on the same volume, this provides an "apples to apples" comparison of spending.

See Exhibit 24.4 for a comparison of the master and flexible budgets based on the ice cream example presented in the previous section. Remember that your budget for ice cream was $0.50 for each unit produced and sold. The master budget cost of $7,500 is based on the 15,000 units you expected to produce ($0.50 × 15,000 = $7,500). The flexible budget cost

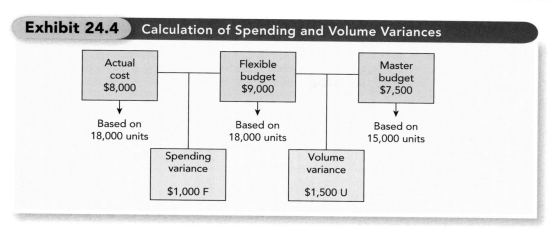

Exhibit 24.4   Calculation of Spending and Volume Variances

of $9,000 is based on the 18,000 units you actually produced and sold ($0.50 × 18,000 = $9,000). The volume variance is the difference between these two amounts ($9,000 − $7,500 = $1,500). In this example, the volume variance is unfavorable because producing more units than expected **should** result in higher ice cream cost. However, this volume variance only considers the cost of the ice cream and ignores other production costs, as well as the additional revenue you would get from increased sales. From an overall company perspective, selling more units than expected is favorable so long as the sales price is high enough to cover the increased variable costs. We do not consider revenue variances in this chapter as they are covered in more advanced managerial accounting texts.

Exhibit 24.4 also includes a comparison of actual ice cream costs to the flexible budget. Recall that you actually spent $8,000 on ice cream to produce 18,000 units. The flexible budget shows that it **should** have cost $9,000 to produce 18,000 units (18,000 × $0.50). The difference is a favorable spending variance of $1,000 ($9,000 − $8,000). It is favorable because you spent less on ice cream than the flexible budget allowed. Notice that volume is held constant between these two numbers at 18,000 units. So the entire variance can be attributed to your **spending** on ice cream, as opposed to the number of units produced. There are several possible explanations for this favorable spending variance. Perhaps you were able to negotiate a reduced price for the ice cream. Or perhaps employees skimped on the amount of ice cream they put into each Cold Stone Creation. In the next section we will calculate price and quantity variances that break the overall spending variance into more detailed components, so that we can hold a specific manager responsible for it.

DIRECT MATERIALS AND DIRECT LABOR VARIANCES

Direct material and direct labor costs are those that can be directly attributed to each unit produced. We can use the same basic framework to analyze these direct costs. This framework allows us to divide the overall spending variance into two unique components: a price variance and a quantity variance.

Variance Framework

The price variance relates to the amount **paid** for a particular **input** that goes into the final product. For Cold Stone Creamery, the direct inputs to the final product are ice cream, mix-in ingredients, and employee time. The price variance compares the price we actually paid for each of these inputs to the price we **should have** paid. Notice that when we talk about price in this context, we are talking about the amount paid for something (cost), not the price we charged the final customer (revenue). Thus, the price variance is actually a cost variance.

The quantity variance relates to the quantity of **input** used to make the final product. For Cold Stone, the quantity of input can be measured in terms of **ounces** of ice cream and mix-in ingredients, or **hours** of employee time. For simplicity, we assume that the quantity of input purchased equals the quantity used. That way we won't need to worry about changes in inventory, which complicates the calculations.

Exhibit 24.5 illustrates the framework we will use to analyze the direct cost variances.

Coach's Tip

In calculating variances, we always isolate the effect of a single factor while holding all other factors constant. Doing so makes it easier to assign responsibility to the manager who has control over that factor.

Exhibit 24.5   Calculation of Direct Cost Variances

```
                                          Total
                                         spending
                                         variance

Approach 1:
Calculate the total cost in each
of the three boxes to the right.      Actual cost         SP × AQ        Flexible budget        Master budget
Then compare the values in             AP × AQ                              SP × SQ           (not used to calculate
each box to get the variances.                                                                spending variances)


Approach 2:
Compute the variances directly
using the formulas provided to        Price variance        Quantity variance      Based on            Based on
the right.                            AQ × (SP − AP)         SP × (SQ − AQ)          actual             budgeted
                                                                                     units               units
```

AP: Actual price per unit of input
AQ: Actual quantity of input
SP: Standard price per unit of input
SQ: Standard quantity of input allowed to achieve the actual units of output

Coach's Tip

Spending variances are calculated by comparing actual costs to the flexible budget. The master budget is used to calculate volume variances, so it is shown outside the box in this diagram.

Exhibit 24.5 shows that direct cost variances can be calculated in two ways. The first approach is to calculate the total cost in each of the orange boxes shown in Exhibit 24.5. Then calculate the difference (variance) between each box by subtracting one value from the other. The second approach is to use the formulas that are shown in the blue boxes. Either of these approaches will provide the same answer, because the variance formulas were derived by subtracting the equations in the orange boxes from one another, as follows:

$$\text{Price variance} = [(SP \times AQ) − (AP \times AQ)] = AQ \times (SP − AP)$$
$$\text{Quantity variance} = [(SP \times SQ) − (SP \times AQ)] = SP \times (SQ − AQ)$$

Notice that each variance formula allows only one factor (either price or quantity) to vary, while holding the other factor constant. Isolating the variance this way allows managers to identify the specific cause of the variance so that a specific manager can be held responsible for it.

Direct Materials Variances

Learning Objective 3

Calculate and interpret the direct materials price and quantity variances.

In an earlier example, we learned that Cold Stone Creamery had a $1,000 unfavorable spending variance for ice cream. Let's see if we can find the specific cause of that variance. The standard cost information for Cold Stone's ice cream is as follows:

Direct Costs	Standard Quantity	Standard Price	Standard Unit Cost
Ice cream	10 oz.	$0.05 per oz.	$0.50

Cold Stone's actual results were as follows:

Coach's Tip

Try entering these numbers into Exhibit 24.5 to see whether you can calculate the variances yourself. Then look at the answers in Exhibit 24.6.

- Produced and sold 18,000 units.
- Purchased and used 200,000 ounces of ice cream at a total cost of $8,000.

Let's start by identifying the following terms:

Actual price: $8,000 / 200,000 = $0.04 per ounce.

Actual quantity: 200,000 ounces.

Standard price: $0.05 per ounce.

Standard quantity: 10 ounces per unit × 18,000 actual units = 180,000 ounces.

The direct materials price variance is the difference between the actual price and the standard price for direct materials multiplied by the actual quantity of direct materials purchased. In this case, the actual price of the ice cream was $0.04 per ounce; the standard price was $0.05 per ounce. To get the variance, we need to multiply the difference by the 200,000 ounces that were actually purchased.

The direct materials quantity variance is the difference between the actual quantity and the standard quantity of direct materials used, multiplied by the standard price. This variance is sometimes called the **direct materials usage variance.** Because the standard quantity for ice cream is 10 ounces for each unit produced, the standard quantity allowed for 18,000 units is 180,000 ounces. However, the company actually used 200,000 ounces. To get the variance, we need to multiply the difference by the $0.05 standard price.

Entering these numbers into Exhibit 24.5 provides the variances in Exhibit 24.6.

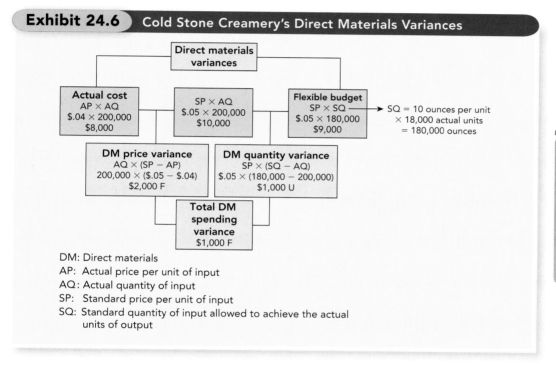

Exhibit 24.6   **Cold Stone Creamery's Direct Materials Variances**

DM: Direct materials
AP: Actual price per unit of input
AQ: Actual quantity of input
SP: Standard price per unit of input
SQ: Standard quantity of input allowed to achieve the actual units of output

Coach's Tip

It may seem odd that we are using the actual number of units to calculate SQ. But remember that SQ is the standard quantity of **input** needed to achieve the actual units of output.

We can draw two conclusions from this diagram. First, the direct materials price variance is $2,000 favorable because the company paid $0.01 less than the standard cost for the 200,000 ounces of materials purchased. **The direct materials purchasing manager is responsible for this favorable direct materials price variance.** A favorable price variance is not always good, however. Although it has a positive effect on short-term spending, it could have a negative effect over the long term if customers can detect a difference in product quality.

What are some potential explanations for this favorable price variance? Perhaps the purchasing manager purchased lower quality ingredients or negotiated a reduced price. Or perhaps the company received a quantity discount that was not factored into the standard price. Maybe the price difference reflects a market fluctuation in the price of ice cream in the same way that dairy prices fluctuate at the grocery store.

Second, the direct materials quantity variance is $1,000 unfavorable because the company used 200,000 ounces of ice cream to make 18,000 units, when only 180,000 ounces were allowed by the standard. **The production manager is typically responsible for the direct materials quantity variance**—in this case, the manager who oversees the employees who make and serve the ice cream creations. What are some potential explanations for this unfavorable usage variance? Perhaps employees put too much ice cream into each unit. Or perhaps the standard quantity does not account for ice cream given away to customers in taste tests or thrown away at the end of the day. Managers would need to investigate further to determine the exact cause, but the variance gives them a starting point for their investigation.

The total direct materials spending variance combines the direct materials price and quantity variances. Because the price variance is $2,000 F and the quantity variance is $1,000 U, we add them together to get a $1,000 favorable spending variance. Notice that this is the same number we calculated in Exhibit 24.4 (page 993) by comparing actual costs to the flexible budget costs. Now, however, we have a better idea of **why** the company spent less money than planned on ice cream. These variances can provide feedback to managers who may need to change their behavior. Alternatively, they may signal that the company's standards need to be updated to reflect new pricing or production methods.

Before you continue, complete the following Self-Study Practice to see whether you can calculate the direct materials variances for Cold Stone Creamery's mix-in ingredients.

SELF-STUDY PRACTICE

Cold Stone Creamery's standard cost card for mix-in ingredients follows:

Direct costs	Standard Quantity	Standard Price	Standard Unit Cost
Mix-in ingredients	2 oz.	$0.10 per oz.	$0.20

Actual results were as follows:

- Produced and sold 18,000 units.
- Purchased and used 35,000 ounces of mix-in ingredients at a total cost of $4,200 ($0.12 per ounce).

Calculate the following variances and label them as favorable (F) or unfavorable (U):

1. Direct materials price variance.
2. Direct materials quantity variance.
3. Total direct materials spending variance.

After you have finished, check your answers with the solutions at the bottom of the page.

Direct Labor Variances

Learning Objective 4

Calculate and interpret the direct labor rate and efficiency variances.

The method for calculating direct labor variances is similar to the one for direct materials variances with a few modifications:

- Because the price of direct labor is called the direct labor rate, **the price variance for labor is called the direct labor rate (not price) variance.**
- Because direct labor quantity is measured in hours, **the quantity variance for labor is called the direct labor efficiency variance.**

Let's use Exhibit 24.7 to analyze Cold Stone Creamery's actual and standard direct labor costs. The labor portion of Cold Stone's standard cost card may be summarized as follows:

Input	Standard Quantity	Standard Price	Standard Unit Cost
Direct labor	.10 hrs.	$8.00 per hr.	$0.80

Cold Stone's actual results were as follows:

- Actual number of units produced was 18,000.
- Actual direct labor costs were $16,500 for 2,000 hours.

Solution to Self-Study Practice

1. DM Price Variance = AQ × (SP − AP) = 35,000 × ($0.10 − $0.12) = $700 U
2. DM Quantity Variance = SP × (SQ − AQ) = $0.10 (36,000 − 35,000) = $100 F
3. Total DM Spending Variance = $700 Unfavorable + $100 Favorable = $600 U

Exhibit 24.7 Calculation of Direct Labor Variances

```
                        Direct labor
                         variances
         ┌──────────────────┼──────────────────┐
   ┌──────────┐        ┌─────────┐        ┌──────────────┐
   │Actual cost│───────│ SR × AH │────────│Flexible budget│
   │  AR × AH  │        └─────────┘        │   SR × SH    │
   └──────────┘                            └──────────────┘
        │                                          │
        │                                     Based on
        │                                     actual units
   ┌──────────────┐   ┌────────────────────┐  produced
   │ DL rate      │   │ DL efficiency      │
   │ variance     │   │ variance           │
   │ AH × (SR − AR)│   │ SR × (SH − AH)     │
   └──────────────┘   └────────────────────┘
```

AR: Actual hourly labor rate
AH: Actual labor hours
SR: Standard hourly labor rate
SH: Standard labor hours allowed to achieve the actual units of output
DL: Direct labor

Coach's Tip

SH is the number of direct labor hours we **should have used** to produce 18,000 actual units of output.

Let's start by filling in the following terms:

Actual labor rate: $16,500 / 2,000 hours = $8.25 per hour.

Actual labor hours: 2,000 hours.

Standard labor rate: $8.00 per hour.

Standard labor hours: 0.10 hours × 18,000 units = 1,800 hours.

Coach's Tip

Try using these numbers in Exhibit 24.7 to see whether you can calculate the variances yourself. Then look at the answers in Exhibit 24.8.

The direct labor rate variance is the difference between the actual labor rate and the standard labor rate multiplied by the actual labor hours used. The direct labor efficiency variance is the difference between the actual number of labor hours used and the standard number of labor hours multiplied by the standard labor rate. Cold Stone's direct labor standard indicates that an employee should take .10 hours (6 minutes) to produce a single unit of output. Because Cold Stone's employees produced 18,000 units, they should have used only 1,800 direct labor hours. Actually, employees worked 2,000 direct labor hours to produce 18,000 units.

Using these numbers in Exhibit 24.7 gives the results in Exhibit 24.8.

The direct labor rate variance is $500 unfavorable because the company paid $0.25 more per hour than the standard labor rate (on average) for the 2,000 labor hours worked. **Holding an individual manager responsible for the direct labor rate variance is difficult** because many factors can influence the variance including labor market conditions, how and when workers were hired and promoted, and turnover rates in the organization. In this case, the variance is unfavorable because the actual labor rate was slightly higher (on average) than the standard rate. The market wage rate may have increased, or the standard wage rate may not have been adjusted to reflect that market reality.

The direct labor efficiency variance is unfavorable because workers took 200 more hours than they **should** have (based on the standard) to produce 18,000 units. When we multiply the 200 extra hours by the standard labor rate of $8.00 per hour, we get an unfavorable efficiency variance of $1,600. **In general, the production manager is responsible for the direct labor efficiency variance.** A variety of factors can affect this variance, including how quickly workers can make the product and how closely production can be matched with customer demand. Unlike a traditional manufacturing firm, which can use inventory to keep production levels stable, Cold Stone Creamery cannot produce its product until a customer walks through the door. If employees are standing around with no customers to serve, it will negatively affect the direct labor efficiency variance. This variance can signal to managers that the staffing schedule should be modified.

The total direct labor spending variance is the sum of the direct labor rate and direct labor efficiency variances. In this case, because both variances are unfavorable, we add them together to arrive at an unfavorable spending variance of $2,100 ($500U + $1,600U = $2,100U).

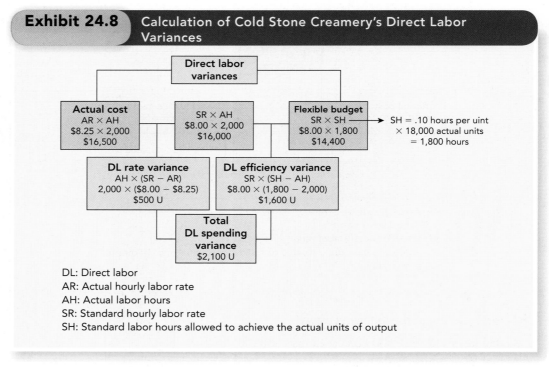

Exhibit 24.8   **Calculation of Cold Stone Creamery's Direct Labor Variances**

DL: Direct labor
AR: Actual hourly labor rate
AH: Actual labor hours
SR: Standard hourly labor rate
SH: Standard labor hours allowed to achieve the actual units of output

MANUFACTURING OVERHEAD COST VARIANCES

Because manufacturing overhead costs cannot be traced directly to specific units, they must be **applied** to products using a predetermined overhead rate and a secondary allocation measure such as direct labor hours. The standard overhead rates are estimated before the accounting period begins based on budgeted costs and budgeted levels of the overhead cost drivers. Overhead is then applied to specific units during the period by multiplying the budgeted (standard) rate by the standard quantity of the cost driver.

This is a key difference between a standard cost system and the "normal" cost system described in Chapter 19. In Chapter 19, we established a budgeted manufacturing overhead rate based on budgeted costs and budgeted levels of the activity drivers. Then we applied overhead cost to products by multiplying the budgeted rate by the **actual** number of units produced. In this chapter, we multiply the budgeted (standard) overhead rate by the **standard** value of the cost driver.

The overall difference (variance) between actual and applied manufacturing overhead is still called over- or underapplied overhead. Now, however, we can break the overall variance down into more detailed variances to gain some insight into **why** manufacturing overhead costs were over- or underapplied. As you will see shortly, our interpretation of these overhead variances changes greatly depending on whether the overhead cost is variable or fixed.

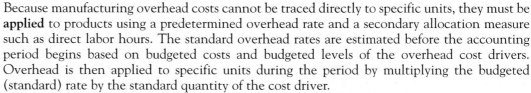

Video 24-3
www.mhhe.com/LLPW1e

Variable Manufacturing Overhead Variances

Learning Objective 5

Calculate and interpret the variable overhead rate and efficiency variances.

Variable manufacturing overhead costs include the costs of indirect materials, such as cleaning supplies and paper products, as well as the power to run machines and other incidental costs that vary with some activity measure. In this chapter, we assume these costs vary in direct proportion to direct labor hours—a realistic assumption for a labor-oriented business such as Cold Stone Creamery. As you learned in earlier chapters, however, overhead costs can vary with many other factors including number of machine hours and nonvolume activity drivers such as the number of setups, materials-handling transactions, and the like. Companies that have activity-based cost systems would do a separate analysis for each major overhead cost driver (a task that is beyond the scope of this book).

Exhibit 24.9   Calculation of Variable Overhead Variances

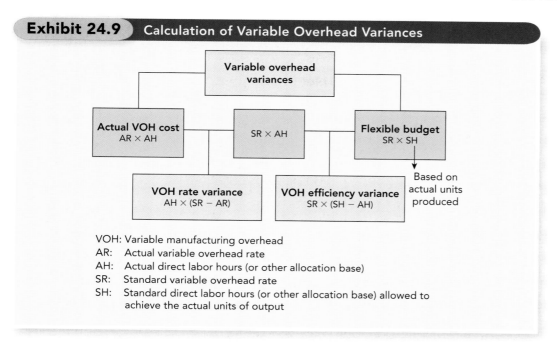

VOH: Variable manufacturing overhead
AR: Actual variable overhead rate
AH: Actual direct labor hours (or other allocation base)
SR: Standard variable overhead rate
SH: Standard direct labor hours (or other allocation base) allowed to achieve the actual units of output

Because we are assuming that variable overhead (VOH) costs are driven by direct labor hours (DLH), we can simply substitute the variable overhead rate for the direct labor rate in the direct labor variance framework (see Exhibit 24.9 for the modified diagram).

Let's apply this framework to our Cold Stone Creamery example. The variable manufacturing overhead standards are as follows:

	Standard Quantity	Standard Price	Standard Unit Cost
Variable manufacturing overhead applied at $1.00 per direct labor hour	0.10 hrs.	$1.00 per hr.	$0.10

The company's actual results were as follows:

- Actual units produced were 18,000.
- Actual direct labor hours were 2,000.
- Actual VOH costs were $1,800.

Let's start by identifying the following terms:

Actual variable overhead rate: $1,800 / 2,000 hours = $0.90 per hour.
Actual DLH: 2,000 hours.
Standard VOH rate: $1.00 per hour.
Standard DLH: .10 hours × 18,000 units = 1,800 hours.

Coach's Tip

Enter these numbers into Exhibit 24.9 to see whether you can calculate the variances yourself. Then look at the answers in Exhibit 24.10.

The **variable overhead (VOH) rate variance** is the difference between the actual variable overhead rate and the standard variable overhead rate multiplied by the actual value of the cost driver (DLH). In this case, the actual cost of VOH is $0.90 per direct labor hour, and the standard variable overhead rate is $1.00 per direct labor hour. The **variable overhead**

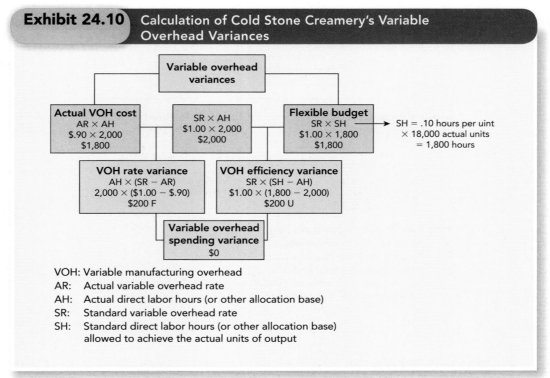

Exhibit 24.10 Calculation of Cold Stone Creamery's Variable Overhead Variances

Coach's Tip

The VOH spending variance is also the amount of over- or underapplied variable overhead. In this case, actual VOH cost is exactly equal to the amount applied based on 18,000 units.

efficiency variance is the difference between the number of actual DLH used and the number of standard DLH, multiplied by the standard variable overhead rate. In this case, the actual number of DLH was 2,000, but according to the standard, only 1,800 hours should have been required to produce 18,000 units.

See Exhibit 24.10 for the results of substituting these numbers into the formulas in Exhibit 24.9.

The variable overhead rate variance is favorable because the actual variable overhead cost per direct labor hour was less than the standard variable overhead rate. When we multiply the $0.10 difference by the 2,000 actual direct labor hours, we get a favorable variable overhead rate variance of $200. What caused this variance? Managers may have paid less for variable overhead items (cleaning supplies, napkins, or power) than the standard allows, or the relationship between the variable overhead cost and the number of direct labor hours may not be perfectly proportional. Even if the variable overhead costs are partially driven by direct labor hours, other factors are likely to influence spending on variable overhead costs.

The variable overhead efficiency variance is unfavorable because the company used 200 more direct labor hours than **should** have been needed to produce 18,000 units. Multiplying the 200 extra hours by the $1.00 standard variable overhead rate gives a $200 unfavorable variable overhead efficiency variance. Although this variance is called the variable overhead efficiency variance, it is really driven by the efficiency (or inefficiency) of the underlying allocation driver (that is, direct labor hours). This variance is a mirror reflection of the direct labor efficiency variance. The assumption is that as managers use more direct labor hours, they also incur additional variable overhead costs.

The total variable overhead spending variance is the sum of the variable overhead rate variance and the variable overhead efficiency variance. In this case, it is zero because the $200 favorable variable overhead rate variance exactly offsets the $200 unfavorable variable overhead efficiency variance.

Before you continue, complete the following Self-Study Practice to make sure you can calculate the direct labor and variable overhead variances.

Papa John's standard cost card for direct labor and variable overhead includes the following costs.

Direct costs	Standard Quantity	Standard Price
Direct labor	.3 hrs.	$10.00 per hr.
Variable overhead	.3 hrs.	2.50 per hr.

Better Ingredients.
Better Pizza.

Actual results were as follows:

- The number of units sold and produced was 15,000.
- The direct labor cost was $38,000 for 4,000 hours ($9.50 per hour).
- The variable overhead cost was $12,000 for 4,000 hours ($3.00 per hour).

Calculate the following variances and label them as favorable or unfavorable:

1. Direct labor rate variance
2. Direct labor efficiency variance
3. Total direct labor spending variance
4. Variable overhead rate variance
5. Variable overhead efficiency variance
6. Total variable overhead spending variance
7. Briefly explain the relationship between the direct labor efficiency variance and the variable overhead efficiency variance.

After you have finished, check your answers with the solutions at the bottom of the page.

Fixed Manufacturing Overhead Variances

The calculation and interpretation of fixed manufacturing overhead variances is completely different from that of the variable manufacturing cost variances. Fixed manufacturing overhead includes costs that are independent of volume, such as supervisors' salaries, rent, equipment depreciation, and insurance.

Although fixed manufacturing overhead costs are unrelated to volume, we must still establish a budgeted (standard) fixed overhead rate based on the budgeted cost and budgeted production volume. For Cold Stone Creamery, we calculated that rate as follows:

Budgeted Fixed Overhead Rate = $6,000 / 15,000 Units = $0.40 per Unit

Solution to
Self-Study Practice

1. DL Rate Variance: AH × (SR − AR) = 4,000 × ($10.00 − $9.50) = $2,000 F
2. DL Efficiency Variance: SR × (SH − AH) = $10.00 × (4,500 − 4,000) = $5,000 F
3. Total DL Spending Variance = $2,000 F + $5,000 F = $7,000 F
4. VOH Rate Variance: AH × (SR − AR) = 4,000 × ($2.50 − $3.00) = $2,000 U
5. VOH Efficiency Variance: SR × (SH − AH) = $2.50 × (4,500 − 4,000) = $1,250 F
6. Total VOH Spending Variance = $2,000 U + $1,250 F = $750 U
7. The direct labor efficiency variance and the variable overhead efficiency variance are both driven by the difference between actual labor hours and standard labor hours. The variable overhead efficiency variance is 25% of the direct labor efficiency variance, because the variable overhead rate is based on the direct labor rate.

Of course, this rate will be accurate only if we correctly estimate the fixed manufacturing overhead cost (in the numerator) and the budgeted number of units (in the denominator).

Refer to Exhibit 24.11 for the calculation of the fixed manufacturing overhead variances. The two variances we calculate for fixed manufacturing overhead relate directly to the numerator and the denominator in the fixed overhead rate. The fixed overhead spending variance, which relates to the numerator, is the difference between the actual fixed manufacturing overhead cost and budgeted fixed manufacturing overhead cost. The fixed overhead volume variance, which relates to the denominator, is the difference between the actual production volume and budgeted production volume. Essentially, if managers produce more units than allowed for in the budget, they will apply too much fixed overhead cost to the product. On the other hand, if they do not produce as many units as allowed for in the budget, they will apply too little fixed overhead cost to the product.

Coach's Tip

Although the model for analyzing fixed manufacturing overhead variances looks similar to the model we used to analyze the variable costs, it is actually quite different. As such, the interpretation of the variances is very different.

Exhibit 24.11   Calculation of Fixed Overhead Variances

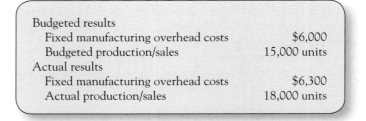

```
                          Fixed overhead
                            variances

   Actual          Budgeted            Applied
   FOH cost        FOH cost            FOH cost
              FOH Rate × Budgeted Units   FOH Rate × Actual Units

      Fixed overhead              Fixed overhead
      spending variance           volume variance

   (Budgeted – Actual FOH Costs)   FOH Rate × (Actual Units – Budgeted Units)
```

FOH: Fixed manufacturing overhead
FOH Rate: Budgeted FOH cost / Budgeted units

To apply the framework in Exhibit 24.11, assume that Cold Stone Creamery's fixed manufacturing costs were as follows:

Budgeted results	
Fixed manufacturing overhead costs	$6,000
Budgeted production/sales	15,000 units
Actual results	
Fixed manufacturing overhead costs	$6,300
Actual production/sales	18,000 units

Substituting these numbers into Exhibit 24.11 produces the results in Exhibit 24.12.

The fixed overhead spending variance is the difference between actual ($6,300) and budgeted ($6,000) fixed overhead cost. It is unfavorable because actual costs were $300 more than budgeted. Perhaps managers failed to anticipate an increase in fixed costs. Even though fixed costs are considered to be independent of volume, they can still change over time as the cost of items such as rent, insurance, and supervision increases.

The fixed overhead volume is driven by the difference in actual production (18,000 units) and budgeted production (15,000 units). Multiplying the 3,000 unit difference by the $0.40 fixed overhead rate results in a $1,200 favorable volume variance. It is favorable because producing more units than expected drives down the cost per unit (getting more volume out of the same cost). But remember that the fixed overhead rate was set in advance based on 15,000 units. The volume variance simply tells managers that they should have been basing the fixed overhead rate on 18,000 units instead of 15,000 units.

Exhibit 24.12 Calculation of Cold Stone Creamery's Fixed Overhead Variances

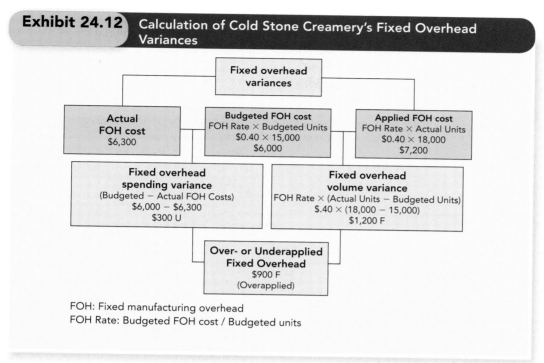

FOH: Fixed manufacturing overhead
FOH Rate: Budgeted FOH cost / Budgeted units

Coach's Tip

Note that the fixed overhead volume variance is the difference between the master budget volume and the flexible budget volume. This is the only time the master budget is used to calculate a cost variance.

Over- or underapplied fixed overhead is the sum of the fixed overhead spending and volume variances. Here, the total fixed overhead variance is $900 favorable because the fixed overhead spending variance was $300 unfavorable and the fixed overhead volume variance was $1,200 favorable ($300 U + $1,200 F = $900 F). This total variance also shows that fixed manufacturing overhead was $900 overapplied, because actual fixed overhead was less than applied. This means that the overhead rate used to apply fixed overhead was too high. Instead of applying fixed overhead cost at the rate of $.40 per unit ($6,000 / 15,000 units), the company **should** have applied it at the rate of $.35 per unit ($6,300 / 18,000 units). In many ways, the fixed overhead variance reflects managers' ability to accurately predict fixed costs and volume, and has very little to do with how well the manager is controlling costs.

Summary of Variances

In this chapter we calculated many different variances. You are probably beginning to suffer from calculation overload. How in the world are you going to remember all those variances and how to calculate them? Exhibit 24.13 provides a summary of all of the variances calculated in this chapter, along with a definition of the terms used in the formulas.

Of course calculating the variance is only part of it. Here are some other tips for understanding and interpreting the variances.

- Variances are always calculated by comparing actual results to budgeted, or standard, results. Variances signal managers that they are (or are not) achieving their plans so they can take corrective action if necessary.

- Companies try to hold specific managers responsible for specific variances, while removing the effects of factors that are beyond managers' control.

- The formulas for variances allow only one factor such as price, quantity, or volume to change, while holding everything else constant at either actual or standard values (depending on the type of variance).

- The driving factor for a variance always appears in parentheses in the formula, as well as in the name of the variance. If you forget the name of a particular variance, just look at the terms in parentheses to figure out the cause of the variance.
- Try not to memorize rules or rely on the formulas to determine whether a variance is favorable or unfavorable; just think about it. Spending or using more of a variable resource is unfavorable. Using more of a fixed resource is favorable because it drives down the fixed cost per unit.

Exhibit 24.13 Summary of Variance Formulas and Terminology

Variance	Formula
DM Price Variance	$AQ \times (SP - AP)$
DM Quantity Variance	$SP \times (SQ - AQ)$
DM Spending Variance	Sum of DM Price and DM Quantity Variances
DL Rate Variance	$AH \times (SR - AR)$
DL Efficiency Variance	$SR \times (SH - AH)$
DL Spending Variance	Sum of DL Rate and DL Efficiency Variances
VOH Rate Variance	$AH \times (SR - AR)$
VOH Efficiency Variance	$SR \times (SH - AH)$
VOH Spending Variance	Sum of VOH Rate and VOH Efficiency Variances
Over or Underapplied VOH	Applied − Actual VOH
FOH Spending Variance	Budgeted − Actual FOH Costs
FOH Budget Variance	Same as FOH Spending Variance
FOH Volume Variance	FOH Rate × (Actual − Budgeted Units)
Over or Under applied FOH	Applied − Actual FOH

Where:

DM:	Direct materials
DL:	Direct labor
VOH:	Variable manufacturing overhead
FOH:	Fixed manufacturing overhead
AP:	Actual price of input
AQ:	Actual quantity of input
SP:	Standard price of input
SQ:	Standard quantity of input allowed for actual units produced
AR:	Actual labor rate (or VOH rate for VOH variances)
AH:	Actual labor hours
SR:	Standard labor rate (or standard VOH rate for VOH variances)
SH:	Standard labor hours allowed for actual units produced

Finally, you need to understand how all of the variances fit together. See Exhibit 24.14 for a summary of all of the manufacturing cost variances calculated in this chapter, and how they can be used to explain the difference in Cold Stone Creamery's actual and budgeted results.

In a standard cost system, all manufacturing costs are initially recorded at the standard amount, in either an inventory or the Cost of Goods Sold account. Recall that Cold Stone's standard unit cost was $2.00. Thus, cost of goods sold for 18,000 units would be $36,000 (18,000 × $2.00). The company's actual manufacturing cost was $36,800. Thus, the overall variance in manufacturing cost was $800 unfavorable.

Throughout the accounting period, the individual variances are accumulated in variance accounts before being closed to the Cost of Goods Sold account at the end of the period. The $800 adjustment to Cost of Goods Sold will increase it from the standard cost of $36,000 to the actual cost of $36,800. The specific journal entries needed to record manufacturing costs and variances in a standard cost system are illustrated in Supplement 24A.

Exhibit 24.14   Summary of Variances for Cold Stone Creamery

COLD STONE CREAMERY

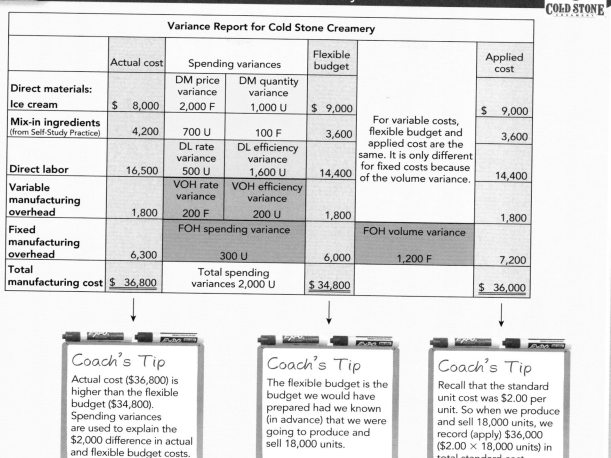

	Actual cost	Spending variances		Flexible budget		Applied cost
		DM price variance	**DM quantity variance**		For variable costs, flexible budget and applied cost are the same. It is only different for fixed costs because of the volume variance.	
Direct materials: Ice cream	$ 8,000	2,000 F	1,000 U	$ 9,000		$ 9,000
Mix-in ingredients (from Self-Study Practice)	4,200	700 U	100 F	3,600		3,600
		DL rate variance	**DL efficiency variance**			
Direct labor	16,500	500 U	1,600 U	14,400		14,400
Variable manufacturing overhead		**VOH rate variance**	**VOH efficiency variance**			
	1,800	200 F	200 U	1,800		1,800
Fixed manufacturing overhead		**FOH spending variance**			**FOH volume variance**	
	6,300	300 U		6,000	1,200 F	7,200
Total manufacturing cost	$ 36,800	Total spending variances 2,000 U		$ 34,800		$ 36,000

Coach's Tip

Actual cost ($36,800) is higher than the flexible budget ($34,800). Spending variances are used to explain the $2,000 difference in actual and flexible budget costs.

Coach's Tip

The flexible budget is the budget we would have prepared had we known (in advance) that we were going to produce and sell 18,000 units.

Coach's Tip

Recall that the standard unit cost was $2.00 per unit. So when we produce and sell 18,000 units, we record (apply) $36,000 ($2.00 × 18,000 units) in total standard cost.

Demonstration Case

Bunko Beds produces bunk beds for children. It sells the beds through Pottery Barn Kids and other retail outlets. The standard cost of producing one of Bunko's most popular beds follows:

STANDARD COST CARD FOR BUNKO BEDS			
	Standard Quantity	Standard Price	Standard Unit Cost
Direct materials (1 × 12″ treated pine)	50 ft.	$ 2.50 per ft.	$125.00
Direct labor	5 hrs.	10.00 per hr.	50.00
Manufacturing overhead costs			
Variable manufacturing overhead (based on direct labor hours)	5 hrs.	5.00 per hr.	25.00
Fixed manufacturing overhead $120,000 / 3,000 units = $40 per unit			40.00
Standard manufacturing cost per unit			$240.00

Bunko's master budget was based on the planned production and sale of 3,000 units. Actual results were as follows:

- Produced 2,500 units.
- Purchased and used 130,000 feet of direct materials at a total cost of $312,000.
- Total direct labor cost was $123,750 for 11,250 hours.
- Variable overhead cost was $54,000.
- Fixed overhead cost was $115,000.

Required:
Calculate the following variances and label them as favorable (F) or unfavorable (U).

1. Direct materials variances:

    a. Direct materials price variance.
    b. Direct materials quantity variance.
    c. Total direct materials spending variance.

2. Direct labor variances:

    a. Direct labor rate variance.
    b. Direct labor efficiency variance.
    c. Total direct labor spending variance.

3. Variable manufacturing overhead variances:

    a. Variable overhead rate variance.
    b. Variable overhead efficiency variance.
    c. Total variable overhead spending variance.

4. Fixed manufacturing overhead variances:

    a. Fixed overhead spending variance.
    b. Fixed overhead volume variance.
    c. Over- or underapplied fixed overhead.

Suggested Solution

1. Direct materials variances:

    AQ = 130,000 ft.
    AP = $312,000 / 130,000 = $2.40 per ft.
    SQ = 50 ft. × 2,500 actual units = 125,000 ft.
    SP = $2.50 per ft.

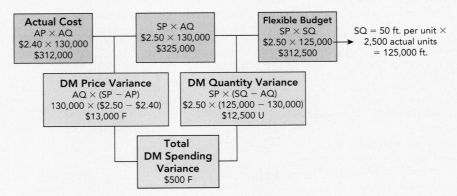

2. Direct labor variances:

    AH = 11,250 hrs.
    AR = $123,750 / 11,250 = $11 per hr.

SH = 5 hrs. × 2,500 actual units = 12,500 hrs.
SR = $10 per hr.

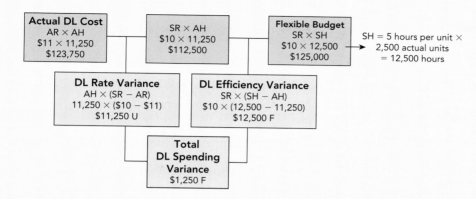

3. Variable manufacturing overhead variances:

AH = 11,250
AR = $54,000 / 11,250 = $4.80 per hour
SH = 5 hrs. × 2,500 units = 12,500
SR = $5.00 per hour

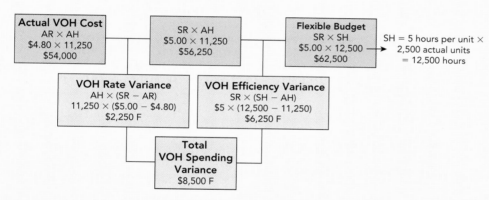

4. Fixed manufacturing overhead variances:

Actual FOH = $115,000
Actual units = 2,500
Budgeted FOH = $120,000
Budgeted Units = 3,000
FOH Rate = $120,000 / 3,000 = $40

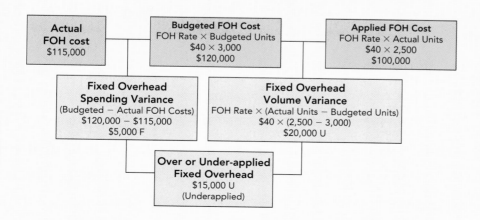

Supplement 24A
Recording Standard Costs and Variances in a Standard Cost System

This supplement focuses on the journal entries used to record the variances generated by a standard cost system. In preparing journal entries for a standard cost system, keep in mind these common rules:

- The initial debit to an inventory account (Raw Materials, Work in Process, or Finished Goods) and the eventual debit to Cost of Goods Sold should be based on the standard, not actual, cost.

- Cash, payables, and other accounts, such as accumulated depreciation or prepaid assets, should be credited for the actual cost incurred.

- The difference between the standard cost (debit) and the actual cost (credit) should be recorded as the cost variance.

- Unfavorable variances should appear as debit entries; favorable variances should appear as credit entries.

- At the end of the accounting period, all variances should be closed to the Cost of Goods Sold account to adjust the standard cost up or down to the actual cost.

Recall from earlier chapters that manufacturing costs are initially recorded in inventory and are later recognized as Cost of Goods Sold as in Exhibit 24A.1.

A standard cost system initially records manufacturing costs at the standard rather than the actual amounts. Thus, the journal entries used to record manufacturing costs always involve a debit to an inventory account or to Cost of Goods Sold for the standard amount.

We illustrate this process using the variances we calculated for Cold Stone Creamery. Because the company does not make the product until a customer orders it, there is no need to keep Work in Process or Finished Goods Inventory accounts. Instead, we can bypass those accounts and transfer raw materials costs directly from the Raw Materials Inventory account to the Cost of Goods Sold account. Similarly, we can record direct labor and manufacturing overhead costs directly in the Cost of Goods Sold account (see Exhibit 24A.2).

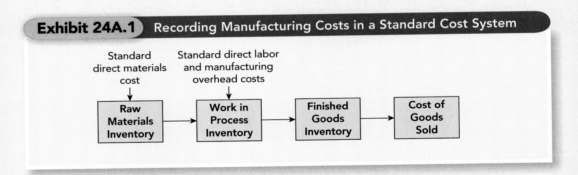

Exhibit 24A.1   Recording Manufacturing Costs in a Standard Cost System

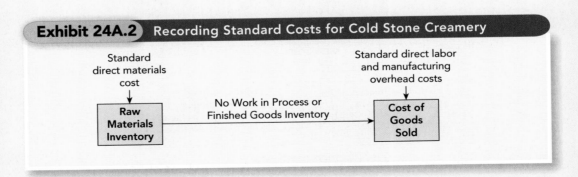

Exhibit 24A.2   Recording Standard Costs for Cold Stone Creamery

Direct Materials Costs

Let's start with the entry to record the purchase of raw materials. Assume Cold Stone's price and quantity standards for ice cream follow:

Direct costs	Standard Quantity	Standard Price	Standard Unit Cost
Ice cream	10 oz.	$0.05 per oz.	$0.50

During the period, the purchasing manager bought 200,000 ounces of ice cream on account for a total of $8,000, at an average actual price of $.04 per ounce. The journal entry to record the purchase of raw materials would be:

	Debit	Credit
Raw Materials Inventory (200,000 × $0.05)	10,000	
Direct Materials Price Variance (200,000 × $0.01)		2,000
Accounts Payable (200,000 × $0.04)		8,000

Coach's Tip

Notice that the variance is the "plug figure" that makes the debits and credits balance. Here the actual cost (credit) is less than the standard cost (debit), resulting in a favorable (credit) variance.

Notice that the debit to Raw Materials Inventory is based on the standard price per unit of $0.05, but the credit to Accounts Payable is based on the actual price of $0.04 per unit. The difference between the actual price and the standard price is the direct materials price variance calculated earlier by multiplying the $0.01 difference in price by 200,000 ounces of ice cream. This variance is favorable because the actual price was less than the standard price.

Next let's record the journal entry to transfer the cost of the ice cream out of Raw Materials Inventory and into Cost of Goods Sold. During the period, Cold Stone's employees used 200,000 ounces of ice cream to produce 18,000 units. The entry to transfer the cost of the ice cream from Raw Materials Inventory to Cost of Goods Sold is:

	Debit	Credit
Cost of Goods Sold (180,000 ounces × $0.05)	9,000	
Direct Materials Quantity Variance (20,000 × $0.05)	1,000	
Raw Materials Inventory (200,000 × $0.05)		10,000

Coach's Tip

A debit entry reflects an unfavorable variance. The quantity of materials actually taken from Raw Materials Inventory (a credit) was more than the standard quantity that should have been used to make 18,000 units (a debit).

Notice that the amount debited to Cost of Goods Sold is based on the flexible budget, or what it **should have cost** the company to produce 18,000 units. Because each unit requires 10 ounces of ice cream, we multiply the standard quantity of 180,000 ounces by the standard price of $0.05 per ounce. The amount that is transferred out of Raw Materials Inventory, however, is based on the 200,000 ounces that were actually used multiplied by the standard price of $0.05. When we multiply the 20,000 ounce difference by the standard price of $0.05, we get an unfavorable direct materials quantity variance of $1,000. Notice that this unfavorable variance appears as a debit entry; a favorable variance would appear as a credit entry.

Before you continue, complete the Self-Study Practice to see whether you can record the purchase and use of Cold Stone Creamery's mix-in ingredients.

SELF-STUDY PRACTICE

Cold Stone Creamery's standard cost card for mix-in ingredients follows.

Direct costs	Standard Quantity	Standard Price	Standard Unit Cost
Mix-in ingredients	2 oz.	$0.10 per oz.	$0.20

Actual results were as follows:

- Purchased 35,000 ounces of mix-in ingredients at a total cost of $4,200, for an average cost of $0.12 per ounce.
- Used 35,000 ounces of mix-in ingredients to produce the 18,000 units sold.

Prepare the journal entries to record the purchase of raw materials and the transfer of their cost to the Cost of Goods Sold account.

After you have finished, check your answers with the solutions at the bottom of the page.

Direct Labor and Manufacturing Overhead Costs

The entries to record direct labor and manufacturing overhead costs are simpler than those to record direct materials costs because the cost can be recorded directly into Cost of Goods Sold. The following journal entries record direct labor, variable manufacturing overhead, and fixed manufacturing overhead costs. The entry to record direct labor costs would be:

	Debit	Credit
Cost of Goods Sold (1,800 hrs. × $8.00 per hr.)	14,400	
Direct Labor Rate Variance [2,000 × ($8.00 − 8.25)]	500	
Direct Labor Efficiency Variance [$8.00 × (1,800 − 2,000)]	1,600	
Wages Payable or Cash (2,000 hrs. × $8.25 per hr.)		16,500

The entry to record variable manufacturing overhead costs would be:

	Debit	Credit
Cost of Goods Sold (1,800 hrs. × $1.00 per hr.)	1,800	
Variable Overhead Efficiency Variance [$1.00 × (1,800 − 2,000)]	200	
Variable Overhead Rate Variance [2,000 × ($1.00 − $0.90)]		200
Wages Payable, Cash, etc. (2,000 hrs. × $0.90 per hr.)		1,800

Solution to
Self-Study Practice

Purchase of Raw Materials

Raw Materials Inventory (35,000 × $0.10)	3,500	
Direct Materials Price Variance	700	
Accounts Payable (35,000 × $0.12)		4,200

Transfer to Cost of Goods Sold When Used

Cost of Goods Sold (36,000 × $0.10)	3,600	
Direct Materials Quantity Variance		100
Raw Materials Inventory (35,000 × $0.10)		3,500

The entry to record fixed manufacturing overhead costs would be:

	Debit	Credit
Cost of Goods Sold (18,000 units × $0.40 per unit)	7,200	
Fixed Overhead Spending Variance ($6,000 − $6,300)	300	
Fixed Overhead Volume Variance (18,000 − 15,000 units) × $0.40		1,200
Salaries Payable or Cash		6,300

Cost of Goods Sold and Cost Variance Summary

After all variances have been recorded, the Cost of Goods Sold and variance summary account[1] will appear as follows:

Cost of Goods Sold		
Ice Cream	9,000	
Mix-ins	3,600	
Direct Labor	14,400	
Var. Mfg. Overhead	1,800	
Fixed Mfg. Overhead	7,200	
Applied/Standard Cost	36,000	
Variance Adjustment	800	
Actual Cost of Goods Sold	36,800	

Cost Variance Summary			
Ice Cream Quantity Variance	1,000	2,000	Ice Cream Price Variance
Mix-in Price Variance	700	100	Mix-in Quantity Variance
DL Rate Variance	500	200	VOH Rate Variance
DL Efficiency Variance	1,600	1,200	FOH Volume Variance
VOH Efficiency Variance	200		
FOH Spending Variance	300		
		Balance	800

Notice that Cost of Goods Sold in the previous T-account is based initially on the standard cost of $36,000. The standard cost card shown at the beginning of this chapter (see Exhibit 24.1 on page 989) indicated that each unit produced should cost $2.00. Because Cold Stone Creamery sold 18,000 units, the cost of goods sold in the T-account is stated initially at $36,000.

The Cost Variance Summary account indicates how much higher or lower the actual costs were compared to the standard costs. Overall, Cold Stone had more unfavorable variances than favorable variances, resulting in a debit (unfavorable) balance of $800. At the end of the accounting period, each individual variance is closed to Cost of Goods Sold, which has the net effect of increasing its amount by $800.

The combined entry to close the variance accounts to Cost of Goods Sold would be:

	Debit	Credit
Ice Cream Price Variance	2,000	
Mix-In Quantity Variance	100	
Variable Overhead Rate Variance	200	
Fixed Overhead Volume Variance	1,200	
Cost of Goods Sold	800	
Ice Cream Quantity Variance		1,000
Mix-In Price Variance		700
Direct Labor Rate Variance		500
Direct Labor Efficiency Variance		1,600
Variable Overhead Efficiency Variance		200
Fixed Overhead Spending Variance		300

Notice that the closing entry debits the favorable variances to eliminate their credit balance and credits the unfavorable variances to eliminate their debit balance. The "plug figure" that makes the debits and credits equal is used to increase or decrease the Cost of Goods Sold account. In this case, we debited (increased) Cost of Goods Sold by $800, which raises it from the standard cost of $36,000 to the actual cost of $36,800.

Adjusting the Cost of Goods Sold account is the easiest and most common method of dealing with variances. However, if Cold Stone had had significant Work in Process or Finished Goods inventory, adjusting those accounts may also have been necessary. That treatment of the variance accounts, which is rare in practice, is beyond the scope of this textbook.

---

[1] For the sake of simplicity, we have shown all variances in a single summary account. In reality, each variance would be accumulated in a separate account so that the manager who is responsible for the variance can monitor it.

Chapter Summary

LO1 Describe the standard-setting process and explain how standard costs relate to budgets and variances. p. 989

- Standard costs, which are set at the beginning of the accounting period to reflect what management believes costs should be, should be set so that they are difficult but not impossible to achieve.
- The two types of standard are price standard and quantity standard.
- The standard price is the amount that **should** be paid for a particular quantity of input.
- The standard quantity is the amount of input that **should** be used to produce a single unit of output.
- Budgeted costs are based on the standard costs for inputs multiplied by a specific level of output.
- Variances are the difference between actual and budgeted or standard costs.

LO2 Prepare a flexible budget and show how total costs change with sales volume. p. 990

- A master budget is a static budget based on the estimated sales volume.
- A flexible budget shows how total costs are expected to change if actual sales are more or less than expected.
- A flexible budget is used to evaluate managerial performance after the fact by separating the effect of spending (that is, cost control) from the effects of volume.
- Spending variances are calculated by comparing actual costs to the flexible budget.
- Volume variances are calculated by comparing the flexible budget to the master budget.

LO3 Calculate and interpret the direct materials price and quantity variances. p. 994

- The direct materials price variance is driven by the difference between the actual and the standard price paid for direct materials.
- The direct materials quantity variance is driven by the difference between the actual quantity and the standard quantity of materials used in production. The standard quantity should be based on the actual volume of output.
- The direct materials purchasing manager is responsible for the direct materials price variance. The production manager is responsible for the direct materials quantity (usage) variance.
- The total direct materials spending variance is the sum of the direct materials price and direct materials quantity variances.

LO4 Calculate and interpret the direct labor rate and efficiency variances. p. 996

- The direct labor rate variance is driven by the difference in the actual direct labor rate and the standard direct labor rate.
- The direct labor efficiency variance is driven by the difference between the actual number of labor hours and the standard number of labor hours allowed for the actual volume of output.
- Assigning direct responsibility for the direct labor rate variance is difficult. The production manager is responsible for the direct labor efficiency variance.
- The total direct labor spending variance is the sum of the direct labor rate and direct labor efficiency variances.

LO5 Calculate and interpret the variable overhead rate and efficiency variances. p. 998

- The variable overhead rate variance is driven by the difference between the actual variable overhead cost and the standard variable overhead cost per unit of the allocation base (such as direct labor hours).
- The variable overhead efficiency variance is driven by the difference between the actual number of labor hours and the standard number of labor hours allowed for production. It is a mirror reflection of the direct labor efficiency variance.
- The total variable overhead spending variance is the sum of the variable overhead rate and the variable overhead efficiency variances.

LO6 Calculate and interpret the fixed overhead spending and volume variances. p. 1001

- The fixed overhead spending variance is the difference between actual fixed overhead cost and budgeted fixed overhead cost.
- The fixed overhead volume variance is driven by the difference between actual production volume and budgeted production volume.
- The fixed overhead volume variance is favorable when a company produces more units than expected because the fixed cost is spread over more units.
- The fixed overhead volume variance is unfavorable when a company produces fewer units than expected because the fixed cost is spread over fewer units.

Key Terms

Direct Labor Efficiency Variance (p. 997)

Direct Labor Rate Variance (p. 997)

Direct Labor Spending Variance (p. 997)

Direct Materials Price Variance (p. 995)

Direct Materials Quantity Variance (p. 995)

Direct Materials Spending Variance (p. 996)

Easily Attainable Standard (p. 988)

Favorable Variance (p. 989)

Fixed Overhead Spending Variance (p. 1002)

Fixed Overhead Volume Variance (p. 1002)

Flexible Budget (p. 990)

Ideal Standard (p. 988)

Over- or Underapplied Fixed Overhead (p. 1003)

Spending Variances (p. 992)

Standard Cost Card (p. 989)

Standard Cost System (p. 988)

Standard Unit Cost (p. 989)

Static Budget (p. 990)

Unfavorable Variance (p. 990)

Variance (p. 987)

Variable Overhead Efficiency Variance (p. 987)

Variable Overhead Rate Variance (p. 999)

Volume Variance (p. 992)

See complete glossary in back of text.

Questions

1. Briefly describe the difference between the budgetary planning and control processes.

2. What are standard costs? When are they set?

3. Explain a standard cost system and how a company uses it.

4. What is the difference between ideal and easily attainable standards?

5. What type of standard is best for motivating individuals to work hard?

6. Briefly describe the two types of standards on which a standard cost system relies.

7. What is a standard cost card and why is it important?

8. How do the terms standard and budget relate to one another and how do they differ?

9. Explain what the terms favorable variance and unfavorable variance mean.

10. How do the master budget, flexible budget, and static budget differ from one another?

11. What type of variance is created by comparing the master budget to the flexible budget?

12. What type of variance is calculated by comparing actual costs to the costs in the flexible budget?

13. The spending variance can be separated into two components. Name and briefly describe them.

14. What are the two direct materials variances? Who is most likely responsible for each of these?

15. What are the two direct labor variances? Who is most likely responsible for each of these?

16. What are the two variable overhead variances? Who is most likely responsible for each of these?

17. What are the two fixed overhead variances? Who is most likely responsible for each of these?

Multiple Choice

1. In general, variances tell managers
   a. Nothing.
   b. Whom to promote and whom to fire.
   c. Whether budgeted goals are being achieved.
   d. Which departments are running at full capacity.

   Quiz 24-1
   www.mhhe.com/LLPW1e

2. In distinguishing between budgets and standards, which of the following is true?
   a. The terms mean exactly the same thing.
   b. Standards are used to develop budgets.
   c. Budgets are used to develop standards.
   d. Budgets and standards are unrelated.

3. Variances are always noted as favorable or unfavorable. What do these terms indicate?
   a. Whether actual costs are more or less than expected costs.
   b. Whether the manager in a particular department is doing a good job.

   c. Whether a company is performing as well as its competitors.
   d. All of the above.

4. What type of budget is an integrated set of operating and financial budgets that reflects managements' expectations for a given sales level, and what type shows how budgeted costs and revenues will change across different levels of sales?
   a. Flexible budget, master budget.
   b. Standard budget, flexible budget.
   c. Master budget, static budget.
   d. Master budget, flexible budget.

5. When evaluating performance in a standard cost system, actual results are compared to
   a. The flexible budget.
   b. The master budget.
   c. The variances.
   d. Last year's actual results.

6. Spending variances may be broken down into
   a. Price and quantity variances.
   b. Price and volume variances.
   c. Volume and quantity variances.
   d. Quantity and quality variances.

7. Temecula Company has calculated its direct materials price variance to be $1,000 favorable and its direct materials quantity variance to be $3,000 unfavorable. Which of the following could explain both of these variances?
   a. The production manager has recently hired more skilled laborers.
   b. The purchases manager found less expensive raw materials but they were also of lesser quality.
   c. A machine in the factory malfunctioned resulting in considerable wasted raw materials.
   d. The purchases manager bought higher quality materials.

8. In producing its product, Ranger Company used 1,500 hours of direct labor at an actual cost of $15 per hour. The standard for Ranger's production level is 1,400 hours at $14 per hour. What is Ranger's direct labor rate variance?
   a. $1,500 favorable.
   b. $1,400 favorable.
   c. $1,500 unfavorable.
   d. $1,400 unfavorable.

9. In producing its product, Ranger Company used 1,500 pounds of direct materials at an actual cost of $1.50 per pound. The standard for Ranger's production level was 1,400 pounds at $1.40 per pound. What is Ranger's direct materials quantity variance?
   a. $150 favorable.
   b. $140 favorable.
   c. $150 unfavorable.
   d. $140 unfavorable.

10. An unfavorable fixed overhead volume variance indicates that a company
    a. manufactured fewer units than it expected.
    b. manufactured more units than it expected.
    c. underestimated its total fixed overhead cost.
    d. overestimated its total fixed overhead cost.

Solutions to Multiple-Choice Questions

1. c   2. b   3. a   4. d   5. a   6. a   7. b
8. c   9. d   10. a

Mini Exercises Available with McGraw-Hill's Homework Manager

LO1   **M24-1 Creating a Grading Scale Based on Ideal, Tight but Attainable and Easily Attainable Standards**

Consider the grading scale for a university class that has 500 possible points. The possible course grades are A, B, C, D, and F. Create a grading scale for the class that would fall into each of the following categories: an ideal standard, an easily attainable standard, and a tight but attainable standard.

LO2   **M24-2 Explaining the Costs That Will Change with Flexible Budget Activity**

When preparing a company's flexible budget, which manufacturing cost(s) will change as the volume increases or decreases? Which manufacturing cost(s) will not change as the volume changes?

LO1   **M24-3 Describing How Standards Are Set in a Standard Cost System**

Dabney Company manufactures widgets and would like to use a standard cost system. Explain how Dabney will determine the standards for direct materials and direct labor to use in its costing system.

LO4   **M24-4 Calculating Unknown Values for Direct Labor Variances**

For each of the following independent cases, fill in the missing amounts in the following table.

Case	Direct Labor Rate Variance	Direct Labor Efficiency Variance	Direct Labor Spending Variance
A	$ 750 F	$1,200 F	$?
B	2,000 U	?	3,500 U
C	1,000 F	?	1,800 U
D	?	500 F	2,500 U
E	?	1,100 U	1,950 U
F	650 F	1,150 U	?

LO3   **M24-5 Interpreting Direct Materials Cost Variances**

Phantom Corp. has calculated its direct materials price and quantity variances to be $500 favorable and $800 unfavorable, respectively. Phantom's production manager believes that these variances indicate that the purchasing department is doing a good job but production is doing a poor job. Explain whether the production manager's conclusions are correct.

M24-6 Calculating Direct Materials Cost Variances
Randolph, Inc., has determined a standard direct materials cost per unit of $6 (2 feet × $3 per foot). Last month, Randolph purchased and used 4,200 feet of direct materials for which it paid $12,180. The company produced and sold 2,000 units during the month. Calculate the direct materials price, quantity, and spending variances.

LO3

M24-7 Calculating Direct Labor Cost Variances
Clayton Corp. has determined a standard labor cost per unit of $12 (1 hour × $12 per hour). Last month, Clayton incurred 1,900 direct labor hours for which it paid $23,940. The company also produced and sold 2,000 units during the month. Calculate the direct labor rate, efficiency, and spending variances.

LO4

M24-8 Calculating Variable Manufacturing Overhead Variances
Montour Company has determined a standard variable overhead rate of $1.10 per direct labor hour and expects 1 labor hour per unit produced. Last month, Montour incurred 1,900 actual direct labor hours in the production of 2,000 units. The company has also determined that its actual variable overhead rate is $1.20 per direct labor hour. Calculate the variable overhead rate and efficiency variances as well as the total amount of over- or underapplied variable overhead.

LO5

M24-9 Calculating Fixed Manufacturing Overhead Variances
LaPaz Company has determined a standard fixed overhead rate of $0.30 per unit based on an expectation of 30,000 units and $9,000 fixed manufacturing overhead. Actual results for the month of October reveal that LaPaz produced 28,000 units and had $9,200 in fixed manufacturing overhead costs. Calculate LaPaz's fixed overhead spending variance, fixed overhead volume variance, and the total amount of over- or underapplied fixed overhead.

LO6

M24-10 Preparing Journal Entries to Record Direct Material Costs and Variances (Supplement)
During May, Willett Corp. purchased direct materials for 4,250 units at a cost of $61,625. Willett's standard materials cost per unit is $14. Prepare the journal entry to record this transaction.

M24-11 Preparing Journal Entries to Record Direct Labor Costs and Variances (Supplement)
Bowman Company reported the following information for the month of November. The standard cost of labor for the month was $38,000, but actual wages paid were $40,000. Bowman has calculated its direct labor rate and efficiency variances to be $2,500 unfavorable and $500 favorable, respectively. Prepare the necessary journal entry to record Bowman's direct labor cost for the month, assuming that standard labor costs are recorded directly to Cost of Goods Sold.

Exercises   Available with McGraw-Hill's Homework Manager

E24-1 Calculating Unknown Values for Direct Materials and Direct Labor Variances
Three Pigs Company manufactures cast-iron barbeque cookware. During a recent windstorm, it lost some of its cost accounting records. Three Pigs has managed to reconstruct portions of its standard cost system database but is still missing a few pieces of information.

LO3, 4

	Direct Materials	Direct Labor
Standard amount per pan produced	2.5 lb.	1.25 hr.
Standard cost	$4.00 per lb.	$16.00 per hr.
Actual amount used per pan produced	2.4 lb.	1.20 hr.
Actual cost	$4.10 per lb.	$15.50 per hr.
Actual number of pans produced and sold	2,500 pans	2,500 pans
Direct materials price variance	?	
Direct materials quantity variance	?	
Direct materials spending variance	?	
Direct labor rate variance		?
Direct labor efficiency variance		?
Direct labor spending variance		?

Required:

Use the information in the table to determine the unknown amounts. You may assume that Three Pigs does not keep any raw materials on hand.

LO2   E24-2 Preparing a Flexible Budget for Manufacturing Costs

Follett Company makes handwoven blankets. The company's master budget appears in the first column of the table.

	Master Budget (5,000 units)	Flexible Budget (4,000 units)	Flexible Budget (6,000 units)	Flexible Budget (7,000 units)
Direct materials	$ 7,500			
Direct labor	20,000			
Variable manufacturing overhead	8,000			
Fixed manufacturing overhead	18,000			
Total manufacturing cost	$53,500			

Required:

Complete the table by preparing Follett's flexible budget for 4,000, 6,000 and 7,000 units.

LO3   E24-3 Interpreting the Direct Materials Price and Quantity Variances

Cody's Collar Company makes custom leather pet collars. The company expects each collar to require 1.5 feet of leather and predicts leather will cost $2.25 per foot. Suppose Cody's made 60 collars during February. For these 60 collars, the company actually averaged 1.6 feet of leather per collar and paid $2.00 per foot for it.

Required:

1. Compute the standard direct materials cost per unit.

2. Without performing any calculations, determine whether the direct materials price variance will be favorable or unfavorable.

3. Without performing any calculations, determine whether the direct materials quantity variance will be favorable or unfavorable.

4. Give a potential explanation for this pattern of variances.

5. Where would you begin to investigate the variances?

6. Calculate the direct materials price and quantity variances.

LO3, 4   E24-4 Calculating Direct Materials and Direct Labor Variances

Rub-a-Dub Dogs is a local pet grooming shop owned by Max Aslett. Max has prepared the following standard cost card for each dog bath given.

	Standard Quantity	Standard Rate	Standard Unit Cost
Direct costs			
Shampoo	2 oz.	$ 0.10 per oz.	$0.20
Water	20 gal.	$ 0.05 per gal.	1.00
Direct labor	.75 hr.	$ 9.00 per hr.	6.75

During the month of July, Max's employees gave 345 baths. The actual results were 725 ounces of shampoo used (total cost $87), 6,500 gallons of water used (cost of $390), and labor costs for 250 hours (cost of $2,300).

Required:

1. Calculate Rub-a-Dub Dogs' direct materials variances for both shampoo and water for the month of July.

2. Calculate Rub-a-Dub Dogs' direct labor variances for the month of July.

3. Identify a possible cause of each variance.

E24-5 Preparing Journal Entries to Record Direct Materials and Direct Labor Costs and Variances (Supplement)

Refer to the information presented in E24-4 regarding Rub-a-Dub Dogs.

Required:

Prepare journal entries to record Rub-a-Dub's July direct materials and labor transactions. (**Hint:** Record all costs directly to Cost of Goods Sold.)

E24-6 Calculating Direct Materials and Direct Labor Variances   LO3, 4

Lucky Charm Company makes handcrafted silver charms that attach to jewelry such as a necklace or bracelet. Each charm is adorned with two crystals of various colors. Standard costs follow.

	Standard Quantity	Standard Price (Rate)	Standard Unit Cost
Direct costs			
Silver	0.25 oz.	$20.00 per oz.	$ 5.00
Crystals	2	$ 0.25 per each	$ 0.50
Direct labor	1.5 hrs.	$15.00 per hr.	$22.50

During the month of January, Lucky Charm made 1,500 charms. The company used 350 ounces of silver (total cost of $7,350), 3,050 crystals (total cost of $701.50), and paid for 2,400 actual direct labor hours (cost of $34,800).

Required:

1. Calculate Lucky Charm's direct materials variances for silver and crystals for the month of January.

2. Calculate Lucky Charm's direct labor variances for the month of January.

3. Identify a possible cause of each variance.

E24-7 Preparing Journal Entries to Record Direct Material and Direct Labor Costs and Variances (Supplement)

Refer to the information in E24-6 regarding Lucky Charm Company.

Required:

Prepare journal entries to record Lucky Charm's January direct materials and labor transactions. (**Hint:** Record all costs directly to Cost of Goods Sold.)

E24-8 Calculating Variable and Fixed Manufacturing Overhead Variances   LO5, 6

Slim Shady Company (SSC) manufactures lamp shades. It applies variable overhead on the basis of the number of direct labor hours used. Information regarding SSC's overhead for the month of August follows.

	Standard Quantity	Standard Rate	Standard Unit Cost
Variable manufacturing overhead	0.5 direct labor hour per shade	$0.80 per direct labor hour	$0.40
Fixed manufacturing overhead ($30,000 / 24,000 units)			1.25

During August, SSC had the following actual results

Units produced and sold	25,000
Actual variable overhead	$ 9,490
Actual direct labor hours	13,000
Actual fixed overhead	$29,000

Required:

1. Compute SSC's variable overhead rate and efficiency variances as well as the over- or underapplied variable overhead.
2. Compute SSC's fixed overhead spending and volume variances as well as its over- or underapplied fixed overhead.

E24-9 Preparing Journal Entries to Record Manufacturing Overhead Cost and Variances (Supplement)
Refer to the information in E24-8 regarding Slim Shady Company.

Required:
Prepare journal entries to record SSC's overhead transactions for August.

LO5, 6

E24-10 Calculating Variable and Fixed Manufacturing Overhead Variances
ClearView Company manufactures clear plastic CD cases. It applies variable overhead based on the number of machine hours used. Information regarding ClearView's overhead for the month of December follows.

	Standard Quantity	Standard Rate	Standard Unit Cost
Variable manufacturing overhead	0.1 machine hours per case	$.50 per machine hour	$0.05
Fixed manufacturing overhead ($180,000 / 600,000 units)			0.30

During December, ClearView had the following actual results.

Number of units produced and sold	625,000
Actual variable overhead cost	$ 30,240
Actual machine hours	63,000
Actual fixed overhead	$ 195,000

Required:

1. Compute ClearView's variable overhead rate and efficiency variances as well as its over- or underapplied variable overhead.
2. Compute ClearView's fixed overhead spending and volume variances as well as its over- or underapplied FOH Fixed overhead.

E24-11 Preparing Journal Entries to Record Manufacturing Overhead Cost and Variances (Supplement)
Refer to the information presented in E24-10 regarding ClearView Company.

Required:
Prepare journal entries to record ClearView's overhead transactions for December.

Problems—Set A   **Available with McGraw-Hill's Homework Manager**

LO3, 4, 5, 6

PA24-1 Calculating Direct Material, Direct Labor, Variable Manufacturing Overhead, and Fixed Manufacturing Overhead Variances
Drink Well, Inc., manufactures custom-ordered commemorative beer steins. Its standard cost information follows.

	Standard Quantity	Standard Price (Rate)	Standard Unit Cost
Direct costs			
Clay	1.5 lbs.	$ 1.60 per lb.	$ 2.40
Direct labor	1.5 hrs.	$12.00 per hr.	18.00
Variable MOH		$ 1.20 per direct labor hour	1.80
Fixed MOH ($250,000 / 100,000 units)			2.50

Drink Well had the following actual results last year.

Number of units produced and sold	110,000
Number of pounds of clay used	180,000
Cost of clay	$ 279,000
Number of labor hours worked	150,000
Direct labor cost	$1,950,000
Variable overhead cost	$ 195,000
Fixed overhead cost	$ 295,000

Required:

1. Calculate Drink Well's direct materials variances.
2. Calculate Drink Well's direct labor variances.
3. Compute Drink Well's variable overhead rate and efficiency variances and its over- or underapplied variable overhead.
4. Compute Drink Well's fixed overhead spending and volume variances and its over- or underapplied fixed overhead.

PA24-2 Preparing Journal Entries to Record Direct Material, Direct Labor, Variable Manufacturing Overhead, and Fixed Manufacturing Overhead Costs and Variances (Supplement)

Refer to the information in PA24-1 for Drink Well. Prepare journal entries to record all its manufacturing costs for last year. Assume the company purchases raw materials as needed and does not maintain any ending inventories.

PA24-3 Calculating Direct Materials, Direct Labor, Variable Manufacturing Overhead, and Fixed Manufacturing Overhead Variances

LO3, 4, 5, 6

www.mhhe.com/LLPW1e

Darting Around Company manufactures dart boards. Its standard cost information follows.

	Standard Quantity	Standard Price (Rate)	Standard Unit Cost
Direct costs			
Corkboard	2.5 sq. ft.	$ 2.00 per sq. ft.	$ 5.00
Direct labor	1 hr.	$14.00 per hr.	14.00
Variable manufacturing overhead		$ .50 per direct labor hour	0.50
Fixed manufacturing overhead ($20,000 / 80,000 units)			0.25

Darting Around had the following actual results for the month of September.

Number of units produced and sold	70,000
Number of square feet of corkboard used	180,000
Cost of corkboard used	$378,000
Number of labor hours worked	75,000
Direct labor cost	$975,000
Variable overhead cost	$ 36,000
Fixed overhead cost	$ 25,000

Required:

1. Calculate Darting Around's direct materials variances.
2. Calculate Darting Around's direct labor variances.
3. Compute Darting Around's variable overhead rate and efficiency variances and its over- or underapplied variable overhead.
4. Compute Darting Around's fixed overhead spending and volume variances and its over- or underapplied fixed overhead.

PA24-4 Preparing Journal Entries to Record Direct Material, Direct Labor, Variable Manufacturing Overhead, and Fixed Manufacturing Overhead Costs and Variances (Supplement)
Refer to the information in PA24-3 for Darting Around Company. Prepare journal entries to record its manufacturing costs for September. Assume the company purchases raw materials as needed and does not maintain any ending inventories.

LO3, 4, 5, 6

www.mhhe.com/LLPW1e

PA24-5 Calculating Direct Materials, Direct Labor, Variable Manufacturing Overhead, and Fixed Manufacturing Overhead Variances
Catch a Wave Company manufactures surf boards. Its standard cost information follows.

	Standard Quantity	Standard Price (Rate)	Standard Unit Cost
Direct costs			
Fiberglass	15 sq. ft.	$ 5 per sq. ft.	$ 75.00
Direct labor	10 hrs.	$15 per hr.	150.00
Variable manufacturing overhead		$ 6 per direct labor hour	60.00
Fixed manufacturing overhead ($20,000 / 250 units)			80.00

Catch a Wave had the following actual results for the month of June.

Number of units produced and sold	260
Number of square feet of fiberglass used	4,100
Cost of fiberglass used	$22,550
Number of labor hours worked	2,550
Direct labor cost	$39,525
Variable overhead cost	$14,790
Fixed overhead cost	$20,500

Required:

1. Calculate Catch a Wave's direct materials variances.
2. Calculate Catch a Wave's direct labor variances.

3. Compute Catch a Wave's variable overhead rate and efficiency variances and its over- or underapplied variable overhead.

4. Compute Catch a Wave's fixed overhead spending and volume variances and its over- or underapplied fixed overhead.

PA24-6 Preparing Journal Entries to Record Direct Materials, Direct Labor, Variable Manufacturing Overhead, and Fixed Manufacturing Overhead Costs and Variances (Supplement)
Refer to the information in PA24-5 for Catch a Wave. Prepare journal entries to record all of its transactions for June. Assume the company purchases raw materials as needed and does not maintain any ending inventories.

Problems—Set B  Available with McGraw-Hill's Homework Manager

PB24-1 Calculating Direct Material, Direct Labor, Variable Manufacturing Overhead, and Fixed Manufacturing Overhead Variances

LO3, 4, 5, 6

CandleGlow, Inc., manufactures scented pillar candles. Its standard cost information for the month of February follows.

	Standard Quantity	Standard Price (Rate)	Standard Unit Cost
Direct costs			
Wax	15 oz.	$ 0.05 per oz.	$0.75
Direct labor	.25 hr.	$14.00 per hr.	3.50
Variable manufacturing overhead		$ 0.40 per direct labor hour	0.10
Fixed manufacturing overhead ($10,000 / 40,000 units)			0.25

CandleGlow had the following actual results for the month of February.

Number of units produced and sold	35,000
Number of ounces of wax purchased and used	530,000
Cost of wax used	$ 31,800
Number of labor hours worked	9,000
Direct labor cost	$123,750
Variable overhead cost	$ 3,300
Fixed overhead cost	$ 9,700

Required:

1. Calculate CandleGlow's direct materials variances.
2. Calculate CandleGlow's direct labor variances.
3. Compute CandleGlow's variable overhead rate and efficiency variances and its over- or underapplied variable overhead.
4. Compute CandleGlow's fixed overhead spending and volume variances and its over- or underapplied fixed overhead.

PB24-2 Preparing Journal Entries to Record Direct Material, Direct Labor, Variable Manufacturing Overhead, and Fixed Manufacturing Overhead Costs and Variances (Supplement)
Refer to the information in PB24-1 for CandleGlow. Prepare journal entries to record its manufacturing costs for February. Assume the company purchases raw materials as needed and does not maintain any ending inventories.

LO3, 4, 5, 6

PB24-3 Calculating Direct Materials, Direct Labor, Variable Manufacturing Overhead, and Fixed Manufacturing Overhead Variances

Gotta Cotta, Inc., manufactures basic terra cotta planters. Its standard cost information for the past year follows.

	Standard Quantity	Standard Price (Rate)	Standard Unit Cost
Direct costs			
Clay	2 lbs.	$ 0.80 per lb.	$1.60
Direct labor	.5 hr.	$12.00 per hr.	6.00
Variable manufacturing overhead		$ 0.40 per direct labor hour	0.20
Fixed manufacturing overhead ($480,000 / 800,000 units)			0.60

Gotta Cotta had the following actual results for the past year.

Number of units produced and sold	750,000
Number of pounds of clay used	1,450,000
Cost of clay purchased and used	$1,087,500
Number of labor hours worked	375,000
Direct labor cost	$3,937,500
Variable overhead cost	$ 157,500
Fixed overhead cost	$ 505,000

Required:

1. Calculate Gotta Cotta's direct materials variances.
2. Calculate Gotta Cotta's direct labor variances.
3. Compute Gotta Cotta's variable overhead rate and efficiency variances and its over- or underapplied variable overhead.
4. Compute Gotta Cotta's fixed overhead spending and volume variances and its over- or underapplied fixed overhead.

PB24-4 Preparing Journal Entries to Record Direct Materials, Direct Labor, Variable Manufacturing Overhead, and Fixed Manufacturing Overhead Costs and Variances (Supplement)

Refer to the information in PB24-3 for Gotta Cotta. Prepare journal entries to record its manufacturing costs for the past year. Assume the company purchases raw materials as needed and does not maintain any ending inventories.

LO3, 4, 5, 6

PB24-5 Calculating Direct Material, Direct Labor, Variable Manufacturing Overhead, and Fixed Manufacturing Overhead Variances

Easy Roller, Inc., manufactures plastic mats for use with rolling office chairs. Its standard cost information for last year follows.

	Standard Quantity	Standard Price (Rate)	Standard Unit Cost
Direct costs			
Plastic	12 sq ft.	$ 0.75 per sq. ft.	$9.00
Direct labor	.25 hr.	$12.00 per hr.	3.00
Variable manufacturing overhead		$ 1.20 per direct labor hour	0.30
Fixed manufacturing overhead ($360,000 / 900,000 units)			0.40

Easy Roller had the following actual results for the past year.

Number of units produced and sold	1,000,000
Number of square feet of plastic used	11,800,000
Cost of plastic purchased and used	$ 8,260,000
Number of labor hours worked	245,000
Direct labor cost	$ 2,891,000
Variable overhead cost	$ 318,500
Fixed overhead cost	$ 355,000

Required:

1. Calculate Easy Roller's direct materials variances.
2. Calculate Easy Roller's direct labor variances.
3. Compute Easy Roller's variable overhead rate and efficiency variances and its over- or underapplied variable overhead.
4. Compute Easy Roller's fixed overhead spending and volume variances and its over- or underapplied fixed overhead.

PB24-6 Preparing Journal Entries to Record Direct Materials, Direct Labor, Variable Manufacturing Overhead, and Fixed Manufacturing Overhead Costs and Variances (Supplement)

Refer to the information in PB24-5 for Easy Roller. Prepare journal entries to record its manufacturing costs for the past year. Assume the company purchases raw materials as needed and does not maintain any ending inventories.

Cases and Projects

CP24-1: Evaluating Managerial Performance by Comparing Actual to Budgeted Results   LO1

Suppose Acore Pharmaceuticals has four sales representatives assigned to the State of Arizona. These sales reps are responsible for visiting physicians in their assigned area, introducing the company's current or upcoming products, providing samples, getting feedback about the products, and generating sales. Each sales rep is given an expense budget that includes samples of Acore's products, travel expenses related to the company vehicle that Acore provides, and entertainment expenses such as buying meals or hosting small "meet and greet" receptions.

The following table includes both budgeted and actual amounts for each sales rep for the first half of the current year. As you can see, each sales rep was allotted the same amount of resources and expected to generate the same amount of sales for the six-month period.

	Samples		Travel		Entertainment		Sales	
Sales Rep	Budget	Actual	Budget	Actual	Budget	Actual	Budget	Actual
Terry	$7,200	$ 4,200	$18,000	$28,000	$4,800	$1,900	$90,000	$ 78,000
Maria	7,200	15,500	18,000	12,000	4,800	9,900	90,000	130,000
Samantha	7,200	2,900	18,000	18,000	4,800	4,600	90,000	43,000
Abraham	7,200	5,300	18,000	16,200	4,800	4,500	90,000	92,000

Required:

1. Calculate the expense and sales variances for each rep. Evaluate each of them and rank them in order of performance. Explain your rationale for these rankings. Suppose $100,000 in bonuses is available to be split among these sales reps. How would you allocate the money to them?

2. Now suppose that you find additional information about the territories to which Acore's Arizona reps are assigned. (If you're not familiar with Arizona, you can find a map at this Web site: www.mapofarizona.net)

- Terry has the northern Arizona territory that includes everything north of Phoenix between the California and New Mexico borders. This territory encompasses a large amount of Native American reservation land as well as the Grand Canyon National Park. Flagstaff is the largest city in the territory.

- Maria has the Phoenix area that includes only the Phoenix metropolitan area including all suburbs of Phoenix such as Glendale, Scottsdale, Mesa, and Sun City.

- Samantha's Southwestern Arizona territory includes all areas south and west of Phoenix. Yuma is the largest city in this region.

- Abraham's southeastern Arizona area includes everything south and east of Phoenix. Tucson is included in this territory.

  Does this new information change your evaluation of Acore's Arizona sales reps? If so, how? Does your allocation of the bonus money change as a result of the additional information? If so, explain how.

3. Do you need any other information to evaluate these employees' performances for the first half of the year?

4. What, if any, adjustments would you make to the budgets for the remainder of the year?

5. Do you think that Acore's policy of allocating the four sales reps the same amount of expenses and expected sales is adequate? What factors would you use in setting budgets for next year?

LO1

CP24-2 Developing Standard Costs Using Time Studies and Incentives to Distort the Standard

For a company to use a standard costing system, it must be able to develop the standards that will serve as the guide for the amount of a resource (e.g., direct materials, direct labor) that should be consumed in the production of a unit. One way to accomplish this is to conduct a time or process study that examines the work of one individual whose results are then used as the standard. This standard serves as a base against which actual results can be compared and ultimately affects performance evaluations.

Suppose you work for an ice packaging service company and your job is to fill each plastic bag with 7 pounds of crushed ice and close the bag with a metal fastener. These bags are then delivered to local grocery and convenience stores for sale. Assume also you were chosen as the subject for a time or process study. Because some amount of spillage is normal, the study will measure the amount of ice each bag has. Your time to fill and fasten each bag will also be measured. These numbers will then serve as company standards for everyone within the company doing your job.

Required:

1. Is there any motivation for you to intentionally spill some ice or to purposefully take longer than normal to fill and/or fasten the bag?

2. How might these standards affect employees (including you) later?

3. How might the company mitigate this problem?

LO1

CP24-3 Investigating the Use of Variance Analysis in Business by Reading a Case Study Article on the Use of Variances in the Construction Industry

Not all companies are manufacturing companies. For that reason, the variances calculated in this chapter are not appropriate for every organization. Industries and/or individual companies must often develop and use variances that make the most sense for evaluating performance within their specific circumstances. The construction industry is one example.

Required:

1. Go to http://www.constructionequipment.com/article/CA6568297.html and read the article that explains how budget variances can be used with respect to construction equipment.

2. Explain how construction equipment costs are separated into owning costs and operating costs.

3. If you were a manager for this company, how would you interpret and evaluate the company's performance for each class of equipment?

4. Does this manner of evaluation make sense for a construction company? Why or why not?

5. Give examples of two other companies or industries that would not necessarily use the variances calculated in this chapter.

25 Decentralized Performance Evaluation

LEARNING OBJECTIVES

After completing this chapter, you should be able to:

LO1 List and explain the advantages and disadvantages of decentralization.

LO2 Describe the different types of responsibility centers and explain how managers in each type are evaluated.

LO3 Compute and interpret an investment center's return on investment.

LO4 Compute and interpret an investment center's residual income.

LO5 Describe the four dimensions of the balanced scorecard and explain how they are used to evaluate managerial performance.

LO6 Explain how transfer prices are set in decentralized organizations.

Lectured slideshow–LP25-1
www.mhhe.com/LLPW1e

Focus Company: BLOCKBUSTER

"Is Opportunity Knocking for You?"

www.blockbuster.com

Think about the last time you rented a movie. Did you go to your neighborhood rental store such as Blockbuster or get it from an online rental service such as Netflix? The battle between Blockbuster and Netflix has been raging for more than a decade. Founded in 1986, Blockbuster Inc. became the world's largest provider of in-home movie entertainment, but now it is struggling to survive in this rapidly changing industry. Many industry experts have predicted the demise of Blockbuster and other "bricks and mortar" rental stores due to competition from online rental services such as Netflix, the increasingly affordable cost of DVDs, and rapid advances in technology for downloadable movies. Although Blockbuster still faces significant challenges in this battle, the company has made major strides and remains a prominent player in the entertainment industry.

As you read this chapter, put yourself in the shoes of a stakeholder at Blockbuster and ask yourself the following questions:

- As a customer of Blockbuster, how would you measure the company's performance?
- If you were a manager at a local Blockbuster store (responsible for all aspects of store management), how would your boss evaluate your performance?
- If you were a manager in Blockbuster's distribution warehouse (responsible for shipping DVDs to individual stores), how would your boss evaluate your performance?
- If you were a senior executive at Blockbuster (responsible for developing and delivering entertainment using new delivery channels), how would your boss evaluate your performance?
- If you owned stock in Blockbuster, how would you measure the company's performance?

Each of these questions involves measuring or evaluating the performance of a manager, a segment of the business, or the entire company. As the questions indicate, performance can be measured in different ways depending on what and who is being evaluated.

In this chapter, we present a variety of methods for measuring the performance of business units and managers. To do so, we apply the techniques to Blockbuster and its various divisions. Although some details and the numbers we use in our examples are hypothetical, they are intended to illustrate the techniques that Blockbuster and other companies use to evaluate the performance of their managers and business units.

ORGANIZATION OF THE CHAPTER

DECENTRALIZATION OF RESPONSIBILITY	RESPONSIBILITY CENTERS	EVALUATION OF INVESTMENT CENTER PERFORMANCE	TRANSFER PRICING
	• Cost Centers • Revenue Centers • Profit Centers • Investment Centers	• Return on Investment (ROI) • Residual Income • Return on Investment versus Residual Income • Limitations of Financial Performance Measures • Balanced Scorecard	• Market-Price Method • Cost-Based Method • Negotiation

DECENTRALIZATION OF RESPONSIBILITY

As children, most of us couldn't wait to grow up and do everything our parents told us we were too young to do—drive a car, stay out late, date, or get a job. It didn't take long, though, to realize that all that freedom comes with a great deal of responsibility. Wikipedia defines responsibility as the "state of being responsible, accountable or answerable." With responsibility comes the authority to make decisions for ourselves, to take action on behalf of others, and ultimately, to be held accountable for both our decisions and our actions.

In business, employees are given the responsibility and authority to make decisions on behalf of their employer. How do organizations make sure that employees act responsibly or make decisions that are in the organization's best interest? The methods they use are not that different from the ones parents use to monitor and control their children, including setting clear rules and guidelines for conduct, directly observing behavior, indirectly measuring the decisions being made, and evaluating the outcome of those decisions.

Think, for example, about how parents teach their children to drive. They establish clear rules of conduct, such as how fast, and when and where to drive, and how many passengers can be in the car. At first, they may insist on being in the car with the new driver (direct observation). Many parents also enroll their children in a driver's education course and receive report cards that assess their children's driving skills (indirect observation). At some point, parents must trust that their children have learned the rules of the road and will drive responsibly. Even so, parents may still check the odometer from time to time, install a GPS unit, or use some other means of indirect monitoring.

Organizations need similar mechanisms to ensure that managers are making responsible decisions—those that are in the best interests of the organization. The approach organizations use depends on how centralized or decentralized the decision-making authority is spread throughout the organization.

Learning Objective 1

List and explain the advantages and disadvantages of decentralization.

In a decentralized organization, decision-making authority is spread throughout the organization, and managers are given a great deal of autonomy to decide how to manage their individual units. In a centralized organization, decision-making authority is kept at the very top of the organization. High-level executives make all strategic and operational decisions and charge lower-level managers with implementing those decisions.

In deciding how much decision-making authority to delegate, organizations must weigh the advantages and disadvantages of decentralization. See Exhibit 25.1 for a summary of the pros and cons of decentralization.

In most organizations, the distinction between centralized and decentralized operations is not an either-or matter but a question of **how much** decision-making authority to delegate.

Exhibit 25.1   Advantages and Disadvantages of Decentralization

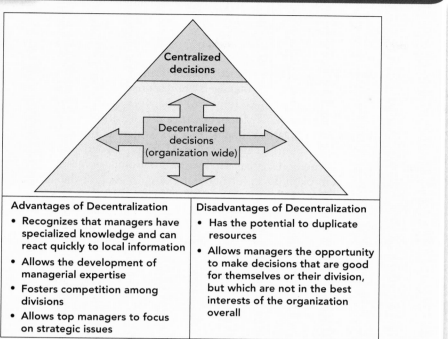

Advantages of Decentralization	Disadvantages of Decentralization
• Recognizes that managers have specialized knowledge and can react quickly to local information • Allows the development of managerial expertise • Fosters competition among divisions • Allows top managers to focus on strategic issues	• Has the potential to duplicate resources • Allows managers the opportunity to make decisions that are good for themselves or their division, but which are not in the best interests of the organization overall

As companies grow, become geographically dispersed, or begin to offer more diversified products and services, keeping all decision-making authority at the top of the organization may not be possible or even desirable.

When decision-making authority has been decentralized, the organization must find a way to monitor and evaluate managerial performance in much the same way that parents monitor and evaluate their children's driving behavior. Ideally, the company's performance measurement system should be designed so that the manager's goals and incentives are aligned with the organization's goals and objectives. Unfortunately, that is much easier said than done and is not always achieved in practice.

In the next section, we use Blockbuster Inc. to illustrate a variety of methods for measuring and evaluating managerial responsibility. Consider the simplified organizational chart for Blockbuster Inc. in Exhibit 25.2 as background. To manage this large, geographically dispersed company, Blockbuster must delegate decision-making responsibility throughout the organization.

Video 25-1
www.mhhe.com/LLPW1e

Exhibit 25.2   Organization Chart for Blockbuster Inc.

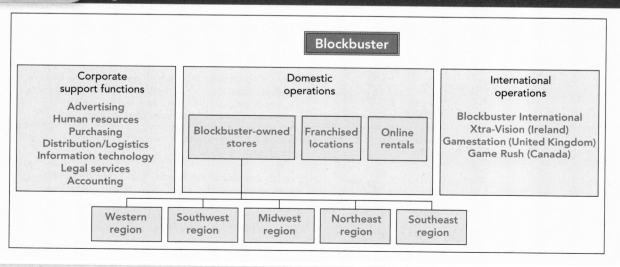

The next section discusses the various methods Blockbuster might use to measure and evaluate managerial performance in these various business segments.

RESPONSIBILITY CENTERS

Responsibility accounting gives managers authority and responsibility for a particular part of the organization and then evaluates them based on the results of that area of responsibility. The part of the organization for which managers are responsible is called a responsibility center. It can be established based on business function, product or service offerings, or geographic area.

As described in Exhibit 25.2, Blockbuster is divided into segments (divisions) based on all three characteristics: business support functions such as human resources, legal services, and accounting; service offerings including Blockbuster-owned stores, franchised stores, and online rentals; and geographic areas such as international, domestic, and regional. Many of these areas could be broken down further. For example, each of the geographic regions could be divided into districts, cities, towns, and individual stores.

One of the most important concepts in responsibility accounting is the controllability principle, which states that managers should be held responsible only for what they can control. The four different types of responsibility centers vary according to what the business managers can control and, thus, what they should be held responsible for:

- The manager of a cost center is responsible for controlling cost.
- The manager of a revenue center is responsible for generating revenue.
- The manager of a profit center is responsible for profit (revenue − cost).
- The manager of an investment center is responsible for profit (revenue − cost) and the investment of assets.

We next discuss each responsibility center and some common measures used to evaluate managerial performance in each.

Cost Centers

Cost center managers have the authority to incur costs to support their areas of responsibility. All of Blockbuster's corporate support functions listed in Exhibit 25.2 would be treated as cost centers: advertising, human resources, purchasing, distribution and logistics, information technology, legal services, and accounting. Note that these centers do not generate revenue directly from customers, although they can have an indirect impact on revenue. For example, dollars spent on advertising should have an impact on the generation of revenue.

To understand the responsibilities of cost center managers, consider the following actual job descriptions posted recently on Blockbuster.com:

Cost Center Managers	Job Description/Responsibilities **Blockbuster**
Distribution Center Manager	• Responsible for the operation and management of the Distribution Center. • Supervise warehouse employees and provide training to ensure that productivity standards are met or exceeded. • Responsible for planning and management of the daily work activities of one or more departments within the warehouse (i.e., processing, returning, and packing) to performance metrics in the areas of throughput, cost, and customer service.
Human Resource Manager	• Manage the field Human Resources function within a specified area of responsibility. • Provide strategic direction and coaching to District Managers on the succession planning and development of employees. • Partner with region, district, and store management on HR related issues and with corporate HR on training and recruiting issues.

One of the primary tools that cost center managers use to manage costs is the budgetary control system described in Chapters 23 and 24. However, cost center managers are responsible for more than just controlling costs. Usually they are also responsible for providing a high level of service to the rest of the organization whether in distribution, human resources, accounting, legal services, or some other internal function. Later in this chapter we discuss the use of the **balanced scorecard** to assess how well managers perform on dimensions other than cost, including internal processes, customer service, and employee satisfaction and turnover.

Revenue Centers

Revenue center managers are responsible for generating revenue within their areas of the organization. The following revenue center positions were posted recently on Blockbuster.com:

Revenue Center Managers	Job Description/ Responsibilities Blockbuster
Sales Manager	• Overall responsibility for meeting sales goals set by the strategic sales plan. • Responsible for implementing sales processes for training, communicating and tracking progress. • Interact with customers in person and on the phone and utilize the computerized point of sale system to complete both credit and cash transactions and maintain member accounts.
Customer Care Associate	• Manage service interactions by exhibiting a superior level of customer service and quality. Win back profitable customers through effective negotiations. • Take personal ownership of meeting average handle time, response time, and contract resolution rates to ensure service level agreements are met while effectively communicating value and service offerings to build and retain current membership base.

Revenue center managers generally receive sales targets or quotas for a particular period and are evaluated based on whether they meet those targets. Later in this chapter, we discuss some other measures for evaluating revenue center managers including customer satisfaction, customer retention, and customer turnover.

Profit Centers

Profit center managers are responsible for generating a profit (revenue − cost) within their area of the business: a store, district, region, division, or other business segment. Because they are responsible for both costs and revenues, profit center managers often supervise revenue and cost center managers. Consider the following profit center positions posted recently on Blockbuster.com:

Profit Center Positions	Job Description/Responsibilities
Store Manager (Tempe, AZ)	• Hire, train and develop store employees. Schedule, organize and direct assignments • Resolve customer problems or complaints by determining optimal solutions • Ensure interior and exterior of store is maintained to company standards • Utilize labor management tools including effective scheduling to maximize productivity, profitability and margins • Analyze store's financial data and take action to grow revenues, control costs, and ensure appropriate inventory management (maintain product and sell-through merchandise inventories) to achieve sales and profit goals.

Regional Director of Operations (Seattle) 	• General Manager responsible for the results of the overall regional business unit. • Responsible for maximizing earnings through the growth of rental and retail sales revenues, effective control of expenses and the use of leadership and mentoring skills to maximize team performance. • Provide coaching, vision and direction to the Region management team, monitor and manage performance, and develop strategies and people to achieve Region growth, service and financial goals.

The most common method of evaluating a profit center manager is by using the segmented income statement, which measures the profitability of a business segment during a particular period. One of the key features of a segmented income statement is that it distinguishes between costs that the segment manager can and cannot control. **Remember that managers should be held accountable only for those costs that are within their control.** The following hypothetical segmented income statement reports on Blockbuster's Seattle District, which includes several retail stores throughout the area:

Coach's Tip

Only these items are controllable by the division's manager, who is evaluated based on the segment margin.

These costs are controlled at the corporate level, so they should be excluded from the segment manager's performance evaluation.

Blockbuster
Segmented Income Statement for Seattle District
For the Quarter Ended March 31, 2010

	Amount	Percentage
Revenues		
Movie and game rental, merchandise sales, etc.	$1,200,000	100%
Less: Variable cost of rentals and merchandise sold	240,000	20
Contribution margin	960,000	80
Less: Direct operating expenses		
Occupancy costs, labor, and supervision costs	300,000	25
Segment margin	**660,000**	**55**
Less: Indirect operating expense (advertising, general and administrative expenses, etc.)	564,000	47
Income from operations	$ 96,000	8%

The most important line on the segmented income statement is the segment margin, which is calculated as revenue minus all costs that are directly traceable to the segment, division, or region. In Blockbuster's segmented income statement for the Seattle district, the variable costs of rentals and merchandise sold plus the direct operating expenses of occupancy costs (rent), labor, and supervision are all directly attributable to the Seattle District. Thus, those costs are deducted from sales revenue to find the segment margin. Notice that indirect costs, such as advertising and general and administrative expenses, are deducted **after** segment margin. Those costs are incurred at corporate headquarters and allocated to the individual divisions, so they should not be included in the segment margin. In short, a profit center manager should be evaluated based on the segment margin, not the profit margin (that is, operating income), because the segment margin includes only those costs that are within the manager's control.

Investment Centers

Investment center managers are responsible for generating a profit (revenue − cost) **and** investing assets. To understand the difference between a profit center manager and an investment center manager, consider the two types of Blockbuster store, company-owned stores and franchised locations. Blockbuster Inc. owns and operates about 80 percent of the individual stores in the United States. For these company-owned stores, senior executives at corporate headquarters make all major investment decisions, including new store openings, store closings, adopting new technologies, and other decisions requiring major investments of capital. Because the lower-level managers at Blockbuster-owned stores do not make decisions concerning the investment of assets, they are profit center managers, not investment center managers.

The other 20 percent of Blockbuster stores are franchised locations owned by other companies or individuals. The owners of these stores pay a franchise fee in exchange for the use of Blockbuster's name, national advertising and promotion, and other benefits, such as access to the company's proprietary software. The owners/managers of these stores are free to make their own decisions about where to locate, how much money to invest in physical assets and local advertising, and how to price their products. The following excerpt is from a recent annual report from Blockbuster.

> Excerpted from:
> **BLOCKBUSTER INC.**
> **FORM 10-K**
> **For the Fiscal Year Ended December 31, 2006**
>
> Our franchisees have control over all operating and pricing decisions at their respective locations. For example, our franchisees have control over whether or not to eliminate extended viewing fees . . . and over whether or not to participate in the BLOCKBUSTER Total Access program. . . . A franchisee has sole responsibility for all financial commitments relating to the development, opening and operation of its stores, including rent, utilities, payroll and other capital and incidental expenses. We cannot offer assurances that our franchisees will be able to achieve profitability levels in their businesses sufficient to pay our franchise fees.

Blockbuster

As the report notes, the owner/manager of a franchised Blockbuster store has significantly more responsibility than the manager of a company-owned Blockbuster store. Because the owner/managers of franchised stores have control over the investment of assets, they are investment center managers.

The next section focuses on the evaluation of an investment center manager's performance. First, complete the following Self-Study Practice to make sure that you understand the differences between the four types of responsibility centers.

SELF-STUDY PRACTICE

Which of the following statements about responsibility centers is true? You may select more than one answer.

1. Cost center managers are responsible for generating sales in their area of the business.
2. Revenue center managers are responsible for controlling costs and generating revenue in their area of the business.
3. Profit center managers are responsible for controlling costs and generating revenue but not for investing assets.
4. Investment center managers are responsible for investing assets but not for controlling costs or generating revenue.
5. None of these statements is true.

After you have finished, check your answers with the solutions at the bottom of the page.

3 is the only true statement

Solution to Self-Study Practice

EVALUATION OF INVESTMENT CENTER PERFORMANCE

As described in the previous section, investment center managers are responsible for generating profit and investing assets. As such, they will be evaluated based on their ability to generate enough profit to compensate for the investment in assets. Next we discuss two common measures for evaluating investment center performance: return on investment and residual income.

Return on Investment (ROI)

The most common method of evaluating investment center performance is by using the rate of return on invested assets. Also called return on invested assets, the **return on investment (ROI)** is calculated as follows:

$$\text{Return on Investment (ROI)} = \frac{\text{Operating Income}}{\text{Invested Assets}}$$

ROI is calculated as the return on the segment's assets (measured by its operating profit) divided by the value of those assets. Thus, the higher a segment's operating profit relative to its investment base, the higher its ROI.

Consider the following sample data for two different segments of Blockbuster.

COMPARISON OF RETURN ON INVESTMENT FOR TWO BLOCKBUSTER BUSINESS SEGMENTS	Blockbuster Western Region	Blockbuster Online Rentals Division
$\dfrac{\text{Operating Income}}{\text{Average invested assets}} =$	$\dfrac{\$\ 120{,}000}{\$2{,}000{,}000}$	$\dfrac{\$\ 600{,}000}{\$2{,}000{,}000}$
Return on Investment	6%	30%

Notice that the two divisions have the same level of investment, with average assets of $2,000,000. Yet Online Rentals generates a much higher operating profit ($600,000) and, thus has a higher ROI (30 percent) than the Western Region (6 percent). This comparison of the two ROIs is a good starting point for evaluating the two investment centers, but it does not provide much information about **why** the Online Rentals Division managed to generate a higher ROI.

To really understand ROI, we need to break it into two separate components, **investment turnover** and **profit margin:**

$$\underset{\substack{\text{Return on} \\ \text{Investment (ROI)}}}{\frac{\text{Operating Income}}{\text{Invested Assets}}} = \underset{\substack{\text{Investment} \\ \text{Turnover}}}{\frac{\text{Sales Revenue}}{\text{Invested Assets}}} \times \underset{\substack{\text{Profit} \\ \text{Margin}}}{\frac{\text{Operating Income}}{\text{Sales Revenue}}}$$

In the preceding formula, investment turnover is the ratio of sales revenue to the invested assets; profit margin is the ratio of operating income to sales revenue. Essentially, this formula states that to increase ROI, managers must either generate more sales revenue from their assets (investment turnover) or keep a larger percentage of sales revenue as profit (profit margin). Developed by executives at DuPont in the early 1900s, the formula is often referred to as the DuPont method.

Applying the DuPont method to Blockbuster's two segments provides the following results:

COMPARISON OF RETURN ON INVESTMENT,
PROFIT MARGIN, AND INVESTMENT TURNOVER
FOR TWO BLOCKBUSTER BUSINESS SEGMENTS

	Blockbuster Western Region	Blockbuster Online Rentals Division
Sales revenue	$3,000,000	$6,000,000
Less: Operating expenses	(2,880,000)	(5,400,000)
Operating income	120,000	600,000
Average invested assets	2,000,000	2,000,000
Investment Turnover $= \dfrac{\text{Sales Revenue}}{\text{Invested Assets}}$	$\dfrac{3,000,000}{2,000,000} = 1.5$	$\dfrac{6,000,000}{2,000,000} = 3$
Profit Margin $= \dfrac{\text{Operating Income}}{\text{Sales Revenue}}$	$\dfrac{120,000}{3,000,000} = 4\%$	$\dfrac{600,000}{6,000,000} = 10\%$
ROI $= \dfrac{\text{Operating Income}}{\text{Invested Assets}}$	$\dfrac{120,000}{2,000,000} = 6\%$	$\dfrac{600,000}{2,000,000} = 30\%$
ROI $= \dfrac{\text{Investment}}{\text{Turnover}} \times \dfrac{\text{Profit}}{\text{Margin}}$	$1.5 \times 4\% = 6\%$	$10\% \times 3 = 30\%$

Coach's Tip

Online Rentals generates more revenue than the Western Region from the same amount of invested assets.

Online Rentals earns more profit (or incurs less cost) than the Western Region for each dollar of sales.

The combined effect is a much higher return on investment for Online Rentals than for the Western Region.

This analysis shows that two factors are driving the difference in ROI for Blockbuster's two segments. The first factor is the amount of sales revenue generated for every dollar of investment. The investment turnover ratio shows how efficiently assets are used to generate sales revenue. The Western Region generates sales equal to 1.5 times its investment base; Online Rental Division generates twice that amount—3 times its investment base—from the same level of investment.

The second factor that drives the difference in ROI is the profit margins of the two business segments. The profit margin shows how much of a segment's sales revenue remains as operating profit after the operating costs have been covered. The Online Rental Division generates $0.10 in operating profit for every dollar of sales; the Western Region generates only $0.04 for every dollar of sales. This difference in profit margin is rooted in the different cost structures of the two segments. Blockbuster's bricks and mortar stores tend to have relatively high fixed costs (for rental space, utilities, and other overhead costs); Online Rentals Division has higher variable costs (for mailing movies back and forth to customers).

Multiplying these two effects gives the ROI, which can be reinvested in the company or paid to the owners. In sum, the Online Rentals Division generates more sales revenue from the same level of investment **and** keeps a higher percentage of the sales revenue as operating profit. The end result is that Online's ROI (30 percent) is much higher than that for the Western Region (6 percent). See these relationships shown in Exhibit 25.3.

To make sure you understand how to calculate ROI, profit margin, and investment turnover, complete the following Self-Study Practice.

SELF-STUDY PRACTICE

Consider the following sample data for Blockbuster's Midwestern Region:

Sales	$1,000,000
Operating expenses	900,000
Operating income	100,000
Invested assets	400,000

1. Compute the region's ROI, profit margin, and investment turnover.
2. Show how the ROI is related to profit margin and investment turnover.

After you have finished, check your answers with the solutions at the bottom of the next page.

Exhibit 25.3 Relationship between Investment Turnover, Profit Margin, and ROI

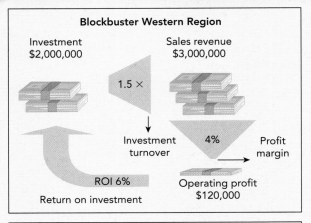

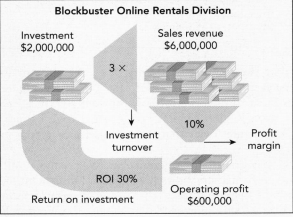

Learning Objective 4

Compute and interpret an investment center's residual income.

Residual Income

An alternative measure for evaluating an investment center's performance, called residual income, involves making a comparison between operating profit and the minimum required rate of return. Recall from Chapter 22 that organizations set the minimum required rate of return on an investment, sometimes called the **hurdle rate.** Residual income is the difference between the operating profit and the minimum profit the organization must earn to cover the hurdle rate as in the following formula:[1]

$$\boxed{\text{Residual Income}} = \boxed{\text{Operating Income}} - \boxed{\text{Invested Assets} \times \text{Hurdle Rate}}$$

Solution to
Self-Study Practice

1. ROI = $100,000 / $400,000 = 25%
   Profit margin = $100,000 / $1,000,000 = 10%
   Investment turnover = $1,000,000 / 400,000 = 2.5
2. ROI = Profit Margin × Investment Turnover = 10% × 2.5 = 25%

---

[1] A closely related technique for evaluating an investment center's performance is known as **economic value added,** or EVA™. This approach, which was devised by Stern, Stewart and Co., measures the economic wealth that is created when a company's operating income exceeds its cost of capital. Conceptually, EVA is very similar to residual income, but it requires a number of complex adjustments that are beyond the scope of this textbook.

Let's compute the residual incomes for two of Blockbuster's segments using a hurdle rate of 10 percent:

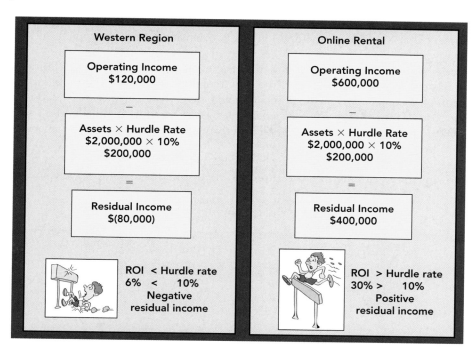

Coach's Tip

Both segments need to earn at least $200,000 in profit to provide a 10% return on invested assets. Anything above that is residual (extra) profit.

Notice that the Western Region has a negative residual income of $(80,000). That is, the region's operating profit is not high enough to cover its 10 percent hurdle rate. The ROI analysis on the previous page showed that the Western Region's ROI was only 6 percent—4 percent less than the hurdle rate. If you multiply the region's $2,000,000 investment by the 4 percent shortfall in its ROI (compared to the hurdle rate), you get the same result: a negative residual income of $(80,000).

The Online Division's residual income is $400,000, which is more than enough to cover the 10 percent required return on investment. The ROI analysis on the previous page showed that the Online Rentals Division was earning a 30 percent ROI. Multiplying the extra 20 percent return (over and above the 10 percent hurdle rate) by the division's $2,000,000 investment gives the same result: a residual income of $400,000. This amount is the additional profit Online Rentals earned over and above the required ROI.

Before you continue, complete the following Self-Study Practice to make sure you understand how to calculate residual income.

SELF-STUDY PRACTICE

Consider the following hypothetical data for Blockbuster's Midwest Region:

Operating income	$100,000
Invested assets	$400,000
ROI	25%

1. Using a hurdle rate of 10 percent, compute the division's residual income.
2. Explain how the residual income is related to the 25 percent ROI.

After you have finished, check your answers with the solutions at the bottom of the page.

---

1. Residual Income = Operating Income − (Invested Assets × Hurdle Rate) = $100,000 − ($400,000 × 10%) = $60,000
2. The 25 percent ROI is higher than the 10 percent hurdle rate
    Excess of 15% × $400,000 Investment = $60,000 Residual Income.

Solution to
Self-Study Practice

Return on Investment versus Residual Income

Return on investment is the most widely used method for evaluating investment center performance. However, it has one major disadvantage: It can sometimes cause managers to reject an investment that would lower the division's ROI, even though the investment might benefit the company as a whole.

To see how that can happen, assume that the manager of Blockbuster's Online Rentals Division has an opportunity to invest in a new technology that would require an up-front investment of $1,000,000. The technology would save the company $150,000 a year in operating costs. Thus, the project's expected ROI is 15 percent. If Blockbuster's minimum required rate of return (hurdle rate) is 10 percent, the project would be an acceptable investment from the company's perspective.

From Online Rentals' perspective, however, the project does not look as promising. The following table summarizes the project's effect on the division's ROI and residual income.

EFFECT OF THE PROPOSED PROJECT ON ONLINE RENTALS' RETURN ON INVESTMENT AND RESIDUAL INCOME

	Status Quo (without project)	Effect of Proposed Project	If Project Is Accepted
Return on investment analysis			
$\dfrac{\text{Operating Income}}{\text{Average Invested Assets}} = $ Return on Investment	$\dfrac{\$600,000}{\$2,000,000} =$	$\dfrac{\$150,000}{\$1,000,000} =$	$\dfrac{\$750,000}{\$3,000,000} =$
	30%	15%	25%
Residual income analysis			
Operating Income	$600,000	$150,000	$750,000
Required Profit (10% of average invested assets)	(200,000)	(100,000)	(300,000)
Residual Income	$400,000	$ 50,000	$450,000

Coach's Tip

Notice that the project would have a negative effect on Online Rentals' ROI because its rate of return would be less than the current ROI of 30%. The project would generate a positive residual income, however, because its return is higher than the company's required rate of return, 10 percent.

Given these numbers, will the manager of Online Rentals want to invest in the project? The answer to this question depends on whether the manager is evaluated based on the division's ROI or its residual income. The proposed project would generate a positive residual income because it would earn more than the required 10 percent hurdle rate. However, it would have a negative impact on the division's ROI because the 15 percent return is less than the division's current ROI of 30 percent. If the manager invests in this project, the division's ROI will drop from 30 percent to 25 percent.

This example shows how a responsibility accounting system can create goal incongruence, or conflict between a manager and the organization as a whole. A manager who is evaluated based on ROI may not be willing to invest in a project that is in the best interest of the company as a whole simply because doing so would have a negative impact on the manager's own performance evaluation. The residual income method helps to align the manager's goals with the organization's objective of earning a minimum ROI of 10 percent. Regardless of the division's current ROI, its residual income will increase as long as the manager invests in projects that exceed the company's minimum required return.

Limitations of Financial Performance Measures

Both ROI and residual income are lagging indicators of financial performance. In other words, they are based on historical information taken from a company's financial statements including past sales revenue, operating income, and assets. These measures tell how a company or a division has done in the past but not necessarily how it will do in the future.

Unfortunately, many of the actions that managers take to improve a company's financial performance in the short run can prove harmful to the organization over the long run. Examples include cutting back on research and development, reducing employee training, and using less expensive materials to make a product. While all of these decisions will improve short-run financial results, they will likely hurt the company in the long term through reduced sales, quality problems, customer complaints, and increased warranty expenses. To avoid these problems, organizations should evaluate and reward managers based on more than just short-term financial results. The next section discusses the balanced scorecard, a performance measurement system designed to focus managers' attention on more than just financial results.

Balanced Scorecard

The balanced scorecard is a comprehensive performance measurement system that translates an organization's vision and strategy into a set of operational performance metrics. The balanced scorecard measures organizational performance on four key dimensions:

- **Customer perspective.**   How do we want our customers to see us?
- **Learning and growth perspective.**   How will we sustain our ability to change and improve?
- **Internal business processes.**   What internal processes will we require to meet the needs of our customers, employees, and shareholders?
- **Financial perspective.**   How do we satisfy our shareholders, regulators, and other stakeholders?

For each of these dimensions, managers must devise specific objectives, measures, and targets that can be used to gauge how well the company is performing and identify what needs to be done to improve performance. Those objectives, measures, and targets should be communicated to managers throughout the organization so that everyone knows what needs to be done to achieve long-term success, not just short-term financial results.

See the sample balanced scorecard for Blockbuster in Exhibit 25.4. Notice that the center of the scorecard is the company's strategic vision. In this example, Blockbuster's strategic vision is to remain the leading provider of in-home movies and gaming. Because of the dynamic nature of this industry, Blockbuster's managers cannot continue to operate as they have in the past, relying primarily on Blockbuster's neighborhood stores. Instead, they must gain market share in the market for online rentals and invest in new technologies that will allow the company to deliver downloadable movies and games.

The four boxes surrounding the center of Exhibit 25.4 represent the four key dimensions of Blockbuster's performance. Notice that each dimension lists specific objectives and measures that managers can use to evaluate the company's performance. For example, one of Blockbuster's internal business processes objectives is to reduce delivery time to customers. A specific measure that managers can use to assess the company's performance on this objective is the percentage of orders that reach customers within one business day. Blockbuster tracks this measure carefully. In a recent annual report, the company noted that its distribution system is set up to reach more than 90 percent of online subscribers within a single business day.

Similar measures must be developed and captured for the other dimensions of the balanced scorecard. For example, customer measures might include the percentage of revenue from online rentals, number of new contracts, and retention of existing customers. Measures for learning and growth might focus on employee education and internal level promotions as well as the amount of money spent on new technology. Measures of financial performance include reductions in operating costs, increase in investment turnover rates, and increases in the company's stock price.

Video 25-2
www.mhhe.com/LLPW1e

Exhibit 25.4   Balanced Scorecard for Blockbuster Inc.   Blockbuster

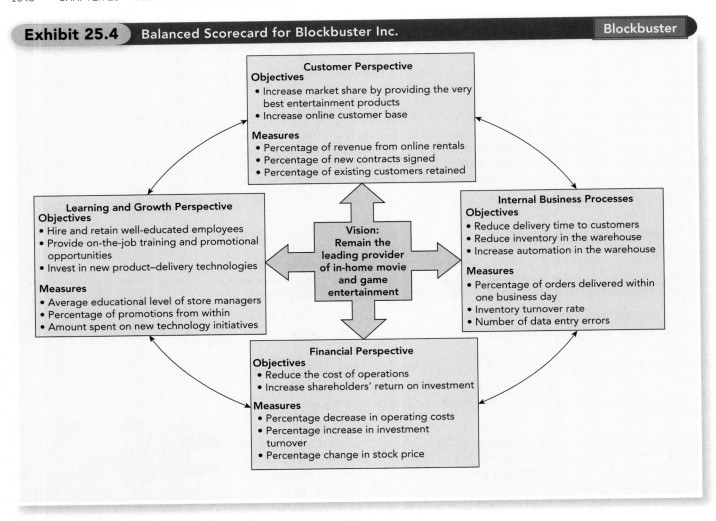

TRANSFER PRICING

The final issue we consider in this chapter is how decentralized organizations deal with the transfer or sale of goods and services between divisions. A transfer price is the amount that one division charges when it sells goods or services to another division in the same company. Transfers happen quite often in today's business environment because many large corporations are composed of several relatively independent business units all owned by the same parent company. Business transactions between units or divisions in the same company are called related-party transactions.

Perhaps the easiest way to think about transfer prices is in terms of the deal you would get if you buy something from a relative. Maybe you want to buy a car from your brother-in-law's dealership, a meal at your cousin's restaurant, or a cut and style at your sister's hair salon. How much would you expect to pay for a product or service when buying from a relative? At a minimum, you should be willing to pay for any variable costs that your relative incurs (floor). For example, if your brother, an auto-mechanic, agrees to repair your car, you should at least be willing to pay for the parts. The maximum amount you should be willing to pay is the going market rate (ceiling) for the product or service. In other words, you should not be willing to pay more for the product or service than you would if you bought it elsewhere. See Exhibit 25.5 for this range of potential transfer prices.

The same rules apply to transfer prices in decentralized organizations. The only difference is that the managers of decentralized business units are not necessarily friendly relatives. In fact, if managers are evaluated based on their ability to control costs and/or generate revenue, their goals may be diametrically opposed even if they do work in the same company. The manager of the selling division is motivated to achieve the highest possible price; the manager of the buying division is motivated to pay the lowest possible price. Although the transfer price

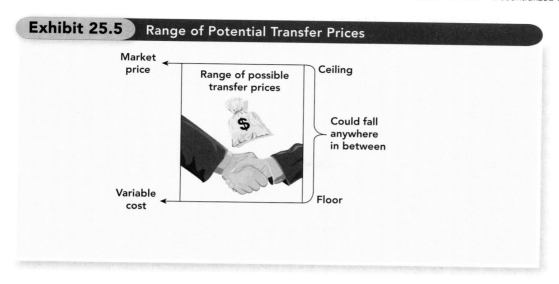

Exhibit 25.5   Range of Potential Transfer Prices

Market price — Range of possible transfer prices — Ceiling — Could fall anywhere in between — Variable cost — Floor

does not really matter from the company's overall perspective,[2] it can make a big difference to individual managers. As in the famous line from the film *The Godfather*, "It's not personal, it's just business."

As a simple example, assume Blockbuster has a controlling interest in the hypothetical company Popcorn Ltd., which manufactures bags of microwave popcorn for sale in large buckets at Blockbuster and other movie rental stores. Because Popcorn Ltd. operates as a free-standing business unit of Blockbucker Inc., its managers are considered profit center managers.

Assume that Popcorn Ltd.'s costs to produce a single case (24 packs) of microwave popcorn are as follows.

> **Popcorn Ltd.**
> **Cost to Produce 1 Case (24 packs)**
> **of Microwave Popcorn**
>
> | | |
> |---|---|
> | Direct materials | $1.00 ⎫ |
> | Direct labor | 0.25 ⎬ $1.50 |
> | Variable overhead | 0.25 ⎭ |
> | Fixed overhead ($350,000 / 100,000 unit capacity) | 3.50 |
> | Full manufacturing cost | $5.00 |
>
> The external market price (for non-Blockbuster buyers) is $10.00.

The manager of Blockbuster's Midwest Region has approached Popcorn Ltd. to buy popcorn for that region. What price should Popcorn Ltd. charge the manager for a case of popcorn?

There are three different ways to determine transfer prices such as this one: the market-price method, the cost-based method, and negotiation.

Market-Price Method

The market price is the price that a company would charge to external customers. It is the maximum price that a buyer should be willing to pay. In this example, the market price is $10 per case of popcorn. The problem with using the market price as a transfer price is that the buyer has no incentive to purchase from within the company and so may consider buying from an outside supplier. Think of buying a car from someone other than your car-dealing brother-in-law because he is unwilling to give you a discount.

Learning Objective 6

Explain how transfer prices are set in decentralized organizations.

---

[2] Transfer prices **can** have a major impact on multinational companies due to variations in tax rates from one country to the next. This issue, which is extremely complex, is beyond the scope of this textbook.

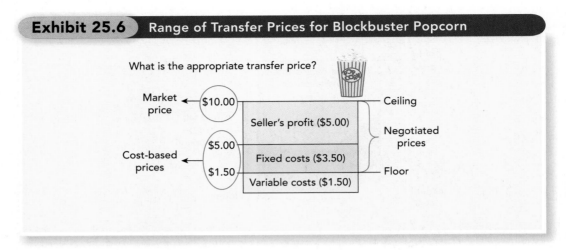

Exhibit 25.6   Range of Transfer Prices for Blockbuster Popcorn

In our example, if the buying division (the Midwest Region) decides to buy from an outside supplier, the selling division (Popcorn Ltd.) loses the opportunity to profit from the sale just as your brother-in-law would lose the opportunity to earn a commission on your new car. As a result, the company as a whole may suffer. The only time that using a market price as a transfer price makes sense is when the selling division is operating at full capacity and cannot fill the order without giving up sales to external customers. If Popcorn Ltd. is already selling all the popcorn it can produce for $10 per case, for example, selling to the Midwest Region at a lower price would not make sense. The company would be losing more profitable business.

If the selling division has **excess capacity,** however, it can make a profit by selling at any price above the variable cost. (Remember that the total fixed cost is constant and does not change depending on the number of units produced and sold, at least within a limited range.) In this example, we assume Popcorn Ltd. has sufficient capacity to fill the Midwest Region's order without incurring additional fixed costs or losing sales to other customers. In that case, Popcorn Ltd. should be willing to sell the popcorn for less than the market price (see Exhibit 25.6). In the next section, we use the cost-based method to determine a transfer price for the popcorn.

Cost-Based Method

The cost-based method uses either the variable cost or the full cost as the basis for setting the transfer price. At a minimum, the selling division should recover the incremental (that is, variable) costs of producing and selling the product. In this example, the transfer price should be set at no less than the variable cost of $1.50 per case of popcorn. Another option is to base the transfer price on the full manufacturing cost of $5.00 per case, which covers both variable and fixed costs.

Many companies have a predetermined "cost-plus" transfer price. For example, Blockbuster might have a policy of making all internal transfers at the full manufacturing cost plus 10 percent. If so, the transfer price per case of popcorn would be $5.00 + (10% of $5.00) = $5.50. If the transfer price were set at $5.50, both buyer and seller would benefit from the transfer. The buying division (Blockbuster's Midwest Region) would pay $5.50 per case, a $4.50 savings compared to the market price of $10.00. The selling division (Popcorn Ltd.) would make $5.50 minus $1.50 in variable costs for an increased profit of $4.00 per case.

Negotiation

A final option is to let divisional managers negotiate transfer prices. In this method, the negotiated price can range anywhere from the variable cost ($1.50) to the full market price ($10.00). As in any negotiation, the final price will depend on the relative power of the buyer and seller, their negotiation skills, and how much inside information each has about the other division's cost, capacity, and demand.

Think of buying a car from a car dealer. You should not be willing to pay more than the market price, which we will assume is the sticker price. The dealer should not be willing to accept less than the variable cost; otherwise, the dealership will lose money on the sale. Knowing the variable cost of the car would certainly help you in your bargaining. On the other hand, if the dealer knows you really want the car and has another customer who is ready to buy it (and no more cars like it on the lot), you will not be in a good bargaining position.

Negotiating transfer prices can be time consuming and can force managers of the same parent company to act as adversaries. To avoid such situations, companies may dictate that the buying and selling divisions split the difference so that each receives an equal benefit from the internal transfer. In our example, the transfer price would be midway between the $10.00 market price and the $1.50 in variable costs, or $5.75. This approach creates a win–win situation for the managers: The buying division saves $4.25 per case ($10.00 − $5.75) by buying from inside, and the selling division makes an extra $4.25 per case ($5.75 − $1.50) in incremental profit.

To make sure you understand how to set transfer prices, complete the following Self-Study Practice.

SELF-STUDY PRACTICE

Kraft Foods owns both Tombstone Pizza and Kraft Cheese. Assume that Tombstone Pizza (the buyer) has approached Kraft Cheese (the seller) to ask for a special deal on the cheese used to produce Tombstone's frozen pizza.
   Which of the following statements is true? You may select more than one answer.

1. If Kraft Cheese is operating at full capacity, the company should be willing to accept less than the market price for the cheese.

2. If Kraft Cheese has excess capacity, the company may be willing to accept less than the variable cost for the cheese.

3. Both statements above are true.

4. None of the statements above are true.

After you have finished, check your answers with the solutions at the bottom of the page.

Demonstration Case

Consider the following data for two divisions of Peter Piper Pizza:

	Northwest Region	Southwest Region
Average invested assets	$ 6,000,000	$6,000,000
Sales revenue	$18,000,000	$9,000,000
Less: Operating expenses	(17,460,000)	(8,100,000)
Operating income	$ 540,000	$ 900,000

Required:

1.   Compute the investment turnover, profit margin, return on investment, and residual income for each division. Assume a 10 percent hurdle rate.

2.   Explain the relationship between each division's residual income and its return on investment.

3.   The manager of the Southwest Region has the opportunity to invest an additional $2,000,000 in a project expected to generate additional operating income of $220,000 per year. Calculate Southwest's new return on investment and residual income if the manager accepts the project.

4.   Would Southwest's manager, who is evaluated based on the region's return on investment, want to invest in the project? If the evaluation were based on the region's residual income? Why or why not?

Solution to
Self-Study Practice

Suggested Solution

1.

		Northwest Region	Southwest Region
Investment Turnover	$= \dfrac{\text{Sales Revenue}}{\text{Invested Assets}}$	$\dfrac{18{,}000{,}000}{6{,}000{,}000} = 3$	$\dfrac{9{,}000{,}000}{6{,}000{,}000} = 1.50$
Profit Margin	$= \dfrac{\text{Operating Income}}{\text{Sales Revenue}}$	$\dfrac{540{,}000}{18{,}000{,}000} = 3\%$	$\dfrac{900{,}000}{9{,}000{,}000} = 10\%$
Return on Investment	$= \dfrac{\text{Operating Income}}{\text{Invested Assets}}$	$\dfrac{540{,}000}{6{,}000{,}000} = 9\%$	$\dfrac{900{,}000}{6{,}000{,}000} = 15\%$
Operating Income		540,000	900,000
Required Profit (10% of assets)		(600,000)	(600,000)
Residual Income		(60,000)	300,000

2. The Northwest Region has a negative residual income because its return on investment, which is 9 percent, is less than the 10 percent hurdle rate, 1 percent of $6,000,000 = $(60,000).

The Southwest Region has a positive residual income because its return on investment, which is 15 percent, is higher than the 10 percent hurdle rate; 5 percent of $6,000,000 = $300,000.

3.

	Southwest Region (before project)	Proposed Project	If Project Is Accepted
Return on Investment Analysis			
$\dfrac{\text{Operating income}}{\text{Average invested assets}} = \text{Return on investment}$	$\dfrac{\$900{,}000}{\$6{,}000{,}000} = 15\%$	$\dfrac{\$220{,}000}{\$2{,}000{,}000} = 11\%$	$\dfrac{\$1{,}120{,}000}{\$8{,}000{,}000} = 14\%$
Residual Income Analysis			
Operating income	$900,000	$220,000	$1,120,000
Required profit (10% of assets)	(600,000)	(200,000)	(800,000)
Residual income	$300,000	$ 20,000	$ 320,000

4. If the evaluation is based on the region's return on investment (ROI), Southwest's regional manager probably would **not** want to invest in the project because it would lower the division's ROI. The project's expected ROI of 11 percent is less than the division's current ROI of 15 percent. Thus, investing the extra $2,000,000 would lower the region's ROI to 14 percent.

However, if the evaluation is based on the region's residual income, the manager **would** want to invest in the project because it would increase the region's residual income. Residual income will increase as long as the project's return (11 percent) is higher than the minimum required rate of return (10 percent).

Chapter Summary

LO1 List and explain the advantages and disadvantages of decentralization. p. 1028

- Decentralization is the delegation of decision-making authority to managers at all levels of the organization.
- The advantages of decentralization include the ability to make decisions more quickly based on local information; the development of managerial expertise; increased competition among managers; and increased opportunity for upper management to focus on strategic issues.
- The disadvantages of decentralization include the potential for duplicating resources and for making suboptimal decisions (those that are not made in the best interests of the organization as a whole).

LO2 Describe the different types of responsibility centers and explain how managers in each type are evaluated. p. 1030

- **Cost center:** Managers are responsible for controlling costs within their area of responsibility, such as distribution, advertising, accounting, or human resources. Cost center managers are evaluated based on their ability to stay within budget and provide the necessary support to the organization.

- **Revenue center:** Managers are responsible for generating sales revenue within their area of responsibility, such as a store, a district, or a region. They are evaluated based on their ability to meet sales quotas and other measures of success, such as customer retention.
- **Profit center:** Managers are responsible for earning a profit within their area of responsibility through both revenue generation and cost control. They are typically evaluated based on a measure such as segment margin, which includes only those costs that are within the segment manager's direct control.
- **Investment center:** Managers are responsible for both profit (revenue − cost) and the investment of assets. They are evaluated based on measures that include both profit and investment, such as return on investment and residual income.

LO3 Compute and interpret an investment center's return on investment. p. 1034

- Return on investment (ROI) is the most common measure for evaluating an investment center's performance.
- ROI equals the investment center's operating profit divided by its average investment in assets.
- The DuPont formula shows that ROI equals the profit margin multiplied by the investment turnover ratio.
- Profit margin is the amount of profit generated for every dollar of sales revenue.
- Investment turnover is the amount of sales revenue generated for every dollar of invested assets.
- Companies can increase ROI by either increasing profit margin (by reducing costs without reducing sales) or increasing asset turnover (by increasing sales without increasing assets).

LO4 Compute and interpret an investment center's residual income. p. 1036

- Residual income is an alternative measure for evaluating an investment center's performance.
- Residual income equals the difference between an investment center's operating profit and the minimum profit it must make to cover its hurdle rate (that is, the minimum rate of return on its assets).
- Managers earn residual income by investing in projects that earn more than the minimum required rate of return (or hurdle rate).

LO5 Describe the four dimensions of the balanced scorecard and explain how they are used to evaluate managerial performance. p. 1039

- The balanced scorecard is a comprehensive performance measurement system that translates the organization's vision and strategy into a set of operational performance measures.
- The balanced scorecard measures operational performances on four key dimensions: consumer perspective, learning and growth perspective, internal business processes, and financial perspective.
- The customer perspective focuses on the customer through measures such as customer retention, customer satisfaction, and market share.
- The learning and growth perspective focuses on the organization's ability to change and improve through measures such as the amount of money spent on research and development and employee education and training.
- The internal business processes focus on the internal processes required to meet customer needs through measures of on-time delivery, quality, and internal process efficiency.
- The financial perspective focuses on traditional financial measures of performance, such as return on investment, residual income, sales revenue, and profit.

LO6 Explain how transfer prices are set in decentralized organizations. p. 1041

- A transfer price is the price charged when one unit or division of a company sells goods or services to another unit or division of the same company.
- The maximum transfer price is the external market price, or the amount that would be charged to an unrelated party. The minimum transfer price is the variable cost (to the seller) of selling to the other division.
- Cost-based transfer prices can be set based on variable cost, full cost, or cost plus some percentage markup.
- Transfer prices can also be set through negotiation between the buying and selling divisions.

Key Terms

Balanced Scorecard (p. 1039)

Centralized Organization (p. 1028)

Controllability Principle (p. 1030)

Cost Center (p. 1030)

Decentralized Organization (p. 1028)

DuPont Method (p. 1034)

Goal Incongruence (p. 1038)

Investment Center (p. 1030)

Investment Turnover (p. 1034)

Profit Center (p. 1030)

Profit Margin (p. 1034)

Related-Party Transactions (p. 1040)

Residual Income (p. 1036)

Responsibility Accounting (p. 1030)

Responsibility Center (p. 1030)

Return on Investment (ROI) (p. 1034)

Revenue Center (p. 1030)

Segmented Income Statement (p. 1032)

Segment Margin (p. 1032)

Transfer Price (p. 1040)

See complete glossary in back of text.

Questions

1. Explain how centralized and decentralized companies differ. What are the advantages and disadvantages of each?

2. How does decentralization create the need for responsibility accounting in an organization?

3. What is the controllability principle and why is it crucial to responsibility accounting?

4. Name the four types of responsibility centers and describe the managers' responsibilities and authority in each.

5. Why are profit center managers evaluated on segment margin instead of overall company income?

6. What role do return on investment and residual income play in responsibility accounting?

7. Return on investment may be separated into two components. Name them and describe what each of these components can tell you.

8. Explain how reliance on return on investment for performance evaluation of investment center managers could lead to goal incongruence.

9. How is residual income calculated?

10. What benefit does residual income offer in comparison to return on investment when evaluating performance?

11. What are the primary limitations of financial measures of performance?

12. Explain the balanced scorecard approach to performance evaluation. What advantages does this approach have over using only financial measurements?

13. What are the four perspective areas of a balanced scorecard? What does each perspective represent?

14. What is a transfer price?

15. Explain the minimum and maximum transfer prices and identify whether each would be determined by the buyer or the seller.

16. What is the market-price method of transfer pricing?

17. What does the term excess capacity mean? How does excess capacity affect a transfer price?

18. Describe the cost-based method of transfer pricing.

19. What are negotiated transfer prices? Explain two possible disadvantages of allowing managers to negotiate a transfer price.

Multiple Choice

1. Sally Thorne is a profit center manager for ABC Company's Phoenix district. Last year, her performance evaluation was based on the operating performance of ABC's entire Southwest region. This is a violation of

Quiz 25-1
www.mhhe.com/LLPW1e

   a. The hurdle rate principle.
   b. The controllability principle.
   c. The balanced scorecard approach.
   d. Negotiated transfer pricing rules.

2. Responsibility centers include
   a. Cost centers.   d. Investment centers.
   b. Revenue centers.   e. All of these.
   c. Profit centers.

3. Which of the following statements is true?
   a. A profit center manager is responsible for investment of company assets.
   b. A cost center manager should be evaluated based on sales revenue.
   c. A profit center manager should be evaluated based on return on investment.
   d. An investment center manager is responsible for costs, revenue, and the investment of assets.

4. Which of the following is most likely to be classified as a cost center manager?
   a. Accounting manager.
   b. Sales manager.
   c. Regional manager.
   d. All of these are cost center managers.

5. Return on investment and residual income are useful in evaluating
   a. Cost center managers.
   b. Revenue center managers.
   c. Profit center managers.
   d. Investment center managers.

6. Return on investment can be separated into
   a. Investment turnover and profit margin.
   b. Profit margin and residual income.
   c. Investment turnover and residual income.
   d. Profit margin and operating income.

7. Raymond Calvin is an investment center manager for XYZ Corp. and is evaluated solely on the return on investment for his division. Which of the following will improve Raymond's evaluation?
   a. Increasing the amount invested in assets while keeping operating income the same.

b. Increasing the amount of operating income while keeping invested assets the same.

c. Decreasing the amount invested in assets while keeping operating income the same.

d. Either b or c.

8. Which of the following statements is true?

a. Return on investment considers a company's hurdle rate for investments.

b. Residual income considers a company's hurdle rate for investments.

c. Projects may be declined based on return on investment even though they produce positive residual income.

d. Both b and c.

9. Which of the following is not a component of the balanced scorecard method of measuring performance?

a. Customer perspective.

b. Management perspective.

c. Learning and growth perspective.

d. Internal business processes.

e. Financial perspective.

10. Transfer price could be based on:

a. Variable costs.

b. Full cost.

c. Market price.

d. Any of the above.

Solutions to Multiple-Choice Questions

1. b   2. e   3. d   4. a   5. d   6. a   7. d   8. d   9. b   10. d

---

Mini Exercises   Available with McGraw-Hill's Homework Manager

M25-1 Describing the Difference in Centralized and Decentralized Organizations   LO1

Lupe Bornes recently graduated from college and received job offers in management from two different companies. The positions are similar in terms of title, salary, and benefits, but the companies vary in organizational structure. Alpha Company is centralized while Beta Company is decentralized. Explain to Lupe what he can infer about each company and how it is likely to affect his position within each one.

M25-2 Describing How Real-World Organizations' Responsibility Centers Are Structured   LO2

Responsibility centers can be created in a variety of ways. Give a real-world example of a company whose responsibility centers would likely be created on the basis of each of the following: functional area, product line, and geographic area.

M25-3 Applying the Balanced Scorecard to a Real-World Company   LO5

Consider the manager of your local Applebee's restaurant. Using a balanced scorecard approach, identify five measures on which upper management could evaluate the manager's performance. At least three of the items listed should be nonfinancial measures.

M25-4 Calculating Return on Investment and Residual Income   LO3, 4

Kettle Company has sales of $450,000, operating income of $250,000, average invested assets of $800,000, and a hurdle rate of 10 percent. What are Kettle's return on investment and its residual income?

M25-5 Calculating Return on Investment and Residual Income   LO3, 4

Lowry Company has sales of $125,000, cost of goods sold of $70,000, operating expenses of $20,000, average invested assets of $400,000, and a hurdle rate of 8 percent. What are Lowry's return on investment and its residual income?

M25-6 Calculating Return on Investment and Residual Income   LO3, 4

Rally Corp's Eastern Division has sales of $190,000, cost of goods sold of $110,000, operating expenses of $35,000, average invested assets of $900,000, and a hurdle rate of 12 percent. What are the Eastern Division's return on investment and its residual income?

M25-7 Describing the Implications of Transfer Pricing   LO2, 6

Assume that your cousin Matilda Flores, manages a local glass shop that was recently bought by a company that produces custom picture frames. As a result, Matilda will soon be providing glass to the Frame Division. She has heard upper management mention a transfer price but does not understand what this term means or how it might affect her division. Briefly explain transfer pricing to Matilda and how it will impact her division's performance in the future.

LO6   **M25-8 Identifying Minimum and Maximum Transfer Prices**

Lancaster Company has two divisions, A and B. Division A manufactures a component that Division B uses. The variable cost to produce this component is $1.50 per unit; full cost is $2.00. The component sells on the open market for $5.00. Assuming Division A has excess capacity, what is the lowest price for which Division A will sell the component? What is the most that Division B will pay for it?

LO6   **M25-9 Calculating a Cost-Plus Transfer Price**

Bellows Company has two divisions, X and Y. Division X manufactures a wheel assembly that Division Y uses. The variable cost to produce this assembly is $4.00 per unit; full cost is $5.00. The component sells on the open market for $9.00. What will the transfer price be if Bellows uses a pricing rule of variable cost plus 40 percent?

Exercises Available with McGraw-Hill's Homework Manager

LO1, 2, 5   **E25-1 Explaining the Relationships among Decentralization, Responsibility Accounting, Controllability, and the Balanced Scorecard**

Assume you are the vice president of operations for a local company. Your company is in the process of converting from a small, centralized company in which its president makes all decisions to a larger, geographically dispersed organization with decentralized decision-making authority.

Required:

Write a brief memo to other company managers explaining how decentralization, responsibility accounting, controllability, and the balanced scorecard method of performance evaluation are all related. Include the most obvious changes the managers are likely to see as this transition takes place and how it will impact their performance evaluations in the future.

LO2   **E25-2 Identifying Types of Responsibility Centers**

Required:

Match the most likely type of responsibility center classification to each of the following positions. You may use a classification once, more than once, or not at all.

Employment Positions	Possible Responsibility Center Classification
_____ Sales manager	a. Cost center
_____ Regional manager	b. Revenue center
_____ Company president	c. Profit center
_____ Purchasing manager	d. Investment center
_____ Human resources manager	
_____ Chief financial officer	
_____ Production facility manager	

LO3   **E25-3 Finding Unknowns Using Return on Investment, Profit Margin, and Investment Turnover**

Tuttle Company recently had a computer malfunction and lost a portion of its accounting records. The company has reconstructed some of its financial performance measurements including components of the return on investment calculations.

Required:

Help Tuttle rebuild its information database by completing the following table.

Return on Investment (percent)	Profit Margin (percent)	Investment Turnover
?	5%	1.1
14	?	2.0
3	4	?
23	?	0.4

E25-4 Finding Unknowns Using Return on Investment, Profit Margin, and Investment Turnover   LO3

Norshon Company recently had a computer malfunction and lost a portion of its accounting records. The company has reconstructed some of its financial performance measurements including components of the return on investment calculations.

Required:

Help Norshon rebuild its information database by completing the following table.

Return on Investment (percent)	Profit Margin (percent)	Investment Turnover	Operating Income	Sales Revenue	Average Invested Assets
?	?	?	$ 35,000	$ 700,000	$1,400,000
?	10	0.40	100,000	?	2,500,000
?	15	1.25	?	2,000,000	?
12	?	2.00	?	500,000	?

E25-5 Calculating Return on Investment and Residual Income and Determining the Effect of Changes in Sales, Expenses, Invested Assets, and the Hurdle Rate on Each   LO3, 4

Mancell Company has sales of $500,000, cost of goods sold of $370,000, other operating expenses of $50,000, invested assets of $1,400,000, and a hurdle rate of 8 percent.

Required:

1. Determine Mancell's return on investment (ROI), investment turnover, profit margin, and residual income.

2. Several possible changes that Mancell could face in the upcoming year follow. Determine each scenario's impact on Mancell's ROI and residual income. (**Note:** Treat each scenario independently.)

   a. Company sales and cost of goods sold increase by 30 percent.
   b. Operating expenses decrease by $10,000.
   c. Operating expenses increase by 20 percent.
   d. Average invested assets increase by $300,000
   e. Mancell changes its hurdle rate to 12 percent.

E25-6 Evaluating Managerial Performance Using Return on Investment and Residual Income   LO3, 4

Francis Corp. has two divisions, Eastern and Western. The following information for the past year is for each division.

	Eastern Division	Western Division
Sales	$ 600,000	$ 900,000
Cost of goods sold and operating expenses	450,000	600,000
Operating Income	$ 150,000	$ 300,000
Average invested assets	$1,000,000	$1,500,000

Francis has established a hurdle rate of 9 percent.

Required:

1. Compute each division's return on investment (ROI) and residual income for last year. Determine which manager seems to be performing better.

2. Suppose Francis is investing in new technology that will increase each division's operating income by $144,000. The total investment required is $1,600,000, which will be split evenly between the two divisions. Calculate the ROI and return on investment for each division after the investment is made.

3. Determine whether both managers will support the investment. Explain how their support will differ depending on which performance measure (ROI or residual investment) is used.

LO5

E25-7 Describing the Objectives and Perspectives of a Balanced Scorecard

Your brother-in-law, Fred Miles, has just taken a new position as the plant manager of a local production facility. He has been told that the company uses a balanced scorecard approach to evaluate its managers. Fred is not familiar with this approach because his previous experience as a production manager focused on only whether the plant met the company's budgeted production.

Required:

1. Briefly explain to Fred how performance evaluations at his new company will differ from those at his previous company.
2. Give Fred five possible objectives that the new company will use in addition to production level in evaluating Fred's performance. For each objective that you identify, be sure to indicate a plausible metric for measuring that item.

LO6

E25-8 Determining Minimum, Maximum, and Negotiated Transfer Prices

Coleman Company is a lumber company that also manufactures custom cabinetry. It is made up of two divisions, Lumber and Cabinetry. Division L is responsible for harvesting and preparing lumber for use; Division C produces custom-ordered cabinetry. The lumber produced by Division L has a variable cost of $1.00 per linear foot and full cost of $1.50. Comparable quality wood sells on the open market for $3.00 per linear foot.

Required:

1. Assume you are the manager of Division C. Determine the maximum amount you would pay for lumber from Division L.
2. Assume you are the manager of Division L. Determine the minimum amount you would charge for the lumber sold to Division C if you have excess capacity. Repeat assuming you have no excess capacity.
3. Assume you were the president of Coleman and wanted to set a mutually beneficial transfer price. Determine the mutually beneficial transfer price.
4. Explain the possible consequences of simply letting the two division managers negotiate a price.

LO6

E25-9 Identifying Minimum and Maximum Transfer Prices and Determining the Effect on Each Division's Profit

Womack Company is made up of two divisions, A and B. Division A produces a widget that Division B uses in the production of its product. Variable cost per widget is $0.50; full cost is $0.70. Comparable widgets sell on the open market for $1.10 each. Division A can produce up to 2,000,000 widgets per year but is currently operating at only 50 percent capacity. Division B expects to use 100,000 widgets in the current year.

Required:

1. Determine the minimum and maximum transfers prices.
2. Calculate Womack Company's total benefit of having the widgets transferred between these divisions.
3. If the transfer price is set at $0.50 per unit, determine how much profit Division A will receive from the transfer. Determine how much Division B will save by not purchasing the widgets on the open market.
4. If the transfer price is set at $1.10 per unit, determine how much profit Division A will receive from the transfer. Determine how much Division B will save by not purchasing the widgets on the open market.
5. What transfer price would you recommend to split the difference?

Problems—Set A   **Available with McGraw-Hill's Homework Manager**

LO3, 4

www.mhhe.com/LLPW1e

PA25-1 Calculating Return on Investment and Residual Income and Determining the Effect of Changes in Sales, Expenses, Invested Assets, and the Hurdle Rate on Each

Longview Company has the following information available for past year.

	Northern Division	Southern Division
Sales	$1,200,000	$1,800,000
Cost of goods sold and operating expenses	900,000	1,300,000
Operating Income	$ 300,000	$ 500,000
Average invested assets	$1,000,000	$1,500,000

The company's hurdle rate is 8 percent.

Required:

1. Calculate return on investment (ROI) and residual income for each division for last year.
2. Recalculate ROI and residual income for each division for each independent situation that follows.

   a. Operating income increase by 10 percent.
   b. Operating income decrease by 10 percent.
   c. The company invests $250,000 in each division, an amount that generates $100,000 additional income per division.
   d. Longview changes its hurdle rate to 6 percent.

PA25-2 Calculating Unknowns and Predicting the Relationship among Return on Investment, Residual Income, and Hurdle Rates   LO3, 4

The following is partial information for Dupre Company's most recent year of operation. Dupre manufactures pet toys and categorizes its operations into two divisions, Cat and Dog.

	Cat Division	Dog Division
Sales revenue	?	$600,000
Average invested assets	$2,000,000	?
Operating income	$ 160,000	$150,000
Profit margin	20%	?
Investment turnover	?	0.2
Return on investment	?	?
Residual income	$ 40,000	$ (30,000)

Required:

1. Without making any calculations, determine whether each division's return on investment is above or below Dupre's hurdle rate. How can you tell?
2. Determine the missing amounts in the preceding table.
3. What is Dupre's hurdle rate?
4. Suppose Dupre has the opportunity to purchase additional assets to help expand the company's market share. The expansion would require an average investment of $2,000,000 and would generate $140,000 in additional income. From Dupre's perspective, is this a viable investment? Why or why not?
5. Suppose the two divisions would equally share the investment and profits from the expansion project. If return on investment is used to evaluate performance, what will each division think about the proposed project?
6. In requirement 5, will either manager's preference change if residual income is used to measure division performance? Explain your answer.

PA25-3 Identifying Minimum, Maximum, and Mutually Beneficial Transfer Prices   LO6

Rideaway Corp. is a high-end bicycle manufacturing company that produces mountain bikes. SoftSaddle, Inc. is a division of Rideaway that manufactures bicycle seats. SoftSaddle's seats are used in Rideaway's bikes and are sold to other bike manufacturers. Cost information per seat follows.

Variable cost	$22.00
Full cost	27.00
Market price	40.00

In addition, its capacity data follow.

Capacity per year	40,000 seats
Current production level	30,000 seats

Required:

1. Assuming Rideaway produces 3,000 bikes per year, determine the overall benefit of using seats from SoftSaddle instead of purchasing them externally.
2. Determine the maximum price that the bike production facility would be willing to pay to purchase the seats from SoftSaddle. How is the overall benefit split between the two divisions if this transfer price is used?
3. Determine the minimum that SoftSaddle will accept as a transfer price. How is the overall benefit split between the two divisions if this transfer price is used?
4. Determine the mutually beneficial transfer price for the bicycle seats.
5. How would your answer change if SoftSaddle were currently operating at capacity?

LO6

PA25-4 Identifying Minimum, Maximum, and Mutually Beneficial Transfer Prices

Travel Well, Inc., manufactures a variety of luggage for use by airline passengers. The company has several luggage production divisions as well as a wholly owned subsidiary, SecureLock, that manufactures small padlocks used on luggage. Each piece of luggage that Duffle Bag Division produces has two padlocks for which it previously paid the going market price of $3 each. Financial information for Travel Well's Duffle Bag Division and for SecureLock follow.

	Duffle Bag Division	SecureLock
Sales		
4,500 bags × $150 each	$675,000	
200,000 locks × $3.00 each		$600,000
Variable expenses		
4,500 units × $85.00 each	382,500	
200,000 × $0.60 each		120,000

SecureLock has a production capacity of 250,000 units.

Required:

1. Determine how much Travel Well will save on each padlock if Duffle Bag Division obtains them from SecureLock instead of an external supplier.
2. Determine the maximum and minimum transfer prices for the padlocks. Who sets these?
3. Suppose Travel Well has set a transfer price policy of variable cost plus 50 percent for all related-party transactions. Determine how much each party will benefit from the internal transfer.
4. Determine the mutually beneficial transfer price.

Problems—Set B   ▦™   Available with McGraw-Hill's Homework Manager

LO3, 4

PB25-1 Calculating Return on Investment and Residual Income and Determining the Effect of Changes in Sales, Expenses, Invested Assets, and the Hurdle Rate on Each

Pascall Company has the following information available for the past year.

	Eastern Division	Western Division
Segment sales	$2,200,000	$1,300,000
Segment cost of goods sold and operating expenses	1,700,000	1,000,000
Segment income	$ 500,000	$ 300,000
Average invested assets	$3,800,000	$2,500,000

The company's hurdle rate is 10 percent.

1. Determine Pascall's return on investment (ROI) and residual income for each division for last year.
2. Recalculate Pascall's ROI and residual income for each division for each independent situation that follows.

   a. Operating income increases by 10 percent.
   b. Operating income decreases by 10 percent.
   c. The company invests $400,000 in each division, an amount that generates $80,000 additional income per division.
   d. Pascall changes its hurdle rate to 15 percent.

3. For each scenario in requirement 2, indicate which division is performing better.

PB25-2 Calculating Unknowns and Predicting the Relationship among Return on Investment, Residual Income, and Hurdle Rates   **LO3, 4**
The following is partial information for Xavier Company's most recent year of operation. Xavier manufactures children's shoes and categorizes its operations into two divisions, Girls and Boys.

	Girls Division	Boys Division
Sales revenue	$2,000,000	?
Average invested assets	?	$1,000,000
Operating income	$ 500,000	$ 300,000
Profit margin	?	15%
Investment turnover	1.0	?
Return on investment	?	?
Residual income	$ 260,000	$ 180,000

Required:

1. Without making any calculations, determine whether each division's return on investment is above or below Xavier's hurdle rate. How can you tell?
2. Determine the missing amounts in the preceding table.
3. What is Xavier's hurdle rate?
4. Suppose Xavier has the opportunity to purchase additional assets to help expand the company's market share. The expansion would require an investment of $4,000,000 and would generate $800,000 in additional income. From Xavier's perspective, is this a viable investment? Why or why not?
5. Suppose the two divisions would equally share the investment and profits from the expansion project. If return on investment is used to evaluate performance, what will each division think about the proposed project?
6. In requirement 5, will either manager's preference change if residual income is used to measure division performance? Explain your answer.

LO6   **PB25-3 Identifying Minimum, Maximum, and Mutually Beneficial Transfer Prices**

Snuggle Up Company produces outdoor gear. ZipIt is a division of Snuggle that manufactures unbreakable zippers used in Snuggle's gear and sold to other manufacturers. Cost information per zipper follows.

Variable cost	$0.80
Full cost	1.10
Market price	3.00

In addition, ZipIt's capacity data follow.

Capacity per year	2,000,000 zippers
Current production level	1,500,000 zippers

Required:

1. Assuming Snuggle produces 300,000 sleeping bags per year, what is the overall benefit of using zippers from ZipIt instead of purchasing them externally?
2. Determine the maximum price that the sleeping bag production facility would be willing to pay to purchase the zippers from ZipIt. How is the overall benefit split between the two divisions if this transfer price is used?
3. Determine the minimum that ZipIt will accept as a transfer price. How is the overall benefit split between the two divisions if this transfer price is used?
4. Determine the mutually beneficial transfer price for the zippers.
5. How would your answer change if ZipIt were currently operating at capacity?

LO6   **PB25-4 Identifying Minimum, Maximum, and Mutually Beneficial Transfer Prices**

H2-Oh! produces bottled water. The company recently purchased PlastiCo., a manufacturer of plastic bottles. In the past, H2-Oh! has purchased plastic bottles on the open market at $0.25 each. Financial information for the past year for H2-Oh! and PlastiCo. follows.

	H2-Oh!	PlastiCo.
Sales		
500,000 units × $2.00 each	$1,000,000	
1,200,000 units × $0.25 each		$300,000
Variable expenses		
500,000 units × $0.25 each	125,000	
1,200,000 × $0.05 each		60,000

PlastiCo has a production capacity of 2,000,000 units.

Required:

1. Determine how much H2-Oh! will save on each bottle if it obtains them from PlastiCo. instead of an external supplier.
2. Determine the maximum and minimum transfer prices for the plastic bottles. Who sets these?
3. Suppose H2-Oh! has determined a transfer price rule of variable cost plus 40 percent for all related-party transactions. Determine how much each party will benefit from the internal transfer.
4. Determine the mutually beneficial transfer price.

Cases and Projects

LO6   **CP25-1 Researching the Effect of Transfer Prices on Taxes**

The problems surrounding transfer pricing are not limited to internal decisions. Companies' transfer prices can have huge implications well beyond departmental profits including significant tax implications.

In September 2006, the U.K.-based pharmaceutical giant, Glaxo SmithKline (GSK), settled an ongoing dispute with the U.S. Internal Revenue Service. In doing so, GSK agreed to pay $3.4 billion dollars in back taxes and interest. This was the largest single tax dispute in U.S. history.

Required:

Research the GSK dispute and write a two-page memo summarizing the central issues of the dispute. Include in your summary the position of each side (IRS and GSK) as well as GSK's explanation for the settlement and any impact on company shareholders.

CP25-2 Researching the Use of the Balanced Scorecard in Business   LO5

This chapter discussed the use of the balanced scorecard for evaluating managerial and organizational performance. Many companies have adopted this performance measurement in recent years.

Required:

Do an Internet search to find an example of a company that has implemented the balanced scorecard and write a brief report of the company's experience. You should include information such as when the company implemented the balanced scorecard, what performance measurement approach it had used previously, any difficulties it experienced with the implementation, and the benefits received from the new method.

CP25-3 Explaining the Impact of Organizational Structure and Budgetary Processes on   LO1
Employee Morale

In the last several chapters, you have learned about many aspects of organizational structure, budgeting, and performance evaluation. None of these characteristics of a company operates in isolation: They all interrelate to form an organization's culture and influence employee morale. The following table has several combinations of organizational structure and budgeting preparation style.

Organizational Structure	Budget Creation Process
Centralized	Administered
Decentralized	Participative
Centralized	Participative
Decentralized	Administered

Required:

For each combination in the table, write a brief paragraph summarizing both the potential advantages and disadvantages for a company using the combination. Consider the impact on managers and other employees as well as the potential impact on outside parties such as customers or other organizational stakeholders.

THE HOME DEPOT, INC. 2007 ANNUAL REPORT*

OUR APRONS, YOUR STORE
2007 Annual Report

* This appendix contains excerpts. Go to the text Web site at www.mhhe.com/LLPW1e for the complete report.

|**DEAR** SHAREHOLDERS, ASSOCIATES, CUSTOMERS, SUPPLIERS AND COMMUNITIES:

This past year was one of the most difficult our company has faced. Year-over-year retail sales declined by 2.1 percent, with comp sales down 6.7 percent. Our operating margin declined 186 basis points and our earnings per share from continuing operations were down 11 percent.

We began the year with the objectives of focusing on our retail business, investing in our associates and stores, and improving our customer service. We stayed true to those objectives despite the economic headwinds and invested over $2 billion in five key priorities: **associate engagement, product excitement, product availability, shopping environment and own the pro.** These investments put additional pressure on earnings in a difficult environment, but we are convinced the right long-term strategy starts with the customer experience in our stores. In each priority area, we made significant progress.

ASSOCIATE ENGAGEMENT:
Our founders emphasized the importance of taking care of our associates who take care of our customers. This is as important today as it was twenty years ago. It is an investment we know will strengthen our market leadership position. This past year, we took significant steps to improve the compensation and recognition of our associates and to build on the expertise in our stores. We implemented a new restricted stock bonus program for our assistant store managers. We are the only retailer of our size to award equity grants at that level of management. For us, it is important that our assistant store managers feel and act like owners. We significantly increased participation and payout of our Success Sharing bonuses for hourly associates and rolled out a new Homer Badge merit program to recognize great customer service. I hope as you shop our stores you will notice the associates who are proudly wearing these badges. We hired more than 2,500 Master Trade Specialists in our plumbing and electrical departments. These associates are licensed plumbers and electricians and provide both knowledgeable service to our customers and great training for associates. As a result of these and other efforts, full time voluntary attrition was down almost 20 percent in 2007.

PRODUCT EXCITEMENT:
Our customers expect great value and exciting products in our stores. In 2007, as in the past, we focused on meeting those expectations. We invested significantly in merchandising resets, drove product innovation through our successful launch of the Ryobi Lithium One+ line of power tools and our Eco Options program, and revamped product lines to drive greater value for our customers. We are particularly proud of the leadership we maintained in a number of categories including appliances, outdoor living, live goods, and paint.

PRODUCT AVAILABILITY:
In 2007, we took an important first step in transforming our supply chain. We piloted a new distribution network and technology - Rapid Deployment Centers (RDCs). The pilot was successful, and we will be rolling out RDCs throughout 2008 and 2009. We are confident that our future supply chain will dramatically improve our supply chain efficiency, improve our in stock levels, improve our asset efficiency, and improve our ability to meet increasingly differentiated customer needs.

SHOPPING ENVIRONMENT:
Our store base is getting older, and we have to protect one of our most important assets. We increased store maintenance in 2007, spending 38 percent more than our 2006 maintenance levels and two times our 2005 maintenance levels. We developed a sustainable programmatic approach to maintenance, with specific schedules for polishing floors, remodeling restrooms, and replacing major equipment such as air conditioners and service desks. As shown through our "Voice of the Customer" surveys, our customers appreciate these investments.

OWN THE PRO:
We know that the professional customer is a critically important customer for us. This year we rolled out several programs aimed at better serving our pros. One of these is our pro bid room, which allows us to better manage large customer orders. Our professional customers look to us for the right products in the right quantities to make their jobs easier. We reinforced our job lot quantity program in our stores and revised our delivery service for better utilization. We are also leveraging our customer data to build stronger relationships with this key customer segment.

INTERNATIONAL:
While discussing progress in 2007, I'd like to give special recognition to our international businesses in Mexico, Canada and China. Our stores in Mexico had double digit positive comps for the year. Our stores in Canada posted positive comps. In China, once we launched our Home Depot brand in August 2007, our stores posted positive comps. Our international stores contributed almost 10 percent of sales and 12 percent of operating profit in 2007. These results demonstrate how well our format translates and the sizable opportunity to

VALUES WHEEL

expand to new areas such as Guam, where we opened our first store this year.

As I complete my first year in this role, I want to thank the Board of Directors for their support and dedication. I would especially like to recognize our directors that are retiring this year: John Clendenin, Claudio González, Mitch Hart, and Ken Langone – one of our founders. Their guidance and counsel has been instrumental in the success of our company.

OUR STRATEGY IS SIMPLE:

We have clearly defined The Home Depot as a retail business. The sale of HD Supply in August of 2007 was the critical step in achieving that clarity and focus. We also defined our capital allocation strategy: We will be focused on improving our return on invested capital and will benchmark all uses of excess cash against the value created for shareholders through share repurchases. With that in mind, we used the proceeds from the sale of HD Supply and cash on hand to buy back $10.7 billion of stock. This puts us approximately halfway through our announced $22.5 billion recapitalization plan. Our cash flow will help determine the timing of the remaining steps in the recapitalization plan, as we look to maintain an adjusted debt/EBITDAR ratio of 2.5 times. We are targeting a payout ratio of 30 percent, amongst the highest ratios in retail.

Our strategy: focus on our retail business, invest in our people, improve our stores, bring great products at great value to our customers, drive a high return on invested capital, and return excess cash to our shareholders.

For 2008, we are expecting a year every bit as challenging as 2007. We plan on opening fewer stores than has been our historical practice as we continue to invest and sharpen our focus on existing stores. We will continue to invest in our business along the five priorities set

out in 2007. As part of our investment plan, we have aggressive plans to build out our U.S. supply chain, to put more associates on the selling floor through a major "aprons on the floor" initiative, and to take the first step in transforming our information technology infrastructure by converting our Canadian business to an Enterprise Resource Planning platform focused on enhancing our merchandising and customer facing activities. As our market improves and as the benefits of these investments in our business take hold, we look forward over the next four years to returning to a double digit operating margin.

We will also continue to build relationships and strengthen ties with our communities. This has been a hallmark of The Home Depot. One of the best parts of my job is hearing about the extraordinary things our associates do to help each other, help our customers and help our communities every day. We are a values based business, and we do our best to live and celebrate the values represented on the wheel depicted on this page. We recognize the self-reinforcing strength of these values builds great customer service. I hope, as you shop in our stores, you will notice our continuing improvement and the value of the investments we are making.

Frank

Francis S. Blake
Chairman & Chief Executive Officer
April 3, 2008

Item 8.   Financial Statements and Supplementary Data.

Management's Responsibility for Financial Statements

The financial statements presented in this Annual Report have been prepared with integrity and objectivity and are the responsibility of the management of The Home Depot, Inc. These financial statements have been prepared in conformity with U.S. generally accepted accounting principles and properly reflect certain estimates and judgments based upon the best available information.

The financial statements of the Company have been audited by KPMG LLP, an independent registered public accounting firm. Their accompanying report is based upon an audit conducted in accordance with the standards of the Public Company Accounting Oversight Board (United States).

The Audit Committee of the Board of Directors, consisting solely of outside directors, meets five times a year with the independent registered public accounting firm, the internal auditors and representatives of management to discuss auditing and financial reporting matters. In addition, a telephonic meeting is held prior to each quarterly earnings release. The Audit Committee retains the independent registered public accounting firm and regularly reviews the internal accounting controls, the activities of the independent registered public accounting firm and internal auditors and the financial condition of the Company. Both the Company's independent registered public accounting firm and the internal auditors have free access to the Audit Committee.

Management's Report on Internal Control over Financial Reporting

Our management is responsible for establishing and maintaining adequate internal control over financial reporting, as such term is defined in Rules 13a-15(f) promulgated under the Securities Exchange Act of 1934, as amended. Under the supervision and with the participation of our management, including our chief executive officer and chief financial officer, we conducted an evaluation of the effectiveness of our internal control over financial reporting as of February 3, 2008 based on the framework in *Internal Control – Integrated Framework* issued by the Committee of Sponsoring Organizations of the Treadway Commission (COSO). Based on our evaluation, our management concluded that our internal control over financial reporting was effective as of February 3, 2008 in providing reasonable assurance regarding the reliability of financial reporting and the preparation of financial statements for external purposes in accordance with generally accepted accounting principles. The effectiveness of our internal control over financial reporting as of February 3, 2008 has been audited by KPMG LLP, an independent registered public accounting firm, as stated in their report which is included on page 32 in this Form 10-K.

/s/ FRANCIS S. BLAKE

Francis S. Blake
Chairman &
Chief Executive Officer

/s/ CAROL B. TOMÉ

Carol B. Tomé
Chief Financial Officer &
Executive Vice President – Corporate
Services

Report of Independent Registered Public Accounting Firm

The Board of Directors and Stockholders
The Home Depot, Inc.:

We have audited The Home Depot Inc.'s internal control over financial reporting as of February 3, 2008, based on criteria established in *Internal Control – Integrated Framework* issued by the Committee of Sponsoring Organizations of the Treadway Commission (COSO). The Home Depot Inc.'s management is responsible for maintaining effective internal control over financial reporting and for its assessment of the effectiveness of internal control over financial reporting, included in the accompanying Management's Report on Internal Control Over Financial Reporting. Our responsibility is to express an opinion on the Company's internal control over financial reporting based on our audit.

We conducted our audit in accordance with the standards of the Public Company Accounting Oversight Board (United States). Those standards require that we plan and perform the audit to obtain reasonable assurance about whether effective internal control over financial reporting was maintained in all material respects. Our audit included obtaining an understanding of internal control over financial reporting, assessing the risk that a material weakness exists, and testing and evaluating the design and operating effectiveness of internal control based on the assessed risk. Our audit also included performing such other procedures as we considered necessary in the circumstances. We believe that our audit provides a reasonable basis for our opinion.

A company's internal control over financial reporting is a process designed to provide reasonable assurance regarding the reliability of financial reporting and the preparation of financial statements for external purposes in accordance with generally accepted accounting principles. A company's internal control over financial reporting includes those policies and procedures that (1) pertain to the maintenance of records that, in reasonable detail, accurately and fairly reflect the transactions and dispositions of the assets of the company; (2) provide reasonable assurance that transactions are recorded as necessary to permit preparation of financial statements in accordance with generally accepted accounting principles, and that receipts and expenditures of the company are being made only in accordance with authorizations of management and directors of the company; and (3) provide reasonable assurance regarding prevention or timely detection of unauthorized acquisition, use, or disposition of the company's assets that could have a material effect on the financial statements.

Because of its inherent limitations, internal control over financial reporting may not prevent or detect misstatements. Also, projections of any evaluation of effectiveness to future periods are subject to the risk that controls may become inadequate because of changes in conditions, or that the degree of compliance with the policies or procedures may deteriorate.

In our opinion, The Home Depot, Inc. maintained, in all material respects, effective internal control over financial reporting as of February 3, 2008, based on criteria established in *Internal Control – Integrated Framework* issued by the Committee of Sponsoring Organizations of the Treadway Commission.

We also have audited, in accordance with the standards of the Public Company Accounting Oversight Board (United States), the Consolidated Balance Sheets of The Home Depot, Inc. and subsidiaries as of February 3, 2008 and January 28, 2007, and the related Consolidated Statements of Earnings, Stockholders' Equity and Comprehensive Income, and Cash Flows for each of the fiscal years in the three-year period ended February 3, 2008, and our report dated March 28, 2008 expressed an unqualified opinion on those consolidated financial statements.

/s/ KPMG LLP

Atlanta, Georgia
March 28, 2008

Report of Independent Registered Public Accounting Firm

The Board of Directors and Stockholders
The Home Depot, Inc.:

We have audited the accompanying Consolidated Balance Sheets of The Home Depot, Inc. and subsidiaries as of February 3, 2008 and January 28, 2007, and the related Consolidated Statements of Earnings, Stockholders' Equity and Comprehensive Income, and Cash Flows for each of the fiscal years in the three-year period ended February 3, 2008. These Consolidated Financial Statements are the responsibility of the Company's management. Our responsibility is to express an opinion on these Consolidated Financial Statements based on our audits.

We conducted our audits in accordance with the standards of the Public Company Accounting Oversight Board (United States). Those standards require that we plan and perform the audit to obtain reasonable assurance about whether the financial statements are free of material misstatement. An audit includes examining, on a test basis, evidence supporting the amounts and disclosures in the financial statements. An audit also includes assessing the accounting principles used and significant estimates made by management, as well as evaluating the overall financial statement presentation. We believe that our audits provide a reasonable basis for our opinion.

In our opinion, the Consolidated Financial Statements referred to above present fairly, in all material respects, the financial position of The Home Depot, Inc. and subsidiaries as of February 3, 2008 and January 28, 2007, and the results of their operations and their cash flows for each of the fiscal years in the three-year period ended February 3, 2008, in conformity with U.S. generally accepted accounting principles.

As discussed in Note 6 to the consolidated financial statements, effective January 29, 2007, the beginning of the fiscal year ended February 3, 2008, the Company adopted Financial Accounting Standards Board Interpretation No. 48, *Accounting for Uncertainty in Income Taxes* . Also, as discussed in Note 3 to the consolidated financial statements, effective January 30, 2006, the beginning of the fiscal year ended January 28, 2007, the Company adopted Securities and Exchange Commission Staff Accounting Bulletin No. 108, *Considering the Effects of Prior Year Misstatements when Quantifying Misstatements in the Current Year Financial Statements* .

We also have audited, in accordance with the standards of the Public Company Accounting Oversight Board (United States), The Home Depot, Inc.'s internal control over financial reporting as of February 3, 2008, based on criteria established in *Internal Control – Integrated Framework* issued by the Committee of Sponsoring Organizations of the Treadway Commission (COSO), and our report dated March 28, 2008 expressed an unqualified opinion on the effectiveness of the Company's internal control over financial reporting.

/s/ KPMG LLP

Atlanta, Georgia
March 28, 2008

THE HOME DEPOT, INC. AND SUBSIDIARIES

CONSOLIDATED STATEMENTS OF EARNINGS

	Fiscal Year Ended [1]		
amounts in millions, except per share data	February 3, 2008	January 28, 2007	January 29, 2006
NET SALES	$ **77,349**	$ 79,022	$ 77,019
Cost of Sales	**51,352**	52,476	51,081
GROSS PROFIT	**25,997**	26,546	25,938
Operating Expenses:			
Selling, General and Administrative	**17,053**	16,106	15,480
Depreciation and Amortization	**1,702**	1,574	1,411
Total Operating Expenses	**18,755**	17,680	16,891
OPERATING INCOME	**7,242**	8,866	9,047
Interest (Income) Expense:			
Interest and Investment Income	**(74)**	(27)	(62)
Interest Expense	**696**	391	142
Interest, net	**622**	364	80
EARNINGS FROM CONTINUING OPERATIONS BEFORE PROVISION FOR INCOME TAXES	**6,620**	8,502	8,967
Provision for Income Taxes	**2,410**	3,236	3,326
EARNINGS FROM CONTINUING OPERATIONS	**4,210**	5,266	5,641
EARNINGS FROM DISCONTINUED OPERATIONS, NET OF TAX	**185**	495	197
NET EARNINGS	$ **4,395**	$ 5,761	$ 5,838
Weighted Average Common Shares	**1,849**	2,054	2,138
BASIC EARNINGS PER SHARE FROM CONTINUING OPERATIONS	$ **2.28**	$ 2.56	$ 2.64
BASIC EARNINGS PER SHARE FROM DISCONTINUED OPERATIONS	$ **0.10**	$ 0.24	$ 0.09
BASIC EARNINGS PER SHARE	$ **2.38**	$ 2.80	$ 2.73
Diluted Weighted Average Common Shares	**1,856**	2,062	2,147
DILUTED EARNINGS PER SHARE FROM CONTINUING OPERATIONS	$ **2.27**	$ 2.55	$ 2.63
DILUTED EARNINGS PER SHARE FROM DISCONTINUED OPERATIONS	$ **0.10**	$ 0.24	$ 0.09
DILUTED EARNINGS PER SHARE	$ **2.37**	$ 2.79	$ 2.72

(1)   Fiscal year ended February 3, 2008 includes 53 weeks. Fiscal years ended January 28, 2007 and January 29, 2006 include 52 weeks.

See accompanying Notes to Consolidated Financial Statements.

THE HOME DEPOT, INC. AND SUBSIDIARIES

CONSOLIDATED BALANCE SHEETS

	February 3, 2008	January 28, 2007
amounts in millions, except share and per share data		
ASSETS		
Current Assets:		
Cash and Cash Equivalents	$ 445	$ 600
Short-Term Investments	12	14
Receivables, net	1,259	3,223
Merchandise Inventories	11,731	12,822
Other Current Assets	1,227	1,341
Total Current Assets	14,674	18,000
Property and Equipment, at cost:		
Land	8,398	8,355
Buildings	16,642	15,215
Furniture, Fixtures and Equipment	8,050	7,799
Leasehold Improvements	1,390	1,391
Construction in Progress	1,435	1,123
Capital Leases	497	475
	36,412	34,358
Less Accumulated Depreciation and Amortization	8,936	7,753
Net Property and Equipment	27,476	26,605
Notes Receivable	342	343
Goodwill	1,209	6,314
Other Assets	623	1,001
Total Assets	$ 44,324	$ 52,263
LIABILITIES AND STOCKHOLDERS' EQUITY		
Current Liabilities:		
Short-Term Debt	$ 1,747	$ —
Accounts Payable	5,732	7,356
Accrued Salaries and Related Expenses	1,094	1,307
Sales Taxes Payable	445	475
Deferred Revenue	1,474	1,634
Income Taxes Payable	60	217
Current Installments of Long-Term Debt	300	18
Other Accrued Expenses	1,854	1,924
Total Current Liabilities	12,706	12,931
Long-Term Debt, excluding current installments	11,383	11,643
Other Long-Term Liabilities	1,833	1,243
Deferred Income Taxes	688	1,416
Total Liabilities	26,610	27,233
STOCKHOLDERS' EQUITY		
Common Stock, par value $0.05; authorized: 10 billion shares; issued 1.698 billion shares at February 3, 2008 and 2.421 billion shares at January 28, 2007; outstanding 1.690 billion shares at February 3, 2008 and 1.970 billion shares at January 28, 2007	85	121
Paid-In Capital	5,800	7,930
Retained Earnings	11,388	33,052
Accumulated Other Comprehensive Income	755	310
Treasury Stock, at cost, 8 million shares at February 3, 2008 and 451 million shares at January 28, 2007	(314)	(16,383)
Total Stockholders' Equity	17,714	25,030
Total Liabilities and Stockholders' Equity	$ 44,324	$ 52,263

See accompanying Notes to Consolidated Financial Statements.

THE HOME DEPOT, INC. AND SUBSIDIARIES

CONSOLIDATED STATEMENTS OF STOCKHOLDERS' EQUITY AND COMPREHENSIVE INCOME

amounts in millions, except per share data	Common Stock		Paid-In Capital	Retained Earnings	Accumulated Other Comprehensive Income (Loss)	Treasury Stock		Stockholders' Equity	Total Comprehensive Income
	Shares	Amount				Shares	Amount		
BALANCE, JANUARY 30, 2005	2,385 $	119 $	6,542 $	23,962 $	227	(200) $	(6,692) $	24,158	
Net Earnings	—	—	—	5,838	—	—	—	5,838	$ 5,838
Shares Issued Under Employee Stock Plans	16	1	409	—	—	—	—	410	
Tax Effect of Sale of Option Shares by Employees	—	—	24	—	—	—	—	24	
Translation Adjustments	—	—	—	—	182	—	—	182	182
Stock Options, Awards and Amortization of Restricted Stock	—	—	174	—	—	—	—	174	
Repurchase of Common Stock	—	—	—	—	—	(77)	(3,020)	(3,020)	
Cash Dividends ($0.40 per share)	—	—	—	(857)	—	—	—	(857)	
Comprehensive Income									$ 6,020
BALANCE, JANUARY 29, 2006	2,401 $	120 $	7,149 $	28,943 $	409	(277) $	(9,712) $	26,909	
Cumulative Effect of Adjustment Resulting from the Adoption of SAB 108, net of tax	—	—	201	(257)	—	—	—	(56)	
ADJUSTED BALANCE, JANUARY 29, 2006	2,401 $	120 $	7,350 $	28,686 $	409	(277) $	(9,712) $	26,853	
Net Earnings	—	—	—	5,761	—	—	—	5,761	$ 5,761
Shares Issued Under Employee Stock Plans	20	1	351	—	—	—	—	352	
Tax Effect of Sale of Option Shares by Employees	—	—	18	—	—	—	—	18	
Translation Adjustments	—	—	—	—	(77)	—	—	(77)	(77)
Cash Flow Hedges	—	—	—	—	(22)	—	—	(22)	(22)
Stock Options, Awards and Amortization of Restricted Stock	—	—	296	—	—	—	—	296	
Repurchase of Common Stock	—	—	—	—	—	(174)	(6,671)	(6,671)	
Cash Dividends ($0.675 per share)	—	—	—	(1,395)	—	—	—	(1,395)	
Other	—	—	(85)	—	—	—	—	(85)	
Comprehensive Income									$ 5,662
BALANCE, JANUARY 28, 2007	2,421 $	121 $	7,930 $	33,052 $	310	(451) $	(16,383) $	25,030	
Cumulative Effect of the Adoption of FIN 48	—	—	—	(111)	—	—	—	(111)	
Net Earnings	—	—	—	4,395	—	—	—	4,395	$ 4,395
Shares Issued Under Employee Stock Plans	12	1	239	—	—	—	—	240	
Tax Effect of Sale of Option Shares by Employees	—	—	4	—	—	—	—	4	
Translation Adjustments	—	—	—	—	455	—	—	455	455
Cash Flow Hedges	—	—	—	—	(10)	—	—	(10)	(10)
Stock Options, Awards and Amortization of Restricted Stock	—	—	206	—	—	—	—	206	
Repurchase of Common Stock	—	—	—	—	—	(292)	(10,815)	(10,815)	
Retirement of Treasury Stock	(735)	(37)	(2,608)	(24,239)	—	735	26,884	—	
Cash Dividends ($0.90 per share)	—	—	—	(1,709)	—	—	—	(1,709)	
Other	—	—	29	—	—	—	—	29	
Comprehensive Income									$ 4,840
BALANCE, FEBRUARY 3, 2008	1,698 $	85 $	5,800 $	11,388 $	755	(8) $	(314) $	17,714	

See accompanying Notes to Consolidated Financial Statements.

THE HOME DEPOT, INC. AND SUBSIDIARIES

CONSOLIDATED STATEMENTS OF CASH FLOWS

	Fiscal Year Ended [1]		
amounts in millions	February 3, 2008	January 28, 2007	January 29, 2006
CASH FLOWS FROM OPERATING ACTIVITIES:			
Net Earnings	$ 4,395	$ 5,761	$ 5,838
Reconciliation of Net Earnings to Net Cash Provided by Operating Activities:			
Depreciation and Amortization	1,906	1,886	1,579
Stock-Based Compensation Expense	207	297	175
Changes in Assets and Liabilities, net of the effects of acquisitions and disposition:			
Decrease (Increase) in Receivables, net	116	96	(358)
Increase in Merchandise Inventories	(491)	(563)	(971)
Decrease (Increase) in Other Current Assets	109	(225)	16
(Decrease) Increase in Accounts Payable and Accrued Liabilities	(465)	531	148
(Decrease) Increase in Deferred Revenue	(159)	(123)	209
(Decrease) Increase in Income Taxes Payable	—	(172)	175
(Decrease) Increase in Deferred Income Taxes	(348)	46	(609)
Increase (Decrease) in Other Long-Term Liabilities	186	(51)	151
Other	271	178	267
Net Cash Provided by Operating Activities	5,727	7,661	6,620
CASH FLOWS FROM INVESTING ACTIVITIES:			
Capital Expenditures, net of $19, $49 and $51 of non-cash capital expenditures in fiscal 2007, 2006 and 2005, respectively	(3,558)	(3,542)	(3,881)
Proceeds from Sale of Business, net	8,337	—	—
Payments for Businesses Acquired, net	(13)	(4,268)	(2,546)
Proceeds from Sales of Property and Equipment	318	138	164
Purchases of Investments	(11,225)	(5,409)	(18,230)
Proceeds from Sales and Maturities of Investments	10,899	5,434	19,907
Net Cash Provided by (Used in) Investing Activities	4,758	(7,647)	(4,586)
CASH FLOWS FROM FINANCING ACTIVITIES:			
Proceeds from (Repayments of) Short-Term Borrowings, net	1,734	(900)	900
Proceeds from Long-Term Borrowings, net of discount	—	8,935	995
Repayments of Long-Term Debt	(20)	(509)	(24)
Repurchases of Common Stock	(10,815)	(6,684)	(3,040)
Proceeds from Sale of Common Stock	276	381	414
Cash Dividends Paid to Stockholders	(1,709)	(1,395)	(857)
Other Financing Activities	(105)	(31)	(136)
Net Cash Used in Financing Activities	(10,639)	(203)	(1,748)
(Decrease) Increase in Cash and Cash Equivalents	(154)	(189)	286
Effect of Exchange Rate Changes on Cash and Cash Equivalents	(1)	(4)	1
Cash and Cash Equivalents at Beginning of Year	600	793	506
Cash and Cash Equivalents at End of Year	$ 445	$ 600	$ 793
SUPPLEMENTAL DISCLOSURE OF CASH PAYMENTS MADE FOR:			
Interest, net of interest capitalized	$ 672	$ 270	$ 114
Income Taxes	$ 2,524	$ 3,963	$ 3,860

(1)   Fiscal year ended February 3, 2008 includes 53 weeks. Fiscal years ended January 28, 2007 and January 29, 2006 include 52 weeks.

See accompanying Notes to Consolidated Financial Statements.

NOTES TO CONSOLIDATED FINANCIAL STATEMENTS

1.   SUMMARY OF SIGNIFICANT ACCOUNTING POLICIES

Business, Consolidation and Presentation

The Home Depot, Inc. and its subsidiaries (the "Company") operate The Home Depot stores, which are full-service, warehouse-style stores averaging approximately 105,000 square feet in size. The stores stock approximately 35,000 to 45,000 different kinds of building materials, home improvement supplies and lawn and garden products that are sold to do-it-yourself customers, do-it-for-me customers, home improvement contractors, tradespeople and building maintenance professionals. In addition, the Company operates EXPO Design Center stores ("EXPO"), which offer products and services primarily related to design and renovation projects. At the end of fiscal 2007, the Company was operating 2,234 stores in total, which included 1,950 The Home Depot stores, 34 EXPO stores, five Yardbirds stores and two THD Design Center stores in the United States, including the territories of Puerto Rico, the Virgin Islands and Guam ("U.S."), 165 The Home Depot stores in Canada, 66 The Home Depot stores in Mexico and 12 The Home Depot stores in China.

Information related to the Company's discontinued HD Supply business is discussed in Note 2. The Consolidated Financial Statements include the accounts of the Company and its wholly-owned subsidiaries. All significant intercompany transactions have been eliminated in consolidation.

Fiscal Year

The Company's fiscal year is a 52- or 53-week period ending on the Sunday nearest to January 31. Fiscal year ended February 3, 2008 ("fiscal 2007") includes 53 weeks and fiscal years ended January 28, 2007 ("fiscal 2006") and January 29, 2006 ("fiscal 2005") include 52 weeks.

Use of Estimates

Management of the Company has made a number of estimates and assumptions relating to the reporting of assets and liabilities, the disclosure of contingent assets and liabilities, and reported amounts of revenues and expenses in preparing these financial statements in conformity with generally accepted accounting principles in the U.S. Actual results could differ from these estimates.

Fair Value of Financial Instruments

The carrying amounts of Cash and Cash Equivalents, Receivables, Short-Term Debt and Accounts Payable approximate fair value due to the short-term maturities of these financial instruments. The fair value of the Company's investments is discussed under the caption "Short-Term Investments" in this Note 1. The fair value of the Company's Long-Term Debt is discussed in Note 5.

Cash Equivalents

The Company considers all highly liquid investments purchased with original maturities of three months or less to be cash equivalents. The Company's Cash Equivalents are carried at fair market value and consist primarily of high-grade commercial paper, money market funds and U.S. government agency securities.

Short-Term Investments

Short-Term Investments are recorded at fair value based on current market rates and are classified as available-for-sale.

Accounts Receivable

The Company has an agreement with a third-party service provider who directly extends credit to customers, manages the Company's private label credit card program and owns the related receivables. We evaluated the third-party entities holding the receivables under the program and concluded that they should not be consolidated by the Company in accordance with the provisions of Financial Accounting Standards Board ("FASB") Interpretation No. 46(R), "Consolidation of Variable Interest Entities." The agreement with the third-party service provider expires in 2011, with the Company having the option, but no obligation, to purchase the receivables at the end of the agreement. The deferred interest charges incurred by the Company for its deferred financing programs offered to its customers are included in Cost of Sales. The interchange fees charged to the Company for the customers' use of the cards and the profit sharing with the third-party administrator are included in Selling, General and Administrative expenses ("SG&A").

In addition, certain subsidiaries of the Company extend credit directly to customers in the ordinary course of business. The receivables due from customers were $57 million and $1.8 billion as of February 3, 2008 and January 28, 2007, respectively, a decrease resulting from the sale of HD Supply. The Company's valuation reserve related to accounts receivable was not material to the Consolidated Financial Statements of the Company as of the end of fiscal 2007 or 2006.

Merchandise Inventories

The majority of the Company's Merchandise Inventories are stated at the lower of cost (first-in, first-out) or market, as determined by the retail inventory method. As the inventory retail value is adjusted regularly to reflect market conditions, the inventory valued using the retail method approximates the lower of cost or market. Certain subsidiaries, including retail operations in Mexico and China, and distribution centers record Merchandise Inventories at the lower of cost (first-in, first-out) or market, as determined by the cost method. These Merchandise Inventories represent approximately 11% of the total Merchandise Inventories balance. The Company evaluates the inventory valued using the cost method at the end of each quarter to ensure that it is carried at the lower of cost or market. The valuation allowance for Merchandise Inventories valued under the cost method was not material to the Consolidated Financial Statements of the Company as of the end of fiscal 2007 or 2006.

Independent physical inventory counts or cycle counts are taken on a regular basis in each store and distribution center to ensure that amounts reflected in the accompanying Consolidated Financial Statements for Merchandise Inventories are properly stated. During the period between physical inventory counts in stores, the Company accrues for estimated losses related to shrink on a store-by-store basis based on historical shrink results and current trends in the business. Shrink (or in the case of excess inventory, "swell") is the difference between the recorded amount of inventory and the physical inventory. Shrink may occur due to theft, loss, inaccurate records for the receipt of inventory or deterioration of goods, among other things.

Income Taxes

The Company provides for federal, state and foreign income taxes currently payable, as well as for those deferred due to timing differences between reporting income and expenses for financial statement purposes versus tax purposes. Federal, state and foreign tax benefits are recorded as a reduction of income taxes. Deferred tax assets and liabilities are recognized for the future tax consequences attributable to temporary differences between the financial statement carrying amounts of existing assets and liabilities and their respective tax bases. Deferred tax assets and liabilities are measured using enacted income tax rates expected to apply to taxable income in the years in which those temporary differences are expected to be recovered or settled. The effect of a change in income tax rates is recognized as income or expense in the period that includes the enactment date.

The Company and its eligible subsidiaries file a consolidated U.S. federal income tax return. Non-U.S. subsidiaries and certain U.S. subsidiaries, which are consolidated for financial reporting purposes, are not eligible to be included in the Company's consolidated U.S. federal income tax return. Separate provisions for income taxes have been determined for these entities. The Company intends to reinvest substantially all of the unremitted earnings of its non-U.S. subsidiaries and postpone their remittance indefinitely. Accordingly, no provision for U.S. income taxes for these non-U.S. subsidiaries was recorded in the accompanying Consolidated Statements of Earnings.

Depreciation and Amortization

The Company's Buildings, Furniture, Fixtures and Equipment are recorded at cost and depreciated using the straight-line method over the estimated useful lives of the assets. Leasehold Improvements are amortized using the straight-line method over the original term of the lease or the useful life of the improvement, whichever is shorter. The Company's Property and Equipment is depreciated using the following estimated useful lives:

	Life
Buildings	10-45 years
Furniture, Fixtures and Equipment	3-20 years
Leasehold Improvements	5-45 years

Capitalized Software Costs

The Company capitalizes certain costs related to the acquisition and development of software and amortizes these costs using the straight-line method over the estimated useful life of the software, which is three to six years. These costs are included in Furniture, Fixtures and Equipment in the accompanying Consolidated Balance Sheets. Certain development costs not meeting the criteria for capitalization are expensed as incurred.

Revenues

The Company recognizes revenue, net of estimated returns and sales tax, at the time the customer takes possession of merchandise or receives services. The liability for sales returns is estimated based on historical return levels. When the Company receives payment from customers before the customer has taken possession of the merchandise or the service has been performed, the amount received is recorded as Deferred Revenue in the accompanying Consolidated Balance Sheets until the sale or service is complete. The Company also records Deferred Revenue for the sale of gift cards and recognizes this revenue upon the redemption of gift cards in Net Sales. Gift card breakage income is recognized based upon historical redemption patterns and represents the balance of gift cards for which the Company believes the likelihood of redemption by the customer is remote. During fiscal 2007, 2006 and 2005, the Company recognized $36 million, $33 million and $52 million, respectively, of gift card breakage income. Fiscal 2005 was the first year in which the Company recognized gift card breakage income, and therefore, the amount recognized includes the gift card breakage income related to gift cards sold since the inception of the gift card program. This income is recorded as other income and is included in the accompanying Consolidated Statements of Earnings as a reduction in SG&A.

Services Revenue

Net Sales include services revenue generated through a variety of installation, home maintenance and professional service programs. In these programs, the customer selects and purchases material for a project and the Company provides or arranges professional installation. These programs are offered through the Company's stores. Under certain programs, when the Company provides or arranges the installation of a project and the subcontractor provides material as part of the installation, both the material and labor are included in services revenue. The Company recognizes this revenue when the service for the customer is complete.

All payments received prior to the completion of services are recorded in Deferred Revenue in the accompanying Consolidated Balance Sheets. Services revenue was $3.5 billion, $3.8 billion and $3.5 billion for fiscal 2007, 2006 and 2005, respectively.

Self-Insurance

The Company is self-insured for certain losses related to general liability, product liability, automobile, workers' compensation and medical claims. The expected ultimate cost for claims incurred as of the balance sheet date is not discounted and is recognized as a liability. The expected ultimate cost of claims is estimated based upon analysis of historical data and actuarial estimates.

Prepaid Advertising

Television and radio advertising production costs, along with media placement costs, are expensed when the advertisement first appears. Included in Other Current Assets in the accompanying Consolidated Balance Sheets are $31 million and $44 million, respectively, at the end of fiscal 2007 and 2006 relating to prepayments of production costs for print and broadcast advertising as well as sponsorship promotions.

Vendor Allowances

Vendor allowances primarily consist of volume rebates that are earned as a result of attaining certain purchase levels and advertising co-op allowances for the promotion of vendors' products that are typically based on guaranteed minimum amounts with additional amounts being earned for attaining certain purchase levels. These vendor allowances are accrued as earned, with those allowances received as a result of attaining certain purchase levels accrued over the incentive period based on estimates of purchases.

Volume rebates and certain advertising co-op allowances earned are initially recorded as a reduction in Merchandise Inventories and a subsequent reduction in Cost of Sales when the related product is sold. Certain advertising co-op allowances that are reimbursements of specific, incremental and identifiable costs incurred to promote vendors' products are recorded as an offset against advertising expense. In fiscal 2007, 2006 and 2005, gross advertising expense was $1.2 billion, $1.2 billion and $1.1 billion, respectively, which was recorded in SG&A. Advertising co-op allowances were $120 million, $83 million and $50 million for fiscal 2007, 2006 and 2005, respectively, and were recorded as an offset to advertising expense in SG&A.

Cost of Sales

Cost of Sales includes the actual cost of merchandise sold and services performed, the cost of transportation of merchandise from vendors to the Company's stores, locations or customers, the operating cost of the Company's sourcing and distribution network and the cost of deferred interest programs offered through the Company's private label credit card program.

The cost of handling and shipping merchandise from the Company's stores, locations or distribution centers to the customer is classified as SG&A. The cost of shipping and handling, including internal costs and payments to third parties, classified as SG&A was $571 million, $545 million and $480 million in fiscal 2007, 2006 and 2005, respectively.

Goodwill and Other Intangible Assets

Goodwill represents the excess of purchase price over the fair value of net assets acquired. The Company does not amortize goodwill, but does assess the recoverability of goodwill in the third quarter of each fiscal year by determining whether the fair value of each reporting unit supports its carrying value. The fair values of the Company's identified reporting units were estimated using the expected present value of discounted cash flows.

The Company amortizes the cost of other intangible assets over their estimated useful lives, which range from 1 to 20 years, unless such lives are deemed indefinite. Intangible assets with indefinite lives are tested in the third quarter of each fiscal year for impairment. The Company recorded no impairment charges for goodwill or other intangible assets for fiscal 2007, 2006 or 2005.

Impairment of Long-Lived Assets

The Company evaluates the carrying value of long-lived assets when management makes the decision to relocate or close a store or other location, or when circumstances indicate the carrying amount of an asset may not be recoverable. A store's assets are evaluated for impairment by comparing its undiscounted cash flows with its carrying value. If the carrying value is greater than the undiscounted cash flows, a provision is made to write down the related assets to fair value if the carrying value is greater than the fair value. Impairment losses are recorded as a component of SG&A in the accompanying Consolidated Statements of Earnings. When a location closes, the Company also recognizes in SG&A the net present value of future lease obligations, less estimated sublease income.

In fiscal 2005 the Company recorded $91 million in SG&A related to asset impairment charges and on-going lease obligations associated with closing 20 of its EXPO stores. Additionally, the Company recorded $29 million of expense in Cost of Sales in fiscal 2005 related to inventory markdowns in these stores. The Company also recorded impairments on other closings and relocations in the ordinary course of business, which were not material to the Consolidated Financial Statements of the Company in fiscal 2007, 2006 and 2005.

Stock-Based Compensation

Effective February 3, 2003, the Company adopted the fair value method of recording stock-based compensation expense in accordance with Statement of Financial Accounting Standards ("SFAS") No. 123, "Accounting for Stock-Based Compensation" ("SFAS 123"). The Company selected the prospective method of adoption as described in SFAS No. 148, "Accounting for Stock-Based Compensation – Transition and Disclosure," and accordingly, stock-based compensation expense was recognized for stock options granted, modified or settled and expense related to the Employee Stock Purchase Plan ("ESPP") after the beginning of fiscal 2003. Effective January 30, 2006, the Company adopted the fair value recognition provisions of SFAS No. 123(R), "Share-Based Payment" ("SFAS 123(R)"), using the modified prospective transition method. Under the modified prospective transition method, the Company began expensing unvested options granted prior to fiscal 2003 in addition to continuing to recognize stock-based compensation expense for all share-based payments awarded since the adoption of SFAS 123 in fiscal 2003. During fiscal 2006, the Company recognized additional stock compensation expense of approximately $40 million as a result of the adoption of SFAS 123(R). Results of prior periods have not been restated.

The per share weighted average fair value of stock options granted during fiscal 2007, 2006 and 2005 was $9.45, $11.88 and $12.83, respectively. The fair value of these options was determined at the date of grant using the Black-Scholes option-pricing model with the following assumptions:

	Fiscal Year Ended		
	February 3, 2008	January 28, 2007	January 29, 2006
Risk-free interest rate	4.4%	4.7%	4.3%
Assumed volatility	25.5%	28.5%	33.7%
Assumed dividend yield	2.4%	1.5%	1.1%
Assumed lives of option	6 years	5 years	5 years

The following table illustrates the effect on Net Earnings and Earnings per Share as if the Company had applied the fair value recognition provisions of SFAS 123(R) to all stock-based compensation in each period (amounts in millions, except per share data):

	Fiscal Year Ended					
		February 3, 2008		January 28, 2007		January 29, 2006
Net Earnings, as reported	$	4,395	$	5,761	$	5,838
Add: Stock-based compensation expense included in reported Net Earnings, net of related tax effects		131		186		110
Deduct: Total stock-based compensation expense determined under fair value based method for all awards, net of related tax effects		(131)		(186)		(197)
Pro forma net earnings	$	4,395	$	5,761	$	5,751
Earnings per Share:						
Basic – as reported	$	2.38	$	2.80	$	2.73
Basic – pro forma	$	2.38	$	2.80	$	2.69
Diluted – as reported	$	2.37	$	2.79	$	2.72
Diluted – pro forma	$	2.37	$	2.79	$	2.68

Derivatives

The Company uses derivative financial instruments from time to time in the management of its interest rate exposure on long-term debt and its exposure on foreign currency fluctuations. The Company accounts for its derivative financial instruments in accordance with SFAS No. 133, "Accounting for Derivative Instruments and Hedging Activities."

Comprehensive Income

Comprehensive Income includes Net Earnings adjusted for certain revenues, expenses, gains and losses that are excluded from Net Earnings under generally accepted accounting principles in the U.S. Adjustments to Net Earnings and Accumulated Other Comprehensive Income consist primarily of foreign currency translation adjustments.

Foreign Currency Translation

Assets and Liabilities denominated in a foreign currency are translated into U.S. dollars at the current rate of exchange on the last day of the reporting period. Revenues and Expenses are generally translated using average exchange rates for the period and equity transactions are translated using the actual rate on the day of the transaction.

Segment Information

The Company operates within a single operating segment primarily within North America. Net Sales for the Company outside of the U.S. were $7.4 billion, $6.3 billion and $5.2 billion for fiscal 2007, 2006 and 2005, respectively. Long-lived assets outside of the U.S. totaled $3.1 billion and $2.5 billion as of February 3, 2008 and January 28, 2007, respectively.

Reclassifications

Certain amounts in prior fiscal years have been reclassified to conform with the presentation adopted in the current fiscal year.

2.   DISPOSITION AND ACQUISITIONS

On August 30, 2007, the Company closed the sale of HD Supply. The Company received $8.3 billion of net proceeds for the sale of HD Supply and recognized a $4 million loss, net of tax, on the sale of the business, subject to the finalization of working capital adjustments. Also in connection with the sale, the Company purchased a 12.5% equity interest in the newly formed HD Supply for $325 million, which is included in Other Assets in the accompanying Consolidated Balance Sheets.

Also in connection with the sale, the Company guaranteed a $1.0 billion senior secured loan ("guaranteed loan") of HD Supply. The fair value of the guarantee, which was determined to be approximately $16 million, is recorded as a liability of the Company and included in Other Long-Term Liabilities. The guaranteed loan has a term of five years and the Company would be responsible for up to $1.0 billion and any unpaid interest in the event of non-payment by HD Supply. The guaranteed loan is collateralized by certain assets of HD Supply.

In accordance with Statement of Financial Accounting Standards No. 144, "Accounting for the Impairment or Disposal of Long-Lived Assets" ("SFAS 144"), the Company reclassified the results of HD Supply as discontinued operations in its Consolidated Statements of Earnings for all periods presented.

The following table presents Net Sales and Earnings of HD Supply through August 30, 2007 which have been reclassified to discontinued operations in the Consolidated Statements of Earnings for fiscal 2007, 2006 and 2005 (amounts in millions):

	Fiscal Year Ended		
	February 3, 2008	January 28, 2007	January 29, 2006
Net Sales	$ 7,391	$ 11,815	$ 4,492
Earnings Before Provision for Income Taxes	$ 291	$ 806	$ 315
Provision for Income Taxes	(102)	(311)	(118)
Loss on Discontinued Operations, net	(4)	—	—
Earnings from Discontinued Operations, net of tax	$ 185	$ 495	$ 197

During fiscal 2007, the Company acquired Ohio Water & Waste Supply, Inc. and Geosynthetics, Inc. These acquisitions operated under HD Supply and were included in the disposition. The aggregate purchase price for acquisitions in fiscal 2007, 2006 and 2005 was $25 million, $4.5 billion and $2.6 billion, respectively, including $3.5 billion for Hughes Supply in fiscal 2006. The Company recorded Goodwill related to the HD Supply businesses of $20 million, $2.8 billion and $1.8 billion for fiscal 2007, 2006 and 2005, respectively, and recorded no Goodwill related to its retail businesses for fiscal 2007 compared to $229 million and $111 million for fiscal 2006 and 2005, respectively, in the accompanying Consolidated Balance Sheets.

3.   STAFF ACCOUNTING BULLETIN NO. 108

In fiscal 2006, the Company adopted Staff Accounting Bulletin No. 108, "Considering the Effects of Prior Year Misstatements when Quantifying Misstatements in Current Year Financial Statements" ("SAB 108"). SAB 108 addresses the process of quantifying prior year financial statement misstatements and their impact on current year financial statements. The provisions of SAB 108 allowed companies to report the cumulative effect of correcting immaterial prior year misstatements, based on the Company's historical method for evaluating misstatements, by adjusting the opening balance of retained earnings in the financial statements of the year of adoption rather than amending previously filed reports. In accordance with SAB 108, the Company adjusted beginning Retained Earnings for fiscal 2006 in the accompanying Consolidated Financial Statements for the items described below. The Company does not consider these adjustments to have a material impact on the Company's consolidated financial statements in any of the prior years affected.

Historical Stock Option Practices

During fiscal 2006, the Company requested that its Board of Directors review its historical stock option granting practices. A subcommittee of the Audit Committee undertook the review with the assistance of independent outside counsel, and it has completed its review. The principal findings of the 2006 review were as follows:

- All options granted in the period from 2002 through the present had an exercise price based on the market price of the Company's stock on the date the grant was approved by the Board of Directors or an officer acting pursuant to delegated authority. During this period, the stock administration department corrected administrative errors retroactively and without separate approvals. The administrative errors included inadvertent omissions of grantees from lists that were approved previously and miscalculations of the number of options granted to particular employees on approved lists.

- All options granted from December 1, 2000 through the end of 2001 had an exercise price based on the market price of the Company's stock on the date of a meeting of the Board of Directors or some other date selected without the benefit of hindsight. The February 2001 annual grant was not finally allocated to recipients until several weeks after the grant was approved. During this period, the stock administration department also corrected administrative errors retroactively and without separate approvals as in the period 2002 to the present.

- For annual option grants and certain quarterly option grants from 1981 through November 2000, the stated grant date was routinely earlier than the actual date on which the grants were approved by a committee of the Board of Directors. In almost every instance, the stock price on the apparent approval date was higher than the price on the stated grant date. The backdating occurred for grants at all levels of the Company. Management personnel, who have since left the Company, generally followed a practice of reviewing closing prices for a prior period and selecting a date with a low stock price to increase the value of the options to employees on lists of grantees subsequently approved by a committee of the Board of Directors.

- The annual option grants in 1994 through 2000, as well as many quarterly grants during this period, were not finally allocated among the recipients until several weeks after the stated grant date. Because of the absence of records prior to 1994, it is unclear whether allocations also postdated the selected grant dates from 1981 through 1993. Moreover, for many of these annual and quarterly grants from 1981 through December 2000, there is insufficient documentation to determine with certainty when the grants were actually authorized by a committee of the Board of Directors. Finally, the Company's stock administration department also retroactively added employees to lists of approved grantees, or changed the number of options granted to specific employees, without authorization of the Board of Directors or a board committee, to correct administrative errors.

- Numerous option grants to rank-and-file employees were made pursuant to delegations of authority that may not have been effective under Delaware law.

- In numerous instances, and primarily prior to 2003, beneficiaries of grants who were required to report them to the SEC failed to do so in a timely manner or at all.

- The subcommittee concluded that there was no intentional wrongdoing by any current member of the Company's management team or its Board of Directors.

The Company believes that because of these errors, it had unrecorded expense over the affected period (1981 through 2005) of $227 million in the aggregate, including related tax items. In accordance with the provisions of SAB 108, the Company decreased beginning Retained Earnings for fiscal 2006 by $227 million within the accompanying Consolidated Financial Statements.

As previously disclosed, the staff of the SEC began in June 2006 an informal inquiry into the Company's stock option practices, and the U.S. Attorney for the Southern District of New York has also requested information on the subject. The Company is continuing to cooperate with these agencies. While the Company cannot predict the outcome of these matters, it does not believe that they will have a material adverse impact on its consolidated financial condition or results of operations.

The Company does not believe that the effect of the stock option adjustment was material, either quantitatively or qualitatively, in any of the years covered by the review of these items. In reaching that determination, the following quantitative measures were considered (dollars in millions):

Fiscal Year	Net After-tax Effect of Adjustment		Reported Net Earnings	Percent of Reported Net Earnings
2005	$	11	$ 5,838	0.19%
2004		18	5,001	0.36
2003		18	4,304	0.42
2002		21	3,664	0.57
1981-2001		159	14,531	1.09
Total	$	227	$ 33,338	0.68%

Vendor Credits

The Company records credits against vendor invoices for various issues related to the receipt of goods. The Company previously identified that it was not recording an allowance for subsequent reversals of these credits based on historical experience. Beginning Retained Earnings for fiscal 2006 was decreased by $30 million in the accompanying Consolidated Financial Statements to reflect the appropriate adjustments to Merchandise Inventories and Accounts Payable, net of tax.

Impact of Adjustments

The impact of each of the items noted above, net of tax, on fiscal 2006 beginning balances are presented below (amounts in millions):

| | Cumulative Effect as of January 30, 2006 | | |
	Stock Option Practices	Vendor Credits	Total
Merchandise Inventories	$ —	$ 9	$ 9
Accounts Payable	—	(59)	(59)
Deferred Income Taxes	11	20	31
Other Accrued Expenses	(37)	—	(37)
Paid-In Capital	(201)	—	(201)
Retained Earnings	227	30	257
Total	$ —	$ —	$ —

4. INTANGIBLE ASSETS

The Company's intangible assets at the end of fiscal 2007 and 2006, which are included in Other Assets in the accompanying Consolidated Balance Sheets, consisted of the following (amounts in millions):

	February 3, 2008	January 28, 2007
Customer relationships	$ 11	$ 756
Trademarks and franchises	83	106
Other	29	67
Less accumulated amortization	(23)	(151)
Total	$ 100	$ 778

The decrease in intangible assets from January 28, 2007 to February 3, 2008 was a result of the sale of HD Supply. Amortization expense related to intangible assets in continuing operations was $9 million, $10 million and less than $1 million for fiscal 2007, 2006 and 2005, respectively. Estimated future amortization expense for intangible assets recorded as of February 3, 2008 is $8 million, $8 million, $8 million, $5 million and $4 million for fiscal 2008 through fiscal 2012, respectively.

5. DEBT

The Company has commercial paper programs that allow for borrowings up to $3.25 billion. All of the Company's short-term borrowings in fiscal 2007 and 2006 were under these commercial paper programs. In connection with the commercial paper programs, the Company has a back-up credit facility with a consortium of banks for borrowings up to $3.0 billion. The credit facility, which expires in December 2010, contains various restrictions, none of which is expected to materially impact the Company's liquidity or capital resources.

Short-Term Debt under the commercial paper program was as follows (dollars in millions):

	February 3, 2008	January 28, 2007
Balance outstanding at fiscal year-end	$ 1,747	$ —
Maximum amount outstanding at any month-end	$ 1,747	$ 1,470
Average daily short-term borrowings	$ 526	$ 300
Weighted average interest rate	5.0%	5.1%

The Company's Long-Term Debt at the end of fiscal 2007 and 2006 consisted of the following (amounts in millions):

	February 3, 2008	January 28, 2007
3.75% Senior Notes; due September 15, 2009; interest payable semi-annually on March 15 and September 15	$ 998	$ 997
Floating Rate Senior Notes; due December 16, 2009; interest payable on March 16, June 16, September 16 and December 16	750	750
4.625% Senior Notes; due August 15, 2010; interest payable semi-annually on February 15 and August 15	998	997
5.20% Senior Notes; due March 1, 2011; interest payable semi-annually on March 1 and September 1	1,000	1,000
5.25% Senior Notes; due December 16, 2013; interest payable semi-annually on June 16 and December 16	1,244	1,243
5.40% Senior Notes; due March 1, 2016; interest payable semi-annually on March 1 and September 1	3,017	2,986
5.875% Senior Notes; due December 16, 2036; interest payable semi-annually on June 16 and December 16	2,959	2,958
Capital Lease Obligations; payable in varying installments through January 31, 2055	415	419
Other	302	311
Total Long-Term Debt	11,683	11,661
Less current installments	300	18
Long-Term Debt, excluding current installments	$ 11,383	$ 11,643

At February 3, 2008, the Company had outstanding interest rate swaps, accounted for as fair value hedges, with notional amounts of $2.0 billion that swap fixed rate interest on the Company's $3.0 billion 5.40% Senior Notes for variable rate interest equal to LIBOR plus 60 to 149 basis points that expire on March 1, 2016. At February 3, 2008, the approximate fair value of these agreements was an asset of $29 million, which is the estimated amount the Company would have received to settle similar interest rate swap agreements at current interest rates.

At February 3, 2008, the Company had outstanding an interest rate swap, accounted for as a cash flow hedge, with a notional amount of $750 million that swaps variable rate interest on the Company's $750 million floating rate Senior Notes for fixed rate interest at 4.36% that expires on December 16, 2009. At February 3, 2008, the approximate fair value of this agreement was a liability of $17 million, which is the estimated amount the Company would have paid to settle similar interest rate swap agreements at current interest rates.

In December 2006, the Company issued $750 million of floating rate Senior Notes due December 16, 2009 at par value, $1.25 billion of 5.25% Senior Notes due December 16, 2013 at a discount of $7 million and $3.0 billion of 5.875% Senior Notes due December 16, 2036 at a discount of $42 million, together the "December 2006 Issuance." The net proceeds of the December 2006 Issuance were used to fund, in part, the Company's common stock repurchases, to repay outstanding commercial paper and for general corporate purposes. The $49 million discount and $37 million of issuance costs associated with the December 2006 Issuance are being amortized to interest expense over the term of the related Senior Notes.

Additionally in October 2006, the Company entered into a forward starting interest rate swap agreement with a notional amount of $1.0 billion, accounted for as a cash flow hedge, to hedge interest rate fluctuations in anticipation of the issuance of the 5.875% Senior Notes due December 16, 2036. Upon issuance of the hedged debt in December 2006, the Company settled its forward starting interest rate swap agreements and recorded an $11 million decrease, net of income taxes, to Accumulated Other Comprehensive Income, which will be amortized to interest expense over the life of the related debt.

In March 2006, the Company issued $1.0 billion of 5.20% Senior Notes due March 1, 2011 at a discount of $1 million and $3.0 billion of 5.40% Senior Notes due March 1, 2016 at a discount of $15 million, together the "March 2006 Issuance." The net proceeds of the March 2006 Issuance were used to pay for the acquisition price of Hughes Supply, Inc. and for the repayment of the Company's 5.375% Senior Notes due April 2006 in the aggregate principal amount of $500 million. The $16 million discount and $19 million of issuance costs associated with the March 2006 Issuance are being amortized to interest expense over the term of the related Senior Notes.

Additionally in March 2006, the Company entered into a forward starting interest rate swap agreement with a notional amount of $2.0 billion, accounted for as a cash flow hedge, to hedge interest rate fluctuations in anticipation of the issuance of the 5.40% Senior Notes due March 1, 2016. Upon issuance of the hedged debt, the Company settled its forward starting interest rate swap agreements and recorded a $12 million decrease, net of income taxes, to Accumulated Other Comprehensive Income, which will be amortized to interest expense over the life of the related debt.

In August 2005, the Company issued $1.0 billion of 4.625% Notes due August 15, 2010 ("August 2005 Issuance") at a discount of $5 million. The net proceeds of $995 million were used to pay for a portion of the acquisition price of National Waterworks, Inc. The $5 million discount and $7 million of issuance costs associated with the August 2005 Issuance are being amortized to interest expense over the term of the related Senior Notes.

The Company also had $1.0 billion of 3.75% Senior Notes due September 15, 2009 outstanding as of February 3, 2008, collectively referred to with the December 2006 Issuance, March 2006 Issuance and August 2005 Issuance as "Senior Notes." The Senior Notes may be redeemed by the Company at any time, in whole or in part, at a redemption price plus accrued interest up to the redemption date. The redemption price is equal to the greater of (1) 100% of the principal amount of the Senior Notes to be redeemed, or (2) the sum of the present values of the remaining scheduled payments of principal and interest to maturity. Additionally, if a Change in Control Triggering Event occurs, as defined by the terms of the December 2006 Issuance, holders of the December 2006 Issuance have the right to require the Company to redeem those notes at 101% of the aggregate principal amount of the notes plus accrued interest up to the redemption date.

The Company is generally not limited under the indenture governing the Senior Notes in its ability to incur additional indebtedness or required to maintain financial ratios or specified levels of net worth or liquidity. However, the indenture governing the Senior Notes contains various restrictive covenants, none of which is expected to impact the Company's liquidity or capital resources.

Interest Expense in the accompanying Consolidated Statements of Earnings is net of interest capitalized of $46 million, $47 million and $51 million in fiscal 2007, 2006 and 2005, respectively. Maturities of Long-Term Debt are $300 million for fiscal 2008, $1.8 billion for fiscal 2009, $1.0 billion for fiscal 2010, $1.0 billion for fiscal 2011, $23 million for fiscal 2012 and $7.5 billion thereafter.

As of February 3, 2008, the market value of the Senior Notes was approximately $10.5 billion. The estimated fair value of all other long-term borrowings, excluding capital lease obligations, was approximately $307 million compared to the carrying value of $302 million. These fair values were estimated using a discounted cash flow analysis based on the Company's incremental borrowing rate for similar liabilities.

6. INCOME TAXES

The components of Earnings From Continuing Operations before Provision for Income Taxes for fiscal 2007, 2006 and 2005 were as follows (amounts in millions):

	Fiscal Year Ended		
	February 3, 2008	January 28, 2007	January 29, 2006
United States	$ 5,905	$ 7,915	$ 8,427
Foreign	715	587	540
Total	$ 6,620	$ 8,502	$ 8,967

The Provision for Income Taxes consisted of the following (amounts in millions):

	Fiscal Year Ended		
	February 3, 2008	January 28, 2007	January 29, 2006
Current:			
Federal	$ 2,055	$ 2,557	$ 3,316
State	285	361	493
Foreign	310	326	155
	2,650	3,244	3,964
Deferred:			
Federal	(242)	(2)	(553)
State	17	(1)	(110)
Foreign	(15)	(5)	25
	(240)	(8)	(638)
Total	$ 2,410	$ 3,236	$ 3,326

The Company's combined federal, state and foreign effective tax rates for fiscal 2007, 2006 and 2005, net of offsets generated by federal, state and foreign tax benefits, were approximately 36.4%, 38.1% and 37.1%, respectively.

The reconciliation of the Provision for Income Taxes at the federal statutory rate of 35% to the actual tax expense for the applicable fiscal years was as follows (amounts in millions):

| | Fiscal Year Ended | | |
	February 3, 2008	January 28, 2007	January 29, 2006
Income taxes at federal statutory rate	$ 2,317	$ 2,976	$ 3,138
State income taxes, net of federal income tax benefit	196	234	249
Other, net	(103)	26	(61)
Total	$ 2,410	$ 3,236	$ 3,326

The tax effects of temporary differences that give rise to significant portions of the deferred tax assets and deferred tax liabilities as of February 3, 2008 and January 28, 2007, were as follows (amounts in millions):

	February 3, 2008	January 28, 2007
Current:		
Deferred Tax Assets:		
Accrued self-insurance liabilities	$ 155	$ 94
Other accrued liabilities	601	603
Current Deferred Tax Assets	756	697
Deferred Tax Liabilities:		
Accelerated inventory deduction	(118)	(137)
Other	(113)	(29)
Current Deferred Tax Liabilities	(231)	(166)
Current Deferred Tax Assets, net	525	531
Noncurrent:		
Deferred Tax Assets:		
Accrued self-insurance liabilities	285	325
State income taxes	105	—
Capital loss carryover	56	—
Net operating losses	52	66
Other	54	—
Valuation allowance	(7)	—
Noncurrent Deferred Tax Assets	545	391
Deferred Tax Liabilities:		
Property and equipment	(1,133)	(1,365)
Goodwill and other intangibles	(69)	(361)
Other	(31)	(74)
Noncurrent Deferred Tax Liabilities	(1,233)	(1,800)
Noncurrent Deferred Tax Liabilities, net	(688)	(1,409)
Net Deferred Tax Liabilities	$ (163)	$ (878)

Current deferred tax assets and current deferred tax liabilities are netted by tax jurisdiction and noncurrent deferred tax assets and noncurrent deferred tax liabilities are netted by tax jurisdiction, and are included in the accompanying Consolidated Balance Sheets as follows (amounts in millions):

	February 3, 2008	January 28, 2007
Other Current Assets	$ 535	$ 561
Other Assets	—	7
Other Accrued Expenses	(10)	(30)
Deferred Income Taxes	(688)	(1,416)
Net Deferred Tax Liabilities	$ (163)	$ (878)

The Company believes that the realization of the deferred tax assets is more likely than not, based upon the expectation that it will generate the necessary taxable income in future periods and, except for certain net operating losses discussed below, no valuation reserves have been provided. As a result of disposition of HD Supply, $139 million of net deferred tax liabilities were transferred to the purchaser.

At February 3, 2008, the Company had state and foreign net operating loss carryforwards available to reduce future taxable income, expiring at various dates from 2010 to 2027. Management has concluded that it is more likely than not that the tax benefits related to the net operating losses will be realized. However, certain foreign net operating losses are in jurisdictions where the expiration period is too short to be assured of utilization. Therefore, a $7 million valuation allowance has been provided to reduce the deferred tax asset related to net operating losses to an amount that is more likely than not to be realized. Total valuation allowances at February 3, 2008 were $7 million.

As a result of its sale of HD Supply, the Company incurred a tax loss, resulting in a net capital loss carryover of approximately $159 million. The tax loss on sale resulted primarily from the Company's tax basis in excess of its book investment in HD Supply. The net capital loss carryover will expire in 2012. However, the Company has concluded that it is more likely than not that the tax benefits related to the capital loss carryover will be realized based on its ability to generate adequate capital gain income during the carryover period. Therefore, no valuation allowance has been provided.

The Company has not provided for U.S. deferred income taxes on approximately $1.3 billion of undistributed earnings of international subsidiaries because of its intention to indefinitely reinvest these earnings outside the U.S. The determination of the amount of the unrecognized deferred U.S. income tax liability related to the undistributed earnings is not practicable; however, unrecognized foreign income tax credits would be available to reduce a portion of this liability.

The Company's income tax returns are routinely under audit by domestic and foreign tax authorities. These audits generally include questions regarding the timing and amount of depreciation deductions and the allocation of income among various tax jurisdictions. In 2005, the U.S. Internal Revenue Service ("IRS") completed its examination of the Company's U.S. federal income tax returns for fiscal years 2001 and 2002. During 2007, the IRS also completed its examination of the Company's fiscal 2003 and 2004 income tax returns. Certain issues relating to the examinations of fiscal years 2001 through 2004 are under appeal, but only years after fiscal 2004 remain subject to future examination. The Mexican government is currently auditing the Mexican operating subsidiaries' fiscal year 2005 returns, although years after 2001 remain subject to audit. The Canadian governments, including various provinces, are currently auditing income tax returns for the years 2001 through 2005. There are also U.S. state and local audits covering tax years 2001 to 2005. At this time, the Company does not expect the results from any income tax audit to have a material impact on the Company's financial statements.

On January 29, 2007, the Company adopted FASB Interpretation No. 48, "Accounting for Uncertainty in Income Taxes – an Interpretation of FASB Statement No. 109" ("FIN 48"). Among other things, FIN 48 requires application of a "more likely than not" threshold to the recognition and derecognition of tax positions. It further requires that a change in judgment related to prior years' tax positions be recognized in the quarter of such change. The adoption of FIN 48 reduced the Company's Retained Earnings by $111 million. As a result of the implementation, the gross amount of unrecognized tax benefits at January 29, 2007 for continuing operations totaled $667 million. A reconciliation of the beginning and ending amount of gross unrecognized tax benefits for continuing operations is as follows (amounts in millions):

	February 3, 2008
Unrecognized tax benefits balance at January 29, 2007	$ 667
Additions based on tax positions related to the current year	66
Additions for tax positions of prior years	25
Reductions for tax positions of prior years	(115)
Reductions due to settlements	(31)
Reductions due to lapse of statute of limitations	(4)
Unrecognized tax benefits balance at February 3, 2008	$ 608

The gross amount of unrecognized tax benefits as of February 3, 2008 includes $368 million of net unrecognized tax benefits that, if recognized, would affect the annual effective income tax rate.

During fiscal 2007, the Company increased its interest accrual associated with uncertain tax positions by approximately $32 million and paid interest of approximately $8 million. Total accrued interest as of February 3, 2008 is $140 million. There were no penalty accruals during fiscal 2007. Interest and penalties are included in net interest expense and operating expenses, respectively. Our classification of interest and penalties did not change as a result of the adoption of FIN 48.

The Company believes that some individual adjustments under appeal for the completed IRS and Canada audits, as well as other state audits, will be agreed upon within the next twelve months. The IRS issues generally concern the useful life of assets and relevant transfer pricing for intangible assets provided to foreign operations. The Canada issues generally concern the relevant transfer pricing for intangible assets provided from the U.S. State issues generally concern related party expense add-back provisions and forced combination filings. The Company has classified approximately $6 million of the reserve for unrecognized tax benefits as a short-term liability in the accompanying Consolidated Balance Sheets. In addition, there is a reasonable possibility that the Company may resolve the Quebec assessment from prior years, which totaled $65 million at February 3, 2008, within the next twelve months. Final settlement of these audit issues may result in payments that are more or less than these amounts, but the Company does not anticipate the resolution of these matters will result in a material change to its consolidated financial position or results of operations.

7.   EMPLOYEE STOCK PLANS

The Home Depot, Inc. 2005 Omnibus Stock Incentive Plan ("2005 Plan") and The Home Depot, Inc. 1997 Omnibus Stock Incentive Plan ("1997 Plan" and collectively with the 2005 Plan, the "Plans") provide that incentive and non-qualified stock options, stock appreciation rights, restricted shares, performance shares, performance units and deferred shares may be issued to selected associates, officers and directors of the Company. Under the 2005 Plan, the maximum number of shares of the Company's common stock authorized for issuance is 255 million shares, with any award other than a stock option reducing the number of shares available for issuance by 2.11 shares. As of February 3, 2008, there were 224 million shares available for future grants under the 2005 Plan. No additional equity awards may be issued from the 1997 Plan after the adoption of the 2005 Plan on May 26, 2005.

Under the Plans, as of February 3, 2008, the Company had granted incentive and non-qualified stock options for 177 million shares, net of cancellations (of which 127 million have been exercised). Under the terms of the Plans, incentive stock options and non-qualified stock options are to be priced at or above the fair market value of the Company's stock on the date of the grant. Typically, incentive stock options and non-qualified stock options vest at the rate of 25% per year commencing on the first anniversary date of the grant and expire on the tenth anniversary date of the grant. The non-qualified stock options also include performance options which vest on the later of the first anniversary date of the grant and the date the closing price of the Company's common stock has been 25% greater than the exercise price of the options for 30 consecutive trading days. The Company recognized $61 million, $148 million and $117 million of stock-based compensation expense in fiscal 2007, 2006 and 2005, respectively, related to stock options.

Under the Plans, as of February 3, 2008, the Company had issued 16 million shares of restricted stock, net of cancellations (the restrictions on 5 million shares have lapsed). Generally, the restrictions on the restricted stock lapse according to one of the following schedules: (1) the restrictions on 100% of the restricted stock lapse at 3, 4 or 5 years, (2) the restrictions on 25% of the restricted stock lapse upon the third and sixth year anniversaries of the date of issuance with the remaining 50% of the restricted stock lapsing upon the associate's attainment of age 62, or (3) the restrictions on 25% of the restricted stock lapse upon the third and sixth year anniversaries of the date of issuance with the remaining 50% of the restricted stock lapsing upon the earlier of the associate's attainment of age 60 or the tenth anniversary date. The restricted stock also includes the Company's performance shares, the payout of which is dependent on the Company's total shareholders return percentile ranking compared to the performance of individual companies included in the S&P 500 index at the end of the three-year performance cycle. Additionally, certain awards may become non-forfeitable upon the attainment of age 60, provided the associate has had five years of continuous service. The fair value of the restricted stock is expensed over the period during which the restrictions lapse. The Company recorded stock-based compensation expense related to restricted stock of $122 million, $95 million and $32 million in fiscal 2007, 2006 and 2005, respectively.

In fiscal 2007, 2006 and 2005, there were 593,000, 417,000 and 461,000 deferred shares, respectively, granted under the Plans. Each deferred share entitles the associate to one share of common stock to be received up to five years after the vesting date of the deferred shares, subject to certain deferral rights of the associate. The Company recorded stock-based compensation expense related to deferred shares of $10 million, $37 million and $10 million in fiscal 2007, 2006 and 2005, respectively.

As of February 3, 2008, there were 2.5 million non-qualified stock options outstanding under non-qualified stock option plans that are not part of the Plans.

The Company maintains two ESPPs (U.S. and non-U.S. plans). The plan for U.S. associates is a tax-qualified plan under Section 423 of the Internal Revenue Code. The non-U.S. plan is not a Section 423 plan. The ESPPs allow associates to purchase up to 152 million shares of common stock, of which 128 million shares have been purchased from inception of the plans. The purchase price of shares under the ESPPs is equal to 85% of the stock's fair market value on the last day of the purchase period. During fiscal 2007, there were 3 million shares purchased under the ESPPs at an average price of $28.25. Under the outstanding ESPPs as of February 3, 2008, employees have contributed $8 million to purchase shares at 85% of the stock's fair market value on the last day (June 30, 2008) of the purchase period. The Company had 24 million shares available for issuance under the ESPPs at February 3, 2008. The Company recognized $14 million, $17 million and $16 million of stock-based compensation in fiscal 2007, 2006 and 2005, respectively, related to the ESPPs.

In total, the Company recorded stock-based compensation expense, including the expense of stock options, ESPPs, restricted stock and deferred stock units, of $207 million, $297 million and $175 million, in fiscal 2007, 2006 and 2005, respectively.

The following table summarizes stock options outstanding at February 3, 2008, January 28, 2007 and January 29, 2006, and changes during the fiscal years ended on these dates (shares in thousands):

	Number of Shares		Weighted Average Exercise Price
Outstanding at January 30, 2005	86,394	$	36.12
Granted	17,721		37.96
Exercised	(11,457)		28.83
Canceled	(8,626)		38.65
Outstanding at January 29, 2006	84,032	$	37.24
Granted	257		39.53
Exercised	(10,045)		28.69
Canceled	(8,103)		40.12
Outstanding at January 28, 2007	66,141	$	38.20
Granted	2,926		37.80
Exercised	(6,859)		28.50
Canceled	(9,843)		40.68
Outstanding at February 3, 2008	52,365	$	38.98

The total intrinsic value of stock options exercised during fiscal 2007 was $63 million.

As of February 3, 2008, there were approximately 52 million stock options outstanding with a weighted average remaining life of five years and an intrinsic value of $30 million. As of February 3, 2008, there were approximately 42 million options exercisable with a weighted average exercise price of $39.43 and an intrinsic value of $28 million. As of February 3, 2008, there were approximately 51 million shares vested or expected to ultimately vest. As of February 3, 2008, there was $84 million of unamortized stock-based compensation expense related to stock options which is expected to be recognized over a weighted average period of two years.

The following table summarizes restricted stock outstanding at February 3, 2008 (shares in thousands):

	Number of Shares		Weighted Average Grant Date Fair Value
Outstanding at January 29, 2006	5,308	$	35.76
Granted	7,575		41.37
Restrictions lapsed	(1,202)		38.03
Canceled	(1,551)		39.00
Outstanding at January 28, 2007	10,130	$	39.20
Granted	7,091		39.10
Restrictions lapsed	(2,662)		39.01
Canceled	(2,844)		39.37
Outstanding at February 3, 2008	11,715	$	39.14

As of February 3, 2008, there was $267 million of unamortized stock-based compensation expense related to restricted stock which is expected to be recognized over a weighted average period of three years.

8.   LEASES

The Company leases certain retail locations, office space, warehouse and distribution space, equipment and vehicles. While most of the leases are operating leases, certain locations and equipment are leased under capital leases. As leases expire, it can be expected that, in the normal course of business, certain leases will be renewed or replaced.

Certain lease agreements include escalating rents over the lease terms. The Company expenses rent on a straight-line basis over the life of the lease which commences on the date the Company has the right to control the property. The cumulative expense recognized on a straight-line basis in excess of the cumulative payments is included in Other Accrued Expenses and Other Long-Term Liabilities in the accompanying Consolidated Balance Sheets.

The Company has a lease agreement under which the Company leases certain assets totaling $282 million. This lease was originally created under a structured financing arrangement and involves two special purpose entities. The Company financed a portion of its new stores opened in fiscal years 1997 through 2003 under this lease agreement. Under this agreement, the lessor purchased the properties, paid for the construction costs and subsequently leased the facilities to the Company. The Company records the rental payments under the terms of the operating lease agreements as SG&A in the accompanying Consolidated Statements of Earnings.

The $282 million lease agreement expires in fiscal 2008 with no renewal option. The lease provides for a substantial residual value guarantee limited to 79% of the initial book value of the assets and includes a purchase option at the original cost of each property. During fiscal 2005, the Company committed to exercise its option to purchase the assets under this lease for $282 million at the end of the lease term in fiscal 2008.

In the first quarter of fiscal 2004, the Company adopted the revised version of FASB Interpretation No. 46(R), "Consolidation of Variable Interest Entities" ("FIN 46"). FIN 46 requires consolidation of a variable interest entity if a company's variable interest absorbs a majority of the entity's expected losses or receives a majority of the entity's expected residual returns, or both. In accordance with FIN 46, the Company was required to consolidate one of the two aforementioned special purpose entities that, before the effective date of FIN 46, met the requirements for non-consolidation. The second special purpose entity that owns the assets leased by the Company totaling $282 million is not owned by or affiliated with the Company, its management or its officers. Pursuant to FIN 46, the Company was not deemed to have a variable interest, and therefore was not required to consolidate this entity.

FIN 46 requires the Company to measure the assets and liabilities at their carrying amounts, which amounts would have been recorded if FIN 46 had been effective at the inception of the transaction. Accordingly, during the first quarter of fiscal 2004, the Company recorded Long-Term Debt of $282 million and Long-Term Notes Receivable of $282 million on the Consolidated Balance Sheets. During fiscal 2007, the liability was reclassified to Current Installments of Long-Term Debt as it is due in fiscal 2008. The Company continues to record the rental payments under the operating lease agreements as SG&A in the Consolidated Statements of Earnings. The adoption of FIN 46 had no economic impact on the Company.

Total rent expense, net of minor sublease income for fiscal 2007, 2006 and 2005 was $824 million, $768 million and $720 million, respectively. Certain store leases also provide for contingent rent payments based on percentages of sales in excess of specified minimums. Contingent rent expense for fiscal 2007, 2006 and 2005 was approximately $6 million, $9 million and $9 million, respectively. Real estate taxes, insurance, maintenance and operating expenses applicable to the leased property are obligations of the Company under the lease agreements.

The approximate future minimum lease payments under capital and all other leases at February 3, 2008 were as follows (in millions):

Fiscal Year	Capital Leases		Operating Leases	
2008	$	79	$	802
2009		80		716
2010		82		644
2011		82		582
2012		82		523
Thereafter through 2097		882		5,664
		1,287	$	8,931
Less imputed interest		872		
Net present value of capital lease obligations		415		
Less current installments		15		
Long-term capital lease obligations, excluding current installments	$	400		

Short-term and long-term obligations for capital leases are included in the accompanying Consolidated Balance Sheets in Current Installments of Long-Term Debt and Long-Term Debt, respectively. The assets under capital leases recorded in Property and Equipment, net of amortization, totaled $327 million and $340 million at February 3, 2008 and January 28, 2007, respectively.

9.   EMPLOYEE BENEFIT PLANS

The Company maintains active defined contribution retirement plans for its employees ("the Benefit Plans"). All associates satisfying certain service requirements are eligible to participate in the Benefit Plans. The Company makes cash contributions each payroll period up to specified percentages of associates' contributions as approved by the Board of Directors.

The Company also maintains a restoration plan to provide certain associates deferred compensation that they would have received under the Benefit Plans as a matching contribution if not for the maximum compensation limits under the Internal Revenue Code. The Company funds the restoration plan through contributions made to a grantor trust, which are then used to purchase shares of the Company's common stock in the open market.

The Company's contributions to the Benefit Plans and the restoration plan were $152 million, $135 million and $122 million for fiscal 2007, 2006 and 2005, respectively. At February 3, 2008, the Benefit Plans and the restoration plan held a total of 22 million shares of the Company's common stock in trust for plan participants.

10.   BASIC AND DILUTED WEIGHTED AVERAGE COMMON SHARES

The reconciliation of basic to diluted weighted average common shares for fiscal 2007, 2006 and 2005 is as follows (amounts in millions):

| | Fiscal Year Ended | | |
	February 3, 2008	January 28, 2007	January 29, 2006
Weighted average common shares	1,849	2,054	2,138
Effect of potentially dilutive securities:			
Stock Plans	7	8	9
Diluted weighted average common shares	1,856	2,062	2,147

Stock plans include shares granted under the Company's employee stock plans as described in Note 7 to the Consolidated Financial Statements. Options to purchase 43.4 million, 45.4 million and 55.1 million shares of common stock at February 3, 2008, January 28, 2007 and January 29, 2006, respectively, were excluded from the computation of Diluted Earnings per Share because their effect would have been anti-dilutive.

11.   COMMITMENTS AND CONTINGENCIES

At February 3, 2008, the Company was contingently liable for approximately $730 million under outstanding letters of credit and open accounts issued for certain business transactions, including insurance programs, trade contracts and construction contracts. The Company's letters of credit are primarily performance-based and are not based on changes in variable components, a liability or an equity security of the other party.

The Company is a defendant in numerous cases containing class-action allegations in which the plaintiffs are current and former hourly associates who allege that the Company forced them to work "off the clock" or failed to provide work breaks, or otherwise that they were not paid for work performed. The complaints generally seek unspecified monetary damages, injunctive relief or both. Class or collective-action certification has yet to be addressed in most of these cases. The Company cannot reasonably estimate the possible loss or range of loss which may arise from these lawsuits. These matters, if decided adversely to or settled by the Company, individually or in the aggregate, may result in a liability material to the Company's consolidated financial condition or results of operations. The Company is vigorously defending itself against these actions.

12. QUARTERLY FINANCIAL DATA (UNAUDITED)

The following is a summary of the quarterly consolidated results of operations from continuing operations for the fiscal years ended February 3, 2008 and January 28, 2007 (dollars in millions, except per share data):

	Net Sales	Gross Profit	Earnings from Continuing Operations	Basic Earnings per Share from Continuing Operations	Diluted Earnings per Share from Continuing Operations
Fiscal Year Ended February 3, 2008:					
First Quarter	$ 18,545	$ 6,263	$ 947	$ 0.48	$ 0.48
Second Quarter	22,184	7,341	1,521	0.78	0.77
Third Quarter	18,961	6,339	1,071	0.59	0.59
Fourth Quarter	17,659	6,054	671	0.40	0.40
Fiscal Year	$ 77,349	$ 25,997	$ 4,210	$ 2.28	$ 2.27
Fiscal Year Ended January 28, 2007:					
First Quarter	$ 19,378	$ 6,636	$ 1,391	$ 0.66	$ 0.66
Second Quarter	22,592	7,456	1,701	0.82	0.82
Third Quarter	19,648	6,604	1,333	0.65	0.65
	17,404	5,850	841	0.42	0.42
Fiscal Year	$ 79,022	$ 26,546	$ 5,266	$ 2.56	$ 2.55

Note: The quarterly data may not sum to fiscal year totals.

10-Year Summary of Financial and Operating Results
The Home Depot, Inc. and Subsidiaries

amounts in millions, except where noted	10-Year Compound Annual Growth Rate	2007 [1]	2006	2005
STATEMENT OF EARNINGS DATA [2]				
Net sales				
Net sales increase (%)	12.3%	$ 77,349	$ 79,022	$ 77,019
Earnings before provision for income taxes	—	(2.1)	2.6	8.3
Net earnings	13.3	6,620	8,502	8,967
Net earnings increase (%)	13.8	4,210	5,266	5,641
Diluted earnings per share ($)	—	(20.1)	(6.6)	14.6
Diluted earnings per share increase (%)	15.9	2.27	2.55	2.63
Diluted weighted average number of common shares	—	(11.0)	(3.0)	18.5
Gross margin – % of sales	(2.1)	1,856	2,062	2,147
Total operating expenses – % of sales	—	33.6	33.6	33.7
Net interest expense (income) – % of sales	—	24.3	22.4	21.9
Earnings before provision for income taxes – % of sales	—	0.8	0.5	0.1
Net earnings – % of sales	—	8.6	10.8	11.6
	—	5.4	6.7	7.3
BALANCE SHEET DATA AND FINANCIAL RATIOS [3]				
Total assets				
Working capital	14.7%	$ 44,324	$ 52,263	$ 44,405
Merchandise inventories	(0.2)	1,968	5,069	2,563
Net property and equipment	12.5	11,731	12,822	11,401
Long-term debt	15.5	27,476	26,605	24,901
Stockholders' equity	24.2	11,383	11,643	2,672
Book value per share ($)	9.6	17,714	25,030	26,909
Long-term debt-to-equity (%)	12.5	10.48	12.71	12.67
Total debt-to-equity (%)	—	64.3	46.5	9.9
Current ratio	—	75.8	46.6	15.2
Inventory turnover [2]	—	1.15:1	1.39:1	1.20:1
Return on invested capital (%) [2]	—	4.2x	4.5x	4.7x
	—	13.9	16.8	20.4
STATEMENT OF CASH FLOWS DATA				
Depreciation and amortization				
Capital expenditures	21.0%	$ 1,906	$ 1,886	$ 1,579
Payments for businesses acquired, net	9.3	3,558	3,542	3,881
Cash dividends per share ($)	(14.3)	13	4,268	2,546
	30.5	0.900	0.675	0.400
STORE DATA				
Number of stores				
Square footage at fiscal year-end	13.6%	2,234	2,147	2,042
Increase in square footage (%)	13.5	235	224	215
Average square footage per store (in thousands)	—	4.9	4.2	7.0
	(0.1)	105	105	105
STORE SALES AND OTHER DATA				
Comparable store sales increase (decrease) (%) [4][5]				
Weighted average weekly sales per operating store (in thousands)	—	(6.7)	(2.8)	3.1
Weighted average sales per square foot ($)	(2.3)%	$ 658	$ 723	$ 763
Number of customer transactions	(2.0)	332	358	377
Average ticket ($)	9.3	1,336	1,330	1,330
Number of associates at fiscal year-end [3]	2.8	57.48	58.90	57.98
	10.3	331,000	364,400	344,800

(1) Fiscal years 2007 and 2001 include 53 weeks; all other fiscal years reported include 52 weeks.

(2) Fiscal years 2003 through 2007 include Continuing Operations only. The discontinued operations prior to 2003 were not material.

(3) Fiscal year 2007 amounts include Continuing Operations only. Fiscal years 1998-2006 amounts include discontinued operations, except as noted.

	2004	2003	2002	2001 [1]	2000	1999	1998
STATEMENT OF EARNINGS DATA [2]							
Net sales	$ 71,100 $	63,660 $	58,247 $	53,553 $	45,738 $	38,434 $	30,219
Net sales increase (%)	11.7	9.3	8.8	17.1	19.0	27.2	25.1
Earnings before provision for income taxes	7,790	6,762	5,872	4,957	4,217	3,804	2,654
Net earnings	4,922	4,253	3,664	3,044	2,581	2,320	1,614
Net earnings increase (%)	15.7	16.1	20.4	17.9	11.3	43.7	31.9
Diluted earnings per share ($)	2.22	1.86	1.56	1.29	1.10	1.00	0.71
Diluted earnings per share increase (%)	19.4	19.2	20.9	17.3	10.0	40.8	29.1
Diluted weighted average number of common shares	2,216	2,289	2,344	2,353	2,352	2,342	2,320
Gross margin – % of sales	33.4	31.7	31.1	30.2	29.9	29.7	28.5
Total operating expenses – % of sales	22.4	21.1	21.1	20.9	20.7	19.8	19.7
Net interest expense (income) – % of sales	—	—	(0.1)	—	—	—	—
Earnings before provision for income taxes – % of sales	11.0	10.6	10.1	9.3	9.2	9.9	8.8
Net earnings – % of sales	6.9	6.7	6.3	5.7	5.6	6.0	5.3
BALANCE SHEET DATA AND FINANCIAL RATIOS [3]							
Total assets	$ 39,020 $	34,437 $	30,011 $	26,394 $	21,385 $	17,081 $	13,465
Working capital	3,818	3,774	3,882	3,860	3,392	2,734	2,076
Merchandise inventories	10,076	9,076	8,338	6,725	6,556	5,489	4,293
Net property and equipment	22,726	20,063	17,168	15,375	13,068	10,227	8,160
Long-term debt	2,148	856	1,321	1,250	1,545	750	1,566
Stockholders' equity	24,158	22,407	19,802	18,082	15,004	12,341	8,740
Book value per share ($)	11.06	9.93	8.38	7.71	6.46	5.36	3.95
Long-term debt-to-equity (%)	8.9	3.8	6.7	6.9	10.3	6.1	17.9
Total debt-to-equity (%)	8.9	6.1	6.7	6.9	10.3	6.1	17.9
Current ratio	1.37:1	1.40:1	1.48:1	1.59:1	1.77:1	1.75:1	1.73:1
Inventory turnover [2]	4.9x	5.0x	5.3x	5.4x	5.1x	5.4x	5.4x
Return on invested capital (%) [2]	19.9	19.2	18.8	18.3	19.6	22.5	19.3
STATEMENT OF CASH FLOWS DATA							
Depreciation and amortization	$ 1,319 $	1,076 $	903 $	764 $	601 $	463 $	373
Capital expenditures	3,948	3,508	2,749	3,393	3,574	2,618	2,094
Payments for businesses acquired, net	727	215	235	190	26	101	6
Cash dividends per share ($)	0.325	0.26	0.21	0.17	0.16	0.11	0.08
STORE DATA							
Number of stores	1,890	1,707	1,532	1,333	1,134	930	761
Square footage at fiscal year-end	201	183	166	146	123	100	81
Increase in square footage (%)	9.8	10.2	14.1	18.5	22.6	23.5	22.8
Average square footage per store (in thousands)	106	107	108	109	108	108	107
STORE SALES AND OTHER DATA							
Comparable store sales increase (decrease) (%) [4][5]	5.1	3.7	(0.5)	—	4	10	7
Weighted average weekly sales per operating store (in thousands)	$ 766 $	763 $	772 $	812 $	864 $	876 $	844
Weighted average sales per square foot ($)	375	371	370	394	415	423	410
Number of customer transactions	1,295	1,246	1,161	1,091	937	797	665
Average ticket ($)	54.89	51.15	49.43	48.64	48.65	47.87	45.05
Number of associates at fiscal year-end [3]	323,100	298,800	280,900	256,300	227,300	201,400	156,700

(4)   Includes Net Sales at locations open greater than 12 months, including relocated and remodeled stores. Stores become comparable on the Monday following their 365 [th] day of operation. Comparable store sales is intended only as supplemental information and is not a substitute for Net Sales or Net Earnings presented in accordance with generally accepted accounting principles.

(5)   Comparable store sales in fiscal years prior to 2002 were reported to the nearest percent.

Corporate and Shareholder Information

STORE SUPPORT CENTER
The Home Depot, Inc.
2455 Paces Ferry Road, NW
Atlanta, GA 30339-4024
Telephone: (770) 433-8211

THE HOME DEPOT WEB SITE
www.homedepot.com

TRANSFER AGENT AND REGISTRAR
Computershare Trust Company, N.A.
P.O. Box 43078
Providence, RI 02490-3078
Telephone: (800) 577-0177
Internet address: www.computershare.com/investor

**INDEPENDENT REGISTERED PUBLIC
ACCOUNTING FIRM**
KPMG LLP
Suite 2000
303 Peachtree Street, NE
Atlanta, GA 30308

STOCK EXCHANGE LISTING
New York Stock Exchange
Trading symbol – HD

ANNUAL MEETING
The Annual Meeting of Shareholders will be held at 9
a.m., Eastern Time, May 22, 2008, at Cobb Galleria Centre
in Atlanta, Georgia.

NUMBER OF SHAREHOLDERS
As of March 24, 2008, there were approximately 160,000
shareholders of record and approximately 1,400,000
individual shareholders holding stock under nominee
security posting listings.

DIVIDENDS DECLARED PER COMMON SHARE

	First Quarter	Second Quarter	Third Quarter	Fourth Quarter
Fiscal 2007	**$0.225**	**$0.225**	**$0.225**	**$0.225**
Fiscal 2006	$0.150	$0.150	$0.225	$0.225

New investors may make an initial investment, and
shareholders of record may acquire additional shares
of our common stock through our direct stock purchase
and dividend reinvestment plan. Subject to certain
requirements, initial cash investments, cash dividends
and/or additional optional cash purchases may be invested
through this plan. To obtain enrollment materials
including the prospectus, access The Home Depot
web site, or call (877) HD-SHARE or (877) 437-4273.
For all other communications regarding these services,
contact Computershare.

**FINANCIAL AND OTHER
COMPANY INFORMATION**
Our Annual Report on Form 10-K for the fiscal year ended February 3, 2008 is available on our web site at www.
homedepot.com under the Investor Relations section. In
addition, financial reports, filing with the Securities and
Exchange Commission, news releases and other information are available on The Home Depot web site.

The Home Depot, Inc. has included as exhibits to its Annual Report on Form 10-K for the fiscal year ended February 3, 2008 certifications of The Home Depot's Chief
Executive Officer and Chief Financial Officer. The Home
Depot's Chief Executive Officer has also submitted to the
New York Stock Exchange (NYSE) a certificate certifying
that he is not aware of any violations by The Home Depot
of the NYSE corporate governance listing standards.

QUARTERLY STOCK PRICE RANGE

	First Quarter	Second Quarter	Third Quarter	Fourth Quarter
Fiscal 2007				
High	**$41.76**	**$40.94**	**$38.31**	**$31.51**
Low	**$36.74**	**$36.75**	**$30.70**	**$24.71**
Fiscal 2006				
High	$43.95	$41.61	$38.24	$41.84
Low	$38.50	$32.85	$33.07	$35.77

Concept and Design: Sagepath (www.sagepath.com)
Photography: Doug Coulter, Craig Bromley, Kim Steele
Printer: Cenveo

LOWE'S COMPANIES, INC. 2007 FORM 10-K ANNUAL REPORT*

* This appendix contains excerpts. Go to the text Web site at www.mhhe.com/LLPW1e for the complete report.

Management's Report on Internal Control Over Financial Reporting

Management of Lowe's Companies, Inc. and its subsidiaries is responsible for establishing and maintaining adequate internal control over financial reporting (Internal Control) as defined in Rule 13a-15(f) under the Securities Exchange Act of 1934, as amended. Our Internal Control was designed to provide reasonable assurance to our management and the board of directors regarding the reliability of financial reporting and the preparation and fair presentation of published financial statements.

All internal control systems, no matter how well designed, have inherent limitations, including the possibility of human error and the circumvention or overriding of controls. Therefore, even those systems determined to be effective can provide only reasonable assurance with respect to the reliability of financial reporting and financial statement preparation and presentation. Further, because of changes in conditions, the effectiveness may vary over time.

Our management, with the participation of the Chief Executive Officer and Chief Financial Officer, evaluated the effectiveness of our Internal Control as of February 1, 2008. In evaluating our Internal Control, we used the criteria set forth by the Committee of Sponsoring Organizations of the Treadway Commission (COSO) in *Internal Control—Integrated Framework* . Based on our management's assessment, we have concluded that, as of February 1, 2008, our Internal Control is effective.

Deloitte & Touche LLP, the independent registered public accounting firm that audited the financial statements contained in this report, was engaged to audit our Internal Control . Their report appears on page 27.

Report of Independent Registered Public Accounting Firm

To the Board of Directors and Shareholders of Lowe's Companies, Inc.
Mooresville, North Carolina

We have audited the accompanying consolidated balance sheets of Lowe's Companies, Inc. and subsidiaries (the "Company") as of February 1, 2008 and February 2, 2007, and the related consolidated statements of earnings, shareholders' equity, and cash flows for each of the three fiscal years in the period ended February 1, 2008. These financial statements are the responsibility of the Company's management. Our responsibility is to express an opinion on these financial statements based on our audits.

We conducted our audits in accordance with the standards of the Public Company Accounting Oversight Board (United States). Those standards require that we plan and perform the audit to obtain reasonable assurance about whether the financial statements are free of material misstatement. An audit includes examining, on a test basis, evidence supporting the amounts and disclosures in the financial statements. An audit also includes assessing the accounting principles used and significant estimates made by management, as well as evaluating the overall financial statement presentation. We believe that our audits provide a reasonable basis for our opinion.

In our opinion, such consolidated financial statements present fairly, in all material respects, the financial position of the Company at February 1, 2008 and February 2, 2007, and the results of its operations and its cash flows for each of the three fiscal years in the period ended February 1, 2008, in conformity with accounting principles generally accepted in the United States of America.

We have also audited, in accordance with the standards of the Public Company Accounting Oversight Board (United States), the Company's internal control over financial reporting as of February 1, 2008, based on the criteria established in *Internal Control—Integrated Framework* issued by the Committee of Sponsoring Organizations of the Treadway Commission and our report dated April 1, 2008 expressed an unqualified opinion on the Company's internal control over financial reporting.

/s/ Deloitte & Touche LLP

Charlotte, North Carolina
April 1, 2008

Report of Independent Registered Public Accounting Firm

To the Board of Directors and Shareholders of Lowe's Companies, Inc.
Mooresville, North Carolina

We have audited the internal control over financial reporting of Lowe's Companies, Inc. and subsidiaries (the "Company") as of February 1, 2008 based on criteria established in *Internal Control — Integrated Framework* issued by the Committee of Sponsoring Organizations of the Treadway Commission. The Company's management is responsible for maintaining effective internal control over financial reporting and for its assessment of the effectiveness of internal control over financial reporting, included in the accompanying Management's Report on Internal Control Over Financial Reporting. Our responsibility is to express an opinion on the Company's internal control over financial reporting based on our audit.

We conducted our audit in accordance with the standards of the Public Company Accounting Oversight Board (United States). Those standards require that we plan and perform the audit to obtain reasonable assurance about whether effective internal control over financial reporting was maintained in all material respects. Our audit included obtaining an understanding of internal control over financial reporting, assessing the risk that a material weakness exists, testing and evaluating the design and operating effectiveness of internal control based on the assessed risk, and performing such other procedures as we considered necessary in the circumstances. We believe that our audit provides a reasonable basis for our opinion.

A company's internal control over financial reporting is a process designed by, or under the supervision of, the company's principal executive and principal financial officers, or persons performing similar functions, and effected by the company's board of directors, management, and other personnel to provide reasonable assurance regarding the reliability of financial reporting and the preparation of financial statements for external purposes in accordance with generally accepted accounting principles. A company's internal control over financial reporting includes those policies and procedures that (1) pertain to the maintenance of records that, in reasonable detail, accurately and fairly reflect the transactions and dispositions of the assets of the company; (2) provide reasonable assurance that transactions are recorded as necessary to permit preparation of financial statements in accordance with generally accepted accounting principles, and that receipts and expenditures of the company are being made only in accordance with authorizations of management and directors of the company; and (3) provide reasonable assurance regarding prevention or timely detection of unauthorized acquisition, use, or disposition of the company's assets that could have a material effect on the financial statements.

Because of the inherent limitations of internal control over financial reporting, including the possibility of collusion or improper management override of controls, material misstatements due to error or fraud may not be prevented or detected on a timely basis. Also, projections of any evaluation of the effectiveness of the internal control over financial reporting to future periods are subject to the risk that the controls may become inadequate because of changes in conditions, or that the degree of compliance with the policies or procedures may deteriorate.

In our opinion, the Company maintained, in all material respects, effective internal control over financial reporting as of February 1, 2008, based on the criteria established in *Internal Control — Integrated Framework* issued by the Committee of Sponsoring Organizations of the Treadway Commission.

We have also audited, in accordance with the standards of the Public Company Accounting Oversight Board (United States), the consolidated financial statements as of and for the fiscal year ended February 1, 2008 of the Company and our report dated April 1, 2008 expressed an unqualified opinion on those financial statements.

/s/ Deloitte & Touche LLP

Charlotte, North Carolina
April 1, 2008

Lowe's Companies, Inc.
Consolidated Statements of Earnings

(In millions, except per share and percentage data) Fiscal years ended on	February 1, 2008	% Sales	February 2, 2007	% Sales	February 3, 2006	% Sales
Net sales (Note 1)	$ 48,283	100.00%	$ 46,927	100.00%	$ 43,243	100.00%
Cost of sales (Notes 1 and 14)	31,556	65.36	30,729	65.48	28,453	65.80
Gross margin	16,727	34.64	16,198	34.52	14,790	34.20
Expenses:						
Selling, general and administrative (Notes 1, 8, 9 and 12)	10,515	21.78	9,738	20.75	9,014	20.84
Store opening costs (Note 1)	141	0.29	146	0.31	142	0.33
Depreciation (Notes 1 and 3)	1,366	2.83	1,162	2.48	980	2.27
Interest - net (Note 15)	194	0.40	154	0.33	158	0.37
Total expenses	12,216	25.30	11,200	23.87	10,294	23.81
Pre-tax earnings	4,511	9.34	4,998	10.65	4,496	10.39
Income tax provision (Notes 1 and 10)	1,702	3.52	1,893	4.03	1,731	4.00
Net earnings	$ 2,809	5.82%	$ 3,105	6.62%	$ 2,765	6.39%
Basic earnings per share (Note 11)	$ 1.90		$ 2.02		$ 1.78	
Diluted earnings per share (Note 11)	$ 1.86		$ 1.99		$ 1.73	
Cash dividends per share	$ 0.29		$ 0.18		$ 0.11	

See accompanying notes to the consolidated financial statements.

Lowe's Companies, Inc.
Consolidated Balance Sheets

(In millions, except par value and percentage data)		February 1, 2008	% Total	February 2, 2007	% Total
Assets					
Current assets:					
Cash and cash equivalents (Note 1)		$ 281	0.9%	$ 364	1.3%
Short-term investments (Notes 1 and 2)		249	0.8	432	1.6
Merchandise inventory - net (Note 1)		7,611	24.6	7,144	25.7
Deferred income taxes - net (Notes 1 and 10)		247	0.8	161	0.6
Other current assets (Note 1)		298	1.0	213	0.8
Total current assets		**8,686**	**28.1**	**8,314**	**30.0**
Property, less accumulated depreciation (Notes 1 and 3)		21,361	69.2	18,971	68.3
Long-term investments (Notes 1 and 2)		509	1.7	165	0.6
Other assets (Note 1)		313	1.0	317	1.1
Total assets		$ **30,869**	**100.0%**	$ **27,767**	**100.0%**
Liabilities and shareholders' equity					
Current liabilities:					
Short-term borrowings (Note 4)		$ 1,064	3.5%	$ 23	0.1%
Current maturities of long-term debt (Note 5)		40	0.1	88	0.3
Accounts payable (Note 1)		3,713	12.0	3,524	12.7
Accrued salaries and wages		424	1.4	425	1.5
Self-insurance liabilities (Note 1)		671	2.2	650	2.4
Deferred revenue (Note 1)		717	2.3	731	2.6
Other current liabilities (Note 1)		1,122	3.6	1,098	3.9
Total current liabilities		**7,751**	**25.1**	**6,539**	**23.5**
Long-term debt, excluding current maturities (Notes 5, 6 and 12)		5,576	18.1	4,325	15.6
Deferred income taxes - net (Notes 1 and 10)		670	2.2	735	2.7
Other liabilities (Note 1)		774	2.5	443	1.6
Total liabilities		**14,771**	**47.9**	**12,042**	**43.4**
Commitments and contingencies (Note 13)					
Shareholders' equity (Note 7) :					
Preferred stock - $5 par value, none issued		-	-	-	-
Common stock - $.50 par value;					
Shares issued and outstanding					
February 1, 2008	1,458				
February 2, 2007	1,525	729	2.3	762	2.7
Capital in excess of par value		16	0.1	102	0.4
Retained earnings		15,345	49.7	14,860	53.5
Accumulated other comprehensive income (Note 1)		8	-	1	-
Total shareholders' equity		**16,098**	**52.1**	**15,725**	**56.6**
Total liabilities and shareholders' equity		$ **30,869**	**100.0%**	$ **27,767**	**100.0%**

See accompanying notes to the consolidated financial statements.

Lowe's Companies, Inc.
Consolidated Statements of
Shareholders' Equity

(In millions)	Common Stock Shares	Common Stock Amount	Capital in Excess of Par Value	Retained Earnings	Accumulated Other Comprehensive Income	Total Shareholders' Equity
Balance January 28, 2005	**1,548** $	**774** $	**1,127** $	**9,597** $	**-** $	**11,498**
Comprehensive income (Note 1):						
Net earnings				2,765		
Foreign currency translation					1	
Total comprehensive income						2,766
Tax effect of non-qualified stock options exercised			59			59
Cash dividends				(171)		(171)
Share-based payment expense (Note 8)			76			76
Repurchase of common stock (Note 7)	(25)	(12)	(762)			(774)
Conversion of debt to common stock (Note 5)	28	14	551			565
Employee stock options exercised and other (Note 8)	15	7	205			212
Employee stock purchase plan (Note 8)	2	1	64			65
Balance February 3, 2006	**1,568** $	**784** $	**1,320** $	**12,191** $	**1** $	**14,296**
Comprehensive income (Note 1):						
Net earnings				3,105		
Foreign currency translation					(2)	
Net unrealized investment gains (Note 2)					2	
Total comprehensive income						3,105
Tax effect of non-qualified stock options exercised			21			21
Cash dividends				(276)		(276)
Share-based payment expense (Note 8)			59			59
Repurchase of common stock (Note 7)	(57)	(28)	(1,549)	(160)		(1,737)
Conversion of debt to common stock (Note 5)	4	2	80			82
Employee stock options exercised and other (Note 8)	7	3	96			99
Employee stock purchase plan (Note 8)	3	1	75			76
Balance February 2, 2007	**1,525** $	**762** $	**102** $	**14,860** $	**1** $	**15,725**
Cumulative effect adjustment (Note 10):				(8)		(8)
Comprehensive income (Note 1):						
Net earnings				2,809		
Foreign currency translation					7	
Total comprehensive income						2,816
Tax effect of non-qualified stock options exercised			12			12
Cash dividends				(428)		(428)
Share-based payment expense (Note 8)			99			99
Repurchase of common stock (Note 7)	(76)	(38)	(349)	(1,888)		(2,275)
Conversion of debt to common stock (Note 5)	1	-	13			13
Employee stock options exercised and other (Note 8)	5	3	61			64
Employee stock purchase plan (Note 8)	3	2	78			80
Balance February 1, 2008	**1,458** $	**729** $	**16** $	**15,345** $	**8** $	**16,098**

See accompanying notes to the consolidated financial statements.

Lowe's Companies, Inc.
Consolidated Statements of Cash Flows

(In millions) Fiscal years ended on	February 1, 2008	February 2, 2007	February 3, 2006
Cash flows from operating activities:			
Net earnings	$ 2,809	$ 3,105	$ 2,765
Adjustments to reconcile earnings to net cash provided by operating activities:			
Depreciation and amortization	1,464	1,237	1,051
Deferred income taxes	2	(6)	(37)
Loss on disposition/writedown of fixed and other assets	51	23	31
Share-based payment expense	99	62	76
Changes in operating assets and liabilities:			
Merchandise inventory - net	(464)	(509)	(785)
Other operating assets	(64)	(135)	(38)
Accounts payable	185	692	137
Other operating liabilities	265	33	642
Net cash provided by operating activities	**4,347**	**4,502**	**3,842**
Cash flows from investing activities:			
Purchases of short-term investments	(920)	(284)	(1,829)
Proceeds from sale/maturity of short-term investments	1,183	572	1,802
Purchases of long-term investments	(1,588)	(558)	(354)
Proceeds from sale/maturity of long-term investments	1,162	415	55
Increase in other long-term assets	(7)	(16)	(30)
Fixed assets acquired	(4,010)	(3,916)	(3,379)
Proceeds from the sale of fixed and other long-term assets	57	72	61
Net cash used in investing activities	**(4,123)**	**(3,715)**	**(3,674)**
Cash flows from financing activities:			
Net increase in short-term borrowings	1,041	23	-
Proceeds from issuance of long-term debt	1,296	989	1,013
Repayment of long-term debt	(96)	(33)	(633)
Proceeds from issuance of common stock under employee stock purchase plan	80	76	65
Proceeds from issuance of common stock from stock options exercised	69	100	225
Cash dividend payments	(428)	(276)	(171)
Repurchase of common stock	(2,275)	(1,737)	(774)
Excess tax benefits of share-based payments	6	12	-
Net cash used in financing activities	**(307)**	**(846)**	**(275)**
Net decrease in cash and cash equivalents	(83)	(59)	(107)
Cash and cash equivalents, beginning of year	364	423	530
Cash and cash equivalents, end of year	**$ 281**	**$ 364**	**$ 423**

See accompanying notes to the consolidated financial statements.

NOTES TO CONSOLIDATED FINANCIAL STATEMENTS
YEARS ENDED FEBRUARY 1, 2008, FEBRUARY 2, 2007 AND FEBRUARY 3, 2006

NOTE 1 - Summary of Significant Accounting Policies:

Lowe's Companies, Inc. and subsidiaries (the Company) is the world's second-largest home improvement retailer and operated 1,534 stores in the United States and Canada at February 1, 2008. Below are those accounting policies considered by the Company to be significant.

Fiscal Year - The Company's fiscal year ends on the Friday nearest the end of January. The fiscal years ended February 1, 2008 and February 2, 2007 contained 52 weeks. The fiscal year ended February 3, 2006 contained 53 weeks. All references herein for the years 2007, 2006 and 2005 represent the fiscal years ended February 1, 2008, February 2, 2007 and February 3, 2006, respectively.

Principles of Consolidation - The consolidated financial statements include the accounts of the Company and its wholly-owned or controlled operating subsidiaries. All material intercompany accounts and transactions have been eliminated.

Use of Estimates - The preparation of the Company's financial statements in accordance with accounting principles generally accepted in the United States of America requires management to make estimates that affect the reported amounts of assets, liabilities, sales and expenses, and related disclosures of contingent assets and liabilities. The Company bases these estimates on historical results and various other assumptions believed to be reasonable, all of which form the basis for making estimates concerning the carrying values of assets and liabilities that are not readily available from other sources. Actual results may differ from these estimates.

Cash and Cash Equivalents - Cash and cash equivalents include cash on hand, demand deposits and short-term investments with original maturities of three months or less when purchased. The majority of payments due from financial institutions for the settlement of credit card and debit card transactions process within two business days and are, therefore, classified as cash and cash equivalents.

Investments - The Company has a cash management program which provides for the investment of cash balances not expected to be used in current operations in financial instruments that have maturities of up to 10 years. Variable-rate demand notes, which have stated maturity dates in excess of 10 years, meet this maturity requirement of the cash management program because the maturity date of these investments is determined based on the interest rate reset date or par value put date for the purpose of applying this criteria.

Investments, exclusive of cash equivalents, with a stated maturity date of one year or less from the balance sheet date or that are expected to be used in current operations, are classified as short-term investments. All other investments are classified as long-term. As of February 1, 2008, investments consisted primarily of money market funds, certificates of deposit, municipal obligations and mutual funds. Restricted balances pledged as collateral for letters of credit for the Company's extended warranty program and for a portion of the Company's casualty insurance and installed sales program liabilities are also classified as investments.

The Company has classified all investment securities as available-for-sale, and they are carried at fair market value. Unrealized gains and losses on such securities are included in accumulated other comprehensive income in shareholders' equity.

Merchandise Inventory - Inventory is stated at the lower of cost or market using the first-in, first-out method of inventory accounting. The cost of inventory also includes certain costs associated with the preparation of inventory for resale and distribution center costs, net of vendor funds.

The Company records an inventory reserve for the loss associated with selling inventories below cost. This reserve is based on management's current knowledge with respect to inventory levels, sales trends and historical experience. Management does not believe the Company's merchandise inventories are subject to significant risk of obsolescence in the near term, and management has the ability to adjust purchasing practices based on anticipated sales trends and general economic conditions. However, changes in consumer purchasing patterns could result in the need for additional reserves. The Company also records an inventory reserve for the estimated shrinkage between physical inventories. This reserve is based primarily on actual shrink results from previous physical inventories. Changes in the estimated shrink reserve may be necessary based on the results of physical inventories. Management believes it has sufficient current and historical knowledge to record reasonable estimates for both of these inventory reserves.

Derivative Financial Instruments - The Company occasionally utilizes derivative financial instruments to manage certain business risks. However, the amounts were not material to the Company's consolidated financial statements in any of the years presented. The Company does not use derivative financial instruments for trading purposes.

Credit Programs - The majority of the Company's accounts receivable arises from sales of goods and services to Commercial Business Customers. In May 2004, the Company entered into an agreement with General Electric Company and its subsidiaries (GE) to sell its then-existing portfolio of commercial business accounts receivable to GE. During the term of the agreement, which ends on December 31, 2016, unless terminated sooner by the parties, GE also purchases at face value new commercial business accounts receivable originated by the Company and services these accounts. The Company accounts for these transfers as sales of accounts receivable. When the Company sells its commercial business accounts receivable, it retains certain interests in those receivables, including the funding of a loss reserve and its obligation related to GE's ongoing servicing of the receivables sold. Any gain or loss on the sale is determined based on the previous carrying amounts of the transferred assets allocated at fair value between the receivables sold and the interests retained. Fair value is based on the present value of expected future cash flows, taking into account the key assumptions of anticipated credit losses, payment rates, late fee rates, GE's servicing costs and the discount rate commensurate with the uncertainty involved. Due to the short-term nature of the receivables sold, changes to the key assumptions would not materially impact the recorded gain or loss on the sales of receivables or the fair value of the retained interests in the receivables.

Total commercial business accounts receivable sold to GE were $1.8 billion in both 2007 and 2006, and $1.7 billion in 2005. During 2007, 2006 and 2005, the Company recognized losses of $34 million, $35 million and $41 million, respectively, on these sales as selling, general and administrative (SG&A) expense, which primarily relates to the fair value of the obligations incurred related to servicing costs that are remitted to GE monthly. At February 1, 2008 and February 2, 2007, the fair value of the retained interests was insignificant and was determined based on the present value of expected future cash flows.

Sales generated through the Company's proprietary credit cards are not reflected in receivables. Under an agreement with GE, credit is extended directly to customers by GE. All credit program-related services are performed and controlled directly by GE. The Company has the option, but no obligation, to purchase the receivables at the end of the agreement in December 2016. Tender costs, including amounts associated with accepting the Company's proprietary credit cards, are recorded in SG&A in the consolidated financial statements.

The total portfolio of receivables held by GE, including both receivables originated by GE from the Company's private label credit cards and commercial business accounts receivable originated by the Company and sold to GE, approximated $6.6 billion at February 1, 2008, and $6.0 billion at February 2, 2007.

Property and Depreciation - Property is recorded at cost. Costs associated with major additions are capitalized and depreciated. Capital assets are expected to yield future benefits and have useful lives which exceed one year. The total cost of a capital asset generally includes all applicable sales taxes, delivery costs, installation costs and other appropriate costs incurred by the Company in the case of self-constructed assets. Upon disposal, the cost of properties and related accumulated depreciation are removed from the accounts, with gains and losses reflected in SG&A expense in the consolidated statements of earnings.

Depreciation is provided over the estimated useful lives of the depreciable assets. Assets are depreciated using the straight-line method. Leasehold improvements are depreciated over the shorter of their estimated useful lives or the term of the related lease, which may include one or more option renewal periods where failure to exercise such options would result in an economic penalty in such amount that renewal appears, at the inception of the lease, to be reasonably assured. During the term of a lease, if a substantial additional investment is made in a leased location, the Company reevaluates its definition of lease term to determine whether the investment, together with any penalties related to non-renewal, would constitute an economic penalty in such amount that renewal appears, at the time of the reevaluation, to be reasonably assured.

Long-Lived Asset Impairment/Exit Activities - The carrying amounts of long-lived assets are reviewed whenever events or changes in circumstances indicate that the carrying amount may not be recoverable.

For long-lived assets held for use, a potential impairment has occurred if projected future undiscounted cash flows expected to result from the use and eventual disposition of the assets are less than the carrying value of the assets. An impairment loss is recognized when the carrying amount of the long-lived asset is not recoverable and exceeds its fair value. The Company estimates fair value based on projected future discounted cash flows.

For long-lived assets to be abandoned, the Company considers the asset to be disposed of when it ceases to be used. Until it ceases to be used, the Company continues to classify the assets as held for use and tests for potential impairment accordingly. If the Company commits to a plan to abandon a long-lived asset before the end of its previously estimated useful life, depreciation estimates are revised.

For long-lived assets held for sale, an impairment charge is recorded if the carrying amount of the asset exceeds its fair value less cost to sell. Fair value is based on a market appraisal or a valuation technique that considers various factors, including local market conditions. A long-lived asset is not depreciated while it is classified as held for sale.

The net carrying value for relocated stores, closed stores and other excess properties that are expected to be sold within the next 12 months are classified as held for sale and included in other current assets in the consolidated balance sheets. Assets held for sale totaled $28 million at February 1, 2008. Assets held for sale at February 2, 2007 were not significant. The net carrying value for relocated stores, closed stores and other excess properties that do not meet the held for sale criteria are included in other assets (non-current) in the consolidated balance sheets and totaled $91 million and $113 million at February 1, 2008 and February 2, 2007, respectively.

When operating leased locations are closed, a liability is recognized for the fair value of future contractual obligations, including property taxes, utilities and common area maintenance, net of estimated sublease income. The liability, which is included in other current liabilities in the consolidated balance sheets, was $11 million and $19 million at February 1, 2008 and February 2, 2007, respectively.

The charge for impairment is included in SG&A expense and totaled $28 million, $5 million and $16 million in 2007, 2006 and 2005, respectively.

Leases - For lease agreements that provide for escalating rent payments or free-rent occupancy periods, the Company recognizes rent expense on a straight-line basis over the non-cancelable lease term and option renewal periods where failure to exercise such options would result in an economic penalty in such amount that renewal appears, at the inception of the lease, to be reasonably assured. The lease term commences on the date that that Company takes possession of or controls the physical use of the property. Deferred rent is included in other long-term liabilities in the consolidated balance sheets.

Assets under capital lease are amortized in accordance with the Company's normal depreciation policy for owned assets or, if shorter, over the non-cancelable lease term and any option renewal period where failure to exercise such option would result in an economic penalty in such amount that renewal appears, at the inception of the lease, to be reasonably assured. The amortization of the assets is included in depreciation expense in the consolidated financial statements. During the term of a lease, if a substantial additional investment is made in a leased location, the Company reevaluates its definition of lease term.

Accounts Payable - In June 2007, the Company entered into a customer-managed services agreement with a third party to provide an accounts payable tracking system which facilitates participating suppliers' ability to finance payment obligations from the Company with designated third-party financial institutions. Participating suppliers may, at their sole discretion, make offers to finance one or more payment obligations of the Company prior to their scheduled due dates at a discounted price to participating financial institutions. The Company's goal in entering into this arrangement is to capture overall supply chain savings, in the form of pricing, payment terms or vendor funding, created by facilitating suppliers' ability to finance payment obligations at more favorable discount rates, while providing them with greater working capital flexibility.

The Company's obligations to its suppliers, including amounts due and scheduled payment dates, are not impacted by suppliers' decisions to finance amounts under this arrangement. However, the Company's right to offset balances due from suppliers against payment obligations is restricted by this arrangement for those payment obligations that have been financed by suppliers. As of February 1, 2008, the Company had placed $77 million of payment obligations on the accounts payable tracking system, and participating suppliers had financed $48 million of those payment obligations to participating financial institutions.

Self-Insurance - The Company is self-insured for certain losses relating to workers' compensation, automobile, property, and general and product liability claims. The Company has stop-loss coverage to limit the exposure arising from these claims. The Company is also self-insured for certain losses relating to extended warranty and medical and dental claims. Self-insurance claims filed and claims incurred but not reported are accrued based upon management's estimates of the discounted ultimate cost for uninsured claims incurred using actuarial assumptions followed in the insurance industry and historical experience. Although management believes it has the ability to reasonably estimate losses related to claims, it is possible that actual results could differ from recorded self-insurance liabilities.

Income Taxes - The Company establishes deferred income tax assets and liabilities for temporary differences between the tax and financial accounting bases of assets and liabilities. The tax effects of such differences are reflected in the balance sheet at the enacted tax rates expected to be in effect when the differences reverse. A valuation allowance is recorded to reduce the carrying amount of deferred tax assets if it is more likely than not that all or a portion of the asset will not be realized. The tax balances and income tax expense recognized by the Company are based on management's interpretation of the tax statutes of multiple jurisdictions.

The Company establishes a reserve for tax positions for which there is uncertainty as to whether or not the position will be ultimately sustained. The Company includes interest related to tax issues as part of net interest in the consolidated financial statements. The Company records any applicable penalties related to tax issues within the income tax provision.

Revenue Recognition - The Company recognizes revenues, net of sales tax, when sales transactions occur and customers take possession of the merchandise. A provision for anticipated merchandise returns is provided through a reduction of sales and cost of sales in the period that the related sales are recorded. Revenues from product installation services are recognized when the installation is completed. Deferred revenues associated with amounts received for which customers have not yet taken possession of merchandise or for which installation has not yet been completed were $332 million and $364 million at February 1, 2008, and February 2, 2007, respectively.

Revenues from stored value cards, which include gift cards and returned merchandise credits, are deferred and recognized when the cards are redeemed. The liability associated with outstanding stored value cards was $385 million and $367 million at February 1, 2008, and February 2, 2007, respectively, and these amounts are included in deferred revenue in the accompanying consolidated balance sheets. The Company recognizes income from unredeemed stored value cards at the point at which redemption becomes remote. The Company's stored value cards have no expiration date or dormancy fees. Therefore, to determine when redemption is remote, the Company analyzes an aging of the unredeemed cards based on the date of last stored value card use.

Extended Warranties - Lowe's sells separately-priced extended warranty contracts under a Lowe's-branded program for which the Company is ultimately self-insured. The Company recognizes revenue from extended warranty sales on a straight-line basis over the respective contract term. Extended warranty contract terms primarily range from one to four years from the date of purchase or the end of the manufacturer's warranty, as applicable. The Company's extended warranty deferred revenue is included in other liabilities (non-current) in the accompanying consolidated balance sheets. Changes deferred revenue for extended warranty contracts are summarized as follows:

(In millions)		2007		2006
Extended warranty deferred revenue, beginning of period	$	315	$	206
Additions to deferred revenue		175		148
Deferred revenue recognized		(83)		(39)
Extended warranty deferred revenue, end of period	$	407	$	315

Incremental direct acquisition costs associated with the sale of extended warranties are also deferred and recognized as expense on a straight-line basis over the respective contract term. Deferred costs associated with extended warranty contracts were $91 million and $81 million at February 1, 2008 and February 2, 2007, respectively. The Company's extended warranty deferred costs are included in other assets (non-current) in the accompanying consolidated balance sheets. All other costs, such as costs of services performed under the contract, general and administrative expenses and advertising expenses are expensed as incurred.

The liability for extended warranty claims incurred is included in self-insurance liabilities in the accompanying consolidated balance sheets. Changes in the liability for extended warranty claims are summarized as follows:

(In millions)	2007	2006
Liability for extended warranty claims, beginning of period	$ 10	$ -
Accrual for claims incurred	41	17
Claim payments	(37)	(7)
Liability for extended warranty claims, end of period	$ 14	$ 10

Cost of Sales and Selling, General and Administrative Expenses - The following lists the primary costs classified in each major expense category:

Cost of Sales	Selling, General and Administrative
■ Total cost of products sold, including: - Purchase costs, net of vendor funds; - Freight expenses associated with moving merchandise inventories from vendors to retail stores; - Costs associated with operating the Company's distribution network, including payroll and benefit costs and occupancy costs; ■ Costs of installation services provided; ■ Costs associated with delivery of products directly from vendors to customers by third parties; ■ Costs associated with inventory shrinkage and obsolescence.	■ Payroll and benefit costs for retail and corporate employees; ■ Occupancy costs of retail and corporate facilities; ■ Advertising; ■ Costs associated with delivery of products from stores to customers; ■ Third-party, in-store service costs; ■ Tender costs, including bank charges, costs associated with credit card interchange fees, and amounts associated with accepting the Company's proprietary credit cards; ■ Costs associated with self-insured plans, and premium costs for stop-loss coverage and fully insured plans; ■ Long-lived asset impairment charges and gains/losses on disposal of assets; ■ Other administrative costs, such as supplies, and travel and entertainment.

Vendor Funds - The Company receives funds from vendors in the normal course of business principally as a result of purchase volumes, sales, early payments or promotions of vendors' products. Based on the provisions of the vendor agreements in place, management develops accrual rates by estimating the point at which the Company will have completed its performance under the agreement and the amount agreed upon will be earned. Due to the complexity and diversity of the individual vendor agreements, the Company performs analyses and reviews historical trends throughout the year to ensure the amounts earned are appropriately recorded. As a part of these analyses, the Company validates its accrual rates based on actual purchase trends and applies those rates to actual purchase volumes to determine the amount of funds accrued by the Company and receivable from the vendor. Amounts accrued throughout the year could be impacted if actual purchase volumes differ from projected annual purchase volumes, especially in the case of programs that provide for increased funding when graduated purchase volumes are met.

Vendor funds are treated as a reduction of inventory cost, unless they represent a reimbursement of specific, incremental and identifiable costs incurred by the customer to sell the vendor's product. Substantially all of the vendor funds that the Company receives do not meet the specific, incremental and identifiable criteria. Therefore, the Company treats the majority of these funds as a reduction in the cost of inventory as the amounts are accrued, and recognizes these funds as a reduction of cost of sales when the inventory is sold.

Advertising - Costs associated with advertising are charged to expense as incurred. Advertising expenses were $788 million, $873 million and $812 million in 2007, 2006 and 2005, respectively. Cooperative advertising vendor funds are recorded as a reduction of these expenses with the net amount included in SG&A expense. Cooperative advertising vendor funds were $5 million in 2007 but insignificant in both 2006 and 2005.

Shipping and Handling Costs - The Company includes shipping and handling costs relating to the delivery of products directly from vendors to customers by third parties in cost of sales. Shipping and handling costs, which include salaries and vehicle operations expenses relating to the delivery of products from stores to customers, are classified as SG&A expense. Shipping and handling costs included in SG&A expense were $307 million, $310 million and $312 million in 2007, 2006 and 2005, respectively.

Store Opening Costs - Costs of opening new or relocated retail stores, which include payroll and supply costs incurred prior to store opening and grand opening advertising costs, are charged to operations as incurred.

Comprehensive Income - The Company reports comprehensive income in its consolidated statements of shareholders' equity. Comprehensive income represents changes in shareholders' equity from non-owner sources and is comprised primarily of net earnings plus or minus unrealized gains or losses on available-for-sale securities, as well as foreign currency translation adjustments. Unrealized gains on available-for-sale securities classified in accumulated other comprehensive income on the accompanying consolidated balance sheets were $2 million at both February 1, 2008 and February 2, 2007. Foreign currency translation gains classified in accumulated other comprehensive income on the accompanying consolidated balance sheets were $6 million at February 1, 2008, and foreign currency translation losses were $1 million at February 2, 2007. The reclassification adjustments for gains/losses included in net earnings for 2007, 2006 and 2005 were insignificant.

Recent Accounting Pronouncements – In September 2006, the Financial Accounting Standards Board (FASB) issued Statement of Financial Accounting Standards (SFAS) No. 157, "Fair Value Measurements". SFAS No. 157 provides a single definition of fair value, together with a framework for measuring it, and requires additional disclosure about the use of fair value to measure assets and liabilities. SFAS No. 157 also emphasizes that fair value is a market-based measurement, not an entity-specific measurement, and sets out a fair value hierarchy with the highest priority being quoted prices in active markets. Under SFAS No. 157, fair value measurements are required to be disclosed by level within that hierarchy. SFAS No. 157 is effective for fiscal years beginning after November 15, 2007, and interim periods within those fiscal years. However, FASB Staff Position (FSP) No. FAS 157-2, "Effective Date of FASB Statement No. 157," issued in February 2008, delays the effective date of SFAS No. 157 for all nonfinancial assets and nonfinancial liabilities, except for items that are recognized or disclosed at fair value in the financial statements on a recurring basis, to fiscal years beginning after November 15, 2008, and interim periods within those fiscal years. The Company does not expect the adoption of SFAS No. 157 to have a material impact on its consolidated financial statements.

In February 2007, the FASB issued SFAS No. 159, "The Fair Value Option for Financial Assets and Financial Liabilities." SFAS No. 159 provides entities with an option to measure many financial instruments and certain other items at fair value, including available-for-sale securities previously accounted for under SFAS No. 115, "Accounting for Certain Investments in Debt and Equity Securities." Under SFAS No. 159, unrealized gains and losses on items for which the fair value option has been elected will be reported in earnings at each subsequent reporting period. SFAS No. 159 is effective for fiscal years beginning after November 15, 2007. The Company does not expect the adoption of SFAS No. 159 to have a material impact on its consolidated financial statements.

In June 2007, the Emerging Issues Task Force (EITF) reached a consensus on Issue No. 06-11, "Accounting for Income Tax Benefits of Dividends on Share-Based Payment Awards." EITF 06-11 states that an entity should recognize a realized tax benefit associated with dividends on nonvested equity shares, nonvested equity share units and outstanding equity share options charged to retained earnings as an increase in additional paid in capital. The amount recognized in additional paid in capital should be included in the pool of excess tax benefits available to absorb potential future tax deficiencies on share-based payment awards. EITF 06-11 should be applied prospectively to income tax benefits of dividends on equity-classified share-based payment awards that are declared in fiscal years beginning after December 15, 2007. The Company does not expect the adoption of EITF 06-11 to have a material impact on its consolidated financial statements.

In December 2007, the FASB issued SFAS No. 141(R), "Business Combinations" and SFAS No. 160, "Noncontrolling Interests in Consolidated Financial Statements – an amendment of ARB No. 51". SFAS No. 141(R) and SFAS No. 160 significantly change the accounting for and reporting of business combinations and noncontrolling interests in consolidated financial statements. Under SFAS No. 141(R), more assets and liabilities will be measured at fair value as of the acquisition date instead of the announcement date. Additionally, acquisition costs will be expensed as incurred. Under SFAS No. 160, noncontrolling interests will be classified as a separate component of equity. SFAS No. 141(R) and SFAS No. 160 should be applied prospectively for fiscal years beginning on or after December 15, 2008, with the exception of the presentation and disclosure requirements of SFAS No. 160, which should be applied retrospectively. The Company does not expect the adoption of SFAS No. 141(R) and SFAS No. 160 to have a material impact on its consolidated financial statements.

Segment Information – The Company's operating segments, representing the Company's home improvement retail stores, are aggregated within one reportable segment based on the way the Company manages its business. The Company's home improvement retail stores exhibit similar long-term economic characteristics, sell similar products and services, use similar processes to sell those products and services, and sell their products and services to similar classes of customers. The amount of long-lived assets and net sales outside the U.S. was not significant for any of the periods presented.

Reclassifications - Certain prior period amounts have been reclassified to conform to current classifications.

NOTE 2 - Investments:

The Company's investment securities are classified as available-for-sale. The amortized costs, gross unrealized holding gains and losses, and fair values of the investments at February 1, 2008, and February 2, 2007, were as follows:

Type (In millions)	Amortized Cost	Gross Unrealized Gains	Gross Unrealized Losses	Fair Value
February 1, 2008				
Municipal obligations	$ 117	$ 1	$ -	$ 118
Money market funds	128	-	-	128
Certificates of deposit	3	-	-	3
Classified as short-term	**248**	**1**	**-**	**249**
Municipal obligations	462	5	-	467
Mutual funds	42	1	(1)	42
Classified as long-term	**504**	**6**	**(1)**	**509**
Total	**$ 752**	**$ 7**	**$ (1)**	**$ 758**

Type (In millions)	Amortized Cost	Gross Unrealized Gains	Gross Unrealized Losses	Fair Value
February 2, 2007				
Municipal obligations	$ 258	$ -	$ (1)	$ 257
Money market funds	148	-	-	148
Corporate notes	26	-	-	26
Certificates of deposit	1	-	-	1
Classified as short-term	**433**	**-**	**(1)**	**432**
Municipal obligations	127	-	-	127
Mutual funds	35	3	-	38
Classified as long-term	**162**	**3**	**-**	**165**
Total	**$ 595**	**$ 3**	**$ (1)**	**$ 597**

The proceeds from sales of available-for-sale securities were $1.2 billion, $412 million and $192 million for 2007, 2006 and 2005, respectively. Gross realized gains and losses on the sale of available-for-sale securities were not significant for any of the periods presented. The municipal obligations classified as long-term at February 1, 2008, will mature in one to 32 years, based on stated maturity dates.

Short-term and long-term investments include restricted balances pledged as collateral for letters of credit for the Company's extended warranty program and for a portion of the Company's casualty insurance and installed sales program liabilities. Restricted balances included in short-term investments were $167 million at February 1, 2008 and $248 million at February 2, 2007. Restricted balances included in long-term investments were $172 million at February 1, 2008 and $32 million at February 2, 2007.

NOTE 3 - Property and Accumulated Depreciation:

Property is summarized by major class in the following table:

(In millions)	Estimated Depreciable Lives, In Years	February 1, 2008	February 2, 2007
Cost:			
Land	N/A	$ 5,566	$ 4,807
Buildings	7-40	10,036	8,481
Equipment	3-15	8,118	7,036
Leasehold improvements	3-40	3,063	2,484
Construction in progress	N/A	2,053	2,296
Total cost		**28,836**	**25,104**
Accumulated depreciation		(7,475)	(6,133)
Property, less accumulated depreciation		**$ 21,361**	**$ 18,971**

Included in net property are assets under capital lease of $523 million, less accumulated depreciation of $294 million, at February 1, 2008, and $533 million, less accumulated depreciation of $274 million, at February 2, 2007.

NOTE 4 - Short-Term Borrowings and Lines of Credit:

In June 2007, the Company entered into an Amended and Restated Credit Agreement (Amended Facility) to modify the senior credit facility by extending the maturity date to June 2012 and providing for borrowings of up to $1.75 billion. The Amended Facility supports the Company's commercial paper and revolving credit programs. Borrowings made are unsecured and are priced at a fixed rate based upon market conditions at the time of funding, in accordance with the terms of the Amended Facility. The Amended Facility contains certain restrictive covenants, which include maintenance of a debt leverage ratio as defined by the Amended Facility. The Company was in compliance with those covenants at February 1, 2008. Seventeen banking institutions are participating in the Amended Facility. As of February 1, 2008, there was $1.0 billion outstanding under the commercial paper program. The weighted-average interest rate on the outstanding commercial paper was 3.92%. As of February 2, 2007, there was $23 million of short-term borrowings outstanding under the senior credit facility, but no outstanding borrowings under the commercial paper program. The interest rate on the short-term borrowing was 5.41%.

In October 2007, the Company established a Canadian dollar (C$) denominated credit facility in the amount of C$50 million, which provides revolving credit support for the Company's Canadian operations. This uncommitted facility provides the Company with the ability to make unsecured borrowings, which are priced at a fixed rate based upon market conditions at the time of funding in accordance with the terms of the credit facility. As of February 1, 2008, there were no borrowings outstanding under the credit facility.

In January 2008, the Company entered into a C$ denominated credit agreement in the amount of C$200 million for the purpose of funding the build out of retail stores in Canada and for working capital and other general corporate purposes. Borrowings made are unsecured and are priced at a fixed rate based upon market conditions at the time of funding in accordance with the terms of the credit agreement. The credit agreement contains certain restrictive covenants, which include maintenance of a debt leverage ratio as defined by the credit agreement. The Company was in compliance with those covenants at February 1, 2008. Three banking institutions are participating in the credit agreement. As of February 1, 2008, there was C$60 million or the equivalent of $60 million outstanding under the credit facility. The interest rate on the short-term borrowing was 5.75%.

Five banks have extended lines of credit aggregating $789 million for the purpose of issuing documentary letters of credit and standby letters of credit. These lines do not have termination dates and are reviewed periodically. Commitment fees ranging from .225% to .50% per annum are paid on the standby letters of credit amounts outstanding. Outstanding letters of credit totaled $299 million as of February 1, 2008, and $346 million as of February 2, 2007.

NOTE 5 - Long-Term Debt:

(In millions) Debt Category	Interest Rates	Fiscal Year of Final Maturity	February 1, 2008	February 2, 2007
Secured debt: [1]				
Mortgage notes	6.00 to 8.25%	2028	$ 33	$ 30
Unsecured debt:				
Debentures	6.50 to 6.88%	2029	694	693
Notes	8.25%	2010	499	498
Medium-term notes - series A	7.35 to 8.20%	2023	20	27
Medium-term notes - series B [2]	7.11 to 7.61%	2037	217	267
Senior notes	5.00 to 6.65%	2037	3,271	1,980
Convertible notes	0.86 to 2.50%	2021	511	518
Capital leases and other		2030	371	400
Total long-term debt			**5,616**	**4,413**
Less current maturities			40	88
Long-term debt, excluding current maturities			$ **5,576**	$ **4,325**

[1] Real properties with an aggregate book value of $47 million were pledged as collateral at February 1, 2008, for secured debt.

[2] Approximately 46% of these medium-term notes may be put at the option of the holder on the twentieth anniversary of the issue at par value. The medium-term notes were issued in 1997. None of these notes are currently putable.

Debt maturities, exclusive of unamortized original issue discounts, capital leases and other, for the next five years and thereafter are as follows: 2008, $10 million; 2009, $10 million; 2010, $501 million; 2011, $1 million; 2012, $552 million; thereafter, $4.3 billion.

The Company's debentures, notes, medium-term notes, senior notes and convertible notes contain certain restrictive covenants. The Company was in compliance with all covenants in these agreements at February 1, 2008.

Senior Notes

In September 2007, the Company issued $1.3 billion of unsecured senior notes, comprised of three tranches: $550 million of 5.60% senior notes maturing in September 2012, $250 million of 6.10% senior notes maturing in September 2017 and $500 million of 6.65% senior notes maturing in September 2037. The 5.60%, 6.10% and 6.65% senior notes were issued at discounts of approximately $2.7 million, $1.3 million and $6.3 million, respectively. Interest on the senior notes is payable semiannually in arrears in March and September of each year until maturity, beginning in March 2008. The discount associated with the issuance is included in long-term debt and is being amortized over the respective terms of the senior notes. The net proceeds of approximately $1.3 billion were used for general corporate purposes, including capital expenditures and working capital needs, and for repurchases of shares of the Company's common stock.

In October 2006, the Company issued $1.0 billion of unsecured senior notes, comprised of two tranches: $550 million of 5.40% senior notes maturing in October 2016 and $450 million of 5.80% senior notes maturing in October 2036. The 5.40% senior notes and the 5.80% senior notes were each issued at a discount of approximately $4.4 million. Interest on the senior notes is payable semiannually in arrears in April and October of each year until maturity, beginning in April 2007. The discount associated with the issuance is included in long-term debt and is being amortized over the respective terms of the senior notes. The net proceeds of approximately $991 million were used for general corporate general corporate purposes, including capital expenditures and working capital needs, and for repurchases of common stock.

In October 2005, the Company issued $1.0 billion of unsecured senior notes comprised of two $500 million tranches maturing in October 2015 and October 2035, respectively. The first $500 million tranche of 5.0% senior notes was sold at a discount of $4 million. The second $500 million tranche of 5.5% senior notes was sold at a discount of $8 million. Interest on the senior notes is payable semiannually in arrears in April and October of each year until maturity, beginning in April 2006. The discount associated with the issuance is included in long-term debt and is being amortized over the respective terms of the senior notes. The net proceeds of approximately $988 million were used for the repayment of $600 million in outstanding notes due December 2005, for general corporate purposes, including capital expenditures and working capital needs, and for repurchases of common stock.

The senior notes issued in 2007, 2006 and 2005 may be redeemed by the Company at any time, in whole or in part, at a redemption price plus accrued interest to the date of redemption. The redemption price is equal to the greater of (1) 100% of the principal amount of the senior notes to be redeemed, or (2) the sum of the present values of the remaining scheduled payments of principal and interest thereon, discounted to the date of redemption on a semiannual basis at a specified rate. The indenture under which the 2007 senior notes were issued also contains a provision that allows the holders of the notes to require the Company to repurchase all or any part of their notes if a change in control triggering event occurs. If elected under the change in control provisions, the repurchase of the notes will occur at a purchase price of 101% of the principal amount, plus accrued and unpaid interest, if any, on such notes to the date of purchase. The indenture governing the senior notes does not limit the aggregate principal amount of debt securities that the Company may issue, nor is the Company required to maintain financial ratios or specified levels of net worth or liquidity. However, the indenture contains various restrictive covenants, none of which is expected to impact the Company's liquidity or capital resources.

Upon the issuance of each of the series of senior notes previously described, the Company evaluated the optionality features embedded in the notes and concluded that these features do not require bifurcation from the host contracts and separate accounting as derivative instruments.

Convertible Notes

The Company has $578.7 million aggregate principal, $497.1 million aggregate carrying amount, of senior convertible notes issued in October 2001 at an issue price of $861.03 per note. Cash interest payments on the notes ceased in October 2006. In October 2021 when the notes mature, a holder will receive $1,000 per note, representing a yield to maturity of approximately 1%. Holders of the notes had the right to require the Company to purchase all or a portion of their notes in October 2003 and October 2006, at a price of $861.03 per note plus accrued cash interest, if any, and will have the right in October 2011 to require the Company to purchase all or a portion of their notes at a price of $905.06 per note. The Company may choose to pay the purchase price of the notes in cash or common stock or a combination of cash and common stock. Holders of an insignificant number of notes exercised their right to require the Company to repurchase their notes during 2003 and 2006, all of which were purchased in cash. The Company may redeem for cash all or a portion of the notes at any time, at a price equal to the sum of the issue price plus accrued original issue discount on the redemption date.

Holders of the senior convertible notes may convert their notes into 34.424 shares of the Company's common stock only if: the sale price of the Company's common stock reaches specified thresholds, or the credit rating of the notes is below a specified level, or the notes are called for redemption, or specified corporate transactions representing a change in control have occurred. The conversion ratio of 34.424 shares per note is only adjusted based on normal antidilution provisions designed to protect the value of the conversion option.

The Company's closing share prices reached the specified threshold such that the senior convertible notes became convertible at the option of each holder into shares of common stock during specified quarters of 2006 and 2007. Holders of an insignificant number of senior convertible notes exercised their right to convert their notes into shares of the Company's common stock during 2007 and 2006. The senior convertible notes will not be convertible in the first quarter of 2008 because the Company's closing share prices did not reach the specified threshold during the fourth quarter of 2007.

The Company has $19.7 million aggregate principal, $13.8 million aggregate carrying amount, of convertible notes issued in February 2001 at an issue price of $608.41 per note. Interest will not be paid on the notes prior to maturity in February 2021, at which time the holders will receive $1,000 per note, representing a yield to maturity of 2.5%. Holders of the notes had the right to require the Company to purchase all or a portion of their notes in February 2004, at a price of $655.49 per note, and will have the right in February 2011 to require the Company to purchase all or a portion of their notes at a price of $780.01 per note. The Company may choose to pay the purchase price of the notes in cash or common stock, or a combination of cash and common stock. Holders of an insignificant number of notes exercised their right to require the Company to purchase their notes during 2004, all of which were purchased in cash.

Holders of the convertible notes issued in February 2001 may convert their notes at any time on or before the maturity date, unless the notes have been previously purchased or redeemed, into 32.896 shares of the Company's common stock per note. The conversion ratio of 32.896 shares per note is only adjusted based on normal antidilution provisions designed to protect the value of the conversion option. During 2007, holders of $18 million principal amount, $13 million carrying amount, of the Company's convertible notes issued in February 2001 exercised their right to convert their notes into 0.6 million shares of the Company's common stock at the rate of 32.896 shares per note. During 2006, holders of $118 million principal amount, $80 million carrying amount, of the Company's convertible notes issued in February 2001 exercised their right to convert their notes into 3.9 million shares of the Company's common stock.

Upon the issuance of each of the series of convertible notes previously described, the Company evaluated the optionality features embedded in the notes and concluded that these features do not require bifurcation from the host contracts and separate accounting as derivative instruments.

NOTE 6 - Financial Instruments:

Cash and cash equivalents, accounts receivable, short-term borrowings, accounts payable and accrued liabilities are reflected in the financial statements at cost, which approximates fair value due to their short-term nature. Short- and long-term investments classified as available-for-sale securities, which include restricted balances, are reflected in the financial statements at fair value. Estimated fair values for long-term debt have been determined using available market information. For debt issues that are not quoted on an exchange, interest rates that are currently available to the Company for issuance of debt with similar terms and remaining maturities are used to estimate fair value. However, considerable judgment is required in interpreting market data to develop the estimates of fair value. Accordingly, the estimates presented herein are not necessarily indicative of the amounts that the Company could realize in a current market exchange. The use of different market assumptions and/or estimation methodologies may have a material effect on the estimated fair value amounts. The fair value of the Company's long-term debt, excluding capital leases and other, is as follows:

(In millions)	February 1, 2008		February 2, 2007	
	Carrying Amount	Fair Value	Carrying Amount	Fair Value
Liabilities:				
Long-term debt (excluding capital leases and other)	$ 5,245	$ 5,406	$ 4,013	$ 4,301

NOTE 7 - Shareholders' Equity:

Authorized shares of common stock were 5.6 billion ($.50 par value) at February 1, 2008 and February 2, 2007.

The Company has 5.0 million ($5 par value) authorized shares of preferred stock, none of which have been issued. The Board of Directors may issue the preferred stock (without action by shareholders) in one or more series, having such voting rights, dividend and liquidation preferences, and such conversion and other rights as may be designated by the Board of Directors at the time of issuance.

NOTE 11 - Earnings Per Share:

Basic earnings per share (EPS) excludes dilution and is computed by dividing the applicable net earnings by the weighted-average number of common shares outstanding for the period. Diluted earnings per share is calculated based on the weighted-average shares of common stock as adjusted for the potential dilutive effect of share-based awards and convertible notes as of the balance sheet date. The following table reconciles EPS for 2007, 2006 and 2005:

(In millions, except per share data)	2007	2006	2005
Basic earnings per share:			
Net earnings	$ 2,809	$ 3,105	$ 2,765
Weighted-average shares outstanding	1,481	1,535	1,555
Basic earnings per share	$ 1.90	$ 2.02	$ 1.78
Diluted earnings per share:			
Net earnings	$ 2,809	$ 3,105	$ 2,765
Net earnings adjustment for interest on convertible notes, net of tax	4	4	11
Net earnings, as adjusted	$ 2,813	$ 3,109	$ 2,776
Weighted-average shares outstanding	1,481	1,535	1,555
Dilutive effect of share-based awards	8	9	10
Dilutive effect of convertible notes	21	22	42
Weighted-average shares, as adjusted	1,510	1,566	1,607
Diluted earnings per share	$ 1.86	$ 1.99	$ 1.73

Stock options to purchase 7.8 million, 6.8 million and 5.6 million shares of common stock for 2007, 2006 and 2005, respectively, were excluded from the computation of diluted earnings per share because their effect would have been antidilutive.

NOTE 12 - Leases:

The Company leases store facilities and land for certain store facilities under agreements with original terms generally of 20 years. For lease agreements that provide for escalating rent payments or free-rent occupancy periods, the Company recognizes rent expense on a straight-line basis over the non-cancelable lease term and any option renewal period where failure to exercise such option would result in an economic penalty in such amount that renewal appears, at the inception of the lease, to be reasonably assured. The lease term commences on the date that the Company takes possession of or controls the physical use of the property. The leases generally contain provisions for four to six renewal options of five years each.

Some agreements also provide for contingent rentals based on sales performance in excess of specified minimums. In 2007, 2006 and 2005, contingent rentals were insignificant.

The Company subleases certain properties that are no longer held for use in operations. Sublease income was not significant for any of the periods presented.

Certain equipment is also leased by the Company under agreements ranging from three to five years. These agreements typically contain renewal options providing for a renegotiation of the lease, at the Company's option, based on the fair market value at that time.

The future minimum rental payments required under capital and operating leases having initial or remaining non-cancelable lease terms in excess of one year are summarized as follows:

NOTE 14 – Related Parties:

A brother-in-law of the Company's Executive Vice President of Business Development is a senior officer of a vendor that provides millwork and other building products to the Company. In both 2007 and 2006, the Company purchased products in the amount of $101 million from this vendor, while in 2005 the Company purchased products in the amount of $84 million from this vendor. Amounts payable to this vendor were insignificant at February 1, 2008 and February 2, 2007.

NOTE 15 - Other Information:

Net interest expense is comprised of the following:

(In millions)		2007		2006		2005
Long-term debt	$	247	$	183	$	171
Capitalized leases		32		34		39
Interest income		(45)		(52)		(45)
Interest capitalized		(65)		(32)		(28)
Other		25		21		21
Net interest expense	$	**194**	$	**154**	$	**158**

Supplemental disclosures of cash flow information:

(In millions)		2007		2006		2005
Cash paid for interest, net of amount capitalized	$	198	$	179	$	173
Cash paid for income taxes	$	1,725	$	2,031	$	1,593

Noncash investing and financing activities:						
Noncash fixed asset acquisitions, including assets acquired under capital lease	$	99	$	159	$	175
Conversions of long-term debt to equity	$	13	$	82	$	565

Lowe's Companies, Inc.
Selected Financial Data (Unaudited)

Selected Statement of Earnings Data:

(In millions, except per share data)	2007	2006	2005*	2004	2003
Net sales	$ 48,283	$ 46,927	$ 43,243	$ 36,464	$ 30,838
Gross margin	16,727	16,198	14,790	12,240	9,533
Earnings from continuing operations	2,809	3,105	2,765	2,167	1,807
Earnings from discontinued operations, net of tax	-	-	-	-	15
Net earnings	2,809	3,105	2,765	2,167	1,822
Basic earnings per share - continuing operations	1.90	2.02	1.78	1.39	1.15
Basic earnings per share – discontinued operations	-	-	-	-	0.01
Basic earnings per share	1.90	2.02	1.78	1.39	1.16
Diluted earnings per share - continuing operations	1.86	1.99	1.73	1.35	1.12
Diluted earnings per share – discontinued operations	-	-	-	-	0.01
Diluted earnings per share	1.86	1.99	1.73	1.35	1.13
Dividends per share	$ 0.29	$ 0.18	$ 0.11	$ 0.08	$ 0.06

Selected Balance Sheet Data:

	2007	2006	2005*	2004	2003
Total assets	$ 30,869	$ 27,767	$ 24,639	$ 21,101	$ 18,667
Long-term debt, excluding current maturities	$ 5,576	$ 4,325	$ 3,499	$ 3,060	$ 3,678

Note: The selected financial data has been adjusted to present the 2003 disposal of the Contractor Yards as a discontinued operation for all periods.
* Fiscal year 2005 contained 53 weeks, while all other years contained 52 weeks.

Selected Quarterly Data:

(In millions, except per share data)	First	Second	Third	Fourth
2007				
Net sales	$ 12,172	$ 14,167	$ 11,565	$ 10,379
Gross margin	4,259	4,883	3,964	3,620
Net earnings	739	1,019	643	408
Basic earnings per share	0.49	0.68	0.44	0.28
Diluted earnings per share	$ 0.48	$ 0.67	$ 0.43	$ 0.28

(In millions, except per share data)	First	Second	Third	Fourth
2006				
Net sales	$ 11,921	$ 13,389	$ 11,211	$ 10,406
Gross margin	4,169	4,478	3,865	3,687
Net earnings	841	935	716	613
Basic earnings per share	0.54	0.61	0.47	0.40
Diluted earnings per share	$ 0.53	$ 0.60	$ 0.46	$ 0.40

TIME VALUE OF MONEY

TIME VALUE OF MONEY

The time value of money is the idea that, quite simply, money received today is worth more than money to be received one year from today (or at any other future date), because it can be used to earn interest. If you invest $1,000 today at 10 percent, you will have $1,100 in one year. So $1,000 in one year is worth $100 less than $1,000 today because you lose the opportunity to earn the $100 in interest.

In some business situations, you will know the dollar amount of a cash flow that occurs in the future and will need to determine its value now. This type of situation is known as a present value problem. The opposite situation occurs when you know the dollar amount of a cash flow that occurs today and need to determine its value at some point in the future. These situations are called future value problems. The value of money changes over time because money can earn interest. The following table illustrates the basic difference between present value and future value problems:

	Now	Future
Present value	?	$1,000
Future value	$1,000	?

Present and future value problems may involve two types of cash flow: a single payment or an annuity (which is the fancy word for a series of equal cash payments). Thus, you need to learn how to deal with four different situations related to the time value of money:

1. Future value of a single payment
2. Present value of a single payment
3. Future value of an annuity
4. Present value of an annuity

Most inexpensive handheld calculators and any spreadsheet program can perform the detailed arithmetic computations required to solve future value and present value problems. In later courses and in all business situations, you will probably use a calculator or computer to solve these problems. At this stage, we encourage you to solve problems using Tables C.1 through C.4 at the end of this appendix. We believe that using the tables will give you a better understanding of how and why present and future value concepts apply to business problems. The tables give the value of a $1 cash flow (single payment or annuity) for different periods (n) and at different interest rates (i). If a problem involves payments other than $1, it is necessary to multiply the value from the table by the amount of the payment.[1] In the final section of this appendix, we explain how to use Excel to compute present values.

COMPUTING FUTURE AND PRESENT VALUES OF A SINGLE AMOUNT

Future Value of a Single Amount

In future value of a single amount problems, you will be asked to calculate how much money you will have in the future as the result of investing a certain amount in the present. If you were to receive a gift of $10,000, for instance, you might decide to put it in a savings account and use the money as a down payment on a house after you graduate. The future value computation would tell you how much money will be available when you graduate.

To solve a future value problem, you need to know three items:

1. Amount to be invested.
2. Interest rate (i) the amount will earn.
3. Number of periods (n) in which the amount will earn interest.

---

[1] Present value and future value problems involve cash flows. The basic concepts are the same for cash inflows (receipts) and cash outflows (payments). No fundamental differences exist between present value and future value calculations for cash payments versus cash receipts.

The future value concept is based on compound interest, which simply means that interest is calculated on top of interest. Thus, the amount of interest for each period is calculated using the principal plus any interest not paid out in prior periods. Graphically, the calculation of the future value of $1 for three periods at an interest rate of 10 percent may be represented as follows:

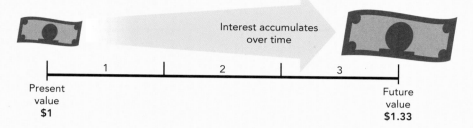

Assume that on January 1, 2009, you deposit $1,000 in a savings account at 10 percent annual interest, compounded annually. At the end of three years, the $1,000 will have increased to $1,331 as follows:

Year	Amount at Start of Year	+	Interest During the Year	=	Amount at End of Year
1	$1,000	+	$1,000 × 10% = $100	=	$1,100
2	1,100	+	1,100 × 10% = 110	=	1,210
3	1,210	+	1,210 × 10% = 121	=	1,331

We can avoid the detailed arithmetic by referring to Table C.1, Future Value of $1, on page C14. For $i = 10\%$, $n = 3$, we find the value 1.3310. We then compute the balance at the end of year 3 as follows:

From Table C.1, Interest rate = 10% n = 3

$$\$1{,}000 \times 1.3310 = \$1{,}331$$

Note that the increase of $331 is due to the time value of money. It is interest revenue to the owner of the savings account and interest expense to the bank.

Present Value of a Single Amount

The present value of a single amount is the worth to you today of receiving that amount some time in the future. For instance, you might be offered an opportunity to invest in a financial instrument that would pay you $1,000 in 3 years. Before you decided whether to invest, you would want to determine the present value of the instrument.

To compute the present value of an amount to be received in the future, we must discount (a procedure that is the opposite of compounding) at i interest rate for n periods. In discounting, the interest is subtracted rather than added, as it is in compounding. Graphically, the present value of $1 due at the end of the third period with an interest rate of 10 percent can be represented as follows:

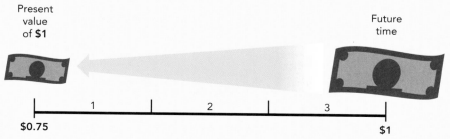

Assume that today is January 1, 2009, and you have the opportunity to receive $1,000 cash on December 31, 2011. At an interest rate of 10 percent per year, how much is the $1,000 payment worth to you on January 1, 2009? You could discount the amount year by year,[2] but it is easier to use Table C.2, Present Value of $1, on pages C14–C15. For $i = 10\%$, $n = 3$, we find that the present value of $1 is 0.7513. The present value of $1,000 to be received at the end of three years can be computed as follows:

From Table C.2,
Interest rate = 10%
n = 3

$$\$1{,}000 \times 0.7513 = \$751.30$$

It is important to learn not only how to compute a present value but also to understand what it means. The $751.30 is the amount you would pay now to have the right to receive $1,000 at the end of three years, assuming an interest rate of 10 percent. Conceptually, you should be indifferent between having $751.30 today and receiving $1,000 in three years. If you had $751.30 today but wanted $1,000 in three years, you could simply deposit the money in a savings account that pays 10% interest and it would grow to $1,000 in three years. Alternatively, if you had a contract that promised you $1,000 in three years, you could sell it to an investor for $751.30 in cash today because it would permit the investor to earn the difference in interest.

What if you could only earn 6 percent during the three-year period from January 1, 2009, to December 31, 2011? What would be the present value on January 1, 2009, of receiving $1,000 on December 31, 2011? To answer this we would take the same approach, using Table C.2, except that the interest rate would change to $i = 6\%$. Referring to Table C.2, we see the present value factor for $i = 6\%$, $n = 3$, is 0.8396. Thus, the present value of $1,000 to be received at the end of three years, assuming a 6 percent interest rate, would be computed as $1,000 × 0.8396 = $839.60. Notice that when we assume a 6 percent interest rate the present value is greater than when we assumed a 10 percent interest rate. The reason for this difference is that, to reach $1,000 three years from now, you would need to deposit more money in a savings account now if it earns 6 percent interest than if it earns 10 percent interest.

SELF-STUDY PRACTICE

1. If the interest rate in a present value problem increases from 8 percent to 10 percent, will the present value increase or decrease?
2. What is the present value of $10,000 to be received 10 years from now if the interest rate is 5 percent, compounded annually?
3. If $10,000 is deposited now in a savings account that earns 5 percent interest compounded annually, how much will it be worth 10 years from now?

After you have finished, check your answers with the solution at the bottom of the next page.

COMPUTING FUTURE AND PRESENT VALUES OF AN ANNUITY

Instead of a single payment, many business problems involve multiple cash payments over a number of periods. An **annuity** is a series of consecutive payments characterized by

1. An equal dollar amount each interest period.
2. Interest periods of equal length (year, half a year, quarter, or month).
3. An equal interest rate each interest period.

---

[2] The detailed discounting is as follows:

Periods	Interest for the Year	Present Value*
1	$1,000 = ($1,000 × 1/1.10) = $90.91	$1,000 − $90.91 = $909.09
2	$909.09 = ($909.09 × 1/1.10) = $82.65	$909.09 − $82.65 = $826.44
3	$826.44 = ($826.44 × 1/1.10) = $75.14[†]	$826.44 − $75.14 = $751.30

*Verifiable in Table C.2.
[†]Adjusted for rounding

Examples of annuities include monthly payments on a car or house, yearly contributions to a savings account, and monthly pension benefits.

Future Value of an Annuity

If you are saving money for some purpose, such as a new car or a trip, you might decide to deposit a fixed amount of money in a savings account each month. The future value of an annuity computation will tell you how much money will be in your savings account at some point in the future.

The future value of an annuity includes compound interest on each payment from the date of payment to the end of the term of the annuity. Each new payment accumulates less interest than prior payments, only because the number of periods remaining in which to accumulate interest decreases. The future value of an annuity of $1 for three periods at 10 percent may be represented graphically as

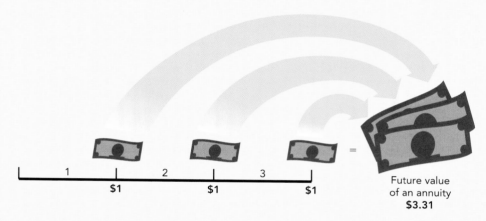

Future value
of an annuity
$3.31

Assume that each year for three years, you deposit $1,000 cash in a savings account at 10 percent interest per year. You make the first $1,000 deposit on December 31, 2009, the second one on December 31, 2010, and the third and last one on December 31, 2011. The first $1,000 deposit earns compound interest for two years (for a total principal and interest of $1,210); the second deposit earns interest for one year (for a total principal and interest of $1,100). The third deposit earns no interest because it was made on the day that the balance is computed. Thus, the total amount in the savings account at the end of three years is $3,310 ($1,210 + $1,100 + $1,000).

To calculate the future value of this annuity, we could compute the interest on each deposit, similar to what is described above. However, a faster way is to refer to Table C.3, Future Value of an Annuity of $1 for i = 10%, n = 3 to find the value 3.3100. The future value of your three deposits of $1,000 each can be computed as follows:

*From Table C.3,
Interest rate = 10%
n = 3*

$1,000 × 3.3100 = $3,310

The Power of Compounding

Compound interest is a remarkably powerful economic force. In fact, the ability to earn interest on interest is the key to building economic wealth. If you save $1,000 per year for the first 10 years of your career, you will have more money when you retire than you would if you had saved $15,000 per year for the last 10 years of your career. This surprising outcome occurs because the money you save early in your career will earn more interest than the money you save at the end of your career. If you start saving money now, the majority of your wealth will not be the money you saved but the interest your money was able to earn.

---

1. The present value will decrease.
2. $10,000 × 0.6139 = $6,139.
3. $10,000 × 1.6289 = $16,289.

Solution to
Self-Study Practice

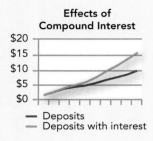

Effects of Compound Interest

$20
$15
$10
$5
$0

— Deposits
— Deposits with interest

The chart in the margin illustrates the power of compounding over a brief 10-year period. If you deposit $1 each year in an account earning 10 percent interest, at the end of just 10 years, only 63 percent of your balance will be made up of money you have saved. The rest will be interest you have earned. After 20 years, only 35 percent of your balance will be from saved money. The lesson associated with compound interest is that even though saving money is hard, you should start now.

Present Value of an Annuity

The present value of an annuity is the value now of a series of equal amounts to be received (or paid out) for some specified number of periods in the future. It is computed by discounting each of the equal periodic amounts. A good example of this type of problem is a retirement program that offers employees a monthly income after retirement. The present value of an annuity of $1 for three periods at 10 percent may be represented graphically as

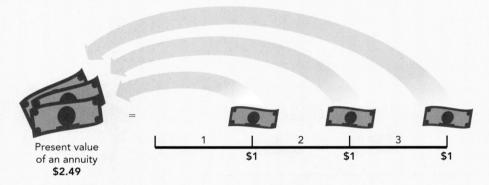

Present value
of an annuity
$2.49

Assume you are to receive $1,000 cash on each December 31, 2009, 2010, and 2011. How much would the sum of these three $1,000 future amounts be worth on January 1, 2009, assuming an interest rate of 10 percent per year? One way to determine this is to use Table C.2 to calculate the present value of each single amount as follows:

		FACTOR FROM TABLE C.2		
Year	Amount		$i = 10\%$		Present Value
1	$1,000	×	0.9091 ($n = 1$)	=	$ 909.10
2	$1,000	×	0.8264 ($n = 2$)	=	826.40
3	$1,000	×	0.7513 ($n = 3$)	=	751.30
			Total present value	=	$2,486.80

Alternatively, we can compute the present value of this annuity more easily by using Table C.4, as follows:

From Table C.4,
Interest rate = 10%
n = 3

$1,000 × 2.4869 = $2,487 (rounded)

Interest Rates and Interest Periods

The preceding illustrations assumed annual periods for compounding and discounting. Although interest rates are almost always quoted on an annual basis, many compounding periods encountered in business are less than one year. When interest periods are less than a year, the values of n and i must be restated to be consistent with the length of the interest compounding period.

To illustrate, 12 percent interest compounded annually for five years requires the use of $n = 5$ and $i = 12\%$. If compounding is quarterly, however, there will be four interest periods per year (20 interest periods in five years), and the quarterly interest rate is one quarter of the annual rate (3 percent per quarter). Therefore, 12 percent interest compounded quarterly for five years requires use of $n = 20$ and $i = 3\%$.

ACCOUNTING APPLICATIONS OF PRESENT VALUES

Many business transactions require the use of future and present value concepts. In finance classes, you will see how to apply future value concepts. In this section, we apply present value concepts to three common accounting cases.

Case A—Present Value of a Single Amount

On January 1, 2009, General Mills bought some new delivery trucks. The company signed a note and agreed to pay $200,000 on December 31, 2010, an amount representing the cash equivalent price of the trucks plus interest for two years. The market interest rate for this note was 12 percent.

1. How should the accountant record the purchase?

Answer: This case requires the computation of the present value of a single amount. In conformity with the cost principle, the cost of the trucks is their current cash equivalent price, which is the present value of the future payment. The problem can be shown graphically as follows:

The present value of the $200,000 is computed as follows:

From Table C.2, Interest rate = 12% n = 2

$$\$200,000 \times 0.7972 = \$159,440$$

This transaction would be recorded with the journal entry shown below.

	Debit	Credit
Delivery Trucks (+A)	159,440	
Note Payable (+L)		159,440

Assets	=	Liabilities	+	Owners' Equity
Delivery Trucks +159,440		Note Payable +159,440		

2. How should the effects of interest be reported at the end of 2009 and 2010?

Answer: Interest expense would be calculated and recorded as follows:

<u>December 31, 2009</u>

$$\text{Interest} = \text{Principal} \times \text{Rate} \times \text{Time}$$
$$= \$159,440 \times 12\% \times 12/12 = \$19,132 \text{ (rounded)}$$

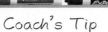

Coach's Tip

The interest is recorded in the Note Payable account because it would be paid as part of the note at maturity.

	Debit	Credit
Interest Expense (+E, −OE)	19,132	
Note Payable (+L)		19,132

Assets	=	Liabilities	+	Owners' Equity
		Note Payable +19,132		Interest Expense (+E) −19,132

December 31, 2010

Interest = Principal × Rate × Time
= ($159,440 + 19,132) × 12% × 12/12 = $21,428 (rounded)

	Debit	Credit
Interest Expense (+E, −OE)	21,428	
Note Payable (+L)		21,428

Assets	=	Liabilities	+	Owners' Equity
		Note Payable +21,428		Interest Expense (+E) −21,428

Note Payable (L)

	159,440 Jan. 1, 2009
	19,132 Interest 2009
	21,428 Interest 2010
200,000 Dec. 31, 2010	

3. **What is the effect of the $200,000 debt payment made on December 31, 2010?**

Answer: At this date the amount to be paid is the balance in *Note Payable*, after it has been updated for interest pertaining to 2010, as shown in the T-account in the margin. Notice that, just prior to its repayment, the balance for the note on December 31, 2010 is the same as the maturity amount on the due date.

The debt payment would be recorded with the journal entry shown below.

	Debit	Credit
Note Payable (−L)	200,000	
Cash (−A)		200,000

Assets		=	Liabilities		+	Owners' Equity
Cash	−200,000		Note Payable	−200,000		

Case B—Present Value of an Annuity

On January 1, 2009, General Mills bought new milling equipment. The company elected to finance the purchase with a note payable to be paid off in three years in annual installments of $163,686. Each installment includes principal plus interest on the unpaid balance at 11 percent per year. The annual installments are due on December 31, 2009, 2010, and 2011. This problem can be shown graphically as follows:

1. What is the amount of the note?

Answer: The note is the present value of each installment payment, $i = 11\%$ and $n = 3$. This is an annuity because the note repayment is made in three equal installments. The amount of the note is computed as follows:

$$\$163,686 \times 2.4437 = \$400,000$$

From Table C.4, Interest rate = 11% n = 3

The acquisition on January 1, 2009, would be accounted for as follows:

	Debit	Credit
Milling Equipment (+A)	400,000	
Note Payable (+L)		400,000

Assets	=	Liabilities	+	Owners' Equity
Milling Equipment +400,000		Note Payable +400,000		

2. How should the payments made at the end of each year be accounted for?

Answer:

December 31, 2009

Each payment includes both interest and principal. The interest part of the first payment is calculated as:

$$\text{Interest} = \text{Principal} \times \text{Rate} \times \text{Time}$$
$$= \$400,000 \times 11\% \times 12/12 = \$44,000$$

Now that we know the interest component, the principal portion of the first payment of $163,686 can be calculated ($163,686 − $44,000 = $119,686). Thus, the first payment on December 31, 2009, would be accounted for as:

	Debit	Credit
Interest Expense (+E, −OE)	44,000	
Note Payable (−L) ($163,686 − $44,000)	119,686	
Cash (−A)		163,686

Assets	=	Liabilities	+	Owners' Equity
Cash −163,686		Note Payable −119,686		Interest Expense (+E) −44,000

December 31, 2010

The interest portion of the second and third payments would be calculated in the same way, although notice that the principal balance in the Note Payable account changes after each payment.

$$\text{Interest} = \text{Principal} \times \text{Rate} \times \text{Time}$$
$$= [(\$400,000 − \$119,686) \times 11\% \times 12/12] = \$30,835$$
$$\text{Principal} = \text{Payment} − \text{Interest}$$
$$= \$163,686 − \$30,835 = \$132,851$$

	Debit	Credit
Interest Expense (+E, −OE)	30,835	
Note Payable (−L)	132,851	
Cash (−A)		163,686

Assets	=	Liabilities	+	Owners' Equity
Cash −163,686		Note Payable −132,851		Interest Expense (+E) −30,835

December 31, 2011

> Interest = Principal × Rate × Time
> = [($400,000 − $119,686 − $132,851) × 11% × 12/12]
> = $16,223 (adjusted to accommodate rounding)
>
> Principal = Payment − Interest
> = $163,686 − $16,223 = $147,463

Note Payable (L)	
	400,000 Jan.1, 2009
Dec. 31, 2009 119,686	
Dec. 31, 2010 132,851	
Dec. 31, 2011 147,463	
0 Dec. 31, 2011	

	Debit	Credit
Interest Expense (+E, −OE)	16,223	
Note Payable (−L)	147,463	
Cash (−A)		163,686

Assets	=	Liabilities	+	Owners' Equity
Cash −163,686		Note Payable −147,463		Interest Expense (+E) −16,223

Case C—Present Value of a Single Amount and an Annuity

On January 1, 2009, General Mills issued 100 four-year, $1,000 bonds. The bonds pay interest annually at a rate of 6 percent of face value. What total amount would investors be willing to pay for the bonds if they require an annual return of: (*a*) 4 percent, (*b*) 6 percent, or (*c*) 8 percent?

Answer: This case requires the computation of the present value of a single amount (the $100,000 face value paid at maturity) plus the present value of an annuity (the annual interest payments of $6,000). The problem can be shown graphically as follows:

Coach's Tip

Each interest payment of $6,000 is calculated as: $100,000 × 6% × 12/12.

(a) 4 Percent Market Interest Rate

The present value of the $100,000 face value is computed as follows:

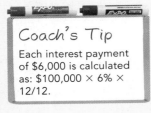

From Table C.2,
Interest rate = 4%
n = 4

$100,000 × 0.8548 = $85,480

The present value of the $6,000 annuity is computed as follows:

> **$6,000 × 3.6299 = $21,780***

> From Table C.4,
> *Interest rate = 4%*
> *n = 4*

*Adjusted to accommodate rounding in the present value factor.

The present value of the total bond payments, computed using the discount rate of 4 percent, is $107,260 (= $85,480 + $21,780).

(b) 6 Percent Market Interest Rate

The present value of the $100,000 face value is computed as follows:

> **$100,000 × 0.7921 = $79,210**

> From Table C.2,
> *Interest rate = 6%*
> *n = 4*

The present value of the $6,000 annuity is computed as follows:

> **$6,000 × 3.4651 = $20,790***

> From Table C.4,
> *Interest rate = 6%*
> *n = 4*

* Adjusted to accommodate rounding in the present value factor.

The present value of the total bond payments, computed using the discount rate of 6%, is $100,000 (= $79,210 + $20,790).

(c) 8 Percent Market Interest Rate

The present value of the $100,000 face value is computed as follows:

> **$100,000 × 0.7350 = $73,503***

> From Table C.2,
> *Interest rate = 8%*
> *n = 4*

* Adjusted to accommodate rounding in the present value factor.

The present value of the $6,000 annuity is computed as follows:

> **$6,000 × 3.3121 = $19,873**

> From Table C.4,
> *Interest rate = 8%*
> *n = 4*

Coach's Tip

The present values in a, b, and c demonstrate the calculation of the bond issue prices used in Chapter 14.

The present value of the total bond payments, computed using the discount rate of 8%, is $93,376 (= $73,503 + $19,873).
The following table summarizes these calculations:

	MARKET INTEREST RATES		
	4%	6%	8%
Present value of $100,000 face value (principal) paid four years from now	$ 85,480	$ 79,210	$73,503
Present value of $6,000 (interest) paid once a year for four years	21,780	20,790	19,873
Amount to pay	**$107,260**	**$100,000**	**$93,376**

Of course, these calculations are just the starting point for understanding how bond liabilities are determined and reported. You'll need to read Chapter 14 for information about how bond liabilities are accounted for.

PRESENT VALUE COMPUTATIONS USING EXCEL

While the present value tables are useful for educational purposes, most present value problems in business are solved with calculators or Excel spreadsheets. Because of the widespread availability of Excel, we will show you how to solve present value problems using Excel. There are slightly different versions of Excel available, depending on the age of the computer. The illustrations in this text are based on Microsoft Office 2007.

Present Value of a Single Payment

The calculation of a present value amount is based on a fairly simple mathematical formula:

$$PV = \text{Payment}/(1+i)^n$$

In this formula, *payment* is the cash payment made at some point in the future, i is the interest rate each period, and n is the number of periods in the problem. We could use this formula to solve all problems involving the present value of a single payment. It is, of course, easier to use a present value table (like the one at the end of this appendix) which is derived by solving the present value formula for various interest rates and numbers of periods. Unfortunately, a table that included all interest rates and numbers of periods actually encountered in business would be too large to work with. As a result, most accountants and analysts use Excel to compute a present value.

To compute the present value of a single payment in Excel, you enter the present value formula in a cell, using the format required by Excel. You should select a cell and enter the following formula:

$$= \text{Payment}/(1+i)\text{^}n$$

To illustrate, if you want to solve for the present value of a $100,000 payment to be made in five years with an interest rate of 10%, you would enter the following in the function field:

$$= 100000/(1.10)\text{^}5$$

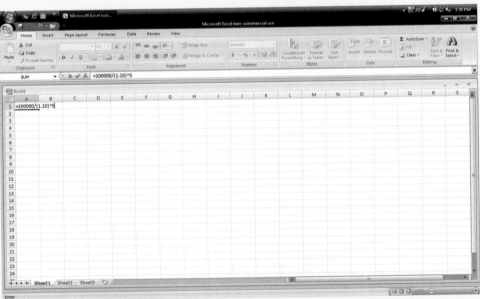

Based on this entry, Excel would compute the present value of $62,092.13. This answer is slightly different from the answer you would have if you used the present value tables at the end of this appendix. The tables are rounded based on four digits. Excel does not round and, therefore, provides a more accurate computation.

Present Value of an Annuity

The formula for computing the present value of an annuity is a little more complicated than the present value of a single payment. As a result, Excel has been programmed to include the formula so that you do not have to enter it yourself.

To compute the present value of an annuity in Excel, select a cell and click on the insert function button (f_x). The following dropdown box will appear:

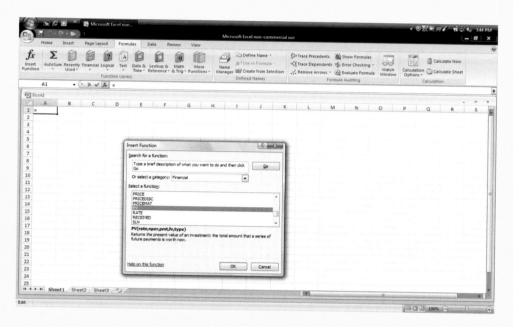

Under the Select Category heading, you should pick "Financial," scroll down under "Select a Function," and click on PV. Then, click on "OK" and a new dropdown box will appear:

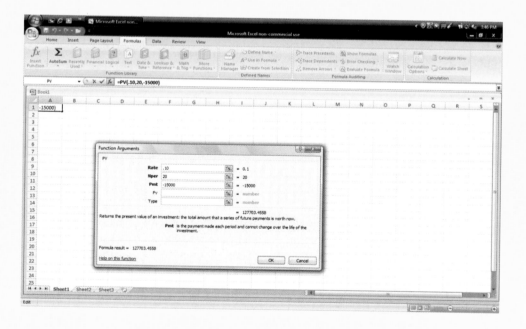

In this box, you should enter the interest rate, 10% in this example, under Rate. Notice that the rate must be entered as a decimal (i.e., 0.10). Enter the number of periods (20) under Nper. Excel has an unusual convention associated with the payment. It must be entered as a negative amount (−15000) under Pmt. Notice also that a comma should not be included in the amount you enter. When you click on OK, Excel will enter the present value in the cell you selected. In this example, the value determined by Excel is $127,703.46.

Table C.1   Future Value of $1

Periods	2%	3%	3.75%	4%	4.25%	5%	6%	7%	8%
0	1.	1.	1.	1.	1.	1.	1.	1.	1.
1	1.02	1.03	1.0375	1.04	1.0425	1.05	1.06	1.07	1.08
2	1.0404	1.0609	1.0764	1.0816	1.0868	1.1025	1.1236	1.1449	1.1664
3	1.0612	1.0927	1.1168	1.1249	1.1330	1.1576	1.1910	1.2250	1.2597
4	1.0824	1.1255	1.1587	1.1699	1.1811	1.2155	1.2625	1.3108	1.3605
5	1.1041	1.1593	1.2021	1.2167	1.2313	1.2763	1.3382	1.4026	1.4693
6	1.1262	1.1941	1.2472	1.2653	1.2837	1.3401	1.4185	1.5007	1.5869
7	1.1487	1.2299	1.2939	1.3159	1.3382	1.4071	1.5036	1.6058	1.7138
8	1.1717	1.2668	1.3425	1.3686	1.3951	1.4775	1.5938	1.7182	1.8509
9	1.1951	1.3048	1.3928	1.4233	1.4544	1.5513	1.6895	1.8385	1.9990
10	1.2190	1.3439	1.4450	1.4802	1.5162	1.6289	1.7908	1.9672	2.1589
20	1.4859	1.8061	2.0882	2.1911	2.2989	2.6533	3.2071	3.8697	4.6610

Periods	9%	10%	11%	12%	13%	14%	15%	20%	25%
0	1.	1.	1.	1.	1.	1.	1.	1.	1.
1	1.09	1.10	1.11	1.12	1.13	1.14	1.15	1.20	1.25
2	1.1881	1.2100	1.2321	1.2544	1.2769	1.2996	1.3225	1.4400	1.5625
3	1.2950	1.3310	1.3676	1.4049	1.4429	1.4815	1.5209	1.7280	1.9531
4	1.4116	1.4641	1.5181	1.5735	1.6305	1.6890	1.7490	2.0736	2.4414
5	1.5386	1.6105	1.6851	1.7623	1.8424	1.9254	2.0114	2.4883	3.0518
6	1.6771	1.7716	1.8704	1.9738	2.0820	2.1950	2.3131	2.9860	3.8147
7	1.8280	1.9487	2.0762	2.2107	2.3526	2.5023	2.6600	3.5832	4.7684
8	1.9926	2.1436	2.3045	2.4760	2.6584	2.8526	3.0590	4.2998	5.9605
9	2.1719	2.3579	2.5580	2.7731	3.0040	3.2519	3.5179	5.1598	7.4506
10	2.3674	2.5937	2.8394	3.1058	3.3946	3.7072	4.0456	6.1917	9.3132
20	5.6044	6.7275	8.0623	9.6463	11.5231	13.7435	16.3665	38.3376	86.7362

Table C.2   Present Value of $1

Periods	2%	3%	3.75%	4%	4.25%	5%	6%	7%	8%
1	0.9804	0.9709	0.9639	0.9615	0.9592	0.9524	0.9434	0.9346	0.9259
2	0.9612	0.9426	0.9290	0.9246	0.9201	0.9070	0.8900	0.8734	0.8573
3	0.9423	0.9151	0.8954	0.8890	0.8826	0.8638	0.8396	0.8163	0.7938
4	0.9238	0.8885	0.8631	0.8548	0.8466	0.8227	0.7921	0.7629	0.7350
5	0.9057	0.8626	0.8319	0.8219	0.8121	0.7835	0.7473	0.7130	0.6806
6	0.8880	0.8375	0.8018	0.7903	0.7790	0.7462	0.7050	0.6663	0.6302
7	0.8706	0.8131	0.7728	0.7599	0.7473	0.7107	0.6651	0.6227	0.5835
8	0.8535	0.7894	0.7449	0.7307	0.7168	0.6768	0.6274	0.5820	0.5403
9	0.8368	0.7664	0.7180	0.7026	0.6876	0.6446	0.5919	0.5439	0.5002
10	0.8203	0.7441	0.6920	0.6756	0.6595	0.6139	0.5584	0.5083	0.4632
20	0.6730	0.5537	0.4789	0.4564	0.4350	0.3769	0.3118	0.2584	0.2145

Table C.2   Present Value of $1 (continued)

Periods	9%	10%	11%	12%	13%	14%	15%	20%	25%
1	0.9174	0.9091	0.9009	0.8929	0.8850	0.8772	0.8696	0.8333	0.8000
2	0.8417	0.8264	0.8116	0.7972	0.7831	0.7695	0.7561	0.6944	0.6400
3	0.7722	0.7513	0.7312	0.7118	0.6931	0.6750	0.6575	0.5787	0.5120
4	0.7084	0.6830	0.6587	0.6355	0.6133	0.5921	0.5718	0.4823	0.4096
5	0.6499	0.6209	0.5935	0.5674	0.5428	0.5194	0.4972	0.4019	0.3277
6	0.5963	0.5645	0.5346	0.5066	0.4803	0.4556	0.4323	0.3349	0.2621
7	0.5470	0.5132	0.4817	0.4523	0.4251	0.3996	0.3759	0.2791	0.2097
8	0.5019	0.4665	0.4339	0.4039	0.3762	0.3506	0.3269	0.2326	0.1678
9	0.4604	0.4241	0.3909	0.3606	0.3329	0.3075	0.2843	0.1938	0.1342
10	0.4224	0.3855	0.3522	0.3220	0.2946	0.2697	0.2472	0.1615	0.1074
20	0.1784	0.1486	0.1240	0.1037	0.0868	0.0728	0.0611	0.0261	0.0115

Table C.3   Future Value of Annuity of $1

Periods*	2%	3%	3.75%	4%	4.25%	5%	6%	7%	8%
1	1.	1.	1.	1.	1.	1.	1.	1.	1.
2	2.02	2.03	2.0375	2.04	2.0425	2.05	2.06	2.07	2.08
3	3.0604	3.0909	3.1139	3.1216	3.1293	3.1525	3.1836	3.2149	3.2464
4	4.1216	4.1836	4.2307	4.2465	4.2623	4.3101	4.3746	4.4399	4.5061
5	5.2040	5.3091	5.3893	5.4163	5.4434	5.5256	5.6371	5.7507	5.8666
6	6.3081	6.4684	6.5914	6.6330	6.6748	6.8019	6.9753	7.1533	7.3359
7	7.4343	7.6625	7.8386	7.8983	7.9585	8.1420	8.3938	8.6540	8.9228
8	8.5830	8.8923	9.1326	9.2142	9.2967	9.5491	9.8975	10.2598	10.6366
9	9.7546	10.1591	10.4750	10.5828	10.6918	11.0266	11.4913	11.9780	12.4876
10	10.9497	11.4639	11.8678	12.0061	12.1462	12.5779	13.1808	13.8164	14.4866
20	24.2974	26.8704	29.0174	29.7781	30.5625	33.0660	36.7856	40.9955	45.7620

Periods*	9%	10%	11%	12%	13%	14%	15%	20%	25%
1	1.	1.	1.	1.	1.	1.	1.	1.	1.
2	2.09	2.10	2.11	2.12	2.13	2.14	2.15	2.20	2.25
3	3.2781	3.3100	3.3421	3.3744	3.4069	3.4396	3.4725	3.6400	3.8125
4	4.5731	4.6410	4.7097	4.7793	4.8498	4.9211	4.9934	5.3680	5.7656
5	5.9847	6.1051	6.2278	6.3528	6.4803	6.6101	6.7424	7.4416	8.2070
6	7.5233	7.7156	7.9129	8.1152	8.3227	8.5355	8.7537	9.9299	11.2588
7	9.2004	9.4872	9.7833	10.0890	10.4047	10.7305	11.0668	12.9159	15.0735
8	11.0285	11.4359	11.8594	12.2997	12.7573	13.2328	13.7268	16.4991	19.8419
9	13.0210	13.5975	14.1640	14.7757	15.4157	16.0853	16.7858	20.7989	25.8023
10	15.1929	15.9374	16.7220	17.5487	18.4197	19.3373	20.3037	25.9587	33.2529
20	51.1601	57.2750	64.2028	72.0524	80.9468	91.0249	102.4436	186.6880	342.9447

* There is one payment each period.

Table C.4 — Present Value of Annuity of $1

Periods*	2%	3%	3.75%	4%	4.25%	5%	6%	7%	8%
1	0.9804	0.9709	0.9639	0.9615	0.9592	0.9524	0.9434	0.9346	0.9259
2	1.9416	1.9135	1.8929	1.8861	1.8794	1.8594	1.8334	1.8080	1.7833
3	2.8839	2.8286	2.7883	2.7751	2.7620	2.7232	2.6730	2.6243	2.5771
4	3.8077	3.7171	3.6514	3.6299	3.6086	3.5460	3.4651	3.3872	3.3121
5	4.7135	4.5797	4.4833	4.4518	4.4207	4.3295	4.2124	4.1002	3.9927
6	5.6014	5.4172	5.2851	5.2421	5.1997	5.0757	4.9173	4.7665	4.6229
7	6.4720	6.2303	6.0579	6.0021	5.9470	5.7864	5.5824	5.3893	5.2064
8	7.3255	7.0197	6.8028	6.7327	6.6638	6.4632	6.2098	5.9713	5.7466
9	8.1622	7.7861	7.5208	7.4353	7.3513	7.1078	6.8017	6.5152	6.2469
10	8.9826	8.5302	8.2128	8.1109	8.0109	7.7217	7.3601	7.0236	6.7101
20	16.3514	14.8775	13.8962	13.5903	13.2944	12.4622	11.4699	10.5940	9.8181

Periods*	9%	10%	11%	12%	13%	14%	15%	20%	25%
1	0.9174	0.9091	0.9009	0.8929	0.8550	0.8772	0.8696	0.8333	0.8000
2	1.7591	1.7355	1.7125	1.6901	1.6681	1.6467	1.6257	1.5278	1.4400
3	2.5313	2.4869	2.4437	2.4018	2.3612	2.3216	2.2832	2.1065	1.9520
4	3.2397	3.1699	3.1024	3.0373	2.9745	2.9137	2.8550	2.5887	2.3616
5	3.8897	3.7908	3.6959	3.6048	3.5172	3.4331	3.3522	2.9906	2.6893
6	4.4859	4.3553	4.2305	4.1114	3.9975	3.8887	3.7845	3.3255	2.9514
7	5.0330	4.8684	4.7122	4.5638	4.4226	4.2883	4.1604	3.6046	3.1611
8	5.5348	5.3349	5.1461	4.9676	4.7988	4.6389	4.4873	3.8372	3.3289
9	5.9952	5.7590	5.5370	5.3282	5.1317	4.9464	4.7716	4.0310	3.4631
10	6.4177	6.1446	5.8892	5.6502	5.4262	5.2161	5.0188	4.1925	3.5705
20	9.1285	8.5136	7.9633	7.4694	7.0248	6.6231	6.2593	4.8696	3.9539

There is one payment each period.

Key Terms

Annuity (p. C4)
Future Value (p. C2)

Present Value (p. C2)

Time Value of Money (p. C2)

See complete glossary in back of text.

Questions

1. Explain the concept of the time value of money.

2. Explain the basic difference between future value and present value.

3. If you deposited $10,000 in a savings account that earns 10 percent, how much would you have at the end of 10 years? Use a convenient format to display your computations.

4. If you hold a valid contract that will pay you $8,000 cash 10 years from now and the going rate of interest is 10 percent, what is its present value? Use a convenient format to display your computations.

5. What is an annuity?

6. Use tables C.1 to C.4 to complete the following schedule:

	TABLE VALUES		
	$i = 5\%, n = 4$	$i = 10\%, n = 7$	$i = 14\%, n = 10$
FV of $1			
PV of $1			
FV of annuity of $1			
PV of annuity of $1			

7. If you deposit $1,000 at the end of each period for 10 interest periods and you earn 8 percent interest, how much would you have at the end of period 10? Use a convenient format to display your computations.

Multiple Choice

1. You are saving up for a Porsche Carrera Cabriolet, which currently sells for nearly half a million dollars. Your plan is to deposit $15,000 at the end of each year for the next 10 years. You expect to earn 5 percent each year. How much will you have saved after 10 years, rounded to the nearest 10 dollars?
    a. $150,000.   c. $495,990.
    b. $188,670.   d. None of the above.

2. Which of the following is a characteristic of an annuity?
    a. An equal dollar amount each interest period.
    b. Interest periods of equal length.
    c. An equal interest rate each interest period.
    d. All of the above are characteristics of an annuity.

3. Which of the following is most likely to be an annuity?
    a. Monthly payments on a credit card bill.
    b. Monthly interest earned on a checking account.
    c. Monthly payments on a home mortgage.
    d. Monthly utility bill payments.

4. Assume you bought a state of the art entertainment system, with no payments to be made until two years from now, when you must pay $6,000. If the going rate of interest on most loans is 5 percent, which table in this appendix would you use to calculate the system's equivalent cost if you were to pay for it today?
    a. Table C.1 (Future Value of $1)
    b. Table C.2 (Present Value of $1)
    c. Table C.3 (Future Value of Annuity of $1)
    d. Table C.4 (Present Value of Annuity of $1)

5. Assuming the facts in question 4, what is the system's equivalent cost if you were to pay for it today?
    a. $5,442   c. $11,100
    b. $6,615   d. $12,300

6. Assume you bought a car using a loan that requires payments of $3,000 to be made at the end of every year for the next three years. The loan agreement indicates the annual interest rate is 6 percent. Which table in this appendix would you use to calculate the car's equivalent cost if you were to pay for it in full today?
    a. Table C.1 (Future Value of $1)
    b. Table C.2 (Present Value of $1)
    c. Table C.3 (Future Value of Annuity of $1)
    d. Table C.4 (Present Value of Annuity of $1)

7. Assuming the facts in question 6, what is the car's equivalent cost if you were to pay for it today? Round to the nearest hundred dollars.
    a. $2,600   c. $8,000
    b. $3,600   d. $9,600

8. Which of the following statements are true?
    a. When the interest rate increases, the present value of a single amount decreases.
    b. When the number of interest periods increase, the present value of a single amount increases.
    c. When the interest rate increases, the present value of an annuity increases.
    d. None of the above are true.

9. Which of the following describes how to calculate a bond's issue price?

	Face Value	Interest Payments
a.	Present value of single amount.	Future value of annuity.
b.	Future value of single amount.	Present value of annuity.
c.	Present value of single amount.	Present value of annuity.
d.	Future value of single amount.	Future value of annuity.

10. If interest is compounded quarterly, rather than yearly, how do you adjust the number of years and annual interest rate when using the present value tables?

	Number of years	Annual interest rate
a.	Divide by 4	Divide by 4
b.	Divide by 4	Multiply by 4
c.	Multiply by 4	Divide by 4
d.	Multiply by 4	Multiply by 4

Solutions to Multiple-Choice Questions

1. b   2. d   3. c   4. b   5. a   6. d   7. c   8. a   9. c   10. c

---

Mini Exercises

MC-1 Computing the Present Value of a Single Payment

What is the present value of $500,000 to be paid in 10 years, with an interest rate of 8 percent?

MC-2 Computing the Present Value of an Annuity

What is the present value of 10 equal payments of $15,000, with an interest rate of 10 percent?

MC-3 Computing the Present Value of a Complex Contract

As a result of a slowdown in operations, Mercantile Stores is offering to employees who have been terminated a severance package of $100,000 cash; another $100,000 to be paid in one year; and an annuity of $30,000 to be paid each year for 20 years. What is the present value of the package, assuming an interest rate of 8 percent?

MC-4 Computing the Future Value of an Annuity

You plan to retire in 20 years. Calculate whether it is better for you to save $25,000 a year for the last 10 years before retirement or $15,000 for each of the 20 years. Assume you are able to earn 10 percent interest on your investments.

Exercises

EC-1 Computing Growth in a Savings Account: A Single Amount

On January 1, 2009, you deposited $6,000 in a savings account. The account will earn 10 percent annual compound interest, which will be added to the fund balance at the end of each year.

Required (round to the nearest dollar):

1. What will be the balance in the savings account at the end of 10 years?
2. What is the interest for the 10 years?
3. How much interest revenue did the fund earn in 2009? 2010?

EC-2 Computing Deposit Required and Accounting for a Single-Sum Savings Account

On January 1, 2009, Alan King decided to transfer an amount from his checking account into a savings account that later will provide $80,000 to send his son to college (four years from now). The savings account will earn 8 percent, which will be added to the fund each year-end.

Required (show computations and round to the nearest dollar):

1. How much must Alan deposit on January 1, 2009?
2. Give the journal entry that Alan should make on January 1, 2009 to record the transfer.
3. What is the interest for the four years?
4. Give the journal entry that Alan should make on (*a*) December 31, 2009, and (*b*) December 31, 2010.

EC-3 Recording Growth in a Savings Account with Equal Periodic Payments

On each December 31, you plan to transfer $2,000 from your checking account into a savings account. The savings account will earn 9 percent annual interest, which will be added to the savings account balance at each year-end. The first deposit will be made December 31, 2009 (at the end of the period).

Required (show computations and round to the nearest dollar):

1. Give the required journal entry on December 31, 2009.
2. What will be the balance in the savings account at the end of the 10th year (i.e., 10 deposits)?
3. What is the total amount of interest earned on the 10 deposits?
4. How much interest revenue did the fund earn in 2010? 2011?
5. Give all required journal entries at the end of 2010 and 2011.

EC-4 Computing Growth for a Savings Fund with Periodic Deposits

On January 1, 2009, you plan to take a trip around the world upon graduation four years from now. Your grandmother wants to deposit sufficient funds for this trip in a savings account for you. On the basis of a budget, you estimate that the trip currently would cost $15,000. Being the generous and sweet lady she is, your grandmother decided to deposit $3,500 in the fund at the end of each of the next four years, starting on December 31, 2009. The savings account will earn 6 percent annual interest, which will be added to the savings account at each year-end.

Required (show computations and round to the nearest dollar):

1. How much money will you have for the trip at the end of year 4 (i.e., after four deposits)?
2. What is the total amount of interest earned over the four years?
3. How much interest revenue did the fund earn in 2009, 2010, 2011, and 2012?

EC-5 Computing Value of an Asset Based on Present Value

You have the chance to purchase an oil well. Your best estimate is that the oil well's net royalty income will average $25,000 per year for five years. There will be no residual value at that time. Assume that the cash inflow occurs at each year-end and that considering the uncertainty in your estimates, you expect to earn 15 percent per year on the investment.

Required:

What should you be willing to pay for this investment right now?

EC-6 Comparing Options Using Present Value Concepts

After hearing a knock at your front door, you are surprised to see the Prize Patrol from a large, well-known magazine subscription company. It has arrived with the good news that you are the big winner, having won "$20 million." You discover that you have three options: (1) you can receive $1 million per year for the next 20 years, (2) you can have $8 million today, or (3) you can have $2 million today and receive $700,000 for each of the next 20 years. Your financial adviser tells you that it is reasonable to expect to earn 10 percent on investments.

Required:
Which option do you prefer? What factors influence your decision?

Problem—Set A

PAC-1 Comparing Options Using Present Value Concepts

After completing a long and successful career as senior vice president for a large bank, you are preparing for retirement. After visiting the human resources office, you have found that you have several retirement options: (1) you can receive an immediate cash payment of $1 million, (2) you can receive $60,000 per year for life (your remaining life expectancy is 20 years), or (3) you can receive $50,000 per year for 10 years and then $70,000 per year for life (this option is intended to give you some protection against inflation). You have determined that you can earn 8 percent on your investments. Which option do you prefer and why?

Problem—Set B

PBC-1 Comparing Options Using Present Value Concepts

After incurring a serious injury caused by a manufacturing defect, your friend has sued the manufacturer for damages. Your friend received three offers from the manufacturer to settle the lawsuit; (1) receive an immediate cash payment of $100,000, (2) receive $6,000 per year for life (your friend's remaining life expectancy is 20 years), or (3) receive $5,000 per year for 10 years and then $7,000 per year for life (this option is intended to compensate your friend for increased aggravation of the injury over time). Your friend can earn 8 percent interest and has asked you for advice. Which option would you recommend and why?

INTERNATIONAL FINANCIAL REPORTING STANDARDS

It has become an old cliché but business really has gone global. Abercrombie is opening stores in Sweden, and Swedish companies like IKEA and H&M are opening stores throughout the United States. Similar trends are occurring in the investing world, where shares of foreign companies like Benetton and British Airways are traded on the New York Stock Exchange (NYSE). Until recently, investors struggled to compare the financial statements of companies like these because different countries used different accounting rules. All this is changing now, with the increasing acceptance of International Financial Reporting Standards (abbreviated IFRS, pronounced "eye-furs").

IFRS are developed by the International Accounting Standards Board (IASB), which is the international counterpart to the Financial Accounting Standards Board (FASB) in the United States. Over 100 different countries including Australia, China, the European Union, South Africa, and New Zealand currently require or permit the use of IFRS, or a local version of IFRS. This number is continuing to grow with IFRS becoming official in the near future in Brazil (2010), Canada (2011), India (2011), and other countries. Although the United States has not yet switched to IFRS, such a change is believed to be coming in the next six years or so. The Securities and Exchange Commission (SEC) has already begun moving in this direction by allowing foreign companies like Benetton and British Airways to issue stock in the United States without having to convert their IFRS-based accounting numbers to U.S. GAAP. The SEC plans to allow some U.S. companies to use IFRS in 2009, and aims to require IFRS starting in 2014. Many foreign-owned private companies in the United States, such as Mack Trucks and Dreyer's Ice Cream, already use IFRS to make it easy to combine their financial statements with their foreign owners' financial statements.

Although IFRS differ from the generally accepted accounting principles currently used in the United States, they do not dramatically alter what you have learned in this course. IFRS use the same system of analyzing, recording, and summarizing the results of business activities that you learned in Chapters 1–4. The most significant differences between IFRS and U.S. GAAP relate to technical issues that are typically taught in intermediate and advanced accounting courses. For the topics discussed in this course, differences between IFRS and U.S. GAAP are limited, which we summarize briefly in the table on the following page.

As we look to the future, it seems clear that U.S. GAAP and IFRS will converge as the FASB and IASB work together to remove differences between the two sets of accounting rules and to develop new rules through joint projects. One of the most exciting of these projects currently being worked on is the development of a new format for organizing items on the financial statements. Although it has not yet been finalized, a current proposal is to separately report the results of operating, investing, and financing activities in each of the financial statements similar to what is currently required for the statement of cash flows. Having learned the differences between typical financing and investing activities (in Chapter 2) and operating activities (in Chapter 3), you will be well-prepared to handle evolutions such as these as they arise during your career.

Chapter Topic	U.S. GAAP	IFRS
7: Inventories	• Allows 4 cost flow methods (p. 307) • LCM rule bases market value on replacement cost (p. 313) • Inventory write-down required but reversal disallowed (p. 314)	• Does not allow LIFO • LCM bases market value on net realizable value (selling price less selling costs) • Both write-down and reversal required
10: Long-Lived Tangible and Intangible Assets	• "Basket purchases" of assets are separated into components (p. 420) • Do not revalue unless impaired (p. 430)	• Individual assets may be separated into significant components • Regular revaluation at fair value permitted
11: Current Liabilities and Payroll	• Contingent liabilities accrued if estimable and probable (p. 477)	• Contingent liabilities accrued if estimable and "more likely than not"
13: Corporations	• Most preferred stock is reported as equity (p. 564)	• Most preferred stock is reported as debt
16: Statement of Cash Flows	• Interest paid, interest received, and dividends received are classified as operating (p. 694) • Dividends paid are classified as financing (p. 694)	• Interest paid can be either operating or financing; interest and dividends received can be either operating or investing • Dividends paid can be either operating or financing

A

Accounting Rate of Return p. 932 Estimated average return on investment that a project is expected to generate over its life cycle.

Active Investments p. 643 Investments in stock of another business to influence or control that business; acquisition of 20 percent or more of the voting stock of a company is presumed to be an active investment.

Activity Based Costing p. 857 Product costing method used by companies that have diverse products to which indirect costs are assigned based on the underlying activities performed.

Activity Cost Driver p. 859 Underlying measure of activity used in activity based costing to assign the indirect cost to products and services.

Actual Manufacturing Overhead p. 806 Actual amount of indirect manufacturing costs incurred during the period.

Administrative Costs p. 773 Costs associated with running the overall organization.

Allocation Base p. 804 Measurable item used to apply indirect overhead costs to products or services.

Amortized Cost p. 644 Cost of bonds adjusted for the amortization of any bond discount or premium.

Annual Rate of Return p. 932 Estimated average return on investment that a project is expected to generate over its life cycle.

Articles of Organization p. 507 Document required in all states to form an LLC; provides important information about its operations and structure.

Authorized Shares p. 567 Shares of stock a corporation can issue as specified in the charter.

Avoidable Cost p. 922 Cost that can be avoided by choosing one decision option instead of another.

B

Balanced Scorecard p. 1039 Comprehensive performance measurement system that translates an organization's vision and strategy into a set of operational performance metrics.

Batch-Level Activities p. 858 Activities performed for a group of units or customers all at once.

Bonds p. 604 Financial instruments that outline future payments a company promises to make in exchange for receiving cash now.

Break-Even Analysis p. 895 One application of cost-volume-profit analysis that determines the point at which fixed costs have been exactly covered and profit is zero.

Break-Even Point p. 895 Point at which total revenue equals total cost, resulting in zero profit; the point at which fixed costs exactly equal the contribution margin.

Budget p. 768 Quantification of the resources and expenditures that will be required during a given period of time to achieve a plan.

Budgeted Balance Sheet p. 962 Balance sheet created from a combination of the financial budgets; shows expected balance of assets, liabilities, and owners' equity at the end of the budget period.

Budgeted Cost of Goods Sold p. 963 Budgeted manufacturing cost per unit multiplied by the number of units of expected sales.

Budgeted Gross Margin p. 964 Budgeted sales less budgeted cost of goods sold.

Budgeted Manufacturing Cost per Unit p. 963 Combination of all budgeted manufacturing costs.

Budgeted Income Statement p. 962 Expectation of income after combining all operating budgets.

Budget Slack p. 961 Cushion that managers may try to build into their budget by understating expected sales or overstating budgeting expenses so that they are more likely to come in under budget for expenses and over budget for revenues.

C

Capital Budgeting p. 920 Decision-making approach aimed at helping managers make decisions about investments in major capital assets.

Capital Budgeting Decisions p. 931 Long-term decisions regarding capital investments.

Capital Deficiency p. 531 Lack of sufficient capital in a partner's capital account to absorb losses resulting from the liquidation of the partnership.

Capital Lease p. 610 Similar to an operating lease, except that virtually all risks and rewards of owning the rented property transfer to the company that obtains the use of the property.

Carrying Value p. 607 Amount at which an item is reported ("carried at") on the balance sheet after considering related contra-accounts.

Cash Budget p. 964 Financial budget that provides information about budgeted cash receipts and disbursements.

Cash-Equivalent Amount p. 600 Amount of cash that would be accepted as full settlement of a liability the moment the liability is created.

Cash Equivalents p. 682 Short-term, highly liquid investments that are both (1) readily convertible to known amounts of cash and (2) so near to maturity that there is little risk their value will change.

Cash Flows from Financing Activities p. 684 Cash inflows and outflows related to financing sources external to the company (owners and lenders).

Cash Flows from Investing Activities p. 684 Cash inflows and outflows related to the purchase or sale of investments and long-lived assets.

Cash Flows from Operating Activities (Cash Flows from Operations) p. 683 Cash inflows and outflows related to components of net income.

Centralized Organization p. 1028 Organization in which decision-making authority is kept at the very top level of the organization.

Common Stock p. 561 Basic voting stock a corporation issues to stockholders.

Consolidated Financial Statements p. 659 Single set of financial statements representing the combination of the operations of two or more companies.

Contributed Capital p. 562 Contributions made directly to a corporation by its owners (stockholders).

Contribution Margin p. 893 Difference between sales revenue and variable costs.

Contribution Margin Income Statement p. 892 Type of income statement that separates costs into variable or fixed costs; used to address many managerial problems.

Contribution Margin Ratio p. 893 Total contribution margin divided by total sales revenue; stated as a percentage of sales.

Control p. 768 One of the key functions of management; involves monitoring actual results to see whether the objectives set in the planning state are being made.

Controllability Principle p. 1030 Concept that managers should be held responsible for only those things that they can control.

Conversion Cost p. 772 Sum of direct labor and manufacturing overhead; total cost incurred to convert direct materials into a finished product.

Cost p. 769 Value given up in exchange for something else.

Cost Behavior p. 884 Describes how total costs change when some measure of activity level changes.

Cost Center p. 1030 Responsibility center in which manager has authority and responsibility for cost.

Cost Driver p. 857 Measure used to allocate or assign indirect costs to products.

Cost Object p. 770 Any item for which one wants to determine cost.

Cost of Goods Completed p. 811   Total amount of cost assigned to goods that were manufactured or completed during an accounting period.

Cost of Goods Manufactured p. 775   Total cost of all units completed during a given time period regardless of whether the units were sold during the current period or not.

Cost of Goods Sold (COGS) p. 806   Expense account including the total cost of jobs or units sold during the period.

Cost-Volume-Profit Analysis p. 894   Analysis that focuses on a specific decision and determines how changes in volume will affect costs and profit.

Cumulative Dividend Preference p. 571   Feature of preferred stock that requires dividends in arrears to be paid before current dividends.

Current Dividend Preference p. 570   Feature of preferred stock that grants priority to preferred dividends over dividends on common stock.

Customer-Level Activities p. 858   Activities performed for a specific customer.

CVP Graph p. 898   Graph that is useful for visualizing the relationship among unit sales volume, total revenue, total cost, and profit.

D

Debt-to-Assets Ratio p. 611   Measures the extent of financing risk by indicating the proportion of total assets financed by liabilities.

Decentralized Organization p. 1028   Organization in which decision-making authority is spread throughout, and managers are responsible for deciding how to manage their particular area of responsibility.

Declaration Date p. 569   Date on which the board of directors officially approves a dividend.

Dependent Variable p. 889   Variable that depends on the level of X.

Differential Analysis p. 921   See *Incremental Analysis*.

Differential Cost p. 922   Cost that differs between decision alternatives.

Direct Costs p. 770   Costs that can be directly attributed or traced to a specific cost object.

Directing/Leading p. 768   One of the key functions of management; involves all actions that managers must take to implement a plan.

Direct Labor p. 772   Costs for labor that can be physically and conveniently traced to the final product.

Direct Labor Budget p. 963   Budget indicating the amount of direct labor needed to meet expected production.

Direct Labor Efficiency Variance p. 997   Variance that calculates the portion of direct labor spending variance driven by the difference in the actual and the standard labor hours, noted as SR × (SH − AH).

Direct Labor Rate Variance p. 997   Variance that calculates the portion of the direct labor spending variance that is driven by the difference in actual and standard labor rate, noted as AH × (SR − AR).

Direct Labor Spending Variance p. 997   Variance that represents the sum of the direct labor rate variance and the direct labor efficiency variances.

Direct Labor Time Ticket p. 803   Source document used to keep track of direct labor costs in a job order cost system.

Direct Materials p. 772   Primary material inputs that can be physically and conveniently traced to the final product.

Direct Materials Price Variance p. 995   Variance that calculates the portion of the direct materials spending variance driven by the difference in actual and standard price of direct materials, noted as AQ × (SP − AP).

Direct Materials Quantity Variance p. 995   Variance that calculates the portion of the direct materials spending variance driven by the difference in actual and standard quantity of direct materials, noted as SP × (SQ − AQ).

Direct Materials Spending Variance p. 996   Sum of the direct materials price variance and the direct materials quantity variances.

Direct Method p. 683   Method of presenting the Operating Activities section of the cash flow statement to report the components of cash flows from operating activities as gross receipts and gross payments.

Discount p. 605   Excess of a bond's face value over its issue price.

Discounted Cash Flow Method p. 932   Decision-making approach that incorporates the time value of money.

Discounting p. 601   Process of calculating the cash-equivalent "present value" of future payments by removing the interest component that is built into future payments.

Dividends in Arrears p. 571   Dividend rights from prior years that must be satisfied before dividends of the current year can be paid.

DuPont Method p. 1034   Formula developed by executives at DuPont in the early 1900s; shows that the return on investment is a function of profit margin and investment turnover.

E

Easily Attainable Standard p. 988   Standard that can be met with relative ease.

Equity Method p. 654   Active investments that are increased (decreased) by the investor's share of the investee's net income or loss (reported as income by the investor) and decreased by the investor's share of the dividends declared by the investee (not reported as income by the investor).

Equivalent Unit p. 851   Measure of the amount of work that occurred during the period.

F

Face Value p. 604   Amount a bond promises to pay on its maturity date.

Facility-Level Activities p. 858   Activities performed for the overall company.

Favorable Variance p. 989   Variance indicating that actual costs were less than budgeted or standard costs.

Financial Accounting p. 766   Area of accounting that prepares information used by external parties, such as investors, creditors, and regulators.

Financial Budget p. 962   Budget that focuses on the financial resources needed to support operations.

Finished Goods Inventory p. 775   Cost of all units that have been completed but have not yet been sold.

Fixed Costs p. 771   Costs that remain the same, in total, regardless of activity level.

Fixed Overhead Spending Variance p. 1002   Variance that represents the difference in actual and budgeted fixed overhead costs.

Fixed Overhead Volume Variance p. 1002   Variance resulting from the difference between actual and budgeted production volume.

Flexible Budget p. 990   Budget showing how budgeted costs and revenues will change for different levels of sales.

G

Goal Incongruence p. 1038   Conflict between a manager and the organization that may cause managers to make decisions that are not in the best interest of the overall organization.

H

High-Low Method p. 890   Method of analyzing mixed costs using the two most extreme activity levels (X values) to estimate fixed and variable costs.

Horizontal (Trend) Analysis p. 732   Comparison of individual financial statement items from year to year with the general goal of identifying significant sustained changes or trends.

Hurdle Rate p. 933   Minimum required rate of return for a project.

I

Ideal Standard p. 988   Standard that can be achieved only under perfect or ideal conditions.

Incremental Analysis p. 921   Short-term decision-making approach that focuses on the differential costs and benefits of alternate decision choices.

Incremental Cost p. 922   See *Differential Costs*.

Independent Variable p. 889   Variable that causes Y to change.

Indirect Costs p. 770   Costs that cannot be traced to a specific cost object or are not worth the effort to trace.

Indirect Materials p. 807   Materials that cannot be directly or conveniently traced to a specific unit and are therefore treated as manufacturing overhead.

Indirect Method p. 683   Method that starts with net income from the income statement and then adjusts it by removing items that do not involve cash but were included in net income and adding items that involved cash but were not yet included in net income.

Internal Rate of Return p. 935   Discount rate at which the present value of cash inflows exactly equals the cash outflows.

Inventoriable Cost p. 773   Cost that is counted as inventory on the balance sheet until the product is sold; another term for product cost.

Inventory Budget p. 963   Budget that shows how much finished goods, work in process, and raw materials inventory are planned at the beginning and end of each budget period.

Investment Center p. 1030   Responsibility center in which manager has authority and responsibility for profit (revenue – cost) and the investment of assets.

Investments for Significant Influence p. 654   Investments in 20 percent or more of the voting stock of other companies to obtain significant influence or control over the financing and operating activities of those companies.

Investments Held to Maturity p. 654   Investments in bonds that management intends and has the ability to hold until the maturity date.

Investment Turnover p. 1034   Ratio of sales revenue to the investment base (assets).

Irrelevant Cost p. 922   Cost that will not impact a particular decision.

Issued Shares p. 867   Shares of stock that have been sold or given to indicate ownership of a corporation.

J

Job Cost Sheet p. 802   Document used to record all of the costs of producing a particular job or servicing a specific customer.

Job Order Costing p. 861   Costing system used by companies that make unique products or provide specialty services.

L

Limited Liability Company (LLC) p. 507   Business organizational form that offers its members limited liability protection and pass-through taxation.

Liquidity p. 736   Ratio indicating the extent to which a company is able to pay its currently maturing obligations.

Long-Term Debt p. 600   Liabilities requiring repayment over more than one year or if longer, the company's operating cycle.

Long-Term Objective p. 959   Specific goal that management wants to achieve over a long-term horizon of more than one year.

M

Managerial Accounting p. 766   Area of accounting that prepares information aimed at managers who are running the business; sometimes called internal reporting because it is used by individuals inside the company.

Manufacturing Firm p. 773   Company that purchases raw materials and uses them to make a finished product to sell to wholesalers, retailers, or customers.

Manufacturing Costs p. 772   Costs incurred to produce a physical product; generally classified as direct materials, direct labor, or manufacturing overhead.

Manufacturing Overhead p. 772   All costs other than direct material and direct labor that must be incurred to manufacture a physical product.

Manufacturing Overhead Budget p. 963   Budget that indicates overhead costs to be incurred to support budgeted production.

Margin of Safety p. 896   Difference between actual or budgeted sales and the break-even point.

Marketing or Selling Costs p. 772   Costs incurred to sell a final product or service to the customer.

Market Interest Rate p. 606   Interest rate that the bond market ultimately obtains by purchasing a bond at a premium, a discount, or face value; represents a company's cost of borrowing.

Market Value Method p. 646   Adjust investments in available for sale and trading securities to market value at the end of each reporting period.

Master Budget p. 962   Integrated set of operating and financial budgets that reflects what management expects to achieve in a future accounting period.

Materials Requisition p. 802   Document used to authorize the issuance of materials

into production; details the cost and quantities of all materials needed to complete specific jobs.

Maturity Date p. 604   Date on which a bond's face value is scheduled to be paid to bondholders.

Merchandising Company p. 773   Company that purchases goods (merchandise) from a supplier and sells them to other businesses or consumers.

Merger p. 659   Event that occurs when one company acquires the assets and liabilities of another company and the acquired company goes out of existence.

Mixed Costs p. 886   Costs that have both a fixed component and a variable component; also known as semivariable costs.

N

Net Present Value (NPV) Method p. 934   Method that compares the present value of the future cash flows for a project to the original investment that is required at the start of the project.

Nondiscounting Methods p. 932   Approaches to management decisions that do not consider the time value of money.

Nonmanufacturing Costs p. 772   Costs associated with running a business and selling a product as opposed to manufacturing a product; generally classified as marketing or selling costs or administrative costs.

Nonvolume-Based Cost Drivers p. 857   Allocation bases not directly related to the number of units produced.

No-Par Value Stock p. 563   Capital stock that has no par value specified in the corporate charter.

O

Operating Agreement p. 507   Document recommended when an LLC is formed to address potential problem areas.

Operating Budgets p. 962   Budgets that cover the organization's planned operating activities for a particular period of time.

Opportunity Cost p. 770   Cost that occurs when you choose not to do something; a forgone benefit or lost opportunity in choosing one alternative instead of another.

Operating Lease p. 610   Rental agreement that allows a company to obtain temporary use of property in exchange for future payments to the property's owner.

Organizing p. 768   One of the key functions of management; involves arranging the necessary resources to carry out the plan.

Out-of-Pocket Costs p. 790   Costs that involve an outlay of cash.

Outstanding Shares p. 567   Issued shares currently held by stockholders, not the corporation itself.

Overapplied Overhead p. 812 Difference between actual and applied overhead when the overhead applied to Work in Process is higher than the actual overhead cost incurred during the period.

Over- or Underapplied Fixed Overhead p. 1003 Sum of the fixed overhead spending variance and the fixed overhead volume variance.

P

Parent Company p. 659 Company acquiring another for control.

Participative Budgeting p. 961 Method that allows employees throughout the organization to have input into the budget-setting process.

Partner Return on Equity p. 533 Ratio that measures a company's efficiency in generating profits from every dollar of equity invested or retained by partners.

Partner's Capital Statement p. 516 Financial statement that replaces the owner's equity statement and shows all changes to capital for each partner in a partnership.

Partnership p. 506 An unincorporated business owned by two or more individuals.

Partnership Agreement p. 506 Recommended document when a partnership is formed to address potential problem areas.

Partnership Dissolution p. 517 When a partner is added, it causes the dissolution of the existing partnership (consisting of the old partners) and the creation of a new partnership (consisting of the new partners).

Partnership Liquidation p. 526 Process to terminate a partnership that involves selling the partnership assets, paying its liabilities, and distributing cash to partners.

Par Value p. 563 Value assigned to each share of capital stock as specified in the charter.

Passive Investments p. 643 Investments in debt and stock instruments for the purpose of earning a return on the funds; acquisition of less than 20 percent of the voting stock of a company is presumed to be a passive investment.

Pass-Through Taxation p. 507 Taxation rule that allows profits from a business to flow directly through to the owners, avoiding taxation at the business level.

Payback Period p. 933 Amount of time it takes to generate enough cash for a project to pay for its original investment.

Payment Date p. 569 Date on which a corporation pays a cash dividend to the stockholders of record.

Period Cost p. 773 Cost that is expensed as soon as it is incurred.

Planning p. 768 Future-oriented aspect of the management process that involves setting long-term goals and objectives and short-term tactics necessary to achieve those goals.

Predetermined Overhead Rate p. 804 Rate estimated before the accounting period begins and used throughout the period to assign overhead costs to products based on actual values of an allocation base.

Preference Decisions p. 932 Decisions that require managers to choose from among a set of alternative capital investment opportunities.

Preferred Stock p. 561 Stock that has specified rights over common stock.

Premium p. 605 Excess of a bond's issue price over its face value.

Prime Cost p. 772 Sum of direct materials and direct labor; represents the costs that can be directly traced to the end product.

Private Companies p. 560 Companies whose stock is bought and sold through private transactions.

Process Costing p. 800 Costing system used by companies that make very homogenous products or services.

Product Costs p. 773 Costs that become a part of the product that is being produced.

Production Budget p. 963 Budget that shows how many units need to be produced each period to meet projected sales.

Production Report p. 855 Essentially a summary of what occurred in the production process during the accounting period.

Product-Level Activities p. 858 Activities performed to support an overall product line.

Profitability p. 736 Profitability is the extent to which a company generates income.

Profit Center p. 1030 Responsibility center in which manager has authority and responsibility for profit (revenue – cost).

Profit Margin p. 1034 Ratio of operating profit to sales revenue.

Public Companies p. 560 Companies whose stock is bought and sold publicly on stock exchanges.

R

Raw Materials Inventory p. 775 Cost of all materials purchased from suppliers that have not yet been used in production.

Raw Materials Inventory Account p. 785 Inventory account that includes the total cost of raw materials purchased but not yet issued to production.

Raw Materials Purchases Budget p. 963 Budget that indicates the quantity of raw materials that must be purchased to meet production and raw materials inventory needs.

Record Date p. 569 Date on which the corporation prepares the list of current stockholders; dividends are paid only to the stockholder who owns stock on this date.

Regression Analysis p. 890 Method of analyzing mixed costs by using a statistical package to calculate the "best-fitting" line using all available data points.

Related-Party Transactions p. 1040 Business transactions between units or divisions of the same company.

Relevant Cost p. 922 Cost that has the potential to influence a particular decision.

Relevant Range p. 884 Range of activity over which assumptions about cost behavior are expected to hold true.

Residual Income p. 1036 Alternative measure for evaluating investment center performance; calculated as the difference between operating income and minimum profit needed to cover the required rate of return (hurdle rate).

Responsibility Accounting p. 1030 Area of accounting in which managers are given authority and responsibility over a particular area of the organization and are then evaluated based on the results of that area of responsibility.

Responsibility Center p. 1030 Area over which managers are given responsibility for specific operations of an organization.

Retained Earnings p. 563 Account used by corporations to accumulate the profits or losses generated each year (minus any dividends declared) since the corporation was first created.

Return on Assets p. 660 Ratio that measures how much the firm earned for each dollar invested in assets.

Return on Investment (ROI) p. 1034 Most common method of evaluating investment center performance; calculated as return (measured by operating profit) / investment (measured by average invested assets).

Revenue Center p. 1030 Responsibility center in which manager has authority and responsibility for revenue.

S

Sales Budget p. 963 Estimate of the number of units to be sold and the total sales revenue to be generated in each budget period; also called the sales forecast.

Scattergraph p. 887 Graph of the relationship between total cost (Y) and activity level (X).

S-Corporation p. 508 Corporation that allows profits to pass through to the owners' personal income tax returns and provides owners limited liability.

Screening Decisions p. 931 Decisions made when managers evaluate a proposed capital investment to determine whether it meets some minimum criteria.

Securities Available for Sale p. 646 Passive investments not actively traded; reported at market value as current and/or noncurrent assets, depending on management's intent; unrealized gains or losses are reported in stockholders' equity on the balance sheet.

Segmented Income Statement p. 1032 Income statement that shows the profitability of individual business segments for a particular period of time.

Segment Margin p. 1032 Calculated as revenue minus all costs that are directly traceable to a particular business segment.

Selling and Administrative Expense Budget p. 963 Budget of expected cost of selling and administration based on the planned level of sales.

Service Company p. 773 Company that provides services to other businesses or consumers.

Short-Term Objective p. 959 Specific goal that management wants to achieve in the short-run; usually no longer than one year.

Solvency p. 736 Solvency is the ability to survive long enough to repay lenders when debt matures.

Spending Variances p. 992 Variances calculated by comparing actual costs to the flexible budget cost.

Standard Cost Card p. 989 Form on which to record a summary of what it should cost to make a single unit of product based on expected production and sales for the upcoming period.

Standard Cost System p. 988 Cost system that records manufacturing costs at standard rather than actual amounts.

Standard Unit Cost p. 989 Expected cost to produce one unit based on standard prices and quantities.

Stated Interest Rate p. 604 Interest rate stated on the face of a bond certificate, which when multiplied by the face value indicates the dollar amount of interest paid each year.

Static Budget p. 990 Budget based on a single estimate of sales volume.

Step Costs p. 885 Costs that are fixed over some range of activity and then increase in a steplike fashion when a capacity limit is reached; can be treated as either step-variable or step-fixed costs.

Step-Fixed Cost p. 886 Step cost with relatively wide steps; typically treated as a fixed cost at least within a relevant range.

Step-Variable Cost p. 885 Step cost with relatively narrow steps; typically treated as a variable cost because multiple steps are encountered across the relevant range.

Stock Dividend p. 572 Distribution of additional shares of a corporation's own stock.

Stockholders p. 560 Owners of a corporation who hold stock certificates indicating their share of ownership.

Stockholders' Equity p. 562 Category of the balance sheet that reports stockholders' claims on the resources of the corporation.

Stock Split p. 573 Increase in the total number of authorized and issued shares by a specified ratio; often is accompanied by a corresponding reduction in the per share value, resulting in no change to the stockholders' equity accounts.

Strategic Plan p. 959 Managers' vision of what they want the organization to achieve over a long-term horizon.

Subsidiary Company p. 659 Company acquired by another company gaining control.

Sunk Cost p. 922 Cost incurred in the past; is not relevant to future decisions.

T

Tactics p. 959 Specific actions or mechanisms that management uses to achieve objectives.

Target Profit Analysis p. 897 CVP analysis that determines the amount of sales necessary to earn a specific profit.

Times Interest Earned Ratio p. 612 Measures the extent to which a company's income before the costs of financing and taxes are sufficient to cover interest expense.

Top-Down Approach p. 961 Method in which top management sets a budget and imposes it on lower levels of the organization.

Trading Securities p. 646 Investments in stocks and bonds that management actively trades; reported at market value in current assets section of balance sheet; unrealized gains or losses are reported on the income statement.

Transfer Price p. 1040 Amount charged when one division sells goods or services to another division of the same company.

Treasury Stock p. 565 Issued shares that the corporation has repurchased.

U

Underapplied Overhead p. 812 Difference in actual and applied overhead that occurs when the overhead applied to Work in Process Inventory is less than the actual overhead cost incurred during the period.

Unfavorable Variance p. 990 Variance indicating that actual costs were more than budgeted or standard costs.

Unit Contribution Margin p. 893 Difference between sales revenue per unit and variable cost per unit; indicates how much each additional unit sold will contribute to fixed costs and profit.

Unit-Level Activities p. 858 Activities performed for each unit or customer (one at a time).

Unrealized Holding Gains or Losses p. 648 Temporary changes in the market value of passive investments.

V

Variable Costs p. 771 Costs that change in total in direct proportion to changes in activity levels.

Variable Overhead Efficiency Variance p. 987 Variance driven by the difference in actual amounts and standard amounts of a cost driver (e.g., direct labor hours) multiplied by the standard variable overhead rate.

Variable Overhead (VOH) Rate Variance p. 999 Variance driven by the difference in actual and standard variable overhead rates.

Variance p. 987 Difference between actual costs and budgeted or standard costs.

Vertical (Common Size) Analysis p. 734 Analytic technique that expresses each line of the income statement (or balance sheet) as a percentage of total sales (or total assets).

Visual Fit Method p. 890 Method of analyzing mixed costs that involves "eyeballing" the data on a scattergraph.

Volume-Based Allocation Measures p. 857 Allocation bases traditionally used to assign indirect costs that are directly related to number of units produced.

Volume Variance p. 992 Variance driven by the difference in actual and budgeted sales volume.

W

Work in Process Inventory p. 775 Cost of units that have been started in the manufacturing operation but are incomplete at the end of an accounting period.

Work in Process Inventory Account p. 785 Inventory account that includes the total cost incurred to manufacture goods that are in process but not yet completed.

Credits

Business Index

Page numbers followed by n indicate footnotes.

A

Aaron Rents, Inc., 592
Abercrombie and Fitch Co., 773, D-1
Activision, Inc., 596, 611
Aeropostale, Inc., 568
AIRBUS, 696
Amazon.com, 773
AMC Theatres, 714
American Airlines, 615
American Eagle Outfitters, 615
American Girl, 919
American Skiing, 572
AMR Corporation, 615
Apple Inc., 714–715, 772
Avis, 610

B

Bausch & Lomb, 985
Benetton, D-1
Big Dog Holdings, 584
Black & Decker Corporation, 614–615, 982–983, 984
Blockbuster, Inc.
    business description, 1027
    decentralization of responsibility, 1028–1030
    evaluation of investment center performance, 1034–1040
    organization chart, 1029
    responsibility centers, 1030–1033
    transfer pricing, 1040–1043
Bloom 'n Flowers
    admission of partner, 517–521
    business description, 505
    division of income (loss), 511–516
    financial statements, 516–517
    formation, 509–510
    partner return on equity, 533–534
    partnership accounting, 509–517
    partnership agreement, 506–507
    partnership liquidation, 526–532
    withdrawal of partner, 521–525
Boeing, 696
British Airways, D-1
Brunswick Corporation, 685, 699–700
Builder's FirstSource, 744

C

Cargill, 560
Cereality, 900
Charmin, 800
The Cheesecake Factory Incorporated, 673
Chevron, 750
Chick-fil-A, 560

Cintas Corporation, 752–753
CK Mondavi Family Vineyards
    activity based costing (ABC), 856–862
    business description, 841–842
    process costing concepts, 842–849
    process costing production report, 849–856
    weighted average process costing, 865–869
Coca-Cola Company, 569, 756, 800–801
Cold Stone Creamery
    budgeted income statement, 969
    budgets in planning and control cycles, 958–961
    business description, 957, 987
    direct labor variances, 996–998, 1010–1011
    direct materials variances, 994–996, 1009–1010
    financial budgets, 970–972
    flexible budgets to calculate cost variances, 990–993
    manufacturing overhead cost variances, 998–1003, 1010–1011
    master budget, 962–964
    operating budget, 964–969
    standard cost system, 988–990, 1008–1011
    strategic vision, 960
    summary of variances, 1003–1005, 1011
The Colgate-Palmolive Company, 670, 714
Constellation Brands Inc., 842
Cybex International, 704–705

D

Dell Computer, 771
Dell Corporation, 569
DiGiorno Pizza, 767, 778
Disney, 659, 716–717
Dollar General Corporation, 754
Dow Jones & Company, Inc., 661
Dreyers Ice Cream, D-1

E

Ernst and Young, 801
Exxon, 800
ExxonMobil, 644n

F

Federal Express Corporation (FedEx), 771
Federated Department Stores, 590–591
Fisher Price, 919
Fitch, 599
Fool.com, 731
Forbes, 770
Ford Motor Company, 626, 774

G

Gannett Co., Inc., 660, 661
The Gap, Inc., 659, 771
General Electric, 560

General Mills, Inc.
    amortization methods, 619–623
    bonds payable, 604–610, 619–623
    business description, 599
    debt-to-assets ratio, 611, 612
    discounted notes, 601–603, 613n, 617–618
    income statement, 608
    lease liabilities, 610–611, 619
    times interest earned ratio, 612
Gibraltar Industries, 716
Glaxo SmithKline, 1054–1055
Grant (W. T.) Company, 685
Gymboree, 714

H

Harley-Davidson, 772, 774
Hasbro, Inc., 759
Hertz, 610
H&M, D-1
The Home Depot, Inc., 595, 637, 677, 724,
    736, 739, 741, 744, 761
    annual report, A-1–A-29
Hoovers.com, 731
Hot Wheels, 919

I

IKEA, D-1
Internet Financial News (IFN), 648, 649

K

Kaplan, Inc., 641
Kellogg's, 611, 612, 613n
Kraft Foods Inc., 630, 765, 767, 796–797,
    800, 1043

L

LA Fitness, 773
Levi's, 774
Lowe's Companies, Inc., 595, 637, 677, 724,
    761
    annual report, B-1–B-19
    balance sheets, 733, 734
    business description, 729
    horizontal (trend) analysis, 732–733
    income statements, 733, 734
    liquidity ratios, 740–742
    profitability ratios, 736–740
    ratio analysis, 736–744
    release of financial information, 730–732
    solvency ratios, 742–743
    vertical (common size) analysis, 734–735

M

Mack Trucks, D-1
Macy's, Inc., 590–591, 668
Marriott International, Inc., 676–677
Matchbox, 919
Mattel, Inc., 759
    business description, 919

    capital budgeting for long-term investment
        decisions, 931–936
    incremental analysis for short-term
        decisions, 923–931
    managerial decision-making process,
        920–922
    relevant/irrelevant costs and benefits,
        922–923
Maytag, 772
McDonald's Corporation, 576–577
Montgomery Ward, 560
Moody's, 599
MSNBC, 559, 641

N

National Beverage Corp., 593
Nautilus Inc.
    balance sheet, 688, 689
    business activities and cash flows of,
        682, 684
    business description, 681
    cash flows from financing activities,
        694–696
    cash flows from investing activities, 693–694
    cash flows from operating activities,
        700–705
    change in current assets and liabilities,
        689–692
    income statement, 688, 689
    statement of cash flows, 696–699, 705–706
Netflix, 1027
Newell Rubbermaid
    income statements, 746
    nonrecurring and other special items,
        746–747
News Corporation, 661
New York Post, 661
Nike, Inc., 712
Northwest Airlines, 696, 697

O

Oscar Mayer, 767

P

Papa John's International, Inc., 991, 1001
PepsiCo, Inc., 715, 756
Pizza Aroma, 765
PMBR, 642
PricewaterhouseCoopers LLC, 767
Procter & Gamble, 753

R

Regis, 773
Rent-A-Center, Inc., 592

S

Safeway, 773
Sam's Club, 773

Sonic Corporation, 582, 674
    balance sheet, 566
    business description, 559
    cash dividends on common stock, 568–570
    earnings per share (EPS), 576
    financial statement reporting, 567–568
    formation of corporation, 561–562
    ownership of, 560
    price/earnings (p/e) ratio, 577
    statement of retained earnings, 575
    stock authorization, 563
    stock sold between investors, 565
Sports Authority, 753
Standard & Poor's, 599
Starbucks Corporation, 603, 671
    business description, 883
    contribution margin, 892–894
    cost behavior patterns, 884–887
    cost-volume-profit analysis, 894–899
    estimating cost behavior, 887–891
State Farm Mutual Automobile Insurance
    Company, 642

T

TheStreet.com, 731
Timberland Company, 670
TJX Companies Inc., 630
Toll Brothers Inc.
    assigning manufacturing costs to jobs,
        801–805
    business description, 799
    cost of goods manufactured/cost of goods
        sold, 815–816
    income statement, 816
    job order costing, 801, 806–812
Tombstone Pizza, 1043
    business description, 765–766
    cost classifications and definitions,
        769–773

functions of management, 768
    managerial accounting and, 766–767,
        769–773
Toni and Guy Hair Salons, 771
Toyota Motor Company, 772, 843
Tribune Company, 660, 661
Trump Industries, 801
20th Century Fox, 661

U

United Parcel Service (UPS), 773
U.S. Department of Defense, 801

V

Vera Wang, 801
Verizon Wireless, 773

W

W. T. Grant Company, 685
The Wall Street Journal, 644n
Wal-Mart Stores, Inc., 765
The Walt Disney Company, 659, 716–717
The Washington Post Company
    balance sheet, 642, 643
    business description, 641
    comparison to benchmarks, 660–661
    consolidated statements, 642–643,
        658–660
    influential investments, 654–660
    notes to financial statements, 642, 654, 659
    passive investments, 642, 643, 644–654
    return on assets (ROA), 660–661
Weiss Ratings, Inc., 761–762

Y

Yahoo!Finance, 560, 731, 738, 740
Yum! Brands, Inc., 659

Subject Index

Page numbers followed by n indicate footnotes.

A

Accounting
 managerial. *See* Managerial accounting
 for stock transactions, 562–568
Accounting communication
 financial reporting in. *See* Financial reporting
 financial statements in. *See* Financial statement(s)
 managerial reporting in. *See* Managerial accounting
Accounting equation. *See* Fundamental accounting equation
Accounting methods, 658
Accounting rate of return, 932–933
Accounting standards. *See also* Generally accepted accounting principles (GAAP)
 Financial Accounting Standards Board (FASB), 683n, D-1
 International Accounting Standards Board (IASB), 654, 744, D-1–D-2
Accounts payable, operating activities and, 691
Accounts receivable
 cash flows from operating activities and, 687, 690
 in partnership formation, 510
 receivables turnover, 737, 740–741
Accrued liabilities, operating activities and, 691
Accumulated depreciation, operating activities and, 687, 689
Accumulated other comprehensive income, 650–651
Active investments
 for control, 642, 643–644, 658–660
 defined, 642, 643
 for significant influence, 642, 643, 644, 654–657
Activity-based costing (ABC), 841, 842, 856–862
 allocation base (cost driver) in, 857, 859–860
 defined, 857
 indirect costs in, 858–859, 860–862
 steps in, 857–862
Actual manufacturing overhead, 806, 809
Additional Paid-In Capital, 564, 567
Administrative costs, 773
American Institute of Certified Public Accountants (AICPA), 683n
Amortization
 of debt investments held to maturity, 644–646
 effective-interest method of, 619–622
 of long-term liabilities, 619–623
 straight-line method of, 622–623

Amortized cost method
 amortized cost, defined, 644
 for debt investments held to maturity, 644–646
Annual rate of return, 932–933
Annual reports
 elements of financial section, 730, 731
 Home Depot, Inc., A-1–A-29
 Lowe's Companies, Inc., B-1–B-19
 release of, 730
 SEC filings, 731
Annuity
 future value of, C-5–C-6, C-15
 present value of, 617, C-6, C-8–C-11, C-12–C-13, C-16
Applied manufacturing overhead, 804–805, 806, 809–810, 812–814
 overapplied, 812–813
 underapplied, 812–813
Arm's-length transactions, 657
Articles of organization, 507
Asset(s). *See also specific assets*
 debt to, 611–612, 737, 742
 depreciation of. *See* Depreciation
 gains (losses) on sale of, 689
Asset turnover, 737, 738
Authorized shares, 567
Avoidable costs, 922

B

Balanced scorecard, 1039–1040
Balance sheet. *See also* Current liabilities; Financial statement(s)
 bonds payable on, 607
 budgeted, 962, 971, 972
 comparative, 685, 688, 732, 733
 consolidated, 643
 fundamental accounting equation and, 686, 687–692
 of manufacturing firms, 775
 of merchandising companies, 775
 partnership, 516–517
 relationships with other financial statements, 685–687, 688
 trend (horizontal) analysis of, 732, 733
 vertical (common size) analysis of, 734–735
Balance sheet equation. *See* Fundamental accounting equation
Batch-level activities, in activity-based costing, 858
Benchmarks
 comparison to, 660–661
 flexible budgets as, 992
Bond investments, 644–646
 interest earned, 645
 principal at maturity, 645
 purchases, 644

Bond pricing, 605–607
    bonds issued at a discount, 606, 608, 619, 621–622, 623
    bonds issued at face value, 604–605, 608, 618
    bonds issued at premium, 606, 608, 618, 619–620, 622–623
    interest periods in, 619
    interest rates and, 607, 619
Bonds payable, 604–610
    bond pricing and, 605–607
    bond retirement, 608–609
    bonds, defined, 604
    interest expense, 607–608
    present value of, 618–619
    reporting bond liabilities, 607
    types of bonds, 609–610
Bonuses
    to existing partners in partnership dissolution, 519
    to exiting partner, 524–525
    to new partners in partnership dissolution, 520–521
    to remaining partners on withdrawal of partner, 523–524
Book (carrying) value, 607
Break-even analysis, 895–896
Break-even point, 895
Budget slack, 961
Budgetary control, 986–1012
    direct labor variances, 996–998
    direct materials variances, 994–996
    flexible budgets to calculate cost variances, 990–993
    manufacturing overhead cost variances, 998–1003
    standard cost systems, 988–990, 1008–1011
    summary of variances, 1003–1005
Budgetary planning, 956–972
    approaches to, 961
    behavioral effects of, 960–962
    benefits of, 959–960, 961
    budget, defined, 959
    ethics and, 962
    financial budget, 962, 970–972
    master budget, 962–964, 990–991
    operating budget, 962, 964–969
    role of budgets, 958–961
Budgeted balance sheet, 962, 971, 972
Budgeted cost of goods sold, 963, 967–968
Budgeted gross margin, 964
Budgeted income statement, 962, 968–969
Budgeted manufacturing cost per unit, 963
Business entities, types of. See Corporations; Partnership(s); Sole proprietorships

C

Callable bonds, 609
Capital budgeting decisions, 931–936
    capital budgeting, defined, 920

    defined, 931
    discounted cash flow methods in, 932, 934–936
    nondiscounting methods in, 932–934
    types of decisions, 931–932
Capital deficiency
    defined, 531
    not paid by partner, 532
    paid by partner, 531
    in partnership liquidation, 529–532
Capital gains. See also Capital losses
    on passive investments, 649–654
    on stock held for significant influence, 656–657
Capital leases
    described, 610–611, 619
    present value of, 619
Capital losses. See also Capital gains
    on passive investments, 649–654
    on stock held for significant influence, 656–657
Carrying (book) value, 607
Cash
    cash flows. See Cash flows
    common stock issued for, 563–564
    dividends and, 570
    excess, investing. See Investment(s)
    net increase (decrease) in, 684
Cash budgets, 964, 970–971
Cash contributions, to partnership, 509–510
Cash dividends
    common stock, 561, 568–570, 574
    compared with stock dividends, 574
    compared with stock splits, 574
    preferred stock, 562, 570–571
Cash-equivalent amount, 600–601
Cash equivalents, defined, 682
Cash flows. See also Statement of cash flows
    from financing activities, 684, 694–696
    from investing activities, 684, 693–694
    from operating activities, 683–684, 687–692, 699–706
    relationship between business activities and, 682–683
Centralized organization, defined, 1028–1029
China, outsourcing to, 927
Clark, Taylor, 883n
Collateralized (secured) bonds, 609
Common size (vertical) analysis, 734–735
Common stock
    authorization of, 563
    cash dividends on, 561, 568–570, 574
    characteristics of, 561
    defined, 561
    earnings per share (EPS), 568, 575, 576–577, 737, 740
    financial statement reporting, 567–568, 574–575
    price/earnings (P/E) ratio, 575, 576, 577, 737, 740
    stock issues, 563–565

Comparative balance sheet, 685, 688, 732, 733
Comparative income statement, 732, 733
Compensation. *See also* Bonuses;
    Partnership(s); Salaries
    stock options used as, 565
    stock used as, 565
Complete income statement, 685, 688
Compounding. *See* Future value
Consolidated financial statements
    balance sheet, 643
    defined, 642
    nature of, 659–660
Continuous budgeting approach, 961
Contra-accounts
    contra-liability accounts, 606
    stockholders' equity, 566
Contributed capital, 562
    cash flows from financing activities and,
      694, 695
Contribution margin, 892–894, 901–903
    contribution margin formula, 893
    contribution margin income statement, 892
    contribution margin ratio, 893–894
    unit, 893
Control. *See also* Budgetary control
    defined, 959
    as function of management, 768
    investing for, 642, 643–644, 658–660
    in planning and control cycle, 959
Controllability principle, 1030
Controlling interests
    control, defined, 643
    investing for, 642, 643–644, 658–660
Conversion cost, 772
    overapplied and underapplied, 848
    in process costing, 845–849
Convertible bonds, 609
Corporate bonds, 609
Corporate charter, 563
Corporate life cycle, 699
Corporations, 558–580
    accounting differences between sole
      proprietorships and, 563
    accounting for stock transactions, 562–568
    cash dividends, 561, 568–572
    characteristics of, 560–562
    common stock. *See* Common stock
    financial statement reporting, 567–568,
      574–575
    financing activities, 562. *See also* Financing
      activities
    formation of, 561–562
    laws concerning, 560–561
    organizational structure, 561
    ownership of, 560
    preferred stock. *See* Preferred stock
    S-Corporations, 508–509
    stock authorization, 563
    stock dividends, 572–573
    stock issues, 563–565
    stock splits, 573–574

taxes and, 560–561
    treasury stock, 565–568, 574–575
Cost
    classifications of, 769–778
    in cost-benefit analysis. *See* Incremental
      analysis
    defined, 769–770
Cost-based method of transfer pricing, 1042
Cost behavior, 884–887
    defined, 884
    estimating costs, 887–891
    fixed costs in, 884–885
    mixed costs in, 886–887, 889–891
    relevant range in, 884
    step costs in, 885–886
    variable costs in, 771, 884, 889–890
Cost-benefit analysis. *See* Incremental analysis
Cost centers
    defined, 1030
    responsibilities of, 1030–1031
Cost drivers
    in activity-based costing, 857, 859–860
    defined, 804, 889
    in job order costing, 804
Cost objects, 770
Cost of goods completed, 811
Cost of goods manufactured report, 775–777,
    815–816
Cost of goods sold (CGS)
    budgeted, 963, 967–968
    converting to cash paid to suppliers,
      701–702, 703
    in job order costing, 806, 811–812,
      815–816
    in process costing, 843
    in standard cost system, 1011
    transferring to finished goods inventory,
      811–812
Cost systems
    activity-based costing, 842, 856–862
    full absorption costing, 901–903
    job order costing, 798–819
    process costing, 800–801, 841–856
    standard costing, 988–990, 1008–1011
    variable costing, 892–894, 901–903
Cost-volume-profit analysis (CVP), 894–899
    assumptions of, 894
    break-even analysis and, 895–896
    CVP graph, 898
    defined, 894
    margin of safety and, 896–897
    multiproduct, 899
    target profit analysis, 897–898
Cumulative dividend preference, 571, 572
Current assets
    in current ratio, 737, 741
    operating activities and, 687, 689–692
Current dividend preference, 570–571
Current liabilities
    accounts payable, 691
    operating activities and, 687, 689–692

Current ratio, 737, 741
Customer(s), customer-level activities, in
    activity-based costing, 858
CVP graph, 898

D

Date of record, 569
Days to collect, 737
Days to sell, 737
Death of partner, 525
Debt. *See also* Notes payable
    equity versus debt financing, 562, 600
Debt securities
    amortized cost method of accounting for,
      644–646
    passive investment in, 643, 644–654
Debt to assets, 611–612, 737, 742
Debt to equity, 742
Decentralized organization. *See also*
    Performance evaluation
    advantages and disadvantages of, 1029
    defined, 1028–1029
Declaration date, 569
Dependent variable, 889
Depreciation, sale of long-term assets, 687, 689
Differential cost, 772
Direct costs, 770–771
Direct cost variances, 994
Directing/leading
    defined, 959
    as function of management, 768
    in planning and control cycle, 958
Direct labor budgets, 963, 966–967
Direct labor cost
    defined, 772
    in job order costing, 801, 809
    in process costing, 844
    in standard cost system, 1010–111
Direct labor standards, 989
Direct labor time tickets, 803
Direct labor variances, 996–998
    calculating, 998
    labor efficiency variances, 997
    labor rate variances, 997
    labor spending variances, 997–998
Direct materials cost, 772
    in job order costing, 801, 808
    in process costing, 843
    in standard cost system, 1009–1010
Direct materials variances, 994–996
    price variances, 995
    quantity variances, 995
    spending variances, 996
Direct method, of reporting cash flows from
    operating activities, 683, 700–705
Disclosure. *See* Financial statement(s)
Discontinued operations, 746–747
Discount(s)
    bonds issued at, 606, 608, 619, 621–622, 623
    defined, 605

Discounted cash flow methods, 934–936
    defined, 932
    internal rate of return, 935–936
    net present value, 934–935
Discounted notes payable
    accounting for, 601–603
    defined, 601
    present value of, 617–618
Discounting. *See also* Present value
    defined, 601, 616
Dividends
    cash, 561–562, 568–572, 574
    on common stock, 561, 568–570, 574
    dividend dates, 569–570
    on preferred stock, 562, 570–571
    requirements for, 570
    on securities purchased, 648, 656
    stock, 572–573, 574
Dividends in arrears, 571, 572
DuPont method, 1034–1035

E

Earning(s)
    on investments for significant influence,
      655–656
    on investments held to maturity, 645
Earnings management, 651
Earnings per share (EPS), 568, 575, 576–577,
    737, 740
Easily attainable standards
    defined, 988
    ideal standards versus, 988
Edison, Thomas, 560
Education, decisions concerning, 770
Effective-interest method, of amortization,
    619–622
Employee compensation. *See* Compensation
Equity. *See also* Common stock; Preferred stock
    active investment in, 643–644
    debt to, 742
    passive investment in, 643, 644, 646–654
Equity financing
    debt financing versus, 562, 600
    nature of, 562
Equity method
    for investments for significant influence,
      654–658
    managers' choice to use, 658
Equivalent units
    defined, 851
    in process costing, 851–853, 866–867
Ethics
    budgeting and, 962
    debt-to-assets ratio and, 612
    improper influence, 657
    stock options as compensation, 565
    subjectivity of net income, 685
Expenses
    change in recognition of, 699
    interest. *See* Interest expense
External reporting, 767

F

Face value
    bonds issued at, 604–605, 608, 618
    of bonds payable, 604–605
    defined, 618
Facility-level activities, in activity-based
    costing, 858
Fair value option, 654
Favorable variances
    causes of, 990
    defined, 989–990
Financial accounting
    defined, 766–767
    managerial accounting versus, 766–767
Financial Accounting Standards Board (FASB),
    683n, D-1
Financial budgets
    defined, 962
    preparing, 970–972
Financial ratios. See Ratio analysis
Financial reporting. See also Financial
        statement(s); Generally accepted
        accounting principles (GAAP)
    bond pricing and, 605–607
    dividends in arrears, 572
    equity securities and earnings
        management, 651
    international differences in accounting
        standards, 654, 744
    passive investments, 651, 654
    selecting accounting methods, 658
Financial statement(s). See also Financial
        reporting; Generally accepted
        accounting principles (GAAP)
    analysis of. See Financial statement analysis
    consolidated, 642, 643, 659–660
    of manufacturing versus nonmanufacturing
        companies, 774–778
    notes to. See Notes to financial statements
    partnership, 516–517
    relationships among, 685–687, 688
    stock reporting and, 567–568, 574–575
    types of. See Balance sheet; Income
        statement; Statement of cash flows
Financial statement analysis, 728–747.
        See also Ratio analysis
    annual reports, 730–731
    discontinued operations, 746–747
    horizontal (trend) analysis, 732–733
    investor information Web sites, 731–732
    Management's Discussion and Analysis
        (MD&A) in, 732–733, 735
    nonrecurring items, 746–747
    other special items, 746–747
    quality of income ratio, 698–699
    quarterly reports, 730, 731
    release of financial information, 730–732
    Securities and Exchange Commission (SEC)
        filings, 731
    vertical (common size) analysis, 734–735

Financing activities
    cash flows from, 684, 694–696
    equity versus debt, 562, 600
    noncash, 696–697
Finished goods inventory, 776
    defined, 775
    in job order costing, 806, 811–812, 815
    in process costing, 843
First-in, first-out (FIFO) inventory method,
    managers' choice of, 658
Fixed assets, fixed asset turnover, 737,
    738–739
Fixed costs
    behavior patterns of, 884–885
    defined, 771, 884–885
Fixed overhead spending variances, 1002
Fixed overhead volume variances, 1002
Fixed-ratio method, 511–512
Flexible budgets, 990–993
    as benchmark, 992
    defined, 990
    master budgets versus, 990–991
    preparing, 991
    static budgets versus, 990
    volume variance versus spending variance,
        992–993
Footnotes. See Notes to financial statements
Form 8-K, 731
Form 10-K, 731
Form 10-Q, 731
Fraud. See Ethics
Free cash flow, 698, 737, 743
Full absorption costing, 901–903
    calculation and uses of, 901
    effect of changes in inventory under, 903
    income statement under, 901, 902
    reconciling income under, 902–903
    variable costing versus, 901
Fundamental accounting equation, changes in
    cash and, 686, 687–692
Future value
    of an annuity, C-5–C-6, C-15
    of a single amount, C-2–C-3, C-14
    tables, C-14, C-15

G

GAAP. See Generally accepted accounting
        principles (GAAP)
Gains, on sale of assets, 689
Generally accepted accounting principles
        (GAAP)
    advantages of, 767
    fair value option for passive investments,
        654
    international standards compared with,
        D-1–D-2
    manufacturing costs in, 848
    subjectivity of net income, 685
Gross profit (gross margin), 811
    budgeted, 964

Gross profit percentage, 737, 738
Growth stocks, 568

H

High-low method, 890–891
Holding gains, 651
Horizontal (trend) analysis, 732–733
Horizontal growth, 658
Hurdle rate, 1036

I

Ideal standards
  defined, 988
  easily attainable standards versus, 988
Improper influence, 657
Income, division of partnership, 511–516,
  534–535
Income (loss) of partnership, 511–516,
  534–535
  fixed-ratio method, 511–512
  interest on partners' capital method, 511,
    512–513
  salaries to partners and interest on partners'
    capital balances method, 511, 514–516
  salaries to partners method, 511, 513–514
Income statement
  budgeted, 962, 968–969
  comparative, 732, 733
  complete, 685, 688
  contribution margin, 892
  under full absorption costing, 901, 902
  gross profit percentage, 737, 738
  of manufacturing firms, 776–778
  of merchandising companies, 776–778
  relationships with other financial
    statements, 685–687, 688
  segmented, 1032
  trend (horizontal) analysis of, 732, 733
  under variable costing, 901, 902
  vertical (common size) analysis of, 734–735
Income stocks, 569
Income taxes. See also Tax reporting
  converting to cash outflow, 702–703
Incremental analysis, 923–931
  defined, 920
  keep-or-drop decisions, 928–930
  make-or-buy decisions, 925–928
  sell-or-process-further decisions, 930–931
  special-order decisions, 923–925
Independent variable, 889
Indirect costs, 770–771
  in activity-based costing, 858–859, 860–862
  in job order costing, 801, 806, 808, 809
Indirect method, of reporting cash flows from
  operating activities, 683, 687–692,
  699–700, 705–706
Industry factors, comparison to benchmarks,
  660–661
Influential investments
  for control, 642, 643–644, 658–660

for significant influence, 642, 643, 654–658
Interest expense
  on bonds payable, 607–608
  converting to cash paid to suppliers, 703
  on discounted notes payable, 602–603
Interest on partners' capital method, 511,
  512–513
Interest periods
  in bond pricing, 619
  time value of money and, C-6–C-7
Interest rates
  bond pricing and, 607
  on bonds payable, 604–605, 618
  quoting, 619
  time value of money and, C-6–C-7
Interest revenue, on bonds, 645
Internal decision makers. See Manager(s)
Internal rate of return (IRR), 935–936
Internal reporting, 767
International Accounting Standards Board
  (IASB), 744, D-1–D-2
International financial reporting standards
  (IFRS), 654, 744, D-1–D-2
Inventoriable costs, 773
Inventory
  cash flows from operating activities and,
    687, 690–691
  types of, 775, 776
Inventory budgets, 963
Inventory costing methods
  first-in, first-out (FIFO) method, 658
  last-in, first-out (LIFO) method, 658
  managers' choice of, 658
Inventory management, inventory turnover
  analysis, 737, 741
Inventory turnover analysis, 737, 741
Investing activities
  cash flows from, 684, 693–694
  noncash, 696–697
Investment(s), 640–665. See also Investing
  activities
  of additional assets in partnership, 518–521
  cash and noncash contributions to partner-
    ship, 509–510
  cash flows from investing activities and,
    684, 693, 694
  consolidated financial statements and, 642,
    643, 659–660
  for control, 642, 643–644, 658–660
  passive, 642, 643, 644–654
  return on assets (ROA), 660–661, 737, 739
  for significant influence, 642, 643, 654–658
Investment centers, 1032–1040
  balanced scorecard, 1039–1040
  defined, 1030
  limitations of financial performance mea-
    sures, 1038–1039
  residual income, 1036–1038
  responsibilities of, 1032–1033
  return on investment (ROI), 1034–1036,
    1038

Investments Held to Maturity, 644–646
Investment turnover, 1034, 1036
Investors. *See also* Stockholders (shareholders)
    corporate ownership and, 560
    investor information Web sites, 731–732
    stock sold between, 565
Irrelevant costs, 772, 922–923
Issued shares, 567

J

Job, defined, 801
Job cost sheet, 801, 802, 803
Job order costing, 798–819
    assignment of manufacturing costs to jobs,
        801–806
    defined, 801
    examples of, 801
    journal entries for, 806–812
    overapplied or underapplied manufacturing
        overhead, 812–814
    process costing versus, 800–801, 842–843
Journal entries. *See also* Special journals
    for job order costing, 806–812
    for partnership formation, 510
    for process costing, 844–848

K

Keep-or-drop decisions, 928–930

L

Labor costs, in job order costing, 808–809
Land, cash flows from investing activities
        and, 694
Last-in, first-out (LIFO) inventory method,
        managers' choice of, 658
Lease liabilities, 610–611
    capital leases, 610–611, 619
    operating leases, 610
Legal issues, for corporations, 560–561
Liabilities
    contra-accounts, 606
    current. *See* Current liabilities
    long-term. *See* Long-term liabilities
    measuring, 600–601
    recording, 600–601
Limited liability companies (LLC), 507–508
    characteristics of, 507–508
    defined, 507
Liquidation of partnership, 526–532, 538–539
    capital deficiency, 529–532
    causes of, 526
    defined, 526
    no capital deficiency, 527–529
    steps in, 527
Liquidity ratios, 736, 737, 740–742
    current ratio, 737, 741
    days to collect, 737
    days to sell, 737

inventory turnover, 737, 741
    quick ratio, 737, 742
    receivables turnover, 737, 740–741
Long-lived assets. *See also* Property, plant,
        and equipment
    cash flows from operating activities and,
        687, 689–692
    depreciation of, 689
    sale of, 689
Long-term debt
    cash flows from financing activities and,
        694, 695
    defined, 600
Long-term liabilities, 598–624
    amortization of, 619–623
    analyzing, 611–612
    bonds payable, 604–610, 618–623
    debt-to-assets ratio, 611–612, 737, 742
    discounted notes payable, 601–603,
        617–618
    discounting future payments, 616–619
    effective-interest method of amortization,
        619–622
    leases, 610–611, 619
    measuring, 600–601, 607
    straight-line method of amortization,
        622–623
    times interest earned ratio, 612, 737,
        742–743
Long-term objectives, 959
Losses
    on division of partnership, 511–516,
        534–535
    on sale of assets, 689

M

Make-or-buy decisions, 925–928
Management's Discussion and Analysis
        (MD&A), 732–733, 735
Manager(s). *See also* Ethics
    choice of inventory costing method, 658
    functions of, 767–768
Managerial accounting, 764–782
    cost classifications in, 769–778
    costs in manufacturing versus
        nonmanufacturing firms, 773–778
    decision-making orientation of, 766
    defined, 766–767
    financial accounting versus, 766–767
    functions of management and, 767–769
    role in organizations, 766–769
Managerial decision-making process, 920–922
    application to personal decision, 921
    incremental analysis in, 923–931
    irrelevant costs in, 722, 922–923
    managerial accounting and, 766
    relevant costs in, 722, 922
    steps in, 920–922
Manufacturing companies
    balance sheets of, 775

cost of goods manufactured report, 775–777

cost systems. *See* Cost systems

financial statements of, 774

income statements of, 776–778

nature of, 773–774

Manufacturing costs. *See also* Cost systems

    assigning to jobs, 801–806

    categories of, 772

    defined, 772

    direct labor time tickets, 803

    job cost sheet, 801, 802, 803

    materials requisition form, 802–803

    nonmanufacturing costs versus, 772–778

    predetermined overhead rates, 804–805

    recording, 806–812

    summary of recorded, 815

Manufacturing overhead, 772

    actual, 806, 809

    applied, 804–805, 806, 809–810, 812–814

    budgets, 963, 967

    fixed overhead variances, 1001–1003

    in job order costing, 801–802, 804–805, 806, 815

    in process costing, 844

    in standard cost system, 1010–1011

    variable overhead variances, 998–1003

Margin of safety, 896–897

Marketing (selling) costs, 772

Market-price method of transfer pricing, 1041–1042

Market value

    managers' choice to use, 658

    of passive investments, 646–650, 658

Master budgets, 962–964

    components of, 962–964

    defined, 962

    flexible budgets versus, 990–991

    preparing, 991

Matching principle, 602, 622

Materials requisition, 802–803

Maturity date

    bond retirement and, 608–609

    of bonds payable, 604–605, 608–609

    debt investments held to maturity, 644–646

Merchandising companies

    balance sheets of, 775

    budgeting and, 972

    defined, 773

    financial statements of, 774

    gross profit percentage, 737, 738

    income statements of, 776–781

Mergers

    consolidated financial statements following, 642, 643, 659–660

    defined, 659

Mixed costs

    behavior patterns of, 886–887

    high-low method for analyzing, 890–891

    linear approaches to analyzing, 889–891

    nature of, 886–887

Mondavi, Cesare, 841–842

Mondavi, Peter, 841–842

Mondavi, Robert, 841–842

Mondavi, Rosa, 841–842

Multiproduct cost-volume-profit analysis, 899

Municipal bonds (munis), 609

N

Negotiation, of transfer pricing, 1042–1043

Net income

    conversion to net cash flow from operating activities, 689

    direct method of reporting cash flows from operating activities, 683, 700–705

    indirect method of reporting cash flows from operating activities, 683, 687–692, 699–700, 705–706

    subjectivity of, 685

Net present value (NPV), 934–935

Net profit margin, 736–738

New York Stock Exchange (NYSE), D-1

Noncash contributions

    common stock issued for, 564

    to corporation, 564

    to partnership, 509–510

Noncash investing and financing activities, 696–697

Nondiscounting methods in capital budgeting, 932–934

    accounting rate of return, 932–933

    defined, 932

    payback period, 933–934

Nonmanufacturing costs

    categories of, 772–773

    defined, 772

    in job order costing, 812–815

    manufacturing costs versus, 772–778

    in process costing, 844

    recording, 812–814

    summary of recorded, 815

Nonvolume-based cost drivers, 857

No-par value stock, 563, 564

Notes payable

    cash flows from financing activities and, 694

    discounted, 601–603, 617–618

Notes to financial statements

    dividends in arrears, 572

    investments in affiliates, 654

    investments in marketable securities, 647

    principles of consolidation, 659–660

O

Operating activities

    accounts affected by, 687

    accrual basis accounting, 691

    cash flows from, 683–684, 687–692, 699–706

    direct method of reporting cash flows from, 683, 700–705

Operating activities—*Cont.*
    impact of change in, 699
    indirect method of reporting cash flows
        from, 683, 687–692, 699–700, 705–706
    quality of income ratio, 698–699
Operating agreement, 507
Operating budgets
    components of, 964–969
    defined, 962
Operating expenses, converting to cash out-
        flow, 702–703
Operating leases, described, 610
Opportunity costs, 770
Organizational forms. *See* Corporations;
        Partnership(s); Sole proprietorships
Organizational structure
    corporation, 561
    decentralized, 1028–1029
Organizing
    defined, 958–959
    as function of management, 768
    in planning and control cycles, 958
Out-of-pocket costs, 770
Outsourcing, 927
Outstanding shares, 567–568
Overapplied manufacturing overhead,
        812–813
    calculating, 812–813
    disposing of, 813–814
    fixed, 1003
Overhead. *See* Manufacturing overhead
Ownership
    corporate, 560
    partnership, 517–525

P

Parent company
    consolidated financial statements following
        merger, 642, 643, 659–660
    defined, 659
Participative budgeting, 961
Partner return on equity, 533–534, 539
Partners' capital statement
    capital deficiency, 529–532
    defined, 516
    no capital deficiency, 527–529
Partnership(s), 504–541
    accounting for, 509–517
    admission of partner, 517–521, 536–537
    characteristics of, 506–507, 508
    death of partner, 525
    defined, 506
    division of income (loss), 511–516,
        534–535
    financial statements, 516–517
    formation of, 509–510
    liquidation of, 526–532, 538–539
    ownership changes, 517–525
    partner return on equity, 533–534, 539

similar forms of business, 507–509
    withdrawal of partner, 521–525, 536–537
Partnership agreement, 506
Partnership dissolution
    admission of partner and, 517–521, 536–537
    bonus to existing partners, 519
    bonus to new partner, 520–521
    defined, 517
Par value, 563
    no-par value stock, 563, 564
    par value common stock issued for cash,
        563–564
Passive investments
    accounting for, 644–654
    amortized cost method and, 644–646
    debt investments held to maturity, 644–646
    in debt securities, 643, 644–650
    defined, 642, 643
    in equity securities, 643, 644, 646–652
    market value method and, 646–650, 658
    sale of stock, 650
    securities available for sale, 646–654
    trading securities, 646, 651
Pass-through taxation
    for limited liability companies (LLC),
        507–508
    for S-Corporations, 508
Payback period, 933–934
Payment date, 569–570
Percentage analysis. *See* Ratio analysis
Performance evaluation, 1026–1045
    budgets in, 961
    decentralization of responsibility,
        1028–1030
    investment centers, 1034–1040
    responsibility centers, 1030–1033
    transfer pricing, 1040–1043
Period costs, 773
Personal decisions
    for education, 770
    managerial decision-making process in, 921
Planning
    budgets in, 961. *See also* Budgetary planning
    defined, 958
    as function of management, 768
    in planning and control cycles, 958
Planning process, 959
Plant and equipment. *See* Property, plant, and
        equipment
Predetermined overhead, 804–805
Preference decisions, 932
Preferred stock
    authorization of, 563
    cash dividends on, 562, 570–571
    characteristics of, 561–562
    cumulative dividend preference, 571, 572
    current dividend preference, 570–571
    defined, 561
    financial statement reporting, 567–568,
        574–575
    stock issues, 564

Premium
    bonds issued at, 606, 608, 618, 619–620,
        622–623
    defined, 605
Prepaid expenses
    converting to cash outflow, 702
    operating activities and, 691
Present value
    accounting applications of, 616–619,
        C-7–C-11
    of an annuity, 617, C-6, C-8–C-11,
        C-12–C-13, C-16
    of bonds payable, 618–619
    of capital leases, 619
    computations using Excel, C-12–C-13
    defined, 601
    of discounted notes payable, 617–618
    of a single amount, 616–617, C-3–C-4,
        C-7–C-8, C-10–C-12, C-14–C-15
    tables, 616, 617, C-14–C-16
Press release, preliminary, 730
Price/earnings (P/E) ratio, 575, 576, 577,
    737, 740
Price standards, 988
Price variances, 993–995
Principal
    on investments held to maturity, 645
    on notes payable, 603
Private companies, 560
Process costing, 800–801, 841–856
    additional factors in, 856
    defined, 800, 841
    examples of, 800
    flow of costs in, 843–844
    formula for, 800–801
    job order costing versus, 800–801,
        842–843
    journal entries for, 844–848
    steps in, 849–856
    weighted average method in, 865–869
Product costing, 773
Production budgets, 963, 964–965
Production report, in process costing, 855,
    868–869
Product-level activities, in activity-based
    costing, 858
Professional standards. See Ethics
Profitability ratios, 736–740
    asset turnover, 737, 738
    earnings per share (EPS), 568, 575,
        576–577, 737, 740
    fixed asset turnover, 737, 738–739
    gross profit percentage, 737, 738
    net profit margin, 736–738
    price/earnings (P/E) ratio, 575, 576, 577,
        737, 740
    return on assets (ROA), 660–661, 737, 739
    return on equity (ROE), 533–534, 539,
        737, 739
    return on partner equity, 533–534, 539

Profit centers
    defined, 1030
    responsibilities of, 1031–1032
Profit margin, 1034, 1036
    net, 736–738
Property, plant, and equipment
    cash flows from investing activities and,
        693, 694
    fixed asset turnover, 737, 738–739
Public companies, 560
Purchases
    of investments for significant influence,
        655
    among partners, 517–518
    among partners on withdrawal of partner,
        522–523
    of securities available for sale, 648
Purchases journal
    in job order costing, 807–808
    in process costing, 844

Q

Qualitative analysis
    of keep-or-drop decisions, 929–930
    of make-or-buy decisions, 927–928
    of special-order decisions, 924–925
Quality control, outsourcing and, 927
Quality of income ratio, 698–699
Quantitative analysis
    of keep-or-drop decisions, 928–929
    of make-or-buy decisions, 926–927
    of special-order decisions, 924
Quantity standards, 988
Quantity variances, 993–995
Quarterly reports
    release of, 730
    SEC filings, 731
Quick ratio, 737, 742

R

Rate of return
    accounting, 932–933
    internal, 935–936
Ratio analysis, 736–744
    accounting decisions and, 744
    comparisons to benchmarks, 660–661
    defined, 736
    investor information Web sites and,
        731–732
    liquidity ratios, 736, 737, 740–742
    profitability ratios, 736–740
    quality of income ratio, 698–699
    solvency ratios, 736, 737, 742–743
Raw materials inventory, 776
    defined, 775
    in job order costing, 806, 815
    in process costing, 843, 844–845
Raw materials purchases budgets, 963,
    965–966

Receivables
  accounts receivable, 687, 690
  receivables turnover analysis, 737, 740–741
Receivables turnover, 737, 740–741
Record date, 569
Regression analysis, 890
Related-party transactions
  defined, 1040
  transfer pricing and, 1040–1043
Relevant costs, 772, 922
Relevant range, 884
Residual claim on assets
  common stock, 561
  preferred stock, 562
Residual income
  measuring, 1036–1037
  return on investment (ROI) versus, 1038
Responsibility
  decentralization of, 1028–1030
  responsibility accounting and, 1030–1033
Responsibility accounting, 1030–1033
Responsibility centers, 1030–1033
  cost centers, 1030–1031
  investment centers, 1030, 1032–1040
  profit centers, 1030, 1031–1032
  revenue centers, 1030, 1031
  transfer pricing and, 1040–1043
Retailers. See Merchandising companies
Retained earnings. See also Statement of
    retained earnings
  cash flows from financing activities and,
      694, 695–696
  defined, 563
  dividends and, 570
  operating activities and, 687
Return on assets (ROA), 660–661, 737
  comparison to benchmarks, 660–661
  defined, 660, 739
Return on equity (ROE), 533–534, 539, 737,
    739
Return on investment (ROI)
  measuring, 1034–1036
  residual income versus, 1038
Revenue(s), impact of change in, 699
Revenue centers
  defined, 1030
  responsibilities of, 1031
Rolling budget approach, 961

S

Salaries. See also Compensation
  salaries to partners and interest on partners'
      capital balances method, 511, 514–516
  salaries to partners method, 511, 513–514
Sales
  corporate life cycle and, 699
  growth of, 699
  revenues from. See Sales revenues
  of stock held for significant influence,
      656–657

Sales budgets, 963
Sales forecast budgets, 964
Sales revenues, converting to cash inflow,
    701, 703
Scattergraphs, 887–889
  defined, 887
  preparing, 887–889
S-Corporations, 508–509
  characteristics of, 508–509
  defined, 508
Screening decisions, 931
SEC. See U.S. Securities and Exchange
    Commission (SEC)
Secured bonds, 609
Securities and Exchange Commission (SEC)
  Electronic Data Gathering and Retrieval
      Service (EDGAR), 731
  filings with, 731
Securities available for sale, 646–650
  accounting for, 647–654
  defined, 646–647
  nature of, 650–651
  trading securities versus, 650–652
Segmented income statement, 1032
Selling and administrative expense budgets,
    963, 968
Sell or process further decisions, 930–931
Semivariable costs. See Mixed costs
Separate entity assumption, 560–561
Service companies
  financial statements of, 774
  nature of, 773
Shareholders' equity. See Stockholders' equity
Short-term objectives, 959
Significant influence
  equity method and, 654–658
  investing for, 642, 643, 644, 654–658
Siler, Julia Flynn, 842n
Single payment
  future value of, C-2–C-3, C-14
  present value of, 616–617, C-3–C-4,
      C-7–C-8, C-10–C-12, C-14–C-15
Sole proprietorships, accounting differences
    between corporations and, 563
Solvency ratios, 736, 737, 742–743
  debt to assets, 611–612, 737, 742
  free cash flow, 698, 737, 743
  times interest earned, 611, 612, 737,
      742–743
Source documents, 802–803
Special journals, purchases, 807–808, 844
Special-order decisions, 923–925
Spending variances
  defined, 992
  volume variances versus, 992–993
Spreadsheet approach, to preparing
    statement of cash flows, 705–706
Standard cost cards, 989
Standard cost systems, 988–990, 1008–1011
  cost of goods sold, 1011
  cost variance summary, 1011

defined, 988
  direct labor overhead costs, 1010–1011
  direct materials costs, 1009–1010
  favorable versus unfavorable variances, 989–990
  ideal versus attainable standards, 988
  manufacturing overhead costs, 1010–1011
  standard cost card, 989
  types of standards, 988–989
Stated interest rate
  on bonds payable, 604–605, 618
  defined, 618
Statement of cash flows, 680–707. *See also* Financial statement(s)
  cash flows from financing activities, 684, 694–696
  cash flows from investing activities, 684, 693–694
  cash flows from operating activities, 683–684, 687–692, 699–706
  categories in, 683
  classifications of, 682–687
  direct method of preparing, 683, 700–705
  format of, 696, 697
  free cash flow, 698, 737, 743
  indirect method of preparing, 683, 687–692, 699–700, 705–706
  net increase (decrease) in cash, 684
  noncash financing activities, 696–697
  noncash investing activities, 696–697
  preparing and evaluating, 696–699
  quality of income ratio, 698–699
  relationship between business activities and cash flows, 682–683
  relationships with other financial statements, 685–687, 688
  spreadsheet approach to preparing, 705–706
  supplemental cash flow information, 698
Statement of earnings. *See* Income statement
Statement of financial position. *See* Balance sheet
Statement of income. *See* Income statement
Statement of operations. *See* Income statement
Statement of retained earnings, 574–575
Static budgets, 990
Step costs, 885–886
Step-fixed costs, 886
Step-variable costs, 885–886
Stock. *See also* Common stock; Preferred stock
  accounting for stock transactions, 562–568
  financial statement reporting and, 567–568, 574–575
  treasury stock, 565–568, 574–575
Stock authorization, 563
Stock dividends, 572–573
  compared with cash dividends, 574
  compared with stock splits, 574

Stock issues
  common stock, 563–565
  preferred stock, 564
Stock options, as compensation, 565
Stock splits, 573–574
Stockholders (shareholders)
  accounting for stock transactions, 562–568
  corporate ownership and, 560
Stockholders' equity
  contra account, 566
  defined, 562
Straight-line method, of amortization, 622–623
Strategic plans, 959, 960
Strips, 609
Subjectivity, of net income, 685
Subsidiary company
  consolidated financial statements following, 659–660
  defined, 659
Sunk costs, 772, 922
Suppliers, cash paid to, 701–702
Synergy, 659

T

Tactics, 959
Tangible assets, fixed asset turnover analysis, 737, 738–739
Target profit analysis, 897–898
Tax reporting. *See also* Income taxes
  corporate, 560–561
  pass-through taxation, 507–508
Time value of money
  computations using Excel, C-12–C-13
  future value of an annuity, C-5–C-6, C-15
  future value of a single amount, C-2–C-3, C-14
  interest periods and, C-6–C-7
  interest rates and, C-6–C-7
  nature of, C-2
  present value of an annuity, 617, C-6, C-8–C-11, C-12–C-13, C-16
  present value of a single amount, 616–617, C-3–C-4, C-7–C-8, C-10–C-12, C-14–C-15
  tables, 616, 617, C-14–C-16
Times interest earned ratio, 611, 612, 737, 742–743
Top-down approach, 961
Total cost, 771
Total fixed costs, 889, 991
Trade accounts payable. *See* Accounts payable
Trading securities
  nature of, 646, 651
  securities available for sale versus, 650–652
Transfer pricing, 1040–1043
  cost-based method, 1042
  defined, 1040
  market-price method, 1041–1042
  negotiation in, 1042–1043

Treasury stock, 565–567
    acquisition of, 566
    defined, 565
    financial statement reporting, 567–568,
        574–575
    reissue of, 566–567
Trend (horizontal) analysis, 732–733
Turnover
    asset, 737, 738
    fixed asset, 737, 738–739
    inventory, 737, 741
    receivables, 737, 740–741

U

Underapplied manufacturing overhead,
    812–813
    calculating, 812–813
    disposing of, 813–814
    fixed, 1003
Unfavorable variances
    causes of, 990
    defined, 989–990
Uniform Partnership Act, 506
Unit contribution margin, 893, 895
U.S. Securities and Exchange Commission
    (SEC), international financial reporting
    standards and, D-1
U.S. Treasury bonds (treasuries), 609
Unit level activities, in activity-based
    costing, 858
Unrealized gain (loss) on investments,
    649–653

V

Valuation
    inventory. See Inventory costing methods
    of passive investments, 649–650
Variable costing, 892–894, 901–903
    calculation and uses of, 901
    effect of changes in inventory under, 903
    full absorption costing versus, 901
    income statement under, 901, 902
    reconciling income under, 902–903
Variable costs
    behavior patterns of, 889–890
    defined, 771, 884
Variable manufacturing costs, 989

Variable manufacturing overhead variances,
    998–1000
Variable overhead (VOH) efficiency variances,
    999–1000
Variable overhead (VOH) rate variances,
    999–1000
Variances
    defined, 998
    direct cost, 994
    direct labor, 996–998
    direct materials, 994–996
    favorable versus unfavorable, 989–990
    flexible budgets to calculate cost, 990–993
    framework for, 993–994
    manufacturing cost, 998–1003
    price, 993–995
    quantity, 993–995
    spending, 996
    in standard cost system, 1008–1011
    summary of, 1003–1005
Vertical (common size) analysis, 734–735
Vertical integration, 658
Visual fit method, 890
Volume-based allocation measures, 857
Volume variance
    defined, 992
    spending variances versus, 992–993
Voting rights
    common stock, 561
    preferred stock, 561

W

Weighted average inventory method, in
    process costing, 865–869
Wholesalers. See Merchandising companies
Withdrawal of partner, 521–525, 536–537
    purchase among partners, 522–523
    withdrawal of assets, 523–525
Work in process inventory, 776
    defined, 775
    in job order costing, 806, 815
    in process costing, 843, 845, 846–849,
        854–855, 867–868

Z

Zero-based budgeting approach, 961
Zero-coupon bonds, 609

Expanded Transaction Analysis Model

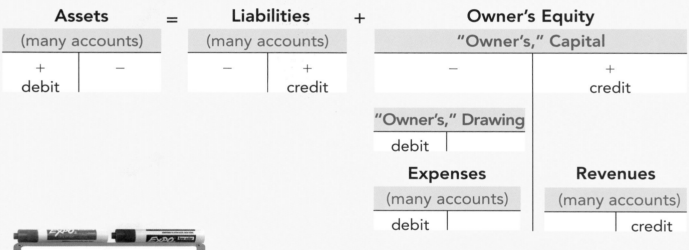

Assets		=	Liabilities		+	Owner's Equity			
(many accounts)			(many accounts)			"Owner's," Capital			
+	−		−	+		−		+	
debit				credit				credit	

"Owner's," Drawing

debit

Expenses			Revenues	
(many accounts)			(many accounts)	
debit				credit

Coach's Tip

Notice that the drawing and expense accounts increase with debits. As these accounts increase, owner's equity decreases.